AA

The 2006
GOLF COURSE
Guid

GW00357704

WIN A GOLF BREAK FOR TWO

with AA Lifestyle Guides
in association with

DE VERE ✦ HOTELS
Hotels of character, run with pride

AA Lifestyle Guides has five golf breaks to give away. We invite you to enter one of five free prize draws*.

The winner of each free prize draw will enjoy a free golf break consisting of a two night break including breakfast and dinner at a De Vere Golf Hotel of their choice PLUS a free round of golf on a specified course.

For more information on golf breaks at De Vere Hotels visit: www.DeVereGolf.co.uk or call 01928 714 068 for a copy of our Golf Leisure Breaks Brochure.
*Terms and conditions apply.
A winner will be drawn from each of the five draws to take place on the first Monday in each of the following months: January, March, May, July, September 2006.

See page 493 for full details

CREDITS

This 20th Edition published 2005
© Automobile Association Developments Limited 2005.

Produced by AA Publishing
Advertisement Sales: advertisingsales@theAA.com
Editorial: lifestyleguides@theAA.com

Prelim and opener pictures have been sourced from Corbis UK

Typeset/repro by Servis Filmsetting Ltd, Manchester
Printed and bound by Trento, Italy

Published by AA Publishing, which is a trading name of Automobile Association Developments Limited, whose registered office is Fanum House, Basingstoke, Hampshire RG21 4EA

Registered number 1878835

A CIP catalogue record for this book is available from the British Library

ISBN-10: 074954 6190

ISBN-13: 978 074954 6190

A02435

Maps prepared by the Cartography Department of The Automobile Association.
© Automobile Association Developments Limited 2005

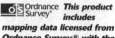 Ordnance Survey® *This product includes mapping data licensed from Ordnance Survey® with the permission of the Controller of Her Majesty's Stationery Office.*
© Crown copyright 2005 All rights reserved. Licence number 399221

 This product includes mapping based upon data licensed from Ordnance Survey of Northern Ireland® reproduced by permission of the Chief Executive, acting on behalf of the Controller of Her Majesty's Stationery Office.
© Crown copyright 2005 Permit number 40463

Republic of Ireland mapping based on Ordnance Survey Ireland Permit number MP000105.
© Ordnance Survey Ireland and Government of Ireland.

How to use the Guide

The directory is arranged in country and county order. Golf courses appear alphabetically by town within each county. The towns are listed in the index.

Sample Entry

1 — **OXFORD** Map 04 SP50

2 —**North Oxford** Banbury Rd OX2 8EZ

3 — ☎ 01865 554924 🖺 01865 515921

4 —**Gently undulating parkland course.**

5 —*18 holes, 5736yds, Par 67, SSS 67, Course record 62. Club membership 700.*

6 — Visitors at weekends & bank holidays may only play after 4pm. **Societies** must contact in advance. **Green Fees** not — 8

7 — confirmed. **Cards** 🖃 💳 🔙 **Prof** Robert Harris **Facilities** — 9

10 — ⊗ 🍴 ⬛ ♨ ♀ ⚒ 🏠 🎯 ⚡ **Conf** Facilities Available — 11

12 — **Location** 3m N of city centre on A423 — 13

Hotel ★★★ 66% The Oxford Hotel, Godstow Rd, Wolvercote Roundabout, OXFORD — 14
☎ 01865 489988 173 en suite

The AA Golf Course Guide provides information about a large selection of courses across Britain and Ireland. The golf courses are selected by the AA and their entry in the Guide is free of charge. The Guide is updated every year for new courses, changes, closures and new features. Entries include the contact details for each course, a brief description of the course, and details of green fees, leisure, club, catering or conference facilities. AA recommended accommodation follows most entries. To avoid disappointment when visiting a golf course we recommend that you telephone in advance; please mention the AA Golf Course Guide when you make an enquiry.

1 Town name and map reference The directory is organised alphabetically by county then town or village name. The atlas and index show the locations of courses. The map reference includes the atlas page number and National Grid reference. The grid references for the Republic of Ireland are unique to this atlas.

2 Club name Where the club name appears in italics we have been unable to verify current course details with the club. You should check any details with the club in advance of your visit.

3 Contact details

4 Description A brief description of the course or courses, with significant features highlighted.

5 Course statistics The number of holes, yardage, par, Standard Scratch Score, Course Record, and number of club members.

6 Visitor information Details of booking requirements or restrictions. A small number of courses included in this guide are not open to visitors, however we have included limited details for information.

7 Society information Details of booking requirements or restrictions for societies.

8 Green fees The most up-to-date green fees are given, including any variations or restrictions. Where green fees are not confirmed you should contact the club for current details. An asterisk * denotes 2005 fees.

9 Credit cards symbols The credit cards accepted by the club.

10 Professional The name of the club professional(s).

11 Facilities Please see the key to symbols on the right.

12 Conference facilities The available conference facilities are noted, and corporate hospitality days.

13 Location The location of the club is given in relation to the nearest town or motorway junction. Many golf courses are in rural locations and we do not provide detailed directions in the Guide. You should contact the club for further details.

14 Accommodation AA recognised hotel or guest accommodation is provided for most entries. This does not imply that the hotel offers special terms for the golf club. The Star or Diamond rating, Quality Assessment (%) score and AA Rosette award appear as applicable. (See page 6 for more details of AA ratings.) Contact details and the number of rooms are given.

Photographs and advertisements
Only golf courses and hotels selected for the Guide can enhance their entry with a photograph or to take a display advertisement.

Recommendations
If you want to recommend a new course for the Guide, please write to:

The Editor
AA Golf Course Guide
Fanum House Floor 14
Basingstoke
Hampshire RG21 4EA

CONTENTS

Key to symbols

☎ Telephone number

🖹 Fax number

€ Euro (Republic of Ireland only)

⊗ Lunch

)Ⅲ Dinner

🍴 Bar snacks

☕ Tea/coffee

⚱ Bar open midday and evenings

🛏 Accommodation at club

⚲ Changing rooms

🏠 Well-stocked shop

🏌 Clubs for hire

🏌 Motorised cart/trolley for hire

🛺 Buggies for hire

🏌 Trolley for hire

𝑓 Driving range

★ AA Star classification for hotels

◉ AA Rosette award

♦ AA Diamond guest house
classification

🏠 Town House Hotel

🏨 Country House Hotel

🏠 Restaurant with rooms

Ⓤ Hotel not yet rated by the AA

⇧ Travel Accommodation

Hotels & guest accommodation

Many golf course entries in the Guide are followed by details of a nearby AA recognised hotel. In some cases the golf course will be in the grounds of the hotel. Most of the hotels fall within the two, three and four-Star classifications. Where there is no nearby AA recognised hotel, AA guest accommodation will be recommended, with a classification from one to five Diamonds.

Where golf courses offer club accommodation the bed symbol appears under Facilities. This is simply listed as an option for readers wishing to stay at the course. Unless the club accommodation has an AA Star or Diamond classification, the only AA recognised accommodation is the hotel or guest house that follows the entry.

Championship courses

Major championship courses have a full-page entry in the Guide with more extensive details. A selection of AA recognised hotels is given for these courses.

Selected courses

Green boxes in the Guide highlight selected courses considered to be of particular merit or interest. These may include historic clubs, particularly testing or enjoyable courses, or those in holiday areas popular with visiting golfers.

The selection is not exhaustive nor totally objective; but it is independent - courses cannot pay to have an entry in the Guide, nor can they pay to have a highlighted entry. Highlighted courses do not represent any formal category on quality or other grounds.

AA classifications and awards

These ratings ensure that your accommodation meets the AA's highest standards of cleanliness with the emphasis on professionalism, proper booking procedures, and a prompt and efficient service.

AA Star classification

★ If you stay in a one-Star hotel you should expect relatively informal yet competent service and an adequate range of facilities, including a television in the lounge or bedroom, and a reasonable choice of hot and cold dishes. The majority of bedrooms are en suite with a bath or shower room always available.

★ ★ A two-Star hotel is run by professionally presented staff and offers at least one restaurant or dining room for breakfast and dinner.

★ ★ ★ Three-Star hotels have direct-dial telephones, a wide selection of drinks in the bar, and last orders for dinner no earlier than 8pm.

★ ★ ★ ★ A four-Star hotel is characterised by uniformed, well-trained staff, additional services, a night porter and a serious approach to cuisine.

★ ★ ★ ★ ★ Finally, and most luxurious of all, the five-Star hotel offers many extra facilities, attentive staff, top-quality rooms and a full concierge service. A wide selection of drinks, including cocktails, are available in the bar, and the impressive menu reflects and complements the hotel's own style of cooking.

The Quality Assessment
score appears after the Star rating for hotels in this Guide. This is an additional assessment made by AA hotel inspectors, covering everything the hotel has to offer, including hospitality. The Quality Assessment score allows a quick comparison between hotels with the same Star rating: the higher the score the better the hotel.

★ AA Top Hotel Awards
The AA Top Hotel Awards recognise the very best hotels in Britain and Ireland across all ratings. Such a hotel will offer outstanding levels of quality, comfort, cleanliness and customer care, and will serve food of at least one-Rosette standard. Top Hotels are identified by their red Stars. No Quality Assessment score is shown for hotels with red Stars.

AA hotel and guest accommodation inspections

The AA inspects and classifies hotels and guest accommodation under quality standards agreed between the AA, VisitBritain and the RAC. Hotels receive a classification from one to five Stars, and guest accommodation establishments receive from one to five Diamonds. AA recognised establishments pay an annual fee that varies according to the classification and the number of bedrooms. The establishments receive an unannounced inspection from a qualified AA inspector who recommends the appropriate classification. Return visits check that standards are maintained; the classification is not transferable if an establishment changes hands. The AA Hotel Guide and AA Bed & Breakfast Guide, published annually, give further details of AA recognised establishments and the classification schemes. Details of AA recognised hotels, guest accommodation, restaurants and pubs can be found at www.theAA.com.

AA Diamond classification

◆ The AA's Diamond awards cover bed and breakfast establishments only, reflecting guest accommodation at five grades of quality, with one Diamond indicating the simplest and five Diamonds the upper end of the scale. The criteria for eligibility are guest care and quality rather than extra facilities. Establishments are visited by qualified AA inspectors to ensure that the accommodation, food and hospitality meet the AA's exacting standards.

Guests should receive a prompt professional check in and check out, comfortable accommodation equipped to modern standards, regularly changed bedding and towels, a sufficient hot water supply at all times, good well-prepared meals, and a full English or continental breakfast.

◆ Red Diamonds indicate the best places among three, four and five-Diamond ratings.

AA Rosette awards

Out of around 40,000 restaurants, the AA awards Rosettes to some 1800 as the best in the UK.

The following is an outline of what to expect from restaurants with AA Rosette awards.

Excellent local restaurants serving food prepared with care, understanding and skill, using good quality ingredients.

The best local restaurants, which aim for and achieve higher standards and better consistency, and where a greater precision is apparent in the cooking. There will be obvious attention to the selection of quality ingredients.

◉ ◉ ◉
Outstanding restaurants that demand recognition well beyond their local area.

Among the very best restaurants in the British Isles, where the cooking demands national recognition.

◉ ◉ ◉ ◉ ◉
The finest restaurants in the British Isles, where the cooking compares with the best in the world.

Driving ranges

ENGLAND

Bedfordshire
BEDFORD
Bedfordshire Golf Club   21
Mowsbury Golf Club   21
The Bedford Golf Club   21
COLMWORTH
Colmworth & North
    Bedfordshire Golf Course   22
LUTON
Stockwood Park Golf Club   23
SHEFFORD
Beadlow Manor Hotel &
    Golf & Country Club   23
TILSWORTH
Tilsworth Golf Centre   24
WYBOSTON
Wyboston Lakes   24

Berkshire
ASCOT
The Berkshire Golf Club   24
Lavender Park Golf Centre   24
Mill Ride Golf Club   24
BINFIELD
Blue Mountain Golf Centre   25
CHADDLEWORTH
West Berkshire Golf Course   25
MAIDENHEAD
Bird Hills Golf Centre   26
MORTIMER
Wokefield Park Golf Club   26
READING
Hennerton Golf Club   27
SINDLESHAM
Bearwood Golf Club   28
WOKINGHAM
Downshire Golf Course   28
Sand Martins Golf Club   28

Bristol
BRISTOL
Bristol and Clifton Golf Club   30

Buckinghamshire
AYLESBURY
Aylesbury Golf Centre   31
BEACONSFIELD
Beaconsfield Golf Club   31
BLETCHLEY
Windmill Hill Golf Centre   31
BURNHAM
The Lambourne Club   32
CHALFONT ST GILES
Oakland Park Golf Club   32
DENHAM
Buckinghamshire Golf Club   33
IVER
Iver Golf Club   34

Richings Park Golf &
    Country Club   34
LITTLE BRICKHILL
Woburn Golf & Country Club   35
LOUDWATER
Wycombe Heights Golf Centre   34
MARLOW
Harleyford Golf Club   34
MENTMORE
Mentmore Golf &
    Country Club   36
MILTON KEYNES
Abbey Hill Golf Club   36
STOKE POGES
Stoke Park Club   36
STOWE
Silverstone Golf Course   36
WAVENDON
Wavendon Golf Centre   37
WEXHAM STREET
Wexham Park Golf Club   37
WING
Aylesbury Vale Golf Club   37

Cambridgeshire
BRAMPTON
Brampton Park Golf Club   38
CAMBRIDGE
The Gog Magog Golf Club   38
HEMINGFORD ABBOTS
Hemingford Abbots
    Golf Course   38
LONGSTANTON
Cambridge Golf Club   38
MELDRETH
Malton Golf Course   39
PETERBOROUGH
Elton Furze Golf Club   39
Peterborough Milton
    Golf Club   39
PIDLEY
Lakeside Lodge Golf Club   39
RAMSEY
Old Nene Golf &
    Country Club   40
ST NEOTS
Abbotsley Golf Hotel &
    Country Club   40
THORNEY
Thorney Golf Centre   40

Cheshire
ANTROBUS
Antrobus Golf Club   41
CHESTER
De Vere Carden Park Hotel
    Golf Resort & Spa   42
Eaton Golf Club   42
Vicars Cross Golf Club   42
DELAMERE
Delamere Forest Golf Club   43
KNUTSFORD
Heyrose Golf Club   44
Mere Golf & Country Club   44
MACCLESFIELD
The Tytherington Club   45
TARPORLEY
Portal Golf & Country Club   47
WILMSLOW
De Vere Mottram Hall   48
Styal Golf Club   49
WINWICK
Alder Root Golf Club   49

Cornwall & Isles of Scilly
BODMIN
Lanhydrock Golf Club   49
CAMELFORD
Bowood Park Hotel &
    Golf Course   50
CONSTANTINE BAY
Trevose Golf Club   50
FALMOUTH
Falmouth Golf Club   51
LAUNCESTON
Trethorne Golf Club   52
LOSTWITHIEL
Lostwithiel Hotel, Golf &
    Country Club   53
MAWGAN PORTH
Merlin Golf Course   53
ROCK
St Enodoc Golf Club   55
ST AUSTELL
Porthpean Golf Club   55
St Austell Golf Club   55
ST MELLION
St Mellion Hotel, Golf &
    Country Club   57
ST MINVER
Roserrow Golf &
    Country Club   56

Driving ranges

Driving ranges

continued

Driving ranges

Driving ranges

Where you'll find a real passion for golf

Those with a passion for golf will love De Vere – nine outstanding four and five star resort hotels, including four-time Ryder Cup host The De Vere Belfry and championship venues such as De Vere Carden Park and De Vere Slaley Hall. Each offers first class golf facilities… as well as heated pools, spas, fine cuisine and much more. So indulge any passions perfectly – with golf breaks at De Vere Hotels.

For your **FREE** BROCHURE, call

01928 714068

quoting AA5
or visit www.DeVereGolf.co.uk

DE VERE HOTELS
Hotels of character, run with pride

England

BEDFORDSHIRE

ASPLEY GUISE   Map 04 SP93

Aspley Guise & Woburn Sands West Hill
MK17 8DX
☎ 01908 583596 📠 01908 583596 (Secretary)
A fine undulating course in expansive heathland interspersed with many attractive clumps of gorse, broom and bracken. Some well-established silver birch are a feature. The really tough 7th, 8th and 9th holes complete the first half.
18 holes, 6079yds, Par 71, SSS 70, Course record 65. Club membership 590.
Visitors with member only weekends. **Societies** Wed, Fri, normally booked six months ahead. **Green Fees** £30 per round weekdays (£46 weekends). **Cards** 💳 💳 💳 **Prof** Colin Clingan **Course Designer** Sandy Herd **Facilities** ⊗ by arrangement 🎿 by arrangement 🏌 ♟ ♨ 🏠 ↑ 🛺 🏌 **Conf** Corporate Hospitality Days available **Location** M1 junct 13, 2m W

Hotel ★★★ 69% Moore Place Hotel, The Square, ASPLEY GUISE ☎ 01908 282000 39 en suite 27 annexe en suite

BEDFORD   Map 04 TL04

Bedford Great Denham Golf Village, Carnoustie Dr, Biddenham MK40 4FF
☎ 01234 320022 📠 01234 320023
e-mail: thebedford@btopenworld.com
American styled course with 89 bunkers, eight large water features and large contoured USPGA specification greens. Built on sand and gravel the course is open all year round.
18 holes, 6471yds, Par 72, SSS 72, Course record 65. Club membership 500.
Visitors contact in advance, weekends after 10.30am **Societies** phone for details. **Green Fees** £30 per 18 holes (£40 weekends). **Cards** 💳 💳 💳 💳 **Prof** Zac Thompson **Course Designer** David Pottage **Facilities** ⊗ 🎿 🏌 ♟ ♨ 🏠 ↑ 🛺 🏌 **Conf** fac available Corporate Hospitality Days available **Location** 2.5m W of Bedford off A428

Hotel ↑ Innkeeper's Lodge Bedford, 403 Goldington Rd, BEDFORD ☎ 0870 243 0500 & 01234 272707 📠 01234 343926 47 en suite

Bedford & County Green Ln, Clapham MK41 6ET
☎ 01234 352617 📠 01234 357195
A mature undulating parkland course established in 1912 with views over Bedford and surrounding countryside. Beware of the brook that discreetly meanders through the 7th, 10th, 11th and 15th holes. The testing par 4 15th is one of the most challenging holes in the area.
18 holes, 6420yds, Par 70, SSS 70, Course record 66. Club membership 600.
Visitors handicap certificate; with member only weekends. **Societies** Mon, Tue, Thu, Fri; phone in advance. **Green Fees** £32 per day, £26 per round weekdays only. **Prof** R Tattersall **Facilities** ⊗ 🎿 by arrangement 🏌 ♟ ♨ 🏠 🏌 **Conf** Corporate Hospitality Days available **Location** 2m N off A6 in Clapham

Hotel ↑ Premier Travel Inn Bedford, Priory Country Park, Barkers Ln, BEDFORD ☎ 08701 977030 32 en suite

Bedfordshire Spring Ln, Stagsden MK43 8SR
☎ 01234 822555 📠 01234 825052
e-mail: office@bedfordshiregolf.com
A challenging 18-hole course on undulating terrain with established trees and woods and water hazards. Magnificent views in all directions.
18 holes, 6565yds, Par 70, SSS 72, Course record 65. Academy Course: 9 holes, 1354yds, Par 28, SSS 28. Club membership 700.
Visitors contact in advance; not 18-hole course weekends except with member. **Societies** phone in advance or confirm in writing. **Green Fees** £40 per day, £30 per 18 holes; 9-hole course £6 (£8 weekends). **Cards** 💳 💳 💳 **Prof** David Armor **Course Designer** Cameron Sinclair **Facilities** ⊗ 🎿 by arrangement 🏌 ♟ ♨ 🏠 ↑ 🛺 🏌 (**Conf** fac available Corporate Hospitality Days available **Location** 3m W of Bedford on A422 at Stagsden

Hotel ↑ Travelodge Bedford South West, Beancroft Rd Junction, MARSTON MORETAINE ☎ 08700 850 950 54 en suite

Mowsbury Cleat Hill, Kimbolton Rd, Ravensden MK41 8DQ
☎ 01234 771041 & 216374 (pro) 📠 01234 771041
e-mail: mgc@freenet.co.uk
18 holes, 6451yds, Par 72, SSS 71, Course record 66.
Course Designer Hawtree **Location** 2m N of town centre on B660
Telephone for further details

Hotel ↑ Innkeeper's Lodge Bedford, 403 Goldington Rd, BEDFORD ☎ 0870 243 0500 & 01234 272707 📠 01234 343926 47 en suite

CHALGRAVE   Map 04 TL02

Chalgrave Manor Dunstable Rd LU5 6JN
☎ 01525 876556 & 876554 📠 01525 876556
e-mail: chalgravegolf@onetel.net.uk
Undulating parkland course set in 150 acres of Bedfordshire countryside. No two consecutive holes play in the same direction. Four holes have water hazards including the signature tenth hole, playing 130yds across water to a sloping green. The par 5 9th, at 621yds, is one of the longest holes in the country.
18 holes, 6382yds, Par 70, SSS 70, Course record 69. Club membership 550.
Visitors dress code smart casual; after 1pm weekends. **Societies** apply in writing or phone, in advance. **Green Fees** £20 per round (£30 weekends & bank holidays). **Cards** 💳 💳 💳 💳 **Prof** Geoff Swain **Course Designer** M Palmer **Facilities** ⊗ 🏌 ♟ ♨ 🏠 🛺 🏌 **Conf** fac available Corporate Hospitality Days available **Location** M1 junct 12, A5120 through Toddington, signed 1m

Hotel ★★★ 63% Old Palace Lodge, Church St, DUNSTABLE ☎ 01582 662201 68 en suite

> **Booking a tee time is always advisable.**

COLMWORTH
Map 04 TL15

Colmworth & North Bedfordshire
New Rd MK44 2NN
☎ 01234 378181 📠 01234 376678
e-mail: colmworth@btopenworld.com
An easy walking course with well-bunkered greens, opened in 1991. The course is often windy and plays longer than the yardage suggests. Water comes into play on three holes.

18 holes, 6435yds, Par 72, SSS 71, Course record 69. Club membership 200.
Visitors advisable to book in advance; weekends after 9.30am. Societies phone in advance. Cards 🌐 💳 💳 💳
🎾 Prof Graham Bithrey Course Designer John Glasgow Facilities ⊗ ℳ by arrangement 🍴 🍷 ♀ ⛾ 🏠 ᵀ 🏌 🛺
♂ 🏐 Leisure fishing, par 3 course. Conf Corporate Hospitality Days available Location off A1 between Bedford & St Neots

Hotel ★★★ 64% Corus hotel Bedford, Cardington Rd, BEDFORD ☎ 0870 609 6108 48 en suite

DUNSTABLE
Map 04 TL02

Dunstable Downs Whipsnade Rd LU6 2NB
☎ 01582 604472 📠 01582 478700
e-mail: dunstabledownsgc@btconnect.com
A fine downland course set on two levels with far-reaching views and frequent sightings of graceful gliders. The 9th hole is one of the best short holes in the country.
18 holes, 6251yds, Par 70, SSS 70, Course record 64. Club membership 600.
Visitors Mon, Tue, Thu, Fri; with member only weekends; handicap certificate. Societies apply in advance. Green Fees £30 per round. Prof Michael Weldon Course Designer James Braid Facilities ⊗ ℳ 🍴 🍷 ♀ ⛾ 🏠 🛺
♂ Conf Corporate Hospitality Days available Location 2m S off B4541

Hotel ★★★ 63% Old Palace Lodge, Church St, DUNSTABLE ☎ 01582 662201 68 en suite

Griffin Chaul End Rd, Caddington LU1 4AX
☎ 01582 415573 📠 01582 415314
e-mail: griffin@griffingolfclub.fsbusiness.co.uk
A challenging 18-hole course with ponds and lakes on top of Blows Downs.
18 holes, 6240yds, Par 71, SSS 70.
Club membership 470.

Griffin Golf Club

Visitors Mon-Fri & after 2pm weekends. Societies midweek & weekends pm summer, book by phone. Green Fees not confirmed. Facilities ⊗ 🍴 🍷 ♀ ⛾ 🏠 🛺 Conf Corporate Hospitality Days available Location M1 junct 11, after 0.5m exit left at Tesco rdbt, towards Dunstable

Hotel ★★★ 63% Old Palace Lodge, Church St, DUNSTABLE ☎ 01582 662201 68 en suite

LEIGHTON BUZZARD
Map 04 SP92

Leighton Buzzard Plantation Rd LU7 3JF
☎ 01525 244800 (Office) 📠 01525 244801
e-mail: lbgc.secretary1@btopenworld.com
Mature parkland and heathland course with easy walking. The 17th and 18th holes are challenging tree-lined finishing holes with tight fairways. The par 3 11th is signature hole.

18 holes, 6101yds, Par 71, SSS 70, Course record 63. Club membership 700.
Visitors play yellow tees; not Tue (Ladies Day); with member only weekends & bank holidays; handicap certificate unless with member. Societies booking required. Green Fees terms on application. Prof Maurice Campbell Facilities ⊗ ℳ 🍴 🍷 ♀ ⛾ 🏠 🐴 🛺 ♂ Conf fac available Location 1.5m N of town centre off A4146

Hotel ★★★ 63% Old Palace Lodge, Church St, DUNSTABLE ☎ 01582 662201 68 en suite

LOWER STONDON
Map 04 TL13

Mount Pleasant Station Rd SG16 6JL
☎ 01462 850999
e-mail: davidsimsmpgolf@aol.com
Undulating meadowland course with three ponds in play and many tree plantations. A deep ditch, sometimes with water, runs through the middle of the course and is crossed four times per nine holes. The main feature of the course is its presentation and

Continued

Continued

superb greens. The course is seldom closed by bad weather.
9 holes, 6185yds, Par 70, SSS 70, Course record 68.
Club membership 300.
Visitors book from two days in advance, booking advisable weekends & evenings May-Sep. **Societies** phone or apply in writing. **Green Fees** £15 per 18 holes, £8.50 per nine holes (£19/£11 weekends). **Cards** 🌐 💳 💳 💳 🌐 🔲 **Prof** Mike Roberts **Course Designer** Derek Young **Facilities** ⊗ ⫸ ⅃ ⅃ 🏌 ⅃ ⅃ ⅃ 🏌 🏌 **Leisure** undercover driving nets. **Conf** Corporate Hospitality Days available **Location** 0.75m W of A600, 4m N of Hitchin

Hotel ★★★ Menzies Flitwick Manor, Church Rd, FLITWICK ☎ 01525 712242 17 en suite

LUTON   Map 04 TL02

South Beds Warden Hill Rd LU2 7AE
☎ 01582 591500 📠 01582 495381
e-mail: office@southbedsgolfclub.co.uk
An 18-hole and a nine-hole chalk downland course, slightly undulating.
Galley Hill Course: 18 holes, 6438yds, Par 71, SSS 71, Course record 64.
Warden Hill Course: 9 holes, 2425yds, Par 32, SSS 32.
Club membership 1000.
Visitors contact in advance; handicap certificate for Galley Hill Course. **Societies** phone for details. **Green Fees** phone for details. **Cards** 🌐 💳 💳 🌐 **Prof** Eddie Cogle **Facilities** ⊗ ⫸ ⅃ ⅃ 🏌 ⅃ ⅃ 🏌 **Conf** Corporate Hospitality Days available **Location** 3m N of Luton on A6

Hotel ★★★ 60% The Chiltern Hotel, Waller Av, LUTON ☎ 0870 609 6120 91 en suite

Stockwood Park London Rd LU1 4LX
☎ 01582 413704 (pro shop)
Well-laid out municipal parkland course with established trees and several challenging holes.
18 holes, 6049yds, Par 69, SSS 69, Course record 67.
Club membership 600.
Visitors no restrictions. **Societies** Mon, Tue, Thu, phone for application. **Green Fees** not confirmed. **Cards** 🌐 💳 **Prof** Glyn McCarthy **Facilities** ⊗ ⫸ ⅃ ⅃ 🏌 ⅃ ⅃ 🏌 **Location** 1m S

Hotel ★★★ 60% The Chiltern Hotel, Waller Av, LUTON ☎ 0870 609 6120 91 en suite

MILLBROOK   Map 04 TL03

Millbrook Millbrook Village MK45 2JB
☎ 01525 840252 📠 01525 406249
e-mail: info@themillbrook.com
Long parkland course, on rolling countryside high above the Bedfordshire plains. Laid out on well-drained sandy soil with many fairways lined with silver birch, pine and larch. The course provides a continuous test of the tee where length and accuracy pay a huge premium.
18 holes, 7021yds, Par 74, SSS 73, Course record 68.
Club membership 510.
Visitors contact in advance; not am weekends. **Societies** phone for details 01525 402269. **Green Fees** phone for details. **Prof** Geraint Dixon **Course Designer** William Sutherland **Facilities** ⊗ ⫸ ⅃ ⅃ 🏌 ⅃ ⅃ 🏌 **Conf** fac available Corporate Hospitality Days available **Location** M1 junct 12/13, A507 Woburn-Ampthill road

Hotel ★★★ Menzies Flitwick Manor, Church Rd, FLITWICK ☎ 01525 712242 17 en suite

PAVENHAM   Map 04 SP95

Pavenham Park MK43 7PE
☎ 01234 822202 📠 01234 826602
e-mail: kolvengolf@ukonline.co.uk
Mature, undulating parkland course with fast contoured greens.
18 holes, 6400yds, Par 72, SSS 71, Course record 63.
Club membership 790.
Visitors weekdays; with member only weekends. **Societies** phone in advance. **Green Fees** not confirmed. **Cards** 🌐 💳 🔲 **Prof** Zac Thompson **Course Designer** Zac Thompson **Facilities** ⊗ ⫸ ⅃ ⅃ 🏌 ⅃ ⅃ 🏌 **Conf** fac available Corporate Hospitality Days available **Location** 1.5m from A6, N of Bedford

Hotel 🏠 Travelodge Bedford South West, Beancroft Rd Junction, MARSTON MORETAINE ☎ 08700 850 950 54 en suite

SANDY   Map 04 TL14

John O'Gaunt Sutton Park SG19 2LY
☎ 01767 260360 📠 01767 262834
e-mail: admin@johnogauntgolfclub.co.uk
Two magnificent parkland courses - John O'Gaunt and Carthagena - covering a gently undulating and tree-lined terrain. The John O'Gaunt course makes the most of numerous natural features, notably a river which crosses the fairways of four holes. The Carthagena course has larger greens, longer tees and from the back tees is a challenging course.
John O'Gaunt Course: 18 holes, 6513yds, Par 71, SSS 71, Course record 64.
Carthagena Course: 18 holes, 5869yds, Par 69, SSS 69.
Club membership 1500.
Visitors contact in advance. **Societies** booking required **Green Fees** £50 per day, £35 per round (£60 per day/round weekends & bank holidays). **Prof** Lee Scarbrow **Course Designer** Hawtree **Facilities** ⊗ ⫸ ⅃ ⅃ 🏌 ⅃ ⅃ 🏌 **Conf** Corporate Hospitality Days available **Location** 3m NE of Biggleswade on B1040

Hotel ★★ 64% Abbotsley Golf Hotel & Country Club, Potton Rd, Eynesbury Hardwicke, ST NEOTS ☎ 01480 474000 42 annexe en suite

SHEFFORD   Map 04 TL13

Beadlow Manor Hotel & Golf & Country Club SG17 5PH
☎ 01525 860800 📠 01525 861345
e-mail: beadlowmanor@talk21.co.uk
A 36-hole golf and leisure complex. The Baroness Manhattan and the Baron Manhattan courses are undulating with water hazards on numerous holes. These are good challenging courses for both the beginner and low handicap player.
Baroness Course: 18 holes, 6072yds, Par 71, SSS 69, Course record 67.
Baron Course: 18 holes, 6619yds, Par 73, SSS 72, Course record 67.
Club membership 850.
Visitors book in advance; dress code. **Societies** apply in writing or phone in advance. **Green Fees** Baroness: £15 per round (£20 weekends); Baron: £15 per round (£20 weekends). **Cards** 🌐 💳 💳 💳 🌐 🔲 **Prof** Gordon

Morrison **Facilities** ⊗ ⋙ ᒪ 🖴 ♌ ♈ 🖴 ☞ 🖴 ❧ 🖴 🖉 ₹
Conf fac available Corporate Hospitality Days available
Location on A507

Hotel ★★★ Menzies Flitwick Manor, Church Rd,
FLITWICK ☎ 01525 712242 17 en suite

TILSWORTH   Map 04 SP92

Tilsworth Dunstable Rd LU7 9PU
☎ 01525 210721/2 ▤ 01525 210465
e-mail: nick@tilsworthgolf.co.uk
The course is in first-class condition and, although not a
long course, is particularly demanding and challenging
where the key is straight driving. The course has its
own Amen Corner between the 14th and 16th holes,
which will challenge all golfers. Panoramic views of
three counties from the 6th tee.
18 holes, 5306yds, Par 69, SSS 66, Course record 62.
Club membership 400.
Visitors book up to seven days in advance; not before
10am Sun. **Societies** weekdays; apply in advance to G
Brandon-White **Green Fees** £16 for 18 holes (£18
weekends & bank holidays). **Cards** 🖃 📰 📇 🔄 🖳 **Prof**
Nick Webb **Facilities** ⊗ ⋙ ᒪ 🖴 ♌ ♈ 🖴 ☞ 🖴 ❧ 🖴 🖉 ₹
Conf Corporate Hospitality Days available **Location** 0.5m
NE off A5, N of Dunstable

Hotel ★★★ 63% Old Palace Lodge, Church St,
DUNSTABLE ☎ 01582 662201 68 en suite

WYBOSTON   Map 04 TL15

Wyboston Lakes MK44 3AL
☎ 01480 212625 ▤ 01480 223000
e-mail: venue@wybostonlakes.co.uk
Parkland course, with narrow fairways, small greens,
set around four lakes and a river which provide the
biggest challenge on this very scenic course.

18 holes, 5955yds, Par 70, SSS 69, Course record 65.
Club membership 300.
Visitors booking system weekends, book no more than
eight days in advance. **Societies** phone in advance. **Green
Fees** phone for details. **Cards** 🖃 📰 **Prof** Paul Ashwell
Course Designer N Oakden **Facilities** ⊗ ⋙ ᒪ 🖴 ♌ ♈
🖴 ☞ 🖴 ❧ 🖴 🖉 ₹ **Leisure** heated indoor swimming
pool, fishing, sauna, solarium, gymnasium, watersports.
Conf fac available Corporate Hospitality Days available
Location 1m S of St Neots off A1/A428

Hotel ★★★ 64% Corus hotel Bedford, Cardington Rd,
BEDFORD ☎ 0870 609 6108 48 en suite

ASCOT   Map 04 SU96

Berkshire Swinley Rd SL5 8AY
☎ 01344 621495 ▤ 01344 623328
Two classic heathland courses, with splendid tree-lined
fairways, that have remained the same since they were
constructed in 1928. The Red Course, on slightly higher
ground, is a little longer than the Blue. It has an
unusual assortment of holes, six par 3s, six par 4s and
six par 5s, the short holes, particularly the 10th and
16th, being the most intimidating. The Blue Course
starts with a par 3 and shares with the 16th the
reputation of being the finest holes of the 18.
Red Course: 18 holes, 6379yds, Par 72, SSS 71.
Blue Course: 18 holes, 6260yds, Par 71, SSS 71.
Visitors by arrangement **Societies** applications in writing
only & must be registered. **Green Fees** £110 per day, £80
per round. **Cards** 🖃 📰 🖳 **Prof** P Anderson **Course
Designer** H Fowler **Facilities** ⊗ ᒪ 🖴 ♌ ♈ 🖴 ☞ 🖴 ❧ 🖴
🖉 ₹ **Conf** Corporate Hospitality Days available **Location**
M3 junct 3, on A332 2.5m NW

Hotel ★★★★ 66% The Berystede, Bagshot Rd,
Sunninghill, ASCOT ☎ 0870 400 8111 90 en suite

Lavender Park Swinley Rd SL5 8BD
☎ 01344 893344
e-mail: lavenderpark@yahoo.com
Public parkland course, ideal for the short game
featuring challenging narrow fairways. Driving range
with nine-hole par 3 course, floodlit until 10pm.
9 holes, 1102yds, Par 27, SSS 28.
Visitors no restrictions. **Societies** notice preferred. **Green
Fees** not confirmed. **Cards** 🖃 📰 📇 🔄 🖳 **Prof**
David Johnson **Facilities** 🖴 ♌ ♈ 🖴 ☞ 🖉 ₹ **Leisure** snooker.
Location 1.5m W of Ascot, off the A329 on the B3017

Hotel ★★★★ 66% The Berystede, Bagshot Rd,
Sunninghill, ASCOT ☎ 0870 400 8111 90 en suite

Mill Ride Mill Ride SL5 8LT
☎ 01344 886777 ▤ 01344 886820
e-mail: c.sheffield@mill-ride.com
Formerly a prestigious polo club and stud of King
George V, this 18-hole course combines links and
parkland styles. The manicured and cross cut fairways
intermingle with lakes and the mounding and hollows
which gives the course a unique parkland design
coupled with an inland links feel to the starting and
closing holes.

Continued

18 holes, 6807yds, Par 72, SSS 72, Course record 64. Club membership 350.
Visitors restricted weekends; contact in advance. **Societies** apply in advance. **Green Fees** terms on application. **Cards** ▦ ▦ ▦ 🛒 ▦ 🂠 🖭 **Prof** Terry Wild **Course Designer** Donald Steel **Facilities** ⊗ ⅷ ⅃ ☕ ♥ ♀ ⚒ 🏠 🏌 ⚙ 🎱 ⚔ **Leisure** sauna. **Conf** fac available Corporate Hospitality Days available **Location** 2m W of Ascot

Hotel ★★★★ 66% The Berystede, Bagshot Rd, Sunninghill, ASCOT ☎ 0870 400 8111 90 en suite

Royal Ascot Winkfield Rd SL5 7LJ
☎ 01344 625175 🖹 01344 872330
e-mail: golf@royalascotgc.fsnet.co.uk
Heathland course inside Ascot racecourse and exposed to weather.
18 holes, 5716yds, Par 68, SSS 68, Course record 65. Club membership 620.
Visitors with member only **Societies** phone for provisional booking. **Green Fees** £15 per round (£18.50 weekends) with member only. **Prof** Alistair White **Course Designer** JH Taylor **Facilities** ⊗ ⅷ ♥ ♀ ⚒ 🏠 ⚙ **Location** 0.5m N on A330

Hotel ★★★★ 66% The Berystede, Bagshot Rd, Sunninghill, ASCOT ☎ 0870 400 8111 90 en suite

Swinley Forest Coronation Rd SL5 9LE
☎ 01344 874979 (Secretary) 🖹 01344 874733
e-mail: swinleyfgc@aol.com
An attractive and immaculate course of heather and pine situated in the heart of Swinley Forest. The 17th is as good a short hole as will be found, with a bunkered plateau green, and the 12th hole is one of the most challenging par 4s.
18 holes, 6100yds, Par 69, SSS 70, Course record 62. Club membership 350.
Visitors on introduction of a member or by invitation only. **Societies** contact in writing. **Green Fees** not confirmed. **Cards** ▦ ▦ 🖭 **Prof** Stuart Hill **Course Designer** Harry Colt **Facilities** ⊗ ♥ ♀ ⚒ 🏠 ♥ ⚙ ⚔ ⚙ **Leisure** Video studeo. **Conf** Corporate Hospitality Days available **Location** 2m S of Ascot, off 4330

Hotel ★★★★ 66% The Berystede, Bagshot Rd, Sunninghill, ASCOT ☎ 0870 400 8111 90 en suite

Blue Mountain Golf Centre Wood Ln RG42 4EX
☎ 01344 300200 🖹 01344 360960
e-mail: bluemountain@americangolf.uk.com
18 holes, 6097yds, Par 70, SSS 70, Course record 63.
Location M4 junct 10, A329(M) signed Bracknell, B3408 signed Binfield, 2nd rdbt onto 2nd exit, 1st left onto Wood Ln
Telephone for further details

Hotel ★★★★ 73% Coppid Beech, John Nike Way, BRACKNELL ☎ 01344 303333 205 en suite

West Berkshire RG20 7DU
☎ 01488 638574 🖹 01488 638781
Challenging and interesting downland course with views of the Berkshire Downs. The course is bordered by ancient woodland and golfers will find manicured

fairways with well-constructed greens and strategically placed hazards. The testing 627yd 5th hole is one of the longest par 5s in southern England. Bunkers are well placed from tees and around the greens to catch any wayward shots.
18 holes, 7001yds, Par 73, SSS 74. Club membership 650.
Visitors contact in advance; weekends pm only. **Societies** phone in advance. **Green Fees** not confirmed. **Cards** ▦ ▦ ▦ 🖭 **Prof** Paul Simpson **Facilities** ⊗ ♥ ♀ ⚒ 🏠 ⚙ ⚔ **Conf** Corporate Hospitality Days available **Location** 1m S of village off A338

Hotel ★★★ 63% The Chequers Hotel, 6-8 Oxford St, NEWBURY ☎ 01635 38000 46 en suite 11 annexe en suite

Winter Hill Grange Ln SL6 9RP
☎ 01628 527613 (Secretary) 🖹 01628 527479
Parkland course set in a curve of the Thames with wonderful views across the river to Cliveden.

18 holes, 6408yds, Par 72, SSS 71, Course record 63. Club membership 770.
Visitors not weekends am; phone in advance. **Societies** Wed & Fri, phone in advance. **Green Fees** not confirmed. **Cards** ▦ ▦ ▦ 🖭 **Prof** Roger Frost **Course Designer** Charles Lawrie **Facilities** ⊗ ♥ ♀ ⚒ 🏠 ⚙ ⚔ ⚙ **Conf** fac available Corporate Hospitality Days available **Location** 1m NW off B4447

Hotel ★★★★ 71% The Compleat Angler, Marlow Bridge, MARLOW ☎ 0870 400 8100 64 en suite

East Berkshire Ravenswood Ave RG45 6BD
☎ 01344 772041 🖹 01344 777378
e-mail: thesecretary@eastberksgc.fsnet.co.uk
An attractive heathland course with an abundance of heather and pine trees. Walking is easy and the greens are exceptionally good. Some fairways become tight where the heather encroaches on the line of play. The course is testing and demands great accuracy.
18 holes, 6236yds, Par 69, SSS 70. Club membership 766.
Visitors contact in advance; handicap certificate; with member only weekends & bank holidays. **Societies** phone for availability. **Green Fees** £45 per day. **Prof** Jason Brant **Course Designer** P Paxton **Facilities** ⊗ ♥ ♀ ⚒ 🏠 ⚙ 🏌 ⚙ **Location** W side of town centre off B3348

Hotel ★★★★★ Pennyhill Park Hotel & The Spa, London Rd, BAGSHOT ☎ 01276 471774 26 en suite 97 annexe en suite

Continued

DATCHET   Map 04 SU97

Datchet Buccleuch Rd SL3 9BP
☎ 01753 543887 & 541872 🖹 01753 541872
e-mail: secretary@datchetgolfclub.co.uk
Meadowland course, easy walking.
9 holes, 6087yds, Par 70, SSS 69, Course record 63.
Club membership 430.
Visitors not weekends. **Societies** Tue, other times by
arrangement. **Green Fees** not confirmed. **Prof** Ian
Godelman **Facilities** ⊗ ⊪ ⅄ ≡ ♀ ⚐ ⚑ **Location** NW
side of Datchet off B470

....

Hotel ★★★ 74% The Castle Hotel, 18 High St,
WINDSOR ☎ 0870 400 8300 41 en suite 70 annexe
en suite

MAIDENHEAD   Map 04 SU88

Bird Hills Drift Rd, Hawthorn Hill SL6 3ST
☎ 01628 771030 🖹 01628 631023
e-mail: info@birdhills.co.uk
**A gently undulating course with easy walking and many
water hazards. Some challenging holes are the par 5 6th
dog-leg, par 3 9th surrounded by water and bunkers,
and the 16th which is a long uphill par 4 and a two-tier
green.**

18 holes, 6176yds, Par 72, SSS 69, Course record 65.
Club membership 400.
Visitors to book phone seven days in advance; no two balls
weekends am or bank holidays am. **Societies** write or
phone in advance **Green Fees** seasonal charges - ring for
details. **Cards** 📇 📇 📇 💳 🄍 **Prof** Nick Slimming
Facilities ⊗ ⊪ ⅄ ≡ ♀ ⚐ ⚑ 🏸 ⚑ 🏊 **Leisure** pool
tables. **Conf** fac available Corporate Hospitality Days
available **Location** 4m S of M4 junct 8/9 on A330

....

Hotel ★★★ 71% Stirrups Country House, Maidens Green,
BRACKNELL ☎ 01344 882284 30 en suite

Maidenhead Shoppenhangers Rd SL6 2PZ
☎ 01628 624693 🖹 01628 780758
e-mail: manager@maidenheadgolf.co.uk
**A pleasant parkland course with excellent greens and
some challenging holes. The long par 4 4th and short
par 3 13th are only two of the many outstanding aspects
of this course.**
18 holes, 6364yds, Par 70, SSS 70.
Club membership 750.
Visitors not pm Fri or weekends; contact in advance;
handicap certificate. **Societies** contact in writing. **Green
Fees** £35 per day; £30 per round. **Cards** 📇 📇 📇 💳 🄍
Prof Steve Geary **Course Designer** Alex Simpson

Continued

Facilities ⊗ ⅄ ⊪ ≡ ♀ ⚐ ⚑ 🏸 ⚑ **Conf** fac available
Location S side of town centre off A308

....

Hotel ★★★★ Fredrick's Hotel Restaurant Spa,
Shoppenhangers Rd, MAIDENHEAD ☎ 01628 581000
37 en suite

Temple Henley Rd, Hurley SL6 5LH
☎ 01628 824795 🖹 01628 828119
e-mail: templegolfclub@btconnect.com
**An open parkland course offering extensive views over
the Thames Valley. Firm, relatively fast greens, natural
slopes and subtle contours provide a challenging test to
golfers of all abilities. Excellent drainage assures play
during inclement weather.**

18 holes, 6266yds, Par 70, SSS 70.
Club membership 480.
Visitors restricted weekends; contact in advance. **Societies**
contact Secretary for details. **Green Fees** £50 per day; £40
per round (£60/£50 weekends). **Cards** 📇 📇 📇 🄍 **Prof**
James Whiteley **Course Designer** Willie Park (Jnr)
Facilities ⊗ ⅄ ≡ ♀ ⚐ ⚑ 🏸 ⚑ **Conf** Corporate
Hospitality Days available **Location** M4 junct 8/9, A404M
then A4130, signed Henley

....

Hotel ★★★★ 71% The Compleat Angler, Marlow Bridge,
MARLOW ☎ 0870 400 8100 64 en suite

MORTIMER   Map 04 SU66

Wokefield Park Wokefield Park RG7 3AE
☎ 0118 933 4029 🖹 0118 933 4031
e-mail: wokefieldgolf@initialstyle.co.uk
**Set in a prime location amid the peaceful and
picturesque Berkshire countryside. The course
architect has retained the numerous mature trees, and
these, together with the winding streams, nine lakes and
large bunkers, contribute to the beauty and challenge of
this championship course.**
18 holes, 6579yds, Par 72, SSS 72, Course record 65.
Club membership 350.
Visitors subject to availability; phone pro shop 0118 933
4072/4078 to book tee times. **Societies** apply in writing,
phone in advance **Green Fees** £50 per day; £30 per round;
£18 per nine holes (£65/£45/£25 weekends). **Cards** 📇
📇 📇 🄍 **Prof** Gary Smith **Course Designer** Jonathan Gaunt
Facilities ⊗ ⅄ ⊪ ≡ ♀ ⚐ ⚑ 🏸 ⚑ 🏊 **Leisure** hard
tennis courts, heated indoor swimming pool, fishing, sauna,
gymnasium, Jacuzzi. **Conf** fac available Corporate
Hospitality Days available **Location** M4 junct 11, A33
towards Basingstoke. 1st rdbt, 3rd exit towards Grazeley &
Mortimer. After 2.5m & sharp right bend club on right

Continued

Hotel ★★★ 72% Romans Country House Hotel, Little London Rd, SILCHESTER ☎ 0118 970 0421   11 en suite 14 annexe en suite

NEWBURY   Map 04 SU46

Donnington Valley Snelsmore House, Snelsmore Common RG14 3BG
☎ 01635 568140 📠 01635 568141
e-mail: golf@donningtonvalley.co.uk

18 holes, 6353yds, Par 71, SSS 71, Course record 71.
Course Designer Mike Smith **Location** 2m N of Newbury
Telephone for further details

Hotel ★★★★ 77% Donnington Valley Hotel & Golf Course, Old Oxford Rd, Donnington, NEWBURY ☎ 01635 551199   58 en suite

Newbury & Crookham Bury's Bank Rd, Greenham RG19 8BZ
☎ 01635 40035 📠 01635 40045
e-mail: steve.myers@newburygolf.co.uk
A traditional English parkland course, whose tree-lined fairways provide a challenge of consistency and accuracy.
18 holes, 5949yds, Par 69, SSS 68, Course record 63.
Club membership 800.
Visitors with member only weekends & bank holidays; handicap certificate. **Societies** contact in advance. **Green Fees** £40 per day; £35 per round. **Cards** 🔲 **Prof** David Harris **Course Designer** JH Turner **Facilities** ⊗ ⫝̸ ⓛ 🖤 ♀ ⚘ 🏠 𝄔 **Conf** Corporate Hospitality Days available **Location** 4m S of M4 off A339

Hotel ★★★ 63% The Chequers Hotel, 6-8 Oxford St, NEWBURY ☎ 01635 38000   46 en suite   11 annexe en suite

READING   Map 04 SU77

Calcot Park Bath Rd, Calcot RG31 7RN
☎ 0118 942 7124 📠 0118 945 3373
e-mail: info@calcotpark.com
A delightfully sporting, slightly undulating parkland course just outside the town, which celebrates its 75th anniversary in 2005. The subtle borrows on the greens challenge all categories of golfer. Hazards include streams, a lake and many trees. The 6th is a 503yd par 5, with the tee-shot hit downhill over cross-bunkers to a well-guarded green; the 7th (156 yds) is played over the lake to an elevated green and the 13th (also 156yds) requires a carry across a valley to a plateau green.
18 holes, 6216yds, Par 70, SSS 70, Course record 63.
Club membership 730.

Continued

Visitors not weekends & bank holidays; handicap certificate or letter of introduction from club. **Societies** apply in writing. **Green Fees** £50 per day/round. Enquire for off peak rates. **Prof** Mark Grieve **Course Designer** H S Colt **Facilities** ⊗ ⫝̸ ⓛ 🖤 ♀ ⚘ 🏠 𝄔 **Leisure** fishing. **Conf** Corporate Hospitality Days available **Location** 1.5m from M4 junct 12 on A4 towards Reading

Hotel ★★★ 72% The Copper Inn Hotel & Restaurant, PANGBOURNE ☎ 0118 984 2244   14 en suite   8 annexe en suite

Hennerton Crazies Hill Rd, Wargrave RG10 8LT
☎ 0118 940 1000 📠 0118 940 1042
Overlooking the Thames Valley, this course has many existing natural features and a good number of hazards such as bunkers, mature trees and two small lakes. An extended 18-hole course opens autumn 2005.
9 holes, 5460yds, Par 68, SSS 67, Course record 62.
Club membership 450.
Visitors not weekends before 10am; book 48 hours in advance. **Societies** phone or write for information. **Green Fees** £20 per 18 holes; £14 per nine holes (£25/£16 weekends & bank holidays). **Cards** 🔲 🔲 🔲 🔲 **Prof** William Farrow **Course Designer** Col D Beard **Facilities** ⊗ ⓛ 🖤 ♀ ⚘ 🏠 𝄔 𝄖 ҫ **Conf** Corporate Hospitality Days available **Location** signed from A321 Wargrave High St

Hotel ★★★ 67% Red Lion Hotel, Hart St, HENLEY-ON-THAMES ☎ 01491 572161   26 en suite

Mapledurham Chazey Heath, Mapledurham RG4 7UD
☎ 0118 946 3353 📠 0118 946 3363
An 18-hole parkland and woodland course designed by Bob Sandow. Flanked by hedgerows and mature woods, it is testing for players of all levels.
Mapledurham Golf & Health Club: 18 holes, 5700yds, Par 69, SSS 67, Course record 65.
Club membership 750.
Visitors booking required; not am weekends. **Societies** contact in advance. **Green Fees** £20 (£26 weekends) per round. **Cards** 🔲 🔲 🔲 🔲 🔲 **Prof** Tim Gilpin **Course Designer** Robert Sandow **Facilities** ⊗ ⫝̸ ⓛ 🖤 ♀ ⚘ 🏠 𝄔 **Leisure** heated indoor swimming pool, sauna, solarium, gymnasium. **Conf** Corporate Hospitality Days available **Location** on A4074 to Oxford

Hotel ★★★ 78% The French Horn, SONNING ON THAMES ☎ 0118 969 2204   13 en suite   8 annexe en suite

Reading 17 Kidmore End Rd, Emmer Green RG4 8SG
☎ 0118 947 2909 (Secretary) 📠 0118 946 4468
e-mail: secretary@readinggolfclub.com
Pleasant tree-lined parkland course, part hilly and part flat with interesting views and several challenging par 3s. After the opening holes the course moves across the valley. The par 4 5th is played from an elevated tee and although relatively short, the well-placed bunkers and trees come into play. The 470yd par 4 12th is a great hole. It has a slight dog-leg and requires an accurate second shot to hit a well-guarded green. The finishing hole requires two great shots to have any chance of reaching par.
18 holes, 6212yds, Par 70, SSS 70, Course record 65.
Club membership 600.

Continued

Visitors contact the professional; with member only Fri & weekends. **Societies** apply by phone, Tue-Thu. **Green Fees** £45 per day, £30 per round. **Cards** 🌐 💳 💳 💷 📧 🏧 🅿 **Prof** Scott Fotheringham **Course Designer** James Braid **Facilities** ⊗ ⊪ ⎍ ⚑ ♀ ⚲ 🏠 ⚲ **Leisure** indoor nets. **Location** 2m N off B481

Hotel ★★★ 78% The French Horn, SONNING ON THAMES ☎ 0118 969 2204 13 en suite 8 annexe en suite

SINDLESHAM   Map 04 SU76

Bearwood Mole Rd RG41 5DB
☎ 0118 976 0060
e-mail: barrytustin@bearwoodgolf.fsnet.co.uk
Flat parkland course with one water hazard, the 40-acre lake which features on the challenging 6th and 7th holes.
9 holes, 5610yds, Par 70, SSS 68, Course record 66.
Club membership 500.
Visitors not am weekends (contact in advance for weekend bookings). **Societies** apply in writing. **Green Fees** not confirmed. **Cards** 🌐 💳 💳 📧 🅿 **Prof** Barry Tustin **Course Designer** Barry Tustin **Facilities** ⊗ ⎍ ⚑ ♀ ⚲ 🏠 🏧 ⚲ ⚲ **Location** 1m SW on B3030

Hotel ★★★★ 75% Millennium Madejski Hotel Reading, Madejski Stadium, READING
☎ 0118 925 3500 140 en suite

SONNING   Map 04 SU77

Sonning Duffield Rd RG4 6GJ
☎ 0118 969 3332 📠 0118 944 8409
e-mail: secretary@sonning-golf-club.co.uk
A quality parkland course & the scene of many county championships. Wide fairways, not over-bunkered, & very good greens. Holes of changing character through wooded belts. Four challenging par 4s over 450yds.
18 holes, 6366yds, Par 70, SSS 70, Course record 65.
Club membership 750.
Visitors not weekends; handicap certificate or proof of membership of another club. **Societies** Wed, min 16, apply in writing. **Green Fees** £40.50 before 10.30am or £30.50 after 10.30am. **Prof** R McDougall **Course Designer** Hawtree **Facilities** ⊗ ⊪ ⎍ ⚑ ♀ ⚲ 🏠 ⚲ **Conf** fac available Corporate Hospitality Days available **Location** 1m S off A4

Hotel ★★★ 78% The French Horn, SONNING ON THAMES ☎ 0118 969 2204 13 en suite 8 annexe en suite

STREATLEY   Map 04 SU58

Goring & Streatley RG8 9QA
☎ 01491 873229 📠 01491 875224
e-mail: secretary@goringgc.org
A parkland and moorland course that requires negotiating. Four well-known holes lead up to the heights of the 5th tee, to which there is a 300ft climb. Wide fairways, not over-bunkered, with nice rewards on the way home down the last few holes. A delightful course that commands magnificent views of the Ridgeway & the River Thames.
18 holes, 6355yds, Par 71, SSS 70, Course record 65.
Club membership 740.
Visitors contact in advance; with member only weekends;

Continued

handicap certificate. **Societies** phone in advance. **Green Fees** not confirmed. **Cards** 🌐 💳 📧 🏧 🅿 **Prof** Jason Hadland **Course Designer** Tom Morris **Facilities** ⊗ ⊪ ⎍ ⎍ ♀ ⚲ 🏠 ⚲ **Location** N of village off A417

Hotel ★★★★ 69% The Swan at Streatley, High St, STREATLEY ☎ 01491 878800 46 en suite

SUNNINGDALE   See page 29

SUNNINGDALE   Map 04 SU96

Sunningdale Ladies Cross Rd SL5 9RX
☎ 01344 620507
e-mail: ladiesgolf@lineone.net
18 holes, 3616yds, Par 60, SSS 60, Course record 51.
Location 1m S off A30
Telephone for further details

Hotel ★★★★ 66% The Berystede, Bagshot Rd, Sunninghill, ASCOT ☎ 0870 400 8111 90 en suite

WOKINGHAM   Map 04 SU86

Downshire Easthampstead Park RG40 3DH
☎ 01344 302030 📠 01344 301020
e-mail: paul.stanwick@bracknell-forest.gov.uk
Beautiful municipal parkland course with mature trees. Water hazards come into play on the 14th & 18th holes, & especially on the short 7th, a testing downhill 169yds over the lake. Pleasant easy walking. Challenging holes: 7th (par 4), 15th (par 4), 16th (par 3).
18 holes, 6416yds, Par 73, SSS 71.
Club membership 1000.
Visitors must book up to 10 days in advance. **Societies** phone in advance. **Green Fees** £18 (£24 weekends & bank holidays). **Cards** 🌐 💳 💳 📧 🏧 🅿 **Prof** Wayne Owers **Facilities** ⊗ ⎍ ♀ ⚲ 🏠 ⚲ 🏧 ⚲ ⚲ **Leisure** 9 hole pitch & putt. **Location** 3m SW of Bracknell, M4 junct 10 follow signs for Crowthorne

Hotel ★★★★ 73% Coppid Beech, John Nike Way, BRACKNELL ☎ 01344 303333 205 en suite

Sand Martins Finchampstead Rd RG40 3RQ
☎ 0118 9792711 📠 0118 977 0282
e-mail: info@sandmartins.com
Two different nine-hole loops: the front nine is mostly tree-lined with ponds and the back nine is similar to a links course.

18 holes, 6212yds, Par 70, SSS 70, Course record 65.
Club membership 800.
Visitors phone in advance; with member only weekends. **Societies** arrangement by phone. **Green Fees** terms on application. **Cards** 🌐 💳 💳 📧 🏧 🅿 **Prof** Andrew

Continued

Berkshire

Sunningdale

Sunningdale   Map 04 SU96

The Old Course, founded in 1900, was designed by Willie Park. It is a classic course at just 6308yds long, with gorse and pines, silver birch, heather and immaculate turf. The New Course is no less a challenge, created by HS Holt in 1922 at 6443yds. There's a long wait to become a member of this prestigious club, and its location within easy reach of London is an attraction in itself. Visitors playing two rounds have to alternate onto the other course in the afternoon. Short rounds may be played by finishing at the 10th or 13th green on the Old Course, and the 10th or 11th green on the New Course. On Monday one course is designated the two-ball course until 3pm - check when booking a tee time.

Ridgemount Rd SL5 9RR
☎ 01344 621681 Fax 01344 624154
Old Course: 18 holes, 6308yds, Par 70, SSS 70.
New Course: 18 holes, 6443yds, Par 71, SSS 72.
Club membership 1000.
Visitors not Fri-Sun, bank holidays; must contact in advance; handicap certificate (less than 18) & letter of introduction.
Societies Tue, Wed, Thu, by arrangement. **Green Fees** Old Course £145 per round; New Course £110 per round. 36 holes £185. **Cards** 💳 💳 💳 💳 💳 **Prof** Keith Maxwell
Course Designer W Park **Facilities** ⊗ 🏋 🏌 ⛳ 🍴 📠 🏪 ⛳
🏌 **Conf** Corporate Hospitality Days available
Location 1m S off A30

....

Hotels

★ ★ ★ ★ ★ Pennyhill Park Hotel & The Spa,
London Rd, BAGSHOT

☎ 01276 471774 26 en suite 97 annexe en suite

★ ★ ★ ★ 66% The Berystede, Bagshot Rd, Sunninghill, ASCOT

☎ 0870 400 8111 Fax 01344 872301 90 en suite

★ ★ ★ ★ 71% The Royal Berkshire Ramada Plaza, London Rd, Sunninghill, ASCOT

☎ 01344 623322 Fax 01344 627100 63 en suite

★ ★ 66% Brockenhurst Hotel, Brockenhurst Rd, SOUTH ASCOT

☎ 01344 621912 Fax 01344 873252 12 en suite
5 annexe en suite

Hall, Stephen Cox **Course Designer** Edward Fox
Facilities ⊗ ⋙ ⓛ ♨ ♀ ⚘ 🏠 ☜ ⚒ 𝒟 ℓ **Conf** fac
available **Location** 1m S of Wokingham

Hotel ★★★ 68% Corus hotel Bracknell, Duke's Ride,
CROWTHORNE ☎ 0870 609 6111 79 en suite

BRISTOL

BRISTOL   Map 03 ST57

Bristol and Clifton Beggar Bush Ln,
Failand BS8 3TH
☎ 01275 393474 📠 01275 394611
e-mail: mansec@bristolgolf.co.uk
Utilising the aesthetics and hazards of a former quarry,
a valley, stone walls and spinneys of trees, the course is
a stern challenge but one always in tip top condition,
due in summer to the irrigation and in winter to the
natural draining land upon which it is situated. Par 3s
from 120 to 220yds, dog-legs which range from the
gentle to the brutal and a collection of natural obstacles
and hazards add to the charm of the layout.
18 holes, 6387yds, Par 70, SSS 71, Course record 63.
Club membership 850.
Visitors weekends restricted; handicap certificate.
Societies phone to enquire. **Green Fees** £38 per day (£45
weekends). **Cards** 🎫 💳 💳 𝒟 **Prof** Paul Mitchell
Facilities ⊗ ⋙ ⓛ ♨ ♀ ⚘ 🏠 ☜ ⚒ ℓ **Leisure** chipping
green, practice bunkers. **Conf** fac available Corporate
Hospitality Days available **Location** M5 junct 19, A369
for 4m, onto B3129, club 1m on right

Hotel ★★★ 68% Corus hotel Bristol, Beggar Bush Ln,
Failand, BRISTOL ☎ 0870 609 6144 112 en suite

Filton Golf Course Ln, Filton BS34 7QS
☎ 0117 969 4169 📠 0117 931 4359
e-mail: thesecretary@filtongolfclub.co.uk
Challenging parkland course situated on high ground
in a pleasant suburb to the north of the city. Extensive
views can be enjoyed from the course, especially from
the second tee and the clubhouse, where on a clear day
the Cotswolds and the Brecon Beacons can be seen.
18 holes, 6173yds, Par 70, SSS 70, Course record 61.
Club membership 750.
Visitors advisable to contact in advance for availability;
with member only weekends; handicap certificate.
Societies apply in writing, phone or e-mail for details.
Green Fees £28 per round. **Cards** 🎫 💳 𝒟 **Prof** D Kelley
Facilities ⊗ ⋙ ⓛ ♨ ♀ ⚘ 🏠 ℓ **Conf** Corporate
Hospitality Days available **Location** 5m NW off A38

Hotel ⟲ Premier Travel Inn Bristol North (Filton), Shield
Retail Park, Gloucester Rd North, Filton, BRISTOL
☎ 0870 9906456 60 en suite

Henbury Henbury Hill, Westbury-on-Trym BS10 7QB
☎ 0117 950 0044 & 950 2121 (Prof) 📠 0117 959 1928
e-mail: thesecretary@henburygolfclub.co.uk
18 holes, 6007yds, Par 69, SSS 70, Course record 65.
Location 3m NW of city centre on B4055 off A4018
Telephone for further details

Hotel Ⓤ Henbury Lodge Hotel, Station Rd, Henbury,
BRISTOL ☎ 0117 950 2615 12 en suite 9 annexe
en suite

Knowle West Town Ln, Brislington BS4 5DF
☎ 0117 977 0660 📠 0117 972 0615
A parkland course with nice turf. The first five holes
climb up and down hill but the remainder are on a
more even plane.
18 holes, 6006yds, Par 69, SSS 69, Course record 61.
Club membership 700.
Visitors handicap certificate; weekends phone professional
0117 977 9193. **Societies** Thu, apply in writing or phone.
Green Fees not confirmed. **Prof** Robert Hayward **Course
Designer** Hawtree, JH Taylor **Facilities** ⊗ ⋙ ⓛ ♨ ♀ ⚘
🏠 ☜ ⚒ 𝒟 **Location** 3m SE of city centre off A37

Hotel ★★★ ♨♨ 79% Hunstrete House Hotel,
HUNSTRETE ☎ 01761 490490 25 en suite

Mangotsfield Carsons Rd, Mangotsfield BS17 3LW
☎ 0117 956 5501
18 holes, 5337yds, Par 68, SSS 66, Course record 61.
Course Designer John Day **Location** 6m NE of city centre
off B4465
Telephone for further details

Hotel ⟲ Premier Travel Inn Bristol East, 200/202
Westerleigh Rd, Emersons Green, BRISTOL
☎ 08701 977042 40 en suite

Shirehampton Park Park Hill, Shirehampton
BS11 0UL
☎ 0117 982 2083 📠 0117 982 5280
e-mail: info@shirehamptonparkgolfclub.co.uk
A lovely parkland course with views across the Avon
Gorge.
18 holes, 5430yds, Par 67, SSS 66, Course record 63.
Club membership 600.
Visitors not before 2pm weekends; handicap certificate.
Societies weekdays, book through Secretary. **Green Fees**
phone for details. **Cards** 🎫 💳 💳 ⓟ 🎫 💳 𝒟 **Prof**
Brent Ellis **Facilities** ⊗ ⋙ ⓛ ♨ ♀ ⚘ 🏠 ☜ ⚒ 𝒟 **Location**
2m E of junct 18 M5 on B4054

Hotel ★★★ 68% Corus hotel Bristol, Beggar Bush Ln,
Failand, BRISTOL ☎ 0870 609 6144 112 en suite

Woodlands Trench Ln, Almondsbury BS32 4JZ
☎ 01454 619319 📠 01454 619397
e-mail: info@woodlands-golf.com
Situated on the edge of the Severn Valley, bordered by
Hortham Brook and Shepherds Wood, this interesting
parkland course features five testing par 3s set around
the course's five lakes, notably the 206yd 5th hole which
extends over water.
18 holes, 6068yds, Par 70, SSS 69.
Club membership 45.
Visitors no restrictions. **Societies** phone or write in
advance. **Green Fees** £13 per round (£15 weekends &
bank holidays). **Cards** 🎫 💳 𝒟 **Prof** L Riddiford
Facilities ⊗ ⋙ ⓛ ♨ ♀ ⚘ 🏠 ☜ ⚒ 𝒟 **Leisure** fishing.
Conf fac available Corporate Hospitality Days available
Location M5 junct 16, A38 towards Bradley Stoke

Hotel ★★ 68% The Bowl Inn, 16 Church Rd, Lower
Almondsbury, BRISTOL ☎ 01454 612757 11 en suite
2 annexe en suite

BUCKINGHAMSHIRE

AYLESBURY
Map 04 SP81

Aylesbury Golf Centre Hulcott Ln, Bierton
HP22 5GA
☎ 01296 393644
A parkland course with magnificent views to the Chiltern Hills. A good test of golf with out of bounds coming into play on nine of the holes, plus a number of water hazards and bunkers.
18 holes, 5965yds, Par 71, SSS 69.
Club membership 200.
Visitors no restrictions; booking advisable. Societies phone for details. Green Fees not confirmed. Cards ▦ ▦ Prof Richard Wooster Course Designer T S Benwell Facilities ⊗ ⑴ ⑤ ⑨ ⑨ ⑧ ⑧ ⑧ ⑧ Conf Corporate Hospitality Days available Location 1m N of Aylesbury on A418

Hotel ⬧ Premier Travel Inn Aylesbury, Buckingham Rd, AYLESBURY ☎ 08701 977019 64 en suite

Aylesbury Park Andrews Way, Off Coldharbour Way, Oxford Rd HP17 8QQ
☎ 01296 399196 ▤ 01296 336830
e-mail: info@aylesburyparkgolf.com
Parkland course with mature trees, located just south-west of Aylesbury.
18 holes, 6148yds, Par 70, SSS 69, Course record 68.
Club membership 360.
Visitors book up to one week in advance. Societies phone for Society Pack Green Fees £16.50 (£22 weekends). Cards ▦ ▦ ▦ ▦ ▦ Course Designer M Hawtree Facilities ⊗ ⑴ ⑤ ⑨ ⑧ ⑧ ⑧ ⑧ ⑧ Leisure 9 hole par 3 course.
Location 0.5m SW of Aylesbury, on the A418

Hotel ★★★★ ⚑ Hartwell House Hotel Restaurant & Spa, Oxford Rd, AYLESBURY ☎ 01296 747444 30 en suite 16 annexe en suite

Chiltern Forest Aston Hill, Halton HP22 5NQ
☎ 01296 631267 ▤ 01296 632709
e-mail: secretary@chilternforest.co.uk
The course nestles in the Chiltern Hills above Aylesbury with stunning views of the surrounding countryside and meanders around challenging wooded terrain. Although not a long course the tightly wooded holes and smallish greens present a challenge to all standards of golfer.
18 holes, 5765yds, Par 70, SSS 69, Course record 65.
Club membership 650.
Visitors with member only weekends. Societies phone in advance. Green Fees £40 per day, £34 per round. Cards ▦ ▦ ▦ ▦ ▦ Prof A Lavers Facilities ⊗ ⑴ ⑤ ⑨ ⑨ ⑧ ⑧ ⑧ Location off A41 between Tring & Wendover

Hotel ⬧ Innkeeper's Lodge Aylesbury, London Rd, ASTON CLINTON ☎ 01296 632777 11 en suite

Ellesborough Wendover Rd, Butlers Cross HP17 0TZ
☎ 01296 622114 ▤ 01296 622114
e-mail: admin@ellesboroughgolf.co.uk
Once part of the property of Chequers, and under the shadow of the famous Coombe monument at the Wendover end of the Chilterns. A downland course, it

Continued

is rather hilly with most holes enhanced by far-ranging views over the Aylesbury countryside.
18 holes, 6360yds, Par 71, SSS 71, Course record 64.
Club membership 700.
Visitors not weekends; handicap certificate. Societies Wed, Thu, by arrangement with General Manager. Green Fees not confirmed. Prof Mark Squire Course Designer James Braid Facilities ⊗ ⑤ ⑨ ⑨ ⑧ ⑧ ⑧ Conf Corporate Hospitality Days available Location 1m W of Wendover on B4010 towards Princes Risborough

Hotel ⬧ Innkeeper's Lodge Aylesbury South, 40 Main St, Weston Turville, AYLESBURY
☎ 01296 613131 & 0870 243 0500 ▤ 01296 616902 16 en suite

BEACONSFIELD
Map 04 SU99

Beaconsfield Seer Green HP9 2UR
☎ 01494 676545 ▤ 01494 681148
e-mail: secretary@beaconsfieldgolfclub.co.uk
An interesting and, at times, testing tree-lined and parkland course which frequently plays longer than appears on the card. Each hole differs to a considerable degree and here lies the charm. Walking is easy, except perhaps to the 6th and 8th. Well bunkered.
18 holes, 6506yds, Par 72, SSS 71, Course record 63.
Club membership 850.
Visitors not weekends; contact in advance; handicap certificate. Societies phone for details Green Fees £60 per day; £50 per round (with member only weekends & bank holidays). Prof Michael Brothers Course Designer HS Colt Facilities ⊗ ⑴ ⑤ ⑨ ⑨ ⑧ ⑧ ⑧ Conf Corporate Hospitality Days available Location M40 junct 2, next to Seer Green railway station

Hotel ⬧ Innkeeper's Lodge, Aylesbury End, BEACONSFIELD ☎ 01494 671211 32 en suite

BLETCHLEY
Map 04 SP83

Windmill Hill Tattenhoe Ln MK3 7RB
☎ 01908 631113 & 366457 (Sec) ▤ 01908 630034
Long, open-parkland course, the first championship course designed by Henry Cotton, opened in 1972. Proprietary Pay & Play. No winter greens.

18 holes, 6720yds, Par 73, SSS 72, Course record 68.
Club membership 400.
Visitors booking system in operation up to seven days in advance. Societies packages available, contact for details. Green Fees not confirmed. Cards ▦ ▦ ▦ ▦ ▦ Prof Colin Clingan Course Designer Henry Cotton Facilities ⊗ ⑴ ⑤ ⑨ ⑨ ⑧ ⑧ ⑧ ⑧ ⑧ Leisure pool table.

Continued

Conf fac available Corporate Hospitality Days available
Location W side of town centre on A421

Hotel ⭐ Campanile, 40 Penn Rd, Fenny Stratford,
Bletchley, MILTON KEYNES ☎ 01908 649819
80 en suite

BUCKINGHAM　　　　　　　　　Map 04 SP63

Buckingham Tingewick Rd MK18 4AE
☎ 01280 815566 🖹 01280 821812
e-mail: admin@buckinghamgolfclub.co.uk
**Undulating parkland course with a stream and river
affecting eight holes.**
*18 holes, 6082yds, Par 70, SSS 69, Course record 67.
Club membership 740.*
Visitors with member only weekends. **Societies** by
arrangement. **Green Fees** phone for details. **Prof** Greg
Hannah **Facilities** ⊗ ℿ ㄴ ♥ ♀ ♨ 🏠 ╬ ♋ ⚙ **Leisure**
snooker room. **Location** 1.5m W on A421

Hotel ★★★ 65% Buckingham Beales Best Western Hotel,
Buckingham Ring Rd, BUCKINGHAM ☎ 01280 822622
70 en suite

BURNHAM　　　　　　　　　　Map 04 SU98

Burnham Beeches Green Ln SL1 8EG
☎ 01628 661448 🖹 01628 668968
e-mail: enquiries@bbgc.co.uk
**A wooded parkland course on the edge of the historic
Burnham Beeches Forest with a good variety of holes.**
*18 holes, 6449yds, Par 70, SSS 71, Course record 66.
Club membership 670.*
Visitors contact in advance; with member only weekends;
handicap certificate. **Societies** Apr-Oct; write or phone for
information. **Green Fees** £40 per round weekdays. **Prof**
Ronnie Bolton **Facilities** ⊗ ℿ ㄴ ♥ ♀ ♨ 🏠 ╬ ♋ ⚙
Location 0.5m NE of Burnham

Hotel ★★★ 65% Burnham Beeches Hotel, Grove Rd,
BURNHAM ☎ 0870 609 6124 82 en suite

Lambourne Dropmore Rd SL1 8NF
☎ 01628 666755 🖹 01628 663301
**A championship standard 18-hole parkland course.
Undulating terrain with many trees and several lakes,
notably on the tricky 7th hole which has a tightly
guarded green reached via a shot over a lake. Seven
par 4s over 400yds with six picturesque lakes, excellent
drainage and full irrigation.**
*18 holes, 6771yds, Par 72, SSS 73, Course record 67.
Club membership 650.*
Visitors not weekends; contact in advance; handicap
certificate. **Societies** subject to application **Green Fees** not
confirmed. **Cards** 🟦 🟥 🟦 🟥 🟥 🔵 **Prof** David Hart
Course Designer Donald Steel **Facilities** ⊗ ℿ ㄴ ♥ ♀ ㄥ
🏠 ╬ ♋ ⚙ ╏ **Leisure** sauna. **Location** M4 junct 7 or
M40 junct 2, towards Burnham

Hotel ★★★ 65% Burnham Beeches Hotel, Grove Rd,
BURNHAM ☎ 0870 609 6124 82 en suite

CHALFONT ST GILES　　　　　　Map 04 SU99

Harewood Downs Cokes Ln HP8 4TA
☎ 01494 762184 🖹 01494 766869
e-mail: secretary@hdgc.co.uk
**A testing undulating parkland course with sloping
greens and plenty of trees.**

*18 holes, 5958yds, Par 69, SSS 69, Course record 63.
Club membership 600.*
Visitors contact in advance. **Societies** apply in writing or
phone. **Green Fees** £33 per round (£38 weekends). **Prof** G
C Morris **Course Designer** JH Taylor **Facilities** ⊗ ℿ ㄴ
♥ ♀ ㄥ 🏠 ╬ ♋ ⚙ **Conf** Corporate Hospitality Days
available **Location** 2m E of Amersham on A413

Hotel ★★★ 69% The Crown Hotel, 16 High St,
AMERSHAM ☎ 01494 721541 19 en suite 18 annexe
en suite

Oakland Park Threehouseholds HP8 4LW
☎ 01494 871277 & 877333 (pro) 🖹 01494 874692
e-mail: info@oaklandparkgolf.co.uk
**Parkland with mature trees, hedgerows and water
features, designed to respect the natural features of the
land and lakes whilst providing a good challenge for
players at all levels.**
*18 holes, 5246yds, Par 67, SSS 66, Course record 66.
Club membership 650.*
Visitors with member only weekends; advisable to contact
in advance. **Societies** Mon, Wed, Fri; apply in writing.
Green Fees £25 per round (£30 weekends & bank
holidays). **Cards** 🟦 🟥 🟦 🟥 🔵 **Prof** Alistair Thatcher
Course Designer Johnathan Gaunt **Facilities** ⊗ ℿ ㄴ ♥ ♀
ㄥ 🏠 ╬ ♋ ♨ ⚙ ╏ **Conf** Corporate Hospitality Days
available **Location** M40 junct 2, 3m N

Hotel ★★★ 69% The Crown Hotel, 16 High St,
AMERSHAM ☎ 01494 721541 19 en suite 18 annexe
en suite

CHARTRIDGE　　　　　　　　Map 04 SP90

Chartridge Park HP5 2TF
☎ 01494 791772
e-mail: petergibbins@tinyworld.co.uk
**A family run, easy walking parkland course set high in
the beautiful Chiltern Hills, affording breathtaking
views.**
*18 holes, 5516yds, Par 69, SSS 67, Course record 65.
Club membership 700.*
Visitors not before 10.30am weekends. **Societies** phone in
advance. **Green Fees** phone for details. **Cards** 🟦 🟥 🟦
🟥 🟥 🔵 **Prof** Peter Gibbins **Course Designer** John
Jacobs **Facilities** ⊗ ℿ ㄴ ♥ ♀ ㄥ 🏠 ╬ ♋ ♨ ⚙
Location 3m NW of Chesham

Hotel ★★★ 69% The Crown Hotel, 16 High St,
AMERSHAM ☎ 01494 721541 19 en suite 18 annexe
en suite

CHESHAM　　　　　　　　　　Map 04 SP90

Chesham & Ley Hill Ley Hill Common HP5 1UZ
☎ 01494 784541 🖹 01494 785506
e-mail: the.secretary@clhgolfclub.co.uk
Wooded parkland course on hilltop with easy walking.
*9 holes, 5296yds, Par 66, SSS 65, Course record 62.
Club membership 400.*
Visitors Mon, Thu, Wed pm, Fri before 4pm. **Societies**
Thu, Fri, subject to approval. **Green Fees** not confirmed.
Facilities ⊗ ℿ ㄴ ♥ ♀ ㄥ **Leisure** practice net. **Conf** fac
available **Location** 2m E of Chesham, off A41 on B4504
to Ley Hill

Hotel ★★★ 69% The Crown Hotel, 16 High St,
AMERSHAM ☎ 01494 721541 19 en suite 18 annexe
en suite

Continued

DAGNALL   Map 04 SP91

Whipsnade Park Studham Ln HP4 1RH
☎ 01442 842330 ▤ 01442 842090
e-mail: whipsnadeparkgolfc@btopenworld.com
**Parkland course situated on downs overlooking the
Chilterns adjoining Whipsnade Zoo. Easy walking,
good views.**
*18 holes, 6800yds, Par 73, SSS 72, Course record 66.
Club membership 600.*
Visitors with member only weekends; contact in advance.
Societies by arrangement. **Green Fees** not confirmed.
Cards ▦ ▦ 🗐 **Prof** Darren Turner **Facilities** ⊗ ⅷ 🍴 🍺
🍷 🛆 🏌 🚶 🚿 ⚷ **Location** 1m E off B4506 between
Dagnall & Studham
....
Hotel ★★★ 63% Old Palace Lodge, Church St,
DUNSTABLE ☎ 01582 662201 68 en suite

DENHAM   Map 04 TQ08

Buckinghamshire Denham Court Dr UB9 5BG
☎ 01895 835777 ▤ 01895 835210
e-mail: enquiries@buckinghamshiregc.co.uk
**A John Jacobs designed championship-standard course.
Visitors welcome only as guests of members to this
beautiful course in 269 acres of lovely grounds
including mature trees, five lakes and two rivers. The
testing 7th hole requires a 185yd carry over a stream,
followed by a second shot over a river to a green
guarded by a lake.**
*18 holes, 6880yds, Par 72, SSS 73, Course record 70.
Club membership 600.*
Visitors subject to availability; contact 48 hours in
advance. **Societies** contact in advance. **Green Fees** £80 per
18 holes (£90 weekends). **Cards** ▦ ▦ ▦ ▦ 🗐
Prof John O'Leary **Course Designer** John Jacobs
Facilities ⊗ ⅷ 🍴 🍺 🍷 🛆 🏠 🏌 ⚷ ℂ **Conf** Corporate
Hospitality Days available **Location** M25 junct 16, signed
Uxbridge
....
Hotel ★★★ 71% Barn Hotel, West End Rd, RUISLIP
☎ 01895 636057 59 en suite

Denham Tilehouse Ln UB9 5DE
☎ 01895 832022 ▤ 01895 835340
e-mail: club.secretary@denhamgolfclub.co.uk
**A beautifully maintained parkland and heathland
course, home of many county champions. Slightly hilly
and calling for good judgement of distance in the
wooded areas.**
*18 holes, 6462yds, Par 70, SSS 71, Course record 66.
Club membership 790.*
Visitors contact in advance; handicap certificate; with
member only Fri-Sun. **Societies** Tue-Thu, book in advance.
Green Fees £55 per round. **Prof** Stuart Campbell **Course
Designer** HS Colt **Facilities** ⊗ ⅷ 🍴 🍺 🍷 🛆 🏠 🏌 ⚷
Conf Corporate Hospitality Days available **Location** 0.5m
N of North Orbital Road, 2m from Uxbridge
....
Hotel ★★★ 71% Barn Hotel, West End Rd, RUISLIP
☎ 01895 636057 59 en suite

FLACKWELL HEATH   Map 04 SU89

Flackwell Heath Treadaway Rd, High Wycombe
HP10 9PE
☎ 01628 520929 ▤ 01628 530040
e-mail: secretary@flackwellheathgolfclub.co.uk
**Open sloping heath and tree-lined course on hills
overlooking the Chilterns. Some good challenging par
3s and several testing small greens.**
*18 holes, 6211yds, Par 71, SSS 70, Course record 63.
Club membership 700.*
Visitors with member only weekends; contact in advance;
handicap certificate. **Societies** Wed, Thu, by booking.
Green Fees £30 per round. **Prof** Paul Watson **Course
Designer** JH Taylor **Facilities** ⊗ ⅷ 🍴 🍺 🍷 🛆 🏌 ⚷
Conf Corporate Hospitality Days available **Location** E
side of High Wycombe, NE side of town centre
....
Hotel ⚲ Premier Travel Inn High Wycombe, Thanestead
Farm, London Rd, Loudwater, HIGH WYCOMBE
☎ 08701 977135 81 en suite

GERRARDS CROSS   Map 04 TQ08

Gerrards Cross Chalfont Park SL9 0QA
☎ 01753 883263 (Sec) & 885300 (Pro) ▤ 01753 883593
e-mail: secretary@gxgolf.co.uk
**A wooded parkland course which has been modernised
in recent years and is now a very pleasant circuit with
infinite variety. The best part lies on the plateau above
the clubhouse where there are some testing holes.**
*18 holes, 6212yds, Par 69, SSS 70, Course record 64.
Club membership 700.*
Visitors not Tue, weekends, public holidays; contact
professional in advance; handicap certificate. **Societies**
book well in advance; handicap certificates; packages to
suit. **Green Fees** £53 per day, £40 per round. **Cards** ▦
▦ ▦ 🗐 **Prof** Matthew Barr **Course Designer** Bill Pedlar
Facilities ⊗ ⅷ 🍴 🍺 🍷 🛆 🏠 🏌 ⚷ **Location** NE side of
town centre off A413
....
Hotel ★★★ 69% Bull Hotel, Oxford Rd, GERRARDS
CROSS ☎ 01753 885995 123 en suite

HIGH WYCOMBE   Map 04 SU89

Hazlemere Penn Rd, Hazlemere HP15 7LR
☎ 01494 719300 ▤ 01494 713914
e-mail: enquiries@hazlemeregolfclub.co.uk
**Undulating parkland course in beautiful countryside
with water hazards in play on some holes. Two long
par 5s, one long par 3 and a fine par 4 closing hole.**
*18 holes, 5810yds, Par 70, SSS 67, Course record 61.
Club membership 600.*
Visitors weekends by arrangement through pro shop 01494
719306. **Societies** arrange by phone. **Green Fees** phone for
details. **Cards** ▦ ▦ ▦ 🗐 **Prof** Gavin Cousins, Paul
Harrison **Course Designer** Terry Murray **Facilities** ⊗ 🍴
🍺 🍷 🛆 🏠 🏌 🚿 ⚷ **Conf** fac available **Location** on
B474 between Beaconsfield & Hazlemere, 2m NE of High
Wycombe
....
Hotel ★★★ 69% The Crown Hotel, 16 High St,
AMERSHAM ☎ 01494 721541 19 en suite 18 annexe
en suite

**Looking for a new course? Always telephone
ahead to confirm visitor arrangements.**

IVER   Map 04 TQ08

Iver Hollow Hill Ln, Langley Park Rd SL0 0JJ
☎ 01753 655615 📠 01753 654225
**Fairly flat, pay and play parkland course with
challenging par 5s, plenty of hazards - water and
ditches - and strong crosswinds to contend with. Most
greens are elevated with plenty of slopes. The short
par 3 course challenging with very small greens.**
9 holes, 6288yds, Par 72, SSS 72, Course record 66.
Club membership 200.
Visitors weekends competitions, phone to book tee times.
Societies phone in advance. **Green Fees** terms on
application. **Cards** 🔲 🔲 🔄 💲 **Prof** Jim Lynch
Facilities ⊗ ♭ 🖤 ♀ 🛆 🕋 ⚑ ⚕ ℄ **Leisure** bunker &
chipping area, par 3 course. **Location** M4 junct 5, 1.5m
SW off B470

Hotel ★★★★ 70% Slough/Windsor Marriott Hotel, Ditton
Rd, Langley, SLOUGH ☎ 0870 400 7244 382 en suite

Richings Park Golf & Country Club North
Park SL0 9DL
☎ 01753 655370 & 655352(pro shop) 📠 01753 655409
e-mail: info@richingspark.co.uk
**Set among mature trees and attractive lakes, this
testing par 70 parkland course provides a suitable
challenge to golfers of all abilities. Well-irrigated greens
and abundant wildlife. There is an academy course with
five short holes and teaching facilities on the driving
range.**
18 holes, 6144yds, Par 70, SSS 69.
Club membership 594.
Visitors not am weekends. Societies apply in writing or
phone. **Green Fees** not confirmed. **Cards** 🔲 🔲 💳 🔄 💲 **Prof** Robert Mullane **Course Designer** Alan Higgins
Facilities ⊗ 川 ♭ 🖤 ♀ 🛆 🕋 ⚑ 🏹 🔨 ⚕ ℄ **Location** M4
junct 5, A4 towards Colnbrook, left at lights, Sutton Lane,
right at next lights North Park

Hotel ★★★ 69% Courtyard by Marriott Slough/Windsor,
Church St, SLOUGH ☎ 0870 400 7215 150 en suite

Thorney Park Thorney Mill Rd SL0 9AL
☎ 01895 422095 📠 01895 431307
e-mail: sales@thorneypark.com
**An 18-hole parkland course which will test both the
beginner and established golfer. Fairway irrigation
ensures lush green fairways and smooth putting
surfaces. Many interesting holes including the testing
par 4 9th which needs a long drive to the water's edge
and a well-hit iron onto the bunker-guarded green. The
back nine finishes with two water holes, the 17th, a near
island green and the shot of 150yds makes this a
picturesque hole. The 18th has more water than grass.**
18 holes, 5731yds, Par 69, SSS 68, Course record 69.
Club membership 300.
Visitors not before 11am weekends, bank holidays; phone
in advance. Societies phone in advance. **Green Fees** £33
per day, £21.50 per 18 holes (£23.50 per round weekends).
Cards 🔲 🔲 🔄 💲 **Prof** Andrew Killing **Course
Designer** David Walker **Facilities** ⊗ 川 ♭ 🖤 ♀ 🛆 🕋 ⚑
🔨 ⚕ **Conf** fac available Corporate Hospitality Days
available **Location** M4 junct 5, left onto A4, left onto
Sutton Ln, right for Thorney Mill Rd

Hotel ★★★★ 70% Slough/Windsor Marriott Hotel, Ditton
Rd, Langley, SLOUGH ☎ 0870 400 7244 382 en suite

LITTLE BRICKHILL   See page 35

LITTLE CHALFONT   Map 04 SU99

Little Chalfont Lodge Ln HP8 4AJ
☎ 01494 764877 📠 01494 762860
**Gently undulating parkland course surrounded by
mature trees.**
9 holes, 5752yds, Par 70, SSS 68, Course record 66.
Club membership 300.
Visitors phone to check for weekends & competitions.
Societies phone in advance. **Green Fees** £13 per 18 holes
(£15 weekends). **Cards** 🔲 🔲 🔄 **Prof** M Dunne
Course Designer JM Dunne **Facilities** ⊗ 川 ♭ 🖤 ♀ 🛆
🕋 ⚑ ⚕ **Leisure** one motorised cart for hire by
arrangement. **Conf** fac available Corporate Hospitality
Days available **Location** M25 junct 18, on A404 between
Little Chalfont & Chorleywood

Hotel ★★★ 69% The Crown Hotel, 16 High St,
AMERSHAM ☎ 01494 721541 19 en suite 18 annexe
en suite

LOUDWATER   Map 04 SU89

Wycombe Heights Golf Centre Rayners Ave
HP10 9SZ
☎ 01494 816686 📠 01494 816728
*High Course: 18 holes, 6265yds, Par 70, SSS 71, Course
record 64.*
Course Designer John Jacobs **Location** M40 junct 3, A40
towards High Wycombe. 0.5m right onto Rayners Av at
lights
Telephone for further details

Hotel ⭐ Premier Travel Inn High Wycombe, Thanestead
Farm, London Rd, Loudwater, HIGH WYCOMBE
☎ 08701 977135 81 en suite

MARLOW   Map 04 SU88

Harleyford Harleyford Estate, Henley Rd SL7 2SP
☎ 01628 816164 📠 01628 816160
e-mail: info@harleyfordgolf.co.uk
**Set in 160 acres, this Donald Steel designed course,
founded in 1996, makes the most of the natural rolling
contours of the beautiful parkland of the historic
Harleyford Estate. A challenging course to golfers of all
handicaps. Stunning views of the Thames Valley.**

18 holes, 6708yds, Par 72, SSS 72, Course record 68.
Club membership 750.
Visitors not before 10am weekdays & 11.30am weekends;
soft spikes only; contact in advance. Societies phone
Daniel Smith 01628 816163. **Green Fees** £45 per round
(£65 weekends). **Cards** 🔲 🔲 💲 **Prof** Darren Brewer

Continued

Woburn

Buckinghamshire

Little Brickhill

Map 04 SP93

Easily accessible from the M1, Woburn is famed not only for its golf courses but also for the magnificent stately home and wildlife park, which are both well worth a visit. Charles Lawrie of Cotton Pennink designed two great courses here among trees and beautiful countryside. From the back tees they are rather long for the weekend amateur golfer. The Duke's Course is a tough challenge for golfers at all levels. The Duchess Course, although relatively easier, still demands a high level of skills to negotiate the fairways guarded by towering pines. The Duke's has become the home of the increasingly popular Weetabix Women's British Open, held here since 1990. The town of Woburn and the abbey are in Bedfordshire, while the golf and country club are over the border in Buckinghamshire.

Golf & Country Club MK17 9LJ
☎ 01908 370756 Fax 01908 378436
e-mail: enquiries@woburngolf.com

Duke's Course: 18 holes, 6973yds, Par 72, SSS 74, Course record 62.
Duchess Course: 18 holes, 6651yds, Par 72, SSS 72.
Marquess Course: 18 holes, 7214yds, Par 72, SSS 74.
Visitors mid-week by arrangement; handicap certificate required (gentlemen 24, ladies 36). Societies must contact in advance.
Green Fees Duke's/Duchess £66 per round, Marquess £96 per round (Aug-Oct £95/£110 including lunch). 36 holes including lunch: Duke's/Duchess £130, Marquess £150. Cards 💳 💳 💳
💳 💳 💳 Prof Luther Blacklock Course Designer Charles Lawrie Facilities ⊗ 🍺 ♀ 🏊 🍴 ⛳ ➰ 🏌 ✓ ⚑
Leisure heated outdoor swimming pool.
Conf Corporate Hospitality Days available
Location M1 junct 13, 4m W off A5130

....

Hotels

★ ★ ★ Menzies Flitwick Manor, Church Rd, FLITWICK

☎ 01525 712242 17 en suite

★ ★ ★ 73% The Inn at Woburn, George St, WOBURN

☎ 01525 290441 Fax 01525 290432 50 en suite
7 annexe en suite

★ ★ ★ 69% Moore Place Hotel, The Square, ASPLEY GUISE

☎ 01908 282000 Fax 01908 281888 39 en suite
27 annexe en suite

Course Designer Donald Steel Facilities ⊗ ⅷ ᵇ ₩ ♀ ♣ 🏠 ⌒ 🖊 ♿ ⌀ ₵ Conf fac available Corporate Hospitality Days available Location S side A4156 Marlow-Henley road

....

Hotel ★★★★ 77% Danesfield House Hotel & Spa, Henley Rd, MARLOW-ON-THAMES ☎ 01628 891010 87 en suite

MENTMORE   Map 04 SP91

Mentmore Golf & Country Club   LU7 0UA
☎ 01296 662020 📠 01296 662592
Rosebery Course: 18 holes, 6777yds, Par 72, SSS 72, Course record 68.
Rothschild Course: 18 holes, 6700yds, Par 72, SSS 72.
Course Designer Bob Sandow Location 4m S of Leighton Buzzard
Phone for further details

....

Hotel ★★★ 63% Old Palace Lodge, Church St, DUNSTABLE ☎ 01582 662201   68 en suite

MILTON KEYNES   Map 04 SP83

Abbey Hill   Monks Way, Two Mile Ash MK8 8AA
☎ 01908 562408
e-mail: steve.tompkins@ukonline.co.uk
18 holes, 6122yds, Par 71, SSS 69, Course record 71.
Location 2m W of town centre off A5
Phone for further details

....

Hotel ★★★ 65% Quality Hotel & Suites Milton Keynes, Monks Way, Two Mile Ash, MILTON KEYNES ☎ 01908 561666   88 en suite

Three Locks   Great Brickhill MK17 9BH
☎ 01525 270050 📠 01525 270470
e-mail: info@threelocksgolfclub.co.uk
Parkland course offering a challenge to beginners and experienced golfers, with water coming into play on ten holes. Magnificent views.
18 holes, 6036yds, Par 70, SSS 69, Course record 60.
Club membership 300.
Visitors phone 01525 270050 to book tee times. Societies write or phone for details. Green Fees £28 per day, £18.50 per round (£34/£23 weekends & bank holidays). Cards 🗀 🗀 🗀 🗀 Prof G Harding Course Designer MRM Sandown Facilities ⊗ ᵇ ₩ ♀ ♣ 🏠 ⌒ 🖊 ♿ ⌀ Leisure fishing. Location A4146 between Leighton Buzzard & Bletchley

....

Hotel ⛢ Campanile, 40 Penn Rd, Fenny Stratford, Bletchley, MILTON KEYNES ☎ 01908 649819 80 en suite

PRINCES RISBOROUGH   Map 04 SP80

Whiteleaf   Upper Icknield Way, Whiteleaf HP27 0LY
☎ 01844 274058 📠 01844 275551
e-mail: whiteleafgc@tiscali.co.uk
A picturesque nine-hole course on the edge of the Chilterns. Good views over the Vale of Aylesbury. A short challenging course requiring great accuracy.
9 holes, 5391yds, Par 66, SSS 66, Course record 64.
Club membership 300.
Visitors advisable to contact in advance; with member only weekends. Societies Thu, contact secretary in advance. Green Fees £20 per 18 holes. Prof Ken Ward

Facilities ⊗ ⅷ ᵇ ₩ ♀ ♣ 🏠 ⌀ Location 1m NE off A4010

STOKE POGES   Map 04 SU98

Farnham Park   Park Rd SL2 4PJ
☎ 01753 643332 & 647065 📠 01753 643332 & 647065
e-mail: farnhamparkgolfclub@btopenworld.com
Fine, public parkland course in a pleasing setting.
18 holes, 6172yds, Par 71, SSS 70, Course record 68.
Club membership 400.
Visitors phone in advance for tee times. Societies apply in writing. Green Fees not confirmed. Cards 🗀 🗀 🗀 🗀 Prof Paul Warner Course Designer Hawtree Facilities ⊗ ᵇ ₩ ♀ ♣ 🏠 ⌒ ⌀ Location W side of village off B416

....

Hotel ★★★★ 70% Slough/Windsor Marriott Hotel, Ditton Rd, Langley, SLOUGH ☎ 0870 400 7244 382 en suite

Stoke Poges   Stoke Park, Park Rd SL2 4PG
☎ 01753 717171 📠 01753 717181
e-mail: info@stokeparkclub.com
Judgement of the distance from the tee is all important on this classic parkland course. Fairways are wide and the challenge seemingly innocuous - testing par 4s, superb bunkering and fast putting surfaces. The 7th hole is the model for the well-known 12th hole at Augusta.
Course 1: 18 holes, 6721yds, Par 71, SSS 72, Course record 65.
Course 2: 18 holes, 6551yds, Par 72, SSS 73.
Course 3: 18 holes, 6318yds, Par 71, SSS 70.
Club membership 2500.
Visitors contact in advance. Societies phone in advance. Green Fees £125 per 18 holes (£200 weekends). Cards 🗀 🗀 🗀 🗀 🗀 Prof Stuart Collier Course Designer Harry Shapland Colt Facilities ⊗ ⅷ ᵇ ₩ ♀ ♣ 🏠 ⌒ 🖊 ♿ ⌀ ₵ Leisure hard & grass tennis courts, heated indoor swimming pool, fishing, sauna, gymnasium, indoor tennis courts. treatment room spa. Conf fac available Corporate Hospitality Days available Location off A4 at Slough onto B416 Stoke Poges Ln, club 1.5m on left

....

Hotel ★★★★ 70% Slough/Windsor Marriott Hotel, Ditton Rd, Langley, SLOUGH ☎ 0870 400 7244 382 en suite

STOWE   Map 04 SP63

Silverstone   Silverstone Rd MK18 5LH
☎ 01280 850005 📠 01280 850156
e-mail: proshop@silverstonegolfclub.co.uk
Set in the rolling north Buckinghamshire countryside, the course offers an interesting challenge for both experienced players and those with a higher handicap. Fairly flat parkland course with water features on nine holes.
18 holes, 6472yds, Par 72, SSS 71, Course record 65.
Club membership 432.
Visitors no restrictions. Societies weekdays & pm weekends, phone to book. Green Fees terms on application. Cards 🗀 🗀 🗀 🗀 Prof Rodney Holt Course Designer David Snell Facilities ⊗ ⅷ ᵇ ₩ ♀ ♣ 🏠 ♿ ⌀ ₵ Conf fac available Corporate Hospitality Days available Location from Silverstone signs to Grand Prix track. Club 1m past entrance on right

....

Hotel ★★★★ 65% Villiers Hotel, 3 Castle St, BUCKINGHAM ☎ 01280 822444 46 en suite

Continued

WAVENDON   Map 04 SP93

Wavendon Golf Centre Lower End Rd MK17 8DA
☎ 01908 281811 📄 01908 281257
e-mail: wavendon@jack-barker.co.uk

18 holes, 5570yds, Par 69, SSS 68.
Course Designer J Drake, N Elmer **Location** M1 junct 13,
off A421
Phone for further details

Hotel ★★★ 69% Moore Place Hotel, The Square,
ASPLEY GUISE ☎ 01908 282000 39 en suite 27 annexe
en suite

WESTON TURVILLE   Map 04 SP81

Weston Turville Golf New Rd HP22 5QT
☎ 01296 424084 📄 01296 395376
e-mail: westonturnvillegc@btconnect.com
**Parkland course situated at the foot of the Chiltern
Hills and providing an excellent challenge for the
accomplished golfer, yet not too daunting for the higher
handicap player. Flat easy walking with water hazards
and many interesting holes, notably the testing dog-leg
5th (418yds).**
18 holes, 6008yds, Par 69, SSS 69, Course record 68.
Club membership 600.
Visitors advance booking advised **Societies** contact in
advance. **Green Fees** not confirmed. **Cards** 🎫 💳 📇 📱
Prof Gary George **Facilities** ⊗ ⫼ by arrangement 🏌 ⚑ ♀
⛳ 🏠 ⛵ 🛅 ⛴ 🏌 **Conf** fac available Corporate
Hospitality Days available **Location** 2m SE of Aylesbury,
off A41

Hotel ⛺ Innkeeper's Lodge Aylesbury South, 40 Main St,
Weston Turville, AYLESBURY
☎ 01296 613131 & 0870 243 0500 📄 01296 616902
16 en suite

WEXHAM STREET   Map 04 SU98

Wexham Park SL3 6ND
☎ 01753 663271 📄 01753 663318
e-mail: wexhamgolf@freenetname.co.uk
**Gently undulating parkland course. Three courses. One
18-hole, one challenging nine-hole and another nine-
hole suitable for beginners.**
Blue: 18 holes, 5346yds, Par 68, SSS 66.
Red: 9 holes, 2822yds, Par 34.
Green: 9 holes, 2233yds, Par 32.
Club membership 850.
Visitors no restrictions. **Societies** contact in advance.
Green Fees £15 for 18 holes, £8.50 for nine holes
(£19.50/£11 weekends). **Cards** 🎫 💳 📇 📱 **Prof**
John Kennedy **Course Designer** E Lawrence, D Morgan

Facilities ⊗ 🏌 ⚑ ♀ ⛳ 🏠 ⛵ 🛅 ⛴ 🏌 **Conf** Corporate
Hospitality Days available **Location** 0.5m S

Hotel ★★★★ 70% Slough/Windsor Marriott Hotel, Ditton
Rd, Langley, SLOUGH ☎ 0870 400 7244 382 en suite

WING   Map 04 SP82

Aylesbury Vale Stewkley Rd LU7 0UJ
☎ 01525 240196 📄 01525 240848
e-mail: info@avgc.co.uk
**This gently undulating course is set amid tranquil
countryside. There are five ponds to pose the golfer
problems, notably on the par 4 420yd 13th - unlucky for
some - where the second shot is all downhill with an
inviting pond spanning the approach to the green. In
addition there is a practice putting green.**
18 holes, 6612yds, Par 72, SSS 72, Course record 67.
Club membership 515.
Visitors contact in advance; dress code. **Societies** phone to
book. **Green Fees** £24 per day, £19 per round, £10 for 9
holes (£29 per day, £25 per round; £20 after 11am
weekends). **Cards** 🎫 💳 📇 📱 **Prof** Terry Bunyan
Course Designer D Wright **Facilities** ⊗ ⫼ 🏌 ⚑ ♀ ⛳
🏠 ⛵ 🛅 ⛴ 🏌 **Conf** fac available Corporate
Hospitality Days available **Location** 2m NW of Leighton
Buzzard on unclassified Stewkley road, between Wing &
Stewkley

Hotel ★★★ 63% Old Palace Lodge, Church St,
DUNSTABLE ☎ 01582 662201 68 en suite

CAMBRIDGESHIRE

BAR HILL   Map 05 TL36

Cambridgeshire Moat House Moat House Hotel,
Bar Hill CB3 8EU
☎ 01954 780098 & 249971 📄 01954 780010
18 holes, 6734yds, Par 72, SSS 73, Course record 68.
Location M11/A14, onto B1050 (Bar Hill)
Phone for further details

Hotel ★★★★ 76% Hotel Felix, Whitehouse Ln,
CAMBRIDGE ☎ 01223 277977 52 en suite

BOURN   Map 05 TL35

Bourn Toft Rd CB3 7TT
☎ 01954 718958 📄 01954 718908
e-mail: proshop@bourn-golf-club.co.uk
**Meadow and parkland course with many water
features and some very challenging holes.**
18 holes, 6417yds, SSS 71.
Club membership 600.
Visitors Societies apply for booking form. **Green Fees**
terms on application. **Prof** Craig Watson **Course Designer**
J Hull **Facilities** ⊗ ⫼ 🏌 ⚑ ♀ ⛳ 🏠 ⛵ 🛅 ⛴ **Leisure**
heated indoor swimming pool, sauna, solarium,
gymnasium.

Hotel ⛺ Travelodge, Huntingdon Rd, LOLWORTH
☎ 08700 850 950 36 en suite

> **Booking a tee time is always advisable.**

Continued

BRAMPTON   Map 04 TL27

Brampton Park Buckden Rd PE28 4NF
☎ 01480 434700 📠 01480 411145
e-mail: admin@bramptonparkgc.co.uk
**Set in truly attractive countryside, bounded by the
River Great Ouse and bisected by the River Lane.
Great variety with mature trees, lakes and water
hazards. One of the most difficult holes is the 4th, a
par 3 island green, 175yds in length.**
*18 holes, 6300yds, Par 71, SSS 72, Course record 62.
Club membership 650.*
Visitors contact in advance. **Societies** apply in advance.
Green Fees not confirmed. **Cards** 💳 💳 💳 💳 💳 **Prof**
Alisdair Currie **Course Designer** Simon Gidman **Facilities**
⊗ ⅷ ⅃ 🏌 ⅄ 🏠 🛒 ⅋ 🏌 (**Conf** fac available
Corporate Hospitality Days available **Location** signs from
A1 or A14 to RAF Brampton

Hotel ★★★★ 71% Huntingdon Marriott Hotel, Kingfisher
Way, Hinchingbrooke Business Park, HUNTINGDON
☎ 01480 446000 150 en suite

CAMBRIDGE   Map 05 TL45

Gog Magog Shelford Bottom CB2 4AB
☎ 01223 247626 📠 01223 414990
e-mail: secretary@gogmagog.co.uk
**Situated just outside the centre of the university town,
Gog Magog, established in 1901, is known as the
nursery of Cambridge undergraduate golf. The chalk
downland courses are on high ground, and it is said
that if you stand on the highest point and could see far
enough to the east the next highest ground would be the
Ural Mountains. The courses are open but there are
enough trees and other hazards to provide plenty of
problems. Views from the high parts are superb. The
nature of the ground ensures good winter golf. The area
has been designated a Site of Special Scientific Interest.**
*Old Course: 18 holes, 6398yds, Par 70, SSS 70, Course
record 62.*
*Wandlebury: 18 holes, 6735yds, Par 72, SSS 72, Course
record 67.*
Club membership 1400.
Visitors weekends & bank holidays by arrangement with
secretary; contact in advance. **Societies** Tue, Thu, by
reservation. **Green Fees** £44 per day, £37 per round (£60
per round weekends & bank holidays). **Prof** Ian
Bamborough **Course Designer** Hawtree Ltd **Facilities** ⊗
ⅷ ⅃ 🏌 ⅄ 🏠 🛒 🏌 🏌 (**Conf** Corporate
Hospitality Days available **Location** 3m SE on A1307

Hotel ★★★ 71% Gonville Hotel, Gonville Place,
CAMBRIDGE ☎ 01223 366611 & 221111
📠 01223 315470 78 en suite

ELY   Map 05 TL58

Ely City 107 Cambridge Rd CB7 4HX
☎ 01353 662751 (Office) 📠 01353 668636
e-mail: elygolf@lineone.net
**Parkland course slightly undulating with water hazards
formed by lakes and natural dykes. Demanding par 4
5th hole (467yds), often into a headwind, and a testing
par 3 2nd hole (160yds) played over two ponds.
Magnificent views of cathedral.**
*18 holes, 6627yds, Par 72, SSS 72, Course record 65.
Club membership 800.*

Visitors advisable to contact the club in advance; handicap
certificate. **Societies** Tue-Fri, contact club well in advance.
Green Fees £32 per day (£38 weekends). **Prof** Andrew
George **Course Designer** Sir Henry Cotton **Facilities** ⊗ ⅷ
⅃ 🏌 ⅄ 🏠 🛒 🏌 (**Leisure** snooker. **Conf** Corporate
Hospitality Days available **Location** S of city on A10

Hotel ★★★ 67% Lamb Hotel, 2 Lynn Rd, ELY
☎ 01353 663574 31 en suite

GIRTON   Map 05 TL46

Girton Dodford Ln CB3 0QE
☎ 01223 276169 📠 01223 277150
e-mail: secretary@girtongolfclub.sagehost.co.uk
**Flat, open parkland course with many trees and
ditches. Easy walking.**
*18 holes, 6012yds, Par 69, SSS 69, Course record 66.
Club membership 800.*
Visitors with member only weekends; contact professional
in advance 01223 276991. **Societies** apply in writing.
Green Fees £22 weekdays. **Prof** Scott Thomson **Course
Designer** Allan Gow **Facilities** ⊗ ⅷ ⅃ 🏌 ⅄ 🏠 🛒 🏌
Location 3m from Cambridge. Just off junct 31 of A14

Hotel ★★★★ 76% Hotel Felix, Whitehouse Ln,
CAMBRIDGE ☎ 01223 277977 52 en suite

HEMINGFORD ABBOTS   Map 04 TL27

Hemingford Abbots Cambridge Rd PE28 9HQ
☎ 01480 495000 & 493900 📠 01480 4960000
**Interesting nine-hole course featuring a par 5 dog-leg
6th with a testing tapering fairway, two ponds at the
entrance to the 8th green and an island green on the
9th.**
*9 holes, 5468yds, Par 68, SSS 68, Course record 69.
Club membership 170.*
Visitors phone in advance, especially for weekends.
Societies apply by writing or phone. **Green Fees** not
confirmed. **Course Designer** Ray Paton **Facilities** ⊗ ⅃
🏌 ⅄ 🏠 🛒 🏌 (**Conf** fac available **Location** A14
Hemingford Abbots turn, between St Ives & Huntingdon

Hotel ★★★ 78% The Old Bridge Hotel, 1 High St,
HUNTINGDON ☎ 01480 424300 24 en suite

LONGSTANTON   Map 05 TL36

Cambridge Station Rd CB4 5DR
☎ 01954 789388
**An undulating parkland course with bunkers and
ponds.**
*18 holes, 6736yds, Par 72, SSS 73.
Club membership 300.*
Visitors phone in advance to book. **Societies** phone in
advance. **Green Fees** £12 per 18 holes, £8 per nine holes
(£15/£10 weekends). **Cards** 💳 💳 💳 💳 💳 **Prof** Geoff
Huggett, A Engelman **Facilities** ⊗ ⅷ ⅃ 🏌 ⅄ 🏌 🏌
🏌 🏌 (**Leisure** fishing, hot air ballons. **Conf** fac
available

Hotel ⛿ Travelodge Cambridge (West), Cambridge Rd,
SWAVESEY ☎ 08700 850 950 36 en suite

> **Prices may change during the currency of the
> Guide, please check when booking.**

Continued

MARCH   Map 05 TL49

March Frogs Abbey, Grange Rd PE15 0YH
☎ 01354 652364 📠 01354 658142
e-mail: secretary@marchgolfclub.co.uk
Nine-hole parkland course with a particularly
challenging par 3 9th hole, with out of bounds on the
right and high hedges to the left.
9 holes, 6204yds, Par 70, SSS 70, Course record 65.
Club membership 346.
Visitors contact in advance; with member only weekends.
Societies contact in advance. Green Fees terms on
application. Prof Alex Oldham Facilities ⊗ by
arrangement 🏏 by arrangement 🍺♀👤🏠🚲 ♂
Location 0.5m off A141, March bypass

Hotel ★★ 62% Olde Griffin Hotel, High St, MARCH
☎ 01354 652517 21 rms (20 en suite)

MELDRETH   Map 05 TL34

Malton Malton Rd, Malton SG8 6PE
☎ 01763 262200 📠 01763 262209
e-mail: desk@maltongolf.co.uk
Set among 230 acres of beautiful undulating
countryside. The River Cam bisects part of the course
which is surrounded by woodlands and wetlands.
18 holes, 6708yds, Par 72, SSS 72, Course record 67.
Visitors phone in advance. Societies booking form
available on request. Green Fees £10 per 18 holes (£16
weekends & bank holidays). Cards 💳 💳 💳 💳 ⑨ Prof
Bill Lyon Facilities ⊗ 🏏 🖡 🍺♀👤🏠🍴🚲 ♂ ⚐
Location between Orwell & Meldreth

Hotel ★★★ 74% Duxford Lodge Hotel, Ickleton Rd,
DUXFORD ☎ 01223 836444 11 en suite 4 annexe
en suite

PETERBOROUGH   Map 04 TL19

Elton Furze Bullock Rd, Haddon PE7 3TT
☎ 01832 280189 & 280614 (pro shop) 📠 01832 280299
e-mail: secretary@eltonfurzegolfclub.co.uk
Elton Furze Golf Club is set in the picturesque
surroundings of the Cambridgeshire countryside. The
course has been designed in and around mature
woodland with ponds and slopes, which provides the
golfer with an interesting and enjoyable round of golf.
18 holes, 6279yds, Par 70, SSS 71, Course record 66.
Club membership 620.
Visitors weekends by arrangement; phone in advance.
Societies by arrangement, phone for details. Green Fees
£49 per day; £31 per round (£55/£35 weekends). Cards
💳 💳 💳 Prof Glyn Krause Course Designer Roger
Fitton Facilities ⊗ 🏏 🖡 🍺♀👤🏠🚲 ♂ ⚐ Conf fac
available Corporate Hospitality Days available Location
4m SW of Peterborough, off A605/A1

Hotel ★★★★ 67% Peterborough Marriott Hotel,
Peterborough Business Park, Lynchwood,
PETERBOROUGH ☎ 01733 371111 157 en suite

Orton Meadows Ham Ln, Orton Waterville
PE2 5UU
☎ 01733 237478 📠 01733 332774
e-mail: enquiries@ortonmeadowsgolfcourse.co.uk
Picturesque course with trees, lakes and an abundance
of water fowl, providing some challenges with water
featuring on 10 holes.

18 holes, 5269yds, Par 67, SSS 68, Course record 64.
Club membership 650.
Visitors phone for reservations seven days in advance.
Societies apply in advance. Green Fees £12.30 per round
(£16.20 weekends & bank holidays). Cards 💳 💳 💳 💳
⑨ Prof AshleyHoward Course Designer D & R Fitton
Facilities ⊗ 🏏 🖡 🍺♀👤🏠🍴🐴 ⚐ Leisure 12 hole
pitch & putt. Location 3m W of town on A605

Hotel ★★★ 68% Best Western Orton Hall Hotel, Orton
Longueville, PETERBOROUGH ☎ 01733 391111
65 en suite

Peterborough Milton Milton Ferry PE6 7AG
☎ 01733 380489 & 380793 (Pro) 📠 01733 380489
e-mail: miltongolfclub@aol.com
Designed by James Braid, this well-bunkered parkland
course is set in the grounds of the Milton Estate, many
of the holes being played in full view of Milton Hall.
Challenging holes are the difficult dog-leg 10th and
15th. Easy walking.
18 holes, 6479yds, Par 71, SSS 72, Course record 62.
Club membership 800.
Visitors contact in advance; handicap certificate. Societies
bookings by e-mail or phone secretary. Green Fees £40
per 36 holes; £30 per 18 holes. Cards 💳 💳 💳 ⑨ Prof
Mike Gallagher Course Designer James Braid Facilities
⊗ 🏏 🖡 🍺♀👤🏠🍴🐴 ⚐ ⚐ Conf fac available
Corporate Hospitality Days available Location 2m W of
Peterborough on A47

Hotel ⏻ Travelodge Peterborough, Crowlands Rd,
PETERBOROUGH ☎ 08700 850 950 42 en suite

Thorpe Wood Thorpe Wood, Nene Parkway PE3 6SE
☎ 01733 267701 📠 01733 332774
e-mail: enquiries@thorpewoodgolfcourse.co.uk
Gently undulating, parkland course designed by Peter
Alliss and Dave Thomas. Challenging holes include the
5th, the longest hole, usually played with prevailing
wind, and the 14th, which has a difficult approach shot
over water to a two-tier green.
18 holes, 7086yds, Par 73, SSS 74, Course record 68.
Club membership 750.
Visitors phone for reservations seven days in advance.
Societies phone in advance, society bookings taken up to
year ahead. Green Fees £12.30 per round (£16.20
weekends & bank holidays). Cards 💳 💳 💳 💳 ⑨ Prof
Roger Fitton Course Designer Peter Allis, Dave Thomas
Facilities ⊗ 🏏 🖡 🍺♀👤🏠🍴 ⚐ Location 3m W of
city centre on A47

Hotel ★★★ 68% Best Western Orton Hall Hotel, Orton
Longueville, PETERBOROUGH ☎ 01733 391111
65 en suite

PIDLEY   Map 05 TL37

Lakeside Lodge Fen Rd PE28 3DF
☎ 01487 740540 📠 01487 740852
e-mail: info@lakeside-lodge.co.uk
A well-designed, spacious course incorporating eight
lakes, 12,000 trees and a modern clubhouse. The 9th
and 18th holes both finish dramatically alongside a lake
in front of the clubhouse. Also nine-hole par 3, and 25-
bay driving range. The Manor provides an interesting
contrast with its undulating fairways and angular
greens.

Continued   *Continued*

Lodge Course: 18 holes, 6885yds, Par 72, SSS 73.
The Manor: 9 holes, 2601yds, Par 34, SSS 33.
The Church: 12 holes, 3290yds, Par 44.
Club membership 1200.
Visitors tee time booking recommended. **Societies** phone in advance. **Green Fees** £15 per 18 holes (£22 weekends & bank holidays); £7.50 per 9/12 holes (£11 week ends & bank holidays). **Cards** 🖃 🖃 🖃 💶 **Prof** Scott Waterman **Course Designer** A W Headley **Facilities** ⊗ �𝕀𝕀 ㅌ ♥ ♀ ⚑ 🏊🛉🏌️ ✈ 🏖️ ✈ ↻ **Leisure** solarium, ten pin bowling, smart golf simulator. **Conf** fac available Corporate Hospitality Days available **Location** A141 from Huntingdon

Hotel ★★★ 70% Slepe Hall Hotel, Ramsey Rd, ST IVES ☎ 01480 463122 16 en suite

RAMSEY   Map 04 TL28

Old Nene Golf & Country Club Muchwood Ln,
Bodsey PE26 2XQ
☎ 01487 815622 📠 01487 813610
e-mail: info@oldnene.freeserve.co.uk
An easy walking, well-drained course, with water hazards and tree-lined fairways. There are excellent greens and many challenging holes across water in either a head wind or cross wind.
9 holes, 5605yds, Par 68, SSS 68, Course record 64.
Club membership 170.
Visitors book in advance especially for evenings & weekends. Dress code. **Societies** arrange in advance with Secretary. **Green Fees** not confirmed. **Cards** 🖃 🖃 🖃 💶 **Prof** Neil Grant **Course Designer** R Edrich **Facilities** ⊗ ⟋⟋ ㅌ ♥ ♀ ⚑ 🏌️ ✈ 🏖️ ✈ ↻ **Leisure** fishing, practice area. **Conf** Corporate Hospitality Days available **Location** 0.75m N of Ramsey towards Ramsey Mereside

Hotel ★★★ 78% The Old Bridge Hotel, 1 High St, HUNTINGDON ☎ 01480 424300 24 en suite

Ramsey 4 Abbey Ter PE26 1DD
☎ 01487 812600 📠 01487 815746
e-mail: admin@ramseyclub.co.uk
Flat, parkland course with water hazards and well-irrigated greens, mature tees and fairways, assuring a good surface whatever the conditions. It gives the impression of wide-open spaces, but the wayward shot is soon punished.
18 holes, 6163yds, Par 71, SSS 68, Course record 64.
Club membership 600.
Visitors handicap certificate; contact professional in advance 01487 813022; with member only weekends & bank holidays. **Societies** apply in writing. **Green Fees** £25 per 18 holes. **Cards** 🖃 🖃 🖃 🖃 **Prof** Stuart Scott **Course Designer** J Hamilton Stutt **Facilities** ⊗ by arrangement ⟋⟋ by arrangement ㅌ ♥ ♀ ⚑ 🏌️ ✈ 🏖️ ✈ **Leisure** snooker tables, bowls rinks. **Location** 12m SE of Peterborough on B1040

Hotel ★★★ 78% The Old Bridge Hotel, 1 High St, HUNTINGDON ☎ 01480 424300 24 en suite

ST IVES   Map 04 TL37

St Ives (Cambs) Westwood Rd PE27 6DH
☎ 01480 468392 📠 01480 468392
e-mail: stivesgolfclub@zoom.co.uk
9 holes, 6180yds, Par 70, SSS 70, Course record 68.
Location W side of town centre off A1123
Phone for further details

Hotel ★★★ 70% Slepe Hall Hotel, Ramsey Rd, ST IVES ☎ 01480 463122 16 en suite

ST NEOTS   Map 04 TL16

Abbotsley Golf & Squash Club Eynesbury
Hardwicke PE19 6XN
☎ 01480 474000 📠 01480 403280
e-mail: abbotsley@crown-golf.co.uk
Set in 250 acres of idyllic countryside, with two 18-hole courses and a nine-hole par 3. The Cromwell course is the less challenging of the two, offering a contrast to the renowned Abbotsley course with its holes meandering through woods and streams. One of the most memorable holes is the Abbotsley second hole known as the Mousehole, which requires an accurate tee shot to a green that is protected by a stream and shaded by the many trees that surround it.
Abbotsley Course: 18 holes, 6311yds, Par 73, SSS 72, Course record 69.
Cromwell Course: 18 holes, 6087yds, Par 70, SSS 69, Course record 66.
Club membership 550.
Visitors book for weekends. **Societies** booking essential. **Green Fees** Abbotsley:£22 per 18 holes (£30 weekends & bank holidays) Cromwell:£15 per 18 holes (£20 weekends & bank holidays). Reduced winter rates. **Cards** 🖃 🖃 🖃 🖃 🖃 **Prof** Denise Hastings, Steve Connolly **Course Designer** D Young, V Saunders **Facilities** ⊗ ⟋⟋ ㅌ ♥ ♀ ⚑ 🏌️ ✈ 🏖️ ✈ ↻ **Leisure** squash, solarium, gymnasium. **Conf** fac available Corporate Hospitality Days available **Location** 10 mins from A1 & A428

Hotel ★★ 64% Abbotsley Golf Hotel & Country Club, Potton Rd, Eynesbury Hardwicke, ST NEOTS ☎ 01480 474000 42 annexe en suite

St Neots Crosshall Rd PE19 7GE
☎ 01480 472363 📠 01480 472363
e-mail: office@stneots-golfclub.co.uk
Set in picturesque rolling parkland and divided by the river Kym, the course offers a challenge to all standards of golfer with tree-lined fairways, water hazards and outstanding greens.
18 holes, 6033yds, Par 69, SSS 69, Course record 64.
Club membership 630.
Visitors book in advance; with member only weekends. **Societies** contact in advance. **Green Fees** £40 per day; £30 per round. **Cards** 🖃 🖃 🖃 🖃 💶 **Prof** Jason Boast **Course Designer** H Vardon **Facilities** ⊗ ⟋⟋ ㅌ ♥ ♀ ⚑ 🏖️ ✈ **Conf** Corporate Hospitality Days available **Location** A1 onto B1048 into St Neots

Hotel ★★ 64% Abbotsley Golf Hotel & Country Club, Potton Rd, Eynesbury Hardwicke, ST NEOTS ☎ 01480 474000 42 annexe en suite

THORNEY   Map 04 TF20

Thorney English Drove, Thorney PE6 0TJ
☎ 01733 270570 📠 01733 270842
The 18-hole Fen course is ideal for the beginner, while the Lakes Course has a challenging links-style layout with eight holes around water.
Fen Course: 18 holes, 6104yds, Par 70, SSS 69, Course record 66.
Lakes Course: 18 holes, 6402yds, Par 71, SSS 70, Course record 65.
Club membership 500.

Continued   *Continued*

Visitors Fen course: book in advance. Lakes course: retricted weekends. **Societies** contact in advance. **Green Fees** terms on application. **Cards** 🃏 🃏 🃏 🃏 🃏 **Prof** Mark Templeman **Course Designer** A Dow **Facilities** ⊗ 🃏 🃏 🃏 🃏 🃏 🃏 🃏 🃏 🃏 🃏 **Leisure** par 3 course. **Location** off A47, 7m NE of Peterborough

....

Hotel ⬧ Travelodge Peterborough, Crowlands Rd, PETERBOROUGH ☎ 08700 850 950 42 en suite

TOFT
Map 05 TL35

Cambridge National Comberton Rd CB3 7RY
☎ 01223 264700 📄 01223 264701
e-mail: meridian@golfsocieties.com
Set in 207 acres to a Peter Allis and Clive Clark design with sweeping fairways, lakes and well-bunkered greens. The 4th hole has bunker complexes, a sharp dog-leg and a river with the green heavily guarded by bunkers. The 9th and 10th holes challenge the golfer with river crossings.

18 holes, 6651yds, Par 73, SSS 72, Course record 72. Club membership 400.
Visitors contact in advance. **Societies** phone for provisional booking **Green Fees** £16 per 18 holes (£25 weekends). **Cards** 🃏 🃏 🃏 🃏 🃏 **Prof** Jamie Donaldson **Course Designer** Peter Alliss, Clive Clark **Facilities** ⊗ 🃏 🃏 🃏 🃏 🃏 🃏 🃏 🃏 **Conf** Corporate Hospitality Days available **Location** 3m W of Cambridge, on B1046

....

Hotel ★★ 64% Abbotsley Golf Hotel & Country Club, Potton Rd, Eynesbury Hardwicke, ST NEOTS ☎ 01480 474000 42 annexe en suite

CHESHIRE

ALDERLEY EDGE
Map 07 SJ87

Alderley Edge Brook Ln SK9 7RU
☎ 01625 584493
e-mail: honsecretary@aegc.co.uk
Well-wooded, undulating pastureland course. A stream crosses seven of the nine holes.
9 holes, 5823yds, Par 68, SSS 68, Course record 62. Club membership 400.
Visitors Thu by arrangement; not Tue, Sat Mar-Oct. **Societies** Thu, apply in writing or phone. **Green Fees** not confirmed. **Cards** 🃏 🃏 🃏 🃏 🃏 **Prof** Peter Bowring **Facilities** ⊗ 🃏 🃏 🃏 🃏 🃏 🃏 **Location** 1m NW on B5085

....

Hotel ★★★ 77% Alderley Edge Hotel, Macclesfield Rd, ALDERLEY EDGE ☎ 01625 583033 52 en suite

ALDERSEY GREEN
Map 07 SJ45

Aldersey Green CH3 9EH
☎ 01829 782157
e-mail: bradburygolf@aol.com
Exciting, tricky, beautiful parkland course set in 200 acres of countryside. With tree-lined fairways and 14 lakes.
18 holes, 6145yds, Par 70, SSS 69, Course record 72. Club membership 350.
Visitors advisable to book. **Societies** by arrangement. **Green Fees** not confirmed. **Prof** Stephen Bradbury **Facilities** ⊗ 🃏 🃏 🃏 🃏 🃏 🃏 **Location** on A41 Whitchurch Rd, 6m S of Chester

....

Hotel ★★★★ 72% De Vere Carden Park, Carden Park, BROXTON ☎ 01829 731000 113 en suite 79 annexe en suite

ALSAGER
Map 07 SJ75

Alsager Golf & Country Club Audley Rd ST7 2UR
☎ 01270 875700 📄 01270 882207
e-mail: business@alsagergolfclub.com
An 18-hole parkland course situated in rolling Cheshire countryside and offering a challenge to all golfers whatever their standard.
18 holes, 6225yds, Par 70, SSS 70, Course record 67. Club membership 640.
Visitors not pm Fri; contact in advance; with member only weekends. **Societies** contact in advance. **Green Fees** not confirmed. **Prof** Richard Brown **Facilities** 🃏 🃏 🃏 🃏 🃏 🃏 **Leisure** bowling green. **Conf** fac available **Location** 2m NE of M6 junct 16

....

Hotel ★★★ 69% Manor House Hotel, Audley Rd, ALSAGER ☎ 01270 884000 57 en suite

ANTROBUS
Map 07 SJ68

Antrobus Foggs Ln CW9 6JQ
☎ 01925 730890 📄 01925 730100
e-mail: info@antrobusgolfclub.co.uk
Challenging parkland course where water is the main feature with streams and ponds in play on most holes. Large undulating greens.
18 holes, 6220yds, Par 71, SSS 71, Course record 65. Club membership 500.
Visitors not Sat; contact in advance. **Societies** weekdays, Sun after 11am, phone in advance or apply in writing. **Green Fees** £22 per day (£25 Sun). **Cards** 🃏 🃏 🃏 🃏 🃏 **Prof** Paul Farrance **Course Designer** Mike Slater **Facilities** ⊗ 🃏 🃏 🃏 🃏 🃏 🃏 🃏 🃏 **Leisure** fishing. **Conf** fac available **Location** M56 junct 10, A559 towards Northwich, 2nd left after Birch & Bottle pub onto Knutsford Rd, 1st left into Foggs Ln

....

Hotel ★★★ 64% The Floatel, Northwich, London Rd, NORTHWICH ☎ 01606 44443 60 en suite

> **If the name of the club appears in *italics*, details have not been confirmed for this edition of the guide.**

CHESTER

Map 07 SJ46

Chester Curzon Park CH4 8AR
☎ 01244 677760 📠 01244 676667
e-mail: vfcwood@chestergolfclub.co.uk
Meadowland course on two levels contained within a loop of the River Dee. The car park overlooks the racecourse across the river.
18 holes, 6508yds, Par 72, SSS 71, Course record 66.
Club membership 820.
Visitors contact in advance. Societies phone or write in advance. Green Fees £30 per day (£35 weekends). Prof Scott Booth Facilities ⊗ ⅏ ⅃ 💺 ⅃ ☷ 🏠 ⅂ 🏌 Location 1m W of city centre

Hotel ★★★ 72% Grosvenor Pulford Hotel, Wrexham Rd, Pulford, CHESTER ☎ 01244 570560 73 en suite

De Vere Carden Park Hotel Carden Park
CH3 9DQ
☎ 01829 731000 📠 01829 731032
e-mail: golf.carden@devere-hotels.com
A superb golf resort set in 750 acres of beautiful Cheshire countryside. Facilities include the mature parkland Cheshire Course, the Nicklaus Course, the 9-hole par 3 Azalea Course, Golf School and a luxurious clubhouse.

Cheshire: 18 holes, 6891yds, Par 72, SSS 71, Course record 64.
Nicklaus: 18 holes, 7094yds, Par 72, SSS 72, Course record 64.
Club membership 250.
Visitors contact in advance; handicap certificate for Nicklaus Course; metal spikes cannot be worn. Societies contact for details 01829 731594. Green Fees terms on application. Cards 🗎 🗎 🗎 🗎 🗎 Prof Paul Hodgson Course Designer Jack Nicklaus Facilities ⊗ ⅏ ⅃ 💺 ⅃ ☷ 🏠 ⅂ 🏌 🏌 Leisure hard tennis courts, heated indoor swimming pool, sauna, solarium, gymnasium, residential golf school, snooker room, dance studio. Conf fac available Corporate Hospitality Days available Location S of City on A41, right at Broxton rdbt onto A534 signed Wrexham. Situated 1.5m on left

Hotel ★★★★ 72% De Vere Carden Park, Carden Park, BROXTON ☎ 01829 731000 113 en suite   79 annexe en suite

Eaton Guy Ln, Waverton CH3 7PH
☎ 01244 335885 📠 01244 335782
e-mail: office@eatongolfclub.co.uk
A parkland course with a liberal covering of both mature trees and new planting enhanced by natural water hazards.
18 holes, 6562yds, Par 72, SSS 71, Course record 68.
Club membership 550.
Visitors contact in advance particularly for weekends. Societies Mon, Wed-Fri, weekends (pm), contact in advance. Green Fees not confirmed. Prof William Tye Course Designer Donald Steel Facilities ⊗ ⅏ ⅃ 💺 ⅃ ☷ 🏠 ⅂ 🏌 🏌 🏌 Location 3m SE of Chester off A41

Hotel ★★★★★ The Chester Grosvenor & Spa, Eastgate, CHESTER ☎ 01244 324024 80 en suite

Upton-by-Chester Upton Ln, Upton-by-Chester CH2 1EE
☎ 01244 381183 📠 01244 376955
Pleasant, tree-lined, parkland course. Not easy for low-handicap players to score well. Testing holes are 2nd (par 4), 14th (par 4) and 15th (par 3).
18 holes, 5808yds, Par 69, SSS 68, Course record 63.
Club membership 750.
Visitors contact in advance. Societies apply in writing. Green Fees terms on application. Cards 🗎 🗎 🗎 Prof Stephen Dewhurst Course Designer Bill Davies Facilities ⊗ ⅏ ⅃ 💺 ⅃ ☷ 🏠 ⅂ 🏌 🏌 Conf Corporate Hospitality Days available Location N side off A5116

Hotel ★★★★ 70% Mollington Banastre Hotel, Parkgate Rd, CHESTER ☎ 01244 851471 63 en suite

Vicars Cross Tarvin Rd, Great Barrow CH3 7HN
☎ 01244 335595 📠 01244 335686
e-mail: secretary@vcgc.fsnet.co.uk
Tree-lined parkland course, with undulating terrain.
18 holes, 6446yds, Par 72, SSS 71, Course record 64.
Club membership 750.
Visitors not Wed & competition days; advisable to contact in advance. Societies Tue, Thu, book in advance. Green Fees not confirmed. Prof JA Forsythe Course Designer J Richardson Facilities ⊗ ⅏ ⅃ 💺 ⅃ ☷ 🏠 ⅂ 🏌 🏌 Conf fac available Location 4m E on A51

Hotel ★★★ 76% Rowton Hall Country House Hotel, Whitchurch Rd, Rowton, CHESTER ☎ 01244 335262 38 en suite

CONGLETON

Map 07 SJ86

Astbury Peel Ln, Astbury CW12 4RE
☎ 01260 272772 📠 01260 276420
e-mail: admin@astburygolfclub.com
Parkland course in open countryside, bisected by a canal. The testing 12th hole involves a long carry over a tree-filled ravine. Large practice area.
18 holes, 6296yds, Par 71, SSS 70, Course record 61.
Club membership 720.
Visitors weekdays Apr-Nov; member of a recognised golf

Continued

Continued

club; handicap certificate. **Societies** contact for details. **Green Fees** not confirmed. **Prof** Ashley Salt **Facilities** ⊗ ⫼ by arrangement ⬛♀⛺🏠 **Location** 1.5m S between A34 & A527

Inn ♦♦♦♦ Egerton Arms Hotel, Astbury Village, CONGLETON ☎ 01260 273946 6 en suite

Congleton Biddulph Rd CW12 3LZ
☎ 01260 273540
9 holes, 5103yds, Par 68, SSS 65.
Location 1.5m SE on A527
Phone for further details

Inn ♦♦♦♦ Egerton Arms Hotel, Astbury Village, CONGLETON ☎ 01260 273946 6 en suite

CREWE   Map 07 SJ75

Crewe Fields Rd, Haslington CW1 5TB
☎ 01270 584099 ▤ 01270 256482
e-mail: secretary@crewegolfclub.co.uk
Undulating parkland course.
18 holes, 6424yds, Par 71, SSS 71, Course record 63.
Club membership 674.
Visitors not weekends, contact professional for details. **Societies** Tue, by arrangement with the secretary. **Green Fees** not confirmed. **Prof** David Wheeler **Course Designer** James Braid **Facilities** ⊗ ⫼ by arrangement ⬛♀⛺ 🏠✓ **Location** 2.25m NE off A534

Hotel ★★★ 72% Hunters Lodge Hotel, Sydney Rd, Sydney, CREWE ☎ 01270 583440 57 en suite

Queen's Park Queen's Park Dr CW2 7SB
☎ 01270 666724 ▤ 01270 569902
e-mail: crewe@americangolf.co.uk
9 holes, 4920yds, Par 68, SSS 64, Course record 67.
Location signed behind Queen's Park
Phone for further details

Hotel ★★★ 72% Hunters Lodge Hotel, Sydney Rd, Sydney, CREWE ☎ 01270 583440 57 en suite

DELAMERE   Map 07 SJ56

Delamere Forest Station Rd CW8 2JE
☎ 01606 883264 & 883800 ▤ 01606 889444
e-mail: info@delameregolf.co.uk
Played mostly on undulating open heath there is great charm in the way this course drops down into the occasional pine sheltered valley. Six of the first testing nine holes are from 420 to 455yds in length.

18 holes, 6328yds, Par 72, SSS 70, Course record 63.
Club membership 500.

Continued

Visitors contact in advance; only two ball games weekends. **Societies** apply in writing or by phone. **Green Fees** £50 per day; £36 per round weekdays. **Prof** Ellis B Jones **Course Designer** H Fowler **Facilities** ⊗ ⫼ by arrangement ⬛⬛♀⛺🏠🚩🛒✓❀ **Conf** Corporate Hospitality Days available **Location** 1.5m NE, off B5152

Hotel ★★ 64% Hartford Hall, School Ln, Hartford, NORTHWICH ☎ 01606 780320 20 en suite

DISLEY   Map 07 SJ98

Disley Stanley Hall Ln SK12 2JX
☎ 01663 764001 ▤ 01663 762678
e-mail: secretary@disleygolfclub.co.uk
Straddling a hilltop site above Lyme Park, this undulating parkland and moorland course affords good views and requires accuracy of approach to almost all the greens which lie on either a ledge or plateau. Testing holes are the 3rd and 4th.

18 holes, 6015yds, Par 70, SSS 69, Course record 63.
Club membership 650.
Visitors not usually weekends; contact in advance. **Societies** by arrangement. **Green Fees** £25 per day (£30 weekends). **Prof** Andrew Esplin **Facilities** ⊗ ⫼ ⬛⬛♀ ⛺🏠🚩✓ **Location** NW side of village off A6

Hotel ★★★ 61% The County Hotel, Bramhall Ln South, BRAMHALL ☎ 0870 609 6148 65 en suite

ELLESMERE PORT   Map 07 SJ47

Ellesmere Port Chester Rd, Childer Thornton CH66 1QF
☎ 0151 339 7689 ▤ 0151 339 7502
18 holes, 6432yds, Par 71, SSS 70.
Course Designer Cotton, Pennick & Lawrie **Location** NW side of town centre. M53 junct 5, A41 for Chester, club 2m on left
Phone for further details

Hotel ★★★ 69% Quality Hotel Chester, Berwick Rd, Little Sutton, ELLESMERE PORT ☎ 0151 339 5121 75 en suite

FRODSHAM   Map 07 SJ57

Frodsham Simons Ln WA6 6HE
☎ 01928 732159 ▤ 01928 734070
e-mail: office@frodshamgolfclub.co.uk
Undulating parkland course with pleasant views from all parts. Emphasis on accuracy over the whole course, the long and difficult par 5 18th necessitating a drive across water to the green. Crossed by two footpaths so extreme care needed.

Continued

18 holes, 6328yds, Par 70, SSS 70, Course record 63. Club membership 700.
Visitors contact in advance; with member only weekends. **Societies** phone for bookings. **Green Fees** £36 per round (weekdays only). **Cards** 🖃 🖃 🖃 🖃 💷 **Prof** Graham Tonge **Course Designer** John Day **Facilities** ⊗ ⅷ 🌢 💷 ♀ ♨ 🏠 ⛳ ⌀ **Leisure** snooker. **Location** 1.5m SW, M56 junct 12, follow signs for Forest Hills Hotel, Golf Club 1st left on Simons Lane

Hotel ★★★ 70% Forest Hills Hotel Leisure Complex, Overton Hill, FRODSHAM ☎ 01928 735255 58 en suite

HELSBY   Map 07 SJ47

Helsby Towers Ln WA6 0JB
☎ 01928 722021 🖷 01928 725384
e-mail: secathgc@aol.com
This gentle but challenging parkland course was originally designed by James Braid. With a wide variety of trees and natural water hazards interspersed throughout the course, it is an excellent test of golfing ability. The last six holes are reputed to be among the most difficult home stretch in Cheshire, with the last being a par 3 of 205yds to a narrow green guarded by bunkers. A wide variety of wildlife lives around the several ponds which are features to be noted (and hopefully avoided).
18 holes, 6221yds, Par 70, SSS 70, Course record 69. Club membership 640.
Visitors contact in advance; with member only weekends & bank holidays. **Societies** Tue, Thu, booking through Hon Secretary; other days possible by arrangement. **Green Fees** £28 per round. **Prof** Matthew Jones **Course Designer** James Braid (part) **Facilities** ⊗ ⅷ 🌢 💷 ♀ 🏠 ⛳ ⌀ **Conf** Corporate Hospitality Days available **Location** M56 junct 14, 1m. 6m from Chester

Hotel ★★★★★ The Chester Grosvenor & Spa, Eastgate, CHESTER ☎ 01244 324024 80 en suite

KNUTSFORD   Map 07 SJ77

Heyrose Budworth Rd, Tabley WA16 0HZ
☎ 01565 733664 🖷 01565 734578
e-mail: info@heyrosegolfclub.com
An 18-hole course in wooded and gently undulating terrain. The par 3 16th (237yds), bounded by a small river in a wooded valley, is an interesting and testing hole - one of the toughest par 3s in Cheshire. Several water hazards. Both the course and the comfortable clubhouse have attractive views.
18 holes, 6499yds, Par 73, SSS 71, Course record 66. Club membership 600.
Visitors contact pro shop for available times 01565 734267 **Societies** contact in advance. **Green Fees** not confirmed. **Cards** 🖃 🖃 🖃 🖃 💷 **Prof** Paul Affleck **Course Designer** C N Bridge **Facilities** ⊗ ⅷ by arrangement 🌢 💷 ♀ 🏠 ⛳ 🏌 ♨ ⌀ ⚑ **Conf** Corporate Hospitality Days available **Location** 1m from M6 junct 19 follow tourist signs

Hotel ★★★★ 71% Cottons Hotel & Spa, Manchester Rd, KNUTSFORD ☎ 01565 650333 109 en suite

High Legh Park Warrington Rd, Mere & High Legh WA16 0WA
☎ 01565 830888 🖷 01565 830999
Gentle parkland set in 200 acres of a former Anglo-Saxon deer park with 20 lakes and streams. USGA greens for all-year play.

Championship: 18 holes, 6715yds, Par 72. South: 18 holes, 6281yds, Par 70. North: 18 holes, 6472yds, Par 70. Club membership 700.
Visitors phone for details. **Societies** phone for details. **Green Fees** not confirmed. **Cards** 🖃 🖃 🖃 🖃 💷 **Prof** Andrew McKenzie **Facilities** ⊗ by arrangement ⅷ by arrangement 🌢 by arrangement 💷 by arrangement ♀ 🏠 🏠 ♨ ⌀ **Leisure** sauna. **Conf** Corporate Hospitality Days available **Location** M6 junct 20, A50 to High Legh

Knutsford Mereheath Ln WA16 6HS
☎ 01565 633355
9 holes, 6288yds, Par 70, SSS 70.
Location N side of town centre off A50
Phone for details

Hotel ★★★★ 71% Cottons Hotel & Spa, Manchester Rd, KNUTSFORD ☎ 01565 650333 109 en suite

---

Mere Golf & Country Club Chester Rd, Mere WA16 6LJ
☎ 01565 830155 🖷 01565 830713
e-mail: enquiries@meregolf.co.uk
A gracious parkland championship course designed by James Braid in the Cheshire sand belt, with several holes close to a lake. The round has a tight finish with four testing holes.

18 holes, 6817yds, Par 71, SSS 73, Course record 64. Club membership 550.
Visitors not Wed, Fri, Sat, Sun; by arrangement only. **Societies** apply by phone to Karen Gallagher. **Green Fees** £70 per day (£50 Oct-Mar). **Cards** 🖃 🖃 🖃 🖃 💷 **Prof** Peter Eyre **Course Designer** James Braid, George Duncan **Facilities** ⊗ ⅷ 🌢 💷 ♀ 🏠 ⛳ 🏌 🏊 ♨ ⌀ ⚑ **Leisure** hard tennis courts, heated indoor swimming pool, squash, sauna, solarium, gymnasium. **Conf** fac available Corporate Hospitality Days available **Location** M6 junct 19, 1m E. M56 junct 7, 1m W

Hotel ★★★★ 71% Cottons Hotel & Spa, Manchester Rd, KNUTSFORD ☎ 01565 650333 109 en suite

---

Peover Plumley Moor Rd, Lower Peover WA16 9SE
☎ 01565 723337 🖷 01565 723311
e-mail: mail@peovergolfclub.co.uk
Tees and greens have been positioned to maximise the benefits of the natural contours of the land. An excellent mix of holes varying in design and character, with many dog-legs and water hazards, and a river that three of the fairways cross, including the 1st.
18 holes, 6702yds, Par 72, SSS 72, Course record 69. Club membership 400.

Continued   *Continued*

Visitors dress code; book for tee times. **Societies** apply in writing or phone in advance. **Green Fees** not confirmed. **Cards** ⊞ ▦ ▤ ▨ ▦ ▨ ⊘ **Prof** Mark Twiss **Course Designer** PA Naylor **Facilities** ⊗ ⫚ ⬘ ⬛ ♥ ⬛ ⬥ ⬛ ➘ ⬛ ⌀ **Conf** fac available Corporate Hospitality Days available **Location** M6 junct 19, A556 onto Plumley Moor Rd

....

Hotel ★★ 76% The Longview Hotel & Restaurant, 55 Manchester Rd, KNUTSFORD ☎ 01565 632119 13 en suite 13 annexe en suite

LYMM   Map 07 SJ68

Lymm Whitbarrow Rd WA13 9AN
☎ 01925 755020 🖹 01925 755020
e-mail: mail@lymmgolfclub.fsnet.co.uk
First ten holes are gently undulating with the Manchester Ship Canal running alongside the 6th hole. The remaining holes are comparatively flat.
18 holes, 6341yds, Par 71, SSS 70.
Club membership 800.
Visitors with member only weekends. **Societies** Wed, contact in advance. **Green Fees** £28 per round weekdays. **Prof** Steve McCarthy **Facilities** ⊗ ⫚ ⬘ ⬛ ♥ ⬛ ⬥ ⬛ ⌀ **Location** 0.5m N off A6144

....

Hotel ★★★ 68% Lymm Hotel, Whitbarrow Rd, LYMM ☎ 01925 752233 18 rms (15 en suite) 48 annexe en suite

MACCLESFIELD   Map 07 SJ97

Macclesfield The Hollins SK11 7EA
☎ 01625 616952 (Pro) 🖹 01625 260061
e-mail: secretary@maccgolfclub.co.uk
Hillside heathland course situated on the edge of the Pennines with excellent views across the Cheshire Plain. The signature hole is the 410yd 3rd, which drops majestically to a plateau green situated above a babbling brook. The temptation is to over-club, thus bringing the out of bounds behind into play. The 7th hole is aptly named Seven Shires as seven counties can be seen on a clear day, as well as the mountains.
18 holes, 5714yds, Par 70, SSS 68, Course record 63.
Club membership 620.
Visitors apply in advance; handicap certificate. **Societies** phone initially. **Green Fees** £30 (£40 weekends & bank holidays). **Prof** Tony Taylor **Course Designer** Hawtree & Son **Facilities** ⊗ ⫚ ⬘ ⬛ ♥ ⬛ ⬥ ⬛ ➘ ⌀ **Conf** Corporate Hospitality Days available **Location** SE side of town centre off A523

....

Hotel ★★★ 70% Best Western Hollin Hall, Jackson Ln, Kerridge, Bollington, MACCLESFIELD ☎ 01625 573246 54 en suite

Shrigley Hall Hotel Shrigley Park, Pott Shrigley SK10 5SB
☎ 01625 575626 🖹 01625 575437
e-mail: shrigleyhall@paramount-hotels.co.uk
Parkland course set in 262-acre estate with breathtaking views over the Peak District and Cheshire Plain. Designed by Donald Steel, this championship standard course provides a real sporting challenge while the magnificent hotel provides a wealth of sporting facilities as well as accommodation and food.
18 holes, 6281yds, Par 71, SSS 71, Course record 68.
Club membership 500.

Shrigley Hall Hotel

Visitors contact in advance by phone. **Societies** contact in advance. **Green Fees** not confirmed. **Cards** ⊞ ▦ ⊘ **Prof** Tony Stevens **Course Designer** Donald Steel **Facilities** ⊗ ⫚ ⬘ ⬛ ♥ ⬛ ⬥ ⬛ ➘ ⬛ ⌀ **Leisure** hard tennis courts, heated indoor swimming pool, squash, fishing, sauna, solarium, gymnasium. **Location** off A523 Macclesfield-Stockport road

....

Hotel ★★★★ 68% Shrigley Hall Hotel Golf & Country Club, Shrigley Park, Pott Shrigley, MACCLESFIELD ☎ 01625 575757 150 en suite

Tytherington Dorchester Way, Tytherington SK10 2JP
☎ 01625 506000 🖹 01625 506040
e-mail: tytherington.events@clubhaus.com
Modern championship course in beautiful, mature parkland setting with eight water features and over 100 bunkers. Testing holes, notably the signature 12th hole (par 5), played from an elevated tee with adjacent snaking ditch and a lake guarding the green.
18 holes, 6765yds, Par 72, SSS 74.
Club membership 4800.
Visitors not am weekends; subject to availability. **Societies** phone & apply in writing. **Green Fees** not confirmed. **Cards** ⊞ ▦ ▤ ▦ ▨ ⊘ **Prof** Gavin Beddon **Course Designer** Dave Thomas, Patrick Dawson **Facilities** ⊗ ⫚ ⬘ ⬛ ♥ ⬛ ⬥ ⬛ ➘ ⬛ ⌀ ⌀ **Leisure** hard tennis courts, heated indoor swimming pool, squash, sauna, solarium, gymnasium. **Location** 1m N of Macclesfield off A523

....

Hotel ★★★★ 68% Shrigley Hall Hotel Golf & Country Club, Shrigley Park, Pott Shrigley, MACCLESFIELD ☎ 01625 575757 150 en suite

NANTWICH   Map 07 SJ65

Reaseheath Reaseheath College CW5 6DF
☎ 01270 625131 🖹 01270 625665
e-mail: chrisb@reaseheath.ac.uk
The course here is attached to Reaseheath College, which is one of the major centres of green-keeper training in the UK. It is a short nine-hole parkland course with challenging narrow fairways, bunkers and a water hazard, all of which make accuracy essential.
9 holes, 1882yds, Par 62, SSS 58, Course record 55.
Club membership 600.
Visitors book in advance. **Societies** apply in writing. **Green Fees** £8 per day. **Course Designer** D Mortram **Facilities** ⬛ **Conf** fac available **Location** 1.5m NE of Nantwich, off A51

....

Hotel ★★★ ♨ Rookery Hall, Main Rd, Worleston, NANTWICH ☎ 01270 610016 30 en suite 16 annexe en suite

Continued

OSCROFT　　　　　　　　　Map 07 SJ56

Pryors Hayes Willington Rd CH3 8NL
☎ 01829 741250 & 740140 ▤ 01829 749077
e-mail: info@pryors-hayes.co.uk
**Picturesque 18-hole parkland course set in the heart of
Cheshire. Gently undulating fairways demand accurate
drives, and numerous trees and water hazards make
the course a challenging test of golf.**
18 holes, 6054yds, Par 69, SSS 69.
Club membership 530.
Visitors no restrictions. **Societies** apply for application
form. **Green Fees** not confirmed. **Cards** ▦ ▦ ▦ ▦ ▦
Prof Martin Redrup **Course Designer** John Day **Facilities**
⊗ ⅷ ▮ ♥ ♀ ♨ ➔ ⚒ ✔ **Location** between A54 &
A51, 6m E of Chester

Hotel ★★★ 66% Blossoms Hotel, St John St, CHESTER
☎ 0870 400 8108　64 en suite

POYNTON　　　　　　　　　Map 07 SJ98

Davenport Worth Hall, Middlewood Rd SK12 1TS
☎ 01625 876951 ▤ 01625 877489
**Gently undulating parkland course. Extensive view
over Cheshire Plain from elevated 5th tee. Testing 17th
hole, par 4. Several long par 3s, water hazards and tree-
lined fairways make this a challenging test of golf.**
18 holes, 6027yds, Par 69, SSS 69, Course record 64.
Club membership 700.
Visitors not Wed, Sat; contact professional in advance
01625 858387. **Societies** Tue, Thu, apply in advance.
Green Fees terms on application. **Prof** Gary Norcott
Facilities ⊗ ⅷ ▮ ♥ ♀ ♨ ✔ **Leisure** snooker.
Location 1m E off A523

Hotel ★★★ 61% The County Hotel, Bramhall Ln South,
BRAMHALL ☎ 0870 609 6148　65 en suite

PRESTBURY　　　　　　　　Map 07 SJ97

Prestbury Macclesfield Rd SK10 4BJ
☎ 01625 828241 ▤ 01625 828241
e-mail: office@prestburygolfclub.com
**Undulating parkland course, with many plateau greens.
The 9th hole has a challenging uphill three-tier green
and the 17th is over a valley. Host to county and inter-
county championships, including hosting an Open
qualifying event annually until 2009.**

18 holes, 6359yds, Par 71, SSS 71, Course record 64.
Club membership 702.
Visitors contact in advance & introduction from own club;
with member only weekends. **Societies** Thu, apply in
writing. **Green Fees** £45 per round. **Cards** ▦ ▦ ▦ ▦

Continued

Prof Nick Summerfield **Course Designer** Harry S Colt
Facilities ⊗ ⅷ ▮ ♥ ♀ ♨ ✔ **Conf** Corporate
Hospitality Days available **Location** S side of village off
A538

Hotel ★★★★ 69% De Vere Mottram Hall, Wilmslow Rd,
Mottram St Andrew, Prestbury,
☎ 01625 828135 132 en suite

RUNCORN　　　　　　　　Map 07 SJ58

Runcorn Clifton Rd WA7 4SU
☎ 01928 574214 ▤ 01928 574214
e-mail: secretary@runcorngolfclub.ltd.uk
**Parkland course with tree-lined fairways and easy
walking. Fine views over Mersey and Weaver valleys.
Testing holes: 7th par 5; 14th par 5; 17th par 4.**
18 holes, 6048yds, Par 69, SSS 69, Course record 63.
Club membership 570.
Visitors with member only weekends; Tue Ladies Day.
Societies phone in advance. **Green Fees** not confirmed.
Prof David Ingman **Facilities** ⊗ ⅷ by arrangement ▮ ♥
♀ ♨ ✔ **Location** 1.25m S of Runcorn station

Hotel ★★★ 70% Lawson House Hotel & Conference
Centre, Moughland Centre, RUNCORN ☎ 01928 593300
30 en suite

SANDBACH　　　　　　　　Map 07 SJ76

Malkins Bank Betchton Rd, Malkins Bank
CW11 4XN
☎ 01270 765931 ▤ 01270 764730
e-mail: davron.hackney@congleton.gov.uk
**This parkland course has a different challenge around
every corner. The four par 3s on the course are all a
challenge, especially the signature hole 14th. Trees in all
directions make the short par 3 a really exciting hole. In
fact, holes 12, 13 and 14 are the Amen Corner of
Malkins Bank. Three very tricky holes, yet for straight
hitters low scores are possible.**
18 holes, 6005yds, Par 70, SSS 69, Course record 65.
Club membership 500.
Visitors no restrictions; advisable to book in advance.
Societies apply to course professional for booking form.
Green Fees £10.50 per 18 holes, £7.70 per nine holes
(£12.50/£7.70 weekends); reduced winter rates. **Cards** ▦
▦ ▦ ▦ **Prof** D Hackney **Course Designer** Hawtree
Facilities ⊗ ⅷ ▮ ♥ ♀ ♨ ⚒ ✔ **Location** 1.5m SE off
A533

Hotel ★★★ 61% The Chimney House Hotel, Congleton
Rd, SANDBACH ☎ 0870 609 6164　48 en suite

SANDIWAY　　　　　　　　Map 07 SJ67

Sandiway Chester Rd CW8 2DJ
☎ 01606 883247 (Secretary) ▤ 01606 888548
e-mail: info@sandiwaygolf.fsnet.co.uk
**Delightful undulating wood and heathland course with
long hills up to the 8th, 16th and 17th holes. Many dog-
legged and tree-lined holes give opportunities for the
deliberate fade or draw. True championship test and
one of the finest inland courses in north-west England.**
18 holes, 6404yds, Par 70, SSS 71, Course record 65.
Club membership 750.
Visitors book through secretary, members have reserved
tees 8.30-9.30am, 12.30-1.30pm (11.30-12.30pm winter);

Continued

handicap certificate. **Societies** book in advance through Secretary/Manager. **Green Fees** £55 per day, £45 per round (£60 per round weekends). **Prof** William Laird **Course Designer** Ted Ray **Facilities** ⊗ ⌇Ⅲ ㄴ ♥ ♀ ㅿ 🖻 ⚐ ♂ **Location** 2m W of Northwich on A556

....

Hotel ★★ 64% Hartford Hall, School Ln, Hartford, NORTHWICH ☎ 01606 780320 20 en suite

SUTTON WEAVER   Map 07 SJ57

Sutton Hall Aston Ln WA7 3ED
☎ 01928 790747 🖹 01928 759174
Undulating parkland course on south facing slopes of the Weaver Valley. Providing a challenge to all levels of play.
18 holes, 6608yds, Par 72, SSS 72, Course record 69.
Club membership 750.
Visitors contact in advance to book tee time. **Societies** write or phone in advance. **Green Fees** terms on application. **Cards** 📟 📠 📟 🖳 📟 📶 💈 **Prof** Jamie Hope **Course Designer** Ace Golf Associates **Facilities** ⊗ ⌇Ⅲ ㄴ ♥ ♀ ㅿ 🖻 🕌 ♂ **Location** M56 junct 12, follow signs for A56 to Warrington, on entering Sutton Weaver take 1st turn right

....

Hotel ★★★ 70% Forest Hills Hotel Leisure Complex, Overton Hill, FRODSHAM ☎ 01928 735255 58 en suite

TARPORLEY   Map 07 SJ56

Portal Golf & Country Club Cobbler's Cross Ln CW6 0DJ
☎ 01829 733933 🖹 01829 733928
e-mail: portalgolf@aol.com

Championship Course: 18 holes, 7037yds, Par 73, SSS 74, Course record 64.
Premier Course: 18 holes, 6508yds, Par 71, SSS 72, Course record 64.
Arderne Course: 9 holes, 1724yds, Par 30.
Course Designer Donald Steel **Location** off A49
Phone for further details

....

Hotel ★★★ 68% The Wild Boar, Whitchurch Rd, Beeston, TARPORLEY ☎ 01829 260309 37 en suite

WARRINGTON   Map 07 SJ68

Birchwood Kelvin Close, Science Park North, Birchwood WA3 7PB
☎ 01925 818819 (Club) & 816574 (Pro) 🖹 01925 822403
e-mail: birchwoodgolfclub.com@lineone.net
Very testing parkland course with many natural water hazards and the prevailing wind creating a problem on each hole. The 11th hole is particularly challenging.

Pilgrims: 18 holes, 6727yds, Par 71, SSS 73, Course record 66.
Progress: 18 holes, 6359yds, Par 71, SSS 72.
Mayflower (ladies course): 18 holes, 5849yds, Par 74, SSS 74.
Club membership 745.
Visitors advisable to check with the professional for availablity. **Societies** Mon, Wed, Thu, apply in writing or phone. **Green Fees** £26 per day; £20 per round (£34 per day weekends & bank holidays). **Cards** 📟 📟 📶 💈 **Prof** Paul McEwan **Course Designer** TJA Macauley **Facilities** ⊗ ⌇Ⅲ ㄴ ♥ ♀ ㅿ 🖻 ♂ **Conf** fac available Corporate Hospitality Days available **Location** M62 junct 11, signs for Science Park North, course 2m

---

Leigh Kenyon Hall, Broseley Ln, Culcheth WA3 4BG
☎ 01925 762943 (Secretary) 🖹 01925 765097
e-mail: golf@leighgolf.fsnet.co.uk
This is a compact parkland course, which has benefited in recent years from an intensive tree planting programme and extra drainage. An interesting course to play with narrow fairways making accuracy from the tees essential.
18 holes, 5853yds, Par 69, SSS 69, Course record 64.
Club membership 850.
Visitors contact professional for details. **Societies** Mon (ex bank holidays), Tue & Fri, apply by phone. **Green Fees** summer £32 (£40 weekends); winter £20 (£27 weekends). **Prof** Andrew Baguley **Course Designer** Harold Hilton **Facilities** ⊗ ⌇Ⅲ ㄴ ♥ ♀ ㅿ 🖻 ♂ **Conf** Corporate Hospitality Days available **Location** 5m NE off A579

....

Hotel ★★★ 72% Fir Grove Hotel, Knutsford Old Rd, WARRINGTON ☎ 01925 267471 52 en suite

---

Poulton Park Dig Ln, Cinnamon Brow, Padgate WA2 0SH
☎ 01925 822802 & 825220 🖹 01925 822802
e-mail: secretary@poultonparkgolfclub.com
A short but rather testing course which runs between houses and the motorway embankment. A range of varied trees have been placed precisely to catch the wayward drive. The seventh hole, in particular, is an excellent test of golf and you can easily lose a couple of shots on this par four. The golfer needs to drive well, keep out of the trees and putt like a champion to play to their handicap.
9 holes, 5179yds, Par 68, SSS 66, Course record 66.
Club membership 350.
Visitors midweek only; contact professional 01925 825220. **Societies** apply in advance. **Green Fees** £18 per day. **Prof** Ian Orrell **Facilities** ⊗ ⌇Ⅲ ㄴ ♥ ♀ ㅿ 🖻 **Conf** Corporate Hospitality Days available **Location** 3m from Warrington on A574

....

Hotel ★★★ 72% Fir Grove Hotel, Knutsford Old Rd, WARRINGTON ☎ 01925 267471 52 en suite

Walton Hall Warrington Rd, Higher Walton WA4 5LU
☎ 01925 263061 (bookings) 🖹 01925 263061
Set in a picturesque parkland setting with fine views from the 13th tee. It boasts many mature trees and a lot of water which comes into play on seven of the holes. Three par 3s are over 200yds.
18 holes, 6647yds, Par 72, SSS 73, Course record 70.
Club membership 250.

Continued

Continued

Visitors must book six days in advance. **Societies** contact in writing. **Green Fees** terms on application. **Prof** John Jackson **Course Designer** Peter Alliss, Dave Thomas **Facilities** ⊗ 🏌 ♀ ⚒ 🏠 ⛳ 🚶 **Location** 2m from junct 11 of M56

Hotel ★★★★ 75% De Vere Daresbury Park, Chester Rd, Daresbury, WARRINGTON
☎ 01925 267331 181 en suite

Warrington Hill Warren, London Rd, Appleton WA4 5HR
☎ 01925 261775 (Secretary) 📠 01925 265933
e-mail: secretary@warrington-golf-club.co.uk
Meadowland, with varied terrain and natural hazards. Major work has recently been carried out on both the clubhouse and the course to ensure high standards. The course is a constant challenge with ponds, trees and bunkers threatening the errant shot.

18 holes, 6305yds, Par 72, SSS 70, Course record 61. Club membership 840.
Visitors contact in advance. **Societies** by arrangement with Secretary. **Green Fees** £35 per day, £27 per round (£30 per round weekend & bank holidays). **Prof** Reay Mackay **Course Designer** James Braid **Facilities** ⊗ 🏌 🏠 🏌 ♀ ⚒ 🏠 ⛳ ✂ **Conf** Corporate Hospitality Days available **Location** 1.5m N of junct 10 of M56 on A49

Hotel ★★★★ 70% The Park Royal Hotel, Stretton Rd, Stretton, WARRINGTON ☎ 01925 730706 142 en suite

Mersey Valley Warrington Rd, Bold Heath WA8 3XL
☎ 0151 4246060 📠 0151 2579097
Parkland course, very easy walking.
18 holes, 6374yds, Par 72, SSS 71, Course record 70. Club membership 500.
Visitors six-day booking system available. **Societies** phone in advance, deposit required. **Green Fees** not confirmed.
Cards 💳 💳 💳 💳 💳 **Prof** Andy Stevenson **Course Designer** R Bush **Facilities** ⊗ 🏌 by arrangement 🏠 🏌 ♀ ⚒ 🏠 ⛳ 🐾 🚶 ✂ **Leisure** fishing. **Location** M62 junct 7, A57 towards Warrington, club 2m on left

Hotel ★★★ 62% The Hillcrest Hotel, 75 Cronton Ln, WIDNES ☎ 0151 424 1616 50 en suite

St Michael Jubilee Dundalk Rd WA8 8BS
☎ 0151 424 6230 📠 0151 495 2124
e-mail: dchapman@aol.com
18 holes, 5925yds, Par 69, SSS 67.
Location W side of town centre off A562
Phone for further details

Widnes Highfield Rd WA8 7DT
☎ 0151 424 2440 & 424 2995 📠 0151 495 2849
e-mail: email@widnes-golfclub.co.uk
Parkland course, easy walking, challenging in parts.

18 holes, 5719yds, Par 69, SSS 68, Course record 64. Club membership 700.
Visitors not before 9am, not before 4pm on competition days, contact in advance. **Societies** contact the secretary in writing. **Green Fees** £19 per 18 holes (£24 weekends). **Prof** J O'Brien **Facilities** ⊗ 🏌 🏠 🏌 ♀ ⚒ 🏠 **Conf** Corporate Hospitality Days available **Location** M62 junct 7, A57 to Warrington, right at lights onto Wilmere Ln, right at T-junct. 1st left at rdbt onto Birchfield Rd, right after 3rd pelican crossing onto Highfield Rd, right before lights

Hotel ⌂ Travelodge, Fiddlers Ferry Rd, WIDNES
☎ 08700 850 950 32 en suite

De Vere Mottram Hall Wilmslow Rd, Mottram St Andrew SK10 4QT
☎ 01625 828135 📠 01625 828950
e-mail: dmh.sales@devere-hotels.com
Championship-standard course - flat meadowland on the front nine and undulating woodland on the back nine, with well-guarded greens. The course is unusual as each half opens and closes with par 5s. Good test for both professional and novice golfers alike.

Mottram Hall: 18 holes, 7006yds, Par 72, SSS 74, Course record 63. Club membership 400.
Visitors not am weekends; may book up to two weeks in advance; handicap certificate. **Societies** contact Golf Co-ordinator in advance. **Green Fees** summer £70 per round; winter £30 per round. **Cards** 💳 💳 💳 💳 💳 💳 💳 💳

Continued *Continued*

Course Designer Dave Thomas **Facilities** ⊗ 〗 🕩 💆 🍴 ⚑ 🏠 🍴 🛎 💺 🏌 🚜 🏌 🏌 **Leisure** hard real tennis courts, heated indoor swimming pool, squash, sauna, solarium, gymnasium, day store & drying room, satellite navigation buggies. **Conf** fac available Corporate Hospitality Days available **Location** on A538 between Wilmslow & Presbury

Hotel ★★★ 69% De Vere Mottram Hall, Wilmslow Rd, Mottram St Andrew, Prestbury, ☎ 01625 828135 132 en suite

Styal Station Rd, Styal SK9 4JN
☎ 01625 531359 📋 01625 416373
e-mail: gtraynor@styalgolf.co.uk
Well-designed flat parkland course with USGA specification greens. Challenging and enjoyable test for all standards of golfer. The par 3 course is widely regarded as one of the finest short courses in the country.
18 holes, 6194yds, Par 70, SSS 70, Course record 63. Club membership 800.
Visitors contact to reserve tee time. **Societies** phone in advance. **Green Fees** £21 per round (£26 weekends). **Cards** 💳 💳 💳 💳 💳 **Prof** Simon Forrest **Course Designer** Tony Holmes **Facilities** ⊗ 〗 🕩 💆 🍴 🏠 🍴 🚜 🏌 🏌 **Leisure** par 3 nine-hole course. **Conf** fac available Corporate Hospitality Days available **Location** M56 junct 5, 5 mins from Wilmslow/Manchester Airport

Hotel ★★★ 66% Belfry House Hotel, Stanley Rd, HANDFORTH ☎ 0161 437 0511 81 en suite

Wilmslow Great Warford, Mobberley WA16 7AY
☎ 01565 872148 📋 01565 872172
e-mail: info@wilmslowgolfclub@co.uk
Peaceful parkland course, in the heart of the Cheshire countryside, offering golf at all levels.
18 holes, 6607yds, Par 72, SSS 72, Course record 62. Club membership 850.
Visitors contact in advance. **Societies** Tue, Thu, application in writing or phone in advance. **Green Fees** £55 per day; £45 per round (£65/£55 weekends & bank holidays). **Cards** 💳 💳 💳 💳 **Prof** John Nowicki **Facilities** ⊗ 〗 🕩 💆 🍴 💺 🏠 🍴 🚜 🏌 **Conf** Corporate Hospitality Days available **Location** 2m SW off B5058

Hotel ★★★ 77% Alderley Edge Hotel, Macclesfield Rd, ALDERLEY EDGE ☎ 01625 583033 52 en suite

Knights Grange Grange Ln CW7 2PT
☎ 01606 552780
e-mail: knightsgrangewinsford@valeroyal.gov.uk
An 18-hole course set in beautiful Cheshire countryside on the town outskirts. The front nine is mainly flat but players have to negotiate water, ditches and other hazards along the way. The back nine takes the player deep into the countryside, with many of the tees offering panoramic views. A lake known as the Ocean is a feature of many holes - a particular hazard for slicers of the ball. There are also many mature woodland areas to catch the wayward drive.
18 holes, 5921yds, Par 70, SSS 68.
Visitors 24 hour booking system for weekly play, after 10am Wed for weekend bookings. **Societies** apply in writing. **Green Fees** £8.65 for 18 holes (£10.80 weekends).

Cards 💳 💳 💳 💳 💳 **Course Designer** Steve Dawson **Facilities** 💆 🏠 🍴 🏌 **Leisure** hard & grass tennis courts. **Location** N side of town off A54

Hotel ✿ Travelodge, M6 Junction 18, A54, MIDDLEWICH ☎ 08700 850 950 32 en suite

Alder Root Alder Root Ln WA2 8R2
☎ 01925 291919 📋 01925 291961
e-mail: admin@alderroot.wanadoo.co.uk
A woodland course, flat in nature but with many undulations. Several holes have water hazards. One of the most testing nine-hole courses in the north west.
9 holes, 5837yds, Par 69, SSS 68, Course record 67. Club membership 400.
Visitors phone for details of dress code. **Societies** phone in advance. **Green Fees** terms on application. **Cards** 💳 💳 💳 **Prof** C McKevitt **Course Designer** Mr Lander, Mr Millington **Facilities** ⊗ 🕩 💆 🍴 🏠 🍴 🏠 🚜 🏌 **Location** M62 junct 9, A49 N for 800yds, left at lights & 1st right into Alder Root Ln

Hotel ★★ 68% Paddington House Hotel, 514 Old Manchester Rd, WARRINGTON ☎ 01925 816767 37 en suite

Lanhydrock Lostwithiel Rd PL30 5AQ
☎ 01208 73600 📋 01208 77325
e-mail: golfing@lanhydrock-golf.co.uk
An acclaimed parkland and moorland course adjacent to the National Trust property of Lanhydrock House. Nestling in a picturesque wooded valley of oak and birch, this undulating course provides an exciting and enjoyable challenge.

18 holes, 6100yds, Par 70, SSS 70, Course record 66. Club membership 300.
Visitors tee time reservation in advance advised. **Societies** phone in advance. **Green Fees** £44 per day, £24-£34 per round. **Cards** 💳 💳 💳 💳 💳 💳 **Prof** Phil Brookes **Course Designer** Hamilton Stutt **Facilities** ⊗ 〗 🕩 💆 🍴 🏠 🍴 🚜 🏌 🏌 **Conf** fac available Corporate Hospitality Days available **Location** 1m S of Bodmin off B3268

Hotel ★★★ 69% Restormel Hotel, Castle Hill, LOSTWITHIEL ☎ 01208 872223 24 en suite 12 annexe en suite

BUDE Map 02 SS20

Bude & North Cornwall Burn View EX23 8DA
01288 352006 01288 356855
e-mail: secretary@budegolf.co.uk
A traditional links course established in 1891. Situated in the centre of Bude with magnificent views to the sea. A challenging course with super greens and excellent drainage enables course to be playable throughout the year off regular tees and greens.
18 holes, 6057yds, Par 71, SSS 70.
Club membership 800.
Visitors restricted tee times weekends; book by phone six days in advance for start time or before six days with deposit. **Societies** apply in writing or by phone or fax. **Green Fees** £27 per day (£27 per round weekends & bank holidays). **Cards** **Prof** John Yeo **Course Designer** Tom Dunn **Facilities** **Leisure** snooker room. **Conf** fac available Corporate Hospitality Days available **Location** N side of town

Hotel ★★★ 68% Camelot Hotel, Downs View, BUDE
01288 352361 24 en suite

BUDOCK VEAN Map 02 SW73

Budock Vean Hotel on the River Mawnan Smith TR11 5LG
01326 250288 (hotel) & 252102 (shop)
01326 250892
e-mail: relax@budockvean.co.uk
Set in 65 acres of mature grounds with a private foreshore to the Helford River, this 18-tee undulating parkland course has a tough par 4 5th hole (456yds) which dog-legs at halfway around an oak tree. The 16th hole measures 572yds, par 5.
9 holes, 5255yds, Par 68, SSS 65, Course record 58.
Club membership 200.
Visitors contact in advance. **Societies** apply in writing or phone in advance. **Green Fees** £20 per day (£25 weekends & bank holidays). **Cards** **Prof** Tony Ramsden **Course Designer** James Braid **Facilities** **Leisure** hard tennis courts, heated indoor swimming pool, fishing, boating facilities. **Location** 1.5m SW of Mawnan Smith

Hotel ★★★★ 73% Budock Vean-The Hotel on the River, MAWNAN SMITH 01326 252100 & 0800 833927
01326 250892 57 en suite

CAMBORNE Map 02 SW64

Tehidy Park TR14 0HH
01209 842208 01209 843680
18 holes, 6241yds, Par 71, SSS 71, Course record 62.
Location on Portreath-Pool road, 2m S of Camborne
Phone for further details

Hotel ★★★ 70% Penventon Park Hotel, REDRUTH
01209 203000 68 en suite

CAMELFORD Map 02 SX18

Bowood Park Hotel Lanteglos PL32 9RF
01840 213017 01840 212622
e-mail: golf@bowoodpark.com
A rolling parkland course set in 230 acres of ancient deer park once owned by the Black Prince; 27 lakes and ponds test the golfer and serve as a haven for wildlife.
Continued

Bowood Park Golf Course

Bowood Park Golf Course: 18 holes, 6736yds, Par 72, SSS 72, Course record 68.
Club membership 3500.
Visitors booking system in operation. **Societies** contact for details. **Green Fees** £30 per round (£40 weekends). **Cards** **Prof** John Phillips **Course Designer** Sandow **Facilities** **Leisure** fishing, masseur available. **Conf** fac available Corporate Hospitality Days available **Location** through Camelford, 0.5m right onto B3266 Tintagel, 1st left at garage

Hotel ★★★ 66% Bowood Park Hotel & Golf Course, Lanteglos, CAMELFORD 01840 213017 31 en suite

CARLYON BAY Map 02 SX05

Carlyon Bay Hotel Sea Rd PL25 3RD
01726 814250 & 814228 (pro shop) 01726 814250
e-mail: golf@carlyonbay.co.uk
Championship-length, cliff-top parkland course running east to west and back again and also uphill and down a fair bit. The fairways stay in excellent condition all year as they have since the course was laid down in 1925. Magnificent views from the course across St Austell Bay; particularly from the ninth green, where an approach shot remotely to the right will plummet over the cliff edge.
18 holes, 6597yds, Par 72, SSS 71, Course record 63.
Club membership 500.
Visitors contact pro shop in advance 01726 814228. **Societies** contact in advance. **Green Fees** from £25-£42 per round depending on season. **Cards** **Prof** Mark Rowe **Course Designer** Hamilton Stutt **Facilities** **Leisure** hard tennis courts, outdoor & indoor heated swimming pools, sauna, solarium, nine-hole par 3 course. **Conf** Corporate Hospitality Days available **Location** 3m SE of St Austell

Hotel ★★★★ 75% Carlyon Bay Hotel, Sea Rd, Carlyon Bay, ST AUSTELL 01726 812304 87 en suite

CONSTANTINE BAY Map 02 SW87

Trevose PL28 8JB
01841 520208 01841 521057
e-mail: info@trevose-gc.co.uk
Well-known links course with early holes close to the sea on excellent springy turf. A championship course affording varying degrees of difficulty appealing to both the professional and higher handicap player. It is a
Continued

good test with well-positioned bunkers, and a meandering stream, and the wind playing a decisive role in preventing low scoring. Self-catering accommodation is available at the club.

Trevose Golf Club

Championship Course: 18 holes, 6863yds, Par 72, SSS 73, Course record 66.
New Course: 9 holes, 3031yds, Par 35.
Short Course: 9 holes, 1360yds, Par 29.
Club membership 1650.
Visitors subject to reservations; handicap certificate for championship course; advisable to contact in advance. **Societies** phone or write to the secretary. **Green Fees** terms on application. **Cards** ⊞ 💳 💳 🔀 💷 **Prof** Peter Green **Course Designer** H S Colt **Facilities** ⊗ 🏶 🖫 💻 ♀ 🏌 🕭 🍴 🎣 🛥 🛺 ✐ 🕯 **Leisure** hard tennis courts, heated outdoor swimming pool, self catering accommodation & a la carte restaurant. **Location** 4m W of Padstow on B3276, to St Merryn, 500yds past x-rds & right turn, signed

FALMOUTH　　　　　　　　　　Map 02 SW83

Falmouth Swanpool Rd TR11 5BQ
☎ 01326 314296 📄 01326 317783
e-mail: falmouthgc@onetel.com
Stunning sea and coastal views. The club is under new ownership and the course has been adjusted to make it fairer, while still a good test of golf. Excellent greens and a well-drained course which rarely closes.

18 holes, 6037yds, Par 71, SSS 70.
Club membership 500.
Visitors book for tee time. **Societies** contact in advance. **Green Fees** £30 per round. **Cards** ⊞ 💳 💳 💳 🔀 💷 **Prof** Nick Rogers **Facilities** ⊗ 🏶 🖫 💻 ♀ 🏌 🕭 🍴 🛥 🛺 ✐ 🕯 **Conf** Corporate Hospitality Days available **Location** SW of town centre

Hotel ★★★★ 72% Royal Duchy Hotel, Cliff Rd, FALMOUTH ☎ 01326 313042　43 en suite

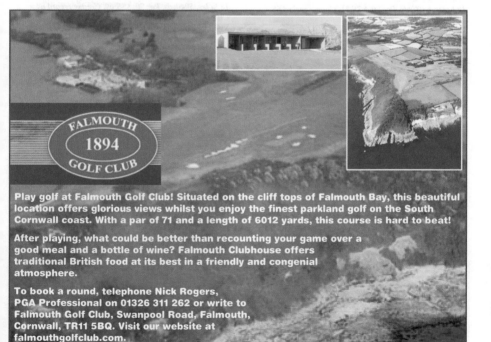

HOLYWELL BAY — Map 02 SW75

Holywell Bay TR8 5PW
☎ 01637 830095 🖹 01637 831000
e-mail: golf@trevornick.co.uk

18 holes, 2784yds, Par 61, Course record 58.
Course Designer Hartley **Location** off A3075 Newquay-Perranporth road
Phone for further details
....

Hotel ★★★ 67% Barrowfield Hotel, Hilgrove Rd, NEWQUAY ☎ 01637 878878 81 en suite 2 annexe en suite

LAUNCESTON — Map 02 SX38

Launceston St Stephens PL15 8HF
☎ 01566 773442 🖹 01566 777506
e-mail: charleshicks@tesco.net
Highly rated course with magnificent views over the historic town and moors. Noted for superb greens and lush fairways.
18 holes, 6407yds, Par 70, SSS 71, Course record 65. Club membership 800.
Visitors not weekends Apr-Oct; contact in advance.
Societies phone in advance. **Green Fees** £30 per day.
Cards 💳 💳 💳 **Prof** John Tozer **Course Designer** Hamilton Stutt **Facilities** ⊗ ⚒ 🖫 🍺 ♀ ⚒ 🏠 ⛳ 🏌 ⚐ **Conf** fac available Corporate Hospitality Days available
Location NW of town centre on B3254
....

Hotel ★★ 65% Eagle House Hotel, Castle St, LAUNCESTON ☎ 01566 772036 14 en suite

Trethorne Kennards House PL15 8QE
☎ 01566 86903 🖹 01566 86929
e-mail: mark@trethornegolfclub.com
18 holes, 6178yds, Par 71, SSS 71, Course record 69.
Course Designer Frank Frayne **Location** off junct A30 & A395, 3m W of Launceston
Phone for further details
....

Hotel ★★ 65% Eagle House Hotel, Castle St, LAUNCESTON ☎ 01566 772036 14 en suite

LELANT — Map 02 SW53

West Cornwall TR26 3DZ
☎ 01736 753401 🖹 01736 753401
e-mail: ian@westcornwallgolfclub.fsnet.co.uk
A seaside links with sandhills and lovely turf adjacent to the Hayle estuary and St Ives Bay. A real test of the player's skill, especially Calamity Corner starting at the 5th on the lower land by the River Hayle.

Continued

West Cornwall Golf Club

18 holes, 5884yds, Par 69, SSS 69, Course record 63. Club membership 813.
Visitors handicap certificate or member of club affiliated to EGU; advisable to contact in advance. **Societies** apply in writing or phone in advance. **Green Fees** not confirmed.
Cards 💳 💳 💳 💳 **Prof** Jason Broadway **Course Designer** Reverend Tyack **Facilities** ⊗ ⚒ 🖫 🍺 ♀ ⚒ 🏠 🏌 ⚐ **Leisure** snooker. **Location** N side of village off A3074
....

Hotel ★★ 72% Pedn-Olva Hotel, West Porthminster Beach, ST IVES ☎ 01736 796222 30 en suite

LOOE — Map 02 SX25

Looe Bindown PL13 1PX
☎ 01503 240239 🖹 01503 240864
Designed by Harry Vardon in 1935, this downland and parkland course commands panoramic views over south-east Cornwall and the coast. Easy walking.
18 holes, 5940yds, Par 70, SSS 69, Course record 64. Club membership 420.
Visitors subject to availability; booking recommended; handicap certificate preferred. **Societies** phone in advance, booking to be confirmed in writing. **Green Fees** not confirmed. **Cards** 💳 💳 💳 💳 **Prof** Jason Bowen **Course Designer** Harry Vardon **Facilities** ⊗ 🖫 🍺 ♀ ⚒ 🏠 🏌 ⚐ 🛒 ⚐ **Conf** Corporate Hospitality Days available **Location** 3.5m NE off B3253
....

Hotel ★★★ 66% Hannafore Point Hotel, Marine Dr, West Looe, LOOE ☎ 01503 263273 37 en suite

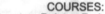
LOSTWITHIEL   Map 02 SX15

Lostwithiel Hotel, Golf & Country Club
Lower Polscoe PL22 0HQ
☎ 01208 873550 📠 01208 873479
e-mail: reception@golf-hotel.co.uk
This 18-hole course is one of the most varied in the
county, designed to take full advantage of the natural
features of the landscape, combining two distinct areas
of hillside and valley. The challenging front nine
rewards you with magnificent views of the surrounding
countryside, while the picturesque back nine runs
through parkland flanked by the river Fowey.

*18 holes, 5984yds, Par 72, SSS 71, Course record 67.
Club membership 500.*
Visitors contact in advance. Societies contact in advance.
Green Fees £30 per day (£34 weekends); reduced winter
rates. Cards ▨ ▨ ▨ ▨ ▨ ▨ 🖲 Prof Tony Nash
Course Designer S Wood Facilities ⊗ ⋔ ▨ ▇ ♀ ♨ 🏠
🍴 🛏 🚲 ✓ ⨂ Leisure hard tennis courts, heated indoor

Continued

swimming pool, fishing, gymnasium. **Conf** fac available
Corporate Hospitality Days available **Location** 1m from
Lostwithiel off A390
....
Hotel ★★★ 65% Lostwithiel Hotel Golf & Country Club,
Lower Polscoe, LOSTWITHIEL ☎ 01208 873550 27 rms
(22 en suite)

MAWGAN PORTH   Map 02 SW86

Merlin TR8 4DN
☎ 01841 540222 📠 01841 541031
18 holes, 6210yds, Par 71, SSS 71.
Course Designer Ross Oliver **Location** on Newquay-
Padstow coast road. After Mawgan Porth signs for St Eval,
course on right
Phone for further details

MAWNAN SMITH

See **Budock Vean**

MULLION   Map 02 SW61

Mullion Cury TR12 7BP
☎ 01326 240685 (sec) & 241176 (pro) 📠 01326 240685
e-mail: secretary@mulliongolfclub.plus.com
Founded in 1895, a clifftop and links course with
panoramic views over Mounts Bay. A steep downhill
slope on 6th and the 10th descends to the beach with a
deep ravine alongside the green. Second most southerly
course in the British Isles.
18 holes, 6083yds, Par 70, SSS 70.
Club membership 750.
Visitors restricted during competitions; advisable to
contact in advance; handicap certificate. *Continued*

Societies contact in advance. **Green Fees** £30 per day, £25 per round (£35/£30 weekends & bank holidays). **Prof** Ian Harris **Course Designer** W Sich **Facilities** ⊗ ⅲ ⅄ 💺 ⅄ ⚒ 🏠 🏌 ⚒ 🏌 ⚒ **Leisure** indoor computerised teaching academy. **Location** 1.5m NW of Mullion, off A3083

Hotel ★★★ 71% Polurrian Hotel, MULLION
☎ 01326 240421 39 en suite

NEWQUAY   Map 02 SW86

Newquay Tower Rd TR7 1LT
☎ 01637 874354 📠 01637 874066
e-mail: info@newquay-golf-club.co.uk
One of Cornwall's finest seaside links with magnificent views over the Atlantic Ocean. Open to the unpredictable nature of the elements and possessing some very demanding greenside bunkers, the prerequisite for good scoring at Newquay is accuracy.
18 holes, 6150yds, Par 69, SSS 69, Course record 63. Club membership 600.
Visitors phone in advance. **Societies** apply in writing or phone. **Green Fees** not confirmed. **Cards** 🔲 🔲 🔲 🔲 🔲 **Prof** Mark Bevan **Course Designer** H Colt **Facilities** ⊗ ⅲ ⅄ 💺 ⅄ 🏠 🏌 ⚒ **Leisure** Snooker. **Conf** Corporate Hospitality Days available **Location** W side of town

Hotel ★★★ 70% Hotel Bristol, Narrowcliff, NEWQUAY
☎ 01637 875181 74 en suite

Treloy TR8 4JN
☎ 01637 878554 📠 01637 871710
e-mail: paull@treloy.freeserve.co.uk
9 holes, 2143yds, Par 32, SSS 31, Course record 63.
Course Designer M R M Sandow **Location** on A3059 Newquay-St Columb Major road
Phone for further details

Hotel ★★ 72% Whipsiderry Hotel, Trevelgue Rd, Porth, NEWQUAY ☎ 01637 874777 20 rms (19 en suite)

PADSTOW

See **Constantine Bay**

PERRANPORTH   Map 02 SW75

Perranporth Budnic Hill TR6 0AB
☎ 01872 573701 📠 01872 573701
e-mail: perranporth@golfclub92.fsnet.co.uk
There are three testing par 5 holes on the links course (2nd, 5th, 11th). This seaside links course has magnificent views of the North Cornwall coastline, and excellent greens. The drainage of the course, being sand-based, is also exceptional.

Continued

Perranporth Golf Club

18 holes, 6272yds, Par 72, SSS 72, Course record 62. Club membership 600.
Visitors contact in advance, no reserved tee times. **Societies** by arrangement. **Green Fees** £25 per round (£30 per round weekends & bank holidays). Additional £5 for extra holes. **Cards** 🔲 🔲 🔲 🔲 **Prof** D Michell **Course Designer** James Braid **Facilities** ⊗ ⅲ ⅄ 💺 ⅄ 🏠 🏌 ⚒ **Conf** Corporate Hospitality Days available **Location** 0.75m NE on B3285

Hotel ★★ 70% Rosemundy House Hotel, Rosemundy Hill, ST AGNES ☎ 01872 552101 46 en suite

PORTWRINKLE   Map 02 SX45

Whitsand Bay Hotel Golf & Country Club
PL11 3BU
☎ 01503 230276 📠 01503 230329
e-mail: golf@whitsandbayhotel.co.uk
Testing seaside course laid out on cliffs overlooking

Continued

Whitsand Bay. Easy walking after first hole. The par 3 3rd hole is acknowledged as one of the most attractive holes in Cornwall.
18 holes, 6030yds, Par 69, SSS 68, Course record 62. Club membership 400.
Visitors advisable to book tee times in advance. **Societies** contact in advance. **Green Fees** £20 weekdays (£28 weekends). **Cards** 🖃 🖩 💳 💷 🖩 💳 💷 **Prof** Steve Dougan **Course Designer** Fernie **Facilities** ⊗ ⍾ ⅃ 🍴 ⛳ ♀ ⅄ 🛏 🛒 🖊 ⛳ 🚗 🏌 **Leisure** heated indoor swimming pool, sauna, solarium, gymnasium. **Conf** Corporate Hospitality Days available **Location** 5m from Torpoint off A374

....
Hotel ★★★ 68% Whitsand Bay Hotel & Golf Club, PORTWRINKLE ☎ 01503 230276 32 en suite

PRAA SANDS

Praa Sands Germoe Cross Roads TR20 9TQ
☎ 01736 763445 📠 01736 763399
e-mail: praasandsgolf@aol.com

9 holes, 4122yds, Par 62, SSS 60, Course record 59.
Course Designer R Hamilton **Location** A394 between Penzance & Helston
Phone for further details
....
Inn ◆◆◆◆ Harbour Inn, Commercal Rd, PORTHLEVEN ☎ 01326 573876 10 en suite

ROCK Map 02 SW97

St Enodoc PL27 6LD
☎ 01208 863216 📠 01208 862976
e-mail: stenodocgolfclub@aol.com
Classic links course with huge sand hills and rolling fairways. James Braid laid out the original 18 holes in 1907 and changes were made in 1922 and 1935. On the Church, the 10th is the toughest par 4 on the course and on the 6th is a truly enormous sand hill known as the Himalayas. The Holywell is not as exacting as the Church; it is less demanding on stamina but still a real test of skill for golfers of any handicap.
Church Course: 18 holes, 6243yds, Par 69, SSS 70, Course record 64.
Holywell Course: 18 holes, 4142yds, Par 63, SSS 61. Club membership 1300.
Visitors not bank holidays; handicap certificate of 24 or below for Church Course; must contain in advance. **Societies** contact by writing or phone. **Green Fees** not confirmed. **Cards** 🖃 🖩 💳 💷 🖩 💳 **Prof** Nick Williams **Course Designer** James Braid **Facilities** ⊗ ⍾ ⅃ ♀ ⅄ 🛏 🛒 🖊 ⛳ 🚗 **Location** W side of village
....
Hotel ★★ 63% The Molesworth Arms Hotel, Molesworth St, WADEBRIDGE ☎ 01208 812055 16 rms (14 en suite)

ST AUSTELL Map 02 SX05

Porthpean Porthpean PL26 6AY
☎ 01726 64613 📠 01726 71643
e-mail: ktuckerpgc@aol.com
A picturesque 18-hole course, the outward holes are in a pleasant parkland setting whilst the return holes command spectacular views over St Austell Bay.
18 holes, 5210yds, Par 67, SSS 66. Club membership 300.
Visitors no restrictions. **Societies** phone in advance. **Green Fees** £16 per day/round; £10 per nine holes. **Cards** 🖃 🖩 🖩 💳 💷 **Facilities** ⊗ 🛏 ♀ ⅄ 🛏 🛒 🖊 ⛳ 🚗 🏌 **Location** 1.5m from St Austell bypass
....
Hotel ★★ 73% The Pier House, Harbour Front, Charlestown, ST AUSTELL ☎ 01726 67955 26 en suite

St Austell Tregongeeves Ln PL26 7DS
☎ 01726 74756 📠 01726 71978
18 holes, 6089yds, Par 69, SSS 69, Course record 64.
Location 1m W of St Austell on A390
Phone for further details
....
Hotel ★★★ 72% Porth Avallen Hotel, Sea Rd, Carlyon Bay, ST AUSTELL ☎ 01726 812802 27 en suite

ST IVES Map 02 SW54

Tregenna Castle Hotel, Golf & Country Club
TR26 2DE
☎ 01736 797381 📠 01736 796066
e-mail: tregennabusiness@hotmail.com
Parkland course surrounding a castellated hotel and overlooking St Ives Bay and harbour.
18 holes, 3260yds, Par 60, SSS 58. Club membership 140.
Visitors no booking required; dress code. **Societies** phone for details. **Green Fees** not confirmed. **Cards** 🖃 🖩 💳 💷 🖩 💳 **Course Designer** Abercrombie **Facilities** ⊗ ⍾ 🛏 ♀ ⅄ 🍴 ⛳ 🚗 🏌 **Leisure** hard tennis courts, outdoor & indoor heated swimming pools, squash, sauna, solarium, gymnasium. **Location** off A30 past Hayle onto A3074
....
Hotel ★★★ 65% Tregenna Castle Hotel, ST IVES ☎ 01736 795254 83 en suite

ST JUST (NEAR LAND'S END) Map 02 SW33

Cape Cornwall Golf & Country Club
Cape Cornwall TR19 7NL
☎ 01736 788611 📠 01736 788611
e-mail: info@capecornwall.com
Coastal parkland, walled course. The walls are an integral part of its design. Britain's first and last 18-hole course overlooking the only cape in England, with views of the north Cornwall coast and old fishing coves. Features a flat front nine followed by a challenging back nine. Extremely scenic views.
18 holes, 5632yds, Par 69, SSS 68, Course record 64. Club membership 750.
Visitors must book tee time; dress code including golf shoes. **Societies** contact in advance. **Green Fees** £22 per round (£25 Fri-Sun). **Cards** 🖃 🖩 💳 💷 🖩 💳 **Prof** Jonathan Lamb **Course Designer** Bob Hamilton **Facilities** ⊗ ⍾ 🛏 ♀ ⅄ 🛏 🛒 🖊 ⛳ 🚗 🏌 **Leisure** heated indoor swimming pool, sauna, solarium, gymnasium. **Conf** fac available Corporate Hospitality Days available **Location** 1m W of St Just

Continued

Hotel ★★ 66% The Old Success Inn, Sennen Cove, SENNEN ☎ 01736 871232 12 en suite

St Mellion   See page 57

St Minver   Map 02 SW97

Roserrow Golf & Country Club
Roserrow PL27 6QT
☎ 01208 863000 📠 01208 863002
e-mail: mail@roserrow.co.uk
Challenging par 72 course in an undulating wooded valley. Stunning views over the Cornish countryside and out to Hayle Bay. Accommodation and numerous facilities on site.

18 holes, 6551yds, Par 72, SSS 72.
Club membership 450.
Visitors by arrangement, must book tee times. **Societies** apply in writing or phone in advance. **Green Fees** terms on application. **Cards** 🖃 💳 💳 💳 🎴 **Prof** Nigel Sears **Facilities** ⊗ ℳ ⓑ ⬛ ♀ ♨ 🏠 🎯 🏕 🐍 ♿ 🏌 ♂ ⓣ **Leisure** hard tennis courts, heated indoor swimming pool, sauna, solarium, gymnasium, outdoor bowling green. **Location** off B3314 between Wadebridge & Polzeath

Hotel ★★ 63% The Molesworth Arms Hotel, Molesworth St, WADEBRIDGE ☎ 01208 812055 16 rms (14 en suite)

Saltash   Map 02 SX45

China Fleet Country Club PL12 6LJ
☎ 01752 848668 📠 01752 848456
e-mail: golf@china-fleet.co.uk
A parkland course with river views. The 14th tee shot has to carry a lake of some 150yds.
18 holes, 6551yds, Par 72, SSS 72, Course record 69.
Club membership 600.
Visitors book up to seven days in advance. **Societies** phone 01752 854664 for provisional booking. **Green Fees** terms on application. **Cards** 🖃 💳 💳 🎴 **Prof** Nick Cook **Course Designer** Hawtree **Facilities** ⊗ ℳ ⓑ ⬛ ♀ ♨ 🏠 🎯 🏕 🐍 ♿ 🏌 ⓣ **Leisure** hard tennis courts, heated indoor swimming pool, squash, sauna, solarium, gymnasium, Beauty & hairdresser. **Conf** fac available Corporate Hospitality Days available **Location** 1m from the Tamar Bridge

Hotel ★★★ 67% China Fleet Country Club, SALTASH ☎ 01752 848668 40 en suite

Truro   Map 02 SW84

Killiow Park Kea TR3 6AG
☎ 01872 270246 📠 01872 240915
e-mail: killiowsec@yahoo.co.uk

Picturesque and testing parkland course set in the grounds of Killiow Estate, with mature trees, water hazards, small greens and tight fairways making this a challenge for golfers of all abilities. Five holes are played across or around water. Floodlit, all-weather driving range and practice facilities.
18 holes, 6132yds, Par 71, SSS 69.
Club membership 500.
Visitors phone to check availability. **Societies** apply in writing or phone. **Green Fees** £21 per 18 holes; reduced winter rates. **Cards** 🖃 💳 💳 💳 🎴 ♨ **Course Designer** Ross Oliver **Facilities** ⊗ ℳ ⓑ ⬛ ♀ ♨ 🐍 ⓣ **Location** 3m SW of Truro, off A39

Hotel ★★★ 75% Alverton Manor, Tregolls Rd, TRURO ☎ 01872 276633 32 en suite

Truro Treliske TR1 3LG
☎ 01872 278684 (manager) 📠 01872 225972
e-mail: trurogolfclub@tiscali.co.uk
Picturesque and gently undulating parkland course with lovely views over the cathedral city of Truro and the surrounding countryside. The 5306yd course offers a great challenge to golfers of all standards and ages. The many trees and shrubs offer open invitations for wayward balls, and with many fairways boasting out of bounds markers, play needs to be safe and sensible. Fairways are tight and the greens small and full of character, making it difficult to play to one's handicap.
18 holes, 5306yds, Par 66, SSS 65, Course record 59.
Club membership 1000.
Visitors handicap certificate; advisable to phone for availability but casual fees welcome. **Societies** phone for details. **Green Fees** £25 per day (£30 weekends & bank holidays). **Prof** Nigel Bicknell **Course Designer** Colt, Alison & Morrison **Facilities** ⊗ ℳ ⓑ ⬛ ♀ ♨ 🐍 ♿ ⓣ **Location** 1.5m W on A390 towards Redruth, adjacent to Treliske Hospital

Hotel ★★★ 75% Alverton Manor, Tregolls Rd, TRURO ☎ 01872 276633 32 en suite

Wadebridge   Map 02 SW97

St Kew St Kew Highway PL30 3EF
☎ 01208 841500 📠 01208 841500
e-mail: fjb@stkewgolfclub.fsnet.co.uk
An interesting, well-laid out nine-hole parkland course with six holes with water and 15 bunkers. In a picturesque setting there are 10 par 4s and eight par 3s. No handicap certificate required but some experience of the game is essential. Nine extra tees have now been provided allowing a different teeing area for the back nine.
9 holes, 4550yds, Par 64, SSS 62, Course record 63.
Club membership 350.
Visitors no restrictions; start time system in operation allowing booking. **Societies** apply in writing, phone or fax. **Green Fees** £15 for 18 holes, £11 for nine holes. **Cards** 💳 💳 ♨ **Prof** David Boyes **Course Designer** David Derry **Facilities** ⊗ ℳ ⓑ ⬛ ♀ ♨ 🏠 🎯 🏕 🐍 ♿ ⓣ **Leisure** fishing, ten pin bowling from end of 2005. **Conf** Corporate Hospitality Days available **Location** 2m N of Wadebridge main A39

Hotel ★★ 63% The Molesworth Arms Hotel, Molesworth St, WADEBRIDGE ☎ 01208 812055 16 rms (14 en suite)

Continued

Cornwall

St Mellion

St Mellion

Map 02 SX36

S et among 450 acres of glorious Cornish countryside, St Mellion with its two outstanding courses is heralded as the premier golf and country club in the south-west. The Old Course is perfect for golfers of all abilities. Complete with well-sited bunkers, strategically tiered greens and difficult water features, this is definitely not a course to be overlooked. But if you really want to test your game, then head to the renowned Nicklaus Course, designed by the great man himself. On its opening in 1998 Jack declared, 'St Mellion is potentially the finest golf course in Europe'. The spectacularly sculptured fairways and carpet greens of the Nicklaus Course are a challenge and an inspiration to all golfers.

Hotel, Golf & Country Club PL12 6SD
☎ **01579 351351 Fax 01579 350537**
e-mail: stmellion@crown-golf.co.uk

Nicklaus Course: 18 holes, 6592yds, Par 72, SSS 74, Course record 63.
The Old Course: 18 holes, 5782yds, Par 68, SSS 68, Course record 60.
Club membership 2850.
Visitors phone in advance 01579 352002. **Societies** apply in writing or phone in advance. **Green Fees** Nicklaus Course £80 per day, £57 per round; Old Course £70 per day, £39 per round. **Cards** 💳 ▬ ▬ 🏧 ▬ ▬ 🏧 🏧 **Prof** David Moon **Course Designer** Old Course HJ Stutt, Jack Nicklaus **Facilities** ⊗ ⊁🏴 🏌 🖥 ☕ 👥 🏠 🕯 🍴 🏑 ⛳ 🏊 🛒 ♨ 🏹 🎾 ℓ **Leisure** hard tennis courts, heated indoor swimming pool, squash, sauna, solarium, gymnasium. **Conf** fac available Corporate Hospitality Days available **Location** A38 to Saltash, onto A388 to Callington

....

Hotels

★★★ 68% St Mellion International, ST MELLION

☎ 01579 351351 39 annexe en suite

★★ Well House Hotel, St Keyne, LISKEARD

☎ 01579 342001 Fax 01579 343891 9 en suite

★★★ 67% China Fleet Country Club, SALTASH

☎ 01752 848668 Fax 01752 848456 40 en suite

CUMBRIA

ALSTON   Map 12 NY74

Alston Moor The Hermitage, Middleton in Teesdale
Rd CA9 3DB
☎ 01434 381675 & 381354 (Sec) 🖹 01434 381675
10 holes, 5518yds, Par 68, SSS 66, Course record 67.
Location 1 S of Alston on B6277
Phone for further details

Hotel ★★ 73% Nenthall Country House Hotel, ALSTON
☎ 01434 381584 18 en suite

APPLEBY-IN-WESTMORLAND   Map 12 NY62

Appleby Brackenber Moor CA16 6LP
☎ 017683 51432 🖹 017683 52773
e-mail: appleby.gc@tiscali.co.uk
**This remotely situated heather and moorland course
offers interesting golf with the rewarding bonus of
several long par 4 holes that will be remembered and
challenging par 3s. There are superb views of the
Pennines and the Lakeland hills. Renowned for the
excellent greens and very good drainage.**
*18 holes, 5901yds, Par 68, SSS 68, Course record 62.
Club membership 800.*
Visitors not before 3pm weekends, competition days;
phone for details. **Societies** contact in advance by letter or
phone. **Green Fees** £25 per day; £20 per round (£30/£24
weekends & bank holidays). **Prof** James Taylor **Course
Designer** Willie Fernie **Facilities** ⊗ ∭ ⊾ ⬛ ♀ ⚘ 🏠 ⛳
⚲ ♐ **Conf** Corporate Hospitality Days available **Location**
2m E of Appleby 0.5m off A66

Hotel ★★★ 78% Appleby Manor Country House Hotel,
Roman Rd, APPLEBY-IN-WESTMORLAND
☎ 017683 51571 23 en suite 7 annexe en suite

ASKAM-IN-FURNESS   Map 07 SD27

Dunnerholme Duddon Rd LA16 7AW
☎ 01229 462675 & 467421 🖹 01229 462675
e-mail: meg@dunnerholme.co.uk
**Unique 10-hole (18-tee) links course with view of the
Cumbrian mountains and Morecambe Bay. Two
streams run through and around the course, providing
water hazards on the 1st, 2nd, 3rd and 9th holes. The
par 3 6th is the feature hole on the course, playing to an
elevated green on Dunnerholme Rock, an imposing
limestone outcrop jutting out into the estuary.**
*10 holes, 6138yds, Par 72, SSS 69.
Club membership 400.*
Visitors restricted Sun. **Societies** apply in writing to the
secretary. **Green Fees** not confirmed. **Facilities** ⬛ ♀ ⚘
Location 1m N on A595

Hotel ★★ 64% Lisdoonie Hotel, 307/309 Abbey Rd,
BARROW-IN-FURNESS ☎ 01229 827312 12 en suite

BARROW-IN-FURNESS   Map 07 SD26

Barrow Rakesmoor Ln, Hawcoat LA14 4QB
☎ 01229 825444 & 832121 (Pro)
e-mail: barrowgolf@supanet.com
**Pleasant course laid out on two levels of meadowland,
with extensive views of the nearby Lakeland fells and
west to the Irish Sea. Upper level is affected by easterly
winds.**

Barrow Golf Club

*18 holes, 6010yds, Par 71, SSS 70, Course record 66.
Club membership 540.*
Visitors member of a recognised golf club or handicap
certificate; advisable to contact the administrator for tee
times; small groups phone administrator for details; groups
over 12 apply to the secretary in advance. **Green Fees** £25
per day (£30 weekends & bank holidays). **Prof** Andy
Whitehall **Course Designer** AM Duncan **Facilities** ⊗ ∭
⊾ ⬛ ♀ ⚘ 🏠 **Location** M6 junct 35, A590 towards
Barrow. 2m to K & C Papermill, left to top of hill

Hotel ★★ 64% Lisdoonie Hotel, 307/309 Abbey Rd,
BARROW-IN-FURNESS ☎ 01229 827312 12 en suite

Furness Central Dr LA14 3LN
☎ 01229 471232
18 holes, 6363yds, Par 71, SSS 71, Course record 65.
Location 1.75 W of town centre off A590 to Walney
Island
Phone for further details

Hotel ★★ 64% Lisdoonie Hotel, 307/309 Abbey Rd,
BARROW-IN-FURNESS ☎ 01229 827312 12 en suite

BOWNESS-ON-WINDERMERE   Map 07 SD49

Windermere Clearbarrow LA23 3NB
☎ 015394 43123 🖹 015394 43123
e-mail: windermeregc@btconnect.com
**Located in the heart of the Lake District, just 2 miles
from Windermere. The course offers some of the finest
views in the country. Not a long course but makes up
for its lack of distance with heather and tight
undulating fairways. The 6th hole has a nerve wracking
but exhilarating blind shots - 160yds over a rocky face
to a humpy fairway with a lake to avoid on the second
shot.**
*18 holes, 5122yds, Par 67, SSS 65, Course record 58.
Club membership 890.*
Visitors 10-12, 1.30-4.30pm, before 9am by arrangement;
contact pro shop seven days before day of play. **Societies**
by arrangement contact the secretary. **Green Fees** £30 per
round (£37 weekends & bank holidays). **Cards** 🖶 💳 🔲
Prof W S M Rooke **Course Designer** G Lowe **Facilities**
⊗ ∭ ⊾ ⬛ ♀ ⚘ 🏠 ⛳ ⚲ ♐ **Leisure** snooker. **Conf**
Corporate Hospitality Days available **Location** B5284
1.5m from Bowness

Hotel ★★★ 68% Famous Wild Boar Hotel, Crook,
WINDERMERE ☎ 015394 45225 36 en suite

> **Booking a tee time is always advisable.**

Continued

BRAMPTON Map 12 NY56

Brampton Tarn Rd CA8 1HN
☎ 016977 2255 🖷 01900 827852
e-mail: secretary@bramptongolfclub.com
Challenging golf across glorious rolling fell country demanding solid driving and many long second shots. A number of particularly fine holes, the pick of which may arguably be the lengthy 3rd and 11th. The challenging nature of the course is complemented by unrivalled panoramic views from a number of vantage points.
18 holes, 6407yds, Par 72, SSS 71, Course record 65. Club membership 800.
Visitors phone in advance for weekends. **Societies** apply in writing to IJ Meldrum (Secretary), 17 Helvellyn Close, Cockermouth, Cumbria CA13 9BJ or phone 01900 827985. **Green Fees** £30 per day £26 round (£38/£32 weekends & bank holidays). **Cards** **Prof** Stewart Wilkinson **Course Designer** James Braid **Facilities** **Leisure** games room. **Conf** Corporate Hospitality Days available **Location** 1.5m SE of Brampton on B6413

Hotel ★★★ Farlam Hall Hotel, BRAMPTON ☎ 016977 46234 11 en suite 1 annexe en suite

CARLISLE Map 11 NY35

Carlisle Aglionby CA4 8AG
☎ 01228 513029 (secretary) 🖷 01228 513303
e-mail: secretary@carlislegolfclub.org
Majestic, long-established parkland course with great appeal providing a secure habitat for red squirrels and deer. A complete but not too severe test of golf, with fine turf, natural hazards, a stream and many beautiful trees; no two holes are similar.
18 holes, 6263yds, Par 71, SSS 70, Course record 63. Club membership 800.
Visitors not before 9am, 12-1.30 & when tee is reserved; very restricted Sun; members only Tue, Sat. **Societies** Mon, Wed, Fri, contact secretary in advance for details 01228 513029. **Green Fees** £45 per day; £35 per round (£45 weekends). **Prof** Graeme Lisle **Course Designer** Mackenzie Ross **Facilities** **Conf** fac available Corporate Hospitality Days available **Location** M6 junct 43, 0.5m E on A69

Hotel ★★★ 71% Crown Hotel, Wetheral, CARLISLE ☎ 01228 561888 49 en suite 2 annexe en suite

Stony Holme Municipal St Aidans Rd CA1 1LS
☎ 01228 625511 🖷 01228 625511
e-mail: stephenli@carlisle-city.gov.uk
Municipal parkland course, bounded on three sides by the River Eden with a backdrop of the Lakeland fells. Water comes into play on 11 holes.
18 holes, 5783yds, Par 69, SSS 68, Course record 64. Club membership 350.
Visitors booking recommended at weekends. **Societies** phone pro shop in advance 01228 625511. **Green Fees** £9.75 per day (£12.50 weekends). **Cards** **Prof** S Ling **Facilities** **Conf** Corporate Hospitality Days available **Location** M6 junct 43, A69, 2m W

Hotel ★★★ 61% The Crown & Mitre, 4 English St, CARLISLE ☎ 01228 525491 74 en suite 20 annexe en suite

COCKERMOUTH Map 11 NY13

Cockermouth Embleton CA13 9SG
☎ 017687 76223 & 76941 🖷 017687 76941
e-mail: secretary@cockermouthgolf.co.uk
A fell course, fenced, with exceptional views of Lakeland hills and valleys and the Solway Firth. A hard climb on the 3rd and 11th holes. Testing holes: 10th and 16th (rearranged by James Braid).
18 holes, 5496yds, Par 69, SSS 66, Course record 62. Club membership 600.
Visitors restricted Wed, Sat & Sun. **Societies** apply in writing to the secretary. **Green Fees** £20 per day (£25 weekends & bank holidays). **Course Designer** J Braid **Facilities** **Conf** Corporate Hospitality Days available **Location** 3m E off A66

Continued

Cockermouth Golf Club

Hotel ★★★ 76% The Trout Hotel, Crown St, COCKERMOUTH ☎ 01900 823591 43 en suite

CROSBY-ON-EDEN   Map 12 NY45

Eden CA6 4RA
☎ 01228 573003 & 573013 ▤ 01228 818435
e-mail: alistair.wannop@virgin.net

18 holes, 6410yds, Par 72, SSS 72, Course record 64.
Location M6 junct 44, 5m on A689 towards Brampton
Phone for further details

Hotel ⌂ Travelodge (Carlisle North), A74 Southbound, Todhills, CARLISLE ☎ 08700 850 950 40 en suite

GRANGE-OVER-SANDS   Map 07 SD47

Grange Fell Fell Rd LA11 6HB
☎ 015395 32536
A fell course with no excessive climbing and dependant on how straight you hit the ball. Fine views in all directions.
9 holes, 5292yds, Par 70, SSS 66, Course record 65.
Club membership 300.
Visitors not Sun. **Green Fees** £15 per day (£20 weekends & bank holidays). **Facilities** ⬛ ♀ ⛆ **Location** 1m W on Grange-Over-Sands/Cartmel

Hotel ★★★ 75% Netherwood Hotel, Lindale Rd, GRANGE-OVER-SANDS ☎ 015395 32552 32 en suite

Grange-over-Sands Meathop Rd LA11 6QX
☎ 015395 33180 or 33754 ▤ 015395 33754
e-mail: dwright@ktdinternet.com
Interesting parkland course with well-sited tree plantations, ditches and water features. The four par 3s are considered to be some of the best in the area.
18 holes, 5958yds, Par 70, SSS 69, Course record 68.
Club membership 650.

Visitors member of golf club or recognised golf society; advisable to contact in advance for weekends. **Societies** apply in writing or by e-mail. **Green Fees** £30 per day; £25 per round (£35/£30 weekends & bank holidays). **Cards** ▦ ▦ ▦ ▧ ▨ **Prof** Andrew Pickering **Course Designer** MacKenzie (part) **Facilities** ⊗ ⽱ ⬛ ♀ ⛆ 🏠 ⛳ ⚑ **Conf** Corporate Hospitality Days available **Location** NE of town centre off B5277

Hotel ★★★ 65% Graythwaite Manor Hotel, Fernhill Rd, GRANGE-OVER-SANDS ☎ 015395 32001 & 33755 ▤ 015395 35549 21 en suite

KENDAL   Map 07 SD59

Carus Green Burneside Rd LA9 6EB
☎ 01539 721097 ▤ 01539 721097
e-mail: info@carusgreen.co.uk
Flat 18-hole course surrounded by the rivers Kent and Mint with an open view of the Kentmere and Howgill fells. The course is a mixture of relatively easy and difficult holes. These rivers come into play on five holes and there are also a number of ponds and bunkers.
Carus Green Golf Course: 18 holes, 5691yds, Par 70, SSS 68, Course record 65.
Club membership 600.
Visitors not during competitions at weekends; check by phone. **Societies** phone for details. **Green Fees** £21 per day, £16 per round (£25/20 weekends & bank holidays). **Prof** D Turner **Course Designer** W Adamson **Facilities** ⬛ ⬛ ♀ ⛆ 🏠 ⛳ ⚑ 🛒 ⚑ **Conf** Corporate Hospitality Days available **Location** 1m from Kendal centre

Hotel ★★★ 60% Riverside Hotel Kendal, Beezon Rd, Stramongate Bridge, KENDAL ☎ 01539 734861 47 en suite

Kendal The Heights LA9 4PQ
☎ 01539 723499 (pro) ▤ 01539 736466
e-mail: secretary@kendalgolfclub.co.uk
Elevated parkland and fell course with breathtaking views of Lakeland fells and the surrounding district.
18 holes, 5796yds, Par 70, SSS 68, Course record 65.
Club membership 552.
Visitors weekends subject to availability; phone to reserve tee-off time; handicap certificate. **Societies** contact in advance. **Green Fees** £26 per day, £22 per round (£32.50/£27.50 weekends). **Cards** ▦ ▦ ▦ ▦ ▧ **Prof** Peter Scott **Facilities** ⊗ ⽱ ⬛ ♀ ⛆ 🏠 ⛳ 🛒 ⚑ **Leisure** Golf clinic with computer analysis. **Location** 1m W of town centre, left at town hall & signed

Hotel ★★★ 77% The Castle Green Hotel in Kendal, KENDAL ☎ 01539 734000 100 en suite

KESWICK   Map 11 NY22

Keswick Threlkeld Hall, Threlkeld CA12 4SX
☎ 017687 79324 ▤ 017687 79861
e-mail: secretary@keswickgolf.com
18 holes, 6225yds, Par 71, SSS 72, Course record 68.
Course Designer Eric Brown **Location** 4m E of Keswick, off A66
Phone for further details

Hotel ★★★ 69% Keswick Country House Hotel, Station Rd, KESWICK ☎ 0845 458 4333 74 en suite

Continued

KIRKBY LONSDALE   Map 07 SD67

Kirkby Lonsdale Scaleber Ln, Barbon LA6 2LJ
☎ 015242 76365 📄 015242 76503
e-mail: KLGolf@Dial.Pipex.com
Parkland course on the east bank of the River Lune and crossed by Barbon Beck. Mainly following the lie of the land, the gently undulating course uses the beck to provide water hazards.
18 holes, 6538yds, Par 72, SSS 72, Course record 67.
Club membership 600.
Visitors restricted Sun; phone in advance or visit pro shop.
Societies apply in writing for society package. **Green Fees**
£28 per day (£33 weekends & bank holidays). **Prof** Chris
Barrett **Course Designer** Bill Squires **Facilities** ⊗ ⏏ 🝔
⏛ ♀ ♿ 🏠 ⛴ ♂ **Conf** Corporate Hospitality Days
available **Location** 3m NE of Kirkby Lonsdale on A683

Hotel ★★ 68% The Whoop Hall, Burrow with Burrow,
KIRKBY LONSDALE ☎ 015242 71284 24 rms
(23 en suite)

MARYPORT   Map 11 NY03

Maryport Bankend CA15 6PA
☎ 01900 812605 📄 815626
e-mail: maryportgcltd@one-tel.com
**A tight seaside links course exposed to Solway breezes.
Fine views across Solway Firth. Course comprises nine
holes links and nine holes parkland and small streams
can be hazardous on several holes. The first three holes
have the seashore on their left and an errant tee shot
can land in the water. Holes 6-14 are parkland in
quality, gently undulating and quite open. Holes 15-18
revert to links.**
18 holes, 6088yds, Par 70, SSS 69, Course record 65.
Club membership 450.
Visitors booking advisable for weekends. **Societies** apply
in writing. **Green Fees** £17 per day (£22 weekends & bank
holidays). **Facilities** ⊗ ⏏ 🝔 ⏛ ♀ ♿ ⛴ ♂ **Location** 1m
N on B5300

Hotel ★★★ 80% Washington Central Hotel, Washington
St, WORKINGTON ☎ 01900 65772 46 en suite

PENRITH   Map 12 NY53

Penrith Salkeld Rd CA11 8SG
☎ 01768 891919 📄 01768 891919
**A beautiful and well-balanced course, always changing
direction, and demanding good length from the tee. It is
set on rolling moorland with occasional pine trees and
some fine views.**
18 holes, 6047yds, Par 69, SSS 69, Course record 63.
Club membership 850.
Visitors contact in advance; handicap certificate. **Societies**
phone in advance. **Green Fees** £31 per day; £26 per round
(£36/£31 weekends). **Prof** Garry Key **Facilities** ⊗ ⏏ 🝔
⏛ ♀ ♿ 🏠 ⛴ ♂ ⏛ **Conf** fac available **Location** M6 junct
41, A6 to Penrith, left after 30mph sign & signed

Hotel ★★ 67% Brantwood Country Hotel, Stainton,
PENRITH ☎ 01768 862748 7 en suite

ST BEES   Map 11 NX91

St Bees Peckmill, Beach Rd CA27 0EJ
☎ 01946 824300
Picturesque 10-hole layout on the cliffs overlooking St

Bees beach with views of the Solway Firth and the Isle
of Man. Not overly long but testing for golfers of all
abilities.
10 holes, 5306yds, Par 66, SSS 66, Course record 64.
Club membership 400.
Visitors not after 4pm Wed, not before 3pm weekends.
Societies apply in writing in advance to club secretary.
Green Fees £12 per day. **Facilities** ⏛ ♀ ♿ **Location**
0.5m W of village off B5345

Hotel ★★★ 70% Ennerdale Country House Hotel,
CLEATOR ☎ 01946 813907 30 en suite

SEASCALE   Map 06 NY00

Seascale The Banks CA20 1QL
☎ 019467 28202 📄 019467 28202
e-mail: seascalegolfclub@aol.com
**A tough links requiring length and control. The natural
terrain is used to give a variety of holes and
considerable character. Undulating greens add to the
challenge. Fine views of the western fells, the Irish Sea
and the Isle of Man.**
18 holes, 6416yds, Par 71, SSS 71, Course record 64.
Club membership 700.
Visitors advisable to book for tee times. **Societies** phone
for provisional booking. **Green Fees** £30 per day; £25 per
round (£35/£30 weekends & bank holidays). **Prof** Sean
Rudd **Course Designer** Willie Campbell **Facilities** ⊗ ⏏ 🝔
⏛ ♀ ♿ 🏠 ⛴ ♂ ⏛ **Conf** fac available **Location** NW side
of village off B5344

Hotel ★★ 76% Low Wood Hall Hotel & Restaurant,
NETHER WASDALE ☎ 01946 726100 6 rms (5 en suite)
6 annexe en suite

SEDBERGH   Map 07 SD69

Sedbergh Dent Rd LA10 5SS
☎ 015396 21551 (Club) 📄 015396 21551
e-mail: info@sedberghgolfclub.co.uk
**A tree-lined grassland course with superb scenery in
the Yorkshire Dales National Park. Feature hole is the
par 3 2nd (110yds) where the River Dee separates the
tee from the green. Undulating fairways, excellent
greens and water features aplenty.**
9 holes, 5624yds, Par 70, SSS 68, Course record 66.
Club membership 250.
Visitors not Sun before 11.30am; advance booking advised
May-Sep. **Societies** contact in advance. **Green Fees** £18
per 18 holes, £12 per nine holes (£20/£14 weekends).
Course Designer W G Squires **Facilities** ⊗ ⏏ 🝔 ⏛ ♀ ♿
🏠 ⛴ ♂ **Leisure** fishing. **Conf** fac available Corporate
Hospitality Days available **Location** 1m S off A683

Hotel ⏛ Premier Travel Inn Kendal (Killington Lake),
Killington Lake, Motorway Service Area, Killington,
KENDAL ☎ 08701 977145 36 en suite

SILECROFT   Map 06 SD18

Silecroft Silecroft, Millom LA18 4NX
☎ 01229 774342 (sec) 📄 01229 774342
**Seaside links course parallel to the coast of the Irish Sea
with spectacular views inland of Lakeland hills. Looks
deceptively easy but an ever present sea breeze ensures
a sporting challenge.**
9 holes, 5896yds, Par 68, SSS 68, Course record 66.
Club membership 275.

Continued   *Continued*

Visitors restricted competition days & bank holidays; contact secretary in advance. **Societies** contact by writing in advance. **Green Fees** £15 per day/round (£20 weekends & bank holidays). **Facilities** ⚑ ♀ ⚐ **Location** 3m W of Millom

SILLOTH   Map 11 NY15

Silloth on Solway The Clubhouse CA7 4BL
☎ 016973 31304 ▤ 016973 31782
e-mail: sillothgolfclub@lineone.net
Billowing dunes, narrow fairways, heather and gorse and the constant subtle problems of tactics and judgement make these superb links on the Solway an exhilarating and searching test. The 13th is a good long hole. Superb views.
18 holes, 6070yds, Par 72, SSS 70, Course record 59. Club membership 700.
Visitors contact in advance. **Societies** phone for times available. **Green Fees** £33 per day (£45 per round weekends). **Cards** 💳 💳 💳 💳 💳 **Prof** J Graham **Course Designer** David Grant, Willie Park Jnr **Facilities** ⊗ ⫟ ⬙ ⚑ ♀ ⚐ 🏠 ♂ **Conf** fac available **Location** S side of village off B5300
· ·
Hotel ★★ 67% Golf Hotel, Criffel St, SILLOTH
☎ 016973 31438   22 en suite

ULVERSTON   Map 07 SD27

Ulverston Bardsea Park LA12 9QJ
☎ 01229 582824 ▤ 01229 588910
e-mail: enquiries@ulverstongolf.co.uk
Inland golf with many medium length holes on undulating parkland. The 17th is a testing par 4. Overlooking Morecambe Bay the course offers extensive views to the Lakeland Fells.
18 holes, 6201yds, Par 71, SSS 70, Course record 64. Club membership 808.
Visitors restricted Tue (Ladies Day); contact in advance; member of an accredited golf club & handicap certificate. **Societies** by arrangement in writing. **Green Fees** terms on application. **Cards** 💳 💳 💳 💳 💳 **Prof** M R Smith **Course Designer** A Herd, HS Colt **Facilities** ⊗ ⫟ ⬙ ⚑ ♀ ⚐ 🏠 ⛳ ♂ **Leisure** practice ball dispensing machine. **Conf** Corporate Hospitality Days available **Location** 2m S off A5087
· ·
Hotel ★★★ 67% Whitewater Hotel, The Lakeland Village, NEWBY BRIDGE ☎ 015395 31133 35 en suite

WINDERMERE

See **Bowness-on-Windermere**

WORKINGTON   Map 11 NY02

Workington Branthwaite Rd CA14 4SS
☎ 01900 67828 ▤ 01900 607123
e-mail: golf@workingtongolfclub.freeserve.co.uk
18 holes, 6217yds, Par 72, SSS 70, Course record 65.
Course Designer James Braid
Location 1.75m E off A596
Phone for further details
· ·
Hotel ★★★ 80% Washington Central Hotel, Washington St, WORKINGTON ☎ 01900 65772   46 en suite

Workington Golf Club Ltd

DERBYSHIRE

ALFRETON   Map 08 SK45

Alfreton Wingfield Rd, Oakerthorpe DE55 7LH
☎ 01773 832070
A small, well-established parkland course with tight fairways and many natural hazards.
11 holes, 5393yds, Par 67, SSS 66, Course record 66. Club membership 350.
Visitors advisable to contact first; weekends by arrangement only. **Societies** apply in writing or phone in advance. **Green Fees** £28 per day; £19 per round. **Facilities** ⊗ by arrangement ⫟ by arrangement ⬙ ⚑ ♀ ⚐ 🏠 **Location** 1m W on A615
· ·
Hotel ★★★★ 70% Renaissance Derby/Nottingham Hotel, Carter Ln East, SOUTH NORMANTON
☎ 01773 812000 158 en suite

ASHBOURNE   Map 07 SK14

Ashbourne Wyaston Rd DE6 1NB
☎ 01335 347960 (pro shop) ▤ 01335 347937
e-mail: sec@ashbournegc.fsnet.co.uk
With fine views over surrounding countryside, the course uses natural contours and water features.
18 holes, 6402yds, Par 71, SSS 71. Club membership 650.
Visitors not competition days; contact professional in advance. **Societies** apply in writing or phone in advance. **Green Fees** £40 per 36 holes, £25 per 18 holes (£30 per 18 holes weekends & bank holidays); reduced winter rates. **Prof** Andrew Smith **Course Designer** D Hemstock **Facilities** ⊗ ⫟ ⬙ ⚑ ♀ ⚐ 🏠 🛒 ♂ **Leisure** snooker table. **Location** off Wyaston Rd
· ·
Hotel ★★★ ⚘ 75% Callow Hall, Mappleton Rd, ASHBOURNE ☎ 01335 300900   16 en suite

BAKEWELL   Map 08 SK26

Bakewell Station Rd DE45 1GB
☎ 01629 812307
Parkland course, hilly, with plenty of natural hazards to test the golfer. Magnificent views across the Wye Valley.
9 holes, 5240yds, Par 68, SSS 66, Course record 68. Club membership 340.
Visitors restricted weekends due to competitions, Ladies Day Thu. **Societies** apply in writing or phone in advance. **Green Fees** terms on application. **Facilities** ⊗ ⫟ ⬙ ⚑ ♀

Continued   *Continued*

Conf Corporate Hospitality Days available
Location E side of town off A6

Hotel ★★★ 68% Rutland Arms Hotel, The Square, BAKEWELL ☎ 01629 812812 18 en suite 17 annexe en suite

BAMFORD Map 08 SK28

Sickleholme Saltergate Ln S33 0BN
☎ 01433 651306 🖷 01433 659498
e-mail: sickleholme.gc@btconnect.com@.
18 holes, 6064yds, Par 69, SSS 69, Course record 62.
Location 0.75m S on A6013
Phone for further details

Hotel ★★ 72% Yorkshire Bridge Inn, Ashopton Rd, Hope Valley, BAMFORD ☎ 01433 651361 14 en suite

BREADSALL Map 08 SK33

Marriot Breadsall Priory Hotel & Country Club Moor Rd, Morley DE7 6DL
☎ 01332 836080 🖷 01332 836036
e-mail: john.winterbottom@marriotthotels.co.uk
Set in 200 acres of mature parkland, the Priory Course is built on the site of a 13th-century priory. Full use has been made of natural features and fine old trees. In contrast the Moorland Course, designed by Donald Steel and built by Brian Piersen, features Derbyshire stone walls and open moors heavily affected by winds. Open when most other clubs are closed in winter.
Priory Course: 18 holes, 6100yds, Par 72, SSS 69, Course record 63.
Moorland Course: 18 holes, 6028yds, Par 70, SSS 69.
Club membership 900.
Visitors contact in advance, 10-day booking service. **Societies** phone in advance. **Green Fees** from £20. **Cards** **Prof** Darren Steels **Course Designer** D Steel **Facilities** **Leisure** hard tennis courts, heated indoor swimming pool, sauna, solarium, gymnasium. **Conf** fac available Corporate Hospitality Days available **Location** 0.75m W

Hotel ★★★★ 67% Marriott Breadsall Priory Hotel & Country Club, Moor Rd, MORLEY ☎ 01332 832235 12 en suite 100 annexe en suite

BUXTON Map 07 SK07

Buxton & High Peak Waterswallows Rd SK17 7EN
☎ 01298 26263 & 23453 🖷 26333
e-mail: admin@bhpgc.co.uk
Bracing, well-drained meadowland course, the highest in Derbyshire. Challenging course where wind direction is a major factor on some holes; others require blind shots to sloping greens.
18 holes, 5966yds, Par 69, SSS 69.
Club membership 650.
Visitors by arrangment only. **Societies** by arrangement only, phone or write to Jane Dobson. **Green Fees** £30 per day, £24 per round (£36/£30 weekends & bank holidays). **Cards** **Prof** Gary Brown **Course Designer** J Morris **Facilities** by arrangement **Conf** fac available Corporate Hospitality Days available **Location** 1m NE off A6

Hotel ★★★★ 66% Palace Hotel, Palace Rd, BUXTON ☎ 01298 22001 122 en suite

Cavendish Gadley Ln SK17 6XD
☎ 01298 79708 🖷 01298 79708
e-mail: admin@cavendishgolfcourse.com
This parkland and moorland course with its comfortable clubhouse nestles below the rising hills. Generally open to the prevailing west wind, it is noted for its excellent surfaced greens which contain many deceptive subtleties. Designed by Dr Alastair McKenzie, good holes include the 8th, 9th and 18th.

18 holes, 5721yds, Par 68, SSS 68, Course record 61.
Club membership 650.
Visitors restricted by competitions weekends, Ladies day Thu; contact in advance. **Societies** phone professional on 01298 25052. **Green Fees** terms on application. **Cards** **Prof** Paul Hunstone **Course Designer** Dr MacKenzie **Facilities** **Location** 0.75m W of town centre off A53

Hotel ★★★ 77% Best Western Lee Wood Hotel, The Park, BUXTON ☎ 01298 23002 35 en suite 5 annexe en suite

CHAPEL-EN-LE-FRITH Map 07 SK08

Chapel-en-le-Frith The Cockyard, Manchester Rd SK23 9UH
☎ 01298 812118 & 813943 (sec) 🖷 01298 814990
e-mail: info@chapelgolf.co.uk
A scenic parkland course surrounded by spectacular mountainous views. A new longer and challenging front nine, a testing short par 4 14th and possibly the best last three-hole finish in Derbyshire.
18 holes, 6434yds, Par 72, SSS 71, Course record 71.
Club membership 676.
Visitors contact professional or secretary in advance. **Societies** apply in advance to Secretary. **Green Fees** terms on application. **Cards** **Prof** David J Cullen **Course Designer** David Williams **Facilities** **Location** on B5470

Hotel ★★★ 77% Best Western Lee Wood Hotel, The Park, BUXTON ☎ 01298 23002 35 en suite 5 annexe en suite

CHESTERFIELD Map 08 SK37

Chesterfield Walton S42 7LA
☎ 01246 279256 🖷 01246 276622
e-mail: secretary@chesterfieldgolfclub.co.uk
A varied and interesting, undulating parkland course with trees picturesquely adding to the holes and the outlook alike. Stream hazard on back nine.
18 holes, 6281yds, Par 71, SSS 70, Course record 65.
Club membership 600.

Continued

Visitors not before 1.30pm Sun; with member only Sat & bank holidays; contact in advance; handicap certificate. **Societies** apply in writing. **Green Fees** £40 per day; £32 per round (£40 per round weekends). **Prof** Mike McLean **Facilities** ⊗ ⅢⅡ ㄴ ♥ ♀ ♐ 🏠 ♂ **Location** 2m SW off A632

Grassmoor Golf Centre North Wingfield Rd,
Grassmoor S42 5EA
☎ 01246 856044 📠 01246 853486
e-mail: enquiries@grassmoorgolf.co.uk
An 18-hole heathland course with interesting and challenging water features, testing greens and testing par 3s.
18 holes, 5723yds, Par 69, SSS 69, Course record 67.
Club membership 450.
Visitors contact Manager in advance; dress code. **Societies** phone Manager in advance. **Green Fees** £12 per 18 holes (£15 weekend & BH). **Cards** 🖃 💳 💳 **Prof** Gary Hagues **Course Designer** Hawtree **Facilities** ⊗ ⅢⅡ ㄴ ♥ ♀ ♐ 🏠 ♂ 🖑 ♣ ♂ **Location** M1 junct 29, 4m off B6038 between Chesterfield & Grassmoor

Stanedge Walton Hay Farm, Stonedge,
Ashover S45 0LW
☎ 01246 566156
e-mail: chrisshaw56@tiscali.co.uk/stanedge
Moorland course in hilly situation open to strong winds. Some tricky short holes with narrow fairways, so accuracy is paramount. Magnificent views over four counties. Extended course now open.
9 holes, 5786yds, Par 69, SSS 68, Course record 68.
Club membership 310.
Visitors tee off before 2pm weekdays; with member only weekends. **Societies** apply in writing. **Green Fees** £15 per round. **Facilities** ♥ ♀ ♐ **Location** 5m SW off B5057 near Red Lion pub

Tapton Park Tapton Park, Tapton S41 0EQ
☎ 01246 239500 & 273887 📠 01246 558024
Municipal parkland course with some fairly hard walking. The 625yd (par 5) 5th is a testing hole.
Tapton Main: 18 holes, 6065yds, Par 71, SSS 69.
Dobbin Clough: 9 holes, 2613yds, Par 34, SSS 34.
Club membership 400.
Visitors contact in advance; no caddies allowed. **Societies** apply in writing or phone in advance. **Green Fees** not confirmed. **Prof** Andrew Carnall **Facilities** ⊗ ⅢⅡ ㄴ ♥ ♀ ♐ 🏠 🖑 ♂ **Conf** fac available Corporate Hospitality Days available **Location** 0.5m E of Chesterfield station

Ormonde Fields Golf & Country Club
Nottingham Rd DE5 9RG
☎ 01773 570043 (Secretary) 📠 01773 742987
Parkland course with undulating fairways and natural hazards. There is a practice area.
18 holes, 6502yds, Par 71, SSS 72, Course record 68.
Club membership 500.
Visitors not before 3pm weekends; contact in advance. **Societies** phone in advance. **Green Fees** £25 per 18 holes (£30 weekend & bank holidays). **Cards** 💳 **Prof** Matthew Myford **Course Designer** John Fearn **Facilities** ⊗ ⅢⅡ ㄴ ♥ ♀ ♐ 🏠 🖑 ♂ **Conf** fac available Corporate Hospitality Days available **Location** 1m SE on A610

Hotel ★★★ 70% Makeney Hall Hotel, Makeney, Milford, BELPER ☎ 0870 609 6136 27 en suite 18 annexe en suite

Allestree Park Allestree Hall, Duffield Rd, Allestree
DE22 2EU
☎ 01332 550616 📠 01332 541195
Public course, picturesque and undulating, set in 300-acre park with views across Derbyshire.
18 holes, 5806yds, Par 68, SSS 68, Course record 61.
Club membership 220.
Visitors start times can be booked by phone. **Societies** apply in writing or by phone in advance. **Green Fees** £12.40 per round. **Cards** 🖃 💳 💳 💳 **Prof** Leigh Woodward **Facilities** ⊗ ⅢⅡ ㄴ ♥ ♀ ♐ 🏠 ♐ ♂ **Leisure** fishing. **Location** N of Derby, A38 onto A6 N, course 1.5m on left

Hotel ★★★★ 67% Marriott Breadsall Priory Hotel & Country Club, Moor Rd, MORLEY ☎ 01332 832235 12 en suite 100 annexe en suite

Mickleover Uttoxeter Rd, Mickleover DE3 9AD
☎ 01332 518662 📠 01332 512092
18 holes, 5702yds, Par 68, SSS 68, Course record 64.
Course Designer J Pennink **Location** 3m W of Derby on A516/B5020
Phone for further details

Hotel ★★★★ 74% Menzies Mickleover Court, Etwall Rd, Mickleover, DERBY ☎ 01332 521234 99 en suite

Sinfin Wilmore Rd, Sinfin DE24 9HD
☎ 01332 766462 📠 01332 769004
Municipal parkland course with tree-lined fairways; an excellent test of golf and famous for its demanding par 4s. Generally a flat course, it is suitable for golfers of all ages.
18 holes, 6163yds, Par 70, SSS 70.
Club membership 244.
Visitors book start time by phone. **Societies** apply in writing or by phone in advance. **Green Fees** £12.40 per round. **Cards** 🖃 💳 💳 💳 **Prof** Daniel Delaney **Facilities** ⊗ ⅢⅡ ㄴ ♥ ♀ ♐ 🏠 ♐ ♂ **Location** 2.5m S of city centre

Hotel ★★★ 63% International Hotel, 288 Burton Rd, DERBY ☎ 01332 369321 41 en suite 21 annexe en suite

Hallowes Hallowes Ln S18 1UR
☎ 01246 411196 📠 01246 413753
Attractive moorland and parkland course in the Derbyshire hills. Several testing par 4s and splendid views.
18 holes, 6302yds, Par 71, SSS 71, Course record 64.
Club membership 630.
Visitors with member only weekends; contact in advance. **Societies** contact in advance, various packages available. **Green Fees** £40 per day; £35 per round. **Prof** Philip Dunn **Facilities** ⊗ ⅢⅡ ㄴ ♥ ♀ ♐ 🏠 🖑 ♂ **Leisure** snooker. **Location** S side of town, off B6057 onto Cemetery Rd & Hallowes Rise/Drive

Hotel ★★★ 65% Sandpiper Hotel, Sheffield Rd, Sheepbridge, CHESTERFIELD ☎ 01246 450550 46 en suite

DUFFIELD   Map 08 SK34

Chevin Golf Ln DE56 4EE
☎ 01332 841864 📠 01332 844028
e-mail: secretary@chevingolf.fsnet.co.uk
A mixture of parkland and moorland, this course is rather hilly which makes for some hard walking, but with most rewarding views of the surrounding countryside. The 8th hole, aptly named Tribulation, requires an accurate tee shot, and is one of the most difficult holes in the country.
18 holes, 6057yds, Par 69, SSS 69, Course record 64.
Club membership 750.
Visitors not before 9.30am or off 1st tee 12.30-2pm; handicap certificate. **Societies** contact in advance. **Green Fees** terms on application. **Prof** Willie Bird **Course Designer** J Braid **Facilities** ⊗ ⅢⅢ ⅏ 🍺 ♀ ⚖ 🏠 ⚑ ♂
Conf fac available Corporate Hospitality Days available **Location** N side of town off A6

Hotel ★★★ 70% Makeney Hall Hotel, Makeney, Milford, BELPER ☎ 0870 609 6136 27 en suite 18 annexe en suite

GLOSSOP   Map 07 SK09

Glossop and District Hurst Ln, off Sheffield Rd SK13 7PU
☎ 01457 865247(clubhouse)
Moorland course in good position, excellent natural hazards. Difficult closing hole (9th & 18th).
11 holes, 5800yds, Par 68, SSS 68, Course record 64.
Club membership 350.
Visitors not weekends. **Societies** apply in writing to professional, steward or secretary. **Green Fees** terms on application. **Prof** Daniel Marsh **Facilities** ⊗ ⅢⅢ ⅏ 🍺 ♀ ⚖ 🏠 ⚑ ♂ **Conf** Corporate Hospitality Days available **Location** 1m E off A57 from town centre

HORSLEY   Map 08 SK34

Horsley Lodge Smalley Mill Rd DE21 5BL
☎ 01332 780838 📠 01332 781118
e-mail: enquiries@horsleylodge.co.uk.
This lush meadowland course set in 180 acres of Derbyshire countryside, has some challenging holes. Also floodlit driving range. USGA world class greens designed by former World Champion Peter McEvoy.

18 holes, 6400yds, Par 71, SSS 71, Course record 65.
Club membership 650.
Visitors not am weekends; contact professional in advance; handicap certificate. **Societies** phone in advance. **Green Fees** not confirmed. **Cards** 💳 💳 💳 💳 💳 💳 **Prof** G Lyall **Course Designer** Bill White **Facilities** ⊗ ⅢⅢ ⅏ 🍺 ♀ ⚖ 🏠 ⚑ 🐴 ♂ **Leisure** fishing. **Conf** fac

available Corporate Hospitality Days available **Location** 4m NE of Derby, off A38 at Belper then follow tourist signs

Hotel ★★★★ 67% Marriott Breadsall Priory Hotel & Country Club, Moor Rd, MORLEY ☎ 01332 832235 12 en suite 100 annexe en suite

KEDLESTON   Map 08 SK34

Kedleston Park DE22 5JD
☎ 01332 840035 📠 01332 840035
e-mail: secretary@kedlestonpark.fsnet.co.uk
The course is laid out in flat mature parkland with fine trees and background views of historic Kedleston Hall (National Trust). Many testing holes are included in each nine and there is an excellent modern clubhouse.
18 holes, 6675yds, Par 72, SSS 72, Course record 64.
Club membership 731.
Visitors contact in advance. **Societies** weekdays, apply in writing. **Green Fees** £55 per day; £45 per round. **Cards** 💳 💳 💳 💳 💳 💳 **Prof** Paul Wesselingh **Course Designer** James Braid **Facilities** ⊗ ⅢⅢ ⅏ 🍺 ♀ ⚖ 🏠 ⚑ ♂ 🐴 ♂ **Leisure** sauna. **Conf** Corporate Hospitality Days available **Location** signed Kedleston Hall from A38

Hotel ★★★ 63% International Hotel, 288 Burton Rd, DERBY ☎ 01332 369321 41 en suite 21 annexe en suite

LONG EATON   Map 08 SK43

Trent Lock Golf Centre Lock Ln, Sawley NG10 2FY
☎ 0115 946 4398 📠 0115 946 1183
e-mail: trentlockgolf@aol.com
Main course has two par 5, five par 3 and eleven par 4 holes, plus water features and three holes adjacent to the river. A challenging test of golf. A 24-bay floodlit golf range is available.
Main Course: 18 holes, 5848yds, Par 69, SSS 68, Course record 67.
9 holes, 2911yds, Par 36.
Club membership 500.
Visitors book for Fri pm-Sun; nine-hole course any time. **Societies** phone in advance. **Green Fees** 18-hole course: £15 per round (£20 weekends). nine-hole course: £6 per round (£7.50 weekends). **Cards** 💳 💳 💳 💳 💳 💳 **Prof** M Taylor **Course Designer** E McCausland **Facilities** ⊗ ⅢⅢ ⅏ 🍺 ♀ ⚖ 🏠 🐴 ♂ ♂ **Conf** fac available Corporate Hospitality Days available

Hotel ★★★ 66% Novotel Nottingham/Derby, Bostock Ln, LONG EATON ☎ 0115 946 5111 108 en suite

MATLOCK   Map 08 SK36

Matlock Chesterfield Rd, Matlock Moor DE4 5LZ
☎ 01629 582191 📠 01629 582135
Moorland course with fine views of the beautiful Peak District.
18 holes, 5996yds, Par 70, SSS 69, Course record 63.
Club membership 700.
Visitors with member only weekends & bank holidays; members only weekdays 12.30-1.30pm. **Societies** by arrangement with Secretary. **Green Fees** not confirmed. **Prof** MA Whithorn **Course Designer** Tom Williamson **Facilities** ⊗ ⅢⅢ ⅏ 🍺 ♀ ⚖ 🏠 ♂ **Location** 1.5m NE of Matlock on A632

Continued

MICKLEOVER   Map 08 SK33

Pastures Social Centre, Hospital Ln DE3 5DQ
☎ 01332 521074
9 holes, 5095yds, Par 64, SSS 65, Course record 67.
Course Designer J F Pennik **Location** 1m SW off A516
Phone for further details

Hotel ★★★ 63% International Hotel, 288 Burton Rd,
DERBY ☎ 01332 369321 41 en suite 21 annexe en suite

MORLEY   Map 08 SK34

Morley Hayes Main Rd DE7 6DG
☎ 01332 780480 & 782000 (shop) ▤ 01332 781094
e-mail: golf@morleyhayes.com
**Peaceful pay and play course set in a splendid valley
and incorporating charming water features and
woodland. Floodlit driving range. Challenging
nine-hole short course (Tower Course).**

*Manor Course: 18 holes, 6726yds, Par 72, SSS 72,
Course record 63.*
Tower Course: 9 holes, 1614yds, Par 30.
Visitors Societies booking essential. **Green Fees** Manor
course: £33 per day, £18 per round (£42/£24 weekends)
Tower course £15 for 18 holes, £8.50 for 9 holes
(£20/£10.50 weekends). **Cards** ▦ ▦ ▦ ▦ ▦ ▦
Prof Mark Marriott **Facilities** ⊗ ⅀ ㄴ ♥ ♀ ㅿ ㅂ ☀ ♣
♂ ℓ **Conf** fac available Corporate Hospitality Days
available **Location** on A608 4m N of Derby

Hotel ★★★★ 67% Marriott Breadsall Priory Hotel &
Country Club, Moor Rd, MORLEY ☎ 01332 832235
12 en suite 100 annexe en suite

NEW MILLS   Map 07 SK08

New Mills Shaw Marsh SK22 4QE
☎ 01663 743485 ▤ 01663 743485
**Moorland course with panoramic views and first-class
greens.**
18 holes, 5604yds, Par 69, SSS 67, Course record 62.
Club membership 483.
Visitors not during competitions; contact secretary or
professional in advance. **Societies** contact secretary or
professional in advance. **Green Fees** terms on application.
Prof Carl Cross **Course Designer** Williams **Facilities** ⊗
⅀ ㄴ ♥ ♀ ㅿ ㅂ ☀ ♥ ♣ ♂ ℓ **Conf** Corporate
Hospitality Days available **Location** 0.5m N off B6101

RENISHAW   Map 08 SK47

Renishaw Park Club House, Mill Ln S21 3UZ
☎ 01246 432044 & 435484 ▤ 01246 432116
Part parkland and part meadowland with easy walking.

18 holes, 6107yds, Par 71, SSS 70, Course record 64.
Club membership 750.
Visitors not competition days; contact professional 01246
435484 for other days. **Societies** phone Secretary's office
to arrange. **Green Fees** not confirmed. **Prof** John Oates
Course Designer Sir George Sitwell **Facilities** ⊗ ⅀ ㄴ ♥
♀ ㅿ ♥ ♂ **Location** 1.5m W of junct 30 M1

Hotel ★★★ 65% Sitwell Arms Hotel, Station Rd,
RENISHAW ☎ 01246 435226 29 en suite

RISLEY   Map 08 SK43

Maywood Rushy Ln DE72 3ST
☎ 0115 939 2306 & 9490043 (pro)
**Wooded parkland course with numerous water
hazards.**
18 holes, 6424yds, Par 72, SSS 71, Course record 70.
Club membership 450.
Visitors not during competitions; advisable to contact in
advance in summer; dress code. **Societies** by arrangement.
Green Fees not confirmed. **Prof** Simon Purcell-Jackson
Course Designer P Moon **Facilities** ⊗ ⅀ ㄴ ♥ ♀ ㅿ ㅂ
☀ ♂ **Location** M1 junct 25

SHIRLAND   Map 08 SK45

Shirland Lower Delves DE55 6AU
☎ 01773 834935 ▤ 01773 832515
**Rolling parkland and tree-lined course with extensive
views of Derbyshire countryside.**
18 holes, 6072yds, Par 71, SSS 70, Course record 67.
Club membership 250.
Visitors contact professional in advance. **Societies** contact
professional. **Green Fees** terms on application. **Cards** ▦
▦ ▦ ▦ **Prof** Neville Hallam **Facilities** ⊗ ⅀ ㄴ ♥ ♀ ㅿ
ㅂ ☀ ♥ ♣ ♂ **Conf** fac available Corporate Hospitality
Days available **Location** S side of village off A61

Hotel ★★★★ 70% Renaissance Derby/Nottingham Hotel,
Carter Ln East, SOUTH NORMANTON
☎ 01773 812000 158 en suite

STANTON BY DALE   Map 08 SK43

Erewash Valley DE7 4QR
☎ 0115 932 3258 ▤ 0115 944 0061
e-mail: secretary@erewashvalley.co.uk
**Parkland and meadowland course overlooking valley
and M1. Unique 4th and 5th in Victorian quarry
bottom; 5th testing par 3.**
18 holes, 6557yds, Par 72, SSS 71, Course record 67.
Club membership 750.
Visitors not during club events. **Societies** contact in
advance. **Green Fees** £40 per day, £30 per round (£40 per
round weekends). **Prof** M J Ronan **Course Designer**
Hawtree **Facilities** ⊗ ⅀ ㄴ ♥ ♀ ㅿ ㅂ ☀ ♥ ♣ ♂ ℓ
Location 1m W. M1 junct 25, 2m

UNSTONE   Map 08 SK37

Birch Hall Sheffield Rd S18 4DB
☎ 01246 291979 ▤ 01246 412912
18 holes, 6379yds, Par 73, SSS 71, Course record 72.
Course Designer D Tucker **Location** off A61 between
Sheffield & Chesterfield, outskirts of Unstone
Phone for further details

Hotel ★★★ 65% Sandpiper Hotel, Sheffield Rd,
Sheepbridge, CHESTERFIELD ☎ 01246 450550
46 en suite

Continued

DEVON

AXMOUTH
Map 03 SY29

Axe Cliff Squires Ln EX12 4AB
☎ 01297 21754 & 24371
e-mail: davidquinn@axecliff.co.uk
Undulating links course with coastal views.

18 holes, 6000yds, Par 70, SSS 70, Course record 64.
Club membership 327.
Visitors contact in advance. **Societies** contact in advance.
Green Fees £15 per round (£20 weekends & bank
holidays). **Cards** 🖃 📰 🖾 **Prof** Mark Dack **Facilities** ⊗
🎢 🖢 💻 ♀ 🛆 🖃 🍸 ♂ **Conf** Corporate Hospitality Days
available **Location** 0.75m S on B3172
....
Hotel ★★ 77% Swallows Eaves, COLYFORD
☎ 01297 553184 8 en suite

BIGBURY-ON-SEA
Map 03 SX64

Bigbury TQ7 4BB
☎ 01548 810557 (secretary) 📄 01548 810207
**Clifftop pasture and parkland course with easy
walking. Exposed to winds, but with fine views over the
sea and River Avon. The 7th hole is particularly tricky.**
18 holes, 6061yds, Par 70, SSS 69, Course record 65.
Club membership 850.
Visitors handicap certificate preferred; must contact pro
shop in advance. **Societies** phone or contact in advance.
Green Fees £30 (£35 weekends). **Prof** Simon Lloyd
Course Designer JH Taylor **Facilities** ⊗ 🎢 by
arrangement 🖢 ♀ 🛆 🖃 🍸 🥄 🐾 ♂ **Conf** Corporate
Hospitality Days available **Location** 1m S on B3392
between Bigbury & Bigbury-on-Sea
....
Hotel ★★★★ 72% Thurlestone Hotel, THURLESTONE
☎ 01548 560382 64 en suite

BLACKAWTON
Map 03 SX85

Dartmouth Golf & Country Club TQ9 7DE
☎ 01803 112650 📄 01803 712628
e-mail: info@dgcc.co.uk
**The nine-hole course and the 18-hole Championship
Course are both worth a visit and not just for the
beautiful views. The Championship is one of the most
challenging courses in the West Country with 12 water
hazards and a daunting par 5 4th hole that visitors will
always remember. The spectacular final hole, looking
downhill and over a water hazard to the green, can be
difficult to judge and has been described as one of the
most picturesque finishing holes in the country.**
*Championship Course: 18 holes, 6663yds, Par 72,
SSS 72, Course record 68.*

Dartmouth Course: 9 holes, 4791yds, Par 66, SSS 64.
Club membership 600.
Visitors subject to availability; contact in advance; dress
code; book tee times for both courses. **Societies** phone in
advance. **Green Fees** Championship: £30 (£40 weekends).
Dartmouth: £13 (£14 weekends). **Cards** 🖃 📰 📰 🖾 🖾 🖾
Course Designer Jeremy Pern **Facilities** ⊗ 🎢 🖢 💻 ♀ 🛆
🖃 🍸 🖾 🐾 ♂ 🍸 **Leisure** heated indoor swimming pool,
sauna, solarium, gymnasium, Massage & beauty
treatments. **Conf** fac available Corporate Hospitality Days
available **Location** on A3122 4m from Dartmouth
....
Hotel ★★★ 68% Stoke Lodge Hotel, Stoke Fleming,
DARTMOUTH ☎ 01803 770523 25 en suite

BUDLEIGH SALTERTON
Map 03 SY08

East Devon Links Rd EX9 6DG
☎ 01395 443370 📄 01395 445547
e-mail: secretary@edge.co.uk
**An interesting course with downland turf, much
heather and gorse, and superb views over the bay. Laid
out on cliffs 250 to 400 feet above sea level, the early
holes climb to the cliff edge. The downhill 17th has a
heather section in the fairway, leaving a good second to
the green. In addition to rare orchids, the course enjoys
an abundance of wildlife including deer and peregrine
falcons.**
18 holes, 6231yds, Par 70, SSS 70, Course record 61.
Club membership 850.
Visitors not before 9am; advisable to contact in advance;
member of a recognised club & handicap certificate.
Societies Thu, contact in advance. **Green Fees** £45 per
27/36 holes; £36 per 18 holes. **Cards** 🖃 📰 📰 🖾 📰 🖾 🖾
Prof Trevor Underwood **Facilities** ⊗ 🎢 🖢 💻 ♀ 🛆 🖃 🍸
♂ **Conf** Corporate Hospitality Days available **Location** W
side of town centre
....
Hotel ★★ 74% Barn Hotel, Foxholes Hill, Marine Dr,
EXMOUTH ☎ 01395 224411 11 en suite

CHITTLEHAMHOLT
Map 03 SS62

Highbullen Hotel EX37 9HD
☎ 01769 540561 📄 01769 540492
e-mail: info@highbullen.co.uk
**Mature parkland course with water hazards and
outstanding scenic views to Exmoor and Dartmoor. An
easy walking course with some outstanding holes.
Excellent greens, which will hold a well-flighted ball,
invite you to shoot for the heart of the green past well-
maintained bunkers that have been intelligently placed
to add to the golfing challenge.**
18 holes, 5755yds, Par 68, SSS 67.
Club membership 150.
Visitors book tee time 01769 540530 daytime, 01769
540561 evenings. **Societies** contact in advance. **Green
Fees** £20 (£24 weekends & BH). **Cards** 🖃 📰 🖾 **Prof**
Paul Weston **Course Designer** M Neil, J Hamilton
Facilities ⊗ 🎢 🖢 💻 ♀ 🛆 🖃 🍸 🖾 🥄 🐾 ♂ **Leisure**
hard & grass tennis courts, outdoor & indoor heated
swimming pools, squash, fishing, sauna, solarium,
gymnasium, golf simulator. **Conf** fac available Corporate
Hospitality Days available **Location** 0.5m S of village
....
Hotel ★★★ 🕭 67% Highbullen Hotel,
CHITTLEHAMHOLT ☎ 01769 540561 12 en suite
25 annexe en suite

Continued

CHRISTOW
Map 03 SX88

Teign Valley EX6 7PA
☎ 01647 253026 📠 01647 253026
e-mail: welcome@teignvalleygolf.co.uk
A scenically spectacular 18-hole course set beside the
River Teign in Dartmoor National Park. Offering a
good challenge to both low and high handicap golfers, it
features two lakeside holes, rolling fairways and fine
views.

18 holes, 5913yds, Par 70, SSS 68.
Club membership 300.
Visitors book by phone. Societies write or phone for
bookings. Green Fees not confirmed. Cards 💳 💳 💳 💳
Prof Scott Amiet Course Designer P Nicholson Facilities
⊗ 🏌 ⓑ 🍴 ♀ ⚐ 🏠 ☂ 🛒 🏌 ♿ Conf fac available
Location A38 Teign Valley exit, Exeter/Plymouth
Expressway & GC signs on B3193

Hotel ★★★★★ 70% Bovey Castle,
MORETONHAMPSTEAD ☎ 01647 445000 65 en suite

CHULMLEIGH
Map 03 SS61

Chulmleigh Leigh Rd EX18 7BL
☎ 01769 580519 📠 01769 580519
e-mail: chulmleighgolf@aol.com
Situated in a scenic area with views to distant
Dartmoor, this undulating meadowland course offers a
good test for the most experienced golfer and is
enjoyable for newcomers to the game. Short 18-hole
summer course with a tricky 1st hole; in winter the
course is changed to nine holes and made longer for
players to extend their game.
Summer course: 18 holes, 2310yds, Par 54, SSS 54,
Course record 49.
Winter course: 9 holes, 2310yds, Par 54, SSS 54, Course
record 53.
Club membership 85.
Visitors Societies phone in advance. Green Fees £8.50 per
18 holes, £7.50 before 10am. Cards 💳 💳 💳 💳 Course
Designer John Goodban Facilities ⓑ 🍴 ♀ ⚐ 🏠 ☂ 🛒 🏌
Location SW side of village just off A377

Hotel ★★★ Northcote Manor, BURRINGTON
☎ 01769 560501 11 en suite

CHURSTON FERRERS
Map 03 SX95

Churston Dartmouth Rd TQ5 0LA
☎ 01803 842751 & 842218 📠 01803 845738
e-mail: manager@churstongc.freeserve.co.uk
18 holes, 6219yds, Par 70, SSS 70, Course record 64.
Location NW side of village on A379
Phone for further details
Continued

Hotel ★★★ 68% Berryhead Hotel, Berryhead Rd,
BRIXHAM ☎ 01803 853225 32 en suite

CREDITON
Map 03 SS80

Downes Crediton Hookway EX17 3PT
☎ 01363 773025 & 774464 📠 01363 775060
e-mail: secretary@downescreditongc.co.uk
Parkland course with water features. Flat front nine.
Hilly and wooded back nine.
18 holes, 5954yds, Par 70, SSS 69.
Club membership 700.
Visitors restricted weekends; contact in advance; handicap
certificate. Societies contact in advance. Green Fees £28
per day (£32 weekends). Cards 💳 💳 💳 💳 💳
Facilities ⊗ 🏌 ⓑ 🍴 ♀ ⚐ 🏠 ☂ 🏌 Conf Corporate
Hospitality Days available Location 1.5m SE off A377

Hotel ★★★ 71% Barton Cross Hotel & Restaurant,
Huxham, Stoke Canon, EXETER ☎ 01392 841245
9 en suite

CULLOMPTON
Map 03 ST00

Padbrook Park EX15 1RU
☎ 01884 38286 📠 01884 34359
e-mail: padbrookpark@fsmail.net
A nine-hole, 18-tee parkland course with many water
and woodland hazards and spectacular views. The dog-
leg 2nd and pulpit 7th are particularly challenging to
golfers of all standards.

9 holes, 6108yds, Par 70, SSS 69, Course record 65.
Club membership 280.
Visitors phone for information pack. Societies apply in
writing or phone for society pack. Green Fees £18 per 18
holes, £13 per nine holes (£21/£16 weekends). Cards 💳
💳 💳 💳 💳 Prof Robert Thorpe Course Designer Bob
Sandow Facilities ⊗ 🏌 ⓑ 🍴 ♀ ⚐ 🏠 ☂ 🛒 🏌 ♿ 🏌
Leisure fishing, solarium, gymnasium, indoor bowling
centre. Conf fac available Corporate Hospitality Days
available Location M5 junct 28, 1m on S edge of town

Hotel Ⓤ Padbrook Park, CULLOMPTON ☎ 01884 38286
40 en suite

DAWLISH WARREN
Map 03 SX97

Warren EX7 0NF
☎ 01626 862255 & 864002 📠 01626 888005
e-mail: secretary@dwgc.co.uk
Typical flat, genuine links course lying on spit between
sea and Exe estuary. Picturesque scenery, a few trees
but much gorse. Testing in windy conditions. The 7th
hole provides the opportunity to go for the green across
a bay on the estuary.
Continued

Warren Golf Club

18 holes, 5912yds, Par 69, SSS 68, Course record 65.
Club membership 600.
Visitors contact in advance; member of golf club.
Societies by arrangement only. **Green Fees** £28 per day
(£31 weekends & bank holidays). Rates exclusive of £1
players' insurance. **Cards** ⊞ 🎫 💳 📇 📠 📶 📎 **Prof**
Darren Prowse **Course Designer** James Braid **Facilities** ⊗
🎫 🍴 ⛳ ♿ 🏠 🕐 ⚷ **Conf** fac available **Location** E side
of village

....

Hotel ★★★ 71% Langstone Cliff Hotel, Dawlish Warren,
DAWLISH ☎ 01626 868000 62 en suite 4 annexe
en suite

DOWN ST MARY   Map 03 SS70

Waterbridge EX17 5LG
☎ 01363 85111
A testing course of nine holes set in a gently sloping
valley. The par of 32 will not be easily gained, with one

par 5, three par 4s and five par 3s, although the course
record holder has par 29. The 3rd hole which is a raised
green is surrounded by water and the 4th (439yds) is
demanding for beginners.
9 holes, 3910yds, Par 64, SSS 64.
Club membership 120.
Visitors no restrictions. **Societies** no restrictions. **Green**
Fees £11.50 per 18 holes; £7 per nine holes (£13.50/£8
weekends & bank holidays). **Cards** ⊞ 🎫 💳 📶 📎 **Prof**
David Ridyard **Course Designer** D Taylor **Facilities** ⊗ 🍴
🎫 🍴 ⛳ 🏠 🕐 ⚷ **Conf** Corporate Hospitality Days
available **Location** A377 from Exeter towards Barnstaple,
1m past Copplestone

....

Hotel ★★★ Northcote Manor, BURRINGTON
☎ 01769 560501 11 en suite

EXETER   Map 03 SX99

Exeter Golf & Country Club Topsham Rd,
Countess Wear EX2 7AE
☎ 01392 874139 📠 01392 874914
e-mail: info@exetergcc.fsnet.co.uk
A sheltered parkland course with some very old trees
and known as the flattest course in Devon. Situated in
the grounds of a fine mansion, which is now the
clubhouse. The 15th and 17th are testing par 4 holes.
Small, well-guarded greens.
18 holes, 6008yds, Par 69, SSS 69, Course record 62.
Club membership 800.
Visitors not during match or competitions; booking
required up to one week in advance; handicap certificate;
phone starter in advance 01392 876303. **Societies** Thu,
booking available by phone to manager 01392 874639.
Green Fees £42 per day; £34 per round (£48 weekends).

Continued   *Continued*

Cards ▦ ▬ ▦ 🌀 **Prof** Gary Milne **Course Designer**
J Braid **Facilities** ⊗ ⅢⅢ ⮂ 🖤 ♀ ⛳ 🏠 ♿ **Leisure** hard
tennis courts, outdoor & indoor heated swimming pools,
squash, sauna, solarium, gymnasium, Jacuzzi. **Conf** fac
available Corporate Hospitality Days available **Location**
SE side of city centre off A379

Hotel ★★★ 64% Buckerell Lodge Hotel, Topsham Rd,
EXETER ☎ 01392 221111 53 en suite

Woodbury Park Hotel, Golf & Country Club Woodbury Castle, Woodbury EX5 1JJ
☎ 01395 233500 📠 01395 233384
e-mail: golfbookings@woodburypark.co.uk
**Irrigated 18-hole Oaks championship course and
excellent nine-hole Acorns course set in 500 acres of
wooded parkland with stunning views.**

*Oaks: 18 holes, 6905yds, Par 72, SSS 72,
Course record 66.
Acorn: 9 holes, 2297yds, Par 32, SSS 32.
Club membership 750.*
Visitors book tee times in advance; handicap certificate for
Oaks course. **Societies** contact in advance 01395 233500.
Green Fees Oaks £45 per 18 holes (£55 weekends).
Acorns £13 per 9 holes. **Cards** ▦ ▬ ▬ ▦ 🌀
Prof Alan Richards **Course Designer** J Hamilton-Stutt
Facilities ⊗ ⅢⅢ ⮂ 🖤 ♀ ⛳ 🏠 ♿ **Leisure**
hard tennis courts, heated indoor swimming pool, squash,
fishing, sauna, gymnasium, health spa. **Conf** fac available
Corporate Hospitality Days available **Location** M5 junct
30, A3052

Hotel ★★★★ 71% Woodbury Park Hotel Golf & Country
Club, Woodbury Castle, WOODBURY ☎ 01395 233382
57 en suite

HIGH BICKINGTON Map 02 SS52

Libbaton EX37 9BS
☎ 01769 560269 & 560167 📠 01769 560342
e-mail: gerald.hemiman@tesco.net
**Parkland course on undulating land with no steep
slopes. Water comes into play on 11 of the 18 holes, as
well as a quarry, ditches, trees and eight raised greens.
Not a heavily bunkered course, but those present are
well positioned and the sharp sand they contain makes
them tricky. Five par 5s could easily get you thinking
this course is only for big hitters but as with many
good courses, sound course management is the key to
success.**
*18 holes, 6481yds, Par 73, SSS 71, Course record 72.
Club membership 500.*
Visitors book in advance; no jeans, trainers or collarless
shirts. **Societies** 6 persons or more, phone to book in

advance. **Green Fees** £20 per 18 holes (£26 weekends).
Cards ▦ ▬ ▬ ▦ 🌀 **Prof** Andrew Norman
Course Designer Col Badham **Facilities** ⊗ ⅢⅢ ⮂ 🖤 ♀ ⛳
🏠 ♿ ♿ ♿ **Conf** fac available Corporate Hospitality
Days available **Location** B3217 1m of High Bickington,
off A377

Hotel ★★★ ♨ 67% Highbullen Hotel,
CHITTLEHAMHOLT ☎ 01769 540561 12 en suite
25 annexe en suite

HOLSWORTHY Map 02 SS30

Holsworthy Killatree EX22 6LP
☎ 01409 253177 📠 01409 253177
e-mail: hgcsecretary@aol.com
**Pleasant parkland course with gentle slopes, numerous
trees and a few strategic sand bunkers. Small greens
offer a good test for players of all abilities.**
*18 holes, 6059yds, Par 70, SSS 69, Course record 64.
Club membership 500.*
Visitors book with professional 01409 254177. **Societies**
by arrangement with secretary or professional. **Green Fees**
terms on application. **Cards** ▦ ▬ ▦ 🌀 **Prof** Alan
Johnston **Facilities** ⊗ ⅢⅢ ⮂ 🖤 ♀ ⛳ 🏠 ♿ ♿ ♿ ♿
Conf fac available Corporate Hospitality Days available
Location 1.5m W on A3072 towards Bude

Hotel ★★★ 72% Falcon Hotel, Breakwater Rd, BUDE
☎ 01288 352005 27 en suite

HONITON Map 03 ST10

Honiton Middlehills EX14 9TR
☎ 01404 44422 & 42943 📠 01404 46383
**Founded in 1896, this level parkland course is situated
on a plateau 850ft above sea level. Easy walking and
good views. The 4th hole is a testing par 3. The 17th and
18th provide a challenging finish.**
*18 holes, 5902yds, Par 69, SSS 68, Course record 65.
Club membership 800.*
Visitors contact in advance; handicap certificate. **Societies**
Thu, by booking. **Green Fees** £25 per day (£30 weekends
& bank holidays). **Prof** Adrian Cave **Facilities** ⊗ ⅢⅢ ⮂ 🖤
♀ ⛳ 🏠 ♿ **Leisure** hardstanding for touring caravans
with services. **Conf** Corporate Hospitality Days available
Location 1.25m SE of Honiton, turn towards Farway at
Tower Cross on A35

Hotel ★★ 71% Home Farm Hotel & Restaurant,
Wilmington, HONITON ☎ 01404 831278 8 en suite
5 annexe en suite

ILFRACOMBE Map 02 SS54

Ilfracombe Hele Bay EX34 9RT
☎ 01271 862176 & 863328 📠 01271 867731
e-mail: ilfracombegolfclub@btinternet.com
**A sporting, clifftop, heathland course with views over
the Bristol Channel and moors from every tee and
green.**
*18 holes, 5596yds, Par 69, SSS 67, Course record 66.
Club membership 520.*
Visitors tee reservation contact pro in advance; members
only before 10am weekends. **Societies** phone in advance.
Green Fees £22 per round (£27 weekends & bank
holidays). **Cards** ▦ ▬ ▬ ▦ 🌀 **Prof** Mark Davies
Course Designer T K Weir **Facilities** ⊗ ⅢⅢ ⮂ 🖤 ♀ ⛳ 🏠
♿ ♿ ♿ ♿ **Location** 1.5m E of Ilfracombe, off A399

Continued *Continued*

Hotel ★★ 71% Elmfield Hotel, Torrs Park,
ILFRACOMBE ☎ 01271 863377 11 en suite 2 annexe
en suite

IPPLEPEN
Map 03 SX86

Dainton Park Totnes Rd, Ipplepen TQ12 5TN
☎ 01803 815000
e-mail: dpgolf@globalnet.co.uk
A challenging parkland course in typical Devon
countryside, with gentle contours, tree-lined fairways
and raised tees. Water hazards make the two opening
holes particularly testing. The 8th, a dramatic 180yd
drop hole totally surrounded by sand, is one of four
tough par 3s on the course.
18 holes, 6302yds, Par 71, SSS 70, Course record 70.
Club membership 650.
Visitors book by phone to guarantee start time. Societies
contact in advance. Green Fees not confirmed. Cards 🔳
🔳 🏧 Prof Martin Tyson Course Designer Adrian Stiff
Facilities ⊗ ⊞ ▙ ⬛ ♀ ⚘ 🏠 ⛳ ↘ ⊘ ⌥ Leisure
gymnasium. Conf Corporate Hospitality Days available
Location 2m S of Newton Abbot on A381

Hotel ★★ 68% Queens Hotel, Queen St, NEWTON
ABBOT ☎ 01626 363133 20 en suite

IVYBRIDGE
Map 02 SX65

Dinnaton Blachford Rd PL21 9HU
☎ 01752 690020 & 892512 🖹 01752 698334
e-mail: info@mccaulays.com
Challenging nine-hole moorland course overlooking the
South Hams. With five par 4 and four par 3 holes, three
lakes and tight fairways; excellent for improving the
short game. Floodlit practice area.
9 holes, 4089yds, Par 64, SSS 60.
Club membership 130.
Visitors no restrictions. Societies no advance arrangements
required. Green Fees Mon-Thu £11 per 18 holes, £7 per
nine holes. Fri-Sun £13/£8. Cards 🔳 🔳 🏧 🔳
Prof Richard Stephenson Course Designer Cotton & Pink
Facilities ⊗ ⊞ ▙ ⬛ ♀ ⚘ ⛳ ⊘ ⌥ Leisure hard tennis
courts, heated indoor swimming pool, squash, sauna,
solarium, gymnasium. Conf fac available Location off
A38 at Ivybridge junct towards town centre, 1st rdbt brown
signs for club 1m

Hotel ★★ 74% Glazebrook House Hotel & Restaurant,
SOUTH BRENT ☎ 01364 73322 10 en suite

MORETONHAMPSTEAD
Map 03 SX78

Bovey Castle TQ13 8RE
☎ 01647 445009 🖹 01647 440961
e-mail: richard.lewis@boveycastle.com
This enjoyable parkland course has enough hazards to
make any golfer think. Most hazards are natural such
as the Rivers Bowden and Bovey which meander
through the first eight holes.
18 holes, 6303yds, Par 70, SSS 70, Course record 63.
Club membership 130.
Visitors contact in advance for start time. Societies phone
for reservation in advance. Green Fees £117.50 per round
any time. Cards 🔳 🔳 🔳 🔳 🔳 🏧 Prof Richard
Lewis Course Designer J Abercrombie Facilities ⊗ ⊞ ▙
⬛ ♀ ⚘ 🏠 ⛳ 🍴 ↘ ⊘ ⌥ Leisure hard & grass tennis
courts, heated indoor plus outdoor swimming pool, fishing,

Continued

sauna, solarium, gymnasium. Conf fac available Corporate
Hospitality Days available Location 2m W of
Moretonhampstead, off B3212

Hotel ★★★★★ 70% Bovey Castle,
MORETONHAMPSTEAD ☎ 01647 445000
65 en suite

MORTEHOE
Map 02 SS44

Mortehoe & Woolacombe EX34 7EH
☎ 01271 870667 & 870566
e-mail: malcolm_wilkinson@northdevon.gov.uk
Easewell: 9 holes, 4690yds, Par 66, SSS 63,
Course record 66.
Course Designer D Hoare Location 0.25m before
Mortehoe on station road
Phone for further details

Hotel ★★★ 81% Watersmeet Hotel, Mortehoe,
WOOLACOMBE ☎ 01271 870333 25 en suite

NEWTON ABBOT
Map 03 SX87

Newton Abbot (Stover) Bovey Rd TQ12 6QQ
☎ 01626 352460 (Secretary) 🖹 01626 330210
e-mail: stovergolfclub@aol.com
Mature wooded parkland course with water coming
into play on eight holes.
18 holes, 5764yds, Par 69, SSS 68, Course record 63.
Club membership 800.
Visitors proof of membership of recognised club or
handicap certificate; advisable to contact in advance.
Societies Thu, by arrangement. Green Fees £32 per
round/day. Cards 🔳 🔳 Prof Malcolm Craig Course
Designer James Braid Facilities ⊗ ⊞ ▙ ⬛ ♀ ⚘ 🏠 ⊘
Conf Corporate Hospitality Days available Location 3m N
of Newton Abbot on A382. Bovey Tracey exit on A38

Hotel ★★ 68% Queens Hotel, Queen St, NEWTON
ABBOT ☎ 01626 363133 20 en suite

OKEHAMPTON
Map 02 SX59

Ashbury Golf Hotel Higher Maddaford EX20 4NL
☎ 01837 55453 🖹 01837 55468
The courses occupy a lightly wooded parkland setting
in rolling Devon countryside on the foothills of
Dartmoor National Park. Extra hazards have been
added to the natural ones already present, with over
100 bunkers and 18 lakes. The courses are open
throughout the year with either larger main greens or
purpose built alternate ones.
Oakwood: 18 holes, 5374yds, Par 68, SSS 66.
Pines: 18 holes, 5628yds, Par 69, SSS 67.
Beeches: 18 holes, 5351yds, Par 68, SSS 66.
Club membership 170.
Visitors contact in advance. Societies phone in advance.
Green Fees £20 per day (£25 weekends). Cards 🔳 🔳
🔳 🔳 🏧 Course Designer David Fensom Facilities ⊗ ▙
⬛ ♀ ⚘ 🏠 ⛳ 🛏 🏑 ⊘ ⌥ Leisure hard tennis courts,
heated indoor swimming pool, fishing, sauna, par 3 course,
indoor bowls, snooker. Location off A3079 Okehampton-
Holsworthy

Hotel ★★ 66% Ashbury Hotel, Higher Maddaford,
Southcott, OKEHAMPTON ☎ 01837 55453 61 en suite
30 annexe en suite

Okehampton Tors Rd EX20 1EF
☎ 01837 52113 📠 01837 52734
e-mail: okehamptongc@btconnect.com
A good combination of moorland, woodland and river makes this one of the prettiest, yet testing courses in Devon.
18 holes, 5268yds, Par 68, SSS 66, Course record 66.
Club membership 600.
Visitors restricted weekends; Sat by arrangement only; booking recommended. **Societies** by arrangement. **Green Fees** £25 per day; £20 per round (£25 weekends). **Cards** ⬗ 🔲 🔳 📇 📠 🖫 **Prof** Ashley Moon **Course Designer** JF Taylor **Facilities** ⊗ ⊪ ⓑ ♥ ♀ ⚲ 🖢 ❏ ⚶ **Location** 1m S off A30, signed from town centre

....

Hotel ★★ 67% White Hart Hotel, Fore St,
OKEHAMPTON ☎ 01837 52730 & 54514
📠 01837 53979   19 en suite

PLYMOUTH   Map 02 SX45

Elfordleigh Colebrook, Plympton PL7 5EB
☎ 01752 336428 (hotel) & 348425 (golf shop)
📠 01752 344581
e-mail: elfordleigh@btinternet.com
18 holes, 5664yds, Par 69, SSS 67, Course record 66.
Course Designer JH Taylor **Location** 2m NE off A374, follow signs from Plympton town centre
Phone for further details

....

Hotel ★★★ 71% Elfordleigh Hotel Golf Leisure,
Colebrook, Plympton, PLYMOUTH ☎ 01752 336428
34 en suite

Staddon Heights Plymstock PL9 9SP
☎ 01752 402475 📠 01752 401998
e-mail: golfclub@btopenworld
18 holes, 5804yds, Par 68, SSS 68, Course record 66.
Course Designer Hamilton Stutt **Location** 5m SW of city centre
Phone for further details

....

Hotel ★★ 73% Langdon Court Hotel, Down Thomas,
PLYMOUTH ☎ 01752 862358   18 en suite

SAUNTON   Map 02 SS43

Saunton EX33 1LG
☎ 01271 812436 📠 01271 814241
e-mail: info@sauntongolf.co.uk
Two traditional championship links courses. Windy, with natural hazards.

East Course: 18 holes, 6427yds, Par 71, SSS 71, Course record 64.

Continued

West Course: 18 holes, 6138yds, Par 71, SSS 70, Course record 63.
Club membership 1450.
Visitors booking recommended; handicap certificate. **Societies** apply in advance; handicap certificates. **Green Fees** £75 per day; £55 per round. **Cards** ⬗ 🔳 🖫 **Prof** AT MacKenzie **Course Designer** F Pennick, WH Fowler **Facilities** ⊗ ⊪ ⓑ ♥ ♀ ⚲ ⚶ 🖢 ⚶ ⚶ **Conf** Corporate Hospitality Days available
Location S side of village off B3231

....

Hotel ★★★★ 74% Saunton Sands Hotel, SAUNTON
☎ 01271 890212   92 en suite

SIDMOUTH   Map 03 SY18

Sidmouth Cotmaton Rd, Peak Hill EX10 8SX
☎ 01395 513451 & 516407 📠 01395 514661
18 holes, 5100yds, Par 66, SSS 65, Course record 59.
Course Designer J H Taylor **Location** W side of town centre
Phone for further details

....

Hotel ★★★★ 75% Victoria Hotel, The Esplanade,
SIDMOUTH ☎ 01395 512651   61 en suite

SOUTH BRENT   Map 03 SX66

Wrangaton (S Devon) Golf Links Rd,
Wrangaton TQ10 9HJ
☎ 01364 73229 📠 01364 73229
e-mail: wrangatongc@tiscali.co.uk
Unique 18-hole course with nine holes on moorland and nine holes on parkland. The course lies within Dartmoor National Park. Spectacular views towards sea and rugged terrain. Natural fairways and hazards include bracken, sheep and ponies.
18 holes, 6083yds, Par 70, SSS 69, Course record 66.
Club membership 680.
Visitors contact in advance. **Societies** write or phone. **Green Fees** terms on application. **Cards** ⬗ 🔳 🔳 **Prof** Glenn Richards **Course Designer** DMA Steel
Facilities ⊗ ⊪ ⓑ ♥ ♀ ⚲ 🖢 ⚶ ⚶ ⚶ **Location** 2.25m SW off A38, between South Brent & Ivybridge

....

Hotel ★★ 74% Glazebrook House Hotel & Restaurant,
SOUTH BRENT ☎ 01364 73322   10 en suite

SPARKWELL   Map 02 SX55

Welbeck Manor & Sparkwell Golf Course
Blacklands PL7 5DF
☎ 01752 837219 📠 01752 837219
9 holes, 2886yds, Par 68, SSS 68, Course record 68.
Course Designer John Gabb **Location** 1m N of A38
Plymouth-Ivybridge road
Phone for further details

....

Hotel ★★ 63% The Moorland Hotel, Wotter, Shaugh Prior, PLYMOUTH ☎ 01752 839228   18 en suite

---

TAVISTOCK   Map 02 SX47

Hurdwick Tavistock Hamlets PL19 0LL
☎ 01822 612746 📠 01822 612746
An executive parkland course with many bunkers and fine views. Executive golf originated in America and the concept is that a round should take no longer than 3 hours while offering a solid challenge.

Continued

18 holes, 5302yds, Par 68, SSS 67, Course record 67. Club membership 110.
Visitors no restrictions. **Societies** contact in advance.
Green Fees not confirmed. **Course Designer** Hawtree
Facilities ⊞ ⚑ ♀ ♫ ⛳ ☁ ⛳ **Location** 1m N of
Tavistock on the Brentor Road

.....

Hotel ★★★ 64% Bedford Hotel, 1 Plymouth Rd,
TAVISTOCK ☎ 01822 613221 30 en suite

Tavistock Down Rd PL19 9AQ
☎ 01822 612344 🖷 01822 612344
e-mail: tavygolf@hotmail.org
Set on Whitchurch Down in south-west Dartmoor with
easy walking and magnificent views over rolling
countryside into Cornwall. Downland turf with some
heather, and interesting holes on undulating ground.
*18 holes, 6495yds, Par 71, SSS 71, Course record 60.
Club membership 700.*
Visitors advisable to contact in advance. **Societies** by
arrangement with secretary. **Green Fees** £28 per day/round
(£35 weekends). **Prof** D Rehaag **Course Designer**
H Fowler **Facilities** ⊗ ⅷ ⊞ ⚑ ♀ ♫ 🛈 ⛳ **Location** 1m
SE of town centre, on Whitchurch Down

.....

Hotel ★★★ 64% Bedford Hotel, 1 Plymouth Rd,
TAVISTOCK ☎ 01822 613221 30 en suite

TEDBURN ST MARY   Map 03 SX89

Fingle Glen EX6 6AF
☎ 01647 61817 🖷 01647 61135
e-mail: fingle.glen@btinternet.com
9 holes, 4818yds, Par 66, SSS 63, Course record 63.
Course Designer Bill Pile **Location** 5m W of Exeter, off
A30
Phone for further details

.....

Hotel ★★★ 72% St Olaves Hotel, Mary Arches St,
EXETER ☎ 01392 217736 15 en suite

TEIGNMOUTH   Map 03 SX97

Teignmouth Haldon Moor TQ14 9NY
☎ 01626 777070 🖷 01626 777304
e-mail: tgc@btconnect.com
This fairly flat heathland course is high up with fine
panoramic views of sea, moors and river valley. Good
springy turf with some heather and an interesting
layout makes for very enjoyable holiday golf. Designed
by Dr MacKenzie, the world famous architect who also
designed Augusta GC USA.
*18 holes, 6200yds, Par 71, SSS 69, Course record 63.
Club membership 900.*
Visitors handicap certificate; phone pro shop to book
01626 772894. **Societies** Thu, phone in advance & confirm
in writing. **Green Fees** £30 per round (£35 weekends).
Cards ▦ ▦ 🛈 **Prof** Rob Selley **Course Designer**
Dr A MacKenzie **Facilities** ⊗ ⅷ ⊞ ⚑ ♀ ♫ 🛈 ⛳ **Conf**
Corporate Hospitality Days available **Location** 2m NW off
B3192

.....

Hotel ★★★ 70% Ness House Hotel, Ness Dr, Shaldon,
TEIGNMOUTH ☎ 01626 873480 7 en suite 5 annexe
en suite

THURLESTONE   Map 03 SX64

Thurlestone TQ7 3NZ
☎ 01548 560405 🖷 01548 562149
e-mail: info@thurlestonegc.co.uk
Situated on the edge of the cliffs with downland turf
and good greens. The course, after an interesting
opening hole, rises to higher land with fine sea views,
and finishes with an excellent 502yd downhill hole to
the clubhouse.
*18 holes, 6340yds, Par 71, SSS 70, Course record 65.
Club membership 770.*
Visitors contact in advance; handicap certificate from
recognised club. **Green Fees** £34 per day/round. **Cards** ▦
▦ ▦ 🛈 **Prof** Peter Laugher **Course Designer** Harry S
Colt **Facilities** ⊗ ⅷ by arrangement ⊞ ⚑ ♀ ♫ 🛈 ⛳ ⛳
Leisure hard & grass tennis courts. **Location** S side of
village

.....

Hotel ★★★★ 72% Thurlestone Hotel, THURLESTONE
☎ 01548 560382 64 en suite

TIVERTON   Map 03 SS91

Tiverton Post Hill EX16 4NE
☎ 01884 252187 🖷 01884 251607
e-mail: tivertongolfclub@lineone.net
A parkland course where the many different species of
tree are a feature and where the lush pastures ensure
some of the finest fairways in the south-west. The
undulating ground provides plenty of variety and there
are a number of interesting holes which visitors will
find a real challenge.
*18 holes, 6236yds, Par 71, SSS 71, Course record 65.
Club membership 750.*
Visitors contact in advance; handicap certificate. **Societies**
apply in writing or phone. **Green Fees** £32 per 18 holes.
Prof Michael Hawton **Course Designer** Braid **Facilities**
⊗ ⅷ by arrangement ⊞ ⚑ ♀ ♫ 🛈 ⛳ **Conf** Corporate
Hospitality Days available **Location** 3m E of Tiverton. M5
junct 27, through Sampford Peverell & Halberton

.....

Hotel ★★★ 70% Tiverton Hotel, Blundells Rd,
TIVERTON ☎ 01884 256120 69 en suite

TORQUAY   Map 03 SX96

Torquay 30 Petitor Rd, St Marychurch TQ1 4QF
☎ 01803 314591 🖷 01803 316116
e-mail: torquaygolfclub@skynow.net
18 holes, 6175yds, Par 69, SSS 69, Course record 63.
Location 1.25m N
Phone for further details

.....

Hotel ★★ 64% Norcliffe Hotel, 7 Babbacombe Downs
Rd, Babbacombe, TORQUAY ☎ 01803 328456
27 en suite

TORRINGTON (GREAT)   Map 02 SS41

Torrington Weare Trees, Great Torrington EX38 7EZ
☎ 01805 622229 & 623878 🖷 01805 623878
e-mail: theoffice@torringtongolf.fsnet.co.uk
Attractive and challenging 9-hole course. Free draining
to allow play all year round. Excellent greens and
outstanding views.
*9 holes, 4423yds, Par 64, SSS 62, Course record 58.
Club membership 420.*

Continued

Visitors not Tue, Wed, weekends & bank holidays am; contact in advance. **Societies** by arrangement. **Green Fees** not confirmed. **Facilities** ⊗)|(⊾ ☕ ♀ ⚲ ⛳ ✓ **Location** 1m W of Torringdon

Hotel ★★★ 69% Royal Hotel, Barnstaple St, BIDEFORD ☎ 01237 472005 32 en suite

WESTWARD HO! Map 02 SS42

Royal North Devon Golf Links Rd EX39 1HD
☎ 01237 473817 🖷 01237 423456
e-mail: info@royalnorthdevongolfclub.co.uk
Oldest links course in England with traditional links features and a museum in the clubhouse.
18 holes, 6716yds, Par 72, SSS 72, Course record 65. Club membership 1150.
Visitors advisable to phone & book tee time; handicap certificate preferred or letter of introduction from club. **Societies** apply in writing or phone. **Green Fees** £44 per day; £38 per round (£50/£44 weekends & bank holidays). **Cards** **Prof** iain Parker **Course Designer** Old Tom Morris **Facilities** ⊗ ⊾ ☕ ♀ ⚲ ⌂ ⛳ ✓ **Leisure** Museum of Golf Memorabilia, snooker. **Location** N side of village off B3236

Guesthouse ♦♦♦♦ Culloden House, Fosketh Hill, WESTWARD HO. ☎ 01237 479421 5 en suite

WOOLSERY Map 02 SS32

Hartland Forest EX39 5RA
☎ 01237 431442 🖷 01237 431734
e-mail: castleacre@btconnect.com
18 holes, 5900yds, Par 70, SSS 68.
Course Designer A Cartwright **Location** 4m S of Clovelly Cross, 1.7m E of A39
Phone for further details

Hotel ★★★ 72% Penhaven Country House, Rectory Ln, PARKHAM ☎ 01237 451388 & 451711 🖷 01237 451878 12 en suite

YELVERTON Map 02 SX56

Yelverton Golf Links Rd PL20 6BN
☎ 01822 852824 🖷 01822 854869
e-mail: secretary@yelvertongc.co.uk
An excellent course on Dartmoor with plenty of gorse and heather. Tight lies in the fairways, fast greens and challenging hazards. Boasts three of the best holes in Devon (12th, 13th and 16th). Outstanding views.
18 holes, 6353yds, Par 71, SSS 71, Course record 64. Club membership 650.

Continued

Yelverton Golf Club

Visitors subject to availability; not Sun; contact in advance; handicap certificate. **Societies** book in advance by phone. **Green Fees** £30 per day. **Cards** **Prof** Tim McSherry **Course Designer** Herbert Fowler **Facilities** ⊗)|(⊾ ☕ ♀ ⚲ ⌂ ⛳ ✓ **Leisure** indoor golf academy. **Conf** fac available Corporate Hospitality Days available **Location** 1m S of Yelverton, off A386

Hotel ★★★ 72% Moorland Links Hotel, YELVERTON ☎ 01822 852245 45 en suite

DORSET

ASHLEY HEATH Map 04 SU10

Moors Valley Horton Rd BH24 2ET
☎ 01425 479776
e-mail: golf@eastdorset.gov.uk
Skilfully designed by Hawtree, this mature heathland and woodland course is scenically set within a wildlife conservation area, exuding peace and tranquillity. Each hole has its own character, the back seven being in particular very special. The course is renowned for its greens.
18 holes, 6357yds, Par 72, SSS 70.
Visitors contact in advance. **Societies** phone for availability. **Green Fees** £20 per round. **Cards** **Prof** James Daniels **Course Designer** Hawtree & Son **Facilities** ⊗)|(⊾ ☕ ♀ ⚲ ⌂ ⛳ ✓ **Leisure** fishing, four-hole game improvement course, bike hire, aerial assault course. **Conf** fac available Corporate Hospitality Days available **Location** signed from A31 Ashley Heath rdbt

Hotel Travelodge, St Leonards, RINGWOOD ☎ 08700 850 950

BEAMINSTER Map 03 ST40

Chedington Court South Perrott DT8 3HU
☎ 01935 891413 🖷 01935 891217
e-mail: admincgc@tiscali.co.uk
This beautiful 18-hole parkland course is set on the Dorset-Somerset borders with mature trees and interesting water hazards. A challenge from the first hole, par 5, blind drive to the elevated tee on the 15th, and the closing holes can be tricky.
18 holes, 5924yds, Par 70, SSS 70, Course record 68. Club membership 400.
Visitors book tee time for weekends. **Societies** apply in writing or phone. **Green Fees** terms on application. **Cards** **Prof** Seven Ritchie **Course Designer**

Continued

David Hemstock, Donald Steel **Facilities** ⊗ ⽫ ㋡ ㉑ ♀ 么
🏠 ⋔ ⛳ ℓ **Conf** Corporate Hospitality Days available
Location 5m NE of Beaminster on A356 Dorchester-
Crewkerne

....

Hotel ★★★ 71% Bridge House Hotel, 3 Prout Bridge,
BEAMINSTER ☎ 01308 862200 9 en suite 5 annexe
en suite

BELCHALWELL   Map 03 ST70

Dorset Heights DT11 0EG
☎ 01258 860900 📠 01258 860900
18 holes, 6138yds, Par 70, SSS 70, Course record 74.
Course Designer David Astill
Phone for further details

....

Hotel ★★★ 71% Crown Hotel, West St, BLANDFORD
FORUM ☎ 01258 456626 32 en suite

BERE REGIS   Map 03 SY89

Dorset Golf & Country Club BH20 7NT
☎ 01929 472244 📠 01929 471294
e-mail: admin@dorsetgolfresort.com
**Lakeland is the longest course in Dorset. Designed by
Martin Hawtree with numerous interconnected water
features, carefully planned bunkers and sculptured
greens. A player who completes a round within
handicap has every reason to celebrate. The Woodland
course, although shorter, is equally outstanding with
rhododendron and tree-lined fairways.**
*Lakeland Course: 18 holes, 6580yds, Par 72, SSS 73,
Course record 69.*
Woodland Course: 9 holes, 5032yds, Par 66, SSS 64.
Club membership 600.
Visitors book in advance. **Societies** apply in advance.
Green Fees Lakeland: £36 (£40 weekends). Woodland:
£24 (£28 weekends). **Cards** 💳 💳 💳 💳 💳 **Prof** Scott
Porter **Course Designer** Martin Hawtree **Facilities** ⊗ ⽫ ㋡
♀ 么 🏠 ⋔ ⛳ ♦ ⛳ ℓ ℓ **Leisure** fishing. **Conf** fac
available Corporate Hospitality Days available **Location**
5m from Bere Regis on Wool Road

....

Hotel ★★ 68% Kemps Country House Hotel, East Stoke,
WAREHAM ☎ 01929 462563 5 rms (4 en suite)
10 annexe en suite

BLANDFORD FORUM   Map 03 ST80

Ashley Wood Wimborne Rd DT11 9HN
☎ 01258 452253 📠 01258 450590
e-mail: generalmanager@ashleywoodgolfclub.com
**The course is one of the oldest in the country. The first
record of play on Keyneston Down was in 1896 and
part of the ancient course is played over Buzbury
Rings, a bronze age hill fort with magnificent views
over the Stour and Tarrant valleys. Constructed on
downland, the fairways are undulating and, apart from
the 3rd hole with a short sharp hill, all holes are easy
walking. Four holes are played within the Ashley
Woods, an ancient woodland. Being natural chalk
downland, the course has excellent drainage.**
18 holes, 6276yds, Par 70, SSS 70, Course record 66.
Club membership 600.
Visitors phone in advance; handicap certificate for
weekends unless with member. **Societies** apply to
Manager. **Green Fees** £42 per day, £26 per 18 holes after
10am (£31.50 per 18 holes weekends). **Prof** Jon Shimmons

Course Designer P Tallack **Facilities** ⊗ ⽫ ㋡ ㉑ ♀ 么 🏠
🐾 ⛳ ℓ **Conf** Corporate Hospitality Days available
Location 2m E on B3082

The Ashley Wood Golf Club

....

Hotel ★★★ 71% Crown Hotel, West St, BLANDFORD
FORUM ☎ 01258 456626 32 en suite

BOURNEMOUTH   Map 04 SZ09

The Club at Meyrick Park Central Dr, Meyrick
Park BH2 6LH
☎ 01202 786000 📠 01202 786020
e-mail: meyrickpark.lodge@clubhaus.com
**Picturesque municipal parkland course founded in
1890.**
*The Club At Meyrick Park: 18 holes, 5600yds, Par 69,
SSS 69.*
Visitors book up to seven days in advance. **Societies** phone
in advance. **Green Fees** from £19 Mon-Fri per round (£22
weekends & bank holidays). **Cards** 💳 💳 💳 💳 💳
Prof Andy Britton **Facilities** ⊗ ⽫ ㋡ ㉑ ♀ 么 🏠 ⋔ ℓ
Leisure heated indoor swimming pool, sauna, solarium,
gymnasium, spa & steam room. **Conf** fac available

....

Hotel ★★★ 63% Burley Court Hotel, Bath Rd,
BOURNEMOUTH ☎ 01202 552824 & 556704
📠 01202 298514 38 en suite

Knighton Heath Francis Av, West Howe BH11 8NX
☎ 01202 572633 📠 01202 590774
e-mail: khgc@btinternet.com
**Undulating heathland course on high ground inland
from Poole.**
18 holes, 6084yds, Par 70, SSS 69.
Club membership 700.
Visitors not play weekend; phone for availability.
Societies book in advance. **Green Fees** not confirmed.
Prof Paul Brown **Facilities** ⊗ ㋡ ♀ 么 🏠 ℓ **Location**
N side of Poole, junct A348 & A3409 signed at rdbt

....

Guesthouse ♦♦♦♦ Ashton Lodge, 10 Oakley Hill,
WIMBORNE ☎ 01202 883423 5 rms (2 en suite)

Open Golf Centres Riverside Av, off Castle Ln East
BH7 7ES
☎ 01202 436436 📠 01202 436400
e-mail: info@opengolfcentres.co.uk
Lakes Course: 18 holes, 6277yds, Par 72, SSS 69.
Course Designer John Jacobs Golf Associates **Location**
off A338 Bournemouth-Southampton road, 2m from town
centre. Cooper Dean rdbt take A3060 towards
Christchurch, over minirdbt, left onto Riverside Av,
500yds on right
Phone for further details

Continued   *Continued*

Hotel ⛉ Innkeeper's Lodge Bournemouth, Cooper Dean
Roundabout, Castle Ln East, BOURNEMOUTH
☎ 01202 390837 28 en suite

Queen's Park Queens Park Dr West BH8 9BY
☎ 01202 396198 ▤ 01202 302611
e-mail: queenspark@bournemouth.gov.uk
A mature parkland course with undulating tree lined
fairways. A demanding test of golf, with each hole
having its own unique character.
18 holes, 6090yds, Par 71, SSS 69, Course record 69.
Club membership 370.
Visitors not Sun pm. Societies book in advance. Green
Fees £15 per round (£18 weekends & bank holidays).
Cards ▥ ▦ ▦ ▨ ▧ Facilities ⊗ ⵙ ⵞ ▣ ♟ ⌇ ⏚
⛿ ♣ ∅ Conf fac available Location 2m NE of
Bournemouth town centre off A338

Hotel ★★★ 68% Queens Hotel, Meyrick Rd, East Cliff,
BOURNEMOUTH ☎ 01202 554415 109 en suite

Solent Meads Rolls Dr, Hengistbury Head BH6 4NA
☎ 01202 420795
e-mail: solentmeads@yahoo.co.uk
An 18-hole par 3 links course overlooking Hengistbury
Head with fine views of Christchurch Harbour and the
Isle of Wight. Expect a sea breeze.
18 holes, 2182yards, Par 54.
Visitors no restrictions. Societies advisable to contact in
advance. Green Fees £7.50 per 18 holes. Prof Warren
Butcher Facilities ⊗ ⵙ ▣ ⏚ ∅ ℓ Leisure 9 hole
pitch & putt. Location A35 onto B3509 signed Tuckton.
Over 2nd rdbt, 1st left (Broadway), 0.75m left onto
Rolls Dr

Hotel ⛉ Premier Travel Inn Christchurch West, Barrack
Rd, CHRISTCHURCH ☎ 08701 977063 42 en suite

Bridport & West Dorset The Clubhouse, Burton
Rd DT6 4PS
☎ 01308 421491 & 421095 ▤ 01308 421095
e-mail: secretary@bridportgolfclub.org.uk
Seaside links course on the top of the east cliff, with fine
views over Lyme Bay and surrounding countryside.
The signature 6th hole, known as Port Coombe, is only
133yds but dropping from the top of the cliff to a green
almost at sea level far below. Fine sea views along the
Chesil Bank to Portland Bill and across Lyme Bay.
18 holes, 5875yds, Par 70, SSS 68.
Club membership 600.
Visitors contact in advance. Societies contact in writing in
advance. Green Fees £24 per day; £18 pm, £12 after 5pm.
Prof David Parsons Course Designer Hawtree Facilities
⊗ ⵙ ▣ ♟ ⏚ ∅ ℓ Leisure pitch & putt (holiday
season). Conf Corporate Hospitality Days available
Location 1m E of Bridport on B3157

Hotel ★★★ 65% Haddon House Hotel, West Bay,
BRIDPORT ☎ 01308 423626 & 425323 ▤ 01308 427348
12 en suite

> **In the hotel entries, the percentage figure refers to
> the AA's most recent Quality Assessment Score.**

Broadstone (Dorset) Wentworth Dr BH18 8DQ
☎ 01202 692595 ▤ 01202 642520
e-mail: admin@broadstonegolfclub.com
Undulating and demanding heathland course with the
2nd, 7th, 13th and 16th being particularly challenging
holes.

18 holes, 6315yds, Par 70, SSS 70, Course record 65.
Club membership 620.
Visitors restricted weekends & bank holidays; contact in
advance; handicap certificate. Societies contact in advance.
Green Fees £70 per 27/36 holes, £45 per round (£55 per
round weekends & bank holidays). Cards ▥ ▦ ▧ ▨
▨ Prof Nigel Tokely Course Designer Colt, Dunn
Facilities ⊗ ⵙ ⵞ ▣ ♟ ⏚ ⌇ ⛿ ∅ Conf Corporate
Hospitality Days available Location N side of village off
B3074

Guesthouse ◆◆◆◆ Ashton Lodge, 10 Oakley Hill,
WIMBORNE ☎ 01202 883423 5 rms (2 en suite)

Dudmoor Farm Dudmoor Farm Rd, off Fairmile Rd
BH23 6AQ
☎ 01202 473826 ▤ 01202 480207
A testing par 3 and 4 woodland course in an Area of
Outstanding Natural Beauty.
9 holes, 1428 metres, Par 31.
Visitors no restrictions. Societies phone in advance.
Green Fees £7.50 per 9/18 holes. Facilities ▣ ♟ ⛿ ∅
Leisure squash, adjoining riding stables. Location private
road off B3073 Christchurch-Hurn road

Hotel ★★★ 74% Waterford Lodge Hotel, 87 Bure Ln,
Friars Cliff, CHRISTCHURCH
☎ 01425 272948 & 278801 ▤ 01425 279130 18 en suite

Came Down Came Down DT2 8NR
☎ 01305 813494 (manager) ▤ 01305 813494
e-mail: manager@camedowngolfclub.co.uk
Scene of the West of England championships on several
occasions, this fine course lies on a high plateau
commanding glorious views over Portland. Three par 5
holes add interest to a round. The turf is of the springy,
downland type.
18 holes, 6255yds, Par 70, SSS 70.
Club membership 750.
Visitors not before 9am weekdays, not before 11am Sun;
advisable to phone in advance; handicap certificate.

Continued

Societies by arrangement **Green Fees** £26 per day weekdays (£30 weekends). **Cards** 🖭 🖭 💳 🖭 🖭 Prof Nick Rodgers **Course Designer** JH Taylor, HS Colt **Facilities** ⊗ ℳ ⅃ ⅃ ♀ 🙏 🖭 𝒸 **Location** 2m S off A354

·····························

Guesthouse ◆◆◆◆◆ Yalbury Cottage Hotel & Restaurant, Lower Bockhampton, DORCHESTER
☎ 01305 262382 8 en suite

FERNDOWN   Map 04 SU00

Dudsbury 64 Christchurch Rd BH22 8ST
☎ 01202 593499 🖹 01202 594555
e-mail: glegg@dudsbury.demon.co.uk
Set in 160 acres of beautiful Dorset countryside rolling down to the River Stour. Wide variety of interesting and challenging hazards, notably water which comes into play on 14 holes. The well-drained greens are protected by large bunkers and water hazards. A feature hole is the 16th where the green is over two lakes; the more aggressive the drive the greater the reward.
Championship Course: 18 holes, 6904yds, Par 71, SSS 73, Course record 64.
Club membership 600.
Visitors by arrangement with secretary or golf professional. **Societies** phone in advance. **Green Fees** £45 per 36 holes; £35 per 18 holes (£50/£40 weekend & bank holidays). **Cards** 🖭 🖭 🖭 🖭 **Prof** Kevin Spurgeon **Course Designer** Donald Steel **Facilities** ⊗ ℳ ⅃ ⅃ ♀ 🙏 🖭 🙏 𝒸 **Leisure** fishing, six-hole par 3 short game academy course. **Conf** fac available Corporate Hospitality Days available **Location** 3m N of Bournemouth on B3073

·····························

Hotel ⬆ Premier Travel Inn Bournemouth/Ferndown, Ringwood Rd, Tricketts Cross, FERNDOWN
☎ 08701 977102 32 en suite

Ferndown 119 Golf Links Rd BH22 8BU
☎ 01202 874602 🖹 01202 873926
e-mail: ferndowngc@lineone.net
Fairways are gently undulating among heather, gorse and pine trees, giving the course a most attractive appearance. There are a number of dog-leg holes.
Championship Course: 18 holes, 6501yds, Par 71, SSS 71, Course record 65.
Presidents Course: 9 holes, 5604yds, Par 70, SSS 68.
Club membership 600.
Visitors not Thu except Presidents course; restricted weekends; contact in advance; handicap certificate. **Societies** Tue, Fri, phone in advance. **Green Fees** Championship: £80 per day, £60 per round (£90/£70 weekends). **Cards** 🖭 🖭 🖭 🖭 **Prof** Neil PIke **Course Designer** Harold Hilton **Facilities** ⊗ ℳ ⅃ ⅃ ♀ 🙏 🖭 🙏 𝒸 **Conf** Corporate Hospitality Days available **Location** S side of town centre off A347

·····························

Hotel ⬆ Premier Travel Inn Bournemouth/Ferndown, Ringwood Rd, Tricketts Cross, FERNDOWN
☎ 08701 977102 32 en suite

Ferndown Forest Forest Links Rd BH22 9QE
☎ 01202 876096 🖹 01202 894095
e-mail: golf@ferndownforestgolf.co.uk
Flat parkland course dotted with mature oak trees, several interesting water features, and some tight fairways.
18 holes, 5068yds, Par 68, SSS 65, Course record 69.
Club membership 400.
Visitors advisable to contact in advance. **Societies** apply in writing. **Green Fees** £13 weekdays (£15 weekends & bank holidays) per day. **Cards** 🖭 🖭 🖭 **Prof** Mike Dodd **Course Designer** Guy Hunt, Richard Graham **Facilities** ⊗ ℳ ⅃ ⅃ ♀ 🙏 🖭 🖭 🙏 𝒸 **Conf** fac available Corporate Hospitality Days available **Location** off A31 N of Ferndown

·····························

Hotel ⬆ Premier Travel Inn Bournemouth/Ferndown, Ringwood Rd, Tricketts Cross, FERNDOWN
☎ 08701 977102 32 en suite

HALSTOCK   Map 03 ST50

Halstock Common Ln BA22 9SF
☎ 01935 891689 & 891968 (pro shop) 🖹 01935 891839
e-mail: halstock.golf@feeuk.com
18 holes, 4481yds, Par 66, SSS 63, Course record 63.
Location 6m S of Yeovil
Phone for further details

·····························

Hotel ★★★ ♨ Summer Lodge, EVERSHOT
☎ 01935 83424 10 en suite 14 annexe en suite

HIGHCLIFFE   Map 04 SZ29

Highcliffe Castle 107 Lymington Rd BH23 4LA
☎ 01425 272210 🖹 01425 272953
Picturesque parkland course with easy walking.
18 holes, 4776yds, Par 64, SSS 63, Course record 58.
Club membership 500.
Visitors handicap certificate & member of recognised club; phone in advance. **Societies** write or phone in advance. **Green Fees** £26 per day (£36 weekends am). **Facilities** ⊗ ℳ ⅃ ⅃ ♀ 🙏 **Conf** Corporate Hospitality Days available **Location** SW side of town on A337

·····························

Hotel ★★★ 74% Waterford Lodge Hotel, 87 Bure Ln, Friars Cliff, CHRISTCHURCH
☎ 01425 272948 & 278801 🖹 01425 279130 18 en suite

HURN   Map 04 SZ19

Parley Parley Green Ln BH23 6BB
☎ 01202 591600 🖹 01202 579043
e-mail: info@parleygolf.co.uk
Flat testing parkland course with few hazards and only two par 5s. Renowned 5th hole, bordering the River Stour.
9 holes, 4938yds, Par 68, SSS 64, Course record 69.
Club membership 200.
Visitors dress code. **Societies** write or phone. **Green Fees** £9.50 for 18 holes, £7 for nine holes (£10.50/£8 weekends). **Cards** 🖭 🖭 🖭 🖭 **Prof** Richard Hill **Course Designer** P Goodfellow **Facilities** ⊗ ℳ by arrangement ⅃ ⅃ ♀ 🙏 🖭 🖭 🙏 𝒸 **Conf** Corporate Hospitality Days available **Location** on B3073 opp Bournemouth airport

·····························

Hotel ⬆ Premier Travel Inn Bournemouth/Ferndown, Ringwood Rd, Tricketts Cross, FERNDOWN
☎ 08701 977102 32 en suite

LYME REGIS
Map 03 SY39

Lyme Regis Timber Hill DT7 3HQ
☎ 01297 442963 ▤ 01297 442963
e-mail: secretary@lymeregisgolfclub.co.uk
Undulating cliff-top course with magnificent views of Golden Cap and Lyme Bay.

18 holes, 6283yds, Par 71, SSS 70, Course record 65.
Club membership 575.
Visitors not Thu, am Sun; contact in advance; handicap certificate or member of recognised golf club. **Societies** Tue, Wed, Fri, contact in writing. **Green Fees** £35 per day, £30 per 18 holes before 2pm, £25 after 2pm. **Prof** Duncan Driver **Course Designer** Donald Steel **Facilities** ⊗ ⅢⅢ ⅃ ⚑ ♀ ⚘ 🏠 ⛟ 🖶 ⚲ **Location** W end of Charmouth bypass (A5), take A3052 to Lyme Regis. 1.5m from A3052-A35 rdbt

Hotel ★★★ 71% Alexandra Hotel, Pound St, LYME REGIS ☎ 01297 442010 25 en suite 1 annexe en suite

LYTCHETT MATRAVERS
Map 03 SY99

Bulbury Woods Bulbury Ln BH16 6HR
☎ 01929 459574 ▤ 01929 459000
e-mail: general@bulbury-woods.co.uk
Parkland course with a mixture of American and traditional style greens and extensive views over the Purbecks and Poole Harbour. A comprehensive programme of tree planting coupled with ancient woodland ensures a round that is picturesque as well as providing interest and challenge.
18 holes, 6002yds, Par 71, SSS 69.
Club membership 450.
Visitors subject to availability; visitors may book seven days in advance. **Societies** contact in advance. **Green Fees** not confirmed. **Cards** 🖶 🖶 🖶 🖶 🖶 **Prof** David Adams **Facilities** ⊗ ⅢⅢ ⅃ ⚑ ♀ ⚘ 🏠 ⛟ 🖶 ⚲ **Conf** fac available Corporate Hospitality Days available **Location** A35 Poole-Dorchester, 3m from Poole centre

Hotel ★★★ 68% Springfield Country Hotel & Leisure Club, Grange Rd, WAREHAM ☎ 01929 552177 48 en suite

POOLE
Map 04 SZ09

Parkstone Links Rd, Parkstone BH14 9QS
☎ 01202 707138 ▤ 01202 706027
e-mail: admin@parkstonegolfclub.co.uk
Very scenic heathland course with views of Poole Bay. Designed in 1909 by Willie Park Jnr and enlarged in 1932 by James Braid. The result of this highly imaginative reconstruction was an intriguing and

Continued

varied test of golf set among pines and heather fringed fairways where every hole presents a different challenge.
18 holes, 6250yds, Par 72, SSS 70, Course record 63.
Club membership 700.
Visitors contact in advance; handicap certificate. **Societies** apply in writing or phone in advance; handicap certificates. **Green Fees** £75 per day; £50 per round (£85/£60 weekends & bank holidays). **Cards** 🖶 🖶 ⚲ **Prof** Martyn Thompson **Course Designer** Willie Park Jnr **Facilities** ⊗ ⅢⅢ ⅃ ♀ ♀ ⚘ 🏠 🖶 ⚲ ⚲ **Conf** Corporate Hospitality Days available **Location** E side of town centre off A35

Hotel ★★★ 64% Salterns Harbourside Hotel, 38 Salterns Way, Lilliput, POOLE ☎ 01202 707321 20 en suite

SHERBORNE
Map 03 ST61

Sherborne Higher Clatcombe DT9 4RN
☎ 01935 814431 ▤ 01935 814218
e-mail: sherbornegc@btconnect.com
Beautiful mature parkland course to the north of Sherborne on the Dorset-Somerset border, with extensive views. Recently extended to 6414yds.
18 holes, 6414yds, Par 72, SSS 71, Course record 62.
Club membership 600.
Visitors contact in advance; handicap certificate. **Societies** Tue, Wed, booking required. **Green Fees** £30 per day, £25 per round (£36 per round weekends). **Prof** Alistair Tresidder **Course Designer** James Braid (part) **Facilities** ⊗ ⅢⅢ ⅃ ♀ ♀ ⚘ 🏠 ⚲ **Location** 2m N off B3145

Hotel ★★★ 72% Eastbury Hotel, Long St, SHERBORNE ☎ 01935 813131 22 en suite

STURMINSTER MARSHALL
Map 03 ST90

Sturminster Marshall Moor Ln BH21 4AH
☎ 01258 858444 ▤ 01258 858262
9 holes, 4882yds, Par 68, SSS 64.
Course Designer John Sharkey, David Holdsworth
Location on A350, signed from village
Phone for further details

Hotel ★★★ 71% Crown Hotel, West St, BLANDFORD FORUM ☎ 01258 456626 32 en suite

SWANAGE
Map 04 SZ07

Isle of Purbeck BH19 3AB
☎ 01929 450361 & 450354 ▤ 01929 450501
e-mail: enquiries@purbeckgolf.co.uk
A heathland course sited on the Purbeck Hills with grand views across Swanage and Poole Harbour. Holes of note include the 5th, 8th, 14th, 15th, and 16th where trees, gorse and heather assert themselves. The very attractive clubhouse is built of the local stone.
Purbeck Course: 18 holes, 6295yds, Par 70, SSS 70, Course record 66.
Dene Course: 9 holes, 4014yds, Par 60.
Club membership 500.
Visitors advisable to phone. **Societies** contact in advance. **Green Fees** not confirmed. **Cards** 🖶 🖶 🖶 ⚲ **Prof** Ian Brake **Course Designer** H Colt **Facilities** ⊗ ⅢⅢ by arrangement ⅃ ♀ ♀ ⚘ 🏠 🖶 ⚲ ⚘ ⚲ **Location** 2.5m N on B3351

Continued

Isle of Purbeck Golf Club

Hotel ★★★ 69% The Pines Hotel, Burlington Rd, SWANAGE ☎ 01929 425211 49 en suite

VERWOOD
Map 04 SU00

Crane Valley The Club House BH31 7LE
☎ 01202 814088 🖹 01202 813407
e-mail: general@crane-valley.co.uk
Two secluded parkland courses set amid rolling Dorset countryside and mature woodland. The 6th nestles in the bend of the River Crane and there are four long par 5s ranging from 499 to 545yds.
Valley: 18 holes, 6445yds, Par 72, SSS 71, Course record 66.
Woodland: 9 holes, 2060yds, Par 33, SSS 30.
Club membership 700.
Visitors contact in advance for Valley course. Woodland course is pay & play. **Societies** phone in advance. **Green Fees** Valley: £25 per round (£35 weekends & bank holidays) Woodland: £10 for 18 holes, £5.50 for 9 holes (£12/£6.50 weekends). **Cards** 🔤 🔤 🔤 🔤 🖾 **Prof** Darrel Ranson **Course Designer** Donald Steel **Facilities** ⊗ ⊪ ⅃ ⅊ ⅂ ⅃ ⌐ ⅋ ⌐ ⌐ **Conf** fac available Corporate Hospitality Days available **Location** 6m W of Ringwood on B3081

Hotel ★★ 64% Candlesticks Inn, 136 Christchurch Rd, RINGWOOD ☎ 01425 472587 8 en suite

WAREHAM
Map 03 SY98

Wareham Sandford Rd BH20 4DH
☎ 01929 554147 🖹 01929 557993
e-mail: admin@warehamgolfclub.com
At the entrance to the Purbeck Hills with splendid views over Poole Harbour and Wareham Forest. A mixture of undulating parkland and heathland fairways. A challenge for all abilities.
18 holes, 5753yds, Par 69, SSS 68, Course record 66.
Club membership 500.
Visitors not before 9.30am weekdays, not before 1pm weekends; handicap certificate preferred. **Societies** weekdays. **Green Fees** not confirmed. **Facilities** ⊗ ⊪ ⅃ ⅊ ⅂ ⅋ ⌐ ⅋ **Location** 0.5m N of Wareham on A351

Hotel ★★★ 68% Springfield Country Hotel Leisure Club, Grange Rd, WAREHAM ☎ 01929 552177 48 en suite

> Looking for a new course? Always telephone ahead to confirm visitor arrangements.

WEYMOUTH
Map 03 SY67

Weymouth Links Rd DT4 0PF
☎ 01305 773981 (Manager) & 773997 (Pro)
🖹 01305 788029
e-mail: weymouthgolfclub@aol.com
Seaside parkland course. The 5th is played off an elevated tee over copse.
18 holes, 5981yds, Par 70, SSS 69, Course record 60.
Club membership 750.
Visitors not weekends; advisable to contact in advance; EGU or LGU handicap required. **Societies** apply by writing, phone, e-mail or fax. **Green Fees** terms on application. **Prof** Des Lochrie **Course Designer** James Braid **Facilities** ⊗ ⊪ ⅃ ⅊ ⅂ ⅃ ⌐ ⅋ ⌐ ⌐ **Conf** Corporate Hospitality Days available **Location** N side of town centre off B3157

Hotel ★★★ 64% Hotel Rex, 29 The Esplanade, WEYMOUTH ☎ 01305 760400 31 en suite

WIMBORNE
Map 03 SZ09

Canford Magna Knighton Ln BH21 3AS
☎ 01202 592552 🖹 01202 592550
e-mail: admin@canfordmagnagc.co.uk
Lying in 350 acres of Dorset countryside, the Canford Magna Golf Club provides 45 holes of challenging golf for the discerning player. The 18-hole Parkland and Riverside courses are quite different and the new nine-hole Knighton course demands the same level of playing skill. For those wishing to improve their handicap, the Golf Academy offers a covered driving range, pitching greens, a chipping green and bunkers, together with a 6-hole par 3 academy course.
Parkland: 18 holes, 6495yds, Par 71, SSS 71, Course record 65.
Riverside: 18 holes, 6214yds, Par 70, SSS 70, Course record 68.
Knighton: 9 holes, 1377yds, Par 27, Course record 26.
Club membership 1000.
Visitors advisable to contact in advance. **Societies** phone in advance. **Green Fees** Parkland £21 per round (£25 weekends). Riverside £17/£20. Knighton £6/£8. **Cards** 🔤 🔤 🔤 🔤 🖾 **Prof** Martin Cummins **Course Designer** Howard Swan **Facilities** ⊗ ⊪ ⅃ ⅊ ⅂ ⅃ ⌐ ⅋ ⌐ ⌐ **Leisure** Golf lessons. **Conf** fac available Corporate Hospitality Days available **Location** on A341

Guesthouse ♦♦♦♦ Ashton Lodge, 10 Oakley Hill, WIMBORNE ☎ 01202 883423 5 rms (2 en suite)

CO DURHAM

BARNARD CASTLE
Map 12 NZ01

Barnard Castle Harmire Rd DL12 8QN
☎ 01833 638355 🖹 01833 695551
e-mail: sec@barnardcastlegolfclub.org.uk
Perched high on the steep bank of the River Tees, the extensive remains of Barnard Castle with its splendid round tower date back to the 12th and 13th centuries. The parkland course is flat and lies in open countryside. Its delightful plantations and natural water features add colour and interest to this classic course.
18 holes, 6406yds, Par 73, SSS 71, Course record 63.
Club membership 650.

Continued

Barnard Castle Golf Club

Visitors restricted weekends; contact in advance; handicap certificate. **Societies** apply in writing. **Green Fees** £22 per round (£32 weekends & bank holidays). **Prof** Darren Pearce **Course Designer** A Watson **Facilities** ⊗ ⅷ ⅼ ☞ ♀ ⚘ 🏠 ⚐ ⚑ ⚒ ✍ **Conf** Corporate Hospitality Days available **Location** 1m N of town centre on B6278

Hotel ★★ Rose & Crown Hotel, ROMALDKIRK
☎ 01833 650213 7 en suite 5 annexe en suite

BEAMISH   Map 12 NZ25

Beamish Park DH9 0RH
☎ 0191 370 1382 🖷 0191 370 2937
e-mail: bpgc@beamishparkgc.fsbusiness.co.uk
Parkland course designed by Henry Cotton and W Woodend.
18 holes, 6183yds, Par 71, SSS 70, Course record 64.
Club membership 630.
Visitors not weekends; contact in advance. **Societies** weekdays, phone in advance. **Green Fees** £28 per day, £22 per round. **Prof** Chris Cole **Course Designer** H Cotton, W Woodend **Facilities** ⊗ ⅷ ⅼ ☞ ♀ ⚘ 🏠 ⚑ ⚒ ✍ **Conf** Corporate Hospitality Days available **Location** 1m NW off A693

Hotel ★★★ 69% Beamish Park Hotel, Beamish Burn Rd, MARLEY HILL ☎ 01207 230666 47 en suite

BILLINGHAM   Map 08 NZ42

Billingham Sandy Ln TS22 5NA
☎ 01642 533816 & 557060 (Pro) 🖷 01642 533816
e-mail: billinghamgc@onetel.com
Undulating parkland course with water hazards.
18 holes, 6346yds, Par 71, SSS 70, Course record 62.
Club membership 1050.
Visitors contact professional in advance 01642 557060; handicap certificate may be requested. **Societies** apply in writing to Secretary/Manager, by phone or e-mail. **Green Fees** £26 per day. **Prof** Michael Ure **Course Designer** F Pennick **Facilities** ⊗ ⅷ ⅼ ☞ ♀ ⚘ 🏠 ⚑ ⚒ ✍ **Location** 1m W of town centre

Hotel ★★★ 72% Parkmore Hotel Leisure Park, 636 Yarm Rd, Eaglescliffe, STOCKTON-ON-TEES
☎ 01642 786815 55 en suite

Wynyard Wellington Dr, Wynyard Park TS22 5QJ
☎ 01740 644399 🖷 01740 644599
e-mail: chris@wynyardgolfclub.co.uk
Built against the delightful backdrop of the Wynyard estate, the Wellington Course combines a fine blend of rolling parkland and mature woodland. It represents

the ultimate in challenge and excitement for both the novice and the highly experienced player.
Wellington: 18 holes, 6851yds, Par 72, SSS 72, Course record 63.
Club membership 350.
Visitors contact in advance for availability. **Societies** phone in advance. **Green Fees** £50 per 18 holes. **Cards** ▭▭ ▭▭ ▭▭ ▭▭ ▭ **Prof** Chris Mounter **Course Designer** Hawtree **Facilities** ⊗ ⅷ ⅼ ☞ ♀ ⚘ 🏠 ⚑ ⚒ ✍ **Leisure** David Leadbetter Golf Academy. **Conf** fac available Corporate Hospitality Days available **Location** off A689 between A19 & A1

BISHOP AUCKLAND   Map 08 NZ22

Bishop Auckland High Plains, Durham Rd DL14 8DL
☎ 01388 661618 🖷 01388 607005
e-mail: enquiries@bagc.co.uk
A rather hilly parkland course with many well-established trees offering a challenging round. A small ravine adds interest to several holes including the short 7th, from a raised tee to a green surrounded by a stream, gorse and bushes. Pleasant views down the Wear Valley and over the residence of the Bishop of Durham. Has the distinction of having three consecutive par 5 holes and two consecutive par 3s.
18 holes, 6379yds, Par 72, SSS 70, Course record 63.
Club membership 950.
Visitors parties must contact in advance; handicap certificate; dress code. **Societies** weekdays, contact in advance. **Green Fees** £24 per round (£30 per round weekends). **Cards** ▭▭ ▭▭ ▭▭ ▭▭ ▭ **Prof** David Skiffington **Course Designer** James Kay **Facilities** ⊗ ⅷ ⅼ ☞ ♀ ⚘ 🏠 ⚒ ✍ **Leisure** snooker. **Location** 1m NE on A689

Hotel ★★★ 74% Whitworth Hall Country Park Hotel, Stanners Ln, SPENNYMOOR ☎ 01388 811772 29 en suite

BURNOPFIELD   Map 12 NZ15

Hobson Hobson NE16 6BZ
☎ 01207 270941 🖷 01207 271069
Meadowland course with very easy walking.
18 holes, 6403yds, Par 69, SSS 68, Course record 65.
Club membership 700.
Visitors book for weekends. **Societies** contact in advance. **Green Fees** £19 per round (£22 weekend). **Cards** ▭▭ ▭▭ ▭▭ ▭▭ ▭ **Prof** Jack Ord **Facilities** ⊗ ⅷ ⅼ ☞ ♀ ⚘ 🏠 ⚑ ✍ **Location** 0.75m S on A692

CHESTER-LE-STREET   Map 12 NZ25

Chester-le-Street Lumley Park DH3 4NS
☎ 0191 388 3218 (Secretary) 🖷 0191 388 1220
e-mail: clsgc@ukonline.co.uk
Parkland course in castle grounds, good views, easy walking.
18 holes, 6437yds, Par 71, SSS 70, Course record 67.
Club membership 650.
Visitors contact in advance; introduction from own club or handicap certificate. **Societies** apply by writing, phone or e-mail. **Green Fees** £30 per day, £25 per round (£35/£30 weekends). **Prof** David Fletcher **Course Designer** JH Taylor **Facilities** ⊗ ⅷ ⅼ ☞ ♀ ⚘ 🏠 ⚑ ⚒ ✍ **Conf** Corporate Hospitality Days available **Location** 0.5m E off B1284

Continued   *Continued*

Hotel ★★★ 72% Ramside Hall Hotel, Carrville,
DURHAM ☎ 0191 386 5282 80 en suite

Roseberry Grange Grange Villa DH2 3NF
☎ 0191 3700670 📇 0191 3700224
**Parkland course providing a good test of golf for all
abilities. Fine panoramic views of County Durham.**
18 holes, 6152yds, Par 71, SSS 69.
Club membership 620.
Visitors not before 11.30am Sun, not before 10.30am Sat
in summer; pay & play Mon-Fri. **Societies** booking form
available on request. **Green Fees** not confirmed. **Cards** 📇
📇 📇 📇 📇 📇 **Prof** Chris Jones **Course Designer**
Durham County Council **Facilities** ⊗ ⅏ ⅃ ⊒ ♀ ⚲ 🕿 ♂
🏌 **Location** 5m W of Chester-le-Street. Off A694 into
West Pelton, signed

Hotel ★★★ 67% George Washington Golf & Country
Club, Stone Cellar Rd, High Usworth, WASHINGTON
☎ 0191 402 9988 103 en suite

CONSETT Map 12 NZ15

Consett & District Elmfield Rd DH8 5NN
☎ 01207 502186 📇 01207 505060
**Undulating parkland and moorland course with views
across the Derwent Valley to the Cheviot Hills.**
18 holes, 6080yds, Par 71, SSS 69, Course record 63.
Club membership 650.
Visitors advised to contact Secretary in advance on 01207
505060. **Societies** apply in writing. **Green Fees** £18 per
day (£26 weekends). **Prof** Shaun Cowell **Course Designer**
Harry Vardon **Facilities** ⊗ ⅏ ⅃ ⊒ ♀ ⚲ 🕿 ⚒ **Leisure**
snooker room. **Location** N side of town on A691

Hotel ★★ 70% Lord Crewe Arms Hotel, BLANCHLAND
☎ 01434 675251 9 en suite 10 annexe en suite

CROOK Map 12 NZ13

Crook Low Jobs Hill DL15 9AA
☎ 01388 762429 📇 01388 762429
**Meadowland and parkland course on elevated position
with natural hazards, varied holes and terrain.
Panoramic views over Durham and the Cleveland Hills.**
18 holes, 6102yds, Par 70, SSS 69, Course record 64.
Club membership 550.
Visitors weekends by arrangement. **Societies** apply in
writing to Secretary or contact professional 01388 768145.
Green Fees terms on application. **Prof** Gordon Cattrell
Facilities ⊗ ⅏ ⅃ ⊒ ♀ ⚲ 🕿 🏌 ⚒ ♂ **Conf** fac
available **Location** 0.5m E off A690

Hotel ★★★ 66% Helme Park Hall Hotel, FIR TREE
☎ 01388 730970 13 en suite

DARLINGTON Map 08 NZ21

Blackwell Grange Briar Close, Blackwell DL3 8QX
☎ 01325 464458 📇 01325 464458
e-mail: secretary@blackwellgrangegolf.com
**One of the most attractive courses in north-east
England. Clever use of the trees on this easy walking
course gives a feeling of having the course to oneself.
Three ponds add to the variety of holes on offer.**
18 holes, 5621yds, Par 68, SSS 67, Course record 63.
Club membership 1000.
Visitors restricted Wed & weekends. **Societies** weekdays
except Ladies Day Wed. **Green Fees** £25 per day; £20 per
round (£30 per round weekends & bank holidays).

Prof Joanne Furby **Course Designer** F Pennink **Facilities**
⊗ ⅏ ⅃ ⊒ ♀ ⚲ 🕿 🏌 ♂ **Conf** Corporate Hospitality
Days available **Location** 1.5m SW off A66 into Blackwell,
signed

Hotel ★★★ 64% The Blackwell Grange Hotel, Blackwell
Grange, DARLINGTON ☎ 0870 609 6121 99 en suite
11 annexe en suite

Darlington Haughton Grange DL1 3JD
☎ 01325 355324 📇 01325 488126
e-mail: darlington.golfclub@virgin.net
18 holes, 6181yds, Par 70, SSS 69, Course record 65.
Course Designer Dr A MacKenzie **Location** N side of
town centre off A1150
Phone for further details

Hotel ★★★ ♨ 75% Headlam Hall Hotel, Headlam,
Gainford, DARLINGTON ☎ 01325 730238 19 en suite
17 annexe en suite

Hall Garth Golf & Country Club Hotel
Coatham Mundeville DL1 3LU
☎ 01325 320246 📇 01325 310083

9 holes, 6621yds, Par 72, SSS 72.
Course Designer Brian Moore **Location** 0.5m from
A1(M) junct 59, off A167
Phone for further details

Hotel ★★★ 73% Hall Garth Golf and Country Club Hotel,
Coatham Mundeville, DARLINGTON ☎ 01325 300400
40 en suite 11 annexe en suite

Headlam Hall Hotel Headlam, Grinford DL2 3HA
☎ 01325 730238 📇 01325 730790
e-mail: admin@headlamhall.co.uk
**Course set over the mature rolling pastureland of
Headlam Hall. Abundance of natural features including
rig and fur', woodland, streams and ponds, making the
course both challenging to the player and pleasing to
the eye. Each hole has its own character but the 7th
Pond Hole is particularly special with a stepped green
protruding into a picturesque pond with woodland
lining the back.**
9 holes, 1806yds, Par 30.
Club membership 200.
Visitors contact hotel/pro shop to book tee time; dress
code. **Societies** phone in advance. **Green Fees** £18 per 18
holes, £12 per nine holes; winter £15/£10. **Prof** Steven
Carpenter **Course Designer** Ralph Givens **Facilities** ⊗ ⅏
⅃ ⊒ ♀ ⚲ 🕿 🏌 ⚑ ♂ 🏌 **Leisure** hard tennis courts,
heated indoor swimming pool, fishing, sauna, gymnasium.
Conf fac available Corporate Hospitality Days available
Location 8m W of Darlington, off A67

Continued

Continued

Hotel ★★★ 🏆 75% Headlam Hall Hotel, Headlam,
Gainford, DARLINGTON ☎ 01325 730238 19 en suite
17 annexe en suite

Stressholme Snipe Ln DL2 2SA
☎ 01325 461002 📠 01325 461002
**Picturesque municipal parkland course, long but wide,
with 98 bunkers and a par 3 hole played over a river.**
18 holes, 6431yds, Par 71, SSS 70, Course record 69.
Club membership 350.
Visitors book seven days in advance. **Societies** phone to
book **Green Fees** not confirmed. **Cards** ▦ ▦ ▦ ▦ ▦
Prof Ralph Givens **Facilities** ⊗ ⏃ ⅏ ⊑ ♀ ♨ 🍴 🏌 ♂ ⎞
Conf fac available Corporate Hospitality Days available
Location SW of town centre on A67

Hotel ★★★ 64% The Blackwell Grange Hotel, Blackwell
Grange, DARLINGTON ☎ 0870 609 6121 99 en suite
11 annexe en suite

DURHAM   Map 12 NZ24

Brancepeth Castle Brancepeth Village DH7 8EA
☎ 0191 378 0075 📠 0191 378 3835
e-mail: brancepethcastle@btclick.com
**Parkland course overlooked at the 9th hole by beautiful
Brancepeth Castle.**
18 holes, 6234yds, Par 70, SSS 70, Course record 64.
Club membership 780.
Visitors restricted weekends; contact in advance. **Societies**
contact in advance. **Green Fees** £35 per day, £30 per round
weekdays. **Cards** ▦ ▦ ▦ ▦ **Prof** David Howdon
Course Designer HS Colt **Facilities** ⊗ ⏃ ⅏ ⊑ ♀ ♨ 🍴 🏌
🍴 ⎞ **Conf** Corporate Hospitality Days available **Location**
4m from Durham A690 towards Crook, left at x-rds in
Brancepath, left at Castle Gates, 400yds

Hotel ★★★★ 72% Durham Marriott Hotel, Royal County,
Old Elvet, DURHAM ☎ 0191 386 6821 142 en suite
8 annexe en suite

Durham City Littleburn, Langley Moor DH7 8HL
☎ 0191 378 0069 📠 0191 378 4265
e-mail: durhamcitygolf@lineone.net
18 holes, 6326yds, Par 71, SSS 70, Course record 67.
Course Designer C Stanton **Location** 2m W of Durham
City, turn left off A690 into Littleburn Ind Est
Phone for further details

Hotel ★★★ 66% Bowburn Hall Hotel, Bowburn,
DURHAM ☎ 0191 377 0311 19 en suite

Mount Oswald South Rd DH1 3TQ
☎ 0191 386 7527 📠 0191 386 0975
e-mail: information@mountoswald.co.uk
**Picturesque parkland course which gently undulates
through the Durham countryside. Easy walking course
which attracts golfers of all levels and abilities.**
18 holes, 5984yds, Par 71, SSS 69.
Club membership 200.
Visitors not before 10am Sun; contact in advance for
weekends & available tee times. **Societies** phone in
advance. **Green Fees** £12.75 per round (£15.50 weekends
& bank holidays); reduced winter rates. **Cards** ▦ ▦ ▦
▦ ▦ **Prof** Chris Calder **Facilities** ⊗ ⏃ ⅏ ⊑ ♀ ♨ 🍴 🏌
♂ 🍴 ⎞ **Conf** fac available Corporate Hospitality Days
available **Location** On A177, 1m SW of city centre

Hotel ★★★ 72% Ramside Hall Hotel, Carrville,
DURHAM ☎ 0191 386 5282 80 en suite

Ramside Hall Carrville DH1 1TD
☎ 0191 386 9514 📠 0191 386 9519
e-mail: golf@ramsidegolfclub.fsnet.co.uk
**Three recently constructed nine-hole parkland courses -
Princes, Bishops, Cathedral - with 14 lakes and
panoramic views surrounding an impressive hotel.
Excellent golf academy and driving range.**

Princes: 9 holes, 3235yds, Par 36, SSS 36.
Bishops: 9 holes, 3285yds, Par 36.
Cathedral: 9 holes, 2874yds, Par 34.
Club membership 450.
Visitors subject to tee availability. **Societies** phone in
advance. **Green Fees** not confirmed. **Cards** ▦ ▦ ▦
▦ ▦ ▦ ▦ **Prof** Robert Lister **Course Designer**
Jonathan Gaunt **Facilities** ⊗ ⏃ ⅏ ⊑ ♀ ♨ 🍴 🏌 🍴 ♂
🍴 ⎞ **Leisure** sauna, steam room. **Conf** fac available
Corporate Hospitality Days available **Location** 500yds
from junct A1 & A690

Hotel ★★★ 72% Ramside Hall Hotel, Carrville,
DURHAM ☎ 0191 386 5282 80 en suite

EAGLESCLIFFE   Map 08 NZ41

Eaglescliffe and District Yarm Rd TS16 0DQ
☎ 01642 780238 (office) 📠 01642 780238
e-mail: eaglescliffegcsec@tiscali.co.uk
**An undulating wooded parkland course with views over
the river Tees to the Cleveland Hills. A tee on the
riverbank makes for a daunting tee shot at the 14th
signature hole.**
18 holes, 6275yds, Par 72, SSS 70, Course record 64.
Club membership 970.
Visitors restricted Tue, Thu, Fri & weekends; contact pro
01642 790122. **Societies** contact in advance, apply to
Secretary 01642 780238. **Green Fees** £40 per day; £30 per
round (£50/£36 weekends). **Prof** Graeme Bell **Course
Designer** J Braid, H Cotton **Facilities** ⊗ ⏃ ⅏ ⊑ ♀ ♨ 🍴
🏌 🍴 ♂ 🍴 **Location** on E side of A135 between Yarm &
Stockton-on-Tees

Hotel ★★★ 72% Parkmore Hotel Leisure Park, 636 Yarm
Rd, Eaglescliffe, STOCKTON-ON-TEES
☎ 01642 786815 55 en suite

HARTLEPOOL   Map 08 NZ53

Castle Eden Castle Eden TS27 4SS
☎ 01429 836510 📠 01429 836510
e-mail: derek.livingston@btinternet.com
*Castle Eden & Peterlee Golf Club: 18 holes, 6262yds,
Par 70, SSS 70, Course record 64.*
Course Designer Henry Cotton **Location** 2m S of Peterlee
on B1281 off A19
Phone for further details

Continued

Hotel ★★ 69% Hardwicke Hall Manor Hotel, Hesleden, PETERLEE ☎ 01429 836326 15 en suite

Hartlepool Hart Warren TS24 9QF
☎ 01429 274398 📠 01429 274129
18 holes, 6200yds, Par 70, SSS 70, Course record 62.
Course Designer Partly Braid **Location** N of Hartlepool, off A1086
Phone for further details

Hotel ⭐ Premier Travel Inn Hartlepool, Maritme Av, Hartlepool Marina, HARTLEPOOL ☎ 08701 977127 40 en suite

MIDDLETON ST GEORGE   Map 08 NZ31

Dinsdale Spa Neasham Rd DL2 1DW
☎ 01325 332297 📠 01325 332297
A mainly flat, parkland course on high land above the River Tees with views of the Cleveland Hills. Water hazards in front of 10th tee and green; the prevailing west wind affects the later holes. There is a practice area by the clubhouse.
18 holes, 6099yds, Par 71, SSS 69, Course record 65.
Club membership 870.
Visitors not Tue, weekends; contact for further details.
Societies not Tue, weekends, apply in writing or phone.
Green Fees £25 per day. **Prof** Neil Metcalfe **Facilities** ⊗ �🍴 🏌 🍺 ♀ ⛳ 🏧 ✦ **Location** 1.5m SW

Hotel ★★★ 69% The Croft, Croft-on-Tees, DARLINGTON ☎ 01325 720319 20 en suite

NEWTON AYCLIFFE   Map 08 NZ22

Oakleaf Golf Complex School Aycliffe Ln DL5 6QZ
☎ 01325 310820 📠 01325 318918
A parkland course in a country setting with established trees, streams and lakes, the signature hole being the 15th. Excellent views.
18 holes, 5568yds, Par 70, SSS 67, Course record 67.
Club membership 450.
Visitors dress code; contact in advance for weekends.
Societies apply in writing or phone. **Green Fees** terms on application. **Cards** 🟰 💳 💳 💳 🟰 💳 **Prof** Ernie Wilson
Facilities ⊗ ⛳ 🏌 🍺 ♀ 🏧 🍴 ✦ **Leisure** squash, fishing. **Location** 6m N of Darlington, off A6072

Hotel ★★★★ 70% Redworth Hall Hotel, REDWORTH ☎ 01388 770600 100 en suite

Woodham Golf & Country Club Burnhill Way DL5 4PN
☎ 01325 320574 (office) 315257 (pro shop)
📠 01325 315254
The course was originally opened in 1981 and the excellent design was by James Hamilton Scott. It is laid out in 229 acres of parkland with the two loops of nine holes starting and finishing at the clubhouse. Mature woodland with large trees and numerous lakes.
18 holes, 6688yds, Par 73, SSS 72, Course record 66.
Club membership 600.
Visitors book one week in advance for Fri-Sun. **Societies** phone or write in advance. **Green Fees** terms on application. **Cards** 🟰 💳 💳 🟰 💳 **Prof** Peter Kelly
Course Designer James Hamilton Stutt **Facilities** ⊗ ⛳ 🏌

Continued

⛳ ♀ 🏌 🏧 🍴 🏧 ✦ **Location** A1 onto A689 towards Bishop Auckland, 0.5m from Rushford

Hotel ⭐ Premier Travel Inn Durham (Newton Aycliffe), Great North Rd, NEWTON AYCLIFFE ☎ 08701 977085 44 en suite

SEAHAM   Map 12 NZ44

Seaham Dawdon SR7 7RD
☎ 0191 5130837 & 5812354
e-mail: seahamgc@onetel.com
Heathland links course with several holes affected by strong winds.
18 holes, 6017yds, Par 70, SSS 69, Course record 64.
Club membership 600.
Visitors contact professional at all times; with member only weekends before 3.30pm. **Societies** apply in advance.
Green Fees £22 per day (£27 weekends). **Prof** Andrew Blunt **Facilities** ⊗ ⛳ by arrangement 🏌 🍺 ♀ 🏧 🍴 🏧 ✦ **Location** 3m E of A19, exit for Seaham

Hotel ★★★★ 69% Sunderland Marriott Hotel, Queen's Pde, Seaburn, SUNDERLAND ☎ 0191 529 2041 82 en suite

SEATON CAREW   Map 08 NZ52

Seaton Carew Tees Rd TS25 1DE
☎ 01429 261040 📠 01429 267952
A championship links course taking full advantage of its dunes, bents, whins and gorse. Renowned for its par 4 17th; just enough fairway for an accurate drive followed by another precise shot to a pear-shape sloping green that is severely trapped.
The Old Course: 18 holes, 6622yds, Par 72, SSS 72.
Brabazon Course: 18 holes, 6857yds, Par 73, SSS 73.
Club membership 761.
Visitors not before 09.30am midweek, not before 10am weekends & bank holidays. **Societies** apply in writing or phone in advance. **Green Fees** terms on application. **Prof** Mark Rogers **Course Designer** MacKenzie **Facilities** ⊗ ⛳ 🏌 🍺 ♀ 🏧 🍴 🏧 🏌 🏧 ✦ **Location** SE side of village off A178

Hotel ⭐ Premier Travel Inn Hartlepool, Maritme Av, Hartlepool Marina, HARTLEPOOL ☎ 08701 977127 40 en suite

SEDGEFIELD   Map 08 NZ32

Knotty Hill Golf Centre TS21 2BB
☎ 01740 620320 📠 01740 622227
e-mail: khgc21@btopenworld.com
The 18-hole Princes Course is set in rolling parkland with many holes routed through shallow valleys. Several holes are set wholly or partially within woodland and water hazards abound. Bishops Course is a developing 18-hole course with varied water features on attractive terrain. Several holes are routed through mature woodland.
Princes Course: 18 holes, 6433yds, Par 72, SSS 71.
Bishops Course: 18 holes, 5976yds, Par 70.
Visitors restricted weekends. **Societies** package available on request. **Green Fees** £12 per round (£13 weekends).
Course Designer C Stanton **Facilities** ⊗ ⛳ 🏌 🍺 🏧 🍴 🏧 ✦ 🏌 **Leisure** gymnasium, tuition range. **Conf** fac available **Location** 1m N of Sedgefield on A177

Hotel ★★★ 75% Hardwick Hall Hotel, SEDGEFIELD ☎ 01740 620253 52 en suite

STANLEY — Map 12 NZ15

South Moor The Middles, Craghead DH9 6AG
☎ 01207 232848 🖹 01207 284616
e-mail: bryandavison@southmoorgc.freeserve.co.uk
Moorland course with natural hazards, designed by
Dr A MacKenzie in 1926 and still one of the most
challenging of its type in north east England. Out of
bounds features on 11 holes from the tee, and the
testing par 5 12th hole is uphill and usually against a
strong headwind.
18 holes, 6271yds, Par 72, SSS 70, Course record 66.
Club membership 550.
Visitors not Sun; contact in advance; handicap certificate
preferred Societies apply in writing to Secretary. Green
Fees £25 per day; £18 per round (£30/20 weekends & bank
holidays). Prof Shaun Cowell Course Designer Dr A
MacKenzie Facilities ⊗ 🎖 🖺 🏌 🖓 🛆 🏠 🍴 🐾 🚣 🏌
Conf Corporate Hospitality Days available Location 1.5m
SE on B6313

Hotel ★★★ 69% Beamish Park Hotel, Beamish Burn Rd,
MARLEY HILL ☎ 01207 230666 47 en suite

STOCKTON-ON-TEES — Map 08 NZ41

Norton Norton TS20 1SU
☎ 01642 676385 🖹 01642 608467
An interesting parkland course with long drives from
the 7th and 17th tees. Several water hazards.
18 holes, 5855yds, Par 70.
Visitors no parties; booked tee times for weekends. Societies
weekdays, apply in advance. Green Fees £11.50 per 18
holes (£13.50 weekends & bank holidays). Cards 🖿
🖿 🖾 🖸 Course Designer T Harper Facilities ⊗ 🎖 🖺 🏌
🏌 🏌 Leisure bowling green. Conf Corporate Hospitality
Days available Location in Norton 2m N off A19

Hotel ★★★ 72% Parkmore Hotel Leisure Park, 636 Yarm
Rd, Eaglescliffe, STOCKTON-ON-TEES
☎ 01642 786815 55 en suite

Teesside Acklam Rd, Thornaby TS17 7JS
☎ 01642 616516 & 673822 (pro) 🖹 01642 676252
e-mail: teesidegolfclub@btconnect.com
Flat parkland course, easy walking.
18 holes, 6535yds, Par 72, SSS 71, Course record 64.
Club membership 700.
Visitors with member only weekdays after 4.30pm,
weekends after 11am. Societies contact in writing. Green
Fees terms on application. Prof Ken Hall Course
Designer Drs McKenzie & Somerville Facilities ⊗ 🎖 🖺
🏌 🏌 🛆 🏠 🏌 Location 1.5m SE on A1130, off A19 at
Mandale interchange

Hotel ★★★ 72% Parkmore Hotel Leisure Park, 636 Yarm
Rd, Eaglescliffe, STOCKTON-ON-TEES
☎ 01642 786815 55 en suite

ESSEX

ABRIDGE — Map 05 TQ49

Abridge Golf and Country Club Epping Ln,
Stapleford Tawney RM4 1ST
☎ 01708 688396 🖹 01708 688550
e-mail: info@abridgegolf.com

Continued

A parkland course with easy walking. The quick drying
course is by no means easy to play. This has been the
venue of several professional tournaments. Abridge is a
golf and country club and has all the attendant
facilities.
18 holes, 6704yds, Par 72, SSS 72, Course record 67.
Club membership 600.
Visitors not Tue & weekends before 2pm; handicap
certificate; contact in advance. Societies Mon, Wed, Fri,
phone in advance. Green Fees £35 per 18 holes (£45
weekends). Cards 🖿 🖿 🖾 🖸 Prof Stuart Layton
Course Designer Henry Cotton Facilities ⊗ 🖺 🏌 🏌 🛆
🏠 🍴 🐾 🚣 🏌 🏌 Leisure heated outdoor swimming pool,
sauna, five short practice holes. Conf fac available
Location 1.75m NE

Hotel ⇧ Premier Travel Inn Romford West, Whalebone
Ln North, Chadwell Heath, ROMFORD ☎ 0870 9906450
40 en suite

BASILDON — Map 05 TQ78

Basildon Clay Hill Ln, Kingswood SS16 5JP
☎ 01268 533297 🖹 01268 284163
e-mail: basildongc@onetel.net.uk
Undulating municipal parkland course. Testing 13th
hole (par 4).
18 holes, 6236yds, Par 72, SSS 70.
Club membership 350.
Visitors contact professional in advance 01268 533532.
Societies contact for details. Green Fees not confirmed.
Prof M Oliver Course Designer A Cotton Facilities ⊗ 🎖
🖺 🏌 🛆 🏠 🍴 🚣 🏌 Location 1m S off A176

Hotel ⇧ Innkeeper's Lodge Basildon/Wickford, Runwell
Rd, WICKFORD ☎ 01268 769671 24 en suite

BENFLEET — Map 05 TQ78

Boyce Hill Vicarage Hill, South Benfleet SS7 1PD
☎ 01268 793625 & 752565 🖹 01268 750497
e-mail: secretary@boycehillgolfclub.co.uk
Hilly parkland course with good views.
18 holes, 6003yds, Par 68, SSS 69, Course record 61.
Club membership 700.
Visitors not weekends; handicap certificate; contact 24
hours in advance. Societies Thu, book well in advance by
phone. Green Fees £45 per 27/36 holes, £35 per 18 holes.
Prof Graham Burroughs Course Designer James Braid
Facilities ⊗ 🎖 🖺 🏌 🏌 🛆 🏠 🐾 🚣 🏌 Location 0.75m
NE of Benfleet station

Hotel ★★ 71% Balmoral Hotel, 34 Valkyrie Rd,
Westcliff-on-Sea, SOUTHEND-ON-SEA
☎ 01702 342947 29 en suite

BILLERICAY — Map 05 TQ69

The Burstead Tye Common Rd, Little Burstead
CM12 9SS
☎ 01277 631171 🖹 01277 632766
*The Burstead Golf Course: 18 holes, 6275yds, Par 71,
SSS 70, Course record 69.*
Course Designer Patrick Tallack Location M25 onto
A127, off A176
Phone for further details

Hotel ★★★ 68% Chichester Hotel, Old London Rd,
Wickford, BASILDON ☎ 01268 560555 2 en suite
32 annexe en suite

Stock Brook Golf & Country Club Queens Park
Av, Stock CM12 0SP
☎ 01277 653616 & 650400 📠 01277 633063
e-mail: events@stockbrook.com
**Set in 250 acres of picturesque countryside the 27 holes
comprise three undulating nines, offering the challenge
of water on a large number of holes. Any combination
can be played, but the Stock and Brook courses make
the 18-hole, 6728yd championship course. There are
extensive clubhouse facilities.**
*Stock & Brook courses: 18 holes, 6728yds, Par 72,
SSS 72, Course record 66.*
Manor Course: 9 holes, 2997yds, Par 35.
Visitors handicap certificate; contact 24 hours in advance.
Societies apply in writing or phone. **Green Fees** not
confirmed. **Cards** 〓 〓 ▦ 🖸 **Prof** Craig Lawrence
Course Designer Martin Gillet **Facilities** ⊗ ⑪ ⓛ 💄 ♀ ♨
📠 ⋔ 🐾 ⇶ ⋔ ♂ **Leisure** hard tennis courts, outdoor &
indoor heated swimming pools, sauna, gymnasium, bowls.
....
Hotel ★★★★ 73% Marygreen Manor Hotel, London Rd,
BRENTWOOD ☎ 01277 225252 4 en suite 40 annexe
en suite

Braintree Kings Ln, Stisted CM77 8DD
☎ 01376 346079 📠 01376 348677
e-mail: manager@braintreegolfclub.freeserve.co.uk
**Parkland course with many unique mature trees. Good
par 3s with the 14th - Devils Lair - regarded as one of
the best in the county.**
18 holes, 6228yds, Par 70, SSS 70, Course record 64.
Club membership 750.
Visitors not am Sun; contact pro shop in advance 01376
343465. **Societies** Wed, Thu, phone in advance, early
booking advised. **Green Fees** £36 per day, £28 per round
(£42 per round weekends & bank holidays). **Prof** Tony
Parcell **Course Designer** Hawtree **Facilities** ⊗ ⑪ ⓛ 💄 ♀
♨ 📠 🐾 🐾 ⇶ ♂ **Conf** Corporate Hospitality Days available
Location 1m E, off A120
....
Hotel ★★★ 65% White Hart Hotel, Bocking End,
BRAINTREE ☎ 01376 321401 31 en suite

Towerlands Panfield Rd CM7 5BJ
☎ 01376 326802 📠 01376 552487
Undulating, grassland course, nine holes with 18 tees.
9 holes, 5559yds, Par 68.
Club membership 250.
Visitors not before 12.30pm weekends, not after 5pm
Wed, dress code; contact in advance. **Societies** contact in
advance by phone. **Green Fees** not confirmed. **Cards** 〓
〓 ▦ 🔂 🖸 **Course Designer** G Shiels **Facilities** ⊗ ⑪ ⓛ
💄 ♀ ♨ ⋔ **Leisure** squash, gymnasium. **Location** on
B1053
....
Hotel ★★★ 65% White Hart Hotel, Bocking End,
BRAINTREE ☎ 01376 321401 31 en suite

Bentley Ongar Rd CM15 9SS
☎ 01277 373179 📠 01277 375097
e-mail: info@bentleygolfclub.com
Parkland course with water hazards.
18 holes, 6709yds, Par 72, SSS 72.
Club membership 545.
Visitors not weekends; contact in advance. **Societies** write
or phone in advance. **Green Fees** £25 per 18 holes. **Cards**

Continued

〓 〓 ▦ 🔂 🖸 **Prof** Nick Garrett **Course Designer** Alec
Swann **Facilities** ⊗ ⑪ ⓛ 💄 ♀ ♨ 📠 🐾 ♂ **Conf**
Corporate Hospitality Days available **Location** 3m NW on
A128
....
Hotel ★★★ 70% Weald Park Hotel, Golf & Country Club,
Coxtie Green Rd, South Weald, BRENTWOOD
☎ 01277 375101 32 annexe en suite

Hartswood King George's Playing Fields, Ingrave Rd
CM14 5AE
☎ 01277 218850 📠 01277 218850
Municipal parkland course, easy walking.
18 holes, 6192yds, Par 70, SSS 69, Course record 68.
Club membership 300.
Visitors book by phone up to five days ahead 01277
214830. **Societies** weekdays, contact in advance. **Green
Fees** not confirmed. **Cards** 〓 〓 ▦ 🔂 🖸 **Prof** Stephen
Cole **Course Designer** H Cotton **Facilities** 💄 ♀ ♨ ⋔
♂ **Location** 0.75m SE of Brentwood town centre on A128
from A127
....
Hotel ★★★ 70% Weald Park Hotel, Golf & Country Club,
Coxtie Green Rd, South Weald, BRENTWOOD
☎ 01277 375101 32 annexe en suite

Warley Park Magpie Ln, Little Warley CM13 3DX
☎ 01277 224891 📠 01277 200679
e-mail: enquiries@warleyparkgc.co.uk
**Parkland course with reasonable walking. Numerous
water hazards. There is also a golf practice ground.**
*1st & 2nd: 18 holes, 5985yds, Par 69, SSS 67,
Course record 66.*
*1st & 3rd: 18 holes, 5925yds, Par 71, SSS 69,
Course record 65.*
*2nd & 3rd: 18 holes, 5917yds, Par 70, SSS 69,
Course record 65.*
Club membership 800.
Visitors not weekends; handicap certificate; contact in
advance. **Societies** phone in advance for provisional
booking. **Green Fees** £50 per day, £36 per round. **Cards**
〓 〓 ▦ 🔂 🖸 **Prof** Kevin Smith **Course Designer** Reg
Plumbridge **Facilities** ⊗ ⑪ ⓛ 💄 ♀ ♨
🐾 🐾 ⇶ ♂ **Conf** fac available Corporate Hospitality Days
available **Location** M25 junct 29, A127 E onto B186, 0.5m
N
....
Hotel ★★★ 70% Weald Park Hotel, Golf & Country Club,
Coxtie Green Rd, South Weald, BRENTWOOD
☎ 01277 375101 32 annexe en suite

Weald Park Hotel, Golf & Country Club
Coxtie Green Rd, South Weald CM14 5RJ
☎ 01277 375101 📠 01277 374888
e-mail: wealdpark@americangolf.uk.com
*Weald Park Golf Club: 18 holes, 6285yds, Par 71,
SSS 70, Course record 65.*
Course Designer Reg Plumbridge **Location** 3m from M25
Phone for further details
....
Hotel ★★★ 70% Weald Park Hotel, Golf & Country Club,
Coxtie Green Rd, South Weald, BRENTWOOD
☎ 01277 375101 32 annexe en suite

BULPHAN — Map 05 TQ68

Langdon Hills Lower Dunton Rd RM14 3TY
☎ 01268 548444 📠 01268 490084
e-mail: info@golflangdon.co.uk
Well situated with the Langdon Hills on one side and dramatic views across London on the other, the centre offers an interchangeable 27-hole course, a floodlit 22-bay driving range and three academy holes.
Langdon & Bulphan Course: 18 holes, 6760yds, Par 72, SSS 72, Course record 67.
Bulphan & Horndon Course: 18 holes, 6537yds, Par 73, SSS 72.
Horndon & Langdon Course: 18 holes, 6279yds, Par 71, SSS 71.
Club membership 800.
Visitors preference to members am weekends; not Langdon course am; cannot book more than five days in advance. **Societies** apply in writing or phone. **Green Fees** not confirmed. **Cards** 〓 〓 〓 〓 🖭 **Prof** Terry Moncur **Course Designer** Howard Swan **Facilities** ⊗ ⊬ ⅃ ⚑ ⅃ ☆ 🏌 **Conf** Corporate Hospitality Days available **Location** off A13 onto B1007

Hotel ★★★★ 73% Marygreen Manor Hotel, London Rd, BRENTWOOD ☎ 01277 225252 4 en suite 40 annexe en suite

BURNHAM-ON-CROUCH — Map 05 TQ99

Burnham-on-Crouch Ferry Rd, Creeksea CM0 8PQ
☎ 01621 782282 📠 01621 784489
e-mail: burnhamgolf@hotmail.com
Undulating meadowland riverside course, easy walking.
18 holes, 6056yds, Par 70, SSS 69, Course record 66.
Club membership 550.
Visitors not weekends; with member only weekends. **Societies** apply in writing or phone. **Green Fees** not confirmed. **Prof** Steven Cardy **Course Designer** Swan **Facilities** ⊗ ⊬ ⅃ ☆ 🏌 **Location** 1.25m W off B1010

CANEWDON — Map 05 TQ99

Ballards Gore Gore Rd SS4 2DA
☎ 01702 258917 📠 01702 258571
A parkland course with several lakes.
18 holes, 6874yds, Par 73, SSS 73, Course record 69.
Club membership 500.
Visitors not Sat & before 2pm Sun; contact in advance. **Societies** apply in advance. **Green Fees** not confirmed. **Cards** 〓 〓 〓 🖭 **Prof** Richard Emery **Course Designer** D & JJ Caton **Facilities** ⊗ ⊬ ⅃ ☆ 🏌 **Leisure** snooker room. **Location** 2m NE of Rochford

Guesthouse ◆◆◆◆ Ilfracombe House Hotel, 9-13 Wilson Rd, SOUTHEND-ON-SEA ☎ 01702 351000 20 en suite

CANVEY ISLAND — Map 05 TQ78

Castle Point Somnes Av SS8 9FG
☎ 01268 696298 (Secretary) & 510830 (Pro)
e-mail: sec@castlepointgolfclub.freeserve.co.uk
18 holes, 6176yds, Par 71, SSS 69, Course record 69.
Location SE of Basildon, A130 to Canvey Island
Phone for further details

Hotel ★★★ 68% Chichester Hotel, Old London Rd, Wickford, BASILDON ☎ 01268 560555 2 en suite 32 annexe en suite

CHELMSFORD — Map 05 TL70

Channels Belstead Farm Ln, Little Waltham CM3 3PT
☎ 01245 440005 📠 01245 442032
e-mail: info@channelsgolf.co.uk
The Channels course is built on land from reclaimed gravel pits, 18 very exciting holes with plenty of lakes providing an excellent test of golf. Belsteads, a nine-hole course, is mainly flat but has three holes where water has to be negotiated.

Channels Course: 18 holes, 6402yds, Par 71, SSS 71, Course record 65.
Belsteads: 9 holes, 2467yds, Par 34, SSS 32.
Club membership 650.
Visitors Channels Course: contact in advance, with member only weekends. Belsteads Course: available anytime. **Societies** phone starter on 01245 443311. **Green Fees** not confirmed. **Cards** 〓 〓 〓 〓 🖭 **Prof** Ian Sinclair **Course Designer** Cotton & Swan **Facilities** ⊗ ⊬ ⅃ ☆ 🏌 **Leisure** fishing, 9-hole pitch & putt course. **Conf** fac available **Location** 2m NE on A130

Hotel ★★★ 71% County Hotel, Rainsford Rd, CHELMSFORD ☎ 01245 455700 53 en suite 8 annexe en suite

Chelmsford Widford Rd CM2 9AP
☎ 01245 256483 📠 01245 256483
e-mail: office@chelmsfordgc.co.uk
An undulating parkland course, hilly in parts, with three holes in woods and four difficult par 4s. From the reconstructed clubhouse there are fine views over the course and the wooded hills beyond.
18 holes, 5981yds, Par 68, SSS 69, Course record 63.
Club membership 650.
Visitors Ladies Day Tue; with member only weekends; contact in advance. **Societies** Wed, Thu, contact in advance. **Green Fees** not confirmed. **Prof** Mark Welch **Course Designer** Tom Dunn **Facilities** ⊗ ⊬ ⅃ ☆ 🏌 **Location** 1.5m S of town centre off A12

Hotel ★★★ 72% Pontlands Park Country Hotel, West Hanningfield Rd, Great Baddow, CHELMSFORD ☎ 01245 476444 36 en suite

Regiment Way Back Ln, Little Waltham CM3 3PR
☎ 01245 362210 & 361100 📠 01245 442032
e-mail: info@channelsgolf.co.uk
A nine-hole course with alternate tee positions, offering a par 64 18-hole course. Fully automatic tee and green irrigation plus excellent drainage ensure play at most times of the year. The course is challenging but at the same time can be forgiving.

Continued

Regiment Way Golf Centre

9 holes, 4887yds, Par 65, SSS 64.
Club membership 265.
Visitors no restrictions. **Societies** min eight players, phone for details. **Green Fees** not confirmed. **Prof** David March **Course Designer** R Stubbings, R Clark **Facilities** ⊗ ⫚ ⻌ ⬛ ♀ ⚘ 🖭 ⛳ 🛺 ∅ ⚑ **Conf** fac available Corporate Hospitality Days available **Location** off A130 N of Chelmsford

....

Hotel ⬚ Premier Travel Inn Chelmsford (Boreham), Main Rd, Boreham, CHELMSFORD ☎ 0870 9906394 78 en suite

CHIGWELL
Map 05 TQ49

Chigwell High Rd IG7 5BH
☎ 020 8500 2059 🖷 020 8501 3410
e-mail: info@chigwellgolfclub.co.uk
18 holes, 6279yds, Par 71, SSS 70, Course record 66.
Course Designer Hawtree, Taylor **Location** 0.5m S on A113
Phone for further details

....

Hotel ⬚ Premier Travel Inn Romford East, Mercury Gardens, ROMFORD ☎ 08701 977220 40 en suite

Woolston Manor Abridge Rd IG7 6BX
☎ 0208 500 2549 🖷 0208 501 5452
e-mail: golf@woolstonmanor.co.uk
Woolston Manor was once owned by William the Conqueror and is mentioned in the Domesday Book. The course, in 200 acres of Essex countryside, built to USGA specifications with superb irrigation, generous teeing areas, dramatic bunker shapes and water coming into play on twelve holes.
Manor Course: 18 holes, 6510yds, Par 72, SSS 72, Course record 67.
Club membership 465.
Visitors book 48 hrs in advance. **Societies** midweek. **Green Fees** £28 per round (£38 weekends pm); reduced winter rates. **Cards** ⊞ ▦ ▤ ▦ 🖸 **Prof** Paul Eady **Course Designer** Neil Coles **Facilities** ⊗ ⫚ ⻌ ⬛ ♀ ⚘ 🖭 🛺 🛺 ∅ **Leisure** outdoor & indoor heated swimming pools, sauna, solarium, gymnasium. **Conf** fac available Corporate Hospitality Days available **Location** M11 junct 5, 1m

....

Hotel ⬚ Premier Travel Inn Romford West, Whalebone Ln North, Chadwell Heath, ROMFORD ☎ 0870 9906450 40 en suite

> **Booking a tee time is always advisable.**

CHIGWELL ROW
Map 05 TQ49

Hainault Forest Romford Rd, Chigwell Row IG7 4QW
☎ 020 8500 2131 🖷 020 8501 5196
e-mail: info@essexgolfcentres.com
Two championship courses with spectacular views of Essex countryside. Parkland courses with modern driving range.
No 1 Course: 18 holes, 5687yds, Par 70, SSS 67, Course record 65.
No 2 Course: 18 holes, 6238yds, Par 71, SSS 71.
Club membership 250.
Visitors booking recommended; dress code. **Societies** please phone, write or e-mail. **Green Fees** not confirmed. **Cards** ⊞ ▦ ▦ 🖸 **Prof** C Hope, B Preston, A Shearn **Course Designer** Taylor & Hawtree **Facilities** ⊗ ⫚ ⻌ ⬛ ♀ ⚘ 🖭 ⛳ 🛺 ∅ ⚑ **Conf** fac available Corporate Hospitality Days available **Location** 0.5m S on A1112

CLACTON-ON-SEA
Map 05 TM11

Clacton West Rd CO15 1AJ
☎ 01255 421919 🖷 01255 424602
e-mail: secretary@clactongolfclub.com
The course covers 110 acres and runs alongside the sea wall and then inland. Easy walking layout, part open and part woodland. A unique feature of the course is the fleets, ditches and streams that cross and border many of the fairways, demanding accuracy and good striking.
18 holes, 6448yds, Par 71, SSS 71.
Club membership 650.
Visitors contact in advance; handicap certificate & member of recognised golf club. **Societies** apply in writing or phone. **Green Fees** £35 per day, £25 per round (£45/£30 weekends & bank holidays). **Prof** S J Levermore **Course Designer** Jack White **Facilities** ⊗ ⫚ ⻌ ⬛ ♀ ⚘ 🖭 🛺 ∅ **Leisure** practice nets available. **Location** 1.25m SW of town centre

....

Hotel ★★ 67% Esplanade Hotel, 27-29 Marine Pde East, CLACTON-ON-SEA ☎ 01255 220450 29 en suite

COLCHESTER
Map 05 TL92

Birch Grove Layer Rd, Kingsford CO2 0HS
☎ 01206 734276
A pretty, undulating course surrounded by woodland - small but challenging with excellent greens. Challenging 6th hole cut through woodland with water hazards and out of bounds.
9 holes, 4532yds, Par 66, SSS 63, Course record 66.
Club membership 250.
Visitors restricted Sun am. **Societies** apply in writing or phone. **Green Fees** £14 for 18 holes; £10 for nine holes. **Course Designer** L A Marston **Facilities** ⊗ ⫚ ⻌ ⬛ ♀ ⚘ 🖭 ∅ **Conf** fac available Corporate Hospitality Days available **Location** 2.5m S on B1026

....

Hotel ★★★ 71% George Hotel, 116 High St, COLCHESTER ☎ 01206 578494 47 en suite

Colchester Braiswick CO4 5AU
☎ 01206 853396 🖷 01206 852698
e-mail: colchester.golf@btinternet.com
A fairly flat, yet scenic, parkland course with tree-lined fairways and small copses. Mainly level walking.

Continued

18 holes, 6347yds, Par 70, SSS 70, Course record 63.
Club membership 700.
Visitors not weekends; by arrangement. **Societies** Mon, Thu, Fri, apply by writing or phone. **Green Fees** not confirmed. **Prof** Mark Angel **Course Designer** James Braid **Facilities** ⊗ ♥ ♀ ♨ 🏠 ⚷ ℂ **Location** 1.5m NW of town centre on B1508 (West Bergholt Rd)

....

Hotel ★★★ 71% George Hotel, 116 High St, COLCHESTER ☎ 01206 578494 47 en suite

Lexden Wood Bakers Ln CO3 4AU
☎ 01206 843333 📠 01206 854775
Challenging 18-hole, parkland course with many water features. A mix of undulating and flat land with testing greens. Also a nine-hole pitch and putt course, and a floodlit driving range.
18 holes, 5500yds, Par 67, Course record 63.
Club membership 500.
Visitors Societies phone for details. **Green Fees** terms on application. **Cards** 💳 💳 💳 💳 💳 **Prof** Phil Grice **Course Designer** J Johnson **Facilities** ⊗ ⅏ ♭ ♥ ♀ ♨ 🏠 ⚷ ⌇ 🏌 ♨ ⚷ ℂ **Leisure** 9 hole par 3. **Conf** Corporate Hospitality Days available **Location** A12 towards Colchester Central, follow tourist signs

....

Hotel ★★★ 74% The Rose and Crown Hotel, East St, COLCHESTER ☎ 01206 866677 31 en suite

Stoke-by-Nayland Keepers Ln, Leavenheath CO6 4PZ
☎ 01206 262836 📠 01206 263356
e-mail: info@golf-club.co.uk

Gainsborough Course: 18 holes, 6498yds, Par 72, SSS 71, Course record 66.
Constable Course: 18 holes, 6544yds, Par 72, SSS 71, Course record 67.
Course Designer Howard Swan **Location** 1.5m NW of Stoke-by-Nayland on B1068
Phone for further details

....

Hotel ★★★ 🍴 Maison Talbooth, Stratford Rd, DEDHAM ☎ 01206 322367 10 en suite

EARLS COLNE   Map 05 TL82

Colne Valley Station Rd CO6 2LT
☎ 01787 224343 & 220770 📠 01787 224126
e-mail: info@colnevalleygolfclub.co.uk
Opened in 1991, this surprisingly mature parkland course belies its tender years. Natural water hazards, and well-defined bunkers, along with USGA standard greens offer year round playability, and a stimulating test for all abilities.
18 holes, 6301yds, Par 70, SSS 71, Course record 68.
Club membership 500.

Visitors not before 10am weekends; dress code; no sharing of clubs; contact in advance. **Societies** apply in writing or phone, min 12 persons. **Green Fees** £25 per 18 holes (£30 weekends). **Cards** 💳 💳 💳 💳 💳 **Prof** Peter Garlick **Course Designer** Howard Swan **Facilities** ⊗ ♭ ♥ ♀ ♨ 🏠 ⌇ 🏌 ♨ ⚷ **Leisure** fishing. **Conf** fac available Corporate Hospitality Days available **Location** off A1124

....

Hotel ★★★ 70% White Hart Hotel, Market End, COGGESHALL ☎ 01376 561654 18 en suite

Essex Golf & Country Club CO6 2NS
☎ 01787 224466 📠 01787 224410
e-mail: essex.retail@clubhaus.com
Created on the site of a World War II airfield, this challenging course contains 10 lakes and strategically placed bunkering. Also a nine-hole course and a variety of leisure facilities.
County Course: 18 holes, 7019yds, Par 73, SSS 73, Course record 67.
Garden Course: 9 holes, 2190yds, Par 34, SSS 34.
Club membership 700.
Visitors contact golf reception for bookings up to seven days in advance. **Societies** apply in writing to the Functions Manager or phone for details. **Green Fees** not confirmed. **Cards** 💳 💳 💳 💳 💳 **Prof** Lee Cocker **Course Designer** Reg Plumbridge **Facilities** ⊗ ⅏ ♭ ♥ ♀ ♨ 🏠 ⌇ 🏌 ➘ ♨ ⚷ ℂ **Leisure** hard tennis courts, heated indoor swimming pool, fishing, sauna, solarium, gymnasium, video golf tuition studio. **Conf** fac available **Location** signed off A120 onto B1024

....

Hotel ★★★ 70% White Hart Hotel, Market End, COGGESHALL ☎ 01376 561654 18 en suite

EPPING   Map 05 TL40

Epping Fluxs Ln CM16 7PE
☎ 01992 572282 📠 01992 575512
e-mail: neilsjoberg@hotmail.com
Undulating parkland course with extensive views over Essex countryside. Incorporates many water features designed to use every club in the bag. Some driveable par 4s, and the spectacular 18th Happy Valley is rarely birdied. The new clubhouse has a bar and restaurant.
18 holes, 5405yds, Par 68, SSS 65, Course record 67.
Club membership 350.
Visitors no restrictions. **Societies** phone in advance. **Green Fees** £18 per day; £12 per round (£21/£15 weekends & bank holidays). **Course Designer** Sjoberg **Facilities** ⊗ ⅏ by arrangement ♭ ♥ ♀ ♨ 🏠 🏌 ➘ ♨ ⚷ ℂ **Leisure** Petanque. **Conf** fac available Corporate Hospitality Days available **Location** M11 junct 7, 2.5m on B1393, left in Epping High Rd towards station

....

Hotel ⌂ Travelodge Harlow East (Stansted), A414 Eastbound, Tylers Green, North Weald, HARLOW ☎ 08700 850 950 60 en suite

Nazeing Middle St, Nazeing EN9 2LW
☎ 01992 893798 📠 01992 893882
Parkland course built with American sand-based greens and tees and five strategically placed lakes. One of the most notable holes is the difficult par 3 13th with out of bounds and a large lake coming into play.
18 holes, 6617yds, Par 72, SSS 72, Course record 68.
Club membership 400.
Visitors contact for weekends & bank holidays pm only. **Societies** by arrangement in writing. **Green Fees** Mon £16

Continued   *Continued*

per round; Tue-Fri £20 (£28 weekends pm). **Cards** **Prof** Robert Green **Course Designer** M Gillete **Facilities** **Conf** fac available Corporate Hospitality Days available **Location** near Waltham Abbey

Hotel ★★★★ 69% Waltham Abbey Marriott Hotel, Old Shire Ln, WALTHAM ABBEY ☎ 01992 717170 162 en suite

FRINTON-ON-SEA Map 05 TM22

Frinton 1 The Esplanade CO13 9EP
☎ 01255 674618 🖷 01255 682450
e-mail: frintongolf@lineone.net
Deceptive, flat seaside links course providing fast, firm and undulating greens that will test the best putters, and tidal ditches that cross many of the fairways, requiring careful placement of shots. Its open character means that every shot has to be evaluated with both wind strength and direction in mind. Easy walking.

Long Course: 18 holes, 6265yds, Par 71, SSS 70, Course record 63.
Short Course: 9 holes, 3062yds, Par 60, SSS 60.
Club membership 850.
Visitors weekends by arrangment; contact in advance. **Societies** Wed, Thu & some Fri, apply in writing to the secretary. **Green Fees** Main course: £32 (£38 weekends). Short course £8/£10. **Cards** **Prof** Peter Taggart **Course Designer** Willy Park Jnr **Facilities** by arrangement **Conf** fac available Corporate Hospitality Days available **Location** SW of town centre

Hotel Premier Travel Inn Clacton-On-Sea, Crown Green Roundabout, Colchester Rd, Weeley, CLACTON-ON-SEA ☎ 08701 977064 40 en suite

GOSFIELD Map 05 TL72

Gosfield Lake The Manor House, Hall Dr CO9 1RZ
☎ 01787 474747 🖷 01787 476044
e-mail: gosfieldlakegc@btconnect.com
Parkland course with bunkers, lakes and water hazards. Designed by Sir Henry Cotton, Howard Swan. The nine-hole course is ideal for beginners and improvers.
Lakes Course: 18 holes, 6615yds, Par 72, SSS 72, Course record 68.
Meadows Course: 9 holes, 4180yds, Par 64, SSS 61.
Club membership 650.
Visitors Lakes Course: contact in advance, not before 3.30pm weekends. Meadows Course: booking advisable. **Societies** by arrangement. **Green Fees** not confirmed. **Prof** Richard Wheeler **Course Designer** Henry Cotton, Howard Swan **Facilities** **Leisure**

Continued

sauna. **Conf** Corporate Hospitality Days available **Location** 1m W of Gosfield off B1017

Hotel ★★★ 65% White Hart Hotel, Bocking End, BRAINTREE ☎ 01376 321401 31 en suite

HARLOW Map 05 TL41

Canons Brook Elizabeth Way CM19 5BE
☎ 01279 421482 🖷 01279 626393
18 holes, 6800yds, Par 73, SSS 72, Course record 65.
Course Designer Henry Cotton **Location** M11 junct 7, 3m NW
Phone for further details

Hotel ★★★ 65% Corus hotel Harlow, Mulberry Green, Old Harlow, HARLOW ☎ 0870 609 6146 55 annexe en suite

North Weald Rayley Ln, North Weald CM16 6AR
☎ 01992 522118 🖷 01992 522881
e-mail: pat.hillier@virgin.net
18 holes, 6377yds, Par 71, SSS 70, Course record 66.
Course Designer David Williams **Location** M11 exit 7, A414 2m towards Chipping Ongar
Phone for further details

Hotel Travelodge Harlow East (Stansted), A414 Eastbound, Tylers Green, North Weald, HARLOW ☎ 08700 850 950 60 en suite

HARWICH Map 05 TM23

Harwich & Dovercourt Station Rd, Parkeston CO12 4NZ
☎ 01255 503616 🖷 01255 503323
Flat parkland course with easy walking. The 234yd par 3 9th hole to an invisible green is a real experience.
9 holes, 5900yds, Par 70, SSS 69, Course record 59.
Club membership 420.
Visitors by arrangement; handicap certificate; with member only weekends. **Societies** arrangement essential. **Green Fees** £20 per 18 holes; £10 per nine holes. **Facilities** **Conf** Corporate Hospitality Days available **Location** off A120 near ferry terminal

Hotel ★★★ 74% The Pier at Harwich, The Quay, HARWICH ☎ 01255 241212 7 en suite 7 annexe en suite

INGRAVE Map 05 TQ69

Thorndon Park CM13 3RH
☎ 01277 810345 🖷 01277 810645
e-mail: tpgc@btclick.com
Course built on clay substructure and playable even at the wettest time of the year. Holes stand on their own surrounded by mature oaks, some of which are more than 700 years old. The lake in the centre of the course provides both a challenge and a sense of peace and tranquillity. The Palladian Thorndon Hall, site of the old clubhouse, is the magnificent backdrop to the closing hole.
18 holes, 6492yds, Par 71, SSS 71, Course record 68.
Club membership 600.
Visitors with member only weekends except after 1pm Sun; contact in advance. **Societies** Mon, Tue, Fri, apply in writing. **Green Fees** terms on application. **Prof** Brian White **Course Designer** Colt, Alison **Facilities** by

Continued

arrangement ⓑ ☕ ♀ ⚐ 🏌 ♂ **Conf** Corporate Hospitality Days available **Location** W side of village off A128

Hotel ★★★ 70% Weald Park Hotel, Golf & Country Club, Coxtie Green Rd, South Weald, BRENTWOOD
☎ 01277 375101   32 annexe en suite

LOUGHTON   Map 05 TQ49

High Beech Wellington Hill IG10 4AH
☎ 020 8508 7323
Short nine-hole course in Epping Forest.
9 holes, 1477, Par 27, Course record 25.
Visitors Green Fees not confirmed. **Prof** Clark Baker
Facilities ☕ ⚐ 🏌 ♂ **Location** M25 junct 26

Loughton Clays Ln, Debden Green IG10 2RZ
☎ 020 8502 2923
Nine-hole parkland course on the edge of Epping Forest. A good test of golf.
9 holes, 4652yds, Par 66, SSS 63, Course record 71.
Club membership 150.
Visitors contact in advance for weekends. **Societies** phone in advance. **Green Fees** not confirmed. **Facilities** ⓑ ☕ ♀ ⚐ 🏌 ♂ **Location** 1.5m SE of Theydon Bois

Hotel ★★★★ 69% Waltham Abbey Marriott Hotel, Old Shire Ln, WALTHAM ABBEY
☎ 01992 717170 162 en suite

MALDON   Map 05 TL80

Forrester Park Beckingham Rd, Great Totham CM9 8EA
☎ 01621 891406 🖷 01621 891406
Set in undulating parkland in the Essex countryside and commanding some beautiful views across the River Blackwater. Accuracy is more important than distance and judgement more important than strength on this traditional club course. There is a separate 10-acre practice ground.
18 holes, 6073yds, Par 71, SSS 69, Course record 69.
Club membership 1000.
Visitors not am weekends & bank holidays; contact in advance. **Societies** apply in advance. **Green Fees** terms on application. **Cards** 💳 💳 💳 💳 **Prof** Gary Pike **Course Designer** TR Forrester-Muir **Facilities** ⊗ ⓑ ☕ ♀ ⚐ 🏌 🛒 ⚒ ♂ ⏐ **Leisure** hard tennis courts. **Conf** fac available **Location** 3m NE of Maldon off B1022

Hotel ★★★ 72% Pontlands Park Country Hotel, West Hanningfield Rd, Great Baddow, CHELMSFORD
☎ 01245 476444   36 en suite

Maldon Beeleigh, Langford CM9 6LL
☎ 01621 853212 🖷 01621 855232
e-mail: maldon.golf@virgin.net
Flat, parkland course in a triangle of land bounded by the River Chelmer and the Blackwater Canal. Small greens provide a test for iron shots and the short game. Testing par 3 14th (166yds) demanding particular accuracy to narrow green guarded by bunkers and large trees.
9 holes, 6253yds, Par 71, SSS 70, Course record 66.
Club membership 380.
Visitors phone to check availability; with member only weekends. **Societies** intially phone then confirm in writing. **Green Fees** £25 per day; £18 per round. **Prof** John

Continued

Edgington **Course Designer** Thompson of Felixstowe
Facilities ⊗ ⧚ by arrangement ⓑ ☕ ♀ ⚐ 🏠 **Location** 1m NW off B1019

Hotel ★★★ 72% Pontlands Park Country Hotel, West Hanningfield Rd, Great Baddow, CHELMSFORD
☎ 01245 476444   36 en suite

ORSETT   Map 05 TQ68

Orsett Brentwood Rd RM16 3DS
☎ 01375 891352 🖷 01375 892471
e-mail: enquiries@orsettgolfclub.co.uk
A very good test of golf - this heathland course with its sandy soil is quick drying and provides easy walking. Close to the Thames estuary it is seldom calm and the main hazards are the prevailing wind and thick gorse. Any slight deviation can be exaggerated by the wind and result in a ball lost in the gorse. The clubhouse has been modernised to very high standards.
18 holes, 6614yds, Par 72, SSS 72, Course record 65.
Club membership 770.
Visitors not weekends; contact in advance; handicap certificate. **Societies** contact in advance. **Green Fees** £30 per round. **Prof** Paul Joiner **Course Designer** James Braid **Facilities** ⊗ ⧚ ⓑ ☕ ♀ ⚐ 🛒 🥢 ⚒ ♂ **Leisure** coaching. **Conf** Corporate Hospitality Days available **Location** junct A13 & A128, S towards Chadwell St Mary

Hotel ★★★ 67% Lakeside Moat House, High Rd, North Stifford, GRAYS ☎ 01708 719988   97 en suite

PURLEIGH   Map 05 TL80

Three Rivers Stow Rd, Cold Norton CM3 6RR
☎ 01621 828631 🖷 01621 828060
e-mail: devers@clubhaus.com
Kings Course: 18 holes, 6449yds, Par 72, SSS 71.
Jubilee Course: 18 holes, 4501yds, Par 64, SSS 62.
Course Designer Hawtree **Location** 2.5m from South Woodham Ferrers
Phone for further details

Hotel ★★★ 72% Pontlands Park Country Hotel, West Hanningfield Rd, Great Baddow, CHELMSFORD
☎ 01245 476444   36 en suite

ROCHFORD   Map 05 TQ89

Rochford Hundred Hall Rd SS4 1NW
☎ 01702 544302 🖷 01702 541343
e-mail: rochfordhundred@rhgc.sagehost.co.uk
Parkland course with ponds and ditches as natural hazards.
18 holes, 6292yds, Par 72, SSS 71, Course record 64.
Club membership 800.
Visitors not am Tue Ladies Day, with member only Sun; handicap certificate. **Societies** contact in writing. **Green Fees** £45 per day, £35 per round. **Prof** Graham Hill **Course Designer** James Braid **Facilities** ⊗ ⧚ ⓑ ☕ ♀ ⚐ 🏠 🥢 ♂ **Location** W on B1013

Guesthouse ◆◆◆◆ Ilfracombe House Hotel, 9-13 Wilson Rd, SOUTHEND-ON-SEA ☎ 01702 351000   20 en suite

SAFFRON WALDEN   Map 05 TL53

Saffron Walden Windmill Hill CB10 1BX
☎ 01799 522786 🖷 01799 520313
e-mail: office@swgc.com

Continued

Undulating parkland course set in the former deer park of Audley End House. Fine views over rolling countryside. Two par 3 signature holes, the 5th and 18th.
18 holes, 6606yds, Par 72, SSS 72, Course record 63.
Club membership 950.
Visitors contact in advance; handicap certificate; with member only weekends. **Societies** contact in advance.
Green Fees terms on application. **Cards** 🖼 🖼 🖼 🖼 💳 **Prof** Philip Davis **Facilities** ⊗ ⫴ ⤶ 💷 ♀ △ 🏠 ♦ ♿ ♂
⛳ **Location** N side of town centre off B184

Hotel ★★★ 69% The Crown House, GREAT CHESTERFORD ☎ 01799 530515 8 en suite 10 annexe en suite

SOUTHEND-ON-SEA   Map 05 TQ88

Belfairs Eastwood Rd North, Leigh on Sea SS9 4LR
☎ 01702 525345 & 520202
Municipal parkland course. Tight second half through thick woods, easy walking.
18 holes, 5840yds, Par 70, SSS 68, Course record 68.
Club membership 350.
Visitors contact for booking; dress code. **Societies** contact 01702 520202. **Green Fees** terms on application. **Prof** Steve Spittles **Course Designer** H S Colt **Facilities** ⊗ ⫴
⤶ 💷 ♀ 🏠 ⌐ ♂ **Leisure** hard tennis courts. **Location** off A127

Hotel ★★ 71% Balmoral Hotel, 34 Valkyrie Rd, Westcliff-on-Sea, SOUTHEND-ON-SEA
☎ 01702 342947 29 en suite

Thorpe Hall Thorpe Hall Av, Thorpe Bay SS1 3AT
☎ 01702 582205 🗐 01702 584498
e-mail: sec@thorpehallgc.co.uk
Tree-lined parkland course with narrow fairways where placement rather than length is essential.
18 holes, 6319yds, Par 71, SSS 71, Course record 62.
Club membership 995.
Visitors contact in advance; handicap certificate; with member only weekends & bank holidays. **Societies** Fri, apply in writing (only a certain number per year). **Green Fees** not confirmed. **Prof** Bill McColl **Course Designer** Various **Facilities** ⊗ ⫴ ⤶ 💷 ♀ △ 🏠 ♦ ♿ ♂ **Leisure** squash, sauna, snooker room. **Conf fac available Location** 2m E off A13

Hotel ★★ 71% Balmoral Hotel, 34 Valkyrie Rd, Westcliff-on-Sea, SOUTHEND-ON-SEA
☎ 01702 342947 29 en suite

SOUTH OCKENDON   Map 05 TQ58

Belhus Park Belhus Park RM15 4QR
☎ 01708 854260 🗐 01708 854260
A well-established 18-hole course set in beautiful parkland.
18 holes, 5589yds, Par 69, SSS 68, Course record 67.
Club membership 200.
Visitors no restrictions; dress code; booking advisable weekends. **Societies** contact in writing or phone. **Green Fees** not confirmed. **Prof** Gary Lunn **Facilities** ⤶ 💷 ♀ △ 🏠 ⌐
♂ ⛳ **Leisure** heated indoor swimming pool, solarium, gymnasium. **Location** off B1335, brown tourist signs to course

Hotel ⭐ Hotel Ibis Thurrock, Weston Av, WEST THURROCK ☎ 01708 686000 102 en suite

Top Meadow Fen Ln, North Ockendon RM14 3PR
☎ 01708 852239
e-mail: info@topmeadow.co.uk
18 holes, 6348yds, Par 72, SSS 71, Course record 68.
Course Designer Burns, Stock **Location** M25 junct 29, A127 towards Southend, B186 towards Ockendon
Phone for further details

Hotel ⭐ Travelodge Brentwood, EAST HORNDON
☎ 08700 850 950 45 en suite

STANFORD LE HOPE   Map 05 TQ68

St Clere's Hall London Rd SS17 0LX
☎ 01375 361565 🗐 01375 361565
18 holes, 6474yds, Par 72, SSS 71, Course record 71.
Course Designer A Stiff **Location** 5m from M25 on A13, Stanford turn towards Linford, St Clere on left
Phone for further details

Hotel ★★★ 67% Lakeside Moat House, High Rd, North Stifford, GRAYS ☎ 01708 719988 97 en suite

STAPLEFORD ABBOTTS   Map 05 TQ59

Stapleford Abbotts Horsemanside, Tysea Hill RM4 1JU
☎ 01708 381108 🗐 01708 386345
e-mail: staplefordabbotts@americangolf.uk.com
Abbotts course provides a challenging test for players of all abilities as mature trees, large greenside bunkers and many lakes are all brought into play. The Priors course with its links-type layout gives a fresh challenge on each hole.
Abbotts Course: 18 holes, 6501yds, Par 72, SSS 71.
Priors Course: 18 holes, 5735yds, Par 70, SSS 69.
Club membership 700.
Visitors not am weekends; book in advance. **Societies** booking required. **Green Fees** not confirmed. **Cards** 🖼
🖼 🖼 🖼 💳 **Prof** Dean Vickerman **Course Designer** Henry Cotton, Howard Swan **Facilities** ⊗ ⫴ ⤶ 💷 ♀ △
🏠 ♦ ♿ ♂ **Leisure** sauna, 9-hole par 3 course.
Location 1m E of Stapleford Abbotts, off B175

Hotel ★★★★ 73% Marygreen Manor Hotel, London Rd, BRENTWOOD ☎ 01277 225252 4 en suite 40 annexe en suite

STOCK   Map 05 TQ69

Crondon Park Stock Rd CM4 9DP
☎ 01277 841115 🗐 01277 841356
e-mail: paul@crondon.com
Undulating parkland course with many water hazards, set in the Crondon Valley.
18 holes, 6585yds, Par 72, SSS 71, Course record 67.
Club membership 700.
Visitors not am weekends; contact in advance.
Societies phone in advance. **Green Fees** terms on application. **Cards** 🖼 🖼 💳 **Prof** Chris Wood, Freddie Sunderland **Course Designer** Mr M Gillet **Facilities** ⊗ ⫴
⤶ 💷 ♀ △ ♿ ♂ ⛳ **Conf fac available Corporate Hospitality Days available Location** on B1007, between Stock & A12

Hotel ★★★★ 73% Marygreen Manor Hotel, London Rd, BRENTWOOD ☎ 01277 225252 4 en suite 40 annexe en suite

THEYDON BOIS   Map 05 TQ49

Theydon Bois Theydon Rd CM16 4EH
☎ 01992 812460 & 813054 📠 01992 813054
e-mail: theydongolf@hotmail.com
The course was originally nine holes built into Epping Forest. It was later extended to 18 holes which were well-planned and well-bunkered but in keeping with the Forest tradition. The old nine in the Forest are short and have two bunkers between them, but even so a wayward shot can be among the trees. The autumn colours here are truly magnificent.

18 holes, 5490yds, Par 68, SSS 67, Course record 64. Club membership 600.
Visitors not Wed, Thu, Sat & am Sun; phone 01992 812460 to confirm tee time. Societies book through the secretary. Green Fees not confirmed. Cards 🔳🔳🔳 🔳📖 Prof R Hall Course Designer James Braid Facilities ⊗ ⅋ 🏌 ⚑ ♨ ♿ 🏠 ⚑ ♿ Location M25 junct 26, 2m

Hotel ⌂ Travelodge Harlow East (Stansted), A414 Eastbound, Tylers Green, North Weald, HARLOW ☎ 08700 850 950 60 en suite

TOLLESHUNT KNIGHTS   Map 05 TL91

Five Lakes Hotel, Golf, Country Club & Spa Colchester Rd CM9 8HX
☎ 01621 868888 & 862426 📠 869696
e-mail: resort@fivelakes.co.uk
Set in 320 acres, the two 18-hole courses both offer their own particular challenges. The Lakes, a PGA championship course, offers generous fairways with water features. The Links has narrow fairways and strategically placed bunkers.

Links Course: 18 holes, 6181yds, Par 71, SSS 70, Course record 67.
Lakes Course: 18 holes, 6751yds, Par 72, SSS 72, Course record 63.
Club membership 430.

Visitors book in advance. Societies contact in advance. Green Fees terms on application. Cards 🔳🔳🔳🔳 🔳📖 Prof Gary Carter Course Designer Neil Coles Facilities ⊗ ⅋ 🏌 ⚑ ♨ ♿ 🏠 ⚑ ♿ Leisure hard tennis courts, heated indoor swimming pool, squash, sauna, solarium, gymnasium, snooker, badminton. Conf fac available Corporate Hospitality Days available Location 1.75m NE on B1026, 15 mins from A12 Kelvedon exit. Brown tourist signs

Hotel ★★★★ 73% Five Lakes Resort, Colchester Rd, TOLLESHUNT KNIGHTS ☎ 01621 868888 114 en suite 80 annexe en suite

TOOT HILL   Map 05 TL50

Toot Hill School Rd CM5 9PU
☎ 01277 365523 📠 01277 364509
18 holes, 6053yds, Par 70, SSS 69, Course record 65.
Course Designer Martin Gillett **Location** 7m SE of Harlow off A414
Phone for further details

Hotel ★★★ 65% Corus hotel Harlow, Mulberry Green, Old Harlow, HARLOW ☎ 0870 609 6146 55 annexe en suite

WITHAM   Map 05 TL81

Benton Hall Wickham Hill CM8 3LH
☎ 01376 502454 📠 01376 521050
e-mail: j.gathercole@theclubcompany.com
Set in rolling countryside surrounded by dense woodland, this challenging course provides a severe test even to the best golfers. The River Blackwater dominates the front nine and natural lakes come into play on five other holes.
18 holes, 6574yds, Par 72, SSS 72, Course record 64. Club membership 600.
Visitors book seven days in advance. Societies phone in advance. Green Fees not confirmed. Cards 🔳🔳🔳🔳 📖 Prof Colin Fairweather Course Designer Alan Walker, Charles Cox Facilities ⊗ ⅋ 🏌 ⚑ ♨ 🏠 ⚑ ♿ Leisure 9-hole par 3 course. Conf fac available Corporate Hospitality Days available Location off A12 at Witham, signed

Hotel ★★★ 65% White Hart Hotel, Bocking End, BRAINTREE ☎ 01376 321401 31 en suite

WOODHAM WALTER   Map 05 TL80

Bunsay Downs Little Baddow Rd CM9 6RU
☎ 01245 222648 📠 01245 223989
9 holes, 2932yds, Par 70, SSS 68.
Badgers: 9 holes, 1319yds, Par 54.
Course Designer John Durham **Location** 2m from Danbury on A414, signed
Phone for further details

Hotel ★★★ 71% County Hotel, Rainsford Rd, CHELMSFORD ☎ 01245 455700 53 en suite 8 annexe en suite

Warren CM9 6RW
☎ 01245 223258 📠 01245 223989
e-mail: enquiries@thewarrengolfclub.co.uk
Attractive parkland course with natural hazards and good views.

Continued   *Continued*

18 holes, 6263yds, Par 70, SSS 70, Course record 62.
Club membership 765.
Visitors not am weekends, not am Wed; contact in advance. **Societies** Mon, Tue, Thu, Fri, arrange by phone, confirm in writing. **Green Fees** not confirmed. **Cards** 💳 💳 💳 💳 **Prof** David Brooks **Facilities** ⊗ 💺 ♀ ⚲ 🏠 🍴 ⚴ 🚗 ♿ ⚘ **Location** 0.5m SW

Hotel ★★★ 71% County Hotel, Rainsford Rd, CHELMSFORD ☎ 01245 455700 53 en suite 8 annexe en suite

GLOUCESTERSHIRE

ALMONDSBURY   Map 03 ST68

Bristol St Swithins Park, Blackhorse Hill BS10 7TP
☎ 01454 620000 ▤ 01454 202700
e-mail: enquiries@bristolgolfclub.co.uk
An undulating parkland course set in 200 acres of parkland with magnificent views over the Severn estuary and surrounding countryside.
18 holes, 6109yds, Par 70, SSS 69, Course record 65.
Club membership 600.
Visitors book in advance. **Societies** contact in advance by phone or writing. **Green Fees** terms on application.
Cards 💳 💳 💳 💳 💳 **Prof** Richard Berry **Course Designer** Pierson **Facilities** ⊗ 💺 ♀ ⚲ 🏠 🍴 ⚴ 🚗 ♿ ⚘ **Leisure** par 3 academy course. **Conf** fac available Corporate Hospitality Days available **Location** M5 junct 17, 100yds

Hotel 🅄 Henbury Lodge Hotel, Station Rd, Henbury, BRISTOL ☎ 0117 950 2615 12 en suite 9 annexe en suite

CHELTENHAM   Map 03 SO92

Cotswold Hills Ullenwood GL53 9QT
☎ 01242 515264 ▤ 01242 515317
e-mail: golf@chgc.freeserve.co.uk
A gently undulating course with open aspects and views of the Cotswolds.
18 holes, 6565yds, Par 72, SSS 71, Course record 67.
Club membership 750.
Visitors not weekends during competitions; phone in advance; handicap certificate. **Societies** apply in writing or phone. **Green Fees** £33 per day (£38 weekends & bank holidays). **Cards** 💳 💳 💳 💳 💳 **Prof** James Latham **Course Designer** MD Little **Facilities** ⊗ 💺 ♀ ⚲ 🏠 🍴 ⚴ 🚗 ♿ ⚘ Corporate Hospitality Days available **Location** 3m SE on A435 & A436

Hotel ★★★★ 65% Cheltenham Park Hotel, Cirencester Rd, Charlton Kings, CHELTENHAM ☎ 01242 222021 33 en suite 110 annexe en suite

Lilley Brook Cirencester Rd, Charlton Kings GL53 8EG
☎ 01242 526785 ▤ 01242 256880
e-mail: secretary@lilleybrookgc.fsnet.co.uk
Undulating parkland course. Magnificent views over Cheltenham and surrounding countryside.
18 holes, 6212yds, Par 69, SSS 70, Course record 61.
Club membership 900.
Visitors not am weekends; advisable to phone; handicap certificate. **Societies** apply in writing. **Green Fees** terms on application. **Cards** 💳 💳 **Prof** Karl Hayler

Course Designer MacKenzie **Facilities** ⊗ 💺 ♀ ⚲ 🏠 🍴 ⚴ 🚗 ♿ ⚘ **Conf** fac available Corporate Hospitality Days available **Location** 2m S of Cheltenham on A435

Hotel ★★★★ 65% Cheltenham Park Hotel, Cirencester Rd, Charlton Kings, CHELTENHAM ☎ 01242 222021 33 en suite 110 annexe en suite

Shipton Shipton Oliffe, Andoverford GL54 4HT
☎ 01242 890237 ▤ 01242 820336
Deceptive, easy walking course situated in the heart of the Cotswolds giving a fair challenge and panoramic views.
9 holes, 2516yds, Par 35, SSS 63, Course record 33.
Visitors pay & play course, no booking required. **Societies** welcome. **Green Fees** not confirmed. **Prof** Noel Boland **Facilities** 💺 ♀ 🏠 🍴 ⚴ ⚘ **Location** on A436, S of A40 junct

Hotel ★★★ 70% Charlton Kings Hotel, London Rd, Charlton Kings, CHELTENHAM ☎ 01242 231061 13 en suite

CHIPPING SODBURY   Map 03 ST78

Chipping Sodbury BS37 6PU
☎ 01454 319042 ▤ 01454 320052
e-mail: info@chippingsodburygolfclub.co.uk
New Course: 18 holes, 6912yds, Par 73, SSS 73, Course record 65.
Course Designer Hawtree **Location** 0.5m N
Phone for further details

Hotel ★★ 71% Compass Inn, TORMARTON ☎ 01454 218242 & 218577 ▤ 01454 218741 26 en suite

CIRENCESTER   Map 04 SP00

Cirencester Cheltenham Rd, Bagendon GL7 7BH
☎ 01285 652465 ▤ 01285 650665
e-mail: info@cirencestergolfclub.co.uk
Undulating open Cotswold course with excellent views.
18 holes, 6055yds, Par 70, SSS 69, Course record 65.
Club membership 800.
Visitors restricted weekends; contact professional shop in advance 01285 656124. **Societies** phone office for details. **Green Fees** £32 per round/day (£38 weekends). **Cards** 💳 💳 💳 💳 💳 **Prof** Ed Goodwin **Course Designer** J Braid **Facilities** ⊗ 💺 ♀ ⚲ 🏠 🍴 ⚴ 🚗 ♿ ⚘ **Leisure** six-hole par 3 academy course. **Conf** fac available Corporate Hospitality Days available **Location** 2m N of Cirencester on A435

Hotel ★★★ 70% Stratton House Hotel, Gloucester Rd, CIRENCESTER ☎ 01285 651761 41 en suite

CLEEVE HILL   Map 03 SO92

Cleeve Hill GL52 3PW
☎ 01242 672025 ▤ 01242 67444
e-mail: hugh.fitzsimons@btconnect.com
Undulating and open heathland course affected by crosswinds. Situated on the highest point of the Cotswolds with fine views over Cheltenham racecourse, the Malvern Hills and the Bristol Channel. An ideal setting to enjoy a challenging round of golf.
18 holes, 6448yds, Par 72, SSS 71, Course record 66.
Club membership 600.

Continued   *Continued*

Visitors restricted weekends; bookings taken seven days in advance. **Societies** phone pro shop in advance 01242 672592. **Green Fees** £15 per round (£18 weekends). **Cards** ⊞ ▣ ▦ ▧ ▨ **Prof** Dave Finch **Facilities** ⊗ ⅶ ⅃ ▬ ♀ ♂ ♨ ⌂ ⌐ ∂ ₵ **Conf** Corporate Hospitality Days available **Location** 1m NE on B4632

....

Hotel ★★★ 63% The Prestbury House Hotel & Oaks Restaurant, The Burgage, Prestbury, CHELTENHAM ☎ 01242 529533 7 en suite 8 annexe en suite

COALPIT HEATH — Map 03 ST68

The Kendleshire Henfield Rd BS36 2UY
☎ 0117 956 7007 ▤ 0117 957 3433
e-mail: info@kendleshire.co.uk
Opened in 1997, the course boasts 27 holes with water coming into play on 18 holes. Notable holes are the 11th, the 16th and the 27th. The 11th is a short hole with an island green set in a 3-acre lake and the 16th has a second shot played over water. The course is never short of interest and the greens have been built to USGA specification.
18 holes, 6550yds, Par 71, SSS 71, Course record 63.
18 holes, 6249yds, Par 71, SSS 70, Course record 68.
18 holes, 6353yds, Par 70, SSS 70, Course record 68.
Club membership 900.
Visitors contact in advance; wear soft spikes. **Societies** phone in advance. **Green Fees** £32 per round (£38 weekends). **Cards** ⊞ ▣ ▦ ▧ ▨ **Prof** Mike Bessell **Course Designer** A Stiff, P McEvoy **Facilities** ⊗ ⅶ ⅃ ▬ ♀ ⌂ ⌐ ∂ ₵ **Conf** fac available Corporate Hospitality Days available **Location** M32 junct 1, on Avon Ring Road
....

Hotel ★★★★ 65% Jurys Bristol Hotel, Prince St, BRISTOL ☎ 0117 923 0333 191 en suite

CODRINGTON — Map 03 ST78

Players Club BS37 6RX
☎ 01454 313029 ▤ 01454 323446
e-mail: enquiries@theplayersgolfclub.com
This Adrian Stiff designed layout can measure up to 7607yds. Often described as an inland links, the rolling sand based fairways encounter an unusual mix of gorse and water.
Championship: 18 holes, 6847yds, Par 72, SSS 72.
Club membership 2000.
Visitors phone in advance for tee time. **Societies** phone in advance. **Green Fees** £70 Mon-Thu, £90 Fri-Sun. 2 for 1 scheme. **Cards** ⊞ ▣ ▦ ▧ ▨ **Prof** Paul Barrington **Course Designer** Adrian Stiff **Facilities** ⊗ ⅶ ⅃ ▬ ♀ ⌂ ⌐ ∂ ₵ **Leisure** fishing, nine-hole par 3 course. **Conf** fac available Corporate Hospitality Days available **Location** M4 junct 18, 1m on B4465
....

Hotel ★★ 71% Compass Inn, TORMARTON
☎ 01454 218242 & 218577 ▤ 01454 218741 26 en suite

COLEFORD — Map 03 SO51

Forest Hills Mile End Rd GL16 7QD
☎ 01594 810620 ▤ 01594 810823
e-mail: foresthills@btopenworld.com
A parkland course on a plateau with panoramic views of Coleford and Forest of Dean. Some testing holes with the par 5 13th hole sitting tight on a water hazard, and the challenging 18th with second shot over large pond

to a green protected by another pond and bunker - all in front of the clubhouse.
18 holes, 6740yds, Par 72, SSS 68, Course record 64.
Club membership 550.
Visitors no restrictions. **Societies** contact in advance. **Green Fees** £17 per day (£25 weekends). **Cards** ⊞ ▣ ▨ **Prof** Richard Ballard **Course Designer** A Stiff **Facilities** ⊗ ⅶ ⅃ ▬ ♀ ⌂ ⌐ ∂ ♨ ∂ ₵ **Leisure** fishing, solarium. **Conf** fac available
....

Hotel ★★★ 67% The Speech House, COLEFORD
☎ 01594 822607 16 en suite 17 annexe rms (16 en suite)

Forest of Dean Golf Club & Bells Hotel Lords Hill GL16 8BE
☎ 01594 832583 ▤ 01594 832584
e-mail: enquiries@bells-hotel.co.uk
18 holes, 6033yds, Par 70, SSS 69, Course record 63.
Course Designer John Day **Location** 0.25m from Coleford town centre on B4431 Coleford-Parkend road
Phone for further details
....

Hotel ★★★ 67% The Speech House, COLEFORD
☎ 01594 822607 16 en suite 17 annexe rms (16 en suite)

DURSLEY — Map 03 ST79

Stinchcombe Hill Stinchcombe Hill GL11 6AQ
☎ 01453 542015 ▤ 01453 549545
e-mail: stinchcombehill@golfers.net
High on the hill with splendid views of the Cotswolds, the River Severn and the Welsh hills. A downland course with good turf, some trees and an interesting variety of greens. Protected greens make this a challenging course in windy conditions.
18 holes, 5734yds, Par 68, SSS 68, Course record 63.
Club membership 550.
Visitors restricted weekends; contact professional in advance 01453 543878. **Societies** apply in advance. **Green Fees** not confirmed. **Prof** Paul Bushell **Course Designer** Arthur Hoare **Facilities** ⊗ ⅶ ⅃ ▬ ♀ ⌂ ⌐ ∂ **Conf** Corporate Hospitality Days available **Location** 1m W off A4135
....

Hotel ★★★ 65% Prince of Wales Hotel, Berkeley Rd, BERKELEY ☎ 01453 810474 43 en suite

DYMOCK — Map 03 SO73

Dymock Grange The Old Grange, Leominster Rd GL18 2AN
☎ 01531 890840 ▤ 01531 890860
A challenging and attractive parkland course set in 75 acres.
Old Course: 9 holes, 5786yds, Par 72, SSS 70, Course record 71.
New Course: 9 holes, 3390yds, Par 60, SSS 60.
Club membership 185.
Visitors contact by phone. **Societies** phone in advance. **Green Fees** £15 per 18 holes. £10 per nine holes. **Cards** ⊞ ▣ ▦ ▨ **Prof** Tim Morgan **Course Designer** Cufingham **Facilities** ⊗ ⅃ ▬ ♀ ⌂ ⌐ ∂ ♨ ∂ ₵ **Conf** Corporate Hospitality Days available **Location** on B4215 Leominster road
....

Hotel ⊞ Three Choirs Vineyards, NEWENT
☎ 01531 890223 8 annexe en suite

Continued

GLOUCESTER   Map 03 SO81

Brickhampton Court Cheltenham Rd, Churchdown
GL2 9QF
☎ 01452 859444 🖹 01452 859333
e-mail: info@brickhampton.co.uk
Rolling parkland courses featuring lakes, streams, strategic white sand bunkers, tree plantations and no steep hills.

Spa: 18 holes, 6449yds, Par 71, SSS 71, Course record 65.
Glevum: 9 holes, 1859yds, Par 31.
Club membership 860.
Visitors advance booking recommended; dress code; evidence of golfing ability preferred. **Societies** contact for information & booking form. **Green Fees** not confirmed. **Cards** 🔲 🔲 🔲 🔲 🔲 **Prof** Bruce Wilson, Chris Gillick **Course Designer** Simon Gidman **Facilities** ⊗ ⅋ ⅃ ⅃ ♥ ♀ ♨ 🏠 ⚲ 🛒 ♿ ⅃ **Conf** fac available Corporate Hospitality Days available **Location** Junct 11 M5, A40 towards Gloucester, at Elmbridge Court rdbt B4063 signed Churchdown, 2m

Hotel ★★★ 62% Hatherley Manor Hotel, Down Hatherley Ln, GLOUCESTER ☎ 01452 730217 52 en suite

Ramada Hotel & Resort Gloucester Matson Ln,
Robinswood Hill GL4 6EA
☎ 01452 525653 🖹 01452 307212
Undulating, wooded course, built around a hill with superb views over Gloucester and the Cotswolds. The 12th is a drive straight up a hill, nicknamed Coronary Hill'.
18 holes, 6170yds, Par 70, SSS 69, Course record 65.
Club membership 600.
Visitors book up to seven days in advance. **Societies** phone in advance. **Green Fees** not confirmed. **Cards** 🔲 🔲 🔲 🔲 **Prof** John Whiddon **Facilities** ⊗ ⅋ ⅃ ⅃ ♥ ♀ ♨ 🏠 ⚲ **Leisure** hard tennis courts, heated indoor swimming pool, squash, sauna, solarium, gymnasium. **Location** 2.5m SE of Gloucester, off B4073

Hotel 🆄 Ramada Hotel & Resort Gloucester, Matson Ln, Robinswood Hill, GLOUCESTER
☎ 01452 525653 107 en suite

Rodway Hill Newent Rd, Highnam GL2 8DN
☎ 01452 384222 🖹 01452 313814
e-mail: jrawl98589@aol.com
A challenging 18-hole course with superb panoramic views. Testing front five holes and the par 3 13th and par 5 16th affected by strong crosswinds off the River Severn.

18 holes, 6040yds, Par 70, SSS 69, Course record 71.
Club membership 400.
Visitors no restrictions. **Societies** phone in advance. **Green Fees** £14 per 18 holes, £7 per nine holes (£16/£9 weekends). **Cards** 🔲 🔲 🔲 🔲 🔲 🔲 **Prof** Chris Murphy **Course Designer** John Gabb **Facilities** ⊗ ⅋ ⅃ ♥ ♀ ♨ 🏠 ⚲ 🛒 ♿ **Conf** Corporate Hospitality Days available **Location** 2m outside Gloucester on B4215

Hotel ★★★ 62% Hatherley Manor Hotel, Down Hatherley Ln, GLOUCESTER ☎ 01452 730217 52 en suite

LYDNEY   Map 03 SO60

Lydney Lakeside Av GL15 5QA
☎ 01594 841186
Flat parkland and meadowland course with prevailing wind along fairways.
9 holes, 5298yds, Par 66, SSS 66, Course record 63.
Club membership 350.
Visitors with member only at weekends & bank holidays. **Societies** apply to Secretary. **Green Fees** not confirmed. **Facilities** ⅃ ♀ ⅃ **Location** SE side of town centre

Hotel ★★★ 67% The Speech House, COLEFORD ☎ 01594 822607 16 en suite 17 annexe rms (16 en suite)

MINCHINHAMPTON   Map 03 SO80

Minchinhampton (New Course) New Course
GL6 9BE
☎ 01453 833866 🖹 01453 837360
e-mail: ian@mgcnew.co.uk
The Cherington course, a South West Regional qualifying course for the Open Championship, is set in undulating upland. Large contoured greens, pot bunkers, and, at times, a stiff breeze present a very fair test of skill. The Avening course has a variety of holes including water on the 10th and 13th.
Avening: 18 holes, 6263yds, Par 70, SSS 70, Course record 61.
Cherington: 18 holes, 6430yds, Par 71, SSS 71, Course record 64.
Club membership 1200.
Visitors contact in advance. **Societies** contact by phone. **Green Fees** £45 per day £35 per round (£52/£42 weekends & bank holidays). **Cards** 🔲 🔲 🔲 🔲 **Prof** Chris Steele **Course Designer** Hawtree & Son **Facilities** ⊗ ⅋ ⅃ ♥ ♀ ♨ 🏠 🛒 ♿ ⅃ **Conf** Corporate Hospitality Days available **Location** B4014 from Nailsworth into Avening, left at Cross pub towards Minchinhampton, club 0.25m on right

Hotel ★★★ 71% Hare & Hounds Hotel, Westonbirt, TETBURY ☎ 01666 880233 & 881000 🖹 01666 880241 24 en suite 7 annexe en suite

Continued

Minchinhampton (Old Course) Old Course
GL6 9AQ
☎ 01453 832642 & 836382 📠 01453 832642
e-mail: mail@minchaldcourse.co.uk
An open grassland course 600ft above sea level. The
numerous humps and hollows around the greens test
the golfer's ability to play a variety of shots - often in
difficult windy conditions. Panoramic Cotswold views.
Two of the par 3s, the 8th and the 16th, often require an
accurate long iron or wood depending on the strength
and direction of the wind.
18 holes, 6019yds, Par 71, SSS 69.
Club membership 650.
Visitors contact in advance. Societies contact in advance.
Green Fees terms on application. Cards 🖾 ▄▄ 🗓
Facilities ⊗ 🦳 🍴 ♀ 🎣 🍴 ⛳ Location 1m NW
....
Hotel ★★ 71% Egypt Mill Hotel, NAILSWORTH
☎ 01453 833449 8 en suite 10 annexe en suite

Naunton Downs GL54 3AE
☎ 01451 850090 📠 01451 850091
e-mail: admin@nauntondowns.co.uk
Naunton Downs course plays over beautiful Cotswold
countryside. A valley running through the course is one
of the main features, creating one par 3 hole that
crosses over it. The prevailing wind adds extra
challenge to the par 5s (which play into the wind),
combined with small undulating greens.
18 holes, 6161yds, Par 71, SSS 69, Course record 67.
Club membership 750.
Visitors contact in advance. Societies phone for details.
Green Fees £23 (£27.50 weekends). Cards 🖾 ▄▄ ▄▄ ▄▄
🗓 Prof Nick Ellis Course Designer J Pott Facilities ⊗ 🦳
🦳 ♀ 🎣 🍴 ⛳ 🐾 🍴 ⛳ Leisure hard tennis courts.
Conf fac available Location B4068 Stow-Cheltenham
....
Hotel ★★★ ♨ Lords of the Manor, UPPER
SLAUGHTER ☎ 01451 820243 27 en suite

Painswick GL6 6TL
☎ 01452 812180
e-mail: painswickgolf@btinternet.com
Downland course set on the Cotswolds at Painswick
Beacon, with fine views. Short course more than
compensated by natural hazards and tight fairways.
18 holes, 4895yds, Par 67, SSS 63, Course record 61.
Club membership 480.
Visitors with member only on Sat pm & Sun. Societies
apply in advance. Green Fees £12-£17.50 per 18 holes
(£20 Sat). Cards 🖾 ▄▄ 🗓 Facilities ⊗ 🦳 🦳 ♀ 🎣 🍴
🍴 ⛳ Conf Corporate Hospitality Days available Location
1m N of Painswick, off A46 to Cheltenham
....
Hotel ★★★ 77% Painswick Hotel and Restaurant, Kemps
Ln, PAINSWICK ☎ 01452 812160 19 en suite

Hilton Puckrup Hall Puckrup GL20 6EL
☎ 01684 271591 📠 01684 271550
Set in 140 acres of undulating parkland with lakes,
existing trees and marvellous views of the Malvern hills.
There are water hazards at the 5th, and a cluster of
bunkers on the long 14th, before the challenging tee
shot across the water to the par 3 18th.
18 holes, 6189yds, Par 70, SSS 70, Course record 63.
Club membership 380.
Visitors not before 11.30am weekends; must be regular
golfer familiar with rules & etiquette; must book a tee time,
up to five days in advance. Societies phone in advance.
Green Fees £30 per round (£35 weekends). Cards 🖾 ▄▄
▄▄ 🦳 ▄▄ ▄▄ Prof Mark Fenning Course Designer
Simon Gidman Facilities ⊗ 🦳 🦳 ♀ 🎣 🍴 🐾 🍴 🐾
⛳ Leisure heated indoor swimming pool, sauna, solarium,
gymnasium. Conf fac available Corporate Hospitality
Days available Location 4m N of Tewkesbury on A38
....
Hotel ★★ 65% Bell Hotel, 57 Church St, TEWKESBURY
☎ 01684 293293 24 en suite

Tewkesbury Park Hotel Golf & Country
Club Lincoln Green Ln GL20 7DN
☎ 01684 295405 📠 01684 292386
e-mail: tewkesburypark@corushotels.com
The course offers many interesting and testing holes,
with wooded areas and water hazards early in the
round, opening up onto spacious fairways on the back
nine holes of the undulating course.

18 holes, 6533yds, Par 73, SSS 72, Course record 66.
Club membership 550.
Visitors book in advance via pro shop or hotel
reservations. Societies phone initially. Green Fees terms
on application. Cards 🖾 ▄▄ ▄▄ 🦳 ▄▄ ▄▄ 🗓 Prof
Charlie Boast Course Designer Frank Pennick Facilities
⊗ 🦳 🦳 ♀ 🎣 🍴 🍴 🐾 🍴 🐾 ⛳ 〔 Leisure hard tennis
courts, heated indoor swimming pool, squash, sauna,
solarium, gymnasium. Conf fac available Corporate
Hospitality Days available Location 1m SW off A38
....
Hotel ★★★ 67% The Tewkesbury Park Hotel Golf &
Country Club, Lincoln Green Ln, TEWKESBURY
☎ 0870 609 6101 80 en suite

Tewkesbury Park Hotel Golf & Country Club

*Lincoln Green Lane, Tewkesbury
Gloucestershire, GL20 7DN*

Tel: 01684 295405   Fax: 01684 292386
Email: tewkesburypark@corushotels.com
www.tewkesburyparkgolfclub.co.uk

A traditional 176 acre parkland course with wooded areas and water early in your round with welcome relief on later holes with spacious fairways.

80 bedroom hotel and full leisure facilities on site.

Thornbury Golf Centre Bristol Rd BS35 3XL
☎ 01454 281144 🖷 01454 281177
e-mail: info@thornburygc.co.uk
Two 18-hole pay and play courses designed by Hawtree and set in undulating terrain with extensive views towards the Severn estuary. The Low 18 is a par 3 with holes ranging from 80 to 207yds and is ideal for beginners. The High course puts to test the more experienced golfer. Excellent 25 bay floodlit driving range.

High Course: 18 holes, 6308yds, Par 71, SSS 69.
Low Course: 18 holes, 2195yds, Par 54.
Club membership 540.
Visitors phone to reserve. **Societies** apply in writing or phone in advance. **Green Fees** terms on application. **Cards** 💳 💳 💳 💳 💳 **Prof** Paul Middleton **Course Designer** Hawtree **Facilities** ⊗ ⅋ ⅃ ⅃ ⅃ ⅃ ⅃ ⅃ ⅃ ⅃ ⅃

Conf fac available Corporate Hospitality Days available
Location M5 junct 16, off A38 towards Gloucester

....

Hotel ★★ 66% Thornbury Golf Lodge, Bristol Rd, THORNBURY ☎ 01454 281144 11 en suite

Westonbirt Westonbirt School GL8 8QG
☎ 01666 880242 & 881338 🖷 01666 880385
e-mail: doyle@westonbirt.gloucs.sch.uk
A parkland course with good views.
9 holes, 4504yds, Par 64, SSS 64.
Club membership 265.
Visitors no restrictions. **Societies** no reserved tees. **Green Fees** £10 per round. **Facilities** ⊗ ⅃ ⅃ ⅃ **Conf** fac available **Location** E side of village off A433

....

Hotel ★★★ 71% Hare & Hounds Hotel, Westonbirt, TETBURY ☎ 01666 880233 & 881000 🖷 01666 880241 24 en suite 7 annexe en suite

The Gloucestershire Tracy Park Estate, Bath Rd BS30 5RN
☎ 0117 937 2251 🖷 0117 937 4288
e-mail: golf@thegloucestershire.com
Two 18-hole championship courses on the south-western escarpment of the Cotswolds, affording fine views. Both courses present a challenge to all levels of player, with water playing a part on a number of occasions. The elegant clubhouse dates from 1600, set in the 221-acre estate of this golf and country club.
Crown Course: 18 holes, 6252yds, Par 69, SSS 70.
Cromwell Course: 18 holes, 6246yds, Par 71, SSS 70.
Club membership 600.
Visitors no restrictions; must book tee time 0117 937 2251. **Societies** phone or write to Robert Ford. **Green Fees** terms on application. **Cards** 💳 💳 💳 💳 💳 **Prof** David Morgan **Facilities** ⊗ ⅋ ⅃ ⅃ ⅃ ⅃ ⅃ ⅃ ⅃ ⅃ ⅃ ⅃ ⅃ **Conf** fac available Corporate Hospitality Days available **Location** S side of village off A420

....

Hotel ★★★ The Queensberry Hotel, Russel St, BATH ☎ 01225 447928 29 en suite

Cotswold Edge Upper Rushmire GL12 7PT
☎ 01453 844167 🖷 01453 845120
e-mail: nnewman@cotswoldedgegolfclub.org.uk
Meadowland course situated in a quiet Cotswold valley with magnificent views. First half flat and open, second half more varied.

Continued   *Continued*

18 holes, 6170yds, Par 71, SSS 71.
Club membership 800.
Visitors preferable to contact in advance; with member only weekends. **Societies** contact in writing or phone in advance. **Green Fees** terms on application. **Prof** Rod Hibbitt **Facilities** ⊗ ⓑ ☕ ♀ ♨ ☜ ♈ ♠ ♂
Location N of town on B4058 Wotton-Tetbury road

Hotel ★★ 71% Egypt Mill Hotel, NAILSWORTH
☎ 01453 833449 8 en suite 10 annexe en suite

GREATER LONDON

Courses that fall within the London Postal District area (i.e. have London postcodes - W1, SW1 etc) are listed under the county heading of **London** in the gazetteer.

ADDINGTON   Map 05 TQ36

The Addington 205 Shirley Church Rd CR0 5AB
☎ 020 8777 1055 📠 020 8777 6661
e-mail: addingtogolf@btconnect.com
This heather and woodland course is possibly one of the best laid out courses in Southern England with the world famous 13th, par 3 at 230yds. A good test of golfing ability with no two holes the same.
18 holes, 6338yds, Par 68, SSS 71, Course record 66.
Visitors handicap certificate. **Societies** weekdays, phone for arrangement. **Green Fees** £75 (£95 weekends after 10.30am). **Cards** 💳 💳 💳 💳 **Course Designer** JF Abercromby **Facilities** ⊗ ⅷ ⓑ ☕ ♀ ♨ ♂ **Conf** Corporate Hospitality Days available **Location** M25 junct 7, 3m from Croydon

Hotel ★★★★ 67% Selsdon Park Hotel & Golf Course, Addington Rd, Sanderstead, CROYDON
☎ 020 8657 8811 204 en suite

Addington Court Featherbed Ln CR0 9AA
☎ 020 8657 0281 (booking) & 8651 5270 (admin)
📠 020 8651 0282
e-mail: addington@americangolf.uk.com
Championship Course: 18 holes, 5577yds, Par 68, SSS 67, Course record 60.
Falconwood: 18 holes, 5472yds, Par 68, SSS 67.
9 holes, 1804yds, Par 31.
Course Designer Hawtree Snr
Location 1m S off A2022
Phone for further details

Hotel ★★★★ 67% Selsdon Park Hotel & Golf Course, Addington Rd, Sanderstead, CROYDON
☎ 020 8657 8811 204 en suite

Addington Palace Addington Park, Gravel Hill CR0 5BB
☎ 020 8654 3061 📠 020 8655 3632
e-mail: david@addingtonpalacegolf.co.uk
Set in the grounds of Addington Palace, which was the home of the Archbishops of Canterbury for a number of years. There are a number of tree-lined fairways and the 17th hole follows one of the original roads into the Palace and has a fine array of horse chestnut trees. The course winds its way through tree-lined fairways for the first nine holes. The second nine holes opens out and needs full concentration to achieve a good score. The 12th hole is one to remember, over a fountain and onto a green bunkered on all sides.

Continued

18 holes, 6339yds, Par 71, SSS 70, Course record 63.
Club membership 700.
Visitors not weekends; phone in advance. **Societies** weekdays only, phone in advance. **Green Fees** £45 per day, £40 per round. **Cards** 💳 💳 💳 💳 **Prof** Roger Williams **Course Designer** JH Taylor **Facilities** ⊗ ⅷ ⓑ ☕ ♀ ♨ ♂ **Conf** Corporate Hospitality Days available **Location** 2m SE of Croydon station on A212

Hotel ★★★★ 67% Selsdon Park Hotel & Golf Course, Addington Rd, Sanderstead, CROYDON
☎ 020 8657 8811 204 en suite

BARNEHURST   Map 05 TQ57

Barnehurst Mayplace Rd East DA7 6JU
☎ 01322 523746 📠 01322 523860
9 holes, 4796yds, Par 70, SSS 67.
Course Designer James Braid **Location** 0.75m NW of Crayford off A2000
Phone for further details

Hotel ★★★★ 67% Bexleyheath Marriott Hotel, 1 Broadway, BEXLEYHEATH
☎ 0870 400 7245 142 en suite

BARNET   Map 04 TQ29

Arkley Rowley Green Rd EN5 3HL
☎ 020 8449 0394 📠 020 8440 5214
e-mail: secretary@arkleygolfclub.co.uk
Wooded parkland course situated on highest spot in Hertfordshire with fine views.
9 holes, 6046yds, Par 69, SSS 69.
Club membership 450.
Visitors with member only weekends. **Societies** contact in advance. **Green Fees** £32 per day, £25 per round. **Prof** Martin Porter **Course Designer** Braid **Facilities** ⊗ ⅷ ⓑ ☕ ♀ ♨ ♂ **Conf** Corporate Hospitality Days available **Location** off A1 at Arkley sign

Hotel ★★★ 67% Corus hotel Elstree, Barnet Ln, ELSTREE ☎ 0870 609 6151 47 en suite

Dyrham Park Country Club Galley Ln EN5 4RA
☎ 020 8440 3361 📠 020 8441 9836
18 holes, 6369yds, Par 71, SSS 70, Course record 65.
Location 3m NW off A1081
Phone for further details

Hotel ⓤ Innkeeper's Lodge Borehamwood, Studio Way, BOREHAM WOOD ☎ 020 8905 1455 55 en suite

Old Fold Manor Old Fold Ln, Hadley Green EN5 4QN
☎ 020 8440 9185 📠 020 8441 4863
e-mail: manager@oldfoldmanor.co.uk
Superb heathland course with some of the finest greens in Hertfordshire, breathtaking views and a challenge for all levels of golfer. Slightly undulating in parts, the course meanders around a historic battle site and gets progressively tougher as it develops.
18 holes, 6447yds, Par 71, SSS 71, Course record 66.
Club membership 560.
Visitors with member only weekends & bank holidays. **Societies** apply in writing or phone in advance. **Green Fees** £38 per 36 holes, £34 per 27 holes, £30 per 18 holes. **Cards** 💳 💳 💳 💳 💳 **Prof** Peter McEvoy **Facilities** ⊗ ⅷ by arrangement ⓑ ☕ ♀ ♨ ☜ ♠ ♂ **Conf** Corporate Hospitality Days available **Location** off A1000 between Barnet & Potters Bar

Continued

Hotel ★★★★ ♨ 73% West Lodge Park Hotel,
Cockfosters Rd, HADLEY WOOD ☎ 020 8216 3900
46 en suite 13 annexe en suite

BECKENHAM   Map 05 TQ36

Beckenham Place Park The Mansion,
Beckenham Place Park BR3 5BP
☎ 020 8650 2292 📠 020 8663 1201
18 holes, 5722yds, Par 68, SSS 69.
Location off A2015
Phone for details

Hotel ★★★ 71% Bromley Court Hotel, Bromley Hill,
BROMLEY ☎ 020 8461 8600 114 en suite

Langley Park Barnfield Wood Rd BR3 6SZ
☎ 020 8658 6849 📠 020 8658 6310
e-mail: manager@langleyparkgolf.co.uk
This is a pleasant, but difficult, well-wooded, parkland
course with natural hazards including a lake at the
par 3 18th hole. Although most fairways are bordered
by woodland, they are wide with forgiving rough and
friendly bunkers.
18 holes, 6488yds, Par 69, SSS 71, Course record 65.
Club membership 700.
Visitors not weekends; contact in advance. **Societies** Wed,
Thu or by arrangement, phone to book. **Green Fees** £45
per day, £35 per round. **Cards** 🖭 🖳 🖃 💳 🖭 🖳 💳
Prof Colin Staff **Course Designer** J H Taylor **Facilities** ⊗
🎤 ⅃ 🍴 🖤 ♀ ⅄ 🏠 🍴 𝒻 **Conf** Corporate Hospitality Days
available **Location** 0.5 N of Beckenham on B2015

Hotel ★★★ 71% Bromley Court Hotel, Bromley Hill,
BROMLEY ☎ 020 8461 8600 114 en suite

BEXLEYHEATH   Map 05 TQ47

Bexleyheath Mount Rd DA6 8JS
☎ 020 8303 6951
Undulating course.
9 holes, 5162yds, Par 66, SSS 66, Course record 65.
Club membership 330.
Visitors not weekends; contact Secretary in advance.
Societies phone in advance. **Green Fees** terms on
application. **Facilities** ⊗ 🎤 ⅃ 🖤 ♀ ⅄ **Location** 1m SW

Hotel ★★★★ 67% Bexleyheath Marriott Hotel, 1
Broadway, BEXLEYHEATH
☎ 0870 400 7245 142 en suite

BIGGIN HILL   Map 05 TQ45

Cherry Lodge Jail Ln TN16 3AX
☎ 01959 572250 📠 01959 540672
e-mail: info@cherrylodgegc.co.uk
Undulating parkland course set 600 feet above sea level
with panoramic views of the surrounding countryside.
An enjoyable test of golf for all standards. The 14th is
434yds across a valley and uphill, requiring two good
shots to reach the green.
18 holes, 6593yds, Par 72, SSS 73, Course record 66.
Club membership 700.
Visitors contact pro shop for weekday reservation; with
member only weekends. **Societies** phone in advance.
Green Fees £40 per 18 holes. **Cards** 🖭 🖳 🖃 💳 **Prof**
Nigel Child **Course Designer** John Day **Facilities** ⊗ ⅃
🖤 ♀ ⅄ 🏠 🍴 𝒻 ſ **Location** 1m E

Hotel ★★★ 71% Donnington Manor, London Rd, Dunton
Green, SEVENOAKS ☎ 01732 462681 60 en suite

BROMLEY   Map 05 TQ46

Bromley Magpie Hall Ln BR2 8JF
☎ 020 8462 7014 📠 020 8462 6916
9 holes, 2745yds, Par 70, SSS 67.
Location 2m SE off A21
Phone for further details

Hotel ★★★ 71% Bromley Court Hotel, Bromley Hill,
BROMLEY ☎ 020 8461 8600 114 en suite

Sundridge Park Garden Rd BR1 3NE
☎ 020 8460 0278 📠 020 8289 3050
e-mail: gm@spgc.co.uk
The East Course is longer than the West but many
think the shorter of the two courses is the more
difficult. The East is surrounded by trees while the
West is more hilly, with good views. Both are certainly
a good test of golf. An Open qualifying course with year
round irrigation of fairways.
East Course: 18 holes, 6516yds, Par 71, SSS 71,
Course record 63.
West Course: 18 holes, 6019yds, Par 69, SSS 69,
Course record 65.
Club membership 1200.
Visitors not weekends; contact in advance; handicap
certificate; no booking necessary. **Societies** contact well in
advance. **Green Fees** £85 per day, £65 per round -
weekdays only. **Cards** 🖭 🖃 💳 **Prof** Stuart Dowsett
Course Designer Willie Park **Facilities** ⊗ 🎤 ⅃ 🖤 ♀ ⅄
🏠 🍴 🕊 🏌 𝒻 **Conf** fac available Corporate Hospitality
Days available **Location** N side of town centre off A2212

Hotel ★★★ 71% Bromley Court Hotel, Bromley Hill,
BROMLEY ☎ 020 8461 8600 114 en suite

CARSHALTON   Map 04 TQ26

Oaks Sports Centre Woodmansterne Rd SM5 4AN
☎ 020 8643 8363 📠 020 8770 7303
e-mail: golf@oaks.sagehost.co.uk
Public parkland course with floodlit, covered driving
range.

18 holes, 6054yds, Par 70, SSS 69, Course record 65.
9 holes, 1497yds, Par 28, SSS 28.
Club membership 477.
Visitors not weekends. **Societies** apply in writing. **Green**
Fees £17.40 for 18 holes, £8.70 for nine holes (£21/£10.50
weekends). **Prof** Horley, Russell, Pilkington
Facilities 🎤 ⅃ 🖤 ♀ ⅄ 🏠 🍴 🕊 𝒻 ſ **Conf** fac available
Location 0.5m S on B278

Continued   Continued

Hotel ★★★ 69% Aerodrome Hotel, Purley Way,
CROYDON ☎ 020 8710 9000 84 en suite

CHESSINGTON   Map 04 TQ16

Chessington Garrison Ln KT9 2LW
☎ 020 8391 0948 ▯ 020 8397 2068
e-mail: info@chessingtongolf.co.uk
**Tree-lined parkland course designed by Patrick Tallack,
with panoramic views over the Surrey countryside.**
9 holes, 1679yds, Par 30, SSS 28.
Club membership 90.
Visitors not before 10am Sun. **Societies** phone in advance.
Green Fees £8.50 per round (£10 weekends & bank
holidays). **Cards** 🎫 💳 📶 📶 💷 **Prof** Mark Janes
Course Designer Patrick Tallack **Facilities** ⊗ ▆ 💷 ♀ 🍴
🍴 🐾 ⚒ ⚑ **Leisure** animated ball teeing facility on
driving range. **Location** M25 junct 9, 3m N on A243

Hotel ☆ Premier Travel Inn Chessington, Leatherhead Rd,
CHESSINGTON ☎ 08701 977057 42 en suite

CHISLEHURST   Map 05 TQ47

Chislehurst Camden Park Rd BR7 5HJ
☎ 020 8467 6798 ▯ 020 8295 0874
e-mail: thesecretary@chislehurstgolfclub.co.uk
**The course was established in 1894 and is dominated by
an imposing 17th century building of great historical
interest. The challenging parkland course has an
overall area of less than 70 acres and accuracy is always
more important than distance off the tee. There are
trees, hills and dales and the excellent greens are
neither too large or too flat. Only the 7th hole remains
from the original nine-hole course.**
18 holes, 5080yds, Par 66, SSS 65, Course record 61.
Club membership 760.
Visitors with member only weekends; handicap certificate
for weekdays. **Societies** weekdays only, book in advance.
Green Fees £30 per round weekdays only. **Prof** Jonathan
Bird **Course Designer** Park **Facilities** ⊗ ▆ ▆ 💷 ♀ 🍴 🍴
⚒ **Leisure** snooker room. **Conf** fac available

Hotel ★★★ 71% Bromley Court Hotel, Bromley Hill,
BROMLEY ☎ 020 8461 8600 114 en suite

COULSDON   Map 04 TQ25

Coulsdon Manor Hotel Coulsdon Court Rd
CR5 2LL
☎ 020 8668 0414 ▯ 020 8668 3118
e-mail: coulsdonmanor@marstonhotels.com
**Designed by Harry S Colt and set in its own 140 acres
of landscaped parkland.**
18 holes, 6037yds, Par 70, SSS 68.
Visitors phone for tee times. **Societies** phone to book.
Green Fees not confirmed. **Cards** 🎫 📶 💳 💷 📶 📶
💷 **Prof** James Leaver **Course Designer** Harry Colt
Facilities ⊗ ▆ ▆ 💷 ♀ 🍴 🍴 🍴 🐾 🐾 ⚒ **Leisure** hard
tennis courts, squash, sauna, solarium, gymnasium. **Conf**
fac available Corporate Hospitality Days available
Location 0.75m E off A23 on B2030

Hotel ★★★★ 75% Coulsdon Manor, Coulsdon Court Rd,
Coulsdon, CROYDON ☎ 020 8668 0414 35 en suite

> **Looking for a new course? Always telephone
> ahead to confirm visitor arrangements.**

Woodcote Park Meadow Hill, Bridle Way CR5 2QQ
☎ 020 8668 2788 ▯ 020 8660 0918
e-mail: info@woodcotepgc.com
Slightly undulating parkland course.
18 holes, 6720yds, Par 71, SSS 72.
Club membership 700.
Visitors not weekends; book up to seven days in advance;
handicap certificate. **Societies** contact Secretary in
advance. **Green Fees** £45 per day/round. **Prof** Wraith
Grant **Course Designer** H S Colt **Facilities** ⊗ ▆ by
arrangement ▆ 💷 ♀ 🍴 🍴 🐾 ⚒ **Location** 1m N of
town centre off A237

Hotel ★★★ 69% Aerodrome Hotel, Purley Way,
CROYDON ☎ 020 8710 9000 84 en suite

CROYDON   Map 04 TQ36

Croham Hurst Croham Rd CR2 7HJ
☎ 020 8657 5581 ▯ 020 8657 3229
e-mail: secretary@chgc.co.uk
**Parkland course with tree-lined fairways and bounded
by wooded hills. Easy walking.**
18 holes, 6290yds, Par 70, SSS 70.
Club membership 800.
Visitors contact in advance; handicap certificate; with
member only weekends & bank holidays. **Societies** apply
in writing or phone in advance **Green Fees** £40 (£50
weekends). **Prof** Matthew Paget **Course Designer**
Hawtree, Braid **Facilities** ⊗ ▆ ▆ 💷 ♀ 🍴 🍴 ⚒ **Conf**
Corporate Hospitality Days available **Location** 1.5m SE of
Croydon on B269

Hotel ★★★★ 67% Selsdon Park Hotel & Golf Course,
Addington Rd, Sanderstead, CROYDON
☎ 020 8657 8811 204 en suite

Selsdon Park Hotel Addington Rd, Sanderstead
CR2 8YA
☎ 020 8657 8811 ▯ 020 8651 6171
**Parkland course. Full use of hotel's sporting facilities
by residents.**
18 holes, 6473yds, Par 73, SSS 71, Course record 63.
Visitors booking advisable; book one week in advance for
weekends. **Societies** phone in advance. **Green Fees** not
confirmed. **Cards** 🎫 💳 📶 📶 💷 **Prof** Malcolm
Churchill **Course Designer** J H Taylor **Facilities** ⊗ ▆ ▆
💷 ♀ 🍴 🍴 🍴 🐾 🐾 ⚒ ⚑ **Leisure** hard & grass tennis
courts, outdoor & indoor heated swimming pools, squash,
sauna, solarium, gymnasium. **Conf** fac available **Location**
3m S on A2022

Hotel ★★★★ 67% Selsdon Park Hotel & Golf Course,
Addington Rd, Sanderstead, CROYDON
☎ 020 8657 8811 204 en suite

> **Shirley Park** 194 Addiscombe Rd CR0 7LB
> ☎ 020 8654 1143 ▯ 020 8654 6733
> e-mail: secretary@shirleyparkgolfclub.co.uk
> **This parkland course lies amid fine woodland with good
> views of Shirley Hills. The more testing holes come in
> the middle section of the course. The remarkable 7th
> hole calls for a 187yd iron or wood shot diagonally
> across a narrow valley to a shelved green set right-
> handed into a ridge. The 13th hole, 160yds, is considered
> to be one of the finest short holes in the county.**
> *18 holes, 6210yds, Par 71, SSS 70, Course record 64.*
> *Club membership 600.*
>
> *Continued*

Visitors contact in advance; with member only Sat.
Societies by arrangement. Green Fees £40 weekday (£48
Sun). Cards ⊞ ▥ 🖳 ▦ 🔲 🔲 Prof Michael Taylor
Course Designer Tom Simpson, Herbert Fowler Facilities
⊗ ⅏ ᠘ ☕ ♀ ♨ 🏠 ♈ ⛳ Location E of town centre on
A232

Hotel ★★★★ 67% Selsdon Park Hotel & Golf Course,
Addington Rd, Sanderstead, CROYDON
☎ 020 8657 8811 204 en suite

DOWNE — Map 05 TQ46

High Elms High Elms Rd BR6 7JL
☎ 01689 853232 & 858175 bookings 📠 01689 856326
18 holes, 6210yds, Par 71, SSS 70, Course record 68.
Course Designer Hawthorn Location 2m E of A21
Phone for further details

Hotel ★★★ 71% Bromley Court Hotel, Bromley Hill,
BROMLEY ☎ 020 8461 8600 114 en suite

West Kent Milking Ln BR6 7LD
☎ 01689 851323 📠 01689 858693
e-mail: golf@wkgc.co.uk
**Undulating woodland course close to south London but
providing a quiet rural setting in three valleys.**
18 holes, 6426yds, Par 71, SSS 71, Course record 68.
Club membership 700.
Visitors with member only weekends; contact in advance.
Societies apply in writing. Green Fees £55 per day; £40
per round. Cards ⊞ ▥ 🔲 🔲 Prof Chris Forsyth Course
Designer H S Colt Facilities ⊗ ᠘ ☕ ♀ ♨ 🏠 ♨ ⛳
Location M25 junct 4, A21 towards Bromley, left signed
Downe, through village on Luxted road 0.5m, West Hill on
right

Hotel ★★★ 71% Bromley Court Hotel, Bromley Hill,
BROMLEY ☎ 020 8461 8600 114 en suite

ENFIELD — Map 04 TQ39

Crews Hill Cattlegate Rd, Crews Hill EN2 8AZ
☎ 020 8363 6674 📠 020 8363 2343
e-mail: gmchgc@aol.com
Parkland course in country surroundings.
18 holes, 6273yds, Par 70, SSS 70, Course record 65.
Club membership 600.
Visitors Mon 7am-9.30am, Tue-Fri after 2pm, Wed, Fri;
handicap certificate; no use of clubhouse facilities.
Societies Wed-Fri, apply in writing. Green Fees not
confirmed. Cards ⊞ ▥ ▥ 🖳 ▦ 🔲 🔲 Prof Neil
Wichelow Course Designer Harry Colt Facilities ⊗ ⅏ ᠘
☕ ♀ ♨ 🏠 🌿 ♨ ⛳ Conf fac available Corporate
Hospitality Days available Location M25 junct 24, A1005
for Enfield, signed

Hotel ★★★ 75% Royal Chace Hotel, The Ridgeway,
ENFIELD ☎ 020 8884 8181 92 en suite

Enfield Old Park Rd South EN2 7DA
☎ 020 8363 3970 📠 020 8342 0381
e-mail: secretary@enfieldgolfclub.co.uk
**Parkland course with mature tree-lined fairways and a
brook meandering through it, which comes into play on
nine of the holes. There are no hidden or unfair hazards
and, although not easy, the course is highly playable
and always attractive.**
18 holes, 6154yds, Par 72, SSS 70, Course record 61.
Club membership 600.

Visitors contact professional in advance; weekends & bank
holidays by arrangement only. Societies contact
secretary in advance. Green Fees terms on application.
Cards ⊞ ▥ ▥ 🖳 ▦ 🔲 🔲 Course Designer James
Braid Facilities ⊗ ⅏ ᠘ ☕ ♀ ♨ 🏠 🌿 ⛳ Conf fac
available Location M25 junct 24, A1005 to Enfield, rdbt
with church, right down Slades Hill, 1st left to end

Hotel ★★★ 75% Royal Chace Hotel, The Ridgeway,
ENFIELD ☎ 020 8884 8181 92 en suite

Whitewebbs Park Whitewebbs Ln EN2 9HH
☎ 020 8363 4454 📠 020 8366 2257
**This challenging parkland course was first opened for
play in 1932 and is set in over 140 acres of attractive
rolling countryside with mature woodland and the
meandering Cuffley brook that comes into play on four
holes.**
18 holes, 5782yds, Par 68, SSS 68, Course record 67.
Club membership 350.
Visitors book up to seven days in advance. Societies apply
in writing or by phone to Course Manager. Green Fees
£22.50 per day, £13.50 per round (£27.50/£17.50
weekends). Cards ⊞ ▥ ▦ 🔲 🔲 Prof Gary Sherriff
Facilities ⊗ ⅏ ᠘ ☕ ♀ ♨ 🏠 ♨ 🌿 ⛳ Location N of
town centre

Hotel ★★★ 75% Royal Chace Hotel, The Ridgeway,
ENFIELD ☎ 020 8884 8181 92 en suite

GREENFORD — Map 04 TQ18

C & L Golf & Country Club Westend Rd,
Northolt UB5 6RD
☎ 020 8845 5662 📠 020 8841 5515
18 holes, 4458yds, Par 67, SSS 62, Course record 58.
Course Designer Patrick Tallack Location junct Westend
Rd & A40
Phone for further details

Hotel ★★★ 67% The Bridge Hotel, Western Av,
GREENFORD ☎ 020 8566 6246 68 en suite

Ealing Perivale Ln UB6 8SS
☎ 020 8997 0937 📠 020 8998 0756
e-mail: junemackison@hotmail.com
**The home of English and European champions. Inland
parkland course with River Brent providing natural
hazards across several holes.**
18 holes, 6216yds, Par 70, SSS 70, Course record 62.
Club membership 650.
Visitors not weekends; only by application to pro shop.
Societies Mon, Wed & Thu, by arrangement. Green Fees
£35 weekdays. Cards ⊞ ▥ 🔲 Prof Ricky Willison
Course Designer HS Colt Facilities ⊗ ⅏ by arrangement
᠘ ☕ ♀ ♨ 🏠 🌿 ♨ ⛳ Conf Corporate Hospitality Days
available Location off A40

Hotel ★★★ 67% The Bridge Hotel, Western Av,
GREENFORD ☎ 020 8566 6246 68 en suite

Horsenden Hill Whitton Av, Woodland Rise
UB6 0RD
☎ 020 8902 4555 📠 020 8902 4555
**A distinctive picturesque course designed over hilly
landscape. Very challenging comprising eight par 3s
(three over 200yds) and par 4 of 292yds. Overlooks the
London skyline to Canary Wharf and the London Eye.**
9 holes, 1632yds, Par 28, SSS 28.
Club membership 135.

Continued

Continued

Visitors no restrictions. Societies phone for details. Green Fees £7.40 per 18 holes, £4.40 per nine holes (£11.70/£6.40 weekends & bank holidays). Cards ▭▭ ▭▭ ▭▭ ▭▭ ▣ Prof Jeff Quarshie Facilities ⊗ ⅢⅢ ⅃Ⅎ ⅃Ⅎ ⅃Ⅎ Ⅎ ⅃Ⅎ Conf Corporate Hospitality Days available Location 3m NE on A4090

Hotel ★★★ 67% The Bridge Hotel, Western Av, GREENFORD ☎ 020 8566 6246 68 en suite

Lime Trees Park Ruislip Rd, Northolt UB5 6QZ
☎ 020 8842 0442 ▤ 0208 8420542
9 holes, 5836yds, Par 71, SSS 69.
Location 300yds off A40 at Polish War Memorial, A4180 towards Hayes
Phone for further details

Hotel ★★★ 67% The Bridge Hotel, Western Av, GREENFORD ☎ 020 8566 6246 68 en suite

Perivale Park Stockdove Way UB6 8TJ
☎ 020 8575 7116
Parkland course by the river Brent.
9 holes, 2667yds, Par 68, SSS 67.
Club membership 250.
Visitors no restrictions. Green Fees £7 per nine holes (£8.50 weekends & bank holidays). Cards ▭▭ ▭▭ ▭▭ ▭▭ ▣ Prof Peter Bryant Facilities ⅃Ⅎ Ⅎ ⅃Ⅎ ⅃Ⅎ ⅃Ⅎ Ⅎ
Location E of town centre off A40

Hotel ★★★ 68% Best Western Cumberland Hotel, 1 St Johns Rd, HARROW ☎ 020 8863 4111 31 en suite 53 annexe en suite

HADLEY WOOD   Map 04 TQ29

Hadley Wood Beech Hill EN4 0JJ
☎ 020 8449 4328 & 4486 ▤ 020 8364 8633
e-mail: gen.mgr@hadleywoodgc.com
A parkland course on the northwest edge of London. The gently undulating fairways have a friendly width inviting the player to open his shoulders, though the thick rough can be very punishing to the unwary. The course is pleasantly wooded and there are some admirable views.

18 holes, 6514yds, Par 72, SSS 71, Course record 67.
Club membership 600.
Visitors not am Tue & weekends; contact in advance; handicap certificate. Societies contact in advance. Green Fees terms on application. Prof Peter Jones Course Designer Dr A MacKenzie Facilities ⊗ ⅢⅢ ⅃Ⅎ Ⅎ ⅃Ⅎ ⅃Ⅎ ⅃Ⅎ ⅃Ⅎ Ⅎ Conf Corporate Hospitality Days available Location E of village

Hotel ★★★★ ⚐ 73% West Lodge Park Hotel, Cockfosters Rd, HADLEY WOOD ☎ 020 8216 3900 46 en suite 13 annexe en suite

HAMPTON   Map 04 TQ17

Fulwell Wellington Rd, Hampton Hill TW12 1JY
☎ 020 8977 3844 & 020 8977 2733 ▤ 020 8977 7732
18 holes, 6544yds, Par 71, SSS 71.
Location 1.5m N on A311
Phone for further details

Hotel ★★★ 69% The Richmond Hill Hotel, Richmond Hill, RICHMOND UPON THAMES ☎ 020 8940 2247 138 en suite

HAMPTON WICK   Map 04 TQ16

Hampton Court Palace Home Park KT1 4AD
☎ 020 8977 2423 ▤ 020 8614 4747
e-mail: hamptoncourtpalace@americangolf.uk.com
Flat course with easy walking situated in the grounds of Hampton Court Palace. Unique blend of parkland and inland links built on a base of sand and gravel, making it one of the finest winter courses in the south of England.
18 holes, 6584yds, Par 71, SSS 71, Course record 64.
Club membership 650.
Visitors not before 1.30pm weekends & during competitions. Societies phone Society Organiser 020 8977 2423. Green Fees £40 per round Fri, £30 Mon-Thu, (£50 weekends & bank holidays). Cards ▭▭ ▭▭ ▭▭ ▭▭ ▭▭ ▣ Prof Adam Smith Course Designer Willie Park Facilities ⊗ ⅢⅢ ⅃Ⅎ Ⅎ ⅃Ⅎ ⅃Ⅎ ⅃Ⅎ ⅃Ⅎ Ⅎ Conf fac available Corporate Hospitality Days available Location off A308 W from Kingston Bridge

Hotel ★★★ 69% The Richmond Hill Hotel, Richmond Hill, RICHMOND UPON THAMES ☎ 020 8940 2247 138 en suite

HILLINGDON   Map 04 TQ08

Hillingdon 18 Dorset Way UB10 0JR
☎ 01895 233956 & 239810 ▤ 01895 233956
9 holes, 5490yds, Par 68, SSS 67.
Location W of town off A4020
Phone for further details

Hotel ★★★ 69% Novotel London Heathrow, M4 junct 4, Cherry Ln, WEST DRAYTON ☎ 01895 431431 178 en suite

HOUNSLOW   Map 04 TQ17

Airlinks Southall Ln TW5 9PE
☎ 020 8561 1418 ▤ 8813 6284
Meadowland and parkland course. Four water holes.
18 holes, 6000yds, Par 71, SSS 69, Course record 63.
Club membership 550.
Visitors contact in advance. Societies phone in advance. Green Fees terms on application. Cards ▭▭ ▭▭ ▭▭ ▭▭ ▭▭ ▣ Prof Tony Martin, Greg Fenner Course Designer P Alliss, D Thomas Facilities ⊗ ⅢⅢ ⅃Ⅎ Ⅎ ⅃Ⅎ ⅃Ⅎ ⅃Ⅎ ⅃Ⅎ ⅃Ⅎ Ⅎ Leisure hard tennis courts, outdoor & indoor heated swimming pools, squash, sauna, solarium, gymnasium.
Location M4 junct 3, W of Hounslow

Hotel ★★★ 66% Best Western Master Robert Hotel, 366 Great West Rd, HOUNSLOW ☎ 020 8570 6261 96 annexe en suite

> **Looking for a new course? Always telephone ahead to confirm visitor arrangements.**

Hounslow Heath Municipal Staines Rd TW4 5DS
☎ 020 8570 5271 📠 020 8570 5205
18 holes, 5901yds, Par 69, SSS 68, Course record 62.
Course Designer Fraser M Middleton **Location** on A315
towards Bedfont
Phone for further details

....

Hotel ★★★ 66% Best Western Master Robert Hotel, 366
Great West Rd, HOUNSLOW ☎ 020 8570 6261
96 annexe en suite

ILFORD
Map 05 TQ48

Ilford Wanstead Park Rd IG1 3TR
☎ 020 8554 2930 📠 020 8554 0822
e-mail: ilfordgolfclub@btconnect.com
**Fairly flat parkland course with the River Roding
running through it. The river borders four holes, and is
crossed by three holes. While not a particularly long
course, the small greens, and many holes requiring
brains rather than brawn, provide a challenging test to
all.**
18 holes, 5299yds, Par 67, SSS 66, Course record 61.
Club membership 500.
Visitors book in advance 020 8554 0094.
Societies phone for provisional date & booking form.
Green Fees terms on application. **Cards** 🖽 💳 💳 📇 📇
Prof S Jackson **Course Designer** Whitehead **Facilities** ⊗
🕤 🏌 💷 ♀ 🏖 📷 ⚬ **Conf** fac available Corporate
Hospitality Days available **Location** NW of town centre
off A12

ISLEWORTH
Map 04 TQ17

Wyke Green Syon Ln TW7 5PT
☎ 020 8847 0685 (Prof) & 8560 8777 (Sec)
📠 020 8569 8392
e-mail: office@wykegreengolfclub.co.uk
**Fairly flat parkland course. Seven par 4 holes over
420yds.**
18 holes, 6182yds, Par 69, SSS 70, Course record 64.
Club membership 650.
Visitors not before 4pm weekends & bank holidays.
Societies apply in writing or phone in advance. **Green
Fees** £28 per round; (£30 weekends). **Prof** Neil Smith
Course Designer Hawtree **Facilities** ⊗ 🕤 🏌 💷 ♀ 🏖 📷
🏐 🛺 ⚬ **Location** 0.5m N on B454, off A4 at Gillette
Corner

....

Hotel ★★★ 66% Best Western Master Robert Hotel, 366
Great West Rd, HOUNSLOW ☎ 020 8570 6261
96 annexe en suite

KINGSTON UPON THAMES
Map 04 TQ16

Coombe Hill Golf Club Dr, Coombe Ln West
KT2 7DF
☎ 020 8336 7600 📠 020 8336 7601
e-mail: thesecretary@coombehillgolf.demon.co.uk
**A splendid course in wooded terrain. The undulations
and trees make it an especially interesting course of
great charm. And there is a lovely display of
rhododendrons in May and June.**
18 holes, 6293yds, Par 71, SSS 71, Course record 67.
Club membership 550.
Visitors contact in advance; with member only weekends.
Societies book in advance. **Green Fees** weekdays only:
£100 per 36 holes, £80 per 18 holes. **Cards** 🖽 💳 **Prof**
Craig Defoy **Course Designer** JF Abercromby

Continued

Facilities ⊗ 🏌 💷 ♀ 🏖 📷 🏐 🛺 ⚬ **Leisure** sauna. **Conf**
Corporate Hospitality Days available **Location** 1.75m E on
A238

....

Hotel ⟡ Travelodge London Kingston, 21-23 London Rd,
KINGSTON-UPON-THAMES ☎ 08700 850 950
72 en suite

Coombe Wood George Rd, Kingston Hill KT2 7NS
☎ 020 8942 0388 📠 020 8942 5665
e-mail: cwoodgc@ukonline.co.uk
**Mature parkland course with seven varied and
challenging par 3s.**
18 holes, 5299yds, Par 66, SSS 66, Course record 59.
Club membership 700.
Visitors not weekends before 3pm. **Societies** Wed, Thu &
Fri, contact in advance. **Green Fees** £26 per round (£38 per
round weekends). **Prof** Phil Wright **Course Designer** Tom
Williamson **Facilities** ⊗ 🕤 by arrangement 🏌 💷 ♀ 🏖 📷
🏐 ⚬ **Conf** fac available Corporate Hospitality Days
available **Location** 1.25m NE on A308

....

Hotel ⟡ Travelodge London Kingston, 21-23 London Rd,
KINGSTON-UPON-THAMES ☎ 08700 850 950
72 en suite

MITCHAM
Map 04 TQ26

Mitcham Carshalton Rd, Mitcham Junction CR4 4HN
☎ 020 8648 4280 📠 020 8647 4197
e-mail: mitchamgolfclub@hotmail.com
A wooded heathland course on a gravel base.
18 holes, 5935yds, Par 69, SSS 68, Course record 65.
Club membership 500.
Visitors restricted weekends; book in advance. **Societies**
phone in advance. **Green Fees** £15 (£20 weekends, £25
bank holidays). **Cards** 🖽 💳 💳 📇 📇 **Prof** Jeff
Godfrey **Course Designer** T Scott, T Morris **Facilities** ⊗
🏌 💷 ♀ 🏖 📷 🏐 ⚬ **Location** 1m S

....

Hotel ★★★ 69% Aerodrome Hotel, Purley Way,
CROYDON ☎ 020 8710 9000 84 en suite

NEW MALDEN
Map 04 TQ26

Malden Traps Ln KT3 4RS
☎ 020 8942 0654 📠 020 8336 2219
e-mail: maldengc@lwcdial.net
18 holes, 6295yds, Par 71, SSS 70.
Location N of town centre off B283
Phone for further details

....

Hotel ⟡ Travelodge London Kingston, 21-23 London Rd,
KINGSTON-UPON-THAMES ☎ 08700 850 950
72 en suite

NORTHWOOD
Map 04 TQ09

Haste Hill The Drive HA6 1HN
☎ 01923 825224
**Parkland course with stream running through.
Excellent views.**
18 holes, 5787yds, Par 68, SSS 68, Course record 63.
Club membership 250.
Visitors advised to book in advance 01923 825224
Societies apply in advance. **Green Fees** not confirmed.
Cards 🖽 💳 💳 📇 📇 **Prof** Cameron Smilie
Facilities ⊗ 🕤 by arrangement 🏌 💷 ♀ 🏖 📷 🏐 🛺 ⚬
Location 0.5m S off A404

Continued

Haste Hill

Hotel ★★★ 68% Quality Harrow Hotel, 12-22 Pinner Rd, HARROW ☎ 020 8427 3435 79 en suite 23 annexe en suite

Northwood Rickmansworth Rd HA6 2QW
☎ 01923 821384 🖷 01923 840150
e-mail: secretary@northwoodgolf.co.uk
A high quality parkland course in the heart of Middlesex. The course provides a good test of golf to the experienced golfer and can hold many surprises for the unsuspecting. The par 4 10th hole, Death or Glory, has wrecked many good cards in the past, while the long par 4 5th hole requires two very good shots to make par.
18 holes, 6535yds, Par 71, SSS 71, Course record 67.
Club membership 650.
Visitors not weekends; contact in advance. Societies apply in writing or by phone. Green Fees £50 per day, £36 per round. Cards 🖩 🖩 🖩 🖩 💲 Prof CJ Holdsworth Course Designer James Braid Facilities ⊗ ⋔ ⓑ ⚑ ♀ ⌓ 🏠 ⌁ Conf Corporate Hospitality Days available Location on A404

Hotel ★★★ 68% Quality Harrow Hotel, 12-22 Pinner Rd, HARROW ☎ 020 8427 3435 79 en suite 23 annexe en suite

Sandy Lodge Sandy Lodge Ln HA6 2JD
☎ 01923 825429 🖷 01923 824319
e-mail: info@sandylodge.co.uk
A links-type, very sandy, heathland course.
18 holes, 6347yds, Par 71, SSS 71, Course record 64.
Club membership 780.
Visitors not weekends; contact in advance; handicap certificate. Societies phone in advance. Green Fees £40 per round. Cards 🖩 🖩 💲 Prof Jeff Pinsent Course Designer H Vardon Facilities ⊗ ⋔ ⓑ ⚑ ♀ ⌓ 🏠 ⌁ 🛒 ⌁ Conf Corporate Hospitality Days available Location N of town centre off A4125

Hotel ★★★ 67% The White House, Upton Rd, WATFORD ☎ 01923 237316 57 en suite

ORPINGTON   Map 05 TQ46

Chelsfield Lakes Golf Centre Court Rd BR6 9BX
☎ 01689 896266 🖷 01689 824577
18 holes, 6077yds, Par 71, SSS 69, Course record 64.
Warren: 9 holes, 1188yds, Par 27.
Course Designer M Sandow Location M25 junct 4, on A224
Phone for further details

Hotel ★★★ 71% Bromley Court Hotel, Bromley Hill, BROMLEY ☎ 020 8461 8600 114 en suite

Cray Valley Sandy Ln, St Paul's Cray BR5 3HY
☎ 01689 837909 & 871490 🖷 01689 891428
18 holes, 5669yds, Par 70, SSS 67.
nine holes, 2140yds, Par 32.
Location 1m off A20, Critley's Corner junct
Phone for further details

Hotel ★★★ 71% Bromley Court Hotel, Bromley Hill, BROMLEY ☎ 020 8461 8600 114 en suite

Ruxley Park Golf Centre Sandy Ln, St Paul's Cray BR5 3HY
☎ 01689 871490 🖷 01689 891428
18 holes, 5703yds, Par 70, SSS 68, Course record 63.
Location 2m NE on A223
Phone for further details

Hotel ★★★ 71% Bromley Court Hotel, Bromley Hill, BROMLEY ☎ 020 8461 8600 114 en suite

PINNER   Map 04 TQ18

Grims Dyke Oxhey Ln, Hatch End HA5 4AL
☎ 020 8428 4539 🖷 020 8421 5494
e-mail: grimsdykegolfclub@hotmail.com
Pleasant, undulating parkland course.
18 holes, 5596yds, Par 69, SSS 67, Course record 61.
Club membership 500.
Visitors not weekends except with member. Societies apply in writing or by phone, deposit required. Green Fees not confirmed. Cards 🖩 🖩 🖩 🖩 💲 Prof Lee Curling Course Designer James Baird Facilities ⊗ ⓑ ⚑ ♀ ⌓ 🏠 ⌁ 🛒 ⌁ Conf fac available Corporate Hospitality Days available Location 3m N of Harrow on A4008

Hotel ★★★ 68% Best Western Cumberland Hotel, 1 St Johns Rd, HARROW ☎ 020 8863 4111 31 en suite 53 annexe en suite

Pinner Hill Southview Rd, Pinner Hill HA5 3YA
☎ 020 8866 0963 🖷 020 8868 4817
e-mail: pinnerhillgc@uk2.net
18 holes, 6392yds, Par 71, SSS 71.
Course Designer JH Taylor Location 2m NW off A404
Phone for further details

Hotel ★★★ 68% Quality Harrow Hotel, 12-22 Pinner Rd, HARROW ☎ 020 8427 3435 79 en suite 23 annexe en suite

PURLEY   Map 05 TQ36

Purley Downs 106 Purley Downs Rd CR2 0RB
☎ 020 8657 8347 🖷 020 8651 5044
e-mail: info@purleydowns.co.uk
Hilly downland course which is a good test for golfers.
18 holes, 6262yds, Par 70, SSS 70, Course record 64.
Club membership 750.
Visitors contact in advance; with member only weekends. Societies contact in advance. Green Fees terms on application. Cards 🖩 🖩 🖩 🖩 🖩 💲 Prof Graham Wilson Course Designer J Taylor, HS Colt Facilities ⊗ ⋔ ⓑ ⚑ ♀ ⌓ 🏠 🛒 ⌁ Location E of town centre off A235

Hotel ★★★ 69% Aerodrome Hotel, Purley Way, CROYDON ☎ 020 8710 9000 84 en suite

Continued

RICHMOND (UPON THAMES)　　Map 04 TQ17

Richmond Sudbrook Park, Petersham TW10 7AS
☎ 020 8940 4351 (office) & 8940 7792 (shop)
📠 8940 8332/7914
e-mail: admin@richmondgolfclub.co.uk
A beautiful and historic wooded, parkland course on the edge of Richmond Park, with six par 3 holes. The 4th is often described as the best short hole in the south. Low scores are uncommon because cunningly sited trees call for great accuracy. The clubhouse is one of the most-distinguished small Georgian mansions in England.
18 holes, 6100yds, Par 70, SSS 70, Course record 65.
Club membership 650.
Visitors not weekends before 3.30pm. **Societies** apply in writing. **Green Fees** £40/£45 per 18 holes weekday. **Cards** 🖃 📧 🖾 🖾 📶 🔗 **Prof** Steve Burridge **Course Designer** Tom Down **Facilities** ⊗ ⊪ by arrangement ᴸ ♥♣♀⤙☂ ⚑ ♨ ⚐ ℓ **Conf** fac available Corporate Hospitality Days available **Location** 1.5m S off A307

Hotel ★★★ 69% The Richmond Hill Hotel, Richmond Hill, RICHMOND UPON THAMES
☎ 020 8940 2247 138 en suite

Royal Mid-Surrey Old Deer Park TW9 2SB
☎ 020 8940 1894 📠 020 8939 0150
e-mail: secretary@rmsgc.co.uk
A long playing parkland course. The flat fairways are cleverly bunkered. The 1st hole at 245yds from the medal tees is a tough par 3 opening hole. The 18th provides an exceptionally good par 4 finish with a huge bunker before the green to catch the not quite perfect long second. The Inner Course, while shorter than the Outer, offers a fair challenge to all golfers. Again the 18th offers a strong par 4 finish with bunkers threatening from the tee. A long second to a sloping, well-bunkered green will reward the accurate player.
Outer Course: 18 holes, 6343yds, Par 69, SSS 70, Course record 63.
Inner Course: 18 holes, 5544yds, Par 68, SSS 67.
Club membership 1400.
Visitors not weekends; contact in advance; handicap certificate. **Societies** apply in writing. **Green Fees** terms on application. **Cards** 🖃 🖾 📶 🔗 **Prof** Philip Talbot **Course Designer** J H Taylor **Facilities** ⊗ ⊪ ♥♣♀⤙☂ ⚑ ♨ ⚐ ℓ **Conf** fac available Corporate Hospitality Days available **Location** 0.5m N of Richmond off A316

Hotel ★★★ 69% The Richmond Hill Hotel, Richmond Hill, RICHMOND UPON THAMES
☎ 020 8940 2247 138 en suite

ROMFORD　　　　　　　　　　　Map 05 TQ58

Maylands Golf Club & Country Park
Colchester Rd, Harold Park RM3 0AZ
☎ 01708 346466 📠 01708 373080
18 holes, 6361yds, Par 71, SSS 70, Course record 65.
Course Designer H S Colt **Location** M25 junct 28, A12 0.5m towards London, club on right
Phone for further details

Hotel ⇧ Premier Travel Inn Romford East, Mercury Gardens, ROMFORD ☎ 08701 977220 40 en suite

Risebridge Golf Centre Risebridge Chase, Lower Bedfords Rd RM1 4DG
☎ 01708 741429 📠 01708 741429
e-mail: pa.jennings@virgin.net
18 holes, 6000yds, Par 71, SSS 70, Course record 66.
Course Designer Hawtree **Location** between Collier Row & Harold Hill
Phone for further details

Hotel ⇧ Premier Travel Inn East, Mercury Gardens, ROMFORD ☎ 08701 977220 40 en suite

Romford Heath Dr, Gidea Park RM2 5QB
☎ 01708 740986 📠 01708 752157
A many-bunkered parkland course with easy walking. It is said there are as many bunkers as there are days in the year. The ground is quick drying making a good course for winter play when other courses might be too wet.
18 holes, 6410yds, Par 72, SSS 70, Course record 64.
Club membership 693.
Visitors with member only weekends & bank holidays; contact professional in advance; handicap certificate. **Societies** phone in advance. **Green Fees** not confirmed. **Prof** Chris Goddard **Course Designer** H Colt **Facilities** ⊗ ⊪ ⊪ ♥♣♀⤒ ⚐ ℓ **Location** 1m NE on A118

Hotel ⇧ Premier Travel Inn Romford East, Mercury Gardens, ROMFORD ☎ 08701 977220 40 en suite

RUISLIP　　　　　　　　　　　　Map 04 TQ08

Ruislip Ickenham Rd HA4 7DQ
☎ 01895 638081 & 638835 📠 01895 635780

18 holes, 5700yds, Par 69, SSS 68, Course record 65.
Course Designer Sand Herd **Location** 0.5m SW on B466
Phone for further details

Hotel ★★★ 68% Quality Harrow Hotel, 12-22 Pinner Rd, HARROW ☎ 020 8427 3435 79 en suite 23 annexe en suite

SIDCUP　　　　　　　　　　　　Map 05 TQ47

Sidcup 7 Hurst Rd DA15 9AE
☎ 020 8300 2150 📠 0208 3002150
e-mail: sidcupgolfclub@tiscali.co.uk
Easy walking parkland course with two lakes and the river Shuttle running through.
9 holes, 5722yds, Par 68, SSS 68.
Club membership 370.
Visitors not weekends & bank holidays; contact in advance. **Societies** contact in advance. **Green Fees** terms on application. **Course Designer** James Braid **Facilities** ⊗ ⊪ ⊪ ♥♣♀⤒ ⚐ **Location** N of town centre off A222

Continued

Hotel ★★★★ 67% Bexleyheath Marriott Hotel, 1 Broadway, BEXLEYHEATH
☎ 0870 400 7245 142 en suite

SOUTHALL   Map 04 TQ17

West Middlesex Greenford Rd UB1 3EE
☎ 020 8574 3450 ▪ 020 8574 2383
e-mail: westmid.gc@virgin.net
Gently undulating parkland course founded in 1891, the oldest private course in Middlesex designed by James Braid.
18 holes, 6119yds, Par 69, SSS 69, Course record 64.
Club membership 600.
Visitors not before 2pm weekends in summer, not pm in winter; contact in advance. **Societies** apply in advance.
Green Fees Mon £14 per round; Wed £16, Tue, Thu-Fri £25; Sat-Sun £30; summer Fri after 3pm £16. **Cards** ▭ ▭ ▭ ▭ ▯ **Prof** T Talbot **Course Designer** James Braid **Facilities** ⊗ ⊞ ⅃ ⚑ ♀ ☖ ☎ ⚐ **Conf** fac available
Location W of town centre on A4127

Hotel ★★★ 66% Best Western Master Robert Hotel, 366 Great West Rd, HOUNSLOW ☎ 020 8570 6261 96 annexe en suite

STANMORE   Map 04 TQ19

Stanmore 29 Gordon Av HA7 2RL
☎ 020 8954 2599 ▪ 020 8954 2599
e-mail: secretary@stanmoregolfclub.co.uk
Stanmore is a quiet and peaceful parkland course set in the suburbs of north-west London with incredible views over the Thames basin from the 3th and 5th tees. The course is short but very challenging as all the fairways are lined with trees. Accuracy plays a major role and notable holes are the 2nd, 8th, 11th and 13th. The signature hole is the par 4 7th, played over a fir tree from an elevated tee onto the fairway.
18 holes, 5885yds, Par 68, SSS 68, Course record 61.
Club membership 500.
Visitors contact professional 020 8954 2599 **Societies** phone in advance for booking sheet. **Green Fees** Mon & Fri: £17; Tue-Thu: £25, £35 per day weekends after 12.30pm. **Cards** ▭ ▭ ▭ ▭ ▯ **Prof** J Reynolds **Course Designer** Dr A MacKenzie **Facilities** ⊗ ⊞ ⅃ ⚑ ♀ ☖ ☎ ⚐ **Conf** Corporate Hospitality Days available
Location S of town centre between Stanmore & Belmont

Hotel ★★★ 68% Quality Harrow Hotel, 12-22 Pinner Rd, HARROW ☎ 020 8427 3435 79 en suite 23 annexe en suite

SURBITON   Map 04 TQ16

Surbiton Woodstock Ln KT9 1UG
☎ 020 8398 3101 (Sec) ▪ 020 8339 0992
e-mail: gill.whitelock@surbitongolfclub.com
Parkland course with easy walking.
18 holes, 6055yds, Par 70, SSS 69, Course record 63.
Club membership 700.
Visitors not am Tue (Ladies Day); phone in advance; handicap certificate; with member only at weekends & bank holidays. **Societies** Mon, Fri. **Green Fees** not confirmed. **Prof** Paul Milton **Course Designer** Tom Dunn **Facilities** ⊗ ⅃ ⚑ ♀ ☖ ☎ ⚐ **Location** A3 Hook junct, A309 S 2m, left onto Woodstock Ln

Hotel ⭑ Premier Travel Inn Chessington, Leatherhead Rd, CHESSINGTON ☎ 08701 977057 42 en suite

TWICKENHAM   Map 04 TQ17

Amida Staines Rd TW2 5JD
☎ 0845 2309 111 ▪ 020 8783 9475
e-mail: hampton.golf.shop@amidaclubs.com
A nine-hole pay and play course situated within 70 acres of mature parkland with a water feature coming into play on the 2nd and 3rd holes. The course is mature but has undergone extensive recent improvement work, including new tees and greens and the installation of an automated irrigation system.
9 holes, 2788yds, Par 35, SSS 69.
Club membership 100.
Visitors advisable to book in advance for weekends & bank holidays. **Societies** apply in advance by phone or writing. **Green Fees** £8 per nine holes ((£10 weekends & bank holidays). **Cards** ▭ ▭ ▭ ▯ **Prof** Suzy Watt **Facilities** ⊗ ⊞ ⅃ ⚑ ♀ ☖ ☎ ⚐ **Leisure** hard tennis courts, heated indoor swimming pool, squash, sauna, solarium, gymnasium, indoor virtual golf. **Conf** fac available Corporate Hospitality Days available **Location** 2m W on A305

Hotel ★★★ 69% The Richmond Hill Hotel, Richmond Hill, RICHMOND UPON THAMES
☎ 020 8940 2247 138 en suite

Strawberry Hill Wellesley Rd, Strawberry Hill TW2 5SD
☎ 020 8894 0165 ▪ 020 8898 0786
e-mail: secretary@shgc.net
Parkland course with easy walking.
9 holes, 4762yds, Par 64, SSS 63, Course record 59.
Club membership 300.
Visitors contact in advance; with member only at weekends. **Societies** apply in writing. **Green Fees** £25/£18 per day, £18/£11 per 18 holes, £14/£8 per nine holes. **Cards** ▭ **Prof** Peter Buchan **Course Designer** JH Taylor **Facilities** ⊗ ⚑ ⅃ ♀ ☖ ☎ ⚐ **Location** S of town centre off A316

Hotel ★★★ 69% The Richmond Hill Hotel, Richmond Hill, RICHMOND UPON THAMES
☎ 020 8940 2247 138 en suite

UPMINSTER   Map 05 TQ58

Upminster 114 Hall Ln RM14 1AU
☎ 01708 222788 (Secretary) ▪ 01708 222484
e-mail: thesecretary@upminstergolfclub.com
The meandering River Ingrebourne features on several holes of this partly undulating parkland course situated on one side of the river valley. It provides a challenge for golfers of all abilities. The clubhouse is a beautiful Grade II listed building.
18 holes, 6076yds, Par 69, SSS 69, Course record 64.
Club membership 1000.
Visitors not weekends; contact in advance. **Societies** phone initially. **Green Fees** not confirmed. **Prof** Steve Cipa **Course Designer** WG Key **Facilities** ⊗ ⊞ ⅃ ⚑ ♀ ☖ ☎ ⚐ **Location** junct M25 & A127, 2m W

Hotel ⭑ Premier Travel Inn Romford East, Mercury Gardens, ROMFORD ☎ 08701 977220 40 en suite

UXBRIDGE   Map 04 TQ08

Stockley Park Stockley Park UB11 1AQ
☎ 020 8813 5700 📠 020 8813 5655
e-mail: k.soper@stockleyparkgolf.com
**Hilly and challenging parkland championship course
designed by Trent Jones in 1993 and situated within 2m
of Heathrow Airport.**
18 holes, 6548yds, Par 72, SSS 71.
Visitors six day advance reservation facility. **Societies**
phone for details. **Green Fees** £26 per round (£37
weekends). **Cards** ⊞ ▦ ▦ ▦ 🅢 🄎 **Prof** Stuart Birch
Course Designer Robert Trent Jones Snr **Facilities** ⊗ ⓑ
🍺 ♉ ⚘ 🏠 ⛴ ➤ ⚒ ♂ **Conf** Corporate Hospitality Days
available **Location** M4 junct 4, 1m N off A408
∙∙∙∙∙∙∙∙∙∙∙∙∙∙∙∙∙∙∙∙∙∙∙∙∙∙∙∙∙∙∙∙∙∙
Hotel ★★★★ 76% Crowne Plaza London - Heathrow,
Stockley Rd, WEST DRAYTON
☎ 0870 400 9140 458 en suite

Uxbridge The Drive, Harefield Place UB10 8AQ
☎ 01895 237287 📠 01895 813539
e-mail: higolf@btinternet.com

18 holes, 5750yds, Par 68, SSS 68, Course record 66.
Location 2m N off B467
Phone for further details
∙∙∙∙∙∙∙∙∙∙∙∙∙∙∙∙∙∙∙∙∙∙∙∙∙∙∙∙∙∙∙∙∙∙
Hotel ★★★★ 76% Crowne Plaza London - Heathrow,
Stockley Rd, WEST DRAYTON
☎ 0870 400 9140 458 en suite

WEMBLEY   Map 04 TQ18

Sudbury Bridgewater Rd HA0 1AL
☎ 020 8902 3713 📠 020 8902 3713
e-mail: enquiries@sudburygolfclubltd.co.uk
Undulating parkland course near the centre of London.

18 holes, 6282yds, Par 69, SSS 70, Course record 63.
Club membership 650.
Visitors handicap certificate; with member only weekends.
Societies apply in writing. **Green Fees** £25 per 18 holes.

Cards ⊞ ▦ ▦ 🅢 🄎 **Prof** Neil Jordan **Course
Designer** Colt **Facilities** ⊗ ⅏ ⓑ 🍺 ♉ ⚘ 🏠 ⛴ ♂
Conf fac available **Location** SW of town centre on A4090
∙∙∙∙∙∙∙∙∙∙∙∙∙∙∙∙∙∙∙∙∙∙∙∙∙∙∙∙∙∙∙∙∙∙
Hotel ★★★ 67% The Bridge Hotel, Western Av,
GREENFORD ☎ 020 8566 6246 68 en suite

WEST DRAYTON   Map 04 TQ07

Heathpark Stockley Rd UB7 9NA
☎ 01895 444232 📠 01895 444232
9 holes, 2032yds, Par 64, SSS 60, Course record 64.
Course Designer Neal Coles **Location** M4 junct 4, off
A408
Phone for further details
∙∙∙∙∙∙∙∙∙∙∙∙∙∙∙∙∙∙∙∙∙∙∙∙∙∙∙∙∙∙∙∙∙∙
Hotel ★★★★ 76% Crowne Plaza London - Heathrow,
Stockley Rd, WEST DRAYTON
☎ 0870 400 9140 458 en suite

WOODFORD GREEN   Map 05 TQ49

Woodford Sunset Av IG8 0ST
☎ 020 8504 3330 & 8504 0553 📠 020 8559 0504
e-mail: office@woodfordgolfclub.fsnet.co.uk
**Forestland course on the edge of Epping Forest. Views
over the Lea Valley to the London skyline. When
played as 18 holes from dual tees, the course is
comprised of four par 3s, two par 5s and 12
par 4s. Although fairly short, the tree-lined fairways
and subtle undulations provide and excellent test of
golfing skill.**
9 holes, 5806yds, Par 70, SSS 68, Course record 66.
Club membership 350.
Visitors not Sat, am Sun; advisable to contact in advance;
must wear major item of red. **Societies** phone for details.
Green Fees £15 per 18 holes; £9 per nine holes. **Prof** Jon
Robson **Course Designer** Tom Dunn **Facilities** ⊗ 🍺 ♉
⚘ 🏠 **Conf** Corporate Hospitality Days available
Location NW of town centre off A104

GREATER MANCHESTER

ALTRINCHAM   Map 07 SJ78

Altrincham Stockport Rd WA15 7LP
☎ 0161 928 0761 📠 0161 928 8542
e-mail: scott.partington@tclt.co.uk
**Municipal parkland course with easy walking, water on
many holes, rolling contours and many trees. Driving
range in grounds.**
18 holes, 6385yds, Par 71, SSS 69.
Club membership 350.
Visitors book in advance via course office. **Societies** by
arrangement. **Green Fees** £10 per round (£13 weekends &
bank holidays). **Cards** ⊞ ▦ ▦ 🅢 🄎 **Prof** Scott
Partington **Facilities** ⊗ ⅏ ♉ ⚘ 🏠 ⛴ ♂ (**Location**
0.75m E of town centre on A560
∙∙∙∙∙∙∙∙∙∙∙∙∙∙∙∙∙∙∙∙∙∙∙∙∙∙∙∙∙∙∙∙∙∙
Hotel ★★★ 68% Cresta Court Hotel, Church St,
ALTRINCHAM ☎ 0161 927 7272 136 en suite

Dunham Forest Oldfield Ln WA14 4TY
☎ 0161 928 2605 📠 0161 929 8975
e-mail: email@dunhamforestgolfclub.com
**Attractive parkland course cut through magnificent
beech woods.**
18 holes, 6636yds, Par 72, SSS 72.
Club membership 680.

Continued   *Continued*

Visitors not weekends, bank holidays by arrangement. **Societies** apply in writing or phone in advance. **Green Fees** not confirmed. **Cards** ⊞ 💳 🏧 💳 📱 **Prof** Ian Wrigley **Course Designer** Dave Thomas **Facilities** ⊗ ⅏ by arrangement 🛍 🍺♀⏚🏠🍴🐾🚜 ✓ **Leisure** hard tennis courts. **Conf** Corporate Hospitality Days available **Location** 1.5m W off A56

Hotel ★★★ 66% Quality Hotel Altrincham, Langham Rd, Bowdon, ALTRINCHAM ☎ 0161 928 7121 91 en suite

Ringway Hale Mount, Hale Barns WA15 8SW
☎ 0161 980 8432 (pro) & 0161 980 2630
📠 0160 980 4414
e-mail: enquiries@ringwaygolfclub.co.uk
Parkland course, with interesting natural hazards. Easy walking and good views over the Pennines and Peak District.
18 holes, 6482yds, Par 71, SSS 71, Course record 65.
Club membership 800.
Visitors not before 9.30am, 1-2pm & play restricted Tue, Fri-Sun; contact in advance; handicap certificate. **Societies** phone for availability. **Green Fees** £40 (£50 weekends). **Cards** ⊞ 💳 🏧 💳 📱 **Prof** Nick Ryan **Course Designer** Colt **Facilities** ⊗ ⅏ 🛍 🍺♀⏚🏠🐾 ✓ **Conf** Corporate Hospitality Days available **Location** M56 junct 6, A538 for 1m signed Hale, right onto Shay Ln

Hotel ★★★ 68% Cresta Court Hotel, Church St, ALTRINCHAM ☎ 0161 927 7272 136 en suite

ASHTON-IN-MAKERFIELD   Map 07 SJ59

Ashton-in-Makerfield Garswood Park, Liverpool Rd WN4 0YT
☎ 01942 719330 📠 01942 719330
18 holes, 6250yds, Par 70, SSS 70, Course record 63.
Location M6 junct 24, 5m W on A580
Phone for further details

Hotel ⏶ Premier Travel Inn Wigan South, 53 Warrington Rd, Ashton-in-Makerfield, WIGAN ☎ 0870 9906582 28 en suite

ASHTON-UNDER-LYNE   Map 07 SJ99

Ashton-under-Lyne Gorsey Way, Higher Hurst OL6 9HT
☎ 0161 330 1537 📠 0161 330 6673
e-mail: info@ashtongolfclub.co.uk
A testing, varied moorland course, with large greens. Easy walking.
18 holes, 5754yds, Par 69, SSS 68.
Club membership 760.
Visitors contact in advance. **Societies** apply in advance. **Green Fees** £27.50 per day. **Prof** Colin Boyle **Facilities** ⊗ ⅏ 🛍 🍺♀⏚🏠 ✓ **Conf** fac available Corporate Hospitality Days available **Location** N off B6194

Hotel ★★★★ 64% Menzies Avant Hotel, Windsor Rd, Manchester St, OLDHAM ☎ 0161 627 5500 103 en suite

Dukinfield Lyne Edge, Yew Tree Ln SK16 5DB
☎ 0161 338 2340 📠 0161 303 0205
e-mail: dgclub@tiscali.co.uk
Recently extended, tricky hillside course with several challenging par 3s and a very long par 5.
18 holes, 5338yds, Par 67, SSS 66.
Club membership 500.

Visitors not pm Wed; with member only weekends; advisable to contact in advance; must play from yellow blocks. **Societies** apply by writing or phone. **Green Fees** £20 per day. **Prof** David Green **Facilities** ⊗ ⅏ 🛍 🍺♀⏚ 🏠 ✓ **Conf** Corporate Hospitality Days available **Location** S off B6175

Hotel ⏶ Premier Travel Inn Manchester (Mottram), Stockport Rd, Mottram, HYDE ☎ 0870 9906334 83 en suite

BOLTON   Map 07 SD70

Bolton Lostock Park, Chorley New Rd BL6 4AJ
☎ 01204 843067 & 843278 📠 01204 843067
e-mail: boltongolf@lostockpark.fsbusiness.co.uk
This well-maintained heathland course is always a pleasure to visit. The 12th hole should be treated with respect and so too should the final four holes which have ruined many a card.
18 holes, 6237yds, Par 70, SSS 70, Course record 64.
Club membership 612.
Visitors not before 4pm Tue, before 10am, 12-2pm & competition days. **Societies** not Tue, Sat or Sun, write or phone in advance. **Green Fees** £25 (winter £20).
Prof R Longworth **Facilities** ⊗ ⅏ 🛍 🍺♀⏚🏠 ✓ **Conf** fac available Corporate Hospitality Days available **Location** 3m W of Bolton on A673

Hotel ⏶ Premier Travel Inn Bolton, 991 Chorley New Rd, Horwich, BOLTON ☎ 08701 977282 40 en suite

Breightmet Red Bridge, Ainsworth BL2 5PA
☎ 01204 527381
9 holes, 6416yds, Par 72, SSS 71, Course record 68.
Location E of town centre off A58
Phone for further details

Hotel ★★★★ 71% Last Drop Village Hotel & Spa, The Last Drop Village & Hotel, Bromley Cross, BOLTON ☎ 01204 591131 118 en suite 10 annexe en suite

Deane Broadford Rd, Deane BL3 4NS
☎ 01204 61944 (professional) & 651808 (secretary)
📠 01204 652047
Undulating parkland course with small ravines on approaches to some holes.
18 holes, 5652yds, Par 68, SSS 67, Course record 64.
Club membership 470.
Visitors restricted weekends; must be a member of a golf club or with member; contact in advance. **Societies** phone in advance & confirm in writing. **Green Fees** £24 per round (£26 weekends). **Prof** David Martindale **Facilities** ⊗ ⅏ 🛍 🍺♀⏚🏠 ✓ **Location** M61 junct 5, 1m towards Bolton

Hotel ⏶ Premier Travel Inn Bolton, 991 Chorley New Rd, Horwich, BOLTON ☎ 08701 977282 40 en suite

Dunscar Longworth Ln, Bromley Cross BL7 9QY
☎ 01204 303321 📠 01204 303321
e-mail: secretary@dunscargolfclub.fsnet.co.uk
A scenic moorland course with panoramic views.
18 holes, 5982yds, Par 71, SSS 69, Course record 63.
Club membership 600.
Visitors phone in advance 01204 592992; handicap certificate. **Societies** apply in writing. **Green Fees** £25 per round (£35 weekends & bank holidays). **Prof** Gary

Continued   *Continued*

Treadgold **Facilities** ⊗ ⵀ 脇 ☕ 🏆 ⚐ 🍴
Location 2m N off A666

....

Hotel ⇧ Travelodge Bolton West, Bolton West Service
Area, Horwich, BOLTON ☎ 08700 850 950   32 en suite

Great Lever & Farnworth Plodder Ln,
Farnworth BL4 0LQ
☎ 01204 656137 📠 01204 656137
Downland course with easy walking.
18 holes, 6044yds, Par 70, SSS 69, Course record 67.
Club membership 600.
Visitors contact in advance; weekends by arrangement;
handicap certificate. **Societies** contact in advance. **Green
Fees** £25 (£30 weekends & bank holidays). **Prof** Tony
Howarth **Facilities** ⊗ ⵀ 脇 ☕ 🏆 ⚐ 🍴
Location M61 junct 4, 1m

....

Hotel ★★★★ 71% Last Drop Village Hotel & Spa, The
Last Drop Village, Bromley Cross, BOLTON
☎ 01204 591131 118 en suite   10 annexe en suite

Harwood Roading Brook Rd, Harwood BL2 4JD
☎ 01204 522878 & 524233 📠 01204 524233
e-mail: secretary@harwoodgolfclub.co.uk
Mainly flat parkland course.
18 holes, 5813yds, Par 70, SSS 68, Course record 65.
Club membership 590.
Visitors member of golf club & handicap certificate; with
member only weekends. **Societies** contact the Secretary by
phone, e-mail or in writing. **Green Fees** £20 per round.
Prof C Maroney **Course Designer** G Shuttleworth
Facilities ⊗ ⵀ 脇 ☕ 🏆 ⚐ 🍴 **Location** 2.5m NE off
B6196

....

Hotel ⇧ Premier Travel Inn Bolton, 991 Chorley New Rd,
Horwich, BOLTON ☎ 08701 977282   40 en suite

Old Links Chorley Old Rd, Montserrat BL1 5SU
☎ 01204 842307 📠 01204 842307 ext 25
e-mail: mail@boltonoldlinks.co.uk
Championship moorland course.
18 holes, 6469yds, Par 71, SSS 72.
Club membership 600.
Visitors restricted weekends; contact in advance. **Societies**
apply by letter or phone. **Green Fees** £30 per day (£40
weekends & bank holidays). **Prof** Paul Horridge **Course
Designer** Dr A MacKenzie **Facilities** ⊗ ⵀ 脇 ☕ 🏆 ⚐ 🍴
🔧 🍴 **Conf** fac available **Location** NW of town centre on
B6226

....

Hotel ⇧ Travelodge Bolton West, Bolton West Service
Area, Horwich, BOLTON ☎ 08700 850 950   32 en suite

Regent Park Links Rd, Chorley New Rd BL6 4AF
☎ 01204 495421 📠 01204 844620
Parkland course.
18 holes, 6130yds, Par 70, SSS 69, Course record 67.
Club membership 200.
Visitors must book six days in advance. **Societies** phone in
advance 01204 495421. **Green Fees** £10 per round (£12.50
weekends). **Cards** 🖃 🖩 🖃 💳 🖃 🐾 📶 **Prof** Neil
Brazell **Course Designer** James Braid **Facilities** ⊗ ⵀ 脇
☕ 🏆 ⚐ 🍴 🍴 🍴 **Conf** Corporate Hospitality Days
available **Location** M61 junct 6, 1m E off A673

....

Hotel ⇧ Travelodge Bolton West, Bolton West Service
Area, Horwich, BOLTON ☎ 08700 850 950   32 en suite

Turton Wood End Farm, Chapeltown Rd,
Bromley Cross BL7 9QH
☎ 01204 852235
18 holes, 6124yds, Par 70, SSS 69, Course record 68.
Course Designer Alex Herd **Location** 3m N off A666,
signs for Last Drop Village
Phone for further details

....

Hotel ★★★★ 71% Last Drop Village Hotel & Spa,
The Last Drop Village & Hotel, Bromley Cross,
BOLTON ☎ 01204 591131 118 en suite
10 annexe en suite

BRAMHALL   Map 07 SJ88

Bramall Park 20 Manor Rd SK7 3LY
☎ 0161 485 7101 📠 0161 485 7101
e-mail: secretary@bramallparkgolfclub.co.uk
**An attractive parkland course with some testing
lengthy par 4s, especially following the recent
completion of a radical re-bunkering of the whole
course.**
18 holes, 6224yds, Par 70, SSS 70, Course record 63.
Club membership 829.
Visitors contact professional or club secretary.
Societies apply in writing or phone in advance. **Green
Fees** £38 per day, £34 per round (£45/40 weekends & bank
holidays). **Prof** M Proffitt **Course Designer** James Braid
Facilities ⊗ ⵀ 脇 ☕ 🏆 ⚐ 🍴 **Conf** Corporate
Hospitality Days available **Location** NW of town centre
off B5149

....

Hotel ★★★ 61% The County Hotel, Bramhall Ln South,
BRAMHALL ☎ 0870 609 6148   65 en suite

Bramhall Ladythorn Rd SK7 2EY
☎ 0161 439 6092 📠 0161 439 0264
e-mail: office@bramhallgolfclub.com
Undulating parkland course, easy walking.
18 holes, 6340yds, Par 70, SSS 70.
Club membership 700.
Visitors contact in advance. **Societies** apply in writing.
Green Fees terms on application. **Prof** Richard Green
Facilities ⊗ ⵀ by arrangement 脇 ☕ 🏆 ⚐ 🍴 🐾 🍴 **Conf**
Corporate Hospitality Days available **Location** E of town
centre off A5102

....

Hotel ★★★ 61% The County Hotel, Bramhall Ln South,
BRAMHALL ☎ 0870 609 6148   65 en suite

BURY   Map 07 SD81

Bury Unsworth Hall, Blackford Bridge, Manchester Rd
BL9 9TJ
☎ 0161 766 4897 📠 0161 796 3480
**Moorland course, difficult in part. Tight and good test
of golf.**
18 holes, 5961yds, Par 69, SSS 69, Course record 61.
Club membership 650.
Visitors not normally weekends; contact in advance.
Societies phone 0161 766 4897. **Green Fees** £30 (£35
weekends). **Cards** 🖃 **Prof** G Coope **Course Designer**
MacKenzie **Facilities** ⊗ ⵀ 脇 ☕ 🏆 ⚐ 🍴 **Conf** fac
available Corporate Hospitality Days available
Location 2m S on A56

....

Hotel ★★★ 66% Bolholt Country Park Hotel, Walshaw
Rd, BURY ☎ 0161 762 4000 65 en suite

Lowes Park Hilltop, Lowes Rd BL9 6SU
☎ 0161 764 1231 📠 0161 763 9503
e-mail: lowes@parkgc.fsnet.co.uk
Moorland course, with easy walking. Exposed outlook with good views.
9 holes, 6009yds, Par 70, SSS 69, Course record 65.
Club membership 350.
Visitors not Wed, Sat & Sun by appointment; contact in advance. Societies apply in writing. Green Fees £15 (£10 winter). Facilities ⊗ ⫴ ⽤ 🏌 ⛳ ⚑ ⛳ Conf fac available
Location N of town centre off A56
....
Hotel ★★★ 66% Bolholt Country Park Hotel, Walshaw Rd, BURY ☎ 0161 762 4000 65 en suite

Walmersley Garretts Close, Walmersley BL9 6TE
☎ 0161 764 1429 & 0161 764 7770 📠 0161 764 7770
18 holes, 5341yds, Par 69, SSS 66.
Course Designer S Marnoch **Location** 2m N off A56
Phone for further details
....
Hotel ★★★ 66% Bolholt Country Park Hotel, Walshaw Rd, BURY ☎ 0161 762 4000 65 en suite

CHEADLE Map 07 SJ88

Cheadle Cheadle Rd SK8 1HW
☎ 0161 491 4452
e-mail: cheadlegolfclub@msn.com
Parkland course with hazards on every hole, from sand bunkers and copses to a stream across six of the fairways.
9 holes, 5006yds, Par 64, SSS 65.
Club membership 425.
Visitors not Tue, Sat & restricted Sun; contact in advance; handicap certificate & member of golf club. Societies apply in writing to secretary. Green Fees £25 (£28 weekends). Prof D Cain Course Designer T Renouf Facilities ⊗ ⫴ ⽤ 🏌 ⛳ ⚑ ⛳ Location S of village off A5149
....
Hotel ★★ 69% The Wycliffe Hotel, 74 Edgeley Rd, Edgeley, STOCKPORT ☎ 0161 477 5395 18 en suite

DENTON Map 07 SJ99

Denton Manchester Rd M34 2GG
☎ 0161 336 3218 📠 0161 336 4751
e-mail: dentongolfclub@btinternet.com
Easy, flat parkland course with brook running through. One notable hole is called Death and Glory.
18 holes, 6541yds, Par 72, SSS 71, Course record 66.
Club membership 740.
Visitors not weekends in summer; contact in advance. Societies apply in advance. Green Fees terms on application. Prof M Hollingworth Course Designer R McCauley Facilities ⊗ ⽤ 🏌 ⛳ ⚑ ⛳ Location M60 junct 24, 1.5m W on A57
....
Hotel ★★★ 65% Old Rectory Hotel, Meadow Ln, Haughton Green, Denton, MANCHESTER ☎ 0161 336 7516 30 en suite 6 annexe en suite

FAILSWORTH Map 07 SD80

Brookdale Medlock Rd M35 9WQ
☎ 0161 681 4534 📠 0161 688 6872
e-mail: info@brookdalegolfclub.co.uk
Challenging parkland course in the Medlock valley with great Pennine views, although only 5m from the

centre of Manchester. The river Medlock meanders through the course and features on six of the holes.
18 holes, 5864yds, Par 68, SSS 68, Course record 64.
Club membership 700.
Visitors advisable to contact in advance. Societies contact in advance. Green Fees terms on application. Prof Tony Cuppello Facilities ⊗ ⫴ ⽤ 🏌 ⛳ ⚑ ⛳ 🏌 ⛳
Location M60/A62 Oldham exit, towards Manchester, left at Nat West bank, left at road end & sharp right. Right at minirdbt, 0.5m on left
....
Hotel ★★★★ 64% Menzies Avant Hotel, Windsor Rd, Manchester St, OLDHAM ☎ 0161 627 5500 103 en suite

FLIXTON Map 07 SJ79

William Wroe Municipal Pennybridge Ln, Flixton Rd M41 5DX
☎ 0161 748 8680
18 holes, 4395yds, Par 64, SSS 65.
Location E of village off B5158, 3m from Manchester centre
Phone for further details
....
Hotel ⌂ Premier Travel Inn Manchester (Sale), Carrington Ln, Ashton-Upon-Mersey, SALE ☎ 08701 977179 40 en suite

GATLEY Map 07 SJ88

Gatley Waterfall Farm, Styal Rd, Heald Green SK8 3TW
☎ 0161 437 2091
e-mail: enquiries@gatleygolfclub.com
Parkland course. Moderately testing.
9 holes, 5934yds, Par 68, SSS 68, Course record 67.
Club membership 400.
Visitors not Tue, Sat; handicap certificate. Societies apply in writing or phone pro shop. Green Fees £20 per 18 holes. Cards 🟦 🟦 🟦 🟦 🟦 Prof James Matterson Facilities ⊗ ⫴ ⽤ 🏌 ⛳ ⚑ ⛳ Conf Corporate Hospitality Days available Location S of village off B5166
....
Hotel ★★★ 66% Belfry House Hotel, Stanley Rd, HANDFORTH ☎ 0161 437 0511 81 en suite

HAZEL GROVE Map 07 SJ98

Hazel Grove Buxton Rd SK7 6LU
☎ 0161 483 3978
Testing parkland course with tricky greens and water hazards coming into play on several holes. Year round play on the greens.
18 holes, 6310yds, Par 71, SSS 70, Course record 62.
Club membership 600.
Visitors contact in advance 0161 483 7272. Societies Mon Thu, Fri, apply in writing. Green Fees terms on application. Prof J Hopley Course Designer MacKenzie Facilities ⊗ ⫴ ⽤ 🏌 ⛳ ⚑ 🏌 ⛳ Conf fac available Corporate Hospitality Days available Location 1m E off A6
....
Hotel ★★★ 61% The County Hotel, Bramhall Ln South, BRAMHALL ☎ 0870 609 6148 65 en suite

HINDLEY Map 07 SD60

Hindley Hall Hall Ln WN2 2SQ
☎ 01942 255131 📠 01942 253871
18 holes, 5913yds, Par 69, SSS 68, Course record 64.
Location M61 junct 6, 3m, 1m N off A58
Phone for further details

Continued Continued

Hotel ★★★ 65% Quality Hotel Wigan, Riverway, WIGAN ☎ 01942 826888 88 en suite

HYDE
Map 07 SJ99

Werneth Low Werneth Low Rd, Gee Cross
SK14 3AF
☎ 0161 368 2503 336 9496(secretary) 📠 0161 320 0053
e-mail: adfwoodley@ukonline.co.uk
Hard walking but good views of six counties from this undulating moorland course, which is played in a 7-4-7 loop. Exposed to wind with small greens. A good test of golfing skill.
11 holes, 6113yds, Par 70, SSS 70, Course record 64. Club membership 375.
Visitors not am Tue, pm Thu, Sun & Sat by arrangement. **Societies** contact at least 14 days in advance. **Green Fees** terms on application. **Cards** 🃏 💳 📇 💵 **Prof** Tony Bacchus **Facilities** ⊗ ⅏ ᴮ 🍺 ♀ ♨ 🍴 🛒 ♂ **Conf** Corporate Hospitality Days available **Location** 2m S of town centre

Hotel ★★ 78% Wind in the Willows Hotel, Derbyshire Level, GLOSSOP ☎ 01457 868001 12 en suite

KEARSLEY
Map 07 SD70

Manor Moss Ln BL4 8SF
☎ 01204 701027 📠 01204 796914
18 holes, 5010yds, Par 66, SSS 64, Course record 65.
Course Designer Jeff Yates **Location** off A666 Manchester Rd
Phone for further details

Hotel ★★★ 63% Novotel Manchester West, Worsley Brow, WORSLEY ☎ 0161 799 3535 119 en suite

LITTLEBOROUGH
Map 07 SD91

Whittaker Whittaker Ln OL15 0LH
☎ 01706 378310
Moorland course with outstanding views of Hollingworth Lake Countryside Park and the Pennines.
9 holes, 5632yds, Par 68, SSS 67, Course record 61. Club membership 240.
Visitors not pm Tue, Sun. **Societies** apply to Secretary. **Green Fees** £14 per 18 holes (£18 weekend & bank holidays); reduced winter rates. **Facilities** ♀ ♨
Location 1.5m from Littleborough off A58

Hotel ★★★★ 62% Norton Grange Hotel, Manchester Rd, Castleton, ROCHDALE ☎ 01706 630788 51 en suite

MANCHESTER
Map 07 SJ89

Blackley Victoria Ave East, Blackley M9 7HW
☎ 0161 643 2980 & 654 7770 📠 0161 653 8300
18 holes, 6237yds, Par 70, SSS 70.
Location 4m N of city centre on Rochdale Rd
Phone for further details

Hotel ★★★ 76% Malmaison, Piccadilly, MANCHESTER ☎ 0161 278 1000 167 en suite

Chorlton-cum-Hardy Barlow Hall, Barlow Hall Rd, Chorlton-cum-Hardy M21 7JJ
☎ 0161 881 5830 📠 0161 881 4532
e-mail: chorltongolf@hotmail.com
Set in the grounds of Barlow Hall, this challenging parkland course winds its way around the way around

the banks of the Mersey. The testing opening holes lead up to the stroke 1 7th, an impressive 474yd par 4, with its elevated green. The course then meanders through parkland culminating at the par 4 18th.

Chorlton-cum-Hardy Golf Club

18 holes, 6039yds, Par 70, SSS 69, Course record 61. Club membership 750.
Visitors handicap certificate. **Societies** Thu, Fri, by booking. **Green Fees** £26 (£32 weekends & bank holidays). **Prof** David Valentine **Facilities** ⊗ ⅏ ᴮ 🍺 ♀ ♨ 🍴 🎯 ♂ **Conf** Corporate Hospitality Days available **Location** 4m S of Manchester, A5103/A5145

Hotel ★★★ 68% Willow Bank Hotel, 340-342 Wilmslow Rd, Fallowfield, MANCHESTER ☎ 0161 224 0461 117 en suite

Davyhulme Park Gleneagles Rd, Davyhulme
M41 8SA
☎ 0161 748 2260 📠 0161 747 4067
e-mail: davyhulmeparkgolfclub@email.com
Parkland course.
18 holes, 6237yds, Par 72, SSS 70, Course record 64. Club membership 700.
Visitors not Wed, Fri, weekends. **Societies** phone in advance. **Green Fees** terms on application. **Prof** Dean Butler **Facilities** ⊗ ⅏ ᴮ 🍺 ♀ ♨ ♂ **Leisure** snooker. **Conf** Corporate Hospitality Days available **Location** next to Trafford General Hospital

Hotel ⭒ Premier Travel Inn Manchester (Sale), Carrington Ln, Ashton-Upon-Mersey, SALE ☎ 08701 977179 40 en suite

Didsbury Ford Ln, Northenden M22 4NQ
☎ 0161 998 9278 📠 0161 902 3060
e-mail: golf@didsburygolfclub.com
18 holes, 6273yds, Par 70, SSS 70, Course record 60.
Location 6m S of city centre off A5145
Phone for further details

Hotel ⭒ Travelodge Manchester South, Kingsway, DIDSBURY ☎ 08700 850 950 62 en suite

Fairfield Boothdale, Booth Rd, Audenshaw M34 5QA
☎ 0161 301 4528 📠 0161 301 4254
e-mail: secretary@fairfieldgolf.co.uk
Parkland course set around a reservoir. Course demands particularly accurate placing of shots.
18 holes, 4956yds, Par 68, SSS 66, Course record 63. Club membership 450.
Visitors not am weekends, restricted Wed, Thu. **Societies** booking through Secretary. **Green Fees** not confirmed. **Prof** Stephen Pownell **Facilities** ⊗ ⅏ ᴮ 🍺 ♀ ♨ 🍴 ♂
Location 5m E of Manchester off A635

Continued

Continued

Hotel ★★★ 65% Old Rectory Hotel, Meadow Ln, Haughton Green, Denton, MANCHESTER
☎ 0161 336 7516 30 en suite 6 annexe en suite

Marriott Worsley Park Hotel & Country Club Worsley Park, Worsley M28 2QT
☎ 0161 975 2043 📠 0161 975 2058
Set in 200 acres of parkland with a range of tee positions, eight lakes and 70 strategically placed bunkers and providing an exciting challenge to golfers of all abilities, very often requiring brains rather than brawn to make a successful score.
18 holes, 6611yds, Par 71, SSS 72, Course record 61.
Club membership 400.
Visitors handicap certificate; contact in advance. Societies weekdays, phone in advance. Green Fees not confirmed.
Cards 📇 💳 💳 💳 💳 💳 🔋 Prof David Screeton
Course Designer Ross McMurray Facilities ⊗ ⫙ ⑂ ▣ ♀ ⚷ 🏕 🍴 🛏 🚲 ♿ ✓ Leisure heated indoor swimming pool, sauna, solarium, gymnasium, Short game area.
Conf fac available Location M60 junct 13, A585, course 0.5m on left

Hotel ★★★★ 69% Marriott Worsley Park Hotel & Country Club, Worsley Park, Worsley, MANCHESTER
☎ 0161 975 2000 158 en suite

Northenden Palatine Rd, Northenden M22 4FR
☎ 0161 998 4738 📠 0161 945 5592
e-mail: manager@northendengolfclub.com
Parkland course surrounded by the River Mersey.

18 holes, 6432yds, Par 72, SSS 71, Course record 64.
Club membership 800.
Visitors contact professional in advance 0161 945 3386.
Societies Tue, Fri, apply in advance to Secretary. Green Fees £28 per day (£32 weekends & bank holidays).
Prof J Curtis Course Designer Renouf Facilities ⊗ ⫙ ⑂ ▣ ♀ ⚷ 🏕 ✓ Leisure indoor teaching facility.
Conf Corporate Hospitality Days available
Location 6.5m S of city centre on B1567

Hotel ⬧ Travelodge Manchester South, Kingsway, DIDSBURY ☎ 08700 850 950 62 en suite

Withington 243 Palatine Rd, West Didsbury M20 2UE
☎ 0161 445 9544 📠 0161 445 5210
18 holes, 6410yds, Par 71, SSS 71.
Location 4m SW of city centre off B5167
Phone for further details

Hotel ⬧ Travelodge Manchester South, Kingsway, DIDSBURY ☎ 08700 850 950 62 en suite

---

Worsley Stableford Av, Worsley M30 8AP
☎ 0161 789 4202 📠 0161 789 3200
18 holes, 6252yds, Par 71, SSS 70, Course record 65.
Course Designer James Braid Location 6.5m NW of city centre off A572
Phone for further details

Hotel ★★★ 63% Novotel Manchester West, Worsley Brow, WORSLEY ☎ 0161 799 3535 119 en suite

MELLOR   Map 07 SJ98

Mellor & Townscliffe Gibb Ln, Tarden SK6 5NA
☎ 0161 427 2208 (secretary)
Scenic parkland and moorland course, undulating with some hard walking. Good views. Testing 200yd 9th hole, par 3.
18 holes, 5925yds, Par 70, SSS 69.
Club membership 650.
Visitors with member only weekends & bank holidays.
Societies apply by letter or phone. Green Fees £24 per day (£32 weekends & bank holidays). Prof Gary R Broadley
Facilities ⊗ ⫙ ⑂ ▣ ♀ ⚷ 🏕 ✓ Location 7m SE of Stockport off A626

Hotel ★★★ 69% Bredbury Hall Hotel & Country Club, Goyt Valley, BREDBURY ☎ 0161 430 7421 150 en suite

MIDDLETON   Map 07 SD80

Manchester Hopwood Cottage, Rochdale Rd M24 6QP
☎ 0161 643 3202 📠 0161 643 9174
e-mail: mgc@zen.co.uk
Moorland golf of unique character over a spaciously laid out course with generous fairways sweeping along to large greens. A wide variety of holes will challenge the golfer's technique, particularly the testing last three holes.
18 holes, 6519yds, Par 72, SSS 72, Course record 63.
Club membership 650.
Visitors restricted Wed & weekends; contact in advance.
Societies phone in advance. Green Fees not confirmed.
Cards 📇 💳 🔋 Prof Brian Connor Course Designer Shapland Colt Facilities ⊗ ⫙ ⑂ ▣ ♀ ⚷ 🏕 🛏 🚲 ✓ ⚑ Leisure snooker. Conf fac available Corporate Hospitality Days available Location 2.5m N off A664

Hotel ★★★★ 62% Norton Grange Hotel, Manchester Rd, Castleton, ROCHDALE ☎ 01706 630788 51 en suite

New North Manchester Rhodes House, Manchester Old Rd M24 4PE
☎ 0161 643 9033 📠 0161 643 7775
e-mail: secretary@nmgc.co.uk
A delightful moorland and parkland course with several water features. Challenging but fair for the accomplished golfer.
18 holes, 6527yds, Par 72, SSS 72, Course record 66.
Club membership 610.
Visitors not Sat; contact pro shop 0161 643 7094 for availability. Societies apply in writing. Green Fees £30 per day, £28 per round (£35 Sun). Prof Jason Peel Course Designer J Braid Facilities ⊗ ⫙ ⑂ ▣ ♀ ⚷ 🏕 ✓ Leisure 2 full size snooker tables. Location W of town centre off A576

Hotel ★★★★ 64% Menzies Avant Hotel, Windsor Rd, Manchester St, OLDHAM ☎ 0161 627 5500 103 en suite

MILNROW
Map 07 SD91

Tunshill Kiln Ln OL16 3TS
☎ 01706 342095
Testing moorland course with two demanding par 5s and out of bounds features on eight of the nine holes.
9 holes, 5743yds, Par 70, SSS 68, Course record 64. Club membership 300.
Visitors contact in advance; with member only weekends & arranged in advance. **Societies** apply in writing. **Green Fees** £12 weekdays only. **Facilities** ⊗ by arrangement ⫚ by arrangement ⌧ by arrangement ⌣ by arrangement ⌐
⚑ **Location** M62 junct 21, 1m NE off B6225

Hotel ★★★★ 62% Norton Grange Hotel, Manchester Rd, Castleton, ROCHDALE ☎ 01706 630788 51 en suite

OLDHAM
Map 07 SD90

Crompton & Royton Highbarn, Royton OL2 6RW
☎ 0161 624 0986 📠 0161 652 4711
e-mail: secretary@cromptonandroytongolfclub.co.uk
Undulating moorland course.
18 holes, 6214yds, Par 70, SSS 70, Course record 62. Club membership 700.
Visitors not Tue, Sat, restricted pm Sun & Wed; contact in advance. **Societies** apply in advance **Green Fees** not confirmed. **Prof** David Melling **Facilities** ⊗ ⫚ ⌧ ⌐ ⌣
⌣ ⌐ ⌐ **Leisure** practice nets. **Location** 0.5m NE of Royton

Hotel ★★★★ 64% Menzies Avant Hotel, Windsor Rd, Manchester St, OLDHAM ☎ 0161 627 5500 103 en suite

Oldham Lees New Rd OL4 5PN
☎ 0161 624 4986
Moorland course, with hard walking.
18 holes, 5122yds, Par 66, SSS 65, Course record 62. Club membership 320.
Visitors no restrictions. **Societies** contact in advance.
Green Fees £18 (£24 weekends & bank holidays).
Prof R Heginbotham **Facilities** ⊗ ⫚ ⌧ ⌐ ⌣ ⌐ ⌐ ⌐
Location 2.5m E off A669

Hotel ★★★★ 64% Menzies Avant Hotel, Windsor Rd, Manchester St, OLDHAM ☎ 0161 627 5500 103 en suite

Werneth Green Ln, Garden Suburb OL8 3AZ
☎ 0161 624 1190
Semi-moorland course, with a deep gully and stream crossing eight fairways. Testing 3rd hole (par 3).
18 holes, 5363yds, Par 68, SSS 66, Course record 61. Club membership 420.
Visitors not Tue, Thu & weekends by arrangement; contact in advance. **Societies** contact in advance. **Green Fees** £16 per day. **Prof** Roy Penney **Course Designer** Sandy Herd **Facilities** ⊗ ⫚ ⌧ ⌐ ⌣ ⌐ ⌐ **Conf** Corporate Hospitality Days available **Location** S of town ⌐entre off A627

Hotel ★★★★ 64% Menzies Avant Hotel, Windsor Rd, Manchester St, OLDHAM ☎ 0161 627 5500 103 en suite

PRESTWICH
Map 07 SD80

Heaton Park Municipal Heaton Park, Middleton Rd M25 2SW
☎ 0161 654 9899 📠 0161 653 2003
A parkland-style course in historic Heaton Park, with rolling hills and lakes, designed by five times Open

Champion, JH Taylor. It boasts some spectacular holes and is a good test of skill for golfers of all abilities.
Championship: 18 holes, 5755yds, Par 70, SSS 68.
Visitors no restrictions. **Societies** apply in writing or by phone to the centre manager. **Green Fees** £10 (£13.50 weekends). **Cards** ⊟ ▤ ▤ ▧ ⌐ **Course Designer** JH Taylor **Facilities** ⊗ ⫚ ⌐ ⌣ ⌐ ⌐ ⌐ ⌐ ⌐
Leisure fishing, 18-hole par 3 course. **Conf** fac available **Location** N of Manchester near M60 junct 19

Hotel ⌂ Premier Travel Inn Manchester West, East Lancs Rd, SWINTON ☎ 0870 9906480 27 en suite

Prestwich Hilton Ln M25 9XB
☎ 0161 773 1404 📠 0161 772 0700
Well-manicured tree-lined parkland course, near to Manchester city centre. A testing course with small greens.
18 holes, 4846yds, Par 65, SSS 65, Course record 60. Club membership 565.
Visitors weekdays by arrangement, restricted weekends, Ladies Day Tue. **Societies** apply in writing or phone.
Green Fees not confirmed. **Prof** Simon Wakefield
Facilities ⊗ ⫚ ⌐ ⌣ ⌐ ⌣ ⌐ ⌐ **Location** N of town centre on A6044

Hotel ★★★ 63% Novotel Manchester West, Worsley Brow, WORSLEY ☎ 0161 799 3535 119 en suite

ROCHDALE
Map 07 SD81

Castle Hawk Chadwick Ln, Castleton OL11 3BY
☎ 01706 640841 📠 01706 860587
e-mail: teeoff@castlehawk.co.uk
New Course: 9 holes, 2699yds, Par 34, SSS 34, Course record 30.
Old Course: 18 holes, 3189yds, Par 55, SSS 55.
Course Designer T Wilson **Location** M62 junct 20, S of Rochdale
Phone for further details

Hotel ★★★★ 62% Norton Grange Hotel, Manchester Rd, Castleton, ROCHDALE ☎ 01706 630788 51 en suite

Marland Park Springfield Park, Bolton Rd OL11 4RE
☎ 01706 656401 (weekends)
Parkland and moorland course in a valley. The River Roch adds an extra hazard to the course.
18 holes, 5237yds, Par 67, SSS 66, Course record 64. Club membership 300.
Visitors contact professional in advance. **Societies** phone in advance. **Green Fees** not confirmed. **Cards** ⊟ ▤ ▤
⌐ **Prof** David Wills **Facilities** ⌐ ⌐ ⌐ **Location** 1.5m SW off A58

Hotel ★★★★ 62% Norton Grange Hotel, Manchester Rd, Castleton, ROCHDALE ☎ 01706 630788 51 en suite

Rochdale Edenfield Rd OL11 5YR
☎ 01706 643818 📠 01706 861113
e-mail: office@rochdalegolfclub.fsnet.com
Parkland course with enjoyable golf and easy walking.
18 holes, 6050yds, Par 71, SSS 69, Course record 65. Club membership 750.
Visitors phone in advance. **Societies** apply in writing or phone. **Green Fees** £22 per day/round (£27 weekends & bank holidays). **Prof** Andrew Laverty **Course Designer** George Lowe **Facilities** ⊗ ⫚ ⌐ ⌣ ⌐ ⌣ ⌐ ⌐ ⌐ **Conf** fac available Corporate Hospitality Days available **Location** 1.75m W on A680

Continued

Continued

Hotel ★★★★ 62% Norton Grange Hotel, Manchester Rd, Castleton, ROCHDALE ☎ 01706 630788 51 en suite

ROMILEY   Map 07 SJ99

Romiley Goose House Green SK6 4LJ
☎ 0161 430 2392 ▤ 0161 430 7258
e-mail: office@romileygolfclub.org
Semi-parkland course on the edge of the Derbyshire Hills, providing a good test of golf with a number of outstanding holes, notably the 6th, 9th, 14th and 16th. The latter enjoys magnificent views from the tee.

18 holes, 6454yds, Par 70, SSS 71, Course record 66. Club membership 700.
Visitors not Thu, before 4pm Sat; contact in advance. **Societies** Tue, Wed, book in advance. **Green Fees** not confirmed. **Prof** Lee Paul Sullivan **Facilities** ⊗ ⅏ ⓛ ♥ ♀ ⌂ ⌂ ❦ ⌑ **Location** E of town centre off B6104

Hotel ★★ 69% The Wycliffe Hotel, 74 Edgeley Rd, Edgeley, STOCKPORT ☎ 0161 477 5395 18 en suite

SALE   Map 07 SJ79

Ashton on Mersey Church Ln M33 5QQ
☎ 0161 976 4390 & 962 3727 ▤ 0161 976 4390
e-mail: golf@aomgc.fsnet.co.uk
Parkland course with easy walking alongside the River Mersey.
9 holes, 6146yds, Par 71, SSS 69, Course record 66. Club membership 485.
Visitors not Tue, Sat; with member only Sun & bank holidays. **Societies** Apply in writing; not Tue, weekends. **Green Fees** £20.50. **Cards** ▦ **Prof** Mike Williams **Facilities** ⊗ ⅏ ⓛ ♥ ♀ ⌂ ⌂ ❦ **Leisure** sauna. **Conf** fac available **Location** M60 junct 7, 1m W off Glebelands Rd

Hotel ★★★ 68% Cresta Court Hotel, Church St, ALTRINCHAM ☎ 0161 927 7272 136 en suite

Sale Golf Rd M33 2XU
☎ 0161 973 1638 (Office) & 973 1730 (Pro)
▤ 0161 962 4217
e-mail: mail@salegolfclub.com
Tree-lined parkland course. Feature holes are the 13th - Watery Gap - and the par 3 3rd hole of 210yds over water. Four new holes in play from 2005.
18 holes, 6301yds, Par 70, SSS 69, Course record 63. Club membership 700.
Visitors not Sat; contact professional in advance. **Societies** apply by letter. **Green Fees** £28 per day (£33 weekends). **Cards** ▨ **Prof** Mike Stewart **Facilities** ⊗ ⅏ ⓛ ♥ ♀ ⌂ ⌂ ❦ **Conf** Corporate Hospitality Days available **Location** M60 junct 6. 0.5m. NW of town centre off A6144

Hotel ★★★ 68% Cresta Court Hotel, Church St, ALTRINCHAM ☎ 0161 927 7272 136 en suite

SHEVINGTON   Map 07 SD50

Gathurst 62 Miles Ln WN6 8EW
☎ 01257 255235 (Secretary) ▤ 01257 255953
Testing parkland course, slightly hilly.
18 holes, 6016yds, Par 70, SSS 69, Course record 64. Club membership 630.
Visitors not competition days; with member only weekends. **Societies** Mon, Tue, Thu, Fri, apply in writing to Secretary. **Green Fees** £30 per round. **Prof** David Clarke **Course Designer** N Pearson **Facilities** ⊗ ⅏ ⓛ ♥ ♀ ⌂ ⌂ ❦ **Location** M6 junct 27, 1m SW of village on B5375

Hotel ★★★★ 63% Kilhey Court Hotel, Chorley Rd, Standish, WIGAN ☎ 01257 472100 62 en suite

STALYBRIDGE   Map 07 SJ99

Stamford Oakfield House, Huddersfield Rd SK15 3PY
☎ 01457 832126
e-mail: stamford.golfclub@totalise.co.uk
Undulating moorland course.
18 holes, 5701yds, Par 70, SSS 68, Course record 62. Club membership 600.
Visitors restricted weekends after 3pm. **Societies** apply in writing or phone 0161 633 5721. **Green Fees** £20 per day (£25 weekends after 3pm). **Cards** ▦ ▨ ▤ ▨ ▦ ▨ **Prof** Brian Badger **Facilities** ⊗ ⅏ ⓛ ♥ ♀ ⌂ ⌂ ❦ **Conf** fac available Corporate Hospitality Days available **Location** 2m NE off A635

Guesthouse ♦♦♦♦ Mallons Restaurant with Guest Rooms, 792-794 Huddersfield Rd, Austerlands, OLDHAM ☎ 0161 622 1234 5 rms (4 en suite)

STANDISH   Map 07 SD51

Standish Court Rectory Ln WN6 0XD
☎ 01257 425777 ▤ 01257 425777
e-mail: info@standishgolf.co.uk
Undulating 18-hole parkland course, not overly long but provides a good test for all levels of players. Front nine more open with room for errors, back nine very scenic through woodland, a number of tight driving holes. Greens in excellent condition.
18 holes, 4860yds, Par 68, SSS 64. Club membership 375.
Visitors phone up to week in advance for tee time; dress code. **Societies** phone in advance. **Green Fees** Mon-Tue £8.50, Wed-Fri £12 (£16 weekends & bank holidays). **Cards** ▦ ▨ ▤ ▨ ▨ **Prof** Blake Toone **Course Designer** P Dawson **Facilities** ⊗ ⅏ ⓛ ♥ ♀ ⌂ ⌂ ✦ ❦ **Conf** fac available Corporate Hospitality Days available **Location** E of town centre on B5239

Hotel ★★★★ 63% Kilhey Court Hotel, Chorley Rd, Standish, WIGAN ☎ 01257 472100 62 en suite

STOCKPORT   Map 07 SJ89

Heaton Moor Heaton Mersey SK4 3NX
☎ 0161 432 2134 ▤ 0161 432 2134
e-mail: hmgc@ukgateway.net
Pleasantly situated in a gently undulating parkland course with two separate nine holes starting from the clubhouse. Narrow fairways are challenging.

Continued   *Continued*

18 holes, 5968, Par 70, SSS 69, Course record 66.
Club membership 450.
Visitors restricted Tue, bank holidays & Sat in summer.
Societies apply in writing. **Green Fees** terms on
application. **Cards** ▦ ▦ ▦ ▦ **Prof** Simon Marsh
Facilities ⊗ ⅢⅢ ⅃ ▤ ♀ ⅃ ⅋ **Location** N of town
centre off B5169

....

Hotel ★★★ 69% Bredbury Hall Hotel & Country Club,
Goyt Valley, BREDBURY ☎ 0161 430 7421 150 en suite

Houldsworth Houldsworth Park, Reddish SK5 6BN
☎ 0161 442 1712 ▤ 0161 947 9678
e-mail: secretary@houldsworthgolfclub.co.uk
Flat parkland course, tree-lined and with water
hazards. Testing holes 9th (par 5) and 13th (par 5).
18 holes, 6209yds, Par 71, SSS 70, Course record 65.
Club membership 680.
Visitors not weekends & bank holidays unless by
arrangement with professional. **Societies** Mon, Thu, Fri,
phone Secretary. **Green Fees** terms on application.
Prof Steven McLean **Course Designer** Dave Thomas
Facilities ⊗ ⅢⅢ ⅃ ▤ ♀ ⅃ ▤ ⅋ **Location** 4m SE of
city centre off A6

....

Hotel ★★★ 68% Willow Bank Hotel, 340-342 Wilmslow
Rd, Fallowfield, MANCHESTER
☎ 0161 224 0461 117 en suite

Marple Barnsfold Rd, Hawk Green, Marple SK6 7EL
☎ 0161 427 2311 & 427 1195(pro) ▤ 0161 427 2311
e-mail: marple.golf.club@ukgateway-net
Parkland course with several ponds or other water
hazards. Gentle slopes overlooking the Cheshire plains.
18 holes, 5552yds, Par 68, SSS 67, Course record 66.
Club membership 640.
Visitors restricted pm Thu, am Tue & weekend
competition days. **Societies** apply in writing to professional
or apply by phone. **Green Fees** terms on application.
Prof David Myers **Facilities** ⊗ ⅢⅢ ⅃ ▤ ♀ ⅃ ⅋
Leisure snooker. **Conf** Corporate Hospitality Days
available **Location** S of town centre

....

Hotel ★★★ 69% Bredbury Hall Hotel & Country Club,
Goyt Valley, BREDBURY ☎ 0161 430 7421 150 en suite

Reddish Vale Southcliffe Rd, Reddish SK5 7EE
☎ 0161 480 2359 ▤ 0161 480 2359
e-mail: admin@reddishvalegolfclub.co.uk
Undulating heathland course designed by Dr A
MacKenzie and situated in the Tame valley.
18 holes, 6100yds, Par 69, SSS 69, Course record 64.
Club membership 550.
Visitors with member only weekends. **Societies** not
weekends, contact in writing. **Green Fees** £25-£40.
Prof Bob Freeman **Course Designer** Dr A MacKenzie
Facilities ⊗ ⅢⅢ ⅃ ▤ ♀ ⅃ ▤ ⅋ **Conf** Corporate
Hospitality Days available **Location** M6 junct 1/27, off
Reddish Rd

....

Hotel ★★ 69% The Wycliffe Hotel, 74 Edgeley Rd,
Edgeley, STOCKPORT ☎ 0161 477 5395 18 en suite

Stockport Offerton Rd, Offerton SK2 5HL
☎ 0161 427 8369 (Secretary) & 427 2421 (Pro)
▤ 0161 449 8293
e-mail: info@stockportgolf.co.uk
A beautifully situated course in wide open countryside
with views of the Cheshire and Derbyshire hills. It is
not too long but requires that the player *Continued*

plays all the shots, to excellent greens. Demanding holes
include the dog-leg 3rd, 12th and 18th and the 460yd
opening hole is among the toughest in Cheshire.
Regional qualifying course for Open Championship.
18 holes, 6326yds, Par 71, SSS 71, Course record 64.
Club membership 500.
Visitors restricted weekends; contact professional in advance.
Societies Wed & Thu only, apply in writing to Secretary.
Green Fees £50 per day, £40 per 18 holes (£55/£45
weekends). **Prof** Mike Peel **Course Designer** P Barrie,
A Herd **Facilities** ⊗ ⅢⅢ ⅃ ▤ ♀ ⅃ ▤ ⅋ **Conf** Corporate
Hospitality Days available **Location** 4m SE on A627

....

Hotel ★★★ 69% Bredbury Hall Hotel & Country Club,
Goyt Valley, BREDBURY ☎ 0161 430 7421 150 en suite

SWINTON   Map 07 SD70

Swinton Park East Lancashire Rd M27 5LX
☎ 0161 794 0861 ▤ 0161 281 0698
e-mail: info@spgolf.com
One of Lancashire's longest inland courses. Designed
and laid out in 1926 by James Braid.

18 holes, 6472yds, Par 73, SSS 71.
Club membership 600.
Visitors not Thu, weekends; contact in advance; handicap
certificate. **Societies** apply by letter. **Green Fees** £30 per
day/round. **Prof** James Wilson **Course Designer** James
Braid **Facilities** ⊗ ⅢⅢ ⅃ ▤ ♀ ⅃ ▤ ⅋ **Conf** fac available
Location 1m W off A580

....

Hotel ★★★ 63% Novotel Manchester West, Worsley
Brow, WORSLEY ☎ 0161 799 3535 119 en suite

UPPERMILL   Map 07 SD90

Saddleworth Mountain Ash OL3 6LT
☎ 01457 873653 ▤ 01457 820647
e-mail: secretary@saddleworthgolfclub.org.uk
Moorland course, with superb views of Pennines.
18 holes, 6118yds, Par 71, SSS 69, Course record 61.
Club membership 800.
Visitors restricted weekends; contact in advance. **Societies**
contact in advance. **Green Fees** £25 (£35 weekends).
Prof Robert Johnson **Course Designer** George Lowe,
Dr MacKenzie **Facilities** ⊗ ⅢⅢ ⅃ ▤ ♀ ⅃ ▤ ⅋ ⅋ ⅋
Location E of town centre off A670

....

Hotel ★★★ 73% Hotel Smokies Park, Ashton Rd,
Bardsley, OLDHAM ☎ 0161 785 5000 73 en suite

> **Looking for a new course? Always telephone**
> **ahead to confirm visitor arrangements.**

URMSTON   Map 07 SJ79

Flixton Church Rd, Flixton M41 6EP
☎ 0161 748 2116 📠 0161 748 2116
Meadowland course bounded by the River Mersey.
9 holes, 6410yds, Par 71, SSS 71.
Club membership 430.
Visitors contact professional in advance; with member
only weekends & bank holidays. **Societies** apply in writing.
Green Fees £22 (£32 weekends). **Cards** ⬛ ⬛ 🔳 🔲
Prof Gary Coope **Facilities** ⊗ ⅏ 🐴 ♟ ♀ ⚑ 🏠 ⚒
Location S of town centre on B5213
....
Hotel ★★★★ 68% Copthorne Hotel Manchester, Clippers
Quay, Salford Quays, MANCHESTER
☎ 0161 873 7321 166 en suite

WALKDEN   Map 07 SD70

Brackley Municipal M38 9TR
☎ 0161 790 6076
**A mostly flat testing parkland course. The fairways are
forgiving but the greens quite testing.**
9 holes, 3003yds, Par 35, SSS 69.
Club membership 65.
Visitors no restrictions. **Societies** phone in advance. **Green
Fees** terms on application. **Facilities** ♟ ♀
Location 2m NW on A6
....
Hotel ★★★ 63% Novotel Manchester West, Worsley
Brow, WORSLEY ☎ 0161 799 3535 119 en suite

WESTHOUGHTON   Map 07 SD60

Hart Common Wigan Rd BL5 2BX
☎ 01942 813195 📠 01942 840775
e-mail: hartcommon@ukgolfer.org
18 holes, 5719yds, Par 71, SSS 68.
Course Designer Mike Shattock **Location** on A58
between Bolton & Hindley
Phone for further details
....
Hotel ★★★ 65% Quality Hotel Wigan, Riverway,
WIGAN ☎ 01942 826888 88 en suite

Westhoughton Long Island, School St BL5 2BR
☎ 01942 811085 & 608958 📠 01942 811085
e-mail: honsec@westhoughtongc.fsnet.co.uk
Compact downland course.
18 holes, 5918yds, Par 70, SSS 69, Course record 64.
Club membership 325.
Visitors with member only weekends. **Societies** phone in
advance or apply in writing. **Green Fees** £20 weekdays.
Course Designer Jeff Shuttleworth **Facilities** ⊗ ⅏ 🐴 ♟
♀ 🏠 **Leisure** snooker. **Location** 0.5m NW off A58
....
Hotel ★★★ 65% Quality Hotel Wigan, Riverway,
WIGAN ☎ 01942 826888 88 en suite

WHITEFIELD   Map 07 SD80

Stand The Dales, Ashbourne Grove M45 7NL
☎ 0161 766 3197 📠 0161 796 3234
**A semi-parkland course with five moorland holes.
Undulating fairways with views of five counties. A fine
test of golf with a very demanding finish.**
18 holes, 6411yds, Par 72, SSS 71, Course record 66.
Club membership 500.
Visitors contact professional in advance. **Societies** Wed,
Fri, apply by phone. **Green Fees** £30. **Cards** 🔳 🔲

Prof Mark Dance **Course Designer** G Lowe, A Herd
Facilities ⊗ ⅏ 🐴 ♟ ♀ ♟ 🏠 ⚑ ⚒ **Conf** Corporate
Hospitality Days available **Location** 1m W off A667
....
Hotel ★★★ 66% Bolholt Country Park Hotel, Walshaw
Rd, BURY ☎ 0161 762 4000 65 en suite

Whitefield Higher Ln M45 7EZ
☎ 0161 351 2700 📠 0161 351 2712
e-mail: enquiries@whitefieldgolfclub.com
**Fine sporting parkland course with well-watered
greens.**
18 holes, 6063yds, Par 69, SSS 69, Course record 64.
Club membership 540.
Visitors restricted Tue, Sun; booking essential weekends &
bank holidays; contact profesional shop 0161 766 3096.
Societies contact in advance. **Green Fees** not confirmed.
Cards ⬛ ⬛ ⬛ 🔳 🔲 **Prof** Paul Reeves **Facilities**
⊗ ⅏ ♟ ♀ 🏠 ⚑ ⚒ **Leisure** hard tennis courts,
snooker room. **Conf** Corporate Hospitality Days available
Location N of town centre on A665
....
Hotel ★★★ 76% Malmaison, Piccadilly, MANCHESTER
☎ 0161 278 1000 167 en suite

WIGAN   Map 07 SD50

Haigh Hall Golf Complex Copperas Ln, Haigh
WN2 1PE
☎ 01942 831107 📠 01942 831417
e-mail: hhgen@wiganmgc.gov.uk
Balcarres Course: 18 holes, 6300yds, Par 70, SSS 71.
Crawford Course: 9 holes, 1446yds, Par 28.
Course Designer Steve Marnoch **Location** M6 junct
27/M61 junct 5 or 6, signed Haigh Hall
Phone for further details
....
Hotel ★★ 65% Bel-Air Hotel, 236 Wigan Ln, WIGAN
☎ 01942 241410 11 en suite

Wigan Arley Hall, Haigh WN1 2UH
☎ 01257 421360
**Fairly level parkland course with outstanding views
and magnificent trees. The fine old clubhouse is the
original Arley Hall, and is surrounded by a medieval
moat.**
18 holes, 6009yds, Par 70, SSS 69.
Club membership 300.
Visitors not Tue, Sat; contact in advance. **Societies** apply
by phone 9.30-2.30pm. **Green Fees** £30 per round. **Course
Designer** Gaunt & Marnoch **Facilities** ⊗ ⅏ 🐴 ♟ ♀ 🏠
Conf fac available **Location** M6 junct 27, 3m NE off
B5238
....
Hotel ★★★ 65% Quality Hotel Wigan, Riverway,
WIGAN ☎ 01942 826888 88 en suite

WORSLEY   Map 07 SD70

Ellesmere Old Clough Ln M28 7HZ
☎ 0161 799 0554 (office) 📠 0161 790 7322
e-mail: honsec@ellesmeregolf.fsnet.co.uk
**Parkland course with natural hazards and hard walking.
Trees and two streams running through the course make
shot strategy an important aspect of the round. Testing
holes: 3rd (par 5), 9th (par 3), 15th (par 5).**
18 holes, 6248yds, Par 70, SSS 70, Course record 67.
Club membership 700.
Visitors not club competition days & bank holidays.
Societies apply in advance. **Green Fees** £30 per day &

Continued   *Continued*

weekends, £25 per round. **Prof** Terry Morley **Facilities** ⊗ ⅏ ⅃ ⅃ ⅃ ⅃ ⅃ ⅃ **Conf** Corporate Hospitality Days available **Location** N of village off A580

Hotel ★★★ 63% Novotel Manchester West, Worsley Brow, WORSLEY ☎ 0161 799 3535 119 en suite

HAMPSHIRE

ALDERSHOT   Map 04 SU85

Army Laffans Rd GU11 2HF
☎ 01252 337272 📠 01252 337562
e-mail: secretary@armygolfclub.com
The second-oldest course in Hampshire. Picturesque heathland course with three par 3s over 200yds.
18 holes, 6550yds, Par 71, SSS 71, Course record 66.
Club membership 750.
Visitors not weekends. **Societies** phone or apply in writing. **Green Fees** £43 for 36 holes, £34.50 for 18 holes. **Cards** 🔲 🔲 🔲 🔲 🔲 **Prof** Graham Cowley **Facilities** ⊗ ⅏ ⅃ ⅃ ⅃ ⅃ ⅃ **Conf** Corporate Hospitality Days available **Location** 1.5m N of town centre off A323/A325

Hotel ★★★ 66% Potters International Hotel, 1 Fleet Rd, ALDERSHOT ☎ 01252 344000 100 en suite

ALTON   Map 04 SU73

Alton Old Odiham Rd GU34 4BU
☎ 01420 82042
Undulating meadowland course.
9 holes, 5744yds, Par 68, SSS 68, Course record 62.
Club membership 350.
Visitors contact in advance; handicap certificate for weekends; dress code. **Societies** contact in advance. **Green Fees** not confirmed. **Prof** Richard Keeling **Course Designer** James Braid **Facilities** ⊗ ⅃ ⅃ ⅃ ⅃ ⅃ **Location** 2m N of Alton off B3349 at Golden Pot

Hotel ★★★ 66% Alton House Hotel, Normandy St, ALTON ☎ 01420 80033 39 en suite

Worldham Park Cakers Ln, East Worldham GU34 3BF
☎ 01420 543151 📠 01420 84124
The course is in a picturesque parkland setting with an abundance of challenging holes (dog-legs, water and sand). Suitable for all golfing standards.
18 holes, 6209yds, Par 71, SSS 70.
Club membership 500.
Visitors advisable to book in advance for weekends. **Societies** contact in advance. **Green Fees** not confirmed. **Cards** 🔲 🔲 🔲 🔲 **Prof** Jon Le Roux **Course Designer** FJ Whidborne **Facilities** ⊗ ⅏ ⅃ ⅃ ⅃ **Conf** Corporate Hospitality Days available **Location** off B3004

Hotel ★★★ 72% Alton Grange Hotel, London Rd, ALTON ☎ 01420 86565 26 en suite 4 annexe en suite

AMPFIELD   Map 04 SU42

Ampfield Par Three Winchester Rd SO51 9BQ
☎ 01794 368480
18 holes, 2478yds, Par 54, SSS 53, Course record 49.
Course Designer Henry Cotton **Location** 4m NE of Romsey on A31
Phone for further details

Hotel ★★★ 68% Corus hotel Romsey, Winchester Rd, Ampfield, ROMSEY ☎ 0870 609 6155 54 en suite

ANDOVER   Map 04 SU34

Andover 51 Winchester Rd SP10 2EF
☎ 01264 358040 📠 01264 358040
e-mail: secretary@andovergolfclub.co.uk
Undulating downland course combining a good test of golf for all abilities with breathtaking views across Hampshire countryside. Well-guarded greens and a notable par 3 9th (225yds) with the tee perched on top of a hill, 100ft above the green. Excellent drainage on the chalk base.
9 holes, 6096yds, Par 70, SSS 69, Course record 64.
Club membership 450.
Visitors contact professional in advance 01264 324151. **Societies** phone in advance or apply in writing. **Green Fees** £21 per 18 holes (£26 weekends). **Prof** D Lawrence **Course Designer** J H Taylor **Facilities** ⊗ ⅏ ⅃ ⅃ ⅃ ⅃ ⅃ **Conf** fac available Corporate Hospitality Days available **Location** 0.5m S on A3057

Hotel ★★★ 62% Quality Hotel Andover, Micheldever Rd, ANDOVER ☎ 01264 369111 13 en suite 36 annexe en suite

Hampshire Winchester Rd SP11 7TB
☎ 01264 357555 (pro shop) & 356462 (office)
📠 01264 356606
e-mail: enquiry@thehampshiregolfclub.co.uk
A pleasant undulating parkland course with fine views and a backdrop of 35,000 young trees and shrubs. The challenging Manor course has two lakes to catch the unwary. Based on chalk which provides very good drainage, with a superb finishing hole.

Manor: 18 holes, 6382yds, Par 72, SSS 71, Course record 67.
Club membership 650.
Visitors advisable to book three days in advance. **Societies** apply by phone to Jan Miles 01264 356462. **Green Fees** £20 per 18 holes (£27 weekends). **Cards** 🔲 🔲 🔲 🔲 **Prof** Iain Powell **Facilities** ⊗ ⅃ ⅃ ⅃ ⅃ ⅃ ⅃ ⅃ ⅃ ⅃ **Leisure** 9-hole par 3 course. **Conf** fac available Corporate Hospitality Days available **Location** 1.5m S of Andover on A3057

Hotel ★★★ 62% Quality Hotel Andover, Micheldever Rd, ANDOVER ☎ 01264 369111 13 en suite 36 annexe en suite

> **In the hotel entries, the percentage figure refers to the AA's most recent Quality Assessment Score.**

Continued

BARTON-ON-SEA   Map 04 SZ29

Barton-on-Sea Milford Rd BH25 5PP
☎ 01425 615308 🖹 01425 621457
Though not strictly a links course, it is situated on a coastal cliff with views over the Solent to the Isle of Wight. With 27 holes (three loops of nine), sea breezes often add to the test.
9 holes, 3012yds, Par 36.
Needles: 9 holes, 3078yds, Par 35.
Stroller: 9 holes, 2989yds, Par 36.
Club membership 940.
Visitors contact in advance. Societies phone in advance. Green Fees not confirmed. Cards 🔲 🔲 🔲 🔲 🔲 Prof Peter Rodgers Course Designer Hamilton Stutt Facilities ⊗ 🏌 🖺 💷 ♀ 🅿 🏠 🍴 🐦 🛅 ♂ Leisure snooker tables. Conf Corporate Hospitality Days available Location B3058 SE of town

....

Hotel ★★★★★ 🏩 Chewton Glen Hotel, Christchurch Rd, NEW MILTON ☎ 01425 275341 58 en suite

BASINGSTOKE   Map 04 SU65

Basingstoke Kempshott Park RG23 7LL
☎ 01256 465990 🖹 01256 331793
e-mail: enquiries@basingstokegolfclub.co.uk
A well-maintained parkland course with wide and inviting fairways. You are inclined to expect longer drives than are actually achieved - partly on account of the trees. There are many two-hundred-year-old beech trees, since the course was built on an old deer park.
18 holes, 6350yds, Par 70, SSS 70, Course record 66.
Club membership 700.
Visitors not weekends & bank holidays; contact in advance. Societies contact in advance. Green Fees £40 per day. Cards 🔲 🔲 🔲 🔲 Prof Guy Shoesmith Course Designer James Braid Facilities ⊗ 🏌 🖺 💷 ♀ 🅿 🏠 🍴 🐦 🛅 ♂ Conf fac available Corporate Hospitality Days available Location M3 junct 7, 3.5m SW on A30

....

Hotel ★★★★ 70% Apollo Hotel, Aldermaston Roundabout, BASINGSTOKE
☎ 01256 796700 125 en suite

Dummer Dummer RG25 2AR
☎ 01256 397888 (office) & 397950 (pro)
🖹 01256 397889
e-mail: enquiries@dummergolfclub.com
Designed by Peter Alliss and Clive Clark, this course is set in 165 acres of countryside with panoramic views. The course meanders around lakes, mature trees and hedgerows with fine views over the surrounding countryside. The course combines large, level teeing areas, undulating fairways, fast true greens and cleverly positioned bunkers to provide a challenging golf experience.
18 holes, 6500yds, Par 72, SSS 71, Course record 62.
Club membership 650.
Visitors restricted weekends; contact in advance; dress code; handicap certificate. Societies contact in advance. Green Fees £25 per round. Cards 🔲 🔲 🔲 🔲 🔲 Prof Andrew Fannon Course Designer Pete Alliss Facilities ⊗ 🏌 🖺 💷 ♀ 🅿 🏠 🍴 🐦 ♂ ♿ Leisure sauna. Conf fac available Corporate Hospitality Days available Location M3 junct 7, towards Dummer, club 0.25m on left

Dummer Golf Club

....

Hotel 🛏 Premier Travel Inn Basingstoke South, NORTH WALTHAM ☎ 0870 9906476 28 en suite

Weybrook Park Rooksdown Ln RG24 9NT
☎ 01256 320347 🖹 01256 812973
e-mail: weybrookpark@aol.com
A course designed to be enjoyable for all standards of player. Easy walking with fabulous views.
18 holes, 6468yds, Par 71, SSS 71.
Club membership 600.
Visitors phone for availability. Societies phone in for availability & confirm in writing. Green Fees terms on application. Cards 🔲 🔲 🔲 Prof Anthony Dillon Facilities ⊗ 🏌 🖺 💷 ♀ 🅿 🏠 🍴 🐦 ♂ 🍴 Conf fac available Location 2m W of town centre via A339

....

Hotel ★★★★ 70% Apollo Hotel, Aldermaston Roundabout, BASINGSTOKE
☎ 01256 796700 125 en suite

BORDON   Map 04 SU73

Blackmoor Firgrove Rd, Whitehill GU35 9EH
☎ 01420 472775 🖹 01420 487666
e-mail: admin@blackmoorgolf.co.uk
A first-class moorland course with a great variety of holes. Fine greens and wide pine tree-lined fairways are a distinguishing feature. The ground is mainly flat and walking easy.
18 holes, 6164yds, Par 69, SSS 69, Course record 63.
Club membership 750.
Visitors not weekends; contact in advance; handicap certificate. Societies phone in advance. Green Fees £49 per 36 holes; £37 per 18 holes (weekdays only). Cards 🔲 🔲 🔲 🔲 🔲 Prof Stephen Clay Course Designer HS Colt Facilities ⊗ by arrangement 🏌 by arrangement 🖺 💷 ♀ 🅿 🏠 ♂ Conf Corporate Hospitality Days available Location 6m S from Farnham on A325, through Whitehill, right at rdbt

....

Hotel ★★★ 66% Alton House Hotel, Normandy St, ALTON ☎ 01420 80033 39 en suite

BOTLEY   Map 04 SU51

Botley Park Hotel, Golf & Country Club
Winchester Rd, Boorley Green SO32 2UA
☎ 01489 780888 🖹 01489 789242
e-mail: info@botleypark.macdonald.hotels.co.uk
18 holes, 6341yds, Par 70, SSS 70, Course record 67.
Course Designer Ewan Murray Location 1m NW of Botley on B3354
Phone for further details

Continued

Continued

Hotel ★★★★ 69% Botley Park Hotel Golf & Country
Club, Winchester Rd, Boorley Green, BOTLEY
☎ 01489 780888 100 en suite

BROCKENHURST   Map 04 SU20

Brokenhurst Manor Sway Rd SO42 7SG
☎ 01590 623332 (Secretary) 🖹 01590 624140
e-mail: secretary@brokenhurst-manor.org.uk
**An attractive forest course set in the New Forest, with
the unusual feature of three loops of six holes each to
complete the round. Fascinating holes include the short
5th and 12th, and the 4th and 17th, both dog-legged. A
stream also features on seven of the holes.**
*18 holes, 6222yds, Par 70, SSS 70, Course record 63.
Club membership 700.*
Visitors contact in advance, numbers limited; handicap
certificate & member of recognised club; max handicap 24
men 36 ladies. **Societies** Thu, apply in writing. **Green Fees**
not confirmed. **Cards** 🔲 🔲 🔲 🔲 💳 **Prof** Bruce Parker
Course Designer HS Colt **Facilities** ⊗ ⟨ 🍴 ┗ 💺 ♀ 🏌
🏠 ♿ **Location** 1m S on B3055

Hotel ★★ 66% Waterplash Hotel, The Rise,
BROCKENHURST ☎ 01590 622344 23 en suite

BURLEY   Map 04 SU20

Burley Cott Ln BH24 4BB
☎ 01425 402431 & 403737 🖹 01425 404168
e-mail: secretary@burleygolfclub.fsnet.co.uk
**Undulating heather and gorseland. The 7th requires an
accurately placed tee shot to obtain par 4. Played off
different tees on second nine.**
*9 holes, 6151yds, Par 71, SSS 69, Course record 68.
Club membership 520.*
Visitors not before 4pm Sat, 8am Sun; contact in advance;
preferably have a handicap certificate & member of
recognised golf club.. **Societies** phone in advance, max 14
in party. **Green Fees** terms on application. **Facilities** ┗ 💺
♀ ♿ ♿ **Location** E of village

Hotel ★★★ 67% Moorhill House, BURLEY
☎ 01425 403285 31 en suite

CORHAMPTON   Map 04 SU62

Corhampton Shepherds Farm Ln SO32 3GZ
☎ 01489 877279 🖹 01489 877680
e-mail: secretary@corhamptongc.co.uk
**Free draining downland course situated in the heart of
the picturesque Meon Valley.**
*18 holes, 6444yds, Par 71, SSS 71.
Club membership 800.*

Visitors not weekends; contact in advance. **Societies** Mon,
Thu, contact in writing or phone. **Green Fees** not
confirmed. **Prof** Ian Roper **Facilities** ⊗ ⟨ 🍴 ┗ 💺 ♀ ♿ 🏠
🏌 ♿ **Location** 1m W of Corhampton off B3035

Hotel ★★ 70% Old House Hotel & Restaurant, The
Square, WICKHAM ☎ 01329 833049 8 en suite
4 annexe en suite

CRONDALL   Map 04 SU74

Oak Park Heath Ln GU10 5PB
☎ 01252 850850 🖹 01252 850851
e-mail: oakpark@americangolf.uk.com
**Oak Park is a gently undulating parkland course
overlooking a pretty village. Woodland is undulating on
holes 10 to 13. Panoramic views, mature trees, very
challenging; 16-bay floodlit driving range, practice
green and practice bunker.**
*Woodland: 18 holes, 6352yds, Par 70, SSS 70.
Village: 9 holes, 3279yds, Par 36.
Club membership 550.*
Visitors members only 7.30am-noon; all tee times
bookable in advance. **Societies** phone & book in advance,
min 12 persons. **Green Fees** not confirmed. **Cards** 🔲 🔲
🔲 💳 🔲 💳 **Prof** Gary Murton **Course Designer**
Patrick Dawson **Facilities** ⊗ ⟨ 🍴 ┗ 💺 ♀ ♿ 🏠 🏌 🏌 ♿ ⌖
Leisure gymnasium. **Conf** fac available Corporate
Hospitality Days available **Location** 0.5m E of village off
A287 Farnham-Odiham

Hotel ★★★ 62% Farnham House Hotel, Alton Rd,
FARNHAM ☎ 01252 716908 25 en suite

Continued

DENMEAD   Map 04 SU61

Furzeley Furzeley Rd PO7 6TX
☎ 023 92231180
**A well-laid parkland course with many features
including several strategically placed lakes which
provide a good test set in beautiful scenery. Straight
hitting and club selection on the short holes is the key to
manufacturing a low score.**
*18 holes, 4454yds, Par 62, SSS 61, Course record 56.
Club membership 250.*
Visitors book two days in advance. **Societies** phone in
advance & confirm in writing. **Green Fees** not confirmed.
Prof Derek Brown **Course Designer** Mark Sale, Robert
Brown **Facilities** ⊗ ⅢⅢ by arrangement ⓑ ♨ ♀ ♨ 🏠
🏐 ♂ **Location** from Waterlooville NW onto Hambledon
road, signed

Hotel ★★★★ 65% Portsmouth Marriott Hotel,
Southampton Rd, PORTSMOUTH
☎ 0870 400 7285 174 en suite

DIBDEN   Map 04 SU40

Dibden Main Rd SO45 5TB
☎ 023 8020 7508 & 8084 5596
**Municipal parkland course with views over
Southampton Water. A pond guards the green at the
par 5 3rd hole. Twenty bay driving range.**
*Course 1: 18 holes, 5931yds, Par 70, SSS 69,
Course record 64.
Course 2: 9 holes, 1520yds, Par 29.
Club membership 600.*
Visitors book in advance for 18-hole course; 9-hole is pay
& play. **Societies** contact in advance. **Green Fees** £13.50
per 18 holes (£16 weekends); £5.40 per 9 holes (£6.50
weekends). **Cards** 🖾 📰 📳 📳 📳 **Prof** Paul Smith
& John Slade **Course Designer** Hamilton Stutt
Facilities ⊗ ⅢⅢ ⓑ ♨ ♀ ♨ 🏠 🏐 ♂ 🏐 **Location** 2m NW
of Dibden Purlieu, off A326 to Hythe

Hotel ★★★ 66% Forest Lodge Hotel, Pikes Hill, Romsey
Rd, LYNDHURST ☎ 023 8028 3677 28 en suite

EASTLEIGH   Map 04 SU41

East Horton Golf Centre Mortimers Ln, Fair Oak
SO50 7EA
☎ 023 8060 2111 📠 023 8069 6280
e-mail: info@easthortongolf.co.uk
**Courses set out over 260 acres of Hampshire
countryside with parkland fairways and mature trees in
abundance. The Greenwood course sets out across a
stream and around a large woodland, returning to the
stream for the 18th. Fine views from the top holes and
from the 16th tee, even the best golfers need to
concentrate with a 160yd carry over an imposing lake.
The Parkland course has relatively wide fairways and
the stream has to be negotiated a few times. The five
par 3s may not be as easy as they appear.**
*Greenwood: 18 holes, 5960yds, Par 70, SSS 69.
Club membership 700.*
Visitors book tee times up to one week in advance.
Societies phone for details. **Green Fees** £16 per 18 holes,
£9 per 9 holes (£19 per 18 holes weekends). **Prof** Miles
Harding **Course Designer** Trevor Pearce **Facilities** ⊗ ⅢⅢ
ⓑ ♨ ♀ ♨ 🏠 🏐 🏐 ♂ 🏐 **Leisure** par 3 course. **Conf** fac
available Corporate Hospitality Days available
Location off B3037

Continued

Hotel ⛫ Premier Travel Inn Eastleigh, Leigh Rd,
EASTLEIGH ☎ 08701 977090 60 en suite

Fleming Park Passfield Av SO50 9NL
☎ 023 80612797 📠 023 80651686
e-mail: ianwarwick@flemingparkgolfcourse.co.uk
**Parkland and woodland course with stream, Monks
Brook, running through. Good greens.**
*18 holes, 4436yds, Par 65, SSS 62, Course record 62.
Club membership 390.*
Visitors contact in advance. **Societies** contact in advance.
Green Fees terms on application. **Cards** 🖾 📰 📳 📳 📳
Prof Ian Warwick **Course Designer** David Miller
Facilities ⊗ ⅢⅢ ⓑ ♨ ♀ ♨ 🏠 🏐 ♂ **Leisure** hard & grass
tennis courts, heated indoor plus outdoor swimming pool,
squash, sauna, solarium, gymnasium.
Location E of town centre

Hotel ⛫ Travelodge Southampton Eastleigh, Twyford Rd,
EASTLEIGH ☎ 08700 850 950 32 en suite

FAREHAM   Map 04 SU50

Cams Hall Cams Hall Estate PO16 8UP
☎ 01329 827222 📠 01329 827111
e-mail: camshall@americangolf.uk.com
*Creek Course: 18 holes, 6244yds, Par 71, SSS 70,
Course record 69.
Park Course: 9 holes, 3247yds, Par 36, SSS 36.*
Course Designer Peter Alliss **Location** M27 junct 11, A27
Phone for further details

Hotel ★★★ 66% Lysses House Hotel, 51 High St,
FAREHAM ☎ 01329 822622 21 en suite

FARNBOROUGH   Map 04 SU85

Southwood Ively Rd, Cove GU14 0LJ
☎ 01252 548700 📠 01252 549091
18 holes, 5738yds, Par 69, SSS 68, Course record 61.
Course Designer Hawtree & Son **Location** 0.5m W
Phone for further details

Hotel ★★★ 65% Falcon Hotel, 68 Farnborough Rd,
FARNBOROUGH ☎ 01252 545378 30 en suite

FLEET   Map 04 SU85

North Hants Minley Rd GU51 1RF
☎ 01252 616443 📠 01252 811627
e-mail: secretary@north-hants-fleetgc.co.uk
**Picturesque tree-lined course with much heather and
gorse close to the fairways. A comparatively easy par 4
first hole may lull the golfer into a false sense of
security, only to be rudely awakened at the testing holes
which follow. The ground is rather undulating, and
though not tiring, does offer some excellent blind shots,
and more than a few surprises in judging distance.**
*18 holes, 6519yds, Par 70, SSS 72, Course record 66.
Club membership 600.*
Visitors contact at least 48 hours in advance;with member
only weekends. **Societies** Tue, Wed, by booking. **Green
Fees** terms on application. **Prof** Steve Porter **Course
Designer** James Braid **Facilities** ⊗ ⅢⅢ ⓑ ♨ ♀ ♨ 🏠 ♂
Conf Corporate Hospitality Days available **Location**
0.25m N of Fleet station on B3013

Hotel ★★★ 65% Falcon Hotel, 68 Farnborough Rd,
FARNBOROUGH ☎ 01252 545378 30 en suite

Continued

North Hants Golf Club

GOSPORT　　　　　　　　　　Map 04 SZ69

Gosport & Stokes Bay Off Fort Rd, Haslar PO12 2AT
☎ 023 92527941 📠 023 92527941
9 holes, 5999yds, Par 70, SSS 69, Course record 65.
Location A32 S from Fareham, E onto Fort Rd to Haslar
Phone for further details

Hotel ★★★ 66% Lysses House Hotel, 51 High St,
FAREHAM ☎ 01329 822622　21 en suite

HARTLEY WINTNEY　　　　　Map 04 SU75

Hartley Wintney London Rd RG27 8PT
☎ 01252 844211 (Sec/Gen Mgr) 📠 01252 844211
e-mail: office@hartleywintneygolfclub.com
Easy walking parkland and partly wooded course in pleasant countryside. Provides a challenging test for golfers of all abilities with many mature trees and water hazards.

18 holes, 6240yds, Par 71, SSS 71, Course record 63.
Club membership 750.
Visitors restricted weekends; contact in advance. **Societies** Mon, Tue, Thu & Fri only by arrangement. **Green Fees** £45 per day, £30 per 18 holes (£50/£35 weekends & bank holidays). **Cards** 🏧 💳 📲 **Prof** Martin Smith **Facilities** ⊗ ⅷ by arrangement 🏌 💺 ♀ 🛎 🍴 ⛳ **Leisure** indoor teaching studio. **Conf** fac available　Corporate Hospitality Days available **Location** NE of village on A30

Hotel ★★★ 68% The Elvetham, HARTLEY WINTNEY
☎ 01252 844871　41 en suite　29 annexe en suite

HAYLING ISLAND　　　　　　Map 04 SU70

Hayling Links Ln PO11 0BX
☎ 023 92464446 📠 023 92461119
e-mail: hgcltd@aol.com
A delightful links course among the dunes offering fine seascapes and views of the Isle of Wight. Varying sea breezes and sometimes strong winds ensure that the course seldom plays the same two days running. Testing holes at the 12th and 13th, both par 4. Club selection is important.
18 holes, 6531yds, Par 71, SSS 71, Course record 65.
Club membership 1000.
Visitors contact in advance by phone or in writing; handicap certificate; dress code. **Societies** Tue, Wed, half days Mon & Thu, apply in writing or phone. **Green Fees** £60 per day; £45 per round (£60 per round weekends).
Cards 🏧 💳 💳 📲 🅿 **Prof** Raymond Gadd **Course Designer** Taylor 1905, Simpson 1933 **Facilities** ⊗ ⅷ 🏌 💺 ♀ 🛎 🍴 ⛳ **Conf** fac available　Corporate Hospitality Days available **Location** SW side of island at West Town

Hotel ★★★ 69% Brookfield Hotel, Havant Rd,
EMSWORTH ☎ 01243 373363　40 en suite

KINGSCLERE　　　　　　　　Map 04 SU55

Sandford Springs Wolverton RG26 5RT
☎ 01635 296800 & 296808 (pro shop) 📠 01635 296801
e-mail: garye@sandfordspringsgolf.co.uk
The course has unique variety in beautiful surroundings and offers three distinctive loops of nine holes. There are water hazards, woodlands and gradients to negotiate, providing a challenge for all playing categories.

The Park: 9 holes, 2963yds, Par 34.
The Lakes: 9 holes, 3042yds, Par 35.
The Wood: 9 holes, 3180yds, Par 36.
Club membership 700.
Visitors restricted weekends; contact in advance. **Societies** contact in advance. **Green Fees** £45 per day, £35 per 18 holes (£40 per 18 holes weekends). **Cards** 🏧 💳 💳 📲 🅿 **Prof** Rhys ap Iolo **Course Designer** Hawtree & Son **Facilities** ⊗ ⅷ 🏌 💺 ♀ 🛎 🍴 🚜 ⛳ 🏌 **Conf** fac available **Location** on A339 between Basingstoke & Newbury

Hotel ★★★ 63% The Chequers Hotel, 6-8 Oxford St,
NEWBURY ☎ 01635 38000　46 en suite　11 annexe en suite

KINGSLEY
Map 04 SU73

Dean Farm GU35 9NG
☎ 01420 489478
9 holes, 1500yds, Par 29.
Location W of village off B3004
Phone for further details

....

Hotel ★★★ 72% Alton Grange Hotel, London Rd,
ALTON ☎ 01420 86565 26 en suite 4 annexe en suite

LECKFORD
Map 04 SU33

Leckford SO20 6JF
☎ 01264 810320 📠 01264 811122
e-mail: golf@leckfordestate.co.uk
Old Course: 9 holes, 6394yds, Par 72, SSS 71.
New Course: 9 holes, 4562yds, Par 66, SSS 62.
Location 1m SW off A3057
Phone for further details

LEE-ON-THE-SOLENT
Map 04 SU50

Lee-on-the-Solent Brune Ln PO13 9PB
☎ 023 9255 1170 📠 023 9255 4233
e-mail: enquiries@leeonthesolentgolfclub.co.uk
**Predominately heath and oak woodland. Whilst not
long in length, still a good test of golf requiring
accuracy off the tee to score well. Excellent greens.**
18 holes, 5962yds, Par 69, SSS 69, Course record 63.
Club membership 725.
Visitors handicap certificate; contact in advance. **Societies**
contact in advance. **Green Fees** £34 per day/round (£39
weekends). **Cards** 🔲 🔲 🔲 🔲 📶 🔲 **Prof** Rob Edwards
Facilities ⊗ ⅲ 🅱 💺 ⚷ ⚘ 🏌 **Conf** fac available
Corporate Hospitality Days available **Location** 3m S of
Fareham

....

Hotel ★★★ 66% Lysses House Hotel, 51 High St,
FAREHAM ☎ 01329 822622 21 en suite

LIPHOOK
Map 04 SU83

Liphook Wheatsheaf Enclosure GU30 7EH
☎ 01428 723271 & 723785 📠 01428 724853
e-mail: liphookgolfclub@btconnect.com
Heathland course with easy walking and fine views.
18 holes, 6167yds, Par 70, SSS 69, Course record 67.
Club membership 800.
Visitors not Tue & competition days; contact in advance;
handicap certificate. **Societies** Wed-Fri only. Must contact
in advance. **Green Fees** £49 per day, £41 per round
(£51/£61 Sat, £59 Sun & bank holidays pm only). **Prof** Ian
Mowbray **Course Designer** AC Croome **Facilities** ⊗ 🅱
💺 ⚷ ⚘ 🏌 🏌 **Location** 1m S on B2070

....

Hotel ★★★★ 71% Lythe Hill Hotel & Spa, Petworth Rd,
HASLEMERE ☎ 01428 651251 41 en suite

Old Thorns Hotel, Golf & Country Club
Griggs Green GU30 7PE
☎ 01428 724555 📠 01428 725036
e-mail: info@oldthorns.com
**A challenging 18-hole championship course with rolling
hills, undulating greens, demanding water features and
magnificent views. A challenge to any level of golfer.**
18 holes, 6581yds, Par 72, SSS 71, Course record 66.
Club membership 250.

Continued

Visitors subject to availability. **Societies** phone in advance.
Green Fees not confirmed. **Cards** 🔲 🔲 🔲 🔲 🔲 🔲
📶 **Prof** Roger Hyder **Course Designer** Peter Alliss,
Dave Thomas **Facilities** ⊗ ⅲ 🅱 💺 ⚷ ⚘ 🏌 🏌 🏌 ⚷
🎾 **Leisure** hard tennis courts, heated indoor
swimming pool, sauna, solarium, gymnasium.
Location off A3 at Griggs Green, S of Liphook, signed
Old Thorns

Old Thorns Hotel, Golf & Country Club

....

Hotel ★★★ 75% Old Thorns Hotel Golf & Country Club,
Griggs Green, LIPHOOK ☎ 01428 724555 29 en suite
4 annexe rms (3 en suite)

LYNDHURST
Map 04 SU20

Bramshaw Brook SO43 7HE
☎ 023 8081 3433 📠 023 8081 3460
e-mail: golf@bramshaw.co.uk
**Two 18-hole courses. The Manor Course is landscaped
parkland with excellent greens, and features mature
trees and streams. The Forest Course is set amid
beautiful open forest. Easy walking.**

*Manor Course: 18 holes, 6517yds, Par 71, SSS 71,
Course record 65.*
*Forest Course: 18 holes, 5774yds, Par 69, SSS 68,
Course record 65.*
Club membership 950.
Visitors restricted weekends & bank holidays unless with
member or resident of Bell Inn; phone in advance.
Societies apply in writing or phone in advance.
Green Fees not confirmed. **Prof** Clive Bonner **Facilities**
⊗ ⅲ 🅱 💺 ⚷ ⚘ 🏌 🏌 🏌 ⚷ **Conf** Corporate
Hospitality Days available **Location** M27 junct 1, 1m W
on B3079

....

Hotel ★★★ 67% Bell Inn, BROOK ☎ 023 8081 2214
25 en suite

Continued

Bell Inn

New Forest Southampton Rd SO43 7BU
☎ 023 8028 2752 📄 023 8028 4030
e-mail: barbara@nfgc.sagehost.co.uk
This picturesque heathland course is laid out in a typical
stretch of the New Forest on high ground a little above
the village of Lyndhurst. Natural hazards include the
inevitable forest ponies. The first two holes are somewhat
teasing, as is the 485yd (par 5) 9th. Walking is easy.
18 holes, 5742yds, Par 69, SSS 67.
Club membership 500.
Visitors contact in advance; dress code. Societies contact
in advance. Green Fees £13 per 18 holes (£17 weekends).
Cards 💳 💳 💳 💳 Prof Colin Murray Facilities ⊗ 🏌
🍺 ♀ ♿ 🏠 🎯 ⚙ Conf Corporate Hospitality Days
available Location 0.5m NE off A35

Hotel ★★★ 70% Crown Hotel, High St, LYNDHURST
☎ 023 8028 2922 39 en suite

NEW ALRESFORD   Map 04 SU53

Alresford Cheriton Rd, Tichborne Down SO24 0PN
☎ 01962 733746 & 733998 (pro shop) 📄 01962 736040
e-mail: secretary@alresford-golf.demon.co.uk
A testing downland course on well-drained chalk. The
five difficult par 3s, tree-lined fairways and well-
guarded fast greens ensure that the course offers a true
test of skill, even for the most experienced golfer.
18 holes, 5905yds, Par 69, SSS 68, Course record 63.
Club membership 600.
Visitors contact in advance. Societies phone in advance.
Green Fees summer £28 (£35 weekends); winter £22 (£30
weekends). Prof Malcolm Scott Course Designer Scott Webb
Young Facilities ⊗ 🏌 🏌 🍺 ♀ ♿ 🏠 🎯 ⚙ Conf Corporate
Hospitality Days available Location 1m S on B3046

Hotel ★★ 64% Swan Hotel, 11 West St, ALRESFORD
☎ 01962 732302 & 734427 📄 01962 735274 11 rms
(10 en suite) 12 annexe en suite

NEW MILTON   Map 04 SZ29

Chewton Glen Hotel Christchurch Rd BH25 6QS
☎ 01425 275341 📄 01425 272310
e-mail: reservations@chewtonglen.com
A nine-hole, par 3 course within the hotel grounds plus
a practice area. Please note - only open to residents of
the hotel or as a guest of a member of the club.
9 holes, 854yds, Par 27.
Club membership 150.
Visitors day country club membership. Societies contact in
advance. Green Fees not confirmed. Cards 💳 💳 💳
💳 💳 💳 Facilities ⊗ by arrangement 🏌 by arrangement

🍺 ♀ 🎯 🏠 ♿ Leisure hard tennis courts, outdoor & indoor
heated swimming pools, sauna, gymnasium, Spa & health
club. Conf fac available Corporate Hospitality Days
available Location off A337 W of town centre

Hotel ★★★★★ ♨ Chewton Glen Hotel, Christchurch
Rd, NEW MILTON ☎ 01425 275341 58 en suite

OVERTON   Map 04 SU54

Test Valley Micheldever Rd RG25 3DS
☎ 01256 771737 📄 01256 771285
e-mail: info@testvalleygolf.com
A downland course with excellent drainage, fine year-
round greens and prominent water and bunker
features. On undulating terrain with lovely views over
the Hampshire countryside.
18 holes, 6165yds, Par 72, SSS 69.
Club membership 500.
Visitors not before 11.30am weekends & bank holidays;
phone in advance. Societies apply in writing or phone in
advance. Green Fees not confirmed. Cards 💳 💳 💳 💳
Prof Alastair Briggs Course Designer Don Wright
Facilities ⊗ 🏌 🏌 🍺 ♀ 🏠 🎯 ⚙ Conf fac
available Corporate Hospitality Days available
Location 1.5m N of A303 on Overton road

Hotel ★★★★ 73% The Hampshire Centrecourt, Centre
Dr, Chineham, BASINGSTOKE ☎ 01256 816664
90 en suite

OWER   Map 04 SU31

Paultons Golf Centre Old Salisbury Rd SO51 6AN
☎ 023 80813992 📄 023 8081 3993
e-mail: paultons@americangolf.uk.com
A pay and play parkland and woodland 18-hole course
built within the original Paultons parkland which was laid
out by Capability Brown. The water features on four of
the holes and the tree-lined fairways challenge the ability
of all golfers. There is also a nine-hole academy course,
ideal for beginners or players wishing to improve their
short games as well as a 24-bay floodlit driving range.
18 holes, 6238yds, Par 71, SSS 70, Course record 67.
Club membership 500.
Visitors book up to seven days in advance. Societies phone
for details. Green Fees not confirmed. Cards 💳 💳 💳
💳 💳 💳 💳 Prof Mark Williamson, Mark Patience
Course Designer JR Smith Facilities ⊗ 🏌 🏌 🍺 ♀ ♿ 🏠
🎯 🏠 ⚙ Leisure nine-hole academy course.
Conf fac available Corporate Hospitality Days available
Location M27 junct 2, A36 towards Salisbury, 1st rdbt 1st
exit, 1st right at Vine pub

Hotel ★★★ 69% Bartley Lodge, Lyndhurst Rd,
CADNAM ☎ 023 8081 2248 31 en suite

PETERSFIELD   Map 04 SU72

Petersfield (New Course) Tankerdale Ln, Liss
GU33 7QY
☎ 01730 895165 (office) 📄 01730 894713
e-mail: richard@petersfieldgolfclub.co.uk
Gently undulating course of downland and parkland
with mature trees and hedgerows. Very free drainage in
an Area of Outstanding Natural Beauty.
18 holes, 6450yds, Par 72, SSS 71, Course record 68.
Club membership 725.
Visitors not before noon weekends; start times required at
weekends. Societies booking forms & deposit required.

Continued
Continued

Green Fees £40 per day, £28 per round (£35 per round weekends & bank holidays). **Prof** Greg Hughes **Course Designer** M Hawtree **Facilities** ⊗ ⅷ ⅊ 🖢 ♥ ♀ ♨ 🖒 ♦ 🖳 ♂ **Location** off A3(M) southbound between Liss & Petersfield exits

⋯⋯⋯⋯⋯⋯

Hotel ★★★ ♨ 69% Southdowns Country Hotel, Dumpford Ln, Trotton, MIDHURST ☎ 01730 821521 22 en suite

Petersfield (Old Course) Sussex Rd GU31 4EJ
☎ 01730 267732 🖹 01730 894713
Parkland course on level ground in an area of outstanding natural beauty. Numerous trees and water features. Part of Petersfield Golf Club although 1.5m away from the 18-hole New Course.
9 holes, 3005yds, Par 72, SSS 69.
Visitors start times required; pay & play at all times. Societies booking form must be completed & deposit. Green Fees not confirmed. **Prof** Greg Hughes
Facilities ⅊ ♨ ♀ ♂ **Location** off Sussex Rd, B214

⋯⋯⋯⋯⋯⋯

Hotel ★★★ ♨ 69% Southdowns Country Hotel, Dumpford Ln, Trotton, MIDHURST ☎ 01730 821521 22 en suite

PORTSMOUTH   Map 04 SU60

Great Salterns Public Course Burrfields Rd
PO3 5HH
☎ 023 9266 4549 🖹 023 9265 0525
Easy walking, seaside course with open fairways and testing shots onto well-guarded, small greens. Testing 13th hole, par 4, requiring 130yd shot across a lake.
18 holes, 5575yds, Par 70, SSS 67, Course record 64.
Club membership 700.
Visitors book up to 1 week in advance. Societies contact in advance. Green Fees terms on application. Cards 🖽 🖽 🖽 🖽 ⅅ **Prof** Terry Healy **Facilities** ⊗ ⅷ 🖢 🖒 ♀ **Location** NE of town centre on A2030

⋯⋯⋯⋯⋯⋯

Hotel ★★★★ 65% Portsmouth Marriott Hotel, Southampton Rd, PORTSMOUTH ☎ 0870 400 7285 174 en suite

ROMSEY   Map 04 SU32

Dunwood Manor Danes Rd, Awbridge SO51 0GF
☎ 01794 340549 🖹 01794 341215
e-mail: admin@dunwood-golf.co.uk
Undulating parkland course with fine views. Fine holes running through mature woodland.
18 holes, 5767yds, Par 69, SSS 68, Course record 65.
Club membership 620.
Visitors advisable to contact in advance; booking essential weekends after 11am. Societies contact in advance. Green Fees not confirmed. **Prof** Heath Teschner **Facilities** ⊗ ⅷ 🖢 ⅊ ♀ ♨ 🖒 ♀ ♦ ♂ ♨ ♂ **Location** 4m NW of Romsey off A27

⋯⋯⋯⋯⋯⋯

Hotel ★★★ 67% Bell Inn, BROOK ☎ 023 8081 2214 25 en suite

Romsey Romsey Rd, Nursling SO16 0XW
☎ 023 80734637 🖹 023 80741036
e-mail: mike@romseygolf.co.uk
Parkland and woodland course with narrow tree-lined fairways. Six holes are undulating, the rest are sloping. There are superb views over the Test valley. Excellent test of golf for all standards.
18 holes, 5718yds, Par 69, SSS 68, Course record 64.
Club membership 800.
Visitors with member only weekends & bank holidays. Societies Mon, Tue, Thu, must contact in advance. Green Fees £36 per day, £30 per round. **Prof** Mark Desmond **Facilities** ⊗ ⅷ 🖢 ⅊ ♀ ♨ 🖒 ♂ **Conf** fac available Corporate Hospitality Days available **Location** 3m S on A3057

Wellow Ryedown Ln, East Wellow SO51 6BD
☎ 01794 323833 & 322872 🖹 01794 323832
Three nine-hole courses set in 217 acres of parkland surrounding Embley Park, former home of Florence Nightingale.
Ryedown & Embley: 18 holes, 5966yds, Par 70, SSS 69, Course record 65.
Embley & Blackwater: 18 holes, 6295yds, Par 72, SSS 70.
Blackwater & Ryedown: 18 holes, 5819yds, Par 70, SSS 68.
Club membership 600.
Visitors not weekends; advisable to contact in advance. Societies Mon-Fri ex bank holidays, phone in advance,. Green Fees £18 per 18 holes (£22 weekends & bank holidays). Cards 🖽 🖽 🖽 ⅅ **Prof** Neil Bratley **Course Designer** W Wiltshire **Facilities** ⊗ ⅷ 🖢 ⅊ ♀ ♨ 🖒 ♂ ♨ ♂ **Leisure** gymnasium. **Conf** fac available Corporate Hospitality Days available
Location M27 junct 2, A36 towards Salisbury, 1m right

ROTHERWICK   Map 04 SU75

Tylney Park RG27 9AY
☎ 01256 762079 🖹 01256 763079
e-mail: martinkimberley@msn.com
A very scenic parkland course with many trees and a practice area.
18 holes, 6109yds, Par 70, SSS 69, Course record 66.
Club membership 730.
Visitors contact in advance for weekends. Societies apply by phone in advance. Green Fees not confirmed. Cards 🖽 🖽 🖽 🖽 ⅅ **Prof** Chris de Bruin **Course Designer** W Wiltshire **Facilities** ⊗ ⅷ by arrangement 🖢 ⅊ ♀ ♨ 🖒 ♀ ♨ ♂ **Conf** Corporate Hospitality Days available **Location** M3 junct 5, 2m NW of Hook

⋯⋯⋯⋯⋯⋯

Hotel ★★★★ ♨ Tylney Hall Hotel, ROTHERWICK ☎ 01256 764881 35 en suite 77 annexe en suite

> In the hotel entries, the percentage figure refers to the AA's most recent Quality Assessment Score.

> If the name of the club appears in *italics*, details have not been confirmed for this edition of the guide.

> Where to stay, where to eat?
> **Visit www.theAA.com**

ROWLAND'S CASTLE   Map 04 SU71

Rowlands Castle 31 Links Ln PO9 6AE
☎ 023 92412784 ▤ 023 92413649
e-mail: manager@rowlandscastlegolfclub.co.uk
**Reasonably dry in winter, the flat parkland course is a
testing one with a number of tricky dog-legs and
bunkers much in evidence. The par 4 13th is a signature
hole necessitating a drive to a narrow fairway and a
second shot to a two-tiered green. The 7th, at 522yds, is
the longest hole on the course and leads to a well-
guarded armchair green.**
18 holes, 6612yds, Par 72, SSS 72, Course record 68.
Club membership 800.
Visitors not Sat; contact in advance; handicap certificate.
Societies Tue, Thu, contact in writing. **Green Fees** terms
on application. **Cards** ▦ **Prof** Peter Klepacz **Course
Designer** Colt **Facilities** ⊗ ⫪ ⬐ 🖤 ♀ ⛄ 🏠 ➤ 🛺 ⫸
Conf Corporate Hospitality Days available
Location W of village off B2149

Hotel ★★★ 69% Brookfield Hotel, Havant Rd,
EMSWORTH ☎ 01243 373363 40 en suite

SHEDFIELD   Map 04 SU51

Marriott Meon Valley Hotel & Country Club
Sandy Ln SO32 2HQ
☎ 01329 833455 ▤ 01329 834411
**It has been said that a golf-course architect is as good as
the ground on which he has to work. Here Hamilton
Stutt had magnificent terrain at his disposal and a very
good and lovely parkland course is the result. There are
three holes over water. The hotel provides many sports
facilities.**
*Meon Course: 18 holes, 6520yds, Par 71, SSS 71,
Course record 66.*
Valley Course: 9 holes, 2721yds, Par 35, SSS 33.
Club membership 700.
Visitors book up to seven days in advance. **Societies** phone
in advance, written confirmation. **Green Fees** not
confirmed. **Cards** ▦ ▦ ▦ ▦ ▣ **Prof** Rod Cameron
Course Designer Hamilton Stutt **Facilities** ⊗ ⫪ ⬐ 🖤 ♀
⛄ 🏠 ➤ 🐎 ➤ 🛺 ⫸ ⫻ **Leisure** hard tennis courts, heated
indoor swimming pool, sauna, solarium, gymnasium.
Location M27 junct 7, off A334 between Botley &
Wickham

Hotel ★★★★ 66% Marriott Meon Valley Hotel &
Country Club, Sandy Ln, SHEDFIELD
☎ 01329 833455 113 en suite

SOUTHAMPTON   Map 04 SU41

Chilworth Main Rd, Chilworth SO16 7JP
☎ 023 8074 0544 ▤ 023 8073 3166
**A course with two loops of nine holes, with a booking
system to allow undisturbed play. The front nine is
fairly long and undulating and include water hazards.
The back nine is tighter and quite a challenge.**
*Manor Golf Course: 18 holes, 5915yds, Par 69, SSS 69,
Course record 68.*
Club membership 600.
Visitors no restrictions. **Societies** phone in advance &
complete booking form, various packages available. **Green
Fees** terms on application. **Cards** ▦ ▦ ▣ ▦ ▦ ▣
Course Designer J Garner **Facilities** ⊗ ⫪ ⬐ 🖤 ♀ ⛄ 🏠
⫸ ⫻ **Location** A27 between Chilworth & Romsey
Continued

Hotel ★★★ 68% Chilworth Manor, CHILWORTH
☎ 023 8076 7333 95 en suite

Southampton Golf Course Rd, Bassett SO16 7LE
☎ 023 80760478 & 80760546 (booking) ▤ 023 80760472
e-mail: golf.course@southampton.gov.uk
18 holes, 6103yds, Par 69, SSS 70.
9 holes, 2395yds, Par 33.
Course Designer Halmree, AP Taylor **Location** 4m N of
city centre off A33
Phone for further details

Hotel ★★ 68% The Elizabeth House Hotel, 42-44 The
Avenue, SOUTHAMPTON ☎ 023 8022 4327 20 en suite
7 annexe en suite

Stoneham Monks Wood Close, Bassett SO16 3TT
☎ 023 8076 9272 ▤ 023 8076 6320
e-mail: richard.penley-martin@stonehamgolfclub.org.uk
**A hilly, heather course with sand or peat sub-soil; the
fairways are separated by belts of woodland and
heather to present a varied terrain. The interesting 4th
is a difficult par 4 and the fine 11th has cross-bunkers
about 150yds from the tee.**
18 holes, 6392yds, Par 72, SSS 70, Course record 63.
Club membership 800.
Visitors advisable to contact in advance, handicap
certificate. **Societies** Mon, Thu, Fri, phone in advance or
apply in writing. **Green Fees** £45 per day; £40 per round
(£60/£50 weekends & bank holidays). **Cards** ▦ ▦ ▦
▦ ▣ **Prof** Ian Young **Course Designer** Willie Park Jnr
Facilities ⊗ ⫪ ⬐ 🖤 ♀ ⛄ 🏠 ➤ ⫻ **Conf** Corporate
Hospitality Days available **Location** 4m N of city centre
off A27

Hotel ★★★ 68% Chilworth Manor, CHILWORTH
☎ 023 8076 7333 95 en suite

SOUTHWICK   Map 04 SU60

Southwick Park Naval Recreation Centre
Pinsley Dr PO17 6EL
☎ 023 923 80131 ▤ 023 9221 0289
e-mail: southwick.park@ukonline.co.uk
Set in 100 acres of parkland.
18 holes, 5884yds, Par 69, SSS 69, Course record 64.
Club membership 700.
Visitors not before 2pm weekends; contact in advance.
Societies apply in writing or phone in advance. **Green
Fees** terms on application. **Prof** John Green **Course
Designer** C Lawrie **Facilities** ⊗ ⫪ ⬐ 🖤 ♀ ⛄ 🏠 ⫸ ⫻
Location 0.5m SE off B2177

Hotel ★★ 70% Old House Hotel & Restaurant, The
Square, WICKHAM ☎ 01329 833049 8 en suite
4 annexe en suite

TADLEY   Map 04 SU66

Bishopswood Bishopswood Ln RG26 4AT
☎ 0118 9812200 ▤ 0118 9408606
e-mail: david@bishopswoodgolfcourse.co.uk
**Wooded parkland course with numerous water
hazards. Considered to be one of the best nine-hole
courses in the UK and venue of the National 9's
regional finals.**
9 holes, 6474yds, Par 72, SSS 71, Course record 66.
Club membership 420.
Continued

Visitors not weekends or bank holidays; contact in advance. **Societies** contact by phone. **Green Fees** £18 per 18 holes, £12 per 9 holes. **Cards** 🏧 💳 📇 📠 💷 **Prof** Steve Ward **Course Designer** MW Phillips, G Blake **Facilities** ⊗ ⅧⓂ 🍴 🎯 🛒 🏌 **Conf** Corporate Hospitality Days available **Location** 6m N of Basingstoke off A340

Hotel ★★★ 72% Romans Country House Hotel, Little London Rd, SILCHESTER ☎ 0118 970 0421 11 en suite 14 annexe en suite

WATERLOOVILLE　　　　　　　　Map 04 SU60

Portsmouth Crookhorn Ln, Purbrook PO7 5QL
☎ 023 92372210 📠 023 92200766
e-mail: info@portsmouthgc.com
Hilly, challenging course with good views of Portsmouth Harbour. Rarely free from the wind and the picturesque 6th, 17th and 18th holes can test the best.
18 holes, 6139yds, Par 69, SSS 70, Course record 64. Club membership 600.
Visitors book in advance. **Societies** book in advance, by writing or phone. **Green Fees** **Cards** 🏧 💳 📇 📠 💷 **Prof** James Green **Course Designer** Hawtree **Facilities** ⊗ ⅧⓂ 🍴 🎯 🛒 **Conf** fac available **Location** 2m S off A3

Hotel ★★★★ 65% Portsmouth Marriott Hotel, Southampton Rd, PORTSMOUTH ☎ 0870 400 7285 174 en suite

Waterlooville Cherry Tree Av, Cowplain PO8 8AP
☎ 023 92263388 📠 023 92242980
e-mail: secretary@waterloovillegolfclub.co.uk
Parkland course, easy walking. Challenging course with five par 5s over 500yds and featuring four ponds and a stream running through. The 13th hole, at 556yds, with a carry over a pond for a drive and a stream crossing the fairway requires due care.
18 holes, 6602yds, Par 72, SSS 72, Course record 64. Club membership 800.
Visitors restricted weekends; contact in advance; handicap certificate. **Societies** Thu, apply by letter or phone. **Green Fees** £40 per day, £30 per round. **Prof** John Hay **Course Designer** Henry Cotton **Facilities** ⊗ 🍴 🎯 🛒 **Conf** Corporate Hospitality Days available **Location** NE of town centre off A3

Hotel ★★★ 69% Brookfield Hotel, Havant Rd, EMSWORTH ☎ 01243 373363 40 en suite

WICKHAM　　　　　　　　　　Map 04 SU51

Wickham Park Titchfield Ln PO17 5PJ
☎ 01329 833342 📠 01329 834798
e-mail: wpgc@crown-golf.co.uk
An attractive 18-hole parkland course set in the Meon Valley. Ideal for beginners and established golfers alike. The course is not overly demanding but is challenging enough to provide an enjoyable round of golf.
18 holes, 5898yds, Par 69, SSS 68, Course record 69. Club membership 600.
Visitors not before 9.30am weekends; book up to seven days in advance. **Societies** weekdays. **Green Fees** not confirmed. **Cards** 🏧 💳 📇 📠 💷 **Prof** Scott Edwards **Facilities** ⊗ ⅧⓂ 🍴 🎯 🛒 🏌
Leisure driving net, chipping area. **Conf** fac available **Location** M27 junct 9/10

Hotel ★★ 70% Old House Hotel & Restaurant, The Square, WICKHAM ☎ 01329 833049 8 en suite 4 annexe en suite

WINCHESTER　　　　　　　　Map 04 SU42

Hockley Twyford SO21 1PL
☎ 01962 713165 📠 01962 713612
e-mail: secretary@hockleygolfclub.com
Downland course with good views.
18 holes, 6336yds, Par 71, SSS 70, Course record 64. Club membership 750.
Visitors restricted weekends; advisable to phone in advance; handicap certificate. **Societies** phone in advance & confirm in writing with deposit. **Green Fees** £45 per day, £35 per round (£50 weekends). **Prof** Gary Stubbington **Course Designer** James Braid **Facilities** ⊗ Ⅶ 🍴 🎯 🛒 🏌 **Conf** Corporate Hospitality Days available **Location** M3 junct 11, signed to Twyford

Hotel ★★★★ 63% The Wessex, Paternoster Row, WINCHESTER ☎ 0870 400 8126 94 en suite

Royal Winchester Sarum Rd SO22 5QE
☎ 01962 852462 📠 01962 865048
e-mail: manager@royalwinchestergolfclub.com
The Royal Winchester course is a sporting downland course centred on a rolling valley, so the course is hilly in places with fine views over the surrounding countryside. Built on chalk downs, the course drains extremely well and offers an excellent playing surface.
18 holes, 6216yds, Par 71, SSS 70, Course record 65. Club membership 800.
Visitors with member only weekends; contact in advance; handicap certificate. **Societies** contact by writing or phone. **Green Fees** £60 per day, £36 per round. **Cards** 🏧 💳 📇 📠 💷 **Prof** Steven Hunter **Course Designer** JH Taylor **Facilities** ⊗ Ⅶ 🍴 🎯 🛒 🏌 **Conf** Corporate Hospitality Days available **Location** 1.5m W off A3090

Hotel ★★★★ 🏨 Lainston House Hotel, Sparsholt, WINCHESTER ☎ 01962 863588 50 en suite

South Winchester Romsey Rd SO22 5QX
☎ 01962 877800 📠 01962 877900
e-mail: swgc@crown-golf.co.uk
This links style course in two loops of nine holes provides all golfers with a fair challenge. The course undulates between grassy slopes and beside several lakes offering easy walking and excellent views. Excellent drainage on the chalk based surface.
18 holes, 7086yds, Par 72, SSS 74, Course record 68. Club membership 750.
Visitors not before 10.30am weekends. **Societies** contact Richard Adams, Director of Golf, in advance 01962 873542. **Green Fees** terms on application. **Cards** 🏧 💳 📇 📠 💷 **Prof** Richard Adams **Course Designer** Dave Thomas **Facilities** ⊗ ⅧⓂ 🍴 🎯 🛒 🏌 **Conf** fac available Corporate Hospitality Days available **Location** M3 junct 11, on A3090 Romsey road

Hotel ★★★ 70% The Winchester Royal, Saint Peter St, WINCHESTER ☎ 01962 840840 75 en suite

> **Prices may change during the currency of the Guide, please check when booking.**

Continued

HEREFORDSHIRE

CLIFFORD   Map 03 SO24

Summerhill HR3 5EW
☎ 01497 820451 📄 01497 820451
Undulating parkland course set deep in the Wye Valley on the Welsh border overlooking the Black Mountains.
9 holes, 2872yds, Par 70, SSS 67, Course record 71.
Club membership 240.
Visitors not am Sun, Thu evenings. **Societies** contact for information on phone above or 07970 076881. **Green Fees** £12 (£15 weekends & bank holidays). **Prof** Andy Gealy **Course Designer** Bob Sandow **Facilities** ⊗ ⅷ by arrangement ⅃ ♥ ♀ ⅄ 🏠 🆗 ♦ ⅾ **Leisure** 3 hole par 3 course. **Conf** fac available   Corporate Hospitality Days available **Location** 0.5m N from Hay on B4350, on right

....
Inn ◆◆◆◆◆ The Talkhouse, Pontdolgoch, CAERSWS
☎ 01686 688919   3 en suite

HEREFORD   Map 03 SO53

Belmont Lodge Belmont HR2 9SA
☎ 01432 352666 📄 01432 358090
e-mail: info@belmont-hereford.co.uk
Parkland course designed in two loops of nine. The first nine take the higher ground, offering magnificent views over Herefordshire. The second nine run alongside the River Wye with five holes in play against the river.

18 holes, 6511yds, Par 72, SSS 71, Course record 66.
Club membership 450.
Visitors advised to contact in advance for weekends 01432 352666 or 352717. **Societies** phone in advance. **Green Fees** not confirmed. **Cards** 💳 💳 💳 💳 💳 💳 **Prof** Mike Welsh **Course Designer** Bob Sandow **Facilities** ⊗ ⅷ ⅃ ♥ ♀ ⅄ 🏠 🆗 ♥ ⅾ ♦ ⅾ **Leisure** hard tennis courts, fishing. **Conf** fac available   Corporate Hospitality Days available **Location** 2m S off A465

....
Hotel ★★★ 69% Belmont Lodge & Golf, Belmont, HEREFORD ☎ 01432 352666   30 en suite

Burghill Valley Tillington Rd, Burghill HR4 7RW
☎ 01432 760456 📄 01432 761654
e-mail: info@bvgc.co.uk
The course is situated in typically beautiful Herefordshire countryside. The walking is easy on gently rolling fairways with a background of hills and woods and in the distance, the Welsh mountains. Some holes are played through mature cider orchards and there are two lakes to negotiate. A fair but interesting test for players of all abilities.

18 holes, 6239yds, Par 71, SSS 70, Course record 66.
Club membership 700.
Visitors contact in advance. **Societies** apply in writing or phone in advance. **Green Fees** terms on application. **Cards** 💳 💳 💳 💳 💳 **Prof** Keith Preece, Andy Cameron **Course Designer** M Barnett **Facilities** ⊗ ⅷ ⅃ ♥ ♀ ⅄ 🏠 ♥ 🆗 ⅾ **Leisure** chipping practice area.
Location 4m NW of Hereford

....
Hotel ⌂ Premier Travel Inn Hereford, Holmer Rd, Holmer, HEREFORD ☎ 08701 977134   60 en suite

Hereford Municipal Hereford Leisure Centre, Holmer Rd HR4 9UD
☎ 01432 344376 📄 01432 266281
This municipal parkland course is more challenging than first appearance. The well-drained greens are open all year round with good drainage for excellent winter golf.
9 holes, 3060yds, Par 35, SSS 69.
Club membership 195.
Visitors restricted on race days. **Societies** phone in advance. **Green Fees** £7.20 per 18 holes, £5.20 per 9 holes (£7.20/£5.20weekends). **Cards** 💳 💳 💳 💳 💳 **Prof** Gary Morgan **Course Designer** J Leek **Facilities** ⊗ ⅷ ⅃ ♥ ♀ ⅄ 🏠 🆗 ⅾ **Leisure** squash, gymnasium, Leisure centre. **Location** within racecourse on A49 Hereford-Leominster road

....
Hotel ⌂ Premier Travel Inn Hereford, Holmer Rd, Holmer, HEREFORD ☎ 08701 977134   60 en suite

KINGTON   Map 03 SO25

Kington Bradnor Hill HR5 3RE
☎ 01544 230340 (club) & 231320 (pro shop)
📄 01544 230340/231320 (pro)
The highest 18-hole course in England, with magnificent views over seven counties. A natural heathland course with easy walking on mountain turf cropped by sheep. There is bracken to catch any really bad shots but no sand traps. The greens play true and fast and are generally acknowledged as some of the best in the west Midlands.
18 holes, 5980yds, Par 70, SSS 68, Course record 63.
Club membership 510.
Visitors contact the professional, particularly at weekends 01544 231320. **Societies** book in advance through the professional. **Green Fees** not confirmed. **Prof** Andy Gealy **Course Designer** Major CK Hutchison **Facilities** ⊗ ⅷ ⅃ ♥ ♀ ⅄ 🏠 🆗 ♥ 🆗 ⅾ ᵗ **Location** 0.5m N of Kington off B4355

....
Hotel ★★★ 66% Talbot Hotel, West St, LEOMINSTER
☎ 01568 616347   20 en suite

LEOMINSTER   Map 03 SO45

Leominster Ford Bridge HR6 0LE
☎ 01568 610055 📄 01568 610055
e-mail: contact@leominstergolfclub.co.uk
On undulating parkland with the lower holes running alongside the River Lugg and others on the higher part of the course affording fine panoramic views over the surrounding countryside.
18 holes, 6026yds, Par 70, SSS 69.
Club membership 520.
Visitors contact in advance. **Societies** phone in advance. **Green Fees** £20 per day, £15 per round (£30/£25

Continued   *Continued*

weekends & bank holidays). **Cards** 🔲 💳 🔟
Prof Nigel Clarke **Course Designer** Bob Sandow
Facilities ⊗ ⑩ ⓑ 🍽️ ♈ ⚲ 🏠 🚌 ✔️ **Leisure** fishing.
Conf fac available **Location** 3m S of Leominster on A49,
signed

....

Hotel ★★★ 66% Talbot Hotel, West St, LEOMINSTER
☎ 01568 616347   20 en suite

ROSS-ON-WYE   Map 03 SO62

Ross-on-Wye Two Park, Gorsley HR9 7UT
☎ 01989 720267   📠 01989 720212
e-mail: secretary@therossonwyegolfclub.co.uk
**This undulating, parkland course has been cut out of a
silver birch forest. The fairways are well-screened from
each other and tight, the greens good and the bunkers
have been restructured.**
18 holes, 6451yds, Par 72, SSS 71, Course record 68.
Club membership 760.
Visitors contact secretary or professional in advance.
Societies apply in writing or phone in advance. **Green
Fees** £50 per 36 holes; £46 per 27 holes; £40 per round.
Cards 🔲 💳 **Prof** Jon Moody **Course Designer**
CK Cotton **Facilities** ⊗ ⑩ ⓑ 🍽️ ♈ ⚲ 🏠 ♿ ✔️ ₹
Conf Corporate Hospitality Days available
Location M50 junct 3, on B4221 N

....

Hotel ★★★ 74% Pengethley Manor, Pengethley Park,
ROSS-ON-WYE ☎ 01989 730211   11 en suite   14 annexe
en suite

South Herefordshire Twin Lakes HR9 7UA
☎ 01989 780535   📠 01989 740611
e-mail: shgc.golf@clara.co.uk
**Impressive 6672yd parkland course fast maturing
into one of Herefordshire's finest. Magnificent
panoramic views of the Welsh mountains and
countryside. Drains well and is playable in any weather.**

**The landscape has enabled the architect to design 18
individual and varied holes.**
*Twin Lakes: 18 holes, 6672yds, Par 71, SSS 72, Course
record 71.*
Club membership 300.
Visitors contact in advance. **Societies** phone in advance.
Green Fees £20 per day, £15 per round (£25/£20
weekends). **Cards** 🔲 💳 🏧 🔟 **Prof** Edward Litchfield
Course Designer John Day **Facilities** ⊗ ⑩ ⓑ 🍽️ ♈ ⚲ 🏠
♈ ♿ 🚌 ✔️ ₹ **Conf** Corporate Hospitality Days available
Location M50 junct 4, to Upton Bishop, right onto B4224,
1m left

....

Hotel ★★★ 68% Pencraig Court Country House Hotel,
Pencraig, ROSS-ON-WYE ☎ 01989 770306   10 en suite

UPPER SAPEY   Map 03 SO66

Sapey WR6 6XT
☎ 01886 853288 & 853567   📠 01886 853485
e-mail: anybody@sapeygolf.co.uk
**Parkland course with easy walking and views of the
Malvern Hills. Trees, lakes and water hazards. A
mixture of long or short holes, including trees, lakes
and water hazards, offering a demanding challenge for
all golfers.**
*The Rowan: 18 holes, 5935yds, Par 69, SSS 68, Course
record 63.*
The Oaks: 9 holes, 1203yds, Par 27, SSS 27.
Club membership 450.
Visitors contact in advance. **Societies** phone in advance.
Green Fees Rowan: £20 per round (£25 weekends). Oaks:
£6 (£7 weekends). **Cards** 🔲 💳 🏧 🔟 **Prof** Chris
Knowles **Course Designer** R McMurray **Facilities** ⊗ ⑩ ⓑ

Continued   *Continued*

🏁 ♀ ⛳ 🏨 🍴 🎿 🚃 🏌 **Conf** Corporate Hospitality Days available **Location** B4203 Bromyard-Stourport road

Hotel ★★★ 66% Talbot Hotel, West St, LEOMINSTER
☎ 01568 616347 20 en suite

WORMSLEY · · · · · · · · · · · Map 03 SO44

Herefordshire Ravens Causeway HR4 8LY
☎ 01432 830219 & 830465 (pro) 🖹 01432 830095
e-mail: herefordshire.golf@breath.com
Undulating parkland course with expansive views of the Clee Hills to the east and the Black Mountains to the west. Peaceful and relaxing situation.
18 holes, 6078yds, Par 70, SSS 69, Course record 61. Club membership 750.
Visitors not during weekend competitions; contact in advance. **Societies** apply in advance. **Green Fees** £20 (£25 weekends & bank holidays). **Cards** 🔲 🔲 🔲 🔳 🔲
Prof Richard Hemming **Course Designer** James Braid
Facilities ⊗ ⚒ 🖥 ♀ 🏌 ⛳ ⛳
Conf Corporate Hospitality Days available
Location 7m NW of Hereford on B road to Weobley

Hotel ⛳ Premier Travel Inn Hereford, Holmer Rd, Holmer, HEREFORD ☎ 08701 977134 60 en suite

HERTFORDSHIRE

ALDBURY · · · · · · · · · · · · Map 04 SP91

Stocks Hotel & Golf Club Stocks Rd HP23 5RX
☎ 01442 851341 & 851491 (pro) 🖹 01442 861253
e-mail: info@stockshotel.co.uk
This gently undulating course sits in the shadow of the Ashridge Forest and commands attractive views of the Chiltern Hills. It is ideally suited to golfers of all standards, representing a true test of golf.
18 holes, 6804yds, Par 72, SSS 73, Course record 66. Club membership 630.
Visitors not am weekends, bank holidays; book up to five days in advance. **Societies** please phone Golf Club Manager, Robin Darling on 01442 852504 **Green Fees** not confirmed. **Cards** 🔲 🔲 🔲 🔳 🔲 🔲 **Prof** Peter Lane **Course Designer** Mike Billcliffe **Facilities** ⊗ ⚒ 🖥 ♀ 🏨 🍴 🚃 ⛳ **Leisure** chipping green, practice bunker. **Conf** fac available **Location** 2m from A41 at Tring towards Tring station

Hotel ★★★★ 68% Pendley Manor, Cow Ln, TRING
☎ 01442 891891 74 en suite

ALDENHAM · · · · · · · · · · · Map 04 TQ19

Aldenham Golf and Country Club
Church Ln WD25 8NN
☎ 01923 853929 🖹 01923 858472
e-mail: info@aldenhamgolfclub.co.uk
Undulating parkland course with woodlands, water hazards and ditches. Many specimen trees and beautiful views across the countryside.
Old Course: 18 holes, 6480yds, Par 70, SSS 71.
White Course: 9 holes, 2350yds, Par 33, SSS 32.
Club membership 500.
Visitors Old Course: restricted before 1pm weekends. White Course: no restrictions. **Societies** contact in advance. **Green Fees** Old Course: £28 per round (£36 weekends). White Course £10 (£12 weekends). **Cards** 🔲 🔲 🔲 🔳
🔲 **Prof** Tim Dunstan **Facilities** ⊗ ⚒ 🖥 ♀ 🏨 🍴

⛳ **Conf** fac available Corporate Hospitality Days available **Location** M1 junct 5, 0.5m to W of village

Aldenham Golf and Country Club

Hotel ★★★ 67% The White House, Upton Rd, WATFORD ☎ 01923 237316 57 en suite

BERKHAMSTED · · · · · · · · Map 04 SP90

Berkhamsted The Common HP4 2QB
☎ 01442 865832 🖹 01442 863730
e-mail: barryh@berkhamstedgc.co.uk
There are no sand bunkers on this championship heathland course but this does not make it any easier to play. The natural hazards will test the skill of the most able players, with a particularly testing hole at the 11th, 568yds, par 5. Fine greens, long carries and heather and gorse. The clubhouse is very comfortable.
18 holes, 6605yds, Par 71, SSS 72, Course record 65. Club membership 700.
Visitors contact in advance; must be competent golfer. **Societies** contact in advance. **Green Fees** £50 per day, £37 per 18 holes (£45 per 18 holes weekends after 11am). **Cards** 🔲 🔲 🔲 🔲 **Prof** John Clarke **Course Designer** Colt, Braid **Facilities** ⊗ ⚒ 🖥 ♀ 🏨 🍴 ⛳
Location 1.5m E

Hotel ★★★★ 68% Pendley Manor, Cow Ln, TRING
☎ 01442 891891 74 en suite

BISHOP'S STORTFORD · · · · · Map 05 TL42

Bishop's Stortford Dunmow Rd CM23 5HP
☎ 01279 654715 🖹 01279 655215
e-mail: office@bsgc.co.uk
Well-established parkland course, fairly flat, but undulating, with easy walking.

18 holes, 6404yds, Par 71, SSS 71, Course record 64. Club membership 900.
Visitors handicap certificate; with member only weekends; Ladies Day Tue. **Societies** contact in writing.

Continued

Continued

Green Fees £40 per day; £32 per 18 holes. **Cards** 🖃 🖃 🖃 🖃 🖭 **Prof** Stephen M Bryan **Course Designer** James Braid **Facilities** ⊗ ⅏ ⅄ ➡ ♀ ⅄ 🕿 ☂ ➪ ⚲ ⚮ ⅄ **Leisure** snooker tables. **Conf** fac available Corporate Hospitality Days available **Location** M11 junct 8, 0.5m W on A1250

Hotel ★★★ 70% Stansted Manor Hotel, Birchanger Ln, BIRCHANGER ☎ 01279 859800 70 en suite

Great Hadham Golf & Country Club
Great Hadham Rd, Much Hadham SG10 6JE
☎ 01279 843558 📠 01279 842122
e-mail: info@ghgcc.co.uk
An undulating meadowland and links course offering excellent country views and a challenge with its ever present breeze.
18 holes, 6854yds, Par 72, SSS 73, Course record 67.
Club membership 800.
Visitors not am Mon, Wed, am weekends. **Societies** weekdays, by advance booking in writing. **Green Fees** £20 per 18 holes, £12 per 9 holes (£27/£15 weekends pm). **Cards** 🖃 🖃 🖃 🖃 🖭 **Prof** Kevin Lunt **Course Designer** Iain Roberts **Facilities** ⊗ ⅏ ⅄ ➡ ♀ ⅄ 🕿 ☂ ⚲ ⅄ **Leisure** sauna, solarium, gymnasium. **Conf** fac available **Location** on B1004, 3m SW of Bishop's Stortford

Hotel ★★★★ 71% Down Hall Country House Hotel, Hatfield Heath, BISHOP'S STORTFORD
☎ 01279 731441 99 en suite

BRICKENDON   Map 05 TL30

Brickendon Grange Pembridge Ln SG13 8PD
☎ 01992 511258 📠 01992 511411
e-mail: play@brickendongrangegc.co.uk
Undulating parkland course with some fine par 4s. 17th hole reputed to be best in the county.
18 holes, 6458yds, Par 71, SSS 71, Course record 67.
Club membership 680.
Visitors handicap certificate; with member only weekends & bank holidays. **Societies** by arrangement. **Green Fees** £45 per day; £36 per round. **Prof** Graham Tippett **Course Designer** CK Cotton **Facilities** ⊗ ⅏ ⅄ ➡ ♀ ⅄ 🕿 ☂ ➪ ⚲ **Location** W of village

BROOKMANS PARK   Map 04 TL20

Brookmans Park Golf Club Rd AL9 7AT
☎ 01707 652487 📠 01707 661851
e-mail: info@bpgc.co.uk
Brookman's Park is an undulating parkland course, with several cleverly constructed holes. But it is a fair course, although it can play long. The 11th, par 3, is a testing hole which plays across a lake.
18 holes, 6473yds, Par 71, SSS 71, Course record 65.
Club membership 750.
Visitors contact professional in advance 01707 652468; handicap certificate; with member only weekends & bank holidays. **Societies** phone or write in advance. **Green Fees** not confirmed. **Prof** Ian Jelley **Course Designer** Hawtree, Taylor **Facilities** ⊗ ⅏ ⅄ ➡ ♀ ⅄ 🕿 ☂ ⚲ **Location** N of village off A1000

Hotel ★★★ 71% Bush Hall, Mill Green, HATFIELD
☎ 01707 271251 25 en suite

BROXBOURNE   Map 05 TL30

Hertfordshire Broxbournebury Mansion, White Stubbs Ln
☎ 01992 466666 & 441268 (pro shop) 📠 01992 470326
e-mail: hertfordshire@americangolf.uk.com
18 holes, 6314yds, Par 70, SSS 70, Course record 62.
Course Designer Jack Nicklaus II **Location** off A10 for Broxbourne, signs for Paradise Wildlife Park, left at Bell Ln over A10, on right
Phone for further details

BUNTINGFORD   Map 05 TL32

East Herts Hamels Park SG9 9NA
☎ 01920 821922 (pro) 📠 01920 823700
e-mail: secretary@ehgc.fsnet.co.uk
An attractive undulating parkland course with magnificent specimen trees.
18 holes, 6456yds, Par 71, SSS 71, Course record 62.
Club membership 750.
Visitors not Wed, weekends; contact in advance; handicap certificate. **Societies** apply in writing. **Green Fees** terms on application. **Prof** G Culmer **Facilities** ⊗ ⅄ ➡ ♀ ⅄ 🕿 ☂ ➪ ⚲ **Conf** Corporate Hospitality Days available **Location** 1m N of Puckeridge off A10, opp Pearce's Farm Shop

Hotel ★★★ 66% Novotel Stevenage, Knebworth Park, STEVENAGE ☎ 01438 346100 100 en suite

BUSHEY   Map 04 TQ19

Bushey Golf & Country Club High St WD23 1TT
☎ 020 8950 2215 (pro shop) & 8950 2283 (club)
📠 020 8386 1181
e-mail: info@busheycountryclub.com
Undulating parkland with challenging 2nd and 9th holes. The latter has a sweeping dog-leg left, playing to a green in front of the clubhouse. For the rather too enthusiastic golfer, Bushey offers its own physiotherapist.

9 holes, 6120yds, Par 70, SSS 69, Course record 67.
Club membership 475.
Visitors not am Wed, am Thu, am weekends; contact in advance. **Societies** apply in writing or phone. **Green Fees** £18 per 18 holes; £12 per 9 holes (£21/£14 weekends). **Cards** 🖃 **Prof** Grahame Atkinson **Course Designer** Donald Steele **Facilities** ⊗ ⅏ ⅄ ➡ ♀ ⅄ ➪ ⚲ ⅄ **Leisure** sauna, solarium, gymnasium, health & fitness club. **Conf** Corporate Hospitality Days available

Hotel ★★★ 67% Corus hotel Elstree, Barnet Ln, ELSTREE ☎ 0870 609 6151 47 en suite

Bushey Hall Bushey Hall Dr WD23 2EP

☎ 01923 222253 🖹 01923 229759
e-mail: info@golfclubuk.co.uk
Tree-lined parkland course.
18 holes, 6099yds, Par 69, SSS 69, Course record 62.
Club membership 500.
Visitors not before 11am weekends; book 14 days in
advance. Societies contact in writing. Green Fees not
confirmed. Cards 🖃 💳 📷 💷 💷 Prof Ken Wickham
Course Designer J Braid Facilities ⊗ ⅢⅢ by arrangement
🍴 💷 ♀ ♨ 🖥 📡 ⚲ ⚘ ♂ Conf Corporate Hospitality
Days available Location M1 junct 5, A41 to Harrow &
B462 to Bushey, 4th exit at rdbt, club 150yds on left

Hotel ★★★ 67% Corus hotel Elstree, Barnet Ln,
ELSTREE ☎ 0870 609 6151 47 en suite

Hartsbourne Golf & Country Club Hartsbourne
Ave WD2 1JW
☎ 020 8950 1133
18 holes, 6305yds, Par 71, SSS 70, Course record 62.
Location 5m SE of Watford
Phone for further details

Hotel ★★★ 67% Corus hotel Elstree, Barnet Ln,
ELSTREE ☎ 0870 609 6151 47 en suite

Cheshunt Park Cheshunt Park, Park Ln EN7 6QD
☎ 01992 624009 🖹 01992 636403
e-mail: brox.golf@lineone.net
Municipal parkland course, well bunkered with ponds,
easy walking.
18 holes, 6692yds, Par 72, SSS 71.
Club membership 350.
Visitors book tee times through reception in advance.
Societies phone for details. Green Fees not confirmed.
Cards 🖃 💳 📷 💷 💷 Prof David Banks Course
Designer P Wawtry Facilities ⊗ ⅢⅢ 🍴 💷 ♀ ♨ 🖥 📡 ⚲
♂ Leisure Club repair service. Location 1.5m NW off
B156. M25 junct 25, 3m N

Chorleywood Common Rd WD3 5LN
☎ 01923 282009 🖹 01923 286739
e-mail: chorleywood.gc@btclick.com
Very attractive mix of woodland and heathland with
natural hazards and good views.
9 holes, 5686yds, Par 68, SSS 67.
Club membership 300.
Visitors restricted Tue, weekends; contact in advance.
Societies initial contact by phone. Green Fees £20 per
round; £15 per 9 holes (£25/15 weekends). Facilities ⊗ ⅢⅢ
by arrangement 🍴 💷 ♀ ♨ Location M25 junct 18, E of
village off A404

Hotel ★★★ 71% The Bedford Arms, CHENIES
☎ 01923 283301 10 en suite

Elstree Watling St WD6 3AA
☎ 020 8953 6115 or 8238 6941 🖹 020 8207 6390
e-mail: admin@elstree-golf.co.uk
Undulating parkland course with ponds and streams.
18 holes, 6556yds, Par 73, SSS 72.
Club membership 400.

Visitors not before 11am weekends & bank holidays;
advisable to contact in advance; dress code. Societies
information pack available from club secretary. Green
Fees £37 weekdays (£45 weekends). 2 for 1 offers
available weekdays & after 11am weekends/bank holidays.
Cards 🖃 💳 💷 Prof Marc Warwick Course
Designer Donald Steel Facilities ⊗ ⅢⅢ by arrangement 🍴
💷 ♀ ♨ 🖥 📡 ⚲ ⚘ ♂ ♂ Leisure snooker. Conf fac
available Corporate Hospitality Days available
Location A5183 between Radlett & Elstree, next to
Wagon & Horses pub

Hotel ★★★ 67% Corus hotel Elstree, Barnet Ln,
ELSTREE ☎ 0870 609 6151 47 en suite

Hatfield London Country Club Bedwell Park
AL9 6HN
☎ 01707 260360 🖹 01707 278475
e-mail: info@hlccgolf.co.uk
Parkland course with many varied hazards, including
ponds, a stream and a ditch; 19th-century manor
clubhouse.
Old Course: 18 holes, 6808yds, Par 72, SSS 72.
New Course: 18 holes, 6938yds, Par 72, SSS 73.
Club membership 250.
Visitors contact in advance. Societies contact in advance.
Green Fees terms on application. Cards 🖃 💳 📷 💷 💷
Prof Norman Greer Course Designer Fred Hawtry
Facilities ⊗ ⅢⅢ 🍴 💷 ♀ ♨ 🖥 📡 ⚲ ♂ Leisure 9-hole
pitch & putt, Japanese bath. Conf fac available Corporate
Hospitality Days available Location 1m S on B158

Hotel ★★★ 65% Quality Hotel Hatfield, Roehyde Way,
HATFIELD ☎ 01707 275701 76 en suite

Chesfield Downs Jack's Hill SG4 7EQ
☎ 01462 482929 🖹 01462 482930
An undulating, open downland course with an inland
links feel.
18 holes, 6648yds, Par 71, SSS 72.
Club membership 500.
Visitors no restrictions. Societies phone in advance. Green
Fees £21 (£28 weekends). Cards 🖃 💳 📷 💷 💷
Prof Jane Fernley Course Designer J Gaunt Facilities ⊗
ⅢⅢ by arrangement 🍴 💷 ♀ ♨ 🖥 📡 ⚲ ⚘ ♂ ♂ Leisure
par 3 9-hole course. Conf fac available Corporate
Hospitality Days available Location A1 junct 8, B197 to
Graveley

Hotel ⯁ Hotel Ibis Stevenage, Danestrete, STEVENAGE
☎ 01438 779955 98 en suite

Aldwickbury Park Piggottshill Ln AL5 1AB
☎ 01582 760112 🖹 01582 760113
e-mail: enquiries@aldwickburyparkgolfclub.com
Wooded parkland course with lakes and spectacular
views across the Lea valley.
18 holes, 6352yds, Par 71, SSS 70, Course record 66.
Club membership 700.
Visitors not before 1pm weekends; book up to three days
in advance by phone. Societies phone for brochure, various
packages available. Green Fees £27 per 18 holes (£33 Fri-
Sun). Cards 🖃 💳 📷 💷 💷 Prof Robin Turley
Course Designer Ken Brown, Martin Gillett

Facilities ⊗ ⫼ ⮞ ♨ ♀ ♣ 🕋 ⛳ 🍴 ⛟ ♂ **Leisure**
gymnasium, 9-hole par 3 course. **Conf** fac available
Corporate Hospitality Days available **Location** M1 junct 9,
off Wheathampstead Rd between Harpenden &
Wheathampstead

Hotel ★★★ 67% Corus hotel Harpenden, 18 Southdown
Rd, HARPENDEN ☎ 01582 449955　17 en suite
59 annexe en suite

Harpenden Hammonds End, Redbourn Ln AL5 2AX
☎ 01582 712580　📠 01582 712725
e-mail: office@harpendengolfclub.co.uk
Gently undulating parkland course, easy walking.
18 holes, 6381yds, Par 70, SSS 70, Course record 65.
Club membership 800.
Visitors Thu & weekends by arrangement only; contact in
advance. **Societies** apply in writing. **Green Fees** £40 per
day, £30 per round (£40 per round weekends & bank
holidays). **Cards** 📧 💳 🏧 📶 💷 **Prof** Peter Cherry
Course Designer Hawtree & Taylor **Facilities** ⊗ ⫼ ⮞ ♨
♀ ♣ 🕋 ⛟ ♂ ⛳ **Location** 1m S on B487

Hotel ★★★ 67% Corus hotel Harpenden, 18 Southdown
Rd, HARPENDEN ☎ 01582 449955　17 en suite
59 annexe en suite

Harpenden Common Cravells Rd, East Common
AL5 1BL
☎ 01582 711328 (pro shop) 📠 01582 711321
e-mail: manager@hcgc.co.uk
Flat, easy walking, parkland course with good greens.
Golf has been played on the common for well over 100
years.
18 holes, 6214yds, Par 70, SSS 70, Course record 64.
Club membership 710.
Visitors contact in advance. **Societies** phone for
availability **Green Fees** £40 per 36 holes, £24 per round
(£35 per round weekends). 2 for 1 £40, Mon-Fri only.
Cards 📧 💳 **Prof** Danny Fitzsimmons **Course Designer**
K Brown **Facilities** ⊗ ⫼ ⮞ ♨ ♀ ♣ 🕋 ⛳ ♂
Location on A1081 0.5m S of Harpenden

HEMEL HEMPSTEAD　　　　　　Map 04 TL00

Boxmoor 18 Box Ln, Boxmoor HP3 0DJ
☎ 01442 242434
The second-oldest course in Hertfordshire. Challenging,
hilly, moorland course with sloping fairways divided by
trees. Fine views. Testing holes: 3rd (par 3), 4th (par 4).
The 3rd has not been holed in one since the course was
founded in 1890 and the par for the course (64) has only
been broken once.
9 holes, 4812yds, Par 64, SSS 63, Course record 62.
Club membership 280.
Visitors not before 9.30am Sun. **Societies** contact in
advance. **Green Fees** £10 per round. **Facilities** ⮞ ♨ ♀ ♣
Location 2m SW on B4505

Hotel ★★ 72% The Two Brewers, The Common,
CHIPPERFIELD ☎ 01923 265266　20 en suite

Little Hay Box Ln, Bovingdon HP3 0DQ
☎ 01442 833798　📠 01442 831399
e-mail: chris.gordon@dacorum.gov.uk
Semi-parkland, inland links.
18 holes, 6300yds, Par 72, SSS 72.
Visitors advisable to contact in advance. **Societies** phone
for details. **Green Fees** £14 per round (£18.50 weekends).

Cards 📧 💳 🏧 📶 💷 **Prof** N Allen, M Perry **Course**
Designer Hawtree **Facilities** ⊗ ⫼ ⮞ ♨ ♀ ♣ 🕋 ⛟
⛳ ⛳ **Location** 1.5m SW off A41 onto B4505

Hotel ★★★ 67% The Bobsleigh Hotel, Hempstead Rd,
Bovingdon, HEMEL HEMPSTEAD ☎ 01442 833276
30 en suite　15 annexe en suite

Shendish Manor London Rd, Apsley HP3 0AA
☎ 01442 251806　📠 01442 230683
e-mail: tconcannon@shendish.fsnet.co.uk
18 holes, 5660yds, Par 70, SSS 67.
Course Designer D Steel **Location** off A4251
Phone for further details

Hotel ★★★★ 68% Pendley Manor, Cow Ln, TRING
☎ 01442 891891　74 en suite

KNEBWORTH　　　　　　　　　　Map 04 TL22

Knebworth Deards End Ln SG3 6NL
☎ 01438 812752　📠 01438 815216
e-mail: knebworth.golf@virgin.net
Parkland course, easy walking.
18 holes, 6492yds, Par 71, SSS 71, Course record 66.
Club membership 900.
Visitors handicap certificate; with member only weekends.
Societies Mon, Tue & Thu. Must contact in advance.
Green Fees £35 per day/round. (weekdays only).
Cards 📧 💳 🏧 📶 💷 **Prof** Garry Parker
Course Designer W Park (Jun) **Facilities** ⊗ ⫼ ⮞ ♨ ♀
♣ 🕋 ♂ ⛳ **Conf** Corporate Hospitality Days available
Location N of village off B197

Hotel ★★★ 66% The Roebuck Inn, London Rd,
Broadwater, STEVENAGE ☎ 0870 011 9076　54 en suite

LETCHWORTH　　　　　　　　　Map 04 TL23

Letchworth Letchworth Ln SG6 3NQ
☎ 01462 683203　📠 01462 484567
e-mail: letchworthgolfclub@uk2.net
Planned more than 50 years ago by Harry Vardon, this
is an adventurous parkland course. To its variety of
natural and artificial hazards is added an unpredictable
wind.
18 holes, 6450yds, Par 71, SSS 71, Course record 66.
Club membership 750.
Visitors not Tue; with member only weekends; contact in
advance; handicap certificate. **Societies** Wed, Thu, Fri,
phone in advance. **Green Fees** terms on application. **Prof**
Karl Teschner **Course Designer** Harry Vardon **Facilities**
⊗ ⫼ ⮞ ♨ ♀ ♣ 🕋 ⛳ ⛳ **Leisure** 9-hole par 3 course.
Conf Corporate Hospitality Days available **Location** S of
town centre off A505

Hotel ★★★ 63% The Cromwell Hotel, High St, Old
Town, STEVENAGE ☎ 01438 779954　76 en suite

LITTLE GADDESDEN　　　　　　Map 04 SP91

Ashridge HP4 1LY
☎ 01442 842244　📠 01442 843770
e-mail: info@ashridgegolfclub.ltd.uk
Classic wooded parkland in area of outstanding natural
beauty.
18 holes, 6580yds, Par 72, SSS 71, Course record 63.
Club membership 720.
Visitors not weekends & bank holidays; contact in

Continued　　　　　　　　　　　　　　　　　　*Continued*

advance; member of recognised club; handicap certificate.
Societies apply in writing & complete booking form.
Green Fees terms on application. **Cards** ⌨ 💳 💳 📷 🖭
Prof Andrew Ainsworth **Course Designer** Sir G
Campbell, C Hutchinson, NV Hotchkin **Facilities** ⊗ ∭ 🏊
🐴 🖳 🏊 🏠 🍴 🚲 🏌 **Conf** Corporate Hospitality Days
available **Location** 5m N of Berkhamsted on B4506

Hotel ★★★ 67% Corus hotel Harpenden, 18 Southdown
Rd, HARPENDEN ☎ 01582 449955 17 en suite
59 annexe en suite

MUCH HADHAM Map 05 TL41

Ash Valley Little Hadham Rd SG10 6HD
☎ 01279 843253 📠 01279 842389
**Naturally undulating course with good views extending
to Canary Wharf in London on a clear day. Tough
enough for lower handicapped players but forgiving for
the beginner and higher handicapped player.**
18 holes, 6586yds, Par 72, SSS 71, Course record 64.
Club membership 150.
Visitors contact in advance for weekends. **Societies** phone
in advance. **Green Fees** £15 per day, £10 per round (£15
weekends & bank holidays). **Prof** John Hamilton **Course
Designer** Martin Gillett **Facilities** ⊗ 🏊 🖳 🍴 🏊 🏠 🚲 🏌
Leisure par 3 pitch & putt. **Location** 1.5m S of A120
Little Hadham lights

Hotel ★★★ 68% Roebuck Hotel, Baldock St, WARE
☎ 01920 409955 50 en suite

POTTERS BAR Map 04 TL20

Potters Bar Darkes Ln EN6 1DE
☎ 01707 652020 📠 01707 655051
e-mail: info@pottersbargolfclub.com
Undulating parkland course.
18 holes, 6279yds, Par 71, SSS 70.
Club membership 560.
Visitors with member only weekends; Ladies Day am
Wed. **Societies** Mon-Fri (pm Wed), by arrangement with
Secretary. **Green Fees** £26 for 18 holes. **Prof** Gary A'Ris,
Julian Harding **Course Designer** James Braid
Facilities ⊗ 🏊 🖳 🍴 🏊 🏠 🍴 🚲 🏌
Location M25 junct 24, 1m N

Hotel ⬆ Days Inn, Bignells Corner, POTTERS BAR
☎ 01707 665440 74 en suite

RADLETT Map 04 TL10

Porters Park Shenley Hill WD7 7AZ
☎ 01923 854127 📠 01923 855475
e-mail: info@porterspark.fsnet.co.uk
**A splendid, undulating parkland course with fine trees
and lush grass. The holes are all different and
interesting - on many, accuracy of shot to the green is of
paramount importance.**
18 holes, 6313yds, Par 70, SSS 70, Course record 64.
Club membership 700.
Visitors book 24 hours in advance; with member only
weekends. **Societies** Wed & Thu only, must apply in
writing. **Green Fees** terms on application. **Cards** ⌨
💳 💳 📷 🖭 **Prof** David Gleeson **Course Designer**
Braid **Facilities** ⊗ ∭ 🏊 🖳 🍴 🏊 🏠 🍴 🏌 🏌
Location NE of village off A5183

Hotel ⬆ Innkeeper's Lodge Borehamwood, Studio Way,
BOREHAM WOOD ☎ 020 8905 1455 55 en suite

REDBOURN Map 04 TL11

Redbourn Kinsbourne Green Ln AL3 7QA
☎ 01582 793493 📠 01582 794362
e-mail: enquiries@redbourngolfclub.com
**A mature parkland course offering a fair test of golf to
all standards. Water comes into play on a number of
holes.**
*Ver Course: 18 holes, 6506yds, Par 70, SSS 71, Course
record 67.*
Kingsbourne Course: 9 holes, 1361yds, Par 27.
Club membership 800.
Visitors Ver Course: contact up to three days in advance.
Par 3: no restrictions. **Societies** phone in advance. **Green
Fees** not confirmed. **Cards** ⌨ 💳 💳 📷 🖭 **Prof** Stephen
Hunter **Facilities** ⊗ ∭ 🏊 🖳 🍴 🏊 🏠 🍴 🚲 🏌 🏌
Conf Corporate Hospitality Days available
Location 1m N off A5183

Hotel ★★★ 67% Corus hotel Harpenden, 18 Southdown
Rd, HARPENDEN ☎ 01582 449955 17 en suite
59 annexe en suite

RICKMANSWORTH Map 04 TQ09

The Grove Chandler's Cross WD3 4TG
☎ 01923 294266 📠 01923 294268
e-mail: golf@thegrove.co.uk
**A course built to USGA specifications but following the
slopes, ridges and mounds that occur naturally within
the landscape. The fairway grass encourages crisp ball
striking and the greens are superb. Continuous hidden
cart path around all holes.**
18 holes, 7152yds.
Visitors Societies advisable to contact in advance. **Green
Fees** terms on application. **Cards** ⌨ 💳 💳 🖭 **Prof** Blyth
Reid **Course Designer** Kyle Phillips **Facilities** ⊗ ∭ 🏊 🖳
🍴 🏊 🏠 🍴 🐴 🚲 🏌 🏌 **Leisure** hard tennis courts,
outdoor & indoor heated swimming pools, sauna,
gymnasium. **Conf** fac available **Location** M25 junct 20,
A411

Hotel ★★★★★ 74% The Grove, Chandler's Cross,
RICKMANSWORTH ☎ 01923 807807 227 en suite

Moor Park WD3 1QN
☎ 01923 773146 📠 01923 777109
e-mail: enquiries@moorparkgc.co.uk
**Two parkland courses with rolling fairways - High
Course is challenging and will test the best golfer and
West Course demands a high degree of accuracy. The
clubhouse is a grade 1 listed mansion.**
*High Golf Course: 18 holes, 6713yds, Par 72, SSS 72,
Course record 63.*
*West Golf Course: 18 holes, 5815yds, Par 69, SSS 68,
Course record 60.*
Club membership 1700.
Visitors not weekends, bank holidays, before 1pm Tue,
Thu; contact in advance. **Societies** contact in advance.
Green Fees High: £77.50 per round. West: £47.50 per
round. **Cards** ⌨ 💳 💳 📷 🖭 **Prof** Lawrence Farmer
Course Designer HS Colt **Facilities** ⊗ 🏊 🖳 🍴 🏊 🏠 🍴
🐴 🚲 🏌 🏌 **Leisure** hard & grass tennis courts, chipping
green snooker room. **Conf** fac available Corporate
Hospitality Days available **Location** M25 junct 17/18, off
A404 to Northwood

Hotel ★★★ 71% The Bedford Arms, CHENIES
☎ 01923 283301 10 en suite

Rickmansworth Public Course Moor Ln

WD3 1QL

☎ 01923 775278

Undulating, municipal parkland course, short but tests skills to the full.

18 holes, 4656yds, Par 65, SSS 63.

Club membership 240.

Visitors contact in advance, seven day booking; set of clubs per person. **Societies** contact in advance. **Green Fees** £12 per round (£16.50 weekends). **Cards** 🖮 💳 📧 🔳 💷 **Prof** Alan Dobbins **Course Designer** Colt **Facilities** ⊗ ⵊ ⵊ 💷 ♀ 🔽 🏠 ⴲ ⵊ 🔀 ⵊ **Conf** fac available Corporate Hospitality Days available **Location** 2m S of town off A4145

·····

Hotel ★★★ 71% The Bedford Arms, CHENIES
☎ 01923 283301 10 en suite

ROYSTON   Map 05 TL34

Barkway Park Nuthampstead Rd, Barkway SG8 8EN

☎ 01763 849070

An undulating course criss-crossed by ditches which come into play on several holes. The challenging par 3 7th features a long, narrow green with out of bounds close to the right edge of the green.

18 holes, 6997yds, Par 74, SSS 74.

Club membership 380.

Visitors phone in advance for tee times. **Societies** apply for booking form. **Green Fees** not confirmed. **Cards** 🖮 💳 📧 🔳 💷 **Prof** Jamie Bates **Course Designer** Vivien Saunders **Facilities** ⊗ ⵊ ⵊ 💷 ♀ 🔽 🏠 🔀 ⵊ **Location** A10 onto B1368

·····

Hotel ★★★ 74% Duxford Lodge Hotel, Ickleton Rd, DUXFORD ☎ 01223 836444 11 en suite 4 annexe en suite

Heydon Grange Golf & Country Club Heydon

SG8 7NS

☎ 01763 208988 📠 01763 208926

e-mail: enquiries@heydon-grange.co.uk

Three nine-hole parkland courses - the Essex, Cambridgeshire and Hertfordshire - situated in gently rolling countryside. Courses are playable all year round.

Essex: 9 holes, 2891yds, Par 36, SSS 35, Course record 64.

Cambridgeshire: 9 holes, 3057yds, Par 36, SSS 36.

Hertfordshire: 9 holes, 2937yds, Par 36, SSS 36.

Club membership 250.

Visitors contact to book tee times for weekends. **Societies** phone in advance for booking form. **Green Fees** not confirmed. **Cards** 🖮 💳 📧 📱 🔳 💷 **Prof** John O'Leary **Course Designer** Cameron Sinclair **Facilities** ⊗ ⵊ ⵊ 💷 ♀ 🔽 ⵊ **Conf** Corporate Hospitality Days available **Location** M11 junct 10, A505 between Royston & Duxford

·····

Hotel ★★★ 74% Duxford Lodge Hotel, Ickleton Rd, DUXFORD ☎ 01223 836444 11 en suite 4 annexe en suite

Kingsway Cambridge Rd, Melbourn SG8 6EY

☎ 01763 262727 📠 01763 263298

The Melbourn course is short and deceptively tricky. This nine-hole course provides a good test for both beginners and experienced golfers. Out of bounds and strategically placed bunkers come into play on several holes, in particular the tough par 3 7th. The Orchard course is a cleverly designed par 3 course set among

trees. Ideal for sharpening the short game or as a family introduction to golf.

Melbourn Course: 9 holes, 2455yds, Par 33, SSS 32.

Orchard Course: 9 holes, 727yds, Par 27, SSS 27.

Club membership 150.

Visitors Societies phone for details. **Green Fees** not confirmed. **Cards** 🖮 📧 💳 🔳 💷 **Prof** S Brown, D Hastings, M Sturgess **Facilities** ⊗ ⵊ 💷 ♀ 🔽 🏠 ⵊ ⵊ **Location** off A10

·····

Hotel ★★★ 74% Duxford Lodge Hotel, Ickleton Rd, DUXFORD ☎ 01223 836444 11 en suite 4 annexe en suite

Royston Baldock Rd SG8 5BG

☎ 01763 242696 📠 01763 246910

e-mail: roystongolf@btconnect.com

Heathland course on undulating terrain and fine fairways. The 8th, 10th and 15th are the most notable holes on this all weather course.

18 holes, 6052yds, Par 70, SSS 70, Course record 65.

Club membership 850.

Visitors not weekends; subject to availability, contact in advance. **Societies** Mon-Fri, by arrangement. **Green Fees** not confirmed. **Cards** 🖮 💳 📧 🔳 💷 **Prof** Sean Clark **Course Designer** Harry Vardon **Facilities** ⊗ ⵊ 💷 ♀ 🔽 🏠 ⵊ ⵊ **Conf** fac available **Location** 0.5m W of town centre

·····

Hotel ★★★ 74% Duxford Lodge Hotel, Ickleton Rd, DUXFORD ☎ 01223 836444 11 en suite 4 annexe en suite

ST ALBANS   Map 04 TL10

Abbey View Westminster Lodge Leisure Ctr, Holywell

Hill AL1 2DL

☎ 01727 868227 📠 01727 848468

e-mail: abbey.view@leisureconnection.co.uk

Abbey View is a picturesque public course in the centre of the city, suitable for beginners and those wishing to test their short game. Fine views of the cathedral.

9 holes, 1411yds, Par 29, Course record 27.

Club membership 140.

Visitors no sharing clubs; suitable footwear; wide-wheel trolleys; pay & play. **Societies** phone or write in advance. **Green Fees** £6 (£7 weekends). **Prof** Nigel Lawrence **Facilities** ⵊ 🏠 ⵊ ⵊ **Leisure** hard & grass tennis courts, heated indoor swimming pool, sauna, solarium, gymnasium, crazy golf. **Conf** Corporate Hospitality Days available **Location** city centre, off Holywell Hill in Verulamium Park

·····

Hotel ★★★ 78% St Michael's Manor, Fishpool St, ST ALBANS ☎ 01727 864444 22 en suite

Continued

Batchwood Hall Batchwood Dr AL3 5XA
☎ 01727 844250 📠 01727 858506
e-mail: batchwood@leisureconnection.co.uk
Municipal parkland course designed by JH Taylor and opened in 1935.
18 holes, 6487yds, Par 71, SSS 71.
Club membership 350.
Visitors book by phone up to seven days in advance.
Societies contact the events manager by phone or e-mail.
Green Fees terms on application. **Cards** 🆒 💳 💳 💳 💳
Prof Mark Flitton **Course Designer** JH Taylor **Facilities**
⊗ 〠 🧖 💌 ♀ ⚷ ⏋ ⚷ **Leisure** hard tennis courts, squash,
gymnasium, Indoor tennis courts. **Conf** Corporate
Hospitality Days available **Location** 1m NW off A5183
....
Hotel ★★★ 78% St Michael's Manor, Fishpool St, ST
ALBANS ☎ 01727 864444 22 en suite

Verulam London Rd AL1 1JG
☎ 01727 853327 📠 01727 812201
e-mail: gm@verulamgolf.co.uk
**Easy walking parkland course with 14 holes having
out of bounds. Water affects the 12th, 13th and 14th
holes. Samuel Ryder was captain here in 1927 when he
began the now celebrated Ryder Cup competition.**
18 holes, 6448yds, Par 72, SSS 71, Course record 67.
Club membership 720.
Visitors contact pro shop in advance; with member only
weekends. **Societies** contact in advance. **Green Fees** Mon:
£25 per round, Tue-Fri: £30, weekends £40. **Cards** 💳
Prof Nick Burch **Course Designer** Braid **Facilities** ⊗ 〠
by arrangement 🧖 💌 ♀ △ 🏠 ⚷ ⏉ **Conf** fac available
Corporate Hospitality Days available **Location** 0.5m from
St Albans centre on A1081 signed by railway bridge
....
Hotel ★★★★ 72% Sopwell House, Cottonmill Ln,
Sopwell, ST ALBANS ☎ 01727 864477 113 en suite
16 annexe en suite

Manor of Groves Golf & Country Club
High Wych CM21 0JU
☎ 01279 603543 📠 01279 726972
e-mail: golf@manorofgroves.co.uk

18 holes, 6228yds, Par 71, SSS 70, Course record 63.
Course Designer S Sharer **Location** 1.5m west of town
centre
Phone for further details
....
Hotel ★★★ 62% Briggens House Hotel, Stanstead Rd,
STANSTEAD ABBOTTS ☎ 01279 829955 54 en suite

Manor of Groves Hotel, Golf & Country Club is proud to
offer an 18 hole par 71 Championship Golf Course with
US-style sandbedded greens. The course winds its way
around the Hotel and provides a true test of golfing ability.

Our resident PGA Professional is on hand to offer advice
and assistance. In addition to a well-stocked professional
shop, a wide variety of services including tuition, equipment
hire and club repairs are provided for your enjoyment.

Tel: 0870 410 8833   Fax: 0870 417 8833
email: golf@manorofgroves.co.uk

Briggens House Hotel Briggens Park, Stanstead Rd
SG12 8LD
☎ 01279 793742 📠 01279 793685
**An attractive nine-hole course set in the grounds of a
hotel which was once a stately house in 80 acres of
countryside.**
9 holes, 2793yds, Par 36, SSS 69, Course record 31.
Club membership 230.
Visitors not 5-6pm Thu, am Sun; no jeans; own clubs &
shoes (hire available). **Societies** contact in advance. **Green
Fees** £15 per 18 holes (£17 weekends & bank holidays).
Cards 🆒 💳 💳 💳 💳 💳 💳 **Prof** Alan McGinn
Facilities ⊗ 〠 🧖 💌 ♀ △ 🏠 ⏋ 🐾 ⚓ 🚣 ⚷ **Leisure**
hard tennis courts, heated outdoor swimming pool, fishing.
Conf fac available Corporate Hospitality Days available
Location off A414 Stanstead road
....
Hotel ★★★ 62% Briggens House Hotel, Stanstead Rd,
STANSTEAD ABBOTTS ☎ 01279 829955 54 en suite

Stevenage Golf Centre 6 Aston Ln, Aston SG2 7EL
☎ 01438 880223 & 880424 (pro shop) 📠 01438 880040
**Municipal course designed by John Jacobs, with
natural water hazards and some wooded areas.**
*Bragbury Course: 18 holes, 6451yds, Par 72, SSS 71,
Course record 63.*
Aston Course: 9 holes, 880yds, Par 27, SSS 27.
Club membership 600.
Visitors no restrictions. **Societies** contact one week in
advance, deposit required. **Green Fees** not confirmed.

Continued

Cards ⊞ ▬ ▦ ▩ 🗆 **Prof** Steve Barker **Course Designer** John Jacobs **Facilities** ⊗ ⅲ ⓛ 💺 ♀ ☖ 🖻 ✐ ⓣ **Leisure** par 3 course. **Conf** fac available Corporate Hospitality Days available **Location** 4m SE off B5169

....

Hotel ★★★ 66% The Roebuck Inn, London Rd, Broadwater, STEVENAGE ☎ 0870 011 9076 54 en suite

---

WARE   See page 137

WARE   Map 05 TL31

Chadwell Springs Hertford Rd SG12 9LE
☎ 01920 461447 🗅 01920 466596
9 holes, 6418yds, Par 72, SSS 71, Course record 68.
Location 0.75m W on A119
Phone for further details

....

Hotel ★★★ 68% Roebuck Hotel, Baldock St, WARE ☎ 01920 409955 50 en suite

Whitehill Dane End SG12 0JS
☎ 01920 438495 🗅 01920 438891
e-mail: whitehillgolf@btconnect.com
Undulating course providing a good test for both the average golfer and the low handicapper. Several lakes in challenging positions.
18 holes, 6618yds, Par 72, SSS 72.
Club membership 600.
Visitors dress code. **Societies** phone or write for booking form. **Green Fees** £23 (£30 weekends). **Cards** ⊞ ▬ ▦
▩ 🗆 **Prof** David Ling **Facilities** ⊗ ⅲ ⓛ 💺 ♀ ☖ 🖻 ⓣ
➘ ♣ ✐ ⓣ **Conf** Corporate Hospitality Days available

....

Hotel ★★★ 68% Roebuck Hotel, Baldock St, WARE ☎ 01920 409955 50 en suite

---

WATFORD   Map 04 TQ19

West Herts Cassiobury Park WD3 3GG
☎ 01923 236484 🗅 01923 222300
Set in parkland, the course is close to Watford but its tree-lined setting is beautiful and tranquil. The plateau course is exceedingly dry. It also has a very severe finish with the 17th, a hole of 378yds, the toughest on the course. The last hole measures over 480yds.
18 holes, 6528yds, Par 72, SSS 71, Course record 65.
Club membership 700.
Visitors contact in advance. **Societies** phone in advance & confirm in writing. **Green Fees** £38 per 18 holes (£48 weekends). **Cards** ⊞ ▬ 🗆 **Prof** Charles Gough **Course Designer** Tom Morris **Facilities** ⊗ ⅲ ⓛ 💺 ♀ ☖ 🖻 ⓣ
♣ ✐ **Leisure** indoor teaching facility. **Conf** Corporate Hospitality Days available **Location** W of town centre off A412

....

Hotel ★★★ 67% The White House, Upton Rd, WATFORD ☎ 01923 237316 57 en suite

---

WELWYN GARDEN CITY   Map 04 TL21

Mill Green Gypsy Ln AL6 4TY
☎ 01707 276900 & 270542 (pro shop) 🗅 01707 276898
e-mail: millgreen@americangolf.uk.com
18 holes, 6615yds, Par 72, SSS 72, Course record 64.
Course Designer Alliss & Clark **Location** A1(M) junct 4, A414 to Mill Green
Phone for further details

Hotel ★★★ 61% Quality Hotel Welwyn, The Link, WELWYN ☎ 01438 716911 96 en suite

Panshanger Golf & Squash Complex
Old Herns Ln AL7 2ED
☎ 01707 333350 & 333312 🗅 01707 390010
e-mail: r.preece@welhat.gov.uk
Picturesque, mature course overlooking Mimram Valley. Challenging.
18 holes, 6347yds, Par 72, SSS 70, Course record 65.
Club membership 400.
Visitors advisable to book one week in advance by phone; dress code. **Societies** phone for details. **Green Fees** £15 per 18 holes (£19 weekends). **Cards** ⊞ ▬ ▦ ▩ 🗆 **Prof** Bryan Lewis, Mick Corlass **Course Designer** Peter Kirkham **Facilities** ⊗ ⅲ ⓛ 💺 ♀ ☖ ⓣ ➘ ♣ ✐ **Leisure** squash.
Conf fac available Corporate Hospitality Days available **Location** 1m N of town centre signed off B1000

....

Hotel ★★★ 61% Quality Hotel Welwyn, The Link, WELWYN ☎ 01438 716911 96 en suite

Welwyn Garden City Mannicotts, High Oaks Rd
AL8 7BP
☎ 01707 325243 🗅 01707 393213
e-mail: secretary@welwyngardencitygolfclub.co.uk
Undulating parkland course with a ravine. A former course record holder is Nick Faldo.
18 holes, 6074yds, Par 70, SSS 69, Course record 63.
Club membership 930.
Visitors not am Sun; contact in advance. **Societies** contact in advance. **Green Fees** terms on application. **Cards** ⊞
▬ ▩ 🗆 **Prof** Richard May **Facilities** ⊗ ⅲ ⓛ 💺 ♀ ☖
🖻 ➘ ♣ ✐ **Location** A1 junct 6, W of city

....

Hotel ★★★ 61% Quality Hotel Welwyn, The Link, WELWYN ☎ 01438 716911 96 en suite

---

WHEATHAMPSTEAD   Map 04 TL11

Mid Herts Lamer Ln, Gustard Wood AL4 8RS
☎ 01582 832242 🗅 01582 834834
e-mail: secretary@mid-hertsgolfclub.co.uk
Commonland, wooded with heather and gorse-lined fairways.
18 holes, 6060yds, Par 69, SSS 69, Course record 61.
Club membership 760.
Visitors not Tue, pm Wed, weekends. **Societies** contact by writing or phone **Green Fees** not confirmed. **Prof** Barney Puttick **Facilities** ⊗ ⓛ 💺 ♀ ☖ 🖻 ✐ **Conf** fac available **Location** 1m N on B651

....

Hotel ★★★ 67% Corus hotel Harpenden, 18 Southdown Rd, HARPENDEN ☎ 01582 449955 17 en suite 59 annexe en suite

---

KENT

ADDINGTON   Map 05 TQ65

West Malling London Rd ME19 5AR
☎ 01732 844785 🗅 01732 844795
e-mail: mike@westmallinggolf.com
Two 18-hole parkland courses.
Spitfire Course: 18 holes, 6142yds, Par 70, SSS 70, Course record 67.
Hurricane Course: 18 holes, 6281yds, Par 70, SSS 70, Course record 68.

Continued   *Continued*

Marriott Hanbury Manor

Hertfordshire

Ware

Map 05 TL31

There can be few golf venues that combine so successfully the old and the new. The old is the site itself, dominated since the 19th century by Hanbury Manor, a Jacobean-style mansion; the wonderful grounds included a nine-hole parkland course designed by the legendary Harry Vardon. The new is the conversion of the estate into the golf and country club; the manor now offers a five-star country house hotel, while Jack Nicklaus II redesigned the grounds for an 18-hole course. The American-style design took the best of Vardon's original and added meadowland to produce a course that looks beautiful and plays superbly. Hanbury Manor has hosted a number of professional events, including the Women's European Open in 1996 and the Men's European Tour's English Open from 1997 to 1999, won respectively by Per Ulrik Johannson, Lee Westwood and Darren Clarke.

Golf & Country Club SG12 0SD
☎ 01920 487722 Fax 01920 487692
e-mail: golf.hanburymanor@marriotthotels.co.uk

18 holes, 7016yds, Par 72, SSS 74, Course record 61.
Club membership 900.
Visitors handicap certificate; hotel residents & golf day participants only; must contact in advance. **Societies** Mon, Tue, Wed, Thu, must book in advance. **Green Fees** terms on application. **Cards** 💳 **Prof** Richard Booth **Course Designer** Jack Nicklaus II **Facilities** ⊗ 🍽 🏐 🏌 ♀ 🏌 🏐 🥎 🏌 ♂ **Leisure** hard tennis courts, heated indoor swimming pool, sauna, solarium, gymnasium. **Conf** fac available Corporate Hospitality Days available **Location** M25 junct 25, 12m N on A10

....

Hotels

★★★★★ 71% Marriott Hanbury Manor Hotel & Country Club, WARE

☎ 01920 487722 & 0870 400 7222 Fax 01920 487692
134 en suite 27 annexe en suite

★★★ 68% Roebuck Hotel, Baldock St, WARE

☎ 01920 409955 Fax 01920 468016 50 en suite

Visitors not am weekends; contact in advance. **Societies** booking required. **Green Fees** terms on application. **Cards** 🏧 💳 📇 📶 💶 **Prof** Duncan Lambert **Course Designer** Max Falkner **Facilities** ⊗ ⅋ 🍴 💺 ♀ 👟 🏠 🐴 🚵 ♂ ⚑ **Leisure** gymnasium, Jacuzzi & steam room. **Conf** fac available Corporate Hospitality Days available **Location** 1m S off A20

....

Hotel ★★★ 67% Larkfield Priory Hotel, London Rd, Larkfield, MAIDSTONE ☎ 01732 846858 52 en suite

ASH   Map 05 TQ66

The London South Ash Manor Estate TN15 7EN
☎ 01474 879899 📠 01474 879912
e-mail: golf@londongolf.co.uk
Visitors may only play the courses as guests of members or prospective members by invitation. The courses were designed by Jack Nicklaus: both include a number of lakes, generous fairways framed with native grasses and many challenging holes. A state-of-the-art drainage system ensures continuous play.
Heritage Course: 18 holes, 7208yds, Par 72, SSS 75, Course record 67.
International Course: 18 holes, 7005yds, Par 72, SSS 74. Club membership 500.
Visitors with member only & prospective members invited by the membership office. **Societies** write in advance. **Green Fees** International Course : £75 per round (£80 weekends). **Cards** 🏧 💳 📇 📶 💶 **Prof** Paul Stuart **Course Designer** Jack Nicklaus **Facilities** ⊗ ⅋ 💺 ♀ 🛖 🏠 ⚑ 👟 🐴 ♂ ⚑ **Leisure** sauna, spa bath. **Conf** fac available Corporate Hospitality Days available **Location** A20, 2m from Brands Hatch

....

Hotel ★★★ 67% Larkfield Priory Hotel, London Rd, Larkfield, MAIDSTONE ☎ 01732 846858 52 en suite

ASHFORD   Map 05 TR04

Ashford Sandyhurst Ln TN25 4NT
☎ 01233 622655 📠 01233 622655
Parkland course with good views and easy walking. Narrow fairways and tightly bunkered greens ensure a challenging game.
18 holes, 6263yds, Par 71, SSS 70, Course record 65. Club membership 650.
Visitors contact in advance; handicap certificate. **Societies** Tue, Thu, by arrangement. **Green Fees** not confirmed. **Prof** Hugh Sherman **Course Designer** Cotton **Facilities** ⊗ ⅋ by arrangement 💺 ♀ 🛖 🏠 🐴 ♂ **Location** 1.5m NW off A20

....

Hotel ★★★★ 69% Ashford International, Simone Weil Av, ASHFORD ☎ 01233 219988 200 en suite

Homelands Bettergolf Centre Ashford Rd, Kingsnorth TN26 1NJ
☎ 01233 661620
e-mail: isj@bettergolf.co.uk
Challenging nine-hole course designed by Donald Steel to provide a stern test for experienced golfers and for others to develop their game. With four par 3s and five par 4s it demands accuracy rather than length. Floodlit driving range.
9 holes, 2205yds, Par 32, SSS 31, Course record 32. Club membership 400.
Visitors booking essential for weekends & summer evenings. **Societies** by arrangement only. **Green Fees** terms on application. **Cards** 🏧 💳 💶 **Prof** Tony Bowers

Continued

Course Designer Donald Steel **Facilities** 💺 ♀ 🍴 ♀ 🛖 🏠 ⚑ 🐴 ♂ ⚑ **Location** M20 junct 10, A2070, signed from 2nd rdbt to Kingsnorth

....

Hotel ⬦ Premier Travel Inn Ashford Central, Hall Av, Orbital Park, Sevington, ASHFORD ☎ 08701 977305 60 en suite

BARHAM   Map 05 TR25

Broome Park The Broome Park Estate CT4 6QX
☎ 01227 830728 📠 01227 832591
e-mail: golf@broomepark.co.uk
Championship standard parkland course in a valley, with a 17th-century mansion clubhouse.
18 holes, 6580yds, Par 72, SSS 71, Course record 66. Club membership 700.
Visitors not am weekends; advisable to contact in advance; handicap certificate. **Societies** Mon-Fri & Sat-Sun after 1pm, apply by writing or phone. **Green Fees** £40 per round (£50 weekends). **Cards** 🏧 💳 📇 📶 💶 **Prof** Tienne Britz **Course Designer** Donald Steel **Facilities** ⊗ ⅋ 💺 ♀ 🛖 🏠 ⚑ 🐴 ♂ **Leisure** hard tennis courts. **Conf** fac available Corporate Hospitality Days available **Location** 1.5m SE on A260

....

Hotel ★★★ 67% The Falstaff Hotel, 8-10 St Dunstan's St, CANTERBURY ☎ 0870 609 6102 25 en suite 22 annexe en suite

BEARSTED   Map 05 TQ85

Bearsted Ware St ME14 4PQ
☎ 01622 738198 📠 01622 735608
Parkland course with fine views of the North Downs.
18 holes, 6437yds, Par 72, SSS 71. Club membership 780.
Visitors contact in advance; handicap certificate; with member only weekends. **Societies** write for reservation forms. **Green Fees** £42 per 36 holes; £32 per 18 holes. **Prof** Tim Simpson **Facilities** ⊗ ⅋ 💺 ♀ 🛖 🏠 ♂ **Location** M20 junct 7, right at rdbt, left at minirdbt, left at 2nd minirdbt. Pass Bell pub on right, under bridge, on left

....

Hotel ★★★★ 70% Marriott Tudor Park Hotel & Country Club, Ashford Rd, Bearsted, MAIDSTONE ☎ 01622 734334 120 en suite

BIDDENDEN   Map 05 TQ83

Chart Hills Weeks Ln TN27 8JX
☎ 01580 292222 📠 01580 292233
e-mail: info@charthills.co.uk

18 holes, 7107yds, Par 72, SSS 74, Course record 61.
Course Designer Nick Faldo **Location** 1m N of Biddenden off A274
Phone for further details

Continued

Hotel ★★★ 75% London Beach Hotel & Golf Club, Ashford Rd, TENTERDEN ☎ 01580 766279 26 en suite

BOROUGH GREEN   Map 05 TQ65

Wrotham Heath Seven Mile Ln TN15 8QZ
☎ 01732 884800 ▤ 01732 887370
Heathland woodland course with magnificent views of the North Downs.
18 holes, 5954yds, Par 70, SSS 69, Course record 66.
Club membership 550.
Visitors weekends with member only. **Societies** Fri, by arrangement. **Green Fees** not confirmed. **Cards** ▤ **Prof** Harry Dearden **Course Designer** Donald Steel (part) **Facilities** ⊗ ⋔ ⓛ ⓗ ☻ ♀ ♨ ☞ ⓖ **Location** 2.25m E on B2016

Hotel ⬥ Premier Travel Inn Sevenoaks/Maidstone, London Rd, Wrotham Heath, WROTHAM ☎ 08701 977227 40 en suite

BRENCHLEY   Map 05 TQ64

Moatlands Watermans Ln TN12 6ND
☎ 01892 724400 ▤ 01892 723300
e-mail: moatlandsgolf@btinternet.com
18 holes, 6693yds, Par 72, SSS 72, Course record 63.
Course Designer T Saito **Location** 3m N of Brenchley off B2160
Phone for further details

Hotel ★★ 65% Russell Hotel, 80 London Rd, TUNBRIDGE WELLS ☎ 01892 544833 19 en suite 5 annexe en suite

BROADSTAIRS   Map 05 TR36

North Foreland Convent Rd, Kingsgate CT10 3PU
☎ 01843 862140 ▤ 01843 862663
e-mail: office@northforeland.co.uk
A picturesque clifftop course situated above the Thames estuary. One of the few courses where the sea can be seen from every hole. Walking is easy and the wind is deceptive. The 8th and 17th, both par 4, are testing holes. There is also an 18-hole approach and putting course.
18 holes, 6430yds, Par 71, SSS 71, Course record 63.
Club membership 1100.
Visitors Main course: booking required; handicap certificate; not am Mon-Tue, am Sun, restricted weekends. Short course: no restrictions. **Societies** Wed, Fri, by arrangement. **Green Fees** £50 per day; £35 per round (£75/#50 weekends & bank holidays). **Cards** ▤ ▤ ▤ ⓖ **Prof** Darren Parris **Course Designer** Fowler & Simpson **Facilities** ⊗ ⋔ ⓛ ☻ ♀ ♨ ☞ ⓖ
Leisure hard tennis courts, 18-hole par 3 course.
Location 1.5m N off B2052

Hotel ★★★ 68% Royal Albion Hotel, Albion St, BROADSTAIRS ☎ 01843 868071 19 en suite

CANTERBURY   Map 05 TR15

Canterbury Scotland Hills, Littlebourne Rd CT1 1TW
☎ 01227 453532 ▤ 01227 784277
e-mail: cgc@freeola.com
Undulating parkland course, densely wooded in places, with elevated tees and challenging drives on several holes.

Canterbury Golf Club

18 holes, 6272yds, Par 71, SSS 70, Course record 64.
Club membership 700.
Visitors not before 9.30am & during competitions, restricted weekends & bank holidays; handicap certificate. **Societies** by arrangement. **Green Fees** £70 per day, £45 per round; (£50 per round weekends). **Cards** ▤ ▤ ▤ ▤ ▤ ⓖ **Prof** Paul Everard **Course Designer** Harry Colt **Facilities** ⊗ ⋔ ⓛ ☻ ♀ ♨ ☞ ⓖ ☞ ♨ ⓖ **Conf** fac available Corporate Hospitality Days available **Location** 1.5m E on A257

Hotel ★★★ 67% The Falstaff Hotel, 8-10 St Dunstan's St, CANTERBURY ☎ 0870 609 6102 25 en suite 22 annexe en suite

CHART SUTTON   Map 05 TQ84

The Ridge Chartway St, East Sutton ME17 3DL
☎ 01622 844382
18 holes, 6254yds, Par 71, SSS 70, Course record 68.
Course Designer Tyton Design **Location** 5m S of Bearsted off A274
Phone for further details

Hotel ★★★★ 70% Marriott Tudor Park Hotel & Country Club, Ashford Rd, Bearsted, MAIDSTONE ☎ 01622 734334 120 en suite

CRANBROOK   Map 05 TQ73

Hemsted Forest Golford Rd TN17 4AL
☎ 01580 712833 ▤ 01580 714274
e-mail: golf@hemstedforest.co.uk
Scenic, parkland course with easy terrain, backed by Hemstead Forest and close to Sissinghurst Castle and Bodiam Castle. The course lies in a beautiful natural setting and offers a haven of tranquillity. The clubhouse, a converted oast, is the only one of its kind.
18 holes, 6305yds, Par 70, SSS 71, Course record 64.
Club membership 1600.
Visitors not before 8am weekdays, 11am weekends, tee reservations can be booked upto one calendar month in advance. **Societies** phone to book. **Green Fees** £25 per round (£40 weekends). **Cards** ▤ ▤ ▤ ⓖ **Prof** Chris Weston **Course Designer** Commander J Harris **Facilities** ⊗ ⋔ ⓛ ☻ ♀ ♨ ☞ ⓖ **Conf** fac available **Location** 2m E

Hotel ★★★ 75% London Beach Hotel & Golf Club, Ashford Rd, TENTERDEN ☎ 01580 766279 26 en suite

> **If the name of the club appears in *italics*, details have not been confirmed for this edition of the guide.**

Continued

DARTFORD · Map 05 TQ57

Birchwood Park Birchwood Rd, Wilmington
DA2 7HJ
☎ 01322 662038 & 660554 📠 01322 667283
e-mail: info@birchwoodparkgc.co.uk
The main course offers highly challenging play and will
test golfers of all abilities. Beginners and those
requiring a quick game or golfers wishing to improve
their short game will appreciate the Orchard course
where holes range from 96 to 258yds.
*Parkland: 18 holes, 6364yds, Par 71, SSS 70, Course
record 64.*
Orchard: 9 holes, 1349yds, Par 29.
Club membership 600.
Visitors Main Course: contact in advance. Societies phone
for details. Green Fees terms on application. Cards 🔲
🔲 🔲 🔲 Course Designer Howard Swann
Facilities ⊗ �🍴 ⅃ 🖥 ♀ ⛷ 🏠 🐎 🏌 Leisure
sauna, solarium, gymnasium. Conf fac available Corporate
Hospitality Days available Location B258 between
Dartford & Swanley
· · · · · · · · · · · · · · · · ·

Hotel ★★★★ 67% Bexleyheath Marriott Hotel, 1
Broadway, BEXLEYHEATH
☎ 0870 400 7245 142 en suite

Dartford Heath Ln (Upper), Dartford Heath DA1 2TN
☎ 01322 226455 📠 01322 226455
e-mail: dartfordgolf@hotmail.com
Challenging parkland course with tight fairways and
easy walking.
18 holes, 5909yds, Par 69, SSS 69, Course record 61.
Club membership 700.
Visitors not weekends; handicap certificate. Societies
Mon, Fri, by arrangement with Secretary. Green Fees £23
per 18 holes weekdays. Prof John Gregory Course
Designer James Braid Facilities ⊗ ⍦ ⅃ 🖥 ♀ ⛷ 🏠 🏌
Conf Corporate Hospitality Days available
Location 2m from town centre off A2
· · · · · · · · · · · · · · · · ·

Hotel � Campanile, 1 Clipper Boulevard West,
Crossways Business Park, DARTFORD
☎ 01322 278925 125 en suite

DEAL · Map 05 TR35

Royal Cinque Ports Golf Rd CT14 6RF
☎ 01304 374007 📠 01304 379530
e-mail: rcpgcsec@aol.com
Famous championship seaside links, windy but with
easy walking. Outward nine is generally considered the
easier, inward nine is longer and includes the renowned
16th, perhaps the most difficult hole. On a fine day
there are wonderful views across the Channel.
18 holes, 6899yds, Par 72, SSS 73.
Club membership 950.
Visitors restricted Wed am, weekends & bank holidays;
contact in advance; handicap certificate; men max 20
handicap; ladies max 30 handicap. Societies contact in
advance. Green Fees not confirmed. Cards 🔲 🔲 🔲
Prof Andrew Reynolds Course Designer James Braid
Facilities ⊗ ⍦ by arrangement 🖥 🖥 ♀ ⛷ 🏠 🏌
Conf Corporate Hospitality Days available
Location on seafront at N end of Deal
· · · · · · · · · · · · · · · · ·

Hotel ★★★ 75% Wallett's Court Country House Hotel &
Spa, West Cliffe, St Margarets-at-Cliffe, DOVER

Continued

☎ 01304 852424 & 0800 0351628 📠 01304 853430
3 en suite 13 annexe en suite

EDENBRIDGE · · · · · · · · · · · · · · · · Map 05 TQ44

Sweetwoods Park Cowden TN8 7JN
☎ 01342 850729 (pro shop) 📠 01342 850866
e-mail: danhowe@sweetwoodspark.com
An undulating and mature parkland course with very
high quality greens, testing water hazards and fine
views across the Weald from four holes. A good
challenge off the back tees. Signature holes include the
2nd, 4th and 14th.
18 holes, 6617yds, Par 72, SSS 72, Course record 63.
Club membership 700.
Visitors no restrictions. Societies after 9am Mon-Fri & pm
Sat, contact for details. Green Fees £28 per round (£34
weekends). 2 for 1 Mon, Wed pm & Sun after 2pm. Cards
🔲 🔲 🔲 🔲 🔲 🔲 Prof Paul Lyons Course
Designer P Strand Facilities ⊗ ⍦ ⅃ 🖥 ♀ ⛷ 🏠 🐎
🏌 Leisure golf college. Conf fac available Corporate
Hospitality Days available Location 4m E of East
Grinstead on A264
· · · · · · · · · · · · · · · · ·

Hotel ★★★ ♨ Gravetye Manor Hotel, EAST
GRINSTEAD ☎ 01342 810567 18 en suite

EYNSFORD · · · · · · · · · · · · · · · · Map 05 TQ56

Austin Lodge Upper Austin Lodge Rd DA4 0HU
☎ 01322 863000 📠 01322 862406
e-mail: linda@pentlandgolf.co.uk
A well-drained course designed to lie naturally in three
secluded valleys in rolling countryside. Over 7000yds
from the medal tees. Practice ground, nets and a
putting green add to the features.
18 holes, 7026yds, Par 73, SSS 71, Course record 68.
Club membership 400.
Visitors soft spikes only. Societies phone for bookings
0800 2585018. Green Fees £19 per 18 holes (£25
weekends & bank holidays). Cards 🔲 🔲 🔲 🔲 Prof
Greg Haenen Course Designer P Bevan Facilities ⊗ ⍦ ⅃
🖥 ♀ ⛷ 🏠 🐎 🏌 Location 6m S of Dartford
· · · · · · · · · · · · · · · · ·

Hotel ★★★★ 74% Brandshatch Place, Brands Hatch Rd,
Fawkham, BRANDS HATCH ☎ 01474 875000
26 en suite 12 annexe en suite

FAVERSHAM · · · · · · · · · · · · · · · · Map 05 TR06

Boughton Brickfield Ln, Boughton ME13 9AJ
☎ 01227 752277 📠 01227 752361
e-mail: greg@pentlandgolf.co.uk
Rolling parkland and downland course set in 160 acres
of Kent countryside, providing a good test of golf, even
for the more accomplished players.
18 holes, 6469yds, Par 72, SSS 71, Course record 68.
Club membership 350.
Visitors phone in advance. Societies phone for details
freephone 0800 2585018. Green Fees not confirmed.
Cards 🔲 🔲 🔲 🔲 Prof Trevor Dungate Course
Designer P Sparks Facilities ⊗ ⍦ ⅃ 🖥 ♀ ⛷ 🏠 🐎 🏌
🐎 🏌 Location M2 junct 7, Brenley Corner
· · · · · · · · · · · · · · · · ·

Hotel ★★★★ ♨ Eastwell Manor, Eastwell Park,
Boughton Lees, ASHFORD ☎ 01233 213000 23 en suite
39 annexe en suite

Faversham Belmont Park ME13 0HB
☎ 01795 890561 📠 01795 890760
e-mail: themanager@faershamgolf.co.uk
A beautiful inland course laid out over part of a large estate with pheasants walking the fairways quite tamely. Play follows two heavily wooded valleys but the trees affect only the loose shots going out of bounds. Fine views.

18 holes, 5965yds, Par 70, SSS 69, Course record 62. Club membership 800.
Visitors advisable contact in advance; handicap certificate; with member only weekends. Societies contact in advance. Green Fees £30 per round. Prof Stuart Rokes Facilities ⊗ ⊞ ⊾ ⬤ ♀ ♧ ⌂ ⟋ ⬥ 🚣 ♂ Conf Corporate Hospitality Days available Location 3.5m S on Belmont road

Hotel ★★★★ ♨ Eastwell Manor, Eastwell Park, Boughton Lees, ASHFORD ☎ 01233 213000 23 en suite 39 annexe en suite

FOLKESTONE   Map 05 TR23

Etchinghill Canterbury Rd, Etchinghill CT18 8FA
☎ 01303 863863 📠 01303 863210
e-mail: jill@pentlandgolf.co.uk
A varied course incorporating parkland on the outward nine holes and an interesting downland landscape with many challenging holes on the back nine.
27 holes, 6101yds, Par 70, SSS 69, Course record 67. Club membership 600.
Visitors advisable to reserve tee time in advance. Societies phone or write, packages available. Green Fees not confirmed. Cards 🌐 💳 🏦 📇 💳 Prof Chris Hodgson Course Designer John Sturdy Facilities ⊗ ⊞ ⊾ ⬤ ♀ ♧ ⌂ ⟋ ⬥ 🚣 ♂ ⟋ ⎨ Leisure 9 hole par3. Conf fac available Location M20 junct 11/12

Hotel ★★★ 70% Clifton Hotel, The Leas, FOLKESTONE ☎ 01303 851231 80 en suite

GILLINGHAM   Map 05 TQ76

Gillingham Woodlands Rd ME7 2AP
☎ 01634 853017 (office) 📠 01634 574749
e-mail: golf@gillinghamgolf.idps.co.uk
Mature parkland course with views of the estuary.
18 holes, 5495yds, Par 69, SSS 66, Course record 64. Club membership 900.
Visitors contact in advance; weekends only with member; handicap certificate. Societies weekdays, book in advance. Green Fees £28 per day, £20 per round. Prof Steven Green, Andrew Brooks Course Designer James Braid, Steel Facilities ⊗ ⊞ ⊾ ⬤ ♀ ♧ ⌂ ⟋

Leisure small practice area. Conf Corporate Hospitality Days available Location 1.5m SE on A2

Hotel ⬀ Premier Travel Inn Gillingham, Kent, Will Adams Way, GILLINGHAM ☎ 08701 977105 45 en suite

GRAVESEND   Map 05 TQ67

Mid Kent Singlewell Rd DA11 7RB
☎ 01474 568035 📠 01474 564218
e-mail: midkentgolfclub@aol.com
A well-maintained downland course with some easy walking and some excellent greens. The first hole is short, but nonetheless a real challenge. The slightest hook and the ball is out of bounds or lost.
18 holes, 6106yds, Par 70, SSS 69, Course record 60. Club membership 900.
Visitors not weekends; contact in advance; handicap certificate. Societies Tue only, apply in writing. Green Fees £35 per day; £25 per round. Prof Mark Foreman Course Designer Frank Pennick Facilities ⊗ ⊞ by arrangement ⊾ ⬤ ♀ ♧ ⌂ ⟋ ⬥ Location S of town centre off A227

Hotel ⬀ Premier Travel Inn Gravesend, Wrotham Rd, GRAVESEND ☎ 08701 977118 36 en suite

Southern Valley Thong Ln, Shorne DA12 4LF
☎ 01474 568568 📠 01474 360366
e-mail: info@southernvalley.co.uk
All year playing conditions on a course landscaped with gorse, bracken and thorn and designed to enhance the views across the Thames Estuary. The course features undulating greens, large trees and rolling fairways with both the 9th and 18th holes located close to the clubhouse.,
18 holes, 6200yds, Par 69, SSS 69, Course record 62. Club membership 450.
Visitors no restrictions. Societies phone in advance. Green Fees £17.50 (£22 weekends & bank holidays). Cards 🌐 💳 🏦 📇 💳 Prof Larry Batchelor Course Designer Weller, Richardson Facilities ⊗ ⊞ ⊾ ⬤ ♀ ♧ ⌂ ⟋ ⬥ 🚣 ⟋ Conf fac available Corporate Hospitality Days available Location A2 junct 4, off slip-road left onto Thong Ln, continue 1m

Hotel ★★★ 72% Manor Hotel, Hever Court Rd, GRAVESEND ☎ 01474 353100 59 en suite

HALSTEAD   Map 05 TQ46

Broke Hill Sevenoaks Rd TN14 7HR
☎ 01959 533225 📠 01959 532680
e-mail: bhgc@crown-golf.co.uk
A challenging game awaits all golfers. The fairways have strategically placed bunkers, some of which come into play off the tee. Five holes have water hazards, the most significant being the 18th where a lake has to be carried to get onto the green.
18 holes, 6454yds, Par 72, SSS 71, Course record 65. Club membership 650.
Visitors not weekends; book in advance. Societies phone for details. Green Fees not confirmed. Cards 🌐 💳 📇 💳 Prof Cameron McKillop Course Designer David Williams Facilities ⊗ ⊞ ⊾ ⬤ ♀ ♧ ⌂ ⟋ ⬥ 🚣 ⟋ Leisure sauna. Conf fac available Corporate Hospitality Days available Location M25 junct 4, opp Knockholt station

Continued   *Continued*

Hotel ★★★ 71% Donnington Manor, London Rd, Dunton Green, SEVENOAKS ☎ 01732 462681 60 en suite

HAWKHURST   Map 05 TQ73

Hawkhurst High St TN18 4JS
☎ 01580 754074 & 752396 📠 01580 754074
e-mail: hawkhurstgolfclub@tiscali.co.uk
Undulating parkland course.
9 holes, 5751yds, Par 70, SSS 68, Course record 69.
Club membership 450.
Visitors not am weekends. **Societies** apply in advance.
Green Fees £26 per day, £20 per round (£24 per round
weekdays). **Cards** ▭ ▭ ▧ ▨ **Prof** James Walpole
Course Designer WA Baldock **Facilities** ⊗ ⅢI by
arrangement ⓑ ⓦ ♀ ♧ ♤ ♏ ✎ **Leisure** squash.
Conf fac available **Location** W of village off A268

Hotel ★★★ 75% London Beach Hotel & Golf Club,
Ashford Rd, TENTERDEN ☎ 01580 766279 26 en suite

HEADCORN   Map 05 TQ84

Weald of Kent Maidstone Rd TN27 9PT
☎ 01622 890866 📠 01622 890866
e-mail: weald-of-kent@aol.com
**Enjoying delightful views over the Weald, this pay and
play course features a range of natural hazards,
including lakes, trees, ditches and undulating fairways.
A good test to golfers of every standard.**
18 holes, 6240yds, Par 70, SSS 70, Course record 64.
Club membership 450.
Visitors book three days in advance; smart casual dress
code, no jeans. **Societies** apply in writing or by phone.
Green Fees not confirmed. **Cards** ▭ ▭ ▨ ▧ **Prof** Paul
Fosten **Course Designer** John Millen **Facilities** ⊗ ⅢI ⓑ
ⓦ ♀ ♧ ♤ ♏ ✎ **Leisure** training academy.
Conf fac available Corporate Hospitality Days available
Location M20 Leeds Castle junct, through Leeds villag,
A274 towards Headcorn, course on left

Hotel ★★★★ 70% Marriott Tudor Park Hotel & Country
Club, Ashford Rd, Bearsted, MAIDSTONE
☎ 01622 734334 120 en suite

HERNE BAY   Map 05 TR16

Herne Bay Eddington CT6 7PG
☎ 01227 374727
18 holes, 5567yds, Par 68, SSS 68.
Course Designer James Braid **Location** on junct A291 &
A299
Phone for further details

Hotel ★★★ 67% The Falstaff Hotel, 8-10 St Dunstan's St,
CANTERBURY ☎ 0870 609 6102 25 en suite 22 annexe
en suite

HEVER   Map 05 TQ44

Hever Castle Hever Rd, Edenbridge TN8 7NP
☎ 01732 700771 📠 01732 700775
e-mail: mail@hevercastlegolfclub.co.uk
**Originally part of the Hever Castle estate, set in 250
acres, the Kings & Queens championship course has
matured well and, with the addition of the Princes' nine
holes, offers stunning holes to challenge all golfers.
Water plays a prominent part in the design of the
course, particularly around Amen Corner, holes 11
through 13. The golfer is then met with the lengthy**

Continued

stretch home, especially up the 17th, a daunting 644yd
par 5, one of Europe's longest.
*Kings & Queens Course: 18 holes, 6761yds, Par 72, SSS
73, Course record 69.*
Princes Course: 9 holes, 2784yds, Par 35.
Club membership 450.
Visitors Kings & Queens course: not before 11am; contact
in advance. **Societies** apply in writing or by phone. **Green
Fees** not confirmed. **Cards** ▭ ▭ ▭ ▨ ▧ **Prof**
Peter Parks **Course Designer** Dr Nicholas **Facilities** ⊗ ⅢI
ⓑ ⓦ ♀ ♧ ♤ ♏ ↺ ♦ ✎ **Leisure** hard tennis courts.
Conf fac available Corporate Hospitality Days available
Location off B269 between Oxted & Tonbridge, 0.5m
from Hever Castle

Hotel ★★★★ 71% The Spa Hotel, Mount Ephraim,
TUNBRIDGE WELLS ☎ 01892 520331 69 en suite

HILDENBOROUGH   Map 05 TQ54

Nizels Nizels Ln TN11 9LU
☎ 01732 838926 (Bookings) 📠 01732 833764
e-mail: nizels.retail@clubhaus.com
**Woodland course with many mature trees, wildlife and
lakes that come into play on several holes. The 2nd hole
is a 553yd par 5, the green being guarded by bunkers
hidden by a range of hillocks. The par 4 7th has water
on both sides of the fairway and a pitch over water to
the green. The 10th is a 539yd par 5 with a sharp dog-
leg to the right, followed by a very narrow entry
between trees for the second shot.**
18 holes, 6408yds, Par 72, SSS 71, Course record 65.
Club membership 650.
Visitors phone professional shop for tee reservation 01732
838926 at least four days in advance. **Societies** weekdays,
phone initially. **Green Fees** not confirmed. **Cards** ▭ ▭
▭ ▨ ▧ **Prof** Ally Mellor, David Brench **Course
Designer** Donaldson, Edwards Partnership **Facilities** ⊗ ⅢI
ⓑ ⓦ ♀ ♧ ♤ ♏ ↺ ♦ ✎ **Leisure** heated indoor
swimming pool, sauna, solarium, gymnasium.
Location off B245

Hotel ★★★ 67% Rose & Crown Hotel, 125 High St,
TONBRIDGE ☎ 01732 357966 54 en suite

HOO   Map 05 TQ77

Deangate Ridge Dux Court Rd ME3 8RZ
☎ 01634 251180 📠 01634 250537
**Parkland, municipal course designed by Fred Hawtree.
18-hole pitch and putt.**
18 holes, 6300yds, Par 71, SSS 70, Course record 65.
Club membership 500.
Visitors no restrictions. **Societies** phone 01634 254481.
Green Fees not confirmed. **Cards** ▭ ▭ ▨ ▧ **Prof**
Richard Fox **Course Designer** F Hawtree **Facilities** ⊗ ⅢI
ⓑ ⓦ ♀ ♧ ♤ ♏ ↺ ♦ ✎ **Leisure** hard tennis courts,
gymnasium. **Location** 4m NE of Rochester off A228

Hotel ★★★★ 74% Bridgewood Manor, Bridgewood
Roundabout, Walderslade Woods, CHATHAM
☎ 01634 201333 100 en suite

**Looking for a new course? Always telephone
ahead to confirm visitor arrangements.**

HYTHE
Map 05 TR13

Hythe Imperial Princes Pde CT21 6AE
☎ 01303 267441 🖹 01303 264610
e-mail: hytheimperial@marstonhotels.com
A nine-hole 18-tee links course bounded by the Royal Military Canal and the English Channel. Although the course is relatively flat, its aspect offers an interesting and challenging round to a wide range of golfers.
9 holes, 5560yds, Par 68, SSS 66, Course record 62. Club membership 300.
Visitors course closed some Sun until 11am for competitions. **Societies** advisable to phone. **Green Fees** not confirmed. **Cards** ▦ ▦ ▦ 🖥 ▦ ▦ 🖸 **Prof** Gordon Ritchie **Facilities** ⊗ ⅀ ⬛ ⬛ ♟ ♨ ♋ ♈ 🐾 ✓ **Leisure** hard & grass tennis courts, heated indoor swimming pool, squash, sauna, solarium, gymnasium, snooker. **Location** M20 junct 11, towards Hythe centre, right onto Twiss Rd, course in grounds of Hythe Imperial

Hotel ★★★★ 77% The Hythe Imperial, Princes Pde, HYTHE ☎ 01303 267441 100 en suite

Additional hotel ★★★ 70% Stade Court, West Pde, HYTHE ☎ 01303 268263 🖹 01303 261803 42 en suite

Sene Valley Sene CT18 8BL
☎ 01303 268513 (Manager) 🖹 01303 237513
e-mail: svgc@svgc.freeserve.co.uk
A two-level downland course, standing 350ft above the town and providing interesting golf over an undulating landscape with sea views. A typical hole that challenges most players, is the par 3, 11th which combines a stunning sea view with a testing tee shot to a green surrounded by bunkers and gorse.
18 holes, 6271yds, Par 71, SSS 70, Course record 65. Club membership 600.
Visitors contact professional in advance; handicap certificate. **Societies** phone in advance. **Green Fees** £25 weekdays (£30 weekends). **Cards** ▦ ▦ 🖸 **Prof** Nick Watson **Course Designer** Henry Cotton **Facilities** ⊗ ⅀ by arrangement ⬛ ⬛ ♟ ♨ ♋ 🐾 ✓ **Conf** Corporate Hospitality Days available **Location** M20 junct 12, A20 towards Ashford for 3m, left at rdbt, Hythe Rd for 1m

Hotel ★★★★ 77% The Hythe Imperial, Princes Pde, HYTHE ☎ 01303 267441 100 en suite

KINGSDOWN
Map 05 TR34

Walmer & Kingsdown The Leas CT14 8EP
☎ 01304 373256 🖹 01304 382336
e-mail: kingsdown.golf@gtwiz.co.uk
18 holes, 6444yds, Par 72, SSS 71, Course record 66.
Course Designer James Braid **Location** 1.5m E of Ringwould off A258 Dover-Deal road
Phone for further details

Hotel ★★★ 72% Dunkerleys Hotel & Restaurant, 19 Beach St, DEAL ☎ 01304 375016 16 en suite

LAMBERHURST
Map 05 TQ63

Lamberhurst Church Rd TN3 8DT
☎ 01892 890591 🖹 01892 891140
e-mail: secretary@lamberhurstgolfclub.com
Parkland course crossing the river twice. Fine views.
18 holes, 6345yds, Par 72, SSS 70, Course record 65. Club membership 650.
Visitors not am weekends unless with member; handicap certificate; advisable to contact in advance. **Societies** Tue, Wed, Thu, Apr-Oct, by arrangement. **Green Fees** not confirmed. **Cards** ▦ ▦ 🖥 🖸 **Prof** Brian Impett **Facilities** ⊗ ⅀ ⬛ ⬛ ♟ ♋ ♈ 🐾 ✓ **Conf** Corporate Hospitality Days available **Location** N of village on B2162

Hotel ★★★★ 71% The Spa Hotel, Mount Ephraim, TUNBRIDGE WELLS ☎ 01892 520331 69 en suite

LITTLESTONE
Map 05 TR02

Littlestone St Andrew's Rd TN28 8RB
☎ 01797 363355 🖹 01797 362740
e-mail: secretary@littlestonegolfclub.org.uk
Located on Romney Marsh, this fairly flat seaside links course calls for every variety of shot. The 8th, 15th, 16th and 17th are regarded as classics by international golfers. Fast running fairways and faster greens.
18 holes, 6486yds, Par 71, SSS 72, Course record 66. Club membership 550.
Visitors not before 11am weekends & bank holidays; contact in advance. **Societies** apply in advance. **Green Fees** £60 per day; £40 per round (£75/£60 weekends & bank holidays). **Cards** ▦ ▦ 🖸 **Prof** Andrew Jones **Course Designer** Laidlaw Purves **Facilities** ⊗ ⅀ ⬛ ⬛ ♟ ♋ ♈ 🐾 ✓ ✓ **Leisure** hard tennis courts. **Conf** Corporate Hospitality Days available **Location** 1m from New Romney off B2070 Littlestone road

Hotel ★★★★ 77% The Hythe Imperial, Princes Pde, HYTHE ☎ 01303 267441 100 en suite

Romney Warren St Andrews Rd TN28 8RB
☎ 01797 362231 🖹 01797 363511
e-mail: info@romneywarrengolfclub.org.uk
A links-style course, normally very dry. Flat providing easy walking and play challenged by sea breezes. Although not overly long, narrow fairways and small greens place a premium on shot selection and placement.
18 holes, 5126yds, Par 67, SSS 65, Course record 63. Club membership 300.
Visitors contact professional in advance. **Societies** contact in advance. **Green Fees** £33 per day, £19 per round (£36/£25 weekends). **Cards** ▦ ▦ 🖥 🖸 **Prof** Andrew Jones **Facilities** ⊗ ⅀ ⬛ ⬛ ♟ ♋ ♈ 🐾 ✓ **Location** N of Littlestone centre

Hotel ★★★★ 77% The Hythe Imperial, Princes Pde, HYTHE ☎ 01303 267441 100 en suite

LYDD
Map 05 TR02

Lydd Romney Rd TN29 9LS
☎ 01797 320808 🖹 01797 321482
e-mail: info@lyddgolfclub.co.uk
A links-type course on marshland, offering some interesting challenges, including a number of eye-catching water hazards, wide fairways and plenty of semi-rough. A constant breeze makes club selection difficult A good test for experienced golfers and appealing to the complete novice.
18 holes, 6529yds, Par 71, SSS 71, Course record 65. Club membership 490.
Visitors contact in advance; weekends subject to availability. **Societies** phone in advance. **Green Fees** £21 (£30 weekends). **Cards** ▦ ▦ 🖥 🖸

Prof Richard J Perkins **Course Designer** Mike Smith **Facilities** ⊗ ⅏ ⅃ ▐ ♀ ⅄ 🏠 ⅌ 🐾 ⚐ ℓ **Leisure** six-hole academy course. **Conf** Corporate Hospitality Days available **Location** A259 onto B2075 by Lydd Airport

Lydd Golf Club

....

Hotel ★★★ 61% The George, High St, RYE ☎ 01797 222114 22 en suite

MAIDSTONE   Map 05 TQ75

Cobtree Manor Park Chatham Rd, Sandling ME14 3AZ
☎ 01622 753276 📠 01634 262003
An undulating parkland course with some water hazards.
Cobtree Manor Park Golf Club: 18 holes, 5611yds, Par 69, SSS 69, Course record 66.
Club membership 400.
Visitors advisable to phone four days in advance. **Societies** Mon-Fri & pm weekends, phone 01622 751881. **Green Fees** terms on application. **Cards** 🔲 🔲 🔲 🔲 🔲 **Prof** Paul Foston **Facilities** ⊗ ⅃ ▐ ♀ ⅄ 🏠 ⅌ ⚐ **Conf** fac available **Location** M20 junct 6, 0.25m N on A229

....

Hotel ★★★ 69% Russell Hotel, 136 Boxley Rd, MAIDSTONE ☎ 01622 692221 42 en suite

Leeds Castle Ashford Rd ME17 1PL
☎ 01622 767828 & 880467 📠 01622 735616
e-mail: stevepurves@leeds-castle.co.uk
Situated around Leeds Castle, this is one of the most picturesque courses in Britain. Redesigned in the 1980s by Neil Coles, it is a challenging nine-hole course with the added hazard of the castle moat.

9 holes, 2681yds, Par 33, SSS 33, Course record 29.
Visitors bookings from six days in advance. **Societies** phone in advance. **Green Fees** terms on application. **Cards** 🔲 🔲 🔲 **Prof** Steve Purves **Course Designer** Neil Coles **Facilities** ⊗ ▐ ♀ ⅄ 🏠 ⅌ ⚐ **Leisure** Green fees include admission to Leeds Castle's gardens &

attractions. **Conf** Corporate Hospitality Days available **Location** M20 junct 8, 4m E of Maidstone on A20 towards Lenham

....

Hotel ★★★★ 70% Marriott Tudor Park Hotel & Country Club, Ashford Rd, Bearsted, MAIDSTONE ☎ 01622 734334 120 en suite

Marriott Tudor Park Hotel & Country Club
Ashford Rd, Bearsted ME14 4NQ
☎ 01622 734334 📠 01622 735360
e-mail: salesadmin.tudorpark@marriotthotels.co.uk
The course is set in a 220-acre former deer park with the pleasant undulating Kent countryside as a backdrop. The natural features of the land have been incorporated into this picturesque course to form a challenge for those of both high and intermediate standard. The par 5 14th is particularly interesting. It can alter your score dramatically should you gamble with a drive to a narrow fairway. This hole has to be carefully thought out from tee to green depending on the wind direction.

Milgate Course: 18 holes, 6041yds, Par 70, SSS 69, Course record 64.
Club membership 750.
Visitors not am weekends; contact pro shop for bookings 01622 739412. **Societies** please phone Golf Events. **Green Fees** not confirmed. **Cards** 🔲 🔲 🔲 🔲 🔲 🔲 **Prof** Nick McNally **Course Designer** Donald Steel **Facilities** ⊗ ⅏ ⅃ ▐ ♀ ⅄ 🏠 ⅌ 🐟 🐾 ⚐ ℓ **Leisure** hard tennis courts, heated indoor swimming pool, sauna, solarium, gymnasium, steam room & spa bath, golf academy. **Conf** fac available Corporate Hospitality Days available **Location** M20 junct 8, 1.25m W on A20

....

Hotel ★★★★ 70% Marriott Tudor Park Hotel & Country Club, Ashford Rd, Bearsted, MAIDSTONE ☎ 01622 734334 120 en suite

NEW ASH GREEN   Map 05 TQ66

Redlibbets Manor Ln, West Yoke TN15 7HT
☎ 01474 879190 📠 01474 879290
e-mail: redlibbets@golfandsport.co.uk
Delightful rolling Kentish course cut through an attractive wooded valley.
18 holes, 6639yds, Par 72, SSS 72, Course record 67.
Club membership 500.
Visitors not weekends. **Societies** Mon, Tue, Thu, apply by phone. **Green Fees** £40. **Cards** 🔲 🔲 🔲 🔲 🔲 🔲 **Prof** Ross Taylor **Course Designer** Jonathan Gaunt **Facilities** ⊗ ⅏ ⅃ ▐ ♀ ⅄ 🏠 ⅌ 🐾 ⚐ ℓ **Conf** fac available Corporate Hospitality Days available **Location** off A20 near Brand's Hatch

Continued

RAMSGATE
Map 05 TR36

St Augustine's Cottington Rd, Cliffsend CT12 5JN
☎ 01843 590333 🖹 01843 590444
e-mail: sagc@ic24.net
18 holes, 5254yds, Par 69, SSS 66, Course record 61.
Course Designer Tom Vardon **Location** off A256
Ramsgate-Sandwich
Phone for further details
....
Hotel ★★★ 68% Royal Albion Hotel, Albion St,
BROADSTAIRS ☎ 01843 868071 19 en suite

ROCHESTER
Map 05 TQ76

Rochester & Cobham Park Park Pale ME2 3UL
☎ 01474 823411 🖹 01474 824446
e-mail: rcpgc@talk21.com
**A first-rate course of challenging dimensions in
undulating parkland. All holes differ and each requires
accurate drive placing to derive the best advantage.**
18 holes, 6597yds, Par 71, SSS 72, Course record 64.
Club membership 640.
Visitors not weekends; contact in advance; handicap
certificate. **Societies** apply in advance. **Green Fees** £45 per
day, £35 per round. **Prof** Iain Higgins **Course Designer**
Donald Steel **Facilities** ⊗)〲 ⅃ ♥ ♀ ⅄ 🏠 ♥ 🛒 ♂ 〔
Conf Corporate Hospitality Days available
Location 2.5m W on A2
....
Hotel ★★★★ 74% Bridgewood Manor, Bridgewood
Roundabout, Walderslade Woods, CHATHAM
☎ 01634 201333 100 en suite

SANDWICH
See page 147

SANDWICH
Map 05 TR35

Prince's Prince's Dr, Sandwich Bay CT13 9QB
☎ 01304 611118 🖹 01304 612000
e-mail: office@princesgolfclub.co.uk
**With 27 championship holes, Prince's Golf Club has a
world-wide reputation as a traditional links of the finest
quality and is a venue that provides all that is best in
modern links golf. One of only 14 courses to be selected
to host the Open Championship.**

Dunes: 9 holes, 3343yds, Par 36, SSS 36.
Himalayas: 9 holes, 3163yds, Par 35, SSS 35.
Shore: 9 holes, 3347yds, Par 36, SSS 36.
Club membership 250.
Visitors contact in advance. **Societies** contact in advance
by writing, e-mail or phone. **Green Fees** terms on

Continued

application. **Cards** 🔤 💳 💷 📇 📲 **Prof** Derek Barbour
Course Designer (1951 Sir Guy Campbell & JSF
Morrison) **Facilities** ⊗)〲by arrangement ⅃ ♥ ♀ ⅄ 🏠
〓 ♥ 🛒 ♂ 〔 **Leisure** private beach area. **Conf** fac
available Corporate Hospitality Days available
Location 2m E via toll road, signs from Sandwich
....
Hotel ★★★ 72% Dunkerleys Hotel & Restaurant, 19
Beach St, DEAL ☎ 01304 375016 16 en suite

SEAL
Map 05 TR36

Wildernesse Park Ln TN15 0JE
☎ 01732 761199 🖹 01732 763809
e-mail: golf@wildernesse.co.uk
**A tight inland course, heavily wooded with tree-lined
fairways. Straight driving and attention to the well-
placed bunkers is essential. With few slopes and easy
walking, it is difficult to beat par.**
18 holes, 6501yds, Par 72, SSS 71.
Club membership 720.
Visitors not weekends; contact in advance. **Societies** Mon,
Thu, Fri. **Green Fees** £46 per round weekdays. **Cards** 🔤
💷 **Prof** Craig Walker **Facilities** ⊗ ⅃ ♥ ♀ ⅄ 🏠 〓 ♥
🛒 ♂ **Conf** Corporate Hospitality Days available
....
Hotel ★★★ 71% Donnington Manor, London Rd, Dunton
Green, SEVENOAKS ☎ 01732 462681 60 en suite

SEVENOAKS   Map 05 TQ55

Knole Park Seal Hollow Rd TN15 0HJ
☎ 01732 452150 📠 01732 463159
e-mail: secretary@knolepark.fsnet.co.uk
The course is laid out within the grounds of the Knole
Estate and can rightfully be described as a natural
layout. The course designer has used the contours of
the land to produce a challenging course in all
weather conditions and throughout all seasons. While,
for most of the year, it may appear benign, in summer,
when the bracken is high, Knole Park represents a
considerable challenge but always remains a fair test of
golf.
18 holes, 6246yds, Par 70, SSS 70, Course record 62.
Club membership 750.
Visitors not weekends & bank holidays; contact secretary
in advance; handicap certificate. Societies phone initially.
Green Fees £45 per day, £35 per round. Cards 💳 💳 💳
💳 🔳 Prof Phil Sykes Course Designer JA Abercromby
Facilities ⊗ ⊪ ⅃ ♥ ♀ ⚐ ✓ Leisure squash. Conf
Corporate Hospitality Days available Location NE of town
centre off B2019

....

Hotel ★★★ 71% Donnington Manor, London Rd, Dunton
Green, SEVENOAKS ☎ 01732 462681 60 en suite

SHEERNESS   Map 05 TQ97

Sheerness Power Station Rd ME12 3AE
☎ 01795 662585 📠 01795 668100
e-mail: thesecretary@sheernessgc.freeserve.co.uk
Part links, marshland course, few bunkers, but many
ditches and water hazards.
18 holes, 6460yds, Par 72, SSS 71, Course record 66.
Club membership 650.
Visitors with member only weekends. Societies weekdays,
book in advance. Green Fees £28 per day, £20 per 18
holes. Prof L Stanford Facilities ⊗ ⊪ by arrangement ⅃
♥ ♀ ⚐ ⚐ ✓ Location 1.5m E off A249

....

Hotel ★★★★ 74% Bridgewood Manor, Bridgewood
Roundabout, Walderslade Woods, CHATHAM
☎ 01634 201333 100 en suite

SHOREHAM   Map 05 TQ56

Darenth Valley Station Rd TN14 7SA
☎ 01959 522944 📠 01959 525089
e-mail: darenthvalleygolfcourse@shoreham2000.fsbusiness.
co.uk
Gently undulating picturesque parkland course in a
beautiful Kentish valley, with excellent well-drained
greens. The course has matured and developed to
become a challenge to both high and low handicap
golfers.
18 holes, 6258yds, Par 72, SSS 71, Course record 64.
Visitors advisable to book in advance. Societies contact in
advance. Green Fees not confirmed. Cards 💳 💳 💳 🔳
🔳 Prof David J Copsey Facilities ⊗ ⊪ ⅃ ♥ ♀ ⚐ ⚐ ✓
✓ Conf fac available Corporate Hospitality Days
available Location 3m N of Sevenoaks off A225 between
Otford & Eynsford

....

Hotel ★★★ 71% Donnington Manor, London Rd, Dunton
Green, SEVENOAKS ☎ 01732 462681 60 en suite

Darenth Valley Golf Course

SITTINGBOURNE   Map 05 TQ96

The Oast Golf Centre Church Rd, Tonge
ME9 9AR
☎ 01795 473527
e-mail: rmail@oastgolf.co.uk
A par 3 approach course of nine holes with 18 tees
augmented by a 17-bay floodlit driving range and a
putting green.
9 holes, 1664yds, Par 54, SSS 54.
Visitors no restrictions. Societies phone in advance. Green
Fees £7 for 18 holes, £5 for nine holes. Prof D Chambers
Course Designer D Chambers Facilities ⅃ ♥ ♀ ⚐ ✓
✓ ♺ Location 2m NE, A2 between Bapchild & Teynham

....

Hotel ★★★★ 74% Bridgewood Manor, Bridgewood
Roundabout, Walderslade Woods, CHATHAM
☎ 01634 201333 100 en suite

Sittingbourne & Milton Regis Wormdale,
Newington ME9 7PX
☎ 01795 842261 📠 01795 844117
e-mail: sittingbournegc@btconnect.com
A downland course with pleasant vistas and renowned
for its greens. There are a few uphill climbs, but the
course is far from difficult. The back nine holes are
very testing.
18 holes, 6291yds, Par 71, SSS 70, Course record 63.
Club membership 715.
Visitors not weekends; contact in advance. Societies Tue,
Thu, apply in advance. Green Fees £40 per 36 holes, £30
per 18 holes. Cards 💳 💳 💳 🔳 🔳 Prof John Hearn
Course Designer Donald Steel Facilities ⊗ ⊪ ⅃ ♥ ♀ ⚐
⚐ ✎ ♺ ✓ Conf Corporate Hospitality Days available
Location off Chestnut St at Danaway

....

Hotel ★★★★ 74% Bridgewood Manor, Bridgewood
Roundabout, Walderslade Woods, CHATHAM
☎ 01634 201333 100 en suite

Upchurch River Valley Golf Centre Oak Ln,
Upchurch ME9 7AY
☎ 01634 379592 📠 01634 387784
Undulating parkland course set in picturesque
countryside. Testing water hazards on several holes.
Excellent winter course. The nine-hole course is ideal
for beginners and for those keen to sharpen up their
short game.
18 holes, 6237yds, Par 70, SSS 70.
Club membership 752.
Visitors book for weekends five days in advance,
weekdays two days in advance. Societies phone for details
01634 360626. Green Fees £12.95 (£16.45 weekends).

Continued   *Continued*

Kent

Royal St George's

Sandwich

Map 05 TR35

Consistently ranked among the leading golf courses in the world, Royal St George's occupies a unique place in the history of golf, playing host in 1894 to the first Open Championship outside Scotland. Set among the dunes of Sandwich Bay, the links provide a severe test for the greatest of golfers. Only two Open winners (Bill Rogers in 1981 and Greg Norman in 1993) have managed to under par after 72 holes. The undulating fairways, the borrows on the greens, the strategically placed bunkers, and the prevailing winds that blow on all but the rarest of occasions, these all soon reveal any weakness in the player; there are few over the years who have mastered all the vagaries in one round. It hosted its thirteenth Open Championship in 2003, dramatically won by outsider Ben Curtis.

CT13 9PB
☎ 01304 613090 Fax 01304 611245
e-mail: secretary@royalstgeorges.com

18 holes, 7102yds, Par 70, SSS 74, Course record 67.
Club membership 750.
Visitors not weekends; three & four-ball golf Tue only; must contact in advance; handicap certificate of 18 or under.
Societies Mon, Tue, Thu, must apply in writing. **Green Fees** £150 per 36 holes, £115 per 18 holes; reduced winter rates.
Cards 🖃 🖃 🖃 🖅 🖂 **Prof** A Brooks **Course Designer** Dr Laidlaw Purves **Facilities** ⊗ 🖫 🖳 ♀ 🏌 🍴 ✂ 🛒 🏌 ♂ ⛳ **Conf** Corporate Hospitality Days available **Location** 1.5m E of Sandwich. Enter town & signs for golf courses

....

Hotels

★★★ 72% Dunkerleys Hotel & Restaurant,
19 Beach St, DEAL

☎ 01304 375016 16 en suite

★★★ 67% The Falstaff Hotel, 8-10 St Dunstan's St,
CANTERBURY

☎ 0870 609 6102 Fax 01227 463525 25 en suite
22 annexe en suite

★★ 70% The Bow Window Inn, 50 High St, Littlebourne,
CANTERBURY

☎ 01227 721264 Fax 01227 721250 11 annexe en suite

Cards 🖪 **Prof** Roger Cornwell **Course Designer** David
Smart **Facilities** ⊗ ⅢⅢ ⅛ 🖳 ♀ 🛆 🖻 ➘ 🛲 ✓ ↾
Leisure heated outdoor swimming pool.
Location A2 between Rainham & Newington

....

Hotel ★★★ 69% Russell Hotel, 136 Boxley Rd,
MAIDSTONE ☎ 01622 692221 42 en suite

SNODLAND   Map 05 TQ76

Oastpark Malling Rd ME6 5LG
☎ 01634 242661 🖹 01634 240744
A challenging parkland course for golfers of all
abilities. The course has water hazards and orchards.
Construction of a further nine holes is planned for
2006.
9 holes, 3150yds, Par 35, SSS 35, Course record 71.
Club membership 60.
Visitors book seven days in advance. **Societies** early
booking with deposits required. **Green Fees** £7 per day
(weekends: £14 per 18 holes, £8 per 9 holes). **Cards** 🖃
🖃 🖪 🗓 **Prof** David Porthouse **Course Designer**
JD Banks **Facilities** ⅛ 🖳 ♀ 🛆 🖻 ✓ ↾
Location M20 junct 4

....

Hotel ★★★ 67% Larkfield Priory Hotel, London Rd,
Larkfield, MAIDSTONE ☎ 01732 846858 52 en suite

TENTERDEN   Map 05 TQ83

London Beach Hotel & Golf Club Ashford Rd
TN30 6HX
☎ 01580 766279 🖹 01580 763884
e-mail: enquiries@londonbeach.com
Located in a mature parkland setting in the Weald. A
test of golf for all abilities of golfer with its rolling
fairways and undulating greens.
9 holes, 5860yds, Par 70, SSS 69, Course record 66.
Club membership 250.
Visitors book in advance. **Societies** apply in writing.
Green Fees £20 per 18 holes, £18 per 9 holes (£25/£20
weekends & bank holidays). **Cards** 🖃 🖃 🖃 🖃 🖃 🖃
🗓 **Prof** Mark Chilcott **Course Designer** Golf Landscapes
Facilities ⊗ ⅢⅢ ⅛ 🖳 ♀ 🛆 🖻 ➘ 🛲 ➘ ✓ ↾
Leisure fishing, pitch & putt clay pigeon shooting.
Conf fac available Corporate Hospitality Days available
Location M20 Junct 9, A28 towards Tenterden, hotel on
right 1m before Tenterden

....

Hotel ★★★ 75% London Beach Hotel & Golf Club,
Ashford Rd, TENTERDEN ☎ 01580 766279 26 en suite

Tenterden Woodchurch Rd TN30 7DR
☎ 01580 763987 (sec) 🖹 01580 763430
e-mail: enquiries@tenterdengolfclub.co.uk
Set in tranquil undulating parkland with beautiful
views, the course is challenging with several difficult
holes.
18 holes, 6071yds, Par 70, SSS 69, Course record 61.
Club membership 600.
Visitors contact secretary; with member only weekends &
bank holidays; handicap certificate. **Societies** contact
secretary, details on request. **Green Fees** £30 per round
(winter £20). **Cards** 🖃 🖃 **Prof** Kyle Kelsall
Facilities ⊗ ⅢⅢ ⅛ 🖳 ♀ 🛆 ➘ 🛲 ✓ **Location** 0.75m E
on B2067

....

Hotel ★★★ 75% London Beach Hotel & Golf Club,
Ashford Rd, TENTERDEN ☎ 01580 766279 26 en suite

TONBRIDGE   Map 05 TQ54

Poultwood Higham Ln TN11 9QR
☎ 01732 364039 & 366180 🖹 01732 353781
There are two public pay and play parkland courses in
an idyllic woodland setting. The courses are ecologically
designed, over predominantly flat land offering
challenging hazards and interesting playing conditions
for all standards of golfer.
18 holes, 5524yds, Par 68, SSS 66.
9 holes, 2562yds, Par 28.
Visitors non-registered golfers can book up to five days in
advance for 18-hole course or take available tee times; pay
& play nine-hole course. **Societies** apply in writing to
clubhouse manager. **Green Fees** 18-hole course £14
(£19.50 weekends & bank holidays); 9-hole course
£5.50/£7. **Cards** 🖃 🖃 🖃 🖃 🗓 **Prof** Bill Hodkin
Course Designer Hawtree **Facilities** ⊗ ⅢⅢ ⅛ 🖳 ♀ 🛆 🖻
🛲 ✓ **Leisure** squash. **Conf** fac available Corporate
Hospitality Days available **Location** off A227 3m N of
Tonbridge

....

Hotel ★★★ 67% Rose & Crown Hotel, 125 High St,
TONBRIDGE ☎ 01732 357966 54 en suite

TUNBRIDGE WELLS (ROYAL)   Map 05 TQ53

Nevill Benhall Mill Rd TN2 5JW
☎ 01892 525818 🖹 01892 517861
e-mail: manager@nevillgolfclub.co.uk
The Kent-Sussex border forms the northern perimeter
of the course. Open undulating ground, well-wooded
with some heather and gorse for the first half. The
second nine holes slope away from the clubhouse to a
valley where a narrow stream hazards two holes.
18 holes, 6349yds, Par 71, SSS 70, Course record 64.
Club membership 800.
Visitors must contact 48 hours in advance; handicap
certificate required; permission from secretary for
weekends. **Societies** apply in writing one month in
advance. **Green Fees** £45 per day; £30 per round (£50/£40
weekends). **Prof** Paul Huggett **Course Designer** Henry
Cotton **Facilities** ⊗ ⅢⅢ ⅛ 🖳 ♀ 🛆 🖻 ✓
Location S of Tunbridge Wells

....

Hotel ★★★★ 71% The Spa Hotel, Mount Ephraim,
TUNBRIDGE WELLS ☎ 01892 520331 69 en suite

Tunbridge Wells Langton Rd TN4 8XH
☎ 01892 523034 🖹 01892 536918
e-mail: info@tunbridgewellsgolfclub.co.uk
Somewhat hilly, well-bunkered parkland course with
lake; trees form natural hazards.
9 holes, 4725yds, Par 65, SSS 62, Course record 59.
Club membership 470.
Visitors contact in advance; restricted weekends. **Societies**
weekdays subject to availability, apply in advance. **Green
Fees** not confirmed. **Cards** 🖃 🖃 🖃 🗓 **Prof** Mike
Barton **Facilities** ⊗ ⅢⅢ by arrangement ⅛ 🖳 ♀ 🛆 🖻
🛲 ✓ **Location** 1m W on A264

....

Hotel ★★★★ 71% The Spa Hotel, Mount Ephraim,
TUNBRIDGE WELLS ☎ 01892 520331 69 en suite

> **Prices may change during the currency of the
> Guide, please check when booking.**

WESTERHAM   Map 05 TQ45

Park Wood Chestnut Av, Tatsfield TN16 2EG
☎ 01959 577744 & 577177 (pro-shop) 📠 01959 572702
e-mail: mail@parkwoodgolf.co.uk
**Situated in an Area of Outstanding Natural
Beauty, flanked by an ancient woodland with superb
views across Kent and Surrey countryside. An
undulating course, tree lined and with some
interesting water features. Playable in all weather
conditions.**

*18 holes, 6835yds, Par 72, SSS 72, Course record 66.
Club membership 500.*
Visitors not bank holidays; phone in advance. **Societies**
apply in writing or phone in advance. **Green Fees** terms on
application. **Cards** 🔳 🔳 🔳 **Prof** Nick Terry
Facilities ⊗ ⅢⅡ ⅡⅡ ⅡⅡ ⚐ 🕰 ⚑ ⛳ 🗡 **Conf** fac available
Corporate Hospitality Days available **Location** A25 onto
B2024 Croydon Rd & Clarks Ln, at Church Hill junct onto
Chestnut Av
....
Hotel ★★★ 71% Donnington Manor, London Rd,
Dunton Green, SEVENOAKS ☎ 01732 462681
60 en suite

Westerham Valence Park, Brasted Rd TN16 1LJ
☎ 01959 567100 📠 01959 567101
e-mail: jon.wittenberg@westerhamgc.co.uk
**Originally forestry land with thousands of mature
pines. The storms of 1987 created natural fairways and
the mature landscape makes the course both
demanding and spectacular. A clubhouse with first-
class facilities and magnificent views.**

*18 holes, 6272yds, Par 72, SSS 72.
Club membership 700.*
Visitors not am weekends. **Societies** phone events office
for details. **Green Fees** not confirmed. **Cards** 🔳 🔳 🔳
🔳 🔳 🔳 **Prof** J Marshal **Course Designer** D Williams
Facilities ⊗ ⅢⅡ ⅡⅡ ⅡⅡ ⚐ 🕰 ⚑ 🗡 **Leisure** short
game practice area. **Conf** fac available Corporate

Hospitality Days available **Location** A25 between
Westerham & Brasted
....
Hotel ★★★ 71% Donnington Manor, London Rd, Dunton
Green, SEVENOAKS ☎ 01732 462681 60 en suite

WESTGATE ON SEA   Map 05 TR37

Westgate and Birchington 176 Canterbury Rd
CT8 8LT
☎ 01843 831115
e-mail: wandbgc@btopenworld.com
**A fine blend of inland and seaside holes which provide a
good test of the golfer despite the apparently simple
appearance of the course.**
*18 holes, 4926yds, Par 64, SSS 64, Course record 60.
Club membership 350.*
Visitors not before 10am Mon-Sat, not before 11am Sun &
bank holidays. **Societies** contact secretary. **Green Fees** not
confirmed. **Prof** Roger Game **Facilities** ⊗ by arrangement
ⅢⅡ by arrangement ⅡⅡ ⚐ 🕰 🗡 **Conf** Corporate
Hospitality Days available **Location** E of town centre off
A28
....
Hotel ★★★ 68% Royal Albion Hotel, Albion St,
BROADSTAIRS ☎ 01843 868071 19 en suite

WEST KINGSDOWN   Map 05 TQ56

Woodlands Manor Tinkerpot Ln, Otford TN15 6AB
☎ 01959 523806 📠 01959 524398
e-mail: woodlandsgolf@aol.com
**Two nine-hole layouts with views over an area of
outstanding natural beauty. The course is challenging
but fair with varied and memorable holes of which the
7th, 10th and 18th stand out. Good playing conditions
all year round.**
*18 holes, 6015yds, Par 69, SSS 69.
Club membership 600.*
Visitors not am Tue & before 1pm weekends; by
arrangement. **Societies** apply in advance. **Green Fees** not
confirmed. **Cards** 🔳 🔳 🔳 🔳 **Prof** Philip Womack
Course Designer Lyons, Coles **Facilities** ⊗ ⅢⅡ ⅡⅡ ⚐ ⅡⅡ
🕰 ⚑ 🗡 🗡 **Location** A20 through West Kingsdown,
right opp Portbello Inn onto School Ln & Tinkerpot Ln,
clubhouse left
....
Hotel ⛺ Premier Travel Inn Sevenoaks/Maidstone,
London Rd, Wrotham Heath, WROTHAM
☎ 08701 977227 40 en suite

WEST MALLING   Map 05 TQ65

Kings Hill Fortune Way, Discovery Dr, Kings Hill
ME19 4AG
☎ 01732 875040 📠 01732 875019
e-mail: khatkhgolf@aol.com
18 holes, 6622yds, Par 72, SSS 72.
Course Designer David Williams Partnership **Location**
M20 junct 4, A228 towards Tonbridge
Phone for further details
....
Hotel ⛺ Premier Travel Inn Maidstone (Leybourne),
Castle Way, LEYBOURNE ☎ 08701 977170 40 en suite

> **If the name of the club appears in *italics*, details
> have not been confirmed for this
> edition of the guide.**

Continued

WHITSTABLE   Map 05 TR16

Chestfield (Whitstable) 103 Chestfield Rd,
Chestfield CT5 3LU
☎ 01227 794411 & 792243 ▤ 01227 794454
e-mail: secretary@chestfield-golfclub.co.uk
**Recent changes have been made to this parkland course
with undulating fairways and fine views of the sea and
countryside. These consist of six new greens and five
new tees. The ancient clubhouse, dating back to the
15th century, is reputed to be the oldest building in the
world used for this purpose.**
*18 holes, 6200yds, Par 70, SSS 70, Course record 66.
Club membership 725.*
Visitors not am Sun; contact for times. **Societies** apply in
writing or phone. **Green Fees** £35 per day, £28 per round.
Cards ▦ ▦ ▦ ▦ ▨ **Prof** John Brotherton **Course
Designer** D Steel, James Braid **Facilities** ⊗ ⅋ 🏌 🏐 ⚑ ♨ ☖
🏠 ➘ ♨ ⚐ **Leisure** half-way house providing
snacks/refreshments. **Location** 0.5m S by Chestfield
railway station, off A2990

Hotel ⮑ Premier Travel Inn Whitstable, Thanet Way,
WHITSTABLE ☎ 08701 977269 40 en suite

Whitstable & Seasalter Collingwood Rd CT5 1EB
☎ 01227 272020 ▤ 01227 280822
9 holes, 5357yds, Par 66, SSS 63, Course record 62.
Location W of town centre off B2205
Phone for further details

Hotel ⮑ Premier Travel Inn Whitstable, Thanet Way,
WHITSTABLE ☎ 08701 977269 40 en suite

LANCASHIRE

ACCRINGTON   Map 07 SD72

Accrington & District Devon Av, Oswaldtwistle
BB5 4LS
☎ 01254 381614 ▤ 01254 233273
e-mail: info@accrington-golf-club.fsnet.co.uk
**Moorland course with pleasant views of the Pennines
and surrounding areas. The course is a real test for
even the best amateur golfers and has hosted many
county matches and championships over its 100 plus
years of history.**
*18 holes, 6060yds, Par 70, SSS 69, Course record 63.
Club membership 600.*
Visitors contact in advance; handicap certificate. **Societies**
contact in advance. **Green Fees** £24 daily Mon-Thu, £30
Fri-Sun. **Prof** Bill Harling **Course Designer** J Braid
Facilities ⊗ ⅋ 🏌 🏐 ⚑ ♨ ☖ 🏠 ➘ ♨ ⚐ **Location** between
Accrington & Blackburn

Hotel ★★★★ 62% Dunkenhalgh Hotel & Spa, Blackburn
Rd, Clayton-le-Moors, ACCRINGTON ☎ 01254 398021
53 en suite 69 annexe en suite

Baxenden & District Top o' th' Meadow,
Baxenden BB5 2EA
☎ 01254 234555
e-mail: baxgolf@hotmail.com
Moorland course with a long par 3 to start.
*9 holes, 5740yds, Par 70, SSS 68, Course record 65.
Club membership 340.*
Visitors with member only Sat, Sun & bank holidays.
Societies contact in advance. **Green Fees** terms on

application. **Facilities** ⊗ ⅋ 🏌 ⚑ ♨ ☖ **Conf** fac available
Corporate Hospitality Days available **Location** 1.5m SE
off A680

Hotel ★★★★ 62% Dunkenhalgh Hotel & Spa, Blackburn
Rd, Clayton-le-Moors, ACCRINGTON ☎ 01254 398021
53 en suite 69 annexe en suite

Green Haworth Green Haworth BB5 3SL
☎ 01254 237580 & 382510 ▤ 01254 396176
e-mail: golf@greenhaworth.freeserve.co.uk
9 holes, 5522yds, Par 68, SSS 67, Course record 66.
Location 2m S off A680
Phone for further details

Hotel ★★★★ 62% Dunkenhalgh Hotel & Spa, Blackburn
Rd, Clayton-le-Moors, ACCRINGTON ☎ 01254 398021
53 en suite 69 annexe en suite

BACUP   Map 07 SD82

Bacup Maden Rd OL13 8HY
☎ 01706 873170 ▤ 01706 877726
e-mail: secretary@bacupgolfltd.co.uk
**Tree-lined moorland course, predominantly flat except
climbs to 1st and 10th holes.**
*9 holes, 6018yds, Par 70, SSS 69.
Club membership 350.*
Visitors not during competitions on Sat & some Sun;
advisable to contact in advance. **Societies** contact in
writing. **Green Fees** terms on application. **Facilities** ⊗ by
arrangement ⅋ by arrangement 🏐 ♨ ☖
Conf Corporate Hospitality Days available
Location W of town off A671

Hotel ★★★ 70% Rosehill House Hotel, Rosehill Av,
BURNLEY ☎ 01282 453931 30 en suite

BARNOLDSWICK   Map 07 SD84

Ghyll Skipton Rd BB18 6JH
☎ 01282 842466
e-mail: secretary@ghyllgc.freeserve.com
**Excellent parkland course with outstanding views,
especially from the 8th tee where you can see the Three
Peaks. Testing 8th hole is an uphill par 4. Eleven holes
in total, nine in Yorkshire and two in Lancashire.**
*11 holes, 5790yds, Par 68, SSS 66, Course record 62.
Club membership 345.*
Visitors not Tue, after 4.30pm Fri & Sun. **Societies** contact
in writing. **Green Fees** not confirmed. **Facilities** 🏐 ♨ ☖
Location NE of town on B6252

Hotel ★★ 68% Herriots Hotel, Bar & Dining Rooms,
Broughton Rd, SKIPTON ☎ 01756 792781 24 en suite

BICKERSTAFFE   Map 07 SD40

Mossock Hall Liverpool Rd L39 0EE
☎ 01695 421717 ▤ 01695 424961
**Relatively flat parkland course with scenic views.
USGA greens and water features on four holes.**
*18 holes, 6492yds, Par 71, SSS 70, Course record 68.
Club membership 580.*
Visitors contact in advance. **Societies** write or phone in
advance. **Green Fees** not confirmed. **Prof** Phil Atkiss
Course Designer Steve Marnoch **Facilities** ⊗ ⅋ 🏌 🏐 ♨
☖ 🏠 ⚐ **Location** M58 junct 3

Hotel ★★★ 60% Lancashire Manor Hotel, Prescott Rd,
UPHOLLAND ☎ 01695 720401 55 en suite

Continued

BLACKBURN Map 07 SD62

Blackburn Beardwood Brow BB2 7AX
☎ 01254 51122 🖷 01254 665578
e-mail: sec@blackburngolfclub.com
Parkland course on a high plateau with stream and hills. Superb views of Lancashire coast and the Pennines.
18 holes, 6144yds, Par 71, SSS 70, Course record 62. Club membership 550.
Visitors contact professional in advance. **Societies** contact in advance. **Green Fees** £26 per day (£30 weekends). **Prof** Alan Rodwell **Facilities** **Conf** fac available **Location** 1.25m NW of town centre off A677

Hotel ★★ 78% The Millstone at Mellor, Church Ln, Mellor, BLACKBURN ☎ 01254 813333 18 en suite 6 annexe en suite

BLACKPOOL Map 07 SD33

Blackpool North Shore Devonshire Rd FY2 0RD
☎ 01253 352054 🖷 01253 591240
e-mail: office@blackpoolnorthshoregolfclub.com
Undulating parkland course.

18 holes, 6432yds, Par 71, SSS 71, Course record 64. Club membership 900.
Visitors not Thu, Sat; advisable to contact in advance. **Societies** contact in advance. **Green Fees** £32 per day, £25 per round (£38/£30 weekends & bank holidays). **Cards** **Prof** Brendan Ward **Course Designer** HS Colt **Facilities** **Conf** Corporate Hospitality Days available **Location** on A587 N of town centre

Hotel ★★ 70% Hotel Sheraton, 54-62 Queens Promenade, BLACKPOOL ☎ 01253 352723 104 en suite

Blackpool Park North Park Dr FY3 8LS
☎ 01253 397916 🖷 01253 397916
e-mail: secretary@bpgc.org.uk
The course, situated in Stanley Park, is municipal. The golf club (Blackpool Park) is private but golfers may use the clubhouse facilities if playing the course. An abundance of grassy pits, ponds and open dykes.
18 holes, 6087yds, Par 70, SSS 69, Course record 64. Club membership 650.
Visitors not Sat; must apply to Mrs A Hirst, Town Hall, Talbot Square, Blackpool. **Societies** phone for details 01253 478478. **Green Fees** £16.50 per round (£19 weekends & bank holidays). **Cards** **Prof** Brian Purdie **Course Designer** Dr A MacKenzie **Facilities** **Location** 1m E of Blackpool Tower

Continued

Hotel ★★★ 70% Carousel Hotel, 663-671 New South Prom, BLACKPOOL ☎ 01253 402642 92 en suite

De Vere Herons Reach East Park Blackpool FY3 8LL
☎ 01253 766156 & 838866 🖷 01253 798800
e-mail: dot.kilbride@devere-hotels.com
The course was designed by Peter Alliss and Clive Clarke. There are 10 man-made lakes and several existing ponds. Built to a links design, well mounded but fairly easy walking. Water comes into play on nine holes, better players can go for the carry or shorter hitters can take the safe route. Extensive plantation and landscaping have been carried out as the course matures. The course provides an excellent and interesting challenge for golfers of all standards.

18 holes, 6628yds, Par 72, SSS 71, Course record 64. Club membership 450.
Visitors can book up to two weeks in advance 01253 766156 (hotel guest/visiting society no limit to how far in advance bookings can be made); handicap certificate; dress code. **Societies** phone or write to golf sales office 01253 838866. **Green Fees** not confirmed. **Cards** **Prof** Richard Bowman **Course Designer** Peter Alliss, Clive Clark **Facilities** **Leisure** hard tennis courts, heated indoor swimming pool, squash, sauna, solarium, gymnasium, health & beauty facilities. **Conf** fac available Corporate Hospitality Days available **Location** off A587 next to Stanley Park & Zoo

Hotel ★★★★ 68% De Vere Herons' Reach, East Park Dr, BLACKPOOL ☎ 01253 838866 172 en suite

BURNLEY Map 07 SD83

Burnley Glen View BB11 3RW
☎ 01282 421045 & 451281 🖷 01282 451281
e-mail: burnleygolfclub@onthegreen.co.uk
Challenging moorland course with exceptional views.
18 holes, 5939yds, Par 69, SSS 69, Course record 62. Club membership 700.
Visitors restricted Sat in summer; contact in advance. **Societies** apply in writing or phone for details. **Green Fees** £20 per day (£25 weekends & bank holidays). **Prof** Paul McEvoy **Facilities** **Leisure** snooker table. **Conf** fac available Corporate Hospitality Days available **Location** S of town off A646

Hotel ★★★ 70% Rosehill House Hotel, Rosehill Av, BURNLEY ☎ 01282 453931 30 en suite

Towneley Towneley Park, Todmorden Rd BB11 3ED
☎ 01282 438473
18 holes, 5811yds, Par 70, SSS 68, Course record 67.
Location 1m SE of town centre on A671
Phone for further details
....
Hotel ★★★ 74% Oaks Hotel, Colne Rd, Reedley,
BURNLEY ☎ 01282 414141 50 en suite

CHORLEY
Map 07 SD51

Charnock Richard Preston Rd, Charnock Richard
PR7 5LE
☎ 01257 470707 📄 01257 791196
e-mail: mail@charnockrichardgolfclub.co.uk
**Flat parkland course with plenty of American-style
water hazards. Signature hole the 6th par 5 with an
island green.**
*18 holes, 6239yds, Par 71, SSS 70, Course record 68.
Club membership 550.*
Visitors members' times 8.30-9.30pm, 12.00-1.00pm
weekdays; phone for weekends; dress code. **Societies**
contact club secretary in writing. **Green Fees** £30 per round
(£40 weekend). **Cards** 🟦 🟥 💳 💷 **Prof** Lee Taylor, Alan
Lunt **Course Designer** Martin Turner **Facilities** ⊗ ⋔ ⅃
💺 ♀ ⚲ 🏠 ⛳ 🎯 ⛟ ⛾ **Leisure** 9 hole pitch & putt.
Conf fac available Corporate Hospitality Days available
Location on A49, 0.25m from Camelot Theme Park
....
Hotel ★★★ 68% Park Hall Hotel, Park Hall Rd, Charnock
Richard, CHORLEY ☎ 01257 455000 56 en suite
84 annexe en suite

Chorley Hall o' th' Hill, Heath Charnock PR6 9HX
☎ 01257 480263 📄 01257 480722
e-mail: secretary@chorleygolfclub.freeserve.co.uk
**A splendid moorland course with plenty of fresh air.
The well-sited clubhouse affords some good views of the
Lancashire coast and of Angelzarke, a local beauty
spot. Beware of the short 3rd hole with its menacing out
of bounds.**
*18 holes, 6269yds, Par 71, SSS 70, Course record 62.
Club membership 550.*
Visitors not weekends or bank holidays; contact in
advance; must play from yellow tees. **Societies** Tue-Fri,
contact in advance. **Green Fees** not confirmed. **Prof** Mark
Bradley **Course Designer** JA Steer **Facilities** ⊗ ⅃ 💺 ♀
⚲ 🏠 ⛟ ⛾ **Location** 2.5m SE on A673
....
Hotel ★★★ 72% Pines Hotel, 570 Preston Rd, Clayton-
Le-Woods, CHORLEY ☎ 01772 338551 37 en suite

Duxbury Jubilee Park Duxbury Hall Rd PR7 4AT
☎ 01257 265380 📄 01257 274500
18 holes, 6390yds, Par 71, SSS 70.
Course Designer Hawtree & Sons **Location** 2.5m S off A6
Phone for further details
....
Hotel ⛴ Welcome Lodge, Welcome Break Service Area,
CHORLEY ☎ 01257 791746 100 en suite

Shaw Hill Hotel Golf & Country Club Preston
Rd, Whittle-Le-Woods PR6 7PP
☎ 01257 269221 📄 01257 261223
e-mail: info@shaw-hill.co.uk
18 holes, 6246yds, Par 72, SSS 70, Course record 65.
Course Designer Harry Vardon
Location 1.5m N on A6
Phone for further details

CLITHEROE
Map 07 SD74

Clitheroe Whalley Rd, Pendleton BB7 1PP
☎ 01200 422292 📄 01200 422292
e-mail: secretary@clitheroegolfclub.com
**One of the best inland courses in the country. Clitheroe
is a parkland-type course with water hazards and good
scenic views, particularly towards Longridge, and
Pendle Hill.**
*18 holes, 6326yds, Par 71, SSS 71, Course record 63.
Club membership 750.*
Visitors contact in advance. **Societies** contact in advance.
Green Fees £33-£45. **Prof** Paul McEvoy **Course Designer**
James Braid **Facilities** ⊗ ⋔ ⅃ 💺 ♀ ⚲ 🏠 ⛳ ⛟ ⛾
Conf Corporate Hospitality Days available
Location 2m S of Clitheroe
....
Hotel ★★ 70% Shireburn Arms Hotel, Whalley Rd, Hurst
Green, CLITHEROE ☎ 01254 826518 18 en suite

COLNE
Map 07 SD84

Colne Law Farm, Skipton Old Rd BB8 7EB
☎ 01282 863391
9 holes, 5961yds, Par 70, SSS 69, Course record 63.
Location 1m E off A56
Phone for further details
....
Hotel ★★★ 74% Oaks Hotel, Colne Rd, Reedley,
BURNLEY ☎ 01282 414141 50 en suite

DARWEN
Map 07 SD62

Darwen Winter Hill BB3 0LB
☎ 01254 701287 (club) & 704367 (office)
📄 01254 773833
e-mail: admin@darwengolfclub.com
18 holes, 5863yds, Par 69, SSS 68, Course record 63.
Location 1m NW
Phone for further details
....
Hotel ⛴ Travelodge Blackburn, Darwen Motorway
services, DARWEN ☎ 08700 850 950

FLEETWOOD
Map 07 SD34

Fleetwood Princes Way FY7 8AF
☎ 01253 873661 & 773573 📄 01253 773573
e-mail: fleetwoodgc@aol.com
**Championship length, flat seaside links where the
player must always be alert to changes of direction or
strength of the wind.**

*18 holes, 6723yds, Par 72, SSS 72.
Club membership 600.*

Continued

Visitors not competition days, after 11am Tue. **Societies** contact in advance, deposit £5 per player. **Green Fees** terms on application. **Prof** S McLaughlin **Course Designer** JA Steer **Facilities** ⊗ ⽉ ⽚ ⽚ ⽚ ⽚ ⽚ ⽚ **Location** W of town centre

Hotel ⇧ Premier Travel Inn Blackpool (Bispham), Devonshire Rd, Bispham, BLACKPOOL ☎ 08701 977033 39 en suite

GARSTANG
Map 07 SD44

Garstang Country Hotel & Golf Club
Garstang Rd, Bowgreave PR3 1YE
☎ 01995 600100 ⬚ 01995 600950
e-mail: reception@garstanghotelandgolf.co.uk

18 holes, 6050yds, Par 68, SSS 68.
Course Designer Richard Bradbeer **Location** 1m S of Garstang on B6430
Phone for further details

Hotel ★★★ 70% Garstang Country Hotel & Golf Club, Garstang Rd, Bowgreave, GARSTANG ☎ 01995 600100 32 en suite

GREAT HARWOOD
Map 07 SD73

Great Harwood
Harwood Bar, Whalley Rd BB6 7TE
☎ 01254 884391
Flat parkland course with fine views of the Pendle region.
9 holes, 6404yds, Par 73, SSS 71, Course record 68.
Club membership 400.
Visitors contact in advance. **Societies** mid-week, apply in writing. **Green Fees** not confirmed. **Facilities** ⽚ ⽚ ⽚ ⽚ **Location** E of town centre on A680

Hotel ★★★★ 62% Dunkenhalgh Hotel & Spa, Blackburn Rd, Clayton-le-Moors, ACCRINGTON ☎ 01254 398021 53 en suite 69 annexe en suite

HASLINGDEN
Map 07 SD72

Rossendale
Ewood Ln Head BB4 6LH
☎ 01706 831339 (Secretary) & 213616 (Pro)
⬚ 01706 228669
e-mail: rgc@golfers.net
Surprisingly flat parkland course, situated on a plateau with panoramic views and renowned for excellent greens.
18 holes, 6293yds, Par 72, Course record 64.
Club membership 700.
Visitors with member only Sat; contact in advance. **Societies** phone in advance & confirm in writing. **Green Fees** not confirmed. **Prof** Stephen Nicholls **Facilities** ⊗ ⽉

⽚ ⽚ ⽚ (ex Mon) ⽚ ⽚ ⽚ **Conf** Corporate Hospitality Days available **Location** 0.5m S off A56

Hotel ★★ 78% The Millstone at Mellor, Church Ln, Mellor, BLACKBURN ☎ 01254 813333 18 en suite 6 annexe en suite

HEYSHAM
Map 07 SD46

Heysham
Trumacar Park, Middleton Rd LA3 3JH
☎ 01524 851011 (Sec) & 852000 (Pro) ⬚ 01524 853030
e-mail: secretary@heyshamgolf.freeserve.co.uk
Seaside parkland course, partly wooded. The 15th is a 459yd par 4 hole nearly always played into the prevailing south west wind.
18 holes, 5999yds, Par 68, SSS 69.
Club membership 930.
Visitors restricted weekends; book in advance via the professional. **Societies** contact in advance. **Green Fees** £30 per day; £25 per round (£40 weekends & bank holidays). **Cards** ⬚ ⬚ ⬚ ⬚ ⬚ **Prof** Ryan Done **Course Designer** Alex Herd **Facilities** ⊗ ⽉ ⽚ ⽚ ⽚ ⽚ ⽚ ⽚ ⽚ ⽚ ⽚ **Leisure** snooker. **Location** 0.75m S off A589

Hotel ★★★ 65% Clarendon Hotel, 76 Marine Rd West, West End Promenade, MORECAMBE ☎ 01524 410180 29 en suite

Continued

KNOTT END-ON-SEA   Map 07 SD34

Knott End Wyreside FY6 0AA
☎ 01253 810576 📠 01253 813446
e-mail: louise@knottendgolfclub.com
**Scenic links and parkland course situated next to the
Wyre estuary with the opening five holes running along
the banks of the river and boasting the most spectacular
views on the Fylde Coast. Although the course is quite
short, the prevailing winds can add to one's score. Over-
clubbing can be disastrous with trouble behind most of
the smallish and well-guarded greens.**
*18 holes, 5849yds, Par 69, SSS 68, Course record 63.
Club membership 500.*
Visitors book via professional up to seven days in advance.
Societies contact in advance. **Green Fees** £31 per day, £29
per round (£41/£37 weekends). **Cards** 🖃 💳 💳 💳 💳 **Prof** Paul Walker **Course Designer** Braid **Facilities** ⊗ 🏲
🏠 💷 ♀ ⚲ 🏠 ⚲ 🥢 **Location** W of village off B5377

Hotel ⬧ Travelodge Lancaster Forton, White Carr Ln,
Bay Horse, FORTON ☎ 08700 850 950 53 en suite

LANCASTER   Map 07 SD46

Lancaster Golf Club Ashton Hall, Ashton-with-
Stodday LA2 0AJ
☎ 01524 751247 📠 01524 752742
**This parkland course is unusual as it is exposed to
winds from the Irish Sea. It is situated on the Lune
estuary and has some natural hazards and easy
walking. There are several fine holes among woods near
the old clubhouse. Fine views towards the Lake District.**
*18 holes, 6282yds, Par 71, SSS 71, Course record 66.
Club membership 925.*
Visitors with member or resident only weekends; must
contact in advance; handicap certificate. Societies Mon-Fri,
must contact in advance; handicap certificates. **Green Fees**
£42 per day, £35 per round. **Cards** 🖃 💳 💳 💳 **Prof**
David Sutcliffe **Course Designer** James Braid **Facilities**
⊗ 🏲 🏠 💷 ♀ ⚲ 🏠 🚄 ⚲ **Conf** Corporate Hospitality
Days available **Location** 3m S on A588

Hotel ★★★★ 71% Lancaster House Hotel, Green Ln,
Ellel, LANCASTER ☎ 01524 844822 80 en suite

Lansil Caton Rd LA1 3PE
☎ 01524 61233
e-mail: lansilsportsgolfclub@onetel.net
Challenging parkland course.
*9 holes, 5540yds, Par 70, SSS 67, Course record 68.
Club membership 375.*
Visitors not before 1pm Sun; contact in advance. Societies
weekdays; must contact in writing. **Green Fees** £12 per 18
holes. **Facilities** ⊗ by arrangement 🏲 by arrangement 🏠
💷 ♀ **Location** N of town centre on A683

Hotel ★★★★ 71% Lancaster House Hotel, Green Ln,
Ellel, LANCASTER ☎ 01524 844822 80 en suite

LANGHO   Map 07 SD73

Mytton Fold Hotel & Golf Complex Whalley
Rd BB6 8AB
☎ 01254 245392 📠 01254 248119
18 holes, 6082yds, Par 72, SSS 70, Course record 69.
Course Designer Frank Hargreaves **Location** on A59
between Langho & Whalley
Phone for further details

Continued

Hotel 🏠 Northcote Manor, Northcote Rd, LANGHO
☎ 01254 240555 14 en suite

LEYLAND   Map 07 SD52

Leyland Wigan Rd PR25 2UD
☎ 01772 436457 📠 01772 435605
e-mail: manager@leylandgolfclub.com
Parkland course, fairly flat and usually breezy.
*18 holes, 6256yds, Par 70, SSS 70, Course record 68.
Club membership 750.*
Visitors with member only weekends; contact in advance.
Societies contact in advance; official handicap. **Green
Fees** £30 per day. **Cards** 🖃 💳 💳 💳 **Prof** Colin
Burgess **Facilities** ⊗ 🏲 🏠 💷 ♀ ⚲ 🏠 ⚲ 🥢 **Conf** fac
available Corporate Hospitality Days available
Location M6 junct 28, 0.75m

Hotel ★★★ 72% Pines Hotel, 570 Preston Rd, Clayton-
Le-Woods, CHORLEY ☎ 01772 338551 37 en suite

LONGRIDGE   Map 07 SD63

Longridge Fell Barn, Jeffrey Hill PR3 2TU
☎ 01772 783291 📠 01772 783022
e-mail: secretary@longridgegolfclub.fsnet.co.uk
**One of the oldest clubs in England, which celebrated its
125th anniversary in 2002. A moorland course with
panoramic views of the Trough of Bowland, the Fylde
Coast and Welsh mountains. Small, sloping greens,
difficult to read.**

*18 holes, 5975yds, Par 70, SSS 69, Course record 63.
Club membership 600.*
Visitors restricted weekends Jul-Aug; contact in advance.
Societies by arrangement. **Green Fees** £28 per day
including bar meal (£22 per round weekends). 2 for 1 by
arrangement. **Cards** 🖃 💳 💳 💳 💳 **Prof** Stephen Taylor
Facilities ⊗ 🏲 🏠 💷 ♀ ⚲ 🏠 🔾 🦲 ⚲ 🥢
Leisure 9 hole par 3 course. **Conf** fac available Corporate
Hospitality Days available **Location** 8m NE of Preston off
B6243

Hotel ★★ 70% Shireburn Arms Hotel, Whalley Rd, Hurst
Green, CLITHEROE ☎ 01254 826518 18 en suite

LYTHAM ST ANNES   Map 07 SD32

Fairhaven Lytham Hall Park, Ansdell FY8 4JU
☎ 01253 736741 (Secretary) 📠 01253 731461
18 holes, 6883yds, Par 74, SSS 73, Course record 64.
Course Designer JA Steer **Location** E of town centre off
B5261
Phone for further details

Hotel ★★★ 69% Bedford Hotel, 307-311 Clifton Dr
South, LYTHAM ST ANNES ☎ 01253 724636
45 en suite

Championship Course

Lancashire

Royal Lytham & St Annes

Lytham St Annes

Map 07 SD32

Founded in 1886, this huge links course can be difficult, especially in windy conditions. Unusually for a championship course, it starts with a par 3, the nearby railway line and red-brick houses creating distractions that add to the challenge. The course has hosted 10 Open Championships with some memorable victories: amateur Bobby Jones famously won the first here in 1926; Bobby Charles of New Zealand became the only left-hander to win the title; in 1969 Tony Jacklin helped to revive British golf with his win; and the most recent in 2001 was won by David Duval.

Links Gate FY8 3LQ
☎ 01253 724206 Fax 01253 780946
e-mail: bookings@royallytham.org

18 holes, 6882yds, Par 71, SSS 74, Course record 64.
Club membership 850.
Visitors not Tue, Wed, Fri, weekends unless a guest in the Dormy House; handicap certificate (max 21 men, max 30 women).
Societies must contact secretary in advance; large groups Thu only. **Green Fees** £165 per 36 holes, £110 per 18 holes (limited play Sun £165 per 18 holes). **Cards**
Prof Eddie Birchenough **Course Designer** George Lowe
Facilities **Leisure** caddies available. **Conf** Corporate Hospitality Days available
Location 0.5m E of St Annes

Hotels

★★★★ 70% Clifton Arms Hotel, West Beach, Lytham, LYTHAM ST ANNES

☎ 01253 739898 48 en suite

★★★ 69% Chadwick Hotel, South Promenade, LYTHAM ST ANNES

☎ 01253 720061 Fax 01253 714455 75 en suite

★★★ 69% Bedford Hotel, 307-311 Clifton Dr South, LYTHAM ST ANNES

☎ 01253 724636 Fax 01253 729244 45 en suite

★★★ 64% The Best Western Glendower Hotel, North Promenade, LYTHAM ST ANNES

☎ 01253 723241 Fax 01253 640069 60 en suite

Lytham Green Drive Ballam Rd FY8 4LE
☎ 01253 737390 📄 01253 731350
e-mail: sec@greendrive.fsnet.co.uk
**Green Drive provides a stern but fair challenge for even
the most accomplished golfer. Tight fairways,
strategically placed hazards and small tricky greens are
the trademark of this testing course which meanders
through pleasant countryside and is flanked by woods,
pastures and meadows. The course demands accuracy
in spite of the relatively flat terrain.**
*18 holes, 6363yds, Par 70, SSS 70, Course record 64.
Club membership 700.*
Visitors weekends by arrangement only; contact in
advance. **Societies** phone to book in advance. **Green Fees**
£40 per day; £33 per round. **Cards** 🔲 🔲 🔲 🔲 **Prof**
Andrew Lancaster **Course Designer** Steer **Facilities** ⊗)🎏
🏌 💺♀🏌🏌🏌🏌 **Conf** Corporate Hospitality Days
available **Location** E of town centre off B5259

Hotel ★★★★ 70% Clifton Arms Hotel, West Beach,
Lytham, LYTHAM ST ANNES ☎ 01253 739898
48 en suite

St Annes Old Links Highbury Rd East FY8 2LD
☎ 01253 723597 📄 01253 781506
e-mail: secretary@coastalgolf.co.uk
**Seaside links, qualifying course for Open
Championship; compact and of very high standard,
particularly greens. Windy, very long 5th, 17th and
18th holes. Famous hole: 9th (171yds), par 3. Excellent
club facilities.**

*18 holes, 6616yds, Par 72, SSS 72, Course record 63.
Club membership 750.*
Visitors not before 9.30am, noon-1.30pm weekdays & not
Sat; Sun phone on day; handicap certificate. **Societies**
contact in advance. **Green Fees** £45 per day; £30 per 18
holes (£50 weekends & bank holidays). Reduced winter
rates. **Cards** 🔲 🔲 🔲 🔲 **Prof** DJ Webster **Course
Designer** George Lowe **Facilities** ⊗)🎏 🏌 💺♀🏌🏌🏌
🏌 **Leisure** snooker room. **Conf** Corporate Hospitality
Days available **Location** N of town centre

Hotel ★★★ 69% Bedford Hotel, 307-311 Clifton Dr
South, LYTHAM ST ANNES ☎ 01253 724636
45 en suite

**If the name of the club appears in *italics*, details
have not been confirmed for this
edition of the guide.**

The Chadwick Hotel

**South Promenade
Lytham St Annes, FY8 1NP**

AA ★★★

Tel: (01253) 720061
Email: sales@thechadwickhotel.com
www.thechadwickhotel.com

*A modern family run hotel and leisure complex close to all the
Fylde Coast Golf Courses and only 1/2 mile from the famous
Royal Lytham. Renowned for its good food, friendly personal
service, comfortable en suite bedrooms and a Bar which boasts
over 100 Malt Whiskys. After your Golf you can relax in the
Health complex which features an indoor pool, sauna, Turkish
bath, jacuzzi, solarium and Gymnasium. An ideal Hotel to stay
for your golfing break with prices starting from only £41.50 per
person per night for Dinner, Bed and Breakfast.*

LYTHAM ST ANNES   See page 155

Hotel ★★★ 69% Chadwick Hotel, South Promenade,
LYTHAM ST ANNES ☎ 01253 720061 📄 01253 714455
75 en suite

MORECAMBE   Map 07 SD46

Morecambe Bare LA4 6AJ
☎ 01524 412841 📄 01524 400088
e-mail: secretary@morecambegolfclub.com
**Holiday golf at its most enjoyable. The well-maintained,
wind-affected seaside parkland course is not long but
full of character. Even so the panoramic views of
Morecambe Bay, the Lake District and the Pennines
make concentration difficult. The 4th is a testing hole.**
*18 holes, 5750yds, Par 67, SSS 69, Course record 69.
Club membership 850.*

Continued

Visitors play from yellow tees; must contact in advance.
Societies contact in advance. Green Fees terms on
application. Cards ⬚ 🟦 🟦 🟥 🟦 Prof Simon Fletcher
Course Designer Dr A MacKenzie Facilities ⊗ ⫘ �🏌 ▬
🏌 ⛳ 🏠 ⚷ Location N of town centre on A5105

Hotel ★★★ 63% Elms Hotel, Bare Village,
MORECAMBE ☎ 01524 411501 39 en suite

NELSON   Map 07 SD83

Marsden Park Townhouse Rd BB9 8DG
☎ 01282 661912
18 holes, 5813yds, Par 70, SSS 68, Course record 66.
Location E of town centre off A56
Phone for further details

Hotel ★★★ 74% Oaks Hotel, Colne Rd, Reedley,
BURNLEY ☎ 01282 414141 50 en suite

Nelson King's Causeway, Brierfield BB9 0EU
☎ 01282 611834 ▤ 01282 611834
e-mail: nelsongc@onetel.net.uk
**Moorland course. Dr MacKenzie, who laid out the
course, managed a design that does not include any
wearisome climbing and created many interesting holes
with wonderful panoramic views of the surrounding
Pendle area.**
18 holes, 6007yds, Par 70, SSS 69, Course record 64.
Club membership 580.
Visitors not before 9.30am, 12.30-1.30pm; phone in
advance 01282 617000/611834. Societies contact in
advance. Green Fees £30 per day (£35 weekends & bank
holidays). Prof Neil Reeves Course Designer Dr
MacKenzie Facilities ⊗ ⫘ �🏌 ▬ 🏌 ⛳ 🏠 ⚷
Conf Corporate Hospitality Days available
Location M65 junct 12, A682 to Brierfield, left at lights
onto Halifax Rd & Kings Causeway

Hotel ★★★ 74% Oaks Hotel, Colne Rd, Reedley,
BURNLEY ☎ 01282 414141 50 en suite

ORMSKIRK   Map 07 SD40

Hurlston Hall Hurlston Ln, Southport Rd, Scarisbrick
L40 8HB
☎ 01704 840400 & 841120 (pro shop) ▤ 01704 841404
e-mail: info@hurlstonhall.co.uk
**Designed by Donald Steel, this gently undulating course
offers fine views of the Pennines and Bowland Fells.
With generous fairways, large tees and greens, two
streams and seven lakes, it provides a good test of golf
for players of all standards. Luxurious colonial-style
clubhouse.**
18 holes, 6746yds, Par 72, SSS 72, Course record 66.
Club membership 650.
Visitors contact in advance Societies registered golf
societies & others approved by club, write or phone for
details. Green Fees £35 per 18 holes (£40 weekends).
Cards ⬚ 🟦 🟦 🟦 🟥 🟦 Course Designer Donald
Steel Facilities ⊗ ⫘ �🏌 ▬ 🏌 ⛳ 🏠 🛒 ⚷ ⟨ Leisure
heated indoor swimming pool, fishing, gymnasium.
Conf fac available Corporate Hospitality Days available
Location 2m from Ormskirk on A570

Hotel ★★★ 66% Beaufort Hotel, High Ln, Burscough,
ORMSKIRK ☎ 01704 892655 20 en suite

Ormskirk Cranes Ln, Lathom L40 5UJ
☎ 01695 572227 ▤ 01695 572227
e-mail: ormskirk@ukgolfer.org
**A pleasantly secluded, fairly flat, parkland course with
much heath and silver birch. Accuracy from the tees
will provide an interesting variety of second shots.**
18 holes, 6358yds, Par 70, SSS 71, Course record 63.
Club membership 300.
Visitors restricted Sat. Societies phone or contact in
writing. Green Fees terms on application. Prof Jack
Hammond Course Designer Harold Hilton Facilities ⊗ ⫘
🏌 ▬ 🏌 ⛳ 🏠 ⚷ Conf Corporate Hospitality Days
available Location 1.5m NE

Hotel ★★★ 66% Beaufort Hotel, High Ln, Burscough,
ORMSKIRK ☎ 01704 892655 20 en suite

PLEASINGTON   Map 07 SD62

Pleasington BB2 5JF
☎ 01254 202177 ▤ 01254 201028
e-mail: secretary.manager@pleasington-golf.co.uk
**Plunging and rising across lovely parkland and
heathland turf, this course tests judgement of distance
through the air to greens of widely differing levels. The
11th and 4th are testing holes.**
18 holes, 6417yds, Par 70, SSS 70.
Club membership 700.
Visitors not Tue, weekends. Societies contact in advance.
Green Fees £55 per day, £44 per round. Prof Ged Furey
Course Designer George Lowe Facilities ⊗ ⫘ �🏌 ▬ 🏌
⛳ 🏠 ⚷ ⟨ Conf fac available Location M65 junct 3,
signed for Blackburn

Hotel ★★ 78% The Millstone at Mellor, Church Ln,
Mellor, BLACKBURN ☎ 01254 813333 18 en suite
6 annexe en suite

POULTON-LE-FYLDE   Map 07 SD33

Poulton-le-Fylde Breck Rd FY6 7HJ
☎ 01253 892444 & 893150 ▤ 01253 892444
9 holes, 4454yds, Par 71, SSS 68.
Course Designer E Astbury Location M55 junct 3, A585
to Poulton, club signed
Phone for further details

Hotel ★★ 70% Hotel Sheraton, 54-62 Queens Promenade,
BLACKPOOL ☎ 01253 352723 104 en suite

PRESTON   Map 07 SD52

Ashton & Lea Tudor Av, Lea PR4 0XA
☎ 01772 735282 ▤ 01772 735762
e-mail: ashtonleagolf@supanet.com
**Fairly flat, well-maintained parkland course with
natural water hazards, offering pleasant walks and
some testing holes for golfers of all standards. Water
comes into play on seven of the last nine holes. The
course has three challenging par 3s.**
18 holes, 6334yds, Par 71, SSS 70, Course record 65.
Club membership 650.
Visitors contact professional 01772 720374 or secretary
01772 735282. Societies contact in writing or by phone.
Green Fees £30 per 18 holes (£40 weekends & bank
holidays). Prof M Greenough Course Designer J Steer
Facilities ⊗ ⫘ �🏌 ▬ 🏌 ⛳ 🏠 ⚷ Leisure snooker table.
Conf fac available Corporate Hospitality Days available
Location 3m W of Preston on A5085

Fishwick Hall Glenluce Dr, Farringdon Park
PR1 5TD
☎ 01772 798300 📠 01772 704600
e-mail: fishwickhallgolfclub@supanet.com
Meadowland course overlooking River Ribble. Natural hazards.
18 holes, 6045yds, Par 70, SSS 69, Course record 66.
Club membership 750.
Visitors advisable to contact in advance. Societies contact in advance. Green Fees terms on application. Cards ▦ 🟥 🟥 📶 🟊 Prof Martin Watson Facilities ⊗ 🍴 🍔 ☕ ♀ 🛄 🍴 🛒 Conf Corporate Hospitality Days available Location M6 junct 31
....
Hotel ★★★ 67% Tickled Trout, Preston New Rd, Samlesbury, PRESTON ☎ 01772 877671 102 en suite

Ingol Tanterton Hall Rd, Ingol PR2 7BY
☎ 01772 734556 📠 01772 729815
e-mail: ingol@golfers.net
Championship-designed course with natural water hazards, set in 250 acres of beautiful parkland. A good test for any golfer.

18 holes, 6294yds, Par 72, SSS 70, Course record 68.
Club membership 650.
Visitors contact booking office in advance. Societies contact in advance. Green Fees terms on application. Cards ▦ 🟥 🟥 📶 🟊 Prof Ryan Grimshaw Course Designer Henry Cotton Facilities ⊗ 🍴 🍔 ☕ ♀ 🛄 🍴 🛒 🚜 ✂ Leisure squash, Snooker & Pool. Conf fac available Location A5085 onto B5411, signs to Ingol
....
Hotel ⬆ Premier Travel Inn Preston East, Bluebell Way, Preston East Link Rd, Fulwood, PRESTON ☎ 08701 977215 65 en suite

Penwortham Blundell Ln, Penwortham PR1 0AX
☎ 01772 744630 📠 01772 740172
e-mail: penworthamgolfclub@supanet.com
A progressive golf club set close to the banks of the River Ribble. The course has tree-lined fairways, excellent greens, and provides easy walking. Testing holes include the 175 yd, par 3 3rd, the 483 yd, par 5 6th, and the 385 yd par 4 16th.
18 holes, 5877yds, Par 69, SSS 69, Course record 65.
Club membership 1100.
Visitors restricted Tue, weekends; contact in advance. Societies apply in writing or phone in advance. Green Fees not confirmed. Prof Darren Hopwood Facilities ⊗ 🍴 🍔 ☕ ♀ 🛄 🍴 🛒 ✂ Conf Corporate Hospitality Days available Location 1.5m W of town centre off A59
....
Hotel ★★★ 67% Tickled Trout, Preston New Rd, Samlesbury, PRESTON ☎ 01772 877671 102 en suite

Preston Fulwood Hall Ln, Fulwood PR2 8DD
☎ 01772 700011 📠 01772 794234
e-mail: secretary@prestongolfclub.com
Pleasant inland golf at this course set in very agreeable parkland. There is a well-balanced selection of holes, undulating among groups of trees, and not requiring great length.
18 holes, 6312yds, Par 71, SSS 71, Course record 68.
Club membership 800.
Visitors midweek only; must contact in advance; handicap certificate. Societies contact in writing or phone. Green Fees £43 per day; £38 per round. Prof Andrew Greenbank Course Designer James Braid Facilities ⊗ 🍴 🍔 ☕ ♀ 🛄 🍴 🛒 ✂ 🎯 Conf fac available Location 1m N of city centre on A6, right at lights onto Watling St, left onto Fulwood Hall Ln, course 300yds on left
....
Hotel ★★★★ 68% Preston Marriott Hotel, Garstang Rd, Broughton, PRESTON ☎ 01772 864087 150 en suite

Rishton Eachill Links, Hawthorn Dr BB1 4HG
☎ 01254 884442 📠 01254 887701
e-mail: rishtongc@onetel.net
Undulating moorland course with some interesting holes and fine views of East Lancashire.
Eachill Links: 10 holes, 6097yds, Par 70, SSS 69, Course record 68.
Club membership 270.
Visitors with member only weekends & bank holidays. Societies contact in writing. Green Fees £20 weekdays only. Course Designer Peter Alliss, Dave Thomas Facilities ⊗ 🍴 🍔 ☕ ♀ by arrangement 🛄 Conf Corporate Hospitality Days available Location M65 junct 6/7, club 1m. Signed from Station Rd in Rishton
....
Hotel ★★★★ 62% Dunkenhalgh Hotel & Spa, Blackburn Rd, Clayton-le-Moors, ACCRINGTON ☎ 01254 398021 53 en suite 69 annexe en suite

Silverdale Redbridge Ln LA5 0SP
☎ 01524 701300 📠 01524 702074
e-mail: silverdalegolfclub@ecosse.net
Challenging heathland course with rock outcrops, set in an Area of Outstanding Natural Beauty with spectacular views of the Lake District hills and Morecambe Bay. It is a course of two halves, being either open fairways or tight hilly limestone valleys. The 13th hole has been described as one of Britain's 100 extraordinary golf holes.
18 holes, 5535yds, Par 70, SSS 68, Course record 68.
Club membership 500.
Visitors not Sun Apr-Sep; phone to book tee 01524 701300. Societies contact by writing, e-mail or phone. Green Fees £25 per day; £20 per round (£30/£25 weekends). Facilities ⊗ 🍴 🍔 ☕ ♀ 🛄 🍴 ✂ Location opp Silverdale station & Leighton Moss RSPB nature reserve
....
Hotel ★★ 65% Royal Station Hotel, Market St, CARNFORTH ☎ 01524 732033 & 733636 📠 01524 720267 13 en suite

PHOLLAND
Map 07 SD50

eacon Park Beacon Ln WN8 7RU
☎ 01695 622700 📠 01695 633066
8 holes, 6000yds, Par 72, SSS 69, Course record 68.
ourse Designer Donald Steel **Location** S of Ashurst
eacon Hill
hone for further details
....
otel ★★★ 66% Beaufort Hotel, High Ln, Burscough,
RMSKIRK ☎ 01704 892655 20 en suite

ean Wood Lafford Ln WN8 0QZ
☎ 01695 622219 📠 01695 622245
-mail: dwgc1922secretary@freenet.co.uk
**his parkland course has a varied terrain - flat front
ine, undulating back nine. Beware the par 4 11th and
7th holes, which have ruined many a card. If there
ere a prize for the best maintained course in
ancashire, Dean Wood would be a strong contender.**
8 holes, 6148yds, Par 71, SSS 70, Course record 65.
lub membership 730.
isitors with member only Tue, Wed. **Societies** contact in
dvance. **Green Fees** £30 per day. **Prof** Stuart Danchin
ourse Designer James Braid **Facilities** ⊗ ∭ ⓑ ⯊ ♉ ☖
☗ ⌖ ✐ **Conf** Corporate Hospitality Days available
ocation M6 junct 26, 1m on A577
....
otel ★★★ 60% Lancashire Manor Hotel, Prescott Rd,
PHOLLAND ☎ 01695 720401 55 en suite

HALLEY
Map 07 SD73

halley Long Leese Barn, Clerk Hill Rd BB7 9DR
☎ 01254 822236
**arkland course near Pendle Hill, overlooking the
bble Valley. Superb views. Ninth hole over pond.**
holes, 6258yds, Par 72, SSS 71, Course record 69.
lub membership 450.
isitors phone in advance 01254 822236. **Societies** apply
writing. **Green Fees** £25 per day (£30 weekends & bank
olidays). **Prof** Jamie Hunt **Facilities** ⊗ ∭ ⓑ ⯊ ♉ ☖ 🏠
Conf Corporate Hospitality Days available
ocation 1m SE off A671
....
otel ★★★★ 66% Clarion Hotel & Suites Foxfields,
halley Rd, Billington, CLITHEROE ☎ 01254 822556
4 en suite

HITWORTH
Map 07 SD81

obden Lobden Moor OL12 8XJ
☎ 01706 343228 & 345598 📠 01706 343228
**oorland course, with hard walking. Windy with
perb views of surrounding hills. Excellent greens.**
holes, 5697yds, Par 70, SSS 68, Course record 63.
lub membership 250.
isitors not Sat. **Societies** apply in writing to Secretary.
reen Fees terms on application. **Facilities** ⊗ ∭ ⓑ ⯐
☖ **Location** E of town centre off A671
....
otel ★★★★ 62% Norton Grange Hotel, Manchester Rd,
astleton, ROCHDALE ☎ 01706 630788 51 en suite

> **Prices may change during the currency of the
> Guide, please check when booking.**

WILPSHIRE
Map 07 SD63

Wilpshire Whalley Rd BB1 9LF
☎ 01254 248260 📠 01254 248260
18 holes, 5971yds, Par 69, SSS 69, Course record 65.
Course Designer James Braid **Location** 2m NE of
Blackburn on A666 towards Clitheroe
Phone for further details
....
Hotel ★★★ 67% Sparth House Hotel, Whalley Rd,
Clayton Le Moors, ACCRINGTON ☎ 01254 872263
16 en suite

LEICESTERSHIRE

ASHBY-DE-LA-ZOUCH
Map 08 SK31

Willesley Park Measham Rd LE65 2PF
☎ 01530 414596 📠 01530 564169
e-mail: info@willesleypark.com
**Undulating heathland and parkland course with quick
draining sandy subsoil.**
18 holes, 6304yds, Par 70, SSS 70, Course record 63.
Club membership 600.
Visitors restricted weekends; contact in advance; handicap
certificate. **Societies** Wed-Fri, must apply in writing.
Green Fees not confirmed. **Prof** Ben Hill **Course
Designer** J Braid **Facilities** ⊗ ∭ ⓑ ⯊ ♉ ☖ 🏠 ✐
Location SW of town centre on B5006
....
Hotel ★★ 62% Charnwood Arms Hotel, Beveridge Ln,
Bardon Hill, COALVILLE ☎ 01530 813644 34 en suite

BIRSTALL
Map 04 SK50

Birstall Station Rd LE4 3BB
☎ 0116 267 4322 📠 0116 267 4322
e-mail: suechilton@btconnect.com
**Parkland course with trees, shrubs, ponds and ditches,
adjacent to Great Central Railway Steam Train line.**
18 holes, 6213yds, Par 70, SSS 70.
Club membership 650.
Visitors weekdays by arrangement; contact professional
for weekends. **Societies** apply in writing. **Green Fees** £35
per day; £30 per round. **Prof** David Clark **Facilities** ⊗ ∭
ⓑ ⯊ ♉ ☖ 🏠 ✐ **Leisure** billiard room. **Conf** Corporate
Hospitality Days available **Location** 3m N of Leicester on
A6
....
Hotel ★★★ 66% Rothley Court, Westfield Ln,
ROTHLEY ☎ 0116 237 4141 13 en suite 21 annexe
en suite

BOTCHESTON
Map 04 SK40

Forest Hill Markfield Ln LE9 9FJ
☎ 01455 824800 📠 01455 828522
18 holes, 6039yds, Par 72, SSS 69.
Phone for further details
....
Hotel ★★ 63% Castle Hotel & Restaurant, Main St,
KIRBY MUXLOE ☎ 0116 239 5337 22 en suite

COSBY
Map 04 SP59

Cosby Chapel Ln, Broughton Rd LE9 1RG
☎ 0116 286 4759 📠 0116 286 4484
e-mail: secretary@cosby-golf-club.co.uk
**Undulating parkland course with a number of tricky,
tight driving holes. Challenging holes include the**
Continued

par 4 1st with an unseen meandering brook, the deceptively long par 4 3rd, the 12th from an elevated tee and the hogs-back shape par 3 14th, both affected by the prevailing wind.
18 holes, 6410yds, Par 71, SSS 71, Course record 65. Club membership 750.
Visitors not after 4pm weekdays, not weekends; recommended to phone in advance; handicap certificate. **Societies** Mon-Fri, book with secretary in advance. **Green Fees** not confirmed. **Prof** Martin Wing **Course Designer** Hawtree **Facilities** ⊗ ⅷ ┗ ♥ ♀ ⚑ ☝ ♪ ♂
Conf fac available **Location** M1 junct 21, B4114 to L-turn at BP service station, signed Cosby

···

Hotel ★★★★ 74% Sketchley Grange Hotel, Sketchley Ln, Burbage, HINCKLEY ☎ 01455 251133 52 en suite

EAST GOSCOTE — Map 08 SK61

Beedles Lake 170 Broome Ln LE7 3WQ
☎ 0116 260 4414 ▤ 0116 260 4414
e-mail: les@jelson.co.uk
Fairly flat parkland course with easy walking and ditches, streams and rivers coming into play on many holes. Older trees and thousands of newly planted ones give the course a mature feel. Many challenging holes where you can ruin a good score.
18 holes, 6641yds, Par 72, SSS 72, Course record 71. Club membership 430.
Visitors phone booking for weekends (by Thu). **Societies** Mon-Fri. **Green Fees** £13 (£18 weekends & bank holidays). **Cards** ⬚ ⬚ ⬚ ⬚ ⬚ **Prof** Sean Byrne **Course Designer** D Tucker **Facilities** ⊗ ⅷ ┗ ♥ ♀ ⚑ ☝ ♪ ♂ ⚘ **Leisure** fishing. **Conf** fac available Corporate Hospitality Days available **Location** off A607

···

Hotel ★★★ 66% Rothley Court, Westfield Ln, ROTHLEY ☎ 0116 237 4141 13 en suite 21 annexe en suite

ENDERBY — Map 04 SP59

Enderby Mill Ln LE19 4LX
☎ 0116 284 9388 ▤ 0116 284 9388
A gently undulating nine-hole course at which beginners are especially welcome. The longest hole is the 2nd at 407yds and there are five par 3s.
9 holes, 2856yds, Par 72, SSS 71, Course record 71. Club membership 150.
Visitors Societies phone in advance. **Green Fees** terms on application. **Prof** Chris D'Araujo **Course Designer** David Lowe **Facilities** ⊗ ⅷ ┗ ♥ ♀ ⚑ ☝ ♂ **Leisure** heated indoor swimming pool, squash, sauna, solarium, gymnasium, indoor bowls snooker badminton.
Location M1 junct 21, 2m S on Narborough road, right at Toby Carvery rdbt, 0.5m on left

···

Hotel ★★★ 68% Corus hotel Leicester, Enderby Rd, Blaby, LEICESTER ☎ 0116 278 7898 & 0870 609 6106 ▤ 0116 278 1974 48 en suite

HINCKLEY — Map 04 SP49

Hinckley Leicester Rd LE10 3DR
☎ 01455 615124 & 615014 ▤ 01455 890841
e-mail: proshop@hinckleygolfclub.com
Parkland course with a good variety of holes to test all abilities. Water comes into play on a number of holes.
18 holes, 6467yds, Par 71, SSS 71, Course record 65. Club membership 750.

Visitors not Tue; with member only weekends & bank holidays; must contact in advance; handicap certificate. **Societies** Mon & Wed, must contact in advance. **Green Fees** £40 per day; £30 per round. **Cards** ⬚ ⬚ ⬚ ⬚ ⬚ **Prof** Richard Jones **Course Designer** Southern Golf Ltd **Facilities** ⊗ ⅷ ┗ ♥ ♀ ⚑ ☝ ♪ ♂ **Leisure** snooker. **Conf** fac available Corporate Hospitality Days available **Location** 1.5m NE on B4668

···

Hotel ★★★ 66% Weston Hall Hotel, Weston Ln, Bulkington, NUNEATON ☎ 024 7631 2989 40 en suite

KIBWORTH — Map 04 SP69

Kibworth Weir Rd, Beauchamp LE8 0LP
☎ 0116 279 2301 ▤ 0116 279 6434
e-mail: secretary@kibworthgolfclub.freeserve.co.uk
Parkland course with easy walking. A brook affects a number of fairways
18 holes, 6113yds, Par 71, SSS 70. Club membership 700.
Visitors with member only weekends; contact in advance. **Societies** contact in advance. **Green Fees** £35 per day; £27 per round. **Prof** Mike Herbert **Facilities** ⊗ ⅷ ┗ ♥ ♀ ⚑ ☝ ♂ **Location** S of village off A6

···

Hotel ★★★ 70% Three Swans Hotel, 21 High St, MARKET HARBOROUGH ☎ 01858 466644 18 en suite 43 annexe en suite

KIRBY MUXLOE — Map 04 SK50

Kirby Muxloe Station Rd LE9 2EP
☎ 0116 239 3457 ▤ 0116 238 8891
e-mail: kirbymuxloegolf@btconnect.com
Pleasant parkland course with a lake in front of the 17th green and a short 18th.
18 holes, 6351yds, Par 71, SSS 70, Course record 62. Club membership 870.
Visitors not Tue, weekends; contact in advance; handicap certificate. **Societies** contact in advance. **Green Fees** £35 per day, £30 per round. **Prof** Bruce Whipham **Facilities** ⊗ ⅷ ┗ ♥ ♀ ⚑ ☝ ♪ ♂ **Conf** Corporate Hospitality Days available **Location** S of village off B5380

···

Hotel ★★ 63% Castle Hotel & Restaurant, Main St, KIRBY MUXLOE ☎ 0116 239 5337 22 en suite

LEICESTER — Map 04 SK50

Humberstone Heights Gypsy Ln LE5 0TB
☎ 0116 276 3680 & 299 5570 (pro) ▤ 0116 299 5569
e-mail: hhmgolfclub@freeserve.co.uk
Municipal parkland course with varied layout.
18 holes, 6343yds, Par 70, SSS 70, Course record 66. Club membership 400.
Visitors phone in advance for weekends. **Societies** phone in advance. **Green Fees** terms on application. **Cards** ⬚ **Prof** Phil Highfield **Course Designer** Hawtry & Sons **Facilities** ⊗ ┗ ♥ ♀ ⚑ ☝ ♪ ♂ **Leisure** 9-hole pitch & putt course. **Location** 2.5m NE of city centre

···

Hotel ★★★ 74% Belmont House Hotel, De Montfort St, LEICESTER ☎ 0116 254 4773 77 en suite

Leicestershire Evington Ln LE5 6DJ
☎ 0116 273 8825 ▤ 0116 249 8799
e-mail: enquiries@thelgc.co.uk
Pleasantly undulating parkland course.
18 holes, 6134yds, Par 68, SSS 70. Club membership 800.

Continued

Continue

Visitors not Sat; contact in advance; handicap certificate.
Societies contact in advance. **Green Fees** £40 per day
weekdays only), £35 per 18 holes. **Prof** Darren Jones
Course Designer Hawtree **Facilities** ⊗ ⍫ ⅃ 𝄢 ♟ ♀ ⚘ 🛆
♀ **Conf** Corporate Hospitality Days available
Location 2m E of city off A6030

....

Hotel ★★★ 68% Regency Hotel, 360 London Rd,
LEICESTER ☎ 0116 270 9634 32 en suite

Western Scudamore Rd, Braunstone Frith LE3 1UQ
☎ 0116 299 5566 📠 0116 299 5568
18 holes, 6518yds, Par 72, SSS 71.
Location 1.5m W of city centre off A47
Phone for further details

....

Hotel ★★ 63% Castle Hotel & Restaurant, Main St,
KIRBY MUXLOE ☎ 0116 239 5337 22 en suite

LOUGHBOROUGH   Map 08 SK51

Longcliffe Snell's Nook Ln, Nanpantan LE11 3YA
☎ 01509 239129 📠 01509 231286
e-mail: longcliffegolf@btconnect.com
Course of natural heathland, tree lined fairways with
water in play on the 14th and 15th holes. This course is
recognised by the English Golf Championship.

18 holes, 6625yds, Par 72, SSS 72, Course record 65.
Club membership 660.
Visitors contact in advance; handicap certificate. **Societies**
phone in advance for availability; handicap certificates.
Green Fees terms on application. **Cards** 💳 💳 💳 **Prof**
David Mee **Course Designer** Williamson **Facilities** ⊗ ⍫
🝆 ♀ ⚘ 🛆 ♀ **Conf** Corporate Hospitality Days
available **Location** M1 junct 23, off A512 1.5m

....

Hotel ★★★ 65% Quality Hotel & Suites Loughborough,
New Ashby Rd, LOUGHBOROUGH ☎ 01509 211800
94 en suite

LUTTERWORTH   Map 04 SP58

Kilworth Springs South Kilworth Rd, North
Kilworth LE17 6HJ
☎ 01858 575082 📠 01858 575078
e-mail: kilworthsprings@ukonline.co.uk
An 18-hole course of two loops of nine: the front nine is
links style while the back nine is in parkland with four
lakes. On a windy day it is a very challenging course
and the 6th hole well deserves its nickname the Devil's
Toenail.
18 holes, 6543yds, Par 72, SSS 71, Course record 66.
Club membership 850.

Visitors subject to availability. **Societies** please contact for
details 01858 575082. **Green Fees** £22 weekdays per 18
holes (£25 weekends). **Cards** 💳 💳 💳 💳 **Prof**
Anders Mankert **Course Designer** Ray Baldwin **Facilities**
⊗ ⍫ 🝆 ♀ ⚘ 🛆 ♀ ⚐ **Conf** Corporate
Hospitality Days available **Location** M1 junct 20, 4m E
A4304 to Market Harborough

....

Hotel ★★ 72% The Sun Inn, Main St, MARSTON
TRUSSELL ☎ 01858 465531 20 en suite

Lutterworth Rugby Rd LE17 4HN
☎ 01455 552532 📠 01455 553586
Hilly course with the River Swift running through.
18 holes, 6226yds, Par 70, SSS 70.
Club membership 700.
Visitors with member only weekends. **Societies** contact in
advance. **Green Fees** £30 per day; £22 per 18 holes. **Prof**
Roland Tisdall **Facilities** ⊗ ⍫ 🝆 ♀ ⚘ 🛆 🎏 ⚐
Conf Corporate Hospitality Days available
Location M1 junct 20, 0.25m

....

Hotel ★★★ 67% Brownsover Hall Hotel, Brownsover Ln,
Old Brownsover, RUGBY ☎ 0870 609 6104 27 en suite
20 annexe en suite

MARKET HARBOROUGH   Map 04 SP78

Market Harborough Oxendon Rd LE16 8NF
☎ 01858 463684 📠 01858 432906
A parkland course close to the town. Undulating and in
parts hilly. There are wide-ranging views over the
surrounding countryside. Lakes feature on four holes;
challenging last three holes.
18 holes, 6070yds, Par 70, SSS 69, Course record 61.
Club membership 650.
Visitors with member only weekends. **Societies** apply in
writing. **Green Fees** £25 per round. **Prof** Frazer Baxter
Course Designer H Swan **Facilities** ⊗ ⍫ 🝆 ♀ ⚘ 🛆
♀ **Conf** Corporate Hospitality Days available
Location 1m S on A508

....

Hotel ★★★ 70% Three Swans Hotel, 21 High St,
MARKET HARBOROUGH ☎ 01858 466644 18 en suite
43 annexe en suite

Stoke Albany Ashley Rd, Stoke Albany LE16 8PL
☎ 01858 535208 📠 01858 535505
e-mail: info@stokealbanygolfclub.co.uk
Parkland course in the picturesque Welland valley.
Affording good views, the course should appeal to the
mid-handicap golfer, and provide an interesting test to
the more experienced player. The greens are
individually contoured, adding to the golfing challenge.
18 holes, 6175yds, Par 71, SSS 70.
Club membership 500.
Visitors all times. **Societies** please phone secretary. **Green**
Fees £17 per 18 holes (£20 weekends). **Cards** 💳 💳 💳
💳 💳 ⚐ **Prof** Adrian Clifford **Course Designer**
Hawtree **Facilities** ⊗ ⍫ 🝆 ♀ ⚘ 🛆 ♀ **Conf** fac
available **Location** N off A427 Market Harborough-Corby
road, follow Stoke Albany 500yds towards Ashley

....

Hotel ★★★ 70% Three Swans Hotel, 21 High St,
MARKET HARBOROUGH ☎ 01858 466644 18 en suite
43 annexe en suite

> **Booking a tee time is always advisable.**

Continued

MELTON MOWBRAY
Map 08 SK71

Melton Mowbray Waltham Rd, Thorpe Arnold
LE14 4SD
☎ 01664 562118 📠 01664 562118
e-mail: mmgc@le144sd.fsbusiness.co.uk
Easy walking heathland course.

18 holes, 6222yds, Par 70, SSS 70, Course record 65.
Club membership 650.
Visitors contact professional 01664 569629. **Societies**
contact in advance. **Green Fees** £35 per day, £25 per round
(£30 per round weekends & bank holidays). **Cards** 🏧 💳
🖥 **Prof** Neil Curtis **Facilities** ⊗ ⅢⅡ ⬥ 🍺 ♀ ♨ 🏠 ⛳ ⚑
🛒 ⚙ 🏌 **Location** 2m NE of Melton Mowbray on A607

························

Hotel ★★★ 73% Sysonby Knoll Hotel, Asfordby Rd,
MELTON MOWBRAY ☎ 01664 563563 23 en suite
7 annexe en suite

Stapleford Park Stapleford LE14 2EF
☎ 01572 787000 📠 01572 787001
e-mail: clubs@stapleford.co.uk
Set in 500 acres of parkland, lake and woods.
Reminiscent of some Scottish links, the course wraps
around the heart of the estate in two extended loops.
Never more than two holes wide, the whole course is
spacious and tranquil. The beauty of the surrounding
countryside is the perfect backdrop.
18 holes, 6944yds, Par 73, SSS 73.
Club membership 300.
Visitors not weekends; contact in advance. **Societies** phone
01572 787070 or e-mail. **Green Fees** £50-£75 per day
seasonal rate. **Cards** 🏧 💳 📇 💳 🖥 **Prof** Richard
Alderson **Course Designer** Donald Steel **Facilities** ⊗ Ⅲ
⬥ 🍺 ♀ ♨ 🏠 ⛳ 🏌 🛒 ⚙ 🏌 **Leisure** hard tennis
courts, heated indoor swimming pool, fishing, sauna,
solarium, gymnasium, shooting, falconry, offroading,
horseriding, archery. **Conf** fac available Corporate
Hospitality Days available **Location** 4m E of Melton
Mowbray off B676

························

Hotel ★★★★ Stapleford Park, Stapleford, MELTON
MOWBRAY ☎ 01572 787522 44 en suite 8 annexe
en suite

OADBY
Map 04 SK60

Glen Gorse Glen Rd LE2 4RF
☎ 0116 271 4159 📠 0116 271 4159
e-mail: secretary@gggc.co.uk
Fairly flat 18-hole parkland course with strategically
placed trees encountered on every hole, rewarding the
straight hitter. The long approaches and narrow greens
require the very best short game. However, a premium
is placed on accuracy and length, and no more so than

over the closing three holes, considered to be one of the
finest finishes in the county.
18 holes, 6648yds, Par 72, SSS 72, Course record 64.
Club membership 730.
Visitors with member only weekends; contact in advance.
Societies phone secretary in advance. **Green Fees** terms on
application. **Prof** Dominic Fitzpatrick **Facilities** ⊗ Ⅲ ⬥
🍺 ♀ ♨ 🏠 🛒 🏌 ⚙ **Leisure** snooker room. **Conf**
Corporate Hospitality Days available **Location** on A6
between Oadby & Great Glen, 5m S of Leicester

························

Hotel ★★★ 68% Regency Hotel, 360 London Rd,
LEICESTER ☎ 0116 270 9634 32 en suite

Oadby Leicester Rd LE2 4AJ
☎ 0116 270 9052
e-mail: oadbygolf@supanet.com
Flat municipal parkland course.
18 holes, 6376yds, Par 72, SSS 70, Course record 69.
Club membership 300.
Visitors no restrictions. **Societies** by arrangement, contact
pro shop. **Green Fees** £11 (£14 weekends). **Prof** Andrew
Wells **Facilities** ⊗ Ⅲ ⬥ 🍺 ♀ ♨ 🏠 ⛳ 🏌 ⚙ **Leisure**
squash, sauna, gymnasium, snooker. **Conf** fac available
Location W of Oadby off A6

························

Hotel ★★★ 68% Regency Hotel, 360 London Rd,
LEICESTER ☎ 0116 270 9634 32 en suite

ROTHLEY
Map 08 SK51

Rothley Park Westfield Ln LE7 7LH
☎ 0116 230 2809 📠 0116 230 2809
e-mail: secretary@rothleypark.co.uk
Parkland course in picturesque situation.
18 holes, 6477yds, Par 71, SSS 71, Course record 67.
Club membership 600.
Visitors not Tue; with member only weekends & bank
holidays; contact professional 0116 230 3023. **Societies**
apply in writing to secretary. **Green Fees** not confirmed.
Prof D Spillane **Facilities** ⊗ Ⅲ ⬥ 🍺 ♀ ♨ 🏠 ⛳ ⚙
Conf Corporate Hospitality Days available
Location N of Leicester, W off A6

························

Hotel ★★★ 66% Rothley Court, Westfield Ln,
ROTHLEY ☎ 0116 237 4141 13 en suite 21 annexe
en suite

SCRAPTOFT
Map 04 SK60

Scraptoft Beeby Rd LE7 9SJ
☎ 0116 241 9000 📠 0116 241 9000
e-mail: info@scraptoft-golf.co.uk
18 holes, 6166yds, Par 70, SSS 70.
Location 1m NE
Phone for further details

························

Hotel ★★★ 74% Belmont House Hotel, De Montfort St,
LEICESTER ☎ 0116 254 4773 77 en suite

SEAGRAVE
Map 08 SK61

Park Hill Park Hill LE12 7NG
☎ 01509 815454 📠 01509 816062
e-mail: mail@parkhillgolf.co.uk
Nestled in the heart of Leicestershire, overlooking the
Charnwood Forest and beyond, Park Hill Golf Club
boasts an 18-hole championship length course that
utilises the land's natural features to ensure that no two
holes are the same. The combination of water features

Continued

Continued

and precisely positioned bunkers provide for a challenging, yet enjoyable course, with excellent playing conditions all year round.

18 holes, 7219yds, Par 73, SSS 75, Course record 71. Club membership 500.

Visitors not before 9am weekends. **Societies** apply in advance. **Green Fees** £22 (£26 weekends & bank holidays). **Cards** ⊞ 🔟 💳 🔤 📶 💷 **Prof** Matthew Ulyett **Facilities** ⊗ ⑪ ⓑ 💺 ♀ 🔼 🏠 🦃 🚜 ⚷ ⓣ **Conf** fac available Corporate Hospitality Days available **Location** 3m N of Leicester off A46, signs to Seagrave

Hotel ★★★ 65% Quality Hotel & Suites Loughborough, New Ashby Rd, LOUGHBOROUGH ☎ 01509 211800 94 en suite

SIX HILLS   Map 08 SK62

Six Hills Six Hills Rd LE14 3PR
☎ 01509 881225 🖨 01509 881846
Flat parkland course.
18 holes, 5758yds, SSS 69.
Visitors advisable to contact in advance **Societies** book in advance. **Green Fees** £14 per 18 holes (£17 weekends & bank holidays). **Cards** ⊞ 🔤 🔤 📶 💷 **Prof** James Hawley **Facilities** ⊗ ⑪ ⓑ 💺 ♀ 🏠 🦃 🚜 ⚷ ⓣ **Location** on B676 between Melton Mowbray & Loughborough

Hotel ⏻ Travelodge Leicester North, THRUSSINGTON ☎ 08700 850 950 32 en suite

ULLESTHORPE   Map 04 SP58

Ullesthorpe Frolesworth Rd LE17 5BZ
☎ 01455 209023 🖨 01455 202537
e-mail: bookings@ullesthorpecourt.co.uk
Set in 130 acres of parkland surrounding a 17th-century manor house, this championship length course can be very demanding and offers a challenge to both beginners and professionals. Excellent leisure facilities. Water plays a part on three holes.

18 holes, 6662yds, Par 72, SSS 72, Course record 67. Club membership 650.
Visitors not Sun; with member only Sat; contact in advance. **Societies** contact well in advance. **Green Fees** £30 per day; £22 per round Mon-Fri. **Cards** ⊞ 🔤 🔤 🔳 🔤 📶 💷 **Prof** David Bowring **Facilities** ⊗ ⑪ ⓑ 💺 ♀ 🔼 🏠 🦃 🐎 🦃 🚜 ⚷ **Leisure** hard tennis courts, heated indoor swimming pool, sauna, solarium, gymnasium. **Conf** fac available Corporate Hospitality Days available **Location** M1 junct 20, 5m

Hotel ★★★ 70% Ullesthorpe Court Country Hotel & Golf Club, Frolesworth Rd, ULLESTHORPE ☎ 01455 209023 38 en suite

WHETSTONE   Map 04 SP59

Whetstone Cambridge Rd, Cosby LE9 1SJ
☎ 0116 286 1424 🖨 0116 286 1424
18 holes, 5795yds, Par 68, SSS 68, Course record 63.
Course Designer E Calloway **Location** 1m S of village
Phone for further details

Hotel ★★★ 68% Corus hotel Leicester, Enderby Rd, Blaby, LEICESTER ☎ 0116 278 7898 0870 609 6106 🖨 0116 278 1974 48 en suite

WILSON   Map 08 SK42

Breedon Priory Green Ln DE73 1AT
☎ 01332 863081 🖨 01332 865319
18 holes, 5777yds, Par 69, SSS 68, Course record 67.
Course Designer David Snell **Location** off A453 into Breedon
Phone for further details

Hotel ★★★★ 74% The Priest House on the River, Kings Mills, Castle Donington, ☎ 01332 810649 24 en suite 18 annexe en suite

WOODHOUSE EAVES   Map 08 SK51

Charnwood Forest Breakback Ln LE12 8TA
☎ 01509 890259 🖨 01509 890925
e-mail: secretary@charnwoodforestgc.co.uk
Hilly heathland course with hard walking, but no bunkers. Play is round volcanic rock giving panoramic views over the Charnwood Forest area.
9 holes, 5960yds, Par 69, SSS 69, Course record 64. Club membership 360.
Visitors restricted weekends; contact in advance. **Societies** Wed-Fri, must contact in advance; Mon by special arrangement. **Green Fees** £23 (£28 weekends). **Course Designer** James Braid **Facilities** ⊗ ⑪ ⓑ 💺 ♀ 🔼 **Conf** fac available Corporate Hospitality Days available **Location** M1 junct 22/23, 3m

Hotel ★★★★ 70% Quorn Country Hotel, Charnwood House, 66 Leicester Rd, QUORN ☎ 01509 415050 30 en suite

Lingdale Joe Moore's Ln LE12 8TF
☎ 01509 890703 🖨 01509 890703
Parkland course located in Charnwood Forest with some hard walking at some holes. The par 3 3rd and par 5 8th are testing holes. Several holes have water hazards and the blend of strategic holes requires good club selection.
18 holes, 6545yds, Par 71, SSS 71, Course record 68. Club membership 659.
Visitors phone professional in advance. **Societies** contact in advance. **Green Fees** not confirmed. **Prof** Peter Sellears **Course Designer** David Tucker **Facilities** ⊗ ⑪ ⓑ 💺 ♀ 🔼 🏠 ⚷ **Location** 1.5m S off B5330

Hotel ★★★★ 70% Quorn Country Hotel, Charnwood House, 66 Leicester Rd, QUORN ☎ 01509 415050 30 en suite

> **If the name of the club appears in *italics*, details have been confirmed for this edition of the guide.**

LINCOLNSHIRE

BELTON
Map 08 SK93

De Vere Belton Woods Hotel NG32 2LN
☎ 01476 593200 🗎 01476 574547
e-mail: belton.woods@devere-hotels.com
Two challenging 18-hole courses, a nine-hole par 3 and a driving range. The Lakes Course has 13 lakes, while The Woodside boasts the third-longest hole in Europe at 613yds. Many leisure facilities.

The Lakes Course: 18 holes, 6831yds, Par 72, SSS 73, Course record 66.
The Woodside Course: 18 holes, 6623yds, Par 73, SSS 72, Course record 67.
Red Arrows Course: 9 holes, 1010yds, Par 27, SSS 27.
Club membership 600.
Visitors book tee times in advance with exception of the Red Arrows; dress code. **Societies** all week, reservations by phone or letter. **Green Fees** Lakes £40 per round, Woodside £30, Red Arrows £6. **Cards** 🖃 ▆▆ ▆▆ ▆ ▆▆ 🖃 🄳 **Prof** Steve Sayers **Facilities** ⊗ ⅢⓁ ♨♀♨♨♨🛖♈ 🍴🏊 🏐 ♢ ⓲ **Leisure** hard tennis courts, heated indoor swimming pool, squash, fishing, sauna, solarium, gymnasium. **Conf** fac available Corporate Hospitality Days available **Location** On A607 2m N of Grantham
....
Hotel ★★★★ 75% De Vere Belton Woods, BELTON
☎ 01476 593200 136 en suite

BLANKNEY
Map 08 TF06

Blankney LN4 3AZ
☎ 01526 320202 🗎 01526 322521
Parkland course in pleasant surroundings with mature trees and testing greens offering a challenging test of golf. Set in the Blankney estate and 2004 was the centenary year.
18 holes, 6634yds, Par 72, SSS 73, Course record 69.
Club membership 700.
Visitors not am Wed, restricted weekends; contact in advance. **Societies** not am Wed, booking required. **Green Fees** terms on application. **Prof** Graham Bradley **Course Designer** C Sinclair **Facilities** ⊗ ⅢⓁ ♨♀♨♨🛖♈ ♈ 🏐 ♢ **Leisure** snooker. **Conf** fac available Corporate Hospitality Days available **Location** 10m SW on B1188
....
Hotel ★★★ 71% Branston Hall Hotel, Branston Park, Branston, LINCOLN ☎ 01522 793305 43 en suite 7 annexe en suite

> In the hotel entries, the percentage figure refers to the AA's most recent Quality Assessment Score.

BOSTON
Map 08 TF34

Boston Cowbridge, Horncastle Rd PE22 7EL
☎ 01205 350589 🗎 01205 367526
e-mail: steveshaw@bostongc.co.uk
Parkland course with water coming into play on a number of holes. Renowned for the quality of the greens.
18 holes, 6415yds, Par 72, SSS 71, Course record 68.
Club membership 650.
Visitors handicap certificate may be requested; contact in advance for tee time. **Societies** apply in writing or phone. **Green Fees** £30 per day; £22.50 per round (£30/£27.50 weekends & bank holidays). **Prof** Nick Hiom **Facilities** ⊗ ⅢⓁ ♨♀♨♨🛖♈ ♈ 🏐 ♢ ⓲ **Conf** Corporate Hospitality Days available **Location** 2m N of Boston on B1183
....
Hotel ★★ 65% Comfort Inn, Donnington Rd, Bicker Bar Roundabout, BOSTON ☎ 01205 820118 55 en suite

Boston West Golf Centre Hubbert's Bridge
PE20 3QX
☎ 01205 290670 🗎 01205 290725
e-mail: info@bostonwestgolfclub.co.uk
A course that is maturing quickly and seems older than 10 years. The original nine holes (10-18) are now a great test. With water featuring on nine holes, it is necessary to think carefully on position with each shot. Play to your handicap on the first five holes and you're doing well. The course drains well.

18 holes, 6333yds, Par 72, SSS 70, Course record 68.
Club membership 650.
Visitors advisable to book up to seven days in advance 01205 290770; dress code. **Societies** phone for details. **Green Fees** £16 (£18 weekends). **Cards** 🖃 ▆▆ ▆▆ 🖃 🄳 **Prof** Simon Collingwood **Course Designer** Michael Zara **Facilities** ⊗ ⅢⓁ ♨♀♨♨🛖♈ ♈ 🏐 ♢ ⓲ **Leisure** 6-hole academy course. **Conf** fac available Corporate Hospitality Days available **Location** 2m W of Boston on A1121-B1192 x-rds
....
Hotel ★★★ 63% Golf Hotel, The Broadway, WOODHALL SPA ☎ 01526 353535 50 en suite

Kirton Holme Holme Rd, Kirton Holme PE20 1SY
☎ 01205 290669
A young parkland course designed for mid to high handicappers. It is flat but has 2500 young trees, two natural water courses plus water hazards. The 2nd is a challenging, 386yd par 4 dog-leg.
9 holes, 5778yds, Par 70, SSS 68, Course record 66.
Club membership 320.
Visitors booking advisable weekends & summer evenings. **Societies** by arrangement. **Green Fees** £9 per day, £5.50

Continued

per round (£10/£6.50 weekends). **Course Designer** DW Welberry **Facilities** ⊗ ⓑ ▆ ⚲ ⚷ ⚒ ⚌ **Conf** Corporate Hospitality Days available **Location** 4m W of Boston off A52

Hotel ★★ 65% Comfort Inn, Donnington Rd, Bicker Bar Roundabout, BOSTON ☎ 01205 820118 55 en suite

BOURNE   Map 08 TF02

Toft Hotel Toft PE10 0JT
☎ 01778 590616 📠 01778 590264

18 holes, 6486yds, Par 72, SSS 71, Course record 63.
Course Designer Roger Fitton **Location** on A6121 Bourne-Stamford road
Phone for further details

Hotel ★★★ 80% The George of Stamford, 71 St Martins, STAMFORD ☎ 01780 750750 & 750700 (Res) 📠 01780 750701 47 en suite

Boston West Golf Centre

Boston West Golf Centre, Hubert's Bridge, Boston, Lincolnshire, PE20 3QX
Tel: 01205 290670 Fax: 01205 290725

Boston West Golf Centre is a Proprietary club, which prides itself on its friendly, family atmosphere.

The 18-hole course at Boston West is a real test of every part of your game with water playing a big part on a lot of holes and very well positioned bunkers.

Web: www.bostonwestgolfclub.co.uk
E-mail: info@bostonwestgolfclub.co.uk

CLEETHORPES   Map 08 TA30

Cleethorpes Kings Rd DN35 0PN
☎ 01472 816110 📠 01472 814060
e-mail: secretary@cleethorpesgolfclub.co.uk
A mature coastal course founded in 1894. Slight undulations give variety but the flat landscape makes for easy walking. The course provides a challenge to all levels of player, especially when the wind blows.

18 holes, 6351yds, Par 70, SSS 70, Course record 65. Club membership 650.
Visitors not after 12.30pm Wed; handicap certificate preferred, must be member of golf club. **Societies** Mon, Thu, Fri, Sun, must phone in advance. **Green Fees** £25 per day (£30 weekends). **Prof** Paul Davies **Course Designer** Harry Vardon **Facilities** ⊗ ⌘ ⓑ ▆ ⚲ ⚷ 🏠 ⚒ **Location** 2m SE of Cleethorpes near theme park

Hotel ★★★ 69% Kingsway Hotel, Kingsway, CLEETHORPES ☎ 01472 601122 49 en suite

Tetney Station Rd, Tetney DN36 5HY
☎ 01472 211644 📠 01472 211644
An 18-hole parkland course at the foot of the Lincolnshire Wolds, noted for its challenging water features.
18 holes, 6245yds, Par 71, SSS 69, Course record 65. Club membership 300.
Visitors contact for start time. **Societies** apply in writing. **Green Fees** not confirmed. **Cards** 🃏 🃏 🃏 🃏 🃏 **Prof** Jason Abrams **Course Designer** JS Grant **Facilities** ⊗ ⌘ ⓑ ▆ ⚲ ⚷ 🏠 ⚒ ⚒ ⚒ **Conf** fac available **Location** 1m off A16 Louth-Grimsby road

Hotel ★★★ 69% Kingsway Hotel, Kingsway, CLEETHORPES ☎ 01472 601122 49 en suite

CROWLE   Map 08 SE71

The Lincolnshire DN17 4BU
☎ 01724 711619 📠 01724 711619
Traditional flat parkland course. Generous greens with discreet use of water and bunkers. Redeveloped greatly in the last few years offering a good test to all standards of golfer.
18 holes, 6283yds, Par 71, SSS 70. Club membership 420.
Visitors no restrictions. **Societies** welcome any time. **Green Fees** not confirmed. **Cards** 🃏 🃏 **Course Designer** Stubley, Byrne **Facilities** ⊗ ⌘ ⓑ ▆ ⚲ ⚷ 🏠 ⚒ ⚒ **Conf** Corporate Hospitality Days available **Location** M180 junct 2, 0.5m on Crowle road

Hotel ★★★ 64% Belmont Hotel, Horsefair Green, THORNE ☎ 01405 812320 23 en suite

ELSHAM
Map 08 TA01

Elsham Barton Rd DN20 0LS
☎ 01652 680291(Sec) 🖷 01652 680308
e-mail: manager@elshamgolfclub.co.uk
Gently undulating, mature parkland and heathland
course in a rural setting with a variety of wildlife,
including many pheasants. Each hole is different and
has its own challenge. Very secluded with easy walking
and a reservoir to maintain irrigation.

18 holes, 6426yds, Par 71, SSS 71, Course record 67.
Club membership 600.
Visitors with member only weekends & bank holidays;
contact in advance. **Societies** apply in writing or phone in
advance **Green Fees** £33 per 36 holes; £25 per 18 holes.
Prof Stuart Brewer **Course Designer** Various **Facilities** ⊗
🍽 🍴 💺 ♀ ⚘ 🏌 🖴 ∂ **Conf** fac available Corporate
Hospitality Days available **Location** 2m NE of Brigg on
B1206

Hotel ★★★ 67% Wortley House Hotel, Rowland Rd,
SCUNTHORPE ☎ 01724 842223 38 en suite

GAINSBOROUGH
Map 08 SK88

Gainsborough Thonock DN21 1PZ
☎ 01427 613088 🖷 01427 810172
e-mail: gainsboroughgc.co.uk
Thonock Park: 18 holes, 6266yds, Par 70, SSS 70,
Course record 63.
Karsten Lakes: 18 holes, 6721yds, Par 72, SSS 72,
Course record 65.
Course Designer Neil Coles **Location** 1m N off A159.
Signed off A631
Phone for further details

Hotel ★★★ 64% The West Retford Hotel, 24 North Rd,
RETFORD ☎ 0870 609 6162 62 annexe en suite

GEDNEY HILL
Map 08 TF31

Gedney Hill West Drove PE12 0NT
☎ 01406 330922 🖷 01406 330323
e-mail: d.t.h@fsddail.co.uk
18 holes, 5493yds, Par 70, SSS 66, Course record 67.
Course Designer Monkwise Ltd **Location** 5m SE of
Spalding
Phone for further details

Hotel ★★★ 68% Elme Hall Hotel, Elm High Rd,
WISBECH ☎ 01945 475566 7 en suite

Prices may change during the currency of the
Guide, please check when booking.

GRANTHAM
Map 08 SK93

Belton Park Belton Ln, Londonthorpe Rd NG31 9SH
☎ 01476 567399 🖷 01476 592078
e-mail: greatgolf@beltonpark
Three nine-hole courses set in classic mature parkland
of Lord Brownlow's country seat, Belton House. Gently
undulating with streams, ponds, plenty of trees and
beautiful scenery, including a deer park. Famous holes:
5th, 12th, 16th and 18th. Combine any of the three
courses for a testing 18-hole round.

Brownlow: 18 holes, 6472yds, Par 71, SSS 71, Course
record 64.
Ancaster: 18 holes, 6325yds, Par 70, SSS 70.
Belmont: 18 holes, 6075yds, Par 69, SSS 69.
Club membership 850.
Visitors contact professional for tee times; no green fees
Tue before 3pm. **Societies** apply in advance. **Green Fees**
£38 per day; £32 per round (£44/38 weekends). **Cards** 🌐
💳 💳 ⊘ **Prof** Simon Williams **Course Designer**
Williamson, Allis **Facilities** ⊗ 🍽 🍴 💺 ♀ ⚘ 🏠 🍴 ♀ 🖴
∂ **Conf** fac available Corporate Hospitality Days
available **Location** 1.5m NE of Grantham

Hotel ★★★ 70% Kings Hotel, North Pde, GRANTHAM
☎ 01476 590800 21 en suite

Sudbrook Moor Charity St, Carlton Scroop
NG32 3AT
☎ 01400 250796
A testing nine-hole parkland and meadowland course in
a picturesque valley setting with easy walking.
9 holes, 4811yds, Par 66, SSS 64, Course record 64.
Club membership 600.
Visitors advisable to phone in advance. **Green Fees** £7-£9
(£9-£12 weekends & bank holidays). **Cards** 🌐 💳 💳
💳 💳 ⊘ **Prof** Tim Hutton **Course Designer** Tim Hutton
Facilities 🍴 💺 🏠 🍴 ∂ ⛳ **Location** 6m NE of
Grantham on A607

Hotel ★★★ 70% Kings Hotel, North Pde, GRANTHAM
☎ 01476 590800 21 en suite

GRIMSBY
Map 08 TA21

Grimsby Littlecoates Rd DN34 4LU
☎ 01472 342630 🖷 01472 342630
e-mail: secretary@grimsby.fsnet.co.uk
Mature undulating parkland course, not particularly
long, but demanding and a good test of golf. The par 3s
are all feature holes, not a common feature on most
courses. The summer greens are fast and quite small.
18 holes, 6057yds, Par 70, SSS 69, Course record 65.
Club membership 730.

Continued

Visitors contact in advance. Societies Mon, Fri by arrangement with secretary. Green Fees £25 per day (£30 weekends & bank holidays). Prof Richard Smith Course Designer Colt Facilities ⊗ ⊪ ⅃ ┗ ■ ♀ ⅄ 🏠 ⤵ 🔧 ✿ Conf Corporate Hospitality Days available Location 1m from A180. 1m from A46
....

Hotel ★★★ 66% Hotel Elizabeth Grimsby, Littlecoates Rd, GRIMSBY ☎ 01472 240024   52 en suite

Waltham Windmill Cheapside, Waltham
DN37 0HT
☎ 01472 824109 🖷 01472 828391
Nestling in 125 acres of Lincolnshire countryside, the natural springs have been used to great effect giving individuality and challenge to every shot. The course has a mixture of long par 5s and water comes into play on nine holes.
18 holes, 6442yds, Par 71, SSS 71.
Club membership 620.
Visitors booking advisable Societies weekdays, booking required. Green Fees £22 per round (£30 weekends). Reduced winter rates. Cards ▦ ▰ ▰ ▨ ▨ ▰ 🗒
Prof Nigel Burkitt Course Designer J Payne Facilities ⊗ ⊪ ⅃ ■ ♀ ⅄ 🏠 ⟍ ⤵ ✿ 🍴 Conf fac available Corporate Hospitality Days available Location 1m off A16
....

Hotel ★★★ 66% Beeches Hotel, 42 Waltham Rd, Scartho, GRIMSBY ☎ 01472 278830   18 en suite

HORNCASTLE   Map 08 TF26

Horncastle West Ashby LN9 5PP
☎ 01507 526800
18 holes, 5717yds, Par 70, SSS 68, Course record 71.
Course Designer EC Wright Location off A153 at West Ashby
Phone for further details
....

Hotel ★★ 71% Admiral Rodney Hotel, North St, HORNCASTLE ☎ 01507 523131   31 en suite

IMMINGHAM   Map 08 TA11

Immingham St Andrews Ln, off Church Ln
DN40 2EU
☎ 01469 575298 🖷 01469 577636
e-mail: admin@immgc.force9.co.uk
An excellent, flat parkland course. The natural exaggerated undulations on the fairways form one of the best local examples of medieval strip farming methods. They are a natural phenomenon to the course, particularly noticeable on the front nine holes and require concentration on fairway play. The Lincolnshire drainage channel, which meanders

through the course and comes into play on over half of the holes, can catch the unwary golfer.
18 holes, 6215yds, Par 71, SSS 70, Course record 69.
Club membership 700.
Visitors phone in advance. Societies phone to arrange date. Green Fees £18 per round (£25 weekends & bank holidays). Prof Nick Harding Course Designer Hawtree & Son Facilities ⊗ ⊪ ⅃ ■ ♀ ⅄ 🏠 ⟊ ⤵ ✿ Conf fac available   Corporate Hospitality Days available Location 7m NW of Grimsby
....

Hotel ★★★ 66% Hotel Elizabeth Grimsby, Littlecoates Rd, GRIMSBY ☎ 01472 240024   52 en suite

LACEBY   Map 08 TA20

Manor Barton St, Laceby Manor DN37 7EA
☎ 01472 873468 (shop) 🖷 01472 276706
e-mail: judith@manorgolf.com
The first seven holes played as a parkland course lined with mature trees. The second nine are more open fairways with water courses running alongside and through the holes. The 16th hole green is surrounded by water. Holes 17 and 18 are tree-lined like the first seven holes.
18 holes, 6354yds, Par 71, SSS 70.
Club membership 550.
Visitors booked tee system at all times; visitors may book six days in advance. Societies phone in advance. Green Fees £18 per round (£20 weekends). Cards ▦ ▰ ▰ ▰ 🗒 Prof Neil Laybourne Facilities ⊗ ⊪ ⅃ ■ ♀ ⅄ 🏠 ⤵ ✿ Leisure fishing. Conf fac available   Corporate Hospitality Days available Location A18 Laceby-Louth
....

Hotel ★★★ 66% Hotel Elizabeth Grimsby, Littlecoates Rd, GRIMSBY ☎ 01472 240024   52 en suite

Continued

LINCOLN   Map 08 SK97

See also **Torksey**, Lincolnshire

Canwick Park Canwick Park, Washingborough Rd LN4 1EF
☎ 01522 542912 ▤ 01522 526997
e-mail: manager@canwickpark.co.uk
Parkland course 2 miles east of the city centre with panoramic views of Lincoln Cathedral. The 5th and 13th holes are testing par 3s both nearly 200yds in length.
18 holes, 6160yds, Par 70, SSS 69, Course record 65. Club membership 650.
Visitors subject to availability; contact club professional 01522 536870. **Societies** weekdays only by arrangement. **Green Fees** £20 (£21 weekends). **Prof** S Williamson **Course Designer** Hawtree & Sons **Facilities** ⊗ ℿ ⅃ ⅃ ⅃ ♟ ⚑ 🏌 ✎ **Conf** Corporate Hospitality Days available **Location** 1m E of Lincoln

---

Hotel ★★★ 68% The Lincoln Hotel, Eastgate, LINCOLN ☎ 01522 520348 72 en suite

Carholme Carholme Rd LN1 1SE
☎ 01522 523725 ▤ 01522 533733
e-mail: info@carholme-golf-club.co.uk
Parkland course where prevailing west winds can add interest. Good views. First hole out of bounds left and right of fairway, pond in front of bunkered green at 5th, lateral water hazards across several fairways.
18 holes, 6215yds, Par 71, SSS 70, Course record 67. Club membership 625.
Visitors not before 2.30pm weekends; contact in advance. **Societies** apply in writing or phone in advance. **Green Fees** not confirmed. **Course Designer** Willie Park Jnr **Facilities** ⊗ ℿ ⅃ ⅃ ♟ ⚑ 🏌 ✎ **Conf** Corporate Hospitality Days available **Location** 1m W of city centre on A57

Hotel ★★★ 66% The White Hart, Bailgate, LINCOLN ☎ 01522 526222 48 en suite

LOUTH   Map 08 TF38

Kenwick Park Kenwick Park LN11 8NY
☎ 01507 605134 ▤ 01507 606556
e-mail: golfatkenwick@nascr.net
Situated on the edge of the Lincolnshire Wolds with panoramic views. Course features a mixture of parkland and woodland holes, complemented by a network of lakes.
18 holes, 6782yds, Par 72, SSS 73, Course record 71. Club membership 520.
Visitors phone pro shop to book tee time 01507 607161. **Societies** phone in advance. **Green Fees** £30 per 18 holes (£40 weekends & bank holidays). 2 for 1 Tue. **Cards** 💳 💳 💳 💳 **Prof** Eric Sharp **Course Designer** Patrick Tallack **Facilities** ⊗ ℿ by arrangement ⅃ ♟ ⅃ ♟ ⚑ 🏌 ✎ ⅃ **Conf** Corporate Hospitality Days available **Location** 2m S of Louth on A157 (Louth bypass)

Hotel ★★★ 70% Kenwick Park Hotel, Kenwick Park Estate, LOUTH ☎ 01507 608806 29 en suite 5 annexe en suite

Louth Crowtree Ln LN11 9LJ
☎ 01507 603681 ▤ 01507 608501
e-mail: enquiries@louthgolfclub.com
Undulating parkland course, fine views in an area of outstanding natural beauty. No winter greens, offering quality golf throughout the year.

Lincoln Golf Club

Torksey, Lincoln, LN1 2EG
email: info@lincolngc.co.uk
web: www.lincolngc.co.uk

Lincoln Golf Club was founded in Lincoln City in 1891 and moved to its present site at Torksey near Lincoln, in 1903.

With it's mature trees, easy walking fairways and just a touch of water, the course offers a true test of golf to members and visitors alike, and is a delight to play.

The course has been played by many famous golfers and Mark James, of Ryder Cup fame, achieved a course record of 65 whilst playing in the Lincolnshire Open.

---

18 holes, 6430yds, Par 72, SSS 71, Course record 66. Club membership 700.
Visitors not Sat; contact in advance to ensure tee is not reserved for competition. **Societies** booking form will be sent on request. **Green Fees** £30 per day, £24 per round (£36/£30 weekends & bank holidays). **Cards** 💳 💳 💳 💳 💳 **Prof** A Blundell **Facilities** ⊗ ℿ ⅃ ⅃ ♟ ⅃ ♟ ⚑ 🏌 ✎ **Leisure** squash. **Conf** fac available Corporate Hospitality Days available **Location** W of Louth between A157 & A153

Hotel ★★★ 69% Beaumont Hotel, 66 Victoria Rd, LOUTH ☎ 01507 605005 16 en suite

MARKET RASEN   Map 08 TF18

Market Rasen & District Legsby Rd LN8 3DZ
☎ 01673 842319
Picturesque, well-wooded heathland course, easy walking, breezy with becks forming natural hazards. Good views of Lincolnshire Wolds.

Continued   *Continued*

18 holes, 6239yds, Par 71, SSS 70, Course record 65.
Club membership 600.
Visitors with member only weekends; must contact in advance. **Societies** weekdays, must contact in advance. **Green Fees** £33 per day, £22 per round. **Prof** AM Chester **Course Designer** Hawtree Ltd **Facilities** ⊗ ⅏ ⅃ ⌑ ♀ ⚎ ⌂ ⚘ ⚒ ⚐ **Location** 1m E, A46 onto A631

Hotel ★★★ 69% Beaumont Hotel, 66 Victoria Rd, LOUTH ☎ 01507 605005 16 en suite

Market Rasen Race Course (Golf Course)
Legsby Rd LN8 3EA
☎ 01673 843434 📠 01673 844532
e-mail: marketrasen@rht.net
This is a public course set within the bounds of Market Rasen race course - the entire racing area is out of bounds. The longest hole is the 4th at 454yds with the race course providing a hazard over the whole length of the drive.
9 holes, 2532yds, Par 32.
Visitors closed racedays (open until noon evening meetings). **Societies** phone in advance to arrange. **Green Fees** £5 per round (£6 weekends). **Course Designer** Edward Stenton **Facilities** ⚐ ⚒ **Leisure** caravan site. **Conf** fac available **Location** 1m E of Market Rasen

Hotel ★★★ 69% Beaumont Hotel, 66 Victoria Rd, LOUTH ☎ 01507 605005 16 en suite

Normanby Hall Normanby Park DN15 9HU
☎ 01724 720226 (pro shop)
Well-maintained course set in secluded mature parkland. A challenge to golfers of all abilities.
18 holes, 6561yds, Par 72, SSS 71, Course record 66.
Club membership 500.
Visitors book in advance by contacting professional. **Societies** contact professional in advance. **Green Fees** not confirmed. **Cards** ⚎ ⚎ ⚎ **Prof** Christopher Mann **Course Designer** Hawtree & Son **Facilities** ⊗ ⅏ ⅃ ⌑ ♀ ⚎ ⌂ ⚐ ⚘ ⚒ ⚐ **Location** 3m N of Scunthorpe on B1130 next to Normanby Hall

Hotel ★★★ 67% Wortley House Hotel, Rowland Rd, SCUNTHORPE ☎ 01724 842223 38 en suite

Ashby Decoy Burringham Rd DN17 2AB
☎ 01724 866561 📠 01724 271708
e-mail: ashby.decoy@btclick.com
Pleasant, flat parkland course to satisfy all tastes, yet test the experienced golfer.
18 holes, 6281yds, Par 71, SSS 71, Course record 66.
Club membership 650.
Visitors not before 2pm Tue, weekends, bank holidays; handicap cerificate. **Societies** apply in advance. **Green Fees** not confirmed. **Prof** A Miller **Facilities** ⊗ ⅏ ⅃ ⌑ ♀ ⚎ ⌂ ⚘ ⚒ ⚐ **Conf** fac available Corporate Hospitality Days available **Location** 2.5m SW on B1450 near Asda store

Hotel ★★★ 67% Wortley House Hotel, Rowland Rd, SCUNTHORPE ☎ 01724 842223 38 en suite

> **Booking a tee time is always advisable.**

Forest Pines Hotel Ermine St, Broughton
DN20 0AQ
☎ 01652 650770 📠 01652 650495
e-mail: enquiries@forestpines.co.uk
Set in 185 acres of mature parkland and open heathland and constructed in a similar design to that of Wentworth or Sunningdale, Forest Pines offers three challenging nine-hole courses - Forest, Pines and Beeches. Any combination can be played. Facilities include a 17-bay driving range and a spacious clubhouse.

Forest Course: 9 holes, 3291yds, Par 36, SSS 36.
Pines Course: 9 holes, 3568yds, Par 37, SSS 37.
Beeches: 9 holes, 3291yds, Par 36, SSS 36.
Club membership 330.
Visitors soft spikes only on all courses. **Societies** phone in advance. **Green Fees** £50 per day; £40 per round. **Cards** ⚎ ⚎ ⚎ ⚎ ⚎ ⚎ ⚎ **Prof** David Edwards **Course Designer** John Morgan **Facilities** ⊗ ⅏ ⅃ ⌑ ♀ ⚎ ⌂ ⚐ ⚘ ⚒ ⚐ ⚐ **Leisure** heated indoor swimming pool, sauna, solarium, gymnasium. **Conf** fac available Corporate Hospitality Days available **Location** M180 junct 4, 200yds

Hotel ★★★★ 74% Forest Pines Hotel, Ermine St, Broughton, SCUNTHORPE ☎ 01652 650770 114 en suite

Grange Park Butterwick Rd, Messingham DN17 3PP
☎ 01724 762945 📠 01724 762945
e-mail: info@grangepark.com
Parkland course with challenging water hazards and impressive stone raised teeing areas.
18 holes, 6146yds, Par 70, SSS 69, Course record 64.
Club membership 320.
Visitors Societies phone for information pack. **Green Fees** £14.50 per 18 holes (£16.50 weekends). **Cards** ⚎ ⚎ ⚎ ⚎ **Prof** Jonathan Drury **Course Designer** R Price **Facilities** ⊗ ⅏ ⅃ ⌑ ♀ ⚎ ⌂ ⚐ ⚘ ⚒ ⚐ **Leisure** hard tennis courts, fishing. **Conf** fac available Corporate Hospitality Days available **Location** 1.5m W of Messingham towards East Butterwick

Hotel ★★★ 67% Wortley House Hotel, Rowland Rd, SCUNTHORPE ☎ 01724 842223 38 en suite

Holme Hall Holme Ln, Bottesford DN16 3RF
☎ 01724 862078 📠 01724 862078
e-mail: secretary@holmehallgolf.co.uk
Natural heathland course with gorse and heather and sandy subsoil. Easy walking. Tight driving holes and good greens.
18 holes, 6404yds, Par 71, SSS 71, Course record 65.
Club membership 650.
Visitors with member only weekends & bank holidays; must contact in advance. **Societies** contact in advance. **Green Fees** £35 per day; £25 per round. **Cards** ⚎ ⚎ ⚐

Continued

Prof Richard McKiernan **Facilities** ⊗ ⅶ ⅃ ⅃ ♟ ⚐ ⌂ ⛤ ⚑ ⚒ ♂ **Conf** Corporate Hospitality Days available **Location** M180 junct 4, 4m SE of Scunthorpe

Hotel ★★★ 67% Wortley House Hotel, Rowland Rd, SCUNTHORPE ☎ 01724 842223 38 en suite

SKEGNESS   Map 09 TF56

North Shore Hotel & Golf Club North Shore Rd PE25 1DN
☎ 01754 763298 ▤ 01754 761902
e-mail: golf@north-shore.co.uk

Part links, part parkland, with two of the nine holes situated next to the sea. A challenging course with both greens in front of the main bar.

18 holes, 6200yds, Par 71, SSS 71, Course record 68. Club membership 450.
Visitors book tee times. **Societies** write or phone in advance. **Green Fees** £38 per day; £28 per round (£48/£35 weekends). **Cards** ▦ ▦ ▦ ▦ ▨ **Prof** J Cornelius **Course Designer** James Braid **Facilities** ⊗ ⅶ ⅃ ⅃ ♟ ⚐ ⌂ ⛨ ⚒ ♂ **Leisure** snooker. **Conf** fac available Corporate Hospitality Days available **Location** 1m N of town centre off A52, opp North Shore Holiday Centre

Hotel ★★ 67% North Shore Hotel & Golf Course, North Shore Rd, SKEGNESS ☎ 01754 763298 33 en suite 3 annexe en suite

Seacroft Drummond Rd, Seacroft PE25 3AU
☎ 01754 763020 ▤ 01754 763020
e-mail: richard@seacroft-golfclub.co.uk

A championship seaside links traditionally laid out with tight undulations and hogsback fairways. Adjacent to Gibraltar Point Nature Reserve.

18 holes, 6479yds, Par 71, SSS 71, Course record 65. Club membership 590.
Visitors must be a member of an affiliated golf club or society. **Societies** contact in advance. **Green Fees** terms on
Continued

application. **Cards** ▦ ▦ ▦ ▦ ▨ **Prof** Robin Lawie **Course Designer** Tom Dunn, Willie Fernie **Facilities** ⊗ ⅶ ⅃ ⅃ ♟ ⌂ ⚐ ⚒ ♂ **Hospitality** Days available **Location** S of town centre towards Gibralter Point Nature Reserve

Hotel ★★★ 65% Crown Hotel, Drummond Rd, Seacroft, SKEGNESS ☎ 01754 610760 30 en suite

SLEAFORD   Map 08 TF04

Sleaford Willoughby Rd, South Rauceby NG34 8PL
☎ 01529 488273 ▤ 01529 488326
e-mail: sleafordgolfclub@btinternet.com

Inland links-type course, moderately wooded and fairly flat with sandy well-draining soil, which supports a variety of trees and shrubs. The lowest index hole is the awkward dog-leg 4th, while the 2nd hole requires two mighty hits to be reached. The feature hole is the 12th, where the green is totally protected by a copse of pine trees. A stream running through the course provides water hazards on several holes.
18 holes, 6503yds, Par 72, SSS 71, Course record 64. Club membership 630.
Visitors not Sun in winter; contact in advance. **Societies** phone professional & written confirmation required. **Green Fees** £32 per day; £25 per round (£36 weekends). **Prof** James Wilson **Course Designer** T Williamson **Facilities** ⊗ ⅶ ⅃ ⅃ ♟ ⌂ ⚐ ⛨ ⚒ ♂ **Conf** fac available Hospitality Days available **Location** 2m W of Sleaford off A153

Hotel ★★★ 70% Kings Hotel, North Pde, GRANTHAM ☎ 01476 590800 21 en suite

SOUTH KYME   Map 08 TF14

South Kyme Skinners Ln LN4 4AT
☎ 01526 861113 ▤ 01526 861113
e-mail: southkymegc@hotmail.com

A challenging fenland course in a tranquil location, described as an inland links with water hazards, trees and fairway hazards.
18 holes, 6482yds, Par 72, SSS 71, Course record 67. Club membership 470.
Visitors advisable to phone in advance for availability. **Societies** phone for booking form. **Green Fees** from £15 per round, £7.50 per 9 holes. **Cards** ▦ ▦ ▦ ▦ ▨ **Prof** Peter Chamberlain **Facilities** ⊗ ⅶ ⅃ ⅃ ♟ ⌂ ⚐ ⛤ ⚒ ♂ **Leisure** 6 hole short course. **Conf** Corporate Hospitality Days available **Location** off B1395 into South Kyme

Hotel ⌂ Travelodge, Holdingham, SLEAFORD ☎ 08700 850 950 40 en suite

SPALDING   Map 08 TF22

Spalding Surfleet PE11 4EA
☎ 01775 680386 (office) & 680474 (pro)
▤ 01775 680988

A pretty, well-laid out course in a fenland area. The River Glen runs beside the 1st, 2nd and 4th holes, and ponds and lakes are very much in play on the 9th, 10th and 11th holes. Challenging holes include the river dominated 2nd and the 10th which involves a tight drive and dog-leg left to reach a raised three-tier green. Positional play is a must on some of the tree lined holes.
Continued

Spalding Golf Club

18 holes, 6478yds, Par 72, SSS 71, Course record 62. Club membership 750.

Visitors contact in advance; handicap certificate. **Societies** Tue pm, Thu, write to the secretary. **Green Fees** £30 per day; £25 per round (£30 per round weekends & bank holidays). **Prof** John Spencer, Chris Huggins **Course Designer** Price, Spencer, Ward **Facilities** ⊗ ⅢI ⅃ 🝱 ♀ ⚘ 🝐 ♤ 🝘 ♂ ⚏ **Conf** Corporate Hospitality Days available **Location** 4m N of Spalding next to A16

Hotel ★★ 70% Cley Hall Hotel, 22 High St, SPALDING ☎ 01775 725157 4 en suite 8 annexe en suite

STAMFORD
Map 04 TF00

Burghley Park St Martins PE9 3JX
☎ 01780 762100 (pro) & 753789 (Sec) 🖷 01780 753789
e-mail: burghley.golf@lineone.net
A compact parkland layout. Tree planting, the introduction of sand and water hazards and the maintenance of fair but punishing rough, have made the course a real challenge. Free draining fairways and greens give first class playing all year.
18 holes, 6236yds, Par 70, SSS 70, Course record 65. Club membership 775.
Visitors with member only weekends; must contact in advance; handicap certificate. **Societies** by arrangement in writing, preferably by 1 Dec previous year. **Green Fees** £30 per day; £18 twilight (noon winter, 5pm summer). **Prof** Glenn Davies **Course Designer** Rev J Day (1938) **Facilities** ⊗ ⅢI ⅃ 🝱 ♀ ⚘ 🝐 ♤ ♂ **Conf** Corporate Hospitality Days available **Location** 1m S of town on B1081

Hotel ★★★ 80% The George of Stamford, 71 St Martins, STAMFORD ☎ 01780 750750 & 750700 (Res) 🖷 01780 750701 47 en suite

STOKE ROCHFORD
Map 08 SK92

Stoke Rochford NG33 5EW
☎ 01476 530275 🖷 01476 530237
Parkland course designed by C Turner and extended in 1936 to 18 holes by Major Hotchkin.
18 holes, 6252yds, Par 70, SSS 70, Course record 65. Club membership 525.
Visitors not before 9am weekdays; weekends by arrangement; contact professional in advance. **Societies** contact one year in advance, in writing. **Green Fees** terms on application. **Cards** ▦ ▦ 🝐 **Prof** Angus Dow **Course Designer** Major Hotchkin **Facilities** ⊗ ⅢI ⅃ 🝱 ♀ ⚘ 🝐 ⚏ ♂ **Location** 5m S of Grantham off A1 southbound signed Stoke Rochford, onto A1 northbound, enter club via BP service station

Continued

SUTTON BRIDGE
Map 09 TF42

Sutton Bridge New Rd PE12 9RQ
☎ 01406 350323
Established in 1914, the nine holes are played along, over and in a Victorian dock basin which was abandoned as a dock in 1881. The original walls of the dock are still intact and help to make the course one of the most interesting courses in the region. The greens are recognised as among the best in Lincolnshire.
9 holes, 5724yds, Par 70, SSS 68, Course record 64. Club membership 350.
Visitors with member only weekends; must contact in advance; handicap certificate. **Societies** write or phone in advance. **Green Fees** Apr-Sep £20 per day; Oct-Mar £15. **Prof** Antony Lowther **Facilities** ⊗ ⅢI ⅃ 🝱 ♀ ⚘ 🝐 ⚏ 🝘 **Conf** Corporate Hospitality Days available **Location** E of village off A17

Hotel ⌂ Travelodge Kings Lynn, Wisbech Rd, LONG SUTTON ☎ 08700 850 950 40 en suite

SUTTON ON SEA
Map 09 TF58

Sandilands Roman Bank LN12 2RJ
☎ 01507 441432 🖷 01507 441617
Well-manicured links course next to the sea. Renowned for the standard of its greens.
18 holes, 6173yds, Par 70, SSS 68, Course record 64. Club membership 230.
Visitors Societies phone in advance. **Green Fees** £25 per day; £18 per round (£30/£20 weekends). Reduced winter rates. **Cards** ▦ ▦ ▦ ▩ 🝐 **Prof** Simon Sherratt **Facilities** ⊗ ⅢI ⅃ 🝱 ♀ ⚘ 🝐 ⚏ 🝘 🝐 ♂ **Leisure** hard & grass tennis courts, gymnasium. **Conf** fac available **Location** 1.5m S off A52

Hotel ★★★ 69% Grange & Links Hotel, Sea Ln, Sandilands, SUTTON-ON-SEA ☎ 01507 441334 23 en suite

TORKSEY
Map 08 SK87

Lincoln LN1 2EG
☎ 01427 718721 🖷 718721
e-mail: info@lincolngc.co.uk
A mature championship standard course offering a variety of holes, links style to parkland.

18 holes, 6438yds, Par 71, SSS 71, Course record 65. Club membership 750.
Visitors all times. **Societies** book in advance. **Green Fees** £38 per day; £30 per round. **Prof** Ashley Carter **Course**

Continued

Designer JH Taylor **Facilities** ⊗ ⊪ ⊫ ⊑ ♀ ⚘ 🏠 ⚑ ⚒
♂ **Leisure** 3 hole practice course. **Conf** fac available
Corporate Hospitality Days available **Location** NE of
village off A156

Hotel ★★★ 66% The White Hart, Bailgate, LINCOLN
☎ 01522 526222 48 en suite

Millfield Laughterton LN1 2LB
☎ 01427 718255 ▯ 01427 718473
e-mail: secretary@millfieldgolfclub.fsnet.co.uk
**This golf complex offers a range of facilities to suit
every golfer. The Millfield is designed to suit the more
experienced golfer and follows the natural contours of
the landscape. The Grenville Green is designed for
more casual golfers and the par 3 is suitable for
beginners, family games or for warm-up and practice
play.**
*The Millfield: 18 holes, 6004yds, Par 72, SSS 69, Course
record 68.*
The Grenville Green: 18 holes, 4485yds, Par 65.
Visitors Millfield: shoes must be worn, dress code.
Grenville Green: no restrictions. Par 3 9-hole: no
restrictions. **Societies** phone in advance. **Green Fees** not
confirmed. **Prof** Brian Cummings **Course Designer**
CW Watson **Facilities** ⊗ ⊪ ⊑ ⚘ 🏠 ⚑ ⚒ ♂ ⚐
Leisure grass tennis courts. **Location** on A1133 1m N of
A57

Hotel ★★★ 66% The White Hart, Bailgate, LINCOLN
☎ 01522 526222 48 en suite

WOODHALL SPA   See page 173

WOODTHORPE   Map 09 TF48

Woodthorpe Hall LN13 0DD
☎ 01507 450000 ▯ 01507 450000
e-mail: secretary@woodthorpehallgolfclub.fsnet.co.uk
18 holes, 5140yds, Par 67, SSS 65, Course record 68.
Location 3m N of Alford on B1373
Phone for further details

Hotel ★★★ 69% Grange & Links Hotel, Sea Ln,
Sandilands, SUTTON-ON-SEA ☎ 01507 441334
23 en suite

LONDON

Courses within the London Postal District (i.e. those that
have London postcodes - W1, SW1 etc) are listed in postal
district order commencing East then North, South and
West. Courses outside the London Postal District, but
within Greater London are listed under the county of
Greater London.

E4 CHINGFORD

Royal Epping Forest Forest Approach, Chingford
E4 7AZ
☎ 020 8529 2195 ▯ 020 8559 4664
e-mail: office@refgc.co.uk
Woodland course. Red garments must be worn.
18 holes, 6342yds, Par 71, SSS 70, Course record 64.
Club membership 400.
Visitors booking system in operation 020 8529 5708.
Societies contact secretary in advance. **Green Fees** not
confirmed. **Cards** ▭ ▭ ▭ ▭ ▭ ▭ ▯ **Prof**
A Traynor **Course Designer** JG Gibson **Facilities** ⊗ by

arrangement ⊪ by arrangement ⊫ by arrangement ⊑ ♀
⚘ 🏠 ⚑ ⚒ ♂ **Conf** fac available **Location** 300yds E of
Chingford station on Chingford Plain

West Essex Bury Rd, Sewardstonebury, Chingford
E4 7QL
☎ 020 8529 7558 ▯ 020 8524 7870
e-mail: sec@westessexgolfclub.co.uk
**Testing parkland course within Epping Forest with
spectacular views over Essex and Middlesex. Created
by James Braid in 1900 and designed to make full use
of the landscape's natural attributes. The front nine is
the shorter of the two and provides a test of accuracy
with tree lined fairways that meander through the
undulating countryside. The back nine is equally
challenging although slightly longer and requiring more
long iron play.**
18 holes, 6289yds, Par 71, SSS 70, Course record 63.
Club membership 710.
Visitors not am Tue, weekends; handicap certificate.
Societies contact in advance. **Green Fees** £40. **Prof** Robert
Joyce **Course Designer** James Braid **Facilities** ⊗ ⊪ ⊪ ⊑
♀ ⚘ 🏠 ⚑ ⚒ ♂ (**Conf** Corporate Hospitality Days
available **Location** M25 junct 26, 1.5m N of Chingford
station

Hotel ★★★★ 65% Menzies Prince Regent,
Manor Rd, WOODFORD BRIDGE ☎ 020 8505 9966
61 en suite

E11 LEYTONSTONE & WANSTEAD

Wanstead Overton Dr, Wanstead E11 2LW
☎ 020 8989 3938 ▯ 020 8532 9138
e-mail: wgclub@aol.com
**A flat, picturesque parkland course with many trees
and shrubs and providing easy walking. The par 3 16th
involves driving across a lake.**
18 holes, 6015yds, Par 69, SSS 69, Course record 62.
Club membership 600.
Visitors not Wed, Thu, weekends; contact in advance.
Societies by arrangement. **Green Fees** not confirmed.
Cards ▭ ▭ ▭ ▯ **Prof** David Hawkins **Course
Designer** James Braid **Facilities** ⊗ ⊪ ⊪ ⊑ ♀ ⚘ 🏠 ⚑ ⚒ ♂
Leisure fishing. **Conf** fac available Corporate Hospitality
Days available **Location** off A12 in Wanstead

N2 EAST FINCHLEY

Hampstead Winnington Rd N2 0TU
☎ 020 8455 0203 ▯ 020 8731 6194
Undulating parkland course with many mature trees.
9 holes, 5822yds, Par 68, SSS 68, Course record 64.
Club membership 526.
Visitors restricted Tue & weekends; contact professional
in advance 020 8455 7089; handicap certificate. **Green
Fees** not confirmed. **Prof** Peter Brown **Course Designer**
Tom Dunn **Facilities** ⊗ ⊪ ⊑ ♀ ⚘ 🏠 ⚑ ⚒ ♂
Location off Hampstead Ln

Guesthouse ◆◆◆◆ Langorf Hotel, 20 Frognal,
Hampstead, LONDON ☎ 020 7794 4483
31 en suite

> Booking a tee time is always advisable.

Continued

Lincolnshire

Woodhall Spa

Woodhall Spa   Map 8 TF16

The Championship Course at Woodhall Spa, now known as the Hotchkin, is arguably the best inland course in Britain. This classic course has cavernous bunkers and heather-lined fairways. Golf has been played here for over a century and the Hotchkin has hosted most of the top national and international amateur events. The English Golf Union acquired Woodhall Spa in 1995 to create a centre of excellence. A second course, the Bracken, has been built, along with extensive practice facilities including one of Europe's finest short-game practice areas. The English Golf Union actively encourages visits to the National Golf Centre throughout the year, to experience the facilities and to enjoy the unique ambience.

The Broadway LN10 6PU
☎ 01526 352511 Fax 01526 351817
e-mail: booking@englishgolfunion.org

The Hotchkin: 18 holes, 7080yds, Par 73, SSS 75, Course record 66.
The Bracken: 18 holes, 6735yds, Par 72, SSS 74, Course record 68.
Club membership 520.
Visitors must contact in advance; handicap certificate.
Societies apply by phone initially. Green Fees Hotchkin £100 per day, £65 per round; Bracken £75 per day, £50 round. £90 per day playing both courses. Cards ▭ ▭ ▦ ◩ Prof A Hare Course Designer Col S V Hotchkin Facilities ⊗ ⊪ ⅃ ☕ ♀ ♨ 🖻 🏌 ✍ ℓ Conf fac available Corporate Hospitality Days available Location NE of village off B1191

....

Hotels

★★★ 68% Petwood Hotel, Stixwould Rd, WOODHALL SPA

☎ 01526 352411 53 en suite

★★★ 63% Golf Hotel, The Broadway, WOODHALL SPA

☎ 01526 353535 Fax 01526 353096 50 en suite

★★ 65% Eagle Lodge Hotel, The Broadway, WOODHALL SPA

☎ 01526 353231 Fax 01526 352797 23 en suite

N6 HIGHGATE

Highgate Denewood Rd N6 4AH
☎ 020 8340 3745 📄 020 8348 9152
e-mail: nigel@highgategc.co.uk
Parkland course with fine views over London. The
nearest 18-hole course north of the river from Marble
Arch. Many interesting holes with a premium on
accuracy. The 15th and 16th holes are very demanding
par 4s.
18 holes, 5985yds, Par 69, SSS 69, Course record 66.
Club membership 700.
Visitors not Wed, weekends, bank holidays. Societies by
arrangement. Green Fees £45 per day, £32 per round.
Cards 🔲 🔲 🔲 🔲 📄 Prof Robin Turner Course
Designer Cuthbert Butchart Facilities ⊗ �🝆 🔩 ▉ ♀ ♨ 🏠
🍴 𝒸 Conf fac available Corporate Hospitality Days
available Location off B519 Hampstead Ln
....
Hotel ★★★★ 73% London Marriott Hotel Regents
Park, 128 King Henry's Rd, LONDON
☎ 0870 400 7240 303 en suite

N9 LOWER EDMONTON

Lee Valley Leisure Lee Valley Leisure Centre,
Meridian Way, Edmonton N9 0AS
☎ 020 8803 3611
Tricky municipal parkland course with some narrow
fairways and the River Lea providing a natural hazard.
18 holes, 4974yds, Par 66, SSS 64, Course record 66.
Club membership 200.
Visitors phone for advance bookings. Societies phone in
advance. Green Fees terms on application. Prof R Gerken
Facilities ▉ 🏠 🍴 𝒸

N14 SOUTHGATE

Trent Park Bramley Rd, Oakwood N14 4XS
☎ 020 8367 4653 📄 0208 366 4581
e-mail: trentpark@americangolf.uk.com
18 holes, 6381yds, Par 70, SSS 69, Course record 64.
Course Designer D McGibbon Location opp Oakwood
tube station
Phone for further details
....
Hotel ★★★★ ♨ 73% West Lodge Park Hotel,
Cockfosters Rd, HADLEY WOOD ☎ 020 8216 3900
46 en suite 13 annexe en suite

N20 WHETSTONE

North Middlesex The Manor House,
Friern Barnet Ln, Whetstone N20 0NL
☎ 020 8445 1604 & 020 8445 3060 📄 020 8445 5023
e-mail: office@northmiddlesexgc.co.uk
Short parkland course renowned for its tricky greens.
18 holes, 5594yds, Par 69, SSS 67, Course record 64.
Club membership 520.
Visitors advisable to contact in advance. Societies
bookings in advance; winter offers & summer packages by
arrangement. Green Fees not confirmed. Cards 🔲 🔲
🔲 🔲 📄 Prof Freddy George Course Designer Willie
Park Jnr Facilities ⊗ ⍂ 🔩 ▉ ♀ ♨ 🏠 𝒸 Conf fac
available Corporate Hospitality Days available
Location M25 junct 23, 5m S
....
Hotel ★★★ 67% Corus hotel Elstree, Barnet Ln,
ELSTREE ☎ 0870 609 6151 47 en suite

South Herts Links Dr, Totteridge N20 8QU
☎ 020 8445 2035 📄 020 8445 7569
e-mail: secretary@southhertsgolfclub.co.uk
An open undulating parkland course perhaps most
famous for the fact that two of the greatest of all British
professionals, Harry Vardon and Dai Rees CBE, were
professionals at the club. The course is testing, over
rolling fairways, especially in the prevailing south-west
wind.
18 holes, 6432yds, Par 72, SSS 71, Course record 63.
Club membership 850.
Visitors not weekends; member of recognised golf club;
handicap certificate of 24 or less. Societies Wed-Fri, must
apply in writing. Green Fees terms on application. Prof
Bobby Mitchell Course Designer Harry Vardon Facilities
⊗ ⍂ 🔩 ▉ ♀ ♨ 🏠 🍴 🔩 🚗 𝒸 ℂ Conf Corporate
Hospitality Days available Location 2m E of A1 at Apex
Corner
....
Hotel ⋂ Innkeeper's Lodge Southgate, 22 The Green,
Southgate, LONDON ☎ 020 8447 8022 19 en suite

N21 WINCHMORE HILL

Bush Hill Park Bush Hill, Winchmore Hill N21 2BU
☎ 020 8360 5738 📄 020 8360 5583
Pleasant parkland course. The holes set a challenge due
to the vast array of mature trees, which make it an
enjoyable course to play. The course offers all players
unlimited opportunities to play a round of golf with a
real sense of achievement. Natural obstacles include a
large pond and an avenue of trees to thread your drive
through.
18 holes, 5809yds, Par 70, SSS 68.
Club membership 700.
Visitors not am Wed, weekends, bank holidays; handicap
certificate; tee booking. Societies by arrangement. Green
Fees £30 per 18 holes weekdays. Prof Lee Fickling
Course Designer Braid Facilities ⊗ 🔩 ▉ ♀ ♨ 🏠 𝒸
Conf Corporate Hospitality Days available Location 1m S
of Enfield off A105
....
Hotel ★★★ 75% Royal Chace Hotel, The Ridgeway,
ENFIELD ☎ 020 8884 8181 92 en suite

N22 WOOD GREEN

Muswell Hill Rhodes Av, Wood Green N22 7UT
☎ 020 8888 1764 📄 020 8889 9380
e-mail: muswellhillgc@msn.com
Undulating parkland course with a brook running
through the centre, set in 87 acres.
18 holes, 6438yds, Par 71, SSS 71, Course record 65.
Club membership 560.
Visitors restricted weekends; contact in advance. Societies
apply in writing or phone. Green Fees not confirmed.
Prof David Wilton Course Designer Braid, Wilson
Facilities ⊗ ⍂ by arrangement 🔩 ▉ ♀ ♨ 🏠 🍴 🚗 𝒸
Location off N Circular Rd at Bounds Green
....
Hotel ★★★ 66% Days Hotel, Welcome Break Service
Area, LONDON ☎ 020 8906 7000 200 en suite

Where to stay, where to eat?

Visit www.theAA.com

NW4 HENDON   Map 04 TQ28

The Metro Golf Centre Barnet Copthall Sports
Centre, Gt North Way NW4 1PS
☎ 020 8202 1202 🗋 020 8203 1203
e-mail: golf@metrogolf.btinternet.com
9 holes, 898yds, Par 27, SSS 27, Course record 24.
Course Designer Cousells **Location** M1 junct 2, off
A41/A1, in Barnet Copthall sports complex
Phone for further details

Hotel ★★★★ 73% London Marriott Hotel Regents
Park, 128 King Henry's Rd, LONDON
☎ 0870 400 7240 303 en suite

NW7 MILL HILL

Finchley Nether Court, Frith Ln, Mill Hill NW7 1PU
☎ 020 8346 2436 🗋 020 8343 4205
e-mail: secretary@finchleygolfclub.co.uk
**Compact course with rolling parkland. Tree-lined
fairways and heavily contoured greens.**

18 holes, 6411yds, Par 72, SSS 71.
Club membership 500.
Visitors contact in advance. **Societies** apply in writing.
Green Fees £40 per day, £30 per 18 holes (£50/£40
weekends & bank holidays). **Cards** 🗱 🗱 📇 **Prof** David
Brown **Course Designer** James Braid **Facilities** ⊗ ⅢⅢ ᴸⱼ
🖳 ♀ ⚘ 🏠 ⛳ ᐟ ♨ ⚸ ᶜ **Conf** fac available Corporate
Hospitality Days available **Location** near Mill Hill East
tube station

Hotel ★★★ 67% Corus hotel Elstree, Barnet Ln,
ELSTREE ☎ 0870 609 6151 47 en suite

Hendon Ashley Walk, Devonshire Rd, Mill Hill
NW7 1DG
☎ 020 8346 6023 🗋 020 8343 1974
e-mail: hendongolfclub@globalnet.co.uk
**Easy walking, parkland course with a good variety of
trees, and providing testing golf.**
18 holes, 6289yds, Par 70, SSS 70, Course record 63.
Club membership 560.
Visitors restricted weekends & bank holidays; must
contact professional in advance 020 8346 8990. **Societies**
Tue-Fri, must contact in advance. **Green Fees** £35 (£40 per
round weekends); winter £25/£33. **Cards** 🗱 🗱 🗱 📇
Prof Matt Deal **Course Designer** HS Colt **Facilities** ⊗ ⅢⅢ
ᴸⱼ 🖳 ♀ ⚘ 🏠 ⛳ ᐟ ♨ ⚸ ᶜ **Conf** fac available Corporate
Hospitality Days available **Location** M1 junct 2
southbound

Hotel ★★★ 67% Corus hotel Elstree, Barnet Ln,
ELSTREE ☎ 0870 609 6151 47 en suite

Mill Hill 100 Barnet Way, Mill Hill NW7 3AL
☎ 020 8959 2339 🗋 020 8906 0731
e-mail: haslehurstd@aol.com
**Parkland course with tree and shrub lined fairways,
water features strongly on holes 2, 9, 10 and 17.**

18 holes, 6247yds, Par 70, SSS 70, Course record 68.
Club membership 550.
Visitors restricted weekends & bank holidays; must
contact in advance. **Societies** contact in advance. **Green
Fees** £28 per round (£35 weekends). **Cards** 🗱 🗱 **Prof**
David Beal **Course Designer** JF Abercrombie, HS Colt
Facilities ⊗ ᴸⱼ 🖳 ♀ ⚘ 🏠 ⛳ ᐟ ♨ ⚸ ᶜ ᶜ **Leisure**
snooker. **Conf** fac available Corporate Hospitality Days
available **Location** on A1 southbound

Hotel ★★★ 67% Corus hotel Elstree, Barnet Ln,
ELSTREE ☎ 0870 609 6151 47 en suite

SE9 ELTHAM

Eltham Warren Bexley Rd, Eltham SE9 2PE
☎ 020 8850 4477
e-mail: secretary@elthamwarren.idps.co.uk
**Parkland course with narrow fairways, all tree-lined,
and small greens. The course is bounded by the A210
on one side and Eltham Park on the other.**
9 holes, 5874yds, Par 69, SSS 68, Course record 62.
Club membership 440.
Visitors not weekends; must contact in advance; handicap
certificate. **Societies** Thu, must book in advance, deposit
required. **Green Fees** £28 per day. **Prof** Gary Brett **Course
Designer** James Braid **Facilities** ⊗ ᴸⱼ 🖳 ♀ ⚘ 🏠 ⛳
Leisure snooker. **Location** 0.5m from Eltham station on
A210

Hotel ★★★ 71% Bromley Court Hotel, Bromley Hill,
BROMLEY ☎ 020 8461 8600 114 en suite

Royal Blackheath Court Rd SE9 5AF
☎ 020 8850 1795 🗋 020 8859 0150
e-mail: info@rbgc.com
**A pleasant, parkland course of great character as befits
the antiquity of the Club; the clubhouse dates from the
17th century. Many great trees survive and there are
two ponds. The 18th requires a pitch to the green over a
thick clipped hedge, which also crosses the front of the
1st tee. You may wish to visit the club's fine museum of
golf.**
18 holes, 6219yds, Par 70, SSS 70, Course record 66.
Club membership 720.
Visitors mid-week only; contact in advance; handicap
certificate. **Societies** apply in writing. **Green Fees** £60 per
day; £45 per round. **Cards** 🗱 🗱 📇 **Prof** Richard
Harrison **Course Designer** James Braid **Facilities** ⊗ ⅢⅢ ᴸⱼ
Continued

♨ ♀ ⛳ 🏠 🚩 🛥 🚏 ✐ Leisure golf museum. Conf fac available Corporate Hospitality Days available Location M25 junct 3, A20 towards London, 2nd lights right, club 500yds on right

Hotel ★★★ 71% Bromley Court Hotel, Bromley Hill, BROMLEY ☎ 020 8461 8600 114 en suite

SE18 WOOLWICH

Shooters Hill Eaglesfield Rd, Shooters Hill SE18 3DA
☎ 020 8854 6368 ▤ 020 8854 0469
e-mail: shgcltd@aol.com
Hilly and wooded parkland course with good view and natural hazards.
18 holes, 5721yds, Par 69, SSS 68, Course record 63.
Club membership 900.
Visitors with member only weekends; handicap certificate; member of recognised golf club. **Societies** Tue, Thu, by arrangement. **Green Fees** £30 per day, £25 per round. **Prof** David Brotherton **Course Designer** Willie Park **Facilities** ⊗ ☶ ⛳ ♨ ♀ ⛳ 🏠 🚩 🛥 ✐ **Conf** fac available Corporate Hospitality Days available **Location** Shooters Hill road from Blackheath

Hotel ★★ 71% Hamilton House Hotel, 14 West Grove, Greenwich, LONDON ☎ 020 8694 9899 9 en suite

SE21 DULWICH

Dulwich & Sydenham Hill Grange Ln, College Rd
SE21 7LH
☎ 020 8693 3961 ▤ 020 8693 2481
e-mail: secretary@dulwichgolf.co.uk
18 holes, 6008yds, Par 69, SSS 69, Course record 63.
Course Designer HS Colt
Phone for further details

Hotel ★★★ 71% Bromley Court Hotel, Bromley Hill, BROMLEY ☎ 020 8461 8600 114 en suite

SE28 WOOLWICH

Thamesview Fairway Dr, Summerton Way,
Thamesmead SE28 8PP
☎ 020 8310 7975
e-mail: enquiries@thamesview-golf.fsnet.co.uk
9 holes, 5462yds, Par 70, SSS 66.
Course Designer Heffernan **Location** off A2 near Woolwich ferry
Phone for further details

Hotel ★★ 71% Hamilton House Hotel, 14 West Grove, Greenwich, LONDON ☎ 020 8694 9899 9 en suite

SW15 PUTNEY

Richmond Park Roehampton Gate, Priory Ln
SW15 5JR
☎ 020 8876 1795 ▤ 020 8878 1354
e-mail: richmondpark@glendale-services.co.uk
Two public parkland courses.
Princes Course: 18 holes, 5868yds, Par 69, SSS 67.
Dukes Course: 18 holes, 6036yds, Par 69, SSS 68.
Visitors contact in advance for weekends. **Societies** contact in advance. **Green Fees** £19 per 18 holes; (£22 weekends). **Cards** ▦ ▧ ▨ ▩ 🅿 **Prof** Stuart Hill & David Bown **Course Designer** Fred Hawtree

Continued

Facilities ⊗ ☶ ⛳ ♨ ⛳ 🏠 🚩 🛥 ✐ ¶ Conf Corporate Hospitality Days available

Hotel ★★★ 69% The Richmond Hill Hotel, Richmond Hill, RICHMOND UPON THAMES
☎ 020 8940 2247 138 en suite

SW17 WANDSWORTH

Central London Golf Centre Burntwood Ln,
Wandsworth SW17 0AT
☎ 020 8871 2468 ▤ 020 8874 7447
e-mail: clgc@aol.com
9 holes, 2277yds, Par 62, SSS 62.
Course Designer Patrick Tallock **Location** between Garatt Ln & Trinity Rd
Phone for further details

SW19 WIMBLEDON

London Scottish Windmill Enclosure, Wimbledon
Common SW19 5NQ
☎ 020 8788 0135 & 8789 1207 ▤ 020 8789 7517
e-mail: secretary.lsgc@virgin.net
Heathland course. The original course was seven holes around the windmill, laid out by 'Old' Willie Dunn of Musselburgh. His son, Tom Dunn, was the first professional to the club and laid out the 18-hole course.
18 holes, 5458yds, Par 68, SSS 66.
Visitors not weekends, bank holidays; pillar box red tops must be worn. **Societies** advisable to contact in advance. **Green Fees** not confirmed. **Prof** Steve Barr **Course Designer** Tom Dunn **Facilities** ⊗ ☶ ☶ ⛳ ♨ ♀ ⛳ 🏠 🚩 ✐

Hotel Ⓤ Premier Travel Inn London Wimbledon South, Merantum Way, Merton, LONDON POSTAL DISTRICTS ☎ 0870 990 6342

Royal Wimbledon 29 Camp Rd SW19 4UW
☎ 020 8946 2125 ▤ 020 8944 8652
e-mail: secretary@rwgc.co.uk
Third oldest club in England, established in 1865 and steeped in the history and traditions of the game. Mainly heathland with trees and heather, a good test of golf with many fine holes, the 12th being rated as the best.
18 holes, 6350yds, Par 70, SSS 71, Course record 66.
Club membership 1050.
Visitors not weekends; must be guest of current club member or contact club in advance; member of recognised club. **Societies** Wed-Thu, must apply in writing. **Green Fees** £85 per day, £60 per round. **Prof** David Jones **Course Designer** H Colt **Facilities** ⊗ ☶ ☶ ⛳ ♨ ♀ ⛳ 🏠 🚩 🛥 ✐ ¶ **Conf** Corporate Hospitality Days available **Location** 1m from Tibbatt's Corner rdbt on Wimbledon Rd

Hotel Ⓤ Premier Travel Inn London Wimbledon South, Merantum Way, Merton, LONDON POSTAL DISTRICTS ☎ 0870 990 6342

Wimbledon Common 19 Camp Rd SW19 4UW
☎ 020 8946 0294 (pro shop) ▤ 020 8947 8697
e-mail: secretary@wcgc.co.uk
Quick-drying course on Wimbledon Common. Well wooded, with tight fairways, challenging short holes but no bunkers.
18 holes, 5438yds, Par 68, SSS 66, Course record 63.
Club membership 290.

Continued

Visitors with member only weekends, bank holidays.
Societies phone in advance, confirm in writing, 25%
deposit. **Green Fees** not confirmed. **Cards** ⊞ 💳 💳 💳
🔲 **Prof** JS Jukes **Course Designer** Tom & Willie Dunn
Facilities ⊗ ⅏ ⅃ 🖳 ♀ 🛆 🗃 ⁊ ♂ **Leisure** snooker
room. **Conf** fac available Corporate Hospitality Days
available **Location** 0.5m N of Wimbledon village

Hotel Ⓤ Premier Travel Inn London Wimbledon South,
Merantum Way, Merton, LONDON POSTAL DISTRICTS
☎ 0870 990 6342

Wimbledon Park Home Park Rd, Wimbledon
SW19 7HR
☎ 020 8946 1250 🖹 020 8944 8688
e-mail: secretary@wpgc.co.uk
**Easy walking on parkland course. Sheltered lake
provides hazard on three holes.**

*18 holes, 5483yds, Par 66, SSS 66, Course record 59.
Club membership 700.*
Visitors restricted weekends & bank holidays; must
contact in advance; handicap certificate or letter of
introduction. **Societies** apply in writing. **Green Fees** £50
per round. **Cards** ⊞ 💳 🔲 **Prof** Dean Wingrove **Course
Designer** Willie Park Jnr **Facilities** ⊗ ⅏ ⅃ 🖳 ♀ 🛆 🗃 ♂
Conf fac available Corporate Hospitality Days available
Location 400yds from Wimbledon Park station

Hotel ★★★ 69% The Richmond Hill Hotel, Richmond
Hill, RICHMOND UPON THAMES
☎ 020 8940 2247 138 en suite

W7 HANWELL

Brent Valley 138 Church Rd, Hanwell W7 3BE
☎ 020 8567 1287
18 holes, 5426yds, Par 67, SSS 66.
Phone for further details

Hotel ★★★ 66% Best Western Master Robert Hotel, 366
Great West Rd, HOUNSLOW ☎ 020 8570 6261
96 annexe en suite

MERSEYSIDE

BEBINGTON   Map 07 SJ38

Brackenwood Brackenwood Golf Course, Bracken Ln
CH63 2LY
☎ 0151 608 3093
**Municipal parkland course with easy walking, a very
testing but fair course in a fine rural setting, usually in
very good condition.**

*18 holes, 6285yds, Par 70, SSS 70, Course record 66.
Club membership 320.*
Visitors book weekends one week in advance. **Societies**
phone in advance. **Green Fees** not confirmed. **Prof** Ken
Lamb **Facilities** 🖳 🗃 ⁊ ♂ **Location** M53 junct 4, 0.75m
N on B5151

Hotel ★★★★ 70% Thornton Hall Hotel, Neston Rd,
THORNTON HOUGH ☎ 0151 336 3938 63 en suite

BIRKENHEAD   Map 07 SJ38

Arrowe Park Woodchurch CH49 5LW
☎ 0151 677 1527
18 holes, 6435yds, Par 72, SSS 71, Course record 66.
Location M53 junct 3, 1m on A551
Phone for further details

Hotel ★★★ 68% Riverhill Hotel, Talbot Rd, Prenton,
BIRKENHEAD ☎ 0151 653 3773 15 en suite

Prenton Golf Links Rd, Prenton CH42 8LW
☎ 0151 609 3426 🖹 0151 609 3421
e-mail: info@prentongolfclub.co.uk
**Parkland course with easy walking and views of the
Welsh hills.**
*18 holes, 6429yds, Par 71, SSS 71.
Club membership 610.*
Visitors Societies phone in advance & confirm in writing.
Green Fees not confirmed. **Prof** Robin Thompson **Course
Designer** James Braid **Facilities** ⊗ ⅏ ⅃ 🖳 ♀ 🛆 🗃 ♂
Location M53 junct 3, off A552 towards Birkenhead

Hotel ★★★ 68% Riverhill Hotel, Talbot Rd, Prenton,
BIRKENHEAD ☎ 0151 653 3773 15 en suite

Wirral Ladies 93 Bidston Rd CH43 6TS
☎ 0151 652 1255 🖹 0151 653 4323
e-mail: sue.headford@virgin.net
**Compact heathland course with heather and birch,
requiring accurate shots.**
*18 holes, 5185yds, Par 68, SSS 65.
Club membership 590.*
Visitors not before 11am weekends, not Christmas &
Easter holidays. **Societies** Mon-Fri, phone in advance.
Green Fees £25.50 per day. **Prof** Angus Law **Facilities** ⊗
⅏ ⅃ 🖳 ♀ 🛆 🗃 ♂ **Leisure** indoor training suite.
Location W of town centre on B5151

Hotel ★★★ 68% Riverhill Hotel, Talbot Rd, Prenton,
BIRKENHEAD ☎ 0151 653 3773 15 en suite

BLUNDELLSANDS   Map 07 SJ39

West Lancashire Hall Rd West L23 8SZ
☎ 0151 924 1076 🖹 0151 931 4448
e-mail: golf@westlancashiregolf.co.uk
**Challenging, traditional links with sandy subsoil
overlooking the Mersey estuary. The course provides
excellent golf throughout the year. The four short holes
are very fine.**
*18 holes, 6763yds, Par 72, SSS 73, Course record 66.
Club membership 650.*
Visitors not before 9.30am Mon-Fri, not Tue. **Societies**
contact in advance. **Green Fees** £75 per day; £60 per round
(£85/70 weekends). **Cards** ⊞ 💳 💳 💳 🔲 **Prof** Gary
Eoge **Course Designer** CK Cotton **Facilities** ⊗ ⅏ ⅃ 🖳 ♀
🛆 🗃 ♂ ⏚ **Conf** Corporate Hospitality Days available
Location N of village, next to Hall Road station

Continued

BOOTLE   Map 07 SJ39

Bootle 2 Dunnings Bridge Rd L30 2PP
☎ 0151 928 1371 📠 0151 949 1815
e-mail: bootlegolfcourse@btconnect.com
18 holes, 6362yds, Par 70, SSS 70, Course record 64.
Location 2m NE on A5036
Phone for further details

....

Hotel 🏠 Premier Travel Inn Liverpool North, Northern
Perimiter Rd, Bootle, LIVERPOOL ☎ 08701 977158
63 en suite

BROMBOROUGH   Map 07 SJ38

Bromborough Raby Hall Rd CH63 0NW
☎ 0151 334 2155 📠 0151 334 7300
e-mail: enquiries@bromboroughgolfclub.org.uk
Parkland course.
18 holes, 6650yds, Par 72, SSS 72, Course record 65.
Club membership 800.
Visitors advisable to contact professional in advance 0151
334 4499. **Societies** Wed, must apply in advance.
Green Fees not confirmed. **Prof** Geoff Berry **Course
Designer** J Hassall **Facilities** ⊗ ⅏ ⅃ 🍺 💷 ♀ 🍴 🏠 ♨ ✔ ♂
Conf Corporate Hospitality Days available
Location 0.5m W of station

....

Hotel ★★★★ 70% Thornton Hall Hotel, Neston Rd,
THORNTON HOUGH ☎ 0151 336 3938   63 en suite

CALDY   Map 07 SJ28

Caldy Links Hey Rd CH48 1NB
☎ 0151 625 5660 📠 0151 6257394
e-mail: secretarycaldygc@btconnect.com
**A heathland and clifftop links course situated on the
estuary of the River Dee with many of the fairways
running parallel to the river. Of championship length,
the course offers excellent golf all year, but is subject to
variable winds that noticeably alter the day-to-day
playing of each hole. There are excellent views of
Snowdonia.**
18 holes, 6651yds, Par 72, SSS 72, Course record 65.
Club membership 800.
Visitors weekdays by arrangement; not before 3.30pm
Tue, not after 12.30pm Wed. **Societies** phone in advance.
Green Fees £80 per day, £70 per round. **Prof** A Gibbons
Course Designer J Braid **Facilities** ⊗ ⅏ ⅃ 🍺 💷 ♀ 🍴 🏠
♨ ♂ **Conf** Corporate Hospitality Days available
Location signed from Caldy A540 rdbt to Caldy & club

....

Hotel ★★★★ 70% Thornton Hall Hotel, Neston Rd,
THORNTON HOUGH ☎ 0151 336 3938   63 en suite

EASTHAM   Map 07 SJ38

Eastham Lodge 117 Ferry Rd CH62 0AP
☎ 0151 327 3003 📠 0151 327 7574
e-mail: easthamlodge@ukgolfer.org
**A parkland course with many mature trees, recently
upgraded to 18 holes. Most holes have a subtle dog-leg
to left or right. The 1st hole requires an accurate drive
to open up the green which is guarded on the right by a
stand of pine trees.**
18 holes, 5436yds, Par 68, SSS 68.
Club membership 800.
Visitors with member only weekends; phone professional
shop to check availability 0151 327 3008; start times

available up to two weeks in advance. **Societies** Tue, must
apply in writing; other days by arrangement. **Green Fees**
not confirmed. **Prof** N Sargent **Course Designer** Hawtree,
D Hemstock **Facilities** ⊗ ⅏ ⅃ 🍺 💷 ♀ 🍴 🏠 🍴 ♂ **Leisure**
snooker. **Conf** Corporate Hospitality Days available
Location 1.5m N, off A41 to Wirral Metropolitan College
& Eastham Country Park

....

Hotel ★★★ 69% Quality Hotel Chester, Berwick Rd,
Little Sutton, ELLESMERE PORT ☎ 0151 339 5121
75 en suite

FORMBY   Map 07 SD30

Formby Golf Rd L37 1LQ
☎ 01704 872164 📠 01704 833028
e-mail: info@formbygolfclub.co.uk
**Championship seaside links through sandhills and pine
trees. Partly sheltered from the wind by high dunes it
features firm, springy turf, fast seaside greens and
natural sandy bunkers. Well drained it plays well
throughout the year.**

18 holes, 6701yds, Par 72, SSS 72, Course record 65.
Club membership 700.
Visitors not before 3.30pm weekends; contact in advance.
Societies contact well in advance. **Green Fees** not
confirmed. **Cards** 💳 💳 **Prof** Gary Butler **Course
Designer** Park, Colt **Facilities** ⊗ ⅏ ⅃ 🍺 💷 ♀ 🍴 🏠 ♨ ♂
Conf fac available   Corporate Hospitality Days available
Location N of town next to Freshfield railway station

Formby Hall Golf & Country Club Southport
Old Rd L37 0AB
☎ 01704 875699 📠 01704 832134
e-mail: mark@formby-hall.co.uk
**A spectacular parkland course with links style bunkers.
American style design with water on 16 holes. Generous
sized fairways with large undulating greens, many of
which are protected by water.**
18 holes, 6707yds, Par 72, SSS 73.
Club membership 600.
Visitors not before 1pm weekends; contact Director of Golf
in advance. **Societies** by arrangement with Director of Golf
Green Fees £50 per 27 holes, £35 per 18 holes (£40 per 18
holes weekends). **Cards** 💳 💳 💳 💳 **Prof** David
Lloyd **Facilities** ⊗ ⅏ ⅃ 🍺 💷 ♀ 🍴 🏠 🍴 ✔ ♂ ✔
Leisure fishing, clay pigeon shooting, paintball. **Conf** fac
available   Corporate Hospitality Days available **Location**
0.5m off A565 Formby bypass, opp RAF Woodvale

Formby Ladies Golf Rd L37 1YH
☎ 01704 873493 📠 01704 873493
e-mail: secretary@formbyladiesgolfclub.co.uk
Seaside links - one of the few independent ladies' clubs

Continued

Continued

in the country. The course has contrasting hard-hitting holes in flat country and tricky holes in sandhills and woods.

18 holes, 5374yds, Par 71, SSS 71, Course record 60. Club membership 570.

Visitors not Thu, before 11am weekends; contact in advance. **Societies** apply in advance; handicap certificate. **Green Fees** not confirmed. **Prof** Gary Butler **Facilities** ⊗ ⓛ ⚑ ♀ ♣ 🏠 ⚐ **Location** N of town centre

HESWALL   Map 07 SJ28

Heswall Cottage Ln CH60 8PB
☎ 0151 342 1237 🖩 0151 342 6140
e-mail: dawn@heswallgolfclub.com

A pleasant parkland course in soft undulating country overlooking the estuary of the River Dee. There are excellent views of the Welsh hills and coastline, and a good test of golf.

18 holes, 6492yds, Par 72, SSS 72, Course record 62. Club membership 940.

Visitors contact in advance. **Societies** apply in advance. **Green Fees** not confirmed. **Prof** Alan Thompson **Facilities** ⊗ ⓜ ⓛ ⚑ ♀ ♣ 🏠 ⚐ **Location** 1m S off A540

Hotel ★★★★ 70% Thornton Hall Hotel, Neston Rd, THORNTON HOUGH ☎ 0151 336 3938 63 en suite

HOYLAKE   See page 181

HOYLAKE   Map 07 SJ28

Hoylake Carr Ln, Municipal Links CH47 4BG
☎ 0151 632 2956

Flat, generally windy semi-links course. Tricky fairways, with some very deep bunkers.

18 holes, 6313yds, Par 70, SSS 70, Course record 67. Club membership 303.

Visitors book tee times with professional; weekend bookings one week in advance. **Societies** phone club steward 0151 632 4883 or club professional 0151 632 2956. **Green Fees** not confirmed. **Cards** 🔲 🔲 🔲 **Prof** Simon Hooton **Course Designer** James Braid **Facilities** ⊗ ⓜ ⓛ ⚑ ♀ ♣ 🏠 ⚐ ⌚ ⚐ **Location** SW of town off A540

Hotel ★★★ 69% Leasowe Castle Hotel, Leasowe Rd, MORETON ☎ 0151 606 9191 47 en suite

HUYTON   Map 07 SJ49

Bowring Roby Rd L36 4HD
☎ 0151 443 0424 489 1901
e-mail: bowringpark@knowsley.gov.uk
18 holes, 6082yds, Par 70.
Location M62 junct 5, on A5080
Phone for further details

Hotel ✿ Premier Travel Inn Liverpool (Roby), Roby Rd, Huyton, LIVERPOOL ☎ 0870 9906596 53 en suite

Huyton & Prescot Hurst Park, Huyton Ln L36 1UA
☎ 0151 489 3948 🖩 0151 489 0797

An easy walking, parkland course providing excellent golf.

18 holes, 5779yds, Par 68, SSS 68, Course record 65. Club membership 700.

Visitors contact in advance & arrange with secretary,

Societies apply in writing. **Green Fees** not confirmed. **Prof** John Fisher **Facilities** ⊗ ⓜ ⓛ ⚑ ♀ ♣ 🏠 ⚐ **Conf** fac available Corporate Hospitality Days available **Location** 1.5m NE off B5199

Huyton & Prescot Golf Club

Hotel ✿ Premier Travel Inn Liverpool (Tarbock), Wilson Rd, Tarbock, LIVERPOOL ☎ 08701 977159 40 en suite

LIVERPOOL   Map 07 SJ39

Allerton Park Allerton Manor Golf Estate, Allerton Rd L18 3JT
☎ 0151 428 7490 🖩 428 7490
Parkland course.
18 holes, 5494yds, Par 67, SSS 66.
Visitors book with professional in advance for 18-hole course. **Societies** apply in writing to golf professional. **Green Fees** £8 (£9 weekends & bank holidays). **Prof** Barry Large **Facilities** ⚑ 🏠 ⌚ ⚐ **Leisure** 9 hole par 3 course. **Location** 5.5m SE of city centre off A562 & B5180

Hotel ★★★ 68% The Royal Hotel, Marine Ter, Waterloo, LIVERPOOL ☎ 0151 928 2332 25 en suite

The Childwall Naylors Rd, Gateacre L27 2YB
☎ 0151 487 0654 🖩 0151 487 0882
e-mail: office@childwallgolfclub.co.uk

Parkland golf is played here over a testing course, where accuracy from the tee is well-rewarded. The course is very popular with visiting societies for the clubhouse has many amenities. Course designed by James Braid.

18 holes, 6425yds, Par 72, SSS 71, Course record 66. Club membership 650.

Visitors contact in advance. **Societies** not Tue, weekends & bank holidays, apply in writing. **Green Fees** £35 (£40 weekends & bank holidays). **Prof** Nigel M Parr **Course Designer** James Braid **Facilities** ⊗ ⓜ ⓛ ⚑ ♀ ♣ 🏠 ⌚ ⚐ **Conf** fac available Corporate Hospitality Days available **Location** 7m E of city centre off B5178

Hotel ✿ Premier Travel Inn Liverpool (Roby), Roby Rd, Huyton, LIVERPOOL ☎ 0870 9906596 53 en suite

Kirkby-Liverpool Municipal Ingoe Ln, Kirkby L32 4SS
☎ 0151 546 5435
18 holes, 6704yds, Par 72, SSS 72, Course record 68.
Location 7.5m NE of city centre on A506
Phone for further details

Hotel ★★★ 68% The Royal Hotel, Marine Ter, Waterloo, LIVERPOOL ☎ 0151 928 2332 25 en suite

Continued

Lee Park
Childwall Valley Rd L27 3YA
☎ 0151 487 3882 📠 0151 498 4666
e-mail: lee.park@virgin.net
Easy walking parkland course with plenty of trees, ponds in places and nine dog-legs. A test for the short game; being in the right position to attack the pins is a premium.
18 holes, 6016yds, Par 71, SSS 69, Course record 66. Club membership 600.
Visitors dress code; contact in advance. **Societies** contact in advance. **Green Fees** £25 per day (£30 weekends & bank holidays). **Prof** Chris Crowder **Course Designer** G Cotton **Facilities** ⊗ ℳ ☒ ☻ ♀ ☖ ∂ **Leisure** snooker room. **Conf** Corporate Hospitality Days available **Location** 7m E of city centre off B5178
....
Hotel ⌂ Premier Travel Inn Liverpool (Roby), Roby Rd, Huyton, LIVERPOOL ☎ 0870 9906596 53 en suite

West Derby
Yew Tree Ln, West Derby L12 9HQ
☎ 0151 254 1034 📠 0151 259 0505
e-mail: pmilne@westderbygc.freeserve.co.uk
A parkland course always in first-class condition, and so giving easy walking. The fairways are well-wooded. Care must be taken on the first nine holes to avoid the brook which guards many of the greens.
18 holes, 6277yds, Par 72, SSS 70, Course record 65. Club membership 550.
Visitors not before 9.30am; weekends by arrangement. **Societies** not weekends & bank holidays; must contact in advance. **Green Fees** £29.50 per day/round (£37 weekends). **Prof** Andrew Witherup **Facilities** ⊗ ℳ ☒ ☻ ♀ ☖ 🏠 ∂ **Conf** fac available Corporate Hospitality Days available **Location** 4.5m E of city centre off A57
....
Hotel ★★★ 68% The Royal Hotel, Marine Ter, Waterloo, LIVERPOOL ☎ 0151 928 2332 25 en suite

Woolton
Doe Park, Speke Rd, Woolton L25 7TZ
☎ 0151 486 2298 📠 0151 486 1664
e-mail: golf@wooltongolf.co.uk
Parkland course providing a good round of golf for all standards. A members-owned course that includes two par 5s and five par 3s.
18 holes, 5717yds, Par 69, SSS 68, Course record 63. Club membership 600.
Visitors restricted weekends; contact in advance. **Societies** contact in advance. **Green Fees** £26 per 18 holes (£40 weekends). **Prof** Dave Thompson **Facilities** ⊗ ℳ ☒ ☻ ♀ ☖ ☻ ♨ **Leisure** Indoor teaching unit. **Conf** fac available Corporate Hospitality Days available **Location** 7m SE of city centre off A562, near Liverpool airport
....
Hotel ★★★ 68% The Royal Hotel, Marine Ter, Waterloo, LIVERPOOL ☎ 0151 928 2332 25 en suite

NEWTON-LE-WILLOWS   Map 07 SJ59

Haydock Park
Newton Ln WA12 0HX
☎ 01925 228525 📠 01925 224984
A well-wooded parkland course, close to the well-known racecourse, and always in excellent condition. The pleasant undulating fairways offer some very interesting golf and the 6th, 9th, 11th and 13th holes are particularly testing.
18 holes, 6058yds, Par 70, SSS 69, Course record 65. Club membership 560.

Continued

Visitors not Tue; with member only weekends & bank holidays; must contact in advance. **Societies** contact in advance. **Green Fees** not confirmed. **Prof** Peter Kenwright **Course Designer** James Braid **Facilities** ⊗ ℳ ☒ ☻ ♀ ☖ 🏠 ∂ **Location** 0.75m NE off A49
....
Hotel ★★ 65% Kirkfield Hotel, 2-4 Church St, NEWTON LE WILLOWS ☎ 01925 228196 20 en suite

RAINHILL   Map 07 SJ49

Blundells Hill
Blundells Ln L35 6NA
☎ 0151 4309551 (secretary) & 4300100 (pro)
📠 0151 4265256
e-mail: information@blundellshill.co.uk
18 holes, 6256yds, Par 71, SSS 70, Course record 69.
Course Designer Steve Marnoch **Location** M62 junct 7, A57 towards Prescot, left after garage, 2nd left into Blundells Ln
Phone for further details
....
Hotel ⌂ Premier Travel Inn Liverpool (Rainhill), 804 Warrington Rd, Rainhill, LIVERPOOL ☎ 0870 9906446 34 en suite

Eccleston Park
Rainhill Rd L35 4PG
☎ 0151 493 0033 📠 0151 493 0044
e-mail: eccleston-sales@crown-golf.co.uk
A tough parkland course designed to test all golfing abilities. Strategically placed water features, bunkers and mounding enhance the beauty and difficulty of this manicured course.
18 holes, 6296yds, Par 70, SSS 72. Club membership 700.
Visitors booking seven days in advance. **Societies** phone in advance. **Green Fees** not confirmed. **Cards** ☷ ▦ ▦ ▦ 🔲 **Prof** Chris McKinney **Facilities** ⊗ ℳ ☒ ☻ ♀ ☖ 🏠 ♨ ∂ **Conf** fac available Corporate Hospitality Days available **Location** M62 junct 7, A57 to Prescot, at hump bridge right at lights, course 1m on left
....
Hotel ⌂ Premier Travel Inn Liverpool (Rainhill), 804 Warrington Rd, Rainhill, LIVERPOOL ☎ 0870 9906446 34 en suite

ST HELENS   Map 07 SJ59

Grange Park
Prescot Rd WA10 3AD
☎ 01744 26318 📠 01744 26318
e-mail: gpgc@ic24.net
A course of Championship length set in pleasant country surroundings - playing the course it is hard to believe that industrial St Helens lies so close at hand. The course is a fine test of golf and there are many attractive holes liable to challenge all grades.
18 holes, 6446yds, Par 72, SSS 71, Course record 65. Club membership 730.
Visitors not Tue & weekends; advisable to contact professional in advance 01744 28785. **Societies** apply in writing. **Green Fees** not confirmed. **Prof** Paul Roberts **Course Designer** James Braid **Facilities** ⊗ ℳ ☒ ☻ ♀ ☖ 🏠 ∂ **Location** 1.5m SW on A58
....
Hotel ★★ 65% Kirkfield Hotel, 2-4 Church St, NEWTON LE WILLOWS ☎ 01925 228196 20 en suite

Lincolnshire

Woodhall Spa

Woodhall Spa   Map 8 TF16

The Championship Course at Woodhall Spa, now known as the Hotchkin, is arguably the best inland course in Britain. This classic course has cavernous bunkers and heather-lined fairways. Golf has been played here for over a century and the Hotchkin has hosted most of the top national and international amateur events. The English Golf Union acquired Woodhall Spa in 1995 to create a centre of excellence. A second course, the Bracken, has been built, along with extensive practice facilities including one of Europe's finest short-game practice areas. The English Golf Union actively encourages visits to the National Golf Centre throughout the year, to experience the facilities and to enjoy the unique ambience.

The Broadway LN10 6PU
☎ 01526 352511   Fax 01526 351817
e-mail: booking@englishgolfunion.org

The Hotchkin: 18 holes, 7080yds, Par 73, SSS 75, Course record 66.
The Bracken: 18 holes, 6735yds, Par 72, SSS 74, Course record 68.
Club membership 520.
Visitors must contact in advance; handicap certificate.
Societies apply by phone initially. **Green Fees** Hotchkin £100 per day, £65 per round; Bracken £75 per day, £50 round. £90 per day playing both courses. **Cards** ▨ ▨ ▨ ▨ **Prof** A Hare **Course Designer** Col S V Hotchkin **Facilities** ⊗ ⅏ ⅃ ♥ ♀ ⌂ 🍴 ⊨ ♂ ╲ **Conf** fac available Corporate Hospitality Days available **Location** NE of village off B1191

....

Hotels

★ ★ ★   68% Petwood Hotel, Stixwould Rd, WOODHALL SPA
☎ 01526 352411 53 en suite

★ ★ ★   63% Golf Hotel, The Broadway, WOODHALL SPA
☎ 01526 353535 Fax 01526 353096 50 en suite

★ ★   65% Eagle Lodge Hotel, The Broadway, WOODHALL SPA
☎ 01526 353231 Fax 01526 352797 23 en suite

Houghwood Golf Billinge Hill, Crank Rd, Crank WA11 8RL
☎ 01744 894444 & 894754 ▤ 01744 894754
e-mail: houghwoodgolf@btinternet.com

From the course's highest point, the 12th tee, there are panoramic views over the Lancashire plain to the Welsh hills. All greens built to USGA specification with a permanent track around the entire course for buggies and trolleys.

18 holes, 6268yds, Par 70, SSS 69, Course record 67. Club membership 680.
Visitors dress code. **Societies** phone enquiries welcome, deposit secures booking. **Green Fees** £25 per round (£35 weekends & bank holidays). **Cards** ▦ ▦ ▦ ▦ **Prof** Paul Dickenson **Course Designer** Neville Pearson **Facilities** ⊗ ⅲ ⅃ ᴸ ♥ ♀ ⅄ 🗑 ♥ ♣ ♂ **Leisure** snooker table. **Conf** fac available Corporate Hospitality Days available **Location** 3.5m N of St Helens off B5205
·····························

Hotel ⏏ Travelodge, Piele Rd, HAYDOCK
☎ 08700 850 950 62 en suite

Sherdley Park Sherdley Rd WA9 5DE
☎ 01744 813149 ▤ 01744 817967
Fairly hilly, challenging, pay and play parkland course with ponds in places. Excellent greens.
18 holes, 5974yds, Par 71, SSS 69.
Visitors Societies not before 1.30pm weekends; phone or write for application form. **Green Fees** not confirmed. **Prof** Danny Jones **Course Designer** Peter Parkinson **Facilities** ⊗ ⅲ ⅃ ᴸ ♥ ♀ ⅄ ♂ ♣ **Location** 2m S of St Helens off A570
·····························

Hotel ★★ 65% Kirkfield Hotel, 2-4 Church St, NEWTON LE WILLOWS ☎ 01925 228196 20 en suite

SOUTHPORT   See page 183

SOUTHPORT   Map 07 SD31

The Hesketh Cockle Dick's Ln, off Cambridge Rd PR9 9QQ
☎ 01704 536897 ▤ 01704 539250
e-mail: secretary@heskethgolfclub.co.uk
The Hesketh is the oldest of the six clubs in Southport, founded in 1885. Set at the northern end of south-west Lancashire's dune system, the course sets a unique challenge with half of the holes threaded through tall dunes while the other holes border the Ribble estuary. The course is next to a renowned bird reserve and across the estuary are fine views of the mountains of Lancashire, Cumbria and Yorkshire. Used as a final qualifying course for the Open Championship.

Continued

18 holes, 6655yds, Par 72, SSS 72, Course record 67. Club membership 600.
Visitors not am Tue (Ladies), 12.30-2pm daily, after 2.30pm Sat & after 10.30am Sun; handicap certificate, must contact in advance. **Societies** please contact Martyn G Senior in advance. **Green Fees** £60 per day; £50 per round (£60 per round weekends & bank holidays). **Cards** ▦ ▦ ▦ ▦ ▦ **Prof** Scott Astin **Course Designer** JF Morris **Facilities** ⊗ ⅲ ⅃ ᴸ ♥ ♀ ⅄ 🗑 ♂ ♣ **Conf** Corporate Hospitality Days available **Location** 1m NE of town centre off A565
·····························

Hotel ★★★ 69% Stutelea Hotel Leisure Club, Alexandra Rd, SOUTHPORT ☎ 01704 544220 20 en suite

Hillside Hastings Rd, Hillside PR8 2LU
☎ 01704 567169 ▤ 01704 563192
e-mail: secretary@hillside-golfclub.co.uk
Championship links course with natural hazards open to strong wind.
18 holes, 6850yds, Par 72, SSS 74, Course record 65. Club membership 700.
Visitors not Sat, restricted Tue (Ladies Day) & Sun; must contact in advance through secretary. **Societies** apply to secretary in advance. **Green Fees** £85 per day; £65 per round (£85 per round Sun). **Cards** ▦ ▦ **Prof** Brian Seddon **Course Designer** Hawtree, Steel **Facilities** ⊗ ⅲ ⅃ ᴸ ♥ ♀ ⅄ 🗑 ♂ ♣ ♣ **Conf** Corporate Hospitality Days available **Location** 3m S of town centre on A565
·····························

Hotel ★★★ 65% Royal Clifton Hotel, Promenade, SOUTHPORT ☎ 01704 533771 111 en suite

Southport & Ainsdale Bradshaws Ln, Ainsdale PR8 3LG
☎ 01704 578000 ▤ 01704 570896
e-mail: secretary@sandagolfclub.co.uk
S and A, as it is known in the north, is another of the fine championship courses for which this part of the country is famed. The club has staged many important events and offers golf of the highest order.
18 holes, 6705yds, Par 72, SSS 73, Course record 62. Club membership 815.
Visitors not after 1pm Thu, after 3pm Sat, pm Sun, bank holidays; must contact club in advance; handicap certificate. **Societies** apply in advance. **Green Fees** £60 per 18 holes; £75 per 36 holes (£75 per 18 holes weekends). **Cards** ▦ ▦ **Prof** J Payne **Course Designer** James Braid **Facilities** ⊗ ⅲ ⅃ ᴸ ♥ ♀ ⅄ 🗑 ♂ ♣ **Location** 3m S off A565
·····························

Hotel ★★★ 65% Royal Clifton Hotel, Promenade, SOUTHPORT ☎ 01704 533771 111 en suite

Merseyside

Royal Birkdale

Southport

Map 07 SD31

Founded in 1889, the Royal Birkdale is considered by many to be the ultimate championship venue, having hosted every major event in the game including eight Open Championships, two Ryder Cup matches, the Walker Cup, the Curtis Cup and many amateur events. The 1st hole provides an immediate taste of what is to come, requiring a well-placed drive to avoid a bunker, water hazard and Out of Bounds to leave a reasonably clear view of the green. The 10th, the first of the inward nine is unique in that it is the only hole to display the significant fairway undulations one expects from the classic links course. The 12th is the most spectacular of the short holes on the course, and is considered by Tom Watson to be one of the best par 3s in the world; tucked away in the sand hills it continues to claim its fair share of disasters. The approach on the final hole is arguably the most recognisable in golf with the distinctive clubhouse designed to appear like an ocean cruise liner rising out of the sand hills. It's a par 5 for mere mortals, and played as a par 4 in the Open, but it will provide a memorable finish to any round of golf.

Waterloo Rd, Birkdale PR8 2LX
☎ 01704 567920 Fax 01704 562327
e-mail: secretary@royalbirkdale.com

18 holes, 6726yds, Par 72, SSS 73.
Club membership 800.
Visitors not Sat; restricted Tue, Fri, Sun; must contact in advance; handicap certificate. **Societies** must apply in advance; handicap certificates. **Green Fees** May-Sep £165 per day, £130 per round (£155 per round Sun); Mar, Apr, Oct-Nov £90 per round including soup & sandwiches (£115 Sun); Dec-Feb £70 per round soup & sandwiches (£95 Sun). **Cards** 💳 🏧 💳 💳 🔄 🔄
Prof Brian Hodgkinson **Course Designer** Hawtree
Facilities ⊗ ⦀ by arrangement. 🏌 🏌 🏌 🏌 🏌 🏌 🏌 🏌
Conf Corporate Hospitality Days available
Location 1.75m S of town centre on A565

....

Hotels

★★★ 71% Scarisbrick Hotel, Lord St, SOUTHPORT

☎ 01704 543000 88 en suite

★★★ 69% Stutelea Hotel & Leisure Club, Alexandra Rd, SOUTHPORT

☎ 01704 544220 Fax 01704 500232 20 en suite

★★★ 65% Royal Clifton Hotel, Promenade, SOUTHPORT

☎ 01704 533771 Fax 01704 500657 111 en suite

★★ 71% Balmoral Lodge Hotel, 41 Queens Rd, SOUTHPORT

☎ 01704 544298 & 530751 Fax 01704 501224
15 en suite

Southport Municipal Park Rd West PR9 0JR
☎ 01704 535286
18 holes, 6400yds, Par 70, SSS 69, Course record 67.
Location N of town centre off A565
Phone for further details

Hotel ★★★ 65% Royal Clifton Hotel, Promenade,
SOUTHPORT ☎ 01704 533771 111 en suite

Southport Old Links Moss Ln, Churchtown
PR9 7QS
☎ 01704 228207 📄 01704 505353
e-mail: secretary@solgc.freeserve.co.uk
**Seaside course with tree-lined fairways and easy
walking. One of the oldest courses in Southport, Henry
Vardon won the Leeds Cup here in 1922.**
9 holes, 6378yds, Par 72, SSS 71, Course record 68.
Club membership 450.
Visitors not Wed, Sun; advisable to contact in advance.
Societies apply in writing. **Green Fees** £25 per 18 holes
(£30 weekends). **Prof** Gary Copeman **Facilities** ⊗ ⦀ ⅃
💺 ♀ ⌂ 🏠 ♂ **Conf** Corporate Hospitality Days available
Location NW of town centre off A5267

Hotel ★★ 70% Bold Hotel, 585 Lord St, SOUTHPORT
☎ 01704 532578 23 en suite

> **If the name of the club appears in *italics*, details
> have not been confirmed for this
> edition of the guide.**

Bidston Bidston Link Rd CH44 2HR
☎ 0151 638 3412
**Parkland course, with westerly winds. Flat easy
walking.**
18 holes, 6233yds, Par 70, SSS 70.
Club membership 600.
Visitors groups of four or more must contact in advance.
Societies apply for booking form. **Green Fees** £24.50 per
18 holes (£32.50 weekends). **Prof** Mark Eagle
Facilities ⊗ ⦀ ⅃ 💺 ♀ ⌂ 🏠 ♂ **Location** M53 junct 1,
0.5m W off A551

Hotel ★★★ 69% Leasowe Castle Hotel, Leasowe Rd,
MORETON ☎ 0151 606 9191 47 en suite

Leasowe Moreton CH46 3RD
☎ 0151 677 5852 📄 0151 641 8519
**A semi-links, seaside course which has recently
undergone landscaping on the first five holes, new
mounds removing the former rather flat appearance.**
18 holes, 6151yds, Par 71, SSS 70.
Club membership 637.
Visitors not Sat, am Sun; phone professional 0151 678
5460; handicap certificate. **Societies** contact in advance.
Green Fees £27.50 (£32.50 Sun). **Cards** 🎴 💳 📇 🏧
💳 🔲 **Prof** Andrew Ayres **Course Designer** John Ball Jnr
Facilities ⊗ ⦀ ⅃ 💺 ♀ ⌂ 🏠 ♂ **Conf** Corporate
Hospitality Days available **Location** 2m W on A551

Hotel ★★★ 69% Leasowe Castle Hotel, Leasowe Rd,
MORETON ☎ 0151 606 9191 47 en suite

Wallasey Bayswater Rd CH45 8LA
☎ 0151 691 1024 📄 0151 638 8988
e-mail: wallaseygc@aol.com
**A well-established sporting links, adjacent to the Irish
Sea, with huge sand hills and many classic holes
where a player often requires good fortune. Large,
firm greens and fine views but not for the fainthearted.**
18 holes, 6503yds, Par 72, SSS 72, Course record 65.
Club membership 650.
Visitors contact one month in advance. **Societies** apply in
writing or phone. **Green Fees** not confirmed. **Cards** 🔲
Prof Mike Adams **Course Designer** Tom Morris
Facilities ⊗ ⦀ ⅃ 💺 ♀ ⌂ 🏠 ♂
Location N of town centre off A554

Hotel ★★★ 71% Grove House Hotel, Grove Rd,
WALLASEY ☎ 0151 639 3947 & 0151 630 4558
📄 0151 639 0028 14 en suite

Warren Grove Rd CH45 0JA
☎ 0151 639 8323
e-mail: golfer@warrengc.freeserve.co.uk
**Short, undulating links course with first-class greens
and prevailing winds off the sea.**
9 holes, 5854yds, Par 72, SSS 68, Course record 68.
Club membership 100.
Visitors not Sun 7-11am. **Societies** contact in advance.
Green Fees terms on application. **Prof** Mark Eagles
Facilities ⅃ 💺 🏠 ♂ **Location** N of town centre off A55∢

Hotel ★★★ 69% Leasowe Castle Hotel, Leasowe Rd,
MORETON ☎ 0151 606 9191 47 en suite

NORFOLK

BARNHAM BROOM   Map 05 TG00

Barnham Broom Hotel, Golf, Conference, Leisure Honingham Rd NR9 4DD
☎ 01603 759552 & 759393 📠 01603 758224
e-mail: golfmanager@barnham-broom.co.uk
Course meanders through the Yare valley, parkland and mature trees. Hill Course has wide fairways, heavily guarded greens and spectacular views.
Valley Course: 18 holes, 6483yds, Par 72, SSS 71.
Hill Course: 18 holes, 6495yds, Par 71, SSS 71.
Club membership 500.
Visitors contact in advance 01603 759552. Societies contact in advance 01603 759393/759552. Green Fees £30 or 18 holes (£40 weekends). Cards ▦ ▦ ▦ 🌐 ▦ ▦
Prof Ian Rollett Course Designer Frank Pennink
Facilities ⊗ ⅏ ⅃ ♥ ♀ ⅄ ☎ ⅂ ⚑ ♥ 🚃 ⚘ ⅃ Leisure hard tennis courts, heated indoor swimming pool, squash, sauna, solarium, gymnasium, three academy holes. Golf School. Squash tuition. Conf fac available Corporate Hospitality Days available Location off A47 at Honingham

Hotel ★★★ 75% Barnham Broom Hotel, Golf & Country Club, BARNHAM BROOM ☎ 01603 759393 759522
📠 01603 758224 52 en suite

BAWBURGH   Map 05 TG10

Bawburgh Glen Lodge, Marlingford Rd NR9 3LU
☎ 01603 740404 📠 01603 740403
e-mail: info@bawburgh.com
Undulating course, mixture of parkland and heathland. The main feature is a large hollow that meanders down to the River Yare creating many interesting tee and green locations. Excellent 18th hole to finish requiring a long accurate second shot to clear the lake in front of the elevated green.
18 holes, 6209yds, Par 70, SSS 70, Course record 64.
Club membership 750.
Visitors restricted weekends; contact in advance. Societies contact in advance. Green Fees terms on application.
Cards ▦ ▦ ▦ ▦ 🌐 Prof Chris Potter Course Designer John Barnard Facilities ⊗ ⅃ ♥ ♀ ⅄ ☎ ♥ 🚃
⅃ Conf fac available Corporate Hospitality Days available Location S of Royal Norfolk Showground, off A47 to Bawburgh

Hotel ★★★ 75% Park Farm Hotel, HETHERSETT
☎ 01603 810264 5 en suite 42 annexe en suite

BRANCASTER   Map 09 TF74

Royal West Norfolk PE31 8AX
☎ 01485 210223 📠 01485 210087
A fine links laid out in grand manner characterised by sleepered greens, superb cross bunkers and salt marshes. The tranquil surroundings include a harbour, the sea, farmland and marshland, inhabited by many rare birds. A great part of the year the club is cut off by tidal flooding that restricts the amount of play.
18 holes, 6428yds, Par 71, SSS 71, Course record 66.
Club membership 865.
Visitors restricted weekends & Aug; contact well in advance. Societies contact Secretary in advance.

Continued

Green Fees terms on application. Cards ▦ ▦ ▦ 🌐 🌐
Prof S Rayner Course Designer Holcombe-Ingleby
Facilities ⊗ ⅏ ♥ ♀ ⅄ ☎ ⅂ ⚘ Location off A149 in Brancaster 1m to seafront

Hotel ★★ 76% The White Horse, BRANCASTER STAITHE ☎ 01485 210262 7 en suite 8 annexe en suite

CROMER   Map 09 TG24

Royal Cromer 145 Overstrand Rd NR27 0JH
☎ 01263 512884 📠 01263 512430
e-mail: general.manager@royal-cromer.com
Challenging course with spectacular views out to sea and overlooking the town. Strong sea breezes affect the clifftop holes, the most famous being the 14th (the Lighthouse) in the shadow of a lighthouse.
18 holes, 6508yds, Par 72, SSS 72, Course record 67.
Club membership 700.
Visitors contact in advance; handicap certificate preferred. Societies contact in advance. Green Fees £45 per day (£55 weekends & bank holidays). Cards ▦ ▦ ▦ 🌐 ▦ ▦
🌐 Prof Lee Patterson Course Designer JH Taylor
Facilities ⊗ ⅏ ♥ ♀ ⅄ ☎ ⅂ ♥ 🚃 ⚘
Conf Corporate Hospitality Days available
Location 1m E on B1159

Hotel ★★ 73% Red Lion, Brook St, CROMER
☎ 01263 514964 12 en suite

DENVER   Map 05 TF60

Ryston Park PE38 0HH
☎ 01366 382133 📠 01366 383834
e-mail: rystonparkgc@fsnet.co.uk
Parkland course with two challenging par 4s to open. Water comes into play on holes 5, 6 and 7. The course is well wooded with an abundance of wildlife.
9 holes, 6310yds, Par 70, SSS 70, Course record 66.
Club membership 330.
Visitors not weekends, bank holidays; contact in advance. Societies apply in writing. Green Fees £30 per day; £20 per round. Course Designer James Braid Facilities ⊗ ⅏
♥ ♀ ⅄ ☎ ⅂ ⚘ Conf fac available Corporate Hospitality Days available Location 0.5m S on A10

Hotel ★★ 72% Castle Hotel, High St, DOWNHAM MARKET ☎ 01366 384311 12 en suite

DEREHAM   Map 09 TF91

Dereham Quebec Rd NR19 2DS
☎ 01362 695900 📠 01362 695904
e-mail: derehamgolfclub@dgolfclub.freeserve.co.uk
Parkland course.
9 holes, 6194yds, Par 71, SSS 70, Course record 64.
Club membership 480.
Visitors with member only weekends; contact in advance. Societies apply in writing or phone in advance. Green Fees not confirmed. Prof Neil Allsebrook Facilities ⊗ ⅏
♥ ♀ ⅄ ☎ ⚘ ⚘ Conf Corporate Hospitality Days available Location N of town centre off B1110

Hotel ★★★ 75% Barnham Broom Hotel, Golf & Country Club, BARNHAM BROOM ☎ 01603 759393 759522
📠 01603 758224 52 en suite

The Norfolk Golf & Country Club
Hingham Rd, Reymerston NR9 4QQ
☎ 01362 850297 ▤ 01362 850614
e-mail: ray.norfolkgolf@ukonline.co.uk
**The course meanders through more than 200 acres of
rolling Norfolk countryside, including ancient ditches,
hedges and woodland. Large greens built to USGA
specification.**
*18 holes, 6609yds, Par 72, SSS 72, Course record 69.
Club membership 500.*
Visitors contact Golf reception for advance bookings.
Societies apply in writing to the Society Organiser.
Green Fees £22 (£27 weekends). **Cards** ▦ ▦ ▦ ▦ ▦
Prof Tony Varney **Facilities** ⊗ ⅏ ⏤ ⬛ ♀ ⚴ ⬛ ⛨ ❧ ⛳
❀ ⌘ **Leisure** heated indoor swimming pool, sauna,
solarium, gymnasium, pitch & putt.
Conf fac available Corporate Hospitality Days available
Location off B1135
....
Hotel ★★★ 75% Barnham Broom Hotel, Golf & Country
Club, BARNHAM BROOM ☎ 01603 759393 759522
▤ 01603 758224 52 en suite

FAKENHAM   Map 09 TF92

Fakenham Gallow Sports Centre, The Race Course
NR21 7NY
☎ 01328 863534
9 holes, 6174yds, Par 71, SSS 70, Course record 65.
Course Designer Cotton(UK)
Phone for further details

FRITTON   Map 05 TG40

Caldecott Hall Golf Leisure Caldecott Hall,
Beccles Rd NR31 9EY
☎ 01493 488488 ▤ 01493 488561
e-mail: caldecotthall@supanet
**Facilities at Caldecott Hall include an 18-hole course
with testing dog-leg fairways, a short par 3 nine-hole
course, a floodlit driving range, and good practising
areas.**

*Main Course: 18 holes, 6685yds, Par 73, SSS 72.
Club membership 500.*
Visitors subject to availability. **Societies** arrange in
advance. **Green Fees** not confirmed. **Cards** ▦ ▦ ▦
▦ ▦ ▦ **Prof** Syer Shulver **Facilities** ⊗ ⅏ ⏤ ⬛ ♀ ⚴ ⬛
⛨ ⌘ ❀ **Leisure** heated indoor swimming pool,
fishing, gymnasium, nine-hole par 3 course.
Conf fac available Corporate Hospitality Days available
Location on A143
....
Hotel ★★★ 73% Caldecott Hall Golf Leisure,
Caldecott Hall, Beccles Rd, FRITTON ☎ 01493 488488
8 en suite

GORLESTON ON SEA   Map 05 TG50

Gorleston Warren Rd NR31 6JT
☎ 01493 661911 ▤ 01493 661911
e-mail: manager@gorlestongolfclub.co.uk
**Clifftop course, the most easterly in the British Isles.
One of the outstanding features of the course is the 7th
hole, which was rescued from cliff erosion about 20
years ago. The green, only 8yds from the cliff edge, is at
the mercy of the prevailing winds and club selection is
critical.**
*18 holes, 6391yds, Par 71, SSS 71, Course record 68.
Club membership 860.*
Visitors advisable to contact in advance; handicap
certificate; dress code. **Societies** apply in writing. **Green
Fees** £25 per 18 holes (£30 weekends & bank holidays).
Cards ▦ ▦ ▦ ▦ **Prof** Nick Brown **Course Designer**
JH Taylor **Facilities** ⊗ ⅏ ⏤ ⬛ ♀ ⚴ ⬛ ⛨ ❀ **Conf**
Corporate Hospitality Days available **Location** between
Gt Yarmouth & Lowestoft, signed from A12

GREAT YARMOUTH   Map 05 TG50

Great Yarmouth & Caister Beach House,
Caister-on-Sea NR30 5TD
☎ 01493 728699 ▤ 01493 728831
e-mail: office@caistergolf.co.uk
**A traditional links-style course played over tight and
undulating fairways. A great deal of gorse and marram
grass. The 468yd 8th (par 4) is a testing hole and the 7th
is an extremely fine short hole. A feature of the course
is a number of sleepered bunkers, a line of four
bisecting the 4th.**
*18 holes, 6330yds, Par 70, SSS 70, Course record 65.
Club membership 720.*
Visitors restricted weekends; contact in advance. **Societies**
apply in writing or phone. **Green Fees** £35 per day; £20
after 4pm (£45/£30 weekends & bank holidays). **Cards** ▦
▦ ▦ ▦ **Prof** Martyn Clarke **Course Designer** H Colt
Facilities ⊗ ⅏ ⏤ ⬛ ♀ ⚴ ⬛ ⛳ **Leisure** snooker.
Location 0.5m N off A149, at S end of Caister
....
Hotel ★★★ 71% Imperial Hotel, North Dr, GREAT
YARMOUTH ☎ 01493 842000 39 en suite

HUNSTANTON   Map 09 TF64

Hunstanton Golf Course Rd PE36 6JQ
☎ 01485 532811 ▤ 01485 532319
e-mail: hunstanton.golf@eidosnet.co.uk
**A championship links course set among some of the
natural golfing country in East Anglia. Keep out of the
numerous bunkers and master the fast greens to play to
your handicap - then you only have the wind to contend
with. Good playing conditions all year round.**
*18 holes, 6759yds, Par 72, SSS 73.
Club membership 675.*
Visitors restricted weekends; not bank holiday weekends;
play in two ball format (singles or foursomes); contact in
advance; member of golf club; handicap certificate.
Societies apply in advance. **Green Fees** £65 per day; £40
after 3pm (£75/£50 weekends). **Cards** ▦ ▦ ▦ ▦
Prof James Dodds **Course Designer** James Braid
Facilities ⊗ ⅏ by arrangement ⏤ ⬛ ♀ ⚴ ⬛ ⛨ ❧ ❀ ⌘
Location off A149 in Old Hunstanton, signed
....
Hotel ★★★ 69% Le Strange Arms Hotel, Golf Course Rd
Old Hunstanton, HUNSTANTON ☎ 01485 534411
36 en suite

Searles Leisure Resort South Beach Rd PE36 5BB
☎ 01485 536010 🖷 01485 533815
e-mail: golf@searles.co.uk
This nine-hole par 34 course is designed in a links style
and provides generous fairways with good greens. A
river runs through the 3rd and 4th holes and the par 5
8th follows the ancient reed bed to finish with the lake-
sided par 3 9th in front of the clubhouse. Good views of
Hunstanton and the surrounding countryside.

9 holes, 2773yds, Par 34.
Club membership 200.
Visitors pay & play course. **Societies** phone or e-mail in
advance. **Green Fees** 18 holes £14, 9 holes £8.50
(£15.50/£9.50 weekends & bank holidays). **Cards** 🖅 🖅
🖅 🖻 **Course Designer** Paul Searle **Facilities** ⊗ ⅏ ⬛ ⬛
🖳 ⚐ ☎ ⚐ ⛳ ✈ 🚴 ⚡ ⚑ **Leisure** hard tennis courts,
outdoor & indoor heated swimming pools, fishing, sauna,
solarium, gymnasium, bowls green. **Conf** fac available
Corporate Hospitality Days available **Location** A149 N to
Hunstanton, 2nd left at rdbt, over minirdbt, 1st left signed
Sports and Country Club

Hotel ★★★ 69% Le Strange Arms Hotel, Golf Course Rd,
Old Hunstanton, HUNSTANTON ☎ 01485 534411
36 en suite

KING'S LYNN   Map 09 TF62

Eagles 39 School Rd, Tilney All Saints PE34 4RS
☎ 01553 827147 🖷 01553 829777
e-mail: shop@eagles-golf-tennis.co.uk
Parkland course with a wide variety of trees and shrubs
lining the fairways. A large area of water comes into
play on several holes.
9 holes, 4284yds, Par 64, SSS 61, Course record 64.
Club membership 200.
Visitors dress code. **Societies** apply in writing. **Green Fees**
18 holes £13.75; 9 holes £10 (weekends £16.75/£11).
Cards 🖅 🖅 🖅 🖳 🖅 🖅 ⚐ **Prof** Nigel Pickerell
Course Designer DW Horn **Facilities** ⊗ by arrangement
⅏ ⬛ ⬛ 🖳 ⚐ ☎ ☎ ⛳ ⚡ ⚑ **Leisure** hard tennis courts,
par 3 course. **Conf** Corporate Hospitality Days available
Location off A47 at rdbt to Tilney All Saints, between
Kings Lynn & Wisbech

Hotel ⯃ Premier Travel Inn King's Lynn, Freebridge
Farm, KING'S LYNN ☎ 08701 977149 40 en suite

King's Lynn Castle Rising PE31 6BD
☎ 01553 631654 🖷 631036
e-mail: klgc@eidosnet.co.uk
The course is set among silver birch and fir woodland
and benefits, especially in the winter, from well-drained
sandy soil.

King's Lynn Golf Club

18 holes, 6609yds, Par 72, SSS 73, Course record 64.
Club membership 910.
Visitors contact in advance; handicap certificate. **Societies**
apply in writing or phone in advance. **Green Fees** £45 per
day (£50 weekends). **Prof** John Reynolds **Course**
Designer Thomas & Alliss **Facilities** ⊗ ⅏ ⬛ ⬛ 🖳 ⚐ ☎ ☎
✈ 🚴 ⚡ **Leisure** Snooker. **Conf** fac available Corporate
Hospitality Days available **Location** 4m NE off A149

Hotel ★★★ 70% Knights Hill Hotel, Knights Hill Village,
South Wootton, KING'S LYNN ☎ 01553 675566
43 en suite 18 annexe en suite

MATTISHALL   Map 09 TG01

Mattishall South Green NR20 3JZ
☎ 01362 850111
9 holes, 3300 metres, Par 72, SSS 69.
Course Designer B Todd **Location** 0.75m S of Mattishall
church
Phone for further details

Hotel ★★★ 75% Barnham Broom Hotel, Golf & Country
Club, BARNHAM BROOM ☎ 01603 759393 759522
🖷 01603 758224 52 en suite

MIDDLETON   Map 09 TF61

Middleton Hall Hall Orchards PE32 1RH
☎ 01553 841800 & 841801 🖷 01553 841800
e-mail: middleton-hall@btclick.com
Natural undulations and mature specimen trees offer a
most attractive environment for golf. The
architecturally designed course provides a challenge for
the competent golfer; there is also a covered floodlit
driving range and practice putting green.
18 holes, 5756yds, Par 71, SSS 68, Course record 70.
Club membership 600.
Visitors Societies contact in advance. **Green Fees** £30 per
day; £25 per round (£35/£30 weekends & bank holidays).
Cards 🖅 🖅 🖅 ⚐ **Prof** Steve White **Course Designer**
D Scott **Facilities** ⊗ ⬛ ⬛ 🖳 ⚐ ☎ ☎ ✈ 🚴 ⚡ ⚑ **Conf**
Corporate Hospitality Days available **Location** 4m from
King's Lynn on A47 towards Norwich

Hotel ★★★ Congham Hall Country House Hotel, Lynn
Rd, GRIMSTON ☎ 01485 600250 14 en suite

> **Looking for a new course? Always telephone
> ahead to confirm visitor arrangements.**

Continued

MUNDESLEY   Map 09 TG33

Mundesley Links Rd NR11 8ES
☎ 01263 720279 & 720095 📠 01263 720279
9 holes, 5377yds, Par 68, SSS 66, Course record 64.
Location W of village off B1159
Phone for further details

Hotel ★★ 73% Red Lion, Brook St, CROMER
☎ 01263 514964 12 en suite

NORWICH   Map 05 TG20

Costessey Park Old Costessey NR8 5AL
☎ 01603 746333 & 747085 📠 01603 746185
e-mail: cpgc@ljgroup.com
The course lies in the gently contoured Tud valley,
providing players with a number of holes that bring the
river and man-made lakes into play. The 1st hole starts
a round with a par 3 that requires an accurate drive
across the river, to land the ball on a sculptured green
beside a reed fringed lake. To end the round at the 18th
hole, you need to make a straight drive past the ruined
belfry to allow a second shot back over the river to land
the ball on a recessed green.
18 holes, 5881yds, Par 71, SSS 69, Course record 65.
Club membership 600.
Visitors not competition days; booking required for
weekends. **Societies** welcome by arrangement. **Green Fees**
£35 per day, £20 per round. **Cards** 🖮 💳 📇 📶 💷 **Prof**
Andrew Young **Facilities** ⊗ ⁗ ⅃ 🖢 💷 ♀ ⅄ 🏠 🐦 🚜 ⌀
Conf Corporate Hospitality Days available
Location 4.5m NW of Norwich. A1074 onto Longwater
Ln, left onto West End, club on left

Hotel ★★★ 68% Quality Hotel Norwich, 2 Barnard Rd,
Bowthorpe, NORWICH ☎ 01603 741161 80 en suite

De Vere Dunston Hall Hotel Ipswich Rd
NR14 8PQ
☎ 01508 470444 📠 01508 470689
e-mail: dhreception@devere-hotels.com

18 holes, 6300yds, Par 71, SSS 70, Course record 70.
Course Designer M Shaw **Location** on A140
Phone for further details

Hotel ★★★★ 70% De Vere Dunston Hall, Ipswich Rd,
NORWICH ☎ 01508 470444 130 en suite

Eaton Newmarket Rd NR4 6SF
☎ 01603 451686 & 452881 📠 01603 457539
e-mail: administrator@eatongc.co.uk
An undulating, tree-lined parkland course. Easy opening
par 5 followed by an intimidating par 3 that is well
bunkered with deep rough on both sides.

The challenging 17th hole is uphill to a small hidden
green and always needs more club than expected.

Eaton Golf Club

18 holes, 6118yds, Par 70, SSS 70, Course record 64.
Club membership 800.
Visitors restricted before 11.30am weekends; advisable to
contact in advance. **Societies** contact in advance. **Green
Fees** £35 (£45 weekends). **Cards** 🖮 💳 📇 📶 💷
Prof Mark Allen **Facilities** ⊗ ⁗ by arrangement 🖢 💷 ♀
⅄ 🏠 ⌀ **Location** 1.5m SW of city centre off A11

Hotel ★★★ 75% Park Farm Hotel, HETHERSETT
☎ 01603 810264 5 en suite 42 annexe en suite

**Marriott Sprowston Manor Hotel &
Country Club** Wroxham Rd NR7 8RP
☎ 01603 254290 📠 01603 788884
e-mail: kieron.tuck@marriotthotels.co.uk
Set in 100 acres of parkland, including an impressive
collection of oak trees that provide a backdrop to many
holes. The course benefits from USGA specification tees
and greens.
18 holes, 6543yds, Par 71, SSS 71, Course record 70.
Club membership 600.
Visitors advisable to book in advance. **Societies** contact in
advance. **Green Fees** £39 per round weekdays. **Cards** 🖮
📇 💳 🖳 📶 💷 **Prof** Guy D Ireson **Course Designer**
Ross McMurray **Facilities** ⊗ ⁗ ⅃ 🖢 💷 ♀ ⅄ 🏠 🐦 📷 🐦
🚜 ⌀ ⅃ **Leisure** heated indoor swimming pool, sauna,
gymnasium. **Conf** fac available Corporate Hospitality Days
available **Location** 4m NE from city centre on A1151

Hotel ★★★★ 75% Marriott Sprowston Manor Hotel &
Country Club, Sprowston Park, Wroxham Rd, Sprowston,
NORWICH ☎ 01603 410871 94 en suite

Royal Norwich Drayton High Rd, Hellesdon
NR6 5AH
☎ 01603 429928 & 408459 📠 01603 417945
e-mail: mail@royalnorwichgolf.co.uk
Undulating mature parkland course complimented with
gorse. Largely unchanged since the alterations carried
out by James Braid in 1924. A challenging test of golf.
18 holes, 6506yds, Par 72, SSS 72, Course record 65.
Club membership 640.
Visitors restricted weekends & bank holidays; contact in
advance. **Societies** contact in advance. **Green Fees** £40 per
day; £25 per round weekdays. **Cards** 🖮 💳 📇 📶 💷
Prof Simon Youd **Course Designer** James Braid **Facilities**
⊗ ⁗ by arrangement 🖢 💷 ♀ ⅄ 🏠 ⌀ **Conf** Corporate
Hospitality Days available **Location** 2.5m NW of city
centre on A1067

Hotel ★★★ 68% Quality Hotel Norwich, 2 Barnard Rd,
Bowthorpe, NORWICH ☎ 01603 741161 80 en suite

Continued

Vensum Valley Hotel, Golf & Country Club Beech Av, Taverham NR8 6HP

☎ 01603 261012 ▤ 01603 261664
mail: enqs@wensumvalleyhotel.co.uk

picturesque course situated on the side of a valley.
he greens in particular are very undulating and
lways give the average golfer a testing time. The 12th
ole from a raised tee provides a blind and windy tee
ot and a very sloping green.

*alley Course: 18 holes, 6172yds, Par 72, SSS 70,
ourse record 72.
Vensum Course: 18 holes, Par 71, SSS 69.
lub membership 900.*

isitors advisable to book tee times at weekends. **Societies**
ply in writing or phone. **Green Fees** £20 per day inc £6
eal voucher. Twilight £12. **Cards** ▦ ▬ ▭ ▦
rof Peter Whittle **Course Designer** B Todd **Facilities** ⊗
▮ ▮ ▮ ♀ ⚑ ⛳ 🏳 ⚲ ⚬ ℓ **Leisure** heated
door swimming pool, fishing, sauna, solarium,
ymnasium. **Conf** fac available Corporate
ospitality Days available **Location** 5m N of Norwich off
1067

Hotel ★★ 67% Wensum Valley Hotel Golf & Country
lub, Beech Av, Taverham, NORWICH ☎ 01603 261012
4 en suite

HERINGHAM   Map 09 TG14

heringham Weybourne Rd NR26 8HG
☎ 01263 823488 ▤ 01263 825189
mail: info@sheringhamgolfclub.co.uk

he course is laid out along a rolling, gorse-clad cliff
om where the sea is visible on every hole. The par 4
oles are outstanding with a fine view along the cliffs
om the 5th tee.

*8 holes, 6456yds, Par 70, SSS 71, Course record 64.
lub membership 760.*

isitors restricted weekends; contact in advance; handicap
rtificate. **Societies** book by writing or phone. **Green Fees**
rms on application. **Prof** MW Jubb **Course Designer**
om Dunn **Facilities** ⊗ ▮ ▮ ▮ ♀ ⚑ 🏠 ⛳ ⚬
ocation W of town centre on A149

otel ★★ 71% Beaumaris Hotel, South St,
HERINGHAM ☎ 01263 822370 21 en suite

WAFFHAM   Map 05 TF80

waffham Cley Rd PE37 8AE
☎ 01760 721621 (secretary) ▤ 01760 721621
mail: swaffamgc@supanet.com

8 holes, 6544yds, Par 71, SSS 71.

ourse Designer Jonathan Gaunt **Location** 1.5m SW of
wn centre

hone for further details

otel ★★★ 67% George Hotel, Station Rd, SWAFFHAM
☎ 01760 721238 29 en suite

HETFORD   Map 05 TL88

eltwell Thor Ave, Feltwell IP26 4AY
☎ 01842 827644 ▤ 01842 827644
mail: secretary@feltwellgolfclub.f9.co.uk

spite of being an inland links, this nine-hole course is
ll open and windy.

*holes, 6488yds, Par 72, SSS 71, Course record 71.
lub membership 400.*

Visitors dress code; golf shoes to be worn. **Societies** apply
in writing or phone in advance. **Green Fees** £16 per day
(£25 weekends & bank holidays). **Prof** Christian Puttock
Facilities ⊗ ▮ ▮ ▮ ♀ (closed Mon) ⚑ 🏠 ⚬
Conf Corporate Hospitality Days available
Location on B1112 next to RAF Feltwell

Hotel ★★ 65% The Thomas Paine Hotel, White Hart St,
THETFORD ☎ 01842 755631 13 en suite

Thetford Brandon Rd IP24 3NE

☎ 01842 752169 ▤ 01842 766212
e-mail: sally@thetfordgolfclub.co.uk

**The course has a good pedigree. It was laid out by the
fine golfer CH Mayo, later altered by James Braid and
then again altered by another famous course designer,
Mackenzie Ross. It is a testing heathland course with a
particularly stiff finish.**

*18 holes, 6849yds, Par 72, SSS 73, Course record 66.
Club membership 750.*

Visitors with member only weekends & bank holidays;
booking advisable; handicap certificate. **Societies** Wed-Fri,
contact in advance. **Green Fees** £40 per day, £30 per
round. **Cards** ▦ ▬ ▭ ▦ 🗎 **Prof** Gary Kitley **Course
Designer** James Braid **Facilities** ⊗ ▮ ▮ ▮ ♀ ⚑ 🏠 ⛳ ⚬
Leisure short game area. **Location** 2m W of Thetford on
B1107

Hotel ★★ 65% The Thomas Paine Hotel, White Hart St,
THETFORD ☎ 01842 755631 13 en suite

WATTON   Map 05 TF90

Richmond Park Saham Rd IP25 6EA

☎ 01953 881803 ▤ 01953 881817
e-mail: info@richmondpark.co.uk

**Compact parkland course with mature and young trees
set around the Little Wissey river and spread over 100
acres of Norfolk countryside. The river and other water
hazards create an interesting but not daunting
challenge.**

*18 holes, 6258yds, Par 71, SSS 70, Course record 69.
Club membership 600.*

Societies contact in advance. **Green Fees** terms on
application. **Cards** ▦ ▬ ▭ ▦ 🗎 **Prof** Alan
Hemsley **Course Designer** D Jessup, D Scott **Facilities** ⊗
▮ ▮ ▮ ♀ ⚑ 🏠 ⛳ 🏳 ⚬ ℓ **Leisure** gymnasium.
Conf Corporate Hospitality Days available
Location 500yds NW of town centre

Hotel ★★★ 67% George Hotel, Station Rd, SWAFFHAM
☎ 01760 721238 29 en suite

Continued

WESTON LONGVILLE Map 09 TG11

Weston Park NR9 5JW

01603 872363 01603 873040
e-mail: golf@weston-park.co.uk

Superb, challenging course, set in 200 acres of magnificent, mature woodland and parkland.

18 holes, 6648yds, Par 72, SSS 72, Course record 68.
Club membership 550.

Visitors phone for tee times 01603 872998. **Societies** phone for prices & tee times. **Green Fees** £35 per 18 holes (£45 weekends). **Cards** **Prof** Michael Few **Course Designer** Golf Technology **Facilities** **Leisure** hard tennis courts, croquet lawn. **Conf** fac available Corporate Hospitality Days available
Location brown tourist signs off A1067 or A47

Hotel ★★★ 68% Quality Hotel Norwich, 2 Barnard Rd, Bowthorpe, NORWICH 01603 741161 80 en suite

WEST RUNTON Map 09 TG14

Links Country Park Hotel & Golf Club

NR27 9QH
01263 838215 01263 838264
e-mail: sales@links-hotel.co.uk

Parkland course 500yds from the sea, with superb views overlooking West Runton. The hotel offers extensive leisure facilities.

9 holes, 4842yds, Par 66, SSS 64.
Club membership 300.

Visitors restricted weekends. **Societies** phone in advance. **Green Fees** terms on application. **Cards** **Prof** Nick Catchpole **Course Designer** JH Taylor **Facilities** **Leisure** hard tennis courts, heated indoor swimming pool, sauna, solarium, gymnasium. **Location** S of village off A149

Hotel ★★ 71% Beaumaris Hotel, South St, SHERINGHAM 01263 822370 21 en suite

NORTHAMPTONSHIRE

CHACOMBE Map 04 SP44

Cherwell Edge OX17 2EN

01295 711591 01295 713674
e-mail: enquiries@cherwelledgegolfclub.co.uk

Parkland course over chalk giving good drainage. The back nine is short and tight with mature trees. The front nine is longer and more open. The course is well bunkered with three holes where water can catch the wayward golfer.

Continued

18 holes, 6092yds, Par 70, SSS 69, Course record 64.
Club membership 500.

Visitors restricted weekends; golf shoes to be worn; dress code. **Societies** apply in advance. **Green Fees** Mon-Thu £20 per 18 holes (£25 weekends). **Cards** **Prof** Jason Newman **Course Designer** R Davies **Facilities** **Conf** fac available Corporate Hospitality Days available **Location** M40 junct 11, 0.5m S off B4525, 2m from Banbury

Hotel ★★★ 71% Whately Hall, Banbury Cross, BANBURY 0870 400 8104 69 en suite

COLD ASHBY Map 04 SP67

Cold Ashby Stanford Rd NN6 6EP

01604 740548 01604 740548
e-mail: coldashby.golfclub@virgin.net

Undulating parkland course, nicely matured, with superb views. The 27 holes consist of three loops of nine, which can be interlinked with each other. All three loops have their own challenge and any combination of two loops will give an excellent course. The start of the Elkington loop offers five holes of scenic beauty and testing golf and the 3rd on the Winwick loop is a 200yd par 3 from a magnificent plateau tee.

Ashby-Elkington: 18 holes, 6308yds, Par 72, SSS 71, Course record 68.
Elkington-Winwick: 18 holes, 6293yds, Par 70, SSS 71, Course record 69.
Winwick-Ashby: 18 holes, 6047yds, Par 70, SSS 70, Course record 65.
Club membership 600.

Visitors book start time at weekends. **Societies** contact in advance. **Green Fees** £17 per round (£20 weekends). **Cards** **Prof** Shane Rose **Course Designer** David Croxton **Facilities** **Conf** fac available Corporate Hospitality Days available **Location** M1 junct 18 or A14 junct 1

Hotel Hotel Ibis Rugby East, Parklands, CRICK 01788 824331 111 en suite

COLLINGTREE Map 04 SP75

Collingtree Park Windingbrook Ln NN4 0XN

01604 700000 & 701202 01604 702600
e-mail: info@collingtreeparkgolf.com

An 18-hole resort course designed by former US and British Open champion Johnny Miller. The American-style course has water hazards on 10 holes with a spectacular par 5 18th Island Green. The Golf Academy includes a driving range, practice holes and indoor video teaching room.

Continued

18 holes, 6776yds, Par 72, SSS 72, Course record 66.
Club membership 660.
Visitors contact in advance; handicap certificate. **Societies** contact in advance. **Green Fees** terms on application. **Cards** 🔲🔲🔲🔲🔲🔲 **Prof** G Pook, A Carter **Course Designer** Johnny Miller **Facilities** ⊗ ℍ ⅃ 🍴 ♥ ♀ ⚑ 🏌 ⚐ ⚒ **Leisure** fishing, three-hole academy, indoor teaching room. **Conf** fac available Corporate Hospitality Days available **Location** M1 junct 15, on A508 to Northampton

....

Hotel ★★★★ 70% Northampton Marriott Hotel, Eagle Dr, NORTHAMPTON
☎ 01604 768700 120 en suite

CORBY
Map 04 SP88

Corby Public Stamford Rd, Weldon NN17 3JH
☎ 01536 260756 📄 01536 260756
Municipal course laid out on made-up quarry ground and open to prevailing wind. Played by Priors Hall Club. A real treasure and good value for money.
18 holes, 6677yds, Par 72, SSS 72, Course record 68.
Club membership 600.
Visitors advisable to book in advance. **Societies** contact in advance. **Green Fees** £12 for 18 holes (£15.50 weekends). **Cards** 🔲🔲🔲🔲🔲 **Prof** Jeff Bradbrook **Course Designer** F Hawtree **Facilities** ⊗ ℍ ⅃ ♥ ♀ 🍴 🏌 ⚑ ⚒ **Location** 4m NE on A43

....

Inn ♦♦ Raven Hotel, Rockingham Rd, CORBY
☎ 01536 202313 17 rms (5 en suite)

Collingtree Park Golf Course

Collingtree Park Golf Course was opened in 1990 by designer and former British & US Open Champion, Mr Johnny Miller.

This championship golf course is the first Johnny Miller "Signature" Course in the United Kingdom. Johnny Miller Design transformed the lush 275-acre property into a course that reflects the best of both American and British design concepts. The signature hole is the finishing 18th with a stunning island green, said to be the first of its kind in England.

The undulating American-style fairways and sloping greens are subtly shaped to reward good shots from top professionals and novices alike. Water is also a key feature, coming into play no less than 10 holes and creating hazards that challenge any handicap or reputation.

You too can enjoy playing one of the country's most elite golf courses and take up the incredible Johnny Miller experience.

For more information, please call on 01604 700 000 or visit our website at www.collingtreeparkgolf.com

DAVENTRY
Map 04 SP56

Daventry & District Norton Rd NN11 2LS
☎ 01327 702829
A challenging hilly course with splendid views, which requires a certain amount of accuracy. Some narrow fairways sharpen the skills off the tee.
9 holes, 5812yds, Par 69, SSS 68, Course record 62.
Club membership 350.
Visitors not before 11.30am Sun. **Societies** contact the club secretary. **Green Fees** terms on application.
Facilities ♥ ♀ ⅃ 🍴 **Location** 0.5m E

....

Hotel ★★★★ 63% The Daventry Hotel, Sedgemoor Way, DAVENTRY ☎ 01327 307000 138 en suite

FARTHINGSTONE
Map 04 SP65

Farthingstone Hotel & Golf Course
NN12 8HA
☎ 01327 361291 📄 01327 361645
e-mail: interest@farthingstone.co.uk
A mature and challenging course set in picturesque countryside.

18 holes, 6299yds, Par 70, SSS 70, Course record 68.
Club membership 350.
Visitors contact in advance. **Societies** contact in advance. **Green Fees** terms on application. **Cards** 🔲🔲🔲🔲🔲 **Prof** Luke Brockway **Course Designer** Don Donaldson **Facilities** ⊗ ℍ ⅃ ♥ ♀ 🍴 🏌 ⚑ 🏓 ⚒ **Leisure** squash, Snooker room. **Conf** fac available Corporate Hospitality Days available
Location M1 junct 16, W near Farthingstone

....

Hotel ⭐ Premier Travel Inn Daventry, High St, WEEDON ☎ 0870 9906364 46 en suite

HELLIDON
Map 04 SP55

Hellidon Lakes Hotel & Country Club
NN11 6GG
☎ 01327 262550 📄 01327 262559
e-mail: hellidon@marstonhotels.com
A total 27 holes of interesting and challenging golf set in rolling countryside, designed by David Snell.
18 holes, 6691yds, Par 72, SSS 72.
Club membership 300.
Visitors 18-hole course contact in advance; handicap certificate at weekends; 9 hole open to beginners. **Societies** phone in advance. **Green Fees** not confirmed. **Cards** 🔲🔲🔲🔲🔲🔲 **Prof** Joe Kingstone **Course Designer** D Snell **Facilities** ⊗ ℍ ⅃ ♥ ♀ ⚑ 🍴 🏓 🏌 ⚒ **Leisure** hard tennis courts, heated indoor swimming pool, fishing, solarium, gymnasium, golf simulator, ten pin bowling. **Conf** fac available Corporate

Continued

Hospitality Days available **Location** off A361 into Hellidon, 2nd right

....

Hotel ★★★★ 76% Hellidon Lakes, HELLIDON
☎ 01327 262550 110 en suite

KETTERING   Map 04 SP87

Kettering Headlands NN15 6XA
☎ 01536 511104 📄 01536 511104
e-mail: secretary@kettering-golf.co.uk
A mature woodland course with gentle slopes.
18 holes, 6081yds, Par 69, SSS 69, Course record 63.
Club membership 700.
Visitors with member only weekends & bank holidays.
Societies Wed, Fri, apply in writing. **Green Fees** £29 per round. **Cards** 🔲 🔲 **Prof** Kevin Theobald **Course Designer** Tom Morris **Facilities** ⊗ 🏂 ▟ ▆ ⌣ ▵ 🏠 ⚐ ⚙
Conf Corporate Hospitality Days available
Location S of town centre

....

Pytchley Golf Lodge Kettering Rd, Pytchley NN14 1EY
☎ 01536 511527 📄 01536 519113
Nine-hole pay and play course, designed with complete beginner in mind, but still challenging for better handicap players.
9 holes, 2574yds, Par 34, SSS 65, Course record 70.
Club membership 300.
Visitors pay & play **Societies** phone in advance. **Green Fees** not confirmed. **Prof** Peter Machin **Course Designer** Roger Griffiths Associates **Facilities** ⊗ 🏂 ▟ ▆ ⌣ ▵ 🏠 ⚐ ⚙ ▌ **Location** A14 junct 9, A509 towards Kettering & tourist signs

....

Hotel ★★★★ 76% Kettering Park Hotel & Spa, Kettering Parkway, KETTERING ☎ 01536 416666 119 en suite

NORTHAMPTON   Map 04 SP76

Brampton Heath Sandy Ln, Church Brampton NN6 8AX
☎ 01604 843939 📄 01604 843885
e-mail: slawrence@bhgc.co.uk
18 holes, 6366yds, Par 71, SSS 70, Course record 66.
Course Designer D Snell **Location** signed off A5199 2m N of Kingsthorpe
Phone for further details

....

Hotel ★★★ 72% Lime Trees Hotel, 8 Langham Place, Barrack Rd, NORTHAMPTON ☎ 01604 632188 20 rms (10 en suite) 7 annexe rms

....

Delapre Golf Complex Eagle Dr, Nene Valley Way NN4 7DU
☎ 01604 764036 📄 01604 706378
e-mail: delapre@btinternet.com
Rolling parkland course, part of a municipal golf complex, which includes two nine-hole par 3 courses, pitch and putt, and a 40-bay floodlit driving range.
The Oaks: 18 holes, 6269yds, Par 70, SSS 70, Course record 66.
Hardingstone Course: 9 holes, 2109yds, Par 32, SSS 32.
Club membership 500.
Visitors booking advised for weekends. **Societies** must book & pay full green fees two weeks in advance. **Green**

Fees not confirmed. **Cards** 🔲 🔲 🔲 🔲 ⚙ **Prof** John Cuddihy **Course Designer** John Jacobs, John Corby **Facilities** ⊗ 🏂 🖳 ▟ ▆ ⌣ ▵ 🏠 ⚐ ▌ **Conf** Corporate Hospitality Days available **Location** M1 junct 15, 3m on A508/A45

....

Hotel ★★★ 65% Quality Hotel Northampton, Ashley Way, Weston Favell, NORTHAMPTON ☎ 01604 739955 33 en suite 38 annexe en suite

Kingsthorpe Kingsley Rd NN2 7BU
☎ 01604 710610 📄 01604 710610
e-mail: secretary@kingsthorpe-golf.co.uk
A compact, undulating parkland course set within the town boundary. Not a long course but the undulating terrain provides a suitable challenge for golfers of all standards. While not a hilly course, the valley that runs through it ensures plenty of sloping lies. The 18th hole is claimed to be the longest 400yds in the county when played into wind and is among the finest finishing holes in the area. New clubhouse.
18 holes, 5903yds, Par 69, SSS 69, Course record 63.
Club membership 650.
Visitors with member only weekends; contact in advance. **Societies** contact in advance. **Green Fees** £25 per day (weekdays only). **Cards** 🔲 🔲 🔲 **Prof** Paul Armstrong **Course Designer** Mr Alison, H Colt **Facilities** ⊗ 🏂 🖳 ▟ ▆ ⌣ ▵ 🏠 ⚙ **Conf** fac available Corporate Hospitality Days available **Location** N of town centre on A5095 between racecourse & Kingsthorpe

....

Hotel ★★★ 65% Quality Hotel Northampton, Ashley Way, Weston Favell, NORTHAMPTON ☎ 01604 739955 33 en suite 38 annexe en suite

Northampton Harlestone NN7 4EF
☎ 01604 845155 📄 01604 820262
e-mail: golf@northamptongolfclub.co.uk
Parkland course with water in play on three holes.
18 holes, 6615yds, Par 72, SSS 72, Course record 63.
Club membership 750.
Visitors not Wed; with member only weekends; contact in advance; handicap certificate. **Societies** contact in advance. **Green Fees** not confirmed. **Cards** 🔲 🔲 🔲 🔲 🔲 ⚙ **Prof** Barry Randall **Course Designer** Sinclair Steel **Facilities** ▵ 🏠 ⚙ **Conf** Corporate Hospitality Days available **Location** NW of town centre on A428

....

Hotel ★★★ 72% Lime Trees Hotel, 8 Langham Place, Barrack Rd, NORTHAMPTON ☎ 01604 632188 20 rms (10 en suite) 7 annexe rms

Northamptonshire County Golf Ln, Church Brampton NN6 8AZ
☎ 01604 843025 📄 01604 843463
e-mail: secretary@countrygolfclub.org.uk
A fine, traditional championship course situated on undulating heathland with areas of gorse, heather and extensive coniferous and deciduous woodland. A river and a railway line pass through the course and there is a great variety of holes.
18 holes, 6505yds, Par 70, SSS 72, Course record 65.
Club membership 750.
Visitors not bank holidays, restricted weekends; must contact in advance; handicap certificate. **Societies** Wed, Thu, must contact in advance. **Green Fees** £60 per 36 holes, £50 per 27 holes, £40 per 18 holes. **Prof** Tim Rouse **Course Designer** HS Colt **Facilities** ⊗ 🏂 🖳 ▟ ▆ ⌣ ▵ 🏠

Continued   *Continued*

🏌 ♿ 𝒞 ℐ **Conf** Corporate Hospitality Days available
Location 5m NW of Northampton off A5199

....

Hotel ★★★ 65% Quality Hotel Northampton, Ashley
Way, Weston Favell, NORTHAMPTON ☎ 01604 739955
3 en suite 38 annexe en suite

Overstone Park Billing Ln NN6 0AP
☎ 01604 647666 📄 01604 642635
e-mail: steph@overstonepark.co.uk
18 holes, 6602yds, Par 72, SSS 72, Course record 69.
Course Designer Donald Steel **Location** M1 junct 15,
A45 to Billing Aquadrome turn off, course 2m off A5076
at Billing Way
Phone for further details

Hotel ★★★ 72% Lime Trees Hotel, 8 Langham Place,
Barrack Rd, NORTHAMPTON ☎ 01604 632188 20 rms
10 en suite) 7 annexe rms

OUNDLE   Map 04 TL08

Oundle Benefield Rd PE8 4EZ
☎ 01832 273267 (gen manager), 01832 272273 (pro)
📄 01832 273267
e-mail: office@oundlegolfclub.com
Undulating parkland course set in pleasant countryside.
A stream running through course in play on nine holes.
Small greens demand careful placement from tees and
accurate iron play.
18 holes, 6265yds, Par 72, SSS 70, Course record 63.
Club membership 600.
Visitors with member only before 10.30am weekends;
Ladies Day Tue; must contact in advance. **Societies**
weekdays, apply in advance. **Green Fees** £34 per day;
£25.50 per round (£44 per day/round weekends). **Cards**
🟦 🟥 🟦 📵 📵 **Prof** Richard Keys **Facilities** ⊗ ⅏ 🏌 💺
👌 🍴 🏠 🍽 ♿ **Leisure** Short game practice area.
Conf Corporate Hospitality Days available
Location 1m W on A427

....

Inn ♦♦ Raven Hotel, Rockingham Rd, CORBY
☎ 01536 202313 17 rms (5 en suite)

STAVERTON   Map 04 SP56

Staverton Park Staverton Park NN11 6JT
☎ 01327 302000
18 holes, 6661yds, Par 71, SSS 72, Course record 65.
Course Designer Cmdr John Harris **Location** 0.75m NE
on A425
Phone for further details

....

Hotel ★★★★ 63% The Daventry Hotel, Sedgemoor Way,
DAVENTRY ☎ 01327 307000 138 en suite

WELLINGBOROUGH   Map 04 SP86

Rushden Kimbolton Rd, Chelveston NN9 6AN
☎ 01933 418511 📄 01933 418511
Parkland course with brook running through the
middle.
10 holes, 6335yds, Par 71, SSS 70, Course record 68.
Club membership 400.
Visitors not pm Wed; with member only weekends.
Societies phone in advance. **Green Fees** not confirmed.
Facilities ⊗ ⅏ 🏌 💺 💺 ♿ **Location** 6m E of
Wellingborough off B645

....

Hotel ⌂ Travelodge Wellingborough, Saunders Lodge,
RUSHDEN ☎ 08700 850 950 40 en suite

Wellingborough Great Harrowden Hall NN9 5AD
☎ 01933 677234 📄 01933 679379
e-mail: info@wellingboroughgolfclub.org
**An undulating parkland course with many trees. The
514yd 14th is a testing hole. The clubhouse is a stately
home and the 18th is the signature hole.**

18 holes, 6651yds, Par 72, SSS 72, Course record 68.
Club membership 820.
Visitors not 9am-2.30pm Tue, weekends, bank holidays.
Societies apply in writing. **Green Fees** £48. **Prof** David
Clifford **Course Designer** Hawtree **Facilities** ⊗ ⅏ 🏌 💺 💺
👌 🍴 🏠 🍽 ♿ **Leisure** outdoor swimming pool.
Conf fac available Corporate Hospitality Days available
Location 2m N of Wellingborough on A509

....

Hotel ⌂ Travelodge Wellingborough, Saunders Lodge,
RUSHDEN ☎ 08700 850 950 40 en suite

WHITTLEBURY   Map 04 SP64

Whittlebury Park Golf & Country Club
NN12 8WP
☎ 01327 858092 📄 01327 850001
e-mail: penny@whittlebury.com
**The 36 holes incorporate three loops of tournament-
standard nines plus a short course. The 1905 course is a
reconstruction of the original parkland course built at
the turn of the century, the Royal Whittlewood is a
lakeland course playing around copses and the Grand
Prix, next to Silverstone Circuit, has a strong links feel
playing over gently undulating grassland with
challenging lake features.**

Grand Prix: 9 holes, 3339yds, Par 36, SSS 36.
Royal Whittlewood: 9 holes, 3323yds, Par 36, SSS 36.
1905: 9 holes, 3256yds, Par 36, SSS 36.
Club membership 400.
Visitors contact in advance. **Societies** phone 01327 858092
(ext 227) in advance. **Green Fees** terms on application.
Cards 🟦 🟥 🟦 📵 **Course Designer** Cameron Sinclair
Facilities ⊗ 💺 💺 🍴 🏠 🍽 🍽 👌 🏌 🟦 ℐ 𝒞 ℐ
Location M1 junct 15a, on A413 Buckingham road

Continued

Hotel ★★★ 65% Buckingham Beales Best Western Hotel, Buckingham Ring Rd, BUCKINGHAM ☎ 01280 822622 70 en suite

NORTHUMBERLAND

ALLENDALE   Map 12 NY85

Allendale High Studdon, Allenheads Rd NE47 9DH
☎ 01434 345371
e-mail: rudi@waitrose.com
Challenging and hilly parkland course set 1000ft above sea level with superb views of Tynedale. New clubhouse.
9 holes, 4541yds, Par 66, SSS 62, Course record 69.
Club membership 130.
Visitors not before 3pm Aug bank holiday, not am bank holidays. **Societies** apply to Secretary. **Green Fees** £12 per day (£15 weekends), half-price after 6pm. **Facilities** ⊗ by arrangement ♥ ⚘ **Conf** Corporate Hospitality Days available **Location** 1m S of Allendale on B6295

Hotel ★★★ 68% Beaumont Hotel, Beaumont St, HEXHAM ☎ 01434 602331 25 en suite

ALNMOUTH   Map 12 NU21

Alnmouth Foxton Hall NE66 3BE
☎ 01665 830231 ▤ 01665 830922
e-mail: secretary@alnmouthgolfclub.com
The original course, situated on the Northumberland coast, was established in 1869, being the fourth oldest in England. The existing course, created in 1930, provides a testing and enjoyable challenge.

18 holes, 6429yds, Par 71, SSS 71, Course record 64.
Club membership 800.
Visitors not Fri, Sat **Societies** Mon-Thu, Sun. **Green Fees** £33 per day; £27.50 per round (£35 per round weekends). **Cards** ▦ ▨ ▧ ▨ **Prof** Linzi Hardy **Course Designer** H S Colt **Facilities** ⊗ ⅏ ⓫ ♥ ♀ ⚘ ⌂ ⊟ ♣ ♂ **Leisure** snooker room. **Conf** Corporate Hospitality Days available **Location** 1m NE of Alnmouth

Alnmouth Village Marine Rd NE66 2RZ
☎ 01665 830370
e-mail: golf@alnmouth-village.fsnet.co.uk
Seaside course with part coastal view.
9 holes, 6090yds, Par 70, SSS 70, Course record 63.
Club membership 480.
Visitors not before 11am competition days. **Societies** contact in advance. **Green Fees** 18 holes £16 (weekends & bank holidays £20). Weekly ticket £60.
Course Designer Mungo Park **Facilities** ⊗ ⅏ ⓫ ♥ ♀ ⚘ **Location** E of village

ALNWICK   Map 12 NU11

Alnwick Swansfield Park NE66 1AR
☎ 01665 602632
e-mail: mail@alnwickgolfclub.co.uk
A mixture of mature parkland, open grassland and gorse bushes with panoramic views out to sea 5m away. Offers a fair test of golf.
18 holes, 6284yds, Par 70, SSS 70, Course record 66.
Club membership 400.
Visitors not before 10am weekends, restricted competition days. **Societies** contact secretary in advance. **Green Fees** £25 per day; £20 per round. **Cards** ▦ ▨ ▨ **Course Designer** Rochester, Rae **Facilities** ⊗ ⅏ ⓫ ♥ ♀ ⚘ ♣ **Leisure** small practice area. **Location** S of town centre off B6341

Hotel ★★★ 59% White Swan Hotel, Bondgate Within, ALNWICK ☎ 01665 602109 56 en suite

BAMBURGH   Map 12 NU13

Bamburgh Castle The Club House, 40 The Wynding NE69 7DE
☎ 01668 214378 (club) & 214321 (sec) ▤ 01668 214607
e-mail: bamburghcastlegolfclub@hotmail.com
Superb coastal course with excellent greens that are both fast and true; natural hazards of heather and whin bushes abound. Magnificent views of the Farne Islands, Holy Island, Lindisfarne Castle, Bamburgh Castle and the Cheviot Hills.
18 holes, 5621yds, Par 68, SSS 67, Course record 64.
Club membership 785.
Visitors restricted weekends, bank holidays & competition days; contact in advance. **Societies** weekdays, Sun, apply in writing. **Green Fees** £45 per day, £32 per round (£50/£37 weekends). **Cards** ▦ ▨ ▨ ▨ ▨ **Course Designer** George Rochester **Facilities** ⊗ ⅏ ⓫ ♥ ♀ ⚘ ♣ **Conf** Corporate Hospitality Days available **Location** 6m E of A1 via B1341 or B1342

Hotel ★★ 69% The Lord Crewe, Front St, BAMBURGH ☎ 01668 214243 18 rms (17 en suite)

BEDLINGTON   Map 12 NZ28

Bedlingtonshire Acorn Bank NE22 6AA
☎ 01670 822457 ▤ 01670 823048
Meadowland and parkland course with easy walking. Under certain conditions the wind can be a distinct hazard.
18 holes, 6813yds, Par 73, SSS 73, Course record 64.
Club membership 800.
Visitors not before 9am weekdays, not before 10am weekends & bank holidays; book with professional. **Societies** contact the Secretary in writing or phone. **Green Fees** not confirmed. **Prof** Marcus Webb **Course Designer** Frank Pennink **Facilities** ⊗ ⅏ by arrangement ⓫ ♥ ♀ ⚘ ⌂ ♂ ♣ ♂ **Conf** Corporate Hospitality Days available **Location** 1m SW on A1068

BELFORD   Map 12 NU13

Belford South Rd NE70 7DP
☎ 01668 213232 ▤ 01668 213282
e-mail: thebelford@tiscali.co.uk
A coastland parkland course recently in new ownership. Many new trees have been added and

Continued

nine new tee boxes, allowing golfers to play each
hole from two different angles for a full 18 holes.
The course is overlooked by the 18th-century
Belford Hall and has fine views of Holy Island.
9 holes, 3227yds, Par 71, SSS 71.
Club membership 200.
Visitors not before 10am Sun. **Societies** contact in
advance. **Green Fees** £18 per day, £15 per 18 holes; £10
per 9 holes (£23/£18/£11 weekends & bank holidays).
Cards ⊞ ▦ ▦ ▦ 🔊 🎵 **Course Designer** Nigel
Williams **Facilities** ⊗ 🍴 🖥 💻 🍺 ⛳ 🏠 🛠 🏌 ♿ 🏇 ✓ ℓ
Conf Corporate Hospitality Days available
Location off A1 between Alnwick & Berwick upon Tweed

Hotel ⌂ Purdy Lodge, Adderstone Services, BELFORD
☎ 01668 213000 20 en suite

BELLINGHAM   Map 12 NY88

Bellingham Boggle Hole NE48 2DT
☎ 01434 220530 (Secretary) ▤ 01434 220160
e-mail: admin@bellinghamgolfclub.com
**This highly regarded 18-hole course lies between
Hadrian's Wall and the Scottish border. A rolling
parkland course with many natural hazards. There is
a mixture of testing par 3s, long par 5s and tricky
par 4s.**

18 holes, 6093yds, Par 70, SSS 70, Course record 65.
Club membership 500.
Visitors advisable to contact in advance, starting sheet in
operation. **Societies** contact in advance. **Green Fees** £24
per day/round (£29 per day/round weekends). **Cards** ⊞
▦ ▦ 🔊 🎵 **Course Designer** E Johnson, I Wilson
Facilities ⊗ by arrangement 🍴 by arrangement 🖥 💻 🍺
⛳ 🏇 ✓ ℓ **Location** N of village on B6320

Hotel ★★ 69% Riverdale Hall Hotel, BELLINGHAM
☎ 01434 220254 20 en suite

BERWICK-UPON-TWEED   Map 12 NT95

Berwick-upon-Tweed (Goswick) Goswick
TD15 2RW
☎ 01289 387256 ▤ 01289 387334
e-mail: goswickgc@btconnect.com
18 holes, 6686yds, Par 72, SSS 72, Course record 69.
Course Designer James Braid **Location** 6m S of Berwick
off A1
Phone for further details

Hotel ★★★ 70% Marshall Meadows Country House
Hotel, BERWICK-UPON-TWEED ☎ 01289 331133
19 en suite

Berwick-upon-Tweed (Goswick) Golf Club

Marshall Meadows Country House Hotel

Booking a tee time is always advisable.

Continued

Magdalene Fields
Magdalene Fields TD15 1NE
☎ 01289 306130 🖹 01289 306384
e-mail: mail@magdalene-fields.co.uk
Seaside course on a clifftop with natural hazards formed by bays. All holes open to winds. Testing 8th hole over bay (par 3). Scenic views to Holy Island and north to Scotland.
18 holes, 6407yds, Par 72, SSS 71, Course record 65. Club membership 350.
Visitors contact in advance for weekends. **Societies** contact in advance. **Green Fees** £20 per round (£22 weekends). **Cards** 🖃 🔳 💳 🖳 **Course Designer** Willie Park **Facilities** ⊗ ⊪ ⓑ 🖳 ♀ ♨ 🏠 �🇹 🚿 ✔ **Conf** Corporate Hospitality Days available **Location** 0.5m E of town centre

....

Hotel ★★★ ♨ 76% Tillmouth Park Country House Hotel, CORNHILL-ON-TWEED ☎ 01890 882255 12 en suite 2 annexe en suite

Blyth
New Delaval, Newsham NE24 4DB
☎ 01670 540110 (sec) & 356514 (pro) 🖹 01670 540134
e-mail: clubmanager@blythgolf.co.uk
Course built over old colliery. Parkland with water hazards. Superb greens.
18 holes, 6456yds, Par 72, SSS 71, Course record 63. Club membership 860.
Visitors with member only after 4pm & at weekends before 2pm; can book up to three days in advance. **Societies** apply in writing or phone. **Green Fees** £30 per day; £24 per round (£35/£28 per round weekends). **Cards** 🖃 🔳 🔳 💳 🖳 **Prof** Andrew Brown **Course Designer** Hamilton Stutt **Facilities** ⊗ ⊪ by arrangement ⓑ 🖳 ♀ ♨ 🏠 ✔ **Location** 1m S of town centre

....

Hotel ★★★ 71% Windsor Hotel, South Pde, WHITLEY BAY ☎ 0191 251 8888 69 en suite

Arcot Hall
NE23 7QP
☎ 0191 236 2794 🖹 0191 217 0370
e-mail: arcothall@tiscali.co.uk
A wooded parkland course, reasonably flat.
18 holes, 6380yds, Par 70, SSS 70, Course record 62. Club membership 695.
Visitors not weekends; contact in advance. **Societies** contact in advance. **Green Fees** £28 per day; £23 after 3pm in summer. **Prof** John Metcalfe **Course Designer** James Braid **Facilities** ⊗ ⊪ ⓑ 🖳 ♀ ♨ 🏠 �🇹 ✔ **Conf** fac available **Location** 2m SW off A1

....

Hotel ⓤ Innkeeper's Lodge Cramlington, Blagdon Ln, CRAMLINGTON ☎ 01670 736111 18 en suite

Dunstanburgh Castle
NE66 3XQ
☎ 01665 576562 🖹 01665 576562
e-mail: enquiries@dunstanburgh.com
Rolling links designed by James Braid, adjacent to the beautiful Embleton Bay. Historic Dunstansburgh Castle is at one end of the course and a National Trust lake and bird sanctuary at the other. Superb views.
18 holes, 6298yds, Par 70, SSS 69, Course record 69. Club membership 385.
Visitors advisable to contact in advance for weekends & holiday periods. **Societies** contact in advance. **Green Fees** £22 per day (£32 per day; £26 per round weekends & bank holidays). **Course Designer** James Braid **Facilities** ⊗ ⊪ ⓑ 🖳 ♀ ♨ 🏠 �🇹 ✔ **Conf** fac available **Location** 7m NE of Alnwick off A1

....

Hotel ★★ 71% Dunstanburgh Castle Hotel, EMBLETON ☎ 01665 576111 20 en suite

Burgham Park
NE65 8QP
☎ 01670 787898 (office) & 787978 (pro shop)
🖹 01670 787164
PGA associates designed course, making the most of the gentle rolling landscape with views to the sea and the Northumbrian hills.
18 holes, 6751yds, Par 72, SSS 72, Course record 67. Club membership 560.
Visitors contact for tee times. **Societies** contact secretary for advance booking. **Green Fees** not confirmed. **Cards** 🖃 🔳 🖳 **Prof** David Mather **Course Designer** Andrew Mair **Facilities** ⊗ ⊪ ⓑ 🖳 ♀ ♨ 🏠 �🇹 🐦 ✔ 🏌 **Leisure** par 3 course. **Location** 5m N of Morpeth, 0.5m off A1

....

Hotel ★★★ 74% Linden Hall Hotel, Health Spa & Golf Course, LONGHORSLEY ☎ 01670 500000 50 en suite

Haltwhistle
Wallend Farm CA6 7HN
☎ 016977 47367 🖹 01434 344311
18 holes, 5522yds, Par 69, SSS 67, Course record 70.
Location N on A69 past Haltwhistle on Gilsland road
Phone for further details

....

Hotel ★★★ ♨ Farlam Hall Hotel, BRAMPTON ☎ 016977 46234 11 en suite 1 annexe en suite

De Vere Slaley Hall, Golf Resort & Spa
Slaley NE47 0BX
☎ 01434 673154 🖹 01434 673152
e-mail: slaley.hall@devere-hotels.com
Measuring 7073yds from the championship tees, this Dave Thomas course incorporates forest, parkland and moorland with an abundance of lakes and streams. The challenging par 4 9th (452yds) is played over water through a narrow avenue of towering trees and dense rhododendrons. The Priestman Course designed by Neil Coles is of equal length and standard as the Hunting Course. Opened in spring 1999, it is situated in 280 acres on the western side of the estate, giving panoramic views over the Tyne valley.

Hunting Course: 18 holes, 7073yds, Par 72, SSS 74, Course record 65.

Continued

Continued

*Priestman Course: 18 holes, 7010yds, Par 72, SSS 72,
Course record 64.
Club membership 350.*
Visitors subject to availability; contact in advance.
Societies apply in writing to bookings co-ordinator, small
groups eight or less may book by phone. **Green Fees** terms
on application. **Cards** 🖃 📇 💳 📇 📇 📇 **Prof**
Gordon Robinson **Course Designer** Dave Thomas, Neil
Coles **Facilities** ⊗ ℿ ⅃ ⅃ ⅃ ⅃ ⅃ ⅃ ⅃ ⅃ ⅃ ⅃
Leisure heated indoor swimming pool, fishing, sauna,
solarium, gymnasium. **Conf** fac available
Location 8m S of Hexham off A68

Hotel ★★★★ 72% De Vere Slaley Hall, Slaley,
HEXHAM ☎ 01434 673350 139 en suite

Hexham Spital Park NE46 3RZ
☎ 01434 603072 📠 01434 601865
-mail: info@hexhamgolf.co.uk
**A very pretty, well-drained parkland course with
interesting natural contours. Exquisite views from parts
of the course of the Tyne valley below. As good a
parkland course as any in the north of England.**
*18 holes, 6294yds, Par 70, SSS 68, Course record 64.
Club membership 700.*
Visitors advance booking advisable. **Societies** weekdays,
contact in advance. **Green Fees** £30 per round (£40
weekends & bank holidays). **Cards** 🖃 📇 💳 📇 📇 📇 📇
Prof Martin Forster **Course Designer** Vardon, Caird
Facilities ⊗ ℿ ⅃ ⅃ ⅃ ⅃ ⅃ ⅃ ⅃ **Leisure**
squash, squash courts. **Conf** fac available Corporate
Hospitality Days available **Location** 1m NW on B6531

Hotel ★★★ 68% Beaumont Hotel, Beaumont St,
HEXHAM ☎ 01434 602331 25 en suite

LONGHORSLEY   Map 12 NZ19

Linden Hall NE65 8XF
☎ 01670 500011 📠 01670 500001
-mail: golf@lindenhall.co.uk
**Set within the picturesque Linden Hall Estate on a
mixture of mature woodland and parkland,
established lakes and burns provide interesting water
features to match the peaceful surroundings. This
award-winning course is a pleasure to play for all
standards of golfer.**

*18 holes, 6846yds, Par 72, SSS 73.
Club membership 350.*
Visitors book in advance. **Societies** reasonable standard of
play; dress code; prefer handicap certificates. **Green Fees**
£45 per day; £30 per round (£50/£35 weekends). **Cards**
🖃 📇 💳 📇 📇 📇 **Prof** David Curry **Course Designer**
Jonathan Gaunt **Facilities** ⊗ ℿ ⅃ ⅃ ⅃ ⅃ ⅃ ⅃ ⅃ ⅃

🛆 ⅃ ⅃ **Leisure** hard tennis courts, heated indoor
swimming pool, sauna, solarium, gymnasium. **Conf** fac
available Corporate Hospitality Days available
Location 0.5m N of village off A697

Hotel ★★★ 74% Linden Hall Hotel, Health Spa & Golf
Course, LONGHORSLEY ☎ 01670 500000 50 en suite

MATFEN   Map 12 NZ07

Matfen Hall NE20 0RH
☎ 01661 886400 📠 01661 886055
e-mail: golf@matfenhall.fsnet.co.uk
**An 18-hole parkland course set in beautiful countryside
with many natural and man-made hazards. The course
is an enjoyable test for players of all abilities but it does
incorporate challenging water features in the shape of a
large lake and a fast flowing river. The dry stone wall
presents a unique obstacle on several holes. The 4th,
9th, 12th and 14th holes are particularly testing par 4s,
the dog-leg 16th is the pick of the par 5s but Matfen's
signature hole is the long par 3 17th with its narrow
green teasingly sited just over the river.**
*18 holes, 6569yds, Par 72, SSS 71, Course record 64.
Club membership 500.*
Visitors restricted 8-11am weekends; contact in advance.
Societies phone for details. **Green Fees** not confirmed.
Cards 🖃 📇 💳 📇 📇 **Prof** John Harrison **Course
Designer** Mair, James, Gaunt **Facilities** ⊗ ℿ ⅃ ⅃ ⅃ ⅃
⅃ ⅃ ⅃ ⅃ ⅃ ⅃ **Leisure** heated indoor swimming pool,
gymnasium, nine-hole par 3 course. Leisure complex.
Conf fac available Corporate Hospitality Days available
Location off B6318

Hotel ★★★★ 76% Matfen Hall, MATFEN
☎ 01661 886500 53 en suite

MORPETH   Map 12 NZ28

Morpeth The Clubhouse NE61 2BT
☎ 01670 504942 📠 01670 504918
18 holes, 6206yds, Par 71, SSS 69, Course record 65.
Course Designer Harry Vardon **Location** S of town centre
on A197
Phone for further details

Hotel ★★★ 74% Linden Hall Hotel, Health Spa & Golf
Course, LONGHORSLEY ☎ 01670 500000 50 en suite

NEWBIGGIN-BY-THE-SEA   Map 12 NZ38

Newbiggin-by-the-Sea Prospect Place NE64 6DW
☎ 01670 817344 📠 01670 520236
Seaside-links course.
*18 holes, 6452yds, Par 72, SSS 71, Course record 65.
Club membership 590.*
Visitors not before 10am; contact clubhouse staff on
arrival. **Societies** apply in writing. **Green Fees** £20 (£25
weekends & bank holidays). **Course Designer** Willie Park
Facilities ⊗ ℿ ⅃ ⅃ ⅃ ⅃ ⅃ ⅃ **Leisure** snooker.
Conf fac available **Location** N of town centre

Hotel ★★★ 74% Linden Hall Hotel, Health Spa & Golf
Course, LONGHORSLEY ☎ 01670 500000 50 en suite

> **Prices may change during the currency of the
> Guide, please check when booking.**

Continued

PONTELAND
Map 12 NZ17

Ponteland 53 Bell Villas NE20 9BD
☎ 01661 822689 📠 01661 860077
e-mail: secretary@thepontelandgolfclub.co.uk
Open parkland course offering testing golf and good views.
18 holes, 6524yds, Par 72, SSS 71, Course record 65.
Club membership 720.
Visitors with member only Fri, weekends & bank holidays.
Societies Tue, Thu, must contact in advance. **Green Fees**
not confirmed. **Cards** ▦ **Prof** Alan Robson-Crosby
Course Designer Harry Fernie **Facilities** ⊗ ⅲ ⅊ ⚑ ⚐ ⚑ ⚑
⌂ ⚑ ⚐ ⚐ **Conf** Corporate Hospitality Days available
Location 0.5m E on A696
....
Hotel ★★★ 67% Novotel Newcastle, Ponteland Rd,
Kenton, NEWCASTLE UPON TYNE
☎ 0191 214 0303 126 en suite

PRUDHOE
Map 12 NZ06

Prudhoe Eastwood Park NE42 5DX
☎ 01661 832466 📠 01661 830710
18 holes, 5812yds, Par 69, SSS 69, Course record 60.
Location E of town centre off A695
Phone for further details
....
Hotel ★★★ 69% Gibside Hotel, Front St, WHICKHAM
☎ 0191 488 9292 45 en suite

ROTHBURY
Map 12 NU00

Rothbury Old Race Course NE65 7TR
☎ 01669 621271
Scenic, flat parkland course set alongside the River Coquet and surrounded by Simonside hills and Cragside Hall.
9 holes, 5779yds, Par 68, SSS 67, Course record 65.
Club membership 306.
Visitors weekends by arrangement. **Societies** contact
secretary D Woolley in advance 01669 630378. **Green Fees** not confirmed. **Course Designer** J Radcliffe
Facilities ⚑ ⚐ ⚑ ⚐ **Location** SW of town off B6342
....
Hotel ★★★ 74% Linden Hall Hotel, Health Spa & Golf
Course, LONGHORSLEY ☎ 01670 500000 50 en suite

SEAHOUSES
Map 12 NU23

Seahouses Beadnell Rd NE68 7XT
☎ 01665 720794 📠 01665 721994
e-mail: secretary@seahousesgolf.co.uk
Typical links course with many hazards, including the famous par 3 10th hole, Logans Loch, water hole. Recent changes to the west side of the course have created mounds on the 5th and 7th fairways and further water features. Spectacular views of the coastline from Bamburgh to Beadnell and out to the Farne Islands.
18 holes, 5542yds, Par 67, SSS 67, Course record 63.
Club membership 650.
Visitors contact in advance. **Societies** Mon-Sat, contact in
advance. **Green Fees** £25 per day; £18 per round (£30/£25
weekends & bank holidays). **Facilities** ⊗ ⅲ ⅊ ⚑ ⚐ ⚑ ⚐
Conf Corporate Hospitality Days available
Location S of village on B1340
....
Hotel ★★★ 67% Bamburgh Castle Hotel, SEAHOUSES
☎ 01665 720283 20 en suite

STOCKSFIELD
Map 12 NZ06

Stocksfield New Ridley Rd NE43 7RE
☎ 01661 843041 📠 01661 843046
e-mail: info@sgcgolf.co.uk
Challenging course: parkland (nine holes), woodland (nine holes). Some elevated greens, giving fine views, and water hazards.
18 holes, 5991yds, Par 70, SSS 69, Course record 61.
Club membership 550.
Visitors with member only am Wed & before 4pm Sat.
Societies contact in advance. **Green Fees** £24 per day; £18
per round (£30 per round Sat, £25 per round Sun). **Prof**
Shaun Cowell **Course Designer** Pennick **Facilities** ⊗ ⅲ
by arrangement ⚑ ⚐ ⚑ ⌂ ⚑ ⚐ ⚐ **Leisure** snooker.
Conf Corporate Hospitality Days available
Location 1.5m S off A695
....
Hotel ★★★ 68% Beaumont Hotel, Beaumont St,
HEXHAM ☎ 01434 602331 25 en suite

SWARLAND
Map 12 NU10

Swarland Hall Coast View NE65 9JG
☎ 01670 787010
e-mail: info@swarlandgolf
Parkland course set in mature woodland. There are seven par 4 holes in excess of 400yds.
18 holes, 6335yds, Par 72, SSS 72.
Club membership 400.
Visitors restricted competition days; advance booking
advisable. **Societies** apply in advance. **Green Fees** not
confirmed. **Cards** ▦ ▦ ▦ ▦ ▦ **Facilities** ⊗ ⅲ ⚑
⚑ ⚐ ⚑ ⌂ ⚑ ⚑ ⚐ ⚐ **Conf** Corporate Hospitality
Days available **Location** 1m W of A1
....
Hotel ★★★ 74% Linden Hall Hotel, Health Spa & Golf
Course, LONGHORSLEY ☎ 01670 500000 50 en suite

WARKWORTH
Map 12 NU20

Warkworth The Links NE65 0SW
☎ 01665 711596
Seaside links course, with good views and alternative tees for the back nine. The first hole is a very testing par 3 and skill is required to avoid the out of bounds. The course is not friendly to right-handed slicers with heather and bracken on the eastern side on the way out. The fearsome Killiecrankie Gorge is in play four times during the 18 holes, especially challenging when a north wind is blowing.
9 holes, 5986yds, Par 70, SSS 69, Course record 66.
Club membership 470.
Visitors not Tue, Sat. **Societies** contact in advance.
Green Fees £12 per day (£20 weekends & bank holidays).
Course Designer Tom Morris **Facilities** ⊗ ⚑ ⚑ ⚐ ⚑
Location 0.5m E of village off A1068

WOOLER
Map 12 NT92

Wooler Dod Law, Doddington NE71 6EA
☎ 01668 282135
Hilltop, moorland course with spectacular views over the Glendale valley. Nine greens played from 18 tees. A very challenging course when windy with one par 5 of 580yds. The course is much under used during the week so is always available.
9 holes, 6411yds, Par 72, SSS 71, Course record 69.
Club membership 300.

Continued

Visitors Societies by arrangement with secretary. **Green Fees** not confirmed. **Facilities** ⊗ by arrangement ⟆ by arrangement ⓑ by arrangement ♦ ♦ ♦ ♦ ♦
Location at Doddington on B6525

Hotel ⌂ Purdy Lodge, Adderstone Services, BELFORD ☎ 01668 213000 20 en suite

NOTTINGHAMSHIRE

CALVERTON   Map 08 SK64

Ramsdale Park Golf Centre Oxton Rd
NG14 6NU
☎ 0115 965 5600 ▤ 0115 965 4105
e-mail: info@ramsdaleparkgc.co.uk
The Seely Course is a challenging and comprehensive test for any standard of golf. A relatively flat front nine is followed by an undulating back nine that is renowned as one of the best in the county. The Lee Course is an 18-hole par 3 course which is gaining a similar reputation.
Seely Course: 18 holes, 6546yds, Par 71, SSS 71, Course record 70.
Lee Course: 18 holes, 2844yds, Par 54, SSS 54.
Club membership 400.
Visitors book up to seven days in advance. **Societies** phone for details. **Green Fees** £19.50 (weekends £25). **Cards** ▦ ▦ ▦ ▦ ▦ **Prof** Robert Macey **Course Designer** Hawtree **Facilities** ⊗ ⟆ ⓑ ♦ ♦ ♦ ♦ ♦ ♦ ♦ ♦ ♦ **Leisure** fishing. **Conf** fac available Corporate Hospitality Days available **Location** 8m NE of Nottingham off B6386

Hotel ★★★ 66% Bestwood Lodge, Bestwood Country Park, Arnold, NOTTINGHAM ☎ 0115 920 3011 39 en suite

Springwater Moor Ln NG14 6FZ
☎ 0115 965 2129 (pro shop) & 965 4946
▤ 0115 965 4957
e-mail: springwater@rapidial.co.uk
This attractive course set in rolling countryside overlooking the Trent valley offers an interesting and challenging game of golf to players of all handicaps. The 18th hole is particularly noteworthy, a 183yd par 3 over two ponds
18 holes, 6262yds, Par 71, SSS 71, Course record 68.
Club membership 440.
Visitors five-day advance booking by phone; booking available all week subject to competitions & society/corporate reservations. **Societies** apply in writing or phone for Society Pack. **Green Fees** £20 per round (£25 weekends & bank holidays). **Cards** ▦ ▦ ▦ ▦ ▦

Prof Paul Drew **Course Designer** Neil Footitt, Paul Wharmsby **Facilities** ⊗ ⟆ ⓑ ♦ ♦ ♦ ♦ ♦ ♦ ♦ ♦ ♦ **Leisure** short-game academy. **Conf** fac available Corporate Hospitality Days available
Location off A6097 to Calverton, 600yds on left

Springwater Golf Club

Hotel ★★★ 67% Westminster Hotel, 312 Mansfield Rd, Carrington, NOTTINGHAM ☎ 0115 955 5000 73 en suite

EAST LEAKE   Map 08 SK52

Rushcliffe Stocking Ln LE12 5RL
☎ 01509 852959 ▤ 01509 852688
e-mail: secretary.rushcliffegc@btopenworld.com
Hilly, tree-lined and picturesque parkland course.
18 holes, 6013yds, Par 70, SSS 69, Course record 63.
Club membership 750.
Visitors not Tue, restricted 9.30-11am, 3-4.30pm weekends & bank holidays. **Societies** apply in advance. **Green Fees** terms on application. **Prof** Chris Hall **Facilities** ⊗ ⟆ ⓑ ♦ ♦ ♦ ♦ ♦ **Location** M1 junct 24

Hotel ★★★ 76% Best Western Yew Lodge Hotel, Packington Hill, KEGWORTH, ☎ 01509 672518 98 en suite

HUCKNALL   Map 08 SK54

Leen Valley Golf Centre Wigwam Ln NG15 7TA
☎ 0115 964 2037 ▤ 0115 964 2724
e-mail: leenvalley@btinternet.com
An interesting and challenging parkland course, featuring several lakes, the River Leen and the Baker Brook. Relatively short but can test golfers of all standards.
18 holes, 6150yds, Par 72, SSS 70.
Club membership 300.
Visitors tee times can be booked in advance; advisable to book for Fri, weekends. **Societies** by arrangement. **Green Fees** £11 per round (£16 weekends). **Cards** ▦ ▦ ▦ ▦ ▦ **Prof** James Sawford **Course Designer** Tom Hodgetts **Facilities** ⊗ ⟆ ⓑ ♦ ♦ ♦ ♦ ♦ **Conf** fac available Corporate Hospitality Days available **Location** 0.5m from town centre, signs for railway station, right onto Wigwam Ln

Hotel ⌂ Premier Travel Inn Nottingham North West, Nottingham Rd, HUCKNALL ☎ 0870 9906518 35 en suite

Looking for a new course? Always telephone ahead to confirm visitor arrangements.

Continued

KEYWORTH   Map 08 SK63

Stanton on the Wolds Golf Rd, Stanton-on-the-Wolds NG12 5BH
☎ 0115 937 4885 📠 0115 937 4885
e-mail: swgc@zoom.co.uk
Parkland course, fairly flat with a stream running through four holes.
18 holes, 6369yds, Par 73, SSS 71, Course record 67.
Club membership 705.
Visitors not Tue; with member only weekends; contact in advance. Societies apply in writing. Green Fees £31 per day; £23 per round (weekdays only). Prof Nick Hernon Course Designer Tom Williamson Facilities ⊗ ⅷ by arrangement ⓛ ⬛♀⚲🏠♂ Location E side of village off A606

Hotel ⓤ Premier Travel Inn Nottingham South, Loughborough Rd, Ruddington, NOTTINGHAM ☎ 0870 9906422 42 en suite

KIRKBY IN ASHFIELD   Map 08 SK55

Notts Derby Rd NG17 7QR
☎ 01623 753225 📠 01623 753655
e-mail: nottsgolfclub@hollinwell.fsnet.co.uk
Undulating heathland championship course.
18 holes, 7103yds, Par 72, SSS 75, Course record 64.
Club membership 450.
Visitors with member only weekends & bank holidays; contact in advance; handicap certificate. Societies apply in advance. Green Fees £90 per day; £60 per round. Cards 💳 💳 💳 💳 💳 Prof Mike Bradley Course Designer Willie Park Facilities ⊗ ⅷ ⓛ ⬛♀⚲🏠⚑♣🏌♂🍴 Conf fac available Location 2m SE of Mansfield off A611

Hotel ★★★★ 70% Renaissance Derby/Nottingham Hotel, Carter Ln East, SOUTH NORMANTON ☎ 01773 812000 158 en suite

MANSFIELD   Map 08 SK56

Sherwood Forest Eakring Rd NG18 3EW
☎ 01623 627403 & 627403 📠 01623 420412
e-mail: sherwood@forest43.freeserve.co.uk
As the name suggests, the forest is the main feature of this natural heathland course with its heather, silver birch and pine trees. The homeward nine holes are particularly testing. The 11th to the 14th are notable par 4 holes on this well-bunkered course designed by the great James Braid.
18 holes, 6853yds, Par 71, SSS 74, Course record 67.
Club membership 750.
Visitors weekdays by arrangement with the golf manager. Societies by arrangement with the golf manager. Green Fees £70 per day, £50 per round (weekdays only). Cards 💳 💳 💳 💳 💳 Prof Ken Hall Course Designer WS Colt, James Braid Facilities ⊗ ⅷ ⓛ ⬛♀⚲🏠♣ 🏌♂ Leisure snooker. Conf fac available Corporate Hospitality Days available Location E of Mansfield

Hotel ★★ 68% Pine Lodge Hotel, 281-283 Nottingham Rd, MANSFIELD ☎ 01623 622308 20 en suite

NEWARK-ON-TRENT   Map 08 SK75

Newark Coddington NG24 2QX
☎ 01636 626282 📠 01636 626497
Wooded, parkland course in a secluded position with easy walking.
18 holes, 6458yds, Par 71, SSS 71, Course record 66.
Club membership 650.
Visitors not Tue (Ladies Day); contact in advance; handicap certificate. Societies contact in advance. Green Fees £33 per day, £27 per round (£33 per round weekend & bank holidays). Prof P A Lockley Course Designer T Williamson Facilities ⊗ ⅷ ⓛ ⬛♀⚲🏠♂ Leisure snooker. Conf Corporate Hospitality Days available Location 4m E of Newark on Sleaford road

Hotel ★★★ 71% The Grange Hotel, 73 London Rd, NEWARK ☎ 01636 703399 10 en suite 9 annexe en suite

NOTTINGHAM   Map 08 SK53

Beeston Fields Old Dr, Wollaton Rd, Beeston NG9 3DD
☎ 0115 925 7062 📠 0115 925 4280
e-mail: beestonfieldsgolfclub@supanet.com
Parkland course with sandy subsoil and wide, tree-lined fairways. The par 3 14th has an elevated tee and a small bunker-guarded green.

18 holes, 6402yds, Par 71, SSS 71, Course record 64.
Club membership 600.
Visitors contact professional for availability 0115 925 7062. Societies apply in advance. Green Fees not confirmed. Prof Alun Wardle Course Designer Tom Williamson Facilities ⊗ ⅷ by arrangement ⓛ ⬛♀⚲🏠 ⚑♂ Conf fac available Corporate Hospitality Days available Location 400yds SW off A52 Nottingham-Derby road

Hotel ⓤ Travelodge Nottingham Trowell, TROWELL ☎ 08700 850 950 35 en suite

Bulwell Forest Hucknall Rd, Bulwell NG6 9LQ
☎ 0115 976 3172 (pro shop) 📠 0115 967 1734
e-mail: david@dnehra.co.uk
Municipal heathland course with many natural hazards. Very tight fairways and subject to wind. Five challenging par 3s. Excellent drainage.
18 holes, 5667yds, Par 68, SSS 67, Course record 62.
Club membership 350.
Visitors restricted weekends; contact pro shop 24 hours in advance. Societies apply in advance. Green Fees £12 per round (£15 weekends & bank holidays). Cards 💳 💳 💳 🖼 💳 💳 💳 Course Designer John Doleman Facilities ⊗ ⓛ ⬛♀⚲🏠⚑♂ Leisure hard tennis courts,

Continued

children's playground. **Location** 4m NW of city centre on A611

Hotel ★★★ 66% Bestwood Lodge, Bestwood Country Park, Arnold, NOTTINGHAM ☎ 0115 920 3011 39 en suite

Chilwell Manor Meadow Ln, Chilwell NG9 5AE
☎ 0115 925 8958 ▤ 0115 922 0575
e-mail: chilwellmanorgolfclub@barbox.net
Flat parkland course. Some water, plenty of trees and narrow fairways.
18 holes, 6255yds, Par 70, SSS 71, Course record 66.
Club membership 750.
Visitors with member only weekends; must contact in advance; handicap certificate. **Societies** Mon, must apply in advance. **Green Fees** £30 per day, £25 per round (weekends £30 per round). **Prof** Paul Wilson **Course Designer** Tom Williamson **Facilities** ⊗ ⫫ ⅃ ⅃ ♟ ♀ ⅄ 🖆 ✧ **Location** 4m SW on A6005

Hotel ★★ 60% Europa Hotel, 20-22 Derby Rd, LONG EATON ☎ 0115 972 8481 15 en suite

Edwalton Municipal Wellin Ln, Edwalton NG12 4AS
☎ 0115 923 4775 ▤ 0115 923 1647
Gently sloping nine-hole parkland course. Also a nine-hole par 3 and large practice ground.
9 holes, 3336yds, Par 72, SSS 72, Course record 71.
Club membership 400.
Visitors booking system in operation; book up to seven days in advance **Societies** booking necessary. **Green Fees** not confirmed. **Cards** 🖦 🖦 🖼 ▨ **Prof** Lee Rawlings **Facilities** ⊗ ⅃ ⅃ ♟ ♀ ⅄ 🖆 ⅂ ⅃ ✧ ⅃ **Leisure** par 3 course. **Conf** fac available Corporate Hospitality Days available **Location** S of Nottingham off A606

Hotel ⮝ Premier Travel Inn Nottingham South, Loughborough Rd, Ruddington, NOTTINGHAM ☎ 0870 9906422 42 en suite

Mapperley Central Av, Plains Rd, Mapperley NG3 6RH
☎ 0115 955 6673 ▤ 0115 955 6670
e-mail: info@mapperleygolfclub.org
Hilly meadowland course but with easy walking.
18 holes, 6302yds, Par 71, SSS 70.
Club membership 650.
Visitors not Sat; contact in advance. **Societies** phone in advance. **Green Fees** £22.50 per day/round (£29.50 weekends & bank holidays). **Cards** 🖦 🖦 ▨ 🖼 🖼 🖼 ▨ **Prof** Jasen Barker **Course Designer** John Mason **Facilities** ⊗ ⅃ ⅃ ♟ ♀ ⅄ 🖆 ⅂ ⅃ ✧ **Leisure** pool room. **Location** 3m NE of city centre off B684

Hotel ⮝ Travelodge Nottingham Trowell, TROWELL ☎ 08700 850 950 35 en suite

Nottingham City Lawton Dr, Bulwell NG6 8BL
☎ 0115 927 6916 & 927 2767 ▤ 0115 927 6916
18 holes, 6218yds, Par 69, SSS 70, Course record 63.
Course Designer H Braid **Location** 4m NW of city centre off A6002
Phone for further details

Hotel ★★★ 66% Bestwood Lodge, Bestwood Country Park, Arnold, NOTTINGHAM ☎ 0115 920 3011 39 en suite

Wollaton Park Limetree Av, Wollaton Park NG8 1BT
☎ 0115 978 7574 ▤ 0115 970 0736
e-mail: wollatonparkgc@aol.com
A traditional parkland course on slightly undulating land, winding through historic woodland and set in a historic deer park. Fine views of 16th-century Wollaton Hall.
18 holes, 6445yds, Par 71, SSS 71, Course record 64.
Club membership 700.
Visitors not Wed & competition days. **Societies** apply in advance. **Green Fees** £48 per day; £35 per round (£55/£40 weekends & bank holidays). **Cards** 🖦 🖦 🖦 🖼 ▨ **Prof** John Lower **Course Designer** T Williamson **Facilities** ⊗ ⫫ ⅃ ♟ ♀ ⅄ 🖆 ✧ **Conf** Corporate Hospitality Days available **Location** 2.5m W of city centre off ring road junct A52

Hotel ★★★ 62% Swans Hotel & Restaurant, 84-90 Radcliffe Rd, West Bridgford, NOTTINGHAM ☎ 0115 981 4042 30 en suite

OLLERTON Map 08 SK66

Rufford Park Golf & Country Club Rufford Ln, Rufford NG22 9DG
☎ 01623 825253 ▤ 01623 825254
e-mail: enquiries@ruffordpark.co.uk
Set in the heart of Sherwood Forest, Rufford Park is noted for its picturesque 18 holes with its especially challenging par 3s. From the unique 175yd par 3 17th over water to the riverside 641yd 13th, the course offers everything the golfer needs from beginner to professional.
18 holes, 6286yds, Par 70, SSS 70, Course record 67.
Club membership 650.
Visitors booking recommended. **Societies** society packages on request, booking essential. **Green Fees** £19 per round (weekends £25); winter £16. **Cards** 🖦 🖦 ▨ 🖼 ▨ **Prof** John Vaughan, James Thompson **Course Designer** David Hemstock, Ken Brown **Facilities** ⊗ ⫫ ⅃ ♟ ♀ ⅄ 🖆 ⅂ ⅃ ✧ ⅃ **Conf** fac available Corporate Hospitality Days available **Location** S of Ollerton, off A614 for Rufford Mill

Hotel ★★★ 65% Clumber Park Hotel, Clumber Park, WORKSOP ☎ 01623 835333 48 en suite

OXTON Map 08 SK65

Oakmere Park Oaks Ln NG25 0RH
☎ 0115 965 3545 ▤ 0115 965 5628
e-mail: enquiries@oakmerepark.co.uk
Twenty-seven holes set in rolling parkland in the heart of picturesque Robin Hood country. The par 4 16th and par 5 1st are notable, as are the all weather playing qualities.
Admirals: 18 holes, 6617yds, Par 73, SSS 72,
Course record 64.
Commanders: 9 holes, 6407yds, Par 72, SSS 72.
Club membership 900.
Visitors book for weekends; dress code. **Societies** please apply in writing or phone. **Green Fees** Admirals: £20 per round (£28 weekends). **Cards** 🖦 🖦 🖼 ▨ **Prof** Daryl St-John Jones **Course Designer** Frank Pennick **Facilities** ⊗ ⫫ ⅃ ♟ ♀ ⅄ 🖆 ⅂ ⅃ ✧ ⅃ **Conf** fac available Corporate Hospitality Days available **Location** 1m NW of Oxton off A6097 or A614

Continued

Oakmere Park

Hotel ★★★ 67% Westminster Hotel, 312 Mansfield Rd, Carrington, NOTTINGHAM ☎ 0115 955 5000 73 en suite

RADCLIFFE ON TRENT Map 08 SK63

Cotgrave Place Golf Club Stragglethorpe, Nr Cotgrave Village NG12 3HB
☎ 0115 933 3344 📠 0115 933 4567
e-mail: cotgrave@americangolf.com
The course offers 36 holes of championship golf. The front nine of the Open course is placed around a beautiful lake, man-made ponds and the Grantham Canal. The back nine is set in magnificent parkland with mature trees and wide fairways. Masters has an opening nine set among hedgerows and coppices. The huge greens with their interesting shapes are a particularly challenging test of nerve. The par 5 17th hole is one of the toughest in the country.

Masters: 18 holes, 5933yds, Par 70, SSS 69, Course record 66.
Open: 18 holes, 6302yds, Par 71, SSS 68, Course record 69.
Club membership 850.
Visitors contact sales manager in advance. Societies phone in advance. Green Fees terms on application. Cards 🔳 🔳 🔳 🔳 🔳 Prof Robert Smith Course Designer Peter Aliss, John Small Facilities ⊗ ⊪ ⓛ ⚑ ♀ ♨ 🏠 🏌 🏌 ♂ ⓘ Conf Corporate Hospitality Days available Location 2m SW of Radcliffe off A52

Hotel ★★★ ⚑⚑ 73% Langar Hall, LANGAR ☎ 01949 860559 12 en suite

Radcliffe-on-Trent Dewberry Ln, off Cropwell Rd NG12 2JH
☎ 0115 933 3000 📠 0115 911 6991
e-mail: les.wake@radcliffeontrentgc.co.uk
Fairly flat parkland course with three good finishing

holes: 16th (427yds) par 4; 17th (180yds) through spinney, par 3; 18th (331yds) dog-leg par 4. Excellent views.
18 holes, 6381yds, Par 70, SSS 71, Course record 64.
Club membership 700.
Visitors contact in advance. Societies Wed, must contact in advance. Green Fees £25 per day (£32 weekends & bank holidays). Cards 🔳 🔳 🔳 🔳 🔳 🔳 🔳 Prof Craig George Course Designer Tom Williamson Facilities ⊗ ⊪ ⓛ ⚑ ♀ ♨ 🏠 🏌 ♂ Conf Corporate Hospitality Days available Location 0.5m SE of town centre off A52

Hotel ★★★ 62% Swans Hotel & Restaurant, 84-90 Radcliffe Rd, West Bridgford, NOTTINGHAM ☎ 0115 981 4042 30 en suite

RETFORD Map 08 SK78

Retford Brecks Rd, Ordsall DN22 7UA
☎ 01777 711188 (Secretary) 📠 01777 710412
A wooded, parkland course.
18 holes, 6409yds, Par 72, SSS 72, Course record 67.
Club membership 700.
Visitors with member only weekends & holidays; advisable to contact in advance. Societies apply in writing or phone. Green Fees not confirmed. Prof Craig Morris Course Designer Tom Williamson Facilities ⊗ ⊪ ⓛ ⚑ ♀ ♨ 🏠 🏌 🏌 ♂ Location 1.5m S, A620 between Worksop & Gainsborough

Hotel ★★★ 64% The West Retford Hotel, 24 North Rd, RETFORD ☎ 0870 609 6162 62 annexe en suite

RUDDINGTON Map 08 SK53

Ruddington Grange Wilford Rd NG11 6NB
☎ 0115 921 1951 (pro shop) & 984 6141
📠 0115 940 5165
e-mail: info@ruddingtongrange.com
Undulating parkland course with water hazards on eight holes. Many mature trees. Challenging but fair layout.
18 holes, 6543yds, Par 72, SSS 72, Course record 69.
Club membership 750.
Visitors restricted am Sat & Wed; tee time must be booked in advance. Societies contact in advance. Green Fees £19.50 per 18 holes. Prof Robert Simpson Course Designer E MacAusland, J Small Facilities ⊗ ⊪ ⓛ ⚑ ♀ ♨ 🏠 🏌 🏌 ♂ Conf fac available Corporate Hospitality Days available Location 1m N of town centre on B680

Hotel ★★★ 62% Swans Hotel & Restaurant, 84-90 Radcliffe Rd, West Bridgford, NOTTINGHAM ☎ 0115 981 4042 30 en suite

SERLBY Map 08 SK68

Serlby Park DN10 6BA
☎ 01777 818268
11 holes, 5325yds, Par 66, SSS 66, Course record 63.
Course Designer Viscount Galway Location E of village off A638
Phone for further details

Hotel ★★★ 70% Charnwood Hotel, Sheffield Rd, BLYTH ☎ 01909 591610 34 en suite

Continued

SOUTHWELL   Map 08 SK65

Norwood Park Norwood Park NG25 0PF
☎ 01636 816626
e-mail: mail@norwoodgolf.co.uk
A parkland course that blends perfectly with the
historic setting of Norwood Park and highlights its
natural features. Built to USGA standards, the course
will appeal to all golfers, who will appreciate the well-
shaped fairways, large undulating greens, natural and
man-made water hazards, and fine views over the
surrounding countryside.
18 holes, 6805yds, SSS 72.
Club membership 600.
Visitors advisable to contact in advance. Societies write or
phone in advance to Mr Henry Starkey, General Manager.
Green Fees £26 per day, £18 per 18 holes, £10 per 9 holes
(£28/£20/£12 Fri, £35/£25/£15 weekends & bank
holidays). Cards ⊞ ⊞ ⊞ ⊞ 🖼 Prof Paul Thornton
Course Designer Clyde B Johnston Facilities ⊗ ⊪ 🖳 🖳
🖳 🖳 🖻 🖐 🖐 🖐 🖐 🖐 🖐 Conf fac available Corporate
Hospitality Days available Location 0.5m N of town
centre

Hotel ★★★ 66% Saracens Head Hotel, Market Place,
SOUTHWELL ☎ 01636 812701 27 en suite

SUTTON IN ASHFIELD   Map 08 SK45

Coxmoor Coxmoor Rd NG17 5LF
☎ 01623 557359 🖹 01623 557359
e-mail: coxmoor@freeuk.com
Undulating moorland and heathland course with easy
walking and excellent views. The clubhouse is
traditional with a well-equipped games room. The
course lies adjacent to Forestry Commission land over
which there are several footpaths and extensive views.
18 holes, 6577yds, Par 73, SSS 72, Course record 65.
Club membership 700.
Visitors with member only weekends & bank holidays;
must contact in advance. Societies apply in advance.
Green Fees £55 per day; £40 per round. Cards ⊞ ⊞ ⊞
🖼 Prof David Ridley Facilities ⊗ ⊪ 🖳 🖳 🖳 🖳 🖻 🖐
Leisure snooker. Conf Corporate Hospitality Days
available Location 2m SE off A611

Hotel ★★★★ 70% Renaissance Derby/Nottingham Hotel,
Carter Ln East, SOUTH NORMANTON
☎ 01773 812000 158 en suite

WORKSOP   Map 08 SK57

Bondhay Golf & Country Club Bondhay Ln,
Whitwell S80 3EH
☎ 01909 723608 🖹 01909 720226
e-mail: enquiries@bondhay.com
The wind usually plays quite an active role in making
this pleasantly undulating championship course testing.
Signature holes are the 10th which requires a second
shot over water into a basin of trees; the 11th comes
back over the same expanse of water and requires a
mid to short iron to a long, narrow green; the 18th is a
par 5 with a lake - the dilemma is whether to lay up
short or go for the carry. The par 3s are generally
island-like in design, requiring accuracy to avoid the
many protective bunker features.
Devonshire Course: 18 holes, 6807yds, Par 72, SSS 72,
Course record 67.

Club membership 450.
Visitors contact in advance. Societies phone in advance.
Green Fees 18 holes: Mon-Tue £15; Wed-Fri £18; Sat-Sun
£23. Par 3 Course £5. Cards ⊞ ⊞ ⊞ 🖼 🖼
Prof Michael Ramsden Course Designer Donald Steel
Facilities ⊗ ⊪ 🖳 🖳 🖳 🖳 🖻 🖐 🖐 🖐 🖐 🖐 Leisure
fishing, par 3 family course. Conf fac available Corporate
Hospitality Days available Location M1 junct 30, 5m W of
Worksop off A619

Hotel ★★★ 65% Sitwell Arms Hotel, Station Rd,
RENISHAW ☎ 01246 435226 29 en suite

College Pines Worksop College Dr S80 3AP
☎ 01909 501431 🖹 01909 481227
This course was opened in 1994 and the par 73 layout
covers 150 acres of well-drained land with heathland
characteristics. It is club policy to remain open on full
tees and greens all year round.
18 holes, 6801yds, Par 73, SSS 73, Course record 67.
Club membership 500.
Visitors welcome by appointment. Societies write or
phone in advance, deposit required. Green Fees £20 per
day; £13 per round (£30/£20 weekends & bank holidays).
Prof Charles Snell Course Designer David Snell
Facilities ⊗ ⊪ 🖳 🖳 🖳 🖳 🖻 🖐 🖐 🖐 🖐 Conf
Corporate Hospitality Days available Location M1 junct
30/31, S of Worksop on B6034 Edwinstowe road

Hotel ★★★ 65% Clumber Park Hotel, Clumber Park,
WORKSOP ☎ 01623 835333 48 en suite

Kilton Forest Blyth Rd S81 0TL
☎ 01909 486563
Slightly undulating, parkland course on the north edge
of Sherwood Forest. Includes three ponds. Excellent
conditions all the year round. A true test of golf.
18 holes, 6424yds, Par 72, SSS 71, Course record 66.
Club membership 320.
Visitors not before 10am weekends; contact in advance.
Societies contact in advance. Green Fees not confirmed.
Prof Stuart Betteridge Facilities ⊗ 🖳 🖳 🖳 🖳 🖻 🖐 🖐
🖐 🖐 Leisure bowling. Location 1m NE of town centre
on B6045

Hotel ★★★ 68% Lion Hotel, 112 Bridge St, WORKSOP
☎ 01909 477925 45 en suite

Lindrick Lindrick Common S81 8BH
☎ 01909 475282 🖹 01909 488685
e-mail: lgc@ansbronze.com
Heathland course with some trees and masses of gorse.
18 holes, 6486yds, Par 71, SSS 71, Course record 63.
Club membership 510.
Visitors restricted Tue, weekends; contact in advance;
handicap certificate. Societies not am Tue, weekends, by
arrangement with the Secretary. Green Fees £60 per day,
£50 per 18 holes. Reduced winter rate. Cards ⊞ ⊞ ⊞
🖼 🖼 🖼 Prof John R King Facilities ⊗ ⊪ 🖳 🖳 🖳
🖳 🖻 🖐 Leisure buggies for disabled only.
Conf Corporate Hospitality Days available
Location M1 junct 31, 4m NW of Worksop on A57

Hotel ★★★ 68% Lion Hotel, 112 Bridge St, WORKSOP
☎ 01909 477925 45 en suite

> **Booking a tee time is always advisable.**

Continued

Worksop Windmill Ln S80 2SQ
☎ 01909 477731 📠 01909 530917
e-mail: worksopgolfclub@worksop.co.uk
Adjacent to Clumber Park, this course has heathland terrain with gorse, broom, oak and birch trees. Fast, true greens, dry all year round.
18 holes, 6660yds, Par 72, SSS 72.
Club membership 600.
Visitors by arrangement with the professional 01909 477731. **Societies** apply in advance. **Green Fees** £48 per 36 holes, £35 per 18 holes. **Prof** C Weatherhead **Course Designer** Tom Williamson **Facilities** ⊗ 〗 🏌 🍺 ♀ ♨ 🏠 ➤ 🚲 ♂ **Leisure** snooker. **Conf** fac available Corporate Hospitality Days available **Location** A57 ring road onto B6034 to Edwinstowe

....

Hotel ★★★ 65% Clumber Park Hotel, Clumber Park, WORKSOP ☎ 01623 835333 48 en suite

OXFORDSHIRE

ABINGDON   Map 04 SU49

Drayton Park Steventon Rd, Drayton OX14 4LA
☎ 01235 550607 (pro shop) 📠 01235 525731
Set in the heart of Oxfordshire, an 18-hole parkland course designed by Hawtree. Five lakes and sand-based greens.

18 holes, 6030yds, Par 67, SSS 67, Course record 60.
Club membership 500.
Visitors phone to book; golf shoes to be worn; dress code. **Societies** contact in advance. **Green Fees** £19 (£22.50 weekends). **Cards** ⚌ 🏧 💳 💳 🔳 🌀 **Prof** Martin Morbey **Course Designer** Hawtree **Facilities** ⊗ 〗 🏌 🍺 ♀ ♨ 🏠 ➤ 🚲 ♂ ⊘ **Leisure** 9-hole par 3 course. **Location** off A34 at Didcot

....

Hotel ★★★ 66% Abingdon Four Pillars Hotel, Marcham Rd, ABINGDON ☎ 0800 374 692 62 en suite

BANBURY   Map 04 SP44

See also **Chacombe** (Northamptonshire)

Banbury Aynho Rd, Adderbury OX17 3NT
☎ 01295 810419 & 812880 📠 01295 810056
e-mail: office@banburygolfcentre.co.uk
Undulating wooded course with water features and USGA specification greens.
Red & Yellow: 18 holes, 6557yds, Par 71, SSS 71.
Yellow & Blue: 18 holes, 6603yds, Par 71, SSS 71.
Red & Blue: 18 holes, 6706yds, Par 72, SSS 72.
Club membership 300.
Visitors **Societies** write or phone in advance. **Green Fees**

£17 per 18 holes (£22 weekends). **Cards** ⚌ 🔳 **Prof** Stuart Kier **Course Designer** Reed, Payn **Facilities** ⊗ 〗 🏌 🍺 ♀ ♨ 🏠 ➤ 🚲 ♂ **Conf** Corporate Hospitality Days available **Location** off B4100 between Adderbury & Aynho

....

Hotel ⟐ Premier Travel Inn Banbury, Warwick Rd, Warmington, BANBURY ☎ 0870 9906512 39 en suite

Rye Hill Milcombe OX15 4RU
☎ 01295 721818 📠 01295 720089
e-mail: info@ryehill.co.uk
Well-drained course, set in 200 acres of rolling countryside, with both parkland and heathland features, including wide fairways, large undulating greens, dramatic lakes and fine views.
18 holes, 6919yds, Par 72, SSS 73, Course record 62.
Club membership 575.
Visitors advisable to in advance, especially for weekends. **Societies** phone or e-mail for details of packages. **Green Fees** £40 per day, £25 per round (£55/£32 weekends). **Cards** ⚌ 🏧 💳 🔳 🌀 **Prof** Tony Pennock **Facilities** ⊗ 〗 🏌 🍺 ♀ ♨ 🏠 ➤ 🚲 ♂ **Leisure** fishing, pitch & putt course. **Conf** fac available Corporate Hospitality Days available **Location** M40 junct 11, A361 towards Chipping Norton, signed 1m out of Bloxham

....

Hotel ★★★ 69% Wroxton House Hotel, Wroxton St Mary, BANBURY ☎ 01295 730777 32 en suite

BURFORD   Map 04 SP21

Burford Swindon Rd OX18 4JG
☎ 01993 822583 📠 01993 822801
e-mail: secretary@burfordgc.co.uk
Parkland with mature, tree-lined fairways and high quality greens.
18 holes, 6401yds, Par 71, SSS 71, Course record 64.
Club membership 770.
Visitors restricted Tue, Thu, weekends; contact in advance. **Societies** apply in writing. **Green Fees** £36 per day. **Prof** Michael Ridge **Course Designer** John H Turner **Facilities** ⊗ 〗 🏌 🍺 ♀ ♨ 🏠 ➤ 🚲 ♂ **Location** 0.5m S off A361

....

Hotel ★★ 64% Golden Pheasant Hotel, 91 High St, BURFORD ☎ 01993 823223 11 rms (10 en suite)

CHESTERTON   Map 04 SP52

Bicester Golf & Country Club OX26 1TE
☎ 01869 242023 📠 01869 240754
e-mail: bicestergolf@ukonline.co.uk
18 holes, 6600yds, Par 71, SSS 70, Course record 68.
Course Designer R Stagg **Location** 0.5m W off A4095
Phone for further details

....

Hotel ★★ 72% Jersey Arms Hotel, BICESTER ☎ 01869 343234 6 en suite 14 annexe en suite

CHIPPING NORTON   Map 04 SP32

Chipping Norton Southcombe OX7 5QH
☎ 01608 642383 📠 01608 645422
e-mail: chipping.nortongc@virgin.net
Downland course situated at 800ft above sea level, its undulations providing a good walk. On a limestone base, the course dries quickly in wet conditions. The opening few holes provide a good test of golf made more difficult when the prevailing wind makes the player use the extremes of the course.

Continued   *Continued*

18 holes, 6241yds, Par 71, SSS 70, Course record 62. Club membership 900.
Visitors with member only weekends & bank holidays. **Societies** phone in advance. **Green Fees** not confirmed. **Prof** Neil Rowlands **Facilities** ⊗ ⫞ ⓑ ♥ ⵑ ⴷ ⴶ ⵏ ⵙ ⵏ **Location** 1.5m E on A44

Hotel ★★★ 72% The Mill House Hotel & Restaurant, KINGHAM ☎ 01608 658188 21 en suite 2 annexe en suite

Wychwood Lyneham OX7 6QQ
☎ 01993 831841 📠 01993 831775
e-mail: golf@wychwoodgc.freeserve.co.uk
Wychwood was designed to use the natural features. It is set in 170 acres on the fringe of the Costwolds and blends superbly with its surroundings. Lakes and streams enhance the challenge of the course with water coming into play on eight of the 18 holes. All greens are sand based, built to USGA specification.
18 holes, 6844yds, Par 72, SSS 72, Course record 67. Club membership 750.
Visitors contact in advance. **Societies** apply in advance. **Green Fees** £30 per day, £24 per 18 holes (£37/£28 weekends). **Cards** ▦ ▰ ▱ 🅶 **Prof** James Fincher **Course Designer** DG Carpenter **Facilities** ⊗ ⫞ ⓑ ♥ ⵑ ⴷ ⵏ ⵙ ⵏ ⴶ ⵏ **Conf** fac available Corporate Hospitality Days available **Location** off A361 between Burford & Chipping Norton

Hotel ★★★ 72% The Mill House Hotel & Restaurant, KINGHAM ☎ 01608 658188 21 en suite 2 annexe en suite

Hadden Hill Wallingford Rd OX11 9BJ
☎ 01235 510410 📠 01235 511260
e-mail: info@haddenhillgolf.co.uk
A challenging course on undulating terrain with excellent drainage, so visitors can be sure of playing no matter what the weather conditions have been. Two loops of nine holes. Superb greens and fairways.
18 holes, 6563yds, Par 71, SSS 71, Course record 65. Club membership 400.
Visitors phone pro shop up to one week in advance to book tee times. **Societies** phone to arrange times & receive booking form. **Green Fees** £18 per 18 holes; £11 per 9 holes (£23/£14 weekends). **Prof** Ian Mitchell **Course Designer** Michael V Morley **Facilities** ⊗ ⫞ ⓑ ♥ ⵑ ⴷ ⵏ ⵙ ⵏ ⴶ ⵏ **Leisure** teaching academy. **Conf** Corporate Hospitality Days available **Location** A34 Milton junct onto A4130, course 1m E of Didcot

Hotel ★★★ 66% Abingdon Four Pillars Hotel, Marcham Rd, ABINGDON ☎ 0800 374 692 62 en suite

Carswell Carswell SN7 8PU
☎ 01367 870422 📠 01367 870592
e-mail: info@carswellgolfandcountryclub.co.uk
An attractive course set in undulating wooded countryside close to Faringdon. Mature trees, five lakes and well-placed bunkers add interest to the course. Floodlit driving range.
18 holes, 6183yds, Par 72, SSS 70. Club membership 520.
Visitors advisable to book eight days in advance, no earlier for tee times. **Societies** phone weekdays to check

availability, deposit required. **Green Fees** not confirmed. **Cards** ▦ ▰ ▱ 🅶 **Prof** Steve Parker **Course Designer** J & E Ely **Facilities** ⊗ ⫞ ⓑ ♥ ⵑ ⴷ ⵏ ⵙ ⵏ ⴶ ⵏ **Leisure** sauna, solarium, gymnasium. **Location** off A420

Carswell Golf & Country Club

Hotel ★★★ 70% Sudbury House Hotel & Conference Centre, London St, FARINGDON ☎ 01367 241272 49 en suite

Frilford Heath OX13 5NW
☎ 01865 390864 📠 01865 390823
e-mail: secretary@frilfordheath.co.uk
Fifty-four holes in three distinctive layouts of significantly differing character. The Green Course is a mature heathland course of some 6006yds. The Red Course is of championship length at 6884yds with a parkland flavour and a marked degree of challenge. The Blue Course is of modern design, and at 6728yds, it incorporates water hazards and large shallow sand traps.
Red Course: 18 holes, 6884yds, Par 73, SSS 73, Course record 66.
Green Course: 18 holes, 6006yds, Par 69, SSS 69, Course record 67.
Blue Course: 18 holes, 6728yds, Par 72, SSS 72, Course record 63.
Club membership 1300.
Visitors contact in advance; handicap certificate. **Societies** apply in advance. **Green Fees** £55 per day (£70 weekends). **Cards** ▦ ▰ ▱ 🅶 **Prof** Derek Craik **Course Designer** J Taylor, D Cotton, S Gidman **Facilities** ⊗ ⫞ ⓑ ♥ ⵑ ⴷ ⵏ ⵙ ⵏ ⴶ ⵏ **Conf** fac available Corporate Hospitality Days available **Location** 05m N of Frilford off A338

Hotel ★★★ 66% Abingdon Four Pillars Hotel, Marcham Rd, ABINGDON ☎ 0800 374 692 62 en suite

Badgemore Park Badgemore RG9 4NR
☎ 01491 637300 📠 01491 576899
e-mail: info@badgemorepark.com
Well-established 18-hole parkland course with attractive specimen trees lining the fairways. The signature hole of this easy walking course is the 13th, a tough par 3 played across a valley to a narrow raised green.
18 holes, 6129yds, Par 69, SSS 69, Course record 64. Club membership 700.
Visitors lady members only am Tue; contact professional shop for availability 01491 574175; 48 hours booking min for weekends. **Societies** contact the club secretary to book.

Continued

Continued

Green Fees £26 per round (£36 weekends & bank holidays). Cards ▨ ▨ ▨ ▨ ▨ Prof Jonathan Dunn Course Designer Robert Sandow Facilities ⊗ ⅢⅢ by arrangement ⓛ ♟ ♀ ♙ ⌂ 🏌 ⚑ ➤ ♣ ⚘ Conf fac available Corporate Hospitality Days available Location N from Henley towards Rotherfield Greys, 1.5m on right

Badgemore Park Golf Club

Hotel ★★★ 67% Red Lion Hotel, Hart St, HENLEY-ON-THAMES ☎ 01491 572161 26 en suite

Henley Harpsden RG9 4HG
☎ 01491 575742 📠 01491 412179
e-mail: henleygolfclub@btinternet.com

Designed by James Braid in 1907, the course retains many of his classic features, while being a challenge for all golfers even with modern technology. The first four holes are considered the hardest opening holes of any course in Oxfordshire and possibly the UK.
18 holes, 6329yds, Par 70, SSS 70, Course record 62.
Club membership 700.
Visitors with member only weekends; contact in advance; handicap certificate. Societies Wed, Thu, apply in writing. Green Fees not confirmed. Cards ▨ ▨ ▨ ▨ ▨ Prof Mark Howell Course Designer James Braid Facilities ⊗ ⅢⅢ ⓛ ♟ ♀ ♙ ⌂ 🏌 ⚘ ⟨ Conf Corporate Hospitality Days available Location 1.25m S off A4155

Hotel ★★★ 67% Red Lion Hotel, Hart St, HENLEY-ON-THAMES ☎ 01491 572161 26 en suite

HORTON-CUM-STUDLEY   Map 04 SP51

Studley Wood The Straight Mile OX33 1BF
☎ 01865 351122 & 351144 📠 01865 351166
e-mail: admin@swgc.co.uk.

Gently undulating woodland course set in a former deer park. Tranquil setting with an abundance of wildlife. USGA specification tees and greens, with lakes coming into play on nine holes.
18 holes, 6811yds, Par 73, SSS 72, Course record 65.
Club membership 700.
Visitors not am weekends; must play to handicap standard; tee times booked up to four days in advance. Societies contact secretary for details. Green Fees £36 per round (£46 per round weekends). Cards ▨ ▨ ▨ ▨ ▨ Prof Tony Williams Course Designer Simon Gidman Facilities ⊗ ⅢⅢ ⓛ ♟ ♀ ♙ ⌂ 🏌 ⚘ ⟨ Leisure teaching studio with video facilities. Conf fac available Corporate Hospitality Days available Location 6m NE of Oxford, off B4027 to Horton

Hotel ★★★★ 70% The Oxford Hotel, Godstow Rd, Wolvercote Roundabout, OXFORD
☎ 01865 489952 168 en suite

KIRTLINGTON   Map 04 SP41

Kirtlington OX5 3JY
☎ 01869 351133 📠 01869 351143
e-mail: info@kirtlingtongolfclub.com

An inland links-type course with challenging greens. The course incorporates many natural features and boasts 102 bunkers and a 110yd par 3 19th when an extra hole is required to determine a winner. New clubhouse, academy course and covered bays on the driving range.
18 holes, 6107yds, Par 70, SSS 69, Course record 68.
Academy Course: 9 holes, 1535yds, Par 30, SSS 53.
Club membership 400.
Visitors book for weekends; advisable to book for weekdays. Societies contact for packages. Green Fees 18 holes £22 (weekends £27). nine holes £10 (£12). Cards ▨ ▨ ▨ ▨ ▨ Prof Andy Taylor Course Designer Graham Webster Facilities ⊗ ⓛ ♟ ♀ ♙ ⌂ 🏌 ➤ ♣ ⚘ ⟨ Conf fac available Corporate Hospitality Days available Location M40 junct 9, on A4095 outside Kirtlington

Hotel ★★★ 70% Weston Manor Hotel, WESTON-ON-THE-GREEN ☎ 01869 350621 15 en suite 20 annexe en suite

MILTON COMMON   Map 04 SP60

The Oxfordshire Rycote Ln OX9 2PU
☎ 01844 278300 📠 01844 278003
e-mail: info@theoxfordshiregolfclub.com

Designed by Rees Jones, The Oxfordshire is considered to be one of the most exciting courses in the country. The strategically contoured holes blend naturally into the surrounding countryside to provide a challenging game of golf. With four lakes and 135 bunkers, the course makes full use of the terrain and the natural elements to provide characteristics similar to those of a links course.

18 holes, 7192yds, Par 72, SSS 75, Course record 64.
Club membership 376.
Visitors not before 11am weekends & bank holidays; contact in advance; handicap certificate. Societies apply in writing or phone in advance. Green Fees not confirmed. Cards ▨ ▨ ▨ ▨ ▨ Prof Stephen Gibson Course Designer Rees Jones Facilities ⊗ ⅢⅢ ⓛ ♟ ♀ ♙ ⌂ 🏌 ♣ ⚘ ⟨ Leisure Japanese ofuro baths. Conf fac available Corporate Hospitality Days available
Location M40 junct 7, 1.5m on A329

Hotel ★★★ 74% Spread Eagle Hotel, Cornmarket, THAME ☎ 01844 213661 33 en suite

NUFFIELD
Map 04 SU68

Huntercombe RG9 5SL
☎ 01491 641207 🖹 01491 642060
e-mail: office@huntercombegolfclub.co.uk
This heathland and woodland course overlooks the Oxfordshire plain and has many attractive and interesting fairways and greens. Walking is easy after the 3rd which is a notable hole. The course is subject to wind and grass pot bunkers are interesting hazards.

18 holes, 6271yds, Par 70, SSS 70, Course record 63. Club membership 800.
Visitors contact in advance; handicap certificate. **Societies** contact in advance. **Green Fees** £60 per day; £40 per round (£75/£60 per round weekends & bank holidays). **Cards** 🔲 🔲 🖫 **Prof** Ian Roberts **Course Designer** Willie Park jnr **Facilities** ⊗ ⅲ ᴸ 🖫 🖤 ♀ 🚶 🖙 🏌 🐾 🏌 🌙 ᘎ
Location off A4130 at Nuffield

Hotel ★★★ 68% Shillingford Bridge Hotel, Shillingford, WALLINGFORD ☎ 01865 858567 34 en suite 8 annexe en suite

OXFORD
Map 04 SP50

Hinksey Heights South Hinksey OX1 5AB
☎ 01865 327775 🖹 01865 736930
e-mail: play@oxford-golf.co.uk
Set in an Area of Outstanding Natural Beauty, overlooking the incomparable Dreaming Spires of Oxford and the Thames Valley. The course has a heathland or links feel with several fairways running along the bottom of valleys created by the use of natural and man-made features. Each of the 18 holes is distinctive and there is also a nine-hole par 3 course for golfers of all ages and abilities.

18 holes, 6936yds, Par 74, SSS 73. Club membership 450.
Visitors advisable to phone in advance. **Societies** apply in advance to professional. **Green Fees** £38 per day; £18 per 18 holes (£23 per 18 holes weekends). **Cards** 🔲 🔲 🔲

Continued

🔲 🔲 🖫 **Prof** Dean Davis **Course Designer** David Heads **Facilities** ⊗ ⅲ ᴸ 🖤 ♀ 🚶 🖙 🏌 🐾 🏌 ᘎ **Conf** Corporate Hospitality Days available **Location** on A34 Oxford bypass between Abingdon & Oxford Botley junction

Hotel ★★★ 69% Hawkwell House, Church Way, Iffley Village, OXFORD ☎ 01865 749988 51 en suite

North Oxford Banbury Rd OX2 8EZ
☎ 01865 554924 🖹 01865 515921
e-mail: secretary@nogc.co.uk
Gently undulating parkland course.

18 holes, 5736yds, Par 67, SSS 67, Course record 62. Club membership 700.
Visitors not before 2pm weekends & bank holidays. **Societies** contact in advance. **Green Fees** not confirmed. **Cards** 🔲 🔲 🖫 🖫 **Prof** Robert Harris **Facilities** ⊗ ⅲ ᴸ 🖤 ♀ 🚶 🖙 🏌 🌙 **Conf** Corporate Hospitality Days available **Location** 3m N of city centre on A4165

Hotel ★★★★ 70% The Oxford Hotel, Godstow Rd, Wolvercote Roundabout, OXFORD ☎ 01865 489952 168 en suite

Southfield Hill Top Rd OX4 1PF
☎ 01865 242158 🖹 01865 728544
e-mail: sgcltd@btopenworld.com
Home of the City, University and Ladies Clubs, and well-known to graduates throughout the world. A challenging course, in a varied parkland setting, providing a real test for players.

18 holes, 6325yds, Par 70, SSS 70, Course record 64. Club membership 740.
Visitors all days **Societies** apply in writing. **Green Fees** £35 per day; £25 per round. **Cards** 🔲 🔲 🖫 🔲 🔲 🖫 🖫 **Prof** Tony Rees **Course Designer** HS Colt **Facilities** ⊗ ⅲ ᴸ 🖤 ♀ 🚶 🖙 🏌 🐾 🌙 **Conf** Corporate Hospitality Days available **Location** 1.5m SE of city centre off B480

Hotel ★★★ 67% Eastgate Hotel, 73 High St, OXFORD ☎ 0870 400 8201 64 en suite

SHRIVENHAM   Map 04 SU28

Shrivenham Park Penny Hooks Ln SN6 8EX
☎ 01793 783853
A flat, mature parkland course with excellent drainage,
providing a good challenge for all standards of golfer.
18 holes, 5769yds, Par 69, SSS 69, Course record 64.
Club membership 150.
Visitors phone in advance. **Societies** phone for details.
Green Fees Mon-Thu 18 holes £15; 9 holes £9, Fri-Sun &
bank holidays £20/£12. **Cards** 🖃 🖃 🖃 🖃 🔯
Prof Richard Jefferies **Course Designer** Gordon Cox
Facilities ⊗ ⅷ Ⅼ ♥ ♀ ⌀ ☎ ⅋ ♨ ⌀
Conf fac available Corporate Hospitality Days available
Location 0.5m NE of town centre

Hotel ★★★ 70% Sudbury House Hotel & Conference
Centre, London St, FARINGDON ☎ 01367 241272
49 en suite

TADMARTON   Map 04 SP33

Tadmarton Heath OX15 5HL
☎ 01608 737278 🖶 01608 730548
e-mail: thgc@btinternet.com
A mixture of heath and sandy land on a plateau in the
Cotswolds. The course opens gently before reaching the
scenic 7th hole across a trout stream close to the
clubhouse. The course then progressively tightens
through the gorse before a challenging 430yd dog-leg
completes the round.
18 holes, 5917yds, Par 69, SSS 69, Course record 63.
Club membership 650.
Visitors not am Thu, weekdays by appointment; with
member only weekends. **Societies** by arrangement with
club office. **Green Fees** £45 per day, £35 after 2.30pm,
(weekends £50, £40 after 12pm). **Prof** Tom Jones **Course
Designer** Col CK Hutchinson **Facilities** ⊗ Ⅼ ♥ ♀ ⌀ ☎
⅋ ♨ ⌀ **Leisure** fishing. **Conf** Corporate Hospitality
Days available **Location** 1m SW of Lower Tadmarton off
B4035, 4m from Banbury

Hotel ★★★ 71% Banbury House, Oxford Rd, BANBURY
☎ 01295 259361 63 en suite

WALLINGFORD   Map 04 SU68

Springs Hotel Wallingford Rd, North Stoke
OX10 6BE
☎ 01491 827310 🖶 01491 827312
e-mail: proshop@thespringshotel.com
The 133 acres of parkland are bordered by the River
Thames, within which lie three lakes and challenging
wetland areas. The course has traditional features like a
double green and sleepered bunker with sleepered lake
edges of typical American design.
18 holes, 6470yds, Par 72, SSS 71, Course record 67.
Club membership 580.
Visitors must be handicap standard; dress code. **Societies**
apply by writing, phone or e-mail. **Green Fees** £37 per
day, £29 per 18 holes (£45/£35 weekends & bank
holidays). **Cards** 🖃 🖃 🖃 🖃 🖃 🔯 **Prof** David Boyce
Course Designer Brian Hugget **Facilities** ⊗ ⅷ Ⅼ ♥ ♀
⌀ ☎ ⅋ ♨ ♨ ⌀ **Leisure** heated outdoor swimming
pool, fishing, sauna, croquet lawn. **Conf** fac available
Corporate Hospitality Days available **Location** 2m SE of
town centre over River Thames

The Springs
HOTEL & GOLF CLUB

The Spring Hotel offers:
• 3 Star Tudor-style country house
• 32 en-suite bedrooms
• Lakeside restaurant for lunch
  or dinner
• Conferences, Weddings & Private
  parties
• Golf Breaks
• Sauna & Outdoor swimming pool
• Croquet & Putting
• Riverside fishing & 'Ridgeway'
  country walks

The Spring Golf Club offers:
• A challenging 18 Hole Par 72
  course
• Excellent short game practice
  facilities
• Attractive Tudor-style clubhouse
• Well stocked Pro Shop
• Corporate, Society & Charity
  Days
• Membership

For more information contact the Hotel on
Tel: 01491 836687   Fax: 01491 836877
Or the Pro Shop for Golf on
Tel: 01491 827310   Fax: 01491 827312

Web: www.thespringshotel.com   Email: info@thespringshotel.com
Wallingford Rd (B4009), North Stoke, Wallingford, Oxon, OX10 6BE
15 miles S.East of Oxford and 12 miles N.West of Reading

Springs Hotel & Golf Club

Hotel ★★★ 75% Springs Hotel & Golf Club, Wallingford
Rd, North Stoke, WALLINGFORD ☎ 01491 836687
31 en suite

WATERSTOCK   Map 04 SP60

Waterstock Thame Rd OX33 1HT
☎ 01844 338093 🖶 01844 338036
e-mail: wgc_oxfordgolf@btinternet.com
A 6535yd course designed by Donald Steel with USGA
greens and tees fully computer irrigated. Four par 3s
facing north, south, east and west. A brook and hidden
lake affect six holes, with dog-legs being 4th and 10th
holes. Five par 5s on the course, making it a challenge
for players of all standards.
18 holes, 6535yds, Par 73, SSS 72, Course record 69.
Club membership 500.

Continued   *Continued*

Visitors no restrictions. **Societies** apply by writing, phone or e-mail. **Green Fees** £32.50 per day, £21 per round, £15 twilight, £11.50 per 9 holes (£40.50/£17/£14.50 weekends). **Cards** 🖃 🖃 🖃 🖃 🖃 **Prof** Paul Bryant **Course Designer** Donald Steel **Facilities** ⊗ ⵏ ⅃ 🖳 ⅄ ⵏ 🖃 ⵏ ⵏ ⵏ ⵏ **Leisure** fishing. **Conf** fac available Corporate Hospitality Days available **Location** M40 junct 8/8A, E of Oxford near Wheatley

Hotel ★★★ 74% Spread Eagle Hotel, Cornmarket, THAME ☎ 01844 213661 33 en suite

WITNEY   Map 04 SP31

Witney Lakes Downs Rd OX29 0SY
☎ 01993 893011 🖹 01993 778866
e-mail: golf@witney-lakes.co.uk
Five large lakes come into play on eight holes. An excellent test of golf that will use every club in your bag.
18 holes, 6700yds, Par 71, Course record 67.
Club membership 450.
Visitors not before 10.30am weekends; can book five days in advance. **Societies** phone or write in advance. **Green Fees** £20 per 18 holes (weekends £28). **Cards** 🖃 🖃 🖃 🖃 🖃 **Prof** Adam Souter **Course Designer** Simon Gidman **Facilities** ⊗ ⵏ ⅃ 🖳 ⅄ ⵏ 🖃 ⵏ ⵏ ⵏ ⵏ **Leisure** heated indoor swimming pool, sauna, solarium, gymnasium. **Conf** fac available Corporate Hospitality Days available **Location** 2m W of town centre, off B4047

Hotel ★★★ 70% Witney Four Pillars Hotel, Ducklington Ln, WITNEY ☎ 0800 374 692 83 en suite

RUTLAND

GREAT CASTERTON   Map 04 TF00

Rutland County PE9 4AQ
☎ 01780 460330 🖹 01780 460437
e-mail: info@rutlandcountygolf.co.uk
Inland links-style course with gently rolling fairways, large tees and greens. Playable all year round due to good drainage.
18 holes, 6401yds, Par 71, SSS 71, Course record 64.
Club membership 740 .
Visitors book in advance at the shop 01780 460239.
Societies contact office by phone, must book in advance.
Green Fees terms on application. **Cards** 🖃 🖃 🖃 🖃 🖃 **Prof** Fred Fearn **Course Designer** Cameron Sinclair **Facilities** ⊗ ⵏ ⅃ 🖳 ⅄ 🖃 ⵏ ⵏ ⵏ ⵏ **Leisure** par 3 course. **Conf** fac available Corporate Hospitality Days available **Location** 2m N of Stamford on A1

Hotel ★★ 68% The White Horse Inn, Main St, EMPINGHAM ☎ 01780 460221 & 460521 🖹 01780 460521 4 en suite 9 annexe en suite

GREETHAM   Map 08 SK91

Greetham Valley Wood Ln LE15 7NP
☎ 01780 460004 🖹 01780 460623
e-mail: info@gvgc.co.uk
Set in 267 acres, including mature woodland, undulating natural valley, and water hazards. The Lakes course is an excellent test of golf with numerous bunkers. Water plays a big part with four holes over water finishing with the 18th set between two lakes. The Valley course is picturesque with many holes playing

Continued

across or along the side of North Brook - twelve holes feature water.

Greetham Valley Golf Club

Lakes: 18 holes, 6779yds, Par 72, SSS 72, Course record 65.
Valley: 18 holes, 5595yds, Par 68, SSS 67, Course record 64.
Club membership 1000.
Visitors contact in advance. **Societies** contact in advance. **Green Fees** £30 per day; £25 per round (£35/£30 weekends). **Cards** 🖃 🖃 🖃 🖃 🖃 **Prof** John Pengelly **Course Designer** FE Hinch, B Stephens **Facilities** ⊗ ⵏ ⅃ 🖳 ⅄ ⵏ 🖃 ⵏ 🖃 ⵏ ⵏ ⵏ **Leisure** fishing, bowls green, nine-hole par 3. **Conf** fac available Corporate Hospitality Days available **Location** A1 onto B668 Oakham road, course signed

Hotel ★★★ 75% Barnsdale Lodge Hotel, The Avenue, Rutland Water, North Shore, OAKHAM ☎ 01572 724678 46 en suite

KETTON   Map 04 SK90

Luffenham Heath PE9 3UU
☎ 01780 720205 🖹 01780 722146
e-mail: jringleby@theluffenhamheathgc.co.uk
This undulating heathland course with low bushes, much gorse and many trees, lies in a conservation area for flora and fauna. From the higher part of the course there is a magnificent view across the Chater valley. The course places a premium on accuracy with many demanding driving holes, challenging bunkers and well-guarded greens. The course is not long but there are several outstanding holes.

18 holes, 6315yds, Par 70, SSS 70, Course record 64.
Club membership 550.
Visitors with member only before 2.30pm weekends; contact in advance. **Societies** write or phone in advance. **Green Fees** not confirmed. **Cards** 🖃 🖃 🖃 **Prof** Ian Burnett **Course Designer** James Braid

Continued

Facilities ⊗ ⦙ ⅃ ᴸ ♥ ♀ ᴧ ⌂ ∅ **Conf** Corporate Hospitality Days available **Location** 1.5m SW of Ketton on A6121 by Foster's Bridge

Hotel ★★★ 80% The George of Stamford, 71 St Martins, STAMFORD ☎ 01780 750750 & 750700 (Res) 📄 01780 750701 47 en suite

---

SHROPSHIRE

BRIDGNORTH
Map 07 SO79

Bridgnorth Stanley Ln WV16 4SF
☎ 01746 763315 📄 01746 763315
e-mail: secretary.bgc@tiscali.co.uk
A pleasant parkland course by the River Severn.
18 holes, 6582yds, Par 73, SSS 72, Course record 72.
Club membership 725.
Visitors not Wed, restricted weekends; contact in advance. **Societies** contact by writing or phone. **Green Fees** £30 per day, £24 per round (£40 per round weekends). **Prof** Paul Hinton **Facilities** ⊗ ⦙ ⅃ ᴸ ♥ ♀ ᴧ ⌂ ♦ ⛟ ∅ **Leisure** fishing. **Conf** Corporate Hospitality Days available **Location** 1m N off B4373

Hotel ★★ 63% Falcon Hotel, Saint John St, Lowtown, BRIDGNORTH ☎ 01746 763134 12 en suite

CHURCH STRETTON
Map 07 SO49

Church Stretton Trevor Hill SY6 6JH
☎ 01694 722281 📄 01743 861918
e-mail: secretary@churchstrettongolfclub.co.uk
Hillside course designed by James Braid on the lower slopes of the Long Mynd, with magnificent views and well-drained turf. No temporary greens or tees.
18 holes, 5020yds, Par 66, SSS 65, Course record 63.
Club membership 450.
Visitors tee reserved for members 9-10.30am, 1-2.30pm Sat in summer, 12-1.30pm in winter, before 10.30am, 1-2.30pm Sun in summer, 12-1.30pm in winter. **Societies** contact in advance. **Green Fees** not confirmed. **Cards** ▦ **Prof** J Townsend **Course Designer** James Braid **Facilities** ⊗ ⦙ ⅃ ᴸ ♥ ♀ ᴧ ⌂ ∅ **Location** W of town. From Cardington Valley up steep Trevor Hill

CLEOBURY MORTIMER
Map 07 SO67

Cleobury Mortimer Wyre Common DY14 8HQ
☎ 01299 271112 📄 01299 271468
e-mail: enquiries@cleoburygolfclub.com
Well-designed 27-hole parkland course set in undulating countryside with fine views from all holes. An interesting challenge to golfers of all abilities.

Continued

Foxes Run: 9 holes, 2980yds, Par 34, SSS 34.
Badgers Sett: 9 holes, 3271yds, Par 36, SSS 36.
Deer Park: 9 holes, 3167yds, Par 35, SSS 35.
Club membership 650.
Visitors advisable to book in advance; handicap certificate may be required weekends. **Societies** write or phone in advance. **Green Fees** £30 per day, £20 per 18 holes (weekends £36/£30). **Cards** ▦ ▦ ▦ ▦ 🟡 **Prof** Jon Jones, Martin Payne **Course Designer** EGU **Facilities** ⊗ ⦙ ⅃ ᴸ ♥ ♀ ᴧ ⌂ ♦ ⛟ ∅ ↑ **Leisure** fishing, snooker table. **Conf** fac available Corporate Hospitality Days available **Location** on A4117 1m N of Cleobury Mortimer

Inn ♦♦♦♦ The Crown Inn, Hopton Wafers, CLEOBURY MORTIMER ☎ 01299 270372 7 en suite

LILLESHALL
Map 07 SJ71

Lilleshall Hall TF10 9AS
☎ 01952 603840 & 604776 📄 01952 604776
18 holes, 5906yds, Par 68, SSS 68, Course record 65.
Course Designer HS Colt **Location** 3m SE
Phone for further details

LUDLOW
Map 07 SO57

Ludlow Bromfield SY8 2BT
☎ 01584 856366 📄 01584 856366
A long-established heathland course in the middle of the racecourse. Very flat, quick drying, with broom and gorse-lined fairways.
18 holes, 6277yds, Par 70, SSS 70, Course record 65.
Club membership 700.
Visitors advisable to contact in advance. **Societies** apply in advance. **Green Fees** £28 per round/£35 per day (£35 weekends & bank holidays). **Prof** Russell Price **Facilities** ⊗ ⦙ ⅃ ᴸ ♥ ♀ ᴧ ⌂ ∅ **Conf** Corporate Hospitality Days available
Location 1m N of Ludlow off A49

Hotel ★★★ 67% The Feathers Hotel, The Bull Ring, LUDLOW ☎ 01584 875261 40 en suite

MARKET DRAYTON
Map 07 SJ63

Market Drayton Sutton Ln TF9 2HX
☎ 01630 652266
e-mail: marketdraytongc@btinternet.com
Undulating parkland course with two steep banks in quiet, picturesque surroundings, providing a good test of golf.
18 holes, 6290yds, Par 71, SSS 71, Course record 69.
Club membership 600.
Visitors not Sun; with member only Sat; must contact in advance. **Societies** welcome Mon, Wed, Thu & Fri, must contact in advance. **Green Fees** summer £26 per round; winter £20. **Prof** Russell Clewes **Facilities** ⊗ ⦙ ⅃ ᴸ ♥ ♀ ᴧ ⌂ ⛟ ∅ **Conf** Corporate Hospitality Days available **Location** 1m S off A41/A529

Hotel ★★★ 70% Goldstone Hall, Goldstone, MARKET DRAYTON ☎ 01630 661202 11 en suite

NEWPORT
Map 07 SJ72

Aqualate Golf Centre Stafford Rd TF10 9DB
☎ 01952 811699
A parkland course with gentle gradients and hazards.
9 holes, 5659yds, Par 69, SSS 67, Course record 67.
Club membership 175.
Visitors phone booking preferred. **Societies** phone booking

Continued

preferred. **Green Fees** £10 per 18 holes, £6 per 9 holes (£13/£8 weekends & bank holidays). **Prof** Kevin Short **Facilities** ♨ ♿ ♟ ♂ ⚲ **Conf** Corporate Hospitality Days available **Location** 2m E of town centre on A518, 400yds from junct A41

Hotel ★★ 68% Royal Victoria Hotel, St Mary's St, NEWPORT ☎ 01952 820331 24 rms

OSWESTRY   Map 07 SJ22

Mile End Mile End, Old Shrewsbury Rd SY11 4JE
☎ 01691 671246 ▤ 01691 670580
e-mail: info@mileendgolfclub.co.uk
A gently undulating parkland-type course covering over 135 acres and including a number of water features, notably the 3rd, 8th and 17th holes, which have greens protected by large pools. The longest hole is the par 5, 542yd 14th, complete with its two tiered green.
18 holes, 6292yds, Par 71, SSS 70, Course record 66.
Club membership 700.
Visitors phone in advance to check availability. **Societies** contact in advance, information available. **Green Fees** £16 per round (£25 weekends & bank holidays). **Cards** 🖼 🖼 🖼 🖼 🖼 **Prof** Scott Carpenter **Course Designer** Price, Gough **Facilities** ⊗ ⅷ by arrangement ▥ ♥ ♀ ♨ ♨ ♣ ⚲ ⚲ **Conf** Corporate Hospitality Days available **Location** 1m SE off A5

Hotel ★★★ 70% Wynnstay Hotel, Church St, OSWESTRY ☎ 01691 655261 29 en suite

Oswestry Aston Park SY11 4JJ
☎ 01691 610535 ▤ 01691 610535
e-mail: secretary@oswestrygolfclub.co.uk
Gently undulating mature parkland course set in splendid Shropshire countryside. Free draining soils make Oswestry an ideal year round test of golf.
18 holes, 6024yds, Par 70, SSS 69, Course record 61.
Club membership 960.
Visitors contact in advance; handicap certificate or play with member. **Societies** contact in advance. **Green Fees** £32 per day, £26 per round (Sat £35/£30). **Prof** David Skelton **Course Designer** James Braid **Facilities** ⊗ ⅷ ▥ ♥ ♀ ♨ ♣ ♨ ♣ ⚲ **Conf** Corporate Hospitality Days available **Location** 2m SE on A5

Hotel ★★★ 70% Wynnstay Hotel, Church St, OSWESTRY ☎ 01691 655261 29 en suite

PANT   Map 07 SJ22

Llanymynech SY10 8LB
☎ 01691 830983 & 830542
e-mail: secretary.llanygc@btinternet.com
Upland course on the site of a prehistoric hillfort with far-reaching views. With 15 holes in Wales and three in England, drive off in Wales and putt out in England on 4th hole. Seven of the old shire counties can be seen from the 12th tee.
18 holes, 6114yds, Par 70, SSS 69, Course record 64.
Club membership 700.
Visitors some weekends restricted; contact in advance. **Societies** contact Secretary. **Green Fees** £30 per day/£20 per round (£25 per round weekends & bank holidays). **Prof** Andrew P Griffiths **Facilities** ⊗ ⅷ ▥ ♥ ♀ ♨ ♣ ⚲ **Conf** Corporate Hospitality Days available **Location** 6m S of Oswestry, off A483 in Pant at Cross Guns Inn

Hotel ★★★ 70% Wynnstay Hotel, Church St, OSWESTRY ☎ 01691 655261 29 en suite

SHIFNAL   Map 07 SJ70

Shifnal Decker Hill TF11 8QL
☎ 01952 460330 ▤ 01952 460330
e-mail: secretary@shifnalgolfclub.co.uk
Well-wooded parkland course. Walking is easy and an attractive country mansion serves as the clubhouse.
18 holes, 6468yds, Par 71, SSS 71, Course record 65.
Club membership 700.
Visitors not Thu, weekends; contact in advance. **Societies** contact in advance. **Green Fees** £35 per day, £28 per 18 holes. **Cards** 🖼 🖼 🖼 **Prof** Justin Flanagan **Course Designer** Pennick **Facilities** ⊗ ⅷ ▥ ♥ ♀ ♨ ♣ ⚲ **Conf** Corporate Hospitality Days available **Location** 1m N off B4379

Hotel ★★★★ 68% Park House Hotel, Park St, SHIFNAL ☎ 01952 460128 38 en suite 16 annexe en suite

SHREWSBURY   Map 07 SJ41

Arscott Arscott, Pontesbury SY5 0XP
☎ 01743 860114 ▤ 01743 860881
At 365ft above sea level, the views from Arscott Golf Club of the hills of south Shropshire and Wales are superb. Arscott is set in mature parkland with water features and holes demanding all sorts of club choice. A challenge to all golfers both high and low handicap.
18 holes, 6178yds, Par 70, SSS 69, Course record 67.
Club membership 550.
Visitors most times available by arrangement. **Societies** apply in writing or phone for tee reservation. **Green Fees** £20 per round (£25 weekends & bank holidays). **Cards** 🖼 🖼 🖼 🖼 🖼 **Course Designer** M Hamer **Facilities** ⊗ ⅷ ▥ ♥ ♀ ♨ ♣ ⚲ **Leisure** fishing, sports injury treatment, massage. **Conf** fac available **Location** off A488 S of town

Hotel ★★★ 63% The Lion Hotel, Wyle Cop, SHREWSBURY ☎ 0870 609 6167 59 en suite

Shrewsbury Condover SY5 7BL
☎ 01743 872976 & 872977 (sec) ▤ 01743 874647
e-mail: info@shrewsbury-golf-club.co.uk
Parkland course. First nine flat, second undulating with good views of the Long Mynd. Several holes with water features. Fast putting surfaces.
18 holes, 6300yds, Par 70, SSS 70.
Club membership 872.
Visitors restricted weekends; contact in advance; handicap certificate. **Societies** contact in writing. **Green Fees** terms on application. **Prof** Peter Seal **Facilities** ⊗ ⅷ ▥ ♥ ♀ ♨ ♣ ♟ ♂ ⚲ **Location** 4m S off A49

Hotel ★★★ 73% Prince Rupert Hotel, Butcher Row, SHREWSBURY ☎ 01743 499955 70 en suite

TELFORD   Map 07 SJ60

Shropshire Golf Centre Granville Park, Muxton TF2 8PQ
☎ 01952 677800 ▤ 01952 677622
e-mail: sales@theshropshire.co.uk
This 27-hole course is set in rolling countryside. The three loops of nine make the most of the natural undulations and provide a challenge for golfers of all

Continued   *Continued*

abilities. Ample stretches of water and bullrush lined ditches, wide countered fairways and rolling greens guarded by mature trees, hummocks and vast bunkers. Several elevated tees with spectacular views.

The Shropshire Golf Centre

Blue: 9 holes, 3286yds, Par 35, SSS 35.
Silver: 9 holes, 3303yds, Par 36, SSS 36.
Gold: 9 holes, 3334yds, Par 36, SSS 36.
Club membership 320.
Visitors advisable to book seven days in advance.
Societies min 12, book in advance. **Green Fees** £25 per 27 holes, £18 per 18 holes, £12 per 9 holes (weekends £29/£24/£14). **Cards** 🖅 📇 📇 🖅 🖭 **Prof** Rob Grier **Course Designer** Martin Hawtree **Facilities** ⊗ 〗 ⅃ ☞ ♀ ⚲ 🖭 ⚑ ⚒ ♂ ⚏ **Leisure** par 3 14-hole academy course. **Conf** fac available Corporate Hospitality Days available **Location** M54/A5 onto B5060 towards Donnington, 3rd exit at Granville rdbt

Telford Golf & Country Club Great Hay Dr, Sutton Heights TF7 4DT
☎ 01952 429977 📠 01952 586602
18 holes, 6761yds, Par 72, SSS 72, Course record 66.
Course Designer Harris, Griffiths **Location** 4m S of town off A442
Phone for further details
....
Hotel ★★★ 66% Telford Golf & Country Club, Great Hay Dr, Sutton Heights, TELFORD ☎ 01952 429977 96 en suite

WELLINGTON Map 07 SJ61

Wrekin Ercall Woods, Golf Links Ln TF6 5BX
☎ 01952 244032 📠 01952 252906
e-mail: wrekingolfclub@btconnect.com
Downland course with some hard walking but superb views.

18 holes, 5570yds, Par 67, SSS 66, Course record 62.
Club membership 675.
Visitors restricted weekends & bank holidays; contact in
Continued

advance. **Societies** apply in writing or phone. **Green Fees** terms on application. **Prof** K Housden **Facilities** ⊗ 〗 ⅃ 🖭 ♀ ⚲ 🖮 ♂ **Location** M54 junct 7, 1.25m S off B5061
....
Hotel ★★★★ 67% Buckatree Hall Hotel, The Wrekin, Wellington, TELFORD ☎ 01952 641821 62 en suite

WESTON-UNDER-REDCASTLE Map 07 SJ52

Hawkstone Park Hotel SY4 5UY
☎ 01939 200611 📠 01939 200335
e-mail: info@hawkstone.co.uk
The Hawkstone Course plays through the English Heritage designated Grade I landscape of the historic park and follies, providing a beautiful, tranquil yet dramatic back drop to a round of golf. The Windmill Course utilises many American style features and extensive water hazards and is a challenging alternative.

Hawkstone Course: 18 holes, 6491yds, Par 72, SSS 71, Course record 65.
Windmill Course: 18 holes, 6476yds, Par 72, SSS 72, Course record 64.
Club membership 650.
Visitors advance booking recommended. **Societies** contact in advance by phone. **Green Fees** £34 per round (£44 weekends). **Cards** 🖅 📇 📇 🖭 📇 🖅 🖭 **Prof** Stuart Leech **Course Designer** J Braid **Facilities** ⊗ 〗 ⅃ 🖭 ♀ ⚲ 🖮 ⚑ 📯 ♄ ♂ ⚏ **Leisure** 6-hole, par 3 course, snooker. **Conf** fac available Corporate Hospitality Days available **Location** off A49/A442, between Whitchurch & Shrewsbury

WHITCHURCH Map 07 SJ54

Hill Valley Terrick Rd SY13 4JZ
☎ 01948 663584 & 667788 📠 01948 665927
e-mail: info@hillvalley.co.uk
Emerald: 18 holes, 6628yds, Par 73, SSS 72, Course record 64.
Sapphire: 18 holes, 4800yds, Par 66, SSS 64.
Course Designer Peter Alliss, Dave Thomas
Location 1m N, signed from bypass
Phone for further details
....
Hotel ★★ 70% Crown Hotel & Restaurant, High St, NANTWICH ☎ 01270 625283 18 en suite

WORFIELD Map 07 SO79

Chesterton Valley Chesterton WV15 5NX
☎ 01746 783682
18 holes, 5671yds, SSS 67.
Course Designer Len Vanes **Location** on B4176
Phone for further details
Continued

Hotel ★★★ Old Vicarage Hotel and Restaurant, Worfield, BRIDGNORTH ☎ 01746 716497 10 en suite 4 annexe en suite

Worfield Roughton WV15 5HE
☎ 01746 716372 📠 01746 716302
e-mail: enquiries@worfieldgolf.co.uk
A parkland links mix with three large lakes, many bunkers and large trees giving a challenge to golfers. Superb views and drainage which allows play on full greens and tees all year. Water comes into play on four holes, including the short par 4 18th where it lies in front of the green.
18 holes, 6545yds, Par 73, SSS 72, Course record 68. Club membership 600.
Visitors not before 1pm weekends; contact in advance. **Societies** phone in advance. **Green Fees** £20 per round (£20 weekends after 1pm). **Cards** 🖃 🏧 🖾 📇 💷 **Prof** Steve Russell **Course Designer** T Williams **Facilities** ⊗ ⊪ ⓑ ♥ ♀ ᛋ ⌂ ♥ 🏄 ♂ **Conf** fac available Corporate Hospitality Days available **Location** 3m W of off A454

Hotel ★★★ Old Vicarage Hotel and Restaurant, Worfield, BRIDGNORTH ☎ 01746 716497 10 en suite 4 annexe en suite

SOMERSET

Tall Pines Cooks Bridle Path, Downside BS48 3DJ
☎ 01275 472076 📠 01275 474869
e-mail: tallpinesgc@ukonline.co.uk
Parkland course with views over the Bristol Channel.
18 holes, 6049yds, Par 70, SSS 70, Course record 65. Club membership 500.
Visitors not am weekends; no green fees before 11am unless by arrangement; must book in advance for pm weekends. **Societies** by arrangement, phone for details. **Green Fees** £20 per round. **Prof** Alex Murray **Course Designer** T Murray **Facilities** ⊗ ⊪ ⓑ ♥ ♀ ᛋ ⌂ ⌂ 🏄 ♥ 🏄 ♂ **Conf** Corporate Hospitality Days available **Location** next to Bristol Airport, 1m off A38/A370

Hotel ★★★ 65% Beachlands Hotel, 17 Uphill Rd North, WESTON-SUPER-MARE ☎ 01934 621401 23 en suite

Bath Sham Castle, North Rd BA2 6JG
☎ 01225 463834 📠 01225 331027
e-mail: enquiries@bathgolfclub.org.uk
Considered to be one of the finest courses in the west, this is the site of Bath's oldest golf club. Situated on high ground overlooking the city and with splendid views over the surrounding countryside. The rocky ground supports good quality turf and there are many good holes. The 17th is a dog-leg right past, or over the corner of an out-of-bounds wall, and then on to an undulating green.
18 holes, 6442yds, Par 71, SSS 71, Course record 66. Club membership 750.
Visitors advisable to contact in advance; handicap certificates. **Societies** Wed, Fri, by arrangement. **Green Fees** not confirmed. **Prof** Peter J Hancox **Course Designer** Colt & others **Facilities** ⊗ ⊪ ⓑ ♥ ♀ ᛋ ⌂ 🏄 ♂ **Location** 1.5m SE city centre off A36

Continued

Hotel ★★★ 72% The Francis, Queen Square, BATH ☎ 0870 400 8223 95 en suite

Entry Hill BA2 5NA
☎ 01225 834248
e-mail: timtapley@aol.com
9 holes, 2065yds, Par 33, SSS 30.
Location off A367
Phone for further details

Lansdown Lansdown BA1 9BT
☎ 01225 422138 📠 01225 339252
e-mail: admin@lansdowngolfclub.co.uk
A flat parkland course situated 800ft above sea level, providing a challenge to both low and high handicap golfers.
18 holes, 6316yds, Par 71, SSS 70, Course record 63. Club membership 700.
Visitors contact in advance for availability; handicap certificate. **Societies** apply in writing or phone in advance. **Green Fees** £23 per day, £12 per round (£29/£15 weekends). **Cards** 🖃 🏧 🖾 📇 💷 **Prof** Terry Mercer **Course Designer** CA Whitcombe **Facilities** ⊗ ⊪ ⓑ ♥ ♀ ᛋ ⌂ ♂ **Conf** fac available Corporate Hospitality Days available **Location** M4 junct 18, 6m SW by Bath racecourse

Hotel ★★★ 70% Pratt's Hotel, South Pde, BATH ☎ 01225 460441 46 en suite

Cannington Cannington College, Cannington TA5 2LS
☎ 01278 655050 📠 01278 655055
Nine-hole links-style course with 18 tees, designed by Martin Hawtree of Oxford. The 4th hole is a challenging 464yd par 4, slightly uphill and into the prevailing wind.
9 holes, 6072yds, Par 68, SSS 70. Club membership 280.
Visitors pay & play anytime ex Wed evening. **Societies** apply in writing. **Green Fees** 18 holes £12.50; 9 holes £9.50 (weekends £18.50/£12.50). **Prof** Ron Macrow **Course Designer** Martin Hawtree **Facilities** ♥ ᛋ ⌂ 🏸 ♂ ⌣ **Leisure** Cycle hire. **Location** 4m NW off A39

Hotel ★★ 76% Combe House Hotel, HOLFORD ☎ 01278 741382 17 rms (16 en suite)

Brean Coast Rd, Brean Sands TA8 2QY
☎ 01278 752111(pro shop) 📠 01278 752111
e-mail: proshop@brean.com
Level moorland course with water hazards. Facilities of Brean Leisure Park adjoining.
18 holes, 5715yds, Par 69, SSS 68, Course record 66. Club membership 350.
Visitors not Sat & Sun before 11.30am. Book in advance through professional. **Societies** contact office or professional in advance. **Green Fees** not confirmed. **Cards** 🖃 🏧 🖾 📇 💷 **Prof** David Haines **Course Designer** In House **Facilities** ⊗ ⊪ ⓑ ♥ ♀ ᛋ ⌂ 🏄 🏸 ♥ 🏄 ♂ **Leisure** heated indoor plus outdoor swimming pool, fishing. **Conf** fac available Corporate Hospitality Days available **Location** M5 junct 22, 4m on coast road

Hotel ★★ ⚑ 69% Batch Country Hotel, Batch Ln, LYMPSHAM ☎ 01934 750371 10 en suite

Burnham & Berrow St Christopher's Way TA8 2PE
☎ 01278 785760 🖹 01278 795440
e-mail: secretary@BurnhamandBerrow.golfclub.co.uk
**Natural championship links course with panoramic
views of the Somerset hills and the Bristol Channel,
with the islands of Steepholm and Flatholm against the
background of the Welsh coast.**
*Championship Course: 18 holes, 6606yds, Par 71, SSS
73, Course record 66.*
Channel Course: 9 holes, 6120yds, Par 70, SSS 69.
Club membership 900.
Visitors contact in advance & have handicap certificate (22
or under gentlemen, 30 or under ladies) to play on the
Championship course. Societies phone in advance. **Green
Fees** not confirmed. **Cards** 🔲 🔲 🔲 🔲 **Prof** Mark
Crowther-Smith **Facilities** ⊗ ⅏ ⅃ ⅃ ⅃ ⅃ ⅃ ⅃
🏌 ⚑ **Location** 1m N of town on B3140

Hotel ★★ 72% Woodlands Country House Hotel, Hill Ln,
BRENT KNOLL ☎ 01278 760232 9 en suite

CHARD   Map 03 ST30

Windwhistle Cricket St Thomas TA20 4DG
☎ 01460 30231 🖹 01460 30055
e-mail: info@windwhistlegolf.co.uk
**Parkland course at 735ft above sea level with
outstanding views over the Somerset Levels to the
Bristol Channel and south Wales.**
*East/West Course: 18 holes, 6510yds, Par 73, SSS 71,
Course record 69.*
Club membership 500.
Visitors contact in advance. Societies by arrangement.
Green Fees terms on application. **Cards** 🔲 🔲 🔲 🔲 🔲
Prof Paul Deeprose **Course Designer** Braid & Taylor,
Fisher **Facilities** ⊗ ⅃ ⅃ ⅃ ⅃ ⅃ ⅃ ⅃ ⅃ ⅃ **Leisure**
squash. **Conf** fac available Corporate Hospitality Days
available **Location** 3m E on A30

Hotel ★★★ 68% Shrubbery Hotel, ILMINSTER
☎ 01460 52108 16 en suite

CLEVEDON   Map 03 ST47

Clevedon Castle Rd, Walton St Mary BS21 7AA
☎ 01275 874057 🖹 01275 341228
e-mail: secretary@clevedongolfclub.co.uk
**Situated on the cliff overlooking the Severn estuary
with distant views of the Welsh coast. Excellent
parkland course in first-class condition. Magnificent
scenery and some tremendous drop holes.**
18 holes, 6557yds, Par 72, SSS 72, Course record 68.
Club membership 750.
Continued

Visitors contact in advance. No play Wed am.
Societies not bank holidays, phone or apply in writing.
Green Fees £30 per day (£40 weekends).
Prof Robert Scanlan **Course Designer** S Herd
Facilities ⊗ ⅃ ⅃ ⅃ ⅃ ⅃ ⅃ ⅃ ⅃ ⅃ **Conf** fac available
Corporate Hospitality Days available
Location M5 junct 20, 1m NE of town centre

Hotel ★★★ 67% Walton Park Hotel, Wellington Ter,
CLEVEDON ☎ 01275 874253 40 en suite

CONGRESBURY   Map 03 ST46

Mendip Spring Honeyhall Ln BS49 5JT
☎ 01934 852322 🖹 01934 853021
e-mail: msgc@melhuish9790.fsworld.co.uk
**Set in peaceful countryside with the Mendip Hills as a
backdrop, this 18-hole course includes lakes and
numerous water hazards covering some 12 acres of the
course. The 12th is an island green surrounded by
water and there are long drives on the 7th and 13th.
The nine-hole Lakeside course is easy walking, mainly
par 4. Floodlit driving range.**
*Brinsea Course: 18 holes, 6352yds, Par 71, SSS 70,
Course record 64.*
Lakeside: 9 holes, 2392yds, Par 34, SSS 66.
Club membership 500.
Visitors contact in advance for Brinsea course & handicap
certificate required for weekends. Lakeside is play & pay
anytime. Societies Booking in advance by arrangement.
Green Fees Brinsea £26 (£35 weekends); Lakeside £9
(£9.50 weekends). **Cards** 🔲 🔲 🔲 🔲 🔲 🔲 **Prof** John
Blackburn & Robert Moss **Facilities** ⊗ ⅃ ⅃ ⅃ ⅃ ⅃ ⅃
⅃ 🏌 ⚑ ⅃ ⅃ **Conf** fac available Corporate Hospitality
Days available **Location** 2m S between A370 & A38

Hotel ★★★ ♨ 70% Daneswood House Hotel, Cuck Hill,
SHIPHAM ☎ 01934 843145 & 843945 🖹 01934 843824
14 en suite 3 annexe en suite

ENMORE   Map 03 ST23

Enmore Park TA5 2AN
☎ 01278 671481 (office) & 671519 (pro)
🖹 01278 671740
e-mail: golfclub@enmore.fsnet.co.uk
**Hilly, parkland course with water features on foothills
of the Quantocks. Wooded countryside and views of
the Mendips; 1st and 10th are testing holes.**
18 holes, 6406yds, Par 71, SSS 71, Course record 66.
Club membership 750.
Visitors phone professional for details, must have handicap
certificate for weekends. Societies contact in advance.
Green Fees £30 per round (£40 weekends). **Cards** 🔲 🔲
🔲 🔲 🔲 **Prof** Nigel Wixon **Course Designer** Hawtree
Facilities ⊗ ⅃ ⅃ ⅃ ⅃ ⅃ ⅃ ⅃ ⅃ 🏌 ⚑ ⅃ **Conf**
Corporate Hospitality Days available **Location** 0.5 E of
village, 3.5m SW of Bridgewater

Hotel ★★★ 72% Walnut Tree Hotel, North Petherton,
BRIDGWATER ☎ 01278 662255 33 en suite

> In the hotel entries, the percentage figure refers to
> the AA's most recent Quality Assessment Score.

FARRINGTON GURNEY · · · · · · · · Map 03 ST65

Farrington Golf & Country Club Marsh Ln
BS39 6TS
☎ 01761 451596 📠 01761 451021
e-mail: info@farringtongolfclub.net
USGA greens on both challenging nine and 18-hole
courses. The 18-hole course has computerised
irrigation, six lakes, four tees per hole and excellent
views. Testing holes include the 12th (282yds) with the
green set behind a lake at the base of a 100ft drop, and
the 17th which is played between two lakes.
*Main Course: 18 holes, 6335yds, Par 72, SSS 71,
Course record 66.*
Club membership 750.
Visitors book starting times & have a handicap certificate
to play at weekends. Societies welcome except for
weekends & bank holidays, phone or write in advance.
Green Fees not confirmed. Cards 💳 💳 💳 💳 Prof Jon
Cowgill Course Designer Peter Thompson Facilities ⊗ ※
🏌 ♥ ♨ 🍴 🏠 🛖 🚬 ✓ ⓣ Leisure sauna, solarium,
gymnasium, video teaching studio. Conf fac available
Corporate Hospitality Days available
Location SE of village off A37

Hotel ★★★ 72% Centurion Hotel, Charlton Ln,
MIDSOMER NORTON ☎ 01761 417711 44 en suite

FROME · Map 03 ST74

Frome Golf Centre Critchill Manor BA11 4LJ
☎ 01373 453410
e-mail: fromegolfclub@yahoo.co.uk
Attractive parkland course, founded in 1992, situated in
picturesque valley just outside the town, complete
with practice areas and a driving range.
9 holes, 5466yds, Par 69, SSS 67, Course record 64.
Club membership 360.
Visitors tee times essential at weekends & bank holidays.
Societies phone in advance. Green Fees not confirmed.
Prof L Wilkin, T Isaac Facilities ⊗ 🏌 ♥ ♨ 🍴 🏠 🛖 ✓ ⓣ
Location 1m SE of town centre

Hotel ★★ 65% The George at Nunney, 11 Church St,
NUNNEY ☎ 01373 836458 9 rms (8 en suite)

Orchardleigh BA11 2PH
☎ 01373 454200 & 454206 📠 01373 454202
e-mail: trevor@orchardleighgolf.co.uk
An 18-hole parkland course set amid Somerset
countryside, designed by former Ryder Cup player
Brian Huggett. Water comes into play on seven holes.
9 holes, 6831yds, Par 72, SSS 73, Course record 67.
Club membership 550.
Visitors no visitors before 11am at weekends. Societies
apply in writing or phone in advance. Green Fees £30 per
round (£40 weekends & bank holidays). Cards 💳 💳 💳
💳 💳 💳 💳 Prof Ian Ridsdale Course Designer Brian Huggett
Facilities ⊗ ※ 🏌 ♥ ♨ 🍴 🏠 🛖 🚬 ✓ ⓣ Leisure fishing.
Conf fac available Corporate Hospitality Days available
Location 1m W of Frome on A362

Hotel ★★ 65% The George at Nunney, 11 Church St,
NUNNEY ☎ 01373 836458 9 rms (8 en suite)

GURNEY SLADE · · · · · · · · · · · Map 03 ST64

Mendip BA3 4UT
☎ 01749 840570 📠 01749 841439
e-mail: mendipgolfclub@lineone.net
Undulating downland course offering an interesting test
of golf on superb fairways and extensive views over the
surrounding countryside.
18 holes, 6383yds, Par 71, SSS 71, Course record 65.
Club membership 900.
Visitors Handicap certificates required for play at
weekends & bank holidays. Societies by arrangement with
secretary. Green Fees £26 per round (£35 weekends). Prof
Adrian Marsh Course Designer CK Cotton Facilities ⊗
※ 🏌 ♥ ♨ 🍴 🏠 🛖 ✓ ⓣ Location 1.5m S off A37

Hotel ★★★ 72% Centurion Hotel, Charlton Ln,
MIDSOMER NORTON ☎ 01761 417711 44 en suite

KEYNSHAM · · · · · · · · · · · · · · Map 03 ST66

Stockwood Vale Stockwood Ln BS31 2ER
☎ 0117 986 6505 📠 0117 986 8974
e-mail: stockwoodvalegc@netscapeonline.co.uk
18 holes, 6031yds, Par 71, SSS 69.
Location off Hicks Gate on junct A4 & A4174
Phone for further details

Guesthouse ♦♦♦♦ Grasmere Court Hotel, 22-24 Bath
Rd, KEYNSHAM ☎ 0117 986 2662 16 en suite

LANGPORT · · · · · · · · · · · · · · · Map 03 ST42

Long Sutton Long Sutton TA10 9JU
☎ 01458 241017 📠 01458 241022
e-mail: reservations@longsuttongolf.com
Gentle, undulating, but testing parkland course. Pay
and play course.

LONG SUTTON GOLF CLUB 01458 241017

18 holes, 6369yds, Par 71, SSS 70, Course record 65.
Club membership 750.
Visitors advisable to phone in advance. Societies phone in
advance. Green Fees £30 per day, £20 per 18 holes, £10
per 9 holes (£35/£25/£12.50 weekends). Cards 💳 💳 💳
💳 💳 💳 💳 Prof Andrew Hayes Course Designer
Patrick Dawson Facilities ⊗ ※ 🏌 ♥ ♨ 🍴 🏠 🛖 ✓ ⓣ
Conf fac available Corporate Hospitality Days available
Location 3.5m E of Langport, 0.5m S of Long Sutton on
B3165

Hotel ★★★ 72% The Hollies, Bower Hinton, MARTOCK
☎ 01935 822232 33 annexe en suite

LONG ASHTON
Map 03 ST57

Long Ashton The Clubhouse, Clarken Coombe
BS41 9DW
☎ 01275 392229 ▤ 01275 394395
e-mail: secretary@longashtongolfclub.co.uk
**Wooded parkland course with fine turf, wonderful
views of Bristol and surrounding areas, and a spacious
practice area. Good testing holes, especially the back
nine, in prevailing south-west wind. Good drainage
ensures pleasant winter golf.**

18 holes, 6193yds, Par 70, SSS 70.
Club membership 700.
Visitors with recognised handicap certificate. **Societies**
contact the secretary in advance. **Green Fees** £30 per
round (£35 weekends). **Cards** ▦ ▦ ▨ ▨ **Prof** Mike
Hart **Course Designer** JH Taylor **Facilities** ⊗ ⫴ ⮸ �P ♀
△ ⌂ ⚑ ∂ **Conf** Corporate Hospitality Days available
Location 0.5m N on B3128

Hotel ★★★ 68% Corus hotel Bristol, Beggar Bush Ln,
Failand, BRISTOL ☎ 0870 609 6144 112 en suite

Woodspring Golf & Country Club Yanley Ln
BS41 9LR
☎ 01275 394378 ▤ 01275 394473
e-mail: info@woodspring-golf.com
**Set in 245 acres of undulating Somerset countryside,
featuring superb natural water hazards, protected
greens and a rising landscape. Designed by Peter Alliss
and Clive Clark and laid out by Donald Steel, the
course has three individual nine-hole courses, the Avon,
Severn and Brunel. The 9th hole on the Brunel Course
is a feature hole, with an elevated tee shot over a
natural gorge. In undulating hills south of Bristol, long
carries to tight fairways, elevated island tees and
challenging approaches to greens make the most of the
27 holes.**
Avon Course: 9 holes, 2960yds, Par 35, SSS 34.
Brunel Course: 9 holes, 3320yds, Par 37, SSS 35.
Severn Course: 9 holes, 3267yds, Par 36, SSS 35.
Club membership 550.
Visitors contact in advance, weekends may be limited to
play after midday. Dress codes must be adhered to.
Societies please contact Dave Watson in advance. **Green
Fees** £28 per 18 holes (£32 weekends). **Cards** ▦ ▦ ▨
▨ ▨ **Prof** Kevin Pitts **Course Designer** Clarke, Alliss,
Steel **Facilities** ⊗ ⫴ ⮸ �P ♀ △ ⌂ ⚑ ✎ ⚒ ∂ ♦
Conf fac available Corporate Hospitality Days available
Location off A38 Bridgwater road

Hotel ★★★ 68% Corus hotel Bristol, Beggar Bush Ln,
Failand, BRISTOL ☎ 0870 609 6144 112 en suite

MIDSOMER NORTON
Map 03 ST65

Fosseway Golf Course Charlton Ln BA3 4BD
☎ 01761 412214 ▤ 01761 418357
e-mail: centurion@centurionhotel.co.uk
**Very attractive tree-lined parkland course, not
demanding but with lovely views towards the Mendip
Hills.**
9 holes, 4565yds, Par 67, SSS 61.
Club membership 300.
Visitors not Wed evenings, Sun am & competitions days.
Societies apply in writing or phone. **Green Fees** £15 per
day. **Cards** ▦ ▦ ▦ ▨ ▨ **Course Designer** CK
Cotton, F Pennink **Facilities** ⊗ ⫴ ⮸ �P ♀ △ ⌂ ⚑ ∂
Leisure heated indoor swimming pool, sauna, gymnasium.
Conf fac available Corporate Hospitality Days available
Location SE of town centre off A367

Hotel ★★★ 72% Centurion Hotel, Charlton Ln,
MIDSOMER NORTON ☎ 01761 417711 44 en suite

MINEHEAD
Map 03 SS94

Minehead & West Somerset The Warren
TA24 5SJ
☎ 01643 702057 ▤ 01643 705095
e-mail: secretary@mineheadgolf.co.uk
**Flat seaside links, very exposed to wind, with good turf
set on a shingle bank. The last five holes adjacent to the
beach are testing. The 215yd 18th is wedged between
the beach and the club buildings and provides a good
finish.**
18 holes, 6228yds, Par 71, SSS 70, Course record 65.
Club membership 620.
Visitors contact secretary in advance. **Societies** phone in
advance. **Green Fees** not confirmed. **Cards** ▦ ▦ ▦
▦ ▨ ▨ **Prof** Ian Read **Facilities** ⊗ ⫴ ⮸ �P ♀ △ ⌂
⚑ ∂ **Conf** Corporate Hospitality Days available
Location E end of esplanade

Hotel ★★★ 64% Northfield Hotel, Northfield Rd,
MINEHEAD ☎ 01643 705155 28 en suite

SALTFORD
Map 03 ST66

Saltford Golf Club Ln BS31 3AA
☎ 01225 873513 ▤ 01225 873525
**Parkland course with easy walking and panoramic
views over the Avon valley. The par 4 2nd and 13th are
notable.**
18 holes, 6081yds, Par 71, SSS 71.
Club membership 800.
Visitors contact in advance & have handicap certificate.
Societies phone in advance. **Green Fees** £28 per day;
£24 per round (£32 per round weekends). **Prof** Dudley
Millinstead **Course Designer** Harry Vardon **Facilities** ⊗
⫴ ⮸ �P ♀ △ ⌂ ⚑ ✎ ⚒ ∂ **Conf** fac available
Corporate Hospitality Days available **Location** S of village

Hotel ★★★ ♨ 79% Hunstrete House Hotel,
HUNSTRETE ☎ 01761 490490 25 en suite

SOMERTON
Map 03 ST42

Wheathill Wheathill TA11 7HG
☎ 01963 240667 ▤ 01963 240230
e-mail: wheathill@wheathill.fsnet.co.uk
**A par 68 parkland course with nice views in quiet
countryside. It is flat lying with the 13th hole along the**

Continue

river. There is an academy course and a massive
practice area.

18 holes, 5362yds, Par 68, SSS 66, Course record 61.
Club membership 500.

Visitors phone to book Fri, Sat & Sun. **Societies** phone to
arrange. **Green Fees** £17 per round (£20 weekends & bank
holidays). **Prof** A England **Course Designer** J Pain
Facilities ⊗ ℳ ㅤ ♨ ♀ ⌂ 🏠 ⚑ ➤ 🏌 ⚐ **Leisure**
8-hole academy course. **Conf** fac available Corporate
Hospitality Days available **Location** 5m E of Somerton off
B3153

....

Hotel ★★★ 57% Wessex Hotel, High St, STREET
☎ 01458 443383 49 en suite

TAUNTON   Map 03 ST22

Oake Manor Oake TA4 1BA
☎ 01823 461993 📠 01823 461995
e-mail: russell@oakemanor.com

**A parkland and lakeland course situated in
breathtaking Somerset countryside with views of the
Quantock, Blackdown and Brendon hills. Ten holes
feature water hazards such as lakes, cascades and a
trout stream. The 15th hole (par 5, 476yds) is bounded
by water all down the left with a carry over another
lake on to an island green. The course is challenging yet
great fun for all standards of golfer.**

18 holes, 6109yds, Par 70, SSS 69, Course record 65.
Club membership 600.

Visitors no restrictions but visitors must book start times in
order to avoid disappointment; phone 01823 461993.
Societies contact Golf Manager Russell Gardner by phone
or e-mail. **Green Fees** £23 per 18 holes (£27 weekends).
Cards ▦ ▦ 🟥 ⚑ ⚐ **Prof** R Gardner, J Smallacombe
Course Designer Adrian Stiff **Facilities** ⊗ ℳ ㅤ ♨ ♀ ⌂
🏠 ⚑ ⚐ ⚐ **Leisure** 2-hole academy course, short game
area. **Conf** fac available Corporate Hospitality Days
available **Location** M5 junct 26, A38 towards Taunton &
signs to Oake

....

Hotel ★★★ 73% Rumwell Manor Hotel, Rumwell,
TAUNTON ☎ 01823 461902 10 en suite 10 annexe
en suite

Taunton & Pickeridge Corfe TA3 7BY
☎ 01823 421537 📠 01823 421742
e-mail: admin@tauntongolf.co.uk

**Downland course established in 1892 with extensive
views of the Quantock and Mendip hills. Renowned for
its excellent greens.**

18 holes, 6020yds, Par 69, SSS 69, Course record 66.
Club membership 800.

Visitors handicap certificate. **Societies** phone in advance.
Green Fees £28 per day; £24 per round (£35 weekends).

Continued

Creech Heathfield,
Taunton, Somerset
TA3 5EY

☎ 01823 412220 (Secretary)
☎ 01823 412880 (Pro Shop, Tee Time bookings)
www.tauntonvalegolf.co.uk

Taunton Value is extremely accessible from
J.24 or 25 of the M5. The complex comprises
of 27 holes of parkland courses set amid 156
acres of gently rolling Somerset countryside
with 10 bay floodlit driving range, chipping and
putting area and excellent clubhouse facilities.

Societies and Visitors always welcome with
value for money packages.
Corporate days catered for.

Cards ▦ ▦ ▦ 🟦 ▦ 🟥 ⚐ **Prof** Simon Stevenson
Facilities ⊗ ℳ ㅤ ♨ ♀ ⌂ 🏠 ⚐ **Conf** fac available
Corporate Hospitality Days available
Location 4m S off B3170

....

Hotel ★★★ 73% The Mount Somerset Hotel, Lower
Henlade, TAUNTON ☎ 01823 442500 11 en suite

Taunton Vale Creech Heathfield TA3 5EY
☎ 01823 412220 📠 01823 413583
e-mail: tvgc@easynet.co.uk

**An 18-hole and a nine-hole course in a parkland
complex occupying 156 acres in the Vale of Taunton.
Floodlit driving range.**

Taunton Vale Golf Club

Charlton Course: 18 holes, 6163yds, Par 70, SSS 69.
Durston Course: 9 holes, 2004yds, Par 32.
Club membership 800.
Visitors phone booking essential. Must contact

Continued

Professional **Societies** book in advance. Not am at weekends. **Green Fees** 18-hole course £20 per round (£25 weekends); 9-hole course £10 per round (£15 weekends). **Cards** **Prof** Martin Keitch **Course Designer** John Payne **Facilities** by arrangement **Conf** fac available Corporate Hospitality Days available
Location off A38 between M5 juncts 24 & 25

Hotel ★★★ 73% The Mount Somerset Hotel, Lower Henlade, TAUNTON ☎ 01823 442500 11 en suite

Vivary Park Municipal Fons George TA1 3JU
☎ 01823 333875 01823 352713
e-mail: vivary.golf.course@tauntondeane.gov.uk
18 holes, 4620yds, Par 63, SSS 63, Course record 59.
Course Designer WH Fowler **Location** S of town centre off A38
Phone for further details

Hotel ★★★ 64% Corner House Hotel, Park St, TAUNTON ☎ 01823 284683 28 en suite

WEDMORE — Map 03 ST44

Isle of Wedmore Lineage BS28 4QT
☎ 01934 712452 (pro shop) 01934 713554
e-mail: office@wedmoregc.fsnet.co.uk
Gently undulating course designed to maintain natural environment. Existing woodland and hedgerow enhanced by new planting. Magnificent panoramic views of Cheddar valley and Glastonbury Tor. The par 3 16th hole has a water feature and the signature hole is the par 3 11th with an elevation to the tee.
18 holes, 5850yds, Par 70, SSS 69, Course record 67. Club membership 680.
Visitors phone professional in advance. Not before 9.30am weekends. **Societies** weekdays phone in advance, weekends subject to competitions. **Green Fees** £32 per day, £22 per round. Reduced winter rates. **Cards** **Prof** Graham Coombe **Course Designer** Terry Murray **Facilities**
Leisure indoor teaching studio & custom fitting centre.
Conf fac available Corporate Hospitality Days available
Location 0.5m N of Wedmore

Hotel ★★★ 74% Swan Hotel, Sadler St, WELLS ☎ 01749 836300 50 en suite

WELLS — Map 03 ST54

Wells (Somerset) East Horrington Rd BA5 3DS
☎ 01749 675005 01749 683170
e-mail: secretary@wellsgolfclub99.freeserve.co.uk
Beautiful wooded course with wonderful views. The prevailing SW wind complicates the 448yd 3rd. Good drainage and paths for trolleys are being constructed all round the course.
18 holes, 6053yds, Par 70, SSS 69, Course record 66. Club membership 670.
Visitors contact in advance & have handicap certificate weekends. Tee times restricted at weekends to after 9.30pm **Societies** apply in advance. **Green Fees** £25 per 18 holes (£32 weekends & bank holidays). **Cards** **Prof** Adrian Bishop **Facilities**
Conf Corporate Hospitality Days available
Location 1.5m E off B3139

Hotel ★★★ 74% Swan Hotel, Sadler St, WELLS ☎ 01749 836300 50 en suite

WESTON-SUPER-MARE — Map 03 ST36

Weston-Super-Mare Uphill Rd North BS23 4NQ
☎ 01934 626968 & 633360(pro) 01934 621360
e-mail: wsmgolfclub@eurotelbroadband.com
A compact and interesting layout with the opening hole adjacent to the beach. The sandy, links-type course is slightly undulating and has beautifully maintained turf and greens. The 15th is a testing 455yd par 4. Superb views across the Bristol Channel to Cardiff.

18 holes, 6245yds, Par 70, SSS 70, Course record 65. Club membership 750.
Visitors have handicap certificate to play. **Societies** apply in writing or phone. **Green Fees** £36 per round (£56 weekends). **Cards** **Prof** Mike Laband **Course Designer** T Dunne, Dr MacKenzie **Facilities** **Location** S of town centre off A370

Hotel ★★★ 65% Beachlands Hotel, 17 Uphill Rd North, WESTON-SUPER-MARE ☎ 01934 621401 23 en suite

Worlebury Monks Hill BS22 9SX
☎ 01934 625789 01934 621935
e-mail: secretary@worleburygc.co.uk
Situated on the ridge of Worlebury Hill, this parkland course offers fairly easy walking and extensive views of the Severn estuary and Wales.
18 holes, 5963yds, Par 70, SSS 69, Course record 66. Club membership 650.
Visitors must be recognised golfers, handicap certificate or proof of club membership may be required. **Societies** apply in writing or phone in advance. **Green Fees** terms on application. **Cards** **Prof** Gary Marks **Course Designer** H Vardon **Facilities**
Location 2m NE off A370

Hotel ★★★ 65% Beachlands Hotel, 17 Uphill Rd North, WESTON-SUPER-MARE ☎ 01934 621401 23 en suite

YEOVIL — Map 03 ST51

Yeovil Sherborne Rd BA21 5BW
☎ 01935 422965 01935 411283
e-mail: yeovilgolfclub@yeovilgc.fsnet.co.uk
On the Old Course the opener lies by the River Yeo before the gentle climb to high downs with good views. The outstanding 14th and 15th holes present a challenge, being below the player with a deep railway cutting on the left of the green. The 1st on the Newton Course is played over the river which then leads to a challenging but scenic course.
Old Course: 18 holes, 6150yds, Par 72, SSS 70, Course record 64.

Continued

ewton Course: 9 holes, 4905yds, Par 68, SSS 65,
ourse record 63.
lub membership 1000.
isitors contact in advance. Members only before 9.30am
12.30-2. Handicap certificate required for Old Course.
cieties phone in advance. Green Fees Old Course Apr-
ct £30 (£40 weekends & bank holidays), Nov-Mar £25
30); Newton Course £18 (£20). Cards 🖃 🔲 📰 🔤
of Geoff Kite Course Designer Fowler & Allison
cilities ⊗ ℳ 🖳 🐾 ♀ 🖻 🚩 🐾 🚜 ⚷ ₹
cation 1m E on A30

....

tel ★★★ 74% The Yeovil Court Hotel Limited, West
ker Rd, YEOVIL ☎ 01935 863746 18 en suite
annexe en suite

STAFFORDSHIRE

ROCTON   Map 07 SJ91

rocton Hall ST17 0TH
☎ 01785 661901 📱 01785 661591
mail: broctonsec@aol.com
arkland course with gentle slopes in places, easy
alking.
 holes, 6064yds, Par 69, SSS 69, Course record 66.
ub membership 665.
sitors not competition days. Must contact in advance.
cieties apply in advance. Green Fees £38 per day (£45
eekends & bank holidays). Cards 🖃 🔲 📰 🔤 Prof
vil Bland Course Designer Harry Vardon Facilities ⊗
🖳 🐾 ♀ △ 🖻 🚩 🐾 🚜 ⚷ Leisure snooker.
cation NW of village off A34

....

tel ★★★ 63% The Garth Hotel, Wolverhampton Rd,
ss Pit, STAFFORD ☎ 0870 609 6169 60 en suite

URTON UPON TRENT   Map 08 SK22

elmont Belmot Rd, Needwood DE13 9PH
 01283 814381 📱 01283 814381
nine-hole course with five par 4s, the longest hole
ing 430yds. The course comprises trees, bunkers,
me water and great views.
oles, 2201yds, Par 32, Course record 31.
sitors individual bag of clubs per person & correct dress
de. Societies phone or write in advance. Green Fees £12
 18 holes, £7.50 per 9 holes (£15/£9 weekends). Prof
Coy Facilities 🖳 🐾 ♀ 🖻 🚩 ⚷ ₹ Leisure fishing,
chery. Conf Corporate Hospitality Days available
cation 3m NW of Burton, off B5017 towards Tutbury

....

tel ★★ 72% Riverside Hotel, Riverside Dr, Branston,
URTON UPON TRENT ☎ 01283 511234 22 en suite

ranston Burton Rd, Branston DE14 3DP
 01283 512211 📱 01283 566984
nail: sales@branston-golf-club.co.uk
mi-parkland course adjacent to River Trent, on
dulating ground with natural water hazards on 13
les. A nine-hole course has recently been opened.
 holes, 6697yds, Par 72, SSS 72, Course record 65.
ub membership 800.
sitors not before 12.30pm or at weekends. Must contact
advance. Societies phone in advance. Green Fees not
nfirmed. Cards 🖃 🔲 📰 📰 🔤 Prof Richard Odell
urse Designer G Ramshall Facilities ⊗ ℳ 🖳 🐾 ♀ △

🖻 🚩 🚜 ⚷ ₹ Leisure heated indoor swimming pool,
sauna, solarium, gymnasium, nine-hole course.
Conf fac available Corporate Hospitality Days available
Location 1.5m SW on A5121

Branston Golf & Country Club

....

Hotel ★★ 72% Riverside Hotel, Riverside Dr, Branston,
BURTON UPON TRENT ☎ 01283 511234 22 en suite

Burton-upon-Trent 43 Ashby Rd East DE15 0PS
☎ 01283 544551(sec) & 562240 (pro) 📱 01283 544551
e-mail: burtongolfclub@btinternet.com
**Undulating parkland course with trees a major feature
and water features on two holes. Testing par 3s at 10th
and 12th.**

*18 holes, 6579yds, Par 71, SSS 71, Course record 63.
Club membership 650.*
Visitors contact in advance & have a handicap certificate.
Societies by arrangement with the Secretary. Green Fees
£46 per day; £35 per round (£52/£40 weekends & bank
holidays). Prof Gary Stafford Course Designer HS Colt
Facilities ⊗ ℳ 🖳 🐾 ♀ △ 🖻 🚩 ⚷ Conf Corporate
Hospitality Days available Location 3m E of Burton on
A511

....

Guesthouse ♦♦♦♦ Edgecote Hotel, 179 Ashby Rd,
BURTON UPON TRENT ☎ 01283 568966 11 rms
(5 en suite)

Craythorne Craythorne Rd, Stretton DE13 0AZ
☎ 01283 564329 📱 01283 511908
e-mail: admin@craythorne.co.uk
**A relatively short and challenging parkland course with
tight fairways and views of the Trent valley. Excellent
greens giving all year play. Suits all standards but
particularly good for society players. The course is now
settled and in good condition after major
refurbishment.**
*18 holes, 5645yds, Par 68, SSS 68, Course record 66.
Club membership 500.*

Continued   Continued

Visitors not before 10.30am & must contact in advance. **Societies** apply in writing or phone for details. **Green Fees** £34 per day, £28 per round. **Cards** 💳 💳 💳 💳 **Prof** Steve Hadfield **Course Designer** AA Wright **Facilities** ⊗ 💷 🏌 💷 ♀ 🛆 🏠 🍴 🐟 🛒 ♂ 🍴 **Conf** fac available Corporate Hospitality Days available **Location** off A38 through Stretton, tourist signs

....

Guesthouse ♦♦♦♦ Edgecote Hotel, 179 Ashby Rd, BURTON UPON TRENT ☎ 01283 568966 11 rms (5 en suite)

Hoar Cross Hall Health Spa Resort

Hoar Cross DE13 8QS
☎ 01283 575671 📋 01283 575652
e-mail: info@hoarcross.co.uk
Golf academy located in the grounds of a stately home, now a health spa resort and hotel. Driving range, bunker and practice areas.
Hoar Cross Hall Health Spa Golf Academy:
Club membership 300.
Visitors day guests & residents. **Societies** golfing societies that are resident only. **Green Fees** not confirmed. **Prof** Richard Coy **Course Designer** Geoffrey Collins **Facilities** 🛆 🏠 🍴 🎯 🍴 **Leisure** hard tennis courts, heated indoor swimming pool, sauna, solarium, gymnasium. **Conf** fac available

....

Hotel ⌂ Travelodge, Western Springs Rd, RUGELEY ☎ 08700 850 950 32 en suite

CANNOCK   Map 07 SJ91

Beau Desert Rugeley Rd, Hazelslade WS12 0PJ
☎ 01543 422626 📋 01543 451137
e-mail: beaudesert@btconnect.com
A moorland course with firm and fast fairways and greens, used on many occasions as an Open qualifier course. The course has many varied and testing holes ranging from the 1st over a pit, the 10th over a ravine, to the 18th with a second shot across gorse traversing the fairway.
18 holes, 6310yds, Par 70, SSS 71, Course record 64.
Club membership 650.
Visitors are advised to contact professional in advance. **Societies** contact in advance. **Green Fees** £50 per round (£60 weekends & bank holidays). **Prof** Barrie Stevens **Course Designer** Herbert Fowler **Facilities** ⊗ 💷 🏌 💷 ♀ 🛆 🏠 🍴 🎯 🍴 **Conf** fac available Corporate Hospitality Days available **Location** off A460 NE of Hednesford

....

Hotel ★★★ 64% The Roman Way Hotel, Watling St, Hatherton, CANNOCK ☎ 0870 609 6125 56 en suite

Cannock Park Stafford Rd WS11 2AL
☎ 01543 578850 📋 01543 578850
e-mail: david.dunk@18global.co.uk
Part of a large leisure centre, this parkland-type course plays alongside Cannock Chase. Severe slopes on some greens. Good drainage, open all year.
18 holes, 5149yds, Par 67, SSS 65.
Club membership 200.
Visitors phone pro shop on 01543 578850 to book in advance. **Societies** please phone in advance. **Green Fees** £9.50 per round (£11.50 weekends). **Cards** 💳 💳 💳 **Prof** David Dunk **Course Designer** John Mainland **Facilities** ⊗ 💷 🏌 💷 ♀ 🛆 🏠 🍴 🍴 **Leisure** hard tennis courts, heated indoor swimming pool, sauna, solarium, gymnasium. **Location** 0.5m N of town centre on A34

....

Hotel ★★★ 64% The Roman Way Hotel, Watling St, Hatherton, CANNOCK ☎ 0870 609 6125 56 en suite

ENVILLE   Map 07 SO88

Enville Highgate Common DY7 5BN
☎ 01384 872074 (office) 📋 01384 873396
e-mail: secretary@envillegolfclub.com
Easy walking on two fairly flat woodland and heathlan courses.
Highgate Course: 18 holes, 6556yds, Par 72, SSS 72, Course record 65.
Lodge Course: 18 holes, 6290yds, Par 70, SSS 70, Course record 66.
Club membership 900.
Visitors must play with member at weekends. **Societies** phone initially for details. **Green Fees** £45 per day; £35 per 18 holes. **Prof** Sean Power **Facilities** ⊗ 💷 🏌 💷 ♀ 🛆 🏠 🍴 🛒 🍴 **Conf** Corporate Hospitality Days available **Location** 2m NE of Enville off A458

....

Hotel ★★★★ 66% Mill Hotel & Restaurant, ALVELEY ☎ 01746 780437 41 en suite

GOLDENHILL   Map 07 SJ85

Goldenhill Mobberley Rd ST6 5SS
☎ 01782 234200 📋 01782 234303
Rolling parkland course with water features on six of the back nine holes.
18 holes, 5957yds, Par 71, SSS 69.
Club membership 300.
Visitors advisable to contact in advance. **Societies** apply in writing or phone. **Green Fees** not confirmed. **Facilities** ⊗ 💷 🏌 💷 ♀ 🛆 🍴 🍴 **Location** on A50 4m N of Stoke

....

Hotel ★★★ 69% Manor House Hotel, Audley Rd, ALSAGER ☎ 01270 884000 57 en suite

HIMLEY   Map 07 SO89

Himley Hall Golf Centre Log Cabin, Himley Hall Park DY3 4DF
☎ 01902 895207
Parkland course set in the grounds of Himley Hall Park. Large practice area including a pitch and putt.
9 holes, 6215yds, Par 72, SSS 70, Course record 65.
Club membership 200.
Visitors restricted weekends. **Societies** welcome weekday apply in writing or phone in advance. **Green Fees** summe 18 holes £12; 9 holes £8 (winter: £10/£7). **Prof** Mark Sparrow **Course Designer** A Baker **Facilities** 🏌 💷 🏠 🍴 **Location** 0.5m E on B4176

....

Hotel ★★★ 64% The Himley Country Hotel, School Rd, HIMLEY ☎ 0870 609 6112 73 en suite

LEEK   Map 07 SJ9

Leek Birchall, Cheddleton Rd ST13 5RE
☎ 01538 384779 & 384767 (pro) 📋 01538 384535
e-mail: secretary@leekgolfclub.fsnet.co.uk
Undulating, challenging, mainly parkland course, reputedly one of the best in the area. In its early years the course was typical moorland with sparse tree growth but its development since the 1960s has produced tree-lined fairways which are much appeciated by golfers for their lush playing qualities.
18 holes, 6218yds, Par 70, SSS 70, Course record 63.
Club membership 825.

Continued
Continu

Visitors contact Professional in advance, not after 3pm without a member. **Societies** apply in advance to Hon Secretary. **Green Fees** £26 per day (£32 weekends). **Prof** Paul Toyer **Facilities** **Leisure** snooker. **Conf** Corporate Hospitality Days available **Location** 0.75m S on A520

Westwood (Leek) Newcastle Rd ST13 7AA
☎ 01538 398385 01538 382485
A challenging moorland and parkland course set in beautiful open countryside with an undulating front nine. The back nine is more open and longer with the River Churnet coming into play on several holes.
18 holes, 6207yds, Par 70, SSS 69, Course record 66.
Club membership 700.
Visitors book in advance. **Societies** apply by phone or in writing. **Green Fees** terms on application. **Prof** Darren Squire **Facilities** **Conf** fac available Corporate Hospitality Days available **Location** on A53 S of Leek

LICHFIELD Map 07 SK10

Seedy Mill Elmhurst WS13 8HE
☎ 01543 417333 01543 418098
e-mail: seedymill.sales@theclubcompany.com
A 27 hole course in picturesque parkland scenery. Numerous holes crossed by meandering mill streams. Undulating greens defended by hazards lie in wait for the practised approach.
Mill Course: 18 holes, 6042yds, Par 72, SSS 70, Course record 67.
Club membership 1200.
Visitors must contact no more than three days in advance, weekend time restrictions. **Societies** apply in writing or phone. **Green Fees** Mill Course £26 per 18 holes (£35 weekends); 9 holes £7.50. **Cards** **Prof** Simon Joyce **Course Designer** Hawtree & Son **Facilities** **Leisure** 9-hole par 3 course. **Conf** fac available Corporate Hospitality Days available **Location** 3m N of Lichfield off B5014

Hotel ★★★ 68% Little Barrow Hotel, 62 Beacon St, LICHFIELD ☎ 01543 414500 24 en suite

Whittington Heath Tamworth Rd WS14 9PW
☎ 01543 432317 01543 433962
e-mail: info@whgcgolf.freeserve.co.uk
The 18 magnificent holes wind through heathland and trees, presenting a good test for the serious golfer. Leaving the fairway can be severely punished. The dog-legs are most tempting, inviting the golfer to chance his arm. Local knowledge is a definite advantage. Clear views of the famous three spires of Lichfield Cathedral.
18 holes, 6490yds, Par 70, SSS 71, Course record 64.
Club membership 660.
Visitors not weekends; contact in advance; handicap certificate. **Societies** welcome Wed & Thu, must apply in writing. **Green Fees** £50 per 36 holes; £42 per 27 holes; £35 per 18 holes. **Cards** **Prof** Adrian Sadler **Course Designer** Colt **Facilities** **Conf** Corporate Hospitality Days available **Location** 2.5m SE on A51

Hotel ★★★ 68% Little Barrow Hotel, 62 Beacon St, LICHFIELD ☎ 01543 414500 24 en suite

NEWCASTLE-UNDER-LYME Map 07 SJ84

Keele Golf Centre Newcastle Rd, Keele ST5 5AB
☎ 01782 627596 01782 714555
e-mail: jackbarker_keelegolfcentreltd@hotmail.com
Parkland course with mature trees and great views of Stoke-on-Trent and surrounding area.

18 holes, 6396yds, Par 71, SSS 70, Course record 64.
Club membership 400.
Visitors contact in advance, bookings from seven days in advance. **Societies Green Fees** terms on application. **Cards** **Course Designer** Hawtree **Facilities** **Location** 2m W of Newcastle on A525 opp Keele University

Hotel ★★ 60% Stop Inn Newcastle-under-Lyme, Liverpool Rd, Cross Heath, NEWCASTLE-UNDER-LYME ☎ 01782 717000 43 rms (42 en suite) 24 annexe en suite

Newcastle-Under-Lyme Whitmore Rd ST5 2QB
☎ 01782 617006 01782 617531
e-mail: info@newcastlegolfclub.co.uk
Parkland course.
18 holes, 6404yds, Par 72, SSS 71.
Club membership 600.
Visitors contact in advance. With member only weekends. **Societies** contact in advance. **Green Fees** not confirmed. **Prof** Paul Symonds **Facilities** **Conf** fac available Corporate Hospitality Days available **Location** 1m SW on A53

Hotel ★★ 60% Stop Inn Newcastle-under-Lyme, Liverpool Rd, Cross Heath, NEWCASTLE-UNDER-LYME ☎ 01782 717000 43 rms (42 en suite) 24 annexe en suite

Wolstanton Dimsdale Old Hall, Hassam Pde, Wolstanton ST5 9DR
☎ 01782 622413 (Sec)
A challenging undulating suburban course incorporating six difficult par 3 holes. The 6th hole (par 3) is 233yds from the Medal Tee.
18 holes, 5807yds, Par 68, SSS 68, Course record 63.
Club membership 700.
Visitors not Tue (Ladies Day); with member only weekends & bank holidays; contact in advance. **Societies** contact in advance. **Green Fees** £25 per day. **Cards** **Prof** Simon Arnold **Facilities** **Conf** fac available Corporate Hospitality Days available **Location** 1.5m from town centre, off A34 at McDonald's

Hotel ★★ 60% Stop Inn Newcastle-under-Lyme, Liverpool Rd, Cross Heath, NEWCASTLE-UNDER-LYME ☎ 01782 717000 43 rms (42 en suite) 24 annexe en suite

ONNELEY
Map 07 SJ74

Onneley CW3 5QF
☎ 01782 750577 & 846759
A parkland course offering panoramic views over Cheshire and Shropshire to the Welsh hills.
18 holes, 5728yds, Par 70, SSS 68.
Club membership 410.
Visitors welcome except during competitions. Subject to change - contact secretary. **Societies** packages available apply in writing to secretary, or by phone. **Green Fees** £20 per day. **Course Designer** A Benson, G Marks **Facilities** ⊗ ⅢⅢ by arrangement ㅤ♥ ♀ ♧ **Location** 2m from Woore on A525

Hotel ★★ 60% Stop Inn Newcastle-under-Lyme, Liverpool Rd, Cross Heath, NEWCASTLE-UNDER-LYME ☎ 01782 717000 43 rms (42 en suite) 24 annexe en suite

PATTINGHAM
Map 07 SO89

Patshull Park Hotel Golf & Country Club
WV6 7HR
☎ 01902 700100 📄 01902 700874
e-mail: sales@patshull-park.co.uk
Picturesque course set in 280 acres of glorious Capability Brown landscaped parkland. Designed by John Jacobs, the course meanders alongside trout fishing lakes. Water comes into play alongside the 3rd hole and there is a challenging drive over water on the 13th. Wellingtonia and cedar trees prove an obstacle to wayward drives off several holes. The 12th is the toughest hole on the course and the tee shot is vital, anything wayward and the trees block out the second to the green.

18 holes, 6400yds, Par 72, SSS 71, Course record 64.
Club membership 360.
Visitors contact in advance. **Societies** contact in advance. **Green Fees** not confirmed. **Cards** 🖃 🖿 📟 💷 🖾 🖎 🖫 **Prof** Richard Bissell **Course Designer** John Jacobs **Facilities** ⊗ ⅢⅢ ㅤ ♥ ♀ ♧ 🖼 ㅏ 🖭 🖚 ✓ **Leisure** heated indoor swimming pool, fishing, sauna, solarium, gymnasium. **Conf** fac available Corporate Hospitality Days available **Location** 1.5m W of Pattingham. At Pattingham church onto Patshull Rd, club on right

Hotel ★★★ 68% Patshull Park Hotel Golf & Country Club, Patshull Park, PATTINGHAM ☎ 01902 700100 49 en suite

> **Prices may change during the currency of the Guide, please check when booking.**

PENKRIDGE
Map 07 SJ91

The Chase Pottal Pool Rd ST19 5RN
☎ 01785 712888 📄 01785 712191
e-mail: tcgc@crown-golf.co.uk
Parkland course with links characteristics.
18 holes, 6707yds, Par 72, SSS 74.
Club membership 850.
Visitors book in advance, weekend restrictions apply. **Societies** must book at least four weeks in advance; seasonal restrictions. **Green Fees** terms on application. **Cards** 🖃 🖿 📟 🖎 🖫 **Prof** Ian Sadler **Facilities** ⊗ ⅢⅢ ㅤ♥ ♀ ♧ 🖼 🖚 ✓ ♫ **Conf** fac available Corporate Hospitality Days available **Location** 2m E off B5012

Hotel ★★★ 66% Quality Hotel Stafford, Pinfold Ln, PENKRIDGE ☎ 01785 712459 47 en suite

PERTON
Map 07 SO89

Perton Park Wrottesley Park Rd WV6 7HL
☎ 01902 380103 & 380073 📄 01902 326219
e-mail: golf@swindonperton.fsbusiness.co.uk
Challenging inland links style course set in picturesque Staffordshire countryside.
18 holes, 6520yds, Par 72, SSS 72, Course record 61.
Club membership 500.
Visitors book in advance. **Societies** phone in advance. **Green Fees** £15 per round (£20 weekends & bank holidays). **Cards** 🖃 🖿 **Prof** Jeremy Harrold **Facilities** ⊗ ⅢⅢ ㅤ♥ ♀ ♧ 🖼 ㅏ 🖚 ✓ ♫ **Leisure** hard tennis courts, bowling greens. **Location** SE of Perton off A454

Hotel ★★ 68% Ely House Hotel, 53 Tettenhall Rd, WOLVERHAMPTON ☎ 01902 311311 18 en suite

RUGELEY
Map 07 SK01

St Thomas's Priory Armitage Ln WS15 1ED
☎ 01543 492096 📄 01543 492096
e-mail: rohanlonpro@aol.com
Parkland course with undulating fairways. Excellent drainage facilitates golf all year round. A good test of golf for both pro and amateur players.
18 holes, 5969yds, Par 70, SSS 70, Course record 64.
Club membership 400.
Visitors phone in advance. **Societies** phone in advance. **Green Fees** £30 per round (£40 weekends). **Cards** 🖃 🖿 📟 🖎 🖫 **Prof** Richard O'Hanlon **Course Designer** PL Mulholland **Facilities** ⊗ ⅢⅢ ㅤ♥ ♀ ♧ 🖼 ㅏ 🖚 ✓ **Leisure** fishing. **Conf** fac available **Location** A51 onto A513

Hotel ⛫ Travelodge, Western Springs Rd, RUGELEY ☎ 08700 850 950 32 en suite

STAFFORD
Map 07 SJ92

Stafford Castle Newport Rd ST16 1BP
☎ 01785 223821 📄 01785 223821
Undulating parkland-type course built around Stafford Castle.
9 holes, 6383yds, Par 71, SSS 70, Course record 68.
Club membership 400.
Visitors not am Sun; contact in advance. **Societies** apply in writing or by phone. **Green Fees** £16 per day (£20 weekends ex Sun am). **Facilities** ⊗ ⅢⅢ ㅤ♥ ♀ ♧ **Conf** Corporate Hospitality Days available **Location** SW of town centre off A518

Continued

Hotel ★★★ 63% The Garth Hotel, Wolverhampton Rd, Moss Pit, STAFFORD ☎ 0870 609 6169 60 en suite

STOKE-ON-TRENT   Map 07 SJ84

Burslem Wood Farm, High Ln, Tunstall ST6 7JT
☎ 01782 837006
On the outskirts of Tunstall, a moorland course with
hard walking.
holes, 5354yds, Par 66, SSS 66, Course record 66.
Club membership 250.
Visitors except Sun & with member only Sat & bank
holidays. Societies phone in advance. Green Fees terms on
application. Facilities ⊗ ⍾ ﷼ ⬛ ♀ ⚘ Location 4m N of
ty centre on B5049

Hotel ★★★ 65% Quality Hotel, 66 Trinity St, Hanley,
STOKE-ON-TRENT ☎ 01782 202361 128 en suite
  annexe en suite

Greenway Hall Stanley Rd, Stockton Brook ST9 9LJ
☎ 01782 503158 ▤ 01782 504259
e-mail: greenway@jackbarker.com
Moorland course with fine views of the Pennines.

8 holes, 5678yds, Par 68, SSS 67, Course record 65.
Club membership 300.
Visitors dress code Societies phone for information &
availability. Green Fees £10 (£15 weekends). Cards ▦
▦ ▦ ▣ ▦ ▦ ⑨ Facilities ⊗ ⍾ ﷼ ⬛ ♀ ⚘ 🏠 ♈ ♌
♍ ⚘ Conf Corporate Hospitality Days available
Location 5m NE off A53

Hotel ★★★ 65% Quality Hotel, 66 Trinity St, Hanley,
STOKE-ON-TRENT ☎ 01782 202361 128 en suite
annexe en suite

Trentham 14 Barlaston Old Rd, Trentham ST4 8HB
☎ 01782 658109 ▤ 01782 644024
e-mail: secretary@trenthamgolf.org
Parkland course. The par 3 4th is a testing hole reached
rough a copse of trees.

18 holes, 6644yds, Par 72, SSS 72, Course record 67.
Club membership 600.
Visitors contact in advance. Societies contact in advance.
Green Fees £40 (weekends & bank holidays £50). Cards
▦ ▦ ⑨ Prof Sandy Wilson Course Designer Colt
& Alison Facilities ⊗ ⍾ ﷼ ⬛ ♀ ⚘ 🏠 ♈ ♍ ♌ ⚘ ⚘
Leisure squash. Location off A5035 in Trentham

Hotel ★★★ 66% Haydon House Hotel, Haydon St,
Basford, STOKE-ON-TRENT ☎ 01782 711311
17 en suite 6 annexe en suite

Trentham Park Trentham Park ST4 8AE
☎ 01782 658800 ▤ 01782 658800
e-mail: trevor-berrisford@barbox.net
Fine woodland course. Set in established parkland with
many challenging and interesting holes making
excellent use of water features. The greens have
recently been redesigned and rebunkered.
18 holes, 6425yds, Par 71, SSS 71, Course record 67.
Club membership 850.
Visitors contact in advance. Societies Wed & Fri, must
apply in advance. Green Fees not confirmed. Prof Simon
Lynn Facilities ⊗ ⍾ ﷼ ⬛ ♀ ♀ 🏠 ♈ ♌ ⚘
Conf Corporate Hospitality Days available
Location M6 junct 15, 1m E. 3m SW of Stoke off A34

Hotel ★★★ 66% Haydon House Hotel, Haydon St,
Basford, STOKE-ON-TRENT ☎ 01782 711311
17 en suite 6 annexe en suite

STONE   Map 07 SJ93

Barlaston Meaford Rd ST15 8UX
☎ 01782 372795 & 372867 ▤ 01782 372867
e-mail: barlaston.gc@virgin.net
Picturesque parkland course designed by Peter Alliss. A
number of water features come into play on several
holes.
18 holes, 5800yds, Par 69, SSS 68, Course record 65.
Club membership 650.
Visitors not before 10am or after 4pm Fri, weekends &
bank holidays after 10 am. Societies phone or apply in
writing. Green Fees terms on application. Prof Ian Rogers
Course Designer Peter Alliss Facilities ⊗ ⍾ ﷼ ⬛ ♀ ⚘
🏠 ⚘ ♌ Conf Corporate Hospitality Days available
Location M6 junct 15, 5m S

Hotel ★★★ 70% Stone House Hotel, Stafford Rd, STONE
☎ 0870 609 6140 50 en suite

Izaak Walton Eccleshall Rd, Cold Norton ST15 0NS
☎ 01785 760900 (sec) & 760808 (pro)
A gently undulating meadowland course with streams
and ponds as features.
18 holes, 6298yds, Par 72, SSS 72, Course record 66.
Club membership 450.
Visitors contact in advance for weekends. Societies phone
in advance. Green Fees £18 per round:£25 per day (£22/30
weekends). Prof Paul Brunt Facilities ⊗ ⍾ ﷼ ⬛ ♀ ⚘ 🏠
⚘ ♌ Location on B5026 between Stone & Eccleshall

Hotel ★★★ 70% Stone House Hotel, Stafford Rd, STONE
☎ 0870 609 6140 50 en suite

> **Booking a tee time is always advisable.**

Continued

Stone Filleybrooks ST15 0NB
☎ 01785 813103
e-mail: stonegolfc@onetel.net.uk
Nine-hole parkland course with easy walking and 18 different tees.
9 holes, 6299yds, Par 71, SSS 70, Course record 67.
Club membership 310.
Visitors with member only, weekends & bank holidays.
Societies apply in writing. **Green Fees** £20 per day or round weekdays. **Facilities** ⊗ ⍩ ⮭ ⯑ ⯒ ♀ ⯐ ♂
Location 0.5m W on A34

Hotel ★★★ 70% Stone House Hotel, Stafford Rd, STONE
☎ 0870 609 6140   50 en suite

TAMWORTH   Map 07 SK20

Drayton Park Drayton Park, Fazeley B78 3TN
☎ 01827 251139 ▤ 01827 284035
e-mail: draytonparkgc.co.uk
18 holes, 6439yds, Par 71, SSS 71, Course record 62.
Course Designer James Braid **Location** 2m S on A4091, next to Drayton Manor Leisure Park
Phone for further details

Hotel ★★★★ 75% De Vere Belfry, WISHAW
☎ 0870 900 0066 324 en suite

Tamworth Municipal Eagle Dr, Amington B77 4EG
☎ 01827 709303 ▤ 01827 709305
e-mail: david-warburton@tamworth.gov.uk
First-class municipal parkland course and a good test of golf.
18 holes, 6488yds, Par 73, SSS 72, Course record 63.
Club membership 460.
Visitors book in advance at weekends. **Societies** contact in advance. **Green Fees** not confirmed. **Cards** ⊟ ⬛ ▦ **Prof** Wayne Alcock **Course Designer** Hawtree & Son **Facilities** ⊗ ⍩ ⮭ ⯑ ⯒ ♀ ⯐ ⯓ ⬡ ♂ **Conf** fac available
Corporate Hospitality Days available **Location** 2.5m E off B5000

Hotel ★★ 63% Angel Croft Hotel, Beacon St, LICHFIELD
☎ 01543 258737 10 rms (8 en suite) 8 annexe en suite

UTTOXETER   Map 07 SK03

Manor Leese Hill, Kingstone ST14 8QT
☎ 01889 563234 ▤ 01889 563234
e-mail: manorgc@btinternet.com
A short but tough course set in the heart of the Staffordshire countryside with fine views of the surrounding area.
18 holes, 6060yds, Par 71, SSS 69, Course record 67.
Club membership 400.
Visitors contact in advance. **Societies** phone in advance.
Green Fees £16 per day (£26.50 weekends). **Cards** ⊟ ⬛ ▦ ▦ **Course Designer** Various **Facilities** ⊗ ⍩ ⮭ ⯑
♀ ⯐ ⯒ ⯓ ⬡ ♂ ⯑ **Leisure** fishing. **Conf** Corporate Hospitality Days available **Location** 2m from Uttoxeter on A518 towards Stafford

Hotel ★★★ 70% Stone House Hotel, Stafford Rd, STONE
☎ 0870 609 6140   50 en suite

Uttoxeter Wood Ln ST14 8JR
☎ 01889 564884 (Pro) & 566552 (Office)
▤ 01889 567501
Undulating, challenging course with excellent putting surfaces, manicured fairways, uniform rough and

Continued

extensive views across the Dove valley to the rolling hills of Staffordshire and Derbyshire.
18 holes, 5801yds, Par 70, SSS 69, Course record 64.
Club membership 900.
Visitors restricted weekends & competition days. Advisable to check availability during peak periods.
Societies book in advance. **Green Fees** not confirmed.
Cards ⊟ ⬛ ▦ **Prof** Adam McCandless **Course Designer** G Rothera **Facilities** ⊗ ⍩ ⮭ ⯑ ⯒ ♀ ⯐ ⬡ ⯓ ♂ **Location** near A50, 0.5m beyond main entrance to racecourse

Hotel ★★★ 70% Stone House Hotel, Stafford Rd, STONE
☎ 0870 609 6140   50 en suite

WESTON   Map 07 SJ92

Ingestre Park ST18 0RE
☎ 01889 270845 ▤ 01889 271434
e-mail: ipgc@lineone.net
Parkland course set in the grounds of Ingestre Hall, former home of the Earl of Shrewsbury, with mature trees and pleasant views.
18 holes, 6352yds, Par 70, SSS 70, Course record 67.
Club membership 750.
Visitors with member only weekends & bank holidays.
Must play before 3.30pm weekdays. Advance booking preferred. Handicap certificate required. **Societies** apply in advance. **Green Fees** £32.50 per day; £28 per round. **Prof** Danny Scullion **Course Designer** Hawtree **Facilities** ⊗ ⍩
⮭ ⯑ ⯒ ♀ ⯐ ⬡ ⯓ ⬡ ♂ **Conf** Corporate Hospitality Days available **Location** 2m SE off A51

Hotel ★★★ 75% The Swan Hotel, 46 Greengate St, STAFFORD ☎ 01785 258142 27 en suite

WHISTON   Map 07 SK04

Whiston Hall Mansion Court Hotel ST10 2HZ
☎ 01538 266260 ▤ 01538 266820
e-mail: enquiries@whistonhall.com
A challenging 18-hole course in scenic countryside, incorporating many natural obstacles and providing a test for all golfing abilities.
18 holes, 5742yds, Par 71, SSS 69, Course record 70.
Club membership 400.
Visitors reasonable dress on the course. Must phone in advance at weekends. **Societies** phone for details. **Green Fees** £10 per round. **Cards** ⊟ ▦ ⬛ ⬛ ▦ ▦ ▦ ▦
Course Designer T Cooper **Facilities** ⊗ ⍩ ⮭ ⯑ ♀ ⯐ ⯑
⬡ ♂ **Leisure** fishing, snooker. **Conf** fac available
Corporate Hospitality Days available
Location E of village centre off A52

Guesthouse ♦♦♦♦ Bank House, Farley Ln, OAKAMOOR ☎ 01538 702810 3 rms (2 en suite)

SUFFOLK

ALDEBURGH   Map 05 TM45

Aldeburgh Saxmundham Rd IP15 5PE
☎ 01728 452890 ▤ 01728 452937
e-mail: info@aldeburghgolfclub.co.uk
Good natural drainage provides year round golf in links-type conditions. Accuracy is the first challenge or well-bunkered, gorse-lined holes. Fine views over an Area of Outstanding Natural Beauty.

Continue

8 holes, 6349yds, Par 68, SSS 71, Course record 65.
River Course: 9 holes, 4228yds, Par 64, SSS 61, Course record 62.

Club membership 900.
Visitors contact in advance and have a handicap certificate. two ball/foursomes only. **Societies** contact in advance. **Green Fees** £50 per day; £40 pm (weekends 60/£50). **Cards** ▦ ▆▆ ▆▆ 🅓 **Prof** Keith Preston **Course Designer** Thompson, Fernie, Taylor, Park. **Facilities** ⊗ ⓑ
☕ ⚲ 🍴 ⛳ **Location** 1m W on A1094

Hotel ★★★ 78% Wentworth Hotel, Wentworth Rd, ALDEBURGH ☎ 01728 452312 28 en suite, annexe en suite.

BECCLES   Map 05 TM48

Beccles The Common NR34 9YN
☎ 01502 712244 ▤ 01502 710380
e-mail: becclesgolfclub@aol.com
Commons course with gorse bushes, no water hazards or bunkers.
9 holes, 2779yds, Par 68, SSS 67.
Club membership 50.
Visitors no restrictions. **Societies** phone in advance. **Green Fees** £5 per day (£10 weekends). **Facilities** ☕ ⚲ △ ⛳
Location NE of town centre

BUNGAY   Map 05 TM38

Bungay & Waveney Valley Outney Common NR35 1DS
☎ 01986 892337 ▤ 01986 892222
e-mail: bungaygolf@aol.com
Heathland course, lined with furze and gorse. Excellent greens all-year-round, easy walking.
18 holes, 6044yds, Par 69, SSS 69, Course record 64.
Club membership 730.
Visitors should contact in advance. With member only weekends & bank holidays. **Societies** contact in advance. **Green Fees** not confirmed. **Prof** Andrew Collison **Course Designer** James Braid **Facilities** ⊗ ⓑ ☕ ⚲ △ 🍴 ⛳
Location 0.5m NW on A143

BURY ST EDMUNDS   Map 05 TL86

Bury St Edmunds Tut Hill IP28 6LG
☎ 01284 755979 ▤ 01284 763288
e-mail: info@burygolf.co.uk
A mature, undulating course, full of character with some challenging holes. The nine-hole pay and play course consists of five par 3s and four par 4s with modern construction greens.
18 holes, 6675yds, Par 72, SSS 72, Course record 65.
9 holes, 2217yds, Par 62, SSS 62.

Club membership 850.
Visitors with member only at weekends for 18-hole course. **Societies** apply in writing. **Green Fees** 18-hole course £35 per day; 9-hole course £13 (£16 weekends). **Cards** ▦ ▆▆ ▆▆ 🏧 🅓 **Prof** Mark Jillings **Course Designer** Ted Ray **Facilities** ⊗ 🍴 by arrangement ⓑ ☕ ⚲ △ 🍴 ⛳ **Conf** Corporate Hospitality Days available **Location** 0.5m NW on B1106

Hotel ★★★ 77% Angel Hotel, Angel Hill, BURY ST EDMUNDS ☎ 01284 714000 64 en suite

Swallow Suffolk Golf & Country Club
Fornham St Genevieve IP28 6JQ
☎ 01284 706777 ▤ 01284 706721
e-mail: thelodge@the-suffolk.co.uk
A classic parkland course with the River Lark running through it. Criss-crossed by ponds and streams with rich fairways. Considerable upgrading of the course in recent years and the three finishing holes are particularly challenging.

The Genevieve Course: 18 holes, 6376yds, Par 72, SSS 71, Course record 70.
Club membership 600.
Visitors contact in advance to book tee times. **Societies** phone for details. **Green Fees** not confirmed. **Cards** **Prof** Steve Hall **Facilities** **Leisure** heated indoor swimming pool, fishing, sauna, solarium, gymnasium. **Conf** fac available Corporate Hospitality Days available **Location** off A14 at Bury St Edmunds, W onto B1106 towards Brandon, club 2.5m on right

Hotel ★★★ 75% Ravenwood Hall Hotel, Rougham, BURY ST EDMUNDS ☎ 01359 270345 7 en suite 7 annexe en suite

CRETINGHAM Map 05 TM26

Cretingham IP13 7BA
☎ 01728 685275 01728 685488
Parkland course, tree-lined with numerous water features, including the River Deben which runs through part of the course.
18 holes, 4968yds, Par 68, SSS 66.
Club membership 350.
Visitors booking required for weekends. **Societies** contact in advance. **Green Fees** terms on application. **Cards** **Prof** Neil Jackson **Course Designer** J Austin **Facilities** **Leisure** hard tennis courts, outdoor swimming pool, fishing, pitch & putt, nine-hole course. **Conf** Corporate Hospitality Days available **Location** NE of village off A1120

Hotel ★★ 68% Cedars Hotel, Needham Rd, STOWMARKET ☎ 01449 612668 25 en suite

FELIXSTOWE Map 05 TM33

Felixstowe Ferry Ferry Rd IP11 9RY
☎ 01394 286834 01394 273679
e-mail: secretary@felixstowegolf.co.uk
An 18-hole seaside links with pleasant views and easy walking. Testing 491yd 7th hole. Nine-hole pay and play course; a good test of golf.
Martello Course: 18 holes, 6166yds, Par 72, SSS 70, Course record 66.
Kingsfleet: 9 holes, 2941yds, Par 35, SSS 35.
Club membership 900.
Visitors may play Martello Course weekends after 2.30pm but must contact in advance & have handicap certificate. Kingsfleet course no restrictions. **Societies** All weekdays ex bank holidays, phone in advance. **Green Fees** Martello £35 per day (£25 after 1pm); £40 weekends & bank holidays. Kingsfleet: £10 (£12.50 weekends & bank holidays). **Prof** Ian MacPherson **Course Designer** Henry Cotton **Facilities** by arrangement **Conf** fac available Corporate Hospitality Days available **Location** NE of town centre, signed from A14

Hotel ★★★ 72% Elizabeth Orwell Hotel, Hamilton Rd, FELIXSTOWE ☎ 01394 285511 60 en suite

FLEMPTON Map 05 TL86

Flempton IP28 6EQ
☎ 01284 728291 01284 728468
Breckland course with gorse and wooded areas. Very little water but surrounded by woodland and Suffolk Wildlife Trust lakes.
9 holes, 6240yds, Par 70, SSS 70, Course record 67.
Club membership 250.
Visitors contact in advance & produce handicap certificate. **Societies** limited to small societies - must apply in writing. **Green Fees** £35 per day/£30 per 18 holes. **Prof** Chris Aldred **Course Designer** JH Taylor **Facilities** **Location** 0.5m W on A1101

Hotel ★★★ 74% The Priory Hotel, Tollgate, BURY ST EDMUNDS ☎ 01284 766181 9 en suite 30 annexe en suite

HALESWORTH Map 05 TM37

Halesworth Bramfield Rd IP19 9XA
☎ 01986 875567 01986 874565
e-mail: info@halesworthgc.co.uk
A 27-hole professionally designed parkland complex of one 18-hole membership course and a nine-hole pay and play.
18 holes, 6580yds, Par 72, SSS 72, Course record 71.
9 holes, 2398yds, Par 33, SSS 33.
Club membership 300.
Visitors visitors welcome at all times except for Sun am on the 18-hole course. Handicap certificate required for 18-hole course. **Societies** phone for booking form. **Green Fees** £25 per day/£18 per round (weekends & bank holidays £30/£22); 9-hole course £7/£5 (£8.50/£6). **Prof** Simon Harrison **Course Designer** JW Johnson **Facilities** **Conf** fac available **Location** 0.75m S of town, signed off A144

Hotel ★★★ 74% Swan Hotel, Market Place, SOUTHWOLD ☎ 01502 722186 25 en suite 17 annexe en suite

HAVERHILL   Map 05 TL64

Haverhill Coupals Rd CB9 7UW
☎ 01440 761951 📠 01440 761951
e-mail: haverhillgolf@coupalsroad.fsnet.co.uk
An 18-hole course lying across two valleys in pleasant parkland. The front nine with undulating fairways is complemented by a saucer-shaped back nine, bisected by the River Stour, presenting a challenge to golfers of all standards.
18 holes, 5929yds, Par 70, SSS 69, Course record 67.
Club membership 767.
Visitors phone to check for club competitions (01440 712628) **Societies** contact in advance. Weekdays if available. **Green Fees** terms on application. **Cards** ▨ ▨ ▨ ▨ **Prof** Nick Duc **Course Designer** P Pilgrem, C Lawrie **Facilities** ⊗ � ▤ ♥ ♀ ♿ ⌂ ✓ **Leisure** chipping green. **Conf** fac available Corporate Hospitality Days available **Location** 1m SE off A1017

HINTLESHAM   Map 05 TM04

Hintlesham IP8 3JG
☎ 01473 652761 📠 01473 652750
e-mail: office@hintleshamgolfclub.com
Magnificent championship length course blending harmoniously with the ancient parkland surrounding the hotel. Opened in 1991 but seeded two years beforehand, this parkland course has reached a level maturity that allows it to be rivalled in the area only by a few ancient courses. The signature holes are the 4th and 17th, both featuring water at very inconvenient interludes.

18 holes, 6638yds, Par 72, SSS 72, Course record 63.
Club membership 470.
Visitors contact 24 hours in advance. **Societies** phone in advance. **Green Fees** £36 per round (£44 weekends & bank holidays). **Cards** ▨ ▨ ▨ ▨ ▨ **Prof** Alastair Spink **Course Designer** Hawtree & Sons **Facilities** ⊗ M ▤ ♥ ♀ ♿ ⌂ ✈ ♫ ✓ **Leisure** hard tennis courts, heated outdoor swimming pool, sauna, gymnasium. **Conf** Corporate Hospitality Days available **Location** in village on A1071

Hotel ★★★★ 80% Hintlesham Hall Hotel, George St, HINTLESHAM ☎ 01473 652334 33 en suite

IPSWICH   Map 05 TM14

Alnesbourne Priory Priory Park IP10 0JT
☎ 01473 727393 📠 01473 278372
e-mail: golf@priory-park.com
A fabulous outlook facing due south across the River Orwell is one of the many good features of this course

set in woodland. All holes run among trees with some fairways requiring straight shots. The 8th green is on saltings by the river.
9 holes, 1700yds, Par 29.
Club membership 30.
Visitors closed Tue; 5 Jan-1 Mar. **Societies** Tue only, phone in advance. **Green Fees** £10 (£15 weekends & bank holidays). **Facilities** ⊗ M ▤ ♥ ♀ ♿ ♟ **Leisure** practice net. **Conf** fac available **Location** 3m SE off A14

Hotel ★★★ 71% Courtyard by Marriott Ipswich, The Havens, Ransomes Europark, IPSWICH ☎ 01473 272244 60 en suite

Fynn Valley IP6 9JA
☎ 01473 785267 📠 01473 785632
e-mail: enquiries@fynn-valley.co.uk
Undulating parkland course alongside a protected river valley. The course has matured into an excellent test of golf enhanced by more than 100 bunkers and protected greens that have tricky slopes and contours.

18 holes, 6320yds, Par 70, SSS 71, Course record 65.
Club membership 650.
Visitors members only Sun until 10.30am. Ladies priority Wed am. **Societies** apply in advance. **Green Fees** £26 per 18 holes (£32 weekends). **Cards** ▨ ▨ ▨ ▨ **Prof** P Wilby, A Lucas, S Dainty **Course Designer** Antonio Primavera **Facilities** ⊗ M ▤ ♥ ♀ ♿ ⌂ ✈ ✓ **Leisure** 9-hole par 3 course, practice bunker. **Conf** fac available Corporate Hospitality Days available **Location** 2m N of Ipswich on B1077

Hotel ★★★ 65% Novotel Ipswich, Greyfriars Rd, IPSWICH ☎ 01473 232400 100 en suite

Ipswich Purdis Heath IP3 8UQ
☎ 01473 728941 📠 01473 715236
e-mail: mail@ipswichgolfclub.com
Many golfers are surprised when they hear that Ipswich has, at Purdis Heath, a first-class course. In some ways it resembles some of Surrey's better courses; a beautiful heathland course with two lakes and easy walking.
Purdis Heath: 18 holes, 6439yds, Par 71, SSS 71, Course record 64
9 holes, 1930yds, Par 31.
Club membership 865.
Visitors contact in advance & have a handicap certificate for 18-hole course. **Societies** contact in advance. **Green Fees** 18-hole course £45 per day, £35 per round pm (£50/£40 weekends & bank holidays); 9-hole course £10 per day (£15). **Cards** ▨ ▨ ▨ ▨ **Prof** Stephen Whymark **Course Designer** James Braid **Facilities** ⊗ M

Continued

Continued

🗼 ☕ ♀ ⛳ 🏠 ✒ **Location** 3m SE of town centre off
A1156 on Bucklesham road

Hotel ★★★ 71% Courtyard by Marriott Ipswich, The
Havens, Ransomes Europark, IPSWICH ☎ 01473 272244
60 en suite

Rushmere Rushmere Heath IP4 5QQ
☎ 01473 725648 📠 01473 273852
e-mail: rushmeregolfclub@talk21.com
**Heathland course with gorse and prevailing winds. A
good test of golf.**
18 holes, 6262yds, Par 70, SSS 70, Course record 66.
Club membership 700.
Visitors not before 2.30pm weekends & bank holidays.
Must have a handicap certificate. Must contact in advance.
Societies weekdays by arrangement. **Green Fees** £38.
Cards 🖶 💳 💳 💳 💳 📠 💷 **Prof** K Vince **Facilities**
⊗ 🗼 🗼 ☕ ♀ ⛳ 🏠 ✒ **Conf** fac available Corporate
Hospitality Days available **Location** on A1214
Woodbridge road near hospital, signed

Hotel ★★★ 67% The Hotel Elizabeth, Old London Rd,
Copdock, IPSWICH ☎ 01473 209988 76 en suite

Rookery Park Beccles Rd, Carlton Colville NR33 8HJ
☎ 01502 509190 📠 01502 509191
e-mail: office@rookeryparkgolfclub.co.uk
Parkland course with a nine-hole par 3 adjacent.
18 holes, 6714yds, Par 72, SSS 72.
Club membership 1000.
Visitors must have handicap certificate. **Societies** by
arrangement. **Green Fees** not confirmed. **Cards** 🖶 💳
💳 📠 💷 **Prof** Martin Elsworthy **Course Designer** CD
Lawrie **Facilities** ⊗ 🗼 🗼 ☕ ♀ ⛳ 🏠 ✒ ✒
Leisure 9-hole par 3 course.
ocation 3.5m SW of Lowestoft on A146

West Suffolk Golf Centre New Drove, Beck Row
IP28 8DY
☎ 01638 718972 📠 01353 675447
**This course has been gradually improved to provide a
unique opportunity to play an inland course in all
weather conditions. Situated on the edge of the
Breckland, the dry nature of the course makes for easy
walking with rare flora and fauna.**
12 holes, 6461yds, Par 71, SSS 71.
Visitors welcome. no restrictions **Societies** phone 24hrs in
advance. More notice required for catering arrangements.
Green Fees £10.50 per day (£14 weekends & bank
holidays). **Cards** 🖶 💳 📠 💷 **Prof** Paul Geen **Facilities**
⊗ 🗼 ☕ ♀ ⛳ 🏠 ✒ ✒ (**Leisure** fishing, pitch & putt
practice course. **Conf** Corporate Hospitality Days available
Location A1101 from Mildenhall to Beck Row, 1st left
after Beck Row signed to West Row, 0.5m on right

Hotel ★★★ 68% The Smoke House, Beck Row,
MILDENHALL ☎ 01638 713223 94 en suite 2 annexe
en suite

**Looking for a new course? Always telephone
ahead to confirm visitor arrangements.**

Links Cambridge Rd CB8 0TG
☎ 01638 663000 📠 01638 661476
e-mail: secretary@linksgc.fsbusiness.co.uk
Gently undulating parkland.
*18 holes, 6582yds, Par 72, SSS 72, Course record 66 or,
Par 72.*
Club membership 780.
Visitors must have handicap certificate, not Sun before
11.30am. **Societies** phone secretary in advance. **Green
Fees** £32 per day, £24 per round (£36/£28 weekends). **Prof**
John Sharkey **Course Designer** Col Hotchkin **Facilities** ⊗
🗼 🗼 ☕ ♀ ⛳ 🏠 ✒ ✒ **Location** 1m SW on A1034

Hotel ★★★ 69% Heath Court Hotel, Moulton Rd,
NEWMARKET ☎ 01638 667171 41 en suite

Newton Green Newton Green CO10 0QN
☎ 01787 377217 & 377501 📠 01787 377549
e-mail: info@newtongreengolfclub.co.uk
**Flat 18-hole course with lake. First nine holes are open
with bunkers and trees. Second nine holes are tight with
ditches and gorse.**
18 holes, 5960yds, Par 69, SSS 68.
Club membership 540.
Visitors contact in advance but not Tue before 12.30
Societies apply in advance. **Green Fees** £22 per round
(£25 weekends). **Cards** 🖶 💳 💷 **Prof** Tim Cooper
Facilities ⊗ 🗼 🗼 ☕ ♀ ⛳ 🏠 ✒ ✒
Location W of village on A134

Hotel ★★★ 73% The Bull, Hall St, LONG MELFORD
☎ 01787 378494 25 en suite

Brett Vale Noakes Rd IP7 5LR
☎ 01473 310718
e-mail: info@brettvalegolf.com
**Brett Vale course takes you through a nature reserve
and on lakeside walks, affording views over Dedham
Vale. The excellent fairways demand an accurate tee
and good approach shots; 1, 2, 3, 8, 10 and 15 are all
affected by crosswinds, but once in the valley it is much
more sheltered. Although only 5813yds the course is
testing and interesting at all levels of golf.**
18 holes, 5813yds, Par 70, SSS 69, Course record 65.
Club membership 600.
Visitors book tee times; dress code; soft spikes only.
Societies apply in writing or phone. **Green Fees** £22.50
per 18 holes (£28 weekends & bank holidays).
Cards 🖶 💳 💳 📠 💷 **Course Designer** Howard Swan
Facilities ⊗ 🗼 🗼 ☕ ♀ ⛳ 🏠 ✒ 🏨 ✒ 🏌 ✒ (
Leisure fishing, gymnasium. **Conf** fac available
Corporate Hospitality Days available
Location SW of village off B1070

Hotel ★★★ 🏵 Maison Talbooth, Stratford Rd,
DEDHAM ☎ 01206 322367 10 en suite

Southwold The Common IP18 6TB
☎ 01502 723234
**Commonland course with fine greens and panoramic
views of the sea.**

Continued

holes, 6052yds, Par 70, SSS 69, Course record 67.
Club membership 350.
Visitors restricted on competition days (Ladies-Wed,
Gents-Sun). Contact in advance. **Societies** contact in
advance. **Green Fees** £26 per 18 holes; £13 per 9 holes
(£28/£14 weekends). **Prof** Brian Allen **Course Designer**
Braid **Facilities** ⊗ ⓗ ■ ♀ ㋡ 🏠 ㋡ ⌖ **Conf** Corporate
Hospitality Days available **Location** S of town off A1095

Hotel ★★★ 74% Swan Hotel, Market Place,
SOUTHWOLD ☎ 01502 722186 25 en suite 17 annexe
en suite

STOWMARKET   Map 05 TM05

Stowmarket Lower Rd, Onehouse IP14 3DA
☎ 01449 736473 📠 01449 736826
e-mail: mail@stowmarketgc.sagehost.co.uk
Parkland course.
18 holes, 6107yds, Par 69, SSS 69, Course record 65.
Club membership 630.
Visitors contact in advance, not Wed. **Societies** Thu or Fri,
by arrangement. **Green Fees** not confirmed. **Cards** 🖃 🖾
🖾 **Prof** Duncan Burl **Facilities** ⊗ ⓗ ⓗ ■ ♀ ㋡ 🏠 ㋡ ⌖
🏠 ⌖ ⌖ **Conf** Corporate Hospitality Days available
Location 2.5m SW off B1115

Hotel ★★ 68% Cedars Hotel, Needham Rd,
STOWMARKET ☎ 01449 612668 25 en suite

STUSTON   Map 05 TM17

Diss Stuston IP21 4AA
☎ 01379 641025 📠 01379 644586
e-mail: sec.dissgolf@virgin.net
**This inland commonland and parkland course has a
links feel with small tight greens. Depending on the
direction of the wind, the golfer can find the last three
holes a pleasure or a pain. The signature hole is the long
par 4 13th, a test on any day - the drive must be long to
give any chance of reaching the green in two.**
18 holes, 6206yds, Par 70, SSS 69, Course record 67.
Club membership 750.
Visitors contact in advance for play at weekends & bank
holidays. **Societies** by arrangement. **Green Fees** £36 per
day; £28 per 18 holes, £14 per 9 holes. **Cards** 🖃 🖾
Prof NJ Taylor **Facilities** ⊗ ⓗ ⓗ ■ ♀ ㋡ 🏠 ⌖ ⌖
Conf fac available Corporate Hospitality Days available
Location 1.5m SE on B1118

Inn ♦♦♦♦ The White Horse Inn, Stoke Ash, EYE
☎ 01379 678222 7 annexe en suite

THORPENESS   Map 05 TM45

Thorpeness Golf Club & Hotel Lakeside Av
IP16 4NH
☎ 01728 452176 📠 01728 453868
e-mail: info@thorpeness.co.uk
**A 6271yd coastal heathland course, designed in 1923
by James Braid. The quality of his design combined
with modern green keeping techniques has resulted
in an extremely challenging course for golfers at
all levels. It is also one of the driest courses in the
region.**
18 holes, 6271yds, Par 69, SSS 71, Course record 66.
Club membership 500.
Visitors contact in advance, handicap certificate required.
Societies phone in advance, handicap certificate & deposit

Continued

required. **Green Fees** £33 per day, £22 after 3pm. **Cards**
🖃 🖾 🖾 🔙 ⑨ **Prof** Frank Hill **Course Designer** James
Braid **Facilities** ⊗ ⓗ ⓗ ■ ♀ ㋡ 🏠 ㋡ ⌖ ⌖ ⌖
Leisure hard & grass tennis courts, fishing, snooker room.
Conf fac available Corporate Hospitality Days available
Location off A1094 to Aldeburgh, signed

Thorpeness Hotel & Golf Club

Hotel ★★★ 70% Thorpeness Golf Club & Hotel,
Lakeside Av, THORPENESS ☎ 01728 452176 30 en suite

WALDRINGFIELD   Map 05 TM24

Waldringfield Heath Newbourne Rd IP12 4PT
☎ 01473 736768 📠 01473 736793
e-mail: patgolf1@aol.com
**Easy walking heathland course with long drives on 1st
and 13th (590yds) and some ponds.**
18 holes, 6141yds, Par 71, SSS 69, Course record 67.
Club membership 550.
Visitors welcome Mon-Fri, weekends & bank holidays
pm. Must book tee times in advance **Societies** by
arrangement. **Green Fees** not confirmed. **Cards** 🖃 🖾
🖾 🔙 ⑨ **Course Designer** Phillip Pilgrem **Facilities** ⊗
ⓗ ⓗ ■ ♀ ㋡ 🏠 ㋡ ⌖ **Conf** fac available
Location 1m W of village off A12

Hotel ★★★ ⚲ 76% Seckford Hall Hotel,
WOODBRIDGE ☎ 01394 385678 22 en suite 10 annexe
en suite

WOODBRIDGE   Map 05 TM24

**Best Western Ufford Park Hotel Golf
Leisure** Yarmouth Rd, Ufford IP12 1QW
☎ 01394 383555 📠 01394 383582
e-mail: mail@uffordpark.co.uk
**The 18-hole par 71 course is set in 120 acres of ancient
parkland with 12 water features and voted one of the
best British winter courses. The course enjoys excellent
natural drainage and a large reservoir supplements a
spring feed pond to ensure ample water for irrigation.
The course is host to the Sky Sports PGA Europro Tour**
18 holes, 6312yds, Par 71, SSS 71, Course record 65.
Club membership 350.
Visitors book tee time from golf shop 01394 382836. Must
adhere to dress code. Handicap certificates required for
Sat/Sun am. **Societies** phone in advance to book tee time
on 01394 382836 **Green Fees** £30 per day (£40 weekends).
Cards 🖃 🖾 🖾 🗾 🖾 🔙 ⑨ **Prof** Stuart Robertson
Course Designer Phil Pilgrim **Facilities** ⊗ ⓗ ⓗ ■ ♀ ㋡
🏠 ㋡ ㋡ ⌖ ⌖ ⌖ **Leisure** heated indoor swimming pool,
sauna, solarium, gymnasium.

Continued

Conf fac available Corporate Hospitality Days available
Location A12 onto B1438

Best Western Ufford Park Hotel Golf & Leisure

....

Hotel ★★★ 72% Best Western Ufford Park Hotel Golf
Leisure, Yarmouth Rd, Ufford, WOODBRIDGE
☎ 01394 383555 84 en suite 6 annexe en suite

Seckford Seckford Hall Rd, Great Bealings IP13 6NT
☎ 01394 388000 📠 01394 382818
e-mail: info@seckfordgolf.co.uk
18 holes, 5303yds, Par 68, SSS 66, Course record 62.
Course Designer J Johnson Location 1m W of
Woodbridge off A12, next to Seckford Hall Hotel
Phone for further details

....

Hotel ★★★ ♨♨ 76% Seckford Hall Hotel,
WOODBRIDGE ☎ 01394 385678 22 en suite 10 annexe
en suite

Woodbridge Bromeswell Heath IP12 2PF
☎ 01394 382038 📠 01394 382392
e-mail: woodbridgegc@anglianet.co.uk
**A beautiful course, one of the best in East Anglia. It is
situated on high ground and in different seasons
presents golfers with a great variety of colour. Some say
that of the many good holes the 16th is the best.**

*Main Course: 18 holes, 6299yds, Par 70, SSS 70, Course
record 64.*
Forest Course: 9 holes, 3191yds, Par 70, SSS 70.
Club membership 700.
Visitors Main Course: must contact in advance, handicap
certificate required, with member only weekends. Forest
Course open all days & no handicap certificate required.
Societies by prior phone call or in writing. Green Fees
Main Course £42 per day; Forest Course £18 per day.
Prof Campbell Elliot Course Designer Davie Grant
Facilities ⊗ 🎜 by arrangement 🏐 💺 ♀ ⚷ 🖻 𝄃
Location 2.5m NE off A1152

Continued

....
Iotel ★★★ ♨ 76% Seckford Hall Hotel,
VOODBRIDGE ☎ 01394 385678 22 en suite 10 annexe
n suite

WORLINGTON   Map 05 TL67

Royal Worlington & Newmarket IP28 8SD
☎ 01638 712216 & 717787 ▤ 01638 717787
nland links course, renowned as one of the best nine-
ole courses in the world. Well drained, giving excellent
vinter playing conditions.
* holes, 3105yds, Par 35, SSS 70, Course record 65.
Club membership 325.
Visitors with member only at weekends. Must contact in
dvance & have a handicap certificate. Societies apply in
vriting. Green Fees £55 per day (reductions after 2 pm).
⊗ ᴸ ♥ ♀ ⚞ ⚐ ⚑ ✓ Location 0.5m SE of Worlington
ear Mildenhall
....
Iotel ★★★ 73% Riverside Hotel, Mill St,
MILDENHALL ☎ 01638 717274 17 en suite 6 annexe
n suite

SURREY

ADDLESTONE   Map 04 TQ06

New Zealand Woodham Ln KT15 3QD
☎ 01932 345049 ▤ 01932 342891
-mail: roger.marrett@nzgc.org
8 holes, 6073yds, Par 68, SSS 69, Course record 66.
Course Designer Muir Fergusson, Simpson
Location 1.5m E of Woking
Phone for further details
....
Iotel ★★★ 67% The Ship Hotel, Monument Green,
VEYBRIDGE ☎ 01932 848364 39 en suite

ASHFORD   Map 04 TQ07

Ashford Manor Fordbridge Rd TW15 3RT
☎ 01784 424644 ▤ 01784 424649
-mail: secretary@ashfordmanorgolfclub.fsnet.co.uk
Tree-lined parkland course is built on gravel and drains
vell, never needing temporary tees or greens. A heavy
nvestment in fairway irrigation and an extensive
voodland management programme over the past few
ears have formed a strong future for this course,
riginally built over 100 years ago.
8 holes, 6298yds, Par 70, SSS 71, Course record 65.
Club membership 700.
Visitors advisable to phone in advance, handicap
ertificate required, with member only at weekends but not
ompetition days. Societies welcome weekdays, except
Thu am, must contact in advance. Green Fees £50 per day,
'40 per round (weekdays only). Cards ⚏ ▦ ▭ 🔊
] Prof Ian Campbell Course Designer Tom Hogg
Facilities ⊗ ᴸ ♥ ♀ ⚞ ⚐ ✓ Conf fac available
Corporate Hospitality Days available Location 2m E of
taines via A308 Staines bypass
....
Iotel ★★★ 72% The Thames Lodge, Thames St,
STAINES ☎ 0870 400 8121 78 en suite

BAGSHOT   Map 04 SU96

Pennyhill Park Hotel & Country Club
London Rd GU19 5EU
☎ 01276 471774 ▤ 01276 473217
e-mail: enquiries@pennyhillpark.co.uk
**A nine-hole course set in 11 acres of beautiful parkland.
It is challenging to even the most experienced golfer.**
9 holes, 2055yds, Par 32, SSS 32.
Club membership 100.
Visitors booking required; must be resident at hotel or day
visitor using other hotel facilities. Green Fees
complimentary for hotel residents/day visitor using hotel
facilities. Cards ⚏ ▦ ▭ 🔊 🖸 Facilities ⊗ ᴸ ♥ ♀
⚞ ⚐ ⚑ ✓ Leisure hard tennis courts, outdoor & indoor
heated swimming pools, fishing, sauna, solarium,
gymnasium. Conf fac available Location off A30 between
Camberley & Bagshot
....
Hotel ★★★★★ Pennyhill Park Hotel & The Spa, London
Rd, BAGSHOT ☎ 01276 471774 26 en suite 97 annexe
en suite

Windlesham Grove End GU19 5HY
☎ 01276 452220 ▤ 01276 452290
18 holes, 6650yds, Par 72, SSS 72, Course record 69.
Course Designer Tommy Horton Location junct A30 &
A322
Phone for further details
....
Hotel ★★★★★ Pennyhill Park Hotel & The Spa, London
Rd, BAGSHOT ☎ 01276 471774 26 en suite 97 annexe
en suite

BANSTEAD   Map 04 TQ25

Banstead Downs Burdon Ln, Belmont, Sutton
SM2 7DD
☎ 020 8642 2284 ▤ 020 8642 5252
e-mail: secretary@bansteaddowns.com
**A natural downland course set on a site of botanic
interest. A challenging 18 holes with narrow fairways
and tight lies.**
18 holes, 6194yds, Par 69, SSS 69, Course record 64.
Club membership 902.
Visitors book in advance & have handicap certificate or
letter of introduction. With member only weekends.
Societies Thu by arrangement Green Fees not confirmed.
Prof Ian Golding Course Designer JH Taylor, James
Braid Facilities ⊗ ᴹ by arrangement ᴸ ♥ ♀ ⚞ ⚐ ✓
Conf Corporate Hospitality Days available
Location M25 junct 8, A217 N for 6m
....
Hotel ★★ 63% Thatched House Hotel, 135 Cheam Rd,
SUTTON ☎ 020 8642 3131 32 rms (29 en suite)

Cuddington Banstead Rd SM7 1RD
☎ 020 8393 0952 ▤ 020 8786 7025
e-mail: ds@cuddingtongc.co.uk
**Parkland course with easy walking and good views.
Reputed to have the longest start, over the first three
holes, in Surrey.**
18 holes, 6614yds, Par 71, SSS 71, Course record 64.
Club membership 694.
Visitors contact in advance & have a handicap certificate
or letter of introduction. Societies welcome Thu, must
apply in advance. Green Fees £20-45 per 18 holes (£25-55
weekends). Prof Mark Warner Course Designer HS Colt
Facilities ⊗ ᴹ ᴸ ♥ ♀ ⚞ ⚐ ⚑ ✓ Conf fac available

Continued

231

Corporate Hospitality Days available **Location** N of
Banstead station on A2022

Hotel ★★ 63% Thatched House Hotel, 135 Cheam Rd,
SUTTON ☎ 020 8642 3131 32 rms (29 en suite)

BLETCHINGLEY   Map 05 TQ35

Bletchingley Church Ln RH1 4LP
☎ 01883 744666 ▤ 01883 744284
e-mail: info@bletchingleygolf.co.uk
**Panoramic views create a perfect backdrop for this
course, constructed on rich sandy loam and playable all
year round. The course design has made best use of the
interesting and undulating land features with a variety
of mixed and mature trees providing essential course
definition. A mature stream creates several interesting
water features.**
18 holes, 6169yds, Par 72, SSS 69.
Club membership 550.
Visitors phone pro shop to book (01883 744848). Play
restricted to pm on Tue, Thu & weekends. **Societies** phone
for details. Mon, Wed & Fri all day. Tue, Thu & weekends
pm only. **Green Fees** £30 (£42 weekends). **Cards** ▤ ▤
▤ ▤ ▨ **Prof** Alasdair Dyer **Facilities** ⊗ ▤ ▤ ♀ ☖ ☖
▼ ♦ ⚒ ∅ ℓ **Conf** fac available Corporate Hospitality
Days available **Location** A25 onto Church Ln in
Bletchingley

Hotel ★★★★ 73% Nutfield Priory, Nutfield, REDHILL
☎ 01737 824400 60 en suite

BRAMLEY   Map 04 TQ04

Bramley GU5 0AL
☎ 01483 892696 ▤ 01483 894673
e-mail: secretary@bramleygolfclub.co.uk
**Parkland course, from the high ground picturesque
views of the Wey Valley on one side and the Hog's
Back. Full on course irrigation system with three
reservoirs on the course.**
18 holes, 5990yds, Par 69, SSS 69, Course record 63.
Club membership 850.
Visitors not Tue am (Ladies Morning) & must play with
member at weekends & bank holidays. Must contact
secretary on 01483 892696. **Societies** phone the General
Manager in advance. **Green Fees** £40 per day/round
(weekdays only). **Cards** ▤ ▤ ▨ ▨ **Prof** Gary Peddie
Course Designer James Braid **Facilities** ⊗ �𝕸 ▤ ▤ ♀ ☖
☖ ▼ ♦ ⚒ ∅ ℓ **Location** 3m S of Guildford on A281

Hotel ⏶ Innkeeper's Lodge, Ockford Rd, GODALMING
☎ 01483 419997 19 rms

BROOKWOOD   Map 04 SU95

West Hill Bagshot Rd GU24 0BH
☎ 01483 474365 ▤ 01483 474252
e-mail: secretary@westhill-golfclub.co.uk
**A challenging course with fairways lined with heather
and tall pines, one of Surrey's finest courses. Demands
every club in the bag to be played.**
18 holes, 6343yds, Par 69, SSS 70, Course record 62.
Club membership 500.
Visitors contact in advance & have handicap certificate,
not weekends & bank holidays. **Societies** weekdays only.
Phone in advance. **Green Fees** £75 per day; £55 per round.
Reduced winter rates. **Cards** ▤ ▤ ▨ ▨ ▨ **Prof** John
A Clements **Course Designer** C Butchart, W Parke

Continued

Facilities ⊗ 𝕸 by arrangement ▤ ▤ ♀ ☖ ☖ ▼ ∅
Conf fac available Corporate Hospitality Days available
Location E of village on A322

Hotel ★★★★★ Pennyhill Park Hotel & The Spa, London
Rd, BAGSHOT ☎ 01276 471774 26 en suite 97 annexe
en suite

CAMBERLEY   Map 04 SU86

Camberley Heath Golf Dr GU15 1JG
☎ 01276 23258 ▤ 01276 692505
e-mail: info@camberleyheathgolfclub.co.uk
**One of the great heath and heather courses so
frequently associated with Surrey. Several very good
short holes - especially the 8th. The 10th is a difficult
and interesting par 4, as is the 17th, where the drive
must be held well to the left as trouble lies to the right.
A fairway irrigation system has been installed.**

18 holes, 6147yds, Par 72, SSS 70, Course record 65.
Club membership 600.
Visitors not weekends; must contact in advance. **Societies**
apply in advance. **Green Fees** not confirmed. **Cards** ▤
▤ ▤ ▨ ▤ ▨ ▨ **Prof** Glenn Ralph **Course Designer**
Harry S Colt **Facilities** ⊗ ▤ ▤ ♀ ☖ ☖ ▼ ♦ ⚒ ∅
Conf fac available Corporate Hospitality Days available
Location 1.25m SE of town centre off A325

Hotel ★★★★★ Pennyhill Park Hotel & The Spa, London
Rd, BAGSHOT ☎ 01276 471774 26 en suite 97 annexe
en suite

Pine Ridge Old Bisley Rd, Frimley GU16 9NX
☎ 01276 675444 & 20770 ▤ 01276 678837
e-mail: enquiry@pineridgegolf.co.uk
18 holes, 6458yds, Par 72, SSS 71, Course record 65.
Course Designer Clive D Smith **Location** off B3015, near
A30
Phone for further details

Hotel ★★★ 72% Frimley Hall Hotel & Spa, Lime Av,
CAMBERLEY ☎ 0870 400 8224 86 en suite

CATERHAM   Map 05 TQ35

Surrey National Rook Ln, Chaldon CR3 5AA
☎ 01883 344555 ▤ 01883 344422
e-mail: caroline@surreynational.co.uk
**Opened in May 1999, this American-style course is set
in beautiful countryside and features fully irrigated
greens and fairways. The setting is dramatic with
rolling countryside, thousands of mature trees and
water features.**

Continued

Surrey National Golf Club

18 holes, 6612yds, Par 72, SSS 73, Course record 70.
Club membership 750.
Visitors may play weekdays & weekends & can book in
advance. **Societies** apply in writing or phone in advance.
Green Fees £26 per round (£30 weekends). **Cards** ▦ ▬
▦ ▦ ⚙ **Prof** David Kent, Wayne East **Course Designer**
David Williams **Facilities** ⊗ ⫢ ⓛ 🔫 ♀ ♨ 🏠 ⛳ ❧ ♣
♂ ♣ **Conf** fac available Corporate Hospitality Days
available **Location** M25 junct 7, A22

Hotel ★★★★ 75% Coulsdon Manor, Coulsdon Court Rd,
Coulsdon, CROYDON ☎ 020 8668 0414 35 en suite

CHERTSEY   Map 04 TQ06

Laleham Laleham Reach KT16 8RP
☎ 01932 564211 🖳 01932 564448
e-mail: sec@laleham-golf.co.uk
Well-bunkered parkland and meadowland course. The
prevailing wind and strategic placement of hazards
makes it a fair but testing challenge. Natural drainage
due to the underlying gravel.
18 holes, 6204yds, Par 70, SSS 70.
Club membership 600.
Visitors at weekends after 3pm **Societies** contact in writing
or phone. **Green Fees** £28.50. **Cards** ▦ ▬ ▦ ▦ ⚙
Prof Hogan Stott **Course Designer** Jack White
Facilities ⊗ ⫢ ⓛ 🔫 ♀ ♨ 🏠 ♂ **Conf** fac available
Location M25 junct 11, A320 to Thorpe Park rdbt, exit
Penton Marina, signed

Hotel ★★★ 72% The Thames Lodge, Thames St,
STAINES ☎ 0870 400 8121 78 en suite

CHIDDINGFOLD   Map 04 SU93

Chiddingfold Petworth Rd GU8 4SL
☎ 01428 685888 🖳 01428 685939
e-mail: chiddingfoldgolf@btconnect.com
With panoramic views across the Surrey hills, this
challenging course offers a unique combination of lakes,
nature woodland and wildlife.
18 holes, 5568yds, Par 70, SSS 67.
Club membership 250.
Visitors phone bookings up to one week in advance.
Societies phone booking required. **Green Fees** terms on
application. **Cards** ▦ ▬ ▦ ▦ ⚙ **Prof** John Wells
Course Designer Johnathan Gaunt **Facilities** ⊗ ⫢ ⓛ 🔫 ♀
♨ 🏠 ⛳ ❧ ♣ ♂ ♣ **Conf** fac available Corporate
Hospitality Days available **Location** on A283

Hotel ★★★★ 71% Lythe Hill Hotel & Spa, Petworth Rd,
HASLEMERE ☎ 01428 651251 41 en suite

CHIPSTEAD   Map 04 TQ25

Chipstead How Ln CR5 3LN
☎ 01737 555781 🖳 01737 555404
e-mail: office@chipsteadgolf.co.uk
Hilly parkland course, hard walking, good views.
Testing 18th hole.
18 holes, 5504yds, Par 68, SSS 67, Course record 61.
Club membership 475.
Visitors not am Tue, weekends; contact in advance.
Societies apply in writing or e-mail. **Green Fees** £40 per
day, £30 per round. **Cards** ▦ ▬ ⚙ **Prof** Gary Torbett
Facilities ⊗ ⫢ ⓛ 🔫 ♀ ♨ 🏠 ⛳ ❧ ♣ ♂ **Conf** fac
available Corporate Hospitality Days available
Location 0.5m N of village

Hotel ★★★★ 67% Selsdon Park Hotel & Golf Course,
Addington Rd, Sanderstead, CROYDON
☎ 020 8657 8811 204 en suite

CHOBHAM   Map 04 SU96

Chobham Chobham Rd, Knaphill GU21 2TZ
☎ 01276 855584 🖳 01276 855663
e-mail: chobhamgolfclub.co.uk
Designed by Peter Allis and Clive Clark, Chobham
course sits among mature oaks and tree nurseries
offering tree-lined fairways, together with six man-
made lakes.
18 holes, 5959yds, Par 69, SSS 69, Course record 67.
Club membership 750.
Visitors booking in advance essential. **Societies** Mon-Thu
by arrangement. **Green Fees** not confirmed. **Cards** ▦ ▬
▣ ▦ ⚙ **Prof** Tim Coombes **Course Designer** Peter
Alliss, Clive Clark **Facilities** ⊗ ⫢ by arrangement ⓛ 🔫 ♀
♨ 🏠 ♣ ♂ ♣ **Conf** fac available Corporate Hospitality
Days available **Location** between Chobham & Knaphill

Hotel ★★★ 65% Falcon Hotel, 68 Farnborough Rd,
FARNBOROUGH ☎ 01252 545378 30 en suite

COBHAM   Map 04 TQ16

Silvermere Redhill Rd KT11 1EF
☎ 01932 584300 🖳 01932 584301
e-mail: sales@silvermere-golf.co.uk
A mixture of light heathland on the first six holes and
parkland on holes 7-16, then two signature water holes
at the 17th and 18th, played over the Silvermere Lake.
18 holes, 6430yds, Par 71.
Club membership 600.
Visitors not before 11am weekends; must contact in
advance. **Societies** contact by phone. **Green Fees** £22.50
per 18 holes (£37.50 weekends). **Cards** ▦ ▬ ▦ ▦ ▦
⚙ **Prof** Doug McClelland **Course Designer** Neil Coles
Facilities ⊗ ⫢ ⓛ 🔫 ♀ ♨ 🏠 ♂ ♣ **Leisure** fishing.
Conf fac available Corporate Hospitality Days available
Location M25 junct 10, 0.5m off A245

Hotel ★★★★ 75% Woodlands Park Hotel, Woodlands
Ln, STOKE D'ABERNON ☎ 01372 843933 57 en suite

CRANLEIGH   Map 04 TQ03

Cranleigh Golf and Leisure Club Barhatch Ln
GU6 7NG
☎ 01483 268855 🖳 01483 267251
e-mail: info@cranleighgolfandleisure.co.uk
Scenic woodland and parkland course at the base of the
Surrey hills, easy walking. The golfer should not be

Continued

deceived by the length of the course. Clubhouse in 400-year-old barn.

18 holes, 5644yds, Par 68, SSS 67, Course record 62.
Club membership 1400.

Visitors welcome weekdays but restricted Thu am. For weekends contact professional shop in advance on 01483 277188 **Societies** phone in advance. **Green Fees** £38 per day, £30 per round (£33 per round weekends & bank holidays). Reduced winter/twilight rates. **Cards** 🖃 📇 📖 🔯 🔯 **Prof** Trevor Longmuir **Facilities** ⊗ 🍴 💄 🍷 🎿 🔯 🏌 🚃 ⛳ ♪ **Leisure** hard tennis courts, heated indoor swimming pool, sauna, solarium, gymnasium, steam room, spa bath. **Conf** Corporate Hospitality Days available **Location** 0.5m N of town centre

Hotel ★★★ 61% Gatton Manor Hotel Golf & Country Club, Standon Ln, OCKLEY ☎ 01306 627555 18 en suite

Wildwood Country Club Horsham Rd, Alfold GU6 8JE
☎ 01403 753255 📠 01403 752005

Parkland with stands of old oaks dominating several holes, a stream fed by a natural spring winds through a series of lakes and ponds. The greens are smooth, undulating and large. The 5th and 16th are the most challenging holes.

18 holes, 6655yds, Par 72, SSS 73, Course record 65.
Club membership 600.

Visitors welcome subject to availability & booking. **Societies** apply in writing or phone for enquiries. **Green Fees** terms on application. **Cards** 🖃 📇 📖 🔯 🔯 **Prof** Mark Dowdell **Course Designer** Hawtree & Sons **Facilities** ⊗ 🍴 💄 🍷 🎿 🔯 🏌 🚃 ⛳ ♪ **Leisure** gymnasium, par 3 course. **Location** off A281 3m SW of Cranleigh

Hotel ★★★ 69% Hurtwood Inn Hotel, Walking Bottom, PEASLAKE ☎ 01306 730851 15 en suite 6 annexe en suite

CROYDON

For golf courses in the area, see **Greater London**.

DORKING   Map 04 TQ14

Betchworth Park Reigate Rd RH4 1NZ
☎ 01306 882052 📠 01306 877462
e-mail: manager@betchworthparkgc.co.uk

Established parkland course with beautiful views, on the southern side of the North Downs near Boxhill.
18 holes, 6285yds, Par 69, SSS 70, Course record 64.
Club membership 725.

Visitors weekend play Sun pm only. Must contact in advance. **Societies** apply by writing, phone or fax. **Green Fees** £35 per day (weekends £45 per round). **Cards** 📇 **Prof** Andy Tocher **Course Designer** Harry Colt **Facilities** ⊗ 🍴 💄 🍷 🎿 🔯 🏌 ⛳ **Conf** Corporate Hospitality Days available **Location** 1m E on A25

Hotel ★★★ 68% The White Horse, High St, DORKING ☎ 0870 400 8282 37 en suite 41 annexe en suite

Dorking Chart Park, Deepdene Av RH5 4BX
☎ 01306 886917
e-mail: dorkinggolfclub@ukgateway.net

Undulating parkland course, easy slopes, wind-sheltered. Testing holes: 5th Tom's Puddle (par 4); 7th Rest and Be Thankful (par 4); 9th Double Decker (par 4).
9 holes, 5120yds, Par 66, SSS 65, Course record 62.
Club membership 392.

Continued

Visitors not Wed am & with member only weekends & bank holidays. Contact in advance. **Societies** Tue & Thu, phone in advance. **Green Fees** terms on application. **Cards** 🖃 📇 📖 🔯 🔯 **Prof** Paul Napier **Course Designer** J Braid & others **Facilities** ⊗ 🍴 💄 🍷 🎿 🔯 🏌 🚃 ⛳ **Location** 1m S on A24

Hotel ★★★★ 66% The Burford Bridge, Burford Bridge, Box Hill, DORKING ☎ 0870 400 8283 57 en suite

EAST HORSLEY   Map 04 TQ05

Drift The Drift, off Forest Rd KT24 5HD
☎ 01483 284641 & 284772(shop) 📠 01483 284642
e-mail: info@driftgolfclub.com
18 holes, 6425yds, Par 73, SSS 72, Course record 65.
Course Designer Sir Henry Cotton, Robert Sandow
Location 0.5m N of East Horsley off B2039
Phone for further details

Hotel ★★ 66% Bookham Grange Hotel, Little Bookham Common, Bookham, LEATHERHEAD ☎ 01372 452742 27 en suite

EFFINGHAM   Map 04 TQ15

Effingham Guildford Rd KT24 5PZ
☎ 01372 452203 📠 01372 459959
e-mail: secretary@effinghamgolfclub.com

Easy-walking downland course laid out on 270 acres with tree-lined fairways. It is one of the longest of the Surrey courses with wide subtle greens that provide a provocative but by no means exhausting challenge. Fine views of the London skyline.

18 holes, 6524yds, Par 71, SSS 71, Course record 64.
Club membership 800.

Visitors contact in advance. With member only weekends & bank holidays. **Societies** Wed, Thu & Fri only & must book in advance. **Green Fees** terms on application. **Prof** Steve Hoatson **Course Designer** HS Colt **Facilities** ⊗ 🍴 by arrangement 💄 🍷 🎿 🔯 🏌 🚃 ⛳ ♪ **Leisure** hard tennis courts. **Conf** fac available Corporate Hospitality Days available **Location** W of village on A246

Hotel ★★ 66% Bookham Grange Hotel, Little Bookham Common, Bookham, LEATHERHEAD ☎ 01372 452742 27 en suite

ENTON GREEN   Map 04 SU94

West Surrey GU8 5AF
☎ 01483 421275 📠 01483 41519
e-mail: westsurreygolfclub@btinternet.com
18 holes, 6520yds, Par 71, SSS 71, Course record 65.
Course Designer Herbert Fowler
Location S of village
Phone for further details

Hotel ★★★ 68% The Bush Hotel, The Borough, FARNHAM ☎ 0870 400 8225 & 01252 715237 📠 01252 733530 83 en suite

---

Prices may change during the currency of the Guide, please check when booking.

EPSOM
Map 04 TQ26

Epsom Longdown Ln South KT17 4JR
☎ 01372 721666 📠 01372 817183
e-mail: secretary@epsomgolfclub.co.uk
**Traditional downland course with many mature trees
and fast undulating greens. Thought must be given to
every shot to play to one's handicap.**
18 holes, 5656yds, Par 69, SSS 67, Course record 63.
Club membership 700.
Visitors available any day except Tue, Sat & Sun am.
Societies phone 01372 721666. **Green Fees** £24 per round
am, £20 pm (£30 weekends per round). Prices per day Dec-
Mar. **Cards** 🖃 💳 💳 🖃 🈺 **Prof** Ron Goudie
Course Designer Willie Dunne **Facilities** ⊗ ⊪ 🖪 ☕ ♀
🔼 🏠 🖰 ✐ **Conf** fac available Corporate Hospitality
Days available **Location** SE of town centre on B288

Hotel ★★★★ 75% Woodlands Park Hotel, Woodlands
Ln, STOKE D'ABERNON ☎ 01372 843933 57 en suite

Horton Park Golf & Country Club Hook Rd
KT19 8QG
☎ 020 8393 8400 & 8394 2626 📠 020 8394 1369
e-mail: hortonparkgc@aol.com
Millennium: 18 holes, 6257yds, Par 71, SSS 70.
Course Designer Dr Peter Nicholson
Phone for further details

Hotel ★★★★ 75% Woodlands Park Hotel, Woodlands
Ln, STOKE D'ABERNON ☎ 01372 843933 57 en suite

ESHER
Map 04 TQ16

Moore Place Portsmouth Rd KT10 9LN
☎ 01372 463533
**Public course on attractive, undulating parkland, laid
out some 80 years ago by Harry Vardon. Examples of
most of the trees that thrive in the UK are to be found
on the course. Testing short holes at 8th and 9th.**
9 holes, 2078yds, Par 33, SSS 30, Course record 27.
Club membership 150.
Visitors no restrictions. **Societies** contact in advance.
Green Fees terms on application. **Cards** 🖃 💳 💳 💳
🖃 🈺 **Prof** Nick Gadd **Course Designer** H Vardon,
D Allen, N Gadd **Facilities** ⊗ ⊪ 🖪 ☕ ♀ 🔼 🏠 🖰 ✐ **Conf**
fac available **Location** 0.5m from town centre on A307

Hotel ★★★ 67% The Ship Hotel, Monument Green,
WEYBRIDGE ☎ 01932 848364 39 en suite

Thames Ditton & Esher Portsmouth Rd KT10 9AL
☎ 020 8398 1551
18 holes, 5149yds, Par 66, SSS 65, Course record 63.
Location 1m NE on A307, next to Marquis of Granby pub
Phone for further details

Hotel ⏚ Premier Travel Inn Cobham, Portsmouth Rd,
Fairmile, COBHAM ☎ 0870 9906358 48 en suite

FARLEIGH
Map 05 TQ36

Farleigh Court Old Farleigh Rd CR6 9PX
☎ 01883 627711 📠 01883 627722
e-mail: fcgc@fbd-uk.u-net.com
18 holes, 6409yds, Par 72, SSS 71, Course record 67.
9 holes, 3281yds, Par 36.
Course Designer John Jacobs **Location** 1.5m from Selsdon
Phone for further details

Hotel ★★★★ 67% Selsdon Park Hotel & Golf Course,
Addington Rd, Sanderstead, CROYDON
☎ 020 8657 8811 204 en suite

FARNHAM
Map 04 SU84

Blacknest Binsted GU34 4QL
☎ 01420 22888 📠 01420 22001
**Privately owned pay and play golf centre catering for
all ages and levels of ability. Facilities include a 15-bay
driving range, gymnasium and a challenging 18-hole
course featuring water on 14 holes.**
18 holes, 5938yds, Par 69, SSS 69, Course record 64.
Club membership 450.
Visitors welcome at all times but should phone for tee
times especially weekends. No denims or collarless shirts.
Societies arrangement by phone or writing. **Green Fees**
£20 per round (£25 weekends). **Cards** 🖃 💳 💳 🖃 🈺
Prof Darren Burgess **Course Designer** Mr Nicholson
Facilities ⊗ ⊪ by arrangement 🖪 ☕ ♀ 🔼 🏠 🖰 🏌 ✐ 🏌
Leisure sauna, solarium, gymnasium. **Conf** fac available
Location 5m SW of Farnham off A325

Hotel ★★★ 62% Farnham House Hotel, Alton Rd,
FARNHAM ☎ 01252 716908 25 en suite

Farnham The Sands GU10 1PX
☎ 01252 782109 📠 01252 781185
e-mail: info@farnhamgolfclub.com
**A mixture of meadowland and heath with quick drying
sandy subsoil. Several of the earlier holes have
interesting features.**
18 holes, 6447yds, Par 72, SSS 71, Course record 66.
Club membership 700.
Visitors contact in advance. Must be member of
recognised club & have handicap certificate. With member
only weekends. **Societies** apply in writing. **Green Fees** £50
per day; £45 per round. **Cards** 🖃 💳 🖃 🈺 **Prof**
Grahame Cowlishaw **Course Designer** Donald Steel
Facilities ⊗ ⊪ by arrangement 🖪 ☕ ♀ 🔼 🏠 ✐
Conf Corporate Hospitality Days available
Location 3m E off A31

Hotel ★★★ 68% The Bush Hotel, The Borough,
FARNHAM ☎ 0870 400 8225 01252 715237
📠 01252 733530 83 en suite

Farnham Park Folly Hill, Farnham Park GU9 0AU
☎ 01252 715216
9 holes, 1163yds, Par 27, SSS 48, Course record 48.
Course Designer Henry Cotton **Location** N of town centre
on A287, next to Farnham Castle
Phone for further details

Hotel ★★★ 68% The Bush Hotel, The Borough,
FARNHAM ☎ 0870 400 8225 & 01252 715237
📠 01252 733530 83 en suite

GODALMING
Map 04 SU94

Broadwater Park Guildford Rd, Farncombe
GU7 3BU
☎ 01483 429955 📠 01483 429955
A par 3 public course with floodlit driving range.
9 holes, 1287yds, Par 54, SSS 50.
Club membership 160.
Visitors book for weekends & bank holidays.
Societies phone in advance. **Green Fees** not confirmed.

Continued

Continued

Cards ⊞ ▨ ▨ 🗩 **Prof** Kevin D Milton, Nick English
Course Designer Kevin Milton **Facilities** ⊗ ﻝ 🖤 ♀ 🖝 ⫯
⫯ ⟨ **Conf** Corporate Hospitality Days available
Location NE of Godalming on A3100

....

Hotel ★★★ 69% The Manor, Newlands Corner,
GUILDFORD ☎ 01483 222624 50 en suite

Hurtmore Hurtmore Rd, Hurtmore GU7 2RN
☎ 01483 426492 🗎 01483 426121
A Peter Alliss and Clive Clark pay and play course with
seven lakes and 85 bunkers. The 15th hole is the longest
at 537yds. Played mainly into the wind there are 10
bunkers to negotiate. The 3rd hole at 448yds stroke
Index 1 is a real test. A dog-leg right around a lake and
nine bunkers makes this hole worthy of its stroke index.
18 holes, 5530yds, Par 70, SSS 67, Course record 65.
Club membership 200.
Visitors book by phone up to seven days in advance.
Societies phone in advance. **Green Fees** £13 per 18 holes;
£9 per 9 holes (£19/£12 weekends); Twilight £9 (£11
weekends). **Cards** ⊞ ▨ 🖾 ▨ ▨ 🗩 **Prof** Maxine
Burton **Course Designer** Peter Alliss, Clive Clark
Facilities ⊗ ﻝ 🖤 ♀ 🖎 🖝 ⫯ ⫯ **Leisure** practice nets.
Location 2m NW of Godalming off A3

....

Hotel ★★★ 69% The Manor, Newlands Corner,
GUILDFORD ☎ 01483 222624 50 en suite

GUILDFORD   Map 04 SU94

Guildford High Path Rd, Merrow GU1 2HL
☎ 01483 563941 🗎 01483 453228
e-mail: secretary@guildfordgolfclub.co.uk
The course is on Surrey downland bordered by
attractive woodlands. Situated on chalk, it is
acknowledged to be one of the best all-weather courses
in the area, and the oldest course in Surrey. Although
not a long course, the prevailing winds across the open
downs make low scoring difficult. It is possible to see
four counties on a clear day.
18 holes, 6090yds, Par 69, SSS 70, Course record 64.
Club membership 700.
Visitors contact in advance. With member only weekends
& bank holidays. **Societies** welcome Mon-Fri. Must apply
in advance. **Green Fees** £48 per day; £38 per round. **Prof**
P G Hollington **Course Designer** JH Taylor, Hawtree
Facilities ⊗ ﻝ 🖤 ♀ 🖎 🖝 ⫯ ⫯ **Conf** fac available
Corporate Hospitality Days available **Location** E of town
centre off A246

....

Hotel ★★★ 69% The Manor, Newlands Corner,
GUILDFORD ☎ 01483 222624 50 en suite

Merrist Wood Coombe Ln, Worplesdon GU3 3PE
☎ 01483 238890 🗎 01483 238896
e-mail: mwgc@merristwood-golfclub.co.uk
More parkland than heathland, Merrist Wood has a bit
of everything. Water comes into play on five holes, the
bunkering is fierce, the greens slope and the back nine
has plenty of trees. Two holes stand out especially: the
picturesque par 3 11th with a tee shot through the trees
and the dastardly par 4 17th, including a 210yd carry
over a lake and ditches either side of the green.
18 holes, 6600yds, Par 72, SSS 71, Course record 69.
Club membership 500.
Visitors contact in advance, at weekends only after 11am
Societies apply in writing or by phone **Green Fees** £30 per

18 holes (£35 weekends); winter £25/£30. **Cards** ⊞ ▨
🖾 ▨ 🗩 **Prof** Greg Brodie **Course Designer** David
Williams **Facilities** ⊗ ﻝ ﻝ 🖤 ♀ 🖎 🖝 ⫯ 🖝 ⫯ ⫯
Leisure golf academy. **Conf** fac available Corporate
Hospitality Days available **Location** 3m from Guildford on
A323 to Aldershot

....

Hotel ★★★ 69% The Manor, Newlands Corner,
GUILDFORD ☎ 01483 222624 50 en suite

Milford Station Ln, Milford GU8 5HS
☎ 01483 419200 🗎 01483 419199
e-mail: milford@americangolf.uk.com
The design has cleverly incorporated a demanding
course within existing woodland and meadow.
18 holes, 5960yds, Par 69, SSS 68, Course record 64.
Club membership 750.
Visitors contact in advance, tee booking system, phone
01483 416291 up to 1 week in advance; not am weekends.
Societies phone in advance. **Green Fees** £25 per 18 holes
(weekends £28). **Cards** ⊞ ▨ 🖾 ▨ 🖾 ▨ 🗩 **Prof**
Paul Creamer **Course Designer** Peter Allis, Clive Clark
Facilities ⊗ ﻝ ﻝ 🖤 ♀ 🖎 🖝 ⫯ ⫯ **Conf** fac
available Corporate Hospitality Days available
Location 6m SW Guildford. Off A3 into Milford, E
towards station

....

Hotel ★★★ 69% The Manor, Newlands Corner,
GUILDFORD ☎ 01483 222624 50 en suite

Roker Park Rokers Farm, Aldershot Rd GU3 3PB
☎ 01483 236677 🗎 01483 232324
A pay and play nine-hole parkland course. A
challenging course with two par 5 holes.
9 holes, 3037yds, Par 36, SSS 72.
Club membership 200.
Visitors no restrictions, pay & play, phone for
reservations. **Societies** by arrangement with deposit at least
14 days before, min 12 persons. **Green Fees** not
confirmed. **Prof** Adrian Carter **Course Designer**
WV Roker **Facilities** ⊗ ﻝ ﻝ 🖤 ♀ 🖎 🖝 ⫯ 🖝 🖝 ⫯ ⟨
Location 3m NW of Guildford on A323

....

Hotel ★★★ 69% The Manor, Newlands Corner,
GUILDFORD ☎ 01483 222624 50 en suite

HINDHEAD   Map 04 SU83

Hindhead Churt Rd GU26 6HX
☎ 01428 604614 🗎 01428 608508
e-mail: secretary@the-hindhead-golf-club.co.uk
A picturesque Surrey heath and heather course.
Players must be prepared for some hard walking. The
first nine fairways follow narrow valleys requiring
straight hitting; the second nine are much less
restricted. The Open Championship pre-qualifying
round is played in July.
18 holes, 6356yds, Par 70, SSS 70, Course record 63.
Club membership 610.
Visitors contact in advance & have a handicap certificate.
Societies Wed & Thu only, contact in advance **Green Fees**
£52 per day; £42 per round. **Prof** Ian Benson **Course**
Designer JH Taylor **Facilities** ⊗ ﻝ 🖤 ♀ 🖎 🖝 ⫯ ⫯
Conf Corporate Hospitality Days available
Location 1.5m NW of Hindhead on A287

....

Hotel ★★★★ 71% Lythe Hill Hotel & Spa, Petworth Rd,
HASLEMERE ☎ 01428 651251 41 en suite

Continued

KINGSWOOD   Map 04 TQ25

Kingswood Golf and Country House

Sandy Ln KT20 6NE

☎ 01737 832188 📠 01737 833920

e-mail: sales@kingswood-golf.co.uk

Mature parkland course sited on a plateau with delightful views of the Chipstead valley. The course features lush, shaped fairways, testing bunkers positions and true greens. Recent improvements ensure it plays every inch of its 6904yds.

18 holes, 6904yds, Par 72, SSS 73.

Club membership 700.

Visitors not weekends before 11am; contact professional three days in advance. Societies apply in advance. **Green Fees** terms on application. **Cards** 🔲 🔲 🔲 🔲 🔲 **Prof** Terry Sims **Course Designer** James Braid **Facilities** ⊗ by arrangement ⅷ by arrangement 🖫 ⚊♀🔺🖾👕🐾 🔩 ✂ ♛ **Leisure** squash, three snooker tables.

Conf fac available Corporate Hospitality Days available **Location** 0.5m S of village off A217

Hotel ★★★ 67% Reigate Manor Hotel, Reigate Hill, REIGATE ☎ 01737 240125 50 en suite

Surrey Downs Outwood Ln KT20 6JS

☎ 01737 839090 📠 01737 839080

e-mail: booking@surreydownsgc.co.uk

18 holes, 6303yds, Par 71, SSS 70, Course record 67.

Course Designer Aliss, Clarke **Location** off A217 E onto B2032 at Kingswood for 1m, club on right after Eyhurst Park **Phone for further details**

Hotel ⭐ Premier Travel Inn Epsom South, Brighton Rd, Burgh Heath, TADWORTH ☎ 0870 9906442 78 en suite

LEATHERHEAD   Map 04 TQ15

Leatherhead Kingston Rd KT22 0EE

☎ 01372 843966 & 843956 📠 01372 842241

e-mail: secretary@lgc-golf.co.uk

Undulating, 100-year-old parkland course with tree-lined fairways and strategically placed bunkers. Easy walking.

18 holes, 5795yds, Par 70, SSS 68.

Club membership 630.

Visitors phone pro shop 01372 843956 up to 21 days in advance; not am weekends. Societies phone in advance. **Green Fees** £37.50 per round (£37.50 per round weekends am only). **Cards** 🔲 🔲 🔲 🔲 🔲 **Prof** Simon Norman **Facilities** ⊗ ⅷ 🖫 ⚊♀🔺🖾👕🔩 ✂ **Conf** fac available **Location** M25 junct 9, 0.25m on A243

Hotel ★★ 66% Bookham Grange Hotel, Little Bookham Common, Bookham, LEATHERHEAD ☎ 01372 452742 37 en suite

Pachesham Park Golf Complex Oaklawn Rd

KT22 0BT

☎ 01372 843453

e-mail: enquiries@pacheshamgolf.co.uk

An undulating parkland course starting with five shorter but tight holes on one side of the road, followed by four longer more open but testing holes to finish.

9 holes, 2805yds, Par 70, SSS 67, Course record 67.

Club membership 150.

Visitors book two days in advance by phone. May play weekends Societies apply in advance. **Green Fees** £18 per 18 holes; £10.50 per 9 holes (£21/£12 weekends & bank holidays). **Cards** 🔲 🔲 🔲 🔲 🔲 **Prof** Philip Taylor **Course Designer** Phil Taylor **Facilities** ⊗ ⅷ 🖫 ⚊♀🔺 🖾👕✂ ♛ **Conf** fac available Corporate Hospitality Days available **Location** M25 junct 9, 0.5m off A244 or A245

Hotel ★★★★ 75% Woodlands Park Hotel, Woodlands Ln, STOKE D'ABERNON ☎ 01372 843933 57 en suite

Tyrrells Wood The Drive KT22 8QP

☎ 01372 376025 📠 01372 360836

Parkland course with easy walking.

18 holes, 6282yds, Par 71, SSS 70, Course record 65.

Club membership 700.

Visitors contact in advance. Restricted weekends. Societies apply in advance. **Green Fees** £40 per round weekdays. **Cards** 🔲 🔲 🔲 🔲 🔲 **Prof** Simon Defoy **Course Designer** James Braid **Facilities** ⊗ ⅷ 🖫 ⚊♀🔺 🖾👕✂ **Conf** fac available Corporate Hospitality Days available **Location** 2m SE of town off A24

Hotel ★★★★ 66% The Burford Bridge, Burford Bridge, Box Hill, DORKING ☎ 0870 400 8283 57 en suite

LIMPSFIELD
Map 05 TQ45

Limpsfield Chart
Westerham Rd RH8 0SL

☎ 01883 723405 & 722106

Tight heathland course on National Trust land, well wooded.

9 holes, 5718yds, Par 70, SSS 68, Course record 64.
Club membership 300.

Visitors with member only or by appointment weekends & not before 3.30pm Thu (Ladies Day). **Societies** apply in advance. **Green Fees** terms on application. **Facilities** ♥ ♀ ⌚ **Leisure** putting green, practice area.
Location M25 junct 6, 1m E on A25

....

Hotel ★★★ 71% Donnington Manor, London Rd, Dunton Green, SEVENOAKS ☎ 01732 462681 60 en suite

LINGFIELD
Map 05 TQ34

Lingfield Park
Racecourse Rd RH7 6PQ

☎ 01342 832659 📄 01342 836077

e-mail: cmorley@lingfieldpark.co.uk

Difficult and challenging tree-lined parkland course, set in 210 acres of beautiful Surrey countryside with water features and 60 bunkers.

18 holes, 6473yds, Par 71, SSS 72, Course record 65.
Club membership 700.

Visitors must be accompanied by member am on Sat & Sun. Advisable to phone first. **Societies** phone in advance. **Green Fees** not confirmed. **Cards** ▦ ▦ ▦ ▦ ▦ 🔲 **Prof** Christopher Morley **Facilities** ⊗ ⫢ ♭ ♥ ♀ ⌚ 🏠 ⌙ ➤ ⚒ ♂ ⍓ **Leisure** squash, sauna, solarium, gymnasium, horse racing. **Conf** Corporate Hospitality Days available **Location** M25 junct 6, signs to racecourse

....

Hotel ⌂ Premier Travel Inn East Grinstead, London Rd, Felbridge, EAST GRINSTEAD ☎ 08701 977088 41 en suite

NEWDIGATE
Map 04 TQ14

Rusper
Rusper Rd RH5 5BX

☎ 01293 871871 (shop) 📄 01293 871456

e-mail: jill@ruspergolfclub.co.uk

The 18-hole course is set in countryside and offers golfers of all abilities a fair and challenging test. After a gentle start the holes wind through picturesque scenery, tree lined fairways and natural water hazards.

18 holes, 6724yds, Par 72, SSS 72.
Club membership 350.

Visitors welcome but phone to reserve time, some restrictions if competitions being played. **Societies** phone in advance for details. **Green Fees** £18 per 18 holes, £14 per 9 holes (£23/£16.50 (9 holes pm) weekends & bank holidays). **Cards** ▦ ▦ ▦ 🔲 **Prof** Janice Arnold **Course Designer** A Blunden **Facilities** ⊗ ⫢ ♭ ♥ ♀ ⌚ 🏠 ⍓ ➤ ⚒ ⌙ **Conf** Corporate Hospitality Days available **Location** off A24 between Newdigate & Rusper

....

Hotel ★★★★ 66% The Burford Bridge, Burford Bridge, Box Hill, DORKING ☎ 0870 400 8283 57 en suite

OCKLEY
Map 04 TQ14

Gatton Manor Hotel Golf & Country Club
Standon Ln RH5 5PQ

☎ 01306 627555 📄 01306 627713

e-mail: gattonmanor@enterprise.net

A challenging course and delightful Victorian water gardens. No two holes are alike and each one requires the golfer to consider the hazards - lakes, streams and tree lined fairways.

18 holes, 6629yds, Par 72, SSS 72, Course record 68.
Club membership 300.

Visitors may book up to 10 days in advance. Restricted Sun (am). Tee times to be booked through professional 01306 627557 **Societies** apply in advance. **Green Fees** terms on application. **Cards** ▦ ▦ ▦ 🔲 ▦ ▦ **Prof** Rae Sargent **Course Designer** Henry Cotton **Facilities** ⊗ ⫢ ♭ ♥ ♀ ⌚ 🏠 ⌙ ➤ ⚒ ♂ ⍓ **Leisure** grass tennis courts, fishing, sauna, solarium, gymnasium. **Conf** fac available Corporate Hospitality Days available
Location 1.5m SW off A29

....

Hotel ★★★ 61% Gatton Manor Hotel Golf & Country Club, Standon Ln, OCKLEY ☎ 01306 627555 18 en suite

OTTERSHAW
Map 04 TQ06

Foxhills
Stonehill Rd KT16 0EL

☎ 01932 872050 📄 01932 875200

e-mail: events@foxhills.co.uk

A pair of parkland courses designed in the grand manner with three championship courses. One course is tree-lined, the other, as well as trees, has massive bunkers and artificial lakes which contribute to the interest. Both courses offer testing golf and they finish on the same long double green. Par 3 Manor Course also available.

The Bernard Hunt Course: 18 holes, 6770yds, Par 73, SSS 72, Course record 65.
Longcross Course: 18 holes, 6453yds, Par 72, SSS 71, Course record 70.

Visitors tee times bookable through events office Mon-Fri. Only after midday at weekends **Societies** welcome Mon-Fri, must apply in advance. **Green Fees** not confirmed. **Cards** ▦ ▦ ▦ ▦ 🔲 **Prof** B Hunt, R Summerscales **Course Designer** FW Hawtree **Facilities** ⊗ ⫢ ♭ ♥ ♀ ⌚ 🏠 ⍓ ➤ ⚒ ⌙ **Leisure** hard tennis courts, outdoor & indoor heated swimming pools, squash, sauna, solarium, gymnasium, par 3 course. **Conf** fac available Corporate Hospitality Days available
Location 1m NW of Ottershaw

....

Hotel ★★★★ 71% Foxhills, Stonehill Rd, OTTERSHAW, Surrey ☎ 01932 872050 38 en suite

PIRBRIGHT
Map 04 SU95

Goal Farm
Gole Rd GU24 0PZ

☎ 01483 473183 📄 01483 473205

e-mail: secretary@gfgc.co.uk

Beautiful landscaped parkland pay and play course with excellent greens. A range of enjoyable yet demanding holes over trees and over water with plenty of bunkers to swallow up tee shots.

9 holes, 1273yds, Par 54, SSS 48, Course record 50.
Club membership 350.

Visitors not Sat before 2pm or Thu before 2pm. **Societies** phone in advance. **Green Fees** terms on application. **Cards** ▦ ▦ ▦ ▦ 🔲 **Prof** Peter Fuller **Course Designer** Bill Cox **Facilities** ♭ ♥ ♀ 🏠 ⍓ **Location** 1.5m NW on B3012

....

Hotel ★★★ 65% Falcon Hotel, 68 Farnborough Rd, FARNBOROUGH ☎ 01252 545378 30 en suite

Continued

PUTTENHAM   Map 04 SU94

Puttenham Heath Rd GU3 1AL
☎ 01483 810498 🖹 01483 810988
e-mail: enquiries@puttenhamgolfclub.co.uk
**Mixture of heathland and woodland - undulating layout
with stunning views across the Hog's Back and towards
the South Downs. Sandy subsoil provides free drainage
for year round play.**
18 holes, 6220yds, Par 71, SSS 70.
Club membership 650.
Visitors weekdays by arrangment, tel 01483 810498, with
member only weekends & public holidays. **Societies** apply in
advance to secretary. **Green Fees** £45 per day; £32 per round.
Cards 🔲 🔲 🔲 🔲 🔲 **Prof** Gary Simmons **Facilities** ⊗ 🍴
by arrangement 🥤 💺 🏊 🏌 🛒 **Conf** Corporate
Hospitality Days available **Location** 1m SE on B3000

Hotel ★★★ 68% The Bush Hotel, The Borough,
FARNHAM ☎ 0870 400 8225 & 01252 715237
🖹 01252 733530 83 en suite

REDHILL   Map 04 TQ25

Redhill & Reigate Clarence Rd, Pendelton Rd
RH1 6LB
☎ 01737 244433 🖹 01737 242117
e-mail: mail@rrgc.net
**Flat picturesque tree-lined course, well over 100 years
old.**
18 holes, 5272yds, Par 68, SSS 66, Course record 65.
Club membership 600.
Visitors not before 11am weekends. Must contact in
advance. **Societies** apply in writing or by phone. **Green
Fees** terms on application. **Cards** 🔲 🔲 🔲 🔲 🔲 🔲
Prof Warren Pike **Course Designer** James Braid **Facilities**
⊗ 🍴 🥤 💺 🏊 🏌 🛒 **Conf** fac available Corporate
Hospitality Days available **Location** 1m S on A23

Hotel ★★★ 67% Reigate Manor Hotel, Reigate Hill,
REIGATE ☎ 01737 240125 50 en suite

REIGATE   Map 04 TQ25

Reigate Heath Flanchford Rd RH2 8QR
☎ 01737 242610 & 226793 🖹 01737 249226
e-mail: reigateheath@surreygolf.co.uk
**Gorse, heather, pine and birch trees abound on this
popular nine-hole heathland course. The course is short
by modern standards but is a good test of golf. Playing
18 holes from nine greens, the second nine is quite
different with changes of angle as well as length.**
9 holes, 5658yds, Par 67, SSS 67, Course record 65.
Club membership 550.
Visitors with member only weekends & bank holidays.
Must contact in advance. **Societies** apply in writing. **Green
Fees** £25 per round. **Prof** Barry Davies **Facilities** ⊗ 🍴 🥤
💺 🏊 🏌 🛒 **Conf** Corporate Hospitality Days available
Location 1.5m W off A25

Hotel ★★★ 67% Reigate Manor Hotel, Reigate Hill,
REIGATE ☎ 01737 240125 50 en suite

Reigate Hill Gatton Bottom RH2 0TU
☎ 01737 645577 🖹 01737 642650
18 holes, 6175yds, Par 72, SSS 70, Course record 75.
Course Designer David Williams
Location M25 junct 8, 1m
Phone for further details

SHEPPERTON   Map 04 TQ06

Sunbury Golf Centre Charlton Ln TW17 8QA
☎ 01932 771414 🖹 01932 789300
e-mail: sunbury@americangolf.uk.com
**27 holes of golf catering for all standards of golfer and a
32 bay floodlit driving range. Easy walking.**
18 holes, 5103yds, Par 68, SSS 65, Course record 60.
Academy: 9 holes, 2444yds, Par 33, SSS 32.
Club membership 400.
Visitors no restrictions. **Societies** may play seven days a
week, advance booking necessary. **Green Fees** £16 per 18
holes; £9 per 9 holes (£20/£10 wekends). **Cards** 🔲 🔲
🔲 🔲 🔲 🔲 **Prof** Adrian McColgan **Facilities** ⊗ 🥤 💺 💺
🏊 🏌 🛒 🏌 🛒 **Conf** fac available Corporate
Hospitality Days available **Location** 1m N off A244

Hotel ★★★ 72% The Thames Lodge, Thames St,
STAINES ☎ 0870 400 8121 78 en suite

SUTTON GREEN   Map 04 TQ05

Sutton Green New Ln GU4 7QF
☎ 01483 747898 🖹 01483 750289
e-mail: admin@suttongreengc.co.uk
**Set in the Surrey countryside, a challenging course with
many water features. Excellent year round conditions
with fairway watering. Many testing holes with water
surrounding greens and fairways, making accuracy a
premium.**
18 holes, 6350yds, Par 71, SSS 70, Course record 64.
Club membership 600.
Visitors contact in advance, play after 2pm weekends
Societies Mon-Fri. Call for details. **Green Fees** terms on
application. **Cards** 🔲 🔲 🔲 **Prof** Paul Tedder **Course
Designer** David Walker, Laura Davies **Facilities** ⊗ 🍴 🥤
💺 🏊 🏌 🛒 🏌 🛒 **Conf** fac available Corporate
Hospitality Days available **Location** off A320 between
Woking & Guildford

Hotel ★★★★★ Pennyhill Park Hotel & The Spa, London
Rd, BAGSHOT ☎ 01276 471774 26 en suite 97 annexe
en suite

TANDRIDGE   Map 05 TQ35

Tandridge RH8 9NQ
☎ 01883 712274 🖹 01883 730537
e-mail: secretary@tandridgegolfclub.com
**A parkland course with two loops of nine holes from the
clubhouse. The first nine is relatively flat. The second
nine undulates with outstanding views of the North
Downs.**
18 holes, 6250yds, Par 70, SSS 70, Course record 66.
Club membership 750.
Visitors contact in advance. May play Mon, Wed, Thu
Societies Mon, Wed & Thu, apply in advance. **Green Fees**
£65 per day, £45 pm; winter £35 per round. **Cards** 🔲 🔲
🔲 🔲 🔲 **Prof** Chris Evans **Course Designer** HS Colt
Facilities ⊗ 🥤 💺 🏊 🏌 🛒 🏌 **Conf** Corporate
Hospitality Days available **Location** M25 junct 6, 2m SE
on A25

Hotel ★★★★ 73% Nutfield Priory, Nutfield, REDHILL
☎ 01737 824400 60 en suite

Continued

TILFORD
Map 04 SU84

Hankley Common The Club House GU10 2DD
☎ 01252 792493 📠 01252 795699
A natural heathland course subject to wind. Greens are first rate. The 18th, a long par 4, is most challenging, the green being beyond a deep chasm which traps any but the perfect second shot. The 7th is a spectacular one-shotter.
18 holes, 6702yds, Par 72, SSS 72, Course record 62.
Club membership 700.
Visitors handicap certificate required, restricted pm weekends. **Societies** apply in writing. **Green Fees** £60 per round/£75 per day (£75 per round weekends). **Cards**
📧 📧 📧 🔳 ⑨ **Prof** Peter Stow **Course Designer** James Braid **Facilities** ⊗ 〗⅃ 🍴 ⚑ 🏧 ♂
Location 0.75m SE of Tilford

Hotel ★★★ 68% The Bush Hotel, The Borough, FARNHAM ☎ 0870 400 8225 & 01252 715237 📠 01252 733530 83 en suite

VIRGINIA WATER
See page 241

WALTON-ON-THAMES
Map 04 TQ16

Burhill Burwood Rd KT12 4BL
☎ 01932 227345 📠 01932 267159
e-mail: info@burhillgolf-club.co.uk
The Old Course is a mature tree-lined parkland course with some of the finest greens in Surrey. The New Course, opened in 2001, is a modern course built to USGA specifications has many bunkers and water hazards, including the River Mole.
Old Course: 18 holes, 6479yds, Par 70, SSS 71, Course record 65.
New Course: 18 holes, 6597yds, Par 72, SSS 71.
Club membership 1100.
Visitors no visitors weekends or bank holidays unless introduced by member. Must contact in advance. **Societies** apply in writing. **Green Fees** £85 per day, £62.50 per 18 holes. **Cards** 📧 📧 ⑨ **Prof** Ian Partington **Course Designer** Willie Park, Simon Gidman **Facilities** ⊗ 〗⅃ 🍴 ⚑ 🏧 ♂ **Conf** fac available Corporate Hospitality Days available **Location** M25 junct 10, A3 towards London, 1st exit (Painshill)

Hotel ★★★ 67% The Ship Hotel, Monument Green, WEYBRIDGE ☎ 01932 848364 39 en suite

WALTON-ON-THE-HILL
See page 243

WEST BYFLEET
Map 04 TQ06

West Byfleet Sheerwater Rd KT14 6AA
☎ 01932 343433 📠 01932 340667
e-mail: secretary@wbgc.co.uk
An attractive course set against a background of woodland and gorse. The 13th is the famous pond shot with a water hazard and two bunkers fronting the green. No less than six holes of 420yds or more.
18 holes, 6211yds, Par 70, SSS 70.
Club membership 622.
Visitors contact professional in advance, only with member at weekends. Restricted Thu (Ladies Day). **Societies** apply in writing or phone. **Green Fees** £70 per

Continued

day, £50 per round. **Cards** 📧 📧 📧 🔳 ⑨ **Prof** David Regan **Course Designer** C S Butchart **Facilities** ⊗ 〗⅃ 🍴 ⚑ 🏧 ♂ **Conf** Corporate Hospitality Days available **Location** W of village on A245

Hotel ★★★ 69% The Manor, Newlands Corner, GUILDFORD ☎ 01483 222624 50 en suite

WEST CLANDON
Map 04 TQ05

Clandon Regis Epsom Rd GU4 7TT
☎ 01483 224888 📠 01483 211781
e-mail: office@clandonregis-golfclub.co.uk
High quality parkland course with challenging lake holes on the back nine. European Tour specification tees and greens.
18 holes, 6484yds, Par 72, SSS 71, Course record 66.
Club membership 652.
Visitors contact in advance for weekend play. **Societies** phone in advance. **Green Fees** not confirmed. **Cards** 📧 📧 📧 🔳 ⑨ **Prof** Steve Lloyd **Course Designer** David Williams **Facilities** ⊗ 〗⅃ 🍴 ⚑ 🏧 ♂ **Leisure** sauna. **Conf** fac available Corporate Hospitality Days available **Location** SE of village of A246

Hotel ★★★ 69% The Manor, Newlands Corner, GUILDFORD ☎ 01483 222624 50 en suite

Surrey

Wentworth Club

Virginia Water

Map 04 TQ06

Wentworth Club, the home of the Volvo PGA and Cisco World Match Play championships, is a very special venue for any sporting, business or social occasion. The West Course (7047yds) is familiar to millions of television viewers who have followed the championships here. There are two other 18-hole courses, the East Course (6201yds) and the Edinburgh Course (7004yds), as well as a nine-hole par 3 executive course. The courses cross Surrey heathland with woods of pine, oak and birch. The Club is renowned for its fine English food, and the superb tennis and health facilities include a holistic spa. The centre opened in January 1999 and has 13 outdoor tennis courts with four different playing surfaces, a 25-metre indoor pool and further extensive leisure facilities.

Wentworth Dr GU25 4LS
☎ 01344 842201 Fax 01344 842804
e-mail: reception@wentworthclub.com

West Course: 18 holes, 7047yds, Par 73, SSS 74, Course record 63.
East Course: 18 holes, 6201yds, Par 68, SSS 70, Course record 62.
Edinburgh Course: 18 holes, 7004yds, Par 72, SSS 74, Course record 67.
Visitors not weekends; handicap certificate (men max 24, women max 32); must contact in advance. **Societies** must contact in advance in writing. **Green Fees** West Course £95-£260; Edinburgh Course £80-£155; East Course £75-£125. **Cards** ⊞ ▦ ▭ ▧ ▦ 🖎 ⊘ **Prof** David Rennie **Course Designer** Jacobs, Gallacher, Player **Facilities** ⊗ 🎅 🏋 ▦ ♀ 🏌 🏕 🎯 🏇 🐕 ⚓ 🚴 ℓ **Leisure** hard and grass tennis courts, outdoor and indoor heated swimming pools, fishing, sauna, solarium, gymnasium. **Conf** fac available Corporate Hospitality Days available **Location** on A30, main gate opp turning for A329

....

Hotels

★ ★ 72% The Wheatsheaf, London Rd, VIRGINIA WATER

☎ 01344 842057 17 en suite

★ ★ ★ ★ 73% Runnymede Hotel & Spa, Windsor Rd, EGHAM

☎ 01784 436171 Fax 01784 436340 180 en suite

★ ★ ★ ★ 66% The Berystede, Bagshot Rd, Sunninghill, ASCOT

☎ 0870 400 8111 Fax 01344 872301 90 en suite

★ ★ ★ ★ 71% The Royal Berkshire Ramada Plaza, London Rd, Sunninghill, ASCOT

☎ 01344 623322 Fax 01344 627100 63 en suite

WEST END   Map 04 SU96

Windlemere Windlesham Rd GU24 9QL
☎ 01276 858727

A parkland course, undulating in parts with natural water hazards. There is also a floodlit driving range.
9 holes, 2673yds, Par 34, SSS 33, Course record 30.
Visitors no restrictions. **Societies** advisable to contact in advance. **Green Fees** £11 per 9 holes (£12.50 weekends). **Cards** ▦ ▦ ▦ ▦ ▨ **Prof** David Thomas **Course Designer** Clive Smith **Facilities** �& ♥♀♨♙↑♂(**Leisure** pool & snooker tables. **Location** N of village at junct A319 & A322

Hotel ★★★★★ Pennyhill Park Hotel & The Spa, London Rd, BAGSHOT ☎ 01276 471774 26 en suite 97 annexe en suite

WEYBRIDGE   Map 04 TQ06

St George's Hill Golf Club Rd, St George's Hill KT13 0NL
☎ 01932 847758 ▤ 01932 821564
e-mail: admin@stgeorgeshillgolfclub.co.uk
Comparable and similar to Wentworth, a feature of this course is the number of long and difficult par 4s. To score well it is necessary to place the drive - and long driving pays handsomely. Walking is hard on this undulating, heavily wooded course with plentiful heather and rhododendrons.
Red & Blue: 18 holes, 6513yds, Par 70, SSS 71, Course record 64.
Green: 9 holes, 2897yds, Par 35.
Club membership 600.
Visitors contact in advance & have a handicap certificate. Visitors may only play Wed-Fri. **Societies** apply in writing or phone. **Green Fees** £120 per day; £90 per round. **Prof** AC Rattue **Course Designer** HS Colt **Facilities** ⊗ �& ♥♀♨♙↑♂(**Conf** Corporate Hospitality Days available **Location** 2m S off B374

Hotel ★★★ 67% The Ship Hotel, Monument Green, WEYBRIDGE ☎ 01932 848364 39 en suite

WOKING   Map 04 TQ05

Hoebridge Golf Centre Old Woking Rd GU22 8JH
☎ 01483 722611 ▤ 01483 740369
e-mail: info@hoebridge.co.uk
Three public courses set in parkland on Surrey sand belt. The main course is a championship length challenge course; Shey Copse is a nine-hole course, ideal for the intermediate golfer; and the Maybury an 18-hole par 3 course which is suited to beginners and occasional golfers.
Main Course: 18 holes, 6536yds, Par 72, SSS 71.
Shey Course: 9 holes, 2294yds, Par 33.
Maybury Course: 18 holes, 2230yds, Par 54.
Club membership 600.
Visitors welcome every day, course & reservation desk open dawn to dusk. Credit card reservations six days in advance. **Societies** Mon-Fri only, phone in advance **Green Fees** Main: £21 Mon-Thu, £24 Fri (£27.50 weekends) Shey: £11 (£13 weekends) Maybury: £9 (£11 weekends). **Cards** ▦ ▦ ▦ ▨ **Prof** Crail Butfoy **Course Designer** John Jacobs **Facilities** ⊗ ▦ �& ♥♀♨♙↑♂(**Leisure** gymnasium, health & fitness club. **Conf** fac

available Corporate Hospitality Days available **Location** M25 junct 11, on B382 Old Woking-West Byfleet road

Hotel ★★★★★ Pennyhill Park Hotel & The Spa, London Rd, BAGSHOT ☎ 01276 471774 26 en suite 97 annexe en suite

Pyrford Warren Ln, Pyrford GU22 8XR
☎ 01483 723555 ▤ 01483 729777
e-mail: pyrford@americangolf.uk.com
This inland links-style course was designed by Peter Alliss and Clive Clark. Set between Surrey woodlands, the fairways weave between 23 acres of water courses while the greens and tees are connected by rustic bridges. The signature hole is the par 5 9th at 595yds, with a dog-leg and final approach over water and a sand shelf. Excellent playing conditions all year round.
18 holes, 6256yds, Par 72, SSS 70, Course record 64.
Club membership 650.
Visitors book in advance; not am weekends **Societies** contact in advance. **Green Fees** not confirmed. **Cards** ▦ ▦ ▦ ▦ ▨ **Prof** Darren Brewer **Course Designer** Peter Allis & Clive Clark **Facilities** ⊗ ▦ �& ♥♀♨♙↑♂(**Conf** Corporate Hospitality Days available **Location** off A3 Ripley to Pyrford

Hotel ★★★★★ Pennyhill Park Hotel & The Spa, London Rd, BAGSHOT ☎ 01276 471774 26 en suite 97 annexe en suite

Traditions Pyrford Rd, Pyrford GU22 8UE
☎ 01932 350355 ▤ 01932 350234
e-mail: traditions@americangolf.uk.com
18 holes, 6304yds, Par 71, SSS 70, Course record 67.
Course Designer Peter Alliss **Location** M25 junct 10, A3, signs to RHS Garden Wisley, through Wisley to Pyrford, course 0.5m
Phone for further details

Hotel ★★★★★ Pennyhill Park Hotel & The Spa, London Rd, BAGSHOT ☎ 01276 471774 26 en suite 97 annexe en suite

Woking Pond Rd, Hook Heath GU22 0JZ
☎ 01483 760053 ▤ 01483 772441
e-mail: woking.golf@btconnect.com
An 18-hole course on Surrey heathland with few changes from the original course designed in 1892 by Tom Dunn. Bernard Darwin, a past captain and president, has written 'the beauty of Woking is that there is something distinctive about every hole'.
18 holes, 6340yds, Par 70, SSS 70, Course record 65.
Club membership 600.
Visitors contact secretary at least seven days prior to playing. No visitors weekends & bank holidays. **Societies** phone intially then confirm in writing, normally 12 months notice. **Green Fees** not confirmed. **Cards** ▦ ▦ ▦ ▨ **Prof** Carl Bianco **Course Designer** Tom Dunn **Facilities** ⊗ ▦ �& ♥♀♨♙↑♂(**Conf** Corporate Hospitality Days available **Location** W of town centre in area of St Johns & Hook Heath

Hotel ★★★★★ Pennyhill Park Hotel & The Spa, London Rd, BAGSHOT ☎ 01276 471774 26 en suite 97 annexe en suite

Continued

Walton Heath

Surrey

Walton-on-the-Hill   Map 04 TQ25

Walton Heath, a traditional member club, has two extremely challenging courses. Enjoying an enviable international reputation, the club was founded in 1903. It has played host to over 60 major amateur and professional championships, including the 1981 Ryder Cup and five European Open Tournaments (1991, 1989, 1987, 1980 and 1977); among the many prestigious amateur events, Walton Heath hosted the English Amateur in 2002. The Old Course is popular with visitors, while the New Course is very challenging, requiring subtle shots to get the ball near the hole. Straying from the fairway brings gorse, bracken and heather to test the most patient golfer.

Deans Ln, Walton-on-the-Hill KT20 7TP
☎ 01737 812380 Fax 01737 814225
e-mail: secretary@whgc.co.uk
Old Course: 18 holes, 6836yds, Par 72, SSS 73,
Course record 65.
New Course: 18 holes, 6613yds, Par 72, SSS 72,
Course record 67.
Club membership 1000.
Visitors restricted weekends; must contact in advance; handicap certificate or letter of introduction. Societies must contact in advance. Green Fees £90 before 11.30am, £80 after 11.30am (£100 weekends). Cards ▭ ▬ ▬ ▣ ▧ ▨
Prof Ken Macpherson Course Designer Herbert Fowler
Facilities ⊗ ▶ ➋ ▼ ♀ ♣ 🖱 ⛳ ◗
Conf Corporate Hospitality Days available
Location SE of village off B2032

....

Hotels

★★ 66% Bookham Grange Hotel, Little Bookham Common, Bookham, LEATHERHEAD

☎ 01372 452742 27 en suite

★★★ 73% Chalk Lane Hotel, Chalk Ln, Woodcote End, EPSOM

☎ 01372 721179 Fax 01372 727878 22 en suite

★★★ 67% Reigate Manor Hotel, Reigate Hill, REIGATE

☎ 01737 240125 Fax 01737 223883 50 en suite

★★★★ 66% The Burford Bridge, Burford Bridge, Box Hill, DORKING

☎ 0870 400 8283 Fax 01306 880386 57 en suite

★★★ 68% The White Horse, High St, DORKING

☎ 0870 400 8282 Fax 01306 887241 37 en suite
41 annexe en suite

Worplesdon Heath House Rd GU22 0RA
☎ 01483 472277
e-mail: office@worplesdongc.co.uk
The scene of the celebrated mixed-foursomes competition. Accurate driving is essential on this heathland course. The short 10th across a lake from tee to green is a notable hole, and the 18th provides a wonderfully challenging par 4 finish.
18 holes, 6431yds, Par 71, SSS 71, Course record 64. Club membership 610.
Visitors must play with member at weekends & bank holidays. Must contact in advance & have a handicap certificate. **Societies** contact in writing. **Green Fees** £80 per day; £60 per round (winter £35). **Cards** 💳 💳 💳 💳 💳 **Prof** J Christine **Course Designer** JF Abercromby **Facilities** ⊗ ⓑ 🛒 ♀ ⚒ 🏠 ⛳ ⚘ **Location** 1.5m N of village off A322

Hotel ★★★★★ Pennyhill Park Hotel & The Spa, London Rd, BAGSHOT ☎ 01276 471774 26 en suite 97 annexe en suite

WOLDINGHAM   Map 05 TQ35

North Downs Northdown Rd CR3 7AA
☎ 01883 652057 📠 01883 652832
e-mail: info@northdownsgolfclub.co.uk
Downland course, 850ft above sea level, with several testing holes and magnificent views.
18 holes, 5857yds, Par 69, SSS 68, Course record 64. Club membership 530.
Visitors must play with member weekend am. Must contact in advance. **Societies** phone in advance & confirm in writing. **Green Fees** £40 per day; £30 per round (£30 per round weekends after 3pm summer, noon winter). **Cards** 💳 💳 💳 💳 💳 **Prof** M Homewood **Course Designer** Pennink **Facilities** ⊗ ⍔ ⓑ 🛒 ♀ ⚒ 🏠 🚜 ⚘ **Conf** fac available Corporate Hospitality Days available **Location** 0.75m S of Woldingham

Hotel ★★★ 71% Donnington Manor, London Rd, Dunton Green, SEVENOAKS ☎ 01732 462681 60 en suite

Woldingham Halliloo Valley Rd CR3 7HA
☎ 01883 653501 📠 01883 653502
e-mail: membership@woldingham-golfclub.co.uk
Located in Halliloo Valley and designed by the American architect Bradford Benz, this pleasant course utilises all the contours and features of the valley.

18 holes, 6393yds, Par 71, SSS 70, Course record 64. Club membership 695.
Visitors tee times should be booked in advance with pro shop. Weekends available after 11am for visitors. **Societies** phone to book. **Green Fees** £26 per round (£30 weekends). **Cards** 💳 💳 💳 💳 💳 **Course Designer** Bradford Benz **Facilities** ⊗ by arrangement ⍔ by arrangement ⓑ 🛒 ♀ ⚒ 🏠 ⛳ 🛒 🚜 ⚘ ⛳ **Conf** fac available Corporate Hospitality Days available **Location** M25 junct 6, A22 N, 1st rdbt onto Woldingham Rd & Halliloo Valley Rd, on left

Hotel ★★★ 71% Donnington Manor, London Rd, Dunton Green, SEVENOAKS ☎ 01732 462681 60 en suite

SUSSEX, EAST

BEXHILL   Map 05 TQ70

Cooden Beach Cooden Sea Rd TN39 4TR
☎ 01424 842040 & 843938 (pro shop) 📠 01424 842040
e-mail: enquiries@coodenbeachgc.com
The course is close by the sea, but is not real links. Despite that, it is dry and plays well throughout the year. There are some excellent holes such as the 4th, played to a built-up green, the short 12th, and three good holes to finish. There are added ponds which make the player think more about tee shots and shots to the green.

18 holes, 6504yds, Par 72, SSS 71, Course record 67. Club membership 850.
Visitors must have a handicap certificate. Restricted at weekends. Book in advance with professional 01424 843938. **Societies** contact in advance by telephoning secretary. **Green Fees** £40 per day, £35 per round (£45/£40 weekends). **Cards** 💳 💳 **Prof** Jeffrey Sim **Course Designer** W Herbert Fowler **Facilities** ⊗ ⍔ ⓑ 🛒 ♀ ⚒ 🏠 🛒 🚜 ⚘ ⛳ **Leisure** indoor practice facility. **Conf** fac available Corporate Hospitality Days available **Location** 2m W on A259

Hotel ★★★ ♨ 76% Powder Mills Hotel, Powdermill Ln, BATTLE ☎ 01424 775511 30 en suite 10 annexe en suite

Highwoods Ellerslie Ln TN39 4LJ
☎ 01424 212625 📠 01424 216866
e-mail: highwoods@btconnect.com
Undulating parkland course with water on six holes.
18 holes, 6218yds, Par 70, SSS 70, Course record 63. Club membership 750.
Visitors must play with member on Sun. Must contact in advance & have an introduction from own club. Handicap required. **Societies** advance notice advised. **Green Fees** £32 per 18 holes (weekends £35). **Prof** Mike Andrews **Course Designer** JH Taylor **Facilities** ⊗ ⍔ ⓑ 🛒 ♀ ⚒ 🏠 ⚘ **Location** 1.5m NW

Continued

Continued

Hotel ★★★ 66% Royal Victoria Hotel, Marina, St
Leonards-on-Sea, HASTINGS ☎ 01424 445544
50 en suite

BRIGHTON & HOVE Map 04 TQ30

Brighton & Hove Devils Dyke Rd BN1 8YJ
☎ 01273 556482 01273 554247
e-mail: phil@bhgc68.fsnet.co.uk
Testing nine-hole course with glorious views over the Downs and the sea. Famous drop hole par 3.
9 holes, 5704yds, Par 68, SSS 67, Course record 64.
Club membership 380.
Visitors contact in advance, restricted play Wed, Fri & weekends. **Societies** contact secretary in advance. **Green Fees** £20 per 18 holes; £12 per 9 holes (£25/£15 weekends). **Cards** **Prof** Phil Bonsall **Course Designer** James Braid **Facilities** **Conf** fac available Corporate Hospitality Days available **Location** 4m NW of Brighton, 1m from A27 & A23

Hotel ★★★ 69% The Old Tollgate Restaurant & Hotel, The Street, BRAMBER ☎ 01903 879494 11 en suite 20 annexe en suite

Dyke Devils Dyke, Dyke Rd BN1 8YJ
☎ 01273 857296(office) & 857260(pro shop)
01273 857078
e-mail: secretary@dykegolfclub.org.uk
This downland course has some glorious views both towards the sea and inland. The signature hole on the course is probably the 17th; it is one of those tough par 3s of just over 200yds, and is played across a gully to a high green.
18 holes, 6627yds, Par 72, SSS 72, Course record 66.
Club membership 800.
Visitors advisable to contact in advance; not am Sun. **Societies** apply by phone or in writing. **Green Fees** not confirmed. **Cards** **Prof** Richard Arnold **Course Designer** Fred Hawtree **Facilities** **Conf** Corporate Hospitality Days available **Location** 4m N of Brighton, between A23 & A27

Hotel ★★★ 69% The Old Tollgate Restaurant & Hotel, The Street, BRAMBER ☎ 01903 879494 11 en suite 20 annexe en suite

Hollingbury Park Ditchling Rd BN1 7HS
☎ 01273 552010 (sec) 500086 (pro) 01273 552010/6
e-mail: graemecrompton@sussexgolfcentre.fsnet.co.uk
Municipal course in hilly situation on the South Downs, overlooking the sea.
18 holes, 6500yds, Par 72, SSS 71, Course record 65.
Club membership 300.
Visitors contact in advance. **Societies** phone the secretary for details. **Green Fees** £14 per 18 holes; £22 per day (weekends £19 per round). **Prof** Graeme Crompton **Facilities** **Location** 2m N of town centre

Hotel ★★★ 64% Quality Hotel Brighton, West St, BRIGHTON ☎ 01273 220033 138 en suite

Waterhall Saddlescombe Rd BN1 8YN
☎ 01273 508658
18 holes, 5773yds, Par 69, SSS 68, Course record 66.
Location 2m NE from A27
Phone for further details

Continued

Hotel ★★★ 69% The Old Tollgate Restaurant & Hotel, The Street, BRAMBER ☎ 01903 879494 11 en suite 20 annexe en suite

West Hove Church Farm, Hangleton BN3 8AN
☎ 01273 419738 & 413494 (pro) 01273 439988
e-mail: info@westhovegolf.co.uk
A downland course designed by Hawtree & Sons.
18 holes, 6226yds, Par 71, SSS 70, Course record 65.
Club membership 600.
Visitors tee times by arrangement. **Societies** by arrangement, phone, write or e-mail. **Green Fees** £25 per 18 holes. **Prof** Darren Cook **Course Designer** Hawtree & Sons **Facilities** by arrangement **Conf** fac available **Location** off A27 N of Brighton

Hotel ★★★ 64% The Courtlands, 15-27 The Drive, HOVE ☎ 01273 731055 60 en suite 7 annexe en suite

CROWBOROUGH Map 05 TQ53

Crowborough Beacon Beacon Rd TN6 1UJ
☎ 01892 661511 01892 611988
e-mail: secretary@cbgc.co.uk
Standing some 800ft above sea level, this is a testing heathland course where accuracy off the tee rather than distance is paramount. Panoramic views of the South Downs, Eastbourne and even the sea on a clear day.

18 holes, 6279yds, Par 71, SSS 70, Course record 66.
Club membership 700.
Visitors contact in advance & have handicap certificate but may only play at weekends & bank holidays after 2.30pm. **Societies** phone or apply in writing to secretary. **Green Fees** £50 per round, £60 per day (£60 per round weekends after 2.30pm). **Cards** **Prof** DC Newnham **Facilities** **Location** 9m S of Tunbridge Wells on A26

Hotel ★★★★ 71% The Spa Hotel, Mount Ephraim, TUNBRIDGE WELLS ☎ 01892 520331 69 en suite

Dewlands Manor Cottage Hill, Rotherfield TN6 3JN
☎ 01892 852266 01892 853015
A compact meadowland course built on land surrounding a 15th-century manor. The short par 4 4th can be played by the brave by launching a driver over the trees; the 7th requires accurate driving on a tight fairway; and the final two holes are sweeping par 5s travelling parallel to each other, a small stream guarding the front of the 9th green.
9 holes, 3186yds, Par 36, SSS 70.
Visitors phone in advance. **Societies** phone for availability.

Continued

Green Fees terms on application. **Cards** 🔲 🔲 🔲 🔲 🔲
Prof Nick Godin **Course Designer** RM & NM Godin
Facilities ⊗ 🅱 ♥ ♀ 🛆 🏠 ⸗ ♦ 🚵 ♂ **Leisure** indoor
teaching facilities with computer analysis. **Conf** Corporate
Hospitality Days available **Location** 0.5m S of Rotherfield

Inn ♦♦♦ Plough & Horses Inn, Walshes Rd,
CROWBOROUGH ☎ 01892 652614 15 en suite

DITCHLING   Map 05 TQ31

Mid Sussex Spatham Ln BN6 8XJ
☎ 01273 846567 📠 01273 841835
e-mail: admin@midsussexgolfclub.co.uk
**Mature parkland course with many trees, water
hazards, strategically placed bunkers and superbly
contoured greens. The 14th hole, a spectacular par 5,
demands accurate shotmaking to avoid the various
hazards along its length.**
*18 holes, 6462yds, Par 71, SSS 71, Course record 65.
Club membership 650.*
Visitors phone in advance to book tee times. After 1pm at
weekends. **Societies** advance booking required. **Green
Fees** not confirmed. **Cards** 🔲 🔲 🔲 🔲 🔲 **Prof** Neil
Plimmer **Course Designer** David Williams **Facilities** ⊗ ♨
🅱 ♥ ♀ ♀ 🛆 🏠 ♦ 𝄢 **Leisure** snooker table.
Conf fac available Corporate Hospitality Days available
Location 1m E of Ditchling

Hotel ★★★ 75% Shelleys Hotel, High St, LEWES
☎ 01273 472361 19 en suite

EASTBOURNE   Map 05 TV69

Eastbourne Downs East Dean Rd BN20 8ES
☎ 01323 720827 📠 01323 412506
**This downland course has spectacular views over the
South Downs and Channel. Situated in an Area of
Outstanding Natural Beauty 1m behind Beachy
Head.**
*18 holes, 6601yds, Par 72, SSS 72, Course record 69.
Club membership 650.*
Visitors a handicap certificate is required for weekends;
not before 9.15am weekdays & before 11am weekends
except by arrangement. **Societies** contact secretary in
advance for details. **Green Fees** £23 per day, £18 per
round (£30/£25 weekends & bank holidays). **Cards** 🔲 🔲
Prof T Marshall **Course Designer** JH Taylor **Facilities** ⊗
♨ 🅱 ♥ ♀ ♀ 🛆 🏠 ♦ 𝄢 **Conf** Corporate Hospitality Days
available **Location** 0.5m W of town centre on A259

Hotel ★★★ 74% Lansdowne Hotel, King Edward's Pde,
EASTBOURNE ☎ 01323 725174 101 en suite

Royal Eastbourne Paradise Dr BN20 8BP
☎ 01323 729738 📠 01323 744048
e-mail: sec@regc.co.uk
**A famous club which celebrated its centenary in 1987.
The course plays longer than it measures. Testing holes
are the 8th, a par 3 played to a high green and the 16th,
a par 5 righthand dog-leg.**
*Devonshire Course: 18 holes, 6077yds, Par 70, SSS 69,
Course record 62.
Hartington Course: 9 holes, 2147yds, Par 64, SSS 61.
Club membership 800.*
Visitors contact in advance, not weekends except by
arrangement. Handicap certificate required for Devonshire
course. **Societies** apply in advance. **Green Fees**

Continued

Devonshire: £46 per day, £29 per round (£58/£35
weekends & bank holidays); Hartington: £17 per day.
Cards 🔲 🔲 🔲 🔲 🔲 🔲 **Prof** Alan Harrison **Course
Designer** Arthur Mayhewe **Facilities** ⊗ ♨ by arrangement
🅱 ♥ ♀ 🛆 🏠 ⸗ 🍴 ♦ 🚵 𝄢 **Leisure** snooker table.
Conf Corporate Hospitality Days available
Location 0.5m W of town centre

Hotel ★★★ 74% Lansdowne Hotel, King Edward's Pde,
EASTBOURNE ☎ 01323 725174 101 en suite

Willingdon Southdown Rd, Willingdon BN20 9AA
☎ 01323 410981 📠 01323 411510
e-mail: secretary@willingdongolfclub.co.uk
**Unique, hilly downland course set in an oyster-shaped
amphitheatre.**
*18 holes, 6118yds, Par 69, SSS 69.
Club membership 610.*
Visitors no restrictions. **Societies** apply in advance. **Green
Fees** £25 per day/£20 per round. **Prof** Troy Moore **Course
Designer** J Taylor, Dr MacKenzie **Facilities** ⊗ ♨ 🅱 ♥ ♀
🛆 🏠 ⸗ ♦ 🚵 𝄢 **Location** 0.5m N of town centre off A22

Hotel ★★★ 73% Hydro Hotel, Mount Rd,
EASTBOURNE ☎ 01323 720643 84 rms (83 en suite)

FOREST ROW   Map 05 TQ43

Royal Ashdown Forest Chapel Ln RH18 5LR
☎ 01342 822018 📠 01342 825211
e-mail: office@royalashdown.co.uk
**Old Course is on undulating heathland with no
bunkers. Long carries off the tees and magnificent
views over the Forest. Not a course for the high
handicapper. West Course on natural heathland with
no bunkers. Less demanding than Old Course although
accuracy is at a premium.**
*Old Course: 18 holes, 6477yds, Par 72, SSS 71, Course
record 67.
West Course: 18 holes, 5606yds, Par 68, SSS 67.
Club membership 450.*
Visitors Old Course; some restrictions at weekends & Tue.
Must have a handicap certificate. No restrictions on West
Course. **Societies** contact in advance. **Green Fees** Old
Course: £50 per round (£70 weekends). West Course: £25
per round (£29 weekends). **Cards** 🔲 🔲 🔲 🔲 🔲
Prof Martyn Landsborough **Facilities** ⊗ ♨ 🅱 ♥ ♀ 🛆 🏠
⸗ ♦ 🚵 𝄢 **Location** on B2110 in Forest Row

Hotel ★★★★ Ashdown Park Hotel and Country Club,
Wych Cross, FOREST ROW
☎ 01342 824988 106 en suite

13 Courses to choose from!

Any 2 days - 14th January - 31st December 2005

Your break includes 2 days' free golf (up to 36 holes each day on the same course), accommodation, full English breakfast, light lunch at the golf club, with a 4 course Dinner and coffee at the hotel.

All our 101 rooms are en suite with every modern facility inc. Satellite TV. Sky Sports TV in public room.

The cost of your golf break from 14th Jan.–28th Feb. £160.00: 1st–31st Mar £170.00: 1st Apr.-31st May £179.00: 1st Jun–30th Sept. £184.00: 1st Oct.–31st Dec. £172.00.

You may, subject to availability, play at a selection of 13 golf clubs (all 18-hole) in this lovely area.

Please write or telephone for our Golfing Break folder.

Lansdowne Hotel AA ★★★

King Edward's Parade · Eastbourne BN21 4EE
Tel: (01323) 725174 Fax: (01323) 739721

AILSHAM Map 05 TQ50

Vellshurst Golf & Country Club North St, ellingly BN27 4EE
01435 813456 (pro shop) 01435 812444
mail: info@wellshurst.com
here are outstanding views of the South Downs and e Weald from this well-manicured, undulating 18-le course. There are varied features and some water azards. A practice sand bunker, putting green and iving range are available to improve your golf. The ubhouse and leisure facilities are open to visitors.
holes, 5992yds, Par 70, SSS 68, Course record 64.
lub membership 450.
isitors no restrictions but advisable to book. **Societies** one in advance to book tee times. **Green Fees** £18 per holes (weekends £22). **Cards** **Prof** ark Jarvis **Course Designer** The Golf Corporation **acilities** **eisure** sauna, solarium, gymnasium, spa bath. **onf** fac available Corporate Hospitality Days available **ocation** 2.5m N on A267

otel ★★ 71% The Olde Forge Hotel & Restaurant, agham Down, HAILSHAM 01323 842893 7 en suite

ASTINGS & ST LEONARDS Map 05 TQ80

EN66 Battle Rd TN37 7BP
01424 854243 01424 854244
holes, 6248yds, Par 71, SSS 70, Course record 70.
ocation 3m N of Hastings on A2100
one for further details

Continued

Hotel ★★★ 70% Beauport Park Hotel, Battle Rd, HASTINGS 01424 851222 25 en suite

HEATHFIELD Map 05 TQ52

Horam Park Chiddingly Rd, Horam TN21 0JJ
01435 813477 01435 813677
e-mail: angie@horamgolf.freeserve.co.uk
A pretty, woodland course with lakes and quality fast-running greens.
9 holes, 6128yds, Par 70, SSS 70, Course record 64.
Club membership 350.
Visitors contact for tee times Can book up to two months in advance. **Societies** booking required. **Green Fees** not confirmed. **Cards** **Prof** Giles Velvick **Course Designer** Glen Johnson **Facilities** **Leisure** pitch & putt, video swingbay on range. **Location** off A267 Hailsham to Heathfield

Hotel ★★★ 66% Boship Farm Hotel, Lower Dicker, HAILSHAM 01323 844826 47 annexe en suite

HOLTYE Map 05 TQ43

Holtye TN8 7ED
01342 850635 & 850576 01342 850576
e-mail: secretary@holtye.com
Undulating forest and heathland course with tree-lined fairways providing testing golf. Different tees on the back nine.
9 holes, 5325yds, Par 66, SSS 66, Course record 62.
Club membership 360.
Visitors not am Wed-Thu & weekends. **Societies** Tue & Fri by arrangement. **Green Fees** terms on application. **Cards** **Prof** Kevin Hinton **Facilities** **Location** 4m E of East Grinstead on A264

Hotel Premier Travel Inn East Grinstead, London Rd, Felbridge, EAST GRINSTEAD 08701 977088 41 en suite

LEWES Map 05 TQ41

Lewes Chapel Hill BN7 2BB
01273 483474 01273 483474
e-mail: secretary@lewesgolfclub.fsnet.co.uk
Downland course with undulating fairways. Fine views. Proper greens all-year-round.
18 holes, 6190yds, Par 71, SSS 70, Course record 64.
Club membership 615.
Visitors not weekends before 2pm in summer, before 11am in winter **Societies** contact in advance. **Green Fees** £30 per round. **Prof** Paul Dobson **Course Designer** Jack Rowe **Facilities**
Location E of town centre

Hotel ★★★ 71% Deans Place, Seaford Rd, ALFRISTON 01323 870248 36 en suite

NEWHAVEN Map 05 TQ40

Peacehaven Brighton Rd BN9 9UH
01273 512571 01273 512571
e-mail: golf@peacehavengc.freeserve.co.uk
Downland course, sometimes windy. Testing holes: 1st (par 3), 4th (par 4), 9th (par 3). Attractive views over the South Downs, the River Ouse and Newhaven Harbour.
9 holes, 5488yds, Par 70, SSS 67, Course record 65.

Continued

Club membership 270.
Visitors not before 11am weekends. **Societies** phone in advance. **Green Fees** £15 per 18 holes, £10 per 9 holes (£20/£14 weekends). **Prof** Alan Tyson **Course Designer** James Braid **Facilities** ⓑ ▣ ♀ ♨ 🏠 ♂
Location 0.75m W on A259

Hotel ★★★ 69% The Star Inn, ALFRISTON
☎ 01323 870495 37 en suite

RYE
Map 05 TQ92

Rye New Lydd Rd, Camber TN31 7QS
☎ 01797 225241 🖹 01797 225460
e-mail: ryelinks@btconnect.com
Unique links course with superb undulating greens set among ridges of sand dunes alongside Rye Harbour. Fine views over Romney Marsh and towards Fairlight and Dungeness.
Old Course: 18 holes, 6317yds, Par 68, SSS 71, Course record 64.
Jubilee Course: 9 holes, 3109yds, Par 71, SSS 70.
Club membership 1100.
Visitors must be introduced by a member. **Green Fees** terms on application. **Prof** Michael Lee **Course Designer** HS Colt **Facilities** ⊗ ▣ ♀ ♨ 🏠 ♂ ♂
Location 2.75m SE off A259

Hotel ★★★ 61% The George, High St, RYE
☎ 01797 222114 22 en suite

SEAFORD
Map 05 TV49

Seaford Firle Rd, East Blatchington BN25 2JD
☎ 01323 892442 🖹 01323 894113
e-mail: secretary@seafordgolfclub.co.uk
The great JH Taylor did not perhaps design as many courses as his friend and rival, James Braid, but Seaford's original design was Taylor's. It is a splendid downland course with magnificent views and some fine holes.
18 holes, 6551yds, Par 69, SSS 71.
Club membership 600.
Visitors contact in advance. **Societies** contact in advance.
Green Fees terms on application. **Cards** ▦ ▦ ▦ ▦ 🔘
Prof David Mills, Clay Morris **Course Designer** JH Taylor **Facilities** ⊗ ▥ ⓑ ▣ ♀ ♨ 🏠 ☾ ♂ ♂ ♂
Conf Corporate Hospitality Days available
Location turn inland off A259 at war memorial

Hotel ★★★ 69% The Star Inn, ALFRISTON
☎ 01323 870495 37 en suite

Seaford Head Southdown Rd BN25 4JS
☎ 01323 890139 & 894843
18 holes, 5848yds, Par 71, SSS 68, Course record 63.
Phone for further details

Hotel ★★★ 71% Deans Place, Seaford Rd, ALFRISTON
☎ 01323 870248 36 en suite

SEDLESCOMBE
Map 05 TQ71

Sedlescombe Kent St TN33 0SD
☎ 01424 871700 🖹 01424 871712
e-mail: golf@golfschool.co.uk
18 holes, 6269yds, Par 72, SSS 70.
Location 4m N of Hastings on A21
Phone for further details

Continued

Hotel ★★★ 70% Brickwall Hotel, The Green, Sedlescombe, BATTLE ☎ 01424 870253 25 en suite

TICEHURST
Map 05 TQ63

Dale Hill Hotel & Golf Club TN5 7DQ
☎ 01580 200112 🖹 01580 201249
e-mail: info@dalehill.co.uk
Dale Hill is set in over 350 acres, high on the Weald in an Area of Outstanding Natural Beauty. Offering two 18-hole courses, one of which has been designed by Ian Woosnam to USGA specifications.

Dale Hill: 18 holes, 6106yds, Par 70, SSS 69.
Ian Woosnam: 18 holes, 6512yds, Par 71, SSS 71, Course record 64.
Club membership 850.
Visitors booking only seven days in advance **Societies** contact in advance. **Green Fees** Dale Hill:£30 (£40 weekends). Ian Woosnam £55 (£65 weekends). **Cards** ▦ ▦ ▦ ▦ 🔘 **Prof** Mark Wood **Course Designer** Ian Woosnam **Facilities** ⊗ ▥ ⓑ ▣ ♀ ♨ 🏠 ☾ ♂ ♂ ♂ ♂ **Leisure** heated indoor swimming pool, sauna, gymnasium. **Conf** fac available Corporate Hospitality Days available **Location** A21 onto B2087, 1m on left

Hotel ★★★★ 75% Dale Hill Hotel & Golf Club, TICEHURST ☎ 01580 200112 35 en suite

UCKFIELD
See page 249

UCKFIELD
Map 05 TQ42

Piltdown Piltdown TN22 3XB
☎ 01825 722033 🖹 01825 724192
e-mail: piltdowngolf@lineone.net
A relatively short, but difficult heather and gorse course built on Sussex clay. No bunkers, easy walking, fine views.
18 holes, 6076yds, Par 68, SSS 69, Course record 64.
Club membership 400.
Visitors phone pro shop in advance 01825 722389 & have a handicap certificate. Restricted Tue, Thu & weekends. **Societies** contact in writing. **Green Fees** £42 per day, £32 per round, £25 after 1.30pm, £16 after 4pm. **Prof** Jason Partridge **Facilities** ⊗ ▥ ⓑ ▣ ♀ ♨ 🏠 ☾ ♂ ♂ ♂
Location 2m W of Uckfield off A272, club signed

Hotel ★★★ Horsted Place, Little Horsted, UCKFIELD
☎ 01825 750581 17 en suite 3 annexe en suite

Booking a tee time is always advisable.

East Sussex National

Sussex, East

Uckfield

Map 05 TQ42

E ast Sussex National offers two huge courses ideal for big-hitting professionals. The European Open has been staged here and it is home to the European Headquarters of the David Leadbetter Golf Academy, with indoor and outdoor video analysis. Bob Cupp designed the courses using 'bent' grass from tee to green, resulting in an American-style course to test everyone. The greens on both the East and West courses are immaculately maintained. The West Course, with stadium design and chosen for major events, is reserved for members and their guests; visitors are welcome on the East Course, also with stadium design, and which was the venue for the 1993 and 1994 European Open. The entrance seems daunting for first-time visitors, unprepared for the vast car park, huge red-brick clubhouse, and the suspended corridor from the reception through to the well-stocked professional shop.

Little Horsted TN22 5ES
☎ 01825 880088 Fax 01825 880066
e-mail: golf@eastsussexnational.co.uk

East Course: 18 holes, 7138yds, Par 72, SSS 74, Course record 63.
West Course: 18 holes, 7154yds, Par 72, SSS 74.
Club membership 650.
Visitors phone Advance Reservations 01825 880231.
Societies phone Advance Reservations 01825 880228.
Green Fees £45 per 18 holes (£50 weekends). **Cards** ⬌ 💳 💳 🖥 📠 🏧 🅿 **Prof** Sarah Maclennan, Mike Clark
Course Designer Bob Cupp **Facilities** ⊗ ⅲ ㎯ ♨ ☕ ♀ ⚲ 🏠 🏌 ⛳ 🛥 ⚓ ⚙ 🎱 **Leisure** hard tennis courts, sauna, golf academy. **Conf** fac available Corporate Hospitality Days available
Location 2m S of Uckfield on A22

....

Hotels

★★★★ 76% Buxted Park Country House Hotel, Buxted, **UCKFIELD**

☎ 01825 733333 44 en suite

★★★ Horsted Place, Little Horsted, **UCKFIELD**

☎ 01825 750581 Fax 01825 750459 17 en suite
3 annexe en suite

★★★ Newick Park Hotel & Country Estate, **NEWICK**

☎ 01825 723633 Fax 01825 723969 13 en suite
3 annexe en suite

SUSSEX, WEST

ANGMERING   Map 04 TQ00

Ham Manor BN16 4JE
☎ 01903 783288 📠 01903 850886
e-mail: secretary.ham.manor@tinyonline.co.uk
**Two miles from the sea, this parkland course has fine
springy turf and provides an interesting test in two
loops of nine holes each.**
*18 holes, 6267yds, Par 70, SSS 70, Course record 64.
Club membership 780.*
Visitors must have a handicap certificate. Phone pro shop
in advance 01903 783732. **Societies** phone for details
Green Fees terms on application. **Prof** Simon Buckley
Course Designer Harry Colt **Facilities** ⊗ by arrangement
⫘ by arrangement ⬛ ♟ ♀ ⌕ 🖾 ✆ **Location** off A259

Guesthouse ♦♦♦♦ Kenmore Guest House, Claigmar Rd,
RUSTINGTON ☎ 01903 784634 7 rms (6 en suite)

ARUNDEL   Map 04 TQ00

Avisford Park Yapton Ln, Walberton BN18 0LS
☎ 01243 554611 📠 01243 555580
18 holes, 5703yds, Par 68, SSS 66.
Location off A27 towards Yapton
Phone for further details

Hotel ★★★ 67% Norfolk Arms Hotel, High St,
ARUNDEL ☎ 01903 882101 21 en suite 13 annexe
en suite

BOGNOR REGIS   Map 04 SZ99

Bognor Regis Downview Rd, Felpham PO22 8JD
☎ 01243 821929 (secretary) 📠 01243 860719
e-mail: sec@bognorgolfclub.co.uk
**This flattish, well tree-lined, parkland course has more
variety than is to be found on some other south-coast
courses. The course is open to the prevailing wind and
the River Rife and many water ditches need
negotiation.**
*18 holes, 6238yds, Par 70, SSS 70, Course record 64.
Club membership 700.*
Visitors handicap certificate required. Must contact in
advance (pro shop 01243 865209). **Societies** phone
initially. **Green Fees** not confirmed. **Prof** Stephen Bassil
Course Designer James Braid **Facilities** ⊗ ⫘ ⬛ ♟ ♀ ⌕
🖾 ↧ ⚒ ✆ **Conf** fac available **Location** 0.5m N at
Felpham lights on A259

Hotel ★★ 71% Beachcroft Hotel, Clyde Rd, Felpham
Village, BOGNOR REGIS ☎ 01243 827142 34 en suite

BURGESS HILL   Map 04 TQ31

Burgess Hill Cuckfield Rd RH15 8RE
☎ 01444 258585 📠 01444 47318
e-mail: enquiries@burgesshillgolfcentre.co.uk
**Very challenging nine-hole course. Gently undulating
layout with trees and water.**
9 holes, 1250yds, Par 27.
Visitors no restrictions **Societies** contact in advance.
Green Fees terms on application. **Cards** ▭ ▤ ▦ ▬
▧ ⚏ **Prof** Mark Collins **Course Designer** Donald Steel
Facilities ⊗ ⫘ ⬛ ♟ ♀ ⌕ 🖾 ↱ ✆ ⚑ **Leisure** pitching &

chipping green. **Conf** fac available Corporate Hospitality
Days available **Location** N of town on B2036

Hotel ★★ ♨ 73% Hilton Park Hotel, Tylers Green,
CUCKFIELD ☎ 01444 454555 11 en suite

CHICHESTER   Map 04 SU80

Chichester Hunston PO20 6AX
☎ 01243 533833 📠 01243 539922
e-mail: chigolfclub@mistral.co.uk
**The front nine on this course boasts a 601yd par 5 that
will challenge the best golfer. This is sandwiched
between two formidable par 3s over water. The back
nine is more subtle with two par 5s which can be
reached in two by the most adventurous and the short
but deceptive 15th, framed with 300 Portland stones
and surrounded by sand.**
*Tower Course: 18 holes, 6175yds, Par 72, SSS 69,
Course record 64.*
*Cathedral Course: 18 holes, 6461yds, Par 72, SSS 71,
Course record 65.*
Club membership 600.
Visitors a strict dress code is in operation. Must contact in
advance. Tee reservations up to seven days in advance on
01243 533833. **Societies** contact in advance. **Green Fees**
Tower £16 (£18.50 weekend); Cathedral £22 (£30
weekends). **Cards** ▭ ▦ ▬ ⚏ ▧ ▨ ⚏ **Prof** Richard
Kirby **Course Designer** Philip Saunders **Facilities** ⊗ ⫘ ⬛
⬛ ♀ ⌕ 🖾 ↱ ⚑ ✆ ⚒ **Leisure** minigolf & par 3 course.
Conf fac available Corporate Hospitality Days available
Location 3m S of Chichester on B2145

Hotel ★★★ 63% The Ship Hotel, North St,
CHICHESTER ☎ 01243 778000 36 en suite

COPTHORNE   Map 05 TQ33

Copthorne Borers Arms Rd RH10 3LL
☎ 01342 712033 & 712508 📠 01342 717682
e-mail: info@copthornegolfclub.co.uk
**Despite it having been in existence since 1892, this club
remains one of the lesser known Sussex courses. It is
hard to know why because it is most attractive with
plenty of trees and much variety.**
*18 holes, 6435yds, Par 71, SSS 71, Course record 66.
Club membership 550.*
Visitors advised to contact in advance, not weekends.
Societies contact in advance. **Green Fees** £34 weekdays.
Cards ▭ ▬ ⚏ **Prof** Joe Burrell **Course Designer** James
Braid **Facilities** ⊗ ⬛ ⬛ ♟ ♀ ⌕ 🖾 ✆
Location M23 junct 10, E of village off A264

Hotel ★★★★ 70% Copthorne Hotel London Gatwick,
Copthorne Way, COPTHORNE
☎ 01342 348800 & 348888 📠 01342 348833 227 en suit

Effingham Park The Copthorne Effingham Park,
Hotel, West Park Rd RH10 3EU
☎ 01342 716528 📠 0870 8900 215
Parkland course.
*9 holes, 1822yds, Par 30, SSS 57, Course record 28.
Club membership 230.*
Visitors restricted at weekends before 11am & not after
4pm Tue, Apr-Oct. **Societies** Mon-Fri, & Sat/Sun after
1pm, must write or phone in advance. **Green Fees** not
confirmed. **Cards** ▭ ▦ ▬ ⚏ ▧ ▨ ⚏ **Prof** Mark
Root **Course Designer** Francisco Escario **Facilities** ⊗ ⫘
⬛ ⬛ ♀ ⌕ 🖾 ↱ ⚑ ✆ **Leisure** hard tennis courts,

Continued   *Continu*

ated indoor swimming pool, sauna, solarium, rmnasium. **Conf** fac available Corporate Hospitality ays available **Location** 2m E on B2028

Effingham Park Golf Club

··

otel ★★★★ 66% Copthorne Hotel and Resort ffingham Park, West Park Rd, COPTHORNE ☎ 01342 714994 122 en suite

RAWLEY   Map 04 TQ23

ottesmore Buchan Hill, Pease Pottage RH11 9AT
☎ 01293 528256 (reception) & 535399 (shop)
📠 01293 522819
mail: cottesmore@americangolf.uk.com
ounded in 1974, the Griffin course is a fine test of lfing skill with fairways lined by silver birch, pine, k and rhododendrons. Four holes have lakes as zards.

*riffin: 18 holes, 6248yds, Par 71, SSS 70,
urse record 67.
oenix: 18 holes, 5600yds, Par 69, SSS 67.*
isitors Griffin course not am at weekends. Dress code plies. Advisable to contact in advance. **Societies** phone advance. **Green Fees** not confirmed. **Cards** ▦ ▦ ▦ ▦ 🟦 **Prof** Calum J Callan **Course Designer** Michael J gerson **Facilities** ⊗ ⅏ ⮂ ☕ ♀ ⚘ 🏠 ⛴ 🏐 🚡 ⚌ isure hard tennis courts, heated indoor swimming pool, una, solarium, gymnasium. **Conf** fac available Corporate ospitality Days available cation M23 junct 11, 2m W

··

otel ★★★ Alexander House Hotel, East St, TURNERS LL ☎ 01342 714914 18 en suite

ield Golf & Country Club Rusper Rd, Ifield
H11 0LN
☎ 01293 520222 📠 01293 612973
rkland course.
holes, 6330yds, Par 70, SSS 70, Course record 64.
ub membership 750.*

Visitors contact professional in advance. Must be guest of member at weekends. **Societies** apply in advance. **Green Fees** £45 per day; £32 per round weekdays. **Cards** ▦ ▦ ▦ ▦ 🟦 **Prof** Jonathan Earl **Course Designer** Hawtree & Taylor **Facilities** ⊗ ⅏ ⮂ ☕ ♀ ⚘ 🏠 🏐 🚡 ⚌ **Location** 1m W side of town centre off A23

··

Hotel ★★★ Alexander House Hotel, East St, TURNERS HILL ☎ 01342 714914 18 en suite

Tilgate Forest Golf Centre Titmus Dr RH10 5EU
☎ 01293 530103 📠 01293 523478
e-mail: tilgate@glendale-services.co.uk
Designed by former Ryder Cup players Neil Coles and Brian Huggett, the course has been carefully cut through a silver birch and pine forest. It is possibly one of the most beautiful public courses in the country. The 17th is a treacherous par 5 demanding an uphill third shot to a green surrounded by rhododendrons.
*18 holes, 6359yds, Par 71, SSS 70, Course record 69.
Club membership 200.*
Visitors public course, pay & play at all times. **Societies** phone in advance for details. **Green Fees** 18 holes £16 (£22 weekends); 9 holes £5 (£6 weekends). **Cards** ▦ ▦ ▦ ▦ 🟦 **Prof** Sean Trussell **Course Designer** Neil Coles, Brian Huggett **Facilities** ⊗ ⅏ ⮂ ☕ ♀ ⚘ 🏠 ⛴ 🚡 ⚌ ⚘ ⚉ **Leisure** par 3 9-hole course. **Conf** Corporate Hospitality Days available **Location** 2m E of town centre

··

Hotel ★★★ Alexander House Hotel, East St, TURNERS HILL ☎ 01342 714914 18 en suite

EAST GRINSTEAD   Map 05 TQ33

Chartham Park Felcourt Rd, Felcourt RH19 2JT
☎ 01342 870340 & 870008 (pro shop) 📠 01342 870719
e-mail: b.smith@clubhaus.com
Mature parkland course.

*18 holes, 6680yds, Par 72, SSS 72, Course record 64.
Club membership 740.*
Visitors may book up to seven days in advance. Weekdays anytime, weekends after 2pm. **Societies** weekdays only, phone for details. **Green Fees** not confirmed. **Cards** ▦ ▦ ▦ ▦ 🟦 **Prof** Ben Knight **Course Designer** Neil Coles **Facilities** ⊗ ⅏ ⮂ ☕ ♀ ⚘ 🏠 ⚌ **Conf** Corporate Hospitality Days available **Location** 2m N from town centre towards Felcourt, on right

··

Hotel ★★★ ⚘ Gravetye Manor Hotel, EAST GRINSTEAD ☎ 01342 810567 18 en suite

Continued

GOODWOOD   Map 04 SU80

Marriott Goodwood Park Hotel & Country Club PO18 0QB
☎ 01243 520117 📠 01243 520120
A parkland course set within the 12,000-acre Goodwood estate, home to the dukes of Richmond for over 300 years. Fairly generous over the opening holes but gets progressively harder as you approach the turn.

18 holes, 6579yds, Par 72, SSS 71, Course record 68.
Club membership 700.
Visitors book in advance, tee times subject to availability; course dress & etiquette. Societies phone or write. Green Fees not confirmed. Cards ▦ ▦ ▦ 📷 ▦ 📶 🗂 Prof Adrian Wratting Course Designer Donald Steele Facilities ⊗ ⅏ ⅃ 🍺 ⟈ ⅄ ⌂ ⋔ 🏄 ⅃ ⚓ ∮ ⟨ Leisure hard tennis courts, heated indoor swimming pool, sauna, solarium, gymnasium. Location 3m NE of Chichester in Goodwood House

Hotel ★★★★ 73% Marriott Goodwood Park Hotel & Country Club, GOODWOOD ☎ 0870 400 7225 94 en suite

HASSOCKS   Map 04 TQ31

Hassocks London Rd BN6 9NA
☎ 01273 846630 & 846990 📠 01273 846070
e-mail: hgc@hassocksgolfclub.co.uk
Set against the backdrop of the South Downs, Hassocks is an 18-hole par 70 course designed and contoured to blend naturally with the surrounding countryside. A friendly and relaxed course, appealing to golfers of all ages and abilities.
18 holes, 5698yds, Par 70, SSS 68, Course record 66.
Club membership 400.
Visitors phone pro. shop in advance,01273 846990. Societies apply in writing or phone in advance. Green Fees not confirmed. Cards ▦ ▦ 📶 🗂 Prof Charles Ledger Course Designer Paul Wright Facilities ⊗ ⅏ ⅃ ⟈ ⅄ ⌂ ⋔ 🏄 ∮ ⟨ Conf Corporate Hospitality Days available Location on A273 between Burgess Hill & Hassocks

Hotel ★★★ 62% The Hickstead Hotel, Jobs Ln, Bolney, HICKSTEAD ☎ 01444 248023 49 en suite

HAYWARDS HEATH   Map 05 TQ32

Haywards Heath High Beech Ln RH16 1SL
☎ 01444 414457 📠 01444 458319
e-mail: info@haywardsheathgolfclub.co.uk
Pleasant parkland course with several challenging par 4s and 3s.
18 holes, 6216yds, Par 71, SSS 70, Course record 65.

Club membership 770.
Visitors must have a handicap certificate. Must contact in advance. Societies Wed & Thu only by arrangement with the secretary. Green Fees £27 per 18 holes (£37 weekends). Prof Michael Henning Course Designer James Braid Facilities ⊗ ⅏ by arrangement ⅃ 🍺 ⅃ ⅄ ⌂ ⋔ ∮ ⟨ Conf Corporate Hospitality Days available Location 1.25m N of Haywards Heath off B2028

Hotel ★★★ 69% The Birch Hotel, Lewes Rd, HAYWARDS HEATH ☎ 01444 451565 51 en suite

Paxhill Park East Mascalls Ln, Lindfield RH16 2QN
☎ 01444 484467 📠 01444 482709
e-mail: johnbowen@paxhillpark.fsnet.co.uk
A relatively flat parkland course in two loops of nine in an Area of Outstanding Natural Beauty. Water hazard on 5th, 13th and 14th holes.
18 holes, 6117yds, Par 70, SSS 69, Course record 67.
Club membership 320.
Visitors not weekends & some weekdays am. Societies contact in advance. Green Fees terms on application. Cards ▦ ▦ ▦ 📶 🗂 Course Designer P Tallack Facilities ⊗ 🍺 ⅃ ⟈ ⅄ ⌂ ⋔ ∮ ⟨ Leisure snooker. Conf fac available Location 2m NE of Haywards Heath, E of Lindfield off B2011

Hotel ★★★ 69% The Birch Hotel, Lewes Rd, HAYWARDS HEATH ☎ 01444 451565 51 en suite

HORSHAM   Map 04 TQ13

See also Slinfold, Mannings Heath

Horsham Worthing Rd RH13 7AX
☎ 01403 271525 📠 01403 274528
e-mail: admin@horshamgolfandfitness.co.uk
9 holes, 4122yds, Par 33, SSS 30, Course record 55.
Location A24 rdbt onto B2237, by garage
Phone for further details

Hotel ★★★★ 👥 South Lodge Hotel, Brighton Rd, LOWER BEEDING ☎ 01403 891711 45 en suite

HURSTPIERPOINT   Map 04 TQ21

Singing Hills Albourne BN6 9EB
☎ 01273 835353 📠 01273 835444
e-mail: info@singinghills.co.uk
Three distinct nines (Lake, River and Valley) can be combined to make a truly varied game. Gently undulating fairways and spectacular waterholes make Singing Hills a test of accurate shotmaking. The opening two holes of the River nine have long drives, while the second hole on the Lake course is an island green where the tee is also protected by two bunkers. The Valley course demands long, accurate tee shots.
Lake: 9 holes, 3253yds, Par 35, SSS 35.
River: 9 holes, 2861yds, Par 34, SSS 34.
Valley: 9 holes, 3362yds, Par 36, SSS 34.
Club membership 410.
Visitors no restrictions, but strict dress code observed. Must book tee-time in advance. Societies apply in advance. Green Fees £24 (£32 weekends & bank holiday). Cards ▦ ▦ ▦ 📷 ▦ 📶 🗂 Course Designer MRM Sandow Facilities ⊗ ⅏ 🍺 ⅃ ⟈ ⅄ ⌂ ∮ ⟨ Conf fac available Corporate Hospitality Days available Location A23 onto B2117

Hotel ★★★ 62% The Hickstead Hotel, Jobs Ln, Bolney, HICKSTEAD ☎ 01444 248023 49 en suite

Continued

ITTLEHAMPTON   Map 04 TQ00

ittlehampton 170 Rope Walk, Riverside West
N17 5DL
☎ 01903 717170 🖹 01903 726629
-mail: lgc@talk21.com
**delightful seaside links in an equally delightful setting
and the only links course in the area.**
8 holes, 6226yds, Par 70, SSS 70, Course record 64.
lub membership 600.
isitors contact pro shop for availability 01903 717170
xt 225). **Societies** welcome weekdays; weekends some
strictions apply **Green Fees** terms on application.
rof Guy McQuitty **Course Designer** Hawtree
acilities ⊗ ⍟ ⓑ 🏌 ⛳ 👤 🏠 🥤 ⛳ **Conf** fac available
orporate Hospitality Days available
ocation 1m W off A259

otel ⭐ Travelodge Littlehampton, Worthing Rd,
USTINGTON ☎ 08700 850 950   36 en suite

OWER BEEDING   Map 04 TQ22

Iannings Heath Hotel Winterpit Ln RH13 6LY
☎ 01403 891191 🖹 01403 891499
**nine-hole, 18 tee course with three par 4s set in
lorious countryside.**
holes, 1529yds, Par 31.
lub membership 150.
isitors phone for details. **Societies** phone in advance.
reen Fees not confirmed. **Cards** ▦ ▦ 🟥 🟥 🔄 🟦
rof Jim Debenham **Facilities** ⊗ ⍟ ⓑ 🏌 ⛳ 👤 🏠 🥤
eisure fishing. **Conf** fac available   Corporate Hospitality
ays available **Location** off A281 S of Horsham

otel ⭐⭐⭐⭐ 🏌 South Lodge Hotel, Brighton Rd,
OWER BEEDING ☎ 01403 891711   45 en suite

IANNINGS HEATH   Map 04 TQ22

Iannings Heath Fullers, Hammerpond Rd
H13 6PG
☎ 01403 210228 🖹 01403 270974
mail: enquiries@manningsheath.com
**he Waterfall is a downhill, parkland, part heathland,
hampionship course with streams and trees in
bundance. It boasts three spectacular par 3s but all the
oles are memorably unique. The Kingfisher course is a
odern design with a lake which comes into play.**
*aterfall: 18 holes, 6483yds, Par 72, SSS 71,
ourse record 63.*
*ingfisher: 18 holes, 6217yds, Par 70, SSS 70,
ourse record 66.*
lub membership 700.
isitors book in advance. **Societies** contact in advance.
reen Fees terms on application. **Cards** ▦ ▦ ▦ 🟦
▦ 🔄 🟦 **Prof** Clive Tucker **Course Designer** David
illiams **Facilities** ⊗ ⍟ ⓑ 🏌 ⛳ 👤 🏠 🏠 🥤 ⛳ ⛳
eisure fishing, sauna, chipping practice area.
onf fac available Corporate Hospitality Days available
ocation off A281 on N side of village

otel ⭐⭐⭐⭐ 🏌 South Lodge Hotel, Brighton Rd,
OWER BEEDING ☎ 01403 891711   45 en suite

> **Prices may change during the currency of the
> Guide, please check when booking.**

MIDHURST   Map 04 SU82

Cowdray Park Petworth Rd GU29 0BB
☎ 01730 813599 🖹 01730 815900
e-mail: cowdray-golf@lineone.net
**Undulating parkland course with scenic views of
surrounding countryside, including Elizabethan ruins.
The course is situated in a park designed by Capability
Brown in the 18th century.**

*18 holes, 6212yds, Par 70, SSS 70, Course record 65.
Club membership 720.*
Visitors phone in advance. Handicap certificate preferred.
Societies apply by writing, phone, e-mail or fax. **Green
Fees** £40 per 18 holes. **Cards** ▦ ▦ 🟥 🟦 **Prof** Richard
Gough **Course Designer** Jack White **Facilities** ⊗ ⍟ ⓑ 🏌
👤 🏠 🏠 🥤 ⛳ ⛳ **Conf** fac available   Corporate
Hospitality Days available **Location** 1m E of Midhurst on
A272

Hotel ⭐⭐⭐ 72% The Angel Hotel, North St, MIDHURST
☎ 01730 812421   28 en suite

PULBOROUGH   Map 04 TQ01

West Sussex Golf Club Ln, Wiggonholt RH20 2EN
☎ 01798 872563 🖹 01798 872033
e-mail: secretary@westsussexgolf.co.uk
**An outstanding beautiful heathland course occupying
an oasis of sand, heather and pine in the middle of
attractive countryside, which is predominately clay and
marsh. The 6th and 13th holes are particularly notable.**
*18 holes, 6264yds, Par 68, SSS 70, Course record 61.
Club membership 850.*
Visitors contact in advance; not weekends except by
agreement of the secretary; Fri only with a member.
Societies Wed & Thu only, apply in writing. **Green Fees**
£80 per 36 holes, £65 per 18 holes (£85/£70 weekends).
Prof Tim Packham **Course Designer** Campbell,
Hutcheson **Facilities** ⊗ ⓑ 🏌 👤 🏠 🏠 🥤 ⛳ ⛳
Location 1.5m E of Pulborough off A283

Hotel ⭐⭐⭐ 69% Best Western Roundabout Hotel,
Monkmead Ln, WEST CHILTINGTON ☎ 01798 813838
23 en suite

PYECOMBE   Map 04 TQ21

Pyecombe Clayton Hill BN45 7FF
☎ 01273 845372 🖹 01273 843338
e-mail: pyecombegc@btopenworld.com
**Typical downland course on the inland side of the
South Downs with panoramic views of the Weald.**
*18 holes, 6278yds, Par 71, SSS 70, Course record 65.
Club membership 525.*

Continued

Visitors contact in advance & may only play after 9.15am weekdays & after 2.15pm weekends **Societies** phone secretary in advance. **Green Fees** £25 per round/£30 per day (weekends £30/£35). **Prof** CR White **Course Designer** James Braid **Facilities** ⊗ ⅲ by arrangement ⓑ ➆ ♀ ⌂ 🏠 ⛴ ✓ **Location** E of village on A273

Hotel ★★★ 64% The Courtlands, 15-27 The Drive, HOVE ☎ 01273 731055 60 en suite 7 annexe en suite

SELSEY   Map 04 SZ89

Selsey Golf Links Ln PO20 9DR
☎ 01243 602203 🖷 01243 607101
e-mail: selsey.cc@talk21.com
Fairly difficult seaside course, exposed to wind and has natural ditches.
9 holes, 5834yds, Par 68, SSS 68, Course record 64.
Club membership 360.
Visitors contact in advance. **Societies** contact in advance in writing **Green Fees** not confirmed. **Prof** Peter Grindley **Course Designer** JH Taylor **Facilities** ⊗ ⅲ ⓑ ➆ ♀ ⌂ 🏠 ✓ Leisure hard tennis courts.
Location 1m N off B2145

Hotel ★★★ 63% The Ship Hotel, North St, CHICHESTER ☎ 01243 778000 36 en suite

SLINFOLD   Map 04 TQ13

Slinfold Park Golf & Country Club Stane St RH13 7RE
☎ 01403 791555 🖷 01403 791465
e-mail: info@slinfoldpark.co.uk
Championship Course: 18 holes, 6407yds, Par 72, SSS 71, Course record 64.
Academy Course: 9 holes, 1315yds, Par 28.
Course Designer John Fortune **Location** 4m W on A29
Phone for further details

Hotel ★★★ 69% Hurtwood Inn Hotel, Walking Bottom, PEASLAKE ☎ 01306 730851 15 en suite 6 annexe en suite

WEST CHILTINGTON   Map 04 TQ01

West Chiltington Broadford Bridge Rd RH20 2YA
☎ 01798 812115 (bookings) & 813574 🖷 01798 812631
e-mail: cottongolf@westchiltington.fsbusiness.co.uk
Windmill: 18 holes, 5866yds, Par 70, SSS 69, Course record 66
9 holes, 1360yds, Par 28.
Course Designer Brian Barnes **Location** N of village
Phone for further details

Hotel ★★★ 69% Best Western Roundabout Hotel, Monkmead Ln, WEST CHILTINGTON ☎ 01798 813838 23 en suite

WORTHING   Map 04 TQ10

Hill Barn Hill Barn Ln BN14 9QF
☎ 01903 237301 🖷 01903 217613
e-mail: info@hillbarngolf.com
Downland course with views of both Isle of Wight and Brighton.
18 holes, 6224yds, Par 70, SSS 70.
Club membership 500.
Visitors no restrictions, but advisable to book tee times, seven days in advance. **Societies** phone in advance. **Green Fees** not confirmed. **Cards** 🖃 🖃 🖃 🖃 🖾

Prof F Morley **Course Designer** Fred Hawtree
Facilities ⊗ ⅲ ⓑ ➆ ♀ ⌂ 🏠 ⛴ 🛬 ✓ Leisure croquet.
Conf fac available Corporate Hospitality Days available
Location 1m N at junct A24 & A27

Hotel ★★★ 63% Findon Manor Hotel, High St, Findon, WORTHING ☎ 01903 872733 11 en suite

Worthing Links Rd BN14 9QZ
☎ 01903 260801 🖷 01903 694664
e-mail: worthinggolf@easynet.co.uk
The Upper Course, short and tricky with entrancing views, will provide good entertainment. Lower Course is considered to be one of the best downland courses in the country.
Lower Course: 18 holes, 6505yds, Par 71, SSS 71, Course record 62.
Upper Course: 18 holes, 5211yds, Par 66, SSS 65.
Club membership 1200.
Visitors advisable to contact in advance, not weekends during GMT. **Societies** contact in advance. **Green Fees** terms on application. **Prof** Stephen Rolley **Course Designer** HS Colt **Facilities** ⊗ ⅲ ⓑ ➆ ♀ ⌂ 🏠 ⛴ 🛬 ✓ ⌘ **Location** N of town centre off A27

Hotel ★★★ 72% Ardington Hotel, Steyne Gardens, WORTHING ☎ 01903 230451 45 en suite

TYNE & WEAR

BACKWORTH   Map 12 NZ37

Backworth The Hall NE27 0AH
☎ 0191 268 1048
9 holes, 5930yds, Par 71, SSS 69, Course record 63.
Location W of town on B1322
Phone for further details

Hotel ⛉ Premier Travel Inn Newcastle (Holystone), Holystone Roundabout, NEWCASTLE ☎ 08701 977189 40 en suite

BIRTLEY   Map 12 NZ25

Birtley Birtley Ln DH3 2LR
☎ 0191 410 2207
A nine-hole parkland course. Good test of golf with challenging par 3 and par 4 holes.
9 holes, 5662yds, Par 67, SSS 67, Course record 63.
Club membership 350.
Visitors must play with member at weekends & bank holidays. **Societies** apply in writing, must contact 1 month in advance in summer. **Green Fees** £14 per 18 holes. **Facilities** ⓑ by arrangement ➆ ♀ restricted ⌂

Hotel ⛉ Travelodge (North), Motorway Service Area, Portobello, BIRTLEY ☎ 08700 850 950 31 en suite

BOLDON   Map 12 NZ36

Boldon Dipe Ln, East Boldon NE36 0PQ
☎ 0191 536 5360 & 0191 536 4182 🖷 0191 537 2270
e-mail: info@boldongolfclub.co.uk
Parkland links course, easy walking, distant sea views.
18 holes, 6362yds, Par 72, SSS 70, Course record 67.
Club membership 700.
Visitors not before 2pm at weekends & bank holidays. **Societies** contact in advance. **Green Fees** £20 per day (£2...

Continued

Continue

weekends & bank holidays). **Course Designer** Harry Varden **Facilities** ⊗ ⒨ ⅃ ⏛ ⚑ ⛳ ᴵ ⚐ ⚘ ℐ ℓ **Leisure** snooker. **Location** S of village off A184

Hotel ★★★ 68% Quality Hotel Sunderland, Witney Way, Boldon, SUNDERLAND ☎ 0191 519 1999 82 en suite

CHOPWELL
Map 12 NZ15

Garesfield NE17 7AP
☎ 01207 561309 📠 01207 561309
e-mail: office@garesfieldgc.fsnet.co.uk
Undulating parkland course with good views and picturesque woodland surroundings.
18 holes, 6458yds, Par 72, SSS 70, Course record 68.
Club membership 697.
Visitors weekends after 4.30pm only, unless with member. **Must** contact in advance. **Societies** contact secretary in advance. May play Sun only & max of 24 players. **Green Fees** terms on application. **Prof** David Race **Course Designer** Harry Fernie **Facilities** ⊗ ⒨ ⅃ ⏛ ⚑ ⛳ ⚐ ℐ **Conf** Corporate Hospitality Days available **Location** off B6315 in High Spen at Bute Arms for Chopwell

Hotel ★★★ 64% Quality Hotel Newcastle upon Tyne, Newgate St, NEWCASTLE UPON TYNE ☎ 0191 232 5025 93 en suite

FELLING
Map 12 NZ26

Heworth Gingling Gate, Heworth NE10 8XY
☎ 0191 469 4424 📠 0191 469 9898
Fairly flat, parkland course.
18 holes, 6422yds, Par 71, SSS 71.
Club membership 800.
Visitors not Sat & before 10am Sun, Apr-Sep. **Societies** apply in writing. **Green Fees** £20 per day. **Prof** Adrian Marshall **Facilities** ⊗ ⒨ ⅃ ⏛ ⚑ ⛳ ℐ **Conf** fac available Corporate Hospitality Days available **Location** on A195 0.5m NW of A1(M) junct

Hotel ⇑ Travelodge Newcastle Whitemare Pool, Wardley, Whitemare Pool, WARDLEY ☎ 08700 850 950 1 en suite

GATESHEAD
Map 12 NZ26

Ravensworth Angel View, Longbank, Wrekenton NE9 7NE
☎ 0191 487 6014 📠 0191 487 6014
e-mail: ravensworth.golfclub@virgin.net
Moorland and parkland course 600ft above sea level with fine views. Testing 5th and 7th holes (par 3s).
18 holes, 5966yds, Par 69, SSS 69.
Club membership 700.
Visitors apply in advance. no weekends Apr-Sep. **Societies** apply in writing to secretary. **Green Fees** not confirmed. **Prof** Shaun Cowell **Course Designer** JW Fraser **Facilities** ⊗ ⒨ ⅃ ⏛ ⚑ ⛳ ℐ **Conf** Corporate Hospitality Days available **Location** A1(M) onto A167 (Angel of the North), onto A1295 for 300yds

Hotel ★★★ 71% Eslington Villa Hotel, 8 Station Rd, Low Fell, GATESHEAD ☎ 0191 487 6017 & 420 0666 0191 420 0667 17 en suite

In the hotel entries, the percentage figure refers to the AA's most recent Quality Assessment Score.

GOSFORTH
Map 12 NZ26

Gosforth Broadway East NE3 5ER
☎ 0191 285 3495 & 285 6710(catering) 📠 0191 284 6274
e-mail: gosforth.golf@virgin.net
Parkland course with natural water hazards, easy walking.
18 holes, 6024yds, Par 69, SSS 68, Course record 62.
Club membership 500.
Visitors contact in advance. Restricted play on competition days. **Societies** phone in advance. **Green Fees** not confirmed. **Prof** G Garland **Facilities** ⊗ ⒨ ⅃ ⏛ ⚑ ⛳ ℐ **Conf** Corporate Hospitality Days available **Location** N of town centre off A6125

Hotel ★★★★ 74% Newcastle Marriott Hotel Gosforth Park, High Gosforth Park, Gosforth, NEWCASTLE UPON TYNE ☎ 0191 236 4111 178 en suite

Parklands Gosforth Park Golfing Complex, High Gosforth Park NE3 5HQ
☎ 0191 236 4480 📠 0191 236 3322
Parkland with challenging shots around and sometimes over attractive water hazards. The first nine holes are easier but the second nine test even the most experienced golfer.
18 holes, 6013yds, Par 71, SSS 69, Course record 66.
Club membership 650.
Visitors a daily start sheet operates with bookings taken from 4.30pm the previous day during weekdays, & from 8am Fri & Sat for weekends. **Societies** by arrangement with club secretary. **Green Fees** not confirmed. **Prof** Brian Rumney **Facilities** ⊗ ⒨ ⅃ ⏛ ⚑ ⛳ ℐ ℓ **Conf** Corporate Hospitality Days available **Location** 3m N at end A1 western bypass

Hotel ★★★★ 74% Newcastle Marriott Hotel Gosforth Park, High Gosforth Park, Gosforth, NEWCASTLE UPON TYNE ☎ 0191 236 4111 178 en suite

HOUGHTON-LE-SPRING
Map 12 NZ34

Elemore Elemore Ln, Hetton-le-Hole DH5 0QB
☎ 0191 517 3061 📠 0191 517 3054
Elmore course tests a player's ability in all aspects of the game, with drives over water as well as wedges. The greens are firm all year round and there are well positioned bunkers.
18 holes, 5947yds, Par 69, Course record 68.
Club membership 100.
Visitors no restrictions. Phone to avoid society days. **Societies** apply in writing, phone enquiries welcome. **Green Fees** £10.50 per 18 holes (£14 weekends & bank holidays). **Course Designer** J Gaunt **Facilities** ⊗ ⅃ ⏛ ⚑ ⛳ ⚐ ℐ **Location** 4m S of Houghton le Spring on A182

Hotel ★★ 67% Chilton Country Pub & Hotel, Black Boy Rd, Chilton Moor, Fencehouses, HOUGHTON-LE-SPRING ☎ 0191 385 2694 25 en suite

Houghton-le-Spring Copt Hill DH5 8LU
☎ 0191 584 1198 & 584 0048
18 holes, 6443yds, Par 72, SSS 71, Course record 64.
Location 0.5m E on B1404
Phone for further details

Hotel ★★ 67% Chilton Country Pub & Hotel, Black Boy Rd, Chilton Moor, Fencehouses, HOUGHTON-LE-SPRING ☎ 0191 385 2694 25 en suite

NEWCASTLE UPON TYNE   Map 12 NZ26

City of Newcastle Three Mile Bridge NE3 2DR
☎ 0191 285 1775 🖹 0191 2840700
e-mail: info@cityofnewcastlegolfclub.com
A well-manicured parkland course in the Newcastle suburbs.
18 holes, 6528yds, Par 72, SSS 71, Course record 64.
Club membership 600.
Visitors no restrictions but advisable to phone first.
Societies phone in advance **Green Fees** £34 per day; £28
per round (£35 weekends). **Prof** Steve McKenna
Course Designer Harry Vardon **Facilities** ⊗ ⊤⊪ ⅃ ♥ ♀
♠ 🏠 ⊶ ✔ Conf Corporate Hospitality Days available
Location 3m N on B1318

Hotel ★★★ 68% The Caledonian Hotel, Newcastle, 64
Osborne Rd, Jesmond, NEWCASTLE UPON TYNE
☎ 0191 281 7881 89 en suite

Newcastle United Ponteland Rd, Cowgate NE5 3JW
☎ 0191 286 9998
e-mail: info@www.nugc.co.uk
Moorland course with natural hazards.
18 holes, 6617yds, Par 72, SSS 72, Course record 66.
Club membership 650.
Visitors must play with member at weekends. **Societies**
contact in writing or phone in advance. **Green Fees** terms
on application. **Cards** 💳 **Course Designer** Various
Facilities ⊗ ⊤⊪ ⅃ ♥ ♀ ♠ 🏠 ⊶ ✔ **Leisure** Snooker
table. **Location** 1.25m NW of city centre off A6127

Hotel ★★★ 68% The Caledonian Hotel, Newcastle, 64
Osborne Rd, Jesmond, NEWCASTLE UPON TYNE
☎ 0191 281 7881 89 en suite

Northumberland High Gosforth Park NE3 5HT
☎ 0191 236 2498 🖹 0191 236 2036
e-mail: gun2446@aol.com
**Predominantly a level heathland style course, the firm,
fast greens are a particular feature.**
18 holes, 6683yds, Par 72, SSS 72, Course record 65.
Club membership 580.
Visitors Limited play weekends. Must contact in advance.
Societies apply in writing or phone. **Green Fees** £50 per
day; £40 per round (£50 per round weekends).
Course Designer Colt, Braid **Facilities** ⊗ ⊤⊪ ⅃ ♥ ♀
♠ ✔ Conf Corporate Hospitality Days available
Location 4m N of city centre off A1

Hotel ★★★★ 74% Newcastle Marriott Hotel Gosforth
Park, High Gosforth Park, Gosforth, NEWCASTLE UPON
TYNE ☎ 0191 236 4111 178 en suite

Westerhope Whorlton Grance, Westerhope NE5 1PP
☎ 0191 286 7636 🖹 0191 214 6287
e-mail: wgc@btconnect.com
**Attractive parkland course with tree-lined fairways,
and easy walking. Good open views towards the airport.**
18 holes, 6444yds, Par 72, SSS 71, Course record 64.
Club membership 778.
Visitors with member only at weekends & bank
holidays.Must contact in advance. **Societies** contact
Secretary in advance. **Green Fees** £22 per round. **Cards**
💳 💳 💳 **Prof** Nigel Brown **Facilities** ⊗ ⊤⊪ ⅃ ♥ ♀ ♠
🏠 ⊶ ✔ **Location** 4.5m NW of city centre off B6324

Hotel ★★★★ 74% Newcastle Marriott Hotel Gosforth
Park, High Gosforth Park, Gosforth, NEWCASTLE UPON
TYNE ☎ 0191 236 4111 178 en suite

RYTON   Map 12 NZ16

Ryton Clara Vale NE40 3TD
☎ 0191 413 3737 🖹 0191 413 1642
e-mail: secretary@rytongolfclub.co.uk
Parkland course.
18 holes, 5950yds, Par 70, SSS 69, Course record 67.
Club membership 600.
Visitors with member only at weekends. **Societies** apply in
advance. **Green Fees** £22 per day; £18 per round (£22 per
round weekends). **Facilities** ⊗ ⊤⊪ ⅃ ♥ ♀ ♠
Conf Corporate Hospitality Days available
Location NW of town centre off A695

Hotel ★★★ 69% Gibside Hotel, Front St, WHICKHAM
☎ 0191 488 9292 45 en suite

Tyneside Westfield Ln NE40 3QE
☎ 0191 413 2742 🖹 0191 413 2742
**Open parkland course, water hazard, hilly, practice
area.**
18 holes, 6009yds, Par 70, SSS 69, Course record 65.
Club membership 641.
Visitors contact in advance to play at weekends (after 5pm
Sat, 3pm Sun) **Societies** apply in advance. **Green Fees** £30
per day, £25 per round (£25 per round weekends). **Cards**
💳 💳 🖭 **Prof** Geoff Dixon **Course Designer** HS Colt
Facilities ⊗ ⊤⊪ ⅃ ♥ ♀ ♠ 🏠 ⊶ ✔ Conf Corporate
Hospitality Days available **Location** NW of town centre
off A695

Hotel ★★★ 69% Gibside Hotel, Front St, WHICKHAM
☎ 0191 488 9292 45 en suite

SOUTH SHIELDS   Map 12 NZ36

South Shields Cleadon Hills NE34 8EG
☎ 0191 456 8942 🖹 0191 456 8942
e-mail: thesecretary@south-shields-golf.freeserve.co.uk
**A slightly undulating downland course on a limestone
base ensuring good conditions underfoot. Open to
strong winds, the course is testing but fair. There are
fine views of the coastline.**
18 holes, 6174yds, Par 71, SSS 70, Course record 64.
Club membership 700.
Visitors contact in advance. **Societies** by arrangement.
Green Fees £32-37 per day; £22-27 per round. **Prof** Glyn
Jones **Course Designer** McKenzie-Braid **Facilities** ⊗ ⊤⊪
⅃ ♥ ♀ ♠ 🏠 Conf fac available **Location** SE of town
centre off A1300

Hotel ★★★ 66% Sea Hotel, Sea Rd, SOUTH SHIELDS
☎ 0191 427 0999 32 en suite

Whitburn Lizard Ln NE34 7AF
☎ 0191 529 4944 (Sec) 🖹 0191 529 4944
e-mail: wgsec@ukonline.co.uk
**Parkland course with sea views. Situated on limestone
making it rarely unplayable.**
18 holes, 5899yds, Par 70, SSS 68, Course record 67.
Club membership 700.
Visitors restricted weekends & Tue. Contact
professional/secretary in advance. **Societies** apply in
writing to secretary **Green Fees** terms on application.
Course Designer Colt, Alison & Morrison **Facilities** ⊗ ⊤
⅃ ♥ ♀ ♠ 🏠 ✔ **Location** 2.5m SE off A183

Continued   *Continue*

....

otel ★★★★ 69% Sunderland Marriott Hotel, Queen's
de, Seaburn, SUNDERLAND ☎ 0191 529 2041
2 en suite

UNDERLAND   Map 12 NZ35

Wearside Coxgreen SR4 9JT
☎ 0191 534 2518 🖹 0191 5346186
**pen, undulating parkland course rolling down to the
iver Wear and beneath the shadow of the famous
enshaw Monument. Built on the lines of a Greek
emple it is a well-known landmark. Two ravines cross
ne course presenting a variety of challenging holes.**
8 holes, 6373yds, Par 71, SSS 74, Course record 63.
'lub membership 648.
isitors not before 9.30am, between 12.30-1.30 or after
pm. Societies apply in writing. Green Fees not
onfirmed. Prof Doug Brolls Facilities ⊗ ⅲ ♭ 🖤 ♀ ⅄
ϖ ⌀ Location 3.5m W off A183

....

otel ★★★★ 69% Sunderland Marriott Hotel, Queen's
de, Seaburn, SUNDERLAND ☎ 0191 529 2041
2 en suite

YNEMOUTH   Map 12 NZ36

ynemouth Spital Dene NE30 2ER
☎ 0191 257 4578 🖹 0191 259 5193
mail: secretary@tynemouthgolfclub.com
**Vell-drained parkland course, not physically
emanding but providing a strong challenge to both low
nd high handicap players.**
8 holes, 6359yds, Par 70, SSS 70, Course record 66.
'lub membership 800.
isitors must play with member weekends & bank
olidays. Societies contact by phone Green Fees £22.50
er 18 holes; £25 per day. Cards ▦ ▬ ▬ 📇 ▦ ▦ 🞖
rof J P McKenna Course Designer Willie Park Facilities
⊗ ⅲ ♭ 🖤 ♀ ⅄ 📇 ⌙ 🞖 ⌀ Location 0.5m W

....

otel ★★★ 69% Grand Hotel, Grand Pde,
YNEMOUTH ☎ 0191 293 6666 40 en suite 4 annexe
n suite

VALLSEND   Map 12 NZ26

Vallsend Rheydt Av, Bigges Main NE28 8SU
☎ 0191 262 1973
arkland course.
8 holes, 5935yds, Par 69, SSS 68, Course record 67.
'lub membership 655.
isitors not before 12.30pm weekends. Must book in
dvance Societies apply in writing. Green Fees £15.50 per
und (£18.50 Sun). Prof Ken Phillips Course Designer
Snowball Facilities ♭ 🖤 ♀ ⅄ 📇 ⌀ ⌙
ocation NW of town centre off A193

....

otel ★★★ 68% The Caledonian Hotel, Newcastle, 64
sborne Rd, Jesmond, NEWCASTLE UPON TYNE
☎ 0191 281 7881 89 en suite

VASHINGTON   Map 12 NZ25

George Washington Golf & Country Club
tone Cellar Rd, High Usworth NE37 1PH
☎ 0191 417 8346 🖹 0191 415 1166
mail: reservations@georgewashington.co.uk
**he course is set in 150 acres of rolling parkland. Wide
enerous fairways and large greens. Trees feature on
ost holes, penalising the wayward shot.**

18 holes, 6604yds, Par 73, SSS 71, Course record 68.
Club membership 550.
Visitors all tee times must be reserved. members only
before 10.30 am & 12.30-1.30pm weekends. Societies
book in advance. Green Fees £25 per 18 holes (£30
weekends). Cards ▦ ▬ ▭ ▬ ▩ 🞖 Prof Graeme
Robinson Course Designer Eric Watson Facilities ⊗ ⅲ ♭
🖤 ♀ ⅄ 📇 ⌙ 🐴 ⌙ 🞖 🚿 ⌀ ⌙ Leisure heated indoor
swimming pool, squash, sauna, solarium, gymnasium,
9-hole par 3 course. Conf fac available Corporate
Hospitality Days available Location A194(M) S onto
A195, 1st rdbt right

....

Hotel ★★★ 67% George Washington Golf & Country
Club, Stone Cellar Rd, High Usworth, WASHINGTON
☎ 0191 402 9988 103 en suite

WHICKHAM   Map 12 NZ26

Whickham Hollinside Park, Fellside Rd NE16 5BA
☎ 0191 488 1576 🖹 0191 488 1577
e-mail: enquiries@whickhamgolfclub.co.uk
**Undulating parkland course set in the beautiful
Derwent valley. Its undulating fairways and subtly
contoured greens create an interesting challenge for
players of all abilities.**
18 holes, 5878yds, Par 68, SSS 68, Course record 61.
Club membership 660.
Visitors contact Professional in advance. Societies by
arrangement. Green Fees terms on application.
Prof Andrew Hall Facilities ⊗ ⅲ by arrangement ♭ 🖤 ♀
⅄ 📇 ⌀ Location 1.5m S

....

Hotel ★★★ 69% Gibside Hotel, Front St, WHICKHAM
☎ 0191 488 9292 45 en suite

WHITLEY BAY   Map 12 NZ37

Whitley Bay Claremont Rd NE26 3UF
☎ 0191 252 0180 🖹 0191 297 0030
e-mail: secretary@whitleybaygolfclub.co.uk
**An 18-hole links type course, close to the sea, with a
stream running through the undulating terrain.**
18 holes, 6579yds, Par 71, SSS 71, Course record 66.
Club membership 800.
Visitors not Sat, phone for Sun play. Advisable to contact
in advance. Societies phone initially. Green Fees £33 per
day; £24 per round (weekend £35 per round).
Prof Gary Shipley Facilities ⊗ ⅲ ♭ 🖤 ♀ ⅄ 📇 🐴 ⌀
Location NW of town centre off A1148

....

Hotel ★★★ 71% Windsor Hotel, South Pde, WHITLEY
BAY ☎ 0191 251 8888 69 en suite

WARWICKSHIRE

ATHERSTONE   Map 04 SP39

Atherstone The Outwoods, Coleshill Rd CV9 2RL
☎ 01827 713110 🖹 01827 715686
**Scenic parkland course, established in 1894 and laid out
on hilly ground. Interesting challenge on every hole.**
18 holes, 6006yds, Par 72, SSS 70, Course record 68.
Club membership 495.
Visitors handicap certificate required. With member only
weekends & bank holidays but not Sun except holders of
handicap certificate by permission of Club Secretary.
Societies contact Secretary in advance (01827 892568).
Green Fees £25 per day/round. Course Designer Hawtree

Continued   *Continued*

& Gaunt Mornoch **Facilities** ⊗)Ⅲ ᒪ ⬤ ♀ ᗩ ⬤
Conf Corporate Hospitality Days available
Location 0.5m S, A5 onto B4116

Hotel ⬆ Travelodge, Green Ln, TAMWORTH
☎ 08700 850 950 & 0800 850950 ◳ 01827 260145
62 en suite

BIDFORD-ON-AVON   Map 04 SP15

Bidford Grange Stratford Rd B50 4LY
☎ 01789 490319 ◳ 01789 490998
18 holes, 7233yds, Par 72, SSS 74, Course record 66.
Location E of village off B439
Phone for further details

Hotel ★★★ 63% Bidford Grange, Stratford Rd,
BIDFORD-ON-AVON ☎ 01789 490319 32 en suite
6 annexe en suite

BRANDON   Map 04 SP47

City of Coventry-Brandon Wood Brandon Ln,
Wolston CV8 3GQ
☎ 024 7654 3141 ◳ 024 7654 5108
**Municipal parkland course surrounded by fields and
bounded by River Avon on east side. Floodlit driving
range.**
18 holes, 6610yds, Par 72, SSS 71, Course record 68.
Club membership 400.
Visitors phone for details, advance booking recommended.
Societies phone secretary for details **Green Fees** not
confirmed. **Cards** ▦ ▦ ▦ ▩ ⬛ **Prof** Chris Gledhill
Facilities ⊗ ᒪ ⬤ ♀ ᗩ 🏠 🏌 ⬤ ⬤ 🏌 **Leisure** Pitching
area. **Location** of A45 S

Hotel ★★★ 67% Brandon Hall, Main St, BRANDON
☎ 0870 400 8105 60 en suite

COLESHILL   Map 04 SP28

Maxstoke Park Castle Ln B46 2RD
☎ 01675 466743 ◳ 01675 466185
e-mail: maxstokepark@btinternet.com
**Parkland course with easy walking. Numerous trees
and a lake form natural hazards.**
18 holes, 6442yds, Par 71, SSS 71, Course record 64.
Club membership 720.
Visitors with member only at weekends & bank holidays.
Societies contact in advance. **Green Fees** £30 per 18 holes
(weekdays only). **Prof** Neil McEwan **Course Designer**
various **Facilities** ⊗)Ⅲ ᒪ ⬤ ♀ ᗩ 🏠 🏌 ⬤ ⬤ **Conf**
Corporate Hospitality Days available **Location** 3m E of
Coleshill, off B4114 for Maxstoke

Hotel ★★★ 65% Grimstock Country House Hotel, Gilson
Rd, Gilson, COLESHILL ☎ 01675 462121 & 462161
◳ 01675 467646 44 en suite

HENLEY-IN-ARDEN   Map 04 SP16

Henley Golf & Country Club Birmingham Rd
B95 5QA
☎ 01564 793715 ◳ 01564 795754
e-mail: enquiries@henleygcc.co.uk
**This improving course is maturing well and provides a
good golfing challenge for all handicaps. All facilities
recently upgraded.**
18 holes, 6933yds, Par 73, SSS 73.
Club membership 675.

Henley Golf & Country Club

Visitors may book up to seven days in advance. **Societies**
apply in writing or phone in advance. **Green Fees** £40 per
day, £27 per round (weekends £47/£34). **Cards** ▦ ▦
▦ ▦ ⬛ **Prof** Neale Hyde **Course Designer**
N Selwyn Smith **Facilities** ⊗)Ⅲ ᒪ ⬤ ♀ ᗩ 🏠 ⬤ ⬤ 🏌 ⬤
Leisure hard tennis courts, nine-hole par 3 course, beauty
salon. **Conf** fac available Corporate Hospitality Days
available **Location** on A3400 just N of Henley-in-Arden

Hotel ★★★ 63% Quality Hotel Redditch, Pool Bank,
Southcrest, REDDITCH ☎ 01527 541511 73 en suite

KENILWORTH   Map 04 SP27

Kenilworth Crewe Ln CV8 2EA
☎ 01926 858517 ◳ 01926 864453
e-mail: secretary@kenilworthgolfclub.co.uk
**Parkland course in open hilly situation. Club founded
in 1889.**
18 holes, 6400yds, Par 73, SSS 71, Course record 62.
Club membership 755.
Visitors contact in advance. **Societies** apply in writing.
Green Fees £35 per day/round (weekends £45). **Cards** ▦
▦ ▩ ▦ ▦ ⬛ **Prof** Steve Yates **Course Designer**
Hawtree **Facilities** ⊗)Ⅲ ᒪ ⬤ ♀ ᗩ 🏠 🏌 ⬤ ⬤ ⬤
Leisure par 3 chipping green. **Conf** fac available
Corporate Hospitality Days available **Location** 0.5m NE

Hotel ★★★★ 64% Chesford Grange Hotel, Chesford
Bridge, KENILWORTH ☎ 01926 859331 209 en suite

LEA MARSTON   Map 04 SP29

Lea Marston Hotel & Leisure Complex
Haunch Ln B76 0BY
☎ 01675 470468 ◳ 01675 470871
e-mail: info@leamarstonhotel.co.uk
**The Marston Lakes course was opened in April 2001.
The layout includes many water and sand hazards
through undulating parkland. While short by modern
standards, it is a good test for even low handicap
players, requiring virtually everything in the bag. Tees
and greens have been built to championship course
specifications.**
Marston Lakes: 9 holes, 2054yds, Par 31, SSS 30.
Club membership 150.
Visitors book in advance & dress code applies. **Societies**
phone in advance. **Green Fees** Mon-Thu £12.50 per 18
holes, £7.50 per 9 holes (£16/£12.50 Fri-Sun & bank
holidays). **Cards** ▦ ▦ ▦ ▩ ▦ ▦ ⬛ **Prof** Darren
Lewis **Course Designer** Contour Golf **Facilities** ⊗)Ⅲ ᒪ
⬤ ♀ ᗩ 🏠 🏌 🏌 ⬤ ⬤ ⬤ 🏌 **Leisure** hard tennis courts,
heated indoor swimming pool, sauna, solarium,
gymnasium, golf simulator. **Conf** fac available Corporate

Continued   *Continued*

ospitality Days available **Location** M42 junct 9, A4097
owards Kingsbury, 1m right

Lea Marston Hotel & Leisure Complex

....

otel ★★★★ 67% Lea Marston Hotel Leisure Complex,
launch Ln, LEA MARSTON ☎ 01675 470468
0 en suite

EAMINGTON SPA   Map 04 SP36

eamington & County Golf Ln, Whitnash
V31 2QA
☎ 01926 425961 🖺 01926 425961
-mail: secretary@leamingtongolf.co.uk
ndulating parkland course with extensive views.
8 holes, 6418yds, Par 72, SSS 71, Course record 65.
lub membership 854.
isitors contact in advance. **Societies** phone in advance.
reen Fees £35 per round (£40 per round weekends).
ards 🖃 🖃 🛯 **Prof** Julian Mellor **Course Designer**
S Colt **Facilities** ⊗ ℡ 🖺 ▣ ♀ ♨ 🖨 ♥ 🚜 🏌
eisure snooker. **Conf** Corporate Hospitality Days
vailable **Location** S of town centre

....

otel ★★★ 70% Courtyard by Marriott Leamington Spa,
lympus Av, Tachbrook Park, LEAMINGTON SPA
☎ 01926 425522 91 en suite

ewbold Comyn Newbold Ter East CV32 4EW
☎ 01926 421157
-mail: colin@newcomyngc-20.wanadoo.co.uk
**unicipal parkland course with a hilly front nine. The
ar 4 9th is a 467-yd testing hole. The back nine is
ather flat but include two par 5s. Presently undergoing
xtensive upgrade.**
8 holes, 6315yds, Par 70, SSS 70, Course record 69.
lub membership 280.
isitors no restrictions. **Societies** apply to professional.
reen Fees 18 holes £10.25; 9 holes £6 (weekends
13.10/£9.80). **Cards** 🖃 🖃 🖃 **Prof** Ricky Carvell
acilities ⊗ ℡ 🖺 ▣ ♀ ♨ 🖨 🏌 **Leisure** heated indoor
wimming pool, gymnasium. **Location** 0.75m E of town
entre off B4099

....

otel ★★★ 65% The Best Western Royal Leamington
otel, 64 Upper Holly Walk, LEAMINGTON SPA
☎ 01926 883777 32 en suite

LEEK WOOTTON   Map 04 SP26

The Warwickshire CV35 7QT
☎ 01926 409409 🖺 01926 408409
e-mail: b.fotheringham@clubhaus.com
**Designed by Karl Litten, the 36 holes are laid out as
four loops of nine holes to create two championship
standard courses. Each nine has its own character:
parkland, woodland, inland links and Americano. The
place for golfers of any age or ability.**
*East South Course: 18 holes, 7000yds, Par 72, SSS 72,
Course record 68.*
*North West Course: 18 holes, 7421yds, Par 74, SSS 73,
Course record 70.*
Club membership 1500.
Visitors can book up to seven days in advance. **Societies**
apply to sales office for details. **Green Fees** not confirmed.
Cards 🖃 🖃 🖃 🔄 🖳 **Prof** Mark Dulson **Course
Designer** Karl Litten **Facilities** ⊗ ℡ 🖺 ▣ ♀ ♨ 🖨 🏌 🚜
🏌 🍴 **Location** S of village off A46

....

Hotel ★★★★ 64% Chesford Grange Hotel, Chesford
Bridge, KENILWORTH ☎ 01926 859331 209 en suite

NUNEATON   Map 04 SP39

Nuneaton Golf Dr, Whitestone CV11 6QF
☎ 024 7634 7810 🖺 024 7632 7563
e-mail: nuneatongolfclub@btconnect.com
**Undulating parkland and woodland course with silver
birch lining the fairways. Easy walking.**
18 holes, 6429yds, Par 71, SSS 71.
Club membership 700.
Visitors member of recognised golf club or society, with
member only at weekends. **Societies** apply in writing.
Green Fees not confirmed. **Prof** Craig Phillips **Facilities**
⊗ ℡ 🖺 ▣ ♀ ♨ 🖨 🚜 🏌 **Location** 2m SE off B4114

....

Hotel ★★★ 66% Weston Hall Hotel, Weston Ln,
Bulkington, NUNEATON ☎ 024 7631 2989 40 en suite

Oakridge Arley Ln, Ansley Village CV10 9PH
☎ 01676 541389 & 540542 🖺 01676 542709
e-mail: admin@oakridgegolf.fsnet.co.uk
**The water hazards on the back nine add to the natural
beauty of the countryside. The undulating course is
affected by winter cross winds on several holes. Overall
it will certainly test golfing skills.**
18 holes, 6242yds, Par 71, SSS 70.
Club membership 500.
Visitors contact in advance, with members only at
weekends. **Societies** apply in writing or phone in advance.
Green Fees £18 per day. **Cards** 🖃 🖃 🖃 **Course
Designer** Algy Jayes **Facilities** ⊗ ℡ 🖺 ▣ ♀ ♨ 🖨 🏌 ♥
🚜 🏌 **Conf** Corporate Hospitality Days available
Location 4m W

....

Hotel ★★★ 66% Weston Hall Hotel, Weston Ln,
Bulkington, NUNEATON ☎ 024 7631 2989 40 en suite

Purley Chase Pipers Ln, Ridge Ln CV10 0RB
☎ 024 7639 3118 🖺 024 7639 8015
e-mail: enquiries@purley-chase.co.uk
**Meadowland course with tricky water hazards on eight
holes and undulating greens.**
18 holes, 6772yds, Par 72, SSS 72, Course record 64.
Club membership 550.
Visitors welcome weekends pm & Mon-Fri. **Societies**
phone for provisional booking (Mon-Fri only).

Continued

Green Fees not confirmed. **Cards** 🏧 💳 💳 💷
Prof Gary Carver **Facilities** ⊗ ⅛ 🎱 🏌 🍽 🛒 🛍 🏌
Conf fac available Corporate Hospitality Days available
Location 2m NW off B4114

··

Hotel ★★★ 66% Weston Hall Hotel, Weston Ln,
Bulkington, NUNEATON ☎ 024 7631 2989 40 en suite

RUGBY   Map 04 SP57

Rugby Clifton Rd CV21 3RD
☎ 01788 542306 (Sec) & 575134 (Pro) 📠 01788 542306
e-mail: golf@rugbygc.fsnet.co.uk
**A short parkland course across the undulating Clifton
valley. Clifton brook runs through the lower level of the
course and comes into play on seven holes. Accuracy is
the prime requirement for a good score.**
18 holes, 5457yds, Par 68, SSS 67, Course record 60.
Club membership 700.
Visitors weekends & bank holidays with member only.
Societies apply in writing. **Green Fees** £25 per day, £50
per week. **Prof** David Quinn **Facilities** ⊗ ⅛ 🎱 🏌 🍽
🛍 🛒 🛍 🏌 **Leisure** snooker room.
Conf Corporate Hospitality Days available
Location 1m NE on B5414

··

Hotel ★★★ 65% Grosvenor Hotel Rugby, 81-87 Clifton
Rd, RUGBY ☎ 01788 535686 26 en suite

Whitefields Hotel Golf & Country Club

London Rd, Thurlaston CV23 9LF
☎ 01788 815555 & 817777 📠 01788 817777
e-mail: mail@whitefields-hotel.co.uk
**Whitefields has superb natural drainage. There are
many water features and the 13th has a stunning dog-
leg 442yd par 4 with a superb view across Draycote
Water. The 16th is completely surrounded by water
and is particularly difficult.**

18 holes, 6289yds, Par 71, SSS 70, Course record 66.
Club membership 325.
Visitors advisable to book unless hotel guest, available
seven days, contact secretary on 01788 815555. **Societies**
contact secretary in advance. brochure available **Green
Fees** terms on application. **Cards** 🏧 💳 💳 💷 💳 💳 💷
Prof Mario Luca **Course Designer** Reg Mason **Facilities**
⊗ ⅛ 🎱 🏌 🍽 🛍 🛒 🛍 🏌 **Leisure** gymnasium.
Conf fac available Corporate Hospitality Days available
Location M45 junct 1, 0.5m on A45, on left. W of
Dunchurch

··

Hotel ★★ 69% The Golden Lion Inn, Easenhall, RUGBY
☎ 01788 832265 12 en suite

STONELEIGH   Map 04 SP37

Stoneleigh Deer Park The Clubhouse, The Old
Deer Park, Coventry Rd CV8 3DR
☎ 024 7663 9991 & 7663 9912 📠 024 7651 1533
e-mail: stoneleighdeerpark@ukgateway.net
**Parkland course in old deer park with many mature
trees. The River Avon meanders through the course
and comes into play on four holes. Also nine-hole par 3
course.**
*Tantara Course: 18 holes, 6056yds, Par 71, SSS 69,
Course record 67.*
Club membership 800.
Visitors contact in advance. **Societies** by arrangement.
Green Fees terms on application. **Cards** 🏧 💳 💳 💷
Prof Matt McGuire & Sarah Perkins **Facilities** ⊗ ⅛ 🎱 🏌
🍽 🛍 🛒 🛍 🏌 **Location** 3m NE of Kenilworth

··

Hotel ★★★★ 62% De Montfort Hotel, Abbey End,
KENILWORTH ☎ 01926 855944 108 en suite

STRATFORD-UPON-AVON   Map 04 SP25

Ingon Manor Ingon Ln, Snitterfield CV37 0QE
☎ 01789 731857 📠 01789 731657
**Nestling in the Welcombe Hills, a short distance from
the town. The Manor, dating back to the 14th century,
lies within 171 acres of land. The championship course
is open all year round and has been designed to test all
standards of golfers with a variety of challenging holes.**
18 holes, 6623yds, Par 72.
Club membership 400.
Visitors phone for details **Societies** phone for details
Green Fees not confirmed. **Cards** 🏧 💳 💳 💷 💳 💳
💷 **Prof** Paul Taylor **Facilities** ⊗ ⅛ 🎱 🏌 🍽 🛍 🛒 🛍
🛒 🏌 ₵ **Leisure** caddies available.

Menzies Welcombe Hotel Warwick Rd
CV37 0NR
☎ 01789 295252 📠 01789 414666
e-mail: welcombe.golfpro@menzies-hotels.co.uk
**Wooded parkland course of great character and
boasting superb views of the River Avon and Stratford.
Set within the hotel's 157-acre estate, it has two lakes
and other water features.**
18 holes, 6288yds, Par 70, SSS 69, Course record 64.
Club membership 450.
Visitors contact in advance. **Societies** booking via Hotel or
golf clubhouse. Write, phone or e-mail in advance, **Green
Fees** terms on application. **Cards** 🏧 💳 💳 💷 💳 💳 💷
Prof Matt Nixon **Course Designer** Thomas Macauley
Facilities ⊗ ⅛ 🎱 🏌 🍽 🛍 🛒 🏌 🛒 🛍 🏌 ₵ **Leisure**
hard tennis courts, heated indoor swimming pool, fishing,
solarium, gymnasium, golf lessons for
individual/groups/company days. **Conf** fac available
Corporate Hospitality Days available **Location** 1.5m NE
off A46

··

Hotel ★★★★ 72% Menzies Welcombe Hotel and Golf
Course, Warwick Rd, STRATFORD-UPON-AVON
☎ 01789 295252 73 en suite

Stratford Oaks Bearley Rd, Snitterfield CV37 0EZ
☎ 01789 731980 📠 01789 731981
e-mail: admin@stratfordoaks.co.uk
**American-style, level parkland course with some water
features designed by Howard Swan.**
18 holes, 6135yds, Par 71, SSS 69, Course record 61.
Club membership 700.

Continue

isitors contact in advance. **Societies** phone in advance.
reen Fees not confirmed. **Cards** 🔲 🔲 🔲 🔲 🔲 **Prof**
ndrew Dunbar **Course Designer** H Swann **Facilities** ⊗
🔲 🔲 🔲 🔲 🔲 🔲 🔲 🔲 **Leisure** gymnasium, massage &
ysiotherapy facility. **Location** 4m N of Stratford-upon-
von

otel ★★★★ 72% Stratford Manor, Warwick Rd,
TRATFORD-UPON-AVON
☎ 01789 731173 104 en suite

tratford-upon-Avon Tiddington Rd CV37 7BA
☎ 01789 205749 📄 01789 414909
mail: sec@stratfordgolf.co.uk
eautiful parkland course. The par 3 16th is tricky and
e par 5 17th and 18th provide a tough end.
 holes, 6311yds, Par 72, SSS 70, Course record 63.
lub membership 750.
isitors not before 11.00am weekends. Phone in advance.
ocieties apply in advance. Tue, Thu only. **Green Fees**
0 per day, £40 per 18 holes (£55/£45 weekends). **Prof**
 Sutherland **Course Designer** Taylor **Facilities** ⊗ 🔲 🔲
🔲 🔲 🔲 🔲 🔲 🔲 **Location** 0.75m E on B4086

otel ★★★★ 72% The Alveston Manor, Clopton Bridge,
TRATFORD-UPON-AVON
☎ 0870 400 8181 113 en suite

ANWORTH IN ARDEN   Map 07 SP17

adbrook Park Poolhead Ln B94 5ED
☎ 01564 742264 📄 01564 742909
mail: secretary@ladbrookparkgolf.co.uk
arkland course lined with trees.
 holes, 6427yds, Par 71, SSS 71, Course record 65.
lub membership 700.
isitors welcome weekdays, with member at weekends.
 ust contact in advance & have handicap certificate.
ocieties apply in advance. **Green Fees** £45 per 36 holes,
0 per 27 holes, £30 per 18 holes. **Cards** 🔲 🔲 🔲
🔲 🔲 **Prof** Richard Mountford **Course Designer** HS Colt
acilities ⊗ 🔲 🔲 🔲 🔲 🔲 🔲 🔲
ocation M42 junct 3, 2.5m SE

otel ★★★ 83% Nuthurst Grange Country House Hotel,
uthurst Grange Ln, HOCKLEY HEATH
☎ 01564 783972 15 en suite

PPER BRAILES   Map 04 SP33

railes Sutton Ln, Lower Brailes OX15 5BB
☎ 01608 685633 📄 01608 685205
mail: office@brailes-golf-club.co.uk
ndulating meadowland on 105 acres of Cotswold
ountryside. Sutton Brook passes through the course
nd must be crossed five times. The par 5 17th offers
e most spectacular view of three counties from the
e. Challenging par 3 short holes. Suitable for golfers
all standards.
 holes, 6304yds, Par 71, SSS 70, Course record 67.
lub membership 600.
isitors phone in advance 01608 685633. **Societies** phone
 write for information to the General Manager. **Green**
es not confirmed. **Cards** 🔲 🔲 🔲 🔲 **Prof** Alistair
rown **Course Designer** B A Hull **Facilities** ⊗ 🔲 🔲 🔲 🔲
🔲 🔲 🔲 🔲 🔲 **Location** S of Lower Brailes off B4035

n ♦♦♦♦ The Red Lion Hotel, Main St, Long Compton,
HIPSTON ON STOUR ☎ 01608 684221 5 en suite

WARWICK   Map 04 SP26

Warwick The Racecourse CV34 6HW
☎ 01926 494316
Parkland course with easy walking. Driving range with
floodlit bays.
9 holes, 2682yds, Par 34, SSS 66, Course record 67.
Club membership 150.
Visitors contact in advance; not before 12.30pm Sun.
Societies contact in advance. **Green Fees** terms on
application. **Prof** Mario Luca **Course Designer**
DG Dunkley **Facilities** 🔲 🔲 🔲 🔲 🔲 🔲 🔲
Location W of town centre

Hotel ★★ 64% Warwick Arms Hotel, 17 High St,
WARWICK ☎ 01926 492759 35 en suite

WISHAW   See page 263

WISHAW   Map 07 SP19

Wishaw Bulls Ln B76 9QW
☎ 0121 313 2110 📄 0121 351 7498
Parkland course with one hill on course at 9th and 18th
holes. Course well drained with irrigation on tees and
greens.
18 holes, 5729yards, Par 70, SSS 68, Course record 67.
Club membership 338.
Visitors phone for details **Societies** phone to book. **Green**
Fees not confirmed. **Cards** 🔲 🔲 🔲 🔲 🔲 **Prof** Alan
Partridge **Course Designer** R Wallis **Facilities** ⊗ 🔲 🔲 🔲
🔲 🔲 🔲 🔲 🔲 🔲 **Conf** fac available Corporate
Hospitality Days available **Location** W of village off
A4097

Hotel ★★★★ 75% De Vere Belfry, WISHAW
☎ 0870 900 0066 324 en suite

WEST MIDLANDS

ALDRIDGE   Map 07 SK00

Druids Heath Stonnall Rd WS9 8JZ
☎ 01922 455595 (Office) 📄 01922 452887
Testing, undulating heathland course. Large greens
with subtle slopes.
18 holes, 6661yds, Par 72, SSS 73, Course record 68.
Club membership 660.
Visitors contact in advance recommended. Weekend play
permitted after 2pm, not bank holidays. **Societies** phone
initially. **Green Fees** £32 per day (£40 weekends after
2pm). **Prof** Glenn Williams **Facilities** ⊗ 🔲 🔲 🔲 🔲 🔲
🔲 🔲 **Leisure** snooker.
Location NE of town centre off A454

Continued

261

Hotel ★★★ 76% The Fairlawns at Aldridge, 178 Little Aston Rd, Aldridge, WALSALL ☎ 01922 455122 50 en suite

BIRMINGHAM   Map 07 SP08

Alison Nicholas Golf Academy Host Centre,
Queslett Park, Great Barr B42 2RG
☎ 0121 360 7600 📠 0121 360 7603
e-mail: info@ the hostcorporation.com
This golf academy consists of a nine-hole short game improvement course, a covered floodlit driving range and teaching and training facilities.
9 holes, 905yds, Par 27, SSS 27, Course record 21.
Club membership 800.
Visitors no restrictions Societies apply in advance by phone or in writing. Green Fees not confirmed. Cards 💳 💳 💳 💳 💳 Prof Gary Broadbent Course Designer Alison Nicholas, Francis Colella Facilities ⊗ 🅱 💺 ♀ 🏠 ⌁ 🍴 Conf fac available Location M6 junct 7

Hotel ⏰ Innkeeper's Lodge Birmingham East, Chester Rd, Streetley, SUTTON COLDFIELD ☎ 0121 353 7785 7 en suite 59 annexe en suite

Brandhall Heron Rd, Oldbury, Warley B68 8AQ
☎ 0121 552 2195
18 holes, 5734yds, Par 70, SSS 68, Course record 66.
Location 5.5m W of Birmingham off A4123
Phone for further details

Hotel ★★★ 63% The Plough & Harrow Hotel, 135 Hagley Rd, EDGBASTON ☎ 0870 609 6118 44 en suite

Cocks Moors Woods Alcester Rd South, Kings Heath B14 4ER
☎ 0121 464 3584 📠 0121 441 1305
Although quite short, this tree-lined parkland course has well-maintained greens and offers a good test of golf.
18 holes, 5769yds, Par 69, SSS 68.
Club membership 300.
Visitors no restrictions. Societies contact in advance. Green Fees £10 (£12 weekend). Cards 💳 💳 💳 Prof Steve Ellis Facilities ⊗ 🅼 🅱 💺 ♀ 🛆 🏠 ⌁ Leisure heated indoor swimming pool, solarium, gymnasium. Location M42 junct 3, 4m N on A435

Hotel ★★★ 68% Corus hotel Solihull, Stratford Rd, Shirley, SOLIHULL ☎ 0870 609 6133 111 en suite

Edgbaston Church Rd, Edgbaston B15 3TB
☎ 0121 454 1736 📠 0121 454 2395
e-mail: secretary@edgbastongc.co.uk
Set in 144 acres of woodland, lake and parkland, 2m from the centre of Birmingham, this delightful course utilises the wealth of natural features to provide a series of testing and adventurous holes set in the traditional double loop that starts directly in front of the clubhouse, an imposing Georgian mansion.
18 holes, 6106yds, Par 69, SSS 69, Course record 63.
Club membership 970.
Visitors recommended to contact in advance through golf reservations, must have handicap certificate. Most weekends pm. Societies apply in writing. Green Fees terms on application. Cards 💳 💳 Prof Jamie Cundy Course Designer HS Colt Facilities ⊗ 🅼 🅱 💺 ♀ 🛆 🏠

Continued

🍴 🐾 🚗 ⌁ Conf fac available Corporate Hospitality Days available Location 2m S of city centre on B4217

Hotel ★★★ 63% The Plough & Harrow Hotel, 135 Hagley Rd, EDGBASTON ☎ 0870 609 6118 44 en suite

Great Barr Chapel Ln, Great Barr B43 7BA
☎ 0121 357 5270
Parkland course with easy walking. Pleasant views of Barr Beacon Park.
18 holes, 6523yds, Par 72, SSS 72, Course record 67.
Club membership 600.
Visitors no visitors at weekends. Societies contact in writing. Green Fees not confirmed. Prof Richard Spragg Facilities ⊗ by arrangement 🅼 by arrangement 🅱 💺 ♀ 🛆 🏠 ⌁ Location 6m N of city centre off A 34

Hotel ⏰ Innkeeper's Lodge Birmingham East, Chester Rd, Streetley, SUTTON COLDFIELD ☎ 0121 353 7785 7 en suite 59 annexe en suite

Handsworth 11 Sunningdale Close, Handsworth Wood B20 1NP
☎ 0121 554 0599 & 554 3387 📠 0121 554 3387
e-mail: info@handsworthgolfclub.net
Undulating parkland course with some tight fairways and strategic bunkering.
18 holes, 6289yds, Par 70, SSS 71, Course record 64.
Club membership 730.
Visitors restricted weekends, bank holidays & Xmas. Must contact in advance & have a handicap certificate. Societies contact in advance. Green Fees £40 per day. Prof Lee Bashford Course Designer HS Colt Facilities ⊗ 🅼 🅱 💺 ♀ 🛆 🏠 🚗 ⌁ Leisure squash. Location 3.5m NW of city centre off A4040

Hotel ⏰ Premier Travel Inn West Bromwich, New Gas St, WEST BROMWICH ☎ 08701 977264 40 en suite

Harborne 40 Tennal Rd, Harborne B32 2JE
☎ 0121 427 3058 📠 0121 427 4039
e-mail: harborne@hgolf.fsnet.co.uk
Parkland course in hilly situation, with a brook running through.
18 holes, 6230yds, Par 70, SSS 70, Course record 65.
Club membership 600.
Visitors must have handicap certificate, contact in advance, not weekends except with member, Ladies have priority Tue. Societies Mon, Wed-Fri apply to secretary, by phone or letter. Green Fees £30 per 36/18 holes. Prof Paul Johnson Course Designer Harry Colt Facilities ⊗ 🅼 🅱 💺 ♀ 🛆 🏠 🍴 ⌁ Location 3.5 m SW of city centre off A4040

Hotel ★★★ 63% The Plough & Harrow Hotel, 135 Hagley Rd, EDGBASTON ☎ 0870 609 6118 44 en suite

Harborne Church Farm Vicarage Rd, Harborne B17 0SN
☎ 0121 427 1204 📠 0121 428 3126
Parkland course with two brooks running through. Course is small but tight.
9 holes, 4882yds, Par 66, SSS 64, Course record 62.
Club membership 115.
Visitors contact in advance. Societies phone in advance. Green Fees £9 per 18 holes; £6 per 9 holes (£10.50/£7 weekends). Cards 💳 💳 💳 💳 💳 💳 💳 Prof Paul Johnson Facilities ⊗ 🅼 🅱 💺 ♀ 🛆 🏠 🍴 ⌁

Continued

The Belfry

Warwickshire

Wishaw

Map 07 SP19

The Belfry is unique as the only venue to have staged the biggest golf event in the world, the Ryder Cup matches, an unprecedented four times, most recently in 2002. The Brabazon is regarded throughout the world as a great championship course with some of the most demanding holes in golf; the 10th (Ballesteros's Hole) and the 18th, with its dangerous lakes and its amphitheatre around the final green, are world famous. These remained intact during the £2.4 million redevelopment in 1998, which made the course even more testing. Alternatively, you can pit your wits against a new legend in the making, the PGA National Course, which has won plaudits from near and far. The Dave Thomas and Peter Alliss designed course has been used for professional competition and is already established as one of Britain's leading courses. For those who like their golf a little easier or like to get back into the swing gently, the Derby is ideal and can be played by golfers of any standard. The Bel Air nightclub, the De Vere Club leisure centre, and the Aqua-Spa with its fire and ice bio-thermal treatments offer unique experiences away from the course.

Wishaw B76 9PR
☎ 01675 470301 Fax 01675 470178
e-mail: enquiries@thebelfry.com

The Brabazon: 18 holes, 6724yds, Par 72, SSS 71.
PGA National: 18 holes, 6639yds, Par 71, SSS 70.
The Derby: 18 holes, 6057yds, Par 69, SSS 69.
Club membership 450.
Visitors handicap certificate required for Brabazon course & PGA National (men 24 or better, women & juniors 32 or better); reservations 24 hours in advance for non-residents.
Societies must phone in advance. **Green Fees** Brabazon £140; PGA £75; Derby: £40; reduced winter rates. **Cards** ▭ ▭ ▭ ▭
▭ ▭ **Prof** Simon Wordsworth **Course Designer** Dave Thomas, Peter Alliss **Facilities** ⊗ ⋔ ⋤ ♥ ♀ ⚲ ☖ ⛳ ⛶ ⛳ ⛴
⛳ ⛱ **Leisure** hard tennis courts, heated indoor swimming pool, squash, sauna, solarium, gymnasium, PGA National Golf Academy.
Conf fac available Corporate Hospitality Days available
Location M42 junct 9, 4m E on A446

....

Hotels

★ ★ ★ ★ 75% De Vere Belfry, WISHAW

☎ 0870 900 0066 324 en suite

★ ★ ★ ★ 67% Lea Marston Hotel & Leisure Complex, Haunch Ln, LEA MARSTON

☎ 01675 470468 Fax 01675 470871 80 en suite

★ ★ ★ ★ 68% Moor Hall Hotel, Moor Hall Dr, Four Oaks, SUTTON COLDFIELD

☎ 0121 308 3751 Fax 0121 308 8974 82 en suite

Leisure practice net.
Location 3.5m SW of city centre off A4040

Hotel ★★★ 63% The Plough & Harrow Hotel, 135 Hagley Rd, EDGBASTON ☎ 0870 609 6118 44 en suite

Hatchford Brook Coventry Rd, Sheldon B26 3PY
☎ 0121 743 9821 📄 0121 743 3420
e-mail: idt@hbgc.freeserve.co.uk
Fairly flat, municipal parkland course.
18 holes, 6155yds, Par 69, SSS 70.
Club membership 350.
Visitors are restricted early Sat & Sun. **Societies** contact in advance. **Green Cards** not confirmed. **Cards** ▦ ▦ ▦ ▦ 📄 **Prof** Mark Hampton **Facilities** ⊗ ▟ ⛳ ♀ ⚐ ☂ ⚑ ♂
Location 6m E of city centre on A45

Hotel ★★★ 68% Novotel Birmingham Airport, BIRMINGHAM AIRPORT ☎ 0121 782 7000 195 en suite

Hilltop Park Ln, Handsworth B21 8LJ
☎ 0121 554 4463
A good test of golf with interesting layout, undulating fairways and large greens, located in the Sandwell Valley conservation area.
18 holes, 6208yds, Par 71, SSS 70, Course record 65.
Club membership 400.
Visitors no restrictions but booking necessary. **Societies** Mon-Fri, phone Professional in advance. **Green Fees** 18 holes £10; 9 holes £6 (£12/£7 weekends & bank holidays). **Cards** ▦ ▦ ▦ ▦ ▦ 📄 **Prof** Kevin Highfield **Course Designer** Hawtree **Facilities** ⊗ ⫚ ▟ ⛳ ♀ ⚐ ☂ ⚑ ♂ ♂
Conf fac available Corporate Hospitality Days available
Location M5 junct 1, 1m on A41

Hotel ⌂ Premier Travel Inn West Bromwich, New Gas St, WEST BROMWICH ☎ 08701 977264 40 en suite

Lickey Hills Rosehill, Rednal B45 8RR
☎ 0121 453 3159 📄 0121 457 8779
Hilly municipal course overlooking the city, set in National Trust land.
Rose Hill: 18 holes, 5835yds, Par 68, SSS 68.
Club membership 300.
Visitors not 9am-10.30am weekends. **Societies** contact in advance. **Green Fees** £12 per 18 holes; £6.50 per 9 holes. **Cards** ▦ ▦ ▦ 📄 **Prof** Mark Toombs
Facilities ⛳ ⚐ ☂ ⚑ 🎾 ♂ **Leisure** hard tennis courts.
Conf fac available Corporate Hospitality Days available
Location 10m SW of city centre on B4096

Hotel ★★ 70% Norwood Hotel, 87-89 Bunbury Rd, Northfield, BIRMINGHAM ☎ 0121 411 2202 18 en suite

Moseley Springfield Rd, Kings Heath B14 7DX
☎ 0121 444 4957 📄 0121 441 4662
e-mail: admin@mosgolf.freeserve.co.uk
Parkland course with a lake, pond and stream to provide natural hazards. The par 3 4th goes through a cutting in woodland to a tree and garden-lined amphitheatre, and the par 4 5th entails a drive over a lake to a dog-leg fairway.
18 holes, 6300yds, Par 70, SSS 71, Course record 63.
Club membership 600.
Visitors weekdays only by arrangement; not bank holidays. **Societies** some Wed & Fri by arrangement. **Green Fees** £37 per round. **Prof** Martin Griffin **Course Designer** HS Colt with others **Facilities** ⊗ ⫚ ▟ ⛳ ♀ ⚐ ♂ **Conf** Corporate Hospitality Days available
Location 4m S of city centre on B4146

Continued

Moseley Golf Club

Hotel ★★ 70% Norwood Hotel, 87-89 Bunbury Rd, Northfield, BIRMINGHAM ☎ 0121 411 2202 18 en suite

North Worcestershire Frankley Beeches Rd, Northfield B31 5LP
☎ 0121 475 1047 📄 0121 476 8681
Designed by James Braid and established in 1907, this is a mature parkland course. Tree plantations rather than heavy rough are the main hazards.
18 holes, 5959yds, Par 69, SSS 68, Course record 64.
Club membership 600.
Visitors by arrangement with professional. Must play with member at weekends. All visitors must have handicap. **Societies** apply in advance in writing or by phone to the professional 0121 475 5721. **Green Fees** terms on application. **Prof** Finley Clarke **Course Designer** James Braid **Facilities** ⊗ ⫚ ▟ ⛳ ♀ ⚐ ☂ ⚑ ♂
Location 7m SW of Birmingham city centre, off A38

Hotel ★★ 70% Norwood Hotel, 87-89 Bunbury Rd, Northfield, BIRMINGHAM ☎ 0121 411 2202 18 en suite

Warley Woods The Pavilion, Lightswood Hill, Warley B67 5ED
☎ 0121 429 2440 & 6862619(secretary) 📄 0121 434 4430
Municipal parkland course in Warley Woods. New out of bounds areas and bunkers have tightened the course considerably with further improvement following tree planting.
9 holes, 5346yds, Par 68, SSS 66, Course record 64.
Club membership 200.
Visitors contact in advance. **Societies** booking advised, times very limited for large parties. **Green Fees** not confirmed. **Prof** D Ashington **Facilities** ⊗ ▟ ♀ ⛳ ⚐ ⚑ ♂ **Leisure** practice nets. **Conf** fac available
Location 4m W of city centre off A456

Hotel ★★★ 63% The Plough & Harrow Hotel, 135 Hagley Rd, EDGBASTON ☎ 0870 609 6118 44 en suite

COVENTRY   Map 04 SP37

Ansty Golf Centre Brinklow Rd, Ansty CV7 9JH
☎ 024 7662 1341 📄 024 7660 2568
An 18-hole pay and play parkland course of two nine-hole loops.
18 holes, 6079yds, Par 71, SSS 68, Course record 66.
Club membership 230.
Visitors no restrictions. **Societies** welcome, phone in advance. **Green Fees** £11 per 18 holes (£16 weekends & bank holidays). Academy £4 (£5.50 weekends & bank holidays). **Cards** ▦ ▦ ▦ ▦ 📄 **Prof** Mark Goodwin **Course Designer** David Morgan **Facilities** ⊗ ⫚ ▟ ⛳ ♀ ♀

Continued

⚒ 🏠 ⛳ 🏌 ♨ ♪ ☖ **Leisure** par 3 course. **Conf** fac available   Corporate Hospitality Days available **Location** M6/M69 junct 2, 1m

Hotel ★★★ 64% Novotel Coventry, Wilsons Ln, COVENTRY ☎ 024 7636 5000   98 en suite

Coventry St Martins Rd, Finham Park CV3 6RJ
☎ 024 7641 4152 📠 024 7669 0131
e-mail: coventrygolfclub@hotmail.com
The scene of several major professional events, this undulating parkland course has a great deal of quality. More than that, it usually plays its length, and thus scoring is never easy, as many professionals have found to their cost.
18 holes, 6601yds, Par 73, SSS 73, Course record 66.
Club membership 500.
Visitors contact in advance; not weekends & bank holidays. **Societies** apply in writing or phone. **Green Fees** £35 per day. **Cards** 🃏 🃏 🃏 🃏 🃏 **Prof** Philip Weaver **Course Designer** Vardon Bros, Hawtree **Facilities** ⊗ 🍴 🏌 ♨ ♟ ⚒ 🏠 ♪ ☖ **Conf** Corporate Hospitality Days available **Location** 3m S of city centre on B4113

Hotel ★★★ 66% Best Western Hylands Hotel, Warwick Rd, COVENTRY ☎ 024 7650 1600   61 en suite

Coventry Hearsall Beechwood Av CV5 6DF
☎ 024 7671 3470 📠 024 7669 1534
Parkland course with fairly easy walking. A brook provides an interesting hazard.
18 holes, 6005yds, Par 70, SSS 69.
Club membership 650.
Visitors with member only at weekends. **Societies** apply in writing to secretary. **Green Fees** not confirmed. **Prof** Mike Tarn **Facilities** ⊗ 🍴 🏌 ♨ ♟ ⚒ 🏠 🍴 ♪ ☖ **Leisure** hard & grass tennis courts, outdoor & indoor heated swimming pools. **Location** 1.5m SW of city centre off A429

Hotel ★★★ 66% Best Western Hylands Hotel, Warwick Rd, COVENTRY ☎ 024 7650 1600   61 en suite

Windmill Village Hotel Golf Leisure Club
Birmingham Rd, Allesley CV5 9AL
☎ 024 7640 4041 📠 024 7640 4042
e-mail: sales@windmillvillagehotel.co.uk
An attractive 18-hole course over rolling parkland with plenty of trees and two lakes that demand shots over open water. Four challenging par 5 holes.
18 holes, 5184yds, Par 70, SSS 66, Course record 63.
Club membership 600.
Visitors not weekends 7-10am; contact in advance; pre-payment required at peak times. **Societies** phone for booking form. **Green Fees** terms on application. **Cards** 🃏 🃏 🃏 🃏 🃏 **Prof** Robert Hunter **Course Designer** Robert Hunter **Facilities** ⊗ 🍴 🏌 ♨ ♟ ⚒ 🏠 ♪ 🍴 ☖ **Leisure** hard tennis courts, heated indoor swimming pool, sauna, solarium, gymnasium, beauty suite, practice nets. **Conf** fac available   Corporate Hospitality Days available **Location** 3m W of Coventry on A45

Hotel ★★★ 72% Brooklands Grange Hotel & Restaurant, Holyhead Rd, COVENTRY ☎ 024 7660 1601   31 en suite

Dudley Turner's Hill, Rowley Regis, Warley B65 9DP
☎ 01384 233877 📠 01384 233177
18 holes, 5714yds, Par 69, SSS 68.
Location 2m S of town centre off B4171
Phone for further details

Hotel ★★★ 64% The Himley Country Hotel, School Rd, HIMLEY ☎ 0870 609 6112   73 en suite

Swindon Bridgnorth Rd, Swindon DY3 4PU
☎ 01902 897031 📠 01902 326219
e-mail: golf@swindonperton.fsbusiness.co.uk
Attractive undulating woodland and parkland course, with spectacular views.
Old Course: 18 holes, 6121yds, Par 71, SSS 70.
Club membership 700.
Visitors contact in advance. **Societies** apply in writing. **Green Fees** £20 per round (£30 weekends & bank holidays). **Cards** 🃏 🃏 **Prof** Phil Lester **Facilities** ⊗ 🍴 🏌 ♨ ♟ ⚒ 🏠 ♪ ☖ **Leisure** fishing, par 3 9-hole course. **Location** 4m W of Dudley on B4176

Hotel ★★★ 64% The Himley Country Hotel, School Rd, HIMLEY ☎ 0870 609 6112   73 en suite

Halesowen The Leasowes, Leasowes Ln B62 8QF
☎ 0121 501 3606 📠 0121 501 3606
e-mail: halesowen-gc@msn.com
Parkland course within the only Grade I listed park in the Midlands.
18 holes, 5754yds, Par 69, SSS 69, Course record 66.
Club membership 625.
Visitors welcome weekdays, may only play weekends or bank holidays with member unless previously agreed. **Societies** apply in writing or phone. **Green Fees** £31 per day, £26 per round. **Prof** Jon Nicholas **Facilities** ⊗ 🍴 🏌 ♟ ⚒ 🏠 ♪ ☖ **Conf** Corporate Hospitality Days available **Location** M5 junct 3, 1m E, off Manor Ln

Hotel ★★★ 63% The Plough & Harrow Hotel, 135 Hagley Rd, EDGBASTON ☎ 0870 609 6118   44 en suite

Copt Heath 1220 Warwick Rd B93 9LN
☎ 01564 772650 & 731620 📠 01564 771022/731621
e-mail: golf@copt-heath.co.uk
Flat heathland and parkland course designed by H Vardon.
18 holes, 6517yds, Par 71, SSS 71, Course record 64.
Club membership 700.
Visitors contact in advance & possess official handicap certificate. May play weekends & bank holidays in limited numbers, please contact in advance. **Societies** contact in advance. **Green Fees** £50 per day, £40 per round (£50 per round weekends). **Prof** Brian J Barton **Course Designer** H Vardon **Facilities** ⊗ 🍴 🏌 ♨ ♟ ⚒ 🏠 ♪ ☖ ⚒ **Conf** Corporate Hospitality Days available **Location** M42 junct 5, 0.5m S on A4141

Hotel ★★★★ 70% Renaissance Solihull Hotel, 651 Warwick Rd, SOLIHULL ☎ 0121 711 3000   179 en suite

MERIDEN   See page 267

MERIDEN   Map 04 SP28

North Warwickshire Hampton Ln CV7 7LL
☎ 01676 522259 (shop) & 522915 (sec) 🖹 01676 523004
Parkland course with easy walking.
9 holes, 6390yds, Par 72, SSS 71, Course record 65.
Club membership 425.
Visitors contact in advance. Must play with member at
weekends. **Societies** apply in writing to secretary. **Green
Fees** not confirmed. **Prof** Andrew Bownes **Facilities** ⊗ by
arrangement 🎜 by arrangement 🖺 🍺 🍴 🕂 🖺 ♂
Location 1m SW on B4102
....
Hotel ★★★ 71% Manor Hotel, Main Rd, MERIDEN
☎ 01676 522735 110 en suite

Stonebridge Golf Centre Somers Rd CV7 7PL
☎ 01676 522442 🖹 01676 522447
e-mail: golf.shop@stonebridgegolf.co.uk
**A parkland course set in 170 acres with towering oak
trees, lakes and the River Blythe on its borders.**
18 holes, 6240yds, Par 70, SSS 70, Course record 67.
Club membership 400.
Visitors visitors can book up to seven days in advance in
person or by phone. **Societies** apply in writing or phone in
advance. **Green Fees** £19 per 18 holes Mon-Thu, £20 Fri,
£25 weekends & bank holidays. **Cards** 💳 💳 💳 💳 💳
Prof Emma Clifford **Course Designer** Mark Jones
Facilities ⊗ 🎜 🖺 🍺 🍴 🕂 🖺 ♂
Leisure fishing, golf academy. **Conf** fac available
Corporate Hospitality Days available
Location M42 junct 6, 3m
....
Hotel ★★★ 71% Manor Hotel, Main Rd, MERIDEN
☎ 01676 522735 110 en suite

SEDGLEY   Map 07 SO99

Sedgley Golf Centre Sandyfields Rd DY3 3DL
☎ 01902 880503
e-mail: info@sedgleygolf.co.uk
**Public pay and play course. Undulating contours and
mature trees with extensive views over surrounding
countryside.**
9 holes, 3147yds, Par 72, SSS 70.
Club membership 100.
Visitors booking advisable for weekends. **Societies** contact
in advance. **Green Fees** £7 per 9 holes; £9.50 per 18 holes.
Prof Garry Mercer **Course Designer** W G Cox
Facilities 🍺 🍴 🕂 🖺 ♂ **Location** 0.5m from town
centre off A463
....
Hotel ★★★ 64% The Himley Country Hotel, School Rd,
HIMLEY ☎ 0870 609 6112 73 en suite

SOLIHULL   Map 07 SP17

Olton Mirfield Rd B91 1JH
☎ 0121 704 1936 🖹 0121 711 2010
e-mail: mailbox@oltongolfclub.fsnet.co.uk
**Parkland course, over 100 years old, with prevailing
south-west wind.**
18 holes, 6265yds, Par 69, SSS 71, Course record 63.
Club membership 600.
Visitors contact in advance. No visitors at weekend.
Societies apply in writing. **Green Fees** not confirmed.
Prof Charles Haynes **Course Designer** JH Taylor

Continued

Facilities ⊗ 🎜 🖺 🍺 🍴 🕂 🕂 🖺 ♂ 🕂 🕂 ♂ 🕻
Conf Corporate Hospitality Days available
Location M42 junct 5, A41 for 1.5m
....
Hotel ★★★★ 70% Renaissance Solihull Hotel, 651
Warwick Rd, SOLIHULL ☎ 0121 711 3000
179 en suite

Robin Hood St Bernards Rd B92 7DJ
☎ 0121 706 0061 🖹 0121 700 7502
e-mail: robin.hood.golf.club@dial.pipex.com
**Pleasant parkland course with easy walking and open
to good views. Tree-lined fairways and varied holes,
culminating in two excellent finishing holes.**
18 holes, 6635yds, Par 72, SSS 72, Course record 68.
Club membership 650.
Visitors contact in advance. With member only at
weekends. **Societies** contact in advance. **Green Fees** not
confirmed. **Prof** Alan Harvey **Course Designer** HS Colt
Facilities ⊗ 🎜 🖺 🍺 🍴 🕂 🖺 ♂ **Conf** Corporate
Hospitality Days available **Location** 2m W off B4025
....
Hotel ★★★★ 70% Renaissance Solihull Hotel, 651
Warwick Rd, SOLIHULL ☎ 0121 711 3000 179 en suite

Shirley Stratford Rd, Monkpath, Shirley B90 4EW
☎ 0121 744 6001 🖹 0121 745 8220
e-mail: shirleygolfclub@btclick.com
Fairly flat parkland course.
18 holes, 6510yds, Par 72, SSS 71.
Club membership 600.
Visitors not bank holidays & with member only at
weekends. Handicap certificate is required. **Societies** only
on Thu, must contact in advance. **Green Fees** terms on
application. **Prof** S Bottrill **Facilities** ⊗ 🎜 🖺 🍺 🍴 🕂 🖺
♂ **Conf** fac available Corporate Hospitality Days
available **Location** M42 junct 4, 0.5m N on A34
....
Hotel ★★★ 68% Corus hotel Solihull, Stratford Rd,
Shirley, SOLIHULL ☎ 0870 609 6133 111 en suite

West Midlands Marsh House Farm Ln, Barston
B92 0LB
☎ 01675 444890 🖹 01675 444891
e-mail: westmidlandsgc@aol.com
**Course built to USGA specification with no temporary
greens or tees. The 18th hole is a par 3 to an island
green totally surrounded by water. A continuous buggy
path allows use of buggies all year round.**
18 holes, 6624yds, Par 72, SSS 72.
Club membership 750.
Societies phone for details **Green Fees** £17.50 (£24.95
weekends). **Cards** 💳 💳 💳 💳 💳 💳
Course Designer Nigel & Mark Harrhy, David Griffith
Facilities ⊗ 🎜 🖺 🍺 🍴 🕂 🖺 🕂 ♂ **Leisure** fishing.
Conf fac available Corporate Hospitality Days available
Location from NEC A45 towards Coventry for 0.5m, onto
A452 towards Leamington, club on right
....
Hotel ★★★ 69% Arden Hotel Leisure Club, Coventry Rd,
Bickenhill, SOLIHULL ☎ 01675 443221 216 en suite

Widney Manor Saintbury Dr, Widney Manor
B91 3SZ
☎ 0121 704 0704 🖹 0121 704 7999
**Parkland course, fairly easy walking. Of medium
length, it is ideal for beginners and improvers. Other
facilities include a driving range, all weather greens
built to USGA specification and buggy paths.**

Continued

West Midlands

Marriott Forest of Arden

Meriden　　　　　　　　　　　　　　　　　**Map 04 SP28**

This is one of the finest golf destinations in the UK, with a range of facilities to impress every golfer. The jewel in the crown is the Arden championship parkland course, set in 10,000 acres of the Packington Estate. Designed by Donald Steel, it presents one of the country's most spectacular challenges and has hosted a succession of international tournaments, including the British Masters and English Open. Beware the 18th hole, which is enough to stretch the nerves of any golfer. The shorter Aylesford Course offers a varied and enjoyable challenge, which golfers of all abilities will find rewarding. Golf events are a speciality, and there is a golf academy and extensive leisure facilities.

Marriott Hanbury Manor Golf & Country Club
Maxstoke Ln CV7 7HR
☎ **0870 400 7272　Fax 0870 400 7372**

Arden Course: 18 holes, 6707yds, Par 72, SSS 73, Course record 63.
Aylesford Course: 18 holes, 5801yds, Par 69, SSS 68.
Club membership 800.
Visitors phone to book in advance. **Societies** by arrangement.
Green Fees terms on application. **Cards** ▭ ▦ ▭ ▣ ▨ ▨
Prof Philip Hoye **Course Designer** Donald Steele
Facilities ⊗ ∭ ⛳ ▶ ♀ ⚐ ⚑ ❖ ⚐ ❦ ⚲ ⚹ ♟
Leisure hard tennis courts, heated indoor swimming pool, fishing, sauna, solarium, gymnasium, croquet lawn, health and beauty salon, steam room, Jacuzzi, aerobics studio.
Conf fac available Corporate Hospitality Days available
Location 1m SW on B4102

....

Hotels

★★★★ 73% Marriott Forest of Arden Hotel & Country Club, Maxstoke Ln, **MERIDEN**

☎ 0870 400 7272 214 en suite

★★★ 71% Manor Hotel, Main Rd, **MERIDEN**

☎ 01676 522735 Fax 01676 522186 110 en suite

★★★ 64% Strawberry Bank Hotel, Main Rd, **MERIDEN**

☎ 01676 522117 Fax 01676 523804 47 en suite

18 holes, 5654yards, Par 71, SSS 66.
Club membership 650.
Visitors may book up to seven days in advance. **Societies** phone for details **Green Fees** £10.95 weekday & weekend pm (£14.95 weekend am). **Cards** 🗖 🖿 💳 🖿 🖳 **Prof** Tim Atkinson **Course Designer** Nigel & Mark Harrhy **Facilities** ⊗ 🍴 🖺 💺 ♀ ♨ 🖚 ♂ ⏺ **Leisure** heated indoor swimming pool, sauna, solarium, gymnasium. **Conf** fac available Corporate Hospitality Days available **Location** M42 junct 4, signs to Monkspath & Widney Manor

Hotel ★★★★ 70% Renaissance Solihull Hotel, 651 Warwick Rd, SOLIHULL ☎ 0121 711 3000 179 en suite

STOURBRIDGE   Map 07 SO88

Hagley Golf & Country Club Wassell Grove Ln, Hagley DY9 9JW
☎ 01562 883701 🖷 01562 887518
e-mail: manager@hagleygcc.freeserve.co.uk
Undulating parkland course set beneath the Clent Hills; there are superb views. Testing 15th, par 5, 559 yards, named Monster under Clent Hills.
18 holes, 6353yds, Par 72, SSS 72, Course record 66.
Club membership 700.
Visitors welcome weekdays but restricted Wed (Ladies Day) & with member only at weekends. **Societies** Mon-Fri only, must apply in writing. **Green Fees** £29 per 18 holes; £34 per day (Mon-Fri). **Cards** 🗖 🖿 **Prof** Iain Clark **Course Designer** Garratt & Co **Facilities** ⊗ 🍴 🖺 💺 ♀ 🖙 🖚 ♂ ⏺ **Leisure** squash. **Conf** fac available Corporate Hospitality Days available **Location** 1m E of Hagley off A456

Hotel 🛏 Premier Travel Inn Hagley, Birmingham Rd, HAGLEY ☎ 08701 977123 40 en suite

Stourbridge Worcester Ln, Pedmore DY8 2RB
☎ 01384 395566 🖷 01384 444660
e-mail: secretary@stourbridge-golf-club.co.uk
Parkland course.
18 holes, 6231yds, Par 70, SSS 69, Course record 67.
Club membership 769.
Visitors contact secretary, no casual visitors weekends. Ladies Day Wed. **Societies** apply in writing or by e-mail. **Green Fees** £30 per 18 holes; £37.50 per day. **Prof** M Male **Facilities** ⊗ 🍴 🖺 💺 ♀ 🖙 🖚 ⏺ **Conf** Corporate Hospitality Days available **Location** 2m S of town centre

Hotel 🛏 Premier Travel Inn Hagley, Birmingham Rd, HAGLEY ☎ 08701 977123 40 en suite

SUTTON COLDFIELD   Map 07 SP19

Boldmere Monmouth Dr B73 6JL
☎ 0121 354 3379 🖷 0121 355 4534
Established municipal course with 10 par 3s and a lake coming into play on the 16th and 18th holes.
18 holes, 4493yds, Par 63, SSS 62, Course record 57.
Club membership 300.
Visitors contact in advance. **Societies** midweek only, apply in writing. **Green Fees** terms on application. **Cards** 🗖 🖿 🖿 🖿 **Prof** Trevor Short **Facilities** ⊗ 🖺 💺 ♀ 🖚 🖙 ⏺ **Location** next to Sutton Park

Hotel ★★★★ 68% Moor Hall Hotel, Moor Hall Dr, Four Oaks, SUTTON COLDFIELD ☎ 0121 308 3751 82 en suite

Little Aston Streetly B74 3AN
☎ 0121 353 2942 🖷 0121 580 8387
e-mail: manager@littleastongolf.co.uk
This parkland course is set in the rolling countryside of the former Little Aston Hall and there is a wide variety of mature trees. There are three par 3 holes and three par 5 holes and although the fairways are not unduly narrow there are rewards for accuracy - especially from the tee. The course features two lakes. At the par 5 12th the lake cuts into the green and at the par 4 17th the lake is also adjacent to the green.
18 holes, 6670yds, Par 72, SSS 73, Course record 63.
Club membership 350.
Visitors contact in advance & not Sat. **Societies** apply in writing. **Green Fees** £63 per round/£78 per day. **Cards** 🗖 🖿 🖿 🖿 **Prof** Brian Rimmer **Course Designer** H Vardon **Facilities** ⊗ 🍴 🖺 💺 ♀ 🖙 🖚 ♂ ⏺ **Location** 3.5m NW of Sutton Coldfield off A454

Hotel ★★★★ 68% Moor Hall Hotel, Moor Hall Dr, Four Oaks, SUTTON COLDFIELD ☎ 0121 308 3751 82 en suite

Moor Hall Moor Hall Dr B75 6LN
☎ 0121 308 6130 🖷 0121 308 9560
e-mail: manager@moorhallgolfclub.fsnet.co.uk
Outstanding parkland course with mature trees lining the fairways. The 14th hole is notable and is part of a challenging finish to the round.
18 holes, 6293yds, Par 70, SSS 70, Course record 64.
Club membership 600.
Visitors contact in advance. With member only weekends & bank holidays.Ladies day Thu am. **Societies** apply in writing or phone in advance. **Green Fees** £50 per day, £38 per round. **Cards** 🗖 🖿 🖿 🖿 ⏺ **Prof** Cameron Clark **Course Designer** Hawtree & Taylor **Facilities** ⊗ 🍴 🖺 💺 ♀ 🖙 🖚 ⏺ **Conf** Corporate Hospitality Days available **Location** 2.5m N of town centre off A453

Hotel ★★★★ 68% Moor Hall Hotel, Moor Hall Dr, Four Oaks, SUTTON COLDFIELD ☎ 0121 308 3751 82 en suite

Pype Hayes Eachel Hurst Rd, Walmley B76 1EP
☎ 0121 351 1014 🖷 0121 313 0206
18 holes, 5927yds, Par 71, SSS 69.
Course Designer Bobby Jones **Location** 2.5m S off B4148
Phone for further details

Hotel ★★★★ 68% Moor Hall Hotel, Moor Hall Dr, Four Oaks, SUTTON COLDFIELD ☎ 0121 308 3751 82 en suite

Sutton Coldfield 110 Thornhill Rd, Streetly B74 3EF
☎ 0121 580 7878 🖷 0121 353 5503
e-mail: admin@suttoncoldfieldgc.com
A fine natural, all-weather, heathland course, with tight fairways, gorse, heather and trees. A good challenge for all standards of golfer.
18 holes, 6541yds, Par 72, SSS 71, Course record 65.
Club membership 600.
Visitors contact professional in advance. Restricted at weekends & bank holidays. **Societies** apply in writing. **Green Fees** £40 per day; £30 per round (£40 per round weeekends). **Prof** Jerry Hayes **Course Designer** Dr A MacKenzie **Facilities** ⊗ 🍴 🖺 💺 ♀ 🖙 🖚 ⏺ **Conf** fac available Corporate Hospitality Days available **Location** 2m W of town on B4138

Continue

lotel ★★★★ 68% Moor Hall Hotel, Moor Hall Dr, Four
)aks, SUTTON COLDFIELD ☎ 0121 308 3751 82 en suite

Walmley Brooks Rd, Wylde Green B72 1HR
☎ 0121 373 0029 & 377 7272 🖹 0121 377 7272
-mail: walmleygolfclub@aol.com
**leasant parkland course with many trees. The hazards
re not difficult.**
*8 holes, 6585yds, Par 72, SSS 72, Course record 67.
:lub membership 700.*
Visitors contact in advance. Weekends may only play as
;uest of member. **Societies** contact in advance. **Green Fees**
iot confirmed. **Cards** ▭ ▬ ▬ **Prof** CJ Wicketts
'acilities ⊗ ╟ ᚼ ❦ ♀ ♂ 🖻 ⚏ ♂ **Conf** Corporate
lospitality Days available **Location** 2m S off A5127

lotel ★★★★ 68% Moor Hall Hotel, Moor Hall Dr, Four
)aks, SUTTON COLDFIELD ☎ 0121 308 3751
;2 en suite

Bloxwich Stafford Rd, Bloxwich WS3 3PQ
☎ 01922 476593 ext 20 🖹 01922 493449
-mail: bloxwich.golf-club@virgin.net
**Jndulating parkland course with natural hazards and
ubject to strong north wind.**
*8 holes, 6257yds, Par 71, SSS 71, Course record 68.
:lub membership 680.*
Visitors not at weekends unless guest of member **Societies**
contact in advance. **Green Fees** terms on application.
Prof Richard J Dance **Facilities** ⊗ ╟ ᚼ ❦ ♀ ♂ 🖻 ♂
:onf fac available Corporate Hospitality Days available
.ocation 3m N of town centre on A34

Jotel ★★★ 76% The Fairlawns at Aldridge, 178 Little
\ston Rd, Aldridge, WALSALL ☎ 01922 455122
i0 en suite

Calderfields Aldridge Rd WS4 2JS
☎ 01922 632243 🖹 01922 640540
:-mail: calderfields@bigfoot.com
**icenic parkland course in peaceful setting, enhanced by
i lake.**
*8 holes, 6509yds, Par 73, SSS 71.
:lub membership 480.*
Visitors no restrictions. **Societies** phone 01922 632243 in
dvance. **Green Fees** £15 per 18 holes (£18 weekends).
:ards ▭ ▬ ▬ ▬ ▣ **Prof** Simon Edwin **Course
Jesigner** Roy Winter **Facilities** ⊗ ╟ ᚼ ❦ ♀ ♂ 🖻 ❧
ᚺ ♂ ¿ **Leisure** fishing. **Conf** Corporate Hospitality Days
.vailable **Location** on A454

Jotel ★★★ 76% The Fairlawns at Aldridge, 178 Little
\ston Rd, Aldridge, WALSALL ☎ 01922 455122
i0 en suite

Walsall The Broadway WS1 3EY
☎ 01922 613512 🖹 01922 616460
8 holes, 6300yds, Par 70, SSS 70, Course record 65.
Course Designer Dr A MacKenzie **Location** 1m S of
own centre off A34
hone for further details

Jotel ★★★ 66% Quality Hotel Birmingham North,
Jirmingham Rd, WALSALL ☎ 01922 633609
)6 en suite

Dartmouth Vale St B71 4DW
☎ 0121 588 5746 & 588 2131
**Very tight meadowland course with undulating but
easy walking. The 617yd par 5 1st hole is something of a
challenge.**
*9 holes, 6036yds, Par 71, SSS 71, Course record 66.
Club membership 250.*
Visitors with member only at weekends; not bank holidays
or medal weekends until after 2pm contact pro first.
Societies must apply in writing or phone. **Green Fees** £25
per day/18 holes. **Prof** G Kilmaster **Facilities** ⊗ ╟ ᚼ ❦
♀ ᚺ 🖻 **Location** E of town centre off A4041

Hotel ★★★ 68% Birmingham/West Bromwich Moat
House, Birmingham Rd, WEST BROMWICH
☎ 0121 609 9988 168 en suite

Sandwell Park Birmingham Rd B71 4JJ
☎ 0121 553 4637 🖹 0121 525 1651
e-mail: secretary@sandwellparkgolfclub.co.uk
**A picturesque course wandering over wooded
heathland and utilising natural features. Each hole is
entirely separate, shielded from the others by either
natural banks or lines of trees. A course that demands
careful placing of shots that have been given a great
deal of thought. Natural undulating fairways create
difficult and testing approach shots to the greens.**

*18 holes, 6204yds, Par 71, SSS 71, Course record 65.
Club membership 550.*
Visitors contact in advance; not weekends. **Societies**
contact in advance. **Green Fees** £42 per 27/36 holes; £36
per 18 holes. **Prof** Nigel Wylie **Course Designer** HS Colt
Facilities ⊗ ╟ ᚼ ❦ ♀ ♂ 🖻 ♂ **Leisure** practice
chipping area. **Conf** fac available Corporate Hospitality
Days available **Location** M5 junct 1, 200yds on A41

Hotel ★★★ 63% The Plough & Harrow Hotel, 135
Hagley Rd, EDGBASTON ☎ 0870 609 6118
44 en suite

Oxley Park Stafford Rd, Bushbury WV10 6DE
☎ 01902 773989 🖹 01902 773981
e-mail: secretary@oxleyparkgolfclub.co.uk
**Rolling parkland course with trees, bunkers and water
hazards.**
*18 holes, 6226yds, Par 71, SSS 71, Course record 66.
Club membership 550.*
Visitors contact in advance. **Societies** contact in advance.
Green Fees £36 per day, £31 per 18 holes. **Cards** ▭ ▬
▬ ▦ ▣ **Prof** Les Burlison **Course Designer** HS Colt

Continued

Facilities ⊗ ⵊ by arrangement 🖺 💻 🛇 🍽 🚼 🏌
Leisure snooker. **Location** M54 junct 2, 2m S

....

Hotel ★★ 68% Ely House Hotel, 53 Tettenhall Rd,
WOLVERHAMPTON ☎ 01902 311311 18 en suite

Penn Penn Common, Penn WV4 5JN
☎ 01902 341142 🖹 01902 620504
e-mail: penn-golf.freeserve.co.uk
Heathland course just outside the town.
18 holes, 6487yds, Par 70, SSS 72, Course record 68.
Club membership 650.
Visitors must play with member at weekends. **Societies**
contact in advance. **Green Fees** not confirmed.
Prof B Burlison **Facilities** ⊗ ⵊ 🖺 💻 🛇 🍽 🏌
Location SW of town centre off A449

....

Hotel ★★★ 66% Quality Hotel Wolverhampton, Penn Rd,
WOLVERHAMPTON ☎ 01902 429216 66 en suite
26 annexe en suite

South Staffordshire Danescourt Rd, Tettenhall
WV6 9BQ
☎ 01902 751065 🖹 01902 741753
18 holes, 6513yds, Par 71, SSS 71, Course record 67.
Course Designer Harry Vardon **Location** 3m NW off A41
Phone for further details

....

Hotel ★★ 68% Ely House Hotel, 53 Tettenhall Rd,
WOLVERHAMPTON ☎ 01902 311311 18 en suite

Three Hammers Short Course Old Stafford Rd,
Coven WV10 7PP
☎ 01902 790940
18 holes, 1438yds, Par 54, SSS 54, Course record 43.
Course Designer Henry Cotton **Location** M54 junct 2, on
A449 N
Phone for further details

....

Hotel ★★★ 64% The Roman Way Hotel, Watling St,
Hatherton, CANNOCK ☎ 0870 609 6125 56 en suite

Wergs Keepers Ln, Tettenhall WV6 8UA
☎ 01902 742225 🖹 01902 744748
e-mail: wergs.golfclub@btinternet.com
**Gently undulating parkland course with streams and
ditches. A mix of evergreen and deciduous trees and
large greens.**
18 holes, 6250yds, Par 72, SSS 70.
Club membership 150.
Visitors are advised to contact in advance. **Societies**
contact in advance. **Green Fees** £15 per day/round (£20
weekends & bank holidays). **Cards** 🖃 🖃 🖃 🖃 🖃
Prof Steve Weir **Course Designer** CW Moseley
Facilities ⊗ ⵊ by arrangement 🖺 💻 🛇 🍽 🚼 🏌
Location 3m W of Wolverhampton off A41

....

Hotel ★★ 68% Ely House Hotel, 53 Tettenhall Rd,
WOLVERHAMPTON ☎ 01902 311311 18 en suite

WIGHT, ISLE OF

COWES   Map 04 SZ49

Cowes Crossfield Av PO31 8HN
☎ 01983 292303 (secretary) 🖹 01983 292303
**Fairly level, tight parkland course with difficult par 3s
and Solent views.**

9 holes, 5934yds, Par 70, SSS 68, Course record 66.
Club membership 300.
Visitors restricted Thu & Sun am. **Societies** Mon-Wed,
must contact in advance. **Green Fees** £15 (£18 weekends).
Course Designer Hamilton-Stutt **Facilities** ⊗ ⵊ 🖺 💻 🛇
🛆 🚼 🏌 **Location** NW of town centre next to Cowes High
School

....

Hotel ★★★ 68% New Holmwood Hotel, Queens Rd,
Egypt Point, COWES ☎ 01983 292508 26 en suite

EAST COWES   Map 04 SZ59

Osborne Osborne House Estate PO32 6JX
☎ 01983 295421
**Undulating parkland course in the grounds of Osborne
House. Quiet and peaceful situation.**
9 holes, 6398yds, Par 70, SSS 70, Course record 69.
Club membership 450.
Visitors not Tue am, weekends am & bank holidays before
11am. **Societies** phone initially. **Green Fees** not confirmed.
Facilities ⊗ ⵊ 🖺 💻 🛇 🛆 🍽 🚼 🏌 **Location** E of town
centre off A3021, in Osborne House Estate

....

Hotel ★★★ 68% New Holmwood Hotel, Queens Rd,
Egypt Point, COWES ☎ 01983 292508 26 en suite

FRESHWATER   Map 04 SZ38

Freshwater Bay Afton Down PO40 9TZ
☎ 01983 752955 🖹 01983 752955
e-mail: tr.fbgc@btopenworld.com
18 holes, 5725yds, Par 69, SSS 68.
Course Designer JH Taylor **Location** 0.5m E of village
off A3055
Phone for further details

....

Hotel ★★★ 68% Sentry Mead Hotel, Madeira Rd,
TOTLAND BAY ☎ 01983 753212 14 en suite

NEWPORT   Map 04 SZ58

Newport St George's Down, Shide PO30 3BA
☎ 01983 525076
e-mail: mail@newportgolfclub.co.uk
**Challenging nine-hole course with water hazards, dog
legs and fine views.**
9 holes, 5579yds, Par 68, SSS 68.
Club membership 350.
Visitors not Wed noon-3.30pm or before 3pm Sat & noon
Sun. **Societies** contact in advance. **Green Fees** £18 per 18
holes (£22 weekends). **Course Designer** Guy Hunt
Facilities ⊗ ⵊ 🖺 💻 🛇 🛆 🍽 🏌 🏌 **Location** 1.5m S off
A3020, 200yds past Newport Football Club on left

....

Hotel ★★★ 68% New Holmwood Hotel, Queens Rd,
Egypt Point, COWES ☎ 01983 292508 26 en suite

RYDE   Map 04 SZ59

Ryde Binstead Rd PO33 3NF
☎ 01983 614809 🖹 01983 567418
e-mail: secretary@rydegolfclub.freeserve.co.uk
**Downland course with wide views over the Solent. Very
tight with out of bound areas on most holes and five
dog-legs.**
9 holes, 5772yds, Par 70, SSS 69.
Club membership 575.
Visitors not Wed before 2.15pm, weekdays before
10.15am & weekends before 11am **Societies** contact in
writing. **Green Fees** not confirmed. **Course Designer**

Continued   *Continued*

Hamilton-Stutt **Facilities** ⊗ ⫢ by arrangement ㋡ ⬤ ♀ ⚐
🞾 ♂ **Location** 1m W from town centre on A3054

Hotel ★★★ 65% Yelf's Hotel, Union St, RYDE
🕿 01983 564062 30 en suite

SANDOWN   Map 04 SZ58

Shanklin & Sandown The Fairway, Lake
PO36 9PR
🕿 01983 403217 (office) & 404424 (pro)
📠 01983 403007 (office)/404424 (pro)
An 18-hole county championship course, recognised for
its natural heathland beauty, spectacular views and
challenging qualities. The course demands respect, with
accurate driving and careful club selection the order of
the day.
18 holes, 6062yds, Par 70, SSS 69, Course record 63.
Club membership 700.
Visitors contact in advance & have handicap certificate;
not am Sat or before 9.30am Sun. **Societies** phone 01983
404424 **Green Fees** £29.50 (weekends & bank holidays
£35). **Cards** 🖃 🖃 🖃 🖃 🖃 **Prof** Peter Hammond
Course Designer Braid **Facilities** ⊗ ⫢ ㋡ ⬤ ♀ ⚐ 🖿
🞾 ♂ **Location** from Sandown towards Shanklin past
Heights Leisure Centre, 200yds right into Fairway for 1m

Hotel ★★ 66% Cygnet Hotel, 58 Carter St, SANDOWN
🕿 01983 402930 46 rms (45 en suite)

VENTNOR   Map 04 SZ57

Ventnor Steephill Down Rd PO38 1BP
🕿 01983 853326 & 853388 📠 01983 853326
e-mail: ventnorgolf@lineone.net
Downland course subject to wind. Fine seascapes.
12 holes, 5767yds, Par 70, SSS 68, Course record 64.
Club membership 297.
Visitors not Sun am. **Societies** phone initially. **Green Fees**
£17 per day. **Cards** 🖃 🖃 🖃 **Facilities** ㋡ ⬤ ♀ ⚐ 🞾 ♂
Location 1m NW off B3327, turn at chip shop

Hotel ★★★★ 67% The Royal Hotel, Belgrave Rd,
VENTNOR 🕿 01983 852186 55 en suite

WILTSHIRE

BISHOPS CANNINGS   Map 04 SU06

North Wilts SN10 2LP
🕿 01380 860627 📠 01380 860877
e-mail: secretary@northwiltsgolf.com
Established in 1890 and one of the oldest courses in
Wiltshire, North Wilts is situated high on the
downlands of Wiltshire, with spectacular views over the
surrounding countryside. The chalk base allows free
draining and the course provides a challenge to golfers
of all abilities.
18 holes, 6414yds, Par 71, SSS 71, Course record 65.
Club membership 800.
Visitors a handicap certificate is required at weekends.
Societies book in advance. **Green Fees** £30 per day (£35
per round weekends). **Cards** 🖃 🖃 🖃 🖃 **Prof** Graham
Laing **Course Designer** HS Colt **Facilities** ⊗ ⫢ ㋡ ⬤ ♀
㋡ 🖿 ⚐ 🞾 ⚒ ♂ **Conf** Corporate Hospitality Days
available **Location** 2m NW of Devizes between A4 &
A361

Hotel ★★★ 64% Bear Hotel, Market Place, DEVIZES
🕿 01380 722444 24 en suite

BRADFORD-ON-AVON   Map 03 ST86

Cumberwell Park BA15 2PQ
🕿 01225 863322 📠 01225 868160
e-mail: enquiries@cumberwellpark.com
Set within tranquil woodland, parkland, lakes and
rolling countryside, this 27-hole course comprises three
linked sets of nine holes. A challenge for all levels of
golfer.

Parkland: 9 holes, 6405yds, Par 71, SSS 71,
Course record 63.
Woodland: 9 holes, 6356yds, Par 72, SSS 70.
Lakeland: 9 holes, 6509, Par 71, SSS 71.
Club membership 1300.
Visitors contact in advance. **Societies** phone for details.
Green Fees £50 per day, £27 per 18 holes, £17 per 9 holes
(£60/£33/£23 weekends & bank holidays). **Cards** 🖃 🖃
🖃 🖃 🖃 **Prof** John Jacobs **Course Designer** Adrian Stiff
Facilities ⊗ ⫢ ㋡ ⬤ ♀ ⚐ 🖿 ⚒ ♂ ♂ **Conf** fac
available Corporate Hospitality Days available
Location 1.5m N on A363

Hotel ★★★ ♨ 76% Woolley Grange, Woolley Green,
BRADFORD-ON-AVON 🕿 01225 864705 14 en suite
12 annexe en suite

CALNE   Map 03 ST97

Bowood Golf & Country Club Derry Hill
SN11 9PQ
🕿 01249 822228 📠 01249 822218
e-mail: golfclub@bowood.org
A championship course set in the beautiful
surroundings of Capability Brown's park.

18 holes, 6890yds, Par 72, SSS 73, Course record 63.
Club membership 500.
Visitors welcome except am on Sat & Sun. Booking
essential. **Societies** booking by phone. **Green Fees** £41
(£43 weekends). **Cards** 🖃 🖃 🖃 🖃 🖃 🖃 **Prof**
Max Taylor **Course Designer** Dave Thomas
Facilities ⊗ ⫢ ㋡ ⬤ ♀ ⚐ 🖿 ⚒ ♂ ⚒ ♂ ♂

Continued

Leisure Bowood House and Gardens. **Conf** fac available
Corporate Hospitality Days available
Location 2.5m W of Calne off A4

Hotel ★★★ 68% Lansdowne Strand Hotel, The Strand,
CALNE ☎ 01249 812488 21 en suite 5 annexe en suite

CASTLE COMBE   Map 03 ST87

Manor House Hotel SN14 7JW
☎ 01249 782206 📠 01249 782992
e-mail: enquiries@manorhousegolfclub.com
**Set in a wonderful location within the wooded estate of
the 14th-century Manor House, this course includes five
par 5s and some spectacular par 3s. A special feature is
the River Bybrook, which meanders its way through
many holes, the most memorable being the 17th with a
breathtaking drop to the green.**
18 holes, 6286yds, Par 72, SSS 71, Course record 67.
Club membership 450.
Visitors must have a handicap certificate & must contact in
advance. May only play pm on Wed & weekends.
Societies contact in advance. **Green Fees** summer rates
£70 (£85 Fri-Sun); spring/autumn £60/£75; winter £40 all
week. **Cards** 💳 💳 💳 💳 💳 💳 **Prof** Peter Green **Course
Designer** Peter Alliss, Clive Clark **Facilities** ⊗ ⌱ ⅃ ▣ ♀
⚲ 🏠 ⛳ 🏊 ⚓ ⚒ 🏇 🏌 **Leisure** hard tennis courts, heated
outdoor swimming pool, fishing, sauna, snooker, croquet.
Conf fac available Corporate Hospitality Days available
Location 5m NW of Chippenham on B4039

Hotel ★★★★ 👥 Manor House Hotel and Golf Club,
CASTLE COMBE ☎ 01249 782206 22 en suite
26 annexe en suite

CHIPPENHAM   Map 03 ST97

Chippenham Malmesbury Rd SN15 5LT
☎ 01249 652040 📠 01249 446681
e-mail: chippenhamgc@onetel.com
**Easy walking on downland course. Testing holes at 1st
and 15th.**
18 holes, 5570yds, Par 69, SSS 67, Course record 62.
Club membership 650.
Visitors contact in advance & play from tees of the day
Societies contact in writing, by phone or via e-mail. **Green
Fees** £30 per day, £22 per round (£27 per round weekends
& bank holidays). **Prof** Bill Creamer **Facilities** ⊗ ⌱ ⅃ ▣
♀ ⚲ 🏠 ⛳ 🏌 **Conf** Corporate Hospitality Days available
Location 1m N of Chippenham by A350

Hotel ★★★★ 👥 Manor House Hotel and Golf Club,
CASTLE COMBE ☎ 01249 782206 22 en suite
26 annexe en suite

CRICKLADE   Map 04 SU09

Cricklade Hotel Common Hill SN6 6HA
☎ 01793 750751 📠 01793 751767
e-mail: reception@crickladehotel.co.uk
**A challenging nine-hole course with undulating greens
and beautiful views. Par 3 6th (128yds) signature hole
from an elevated tee to a green protected by a deep pot
bunker.**
9 holes, 1830yds, Par 62, SSS 58, Course record 59.
Club membership 130.
Visitors not weekends or bank holidays unless
accompanied by a member. Must contact in advance.
Societies apply in writing. **Green Fees** £25 per day; £16

Cricklade Hotel

for 18 holes. **Cards** 💳 💳 💳 💳 💳 💳 💳 **Prof** Ian Bolt
Course Designer Ian Bolt, Colin Smith **Facilities** ⊗ ⌱ ⅃
▣ ♀ ⚲ 🏇 🏌 ⛳ **Leisure** hard tennis courts, heated
indoor swimming pool, solarium, gymnasium, snooker,
pool, Jacuzzi, tennis, steam room. **Conf** fac available
Location on B4040 from Cricklade towards Malmesbury

Hotel ★★★ 72% Cricklade Hotel, Common Hill,
CRICKLADE ☎ 01793 750751 25 en suite 21 annexe
en suite

ERLESTOKE   Map 03 ST95

Erlestoke Sands SN10 5UB
☎ 01380 831069 📠 01380 831284
e-mail: info@erlestokesands.co.uk
**The course is set on the lower slopes of Salisbury Plain
with distant views to the Cotswolds and the
Marlborough Downs. The 7th plunges from an elevated
three-tiered tee, high in the woods, to a large green with
a spectacular backdrop of a meandering river and hills.
The course was built to suit every standard of golfer
from the novice to the very low handicapper and its two
tiers offer lakes and rolling downland.**
18 holes, 6406yds, Par 73, SSS 71, Course record 66.
Club membership 720.
Visitors phone for tee booking in advance 01380 830300.
Dress rules apply. **Societies** book in advance. **Green Fees**
£30 per 36 holes, £25 per 18 holes (£40/£30 weekends &
bank holidays). **Cards** 💳 💳 💳 **Prof** Michael Waters
Course Designer Adrian Stiff **Facilities** ⊗ ⌱ ⅃ ▣ ♀ ⚲
🏠 ⛳ ⚒ 🏌 🏇 **Location** on B3098 Devizes-Westbury road

Hotel ★★★ 64% Bear Hotel, Market Place, DEVIZES
☎ 01380 722444 24 en suite

GREAT DURNFORD   Map 04 SU13

High Post SP4 6AT
☎ 01722 782356 📠 01722 782674
e-mail: highpostgolfclub@lineone.net
**An interesting downland course on Wiltshire chalk with
good turf and splendid views over the southern area of
Salisbury Plain. The opening three holes are often
played with the prevailing wind to the round, however,
turning back into the wind on the 2nd and requiring
good concentration. The closing three holes are as
tough a finish as you will find anywhere.**
18 holes, 6305yds, Par 70, SSS 70, Course record 64.
Club membership 625.
Visitors a handicap certificate is required at weekends &
bank holidays. Phone professional in advance 01722
782219. **Societies** apply by phone to manager.

Continued

Continued

High Post Golf Club

reen Fees £40 per day; £32 per round (£50/£42 eekends). **Prof** Tony Isaacs **Course Designer** Hawtree & rs **Facilities** ⊗ ⅲ ⅙ ⬤ ♀ ⚖ 🏠 🚜 ⚒ ¶ onf fac available

ocation on A345 between Sailsbury & Amesbury

otel ★★★ 60% The Rose & Crown Hotel, Harnham Rd, arnham, SALISBURY ☎ 0870 6096163 28 en suite

IGHWORTH   Map 04 SU29

ighworth Community Golf Centre Swindon d SN6 7SJ
☎ 01793 766014 ▤ 01793 766014
holes, 3120yds, Par 35, SSS 35, Course record 29.
ourse Designer T Watt, B Sandry, D Lang
ocation off A361 Swindon-Lechlade road
hone for further details

otel ★★★ 70% Sudbury House Hotel & Conference entre, London St, FARINGDON ☎ 01367 241272) en suite

rag Barn Golf & Country Club Shrivenham d SN6 7QQ
☎ 01793 861327 ▤ 01793 861325
mail: info@wragbarn.com
fast maturing parkland course in an Area of utstanding Natural Beauty with views to the ambourne Hills and Vale of the White Horse. 3 holes, 6633yds, Par 72, SSS 72, Course record 65. lub membership 600.
isitors no restrictions but not am at weekends. **Societies** ntact in advance. **Green Fees** terms on application.
ards ▦ ▦ ▦ ▧ ▨ **Prof** Barry Loughrey **Course** esigner Hawtree **Facilities** ⊗ ⅙ ⬤ ♀ ⚖ 🏠 ¶ ¶ 🚜
¶ **Conf** fac available Corporate Hospitality Days ailable **Location** on B4000 from Highworth, signed

otel ★★★ 66% Stanton House Hotel, The Avenue, anton Fitzwarren, SWINDON ☎ 01793 861777 en suite

INGSDOWN   Map 03 ST86

ingsdown SN13 8BS
☎ 01225 743472 ▤ 01225 743472
airly flat, open downland course with very sparse tree ver but surrounding wood.
holes, 6445yds, Par 72, SSS 71, Course record 64. lub membership 650.
isitors weekends only with a member. Handicap rtificate required weekdays. **Societies** apply by letter.

Green Fees not confirmed. **Prof** Andrew Butler **Facilities** ⊗ ⅲ ⅙ ⬤ ♀ ⚖ 🏠 ¶ ⚒ ¶ **Location** W of village between Corsham & Bath

Hotel ★★★★ ♠♠ Lucknam Park, COLERNE ☎ 01225 742777 23 en suite 18 annexe en suite

LANDFORD   Map 04 SU21

Hamptworth Golf & Country Club
Hamptworth Rd, Hamptworth SP5 2DU
☎ 01794 390155 ▤ 01794 390022
e-mail: info@hamptworthgolf.co.uk
Hamptworth enjoys ancient woodland and an abundance of wildlife in a beautiful setting on the edge of the New Forest. The 14th is one of its most challenging holes with a narrow fairway guarded by established forest oaks. The 2nd is a dog-leg of 543yds and plays differently all year.

18 holes, 6516yds, Par 72, SSS 71, Course record 68. Club membership 600.
Visitors phone to check availability. **Societies** write or phone in advance. **Green Fees** Apr-Sep £30 (£40 weekends); Oct-Mar £20-£25 (£30 weekends). **Cards** ▦ ▦ ▦ ▧ ▨ **Prof** M White **Course Designer** Philip Sanders, Brian Pierson **Facilities** ⊗ ⅲ ⅙ ⬤ ♀ ⚖ 🏠 ¶ ¶ 🚜 ⚒ ¶ **Leisure** gymnasium, croquet lawns. **Conf** fac available Corporate Hospitality Days available **Location** 1.5m W of Landford off B3079

Hotel ★★★ 69% Bartley Lodge, Lyndhurst Rd, CADNAM ☎ 023 8081 2248 31 en suite

MARLBOROUGH   Map 04 SU16

Marlborough The Common SN8 1DU
☎ 01672 512147 ▤ 01672 513164
e-mail: contactus@marlboroughgolfclub.co.uk
Undulating downland course with extensive views over the Og valley and the Marlborough Downs.
18 holes, 6514yds, Par 72, SSS 71, Course record 61. Club membership 900.
Visitors restricted at certain times. Must have a handicap certificate at weekends. Must contact in advance. **Societies** contact in advance. **Green Fees** £38 per day; £28 per round (£50/£35 weekends). **Cards** ▦ ▦ ▦ ▧ ▨ **Prof** S Amor **Facilities** ⊗ ⅲ ⅙ ⬤ ♀ ⚖ 🏠 ¶ 🚜 ⚒ **Conf** fac available Corporate Hospitality Days available **Location** N of town centre on A346

Hotel ★★★ 64% The Castle & Ball, High St, MARLBOROUGH ☎ 01672 515201 34 en suite

Continued

OGBOURNE ST GEORGE
Map 04 SU27

Ogbourne Downs SN8 1TB
☎ 01672 841327 📠 01672 841101

Downland turf and magnificent greens. Wind and slopes make this one of the most challenging courses in Wiltshire. Extensive views.

18 holes, 6363yds, Par 71, SSS 70, Course record 65.
Club membership 800.

Visitors phone in advance. Handicap certificate required. **Societies** apply for booking form in advance. **Green Fees** terms on application. **Cards** 💳 💳 💳 💳 💳 **Prof** Andrew Kirk **Course Designer** JH Taylor **Facilities** ⊗ ⓑ 🍺 ♀ ⚒ 🏠 🚣 ✿ ⚑ **Location** N of village on A346

Hotel ★★★ 64% The Castle & Ball, High St, MARLBOROUGH ☎ 01672 515201 34 en suite

SALISBURY
Map 04 SU12

Salisbury & South Wilts Netherhampton SP2 8PR
☎ 01722 742645 📠 01722 742676
e-mail: mail@salisburygolf.co.uk

Gently undulating and well-drained parkland courses in country setting with panoramic views of the cathedral and surrounding countryside. Never easy with six excellent opening holes and four equally testing closing holes.

Main Course: 18 holes, 6485yds, Par 71, SSS 71, Course record 61.
Bibury Course: 9 holes, 2837yds, Par 34.
Club membership 1150.

Visitors advisable to phone in advance. **Societies** phone, write or e-mail for information park. **Green Fees** Main £32 per day, £26 per 18 holes; Bibury £12 per 18 holes, £10 per 9 holes. **Prof** Geraldine Teschner **Course Designer** JH Taylor, S Gidman **Facilities** ⊗ ⓜ ⓑ 🍺 ♀ ⚒ 🏠 ⚑ ✿ 🚣 ✿ ⚑ **Conf** fac available Corporate Hospitality Days available **Location** 2m SW of Salisbury on A3094

Hotel ★★★ 60% The Rose & Crown Hotel, Harnham Rd, Harnham, SALISBURY ☎ 0870 6096163 28 en suite

SWINDON
Map 04 SU18

Broome Manor Golf Complex Pipers Way
SN3 1RG
☎ 01793 532403 (bookings) 495761 (enquiries)
📠 01793 433255

Two courses and a 34-bay floodlit driving range. Parkland with water hazards, open fairways and short cut rough. Walking is easy on gentle slopes.

18 holes, 5989yds, Par 71, SSS 70, Course record 62.
9 holes, Par 33.
Club membership 800.

Visitors booking necessary six days in advance for 18-hole course. **Societies** booking required. **Green Fees** 18 holes £19.10; 9 holes £11.60. **Cards** 💳 💳 💳 💳 💳 **Prof** Barry Sandry **Course Designer** Hawtree **Facilities** ⊗ ⓜ ⓑ 🍺 ♀ ⚒ 🏠 ⚑ ✿ **Leisure** gymnasium. **Conf** fac available Corporate Hospitality Days available **Location** 1.75m SE of town centre off B4006

Hotel ★★★★ 66% Swindon Marriott Hotel, Pipers Way, SWINDON ☎ 0870 400 7281 156 en suite

---

Prices may change during the currency of the Guide, please check when booking.

TIDWORTH
Map 04 SU24

Tidworth Garrison Bulford Rd SP9 7AF
☎ 01980 842301 📠 01980 842301
e-mail: tidworth@garrison-golfclub.fsnet.co.uk

A breezy, dry downland course with lovely turf, fine trees and views over Salisbury Plain and the surrounding area. The 4th and 12th holes are notable. The 565yd 14th, going down towards the clubhouse, gives the big hitter a chance to let fly.

18 holes, 6320yds, Par 70, SSS 70, Course record 63.
Club membership 800.

Visitors contact in advance, weekend & bank holiday bookings may not be made until Thu prior, handicap certificate required. **Societies** Tue & Thu, bookings required 12-18 months in advance. **Green Fees** £34 per round/day. **Prof** Terry Gosden **Course Designer** Donald Steel **Facilities** ⊗ ⓜ ⓑ 🍺 ♀ ⚒ 🏠 ⚑ 🚣 ✿ **Location** W of village off A338

Hotel ★★★ 62% Quality Hotel Andover, Micheldever Rd, ANDOVER ☎ 01264 369111 13 en suite 36 annexe en suite

TOLLARD ROYAL
Map 03 ST91

Rushmore Park Golf Club SP5 5QB
☎ 01725 516326 📠 01725 516437
e-mail: andrea@rushmoregolfclub.co.uk

Peaceful and testing parkland course situated on Cranborne Chase with far-reaching views. An undulating course with avenues of trees and well-drained greens. With water on seven out of 18 holes, it will test the most confident of golfers.

18 holes, 6172yds, Par 71, SSS 69.
Club membership 679.

Visitors book in advance. Dress code enforced & soft spikes only. **Societies** welcome by appointment, apply in writing or phone. **Green Fees** £22.50 per 18 holes (£27.50 weekends). **Cards** 💳 💳 💳 💳 💳 **Prof** Sean McDonagh **Course Designer** David Pottagem, John Jacobs Developments **Facilities** ⊗ ⓜ by arrangement ⓑ 🍺 ♀ ⚒ 🏠 ⚑ 🚣 ✿ ⚑ **Conf** fac available Corporate Hospitality Days available **Location** N off B3081 between Sixpenny Handley & Tollard Royal

Hotel ★★★ 67% Royal Chase Hotel, Royal Chase Roundabout, SHAFTESBURY ☎ 01747 853355 33 en suite

UPAVON
Map 04 SU15

Upavon Douglas Av SN9 6BQ
☎ 01980 630787 & 635419 📠 01980 635419
e-mail: play@upavongolfclub.co.uk

Free-draining course on chalk downland with panoramic views over the Vale of Pewsey and the Alton Barnes White Horse. A fair test of golf with a good mixture of holes including a 602yd par 5 and an excellent finishing hole, a par 3 of 169yds across a valley.

18 holes, 6402yds, Par 71, SSS 71, Course record 69.
Club membership 600.

Visitors contact in advance & not am at weekends. **Societies** phone in advance. **Green Fees** £26 per day (£36 weekends). **Cards** 💳 💳 💳 💳 💳 **Prof** Richard Blake **Course Designer** Richard Blake **Facilities** ⊗ ⓜ by arrangement ⓑ 🍺 ♀ ⚒ 🏠 ⚑ 🚣 ✿ **Location** 1.5m SE of Upavon on A342

Continued

otel ★★★ 64% Bear Hotel, Market Place, DEVIZES
☎ 01380 722444 24 en suite

WARMINSTER   Map 03 ST84

West Wilts Elm Hill BA12 0AU
☎ 01985 213133 📠 01985 219809
mail: sec@westwiltsgolfclub.co.uk
**hilltop course among the Wiltshire downs on
ownland turf. Free draining, short, but a very good
st of accurate iron play. Excellent greens and
lubhouse facilities.**
*8 holes, 5754yds, Par 70, SSS 68, Course record 60.
lub membership 570.*
isitors not Sat; must contact in advance; handicap
rtificate. **Societies** Wed & Fri only. Apply by letter or
hone **Green Fees** £30 per day; £25 per round (£40/30 Sun
bank holidays). **Cards** 💳 **Prof** Rob Morris **Course
esigner** JH Taylor **Facilities** ⊗ ♒ ⛶ 🍺 ♀ ♨ 🏠 ❜ 𝄐
ocation N of town centre off A350

otel ★★★★ 74% Bishopstrow House, WARMINSTER
☎ 01985 212312 32 en suite

WOOTTON BASSETT   Map 04 SU08

Brinkworth Longmans Farm, Brinkworth SN15 5DG
☎ 01666 510277
9 holes, 5884yds, Par 70, SSS 70.
ourse Designer Jullian Sheppard **Location** off B4042
etween Malmesbury & Wootton Bassett
hone for further details

otel ★★★ 66% Marsh Farm Hotel, Coped Hall,
WOOTTON BASSETT ☎ 01793 848044 11 en suite
0 annexe en suite

Wiltshire Vastern SN4 7PB
☎ 01793 849999 📠 01793 849988
mail: tracey@the-wiltshire.co.uk
**Peter Alliss and Clive Clark design set in rolling
Viltshire downland. A number of lakes add a challenge
r both low and high handicappers.**

*8 holes, 6519yds, Par 72, SSS 72, Course record 67.
lub membership 800.*
isitors contact in advance. **Societies** contact in advance.
reen Fees not confirmed. **Cards** 💳 **Prof** Kevin Pickett **Course Designer** Peter Allis & Clive
lark **Facilities** ⊗ ♒ ⛶ 🍺 ♀ 🏠 ❜ 🐟 🛥 𝄐 ⛳
eisure heated indoor swimming pool, sauna, solarium,
ymnasium, creche, Jacuzzi. **Conf** fac available Corporate
ospitality Days available **Location** off A3102 SW of
ootton Bassett

Hotel ★★★ 69% The Lodge @ Wiltshire Golf & Country
Club, WOOTTON BASSETT ☎ 01793 849999
58 en suite

WORCESTERSHIRE

ALVECHURCH   Map 07 SP07

Kings Norton Brockhill Ln, Weatheroak B48 7ED
☎ 01564 826706 & 826789 📠 01564 826955
e-mail: info@kingsnortongolfclub.co.uk
**Parkland course with water hazards. A 27-hole
championship venue playing as three combinations of
nine holes.**
*Weatheroak: 18 holes, 6748yds, Par 72, SSS 72,
Course record 65.
Brockhill: 18 holes, 6648yds, Par 72, SSS 72.
Wythall: 18 holes, 6612yds, Par 72, SSS 72.
Club membership 1000.*
Visitors contact in advance. No visitors at weekends.
Societies phone in advance. **Green Fees** terms on
application. **Cards** 💳 **Prof** Kevin Hayward
Course Designer F Hawtree **Facilities** ⊗ ♒ ⛶ 🍺 ♀ ♨
🏠 ❜ 🛥 𝄐 **Leisure** par 3 course. **Conf** fac available
Corporate Hospitality Days available
Location M42 junct 3, off A435

Hotel ★★★★ 66% Hanover International Hotel & Club,
Kidderminster Rd, BROMSGROVE
☎ 01527 576600 114 en suite

BEWDLEY   Map 07 SO77

Little Lakes Golf and Country Club Lye Head
DY12 2UZ
☎ 01299 266385 📠 01299 266398
e-mail: marklaing@littlelakesgc.fsnet.co.uk
**A pleasant undulating 18-hole parkland course. A
challenging test of golf with stunning views of the
Worcestershire countryside. Well acclaimed for the use
of natural features.**

*18 holes, 6278yds, Par 71, SSS 70, Course record 68.
Club membership 475.*
Visitors advisable to phone in advance. **Societies** phone in
advance. **Green Fees** not confirmed. **Cards** 💳
🔒 **Prof** Mark A Laing **Course Designer** M Laing
Facilities ⊗ by arrangement ♒ by arrangement ⛶
by arrangement 🍺 by arrangement ♀ ♨ 🏠 🐟 🛥 𝄐 **Leisure**
hard tennis courts, heated outdoor swimming pool, fishing.
Conf fac available **Location** 2.25m W of Bewdley off
A456

Continued

Wharton Park Longbank DY12 2QW
☎ 01299 405163 ▤ 01299 405121
e-mail: enquiries@whartonpark.co.uk
An 18-hole championship-standard course set in 200 acres of beautiful Worcestershire countryside, with stunning views. Some long par 5s such as the 9th (594yds) as well as superb par 3 holes at 3rd, 10th and 15th make this a very challenging course.

18 holes, 6603yds, Par 72, SSS 71, Course record 66. Club membership 500.
Visitors contact in advance; not weekend am. Societies booking required. Green Fees terms on application. Cards ▦ ▦ ▦ ▦ ▣ Prof Angus Hoare Course Designer Howard Swan Facilities ⊗ ⑪ ⮞ ▆ ♀ ⚱ 🛍 ♦ 🏌 ♂ � Conf fac available Corporate Hospitality Days available Location off A456 Bewdley bypass

Vale Golf Club Hill Furze Rd WR10 2LZ
☎ 01386 462781 ▤ 01386 462597
e-mail: vale-sales@crown-golf.co.uk
This course offers an American-style layout, with large greens, trees and bunkers and several water hazards. Its rolling fairways provide a testing round, as well as superb views of the Malvern Hills. Picturesque and peaceful.
International Course: 18 holes, 7174yds, Par 74, SSS 74, Course record 67.
Lenches Course: 9 holes, 5518yds, Par 70, SSS 66. Club membership 700.
Visitors booking up to one week in advance. Some weekend restrictions on International course. Societies apply in advance. Some weekend restrictions. Green Fees not confirmed. Cards ▦ ▦ ▦ ▦ ▦ ▣ Prof Paul Edgcombe Course Designer Bob Sandow Facilities ⊗ ⑪ ⮞ ▆ ♀ ⚱ 🛍 ♦ 🏌 ♂ � Conf fac available Corporate Hospitality Days available Location signed off A44

Hotel ★★★ 72% Salford Hall Hotel, ABBOT'S SALFORD ☎ 01386 871300 14 en suite 19 annexe en suite

Broadway Willersey Hill WR12 7LG
☎ 01386 853683 ▤ 01386 858643
e-mail: secretary@broadwaygolfclub.co.uk
At the edge of the Cotswolds this downland course lies at an altitude of 900ft above sea level, with extensive views. Natural contours and man-made hazards mean that drives have to be placed, approaches carefully judged and the greens expertly read.
18 holes, 6228yds, Par 72, SSS 70, Course record 66. Club membership 850.

Visitors not before 3pm Sat Apr-Sep. Restricted play Sun. Must contact in advance. Societies Wed-Fri, must contact in advance. Green Fees £38 per day, £30 per round (£38 weekends & bank holidays). Cards ▦ ▦ ▦ ▣ Prof Martyn Freeman Course Designer James Braid Facilities ⊗ ⑪ ⮞ ▆ ♀ ⚱ 🛍 🏌 ♂ ♦ 🏌 ♂ � Conf fac available Location 1.5m E on A44

Hotel ★★★ 79% Dormy House Hotel, Willersey Hill, BROADWAY ☎ 01386 852711 25 en suite 23 annexe en suite

Blackwell Agmore Rd, Blackwell B60 1PY
☎ 0121 445 1994 ▤ 0121 445 4911
e-mail: info@blackwellgolfclub.com
Mature undulating parkland, 112 years old, with a variety of mature trees. Laid out in two nine-hole loops.
18 holes, 6080yds, Par 70, SSS 71, Course record 61. Club membership 355.
Visitors contact in advance, must have handicap certificate, not at weekends. Societies contact in advance. Green Fees 18 holes £60; 27/36 holes £70. Prof Nigel Blake Course Designer Herbert Fowler, Tom Simpson Facilities ⊗ by arrangement ⑪ by arrangement ⮞ ▆ ♀ ⚱ 🛍 🏌 ♂ ♦ Conf Corporate Hospitality Days availabl Location 2.5m NE of Bromsgrove off B4184

Hotel ★★★★ 66% Hanover International Hotel & Club, Kidderminster Rd, BROMSGROVE ☎ 01527 576600 114 en suite

Bromsgrove Golf Centre Stratford Rd B60 1LD
☎ 01527 575886 & 570505 ▤ 01527 570964
e-mail: enquiries@bromsgrovegolfcentre.com
This gently undulating course with superb views over Worcestershire is not to be underestimated. Creative landscaping and a selection of well-defined bunkers ensure that the course delivers a uniquely satisfying experience through a variety of challenging, yet enjoyable, holes.

18 holes, 5969yds, Par 68, SSS 69. Club membership 900.
Visitors dress restriction, no T-shirts, jeans, tracksuits etc seven day booking facilities available. Societies packages available, apply in writing or phone. Green Fees £18.70 per 18 holes (£24.70 weekends). Discount scheme available. Cards ▦ ▦ ▦ ▣ Prof Graeme Long, Danny Wall Course Designer Hawtree & Son Facilities ⊗ ⑪ ⮞ ▆ ♀ ⚱ 🛍 🏌 ♂ ♦ 🏌 ♂ � Conf fac available Corporate Hospitality Days available Location 1m from town centre at junct A38 & A448

Continued   *Continue*

Hotel ★★★★ 66% Hanover International Hotel & Club, Kidderminster Rd, BROMSGROVE
☎ 01527 576600 114 en suite

DROITWICH   Map 03 SO86

Droitwich Golf & Country Club Ford Ln
WR9 0BQ
☎ 01905 774344 📠 01905 797290
e-mail: droitwich-golf-club@tiscali.co.uk
Undulating wooded parkland course with scenic views from the highest points.
18 holes, 5976yds, Par 70, SSS 69, Course record 62.
Club membership 732.
Visitors with member only weekends & bank holidays.
Societies apply by phone & letter. Green Fees £26 per day, £18 per round. Prof C Thompson Course Designer Braid, G Franks Facilities ⊗ ⌘ ⓑ ♥ ♀ ♨ 🏠 ✇
Leisure snooker. Conf Corporate Hospitality Days available Location off A38 between Droitwich & M5 junct 5

Hotel ★★★★ 67% Chateau Impney Hotel, DROITWICH SPA ☎ 01905 774411 67 en suite 53 annexe en suite

Gaudet Luce Middle Ln, Hadzor WR9 7DP
☎ 01905 796375 📠 01905 797245
e-mail: info@gaudet-luce.co.uk
18 holes, 6040yds, Par 70, SSS 68.
Course Designer M A Laing Location M5 junct 5, left at Tagwell Rd onto Middle Ln, 1st driveway on left
Phone for further details

Hotel ★★★★ 67% Chateau Impney Hotel, DROITWICH SPA ☎ 01905 774411 67 en suite 53 annexe en suite

Ombersley Bishops Wood Rd, Lineholt, Ombersley
WR9 0LE
☎ 01905 620747 📠 01905 620047
e-mail: enquiries@ombersleygolfclub
Undulating course in beautiful countryside high above the edge of the Severn valley. Covered driving range and putting green.
18 holes, 6139yds, Par 72, SSS 69, Course record 67.
Club membership 750.
Visitors suitable dress expected, no jeans, shirts must have collar. phone in advance Societies phone in advance.
Green Fees £21.50 per 18 holes, £12.75 per 9 holes (£29.65/£17.80 weekends & bank holidays). Cards 💳 💳 💳 💳 💳 Prof G Glenister, N Woodman, D Hall Course Designer David Morgan Facilities ⊗ ⌘ ⓑ ♥ ♀ ♨ 🏠 ⌇ ♣ ♨ ✇ Leisure chipping green & practice bunker. Conf fac available Corporate Hospitality Days available Location 3m W of Droitwich off A449. At Mitre Oak pub A4025 to Stourport, signed 400yds on left

Hotel ★★★★ 65% Raven Hotel, Victoria Square, DROITWICH SPA ☎ 01905 772224 72 en suite

FLADBURY   Map 03 SO94

Evesham Craycombe Links, Old Worcester Rd
WR10 2QS
☎ 01386 860395 📠 01386 861356
e-mail: eveshamgolfclub@talk21.com
Parkland, heavily wooded, with the River Avon running alongside 5th and 14th holes. Good views. Nine greens played from 18 different tees.
9 holes, 6415yds, Par 72, Course record 65.
Club membership 450.

Visitors contact in advance, & have a handicap certificate.
Societies apply in advance by phone or writing. Green Fees not confirmed. Prof Dan Cummins Facilities ⊗ ⌘ ⓑ ♥ ♀ ♨ 🏠 ♣ ✇ Location 0.75m N on A4538

Hotel ★★★ 77% The Evesham Hotel, Coopers Ln, Off Waterside, EVESHAM
☎ 01386 765566 & 0800 716969 (Res) 📠 01386 765443
39 en suite 1 annexe en suite

HOLLYWOOD   Map 07 SP07

Gay Hill Hollywood Ln B47 5PP
☎ 0121 430 8544 & 474 6001 (pro) 📠 0121 436 7796
e-mail: secretary@ghgc.org.uk
Parkland course with some 10,000 trees and a brook running through.
18 holes, 6406yds, Par 72, SSS 72, Course record 64.
Club membership 740.
Visitors contact in advance. Societies phone in advance.
Green Fees £32 per day. Prof Andrew Potter Facilities ⊗ ⌘ ⓑ ♥ ♀ ♨ 🏠 ♥ ✇ Location N of village

Hotel ★★★ 68% Corus hotel Solihull, Stratford Rd, Shirley, SOLIHULL ☎ 0870 609 6133 111 en suite

KIDDERMINSTER   Map 07 SO87

Churchill and Blakedown Churchill Ln,
Blakedown DY10 3NB
☎ 01562 700018 📠 0871 242 2049
e-mail: cbgolfclub@tiscali.co.uk
Mature hilly course, playable all year round, with good views.
9 holes, 6488yds, Par 72, SSS 71.
Club membership 410.
Visitors with member only weekends & bank holidays.
Handicap certificate required. Must contact in advance.
Societies by arrangement through secretary. Green Fees £25 weekdays. Prof G Wright Facilities ⊗ ⌘ ⓑ ♥ ♀ ♨ 🏠 ✇ Conf Corporate Hospitality Days available Location W of village off A456

Hotel ★★★★ 68% Stone Manor Hotel, Stone, KIDDERMINSTER ☎ 01562 777555 52 en suite 5 annexe en suite

Habberley Low Trimpley DY11 5RF
☎ 01562 745756 📠 01562 745756
Very hilly, wooded parkland course.
9 holes, 5401yds, Par 69, Course record 62.
Club membership 152.
Visitors weekends only with member; weekdays by arrangement. Societies phone initially. Green Fees not confirmed. Cards 💳 💳 💳 💳 💳 💳 Facilities ⊗ ⌘ ⓑ ♥ ♀ ♨ Location 2m NW of Kidderminster

Hotel ★★★★ 68% Stone Manor Hotel, Stone, KIDDERMINSTER ☎ 01562 777555 52 en suite 5 annexe en suite

Kidderminster Russell Rd DY10 3HT
☎ 01562 822303 📠 01562 827866
e-mail: info@kiddigolf.com
Pleasant wooded parkland course, mainly flat, but a good test of golf for all levels of player. Two small lakes add to the challenge.

Continued   Continued

Kidderminster Golf Club

The Cottage in the Wood Hotel

18 holes, 6422yds, Par 72, SSS 71, Course record 65.
Club membership 860.
Visitors with member only weekends & bank holidays.
Must have a handicap certificate. **Societies** weekdays only
apply in advance. **Green Fees** £35 per day, £30 per round.
Cards ⊞ ▦ ▩ **Prof** Pat Smith **Facilities** ⊗ ⫪ ⬚ ⬛ ♀
⛳ ⌂ ⛵ ⚓ ⚒ ⚑ **Conf** fac available Corporate
Hospitality Days available **Location** 0.5m SE of town
centre, signed off A449
....
Hotel ★★★★ 68% Stone Manor Hotel, Stone,
KIDDERMINSTER ☎ 01562 777555 52 en suite
5 annexe en suite

Wyre Forest Zortech Av DY11 7EX
☎ 01299 822682 ▤ 01299 879433
e-mail: simon@wyreforestgolf.com
18 holes, 5790yds, Par 70, SSS 68, Course record 68.
Location on A451 between Kidderminster & Stourport,
Phone for further details
....
Hotel ★★★★ 73% Menzies Stourport Manor, Hartlebury
Rd, STOURPORT-ON-SEVERN ☎ 01299 289955
68 en suite

MALVERN WELLS   Map 03 SO74

Worcestershire Wood Farm, Wood Farm Rd
WR14 4PP
☎ 01684 575992 ▤ 01684 893334
e-mail: secretary@theworcestershiregolfclub.co.uk
Fairly easy walking on windy downland course with
trees, ditches and other natural hazards. Outstanding
views of the Malvern Hills and the Severn valley. The
17th hole (par 5) is approached over small lake.
18 holes, 6500yds, Par 71, SSS 72.
Club membership 750.
Visitors handicap certificate required. Phone for
availability **Societies** Apply in advance by phone. **Green**
Fees £35 per day; £28 per round (£40/£34 weekends &
bank holidays). **Prof** Richard Lewis **Course Designer** JH
Taylor **Facilities** ⊗ ⫪ ⬚ ⬛ ♀ ⛳ ⌂ ⚒ **Leisure** indoor
teaching facility. **Conf** Corporate Hospitality Days
available **Location** 2m S of Gt Malvern on B4209
....
Hotel ★★★ ⚑ 74% The Cottage in the Wood Hotel,
Holywell Rd, Malvern Wells, MALVERN
☎ 01684 575859 8 en suite 23 annexe en suite

REDDITCH   Map 07 SP06

Abbey Hotel Golf & Country Club Dagnell
End Rd, Hither Green Ln B98 9BE
☎ 01527 406600 & 406500 ▤ 01527 406514
e-mail: info@theabbeyhotel.co.uk
Parkland course with rolling fairways with many trees
and lakes on several holes. Recent course improvements
have resulted in a course which requires more thought
than before. Pure putting surfaces are a worthy reward
for some solid iron play, allowing the golfer to make the
most of a birdie.

18 holes, 6561yds, Par 72, SSS 72.
Club membership 500.
Visitors contact in advance, dress code applies. **Societies**
apply in writing or by phone. **Green Fees** £18 per round
(£25 Fri-Sun & bank holidays). **Cards** ⊞ ▦ ▩ ▦ ▦
▩ ▩ **Prof** R Davies **Course Designer** Donald Steele
Facilities ⊗ ⫪ ⬚ ⬛ ♀ ⛳ ⌂ ⛵ ⚓ ⚒ ⚑ **Leisure**
heated indoor swimming pool, fishing, sauna, solarium,
gymnasium. **Conf** fac available Corporate Hospitality
Days available **Location** A441 N from town, onto B4101
signed Beoley, right onto Hither Green Ln
....
Hotel ★★★★ 67% The Abbey Hotel Golf & Country
Club, Hither Green Ln, Dagnell End Rd, Bordesley,
REDDITCH ☎ 01527 406600 72 en suite

Pitcheroak Plymouth Rd B97 4PB
☎ 01527 541054 ▤ 01527 65216
9 holes, 4561yds, Par 65, SSS 62.
Location SW of town centre off A448
Phone for further details
....
Hotel ★★★ 63% Quality Hotel Redditch, Pool Bank,
Southcrest, REDDITCH ☎ 01527 541511 73 en suite

Continued

Set amidst a beautiful undulating landscape in North Worcestershire, the Abbey course offers a variety of challenges from wooded areas to water early in your round but many holes offer welcome relief with their spacious fairways. xtensive drainage works have ensured the ourse is playable during all seasons. All guests ave complimentary use of the health club, cluding indoor pool and gymnasium. Packages re available for corporate golf and societies.

**Hither Green Lane, Dagnell End Road,
Redditch, Worcestershire B98 9BE
Tel: 01527 406600 Fax: 01527 406514
www.theabbeyhotel.co.uk**

edditch Lower Grinsty, Green Ln, Callow Hill
97 5PJ
☎ 01527 543079 (sec) 📠 01527 547413
mail: redditchgolfclub@btconnect.com
**arkland course with many tree-lined fairways,
xcellent greens and a particularly tough finish. The
ar 3s are all long and demanding.**
8 holes, 6671yds, Par 72, SSS 72, Course record 68.
lub membership 650.
isitors with member only weekends & bank holidays, no
sitors on competition days, advisable to phone in
lvance. **Societies** apply in writing to secretary.
reen Fees £35 per round/£45 per day. **Prof** David Down
ourse Designer F Pennick **Facilities** ⊗ ⫪ �ᴸ ♥ ⏇ ⚒ ⛟
♨ ∅ **Location** 2m SW
....
otel ★★★ 63% Quality Hotel Redditch, Pool Bank,
outhcrest, REDDITCH ☎ 01527 541511 73 en suite

ENBURY WELLS   Map 07 SO56

admore Lodge Hotel & Country Club
Michaels, Berrington Green WR15 8TQ
☎ 01584 810044 📠 01584 810044
mail: info@cadmorelodge.demon.co.uk
holes, 5132yds, Par 68, SSS 65.
ocation A4112 from Tenbury to Leominster, 2m right for
rrington, 0.75m on left
one for further details
....
otel ★★ 67% Cadmore Lodge Hotel & Country Club,
rrington Green, St Michaels, TENBURY WELLS
☎ 01584 810044 15 rms (14 en suite)

WORCESTER   Map 03 SO85

Bank House Hotel Golf & Country Club
Bransford WR6 5JD
☎ 01886 833545 📠 01886 832461
e-mail: info@bransfordgolfclub.co.uk
**The Bransford Course is designed as a Florida-style
course with fairways weaving between water courses,
13 lakes and sculpted mounds with colourful plant
displays. The 6204yd course has dog-legs, island greens
and tight fairways to challenge all standards of player.
The 10th, 16th and 18th (The Devil's Elbow) are
particularly tricky.**

*Bransford Course: 18 holes, 6204yds, Par 72, SSS 71,
Course record 65.*
Club membership 380.
Visitors all tee times must be booked, no play before
9.30am. **Societies** contact the golf secretary, all tee times
must be booked in advance. **Green Fees** summer £20 per
18 holes (£25 weekends); winter £18 per round (£22
weekends). **Cards** ▦ ▨ ▨ 💳 ▨ 🔳 🔲 **Prof** Scott
Fordyce **Course Designer** Bob Sandow **Facilities** ⊗ ⫪ �ᴸ
♥ ♀ ⚒ 🏠 ⏇ ⋈ ♨ ⛟ ∅ ♟ **Leisure** outdoor swimming
pool, sauna, solarium, gymnasium, spa pool, vertical
sunbed. **Conf** fac available Corporate Hospitality Days
available **Location** M5 Junct 7, club 3m S of Worcester,
A4103

Perdiswell Park Bilford Rd WR3 8DX
☎ 01905 754668 & 457189
**Set in 85 acres of attractive parkland and suitable for
all levels of golfer.**
18 holes, 5297yds, Par 68, SSS 66.
Club membership 285.
Visitors contact in advance. **Societies** phone in advance for
packages. **Green Fees** £9.80 per 18 holes, £6.50 per 9
holes (£13.40/£8.30 weekends). **Cards** ▦ ▨ ▨ 🔳 🔲
Prof Mark Woodward **Facilities** ⊗ ⫪ �ᴸ ♥ ♀ ⚒ 🏠 ♟ ♦
♨ ∅ **Leisure** gymnasium. **Conf** fac available Corporate
Hospitality Days available **Location** N of city centre off
A30
....
Hotel ★★★ 74% Pear Tree Inn & Country Hotel, Smite,
WORCESTER ☎ 01905 756565 24 en suite

Worcester Golf & Country Club Boughton Park
WR2 4EZ
☎ 01905 422555 📠 01905 749090
18 holes, 6251yds, Par 70, SSS 70, Course record 67.
Course Designer Dr A MacKenzie **Location** 1.5m from
city centre on A4103
Phone for further details

WYTHALL   Map 07 SP07

Fulford Heath Tanners Green Ln B47 6BH
☎ 01564 824758 📄 01564 822629
e-mail: secretary@fulfordheath.co.uk
**A mature parkland course encompassing two classic
par threes. The 11th, a mere 149yds, shoots from an
elevated tee through a channel of trees to a well-
protected green. The 16th, a 166yd par 3, elevated
green, demands a 140 yard carry over an imposing
lake.**
18 holes, 5959yds, Par 70, SSS 69.
Club membership 750.
Visitors with member only weekend & bank holidays.
Handicap certificate required. Societies apply in advance.
Green Fees £35 per day/round. Prof Richard Dunbar
Course Designer Braid, Hawtree Facilities ⊗ ⍟ ⮷ 💺 ♀
⚒ 🏠 🚵 ⚗ Conf Corporate Hospitality Days available
Location 1m SE off A435

Hotel ★★★★ 70% Renaissance Solihull Hotel, 651
Warwick Rd, SOLIHULL ☎ 0121 711 3000 179 en suite

YORKSHIRE, EAST RIDING OF

ALLENTHORPE   Map 08 SE85

Allerthorpe Park Allerthorpe Park YO42 4RL
☎ 01759 306686 📄 01759 304308
e-mail: allerthorpepark@aol.com
**A picturesque parkland course, maintained to a high
standard, with many interesting features, including a
meandering beck and the 18th hole over the lake.**
18 holes, 6430yds, Par 70, SSS 70, Course record 67.
Club membership 550.
Visitors advisable to contact in advance. Societies by
arrangement in advance. Please phone. Green Fees £30 per
day, £24 per 18 holes (all week). Cards 💳 💳 💳 💳 💳
Prof James Calam Course Designer JG Hatcliffe &
Partners Facilities ⊗ ⍟ ⮷ 💺 by arrangement ♀ ⚒ 🏠 🚵
⚗ Conf fac available Corporate Hospitality Days
available Location 2m SW of Pocklington off A1079

Hotel ★★ 63% Feathers Hotel, 56 Market Place,
POCKLINGTON ☎ 01759 303155 6 en suite 6 annexe
en suite

AUGHTON   Map 08 SE73

Oaks Aughton Common YO42 4PW
☎ 01757 288577 📄 01757 288232
e-mail: sheila@theoaksgolfclub.co.uk
**The course is built in harmony with its natural wooded
parkland setting, near to the Derwent Ings. The wide
green fairways blend and bend with the gentle
countryside. Seven lakes come into play.**
18 holes, 6792yds, Par 72, SSS 72, Course record 65.
Club membership 700.
Visitors weekdays only. Societies may play weekdays.
Phone in advance. Green Fees £35 per day; £25.per round.
Cards 💳 💳 💳 💳 💳 💳 Prof Graham Walker Course
Designer Julian Covey Facilities ⊗ ⍟ ⮷ 💺 ♀ ⚒ 🏠 🍴
🚵 🚵 ⚗ ⛴ Leisure heated indoor swimming pool, sauna,
solarium, gymnasium, two self-catering cottages with own
putting greens. Conf fac available Corporate Hospitality
Days available Location 1m N of Bubwith on B1228

Hotel ★★★ 73% The Parsonage Country House Hotel,
York Rd, ESCRICK ☎ 01904 728111 12 en suite
34 annexe en suite

BEVERLEY   Map 08 TA03

Beverley & East Riding The Westwood
HU17 8RG
☎ 01482 868757 📄 01482 868757
e-mail: golf@beverleyandeastridinggolfclub.karoo.co.uk
**Picturesque parkland course with some hard walking
and natural hazards - trees and gorse bushes. Only two
fairways adjoining. Also cattle (spring to autumn);
horse-riders are an occasional hazard in the early
morning.**
Westwood: 18 holes, 6127yds, Par 69, SSS 69,
Course record 64.
Club membership 530.
Visitors contact in advance. Societies phone 01482
868757, then written confirmation. Green Fees £21 per
day; £16 per round (£26/£21 weekends). Prof Alex Ashby
Facilities ⊗ ⍟ ⮷ 💺 ♀ ⚒ 🏠 ⛳ ⚗ Location 1m SW on
B1230

Hotel ★★★ 65% The Beverley Arms Hotel, North Bar
Within, BEVERLEY ☎ 0870 609 6149 56 en suite

BRANDESBURTON   Map 08 TA14

Hainsworth Park Burton Holme YO25 8RT
☎ 01964 542362
**A parkland course based on sand and gravel giving
excellent drainage. Demands straight driving due to
mature trees.**
18 holes, 6362yds, Par 71, SSS 71.
Club membership 500.
Visitors contact in advance. Societies phone initially.
Green Fees not confirmed. Cards 💳 💳 💳 💳 💳
Prof Paul Binnington Facilities ⊗ ⍟ ⮷ 💺 ♀ ⚒ 🏠 🍴 ⛴
🍴 🚵 ⚗ Location SW of village on A165

Hotel ★★ 66% Burton Lodge Hotel, BRANDESBURTON
☎ 01964 542847 7 en suite 2 annexe en suite

BRIDLINGTON   Map 08 TA16

Bridlington Belvedere Rd YO15 3NA
☎ 01262 606367 📄 01262 606367
e-mail: enquiries@bridlingtongolfclub.co.uk
**Parkland course alongside Bridlington Bay, with tree-
lined fairways and six ponds. There are many well-
positioned fairway and greenside bunkers which
protect excellent putting surfaces.**
18 holes, 6638yds, Par 72, SSS 72, Course record 66.
Club membership 600.
Visitors contact in advance, professional 01262 674721
limited at weekends. Societies phone bookings in advance
Green Fees not confirmed. Cards 💳 💳 💳 💳
Prof Anthony Howarth Course Designer James Braid
Facilities ⊗ ⍟ ⮷ 💺 ♀ ⚒ 🏠 🍴 🚵 🚵 ⚗
Leisure snooker. Conf Corporate Hospitality Days
available Location 1m S off A165

Hotel ★★★ 70% Revelstoke Hotel, 1-3 Flamborough Rd,
BRIDLINGTON ☎ 01262 672362 26 en suite

> **Looking for a new course? Always telephone
> ahead to confirm visitor arrangements.**

Continued

ridlington Links Flamborough Rd, Marton
O15 1DW
☎ 01262 401584 🖹 01262 401702
ain: 18 holes, 6719yds, Par 72, SSS 72,
ourse record 70.
ourse Designer Swan **Location** on B1255 between
ridlington & Flamborough
hone for further details

otel ★★★ 68% Expanse Hotel, North Marine Dr,
RIDLINGTON ☎ 01262 675347 48 en suite

ROUGH   Map 08 SE92

rough Cave Rd HU15 1HB
☎ 01482 667291 🖹 01482 669873
mail: gt@brough-golfclub.co.uk
arkland course, where accurate positioning of the tee
all is required for good scoring. Testing for the scratch
ayer without being too difficult for the higher
andicap.
holes, 6067yds, Par 68, SSS 69, Course record 62.
lub membership 700.
isitors must have handicap certificate & contact in
vance. **Societies** apply by letter. **Green Fees** £45 per
y: £32 per round (£60/£45 weekends & bank holidays).
rof Gordon Townhill **Facilities** ⊗ ⅋ ⅂ ⅃ ♔ ⅂ ⅄ ⅂ 龠
⅂ ⅃ **Location** 8m W of Hull off A63

otel ★★★ 65% Elizabeth Hotel Hull, Ferriby High Rd,
ORTH FERRIBY ☎ 01482 645212 95 en suite

OTTINGHAM   Map 08 TA03

'ottingham Parks Golf & Country Club
oodhill Way HU16 5RZ
☎ 01482 846030 🖹 01482 845932
mail: jane.wiles@cottinghamparks.co.uk
ently undulating parkland course incorporating many
atural features, including lateral water hazards, several
nds on the approach to greens, and rolling fairways.

holes, 6459yds, Par 72, SSS 71, Course record 66.
lub membership 600.
isitors may book by phone in advance, times available
eekdays & weekends. **Societies** deposit required &
nfirmation in writing. After 2pm weekends. **Green Fees**
0 per round (£28 weekends & bank holidays). **Cards** ▦
⅂ ▦ ▦ ⅃ **Prof** Chris Gray **Course Designer** Terry
tten **Facilities** ⊗ ⅋ ⅂ ⅃ ♔ ⅂ ⅄ 龠 ⅂ ⅃ ⅂ **Leisure**
ated indoor swimming pool, sauna, solarium, gymnasium,
cuzzi Remedial masseur. **Conf** fac available Corporate
ospitality Days available **Location** A164 onto B1233
wards Cottingham, 100yds left onto Woodhill Way

otel ★★ 66% The Rowley Manor Hotel, Rowley Rd,
TTLE WEIGHTON ☎ 01482 848248 16 en suite

DRIFFIELD (GREAT)   Map 08 TA05

Driffield Sunderlandwick YO25 9AD
☎ 01377 253116 🖹 01377 240599
e-mail: info@diffieldgolfclub.com
**An easy walking, mature parkland course set within the
beautiful Sunderlandwick Estate, including numerous
water features, one of which is a renowned trout
stream.**
18 holes, 6215yds, Par 70, SSS 69, Course record 65.
Club membership 693.
Visitors book in advance & adhere to club dress rule.
Societies apply in writing or phone. **Green Fees** £35 per
day, £26 per round;(£45/£35 weekends). **Prof** Kenton
Wright **Facilities** ⊗ ⅋ ⅂ ⅃ ♔ ⅂ ⅄ 龠 ⅂ ⅃ **Leisure**
fishing. **Conf** Corporate Hospitality Days available
Location 2m S off A164

Hotel ★★★ 73% Bell Hotel, 46 Market Place,
DRIFFIELD ☎ 01377 256661 16 en suite

FLAMBOROUGH   Map 08 TA27

Flamborough Head Lighthouse Rd YO15 1AR
☎ 01262 850333 🖹 01262 850279
e-mail: secretary@flamboroughheadgolfclub.co.uk
**Undulating cliff top links type course on the
Flamborough headland.**
18 holes, 6189yds, Par 71, SSS 69, Course record 71.
Club membership 500.
Visitors not before 1pm Sun, Wed between 10 & 1.30, Sat
between 11.30 & 12.30. **Societies** contact in advance.
Green Fees £23 per day, £18 per round (£30/£25
weekends & bank holidays). **Prof** Paul Harrison **Facilities**
⊗ ⅋ ⅂ ⅃ ♔ ⅂ ⅄ 龠 ⅂ ⅃ ⅂ **Location** 2m E off B1259

Hotel ★★ 72% North Star Hotel, North Marine Dr,
FLAMBOROUGH ☎ 01262 850379 7 en suite

HESSLE   Map 08 TA02

Hessle Westfield Rd, Raywell HU16 5YL
☎ 01482 650171 & 650190 (pro) 🖹 01482 652679
e-mail: secretary@hessle-golf-club.co.uk
**Well-wooded downland course with easy walking. The
greens, conforming to USGA specification, are large
and undulating with excellent drainage, enabling play
throughout the year.**
18 holes, 6608yds, Par 72, SSS 72, Course record 65.
Club membership 720.
Visitors not Tue between 9-1 & not before 11.30am on Sat
& Sun. **Societies** by arrangement. **Green Fees** £34 per day;
£26 per round (£34 per round weekends). **Cards** ▦ ▦
▦ ⅂ **Prof** Grahame Fieldsend **Course Designer**
D Thomas, P Allis **Facilities** ⊗ ⅋ ⅂ ⅃ ♔ ⅂ ⅄ 龠 ⅂ ⅃ ⅂
Conf fac available Corporate Hospitality Days available
Location 3m SW of Cottingham

Hotel ★★★ 65% Elizabeth Hotel Hull, Ferriby High Rd,
NORTH FERRIBY ☎ 01482 645212 95 en suite

HORNSEA   Map 08 TA14

Hornsea Rolston Rd HU18 1XG
☎ 01964 532020 🖹 01964 532080
e-mail: hornseagolfclub@aol.com
**Easy walking parkland course renowned for the quality
of its greens.**
18 holes, 6685yds, Par 72, SSS 72, Course record 66.
Club membership 600.

Continued

Visitors with member only at weekends until 3pm Sat, 2pm Sun. Must contact in advance. **Societies** contact Secretary in advance. **Green Fees** £40 per day; £30 per round. **Cards** ⌨ 🏧 💳 🏧 🏧 🏧 🖥 **Prof** Stretton Wright **Facilities** ⊗ ⅷ by arrangement 🍴 🏌 🏊 🛌 ⛳ ♻ **Conf** Corporate Hospitality Days available **Location** 1m S on B1242, signs for Hornsea Freeport

....

Hotel ★★★ 65% The Beverley Arms Hotel, North Bar Within, BEVERLEY ☎ 0870 609 6149 56 en suite

HOWDEN   Map 08 SE72

Boothferry Park Spaldington Ln DN14 7NG
☎ 01430 430364 📄 01430 430567
Pleasant, meadowland course in the Vale of York with interesting natural dykes, creating challenges on some holes. The par 5 9th is a test for any golfer with its dyke coming into play on the tee shot, second shot and approach.
18 holes, 6651yds, Par 73, SSS 72, Course record 64.
Club membership 250.
Visitors contact in advance, tee times bookable. **Societies** contact for booking form. **Green Fees** not confirmed. **Prof** James Major **Course Designer** Donald Steel **Facilities** ⊗ ⅷ 🍴 🏌 🏊 🛌 ⛳ 🐎 ♻ ⚜ **Conf** Corporate Hospitality Days available **Location** M62 junct 37, 2.5m N of Howden off B1228

....

Hotel ⛳ Premier Travel Inn Goole, Rawcliffe Rd, Airmyn, GOOLE ☎ 08701 977177 41 en suite

KINGSTON UPON HULL   Map 08 TA02

Ganstead Park Longdales Ln, Coniston HU11 4LB
☎ 01482 817754 📄 01482 817754
e-mail: secretary@gansteadpark.co.uk
Parkland course, easy walking, with water features.
18 holes, 6801yds, Par 72, SSS 73, Course record 62.
Club membership 500.
Visitors contact in advance. **Societies** phone in advance. **Green Fees** terms on application. **Prof** Michael J Smee **Course Designer** P **Green Facilities** ⊗ ⅷ 🍴 🏌 🏊 🛌 ⛳ 🐎 🐎 ♻ **Conf** Corporate Hospitality Days available **Location** A165 Hull exit, pass Ganstead & sharp right onto B1238 to Bilton, course on right

....

Hotel ★★★ 67% Quality Hotel Royal Hull, 170 Ferensway, HULL ☎ 01482 325087 155 en suite

Hull The Hall, 27 Packman Ln HU10 7TJ
☎ 01482 658919 📄 01482 658919
e-mail: info.hullgolfclub@virgin.net
Attractive mature parkland course.
18 holes, 6242yds, Par 70, SSS 70.
Club membership 768.
Visitors only weekdays. Contact professional 01482 653074. **Societies** Mon, Tue, Thu, Fri by arrangement. **Green Fees** Dec-Feb £21 per day/round; Mar-Nov £32 per day, £26.50 per round. **Cards** ⌨ 🏧 🏧 🖥 **Prof** David Jagger **Course Designer** James Braid **Facilities** ⊗ ⅷ 🍴 🏌 🏊 🛌 ⛳ 🐎 ♻ **Conf** Corporate Hospitality Days available **Location** 5m W of city off A164

....

Hotel ★★★ 73% Willerby Manor Hotel, Well Ln, WILLERBY ☎ 01482 652616 51 en suite

Springhead Park Willerby Rd HU5 5JE
☎ 01482 656309
Municipal parkland course with tight, undulating tree-lined fairways.

18 holes, 6402yds, Par 71, SSS 71.
Club membership 200.
Visitors welcome ex Sun (tee reserved). **Societies** contact on 01482 654875 **Green Fees** £12.50 per round (£14.50 weekends). **Facilities** 🍴 🏌 🏊 🛌 ⛳ 🐎 **Conf** Corporate Hospitality Days available **Location** 5m W off A164

....

Hotel ★★★ 73% Willerby Manor Hotel, Well Ln, WILLERBY ☎ 01482 652616 51 en suite

Sutton Park Salthouse Rd HU8 9HF
☎ 01482 374242 📄 01482 701428
18 holes, 6251yds, Par 70, SSS 69, Course record 67.
Location 3m NE on B1237, off A165
Phone for further details

....

Hotel ★★★ 67% Quality Hotel Royal Hull, 170 Ferensway, HULL ☎ 01482 325087 155 en suite

POCKLINGTON   Map 08 SE84

Kilnwick Percy Kilnwick Percy YO42 1UF
☎ 01759 303090
Parkland course on the edge of the Wolds above Pocklington combines a good walk with interesting golf. Undulating fairways, mature trees, water hazards and breathtaking views from every hole.
18 holes, 6218yards, Par 70, SSS 70.
Club membership 300.
Visitors phone to book tee. May only play after 10am weekends/bank holidays **Societies** phone for details of society packages. **Green Fees** £25 per day; £18 per 18 holes; £12 per 9 holes (£28/£20/£14 weekends & bank holidays). **Prof** Joe Townhill **Course Designer** John Day **Facilities** ⊗ 🍴 🏌 🏊 🛌 ⛳ 🐎 ♻ **Conf** Corporate Hospitality Days available **Location** 1m E of Pocklington off B1246

....

Hotel ★★ 63% Feathers Hotel, 56 Market Place, POCKLINGTON ☎ 01759 303155 6 en suite 6 annexe en suite

SOUTH CAVE   Map 08 SE93

Cave Castle Hotel & Country Club Church Hill, South Cave HU15 2EU
☎ 01430 421286 📄 01430 421118
e-mail: admin@cavecastlegolf.co.uk
An undulating meadow and parkland course at the foot of the Wolds, with superb views.
18 holes, 6524yds, Par 72, SSS 71, Course record 68.
Club membership 450.
Visitors contact in advance, not before 11am weekends/bank holidays. **Societies** by arrangement with Professional or golf administrator. **Green Fees** terms on application. **Cards** ⌨ 🏧 🏧 🖥 **Prof** Stephen MacKinder **Course Designer** Mrs N Freling **Facilities** ⊗ ⅷ 🍴 🏌 🏊 🛌 ⛳ 🐎 🐎 ♻ **Leisure** heated indoor swimming pool, sauna, solarium, gymnasium. **Conf** fac available Corporate Hospitality Days available **Location** 1m from A63

....

Hotel ★★★ 65% Elizabeth Hotel Hull, Ferriby High Rd, NORTH FERRIBY ☎ 01482 645212 95 en suite

> **Booking a tee time is always advisable.**

Continued

WITHERNSEA

Map 08 TA32

Withernsea Chesnut Av HU19 2PG
☎ 01964 612078 & 612258 📄 01964 612078
-mail: golf@withernseagolfclub.fsnet.co.uk
**Exposed seaside links with narrow, undulating
fairways, bunkers and small greens.**
*holes, 6207yds, Par 72, SSS 69.
Club membership 300.*
Visitors with member only at weekends before 3pm.
Societies apply in writing or phone **Green Fees** £12 per 18
oles/per day. **Facilities** ⊗ ⫫ ⬛ ▦ ♀ ⚘ Leisure
enior/junior coaching. **Conf** fac available Corporate
Hospitality Days available **Location** S of town centre off
A1033, signed from Victoria Av

Hotel ★★★ 67% Quality Hotel Royal Hull, 170
erensway, HULL ☎ 01482 325087 155 en suite

YORKSHIRE, NORTH

ALDWARK

Map 08 SE46

Aldwark Manor YO61 1UF
☎ 01347 838353 📄 01347 833991
**An easy walking, scenic 18-hole parkland course with
holes both sides of the River Ure. The course surrounds
the Victorian Aldwark Manor Golf Hotel.**
*8 holes, 6187yds, Par 72, SSS 70, Course record 67.
Club membership 400.*
Visitors contact in advance, restricted weekends. **Societies**
phone in advance. **Green Fees** £35 per day; £25 per round
£40/£30 weekends & bank holiday). **Cards** ▦ ▦
◼ ▦ 🔟 **Facilities** ⊗ ⫫ ⬛ ▦ ♀ ⚘ 🏠 ⚘ ⚘ ⚘
Leisure heated indoor swimming pool, fishing, sauna,
gymnasium. **Conf** fac available Corporate
Hospitality Days available **Location** 5m SE of
oroughbridge off A1

Hotel ★★★★ 77% Aldwark Manor, ALDWARK
☎ 01347 838146 60 en suite

BEDALE

Map 08 SE28

Bedale Leyburn Rd DL8 1EZ
☎ 01677 422451 (sec) 📄 01677 427143
-mail: bedalegolfclub@aol.com
**One of North Yorkshire's most picturesque and
interesting courses. The 18-hole course is in parkland
with mature trees, water hazards and strategically
placed bunkers. Easy walking, no heavy climbs.**

*8 holes, 6610yds, Par 72, SSS 72, Course record 68.
Club membership 600.*

Visitors welcome, contact in advance. **Societies** contact
secretary for details. **Green Fees** £32 per day, £25 per
round (£40/£35 weekends). **Cards** ▦ ▦ ▦ 🔟 **Prof**
Tony Johnson **Course Designer** Hawtree **Facilities** ⊗ ⫫
⬛ ▦ ♀ ⚘ 🏠 ⚘ ⚘ ⚘ ⚘ **Conf** Corporate Hospitality
Days available **Location** A1 onto A684 at Leeming Bar to
Bedale

Hotel ★ 69% Buck Inn, THORNTON WATLASS
☎ 01677 422461 7 rms (5 en suite)

BENTHAM

Map 07 SD66

Bentham Robin Ln LA2 7AG
☎ 01524 62455
e-mail: secretary@benthamgolfclub.co.uk
**Moorland course with glorious views and excellent
greens.**
*18 holes, 6005yds, Par 71, SSS 69, Course record 69.
Club membership 600.*
Visitors contact in advance. **Societies** apply in advance.
Green Fees £30 per day, £26 per round (£35/£30
weekends). **Prof** Alan Watson **Facilities** ⊗ ⫫ ⬛ ▦ ♀ ⚘
🏠 ⚘ ⚘ ⚘ **Conf** Corporate Hospitality Days available
Location N side of High Bentham

Guesthouse ◆◆◆◆ Turnerford Fold, Keasden,
CLAPHAM ☎ 015242 51731 2 en suite

CATTERICK GARRISON

Map 08 SE29

Catterick Leyburn Rd DL9 3QE
☎ 01748 833268 📄 01748 833268
e-mail: grant@catterickgolfclub.co.uk
**Scenic parkland and moorland course of championship
standard, with good views of the Pennines and the
Cleveland Hills. Testing 1st and 6th holes.**
*18 holes, 6329yds, Par 71, SSS 71, Course record 64.
Club membership 700.*
Visitors tee reservation system in operation phone
professional shop 01748 833671; not before 10am
Tue/Thu/weekends & bank holidays. **Societies** by
arrangement. **Green Fees** not confirmed. **Cards** ▦ ▦ 🔟
Prof Andy Marshall **Course Designer** Arthur Day
Facilities ⊗ ⫫ ⬛ ▦ ♀ ⚘ 🏠 ⚘ ⚘ ⚘ ⚘ **Conf** fac
available Corporate Hospitality Days available
Location 0.5m W of Catterick Garrison

Hotel ★★★ 66% King's Head Hotel, Market Place,
RICHMOND ☎ 01748 850220 26 en suite 4 annexe
en suite

COPMANTHORPE

Map 08 SE54

Pike Hills Tadcaster Rd YO23 3UW
☎ 01904 700797 📄 01904 700797
e-mail: thesecretary@pikehills.fsnet.co.uk
**Parkland course surrounding a nature reserve. Level
terrain.**
*18 holes, 6146yds, Par 71, SSS 70, Course record 63.
Club membership 750.*
Visitors welcome weekdays, with member only weekends
& bank holidays. **Societies** apply in advance. **Green Fees**
not confirmed. **Prof** Ian Gradwell **Facilities** ⊗ ⫫ ⬛ ▦ ♀
⚘ 🏠 ⚘ ⚘ ⚘ **Conf** fac available Corporate
Hospitality Days available **Location** 3m SW of York on
A64

Hotel ★★★★ 69% York Marriott Hotel, Tadcaster Rd,
YORK ☎ 01904 701000 108 en suite

Continued

EASINGWOLD Map 08 SE56

Easingwold Stillington Rd YO61 3ET
☎ 01347 821964 (pro) & 822474 (sec) 📠 01347 822474
e-mail: brian@easingwold-golf-club.fsnet.co.uk
Parkland course with easy walking. Trees are a major feature and on six holes water hazards come into play.
18 holes, 6559yds, Par 74, SSS 72.
Club membership 750.
Visitors prior enquiry essential. **Societies** application in writing essential or by phone **Green Fees** £35 per day; £28 per round. **Prof** John Hughes **Course Designer** Hawtree **Facilities**
Conf Corporate Hospitality Days available
Location 1m S of Easingwold

Hotel ★★ 72% George Hotel, Market Place, EASINGWOLD ☎ 01347 821698 15 en suite

FILEY Map 08 TA18

Filey West Av YO14 9BQ
☎ 01723 513293 📠 01723 514952
e-mail: secretary@fileygolfclub.wanadoo.co.uk
Links and parkland course with good views. Stream runs through course. Testing 9th and 13th holes.
18 holes, 6112yds, Par 70, SSS 69, Course record 64
9 holes, 1513yds, Par 30.
Club membership 900.
Visitors phone to reserve tee time. **Societies** contact by phone. **Green Fees** £25 per day (weekends £30 per round). **Cards** **Prof** Gary Hutchinson **Course Designer** Braid **Facilities**
Location 0.5m S of Filey

Hotel ★★ 69% Wrangham House Hotel, 10 Stonegate, HUNMANBY ☎ 01723 891333 8 en suite 4 annexe en suite

GANTON Map 08 SE97

Ganton YO12 4PA
☎ 01944 710329 📠 01944 710922
e-mail: secretary@gantongolfclub.com
Championship course, heathland, gorse-lined fairways and heavily bunkered; variable winds. The opening holes make full use of the contours of the land and the approach to the second demands the finest touch. The 4th is considered one of the best holes on the outward half with its shot across a valley to a plateau green, the surrounding gorse punishing anything less than a perfect shot. The finest hole is possibly the 18th, requiring an accurately placed drive to give a clear shot to the sloping, well-bunkered green.
18 holes, 6734yds, Par 72, SSS 73, Course record 65.
Club membership 500.
Visitors by arrangement. Restricted play at weekends. **Societies** arrangement in writing. **Green Fees** £68 per day/round (£78 weekends & bank holidays). **Cards** **Prof** Gary Brown **Course Designer** Dunn, Vardon, Braid, Colt **Facilities** **Conf** Corporate Hospitality Days available
Location N of village off A64

Hotel ★★★ 62% East Ayton Lodge Country House, Moor Ln, Forge Valley, EAST AYTON ☎ 01723 864227 10 en suite 20 annexe en suite

HARROGATE Map 08 SE35

Harrogate Forest Ln Head, Starbeck HG2 7TF
☎ 01423 862999 📠 01423 860073
e-mail: hon.secretary@harrogate-gc.co.uk
Course on fairly flat terrain with MacKenzie-style greens and tree-lined fairways. While not a long course, the layout penalises the golfer who strays off the fairway. Subtly placed bunkers and copses of trees require the golfer to adopt careful thought and accuracy if par is to be bettered. The last six holes include five par 4s, of which four exceed 400yds.
18 holes, 6241yds, Par 69, SSS 70, Course record 63.
Club membership 700.
Visitors advisable to contact professional in advance, weekend play limited. **Societies** contact in writing or intially by phone. **Green Fees** £36 per day, £30 per round (weekends £40). **Cards** **Prof** Paul Johnson **Course Designer** Sandy Herd **Facilities** **Leisure** snooker. **Conf** Corporate Hospitality Days available **Location** 2.25m N on A59

Hotel ★★★ 74% Grants Hotel, 3-13 Swan Rd, HARROGATE ☎ 01423 560666 42 en suite

Oakdale Oakdale Glen HG1 2LN
☎ 01423 567162 📠 01423 536030
e-mail: sec@oakdale-golfclub.com
A pleasant, undulating parkland course which provides a good test of golf for the low handicap player without intimidating the less proficient. A special feature is an attractive stream which comes in to play on four holes. Excellent views from the clubhouse with good facilities.
18 holes, 6456yds, Par 71, SSS 71, Course record 61.
Club membership 1034.
Visitors no party bookings weekends. **Societies** phone followed by letter. **Green Fees** £40 for 27 holes, £33 per round (£45 per round weekends & bank holidays). **Prof** Clive Dell **Course Designer** Dr MacKenzie **Facilities** **Conf** Corporate Hospitality Days available **Location** N of town centre off A61

Hotel ★★★ 74% Grants Hotel, 3-13 Swan Rd, HARROGATE ☎ 01423 560666 42 en suite

Rudding Park Hotel & Golf Rudding Park, Follifoot HG3 1JH
☎ 01423 872100 📠 01423 873400
e-mail: sales@ruddingpark.com
Running through Rudding Park's mature parkland, originally designed as a deer park. Water comes into play on seven holes, while trees are present on all fairways.

Continued

8 holes, 6883yds, Par 72, SSS 73, Course record 65.
Club membership 600.
Visitors handicap certificate required, tee reservation available seven days in advance. **Societies** apply by phone n advance. **Green Fees** Mon-Thu £40 per day, £28.50 per 8 holes (£50/£35 Fri-Sun). **Cards** 🎴🎴🎴🎴🎴 **Prof** Moore, Hobkinson, Fountain **Course Designer** Martin Hawtree **Facilities** ⊗ ⅏ ⅃ ⚑ ♨ ♨ ♨ **Conf** fac available Corporate Hospitality Days available **Location** 2m SE of Harrogate town centre, off A658, brown tourist signs

Hotel ★★★★ Rudding Park Hotel & Golf, Rudding Park, Follifoot, HARROGATE ☎ 01423 871350 50 en suite

KIRKBYMOORSIDE   Map 08 SE68

Kirkbymoorside Manor Vale YO62 6EG
☎ 01751 430402 📠 01751 433190
e-mail: enqs@kirkbymoorsidegolf.co.uk
Hilly parkland course with narrow fairways, gorse and hawthorn bushes. Beautiful views.
8 holes, 6207yds, Par 69, SSS 69, Course record 65.
Club membership 650.
Visitors are advised to contact in advance, not before 9.30 or between 12.30-1.30. **Societies** apply in advance. **Green Fees** £22 per round/£28 per day (weekends £32). **Cards** 🎴🎴🎴 **Prof** John Hinchliffe **Facilities** ⊗ ⅏ ⅃ ⚑ ♨ **Conf** Corporate Hospitality Days available **Location** N of village

Hotel ★★ 67% George & Dragon Hotel, 17 Market Place, KIRKBYMOORSIDE ☎ 01751 433334 11 en suite ✱ annexe en suite

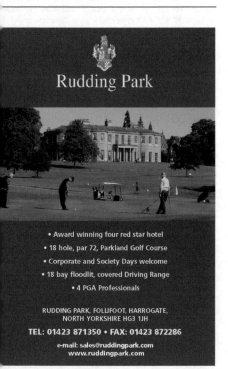
KNARESBOROUGH   Map 08 SE35

Knaresborough Boroughbridge Rd HG5 0QQ
☎ 01423 862690 📠 01423 869345
e-mail: knaresboroughgolfclub@btopenworld.com
Pleasant and well-presented parkland course in a rural setting. The first 11 holes are tree-lined and are constantly changing direction around the clubhouse. The closing holes head out overlooking the old quarry with fine views.
18 holes, 6864yds, Par 72, SSS 72.
Club membership 840.
Visitors restricted start times summer weekends. **Societies** apply by phone, e-mail or letter. **Green Fees** £40 per day, £30 per round (weekends £35). **Prof** Gary J Vickers **Course Designer** Hawtree **Facilities** ⊗ ⅏ ⅃ ⚑ ♨ ♨ ♨ **Conf** Corporate Hospitality Days available **Location** 1.25m N on A6055

Hotel ★★★ 70% Dower House Hotel, Bond End, KNARESBOROUGH ☎ 01423 863302 28 en suite 3 annexe en suite

MALTON   Map 08 SE77

Malton & Norton Welham Park, Norton YO17 9QE
☎ 01653 697912 📠 01653 697912
e-mail: maltonandnorton@btconnect.com
Parkland course, consisting of three nine-hole loops, with panoramic views of the moors. Very testing 1st hole (564yd dog-leg, left) on the Welham Course.
Welham Course: 18 holes, 6456yds, Par 72, SSS 71, Course record 66.
Park Course: 18 holes, 6251yds, Par 72, SSS 70, Course record 67.
Derwent Course: 18 holes, 6295yds, Par 72, SSS 70, Course record 66.
Club membership 880.
Visitors anytime except during competitions, no parties on Sat. **Societies** phone & confirm in writing. **Green Fees** £27 per round/day (£32 weekends & bank holidays). **Cards** 🎴🎴🎴🎴 **Prof** S Robinson **Facilities** ⊗ ⅏ ⅃ ⚑ ♨ ♨ ♨ **Conf** Corporate Hospitality Days available **Location** 0.75m from Malton

Hotel ★★★ 🎖 73% Burythorpe House Hotel, Burythorpe, MALTON ☎ 01653 658200 11 en suite 5 annexe en suite

MASHAM   Map 08 SE28

Masham Burnholme, Swinton Rd HG4 4HT
☎ 01765 688054 & 689379 📠 01765 688054
Flat parkland course crossed by River Burn, which comes into play on six holes.
9 holes, 6068yds, Par 70, SSS 69, Course record 70.
Club membership 290.
Visitors must play with member at weekends & bank holidays. **Societies** write or phone well in advance. **Green Fees** £20 per day £17 per round. **Facilities** ⊗ by arrangement ⅏ by arrangement ⅃ by arrangement ♨ by arrangement ♨ △ **Location** SW of Masham centre off A6108

Hotel ★ 69% Buck Inn, THORNTON WATLASS ☎ 01677 422461 7 rms (5 en suite)

Booking a tee time is always advisable.

MIDDLESBROUGH   Map 08 NZ41

Middlesbrough Brass Castle Ln, Marton TS8 9EE
☎ 01642 311515 📠 01642 319607
e-mail: enquiries@middlesbroughgolfclub.co.uk
**Undulating wooded parkland course, prevailing winds.
Testing 6th, 8th and 12th holes.**
*18 holes, 6278yds, Par 70, SSS 70, Course record 63.
Club membership 1004.*
Visitors restricted Tue & Sat. **Societies** Mon, Wed, Thu &
Fri only. Must contact the club in advance. **Green Fees**
£37 (£42 weekends). **Prof** Don Jones **Course Designer**
Baird **Facilities** ⊗ ⧖ ⛳ ⬛ ♀ ♨ 🏠 ⛳ ⛏ 🛒 ⛱ Leisure
snooker table. **Conf** fac available Corporate Hospitality
Days available **Location** 4m S off A172
....
Hotel ★★★ 72% Parkmore Hotel Leisure Park, 636 Yarm
Rd, Eaglescliffe, STOCKTON-ON-TEES
☎ 01642 786815 55 en suite

Middlesbrough Municipal Ladgate Ln TS5 7YZ
☎ 01642 315533 📠 01642 300726
18 holes, 6333yds, Par 71, SSS 70, Course record 67.
Course Designer Shuttleworth **Location** 2m S of
Middlesbrough on the A174
Phone for further details
....
Hotel ★★★ 72% Parkmore Hotel Leisure Park, 636 Yarm
Rd, Eaglescliffe, STOCKTON-ON-TEES
☎ 01642 786815 55 en suite

NORTHALLERTON   Map 08 SE39

Romanby Yafforth Rd DL7 0PE
☎ 01609 778855 📠 01609 779084
e-mail: mark@romanby.com
**Set in natural undulating terrain with the River Wiske
meandering through the course, it offers a testing
round of golf for all abilities. In addition to the river,
two lakes come into play on the 2nd, 5th and 11th holes.
A 12-bay floodlit driving range.**
*18 holes, 6663yds, Par 72, SSS 72, Course record 72.
Club membership 635.*
Visitors welcome everyday please book tee time in
advance. **Societies** contact Mark Boersma for details
01609 778855. **Green Fees** not confirmed. **Cards** 💳 💳
💳 💳 💳 **Prof** Tim Jenkins **Course Designer** Will
Adamson **Facilities** ⊗ ⧖ ⛳ ⬛ ♀ ♨ 🏠 ⛳ ⛏ 🛒 ⛱ ⛏
Leisure six-hole par 3 academy course. **Conf** fac available
Corporate Hospitality Days available
Location 1m W of Northallerton on B6271

PANNAL   Map 08 SE35

Pannal Follifoot Rd HG3 1ES
☎ 01423 872628 📠 01423 870043
e-mail: secretary@pannalgc.co.uk
**Fine championship course. Moorland turf but well-
wooded with trees closely involved with play. Excellent
views enhance the course.**
*18 holes, 6622yds, Par 72, SSS 72, Course record 62.
Club membership 780.*
Visitors preferable to contact in advance, weekends
limited. Not Tue am **Societies** apply in advance. **Green
Fees** £60 per day, £45 per round (£60 per round
weekends). **Cards** 💳 💳 💳 💳 💳 **Prof** David Padgett
Course Designer Sandy Herd **Facilities** ⊗ ⧖ ⛳ ⬛ ♀ ♨
🏠 ⛳ 🛒 ⛱ ⛏ Leisure snooker.

Continued

Conf Corporate Hospitality Days available
Location E of village off A61
....
Hotel ★★★ 70% The Yorkshire, Prospect Place,
HARROGATE ☎ 01423 565071 80 en suite

RAVENSCAR   Map 08 NZ90

Raven Hall Country House Hotel YO13 0ET
☎ 01723 870353 📠 01723 870072
e-mail: enquiries@ravenhall.co.uk
**Opened by the Earl of Cranbrook in 1898, this nine-
hole clifftop course is sloping and with good quality
small greens. Because of its clifftop position it is subject
to strong winds which make it great fun to play,
especially the 6th hole.**

*9 holes, 1894yds, Par 32, SSS 32.
Club membership 120.*
Visitors contact in advance, busy at weekends, spikes
essential, no jeans & T-shirts. **Societies** phone in advance.
Green Fees not confirmed. **Cards** 💳 💳 💳 💳 **Facilities**
⊗ ⧖ ⛳ ⬛ ♀ ♨ 🏠 Leisure hard tennis courts, heated
indoor plus outdoor swimming pool, sauna, gymnasium,
snooker, croquet, bowls. **Conf** fac available Corporate
Hospitality Days available **Location** A171 from
Scarborough towards Whitby, through Cloughton, right to
Ravenscar, hotel on clifftop
....
Hotel ★★★ 67% Raven Hall Country House Hotel,
RAVENSCAR ☎ 01723 870353 52 en suite

REDCAR   Map 08 NZ62

Cleveland Majuba Rd TS10 5BJ
☎ 01642 471798 📠 01642 471798
e-mail: secretary@clevelandgolfclub.co.uk
**The oldest golf club in Yorkshire playing over the only
links championship course in Yorkshire. A true test of
traditional golf, especially when windy. Flat seaside
links with easy walking.**
*18 holes, 6696yds, Par 72, SSS 72, Course record 67.
Club membership 920.*
Visitors advisable to book in advance. **Societies** initially
phone for details. **Green Fees** not confirmed. **Prof** Craig
Donaldson **Course Designer** Donald Steel (new holes)
Facilities ⊗ ⧖ ⛳ ⬛ ♀ ♨ 🏠 ⛏ **Conf** Corporate
Hospitality Days available **Location** 8m E of
Middlesborough, at N end of Redcar
....
Hotel ★★★ 66% Rushpool Hall Hotel, Saltburn Ln,
SALTBURN-BY-THE-SEA ☎ 01287 624111
21 en suite

Raven Hall
Country House Hotel
& Golf Course

Probably the most stunning views in the UK makes this challenging 9 hole golf course and country house hotel a must for those who enjoy a luxury break with good food, great atmosphere and exercise at just the right pace!

Ravenscar • Scarborough • North Yorkshire • YO13 0ET
Tel: (01723) 870353 • Fax: (01723) 870072
Email: enquiries@ravenhall.co.uk
Website: www.ravenhall.co.uk

Wilton Wilton TS10 4QY
☎ 01642 465265 (Secretary) 🖷 01642 465463
e-mail: secretary@wiltongolfclub.co.uk
Parkland course with some fine views and an abundance of trees and shrubs.
18 holes, 6540yds, Par 70, SSS 69, Course record 64.
Club membership 730.
Visitors phone professional 01642 452730 to check availability, no visitors Sat, Ladies competition priority Tue, tee off 10am or later. **Societies** phone secretary in advance.
Green Fees £24 per day (£30 weekends & bank holidays).
Prof P D Smillie **Facilities** ⊗ ⅏ by arrangement ᗷ 🍽 ♀ ᗷ 🏠 ⛳ ⛴ **Leisure** snooker. **Conf** Corporate Hospitality Days available **Location** 3m W of Redcar on A174

....

Hotel ★★★ 66% Rushpool Hall Hotel, Saltburn Ln, SALTBURN-BY-THE-SEA ☎ 01287 624111 21 en suite

RICHMOND   Map 07 NZ10

Richmond Bend Hagg DL10 5EX
☎ 01748 823231(Secretary) 🖷 01748 821709
Undulating parkland course. Ideal to play 27 holes, not too testing but very interesting.
18 holes, 6073yds, Par 71, SSS 69, Course record 63.
Club membership 600.
Visitors not before 3.30am on Sun. **Societies** contact in writing or phone 01748 822457. **Green Fees** £22 per round/£24 per day (£25/£30 weekends & bank holidays).
Prof Paul Jackson **Course Designer** F Pennink **Facilities** ⊗ ⅏ ᗷ 🍽 ♀ ᗷ 🏠 ⛳ 🚃 ⛴ **Conf** fac available
Location 0.75m N

....

Hotel ★★★ 66% King's Head Hotel, Market Place, RICHMOND ☎ 01748 850220 26 en suite 4 annexe en suite

RIPON   Map 08 SE37

Ripon City Palace Rd HG4 3HH
☎ 01765 603640 🖷 01765 692880
e-mail: office@ripongolf.com
18 holes, 6084yds, Par 70, SSS 69, Course record 66.
Course Designer H Varden **Location** 1m NW on A6108
Phone for further details

....

Hotel ★★★ 69% Ripon Spa Hotel, Park St, RIPON ☎ 01765 602172 40 en suite

SALTBURN-BY-THE-SEA   Map 08 NZ62

Hunley Hall Golf Club & Hotel Ings Ln, Brotton TS12 2QQ
☎ 01287 676216 🖷 01287 678250
e-mail: enquiries@hunleyhall.co.uk
A picturesque 27-hole coastal course with panoramic views of the countryside and coastline, providing a good test of golf and a rewarding game for all abilities.

Morgans: 18 holes, 6918yds, Par 73, SSS 73, Course record 63.
Millennium: 18 holes, 5948yds, Par 68, SSS 68, Course record 69.
Jubilee: 18 holes, 6292yds, Par 71, SSS 70, Course record 66.
Club membership 600.
Visitors please phone for information & availability
Societies phone for availability. **Green Fees** £25 per day (£35 weekends & bank holidays). **Cards** 💳 💳 💳 💳 💳 **Prof** Andrew Brook **Course Designer** John Morgan
Facilities ⊗ ⅏ ᗷ 🍽 ♀ ᗷ 🏠 ⛳ 🛈 🚃 ⛴ ⛴ **Conf** fac available Corporate Hospitality Days available
Location off A174 in Brotton onto St Margarets Way, 700yds to club

....

Hotel ★★ 67% Hunley Hall Golf Club & Hotel, Ings Ln, Brotton, SALTBURN ☎ 01287 676216 8 en suite

Saltburn by the Sea Hob Hill, Guisborough Rd TS12 1NJ
☎ 01287 622812 🖷 01287 625988
e-mail: info@saltburngolf.co.uk
Undulating meadowland course surrounded by woodland. Particularly attractive in autumn. There are fine views of the Cleveland Hills and of Tees Bay.
18 holes, 5846yds, Par 70, SSS 68, Course record 62.
Club membership 900.
Visitors phone in advance, no visitors on Sat. **Societies** apply in advance by writing or phone. **Green Fees** terms on application. **Cards** 💳 💳 💳 **Prof** David Hughes

Continued

Course Designer J Braid **Facilities** ⊗ ⽊ ⓑ ⬛ ♀ ⚒ ⌂ ✐ **Leisure** 2 snooker tables. **Conf** Corporate Hospitality Days available **Location** 0.5m S from Saltburn

Hotel ★★★ 66% Rushpool Hall Hotel, Saltburn Ln, SALTBURN-BY-THE-SEA ☎ 01287 624111 21 en suite

SCARBOROUGH
Map 08 TA08

Scarborough North Cliff North Cliff Av
YO12 6PP
☎ 01723 355397 🖷 01723 362134
e-mail: info@northcliffgolfclub.co.uk
Seaside course beginning on clifftop overlooking North Bay and castle winding inland through parkland with stunning views of the North Yorkshire Moors.
18 holes, 6425yds, Par 71, SSS 71, Course record 66.
Club membership 895.
Visitors must be member of a club with handicap certificate; not before 10.30am Sun. **Societies** booking with secretary for parties of 8-40. **Green Fees** £36 per day; £30 per round (£40/£35 Fri-Sun & bank holidays). **Prof** Simon N Deller **Course Designer** James Braid **Facilities** ⊗ ⽊ ⓑ ⬛ ♀ ⚒ ⌂ ✐ ✎ **Conf** Corporate Hospitality Days available **Location** 2m N of town centre off A165

Hotel ★★★ 66% Esplanade Hotel, Belmont Rd, SCARBOROUGH ☎ 01723 360382 73 en suite

Scarborough South Cliff Deepdale Av YO11 2UE
☎ 01723 374737 🖷 01723 374737
e-mail: secretary@scarboroughgolfclub.co.uk
Parkland and seaside course which falls into two parts, divided from one another by the main road from Scarborough to Filey. On the seaward side of the road lie holes 4 to 10. On the landward side the first three holes and the last eight are laid out along the bottom of a rolling valley, stretching southwards into the hills.
18 holes, 6405yds, Par 72, SSS 71, Course record 68.
Club membership 560.
Visitors contact in advance; not before 9.30am Mon-Fri, 10am Sat & 10.30am Sun. **Societies** contact Secretary in advance. **Green Fees** £30 per day, £25 per round (£35/£30 weekends). **Prof** Tony Skingle **Course Designer** MacKenzie **Facilities** ⊗ ⽊ ⓑ ⬛ ♀ ⚒ ⌂ ✐ ✎ ⚲ ✐ **Location** 1m S on A165

Hotel ★★ 65% Bradley Court Hotel, Filey Rd, South Cliff, SCARBOROUGH ☎ 01723 360476 40 en suite

SELBY
Map 08 SE63

Selby Mill Ln, Brayton YO8 9LD
☎ 01757 228622 🖷 01757 228622
e-mail: selbygolfclub@hotmail.com
Mainly flat, links-type course; prevailing south-west wind. Testing holes including the 3rd, 7th and 16th.
18 holes, 6374yds, Par 71, SSS 71, Course record 68.
Club membership 840.
Visitors contact professional on 01757 228785, members & guests only at weekends. **Societies** welcome Mon-Fri, must apply in advance. **Green Fees** £37 per day, £32 per round. **Cards** 🖿 🖿 💳 **Prof** Nick Ludwell **Course Designer** J Taylor & Hawtree **Facilities** ⊗ ⽊ ⓑ ⬛ ♀ ⚒ ⌂ ✐ ✐ ⚲ **Location** off A63 Selby bypass

Hotel ★★★ ♨ 74% Monk Fryston Hall Hotel, MONK FRYSTON ☎ 01977 682369 29 en suite

SETTLE
Map 07 SD86

Settle Buckhaw Brow, Giggleswick BD24 0DH
☎ 01729 825288 🖷 01729 825288
Picturesque parkland course with a stream affecting play on four holes.
9 holes, 6200yds, Par 72, SSS 72.
Club membership 380.
Visitors not before 2pm on Sun. **Societies** apply in writing or phone four weeks in advance. **Green Fees** not confirmed. **Course Designer** Facilities ⚒ **Location** 1m W of Settle on Kendal Rd

Inn ♦♦♦♦ Golden Lion, 5 Duke St, SETTLE ☎ 01729 822203 12 rms (10 en suite)

SKIPTON
Map 07 SD95

Skipton Short Lee Ln BD23 3LF
☎ 01756 795657 🖷 01756 796665
e-mail: enquiries@skiptongolfclub.co.uk
Undulating parkland course with some water hazards and panoramic views.
18 holes, 6049yds, Par 70, SSS 69, Course record 66.
Club membership 800.
Visitors welcome by arrangement **Societies** apply by phone or in writing. **Green Fees** £30 per day, £24 per 18 holes (£26 per 18 holes weekends). **Prof** Peter Robinson **Facilities** ⊗ ⽊ ⓑ ⬛ ♀ ⚒ ⌂ ✐ **Leisure** snooker. **Conf** Corporate Hospitality Days available **Location** 1m N of Skipton on A59

Hotel ★★★ The Devonshire Arms Country House Hotel, BOLTON ABBEY ☎ 01756 710441 41 en suite

TADCASTER
Map 08 SE44

Cocksford Cocksford, Stutton LS24 9NG
☎ 01937 834253 🖷 01937 834253
e-mail: enquiries@cocksfordgolfclub.freeserve.co.uk
Old Course: 18 holes, 5570yds, Par 71, SSS 69, Course record 68.
Phone for further details

Hotel ★★★★ ♨ 76% Wood Hall Hotel, Trip Ln, Linton, WETHERBY ☎ 01937 587271 14 en suite 30 annexe en suite

Scathingwell Scarthingwell LS24 9PF
☎ 01937 557864 (pro) 557878 (club) 🖷 01937 557909
Testing water hazards and well-placed bunkers and trees provide a challenging test of golf for all handicaps at this scenic parkland course. Easy walking.
18 holes, 6771yds, Par 72, SSS 72.
Club membership 500.
Visitors dress code must be adhered to. May play anytime midweek & Sun, after 2pm Sat. **Societies** golf packages available, book one month in advance. **Green Fees** terms on application. **Prof** Steve Footman **Facilities** ⊗ ⽊ ⓑ ⬛ ♀ ⚒ ⌂ ✐ **Conf** Corporate Hospitality Days available **Location** 4m S of Tadcaster on A162 Tadcaster-Ferrybridge road

Hotel ★★★ 77% Hazlewood Castle, Paradise Ln, Hazlewood, TADCASTER ☎ 01937 535353 9 en suite 12 annexe en suite

HIRSK   Map 08 SE48

hirsk & Northallerton Thornton-le-Street
)7 4AB
☎ 01845 522170 & 525115 🖷 01845 525115
mail: secretary@tngc.co.uk
**ie course has good views of the nearby Hambleton
ills to the east and Wensleydale to the west. Testing
urse, mainly flat.**
holes, 6495yds, Par 72, SSS 71, Course record 66.
ub membership 500.
sitors phone in advance & have handicap certificate. No
ay Sun unless with member. **Societies** apply in writing.
reen Fees £30 per day; £24 per round (£40/£30
eekends). **Prof** Robert Garner **Course Designer** ADAS
cilities ⊗)||| 🖳 💺 ♀ 👤 📁 ⛴ ➹ 🚜 ⚷ **Location** 2m N
A168

otel ★★ 75% Golden Fleece Hotel, 42 Market Place,
HIRSK ☎ 01845 523108 23 en suite

WHITBY   Map 08 NZ81

hitby Low Straggleton, Sandsend Rd YO21 3SR
☎ 01947 600660 🖷 01947 600660
mail: whitby_golf_club@compuserve.com
**aside course with four holes along clifftops and over
vines. Good views and a fresh sea breeze.**
holes, 6134yds, Par 71, Course record 66.
ub membership 600.
sitors not competition days, parties must contact in
vance. **Societies** contact in writing. **Green Fees** £25 per
y (£30 weekends). **Prof** Tony Mason **Facilities** ⊗)||| 🖳
♀ 👤 📁 ⛴ ⚷ **Location** 1.5m NW on A174

otel ★★ 70% White House Hotel, Upgang Ln, West
iff, WHITBY ☎ 01947 600469 10 en suite

ORK   Map 08 SE65

orest of Galtres Moorlands Rd, Skelton YO32 2RF
☎ 01904 766198 🖷 01904 769400
mail: secretary@forestofgaltres.co.uk
**›vel parkland course in the heart of the ancient Forest
Galtres with mature oak trees and interesting water
atures coming into play on the 6th, 14th and 17th
›les. Views towards York Minster.**
holes, 6412yds, Par 72, SSS 70, Course record 63.
ub membership 450.
sitors phone to book, may play anytime subject to
ailability **Societies** not Sat, booking system, phone for
rms. **Green Fees** £25 per day; £20 per round (£32/£27
eekends & bank holidays). **Cards** 🖵 🖵 🖵 🖵 🖵 🖵
of Phil Bradley **Course Designer** Simon Gidman
cilities ⊗)||| by arrangement 🖳 💺 ♀ 👤 📁 ⛴ ⚷ ℓ
›cation 4.5m NW from city centre, off A19 through
elton

otel ★★ 70% Beechwood Close Hotel, 19 Shipton Rd,
ifton, YORK ☎ 01904 658378 14 en suite

orest Park Stockton on the Forest YO32 9UW
☎ 01904 400425 & 400688 🖷 01904 400717
mail: admin@forestparkgolfclub.co.uk
**at parkland 27-hole course with large greens and
rrow tree-lined fairways. The Old Foss beck
eanders through the course, creating a natural hazard
many holes.**
d Foss Course: 18 holes, 6600yds, Par 71, SSS 72,

Course record 73.
The West Course: 9 holes, 3186yds, Par 70, SSS 70.
Club membership 600.
Visitors welcome, subject to tee availability. Advisable to
contact club in advance. **Societies** by arrangement. **Green
Fees** 18 holes £20 (weekends £25); 9 holes £9 (£11).
Cards 🖵 🖵 🖵 **Prof** Mark Winterburn **Facilities** ⊗)||| 🖳
🖳 ♀ 👤 📁 ⛴ ➹ 🚜 ⚷ ℓ **Conf** Corporate Hospitality
Days available **Location** 4m NE of York off A64 York
bypass

Hotel ★★ 67% Jacobean Lodge Hotel, Plainville Ln,
Wigginton, YORK ☎ 01904 762749 8 en suite

Fulford Heslington Ln YO10 5DY
☎ 01904 413579 🖷 01904 416918
e-mail: info@fulfordgolfclub.co.uk
**A flat, parkland and heathland course well-known for
the superb quality of its turf, particularly the greens,
and now famous as the venue for some of the best golf
tournaments in the British Isles in past years.**
18 holes, 6775yds, Par 72, SSS 72, Course record 62.
Club membership 775.
Visitors contact in advance. Not Tue am. Limited
weekends **Societies** not Tue am, book with the manager.
Green Fees £65 per day, £50 per round. **Prof** Martin
Brown **Course Designer** C MacKenzie **Facilities** ⊗)||| 🖳
🖳 ♀ 👤 📁 ➹ ⚷ **Conf** Corporate Hospitality Days
available **Location** 2m S of York off A19

Hotel ★★★ 71% York Pavilion Hotel, 45 Main St,
Fulford, YORK ☎ 01904 622099 🖷 01904 626939
57 en suite

Heworth Muncaster House, Muncastergate YO31 9JY
☎ 01904 422389 🖷 01904 426156
e-mail: golf@heworth-gc.fsnet.co.uk
**A 12-hole parkland course, easy walking. Holes 3 to 7
and 9 played twice from different tees.**
12 holes, 6105yds, Par 69, SSS 69, Course record 68.
Club membership 550.
Visitors advisable to phone the professional in advance, no
catering Mon **Societies** apply in writing or phone
professional 01904 422389 **Green Fees** £20 per day; £15
per round (£25/£20 weekends & bank holidays). **Prof**
Stephen Burdett **Course Designer** B Cheal **Facilities** ⊗)|||
by arrangement 🖳 💺 ♀ 👤 📁 ⛴ ⚷ **Conf** Corporate
Hospitality Days available **Location** 1.5m NE of city
centre on A1036

Hotel ★★★ 70% Monkbar Hotel, Monkbar, YORK
☎ 01904 638086 99 en suite

Continued

Swallow Hall Crockey Hill YO19 4SG
☎ 01904 448889 📄 01904 448219
e-mail: jtscores@hotmail.com
**A small 18-hole, par 3 course with three par 4s.
Attached to a caravan park and holiday cottages.**
*18 holes, 3600yds, Par 57, SSS 56, Course record 58.
Club membership 100.*
Visitors no restrictions. **Societies** phone in advance. **Green
Fees** not confirmed. **Cards** 🔲 🔳 🔳 **Course Designer**
Brian Henry **Facilities** ⊗ ⍟ 🏪 ⚑ ♀ ♨ ⌇ 🏐 🚧 ⚙ 🥂
Leisure hard tennis courts, fishing. **Conf** fac available
Corporate Hospitality Days available **Location** off A19
signed Wheldrake

....

Hotel ★★★ 71% York Pavilion Hotel, 45 Main St,
Fulford, YORK ☎ 01904 622099 57 en suite

York Lords Moor Ln, Strensall YO32 5XF
☎ 01904 491840 (Sec) 490304 (Pro) 📄 01904 491852
e-mail: secretary@yorkgolfclub.co.uk
**A pleasant, well-designed, heathland course with easy
walking. The course is of good length but is flat so not
too tiring. The course is well bunkered with excellent
greens and there are two testing pond holes.**
*18 holes, 6301yds, Par 70, SSS 70, Course record 66.
Club membership 750.*
Visitors with member only Sun, must contact in advance
Sat. **Societies** initial enquiry through professional. **Green
Fees** £45 for 36 holes, £40 for 27 holes, £35 for 18 holes
(weekends £47 for 27 holes, £43 for 18 holes). **Prof** AP
Hoyles **Course Designer** JH Taylor **Facilities** ⊗ ⍟ 🏪 ⚑
♀ ♨ 🥂 ⚙ **Location** 6m NE of York, E of Strensall

....

Hotel ★★★ 77% Dean Court Hotel, Duncombe Place,
YORK ☎ 01904 625082 39 en suite

YORKSHIRE, SOUTH

BARNSLEY   Map 08 SE30

Barnsley Wakefield Rd, Staincross S75 6JZ
☎ 01226 382856 📄 01226 382856
e-mail: barnsleygolfclub@hotmail.com
**Undulating municipal parkland course with easy walking
apart from last four holes. Testing 8th and 18th holes.**
*18 holes, 5951yds, Par 69, SSS 69, Course record 64.
Club membership 450.*
Visitors booking advisable, phone professional on 01226
380358. **Societies** by arrangement, contact club
professional at 01226 380358 **Green Fees** 18 holes £10.50
(weekends & bank holidays £12.50). **Prof** Shaun Wyke
Facilities ⊗ by arrangement ⍟ by arrangement 🏪 by
arrangement ⚑ ♨ 🥂 ⌇ ⚙ **Location** 3m N on A61

....

Hotel ★★★ 73% Ardsley House Hotel & Health Club,
Doncaster Rd, Ardsley, BARNSLEY ☎ 01226 309955
75 en suite

Sandhill Middlecliffe Ln, Little Houghton S72 0HW
☎ 01226 753444 📄 01226 753444
**An attractive, easy walking, parkland course with views
of the surrounding countryside. The course has now
almost reached full maturity and is both rewarding and
challenging to the club member. The 4th hole poses a
challenge, having a deep bunker directly in front of the
green.**
*18 holes, 6257yds, Par 71, SSS 70, Course record 69.
Club membership 420.*

Visitors welcome by booking. **Societies** phone for
availability, write to confirm. **Green Fees** £13 per round
(weekends £18). **Cards** 🔲 🔳 🔳 🔳 🔳 ⚙ **Course
Designer** John Royston **Facilities** ⊗ ⍟ 🏪 ⚑ ♀ ♨ 🥂 🏐
⚙ ⌇ **Location** 5m E of Barnsley off A635

....

Hotel ★★★ 73% Ardsley House Hotel & Health Club,
Doncaster Rd, Ardsley, BARNSLEY ☎ 01226 309955
75 en suite

BAWTRY   Map 08 SK69

Bawtry Cross Ln, Austerfield DN10 6RF
☎ 01302 710841
**Championship moorland course featuring the 618yd
7th and the Postage Stamp 8th. Well drained and easy
walking with attached driving range.**
*18 holes, 6994yds, Par 73, SSS 73, Course record 67.
Club membership 600.*
Visitors phone in advance for weekends. **Societies** phone
in advance. May only play pm at weekends. **Green Fees**
£15 (£20 weekends & bank holidays). **Cards** 🔲 🔳 🔳
🔳 🔳 ⚙ **Prof** Darran Roberts **Facilities** ⊗ ⍟ 🏪 ⚑ ♀ ♨
🥂 🏐 🚧 ⚙ ⌇ **Conf** Corporate Hospitality Days available
Location 2m from Bawtry on A614

....

Hotel ★★★★ 69% Mount Pleasant Hotel, Great North R
ROSSINGTON ☎ 01302 868696 & 868219
📄 01302 865130 45 en suite

CONISBROUGH   Map 08 SK59

Crookhill Park Municipal Carr Ln DN12 2AH
☎ 01709 862979 📄 01709 866455
**A naturally sloping parkland course with many holes
featuring tight dog-legs and small, undulating greens.
The signature hole (11th) involves a fearsome tee shot
over a ditch onto a sloping fairway and final shot to an
elevated green surrounded by tall trees and deep
bunkers.**
*18 holes, 5849yds, Par 70, SSS 68, Course record 64.
Club membership 350.*
Visitors booking system for general play. **Societies**
bookings taken in advance, deposits taken through bookin
system. **Green Fees** £11.25 (£12.50 weekends).
Prof Richard Swaine **Facilities** 🏪 ⚑ ♀ ♨ 🥂 ⌇
Location 1.5m SE on B6094

....

Hotel ★★ 64% Pastures Hotel, Pastures Rd,
MEXBOROUGH ☎ 01709 577707 29 en suite

DONCASTER   Map 08 SE50

Doncaster 278 Bawtry Rd, Bessacarr DN4 7PD
☎ 01302 865632 📄 01302 865994
e-mail: doncastergolf@aol.com
18 holes, 6220yds, Par 69, SSS 70, Course record 66.
Course Designer Mackenzie, Hawtree **Location** 4m SE o
A638
Phone for further details

....

Hotel ★★★★ 69% Mount Pleasant Hotel, Great North R
ROSSINGTON ☎ 01302 868696 & 868219
📄 01302 865130 45 en suite

> If the name of the club appears in *italics*, details
> have not been confirmed for this
> edition of the guide.

Continued

Doncaster Town Moor Bawtry Rd, Belle Vue
DN4 5HU
☎ 01302 535286 (pro shop) & 533167 (bar)
📠 01302 533778
e-mail: dtmgc@btconnect.com
**Easy walking, but testing, heathland course with good
true greens. Notable hole is 11th (par 4), 464yds.
Situated in centre of racecourse.**
18 holes, 6072yds, Par 69, SSS 69, Course record 63.
Club membership 520.
Visitors not Sun am. Contact in advance. **Societies** contact
in advance. **Green Fees** not confirmed. **Prof** Steven Shaw
Facilities ⊗ ⁊ℍ ㇐ 💺 ⅋ ㇇ 🏠 ⚘ **Conf** Corporate
Hospitality Days available **Location** 1.5m E at racecourse
on A638

Hotel ⛫ Campanile, Doncaster Leisure Park, Bawtry Rd,
DONCASTER ☎ 01302 370770 50 en suite

Owston Park Owston Ln, Owston DN6 8EF
☎ 01302 330821
e-mail: will@owstonpark.fsnet.co.uk
9 holes, 2866yds, Par 35, SSS 70.
Course Designer M Parker **Location** 5m N of Doncaster
off A19
Phone for further details

Hotel ★★★ 68% Danum Hotel, High St, DONCASTER
☎ 01302 342261 66 en suite

Thornhurst Park Holme Ln, Owston DN5 0LR
☎ 01302 337799 📠 01302 721495
e-mail: info@thornhurst.co.uk
**Surrounded by Owston Wood, this scenic parkland
course has numerous strategically placed bunkers, and
a lake comes into play at the 7th and 8th holes.**
18 holes, 6490yds, Par 72, SSS 72, Course record 72.
Club membership 160.
Visitors must wear trousers, shirt with collar & golf shoes,
can contact two days in advance. **Societies** phone or write
in advance. **Green Fees** £12 per 18 holes, £7 per 9 holes
(£14/£8 weekends & bank holidays). **Cards** 🌐 💳 🏧 📇
📱 **Prof** Kevin Pearce **Facilities** ⊗ ⁊ℍ ㇐ 💺 ⅋ 🏠 ⚘ ⚘
Conf fac available Corporate Hospitality Days available
Location on A19 between Bentley & Askern

Hotel ★★★ 68% Danum Hotel, High St, DONCASTER
☎ 01302 342261 66 en suite

Wheatley Armthorpe Rd DN2 5QB
☎ 01302 831655 📠 01302 812736
18 holes, 6405yds, Par 71, SSS 71, Course record 64.
Course Designer George Duncan **Location** NE of town
centre off A18
Phone for further details

Hotel ★★★ 68% Regent Hotel, Regent Square,
DONCASTER ☎ 01302 364180 52 en suite

Kings Wood Thorne Rd DN7 6EP
☎ 01405 741343
**A flat course with ditches that come into play on several
holes, especially on the testing back nine. Notable holes
are the 12th par 4, 16th and par 5 18th. Water is a
prominent feature with several large lakes strategically
placed.**
18 holes, 6002yds, Par 70, SSS 69, Course record 67.

Club membership 100.
Visitors visitors are welcome any time. **Societies** or phone
in advance. **Green Fees** not confirmed. **Cards** 🌐 💳 🏧
📇 📱 **Prof** Mark Cunningham **Course Designer** John
Hunt **Facilities** 💺 🏠 ㇐ ⚘ ⚘ **Location** M180 junct 1,
A614 towards Thorne, onto A1146 towards Hatfield for
0.8m

Hotel ★★★ 64% Belmont Hotel, Horsefair Green,
THORNE ☎ 01405 812320 23 en suite

Hickleton Lidgett Ln DN5 7BE
☎ 01709 896081 📠 01709 896083
e-mail: hickleton@hickletongolfclub.freeserve.co.uk
**Undulating, picturesque parkland course designed by
Neil Coles and Brian Huggett offering a good test of
golf and fine views of the eastern Pennines.**
18 holes, 6434yds, Par 71, SSS 71, Course record 67.
Club membership 625.
Visitors weekdays after 9am & weekends after 2.30pm.
Must contact in advance. **Societies** contact in advance.
Green Fees £30 per day, £25 per round (£30 per round
weekends & bank holidays). **Prof** Paul J Audsley **Course
Designer** Huggett, Coles **Facilities** ⊗ ⁊ℍ ㇐ 💺 ⅋ 🏠 🍴
⚘ ⚘ **Conf** fac available Corporate Hospitality Days
available **Location** A1(M) junct 37, 3m W off A635

Hotel ★★★ 68% Danum Hotel, High St, DONCASTER
☎ 01302 342261 66 en suite

Tankersley Park S35 4LG
☎ 0114 246 8247 📠 0114 245 7818
e-mail: secretary@tpgc.freeserve.co.uk
**Rolling parkland course that demands accuracy rather
than length. Lush fairways. The 18th hole considered to
be one of the best last hole tests in Yorkshire.**
18 holes, 6244yds, Par 70, SSS 70, Course record 64.
Club membership 634.
Visitors contact in advance. Restricted play at weekends.
Societies apply in writing. **Green Fees** £36 per day; £27
per round (£36 per round weekends). **Cards** 🌐 💳 🏧
📇 📱 **Prof** Ian Kirk **Course Designer** Hawtree
Facilities ⊗ ⁊ℍ ㇐ 💺 ⅋ 🏠 🍴 ⚘ **Conf** Corporate
Hospitality Days available **Location** A61/M1 onto A616
Stocksbridge bypass

Hotel ★★★★ 75% Tankersley Manor, Church Ln,
TANKERSLEY ☎ 01226 744700 99 en suite

Wath Abdy Ln S62 7SJ
☎ 01709 878609 📠 01709 877097
e-mail: golf@wathgolfclub.co.uk
**Parkland course, not easy in spite of its length. Testing
course with narrow fairways and small greens. Many
dikes crisscross fairways, making playing for position
paramount. Strategically placed copses reward the
golfer who is straight off the tee. Playing over a pond
into a prevailing wind on the 12th hole to a postage
stamp size green, will test the most accomplished
player.**
18 holes, 6123yds, Par 70, SSS 69, Course record 65.
Club membership 650.
Visitors not weekends. Must contact in advance & have a
handicap certificate. **Societies** contact by writing or phone;

Continued   *Continued*

not weekends. **Green Fees** £29 per day; £24 per round.
Prof Chris Bassett **Facilities** ⊗ ⍧ ঌ 🖤 🏐 ♨ 🏌 ⛳ ✓
Conf fac available Corporate Hospitality Days available
Location 2m N of Rotherham on B6089

Hotel ★★★ 65% Carlton Park Hotel, 102/104 Moorgate
Rd, ROTHERHAM ☎ 01709 849955 80 en suite

ROTHERHAM   Map 08 SK49

Grange Park Upper Wortley Rd S61 2SJ
☎ 01709 559497
e-mail: crowncourt@bun.com
18 holes, 6421yds, Par 71, SSS 71, Course record 65.
Course Designer Fred Hawtree **Location** 3m NW off
A629
Phone for further details

Hotel ★★★★ 75% Tankersley Manor, Church Ln,
TANKERSLEY ☎ 01226 744700 99 en suite

Phoenix Pavilion Ln, Brinsworth S60 5PA
☎ 01709 363864 & 382624 🖹 01709 363788
Undulating meadowland course with variable wind.
18 holes, 6182yds, Par 71, SSS 70, Course record 65.
Club membership 930.
Visitors contact in advance. **Societies** apply in writing.
Green Fees summer £24 per day; £18 per round (£32/£24
weekends & bank holidays); winter £15 per round/day (£21
weekends & bank holidays). **Prof** M Roberts **Course
Designer** C K Cotton **Facilities** ⊗ ⍧ ঌ 🖤 🏐 ♨ 🏌 ⛳
✓ ⛳ **Leisure** hard tennis courts, squash, fishing,
gymnasium. **Conf** fac available Corporate Hospitality
Days available **Location** SW of Rotherham off A630

Hotel ★★★ 65% Carlton Park Hotel, 102/104 Moorgate
Rd, ROTHERHAM ☎ 01709 849955 80 en suite

Rotherham Golf Club Ltd Thrybergh Park,
Doncaster Rd, Thrybergh S65 4NU
☎ 01709 859500 🖹 01709 859517
**Parkland course with easy walking along tree-lined
fairways.**
18 holes, 6324yds, Par 70, SSS 70, Course record 65.
Club membership 500.
Visitors contact in advance. **Societies** contact secretary in
advance. **Green Fees** not confirmed. **Prof** Simon Thornhill
Facilities ⊗ ⍧ ঌ 🖤 🏐 ♨ 🏌 ⛳ ✓
Location 3.5m E on A630

Hotel ★★★ 69% Best Western Elton Hotel, Main St,
Bramley, ROTHERHAM ☎ 01709 545681 13 en suite
16 annexe en suite

Sitwell Park Shrogswood Rd S60 4BY
☎ 01709 541046 🖹 01709 703637
e-mail: secretary@sitwellgolf.co.uk
Undulating parkland course.
18 holes, 5960yds, Par 71, SSS 69.
Club membership 450.
Visitors not Sat; contact in advance. **Societies** contact in
advance. **Green Fees** not confirmed. **Prof** Nic Taylor
Course Designer A MacKenzie **Facilities** ⊗ ⍧ ঌ 🖤 🏐
♨ 🏌 ⛳ ✓ **Conf** Corporate Hospitality Days available
Location 2m SE of Rotherham centre off A631

Hotel ★★★ 64% Hellaby Hall Hotel, Old Hellaby Ln,
Hellaby, ROTHERHAM ☎ 01709 702701 90 en suite

SHEFFIELD   Map 08 SK38

Abbeydale Twentywell Ln, Dore S17 4QA
☎ 0114 236 0763 🖹 0114 236 0762
e-mail: abbeygolf@compuserve.com
Undulating parkland course set in the Beauchief Estate.
18 holes, 6261yds, Par 71, SSS 71, Course record 64.
Club membership 696.
Societies larger groups must apply in writing, smaller
groups by phone. **Green Fees** not confirmed. **Prof** Nigel
Perry **Course Designer** Herbert Fowler **Facilities** ⊗ ⍧ ঌ
🖤 🏐 ♨ 🏌 ⛳ ✓ **Conf** fac available **Location** 4m SW
of city centre off A621

Hotel ★★★ 71% The Beauchief Hotel, 161 Abbeydale Rd
South, SHEFFIELD ☎ 0114 262 0500 50 en suite

Beauchief Public Abbey Ln S8 0DB
☎ 0114 236 7274
18 holes, 5469yds, Par 67, SSS 66, Course record 65.
Location 4m SW of city off A621
Phone for further details

Hotel ★★★ 71% The Beauchief Hotel, 161 Abbeydale Rd
South, SHEFFIELD ☎ 0114 262 0500 50 en suite

Birley Wood Birley Ln S12 3BP
☎ 0114 264 7262
e-mail: birley@sivltd.com
**Undulating meadowland course with well-varied
features, easy walking and good views. Practice range
and putting green.**
*Fairway course: 18 holes, 5734yds, Par 69, SSS 67,
Course record 64.*
Birley Course: 18 holes, 5037, Par 66, SSS 65.
Club membership 278.
Visitors apply in advance. **Societies** apply in advance.
Phone 0114 223 3824 **Green Fees** £9.60 per round (£12
weekends). **Cards** 💳 💳 💳 💳 💳 **Prof** Peter Ball
Facilities ⊗ ⍧ ঌ 🖤 🏐 ♨ 🏌 ⛳ ♨ 🏌 ✓
Location 4.5m SE of city off A616

Hotel ★★★ 66% Mosborough Hall Hotel, High St,
Mosborough, SHEFFIELD ☎ 0114 248 4353 52 en suite

Concord Park Shiregreen Ln S5 6AE
☎ 0114 257 7378
**Hilly municipal parkland course with some fairways
wood-flanked, good views, often windy. Seven par 3
holes.**
18 holes, 4872yds, Par 67, SSS 64, Course record 57.
Club membership 150.
Visitors no restrictions. **Societies** pay & play **Green Fees**
terms on application. **Prof** W Allcroft **Facilities** ⊗ ঌ 🖤 🏐
♨ 🏌 ⛳ ✓ ⛳ **Leisure** hard tennis courts, heated
indoor swimming pool, squash, gymnasium. **Conf**
Corporate Hospitality Days available **Location** 3.5m N of
city on B6086, off A6135

Hotel ⛫ Premier Travel Inn Sheffield (Meadowhall),
Sheffield Rd, Meadowhall, SHEFFIELD
☎ 0870 9906440 103 en suite

Dore & Totley Bradway Rd, Bradway S17 4QR
☎ 0114 2366 844 🖹 0114 2366 844
e-mail: dtgc@lineone.net
18 holes, 6265yds, Par 70, SSS 70, Course record 65.
Location 7m S of city on B6054, off A61
Phone for further details

Continued

otel ★★★ 71% The Beauchief Hotel, 161 Abbeydale Rd
uth, SHEFFIELD ☎ 0114 262 0500 50 en suite

Iallamshire Golf Club Ltd Sandygate S10 4LA
☎ 0114 230 2153 📠 0114 230 5413
e-mail: secretary@hallamshiregolfclub.co.uk
tuated on a shelf of land at a height of 850ft.
Iagnificent views to the west. Moorland turf, long
arries over ravine and small and quick greens.
8 holes, 6346yds, Par 71, SSS 71, Course record 65.
Iub membership 600.
isitors contact professional or secretary in advance; tees
served for members 8-10am, noon-2pm; not Sat.
cieties Sun-Fri, book in advance with secretary. **Green
ees** £45 per day/round (£60 weekends & bank holidays).
ards 🔲 🔲 🔲 🔲 💳 **Prof** GR Tickell **Course
esigner** Various **Facilities** ⊗ ⅷ 🖫 💶 ♀ ♿ 🏠 🛉 ✐
onf Corporate Hospitality Days available
cation off A57 at Crosspool onto Sandygate Rd,
ubhouse 0.75m on right

otel ★★★★ 70% Marriott Sheffield, Kenwood Rd,
HEFFIELD ☎ 0870 400 7261 114 en suite

Iillsborough Worrall Rd S6 4BE
☎ 0114 234 9151 (sec) 📠 0114 229 4105
e-mail: admin@hillsboroughgolfclub.co.uk
eautiful moorland and woodland course 500ft above
alevel, reasonable walking. Challenging first four
oles into a prevailing wind and a tight, testing 14th
ole.
8 holes, 6345yards, Par 71, SSS 70, Course record 63.
Iub membership 650.
isitors contact professional in advance; Tue (Ladies
ay), Thu, weekends before 2pm by arrangement.
cieties apply in writing to secretary. **Green Fees** not
nfirmed. **Prof** Lewis Horsman **Facilities** ⊗ ⅷ 🖫 💶 ♀
🏠 🛉 ♿ ✐ 🥂 **Location** 3m NW of city centre off
616

otel ★★★★ 75% Tankersley Manor, Church Ln,
ANKERSLEY ☎ 01226 744700 99 en suite

ees Hall Hemsworth Rd, Norton S8 8LL
☎ 0114 250 7868
8 holes, 6171yds, Par 71, SSS 70, Course record 63.
cation 3.5m S of city centre off A6102
one for further details

otel ★★★★ 70% Marriott Sheffield, Kenwood Rd,
HEFFIELD ☎ 0870 400 7261 114 en suite

other Valley Golf Centre Mansfield Rd, Wales
ar S26 5PQ
☎ 0114 247 3000 📠 0114 247 6000
e-mail: rother-jackbarker@btinternet.com
he challenging Blue Monster parkland course features
variety of water hazards. Notable holes include the
h, with its island green fronted by water and
ominated by bunkers to the rear. Lookout for the
ater on the par 5 18th.
8 holes, 6602yds, Par 72, SSS 72, Course record 70.
Iub membership 500.
isitors 2 days in advance booking format. **Societies** apply
writing or phone in advance. **Green Fees** not confirmed.
ards 🔲 🔲 🔲 🔲 💳 **Prof** Jason Ripley **Course
esigner** Michael Shattock & Mark Roe **Facilities** ⊗ ⅷ 🖫

📍♀♿🏠🛉🥢🛒✐ ⌘ **Location** M1 junct 31, signs to
Rother Valley Country Park

Hotel ★★★ 66% Mosborough Hall Hotel, High St,
Mosborough, SHEFFIELD ☎ 0114 248 4353 52 en suite

Tinsley Park Municipal Golf High Hazels Park,
Darnall S9 4PE
☎ 0114 203 7435
e-mail: tinsleyparkgc@hotmail.com
Undulating parkland course with plenty of trees and
rough. Easy walking. The signature hole is the par 3
17th.
18 holes, 6064yds, Par 70, SSS 68, Course record 66.
Club membership 150.
Visitors booking essential. Societies apply to professional
shop on 0114 203 7435 **Green Fees** £12.50 per round.
Cards 🔲 💳 **Prof** W Yellott **Facilities** ⊗ by arrangement
🖫 💶 ♀ ♿ 🏠 🛉 🥢 ✐ **Leisure** hard tennis courts.
Location 4m E of city centre off A630

Hotel ★★★ 66% Mosborough Hall Hotel, High St,
Mosborough, SHEFFIELD ☎ 0114 248 4353 52 en suite

Silkstone Field Head, Elmhirst Ln S75 4LD
☎ 01226 790328 📠 01226 792653
Parkland and downland course, fine views over the
Pennines. Testing golf.
18 holes, 6069yds, Par 70, SSS 70, Course record 64.
Club membership 530.
Visitors with member only at weekends. Societies contact
in advance. **Green Fees** not confirmed. **Prof** Kevin Guy
Facilities ⊗ ⅷ 🖫 💶 ♀ ♿ 🥢 🛒 ✐ **Conf** Corporate
Hospitality Days available **Location** 1m E off A628

Hotel ★★★ 73% Ardsley House Hotel & Health Club,
Doncaster Rd, Ardsley, BARNSLEY ☎ 01226 309955
75 en suite

Stocksbridge & District Royd Ln, Deepcar S36 2RZ
☎ 0114 288 2003 (office) 📠 0114 283 1460
e-mail: secretary@stocksbridgeanddistrictgolfclub.com
Hilly moorland course.
18 holes, 5200yds, Par 65, SSS 65, Course record 60.
Club membership 470.
Visitors contact the professional. Societies apply to
secretary. **Green Fees** not confirmed. **Cards** 🔲 🔲 💳
Prof Roger Broad **Course Designer** Dave Thomas
Facilities ⊗ ⅷ 🖫 💶 ♀ ♿ ✐ **Location** S of town
centre

Hotel ★★★ 71% Whitley Hall Hotel, Elliott Ln,
Grenoside, SHEFFIELD ☎ 0114 245 4444 20 en suite

Thorne Kirton Ln DN8 5RJ
☎ 01405 812084 📠 01405 741899
Picturesque parkland course with 6000 newly planted
trees. Water hazards on 11th, 14th and 18th holes.
18 holes, 5366yds, Par 68, SSS 66, Course record 62.
Club membership 300.
Visitors no restrictions. Societies phone in advance. **Green
Fees** £9.75 (£10.75 weekends). **Cards** 🔲 🔲 🔲 🔲 💳
Prof Edward Highfield **Course Designer** RD Highfield
Facilities ⊗ ⅷ 🖫 💶 ♀ ♿ 🏠 🛉 🥢 🛒 ✐ **Conf** fac

Continued   *Continued*

available Corporate Hospitality Days available **Location**
M180 Junct 1, A614 into Thorne, left onto Kirton Ln

Hotel ★★★ 64% Belmont Hotel, Horsefair Green,
THORNE ☎ 01405 812320 23 en suite

WORTLEY   Map 08 SK39

Wortley Hermit Hill Ln S35 7DF
☎ 0114 288 8469 📠 0114 288 8469
e-mail: wortley.golfclub@virgin.net
**Well-wooded, undulating parkland course sheltered
from the prevailing wind. Excellent greens in a totally
pastoral setting.**

*18 holes, 6028yds, Par 69, SSS 68, Course record 62.
Club membership 510.*
Visitors not 11.30am-1pm. Must contact professional in
advance & hold a handicap certificate. **Societies** phone in
advance & confirm in writing with deposit. **Green Fees** not
confirmed. **Cards** ▭ ▬ **Prof** Ian Kirk **Facilities** ⊗ ⏸ ⅃
♨ ♀ ♨ 🏠 🎯 ♂ **Conf** Corporate Hospitality Days
available **Location** 0.5m NE of village off A629

Hotel ★★★ 71% Whitley Hall Hotel, Elliott Ln,
Grenoside, SHEFFIELD ☎ 0114 245 4444 20 en suite

YORKSHIRE, WEST

ADDINGHAM   Map 07 SE04

Bracken Ghyll Skipton Rd LS29 0SL
☎ 01943 831207 📠 01943 839453
e-mail: office@brackenghyll.co.uk
**On the edge of the Yorkshire Dales, the course
commands superb views over Ilkley Moor and the
Wharfe valley. The demanding 18-hole layout is a test
of both golfing ability and sensible course management.**
*18 holes, 5600yds, Par 69, SSS 66, Course record 69.
Club membership 350.*
Visitors contact in advance. **Societies** phone for
information **Green Fees** terms on application. **Prof** John
Hammond **Facilities** ⊗ ⏸ ⅃ ♨ ♀ ♨ 🏠 🎯 ♂ ♩ **Conf**
Corporate Hospitality Days available **Location** off A65
between Ilkley & Skipton

Hotel ★★★ 76% Rombalds Hotel & Restaurant, 11 West
View, Wells Rd, ILKLEY ☎ 01943 603201 18 en suite

ALWOODLEY   Map 08 SE24

Alwoodley Wigton Ln LS17 8SA
☎ 0113 268 1680 📠 0113 293 9458
**Natural moorland course with heather, whins and
shrubs. Plentifully and cunningly bunkered with
undulating and interesting greens.** *Continued*

Alwoodley Golf Clu

*18 holes, 6666yds, Par 72, SSS 72.
Club membership 460.*
Visitors contact Secretary in advance. **Societies** apply in
advance. **Green Fees** £65 per day/round (£80 weekends).
Cards ▭ ▬ ▬ 🔲 **Prof** John R Green **Course Designer**
Dr Alistair MacKenzie **Facilities** ⊗ ⏸ ⅃ ♨ ♀ ♨ 🏠 🎯
🛒 ♂ **Conf** Corporate Hospitality Days available
Location 5m N off A61

Hotel ★★★ 70% The Merrion Hotel, Wade Ln, LEEDS
☎ 0113 243 9191 109 en suite

BAILDON   Map 07 SE13

Baildon Moorgate BD17 5PP
☎ 01274 584266
e-mail: sec@baildongolfclub.freeserve.co.uk
**Moorland course set out in links style with outward
front nine looping back to clubhouse. Panoramic views
with testing short holes in prevailing winds. The 2nd
hole has been described as one of Britain's scariest.**

*18 holes, 6225yds, Par 70, SSS 70, Course record 63.
Club membership 750.*
Visitors contact in advance, restricted Tue & weekends.
Societies large numbers apply in writing, small numbers
check with the professional. **Green Fees** 18 holes £20
(weekends £24). **Prof** Richard Masters **Course Designer**
Tom Morris **Facilities** ⊗ ⏸ ⅃ ♨ ♀ ♨ 🏠 🎯 ♂ **Leisure**
snooker tables. **Conf** fac available
Location 3m N of Bradford off A6038 at Shipley

Hotel ★★★★ 70% Marriott Hollins Hall Hotel & Countr
Club, Hollins Hill, Baildon, SHIPLEY
☎ 0870 400 7227 122 en suite

BINGLEY
Map 07 SE13

Bingley St Ives Golf Club House, St Ives Estate, Harden BD16 1AT
☎ 01274 562436 📠 01274 511788
e-mail: bingleyst-ives@harden.freeserve.co.uk
Parkland and moorland course.

18 holes, 6485yds, Par 71, SSS 71, Course record 69.
Club membership 450.
Visitors contact professional on 01274 562506, no green fees Sat. **Societies** phone in advance, the professional 01274 562506. **Green Fees** not confirmed. **Cards** 🔲 🔲
🔲 🔲 **Prof** Ray Firth **Course Designer** A MacKenzie **Facilities** ⊗ 〗 🝝 💻 ♀ 🔺 🏠 🚮 ♂
Location 0.75m W off B6429

....
Hotel ★★ 67% Dalesgate Hotel, 406 Skipton Rd, Utley, KEIGHLEY ☎ 01535 664930 20 en suite

Shipley Beckfoot Ln BD16 1LX
☎ 01274 568652 (Secretary) 📠 01274 567739
e-mail: office@shipleygc.co.uk
Well-established parkland course, founded in 1922, featuring six good par 3s.
18 holes, 6235yds, Par 71, SSS 70, Course record 65.
Club membership 600.
Visitors may play Mon, Wed-Fri & Sun, but Tue only after 2.30pm & Sat after 4pm. **Societies** initial enquiry by phone to professional 01274 563674 or by letter. **Green Fees** £39 per day, £32 per round (£40 Sun & bank holidays).
Cards 🔲 🔲 🔲 🔲 🔲 **Prof** J R Parry **Course Designer** Colt, Allison, Mackenzie, Braid **Facilities** ⊗ 〗 🝝 💻 ♀
🔺 🏠 ⛳ ♂ **Conf** fac available Corporate
Hospitality Days available **Location** 6m N of Bradford on A650

....
Hotel ★★ 67% Dalesgate Hotel, 406 Skipton Rd, Utley, KEIGHLEY ☎ 01535 664930 20 en suite

BRADFORD
Map 07 SE13

Bradford Moor Scarr Hall, Pollard Ln BD2 4RW
☎ 01274 771716 & 771693
Moorland course with tricky undulating greens.
9 holes, 5900yds, Par 70, SSS 68, Course record 65.
Club membership 330.
Visitors no visitors at weekends except with member.
Societies can book starting times by application in writing.
Green Fees £10 weekdays only. **Facilities** 💻 ♀ 🔺
Location 2m NE of city centre off A658

....
Hotel ★★★ 70% Midland Hotel, Forster Square, BRADFORD ☎ 01274 735735 90 en suite

Clayton Thornton View Rd, Clayton BD14 6JX
☎ 01274 880047
Parkland course, difficult in windy conditions.
9 holes, 6300yds, Par 72, SSS 72.
Club membership 250.
Visitors not before 4pm on Sun during summer months
Societies apply in writing to the Secretary or Captain.
Green Fees £17 per 18 holes; £9 per 9 holes.
Facilities ⊗ 〗 🝝 💻 ♀ 🔺 **Location** 2.5m SW of city centre on A647

....
Hotel ★★★ 63% Novotel Bradford, 6 Roydsdale Way, BRADFORD ☎ 01274 683683 119 en suite

East Bierley South View Rd, East Bierley BD4 6PP
☎ 01274 681023 📠 01274 683666
e-mail: rjwelch@hotmail.com
Hilly moorland course with narrow fairways. Two par 3 holes over 200yds.
9 holes, 4700yds, Par 64, SSS 63, Course record 59.
Club membership 300.
Visitors restricted Sat (am), Sun & Mon evening. Must contact in advance. **Societies** apply in writing. **Green Fees** not confirmed. **Prof** J Whittom **Facilities** ⊗ 🝝 💻 ♀ 🔺 🏠
Location 4m SE of city centre off A650

....
Hotel ★★★ 63% Novotel Bradford, 6 Roydsdale Way, BRADFORD ☎ 01274 683683 119 en suite

Headley Headley Ln, Thornton BD13 3LX
☎ 01274 833481 📠 01274 833481
e-mail: honsec-hgc@yahoo.com
9 holes, 4864yds, Par 65, SSS 65, Course record 57.
Location 4m W of city centre off B6145 at Thornton
Phone for further details

....
Hotel ★★★ 70% Midland Hotel, Forster Square, BRADFORD ☎ 01274 735735 90 en suite

Queensbury Brighouse Rd, Queensbury BD13 1QF
☎ 01274 882155 & 816864 📠 01274 882155
e-mail: queensburygolf@supanet.com
Undulating woodland and parkland course.
9 holes, 5024yds, Par 66, SSS 65, Course record 59.
Club membership 380.
Visitors preferable to phone in advance, restricted at weekends. **Societies** apply in writing. **Green Fees** terms on application. **Prof** David Delaney **Course Designer** Jonathan Gaunt **Facilities** ⊗ 〗 🝝 💻 ♀ 🔺 🏠 🚮 ♂
Location 4m from Bradford on A647

....
Hotel ★★★ 70% Midland Hotel, Forster Square, BRADFORD ☎ 01274 735735 90 en suite

South Bradford Pearson Rd, Odsal BD6 1BH
☎ 01274 673346 (pro shop) & 679195 📠 01274 690643
Hilly course with good greens, trees and ditches.
Interesting short 2nd hole (par 3) 200yds, well-bunkered and played from an elevated tee.
9 holes, 6068yds, Par 70, SSS 68, Course record 65.
Club membership 300.
Visitors contact professional in advance. Weekends contact for availability. Tue Ladies Day. **Societies** apply in writing to the secretary. **Green Fees** terms on application.
Cards 🔲 🔲 **Prof** Paul Cooke **Facilities** ⊗ 〗 🝝 💻 ♀ 🔺
🏠 ♂ **Location** 2m S of city centre off A638

....
Hotel ★★★ 63% Novotel Bradford, 6 Roydsdale Way, BRADFORD ☎ 01274 683683 119 en suite

West Bowling
Newall Hall, Rooley Ln BD5 8LB
☎ 01274 393207 (office) & 728036 (pro)
🖹 01274 393207
Undulating, tree-lined parkland course. Testing hole: the Coffin, short par 3, very narrow.
18 holes, 5769yds, Par 69, SSS 67, Course record 65.
Club membership 500.
Visitors apply in writing, very limited at weekends. **Societies** apply in writing or phone in advance. **Green Fees** not confirmed. **Prof** Ian A Marshall **Facilities** ⊗ ⅏ ⅃ ♥ ♀ ♨ 🏠 ⌀ **Conf** Corporate Hospitality Days available **Location** junct M606 & A638 (E)

West Bradford
Chellow Grange Rd, Haworth Rd BD9 6NP
☎ 01274 542767 🖹 01274 482079
e-mail: secretary @westbradfordgolfclub.co.uk
Parkland course, not of great length by modern standards, but provides a good test for golfers of all abilities with its undulating terrain, tree-lined fairways and demanding par 3 holes.
18 holes, 5738yds, Par 69, SSS 68, Course record 63.
Club membership 440.
Visitors restricted Sat & Sun. Tue is Ladies Day (can play if times available). Must phone 01274 542102 to reserve a time. **Societies** contact in advance. **Green Fees** £25 per day/round. **Prof** Nigel M Barber **Facilities** ⊗ by arrangement ⅏ by arrangement ⅃ ♥ ♀ ♨ 🏠 ⌀ **Leisure** snooker room. **Conf** fac available Corporate Hospitality Days available **Location** 3.5 m W of city centre off B6144

Hotel ★★★★ 70% Marriott Hollins Hall Hotel & Country Club, Hollins Hill, Baildon, SHIPLEY
☎ 0870 400 7227 122 en suite

Willow Valley Golf & Country Club
Highmoor Ln, Clifton HD6 4JB
☎ 01274 878624
e-mail: golf@wvgc.co.uk
A championship length 18-hole course offering a unique golfing experience, featuring island greens, shaped fairways and bunkers, and multiple teeing areas. The nine-hole course offers an exciting challenge to less experienced golfers.

South: 18 holes, 6496yds, Par 72, SSS 74, Course record 69.
North: 9 holes, 2039yds, Par 62, SSS 60.
Club membership 350.
Visitors tee times may be booked by phone on payment of green fee by credit/debit card. **Societies** phone in advance for availability & booking form. **Green Fees** summer 18 holes Mon-Fri £23 (£28 weekends), 9 holes £7.50 (£9

weekends); reduced winter rates. **Cards** 🔲 🔲 🔲 🔲 **Prof** Julian Haworth **Course Designer** Jonathan Gaunt **Facilities** ⊗ ⅏ ⅃ ♥ ♀ ♨ 🏠 ⌀ ⌀ **Leisure** three-hole floodlit academy course. **Conf** Corporate Hospitality Days available **Location** M62 junct 25, A644 towards Brighouse, right at rdbt onto A643, course 2m on right

Hotel ★★★ 66% Heals Hall Hotel, Leeds Rd, Liversedge, DEWSBURY ☎ 01924 409112 24 en suite

Cleckheaton & District
Bradford Rd BD19 6BU
☎ 01274 851266 🖹 01274 871382
e-mail: info@cleckheatongolf.fsnet.co.uk
Parkland course with gentle hills. Easy walking. Feature holes at 5th, 16th and 17th.
18 holes, 5706yds, Par 70, SSS 68, Course record 61.
Club membership 550.
Visitors parties must arrange in advance, Sun by arrangement. **Societies** weekdays only; must contact in advance, Sun by arrangement. **Green Fees** May-Sep £30 per round/£35 per day. Nov-Apr £25 per day. **Prof** Mike Ingham **Course Designer** Dr A MacKenzie **Facilities** ⊗ ⅏ ⅃ ♥ ♀ ♨ 🏠 ⌀ **Location** M62 junct 26, towards Oakenshaw, 100yds on left, signed Low Moor

Hotel ★★★ 71% Gomersal Park Hotel, Moor Ln, GOMERSAL ☎ 01274 869386 100 en suite

Hanging Heaton
White Cross Rd WF12 7DT
☎ 01924 461606 🖹 01924 430100
e-mail: ken.wood@hhgc.org
Arable land, easy walking, fine views. Testing 4th hole (par 3).
9 holes, 5836yds, Par 69, SSS 68.
Club membership 500.
Visitors must play with member at weekends & bank holidays. Must contact in advance. **Societies** phone in advance. **Green Fees** not confirmed. **Prof** Gareth Moore **Facilities** ⊗ ⅏ ⅃ ♥ ♀ ♨ 🏠 **Conf** fac available **Location** 0.75m NE off A653

Hotel ★★★ 66% Heals Hall Hotel, Leeds Rd, Liversedge, DEWSBURY ☎ 01924 409112 24 en suite

Elland
Hammerstone, Leach Ln HX5 0TA
☎ 01422 372505 & 374886 (pro)
Nine-hole parkland course played off 18 tees.
9 holes, 5498yds, Par 66, SSS 67, Course record 65.
Club membership 450.
Visitors welcome. **Societies** contact in writing. **Green Fees** £18 per round/day (£30 weekends & bank holidays). **Prof** N Krzywicki **Facilities** ⊗ ⅏ ⅃ ♥ ♀ ♨ 🏠 ⌀ **Location** M62 junct 24, signs to Blackley

Hotel ★★★ 63% The Rock Inn Hotel, Holywell Green, HALIFAX ☎ 01422 379721 30 en suite

Woodsome Hall
HD8 0LQ
☎ 01484 602739 🖹 01484 608260
e-mail: thesecretary@woodsome.co.uk
A parkland course with good views and a historic clubhouse.

Continued   Continued

18 holes, 6096yds, Par 70, SSS 69, Course record 67.
Club membership 800.
Visitors contact in advance. Jacket & tie required in all rooms except casual bar. **Societies** apply in writing. **Green Fees** terms on application. **Cards** ⬜ ▬ ▢ **Prof** M Higginbotton **Facilities** ⊗ ⅷ ⅃ ⅃ ⅃ ⅃ ⅃ ⅃ **Location** 1.5m SW off A629

Hotel ★★★ 69% Bagden Hall, Wakefield Rd, Scissett, HUDDERSFIELD ☎ 01484 865330 16 en suite

GARFORTH Map 08 SE43

Garforth Long Ln LS25 2DS
☎ 0113 286 2021 📠 0113 286 3308
e-mail: garforthgcltd@lineone.net
Gently undulating parkland course with fine views, easy walking.
18 holes, 6304yds, Par 70, SSS 70, Course record 64.
Club membership 600.
Visitors contact in advance & have handicap certificate. With member only weekends & bank holidays. **Societies** apply in advance. **Green Fees** Mon-Fri £36 per round/£42 per day. **Prof** Ken Findlater **Course Designer** Dr A MacKenzie **Facilities** ⊗ ⅷ ⅃ ⅃ ⅃ ⅃ ⅃ ⅃ ⅃ **Conf** Corporate Hospitality Days available **Location** 6m E of Leeds, next to A1/M1 link road

Hotel ★★★ 73% Milford Hotel, A1 Great North Rd, Peckfield, LEEDS ☎ 01977 681800 47 en suite

GUISELEY Map 08 SE14

Bradford (Hawksworth) Hawksworth Ln LS20 8NP
☎ 01943 875570 📠 01943 875570
Set in undulating countryside, the course is a moorland links laid out on the southern slope of a wooded ridge about 650ft above sea level. The spacious greens with their subtle borrows, together with some tough and uncompromising par 4s make this a challenging course. The testing par 4 10th and the par 3 14th require accurate shots to well-protected greens.
Hawksworth: 18 holes, 6303yds, Par 71, SSS 71, Course record 65.
Club membership 650.
Visitors must have a handicap certificate & contact in advance; not Sat. **Societies** by arrangement with manager. **Green Fees** £36 per round (£45 weekends & bank holidays). **Prof** Sydney Weldon **Course Designer** WH Fowler **Facilities** ⊗ ⅷ ⅃ ⅃ ⅃ ⅃ ⅃ **Conf** Corporate Hospitality Days available **Location** SW of town centre off A6038

Hotel ★★★★ 70% Marriott Hollins Hall Hotel & Country Club, Hollins Hill, Baildon, SHIPLEY ☎ 0870 400 7227 122 en suite

HALIFAX Map 07 SE02

Halifax Union Ln, Ogden HX2 8XR
☎ 01422 244171
e-mail: halifax.golfclub@virgin.net
Moorland course crossed by streams, natural hazards and offering fine views of wildlife and the surroundings. Testing 172yd 17th (par 3).
18 holes, 6037yds, Par 70, SSS 69, Course record 65.
Club membership 700.
Visitors contact professional for tee times 01422 240047. Limited play weekend. **Societies** contact secretary for

dates. **Green Fees** £25 per round/£30 per day. **Prof** Michael Allison **Course Designer** A Herd, J Braid **Facilities** ⊗ ⅷ ⅃ ⅃ ⅃ ⅃ ⅃ ⅃ **Conf** fac available Corporate Hospitality Days available **Location** 4m from Halifax on A629 Halifax-Keighley road

Hotel ★★★ 75% Holdsworth House Hotel, Holdsworth, HALIFAX ☎ 01422 240024 40 en suite

Lightcliffe Knowle Top Rd, Lightcliffe HX3 8SW
☎ 01422 202459 204081
A parkland course where positioning of the drive is as important as length. Signature hole is a dog-leg with the second shot over a deep ravine.
9 holes, 5892yds, Par 68, SSS 68.
Club membership 460.
Visitors contact in advance. **Societies** apply in writing. **Green Fees** terms on application. **Prof** Robert Kershaw **Facilities** ⊗ ⅷ ⅃ ⅃ ⅃ ⅃ ⅃ **Location** 3.5m E of Halifax on A58

Hotel ★★★ 75% Holdsworth House Hotel, Holdsworth, HALIFAX ☎ 01422 240024 40 en suite

West End Paddock Ln, Highroad Well HX2 0NT
☎ 01422 341878 📠 01422 341878
e-mail: info@westendgc.co.uk
Semi-moorland course. Tree lined. Two ponds.
18 holes, 5951yds, Par 69, SSS 69, Course record 62.
Club membership 560.
Visitors not Sat; contact in advance. **Societies** apply in writing to Secretary. **Green Fees** not confirmed. **Prof** David Rishworth **Facilities** ⊗ ⅷ ⅃ ⅃ ⅃ ⅃ ⅃ ⅃ **Conf** Corporate Hospitality Days available **Location** W of town centre off A646

Hotel ★★★ 75% Holdsworth House Hotel, Holdsworth, HALIFAX ☎ 01422 240024 40 en suite

HEBDEN BRIDGE Map 07 SD92

Hebden Bridge Mount Skip, Wadsworth HX7 8PH
☎ 01422 842896 & 842732
9 holes, 5242yds, Par 68, SSS 67, Course record 61.
Location 1.5m E off A6033
Phone for further details

Hotel ★★ 71% Old White Lion Hotel, Main St, HAWORTH ☎ 01535 642313 15 en suite

HOLYWELL GREEN Map 07 SE01

Halifax Bradley Hall HX4 9AN
☎ 01422 374108
Moorland and parkland course, tightened by tree planting, easy walking.
18 holes, 6138yds, Par 70, SSS 70, Course record 65.
Club membership 500.
Visitors contact in advance. **Societies** apply in advance. **Green Fees** not confirmed. **Prof** Peter Wood **Facilities** ⊗ ⅷ ⅃ ⅃ ⅃ ⅃ **Location** S on A6112

Hotel ★★★ 63% The Rock Inn Hotel, Holywell Green, HALIFAX ☎ 01422 379721 30 en suite

Looking for a new course? Always telephone ahead to confirm visitor arrangements.

Continued

HUDDERSFIELD   Map 07 SE11

Bagden Hall Hotel & Golf Course Wakefield
Rd, Scissett HD8 9LE
☎ 01484 865330 📄 01484 861001
e-mail: info@bagdenhall.demon.co.uk.
9 holes, 3002yds, Par 56, SSS 55, Course record 60.
Course Designer F O'Donnell, R Braithwaite
Location A636 Wakefield-Denby Dale
Phone for further details

Hotel ★★★ 69% Bagden Hall, Wakefield Rd, Scissett,
HUDDERSFIELD ☎ 01484 865330 16 en suite

Bradley Park Off Bradley Rd HD2 1PZ
☎ 01484 223772 📄 01484 451613
e-mail: parnellreilly@tinyworld.co.uk
**Parkland course, challenging with good mix of long and
short holes. Also 14-bay floodlit driving range and a
nine-hole par 3 course, ideal for beginners. Superb
views.**
*18 holes, 6284yds, Par 70, SSS 70, Course record 65.
Club membership 300.*
Visitors may book by phone for weekends & bank
holidays from the preceeding Thu. No restrictions on other
days. **Societies** welcome midweek, apply in writing to
professional. **Green Fees** not confirmed. **Cards** 💳 💳
💳 💳 💳 **Prof** Parnell E Reilly **Course Designer** Cotton,
Pennick, Lowire & Partners **Facilities** ⊗ �𝍌 🖫 🞗 ♀ ⚲ 🏠
🏌 ⚲ 🏌 ⚮ 🏌 **Leisure** 9-hole par 3 course. **Conf** fac
available Corporate Hospitality Days available
Location M62 junct 25, 2.5m

Hotel ★★★★ 61% Cedar Court Hotel, Ainley Top,
HUDDERSFIELD ☎ 01422 375431 114 en suite

Crosland Heath Felk Stile Rd, Crosland Heath
HD4 7AF
☎ 01484 653216 📄 01484 461079
e-mail: croslandheath@onetel.net.uk
Moorland course with fine views over valley.
*18 holes, 6007yds, Par 70, SSS 69.
Club membership 650.*
Visitors welcome, but advisable to check with
professional; not Sat. **Societies** phone in advance. **Green
Fees** terms on application. **Prof** John Eyre **Course
Designer** Dr. McKenzie **Facilities** ⊗ �𝍌 🖫 🞗 ♀ ⚲ 🏠 ⚮
Conf fac available Corporate Hospitality Days available
Location SW off A62

Hotel ★★★ 66% Pennine Manor Hotel, Nettleton Hill Rd,
Scapegoat Hill, HUDDERSFIELD ☎ 01484 642368
31 en suite

Huddersfield Fixby Hall, Lightridge Rd, Fixby
HD2 2EP
☎ 01484 426203 📄 01484 424623
e-mail: secretary@huddersfield-golf.co.uk
**A testing heathland course of championship standard
laid out in 1891.**
*18 holes, 6399yds, Par 71, SSS 71, Course record 63.
Club membership 760.*
Visitors book tee times with professional. **Societies**
welcome Mon, Wed-Fri by arrangement. **Green Fees** £47
per day, £37 per round (£57/£47 weekends & bank
holidays). **Cards** 💳 💳 💳 💳 💳 **Prof** Paul Carman
Facilities ⊗ �𝍌 🖫 🞗 ♀ ⚲ 🏠 ⚮ 🏌 **Conf** fac available
Corporate Hospitality Days available **Location** 2m N off
A641

Hotel ★★★★ 61% Cedar Court Hotel, Ainley Top,
HUDDERSFIELD ☎ 01422 375431 114 en suite

Longley Park Maple St, Off Somerset Rd HD5 9AX
☎ 01484 422304
9 holes, 5212yds, Par 66, SSS 66, Course record 61.
Location 0.5m SE of town centre off A629
Phone for further details

Hotel ★★★★ 61% Cedar Court Hotel, Ainley Top,
HUDDERSFIELD ☎ 01422 375431 114 en suite

ILKLEY   Map 07 SE14

Ben Rhydding High Wood, Ben Rhydding LS29 8SB
☎ 01943 608759
e-mail: secretary@benrhyddinggc.freeserve.co.uk
**Moorland and parkland course with splendid views
over the Wharfe valley. A compact but testing course.**
*9 holes, 4611yds, Par 65, SSS 63, Course record 64.
Club membership 290.*
Visitors contact in advance. May only play at weekend as
guest of member. **Societies** advance notice in writing. In
view of limited resources requests considered by monthly
committee meeting. **Green Fees** £15 (£20 weekends).
Course Designer William Dell **Facilities** ♀ ⚲
Location SE of town centre. Off Wheatley Ln onto
Wheatley Grove, left onto High Wood, clubhouse on left

Hotel ★★★ 76% Rombalds Hotel & Restaurant, 11 West
View, Wells Rd, ILKLEY ☎ 01943 603201 18 en suite

Ilkley Nesfield Rd, Myddleton LS29 0BE
☎ 01943 600214 📄 01943 816130
e-mail: honsec@ilkleygolfclub.co.uk
**This beautiful parkland course is situated in
Wharfedale and the Wharfe is a hazard on each of the
first seven holes. In fact, the 3rd is laid out entirely on
an island in the river.**
*18 holes, 5953yds, Par 69, SSS 70, Course record 64.
Club membership 450.*
Visitors advisable to contact in advance. **Societies** apply in
writing or phone in advance. **Green Fees** £42 (£50
weekends). **Cards** 💳 💳 💳 💳 💳 💳 **Prof** John L
Hammond **Course Designer** MacKenzie **Facilities** ⊗ �𝍌
🖫 🞗 ♀ ⚲ 🏠 🏌 ⚮ **Leisure** fishing. **Conf** Corporate
Hospitality Days available **Location** W side of town centre
off A65

Hotel ★★★ 76% Rombalds Hotel & Restaurant, 11 West
View, Wells Rd, ILKLEY ☎ 01943 603201 18 en suite

KEIGHLEY   Map 07 SE04

Branshaw Branshaw Moor, Oakworth BD22 7ES
☎ 01535 643235 (sec) 📄 01535 648011
e-mail: branshaw@golfclub.fslife.co.uk
**Picturesque moorland course with fairly narrow
fairways and good greens. Extensive views.**
*18 holes, 5823yds, Par 69, SSS 68, Course record 64.
Club membership 500.*
Visitors welcome most times, restrictions at weekends
advisable to ring. **Societies** apply in writing to
Professional. **Green Fees** £20 per day (£30 weekends).
Prof Simon Jowitt **Course Designer** James Braid
Facilities ⊗ ⯏ 🖫 🞗 ♀ ⚲ ⚮ **Conf** Corporate
Hospitality Days available **Location** 2m SW on B6149,
signed Oakworth

Continued   *Continued*

tel ★★ 67% Dalesgate Hotel, 406 Skipton Rd, Utley,
IGHLEY ☎ 01535 664930 20 en suite

eighley Howden Park, Utley BD20 6DH
01535 604778 📠 01535 604778
mail: manager@keighleygolfclub.com
rkland course is good quality and has great views
wn the Aire valley. The 17th hole has been described
one of the most difficult and dangerous holes in
rkshire golf'. The club celebrated its centenary in
04.
holes, 6141yds, Par 69, SSS 70, Course record 64.
ub membership 650.
sitors restricted Sat & Sun. Must contact in advance.
dies Dday Tue. Societies apply in advance. Green Fees
2 per day; £35 per round (£47/£39 weekends & bank
idays). Cards ▨ ▨ ▨ ▨ ▨ ▨ 🔒 Prof Andrew
odes Facilities ⊗ ﹐ 🍴 💪 ♀ ⚘ 🏠 🛒 🚜 ⚐ Leisure
ooker table. Conf fac available Corporate Hospitality
ys available Location 1m NW of town centre off
265, turn N at Roebuck pub & signed

tel ★★ 67% Dalesgate Hotel, 406 Skipton Rd, Utley,
IGHLEY ☎ 01535 664930 20 en suite

EDS   Map 08 SE33

andon Holywell Ln, Shadwell LS17 8EZ
0113 273 7471
18-hole links type course enjoying varying degrees
rough, water and sand hazards.
holes, 4000yds, Par 63.
sitors pay & play course booking not usually necessary.
cieties phone or write in advance. Green Fees £7.50 per
holes (£8.50 weekends). Prof Carl Robinson Course
signer William Binner Facilities 💪 💪 ⚘ 🏠 🛒 🚜
Location off A58 into Shadwell, onto Main St, right at
d Lion pub

tel ★★★★ 🏠 74% Haley's Hotel & Restaurant, Shire
k Rd, Headingley, LEEDS ☎ 0113 278 4446
en suite 6 annexe en suite

okridge Hall Golf & Country Club
okridge Ln LS16 7NL
0113 2300641 📠 0113 203 0198
mail: cookridgehall@americangolf.uk.com
merican-style course designed by Karl Litten. Expect
nty of water hazards, tees for all standards. Large
nkers and fairways between mounds and young
es.
holes, 6788yds, Par 72, SSS 72.
ub membership 520.
sitors contact in advance. Strict dress code applies.
cieties phone in advance. Green Fees not confirmed.
rds ▨ ▨ ▨ ▨ ▨ Prof Martin Jackson Course
signer Karl Liiten Facilities ⊗ ﹐ 💪 💪 ♀ ⚘ 🏠 🛒 🚜
K Leisure chipping & practice bunker.
nf Corporate Hospitality Days available
cation 6m NW of Leeds, off A660

tel ★★★★ 🏠 74% Haley's Hotel & Restaurant, Shire
k Rd, Headingley, LEEDS ☎ 0113 278 4446
en suite 6 annexe en suite

tts Park Armley Ridge Rd LS12 2QX
0113 231 1896 & 2562994
mail: maurice.gl@sagainternet.co.uk
nicipal parkland course; hilly and windy with

narrow fairways. Some very steep hills to some greens.
A challenging course requiring accuracy rather than
length from the tees.
18 holes, 4960yds, Par 65, SSS 64, Course record 63.
Club membership 200.
Visitors no restrictions.apply directly to Leeds leisure
services. Green Fees not confirmed. Facilities ⊗ 💪 ♀
🏠 🛒 Location 3m W of city centre off A647

Hotel ★★★★ 68% Queens Hotel, City Square, LEEDS
☎ 0113 243 1323 217 en suite

Headingley Back Church Ln, Adel LS16 8DW
☎ 0113 267 9573 📠 0113 281 7334
e-mail: manager@headingleygolfclub.co.uk
An undulating course with a wealth of natural features
offering fine views from higher ground. Its most
striking hazard is the famous ravine at the 18th.
Leeds's oldest course, founded in 1892.
18 holes, 6608yds, Par 71, SSS 72.
Club membership 700.
Visitors contact in advance, restricted at weekends.
Societies phone in advance & confirm in writing. Green
Fees £45 per day; £36 per round (£45 per day/round
weekends). Prof Neil M Harvey Course Designer
Dr MacKenzie Facilities ⊗ ﹐ 💪 💪 ♀ ⚘ 🏠 🛒 ⚐ Conf
Corporate Hospitality Days available Location 5.5m N of
city centre. A660 to Skipton, right at lights junct Farrar Ln
& Church Ln, follow Eccup signs

Hotel 🏠 Premier Travel Inn Leeds/Bradford Airport,
Victoria Av, Yeadon, LEEDS ☎ 08701 977153
40 en suite

Horsforth Layton Rise, Layton Rd, Horsforth
LS18 5EX
☎ 0113 258 6819 📠 0113 258 9336
e-mail: secretary@horsforthgolfclubltd.co.uk
Moorland and parkland course combining devilish
short holes with some more substantial challenges.
Extensive views across Leeds and on a clear day York
Minster can be seen from the 14th tee.
18 holes, 6243yds, Par 71, SSS 70, Course record 65.
Club membership 750.
Visitors restricted Sat & Sun. Must contact professional
0113 258 5200. Societies apply in writing or phone Green
Fees £30 per round (£36 weekends & bank holidays).
Prof Dean Stokes, Simon Booth Course Designer
A MacKenzie Facilities ⊗ ﹐ 💪 💪 ♀ ⚘ 🏠 🚜 ⚐
Conf fac available Corporate Hospitality Days available
Location 6.5m NW of city centre off A65

Hotel 🏠 Travelodge (Leeds Bradford Airport), White
House Ln, LEEDS ☎ 0113 250 3996 48 en suite

Leeds Elmete Ln LS8 2LJ
☎ 0113 265 8775 📠 0113 232 3369
e-mail: leedsgccobble@btconnect.com
Parkland course with pleasant views.
18 holes, 6097yds, Par 69, SSS 69, Course record 63.
Club membership 600.
Visitors with member only weekends. Must book in
advance weekdays. Societies apply in writing. Green Fees
not confirmed. Prof Simon Longster Facilities ⊗ ﹐ 💪 💪
♀ ⚘ 🏠 🛒 🚜 ⚐ Location 5m NE of city centre on
A6120, off A58

Hotel ★★★★ 🏠 74% Haley's Hotel & Restaurant, Shire
Oak Rd, Headingley, LEEDS ☎ 0113 278 4446
22 en suite 6 annexe en suite

Continued

Leeds Golf Centre Wike Ridge Ln, Shadwell LS17 9JW
☎ 0113 288 6000 🖷 0113 288 6185
e-mail: info@leedsgolfcentre.com
The 18-hole Wike Ridge is a traditional heathland course designed by Donald Steel. The sand-based greens are constructed to USGA specification and there are an excellent variety of holes with some very challenging par 5s. The 12-hole Oaks is complemented by a floodlit driving range and other practice facilities. The course is the home of the Leeds Golf Academy.
Wike Ridge Course: 18 holes, 6482yds, Par 72, SSS 71.
Oaks: 12 holes, 1610yds, Par 36.
Club membership 500.
Visitors no restrictions, phone booking advisable. **Societies** tee reservation available in advance. **Green Fees** not confirmed. **Cards** **Prof** Mark Pinkett **Course Designer** Donald Steel **Facilities** **Conf** fac available Corporate Hospitality Days available **Location** 5m N, A58, course on N side of Shadwell

Hotel ★★★★ 74% Haley's Hotel & Restaurant, Shire Oak Rd, Headingley, LEEDS ☎ 0113 278 4446 22 en suite 6 annexe en suite

Middleton Park Municipal Middleton Park, Middleton LS10 3TN
☎ 0113 270 0449 🖷 0113 270 0449
e-mail: lynn@ratcliffel.fsnet.co.uk
18 holes, 5263yds, Par 68, SSS 66, Course record 63.
Location 3m S off A653
Phone for further details

Hotel ★★★★ 68% Queens Hotel, City Square, LEEDS ☎ 0113 243 1323 217 en suite

Moor Allerton Coal Rd, Wike LS17 9NH
☎ 0113 266 1154 🖷 0113 237 1124
e-mail: info@magc.co.uk
The Moor Allerton Club, established in 1923, has 27 holes set in 220 acres of undulating parkland, with testing water hazards and magnificent views extending across the Vale of York. The championship course was designed by Robert Trent Jones, the famous American course architect, and provides a challenge to both high and low handicapped golfers.
Lakes Course: 18 holes, 6470yds, Par 71, SSS 72.
Blackmoor Course: 18 holes, 6673yds, Par 71, SSS 73.
High Course: 18 holes, 6841yds, Par 72, SSS 74.
Club membership 500.
Visitors contact professional (0113 266 5209). **Societies** apply in advance. **Green Fees** £70 per day; £49 per round (£65 weekends). **Cards** **Prof** Richard Lane **Course Designer** Robert Trent Jones **Facilities** **Leisure** sauna. **Conf** fac available Corporate Hospitality Days available **Location** 5.5m N of city centre on A61

Hotel ★★★ 70% The Merrion Hotel, Wade Ln, LEEDS ☎ 0113 243 9191 109 en suite

Moortown Harrogate Rd, Alwoodley LS17 7DB
☎ 0113 268 6521 🖷 0113 268 0986
e-mail: secretary@moortown-gc.co.uk
Championship course, tough but fair. Springy moorland turf, natural hazards of heather, gorse and streams, cunningly placed bunkers and immaculate greens. Original home of Ryder Cup in 1929.
18 holes, 6757yds, Par 72, SSS 73, Course record 64.
Club membership 568.
Visitors contact in advance. **Societies** apply in writing in advance. **Green Fees** £65 per day/round (£75 weekends & bank holidays). Reduced winter rates. **Prof** Martin Heggi **Course Designer** A MacKenzie **Facilities** **Conf** Corporate Hospitality Days available **Location** 6m N of city centre on A61

Hotel ★★★ 70% The Merrion Hotel, Wade Ln, LEEDS ☎ 0113 243 9191 109 en suite

Oulton Park Rothwell LS26 8EX
☎ 0113 282 3152 🖷 0113 282 6290
Hall Course: 9 holes, 3286yds, Par 36, SSS 36.
Park Course: 9 holes, 3184yds, Par 35, SSS 35.
Royds Course: 9 holes, 3169yds, Par 35, SSS 35.
Course Designer Dave Thomas **Location** M62 junct 30
Phone for further details

Hotel ★★★★★ 64% De Vere Oulton Hall, Rothwell Ln Oulton, LEEDS ☎ 0113 282 1000 152 en suite

Roundhay Park Ln LS8 2EJ
☎ 0113 266 2695 & 266 4225
Attractive municipal parkland course, natural hazard easy walking.
9 holes, 5223yds, Par 70, SSS 65, Course record 61.
Club membership 240.
Visitors contact professional at all times. **Societies** phone or write to the professional. **Green Fees** terms on application. **Prof** James Pape **Facilities**
Location 4m NE of city centre off A58

Hotel ★★★★ 74% Haley's Hotel & Restaurant, Shi Oak Rd, Headingley, LEEDS ☎ 0113 278 4446 22 en suite 6 annexe en suite

Sand Moor Alwoodley Ln LS17 7DJ
☎ 0113 268 5180 🖷 0113 266 1105
e-mail: sandmoorgolf@btclick.com
A beautiful, inland course situated next to Eccup reservoir on the north side of Leeds. It has been described as the finest example of golfing paradise being created out of a barren moor. With magnificent views of the surrounding countryside, the course has sandy soil and drains exceptionally well.
18 holes, 6414yds, Par 71, SSS 71, Course record 63.
Club membership 600.

Continued

Contin

isitors restricted weekends & bank holidays. **Societies** ply in advance. **Green Fees** not confirmed. **Cards** ⊞ ⊠ 🗇 **Prof** Frank Houlgate **Course Designer** r A MacKenzie **Facilities** ⊗ ⑪ ⓛ ⓦ ⓟ ⚘ 🖻 ⚐ ⚘ onf Corporate Hospitality Days available ocation 5m N of city centre off A61

otel ★★★★ 64% Cedar Court Hotel, Denby Dale Rd, ⍟AKEFIELD ☎ 01924 276310 151 en suite

outh Leeds Gipsy Ln, Beeston LS11 5TU
☎ 0113 277 1676 (office)
mail: sec@slgc.freeserve.co.uk
arkland course, windy, hard walking, good views. nall undulating greens - a very good test of putting ility.

holes, 5865yds, Par 69, SSS 68, Course record 63.
lub membership 400.
isitors not weekends & competitions. **Societies** apply in vance to professional on 0113 270 2598 **Green Fees** £28 r day, £18 per round (£25 per round weekends). **Prof** urie Turner **Course Designer** Dr A MacKenzie cilities ⊗ ⑪ ⓛ ⓦ ⓟ ⚘ 🖻 ⚘ **Conf** Corporate ospitality Days available **Location** 3m S of city centre f A653

otel ★★★★ 68% Queens Hotel, City Square, LEEDS ☎ 0113 243 1323 217 en suite

emple Newsam Temple-Newsam Rd LS15 0LN
☎ 0113 264 7362
wo parkland courses. Testing long 13th (563yds) on cond course.
ord Irwin: 18 holes, 6460yds, Par 68, SSS 71,
ourse record 66.
ady Dorothy: 18 holes, 6299yds, Par 70, SSS 70,
ourse record 67.
lub membership 520.
isitors booking required for weekends & bank holidays, cieties phone in advance. **Green Fees** £8.50 (£11 eekends & bank holidays). **Cards** ⊞ ▦ ▥ ▦ ⊠ of Adrian Newboult **Facilities** ⊗ ⑪ by arrangement ⓦ ⓛ 🖻 ⚐ ⚒ ⚘ **Conf** fac available Corporate ospitality Days available **Location** 3.5m E of city centre f A63

otel ★★★★ 🏠 74% Haley's Hotel & Restaurant, Shire ak Rd, Headingley, LEEDS ☎ 0113 278 4446 en suite 6 annexe en suite

> **Prices may change during the currency of the Guide, please check when booking.**

MARSDEN
Map 07 SE01

Marsden Mount Rd, Hemplow HD7 6NN
☎ 01484 844253
Moorland course with good views, natural hazards, windy.
9 holes, 5702yds, Par 68, SSS 68, Course record 64.
Club membership 280.
Visitors must play with member at weekends but not before 4pm Sat. **Societies** Mon-Fri; must contact in advance. **Cards** ⊞ ▦ **Prof** David Pendleton-Nash **Course Designer** Dr MacKenzie **Facilities** ⊗ ⑪ ⓛ ⓦ ⓟ ⚘ 🖻 **Leisure** tennis courts. **Location** S side off A62

Hotel ★★ 67% Old Bridge Hotel, HOLMFIRTH
☎ 01484 681212 20 en suite

MELTHAM
Map 07 SE01

Meltham Thick Hollins Hall HD9 4DQ
☎ 01484 850227 (office) & 851521 (pro)
🗎 01484 850227
e-mail: melthamgolf@supanet.com
Parkland course with good views. Testing 548yd 13th hole (par 5).
18 holes, 6139yds, Par 71, SSS 70.
Club membership 756.
Visitors not Sat & Wed (Ladies Day), contact professional in advance. **Societies** apply in writing or phone. **Green Fees** £33 per day; £28 per round (£38/£33 weekends & bank holidays). **Prof** Paul Davies **Course Designer** Alex Herd **Facilities** ⊗ ⑪ ⓛ ⓦ ⓟ ⚘ 🖻 ⚐ ⚘
Location 0.5m E of Meltham on B6107

Hotel ★★ 73% Hey Green Country House Hotel, Waters Rd, MARSDEN ☎ 01484 844235 12 en suite

MIRFIELD
Map 08 SE21

Dewsbury District Sands Ln WF14 8HJ
☎ 01924 492399 & 496030 🗎 01924 492399
e-mail: dewsbury.golf@btconnect.com
Moorland or parkland terrain with panoramic views. Ponds in middle of 3rd fairway, left of 5th green and 17th green. A challenging test of golf.
18 holes, 6360yds, Par 71, SSS 71.
Club membership 700.
Visitors At weekends only after 3pm. Phone in advance. **Societies** phone bookings. **Green Fees** £25 per day; £20 per round (£17.50 weekend after 3pm). **Cards** ⊞ ▦ ⊠ 🗇 **Prof** Nigel P Hirst **Course Designer** Old Tom Morris, Peter Alliss **Facilities** ⊗ ⑪ by arrangement ⓛ ⓦ ⓟ ⚘ 🖻 ⚐ ⚘ **Leisure** snooker tables. **Conf** fac available Corporate Hospitality Days available
Location M62 junct 25, 6m off A644

Hotel ★★★ 66% Healds Hall Hotel, Leeds Rd, Liversedge, DEWSBURY ☎ 01924 409112 24 en suite

MORLEY
Map 08 SE22

Howley Hall Scotchman Ln LS27 0NX
☎ 01924 350100 🗎 01924 350104
e-mail: office@howleyhall.co.uk
Parkland course with easy walking and superb views of the Pennines and the Calder valley.
18 holes, 6092yds, Par 71, SSS 69, Course record 66.
Club membership 700.

Continued

Visitors play from yellow markers; not Sat. **Societies** contact secretary/manager for details. **Green Fees** £36 per day; £30 per round (£40 weekends & bank holidays). **Prof** Gary Watkinson **Course Designer** MacKenzie **Facilities** ⊗ ⅲ ⅱ 🏌 ♀ 👥 🏠 ✓ **Conf** fac available Corporate Hospitality Days available **Location** 1.5m S on B6123

Hotel ★★ 70% Alder House Hotel, Towngate Rd, Healey Ln, BATLEY ☎ 01924 444777 20 en suite

OSSETT
Map 08 SE22

Low Laithes Parkmill Ln, Flushdyke WF5 9AP
☎ 01924 274667 & 266067 🖹 01924 266067
Testing parkland course.
18 holes, 6463yds, Par 72, SSS 71, Course record 65.
Club membership 600.
Visitors not before 9.30am & 12.30-1.30 weekdays & before 10am & 12-2 weekends/bank holidays. **Societies** by arrangement. **Green Fees** £25 per day, £22 per round (£36 weekends & bank holidays). **Prof** Paul Browning **Course Designer** Dr MacKenzie **Facilities** ⊗ ⅲ ⅱ 🏌 ♀ 👥 🏠 🚚 ✓ **Conf** Corporate Hospitality Days available **Location** M1 junct 40, 0.5m on Dewsbury road, signed

Hotel ★★★ 67% Heath Cottage Hotel & Restaurant, Wakefield Rd, DEWSBURY ☎ 01924 465399 23 en suite 6 annexe en suite

OTLEY
Map 08 SE24

Otley Off West Busk Ln LS21 3NG
☎ 01943 465329 🖹 01943 850387
e-mail: office@otley-golfclub.co.uk
An expansive course with magnificent views across Wharfedale. It is well wooded with streams crossing the fairway. The 4th is a fine hole which generally needs two woods to reach the plateau green. The 17th is a good short hole. A test of golf as opposed to stamina.
18 holes, 6237yds, Par 70, SSS 70, Course record 62.
Club membership 700.
Visitors phone to check tee time; not am Tue, Sat. **Societies** phone enquiries welcome, bookings in writing. **Green Fees** £38 per day, £32 per 18/27 holes (£45/£38 weekends & bank holidays). **Cards** 🎫 💳 💳 💳 💳 📷 🗾 **Prof** Steven Tomkinson **Facilities** ⊗ ⅲ ⅱ 🏌 ♀ 👥 🏠 ♈ ✓ ℓ **Leisure** practice bunker. **Conf** fac available Corporate Hospitality Days available **Location** 1m W of Otley off A6038

Hotel ⇪ Premier Travel Inn Leeds/Bradford Airport, Victoria Av, Yeadon, LEEDS ☎ 08701 977153 40 en suite

OUTLANE
Map 07 SE01

Outlane Slack Ln, off New Hey Rd HD3 3FQ
☎ 01422 374762 🖹 01422 311789
An 18-hole moorland course with undulating fairways. Four par 3 holes with an 8th hole of 249yds and a 15th regarded as the hardest par 3 in Yorkshire. The three par 5s may be reachable on a good day in two strokes but in adverse conditions will take more than three. Smaller than average greens on some holes, which makes for accurate second shots.
18 holes, 6015yds, Par 71, SSS 69, Course record 67.
Club membership 600.
Visitors phone in advance, must be correctly equipped & attired. No play Sat, limited Sun am. **Societies** apply in writing. **Green Fees** £19 per day (£29 weekends & bank

holidays). **Prof** David Chapman **Facilities** ⊗ ⅲ ⅱ 🏌 ♀ 👥 🏠 ♈ 🚚 ✓ **Location** M62 junct 23, A640 New Hey Rd through Outlane

Hotel ★★★ 67% The Old Golf House Hotel, New Hey Rd, Outlane, HUDDERSFIELD ☎ 01422 379311 52 en suite

PONTEFRACT
Map 08 SE42

Mid Yorkshire Havercroft Ln, Darrington WF8 3BP
☎ 01977 704522 🖹 01977 600823
e-mail: linda_midyorksgc@btconnect.com

18 holes, 6500yds, Par 72, SSS 71, Course record 68.
Course Designer Steve Marnoch **Location** on A1 0.5m S junct A1/M62
Phone for further details

Hotel ★★★ 74% Wentbridge House Hotel, Wentbridge, PONTEFRACT ☎ 01977 620444 14 en suite 4 annexe en suite

Pontefract & District Park Ln WF8 4QS
☎ 01977 792241 🖹 01977 792241
e-mail: manager@pdgc.co.uk
18 holes, 6227yds, Par 72, SSS 70.
Course Designer A MacKenzie **Location** W of Pontefract A639 onto B6134, club 1m on right
Phone for further details

Hotel ★★★ 74% Wentbridge House Hotel, Wentbridge, PONTEFRACT ☎ 01977 620444 14 en suite 4 annexe en suite

PUDSEY
Map 08 SE23

Calverley Woodhall Ln LS28 5QY
☎ 0113 256 9244 🖹 0113 256 4362
e-mail: golf@cgc1.freeserve.co.uk
Parkland course on gently undulating terrain where accurate approach shots are rewarded to small greens.

Continued

Continue

8 holes, 5590yds, Par 68, SSS 67, Course record 62.*
holes, 3000yds, Par 36.
lub membership 535.
isitors advisable to book 18-hole course; not weekend m. **Societies** contact in writing or phone. **Green Fees** £13 er round (£16 weekends). **Cards** **Prof** Neil Vendel-Jones **Facilities** **Conf** Corporate Hospitality Days available **Location** signed Calverley from A647

Hotel Travelodge Bradford, 1 Mid Point, Dick Ln, UDSEY ☎ 08700 850 950 48 en suite

ulneck LS28 8NT
☎ 0113 256 5191
holes, 5456yds, Par 66, SSS 67, Course record 65.
Location Pudsey, between Leeds & Bradford
hone for further details

Hotel ★★★ 63% Novotel Bradford, 6 Roydsdale Way, BRADFORD ☎ 01274 683683 119 en suite

Voodhall Hills Calverley LS28 5UN
☎ 0113 255 4594 🖹 0113 255 4594
-mail: whhgc@tiscali.co.uk
Meadowland course, recently redeveloped with an improved layout and open ditches around the course. A challenging opening hole, a good variety of par 3s and esting holes at the 6th and 11th.
8 holes, 6184yds, Par 71, SSS 70, Course record 64.
lub membership 550.
isitors any day advise manager/professional in advance, at after 4.30pm; Sun after 9.30am. **Societies** phone in dvance. **Green Fees** not confirmed. **Prof** Warren Lockett **acilities** **Conf** fac available orporate Hospitality Days available **Location** 1m NW off 647

Hotel Travelodge Bradford, 1 Mid Point, Dick Ln, UDSEY ☎ 08700 850 950 48 en suite

RIDDLESDEN Map 07 SE04

Riddlesden Howden Rough BD20 5QN
☎ 01535 602148
ndulating moorland course with prevailing west winds nd beautiful views. Nine par 3 holes and spectacular th and 15th holes played over old quarry sites.
8 holes, 4295yds, Par 63, SSS 61, Course record 59.
lub membership 300.
isitors restricted before 2pm weekends. **Societies** apply y phone or in writing. **Green Fees** £16 per day/round £21 weekends). **Facilities** **Conf** orporate Hospitality Days available **Location** 1m NW

Hotel ★★ 67% Dalesgate Hotel, 406 Skipton Rd, Utley, EIGHLEY ☎ 01535 664930 20 en suite

SCARCROFT Map 08 SE34

carcroft Syke Ln LS14 3BQ
☎ 0113 289 2311 🖹 0113 289 3835
-mail: sge@cwcomm.net
8 holes, 6426yds, Par 71, SSS 69.
ourse Designer Charles Mackenzie **Location** 0.5m N of illage off A58
hone for further details

Hotel ★★★ 70% The Merrion Hotel, Wade Ln, LEEDS
☎ 0113 243 9191 109 en suite

SHIPLEY Map 07 SE13

Marriott Hollins Hall Hotel & Country Club
Hollins Hill, Otley Rd BD17 7QW
☎ 01274 534212 🖹 01274 534220

18 holes, 6671yds, Par 71, SSS 71, Course record 66.
Course Designer Ross McMurray **Location** 3m N on the A6038
Phone for further details

Hotel ★★★★ 70% Marriott Hollins Hall Hotel & Country Club, Hollins Hill, Baildon, SHIPLEY
☎ 0870 400 7227 122 en suite

Northcliffe High Bank Ln BD18 4LJ
☎ 01274 596731 🖹 01274 584148
e-mail: northcliffe@bigfoot.com
Parkland course with magnificent views of moors. Testing 1st hole, dog-leg left over a ravine. The 18th hole is one of the most picturesque and difficult par 3s in the country, with a green 100ft below the tee and protected by bunkers, water and trees.
18 holes, 6104yds, Par 71, SSS 70, Course record 64.
Club membership 700.
Visitors limited access at weekend. **Societies** book via secretary in advance, weekdays only. **Green Fees** £30 per day; £25 per round (£30 per round weekends & bank holidays). **Prof** M Hillas **Course Designer** James Braid **Facilities** **Conf** Corporate Hospitality Days available **Location** 1.25m SW of Shipley, off A650

Hotel ★★★★ 70% Marriott Hollins Hall Hotel & Country Club, Hollins Hill, Baildon, SHIPLEY
☎ 0870 400 7227 122 en suite

SILSDEN Map 07 SE04

Silsden Brunthwaite Ln, Brunthwaite BD20 0ND
☎ 01535 652998 🖹 01535 654273
e-mail: info@silsdengolfclub.co.uk
Tight downland course which can be windy. Good views of the Aire valley.
18 holes, 5062yds, Par 67, SSS 64, Course record 62.
Club membership 350.
Visitors phone in advance for weekend bookings. **Societies** phone in advance or apply in writing. **Green Fees** £20 weekday (£25 weekend & bank holidays). **Facilities** **Conf** fac available **Location** E of town off Howden Rd onto Hawber Ln

Hotel ★★ 67% Dalesgate Hotel, 406 Skipton Rd, Utley, KEIGHLEY ☎ 01535 664930 20 en suite

SOWERBY — Map 07 SE02

Ryburn The Shaw, Norland HX6 3QP
☎ 01422 831355
Moorland course, easy walking. Panoramic views of the Ryburn and Calder valleys.
9 holes, 5127yds, Par 66, SSS 65, Course record 64.
Club membership 300.
Visitors contact in advance. **Societies** apply in writing.
Green Fees not confirmed. **Facilities** ⊗ ⅲ ⅼ ⬤ ♀ ☍
Conf Corporate Hospitality Days available **Location** 1m S of Sowerby Bridge off A58

Hotel ★★★ 63% The Rock Inn Hotel, Holywell Green, HALIFAX ☎ 01422 379721 30 en suite

TODMORDEN — Map 07 SD92

Todmorden Rive Rocks, Cross Stone Rd OL14 8RD
☎ 01706 812986 📠 01706 812986
A tough but fair moorland course with spectacular scenery.
9 holes, 5874yds, Par 68, SSS 68, Course record 67.
Club membership 240.
Visitors restricted Thu & weekends. Advisable to contact in advance. **Societies** apply in writing. **Green Fees** £15 (weekends & bank holidays £20). **Facilities** ⊗ by arrangement ⅲ by arrangement ⅼ ⬤ ♀ ☍
Location NE off A646

Hotel ★★★ 75% Holdsworth House Hotel, Holdsworth, HALIFAX ☎ 01422 240024 40 en suite

WAKEFIELD — Map 08 SE32

City of Wakefield Horbury Rd WF2 8QS
☎ 01924 360282
18 holes, 6319yds, Par 72, SSS 70, Course record 64.
Course Designer JSF Morrison **Location** 1.5m W of city centre on A642
Phone for further details

Hotel ★★★ 75% Waterton Park Hotel, Walton Hall, The Balk, Walton, WAKEFIELD ☎ 01924 257911 & 249800 📠 01924 259686 25 en suite 36 annexe en suite

Lofthouse Hill Leeds Rd WF3 3LR
☎ 01924 823703 📠 01924 823703
e-mail: lofthousehillgolfclub@fsmail.net
New parkland course.
18 holes, 5988yds, Par 70, SSS 69.
Visitors contact in advance **Societies** contact for details.
Green Fees £12 per 18 holes. **Cards** ▭ ▭ ▭ ▭ ▭
Prof Simon Hotham **Facilities** ⊗ ⅲ ⅼ ⬤ ♀ ☍ ☍ 🏌 🛒
Location 4m from Wakefield off A6

Hotel ★★★ 75% Waterton Park Hotel, Walton Hall, The Balk, Walton, WAKEFIELD ☎ 01924 257911 & 249800 📠 01924 259686 25 en suite 36 annexe en suite

Normanton Hatfield Hall, Aberford Rd WF3 4JP
☎ 01924 377943 📠 01924 200777
A championship course occupying 145 acres of the Hatfield Hall Estate. A blend of parkland and elevations, the course incorporates impressive lakes and benefits from the sympathetic preservation of long established trees and wildlife. The large undulating greens are built to USGA standards and are playable all year.
18 holes, 6205yds, Par 72, SSS 71.

Continued

Club membership 1000.
Visitors not weekends. **Societies** weekdays only, apply in writing. **Green Fees** not confirmed. **Cards** ▭ ▭ ▭ ▭ ▭ ▭ **Prof** Gary Pritchard **Facilities** ⊗ ⅲ ⅼ ⬤ ♀ ☍ 🏌 🛒 ✐ **Conf** fac available **Location** M62 junct 30, A642 towards Wakefield, 2m on right

Hotel 🅄 Chasley Hotel, Queen St, WAKEFIELD ☎ 01924 372111 64 en suite

Painthorpe House Painthorpe Ln, Painthorpe, Crigglestone WF4 3HE
☎ 01924 254737 & 255083 📠 01924 252022
Undulating meadowland course, easy walking.
9 holes, 4544yds, Par 62, SSS 62, Course record 63.
Club membership 100.
Visitors pay & play Mon-Sat, after 2.30pm on Sun. **Societies** phone in advance. **Cards** ▭ ▭ **Facilities** ⊗ ⅲ ⅼ ⬤ ♀ ☍ **Leisure** bowling green. **Location** 2m S off A636

Hotel ★★★★ 64% Cedar Court Hotel, Denby Dale Rd, WAKEFIELD ☎ 01924 276310 151 en suite

Wakefield Woodthorpe Ln, Sandal WF2 6JH
☎ 01924 258778 (sec) 📠 01924 242752
A well-sheltered meadowland and parkland course with easy walking and good views.
18 holes, 6653yds, Par 72, SSS 72, Course record 67.
Club membership 540.
Visitors contact must be made in advance. Visitors Wed, Thu & Fri only. **Societies** apply in writing. **Green Fees** £32 per round/£37 per day (weekends £40). **Prof** Ian M Wright **Course Designer** A MacKenzie, S Herd **Facilities** ⊗ ⅲ ⅼ ⬤ ♀ ☍ 🏠 ✐ **Conf** Corporate Hospitality Days available **Location** 3m S of Wakefield off A61

Hotel ★★★ 69% Hotel St Pierre, Barnsley Rd, Newmillerdam, WAKEFIELD ☎ 01924 255596 54 en suite

WETHERBY — Map 08 SE44

Wetherby Linton Ln LS22 4JF
☎ 01937 580089 📠 01937 581915
e-mail: info@wetherbygolfclub.co.uk
A medium length parkland course renowned for its lush fairways. Particularly memorable holes are the 7th, a par 4 which follows the sweeping bend of the River Wharfe, and the 14th (the quarry hole), an intimidating par 3.
18 holes, 6213yds, Par 71, SSS 70, Course record 63.
Club membership 950.
Visitors not Mon am, Tue am; contact in advance. **Societies** apply in writing, e-mail or phone in advance. **Green Fees** £39 per day, £32 per round (£44 per day/round). **Prof** Mark Daubney **Facilities** ⊗ ⅲ ⅼ ⬤ ♀ ☍ 🏠 🏌 🛒 ✐ ⓣ **Conf** fac available Corporate Hospitality Days available **Location** 1m W off A661

Hotel ★★★★ ♨ 76% Wood Hall Hotel, Trip Ln, Linton, WETHERBY ☎ 01937 587271 14 en suite 30 annexe en suite

In the hotel entries, the percentage figure refers to the AA's most recent Quality Assessment Score.

WIKE
Map 08 SE34

The Village Golf Course Backstone Gill Ln
S17 9JU
☎ 0113 273 7471

nine-hole pay and play course in an elevated position
njoying long panoramic views. The holes are par 3, 4
nd 5s and include water hazards and shaped large
reens. There are now three extra optional holes (no
xtra charge), all par 3s over water.
2 holes, 5780yds, Par 75, SSS 68, Course record 66.
isitors smart casual wear **Societies** contact in advance by
tter or phone **Green Fees** not confirmed. **Course
esigner** William Binner **Facilities** ⊗ ⅲ ⓛ ☑ ⁎ ⌀
eisure fishing. **Conf** fac available   Corporate Hospitality
ays available **Location** signed, 1m off A61, 2m off A58

otel ★★★ 68% Jurys Inn Leeds, Kendell St, Brewery
ace, Brewery Wharf, LEEDS
☎ 0113 283 8800 248 en suite

WOOLLEY
Map 08 SE31

Woolley Park New Rd WF4 2JS
☎ 01226 380144 📄 01226 390295

demanding course set in a mature wooded parkland.
With many water features in play and undulating
reens, the course offers a challenge to all golfers.
8 holes, 6636yds, Par 71, SSS 72.
isitors bookings accepted from Thu prior to play;
eekends restricted. **Societies** apply in writing for
formation pack. **Green Fees** £18.50 per 18 holes (£25
eekends). **Cards** 🖩 ▨ ▨ ▨ 🖾 **Prof** Jon Baldwin
ourse Designer M Shattock **Facilities** ⊗ ⅲ by
rangement ⓛ ☑ ♀ ☖ ☋ ⁎ ⛾ ⌀ **Conf** Corporate
ospitality Days available **Location** M1 junct 38, off A61
tween Wakefield & Barnsley

otel ★★★★ 64% Cedar Court Hotel, Denby Dale Rd,
WAKEFIELD ☎ 01924 276310 151 en suite

CHANNEL ISLANDS

ALDERNEY

ALDERNEY
Map 16

Alderney Route des Carrieres GY9 3YD
☎ 01481 822835

ndulating seaside course with sea on all sides, offering
agnificent views from its high tees and greens.
holes, 5006yds, Par 64, SSS 65, Course record 65.
lub membership 400.
isitors not before 10am at weekends. Advisable to
ntact in advance. **Societies** contact in advance. **Green
ees** £28 per day (£20 per 18 or 9 holes weekends & bank
olidays). **Cards** 🖩 ▨ ▨ ▨ 🖾 **Facilities** ⊗ by
rangement ⓛ ☑ ♀ ☖ ☋ ⁎ ⌀
ocation 1m E of St Annes

> If the name of the club appears in *italics*, details
> have not been confirmed for this
> edition of the guide.

GUERNSEY

L'ANCRESSE VALE
Map 16

Royal Guernsey GY3 5BY
☎ 01481 246523 📄 01481 243960
e-mail: bobby@rggc.fsnet.co.uk
**Not quite as old as its neighbour Royal Jersey, Royal
Guernsey is a sporting course which was redesigned
after World War II by Mackenzie Ross, who has many
fine courses to his credit. It is a pleasant links, well-
maintained, and administered by the States of
Guernsey. The 8th hole, a good par 4, requires an
accurate second shot to the green set among the gorse
and thick rough. The 18th, with lively views, needs a
strong shot to reach the green well down below. The
course is windy, with hard walking.**
18 holes, 6215yds, Par 70, SSS 70, Course record 64.
Club membership 934.
Visitors must have a handicap certificate; not Thu, Sat pm
& Sun. **Green Fees** £44 per day/round.
Prof Norman Wood **Course Designer** Mackenzie Ross
Facilities ⊗ ⅲ ⓛ ☑ ♀ ☖ ☋ ⁎ ⌀ ⓵
Location 3m N of St Peter Port

Hotel ★★★★ 66% St Pierre Park Hotel, Rohais, ST
PETER PORT ☎ 01481 728282 131 en suite

CASTEL
Map 16

La Grande Mare Golf & Country Club
Vazon Bay GY5 7LL
☎ 01481 253544 📄 01481 255197
e-mail: golf@lagrandemare.com
**This hotel and golf complex is set in over 120 acres of
grounds. The Hawtree designed parkland course
opened in 1994 and was originally designed around 14
holes with four double greens. The course was extended
to a full 18 holes in 2001. Water hazards on 15 holes.**
18 holes, 4755yards, Par 64, SSS 64, Course record 65.
Club membership 800.
Visitors may book a tee time up to two days in advance.
Societies book in advance, **Green Fees** £32 per 18 holes
(£36 weekends). **Cards** 🖩 ▨ ▨ ▨ 🖾 **Prof** Matt
Groves **Course Designer** Hawtree **Facilities** ⊗ ⅲ ⓛ ☑ ♀
☖ ⁎ ⌀ ⓵ **Leisure** hard tennis courts, outdoor &
indoor heated swimming pools, fishing, sauna,
gymnasium, sports massage. **Conf** Corporate Hospitality
Days available

Hotel ★★★ 70% Hotel Hougue du Pommier, Hougue du
Pommier Rd, CASTEL ☎ 01481 256531 37 en suite
6 annexe en suite

ST PETER PORT
Map 16

St Pierre Park Golf Club Rohais GY1 1FD
☎ 01481 728282 📄 01481 712041
e-mail: stppark@itl.net
**Par 3 parkland course with delightful setting, with
lakes, streams and many tricky holes.**
9 holes, 2610yds, Par 54, SSS 50, Course record 52.
Club membership 200.
Visitors book tee times. Strict dress code, contact club in
advance for datails. **Societies** contact in advance. **Green
Fees** terms on application. **Cards** 🖩 ▨ ▨ ▨ 🖾 🖾

Continued

Prof Roy Corbet **Course Designer** Jacklin **Facilities** ⊗ ⫙ ⓑ ♣ ♀ 🛆 🏠 🇶 ⌿ ⌀ ⦗ **Leisure** hard tennis courts, heated indoor swimming pool, sauna, solarium, gymnasium. **Conf** fac available **Location** 1m W off Rohais Rd

Hotel ★★★★ 66% St Pierre Park Hotel, Rohais, ST PETER PORT ☎ 01481 728282 131 en suite

JERSEY

GROUVILLE   Map 16

Royal Jersey Le Chemin au Greves JE3 9BD
☎ 01534 854416 📠 01534 854684
e-mail: thesecretary@royaljersey.com
A seaside links - its centenary was celebrated in 1978. It is also famous for the fact that Britain's greatest golfer, Harry Vardon, was born in a little cottage on the edge of the course and learned his golf here.
18 holes, 6100yds, Par 70, SSS 70, Course record 63. Club membership 1234.
Visitors restricted to 10am-noon & 2pm-4pm Mon-Fri & after 2.30pm weekends & bank holidays. **Societies** welcome Mon-Fri. Must apply in writing. **Green Fees** not confirmed. **Cards** 🖶 💳 💳 💳 💷 **Prof** David Morgan
Facilities ⊗ ⫙ ⓑ ♣ ♀ 🛆 🏠 🇶 ⌿
Location 4m E of St Helier off coast road

Hotel ★★★ 69% Old Court House Hotel, GOREY
☎ 01534 854444 58 en suite

LA MOYE   Map 16

La Moye La Route Orange JE3 8GQ
☎ 01534 743401 📠 01534 747289
Seaside championship links course (venue for the Jersey Seniors Open) situated in an exposed position on the south western corner of the island overlooking St Ouen's Bay. Offers spectacular views, two start points, full course all year - no temporary greens.
18 holes, 6664yds, Par 72, SSS 73, Course record 65. Club membership 1300.
Visitors contact Course Ranger in advance 01534 747166. Visitors may play after 2.30pm weekends & bank holidays. **Societies** apply in writing. **Green Fees** 18 holes £50 (weekends & bank holidays £55). **Cards** 🖶 💳 💳 💳 💷 **Prof** Mike Deeley **Course Designer** James Braid
Facilities ⊗ ⫙ ⓑ ♣ ♀ 🛆 🏠 🇶 ⌿ ⦗
Location W of village off A13

Hotel ★★★★ The Atlantic Hotel, Le Mont de la Pulente, ST BRELADE ☎ 01534 744101 50 en suite

ST CLEMENT   Map 16

St Clement Jersey Recreation Grounds JE2 6PN
☎ 01534 721938 📠 01534 721012
Very tight moorland course. Impossible to play to scratch. Suitable for middle to high handicaps.
9 holes, 2244yds, Par 30, SSS 31, Course record 30. Club membership 500.
Visitors not Sun am or Tue am. **Green Fees** terms on application. **Cards** 🖶 💳 💳 💳 💷 **Prof** Lee Elstone
Facilities ⊗ ⫙ ♣ ♀ 🛆 🇶 ⌿ ⦗ **Leisure** hard tennis courts, squash, bowls. **Location** E of St Helier on A5

Hotel ★★★★ 🏵 Longueville Manor Hotel, ST SAVIOUR ☎ 01534 725501 29 en suite 1 annexe en suite

ST OUEN   Map 16

Les Mielles Golf & Country Club JE3 7FQ
☎ 01534 482787 📠 01534 485414
e-mail: enquiry@lesmielles.co.je
Challenging championship course with bent grass greens, dwarf rye fairways and picturesque ponds situated in the Island's largest conservation area within St Ouen's Bay.

18 holes, 5261yds, Par 70, SSS 68, Course record 65. Club membership 1500.
Visitors welcome all times; booking recommended. **Societies** book in advance to avoid disappointment. **Green Fees** terms on application. **Cards** 🖶 💳 💳 💳 💷 **Prof** W Osmand, L Cummins, A Jones **Course Designer** J Le Brun, R Whitehead **Facilities** ⊗ ⫙ ⓑ ♣ ♀ 🛆 🏠 🇶 🛒 ⌿ ⦗ **Leisure** Laser clay pigeon shooting, Breakers realistic golf course. **Conf** fac available Corporate Hospitality Days available **Location** centre of St Ouen's Bay

Hotel ★★★★ 76% Hotel L'Horizon, St Brelade's Bay, ST BRELADE ☎ 01534 743101 106 en suite

ISLE OF MAN

CASTLETOWN   Map 06 SC26

Castletown Golf Links Fort Island, Derbyhaven IM9 1UA
☎ 01624 822220 📠 01624 829661
e-mail: 1sttee@manx.net
Set on the Langness peninsula, this superb championship course is surrounded on three sides by the sea, and holds many surprises from its Championship tees.
18 holes, 6707yds, Par 72, SSS 72, Course record 64. Club membership 600.
Visitors contact in advance. Sat reserved for hotel residents & club members, Wed for Ladies, but times may be available on both days. **Societies** phone in advance. **Green Fees** £37 Mon-Thu (£43 Fri-Sun & bank holidays). **Cards** 🖶 💳 💳 💳 💷 **Prof** Murray Crowe **Course Designer** McKenzie Ross **Facilities** ⊗ ⫙ ⓑ ♣ ♀ 🛆 🏠 🇶 🛒 ⌿ ⦗ **Leisure** heated indoor swimming pool, sauna. **Conf** fac available Corporate Hospitality Days available

Hotel ★★ 65% Falcon's Nest, The Promenade, PORT ERIN ☎ 01624 834077 35 en suite

Continued

OUGLAS   Map 06 SC37

ouglas Pulrose Park IM2 1AE
☎ 01624 675952
mail: mikevipondgolf@aol.com
8 holes, 5937yds, Par 69, SSS 69, Course record 62.
ourse Designer Dr A MacKenzie **Location** 1m from
ouglas on Castletown road on Pulrose Estate
hone for further details
....
otel ★★★ 68% The Empress Hotel, Central Promenade,
OUGLAS ☎ 01624 661155 102 en suite

Iount Murray Hotel & Country Club
ount Murray, Santon IM4 2HT
☎ 01624 661111 ▤ 01624 611116
mail: hotel@mountmurray.com
challenging course with many natural features, lakes,
reams etc. Six par 5s, five par 3s and the rest par 4.
ine views over the whole island.

8 holes, 6664yds, Par 73, SSS 73, Course record 69.
lub membership 378.
isitors contact in advance; not before 9.30am weekends.
ocieties phone in advance. **Green Fees** not confirmed.
ards ▦ ▦ ▦ 📇 📖 **Prof** Andrew Dyson **Course**
esigner Bingley Sports Research **Facilities** ⊗ ▥ ▙ 🖴 ♀
▚ 🖻 ⚑ 🍴 ➶ 🏌 🖢 ✓ **Leisure** hard tennis courts, heated
door swimming pool, squash, sauna, solarium,
mnasium. **Conf** fac available Corporate Hospitality
ays available **Location** 5m from Douglas towards airport
....
otel ★★★★ 70% Mount Murray Hotel & Country Club,
anton, DOUGLAS ☎ 01624 661111 90 en suite

NCHAN   Map 06 SC47

ing Edward Bay Golf & Country Club
owstrake, Groudle Rd IM3 2JR
☎ 01624 672709 620430
mail: mail@kebgc.com
illy seaside links with natural hazards and good views.
hough a short course, it is a fair test of golf.
8 holes, 5492yds, Par 67, SSS 65, Course record 58.
lub membership 350.
isitors must have a handicap certificate & contact in
vance. **Societies** contact in advance. **Green Fees** not
nfirmed. **Prof** Donald Jones **Course Designer** Tom
orris **Facilities** ⊗ ▥ ▙ 🖴 ♀ ▚ 🖻 ⚑ 🍴 ➶ ✓ **Conf** fac
ailable **Location** E of town off A11
....
otel ★★★★ 72% Sefton Hotel, Harris Promenade,
OUGLAS ☎ 01624 645500 100 en suite

PEEL   Map 06 SC28

Peel Rheast Ln IM5 1BG
☎ 01624 842227 & 843456 ▤ 01624 843456
e-mail: lcullen@peelgolfclub.idps.co.uk
18 holes, 5850yds, Par 69, SSS 69, Course record 64.
Course Designer James Braide **Location** SE of town
centre on A1
Phone for further details
....
Hotel ★★★ 68% The Empress Hotel, Central Promenade,
DOUGLAS ☎ 01624 661155 102 en suite

PORT ERIN   Map 06 SC16

Rowany Rowany Dr IM9 6LN
☎ 01624 834108 or 834072 ▤ 01624 834072
e-mail: rowany@iommail.net
Undulating seaside course with testing later holes,
which cut through gorse and rough. However, those
familiar with this course maintain that the 7th and 12th
holes are the most challenging.
18 holes, 5840yds, Par 70, SSS 69, Course record 62.
Club membership 500.
Visitors contact in advance. **Societies** phone in advance.
Green Fees terms on application. **Course Designer** G
Lowe **Facilities** ⊗ ▥ by arrangement ▙ ▆ ♀ ▚ 🖻 ⚑ 🖢
➶ ✓ **Conf** Corporate Hospitality Days available
Location N of village off A32
....
Hotel ★★★ 67% Ocean Castle Hotel, The Promenade,
PORT ERIN ☎ 01624 836399 40 en suite

PORT ST MARY   Map 06 SC26

Port St Mary Kallow Point Rd
☎ 01624 834932
Slightly hilly course with beautiful scenic views over
Port St Mary and the Irish Sea.
9 holes, 5702yds, Par 68, SSS 68, Course record 62.
Club membership 324.
Visitors not 8-10.30am weekends. **Societies** contact for
details. **Green Fees** terms on application. **Cards** ▦ ▦
▦ 📇 **Course Designer** George Duncan **Facilities** ⊗ ▥
▙ ▆ ♀ ▚ ⚑ 🖢 ➶ ✓ **Leisure** hard tennis courts, Croquet
lawn. **Conf** Corporate Hospitality Days available
Location signed entering Port St Mary, one-way system,
2nd left to end & right, 1st right
....
Hotel ★★★ 67% Ocean Castle Hotel, The Promenade,
PORT ERIN ☎ 01624 836399 40 en suite

RAMSEY   Map 06 SC49

Ramsey Brookfield IM8 2AH
☎ 01624 812244 ▤ 01624 815833
e-mail: ramseygolfclub@manx.net
Parkland course, with easy walking. Windy. Good
views. Testing holes: 1st, par 5; 18th, par 3.
18 holes, 5960yds, Par 70, SSS 69, Course record 63.
Club membership 1000.
Visitors contact in advance; not before 10am weekdays.
Societies apply in advance. **Green Fees** £25 per day (£35
weekends & bank holidays). Reduced winter rates. **Cards**
▦ ▦ 📇 **Prof** Andrew Dyson **Course Designer** James
Braid **Facilities** ⊗ ▥ by arrangement ▙ ▆ ♀ ▚ 🖻 ⚑ ✓
Conf Corporate Hospitality Days available
Location SW of town centre
....
Hotel ★★★ 68% The Empress Hotel, Central Promenade,
DOUGLAS ☎ 01624 661155 102 en suite

Scotland

ABERDEEN CITY

ABERDEEN   Map 15 NJ90

Auchmill Bonnyview Rd, West Heatheryfold
AB16 7FQ
☎ 01224 714577 📠 01224 648693
18 holes, 5123metres, Par 70, SSS 67, Course record 67.
Course Designer Neil Coles, Brian Hugget
Location outskirts Aberdeen, A96 Aberdeen-Inverness
Phone for further details

....

Hotel ★★★ 70% The Craighaar Hotel, Waterton Rd,
Bucksburn, ABERDEEN ☎ 01224 712275 55 en suite

Balnagask St Fitticks Rd AB11 3QT
☎ 01224 876407 📠 01224 648693
Links course. Used by the Nigg Bay Club.
18 holes, 5986yds, Par 70, SSS 69.
Visitors book in person on day of play. **Societies** apply to
council tel 01224 522000. **Green Fees** not confirmed.
Facilities ⊗ ⅷ ⅃ 💺 ⅀ 🏊 🏌 **Leisure** 9-hole pitch & putt
course. **Location** 2m E of city centre

....

Hotel ★★★ 68% Maryculter House Hotel, South Deeside
Rd, Maryculter, ABERDEEN ☎ 01224 732124
23 en suite

Craibstone Golf Centre Craibstone Estate,
Bucksburn AB21 9YA
☎ 01224 716777 & 711012 📠 01224 711298
e-mail: craibstonegolf@sac.co.uk
*This 18-hole, par 69 parkland course is a fair and
enjoyable test for all golfers. The course rewards
accuracy off the tee, with the difficult 11th, 12th and
13th holes, and true and fast greens.*
18 holes, 5757yds, Par 69, SSS 69, Course record 66.
Club membership 425.
Visitors seven day booking system. 50% of prime times
for visitors. **Societies** phone in advance **Green Fees** £17
per round (£22 weekends). **Cards** 📇 💳 📶 🏧 **Prof** Iain
Buchan **Facilities** ⊗ ⅷ ⅃ 💺 ⅀ 🏊 🏕 🏓 🎣 🚴 🍴
Leisure sauna, gymnasium, floodlit astroturf sports area.
Conf fac available **Location** NW of city off A96
Aberdeen-Inverness road. A96 through Bucksburn. Before
next rdbt left signed Forrit Brae. At top of road club signed

....

Hotel ★★★★ 67% Aberdeen Marriott Hotel, Overton
Circle, Dyce, ABERDEEN ☎ 01224 770011 155 en suite

Deeside Golf Rd, Bieldside AB15 9DL
☎ 01224 869457 📠 01224 869457
e-mail: admin@deesidegolfclub.com
*An interesting riverside course with several tree-lined
fairways. A stream comes into play at nine of the 18
holes on the main course. In recent years major
reconstruction work has taken place to provide a
testing course in which only five of the original holes
are virtually unchanged. These include the 15th (the old
4th) which bears the name of James Braid who advised
the club during previous course alterations. Various
water features are incorporated into the course
including pools at the 4th, 10th and 17th.*
Haughton: 18 holes, 6286yds, Par 70, SSS 71.
Blairs: 9 holes, 5889yds, Par 70, SSS 67.
Club membership 1000.

Visitors contact in advance **Societies** apply in writing.
Green Fees not confirmed. **Cards** 📇 💳 📶 🏧 🏧
Prof Frank J Coutts **Course Designer** Archie Simpson
Facilities ⊗ ⅷ ⅃ 💺 ⅀ 🏊 🏕 🎣 **Conf** Corporate
Hospitality Days available **Location** 3m W of city centre
off A93

....

Hotel ★★★★ 74% Ardoe House, South Deeside Rd,
Blairs, ABERDEEN ☎ 01224 860600 117 en suite

Hazelhead Public Hazlehead AB1 8BD
☎ 01224 321830 📠 01224 648693
18 holes, 6211yds, Par 70, SSS 70.
18 holes, 5742yds, Par 67, SSS 67.
Location 4m W of city centre off A944
Phone for further details

....

Hotel ★★★★ 74% Ardoe House, South Deeside Rd,
Blairs, ABERDEEN ☎ 01224 860600 117 en suite

Kings Links AB24 1RZ
☎ 01224 632269 📠 01224 648693
18 holes, 6384yds, Par 72, SSS 71.
Location 0.75m NE of city centre
Phone for further details

Murcar Bridge of Don AB23 8BD
☎ 01224 704354 📠 01224 704354
e-mail: golf@murcar.co.uk
*Seaside links course with a prevailing south-west wind.
Its main attraction is the challenge of playing round
and between gorse, heather and sand dunes. The
additional hazards of burns and out of bounds give any
golfer a testing round of golf.*
*Murcar: 18 holes, 6314yds, Par 71, SSS 72,
Course record 64.*
Strabathie: nine holes, 2680yds, Par 35, SSS 35.
Club membership 850.
Visitors contact in advance & observe club dress code
Societies advance booking required. **Green Fees** £75 per
day, £55 per round (£85/£65 weekends & bank holidays).
Strabathie: £30 per day, £12 per 9 holes (£40/£20
weekends & bank holidays). **Cards** 📇 💳 📶 🏧 **Prof**
Gary Forbes **Course Designer** Archie Simpson, James
Braid **Facilities** ⊗ ⅷ ⅃ 💺 ⅀ 🏊 🏕 🎣
Location 5m NE of city centre off A90

....

Hotel ★★★ 70% The Craighaar Hotel, Waterton Rd,
Bucksburn, ABERDEEN ☎ 01224 712275 55 en suite

Royal Aberdeen Links Rd, Balgownie, Bridge of Don
AB23 8AT
☎ 01224 702571 📠 01224 826591
e-mail: admin@royalaberdeengolf.com
*Championship links course with undulating dunes.
Windy, easy walking.*
*Balgownie Course: 18 holes, 6504yds, Par 71, SSS 71,
Course record 63.*
Silverburn Course: 18 holes, 4066yds, Par 60, SSS 60.
Club membership 500.
Visitors 10-11.30am, 2-3.30pm weekdays, after 3.30pm
weekends. Must contact in advance. **Societies** apply in
writing. **Green Fees** not confirmed. **Cards** 📇 💳 **Prof**
Ronnie MacAskill
Course Designer Baird & Simpson **Facilities** ⊗ ⅃ 💺 ⅀
🏊 🏕 🎣 **Location** 2.5m N of city centre off A92

Continued

Westhill Westhill Heights, Westhill AB32 6RY
☎ 01224 740159 🗎 01224 749124
e-mail: westhillgolfclub@btinternet.com
A challenging parkland course.
18 holes, 5921yds, Par 69, SSS 69, Course record 65.
Club membership 808.
Visitors no restrictions **Societies** phone in advance. **Green
Fees** £14 per round (£20 weekends). **Cards** 💳 💳 💳 💳
Prof George Bruce **Course Designer** Charles Lawrie
Facilities ⊗ ⊪ ⅋ ▆ ♀ 🏌 🏠 🍴 🏌 ⚡
Leisure Snooker table. **Conf** fac available
Corporate Hospitality Days available
Location 7m NW of city centre off A944

PETERCULTER   Map 15 NJ80

Peterculter Oldtown, Burnside Rd AB14 0LN
☎ 01224 734994 (shop) & 735245 (office)
🗎 01224 735580
e-mail: info@peterceltergolfclub.co.uk
**Five new holes were brought into play in 2001.
Surrounded by wonderful scenery and bordered by the
River Dee, a variety of birds, deer and foxes may be
seen on the course, which also has superb views up the
Dee Valley.**
18 holes, 6207yds, Par 71, SSS 70, Course record 64.
Club membership 1035.
Visitors contact three days in advance, welcome between
10am-3.15pm weekdays, 11am-6pm weekends. **Societies**
contact up to seven days in advance. **Green Fees** £22 per
round/£30 per day (weekend £27/£35). **Cards** 💳 💳 💳
💳 💳 **Prof** Dean Vannet **Course Designer** Greens of
Scotland **Facilities** ⊗ ⊪ ⅋ ▆ ♀ 🏌 🏠 🍴 🏌 ⚡
Location On A93

ABERDEENSHIRE

ABOYNE   Map 15 NO59

Aboyne Formaston Park AB34 5HP
☎ 013398 86328 🗎 013398 87592
e-mail: aboynegolfclub@btinternet.com
**Beautiful parkland with outstanding views. Two lochs
on course.**
18 holes, 5975yds, Par 68, SSS 69, Course record 62.
Club membership 930.
Visitors no restrictions. Advisable to contact in advance.
Societies booking essential. **Green Fees** £22 per round/£30
per day (weekend £25/£35). **Cards** 💳 💳 💳 **Prof** Stephen
Moir **Facilities** ⊗ ⊪ ⅋ ▆ ♀ 🏠 🍴 ⚡ **Location** E side
of village, N of A93

....

Hotel ★★ 73% Loch Kinord Hotel, Ballater Rd, Dinnet,
BALLATER ☎ 01339 885229 21 rms (19 en suite)

ALFORD   Map 15 NJ51

Alford Montgarrie Rd AB33 8AE
☎ 019755 62178 🗎 019755 64910
e-mail: info@alford-golf-club.co.uk
**A flat parkland course in scenic countryside. Divided
into sections by a road, a narrow-gauge railway and a
burn. The course is challenging, testing golfers of all
skills and abilities.**
18 holes, 5483yds, Par 69, SSS 65, Course record 64.
Club membership 800.
Visitors advisable to contact in advance. **Societies** phone,
e-mail or write in advance. **Green Fees** £20 per round/£25

per day (weekends £25/£30). **Cards** 💳 💳 💳
Facilities ⊗ ⊪ ⅋ ▆ ♀ 🏠 🍴 🏌 🏌 ⚡ **Conf** Corporate
Hospitality Days available **Location** in village centre on
A944

....

Hotel ★★ 63% Gordon Arms Hotel, The Square,
HUNTLY ☎ 01466 792288 13 en suite

AUCHENBLAE   Map 15 NO77

Auchenblae AB30 1WQ
☎ 01561 320002
**Short but demanding course set in spectacular scenery
and renowned for its excellent greens. A mixture of
short and long holes, small and large greens add to the
challenge and enjoyment of the course.**
9 holes, 2217yds, Par 32, SSS 61, Course record 60.
Club membership 450.
Visitors anytime except club nights during peak season
but phone to confirm. **Societies** phone in advance.
Green Fees £10 per day (£12 weekends). **Course
Designer** Robin Hiseman **Facilities** ▆ ⅋ ⚡
Leisure hard tennis courts.
Location 5m NW of Laurencekirk off A90

....

Hotel ★★ 66% County Hotel & Squash Club, Arduthie
Rd, STONEHAVEN ☎ 01569 764386 14 en suite

BALLATER   Map 15 NO39

Ballater Victoria Rd AB35 5QX
☎ 013397 55567
e-mail: sec@ballatergolfclub.co.uk
**Heather covered course with testing long holes and
beautiful scenery.**
18 holes, 5638yds, Par 67, SSS 67, Course record 62.
Club membership 750.
Visitors advisable to contact in advance. **Societies** booking
recommended. **Green Fees** £23 per round (weekend £27).
Cards 💳 💳 💳 💳 **Prof** Bill Yule **Facilities** ⊗ ⊪ ⅋
♀ 🏠 🍴 🏌 🏌 ⚡ **Leisure** hard tennis courts, fishing,
snooker. **Conf** Corporate Hospitality Days available
Location W side of town

....

Hotel ★★★ Darroch Learg Hotel, Braemar Rd,
BALLATER ☎ 01339 755443 12 en suite 5 annexe
en suite

BALMEDIE   Map 15 NJ91

East Aberdeenshire Golf Centre Millden
AB23 8YY
☎ 01358 742111 🗎 01358 742123
e-mail: info@eagolf.com
**Designed as two loops of nine holes each, starting and
finishing outside the clubhouse. Skilful use of 130 acres
of rolling Buchan farmland has resulted in a
challenging course of 6276yds in length. Even in the
short history of the course, the par 3 holes have gained
the reputation of being equal to any in the north of
Scotland.**
18 holes, 6276yds, Par 71, SSS 71, Course record 69.
Club membership 400.
Visitors phone pro shop to book tee time on 01358 742111
(ext 21) **Societies** write or phone to Sandra Watson. **Green
Fees** £17 (£22 weekends & bank holidays). **Cards** 💳 💳
💳 💳 **Prof** Ian Bratton **Course Designer** Ian Cresswell
Facilities ⊗ ⊪ ⅋ ▆ ♀ 🏠 🍴 🏌 🏌 ⚡ ⚡ **Conf** fac
available Corporate Hospitality Days available

Continued

BANCHORY   Map 15 NO69

Banchory Kinneskie Rd AB31 5TA
☎ 01330 822365 📠 01330 822491
-mail: info@banchorygolfclub.co.uk
Sheltered parkland course situated beside the River
Dee, with easy walking and woodland scenery. Twelfth
nd 13th holes are testing.
8 holes, 5781yds, Par 69, SSS 68, Course record 63.
Club membership 975.
Visitors contact in advance, phone for details on 01330
'22447 **Societies** book in advance. **Green Fees** not
onfirmed. **Cards** 🖅 💳 📇 💷 **Prof** David Naylor
Facilities ⊗ ⊪ ⏄ ⛳ ♀ ⚞ 🏠 ⛵ ♨ ✐ ♂
Location A93, 300yds from W end of High St

Hotel ★★★ ♨ 71% Banchory Lodge Hotel,
BANCHORY ☎ 01330 822625 22 en suite

Inchmarlo Golf Centre Inchmarlo AB31 4BQ
☎ 01330 826422 📠 01330 826425
-mail: info@inchmarlo.com
The Laird's (18-hole course) is laid out on the gentle
arkland slopes of the Inchmarlo Estate and the
designer has taken advantage of the natural contours of
he land and its many mature trees. The nine-hole
acility is a tricky and testing course with ponds,
meadering burns and dry stone wall combined with the
more traditional bunkers to test the skill of even the
most accomplished player.
Laird's Course: 18 holes, 6218yds, Par 71, SSS 71,
Course record 66.
9 holes, 2150yds, Par 32, SSS 31.
Club membership 900.
Visitors booking in advance preferred. **Societies** book in
dvance **Green Fees** Laird's Course £30 per round (£35
weekends); 9-hole course £16 per 18 holes; £11 per 9 holes
£18/£12 weekends). **Cards** 🖅 💳 📇 💷 📇 📇 💷 **Prof**
Patrick Lovie **Course Designer** Graeme Webster
Facilities ⊗ ⊪ ⏄ ⛳ ♀ ⚞ 🏠 ⛵ ♨ ✐ ♂ ⚑ **Conf** fac
available Corporate Hospitality Days available
Location 0.5m from A93 Aberdeen-Braemar road

Hotel ★★★ 78% Tor-na-Coille Hotel, BANCHORY
☎ 01330 822242 22 en suite

BANFF   Map 15 NJ66

Duff House Royal The Barnyards AB45 3SX
☎ 01261 812062 📠 01261 812224
-mail: duff-house-royal@btinternet.com
Well-manicured flat parkland, bounded by woodlands
nd the River Deveron. Well bunkered and renowned
or its large, two-tier greens. The river is a hazard for
hose who wander off the tee at the 7th, 16th and 17th
oles.
8 holes, 6161yds, Par 68, SSS 70, Course record 62.
Club membership 1000.
Visitors phone professional in advance, handicap
ertificate is preferred. Restrictions at weekends during
ummer. **Societies** apply in writing. **Green Fees** £31 per
ay, £25 per round (£37/£32 weekends). **Cards** 💷 **Prof**
ob Strachan **Course Designer** Dr MacKenzie
Facilities ⊗ ⊪ ⏄ ⛳ ♀ ⚞ 🏠 ♨ ♂ **Conf** fac available
Location 0.5m S on A98

Hotel ★★★ 71% Banff Springs Hotel, Golden Knowes
d, BANFF ☎ 01261 812881 31 en suite

BRAEMAR   Map 15 NO19

Braemar Cluniebank Rd AB35 5XX
☎ 013397 41618 📠 013397 41400
**Flat course, set amid beautiful countryside on Royal
Deeside, with River Clunie running through several
holes. The 2nd hole is one of the most testing in the area.**
18 holes, 5000yds, Par 65, SSS 64, Course record 59.
Club membership 450.
Visitors are advised to book 24 hours in advance to play at
weekends. Tee reserved until 12.30 on Sat for members
only. **Societies** contact secretary in advance 013397 41595.
Green Fees not confirmed. **Course Designer** Joe
Anderson **Facilities** ⊗ ⊪ ⏄ ⛳ ♀ ⚞ 🏠 ⛵ ♂
Location 0.5m S

CRUDEN BAY   Map 15 NK03

Cruden Bay Aulton Rd AB42 0NN
☎ 01779 812285 📠 01779 812945
e-mail: cbaygc@aol.com
**A typical links course which epitomises the old fashioned
style of rugged links golf. The drives require accuracy
with bunkers and protecting greens, blind holes and
undulating greens. The 10th provides a panoramic view
of half the back nine down at beach level, and to the east
can be seen the outline of the spectacular ruin of Slains
Castle featured in Bram Stoker's Dracula. The figure
eight design of the course is quite unusual.**
*Main Course: 18 holes, 6395yds, Par 70, SSS 72, Course
record 65.*
St Olaf Course: 9 holes, 5106yds, Par 64, SSS 65.
Club membership 1100.
Visitors welcome on weekdays, at weekends only when
there are no competitions, must book. **Societies** weekdays,
phone in advance. **Green Fees** £55 per round/£75 per day
(weekend £65 per round). **Cards** 🖅 💳 📇 📇 💷
Prof Robbie Stewart **Course Designer** Thomas Simpson
Facilities ⊗ ⊪ ⏄ ⛳ ♀ ⚞ 🏠 ⛵ ♂ ✐ ♂ **Conf** Corporate
Hospitality Days available **Location** SW side of village on
A975

Hotel ★★ 66% Red House Hotel, Aulton Rd, CRUDEN
BAY ☎ 01779 812215 6 rms (5 en suite)

ELLON   Map 15 NJ93

McDonald Hospital Rd AB41 9AW
☎ 01358 720576 📠 01358 720001
e-mail: mcdonald.golf@virgin.net
Tight, parkland course with streams.
18 holes, 5986yds, Par 70, SSS 70, Course record 62.
Club membership 710.
Visitors advisable to book in advance **Societies** phone in
advance. **Green Fees** not confirmed. **Cards** 🖅 💳 📇 💷
Prof Ronnie Urquhart **Facilities** ⊗ ⊪ ⏄ ⛳ ♀ ⚞ 🏠 ⛵ ♂
Conf Corporate Hospitality Days available
Location 0.25m N on A948

FRASERBURGH   Map 15 NJ96

Fraserburgh AB43 8TL
☎ 01346 516616 📠 01346 516616
e-mail: fburghgolf@aol.com
Corbie: 18 holes, 6308yds, Par 70, SSS 71,
Course record 63.
Rosehill: 9 holes, 2416yds, Par 66, SSS 63.
Course Designer James Braid **Location** 1m SE on B9033
Phone for further details

HUNTLY   Map 15 NJ53

Huntly Cooper Park AB54 4SH
☎ 01466 792643 📠 01466 792643
e-mail: huntlygc@tinyworld.co.uk
**A parkland course lying between the rivers Deveron
and Bogie.**
18 holes, 5399yds, Par 67, SSS 66.
Club membership 850.
Visitors not before 8am. Societies contact the secretary.
Green Fees not confirmed. Facilities ⊗ � ⅃ 🏌 🍴 ♀ ⅍ 🏠
⅄ ♟ Location N side of Huntly, turn off A96 at bypass
rdbt
....
Hotel ★★ 63% Gordon Arms Hotel, The Square,
HUNTLY ☎ 01466 792288 13 en suite

INSCH   Map 15 NJ62

Insch Golf Ter AB52 6JY
☎ 01464 820363 📠 01464 820363
e-mail: inschgolf@tiscali.co.uk
**A challenging 18-hole course, a mixture of flat
undulating parkland, with trees, stream and pond. The
most challenging hole of the course is the 9th, a testing
par 5 of 536yds requiring long and accurate play. This
follows the par 3 8th, a hole which demands a well-
positioned tee shot played over a large water hazard to
a long narrow green. Although a relatively short course,
the natural woodland, water hazards and large
contoured greens require accurate play.**
18 holes, 5350yds, Par 69, SSS 67.
Club membership 400.
Visitors restricted during club competitions; Mon Ladies
night, Tue Mens night, Wed juniors; phone clubhouse
01464 820363 for information; booking is advised.
Societies apply in writing or phone, bookings accepted.
Green Fees £16 per day (£20 weekends) reductions during
winter. Cards 💳 💳 💳 🏌 Course Designer Greens of
Scotland Facilities ⊗ by arrangement � by arrangement
🏌 🍴 ♀ ⅍ 🍴 🏠 ♟ Conf Corporate Hospitality Days
available Location A96
....
Hotel ★★★ 65% Strathburn Hotel, Burghmuir Dr,
INVERURIE ☎ 01467 624422 25 en suite

INVERALLOCHY   Map 15 NK06

Inverallochy Whitelink AB43 8XY
☎ 01346 582000
**Seaside links course with natural hazards, tricky par 3s
and easy walking.**
18 holes, 5351yds, Par 67, SSS 66, Course record 57.
Club membership 600.
Visitors restricted at weekends and competition days,
contact for availability. Societies apply in writing or phone
in advance. Green Fees Sun-Fri £15, Sat £20.
Facilities ⊗ � 🏌 🍴 ♀ ⅍ 🏠 ♟ Leisure Bowling green.
Location E side of village off B9107

INVERURIE   Map 15 NJ72

Inverurie Blackhall Rd AB51 5JB
☎ 01467 624080 📠 01467 672869
e-mail: administrator@inveruriegc.co.uk
**Parkland course, part of which is through a wooded
area.**
18 holes, 5711yds, Par 69, SSS 68, Course record 63.
Club membership 750.
Visitors book tee time through shop up to 24 hrs in

advance 01467 672863 **Societies** phone administrator.
Green Fees £24 per day; £20 per round (£30/£24
weekends). Prof John Logue Facilities ⊗ � 🏌 🍴 ♀ ⅍
🏠 ♟ ♟ Location Easily accessible from Blackhall rdbt
off A96 bypass
....
Hotel ★★★ 65% Strathburn Hotel, Burghmuir Dr,
INVERURIE ☎ 01467 624422 25 en suite

KEMNAY   Map 15 NJ71

Kemnay Monymusk Rd AB51 5RA
☎ 01467 642225 (shop) 📠 01467 643746
e-mail: administrator@kemnaygolfclub.co.uk
**A parkland course with stunning views, incorporating
both tree lined and open fairways and a stream crossing
four holes. The course is not physically demanding but
a challenge is presented to every level of golfer due to
the diverse characteristics of each hole.**
18 holes, 6362yds, Par 71, SSS 71, Course record 66.
Club membership 800.
Visitors phone shop for booking. Societies phone in
advance. Green Fees £26 per day; £20 per round (£30/£24
weekends). Cards 💳 💳 💳 🏌 Prof Ronnie McDonald
Course Designer Greens of Scotland Facilities ⊗ � 🏌
🍴 ♀ ⅍ 🏠 🍴 🏠 ♟ Conf Corporate Hospitality Days
available Location W side of village on B993

KINTORE   Map 15 NJ71

Kintore Balbithan AB51 0UR
☎ 01467 632631 📠 01467 632995
e-mail: kintoregolfclub@lineone.net
**The course covers a large area of ground, from the Don
Basin near the clubhouse, to mature woodland at the
far perimeter. The 1st is one of the toughest opening
holes in the North East, and the 7th requires an
accurate drive followed by a second shot over a burn
which runs diagonally across the front of the green. The
11th is the longest hole on the course, made longer by
the fact that it slopes upwards all the way to the green.
The final holes are short, relatively hilly and quite
tricky but offer spectacular views to the Bennachie and
Grampian hills.**
18 holes, 6019yds, Par 70, SSS 69, Course record 62.
Club membership 700.
Visitors during season booking system is in operation &
slots for visitors are available. Other times can be booked
24 hours in advance. Societies apply in writing or phone.
Green Fees terms on application. Cards 💳 💳 🏌
Facilities ⊗ � 🏌 🍴 ♀ ⅍ 🏠 ♟ Conf Corporate
Hospitality Days available Location 1m from village
centre on B977

MACDUFF   Map 15 NJ76

Royal Tarlair Buchan St AB44 1TA
☎ 01261 832897 📠 01261 833455
e-mail: info@royaltarlair.co.uk
Seaside clifftop course. Testing 13th, Clivet (par 3).
18 holes, 5866yds, Par 71, SSS 68, Course record 62.
Club membership 520.
Visitors no restrictions. Societies apply in writing. Green
Fees £15 per round; £20 per day (weekends £18/£22).
Facilities ⊗ � 🏌 🍴 ♀ ⅍ 🏠 🍴 ♟ Conf Corporate
Hospitality Days available Location 0.75m E off A98
....
Hotel ★★★ 71% Banff Springs Hotel, Golden Knowes
Rd, BANFF ☎ 01261 812881 31 en suite

Continued

NEWBURGH   Map 15 NJ92

Newburgh on Ythan Beach Rd AB41 6BE
☎ 01358 789058 📠 01358 788104
e-mail: secretary@newburgh-on-ythan.co.uk
This seaside course was founded in 1888 and is adjacent
to a bird sanctuary. The course was extended in 1996
and the nine new holes, the outward half, are
characterised by undulations and hills, with elevated
tees and greens requiring a range of shot making. The
original inward nine demands accurate golf from tee to
green. Testing 550yd dog-leg (par 5).
18 holes, 6162yds, Par 72, SSS 71, Course record 68.
Club membership 800.
Visitors contact in advance; not before 1pm Sat. Societies
apply in advance. Green Fees not confirmed. Cards ▦
▦ ▦ ▧ Facilities ⊗ ⅋ ▥ 💷 ♀ 🅿 🏧 ⚐ ⚑ ✓ 𝄞
Leisure hard tennis courts. Conf Corporate Hospitality
days available Location 10m N of Aberdeen on A975

NEWMACHAR   Map 15 NJ81

Newmachar Swailend AB21 7UU
☎ 01651 863002 📠 01651 863055
e-mail: info@newmachargolfclub.co.uk
Hawkshill is a championship-standard parkland course
designed by Dave Thomas. Several lakes affect five of
the holes and there are well-developed birch and Scots
pine trees. Swailend is a parkland course, also designed
by Dave Thomas and opened in 1997. It provides a test
of its own with some well-positioned bunkering and
putting greens.
Hawkshill Course: 18 holes, 6659yds, Par 72, SSS 74,
Course record 67.
Swailend Course: 18 holes, 6388yds, Par 72, SSS 71,
Course record 67.
Club membership 900.
Visitors contact in advance & must have handicap
certificate for Hawkshill course. Societies apply in writing.
Green Fees terms on application. Cards ▦ ▦ ▦ ▧
Prof Gordon Simpson Course Designer Dave Thomas,
Peter Allis Facilities ⊗ ⅋ ▥ 💷 ♀ 🅿 🏧 ⚐ ⚑ 🏌 ✓ 𝄞
Location 2m N of Dyce, off A947

Hotel ★★★ 65% Strathburn Hotel, Burghmuir Dr,
INVERURIE ☎ 01467 624422 25 en suite

OLDMELDRUM   Map 15 NJ82

Old Meldrum Kirk Brae AB51 0DJ
☎ 01651 872648 📠 01651 872896
e-mail: admin@oldmeldrumgolf.co.uk
Parkland course with tree-lined fairways and superb
views. Challenging 196yd, par 3 11th over two ponds to
a green surrounded by bunkers.
18 holes, 5988yds, Par 70, SSS 69, Course record 66.
Club membership 850.
Visitors not during Club competitions. Must contact in
advance Societies apply in writing to secretary Green Fees
£22 per round (weekend £26). Prof Hamish Love Course
Designer Various Facilities ⊗ ⅋ ▥ 💷 ♀ 🅿 🏧 ⚐ ⚑ ✓
Location E side of village off A947

Hotel ★★★ 65% Strathburn Hotel, Burghmuir Dr,
INVERURIE ☎ 01467 624422 25 en suite

> **Booking a tee time is always advisable.**

PETERHEAD   Map 15 NK14

Peterhead Craigewan Links, Riverside Dr AB42 1LT
☎ 01779 472149 & 480725 📠 01779 480725
e-mail: phdgc@freenetname.co.uk
The Old Course is a natural links course bounded by
the sea and the River Ugie. Varying conditions of play
depending on wind and weather. The New Course is
more of a parkland course.
Old Course: 18 holes, 6173yds, Par 70, SSS 71,
Course record 64.
New Course: 9 holes, 2228yds, Par 31.
Club membership 650.
Visitors welcome any day apart from Sat, restricted times
on the Old Course. Phone for details. Societies apply in
writing, restricted Sat. Green Fees £30 per round/£40 per
day (weekend £38/£48). Cards ▦ Course Designer
W Park, L Auchterconie, J Braid Facilities ⊗ ⅋ ▥ 💷 ♀
🅿 ⚑ ✓ Location N side of town centre off A90

PORTLETHEN   Map 15 NO99

Portlethen Badentoy Rd AB12 4YA
☎ 01224 782575 & 781090 📠 01224 783383
e-mail: info@portlethengc.fsnet.co.uk
Set in pleasant parkland, this new course features
mature trees and a stream which affects a number of
holes.
18 holes, 6707yds, Par 72, SSS 72, Course record 63.
Club membership 1200.
Visitors not Sat. Contact in advance. Societies apply in
advance. Green Fees £22 per day; £15 per round (£22
weekends & bank holidays). Cards ▦ ▦ ▦ ▧
Prof Muriel Thomson Course Designer Cameron Sinclair
Facilities ⊗ ⅋ ▥ 💷 ♀ 🅿 🏧 🏌 ✓ 𝄞 Conf fac available
Location Off A90 S of Aberdeen

Hotel ★★ 66% County Hotel & Squash Club, Arduthie
Rd, STONEHAVEN ☎ 01569 764386 14 en suite

STONEHAVEN   Map 15 NO88

Stonehaven Cowie AB39 3RH
☎ 01569 762124 📠 01569 765973
e-mail: stonehaven.golfclub@virgin.net
Challenging meadowland course overlooking sea with
three gullies and splendid views.
18 holes, 5103yds, Par 66, SSS 65, Course record 61.
Club membership 850.
Visitors prefer booking; not before 4pm Sat. Societies
phone or fax in advance to WA Donald. Green Fees not
confirmed. Cards ▦ ▦ ▧ Course Designer
C Simpson Facilities ⊗ ⅋ ▥ 💷 ♀ 🅿 🏧 ⚐ ✓
Leisure snooker. Location 1m N off A92

Hotel ★★ 66% County Hotel & Squash Club, Arduthie
Rd, STONEHAVEN ☎ 01569 764386 14 en suite

TARLAND   Map 15 NJ40

Tarland Aberdeen Rd AB34 4TB
☎ 013398 81000 📠 013398 81000
e-mail: telward@aol.com
Difficult upland course, but easy walking. Some
spectacular holes, mainly 4th (par 4) and 5th (par 3)
and fine scenery. A challenge to golfers of all abilities.
9 holes, 5888yds, Par 67, SSS 68, Course record 65.
Club membership 392.
Visitors contact in advance. Societies phone in advance.
Green Fees £15 per day (£20 weekends). Course

Continued

Designer Tom Morris **Facilities** ⊗ ⅢⅢ ⓑ ℡ ♀ ♈ ☎ ✓
Conf Corporate Hospitality Days available
Location E side of village off B9119

Hotel ★★ 73% Loch Kinord Hotel, Ballater Rd, Dinnet,
BALLATER ☎ 01339 885229 21 rms (19 en suite)

TORPHINS   Map 15 NJ60

Torphins Bog Rd AB31 4JU
☎ 013398 82115 & 82402 (Sec) 🗎 013398 82402
e-mail: stuart@macgregor5.fsnet.co.uk
**Heathland and parkland course built on a hill with
views of the Cairngorms.**
*9 holes, 4800yds, Par 64, SSS 64, Course record 59.
Club membership 380.*
Visitors restricted competition days (alternate Sat & Sun)
Societies apply in advance. **Green Fees** £13 per day (£14
weekends); £7 per 9 holes. **Facilities** ⊗ ⓑ ℡ ♈
Location 0.25m W of village off A980

Hotel ★★★ 78% Tor-na-Coille Hotel, BANCHORY
☎ 01330 822242 22 en suite

TURRIFF   Map 15 NJ75

Turriff Rosehall AB53 4HD
☎ 01888 562982 🗎 01888 568050
e-mail: grace@turriffgolf.sol.co.uk
**An inland course with tight fairways, well-paced greens
and well-sighted bunkers to test all golfers. The par 5
12th hole sets a challenge for the longest driver while
the short par 3 4th, with its green protected by bunkers
is a challenge in its own right.**

*18 holes, 5664yds, Par 68, SSS 68.
Club membership 650.*
Visitors not before 10am weekends. Must contact in
advance. **Societies** apply in writing to the secretary. **Green
Fees** £25 per day, £21 per day (£31/£25 weekends &
holidays). **Prof** John Black **Facilities** ⊗ ⅢⅢ ⓑ ℡ ♀ ♈ ☎
✓ **Location** 1m W off B9024

Hotel ★★★ 71% Banff Springs Hotel, Golden Knowes
Rd, BANFF ☎ 01261 812881 31 en suite

ANGUS

ARBROATH   Map 12 NO64

Arbroath Elliot DD11 2PE
☎ 01241 875837 🗎 01241 875837
e-mail: golfshop@fsmail.net
**This predominantly flat course has wide undulating
fairways and the controlled rough flatters to deceive.
Sea breezes combined with fast greens and difficult**

approaches catch out the unwary, as will the subtly
positioned bunkers.
*18 holes, 6185yds, Par 70, SSS 69, Course record 64.
Club membership 550.*
Visitors contact professional 01241 875837. **Societies**
contact professional 01241 875837. **Green Fees** not
confirmed. **Cards** 🎫 🎫 💳 **Prof** Lindsay Ewart **Course
Designer** Braid **Facilities** ⊗ ⅢⅢ ⓑ ℡ ♀ ♈ ☎ ✈ ✓
Location 2m SW on A92

Hotel ★★ 65% Hotel Seaforth, Dundee Rd, ARBROATH
☎ 01241 872232 19 en suite

Letham Grange Colliston DD11 4RL
☎ 01241 890373 & 809377 🗎 01241 890725
e-mail: lethamgrange@sol.co.uk
*Old Course: 18 holes, 6632yds, Par 73, SSS 73,
Course record 68.
Glens Course: 18 holes, 5528yds, Par 68, SSS 68,
Course record 63.*
Course Designer GK Smith, Donald Steel
Location 4m N on A933
Phone for further details

Hotel ★★ 65% Hotel Seaforth, Dundee Rd, ARBROATH
☎ 01241 872232 19 en suite

BARRY   Map 12 NO53

Panmure Burnside Rd DD7 7RT
☎ 01241 855120 🗎 01241 859737
e-mail: secretary@panmuregolfclub.co.uk

18 holes, 6317yds, Par 70, SSS 71, Course record 62.
Location S side of village off A930
Phone for further details

Hotel ⛨ Premier Travel Inn Dundee East, 115-117 Lawe
Dr, Panmurefield Village, BROUGHTY FERRY
☎ 0870 9906324 60 en suite

BRECHIN   Map 15 NO56

Brechin Trinity DD9 7PD
☎ 01356 622383 & 625270 🗎 01356 625270
e-mail: brechingolfclub@btconnect.com
**Rolling parkland course, with easy walking and good
views of the Grampian mountains. Set among many
tree-lined fairways with excellent greens and lush gree
fairways. A wide variation of holes with dog legs, long
par 3s, tricky par 4s and reachable in two par 5s,
where the longer hitters can take a more challenging t
shot.**
*18 holes, 6092yds, Par 72, SSS 70, Course record 66.
Club membership 850.*

Continued

Continue

Visitors contact Professional on 01356 625270 in advance. Restricted weekends. **Societies** contact club steward in advance. **Green Fees** £33 per day, £25 per round (£40/£30 weekends). **Cards** 🖻 💳 💷 **Prof** Stephen Rennie **Course Designer** James Braid (partly) **Facilities** ⊗ 沥 ⓑ 💺 ♀ ⅄ 🖻 ⚐ ☜ ♣ ♂ **Leisure** squash. **Conf** Corporate Hospitality Days available **Location** 1m N on B966

Hotel ★★★ 65% Glenesk Hotel, High St, EDZELL
🕾 01356 648319 24 en suite

CARNOUSTIE   See page 317

EDZELL   Map 15 NO66

Edzell High St DD9 7TF
🕾 01356 647283 (Secretary) 🖺 01356 648094
e-mail: secretary@edzellgolfclub.net
This delightful, gentle, flat course is situated in the foothills of the Highlands and provides good golf as well as conveying a feeling of peace and quiet to everyone who plays here. The village of Edzell is one of the most picturesque in Scotland.
18 holes, 6367yds, Par 71, SSS 71, Course record 62.
West Water: 9 holes, 2057yds, Par 32, SSS 31.
Club membership 855.
Visitors not 4.45-6.15pm weekdays, 7.30-10am, 12-2pm weekends. **Societies** contact secretary at least 14 days in advance. **Green Fees** £38 per day; £28 per round (£48/£34 weekends). West Water £15 per 18 holes, £10 per 9 holes.
Cards 🖻 💳 💳 📷 💷 **Prof** AJ Webster
Course Designer Bob Simpson **Facilities** ⊗ 沥 ⓑ 💺 ♀ ⅄ 🖻 ⚐ ♣ ♂ ☜ **Location** on B966, S end of Edzell

Hotel ★★★ 65% Glenesk Hotel, High St, EDZELL
🕾 01356 648319 24 en suite

FORFAR   Map 15 NO45

Forfar Cunninghill, Arbroath Rd DD8 2RL
🕾 01307 463773 🖺 01307 468495
e-mail: forfargolfclub@uku.co.uk
Moorland course with wooded, undulating fairways, excellent greens and fine views.
18 holes, 6066yds, Par 69, SSS 70, Course record 61.
Club membership 850.
Visitors not before 2.30pm Sat. Advance booking required.
Societies contact in advance. **Green Fees** not confirmed.
Cards 🖻 💳 💷 📷 💷 **Prof** Peter McNiven
Course Designer James Braid **Facilities** ⊗ 沥 ⓑ 💺 ♀ ⅄ 🖻 ⚐ ♂ ☜ **Conf** Corporate Hospitality Days available **Location** 1.5m E of Forfar on A932

Hotel ★★★ ⚓ Castleton House Hotel, Castleton of Eassie, GLAMIS 🕾 01307 840340 6 en suite

KIRRIEMUIR   Map 15 NO35

Kirriemuir Shielhill Rd, Northmuir DD8 4LN
🕾 01575 573317 🖺 01575 574608
e-mail: kirriemuirgc@aol.com
18 holes, 5553yds, Par 68, SSS 67, Course record 62.
Course Designer James Braid **Location** 1m N off B955
Phone for further details

Hotel ★★★ ⚓ Castleton House Hotel, Castleton of Eassie, GLAMIS 🕾 01307 840340 6 en suite

MONIFIETH   Map 12 NO43

Monifieth Princes St DD5 4AW
🕾 01382 532767 (Medal) & 532967 (Ashludie)
🖺 01382 535816
The chief of the two courses at Monifieth is the Medal Course. It has been one of the qualifying venues for the Open Championship on more than one occasion. A seaside links, but divided from the sand dunes by a railway which provides the principal hazard for the first few holes. The 10th hole is outstanding, the 17th is excellent and there is a delightful finishing hole. The other course here is the Ashludie, and both are played over by a number of clubs who share the links.

Medal Course: 18 holes, 6655yds, Par 71, SSS 72, Course record 63.
Ashludie Course: 18 holes, 5123yds, Par 68, SSS 66.
Club membership 1750.
Visitors contact in advance. Restricted to after 2pm Sat, 10am Sun & after 9.30pm Mon-Fri. **Societies** contact in advance by phone or writing to Medal Starter's Box, Princes St, Monifieth. **Green Fees** terms on application.
Cards 🖻 💳 📷 💷 **Prof** Ian McLeod **Facilities** ⊗ 沥 by arrangement ⓑ 💺 ♀ ⅄ 🖻 ⚐ ♂ **Location** NE side of town on A930

Hotel ⚐ Premier Travel Inn Dundee East, 115-117 Lawers Dr, Panmurefield Village, BROUGHTY FERRY
🕾 0870 9906324 60 en suite

MONTROSE   Map 15 NO75

Montrose Golf Links Traill Dr DD10 8SW
🕾 01674 672932 🖺 01674 671800
e-mail: secretary@montroselinks.co.uk
The links at Montrose like many others in Scotland are on commonland and are shared by three clubs. The Medal Course at Montrose - the fifth oldest in the world - is typical of Scottish links, with narrow, undulating fairways and problems from the first hole to the last. The Broomfield course is flatter and easier.
Medal Course: 18 holes, 6544yds, Par 71, SSS 72, Course record 63.
Broomfield Course: 18 holes, 4830yds, Par 66, SSS 63.
Club membership 1300.
Visitors not Medal Course on Sat before 2.45pm & before 10am on Sun. Must have a handicap certificate for Medal Course. Contact in advance. No restrictions on Broomfield Course. Must contact in advance. **Societies** contact secretary in advance. **Green Fees** Medal £50 per day, £40 per round (£58/£44 weekends); Broomfield £18 per round (£20 weekends). **Cards** 🖻 💳 💷 📷 💷

Continued

Prof Jason J Boyd **Course Designer** W Park, Tom Morris
Facilities ⊗ ⑪ ⓑ 🖳 ♀ ⌂ 🏠 ⛳ 🚶 ⛳ **Location** NE side
of town off A92

Montrose Golf Links Ltd

Hotel ★★★ 74% Best Western Links Hotel, Mid Links,
MONTROSE ☎ 01674 671000 25 en suite

If the name of the club appears in *italics*, details
have not been confirmed for this
edition of the guide.

ARGYLL & BUTE

CARDROSS
Map 10 NS37

Cardross Main Rd G82 5LB
☎ 01389 841754 📄 01389 842162
e-mail: golf@cardross.com
Undulating, testing parkland course with good views.
18 holes, 6469yds, Par 71, SSS 72, Course record 64.
Club membership 800.
Visitors not weekends unless introduced by member.
Contact professional in advance 01359 841350. **Societies**
contact in writing. **Green Fees** £30 per round/£45 per day.
Reduced winter rates. **Cards** 🔲 🔲 📳 **Prof** Robert Farrell
Course Designer James Braid **Facilities** ⊗ ⑪ ⓑ 🖳 ♀ ⌂
🏠 ⛳ ⛳ **Conf** Corporate Hospitality Days available
Location in village centre on A814

Hotel ★★★★★ 72% De Vere Cameron House,
BALLOCH ☎ 01389 755565 96 en suite

CARRADALE
Map 10 NR83

Carradale The Arch PA28 6QT
☎ 01583 431321
**Pleasant seaside course built on a promontory
overlooking the Isle of Arran. Natural terrain and small
greens are the most difficult natural hazards. Described
as the most sporting nine-hole course in Scotland.
Testing 7th hole (240yds), par 3.**
9 holes, 2358yds, Par 65, SSS 64, Course record 62.
Club membership 320.
Visitors no restrictions, advisable to contact at weekends
during summer months. **Societies** contact in advance.
Green Fees £12 per day. **Facilities** ⌂ ⛳ **Location** S side
of village on B842

DALMALLY
Map 10 NN12

Dalmally Old Saw Mill PA33 1AE
☎ 01838 200370
e-mail: golfclub@lock-awe.com
**A nine-hole flat parkland course bounded by the River
Orchy and surrounded by mountains. Many water
hazards and bunkers.**
9 holes, 2257yds, Par 64, SSS 63, Course record 64.
Club membership 130.
Visitors not Sun 9-10am, 1-2pm & Mon 5.45-6.15pm
Societies phone in advance. **Green Fees** £12 per
day/round. **Course Designer** MacFarlane Barrow Co
Facilities ⊗ by arrangement ⓑ by arrangement 🖳 by
arrangement ♀ ⌂ ⛳ ⛳ **Location** on A85, 1.5m W of
Dalmally

Hotel ★★★ 68% Loch Fyne Hotel Leisure Club,
INVERARAY ☎ 01499 302148 80 en suite

DUNOON
Map 10 NS17

Cowal Ardenslate Rd PA23 8LT
☎ 01369 705673 📄 01369 705673
e-mail: secretary@cowalgolfclub.com
**Moorland course. Panoramic views of the Clyde estuary
and surrounding hills.**
18 holes, 6063yds, Par 70, SSS 70, Course record 63.
Club membership 900.
Visitors advisable to book in advance. **Societies** phone in
advance. **Green Fees** terms on application. **Cards** 🔲 🔲
📳 **Prof** Russell Weir **Course Designer** James Braid
Facilities ⊗ ⑪ ⓑ 🖳 ♀ ⌂ 🏠 ⛳ ⛳ **Location** 1m N

Continued

Carnoustie Golf Links

Angus

Carnoustie   Map 12 NO53

This Championship Course has been voted the top course in Britain by many golfing greats and described as Scotland's ultimate golfing challenge. The course developed from origins in the 1560s; James Braid added new bunkers, greens and tees in the 1920s. The Open Championship first came to the course in 1931 and Carnoustie hosted the Scottish Open in 1995 and 1996, and was the venue for the 1999 Open Championship. The Burnside Course (6028yds) is enclosed on three sides by the Championship Course and has been used for Open Championship qualifying rounds. The Buddon Course (5420yds) has been extensively remodelled, making it ideal for mid to high handicappers.

Links Pde DD7 7JE
☎ 01241 853789 bookings
Fax 01241 852720
e-mail: golf@carnoustiegolflinks.co.uk

Championship: 18 holes, 6941yds, Par 72, SSS 75, Course record 64.
Burnside: 18 holes, 6028yds, Par 68, SSS 69.
Buddon Links: 18 holes, 5420yds, Par 66, SSS 67.
Visitors not before 2pm Sat, not before 11.30am Sun; must contact in advance; handicap certificate for Championship Course. Societies write or phone in advance. Green Fees terms on application. Cards ▨ ▨ ▨ ▨ ▨ ▨ ▨ Prof Colin Sinclair Course Designer James Braid Facilities ⊗ ⅷ ㋡ ▨ ♀ ⚲ ▤ ⏏ ↝ ♂ Leisure heated indoor swimming pool, sauna, solarium, gymnasium. Location SW of town centre off A930

....

Hotels

★★ 65% Hotel Seaforth, Dundee Rd, ARBROATH

☎ 01241 872232 19 en suite

★★★★ 76% Apex City Quay Hotel & Spa, 1 West Victoria Dock Rd, DUNDEE

☎ 01382 202404 & 0845 608 3456 Fax 01382 201401 153 en suite

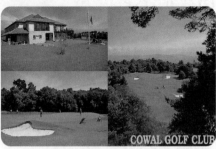

Cowal Golf Club

Hotel ★★ 66% Selborne Hotel, Clyde St, West Bay, DUNOON ☎ 01369 702761 98 en suite

ERISKA   Map 10 NM94

Isle of Eriska PA37 1SD
☎ 01631 720371 🖹 01631 720531
e-mail: gc@eriska-hotel.co.uk
This remote and most beautiful six-hole course, set around the owners' hotel, is gradually being upgraded to a testing nine-hole challenge, complete with stunning views. The signature 5th hole provides a 140yd carry to a green on a hill surrounded by rocks and bunkers.
6 holes, 1588yds, Par 22.
Club membership 40.
Visitors contact in advance. **Green Fees** £10 per day.
Cards 🖿 🖿 🖿 🖿 🖿 🖿 **Course Designer** H Swan
Facilities ⊗ 🛏 ▼ ♀ ⚘ ⚘ ⚘ ⚘ ⚘ **Leisure** hard tennis courts, heated indoor swimming pool, sauna, gymnasium.
Location A828 Connel-Fort William, signed 4m N of Benderloch

Hotel ★★★★ ≜≜ Isle of Eriska, Eriska, Ledaig, BY OBAN ☎ 01631 720371 17 en suite

GIGHA ISLAND   Map 10 NR64

Isle of Gigha PA41 7AA
☎ 01583 505242 🖹 01583 505244
A nine-hole course with scenic views of the Sound of Gigha and Kintyre. Ideal for the keen or occasional golfer.
9 holes, 5042yds, Par 66, SSS 65.
Club membership 40.
Visitors no restrictions. **Societies** phone for details. **Green Fees** £10 per day/round. **Course Designer** Members
Facilities ⚘ ⚘ **Location** short distance from ferry landing

HELENSBURGH   Map 10 NS28

Helensburgh 25 East Abercromby St G84 9HZ
☎ 01436 674173 🖹 01436 671170
e-mail: thesecretary@helensburghgolfclub.org.uk
Sporting moorland course with superb views of Loch Lomond and River Clyde.
18 holes, 6104yds, Par 69, SSS 70, Course record 64.
Club membership 875.
Visitors not weekends. **Societies** weekdays only, must contact in writing. **Green Fees** £40 per day; £30 per round.
Prof David Fotheringham **Course Designer** Old Tom Morris **Facilities** ⊗ ⚘ 🛏 ▼ ♀ ⚘ ⚘ ⚘ **Conf** Corporate Hospitality Days available **Location** NE side of town off B832

Hotel ★★★★★ 72% De Vere Cameron House, BALLOCH ☎ 01389 755565 96 en suite

INNELLAN   Map 10 NS17

Innellan Knockamillie Rd PA23 7SG
☎ 01369 830242 & 702573
Situated above the village of Innellan, this undulating hilltop, parkland course has extensive views of the Firth of Clyde.
9 holes, 4683yds, Par 64, SSS 64, Course record 63.
Club membership 199.
Visitors not after 5pm Mon. **Societies** phone initially.
Green Fees £9 per round (£12 per day). **Facilities** 🛏 ▼ ♀ ⚘ **Location** 4m S of Dunoon

Hotel ★★ 73% Royal Marine Hotel, Hunters Quay, DUNOON ☎ 01369 705810 31 en suite 10 annexe en suite

INVERARAY   Map 10 NN00

Inveraray North Cromalt PA32 8XT
☎ 01499 302116
Testing parkland course with beautiful views overlooking Loch Fyne.
9 holes, 5628yds, Par 70, SSS 68, Course record 69.
Club membership 160.
Visitors no restrictions. **Societies** write or phone to the secretary. **Green Fees** £15 per day. **Facilities** ⚘ ⚘
Location 1m S of Inveraray

Hotel ★★★ 68% Loch Fyne Hotel Leisure Club, INVERARAY ☎ 01499 302148 80 en suite

LOCHGILPHEAD   Map 10 NR88

Lochgilphead Blarbuie Rd PA31 8LE
☎ 01546 602340 & 510383
A varied and challenging scenic course with a spectacular par 3 finishing hole.

9 holes, 2242yds, Par 64, SSS 63, Course record 58.
Club membership 250.
Visitors restricted during weekend club competitions.
Societies apply in advance, restricted weekends. **Green Fees** not confirmed. **Course Designer** Dr I McCamond
Facilities 🛏 ▼ ♀ ⚘ 🏠 ⚘ ⚘ **Location** next to hospital, signed from village

Hotel ★★ 66% Stag Hotel, 47 Argyll St, LOCHGILPHEAD ☎ 01546 602496 18 en suite

In the hotel entries, the percentage figure refers to the AA's most recent Quality Assessment Score.

Continued

LUSS   Map 10 NS39

Loch Lomond Rossdhu House G83 8NT
☎ 01436 655555 📠 01436 655500
e-mail: info@lochlomond.com
A stunning and challenging course set in the heart of some of the most beautiful Scottish scenery. The exclusive club is strictly for members only. Nick Faldo called it the finest new course in Europe. It was designed by two Americans, Jay Morrish and Tom Weiskopf and was founded in 1993. There is a putting green, practice area and driving range. The clubhouse used to be the home of the chiefs of Clan Colquhoun.
Loch Lomond: 18 holes, 7100yds, Par 71,
Course record 62.
Club membership 650.
Visitors no visitors strictly private **Green Fees** terms on application. **Prof** Colin Campbell **Course Designer** Tom Weiskopf **Facilities** 🏌 🏠 🍴 ✓ ♨ **Leisure** fishing. **Location** Off A82 at Luss

....
Hotel ★★★★★ 72% De Vere Cameron House, BALLOCH ☎ 01389 755565 96 en suite

MACHRIHANISH   Map 10 NR62

Machrihanish PA28 6PT
☎ 01586 810213 📠 01586 810221
e-mail: secretary@machgolf.com
Magnificent natural links of championship status. The 1st hole is the famous drive across the Atlantic. Sandy soil allows for play all year round. Large greens, easy walking, windy.
18 holes, 6225yds, Par 70, SSS 71.
Club membership 1300.
Visitors no restrictions. **Societies** apply in writing. **Green Fees** Sun-Fri £40 per round/£60 per day, Sat £50/£75. 9-hole course £12 per day. **Cards** 🔲 🔲 🔲 🔲 **Prof** Ken Campbell **Course Designer** Tom Morris **Facilities** ⊗ 🍴 🛒 🍴 ♨ 🏠 🍴 🛒 ✓ **Location** 5m W of Campbeltown on B843

OBAN   Map 10 NM83

Glencruitten Glencruitten Rd PA34 4PU
☎ 01631 564604
There is plenty of space and considerable variety of hole on this downland course - popular with holidaymakers. In a beautiful, isolated situation, the course is hilly and testing, particularly the 1st and 12th (par 4s) and 10th and 17th (par 3s).
18 holes, 4452yds, Par 61, SSS 63, Course record 55.
Club membership 500.
Visitors restricted Thu & weekends. **Societies** contact in writing. **Green Fees** not confirmed. **Course Designer** James Braid **Facilities** ⊗ 🍴 🛒 🍴 ♨ 🏠 🍴 ✓ **Location** NE side of town centre off A816

....
Hotel ★★★ 72% Manor House Hotel, Gallanach Rd, OBAN ☎ 01631 562087 11 en suite

SOUTHEND   Map 10 NR60

Dunaverty PA28 6RW
☎ 01586 830677 📠 01586 830677
e-mail: dunavertygc@aol.com
Undulating, seaside course with spectacular views of Ireland and the Ayrshire coast.

18 holes, 4799yds, Par 66, SSS 63, Course record 58.
Club membership 400.
Visitors limited Sat, contact in advance. **Societies** apply in advance. **Green Fees** not confirmed. **Facilities** ⊗ 🍴 🛒 🍴 🏠 🍴 ✓ **Leisure** fishing. **Location** 10m S of Campbeltown on B842

TARBERT   Map 10 NR86

Tarbert PA29 6XX
☎ 01546 606896
Hilly parkland course with views over West Loch Tarbert.
9 holes, 4460yds, Par 66, SSS 63, Course record 62.
Visitors not Sat pm. **Societies** apply in writing. **Green Fees** £10 per round (£20 per day). **Location** N1m W on B8024

TIGHNABRUAICH   Map 10 NR97

Kyles of Bute PA212AB
☎ 01700 811603
Moorland course which is hilly and exposed. Fine mountain and sea views. Heather, whin and burns provide heavy penalties for inaccuracy. Wildlife abounds.
9 holes, 4778yds, Par 66, SSS 64, Course record 62.
Club membership 150.
Visitors not Wed 6pm or Sun am. **Societies** phone in advance. **Green Fees** £10 per day/round.
Facilities 🏌 🍴 ✓ **Location** 1.25m S off B8000

....
Hotel ★★ 79% The Royal at Tighnabruaich, Shore Rd, TIGHNABRUAICH ☎ 01700 811239 11 en suite

CITY OF EDINBURGH

EDINBURGH   See page 321

EDINBURGH   Map 11 NT27

Baberton 50 Baberton Av, Juniper Green EH14 5DU
☎ 0131 453 4911 📠 0131 453 4678
e-mail: babertongolfclub@btinternet.com
Parkland course offering the golfer a variety of interesting and challenging holes. The outward half follows the boundary of the course and presents some demanding par 3 and 4 holes over the undulating terrain. The inward half has some longer, equally challenging holes contained within the course and presents some majestic views of the Pentland Hills and the Edinburgh skyline.
18 holes, 6129yds, Par 69, SSS 70, Course record 64.
Club membership 900.
Visitors not before 3.30pm weekdays, after 1pm weekends; contact professional in advance. **Societies** contact in advance. **Green Fees** not confirmed. **Cards** 🔲 🔲 **Prof** Ken Kelly **Course Designer** Willie Park Jnr **Facilities** ⊗ 🍴 🛒 🍴 ♨ 🏠 🍴 ✓ **Conf** Corporate Hospitality Days available **Location** 5m W of city centre off A70

....
Hotel ★★★★ 69% Edinburgh Marriott Hotel, 111 Glasgow Rd, EDINBURGH
☎ 0870 400 7293 245 en suite

Booking a tee time is always advisable.

Braid Hills Braid Hills Approach EH10 6JZ
☎ 0131 447 6666 📠 0131 651 2299
e-mail: golf@edinburghleisure.co.uk
Municipal heathland course with superb views of Edinburgh and the Firth of Forth, quite challenging.

18 holes, 5345yds, Par 70, SSS 66.
Visitors contact in advance. **Societies** contact in advance
Green Fees not confirmed. **Cards** ▦ ▬ ▧ 🌀 **Course Designer** Peter McEwan & Bob Ferguson **Facilities** 🛆 ⛳
♂ **Conf** fac available **Location** 2.5m S of city centre off A702
....

Hotel ★★★ 70% Braid Hills Hotel, 134 Braid Rd, EDINBURGH ☎ 0131 447 8888 67 en suite

Bruntsfield Links Golfing Society
32 Barnton Av EH4 6JH
☎ 0131 336 1479 📠 0131 336 5538
e-mail: secretary@bruntsfield.sol.co.uk
Mature parkland course with magnificent views over the Firth of Forth and to the west. Greens and fairways are generally immaculate. Challenging for all categories of handicap.
18 holes, 6407yds, Par 71, SSS 71, Course record 64.
Club membership 1180.
Visitors phone in advance. 0131 336 4050 or 0131 336 1479 **Societies** apply in writing. **Green Fees** £70 per day; £50 per round (£75/£55 weekends). **Cards** ▦ ▬ ▧ **Prof** Brian Mackenzie **Course Designer** Willie Park Jr, Dr A MacKenzie, Hawtree **Facilities** ⊗ 〗 ▮ ♀ 🛆 🏠 ⛳ 🛒
♂ ℄ **Conf** Corporate Hospitality Days available
Location 4m NW of city centre off A90
....

Hotel ★★★★ 70% Menzies Belford Hotel, 69 Belford Rd, EDINBURGH ☎ 0131 332 2545 146 en suite

Carrick Knowe Carrick Knowe, Glendevon Park EH12 5UZ
☎ 0131 337 1096 📠 0131 651 2299
e-mail: golf@edinburghleisure.co.uk
18 holes, 5697yds, Par 70, SSS 69.
Location 3m W of city centre, S of A8
Phone for further details
....

Hotel ★★★ 66% Greens Hotel, 24 Eglinton Crescent, Haymarket, EDINBURGH ☎ 0131 337 1565 55 en suite

Craigentinny Fillyside Rd EH7 6RG
☎ 0131 554 7501 📠 0131 651 2299
e-mail: golf@edinburghleisure.co.uk
An interesting mix of holes on an undulating parkland layout. From some tricky par 3s to some testing par 4s, this relatively short course will suit all abilities. The greens are surrounded by some awkward bunkers, requiring a great deal of forethought and an amount of accuracy to make par. The dog-leg 414yd par 4 10th requires a long tee shot to beyond the trees and an equally long second to the front of the green.
18 holes, 5205yds, Par 67, SSS 65.
Visitors contact in advance. **Societies** contact in advance
Green Fees £12 per round (£14 weekends & public holidays). **Cards** ▦ ▬ ▧ 🌀 **Prof** Steve Craig
Facilities 🛆 ⛳ ♂ **Location** NE side of city, between Leith & Portobello
....

Hotel ★★★ 69% Kings Manor, 100 Milton Rd East, EDINBURGH ☎ 0131 669 0444 67 en suite

Championship Course

Marriott Dalmahoy Hotel

Kirknewton

Map 11 NT27

The Championship East Course has hosted many major events including the Solheim Cup, the Scottish Seniors Open Championship and the PGA Championship of Scotland. The greens are large with immaculate putting surfaces and many of the long par 4 holes offer a serious challenge to any golfer. The short holes are well bunkered and the 15th hole in particular, known as the Wee Wrecker, will test your nerve and skill. The shorter West Course offers a different test with small greens requiring accuracy from a player's short game. The finishing holes with the Golgar burn meandering through the fairway create a tough finish.

Golf & Country Club
Kirknewton EH27 8EB
☎ 0131 3358010 Fax 0131 335 3577
e-mail: golf.dalmahoy@marriotthotels.co.uk

East Course: 18 holes, 7475yds, Par 72, SSS 72, Course record 62.
West Course: 18 holes, 5168yds, Par 68, SSS 66, Course record 60.
Visitors subject to availability; weekends by application; phone to book tee times. **Societies** Mon–Fri, phone or write for information. **Green Fees** East Course £65 per 18 holes (£80 weekends & bank holidays); West Course £35 (£40 weekends & bank holidays). **Cards** 🖃 ▒▒ ▒▒ ▒ 🖩 **Prof** Neal Graham **Course Designer** James Braid **Facilities** ⊗ ⅷ ⅼ 🖤 ♀ ⚒ 🏠 ⌐ 🏐 🏌 ⚐ 🍴 **Leisure** hard tennis courts, heated indoor swimming pool, sauna, solarium, gymnasium, beauty & hairdressing salon, fitness studio. **Conf** fac available Corporate Hospitality Days available **Location** 7m W of city on A71

....

Hotels

★★★★ 72% Marriott Dalmahoy Hotel & Country Club, Kirknewton, EDINBURGH

☎ 0870 400 7299 43 en suite 172 annexe en suite

★★★★ 68% Houstoun House, UPHALL

☎ 01506 853831 Fax 01506 854220 24 en suite 47 annexe en suite

★★★★ 69% Edinburgh Marriott Hotel, 111 Glasgow Rd, EDINBURGH

☎ 0870 400 7293 Fax 0870 400 7393 245 en suite

Craigmillar Park
1 Observatory Rd EH9 3HG
☎ 0131 667 0047 📠 0131 662 8091
e-mail: secretary@craigmillarpark.co.uk
Parkland course, with good views.
18 holes, 5851yds, Par 70, SSS 69, Course record 63.
Club membership 750.
Visitors Mon-Fri & Sun after 2.30pm; contact in advance.
Societies contact in writing. **Green Fees** £30 per day, £20
per round (£30 per round Sun after 3pm). **Cards** 🎴 🎴
🎴 🎴 **Prof** Scott Gourlay **Course Designer** James Braid
Facilities ⊗ ⊪ ⅙ 🍷 ♀ 🏖 ┱ 🛒 𝒞 **Location** 2m S of
city centre off A7

Hotel ★★★ 70% Braid Hills Hotel, 134 Braid Rd,
EDINBURGH ☎ 0131 447 8888 67 en suite

Duddingston
Duddingston Rd West EH15 3QD
☎ 0131 661 4301 📠 0131 661 4301
e-mail: generalmanager@duddingston-golf-club.com
Parkland course with burn as a natural hazard. Testing
11th hole. Easy walking.
18 holes, 6473yds, Par 72, SSS 72, Course record 63.
Club membership 700.
Visitors limited availability at weekends - booking
advised. **Societies** Mon, Tue & Thu. Must contact in
advance. **Green Fees** £35 per day/round. **Cards** 🎴 🎴 💳
Prof Alastair McLean **Course Designer** Willie Park Jnr
Facilities ⊗ ⊪ ⅙ 🍷 ♀ 🏖 🏠 ┱ 🛒 𝒞 **Conf** fac
available Corporate Hospitality Days available
Location 2.5m SE of city centre off A1

Hotel ★★★ 69% Kings Manor, 100 Milton Rd East,
EDINBURGH ☎ 0131 669 0444 67 en suite

Kingsknowe
326 Lanark Rd EH14 2JD
☎ 0131 441 1145 (Secretary) 📠 0131 441 2079
e-mail: kingsknowe.golfclub@virgin.net
Picturesque parkland course set amid gently rolling
hills. This course provides a varied and interesting
challenge for all levels of golfers.

18 holes, 5981yds, Par 69, SSS 69, Course record 63.
Club membership 930.
Visitors contact in advance & subject to availability of tee
times. Not weekends. **Societies** apply in writing or phone
secretary. **Green Fees** £30 per day; £23 per round (£35 per
round weekends). **Prof** Chris Morris **Course Designer**
A Herd, James Braid **Facilities** ⊗ ⊪ ⅙ 🍷 ♀ 🏖 🏠 ┱ 🛒
┱ 𝒞 **Leisure** Indoor teaching/practice facility.
Conf Corporate Hospitality Days available
Location 4m SW of city centre on A70

Hotel ★★★ 76% Best Western Bruntsfield Hotel, 69/74
Bruntsfield Place, EDINBURGH ☎ 0131 229 1393
73 en suite

Liberton
297 Gilmerton Rd EH16 5UJ
☎ 0131 664 3009 (sec) 📠 0131 666 0853
e-mail: info@libertongc.co.uk
Undulating, wooded parkland course.
18 holes, 5170yds, Par 67, SSS 65, Course record 61.
Club membership 846.
Visitors contact in advance. **Societies** contact in writing.
Green Fees £20 per round/£36 two rounds (weekends
£30). **Cards** 💳 **Prof** Iain Seath **Facilities** ⊗ ⊪ ⅙ 🍷 ♀
🏖 🏠 𝒞 **Location** 3m SE of city centre on A7

Hotel ★★★ 75% Dalhousie Castle and Aqueous Spa,
Bonnyrigg, EDINBURGH ☎ 01875 820153 27 en suite
6 annexe en suite

Lothianburn
106A Biggar Rd, Fairmilehead
EH10 7DU
☎ 0131 445 2288 (pro) & 445 5067 (sec)
📠 0131 445 7067
e-mail: info@lothianburngc.co.uk
Situated to the south-west of Edinburgh, on the slopes
of the Pentland Hills, the course rises from the
clubhouse some 300ft to its highest point at the 13th
green. There is only one real climb of note, after playing
the 2nd shot to the 9th green. The course is noted for its
excellent greens, and challenging holes include the 5th,
where one drives for position in order to pitch at almost
right angles to a plateau green; and the 14th, longest
hole on the course, three-quarters of which is downhill
with out of bounds on both sides of the fairway.
18 holes, 5662yds, Par 71, SSS 68, Course record 64.
Club membership 850.
Visitors weekends after 3.30pm contact professional,
weekdays up to 4pm. **Societies** apply to the secretary or
phone in the first instance. **Green Fees** £18.50 per round
(weekend £24.50 per round). **Prof** Kurt Mungall **Course**
Designer J Braid (redesigned 1928) **Facilities** ⊗ ⊪ ⅙ 🍷 ♀
🏖 🏠 ┱ 🛒 𝒞 **Location** 4.5m S of city centre on A702

Hotel ★★★ 70% Braid Hills Hotel, 134 Braid Rd,
EDINBURGH ☎ 0131 447 8888 67 en suite

Merchants of Edinburgh
10 Craighill Gardens
EH10 5PY
☎ 0131 447 1219 📠 0131 446 9833
e-mail: admin@merchantsgolf.com
Testing hill course with fine views over the city and the
surrounding countryside.
18 holes, 4889yds, Par 65, SSS 64, Course record 59.
Club membership 980.
Visitors contact Secretary in advance. **Societies** contact
secretary in writing or phone 48 hours in advance. **Green**
Fees not confirmed. **Cards** 🎴 🎴 🎴 **Prof** Neil
Colquhoun **Course Designer** Ben Sayers **Facilities** ⊗ ⊪
⅙ 🍷 ♀ 🏖 🏠 ┱ 𝒞 **Leisure** snooker room. **Conf** fac
available Corporate Hospitality Days available
Location 2m SW of city centre off A702

Hotel ★★★ 70% Braid Hills Hotel, 134 Braid Rd,
EDINBURGH ☎ 0131 447 8888 67 en suite

Mortonhall
231 Braid Rd EH10 6PB
☎ 0131 447 6974 📠 0131 447 8712
e-mail: clubhouse@mortonhallgc.co.uk
Moorland and parkland course with views over
Edinburgh.
18 holes, 6502yds, Par 72, SSS 72, Course record 66.
Club membership 525.
Visitors advisable to contact by phone. **Societies** not

Continued

veekends; must contact in writing. **Green Fees** not onfirmed. **Cards** 🔲 **Prof** Malcolm Leighton **Course Designer** James Braid, F Hawtree **Facilities** ⊗ 🖪 💻 🏆 ♨ 🕈 ⚒ ⚐ **Location** 3m S of city centre off A702

Hotel ★★★ 70% Braid Hills Hotel, 134 Braid Rd, EDINBURGH ☎ 0131 447 8888 67 en suite

Murrayfield 43 Murrayfield Rd EH12 6EU
☎ 0131 337 3478 📠 0131 313 0721
e-mail: marjorie@murrayfieldgolfclub.ltd.uk
Parkland course on the side of Corstorphine Hill, with fine views.
18 holes, 5725yds, Par 70, SSS 69.
Club membership 815.
Visitors contact in advance; not weekends. **Societies** apply in writing **Green Fees** £35 per round/£40 per day.
Cards 🔲 ⚐ **Prof** K Stevenson **Facilities** ⊗ 🖪 💻 🏆 🖫 ⚒ 🕈 ⚐ **Location** 2m W of city centre off A8

Hotel ★★★ 66% Greens Hotel, 24 Eglinton Crescent, Haymarket, EDINBURGH ☎ 0131 337 1565 55 en suite

Portobello Stanley St EH15 1JJ
☎ 0131 669 4361 & 557 5457(bookings)
📠 0131 557 5170
Public parkland course, easy walking.
9 holes, 2252yds, Par 32, SSS 32.
Club membership 55.
Visitors advanced booking recommended. Contact Edinburgh Leisure. **Societies** contact in advance, phone 131 557 5457 or write to Edinburgh Leisure, 23 Waterloo Place EH1 3BH. **Green Fees** not confirmed. **Cards** 🔲 🔲 ⚐ **Facilities** 🖪 ♨ 🕈 ⚐ **Location** 3m E of city centre off A1

Hotel ★★★ 69% Kings Manor, 100 Milton Rd East, EDINBURGH ☎ 0131 669 0444 67 en suite

Prestonfield 6 Priestfield Rd North EH16 5HS
☎ 0131 667 9665 📠 0131 667 9665
e-mail: generalmanager@prestonfieldgolfclub.co.uk
Parkland course with beautiful views.
18 holes, 6212yds, Par 70, SSS 70, Course record 66.
Club membership 850.
Visitors contact secretary in advance; not Sat before 10.30am or 12pm-1.30pm & Sun before 11.30am. **Societies** contact general manager **Green Fees** £28 per round (£38 per day). **Cards** 🔲 🔲 🔲 ⚐ **Prof** Gavin Cook **Course Designer** James Braid **Facilities** ⊗ 🎮 🖪 💻 🏆 🖫 ♨ 🕈 ⚒ ⚐ **Conf** fac available Corporate Hospitality Days available **Location** 1.5m S of city centre off A68

Hotel ★★★★ Prestonfield, Priestfield Rd, EDINBURGH ☎ 0131 225 7800 26 en suite

Ravelston 24 Ravelston Dykes Rd EH4 3NZ
☎ 0131 315 2486 📠 0131 315 2486
Parkland course on the north-east side of Corstorphine Hill, overlooking the Firth of Forth.
9 holes, 5230yds, Par 66, SSS 66, Course record 64.
Club membership 610.
Visitors contact in advance; not weekends & bank holidays. **Green Fees** terms on application. **Course Designer** James Braid **Facilities** 🖪 💻 🖫 **Location** 3m W of city centre off A90

Hotel ★★★★ 69% Edinburgh Marriott Hotel, 111 Glasgow Rd, EDINBURGH ☎ 0870 400 7293 245 en suite

Royal Burgess 181 Whitehouse Rd, Barnton EH4 6BU
☎ 0131 339 2075 📠 0131 339 3712
e-mail: secretary@royalburgess.co.uk
No mention of golf clubs would be complete without the Royal Burgess, which was instituted in 1735 and is the oldest golfing society in the world. Its course is a pleasant parkland, and one with a great deal of variety. A club which anyone interested in the history of the game should visit.
18 holes, 6111yds, Par 68, SSS 69.
Club membership 620.
Visitors contact in advance; not weekends. **Societies** contact in advance. **Green Fees** terms on application.
Cards 🔲 🔲 🔲 📇 ⚐ **Prof** Steven Brian **Course Designer** Tom Morris **Facilities** ⊗ 🖪 💻 🏆 🖫 ♨ 🕈 ⚐ **Conf** Corporate Hospitality Days available **Location** 5m W of city centre off A90

Hotel ★★★★ 70% Menzies Belford Hotel, 69 Belford Rd, EDINBURGH ☎ 0131 332 2545 146 en suite

Silverknowes Silverknowes, Parkway EH4 5ET
☎ 0131 336 3843 📠 0131 651 2299
e-mail: golf@edinburghleisure.co.uk
Public links course on coast overlooking the Firth of Forth with magnificent views, generous fairways and expansive greens. The 601yd 18th will be a final test that will make or break your game. The ball needs to be kept low against the prevailing westerlies.
18 holes, 6070yds, Par 71, SSS 70.
Visitors advanced booking recommended in summer **Societies** contact in advance **Green Fees** terms on application. **Cards** 🔲 🔲 📇 ⚐ **Facilities** ⊗ 🎮 🖪 💻 🏆 ♨ 🖫 ⚒ 🕈 ⚐ **Location** 4m NW of city centre, easy access from city bypass

Hotel ★★★★ 70% Menzies Belford Hotel, 69 Belford Rd, EDINBURGH ☎ 0131 332 2545 146 en suite

Swanston 111 Swanston Rd, Fairmilehead EH10 7DS
☎ 0131 445 2239 📠 0131 445 2239
Hillside course with steep climb at 12th and 13th holes.
18 holes, 5024yds, Par 66, SSS 65, Course record 63.
Club membership 600.
Visitors not competition days, weekends restricted; contact in advance. **Societies** contact in advance 0131 445 4002.
Green Fees not confirmed. **Prof** Stu Pardoe **Course Designer** Herbert More **Facilities** ⊗ 🎮 🖪 💻 🏆 🖫 ⚒ 🕈 ♨ ⚐ **Conf** Corporate Hospitality Days available **Location** 4m S of city centre off B701

Hotel ★★★ 70% Braid Hills Hotel, 134 Braid Rd, EDINBURGH ☎ 0131 447 8888 67 en suite

Torphin Hill Torphin Rd, Colinton EH13 0PG
☎ 0131 441 1100 📠 0131 441 7166
e-mail: info@torphinhillgc.co.uk
Beautiful hillside, heathland course, with fine views of Edinburgh and the Forth estuary. From 600 to 700ft above sea level with 14 holes set on a relatively flat plateau.
18 holes, 5286yds, Par 68, SSS 67, Course record 64.
Club membership 550.
Visitors contact in advance, limited access Sat & Sun (only after 2pm) **Societies** contact in advance. **Green Fees** terms on application. **Cards** 🔲 🔲 **Prof** Jamie Browne

Continued

Facilities ⊗ ⅉ ⅊ ⅋ ♁ ⚘ ⛳ ⚐ ⚑ ✓ Conf Corporate
Hospitality Days available **Location** 5m SW of city centre
S of A720

Hotel ★★★ 70% Braid Hills Hotel, 134 Braid Rd,
EDINBURGH ☎ 0131 447 8888 67 en suite

Turnhouse 154 Turnhouse Rd EH12 0AD
☎ 0131 339 1014
e-mail: secretary@turnhousegc.com
**Challenging tree lined course with numerous par 4s in
excess of 400yds. Large sloping greens give a real
challenge and the golfer is virtually guaranteed to use
all the clubs in the bag.**
18 holes, 6171yds, Par 69, SSS 70, Course record 62.
Club membership 800.
Visitors restricted Sat. Must contact professional in
advance. **Societies** contact in writing to secretary. **Green
Fees** £30 per day (£38 per day, £25 per 18 holes
weekends). **Cards** ▦ ▦ ▦ ▦ Ⓡ **Prof** John Murray
Course Designer J Braid **Facilities** ⊗ ⅉ ⅊ ⅋ ♁ ⚘ ⛳
⚐ ✓ **Conf** fac available Corporate Hospitality Days
available **Location** 6m W of city centre N of A8

Hotel ★★★★ 69% Edinburgh Marriott Hotel, 111
Glasgow Rd, EDINBURGH
☎ 0870 400 7293 245 en suite

RATHO   Map 11 NT17

Ratho Park EH28 8NX
☎ 0131 335 0068 & 335 0068 ⓘ 0131 333 1752
e-mail: secretary.rpgc@btconnect.com
**Easy walking, parkland course with converted mansion
as the clubhouse.**
18 holes, 5960yds, Par 69, SSS 68, Course record 62.
Club membership 850.
Visitors contact in advance. **Societies** contact in writing.
Only able to play Mon-Fri **Green Fees** £36 per day, £26
per round (£36 per round weekends). **Cards** ▦ ▦ Ⓡ
Prof Alan Pate **Course Designer** James Braid **Facilities** ⊗
ⅉ ⅊ ⅋ ♁ ⚘ ⛳ ⚐ ⚑ ✓ **Location** 0.75m E, N of A71

Hotel ★★★★ 78% Norton House Hotel & Restaurant,
Ingliston, EDINBURGH ☎ 0131 333 1275 47 en suite

SOUTH QUEENSFERRY   Map 11 NT17

Dundas Parks Dundas Estate EH30 9SS
☎ 0131 331 4252
**Parkland course situated on the estate of Dundas
Castle, with excellent views. For 18 holes, the nine are
played twice.**
9 holes, 6056yds, Par 70, SSS 69, Course record 62.
Club membership 500.
Visitors contact in advance; not weekends. **Societies**
contact in writing. **Green Fees** £12. **Facilities** by
arrangement ⅊ ♁ **Location** 0.5m S on A8000

Hotel ⬙ Premier Travel Inn (South Queensferry),
Builyeon Rd, SOUTH QUEENSFERRY ☎ 08701 977094
46 en suite

CITY OF GLASGOW

GLASGOW   Map 11 NS56

Alexandra Alexandra Park, Alexandra Pde G31 8SE
☎ 0141 556 1294
Parkland course, hilly with some woodland. Many
Continued

bunkers and a barrier of trees between 1st and 9th
fairway.
9 holes, 2800yds, Par 31, Course record 25.
Club membership 85.
Visitors no restrictions. **Societies** phone 24 hrs in advance
or by writing one week in advance. **Green Fees** £3.60.
Course Designer G McArthur **Facilities** ♁ **Leisure**
bowling green. **Location** 2m E of city centre off M8/A8

Hotel ★★★ 73% Holiday Inn, 161 West Nile St,
GLASGOW ☎ 0141 352 8300 113 en suite

Cowglen Barrhead Rd G43 1AU
☎ 0141 632 0556 ⓘ 01505 503000
e-mail: r.jamieson-accountants@rsmail.net
**Undulating and challenging parkland course with good
views over the Clyde valley to the Campsie Hills. Club
and line selection is most important on many holes due
to the strategic placing of copses on the course.**

18 holes, 6053yds, Par 70, SSS 69, Course record 64.
Club membership 805.
Visitors play on shorter course. Must contact secretary for
times in advance & have a handicap certificate. No visitors
Tue, Fri & weekends. **Societies** booking in writing to
secretary. **Green Fees** £35 per day; £27.50 per round. **Prof**
Simon Payne **Course Designer** David Adams, James Braid
Facilities ⊗ ⅉ ⅊ ⅋ ♁ ⚘ ⛳ ✓ ⛳ **Conf** fac available
Corporate Hospitality Days available **Location** M77 S from
Glasgow, Pollok/Barrhead slip road, left at lights club 0.5m
right

Hotel ⬙ Travelodge (Glasgow Paisley Road), 251 Paisley
Rd, GLASGOW ☎ 08700 850 950 75 en suite

Haggs Castle 70 Dumbreck Rd, Dumbreck G41 4SN
☎ 0141 427 1157 ⓘ 0141 427 1157
e-mail: secretary@haggscastlegolfclub.com
**Wooded, parkland course where Scottish National
Championships and the Glasgow and Scottish Open
have been held.**
18 holes, 6426yds, Par 72, SSS 71, Course record 63.
Club membership 900.
Societies apply in writing. **Green Fees** £40 per round; £50
per day. **Cards** ▦ ▦ ▦ Ⓡ **Prof** Campbell Elliott
Course Designer James Braid **Facilities** ⊗ ⅉ ⅊ ⅋ ♁ ⚘
⚐ ⚑ ⛳ ✓ **Conf** Corporate Hospitality Days available
Location 2.5m SW of city centre off M77 junct 1

Kirkhill Greenless Rd, Cambuslang G72 8YN
☎ 0141 641 8499 ⓘ 0141 641 8499
e-mail: carol.downes@virgin.net
Meadowland course designed by James Braid.
18 holes, 6030yds, Par 70, SSS 70, Course record 63.
Club membership 650.
Continue

isitors must play with member at weekends. **Societies** ontact in advance. **Green Fees** terms on application. rof Duncan Williamson **Course Designer** J Braid acilities ⊗ ⊞ ᒪ 🍺 ♀ ⚲ 🏠 ⚒ **Location** 5m SE of city ntre off A749

....

otel ★★★ 68% Bothwell Bridge Hotel, 89 Main St, OTHWELL ☎ 01698 852246 90 en suite

nightswood Lincoln Av G13 5QZ
☎ 0141 959 6358
lat parkland course within easy reach of city. Two og-legs.
holes, 5586yds, Par 68, SSS 67.
lub membership 40.
isitors reserved tee Wed & Fri am. Bookings 1 day in lvance, no other restrictions. **Societies** welcome, must ook 1 day in advance. **Green Fees** not confirmed. acilities ⚲ **Location** 4m W of city centre off A82

....

otel ★★★ 63% Jurys Glasgow Hotel, Great Western Rd, LASGOW ☎ 0141 334 8161 137 en suite

ethamhill 1240 Cumbernauld Rd, Millerston
33 1AH
☎ 0141 770 6220 & 0141 770 7135 📠 1041 770 0520
Iunicipal parkland course.
holes, 5859yds, Par 70, SSS 69.
isitors contact in advance. **Societies** contact in advance.
reen Fees not confirmed. **Cards** ⊞ ▬ ▬ 💲 **Prof**
ary Taggart **Facilities** ⚲ **Location** 3m NE of city centre A80

....

otel ★★★★ 73% Millennium Hotel Glasgow, George quare, GLASGOW ☎ 0141 332 6711 117 en suite

inn Park Simshill Rd G44 5EP
☎ 0141 633 0377
holes, 4952yds, Par 65, SSS 65, Course record 61.
ocation 4m S of city centre off B766
none for further details

ollok 90 Barrhead Rd G43 1BG
☎ 0141 632 4351 📠 0141 649 1398
mail: secretary@pollokgolf.com
arkland course with woods and river. Gentle walking ntil the 18th hole.
holes, 6358yds, Par 71, SSS 71, Course record 62.
lub membership 620.
isitors members only until 2pm weekends. Must contact advance. **Societies** contact in writing for large parties, one for up to 4 **Green Fees** £50 per round weekdays. ards ⊞ ▬ 💲 **Course Designer** J Douglas & Dr A acKenzie **Facilities** ⊗ ⊞ by arrangement ᒪ 🍺 ♀ ⚲ ⚒ ⚒ **Conf** fac available **Location** M77 junct 2, S to A762 rrhead Rd, club 1m E

illiamwood Clarkston Rd G44 3YR
☎ 0141 637 1783 📠 0141 571 0166
ndulating parkland course with mature woodlands.
holes, 5878yds, Par 68, SSS 69, Course record 61.
ub membership 800.
isitors apply in writing to secretary, no weekend play. cieties midweek bookings only, apply in writing to cretary. **Green Fees** £40 per day; £30 per round. **Cards** ⊞ **Prof** Stewart Marshall **Course Designer** James Braid cilities ⊗ ⊞ ᒪ 🍺 ♀ ⚲ 🏠 ⚒ **Location** 5m S of city ntre on B767

ALLOA   Map 11 NS89

Alloa Schawpark, Sauchie FK10 3AX
☎ 01259 724476 📠 01259 724476
e-mail: bellville51@hotmail.com
Set in 150 acres of rolling parkland beneath the Ochil Hills, this course will challenge the best golfers while offering great enjoyment to the average player. The challenging finishing holes, 15th to 18th, consist of two long par 3s split by two long and demanding par 4s which will test any golfer's ability. Privacy provided by mature tree lined fairways.
18 holes, 6229yds, Par 69, SSS 71, Course record 63.
Club membership 910.
Visitors 7 day booking system through professional. Advised to book especially at weekends. **Societies** apply in writing or phone. **Green Fees** £36 per day Mon-Fri £26 per round (£30 per round weekends). **Cards** ⊞ ▬ 🍺 💲 **Prof** Bill Bennett **Course Designer** James Braid **Facilities** ⊗ ⊞ ᒪ 🍺 ♀ ⚲ 🏠 ⚒ ⚒ **Conf** Corporate Hospitality Days available **Location** 1.5m NE on A908

Braehead Cambus FK10 2NT
☎ 01259 722078 📠 01259 214070
e-mail: braehead.gc@btinternet.com
Attractive parkland course at the foot of the Ochil Hills, and offering spectacular views.
18 holes, 6086yds, Par 70, SSS 69, Course record 64.
Club membership 800.
Visitors advisable to phone in advance. **Societies** contact the professional in advance on 01259 722078 **Green Fees** not confirmed. **Cards** ⊞ ▬ ▬ 🍺 💲 **Prof** Jamie Stevenson **Course Designer** Robert Tait **Facilities** ⊗ ⊞ ᒪ 🍺 ♀ ⚲ 🏠 ⚒ ⚒ **Conf** Corporate Hospitality Days available **Location** 1m W on A907

ALVA   Map 11 NS89

Alva Beauclerc St FK12 5LD
☎ 01259 760431
e-mail: alva@alvagolfclub.wanadoo.com
A nine-hole course at the foot of the Ochil Hills which gives it its characteristic sloping fairways and fast greens.
9 holes, 2423yds, Par 66, SSS 64, Course record 63.
Club membership 318.
Visitors not during medal competitions or Thu evening (Ladies night). **Societies** apply in writing or phone in advance. **Green Fees** not confirmed. **Facilities** ᒪ 🍺 ♀ ⚲ **Location** 7m from Stirling, A91 Stirling-St Andrews

....

Hotel ★★★ 68% Royal Hotel, Henderson St, BRIDGE OF ALLAN ☎ 01786 832284 32 en suite

DOLLAR   Map 11 NS99

Dollar Brewlands House FK14 7EA
☎ 01259 742400 📠 01259 743497
e-mail: dollargc@brewlandshousefreeserve.co.uk
Compact hillside course with magnificent views along the Ochil Hills.
18 holes, 5242yds, Par 69, SSS 66, Course record 60.
Club membership 450.
Visitors weekdays course available but restricted Wed Ladies day, weekends advised to contact in advance. **Societies** write or phone in advance. **Green Fees** not confirmed. **Course Designer** Ben Sayers

Continued

Facilities ⊗ ⍲ 🛏 ♨ ♀ ⛱ 🏌 ♪ **Leisure** snooker table.
Conf Corporate Hospitality Days available **Location** 0.5m
N off A91

Hotel ★★★ 68% Royal Hotel, Henderson St, BRIDGE OF
ALLAN ☎ 01786 832284 32 en suite

MUCKHART   Map 11 NO00

Muckhart FK14 7JH
☎ 01259 781423 & 781493 🖷 01259 781544
e-mail: enquiries@muckhartgolf.com
Scenic heathland and downland course comprising
27 holes in three combinations of nine, all of which start
and finish close to the clubhouse. Each of the nine holes
requires a different approach, demanding tactical
awareness and a skilful touch with all the clubs in the
bag. There are superb views from the course's many
vantage points, including the aptly named 5th Top of
the World.
Cowden: 9 holes, 3251yds, Par 36.
Naemoor: 9 holes, 3234yds, SSS 36.
Arndean: 9 holes, 2835yds, Par 35.
Club membership 750.
Visitors phone to book - 01259 781423 or professional
01259 781493.Correct attire to be worn at all times.
Societies by arrangement. **Green Fees** terms on
application. **Cards** 🌐 📇 🖸 **Prof** Keith Salmoni
Facilities ⊗ ⍲ 🛏 ♨ ♀ ⛱ 🏠 🏌 ♪ **Location** S of village
between A91 & A823

Hotel ★★ 72% Castle Campbell Hotel, 11 Bridge St,
DOLLAR ☎ 01259 742519 8 en suite

TILLICOULTRY   Map 11 NS99

Tillicoultry Alva Rd FK13 6BL
☎ 01259 750124 🖷 01259 750124
e-mail: miket@tillygc.freeserve.co.uk
Parkland course at foot of the Ochil Hills entailing
some hard walking but affording fine views.
9 holes, 5472yds, Par 68, SSS 67, Course record 64.
Club membership 400.
Visitors contact in advance. **Societies** apply to the
secretary. **Green Fees** £12 per 18 holes (£17 weekends &
bank holidays). **Facilities** 🛏 ♨ ♀ ⛱ **Conf** Corporate
Hospitality Days available **Location** A91, 9m E of Stirling

Hotel ★★★ 68% Royal Hotel, Henderson St, BRIDGE OF
ALLAN ☎ 01786 832284 32 en suite

DUMFRIES & GALLOWAY

CASTLE DOUGLAS   Map 11 NX76

Castle Douglas Abercromby Rd DG7 1BA
☎ 01556 502801 & 502877
Parkland course, one severe hill.
9 holes, 2704yds, Par 68, SSS 66, Course record 61.
Club membership 400.
Visitors welcome except Tue & Thu after 4pm & during
competitions. Must contact secretary or steward in
advance. **Societies** apply by writing to secretary. **Green
Fees** £15 per round/day. **Facilities** ⊗ ⍲ 🛏 ♨ ♀ ⛱
Conf Corporate Hospitality Days available
Location W side of town

Hotel ★★ 67% Imperial Hotel, 35 King St, CASTLE
DOUGLAS ☎ 01556 502086 12 en suite

COLVEND   Map 11 NX85

Colvend Sandyhills DG5 4PY
☎ 01556 630398 🖷 01556 630495
e-mail: thesecretary@colvendgolfclub.co.uk
Picturesque and challenging course on the Solway
coast. Superb views.
18 holes, 5250yds, Par 68, SSS 67, Course record 64.
Club membership 490.
Visitors restricted Apr-Sep on Tue, 1st tee reserved for
weekly Medal 1-1.30 & 4-6pm & some weekends for open
competitions. **Societies** phone in advance. **Green Fees** £22
per day. **Course Designer** Allis & Thomas **Facilities** ⊗ ⍲
🛏 ♨ ♀ ⛱ 🏌 ♪ 🚜 ♪ **Location** 6m SE from Dalbeattie
on A710

CUMMERTREES   Map 11 NY16

Powfoot DG12 5QE
☎ 01461 700276 🖷 01461 700276
e-mail: bsutherland@powfootgolfclub.fsnet.co.uk
This British Championship course is on the Solway
Firth, playing at this delightfully compact semi-links
seaside course is a scenic treat. Lovely holes include the
2nd, the 8th and the 11th, also 9th with a second world
war bomb crater.
18 holes, 6283yds, Par 71, SSS 70, Course record 63.
Club membership 950.
Visitors contact in advance; not before 9am, 11am-1pm &
after 3.30pm weekdays, not Sat or before 1pm Sun. **Societies**
book in advance. **Green Fees** not confirmed. **Cards** 📇 🖸
Prof Stuart Smith **Course Designer** J Braid **Facilities** ⊗ ⍲
🛏 ♨ ♀ ⛱ 🏠 🚜 ♪ **Location** 0.5m off B724

Hotel ★★★ 68% Hetland Hall Hotel,
CARRUTHERSTOWN ☎ 01387 840201 14 en suite
15 annexe en suite

DALBEATTIE   Map 11 NX86

Dalbeattie 60 Maxwell Park DG5 4LR
☎ 01556 610666
e-mail: ocm@associates-ltd.fsnet.co.uk
This nine-hole course provides an excellent challenge
for golfers of all abilities. There are a few gentle slopes
to negotiate but compensated by fine views along the
Urr Valley. The 363yd 4th hole is a memorable par 4.
A good straight drive is required to the corner of the
course where a right angle dog-leg is taken for a pitch
to a smallish green.
9 holes, 5710yds, Par 68, SSS 68.
Club membership 250.
Visitors welcomed any day, effort made to accomodate on
club competitions days **Societies** apply in writing to
Secretary or phone 01556 610666 **Green Fees** £16 for
18holes/£20 per day (£10 per 9 holes). **Facilities** ⊗ 🛏 ♨
♀ ⛱ 🚜 ♪ **Location** signed off B794

Hotel ★★ 68% King's Arms Hotel, St Andrew's St,
CASTLE DOUGLAS ☎ 01556 502626 10 rms (9 en suit

DUMFRIES   Map 11 NX9

Dumfries & County Nunfield, Edinburgh Rd
DG1 1JX
☎ 01387 253585 🖷 01387 253585
e-mail: dumfriesc@aol.com
Parkland course alongside River Nith, with views over th
Queensberry Hills. Greens built to USPGA specification

Continu

The Dumfries & County Golf Club

...unfield: 18 holes, 5918yds, Par 69, SSS 69, Course ...cord 61.
...ub membership 800.
...sitors contact in advance; not Sat & during competitions ... Sun. **Societies** phone professional in advance 01387 ...8918. **Green Fees** £37 per 36 holes, £33 per 27 holes, ...7 per round (£37 per 27/36 holes, £33 per round ...eekends). **Cards** 🔲 🔲 💳 **Prof** Stuart Syme ...ourse Designer William Fernie **Facilities** ⊗ Ⅲ ⅃ ♨ 🍺 ♀ ⬚ 🍴 ⛳ 🏌 🛺 ⚐ **Conf** Corporate Hospitality Days ...ailable **Location** 1m NE of Dumfries on A701

...umfries & Galloway 2 Laurieston Av DG2 7NY ☎ 01387 263848 🖷 01387 263848
...mail: info@dandggolfclub.co.uk
...ttractive parkland course, a good test of golf but not ...ysically demanding.
...holes, 6309yds, Par 70, SSS 71.
...ub membership 800.
...sitors not competition days. Must contact in advance. ...o visitors on Sat during season. Some Sun not available. ...ocieties apply in writing. **Green Fees** £25 per round/£27 ...r day (weekend £30/£33). **Prof** Joe Fergusson ...ourse Designer W Fernie **Facilities** ⊗ Ⅲ ⅃ ♨ 🍺 ♀ 🍴 🛺 ⚐ **Location** W of town centre on A75

...otel ★★★ 69% Station Hotel, 49 Lovers Walk, ...UMFRIES ☎ 01387 254316 32 en suite

...nes Golf Centre Lockerbie Rd DG1 3PF ☎ 01387 247444 🖷 01387 249600
...mail: admin@pinesgolf.com
...mixture of parkland and woodland with numerous ...ter features and dog-legs. Excellent greens.
...holes, 5604yds, Par 68, SSS 67, Course record 66.
...ub membership 280.
...sitors visitors welcome at all times. **Societies** phone in ...vance. **Green Fees** not confirmed. **Prof** Brian Gemmell, ...uce Gray **Course Designer** Duncan Gray **Facilities** ⊗ ⅃ ♨ ♀ 🛺 🍴 🏌 🛺 ⛳ **Conf** Corporate Hospitality ...ys available

...ATEHOUSE OF FLEET   Map 11 NX55

...atehouse Laurieston Rd DG7 2BE ☎ 01644 450260 🖷 01644 450260
...mail: gatehousegolf@sagainternet.co.uk
...t against a background of rolling hills with scenic ...ews of Fleet Bay and the Solway Firth.
...oles, 2521yds, Par 66, SSS 66, Course record 62.
...ub membership 300.
...sitors restricted Sun before 11.30am. **Societies** phone in ...vance. **Green Fees** not confirmed. **Course Designer** ...m Fernie **Facilities** ⚲ **Location** 0.25m N of town

....
Hotel ★★★★ 73% Cally Palace Hotel, GATEHOUSE OF FLEET ☎ 01557 814341 55 en suite

GLENLUCE   Map 10 NX15

Wigtownshire County Mains of Park DG8 0NN ☎ 01581 300420 🖷 01581 300420
e-mail: enquiries@wigtownshirecountygolfclub.com
Seaside links course on the shores of Luce Bay, easy walking but affected by winds. The 12th hole, a dog-leg with out of bounds to the right, is named after the course's designer, Gordon Cunningham.
18 holes, 5904yds, Par 70, SSS 69, Course record 63.
Club membership 450.
Visitors all days by arrangement; not competition days.
Societies contact in advance. **Green Fees** £30 per day; £23 per round (£32/£25 weekends). **Course Designer** W Gordon Cunningham **Facilities** ⊗ Ⅲ ⅃ ♨ 🍺 ♀ 🛺 🍴 🏌 🛺

Continued   *Continued*

🏌 ♂ **Conf** Corporate Hospitality Days available
Location 1.5m W off A75, 200yds off A75 on shores of
Luce Bay

GRETNA · Map 11 NY36

Gretna Kirtle View DG16 5HD
☎ 01461 338464 📄 01461 337362
A nice parkland course on gentle hills. It offers a good
test of skill.
9 holes, 3214yds, Par 72, SSS 71, Course record 71.
Club membership 200.
Visitors no restrictions. **Societies** phone in advance. **Green
Fees** £5 per 9 holes; £10 per day. **Cards** ▦ ▦ ▦ ▦ 🄯
Prof Mr Gareth Dick **Course Designer** N Williams
Facilities ⊗ Ⅲ ⅃ 🖵 ♀ ♧ ⚑ 🏌 ♂ ♱ **Conf** fac available
Location 0.5m W of Gretna on B721, signed

Hotel ★★★ 67% Garden House Hotel, Sarkfoot Rd,
GRETNA ☎ 01461 337621 38 en suite

KIRKCUDBRIGHT · Map 11 NX65

Brighouse Bay Brighouse Bay, Borgue DG6 4TS
☎ 01557 870409 📄 01557 870409
e-mail: leisureclub@brighouse-bay.co.uk
A beautifully situated scenic maritime course on free
draining coastal grassland and playable all year.
Making use of many natural features - water, gullies
and rocks - it provides a testing challenge to golfers of
all handicaps.
18 holes, 6366yds, Par 73, SSS 73.
Club membership 170.
Visitors pay as you play - payment at adjacent Golf
Leisure Club. Phoning in advance recommended. **Societies**
by arrangement necessary. **Green Fees** not confirmed.
Cards ▦ ▦ ▦ ▦ **Course Designer** D Gray **Facilities**
⊗ Ⅲ⅃ 🖵 ♀ ♧ ⚑ ♱ ⛳ ⚑ 🏌 ♱ **Leisure** heated
indoor swimming pool, fishing, sauna, gymnasium,
Turkish steam room, Jacuzzi, pool tables.
Conf fac available Corporate Hospitality Days available
Location 3m S of Borgue off B727

Hotel ★★ 67% Arden House Hotel, Tongland Rd,
KIRKCUDBRIGHT ☎ 01557 330544 9 rms (8 en suite)

Kirkcudbright Stirling Crescent DG6 4EZ
☎ 01557 330314 📄 01557 330314
e-mail: david@kirkcudbrightgolf.co.uk
Parkland course. Hilly, with good views over the
harbour town of Kirkcudbright and the Dee estuary.
18 holes, 5739yds, Par 69, SSS 69, Course record 63.
Club membership 500.
Visitors advisable to contact in advance. **Societies** contact
in advance. **Green Fees** £25 per day; £20 per round.
Facilities ⊗ Ⅲ⅃ 🖵 ♀ ♧ ⚑ ♱ ⚑ 🏌 **Location** NE side
of town off A711

Hotel ★★ 67% Arden House Hotel, Tongland Rd,
KIRKCUDBRIGHT ☎ 01557 330544 9 rms (8 en suite)

LANGHOLM · Map 11 NY38

Langholm Whiteside DG13 0JR
☎ 013873 81247
e-mail: golf@langholmgolfclub.co.uk
Hillside course with fine views, easy to medium
walking.
9 holes, 6180yds, Par 70, SSS 70, Course record 65.
Club membership 200.

Visitors restricted Sat & Sun. **Societies** apply in writing to
secretary. **Green Fees** not confirmed. **Facilities** ⊗ by
arrangement ⅢⅡ by arrangement ⅃ by arrangement ♀
Location E side of village off A7

Guesthouse ♦♦♦♦ Whitecroft Hotel, 81 High St,
LANGHOLM ☎ 01387 381343 5 en suite

LOCHMABEN · Map 11 NY08

Lochmaben Castlehillgate DG11 1NT
☎ 01387 810552
e-mail: lochmabengc@aol.com
Attractive parkland course surrounding the Kirk Loch
excellent views on this well-maintained course.
18 holes, 5890yds, Par 70, SSS 69, Course record 60.
Club membership 850.
Visitors advised to contact in advance 01387 810552,
weekdays up to 5pm, weekends available **Societies** contact
in advance 01387 810552 **Green Fees** £28 per day; £25 per
round (£35/£30 weekends). **Course Designer** James Braid
Facilities ⊗ Ⅲ⅃ 🖵 ♀ ♧ ⚑ 🏌 **Leisure** fishing.
Conf Corporate Hospitality Days available **Location**
4m from Lockerbie on A74. S side of village off A709

Hotel ★★★ 80% The Dryfesdale Country House Hotel,
Dryfebridge, LOCKERBIE ☎ 01576 202427 16 en suite

LOCKERBIE · Map 11 NY18

Lockerbie Corrie Rd DG11 2ND
☎ 01576 203363 📄 01576 203363
18 holes, 5614yds, Par 68, SSS 67, Course record 64.
Course Designer James Braid **Location** E side of town
centre off B7068
Phone for further details

Hotel ★★★ 80% The Dryfesdale Country House Hotel,
Dryfebridge, LOCKERBIE ☎ 01576 202427 16 en suite

MOFFAT · Map 11 NT00

Moffat Coatshill DG10 9SB
☎ 01683 220020 📄 01683 221802
e-mail: bookings@moffatgolfclub.co.uk
Scenic moorland course overlooking the town, with
panoramic views of southern uplands.
18 holes, 5259yds, Par 69, SSS 67, Course record 60.
Club membership 350.
Visitors advised to contact in advance, no visitors after
3pm on Wed. **Societies** apply in writing or phone the
clubmaster. **Green Fees** £25 per day, £19.50 per round
(£34/£28 weekends & bank holidays). **Cards** ▦ ▦ ▦
▦ ▦ **Course Designer** Ben Sayers **Facilities** ⊗ Ⅲ⅃ 🖵
♀ ♧ ⛳ ♱ **Leisure** snooker. **Conf** Corporate
Hospitality Days available **Location** A74(M) junct 15,
A701 to Moffat, course signed on left after 30mph sign

Hotel ★★★ 69% Moffat House Hotel, High St, MOFFAT
☎ 01683 220039 21 en suite

MONREITH · Map 10 NX34

St Medan DG8 8NJ
☎ 01988 700358
Scotland's most southerly course. This links nestles in
Monreith Bay with panoramic views across to the Isle
of Man. The testing nine-hole course is a challenge to
both high and low handicaps.
9 holes, 4520yds, Par 64, SSS 64, Course record 60.
Club membership 300.

Continued

Continu

Visitors no restrictions. Societies apply in advance by phone or writing Green Fees £24 per day; £15 per 18 holes; £10 per 9 holes. Course Designer James Braid Facilities ⬛ 🍺 🎱 ⛳ ⚑ ✐ Location 3m S of Fort William off A747

Hotel ★★ 67% Kelvin House Hotel, 53 Main St, GLENLUCE ☎ 01581 300303 6 rms (5 en suite)

NEW GALLOWAY   Map 11 NX67

New Galloway High St DG7 3RN
☎ 01644 420737 & 450685 📠 01644 450685
Set on the edge of the Galloway Hills and overlooking Loch Ken, the course has excellent tees, no bunkers and first class greens. The course rises through the first two fairways to a plateau with all round views that many think unsurpassed.
9 holes, 5006yds, Par 68, SSS 67, Course record 64.
Club membership 350.
Visitors restricted on Sun (competition days). All visitors play off yellow markers. Contact Secretary in advance. Smart/casual dress. Societies contact secretary in advance. Green Fees £18 per day. Course Designer James Braid Facilities ⬛ 🍺 🎱 ⛳ ⚑ ✐ Conf Corporate Hospitality Days available Location S side of town on A762

Hotel ★★ 67% Imperial Hotel, 35 King St, CASTLE DOUGLAS ☎ 01556 502086 12 en suite

NEWTON STEWART   Map 10 NX46

Newton Stewart Kirroughtree Av, Minnigaff
DG8 6PF
☎ 01671 402172 📠 01671 402172
e-mail: email@newtonstewartgolfclub.com
Parkland course in picturesque setting. A good test for all standards of golfer with a variety of shots required. Many mature trees on the course and the five short holes have interesting features.
18 holes, 5840yds, Par 69, SSS 70, Course record 66.
Club membership 380.
Visitors contact in advance. Societies contact in advance. Green Fees £24 per round (£27 weekends). Facilities ⊗ ⬛ 🎱 ⛳ ⚑ 🏌 ✐ Location 0.5m N of town centre off A75

Hotel ★★★ 🏌 Kirroughtree House, Minnigaff, NEWTON STEWART ☎ 01671 402141 17 en suite

PORTPATRICK   Map 10 NX05

Portpatrick Golf Course Rd DG9 8TB
☎ 01776 810273 📠 01776 810811
e-mail: enquiries@portpatrickgolfclub.com
Seaside links-type course, set on cliffs overlooking the Irish Sea, with magnificent views.
Dunskey Course: 18 holes, 5908yds, Par 70, SSS 69, Course record 63.
Dinvin Course: 9 holes, 1504yds, Par 27, SSS 27, Course record 23.
Club membership 750.
Visitors contact in advance. £5 deposit required Societies contact in advance. Green Fees £38 per day; £28 per round (£43/£33 weekends). Cards ▦ ▬ 🔀 🌀 Course Designer Charles Hunter Facilities ⊗ ⍭ ⬛ 🍺 🎱 ⛳ 📠 ⚑ 🏌 ✐ Location entering village fork right at war memorial, signed 300yds

Hotel ★★★ 74% Fernhill Hotel, Heugh Rd, PORTPATRICK ☎ 01776 810220 27 en suite 9 annexe en suite

SANQUHAR   Map 11 NS70

Sanquhar Euchan Golf Course, Blackaddie Rd DG4 6JZ
☎ 01659 50577
e-mail: tich@rossirence.fsnet.co.uk
Parkland course, fine views, easy walking. A good test for all standards of golfer.
9 holes, 5594yds, Par 70, SSS 68, Course record 66.
Club membership 200.
Visitors no restrictions. Societies booking required. Green Fees £10 per day (£12 weekends). Course Designer Willie Fernie Facilities 🎱 ⛳ Leisure snooker, pool.
Conf Corporate Hospitality Days available
Location 0.5m SW off A76

Hotel ★★ 67% Blackaddie House Hotel, Blackaddie Rd, SANQUHAR ☎ 01695 50270 9 en suite

SOUTHERNESS   Map 11 NX95

Southerness DG2 8AZ
☎ 01387 880677 📠 01387 880644
e-mail: admin@southernessgc.sol.co.uk
Natural links, championship course with panoramic views. Heather and bracken abound.
18 holes, 6566yds, Par 69, SSS 73, Course record 64.
Club membership 830.
Visitors must have handicap certificate & contact in advance. May only play from yellow markers. Societies contact in advance. Green Fees £42 per day (£52 weekends & bank holidays). Cards ▦ ▬ 🔀 🌀 Course Designer McKenzie Ross Facilities ⊗ ⍭ ⬛ 🍺 🎱 ⛳ ✐ Location 3.5m S of Kirkbean off A710

STRANRAER   Map 10 NX06

Stranraer Creachmore DG9 0LF
☎ 01776 870245 📠 01776 870445
e-mail: stranraergolf@btclick.com
Parkland course with beautiful views overlooking Loch Ryan to Ailsa Craig, Arran and beyond. Several notable holes including the 3rd, where a winding burn is crossed three times to a green set between a large bunker and a steep bank sloping down to the burn; the scenic 5th with spectacular views; the 11th requiring a demanding tee shot with trees and out of bounds to the left, then a steep rise to a very fast green. The 15th is a difficult par 3 where accuracy is paramount with ground sloping away either side of the green.

Continued   Continued

18 holes, 6308yds, Par 70, SSS 72, Course record 66.
Club membership 700.
Visitors contact in advance. Members times reserved
throughout year. **Societies** phone in advance.
Green Fees Terms on application. **Cards** 🖃 ▦ 🔳 💷
Course Designer James Braid **Facilities** ⊗ ⅢⅢ ⅃ 🖳 ♀ ♨
🖦 ㇌ ⅂ ㅅ ⚘ ✐ **Location** 2.5m NW on A718 from
Stranraer

Thornhill Blacknest DG3 5DW
☎ 01848 331779 & 330546
e-mail: thornhillgc@fsmail.net
**Moorland and parkland course with fine views over the
southern uplands.**
*18 holes, 6085yds, Par 71, SSS 70, Course record 67.
Club membership 560.*
Visitors apply in advance, restricted competition days.
Societies apply in writing. **Green Fees** £21 per round/£30
per day (weekends £25/£35). **Course Designer** Willie
Fernie **Facilities** ⊗ ⅢⅢ ⅃ 🖳 ♀ ㅅ ㇌ ✐ **Location** 1m E
of town off A76

Hotel ★★ 75% Trigony House Hotel, Closeburn,
THORNHILL ☎ 01848 331211   8 en suite

Wigtown & Bladnoch Lightlands Ter DG8 9DY
☎ 01988 403354
**Slightly hilly parkland course with fine views over
Wigtown Bay to Galloway Hills.**
*9 holes, 5462yds, Par 68, SSS 67, Course record 62.
Club membership 150.*
Visitors advisable to contact in advance for weekend play.
Course closed to visitors during open competitions.
Societies contact secretary in advance. **Green Fees** £15 for
18 holes/£10 for 9 holes. **Course Designer** W Muir
Facilities 🖳 ♀ ㅅ ✐ **Location** SW on A714

Hotel ★★★ ♨ Kirroughtree House, Minnigaff,
NEWTON STEWART ☎ 01671 402141   17 en suite

Caird Park Mains Loan DD4 9BX
☎ 01382 438871   📄 01382 433211
e-mail: la.bookings@dundeecity.gov.uk
**A pay and play course situated in extensive parkland in
the heart of Carnoustie countryside. A reasonably easy
start belies the difficulty of the middle section (holes 7-
13) and the back nine cross the Gelly Burn four times.**
*18 holes, 6280yds, Par 72, SSS 69, Course record 67.
Club membership 1800.*
Visitors no restrictions. **Societies** contact in advance 01382
433036 **Green Fees** £20 Mon-Fri (£25 weekends).
Prof J Black **Facilities** ⅃ 🖳 ♀ ㅅ 🖦 ㇌ ✐
Location off Kingsway (A90) onto Forfar Rd, left onto
Claverhouse Rd, 1st left into Caird Park

Hotel ★★★★ 76% Apex City Quay Hotel & Spa, 1 West
Victoria Dock Rd, DUNDEE
☎ 01382 202404 & 0845 608 3456
📄 01382 201401   153 en suite

Camperdown Camperdown Park, Coupar Angus Rd
DD2 4TF
☎ 01382 432688
18 holes, 6548yds, Par 71, SSS 72.
Location Kingsway (A90) onto Coupar Angus Rd (A923)
left into Camperdown Park
Phone for further details

Downfield Turnberry Av DD2 3QP
☎ 01382 825595   📄 01382 813111
e-mail: downfieldgc@aol.com
**A course with championship credentials providing an
enjoyable test for all golfers.**
*18 holes, 6803yds, Par 73, SSS 73, Course record 65.
Club membership 750.*
Visitors contact in advance, no visitors at weekends.
Societies contact in advance. **Green Fees** £38 per 18 holes
(£47 per 36 holes). **Cards** 🖃 🔳 ▦ 🔳 💷 **Prof** Kenny
Hutton **Course Designer** James Braid **Facilities** ⊗ ⅢⅢ ⅃
🖳 ♀ ㅅ 🖦 ㇌ ⅂ ㅅ ⚘ ✐ **Leisure** snooker room. **Conf**
Corporate Hospitality Days available **Location** N of city
centre, signed on junct A90 & A923

Loudoun Edinburgh Rd KA4 8PA
☎ 01563 821993   📄 01563 820011
e-mail: secy@loudoungowfclub.co.uk
**Pleasant, fairly flat parkland course with many mature
trees, located in the Irvine valley in the rural heart of
Ayrshire.**
*18 holes, 6005yds, Par 68, SSS 69, Course record 60.
Club membership 850.*
Visitors contact in advance. Weekdays only, must play
with member at weekends/public holidays **Societies** phone
in advance. **Green Fees** £35 per day, £25 per 18 holes.
Cards 🖃 🔳 ㇌ 💷 **Facilities** ⊗ ⅢⅢ ⅃ 🖳 ♀ ㅅ 🖦 ㇌ ✐
Conf Corporate Hospitality Days available
Location NE side of town on A71

Hotel ★★★ 74% Strathaven Hotel, Hamilton Rd,
STRATHAVEN ☎ 01357 521778   22 en suite

Annanhill Irvine Rd KA1 2RT
☎ 01563 521644 & 521512
Municipal, tree-lined parkland course.
*18 holes, 6269yds, Par 71, SSS 70, Course record 66.
Club membership 274.*
Visitors book at starters office 01563-521512. Parties by
arrangement. **Societies** apply in writing. **Green Fees** terms
on application. **Course Designer** Jack McLean
Facilities 🖳 ㅅ ㇌ **Location** 1m N on B7081

Hotel ⚲ Premier Travel Inn Kilmarnock, Annadale,
KILMARNOCK ☎ 08701 977148   40 en suite

> **Looking for a new course? Always telephone
> ahead to confirm visitor arrangements.**

aprington Ayr Rd KA1 4UW
☎ 01563 523702 & 521915 (Gen Enq)
holes, 5810yds, Par 68, SSS 68.
ocation 1.5m S on B7038
one for further details

....

tel ♿ Travelodge, Kilmarnock Bypass,
LMARNOCK ☎ 08700 850 950   40 en suite

AUCHLINE   Map 11 NS42

allochmyle Catrine Rd KA5 6LE
☎ 01290 550469 ▤ 01290 553657
nail: secretary@ballochmyle.freeserve.co.uk
arkland course.
holes, 5972yds, Par 70, SSS 69, Course record 64.
ub membership 730.
sitors not Sat. **Societies** apply in writing or phone.
een Fees £20 per 18 holes, £30 per 36 holes (weekends
5/£35). **Cards** ▤▤ ▤▤ ▤ **Facilities** ⊗ ⏽ ⮭ ♥ ♀ ⬒
⛳ **Leisure** snooker. **Location** 1m SE on B705

....

tel ♿ Travelodge, Kilmarnock Bypass,
LMARNOCK ☎ 08700 850 950   40 en suite

EW CUMNOCK   Map 11 NS61

ew Cumnock Lochhill, Cumnock Rd KA18 4PN
☎ 01290 338848
holes, 5176yds, Par 68, SSS 68, Course record 63.
ourse Designer Willie Fernie **Location** 0.75m N on A76
one for further details

....

tel ★★ 67% Blackaddie House Hotel, Blackaddie Rd,
ANQUHAR ☎ 01695 50270   9 en suite

ATNA   Map 10 NS41

oon Valley Hillside Park KA6 7JT
☎ 01292 531607
**tablished parkland course located on an undulating
llside.**
holes, 5886yds, Par 70, SSS 70, Course record 56.
ub membership 100.
sitors no restrictions mid week, advisable to contact in
vance for weekends. **Societies** phone to arrange. **Green
es** £10 per 18 holes. **Facilities** ♀ ⬒ **Leisure** fishing,
ness & games hall nearby. **Location** 10m S of Ayr on the
13

....

tel ★★ Ladyburn, MAYBOLE ☎ 01655 740585
en suite

EAST DUNBARTONSHIRE

ALMORE   Map 11 NS57

almore Golf Course Rd G64 4AW
☎ 01360 620284 ▤ 01360 622742
nail: secretary@balmoregolfclub.co.uk
arkland course with fine views.
holes, 5530yds, Par 66, SSS 67, Course record 61.
ub membership 700.
sitors contact in advance; not weekends. **Societies** apply
writing. **Green Fees** £40 per day; £30 per round.
of Kevin Craggs **Course Designer** Harry Vardon
cilities ⊗ ⏽ ⮭ ♥ ♀ ⬒ ⮥ ⛳ **Location** N off A807

....

tel ♿ Premier Travel Inn Glasgow (Bearsden),
llngavie Rd, BEARSDEN ☎ 0870 9906532   61 en suite

BEARSDEN   Map 11 NS57

Bearsden Thorn Rd G61 4BP
☎ 0141 586 5300
e-mail: secretary@bearsdengolfclub.com
**Parkland course, with 16 greens and 11 teeing grounds.
Easy walking and views over city and Campsie Hills.**
9 holes, 6014yds, Par 68, SSS 69, Course record 64.
Club membership 600.
Visitors with member only. **Societies** apply by writing.
Green Fees terms on application. **Facilities** ⊗ ⏽ ⮭ ♥ ♀
⬒ **Location** 1m W off A809

....

Hotel ♿ Premier Travel Inn Glasgow (Bearsden),
Milngavie Rd, BEARSDEN ☎ 0870 9906532   61 en suite

Douglas Park Hillfoot G61 2TJ
☎ 0141 942 2220 (Clubhouse) ▤ 0141 942 0985
e-mail: secretary@douglasparkgolfclub.net
Parkland course with wide variety of holes.
18 holes, 5962yds, Par 69, SSS 69, Course record 64.
Club membership 900.
Visitors must be accompanied by member or must contact
in advance, Wed & Thu for visiting parties only. **Societies**
Wed & Thu. Must phone in advance. **Green Fees** £31 per
day; £23 per round. **Prof** David Scott **Course Designer**
Willie Fernie **Facilities** ⊗ ⏽ ⮭ ♥ ♀ ⬒ 🏠 🛒 ⛳
Location E side of town on A81

....

Hotel ♿ Premier Travel Inn Glasgow (Bearsden),
Milngavie Rd, BEARSDEN ☎ 0870 9906532   61 en suite

Glasgow Killermont G61 2TW
☎ 0141 942 2011 ▤ 0141 942 0770
e-mail: secretary@glasgow-golf.com
One of the finest parkland courses in Scotland.
18 holes, 5968yds, Par 70, SSS 69.
Club membership 800.
Visitors contact secretary in advance & have handicap
certificate. Not at weekends. **Societies** apply to secretary
Green Fees £70 per day; £55 per round. **Cards** ▤▤ ▤▤ ▤▤
▤ **Prof** J Steven **Course Designer** Tom Morris Snr
Facilities ⊗ ⏽ ⮭ ♥ ♀ (members guest only) ⬒ 🏠 🏳
🏴 ⛳ **Conf** Corporate Hospitality Days available
Location SE side off A81

Windyhill Baljaffray Rd G61 4QQ
☎ 0141 942 2349 ▤ 0141 942 5874
e-mail: secretary@windyhill.co.uk
**Interesting parkland and moorland course with
panoramic views of Glasgow and beyond; testing 12th
hole.**
18 holes, 6254yds, Par 71, SSS 70, Course record 64.
Club membership 800.
Visitors not weekends; must contact professional in
advance; handicap certificate. **Societies** apply in writing.
Green Fees £25 per round/£35 per day. **Cards** ▤▤ ▤▤ ▤
Prof Chris Duffy **Course Designer** James Braid **Facilities**
⊗ ⏽ ⮭ ♥ ♀ ⬒ 🏠 🏳 ⛳ **Location** 2m NW off B8050,
1.5m from Bearsden cross, just off Drymen road

....

Hotel ♿ Premier Travel Inn Glasgow (Bearsden),
Milngavie Rd, BEARSDEN ☎ 0870 9906532   61 en suite

> **In the hotel entries, the percentage figure refers
> to the AA's most recent Quality Assessment Score.**

BISHOPBRIGGS   Map 11 NS67

Bishopbriggs Brackenbrae Rd G64 2DX
☎ 0141 772 1810 772 8938 ▤ 7622532
e-mail: secretarybgc@yahoo.co.uk
Parkland course with views to Campsie Hills.
18 holes, 6041yds, Par 69, SSS 69, Course record 63.
Club membership 800.
Visitors contact in advance; not weekends. Societies apply
in writing in advance. Green Fees not confirmed. Course
Designer James Braid Facilities ⊗ ⅢⅢ ㅂ ♥ ♀ ㅅ �📷
Conf fac available Corporate Hospitality Days available
Location 0.5m NW off A803
....
Hotel ★★★★ 68% Glasgow Marriott Hotel, 500 Argyle
St, Anderston, GLASGOW ☎ 0870 400 7230 300 en suite

Cawder Cadder Rd G64 3QD
☎ 0141 761 1281 ▤ 0141 761 1285
e-mail: secretary@cawdergolfclub.org.uk
**Two parkland courses: Cawder Course is hilly, with the
5th, 9th, 10th and 11th testing holes; Keir Course is flat.**
*Cawder Course: 18 holes, 6295yds, Par 70, SSS 71,
Course record 63.*
Keir Course: 18 holes, 5877yds, Par 68, SSS 68.
Club membership 1150.
Visitors contact in advance & may play on weekdays only.
Societies contact in writing, not bank holidays Green Fees
£30 per round/£40 per day. Cards ▭ ▭ ▩ ▨ Prof Ken
Stevely Course Designer James Braid Facilities ⊗ ⅢⅢ ㅂ
♥ ♀ ㅅ 📷 ⌁ ⌀ Conf Corporate Hospitality Days
available Location 5 m NE off A803
....
Hotel ★★★★ 68% Glasgow Marriott Hotel, 500 Argyle
St, Anderston, GLASGOW ☎ 0870 400 7230 300 en suite

Littlehill Auchinairn Rd G64 1UT
☎ 0141 772 1916
18 holes, 6240yds, Par 70, SSS 70.
Location 3m NE of Glasgow city centre on A803
Phone for further details
....
Hotel ★★★★ 68% Glasgow Marriott Hotel, 500 Argyle
St, Anderston, GLASGOW ☎ 0870 400 7230 300 en suite

KIRKINTILLOCH   Map 11 NS67

Hayston Campsie Rd G66 1RN
☎ 0141 776 1244 ▤ 0141 7769030
e-mail: secretary@haystongolf.com
An undulating, tree-lined course with a sandy subsoil.
18 holes, 6042yds, Par 70, SSS 70, Course record 60.
Club membership 800.
Visitors apply in advance; not weekends. Societies Tue &
Thu, apply in writing Green Fees terms on application. Prof
Steven Barnett Course Designer James Braid Facilities ⊗
ⅢⅢ ㅂ ♥ ♀ ㅅ 📷 Location 1m NW off A803
....
Hotel ★★★★ 69% The Westerwood Hotel, 1 St Andrews
Dr, Westerwood, CUMBERNAULD
☎ 01236 457171 100 en suite

Kirkintilloch Campsie Rd G66 1RN
☎ 0141 776 1256 & 775 2387 ▤ 0141 775 2424
**A rolling parkland course in the foothills of the
Campsie Fells. The course was extended some years ago
giving testing but enjoyable holes over the whole 18.**
18 holes, 5860yds, Par 70, SSS 69.
Club membership 650.

Visitors must be introduced by member. Societies apply in
writing. Green Fees terms on application. Course Designer
James Braid Facilities ⊗ ⅢⅢ ㅂ ♥ ♀ ㅅ 📷 Conf Corporate
Hospitality Days available Location 1m NW off A803
....
Hotel ★★★★ 69% The Westerwood Hotel,
1 St Andrews Dr, Westerwood, CUMBERNAULD
☎ 01236 457171 100 en suite

LENNOXTOWN   Map 11 NS67

Campsie Crow Rd G66 7HX
☎ 01360 310244 ▤ 01360 310244
e-mail: campsiegolfclub@aol.com
Scenic hillside course.
18 holes, 5507yds, Par 70, SSS 68, Course record 69.
Club membership 620.
Visitors preferred weekdays. Weekends only by
arrangement, contact professional 01360 310920. Societies
written application. Green Fees £25 per day, £20 per
round (£25 per round weekends). Prof Mark Brennan
Course Designer W Auchterlonie Facilities ⊗ ⅢⅢ ㅂ ♥ ♀
ㅅ 📷 Conf Corporate Hospitality Days available
Location 0.5m N on B822
....
Hotel ★★★★ 69% The Westerwood Hotel,
1 St Andrews Dr, Westerwood, CUMBERNAULD
☎ 01236 457171 100 en suite

LENZIE   Map 11 NS67

Lenzie 19 Crosshill Rd G66 5DA
☎ 0141 776 1535 & 812 3018 ▤ 0141 777 7748
or 0141 812 3018
e-mail: scottdavidson@lenziegolfclub.demon.co.uk
**The course is parkland and prominent features include
the old beech trees, which line some of the fairways
together with thorn hedges and shallow ditches.
Extensive larch and fir plantations have also been
created. The course is relatively flat apart from a steep
hill to the green at the 5th hole.**
18 holes, 5984yds, Par 69, SSS 69, Course record 64.
Club membership 890.
Visitors contact in advance. Societies apply in writing or
phone in advance. Green Fees £26 per round, £30 per day
Prof Jim McCallum Facilities ⊗ ⅢⅢ ㅂ ♥ ♀ ㅅ 📷 ⌁ ⌀
Conf fac available Location N of Glasgow, 15 mins from
Glasgow city centre, Kirkintilloch turn off M80
....
Hotel ★★★★ 69% The Westerwood Hotel,
1 St Andrews Dr, Westerwood, CUMBERNAULD
☎ 01236 457171 100 en suite

MILNGAVIE   Map 11 NS57

Clober Craigton Rd G62 7HP
☎ 0141 956 1685 ▤ 0141 955 1416
e-mail: clobergolfclub@btopenworld.com
**Short parkland course that requires skill in chipping
with eight par 3s. Testing 5th hole, par 3 with out of
bounds left and right and a burn in front of the tee.**
18 holes, 4824yds, Par 66, SSS 65, Course record 61.
Club membership 600.
Visitors not after 4pm Mon-Fri. Must play with member
weekends & bank holidays. Societies contact in advance.
Green Fees £18 per round, £30 per day. Cards ▭ ▭ ♥ ㅅ
▩ ▨ ▨ Prof J McFadyen Facilities ⊗ ⅢⅢ ㅂ ♥ ♀ ㅅ
⌁ ⌀ Location NW side of town
....
Hotel ⇧ Premier Travel Inn Glasgow (Milngavie),
103 Main St, MILNGAVIE ☎ 08701 977112 60 en suite

Continued

sporta, Dougalston Strathblane G62 8HJ
☏ 0141 955 2404 & 955 2434 📠 0141 955 2406
✉ mail: hilda.everett@esporta.com
course of tremendous character set in 300 acres of
autiful woodland dotted with drumlins, lakes and
iss-crossed by streams and ditches. The course makes
cellent use of the natural features to create mature,
ee-lined fairways.
 holes, 6120yds, Par 70, SSS 71, Course record 65.
'ub membership 800.
isitors book tee time 1 week in advance. May play at
eekends after 2pm subject to availability. **Societies**
eekdays only, phone in advance. **Green Fees** terms on
plication. **Cards** 🎴 💳 💳 **Prof** Craig Everett **Course**
esigner Commander Harris **Facilities** ⊗ �🅙 🄻 ▆ ♀ 🄰
🚩 ⚲ ⚓ ⚌ **Leisure** hard tennis courts, heated indoor
imming pool, sauna, solarium, gymnasium.
onf Corporate Hospitality Days available
ocation NE side of town on A81

⸱⸱⸱⸱⸱⸱⸱⸱⸱⸱⸱⸱⸱⸱⸱⸱⸱⸱⸱⸱⸱⸱⸱⸱⸱⸱⸱⸱

ilton Park Auldmarroch Estate, Stockiemuir Rd
62 7HB
☏ 0141 956 4657 📠 0141 956 4657
✉ mail: info@hiltonparkgolfclub.fsnet.co.uk
oorland courses set amid magnificent scenery.
ilton Course: 18 holes, 6054yds, Par 70, SSS 70, Course
cord 65.
'lander Course: 18 holes, 5487yds, Par 69, SSS 67,
urse record 65.
'ub membership 1200.
isitors contact in advance; not weekends. **Societies** apply
advance to secretary. **Green Fees** £25 per round/£35 per
y. **Prof** W McCondichie **Course Designer** James Braid
acilities ⊗ �🅙 🄻 ▆ ♀ 🄰 📠 🚩 ⚲ ⚌ **Location** 3m NW
Milngavie, on A809

⸱⸱⸱⸱⸱⸱⸱⸱⸱⸱⸱⸱⸱⸱⸱⸱⸱⸱⸱⸱⸱⸱⸱⸱⸱⸱⸱⸱

otel ⌂ Premier Travel Inn Glasgow (Milngavie), 103
ain St, MILNGAVIE ☏ 08701 977112 60 en suite

⸱⸱⸱⸱⸱⸱⸱⸱⸱⸱⸱⸱⸱⸱⸱⸱⸱⸱⸱⸱⸱⸱⸱⸱⸱⸱⸱⸱

'ilngavie Laighpark G62 8EP
☏ 0141 956 1619 📠 0141 956 4252
 holes, 5818yds, Par 68, SSS 68, Course record 59.
urse Designer The Auchterlonie Brothers
ocation 1.25m N
one for further details

⸱⸱⸱⸱⸱⸱⸱⸱⸱⸱⸱⸱⸱⸱⸱⸱⸱⸱⸱⸱⸱⸱⸱⸱⸱⸱⸱⸱

otel ⌂ Premier Travel Inn Glasgow (Milngavie),
3 Main St, MILNGAVIE ☏ 08701 977112 60 en suite

EAST LOTHIAN

BERLADY   Map 12 NT47

ilspindie EH32 0QD
☏ 01875 870358 📠 01875 870358
✉ mail: kilspindie@btconnect.com
aditional Scottish seaside links, short but good
allenge of golf and well-bunkered. Situated on the
ores of the River Forth with panoramic views.
 holes, 5480yds, Par 69, SSS 66, Course record 59.
'ub membership 800.
isitors contact in advance, preferred days for visitors
on-Fri, but tee times available at weekends. **Societies**
ntact secretary in advance. **Green Fees** £47.50 per day,
9.50 per round (£57.50/£38 weekends). **Cards** 🎴 💳

🎴 📧 💳 **Prof** Graham J Sked **Course Designer** Various
Facilities ⊗ �🅙 🄻 ▆ ♀ 🄰 📠 🚩 ⚲ ⚌
Conf Corporate Hospitality Days available
Location N side of village off A198, private road access
located at eastern end of village of Aberlady

⸱⸱⸱⸱⸱⸱⸱⸱⸱⸱⸱⸱⸱⸱⸱⸱⸱⸱⸱⸱⸱⸱⸱⸱⸱⸱⸱⸱

Hotel ★★★ 🄰🄰 Greywalls Hotel, Muirfield, GULLANE
☏ 01620 842144 17 en suite 5 annexe en suite

Luffness New EH32 0QA
☏ 01620 843336 📠 01620 842933
e-mail: secretary@luffnessnew.com
**Links course, national final qualifying course for the
Open Championship.**
*18 holes, 6122yds, Par 69, SSS 70, Course record 61.
Club membership 750.*
Visitors contact in advance; not weekends & public
holidays. **Societies** phone for application form. **Green Fees**
£66 per day; £46 per round. **Course Designer** Tom Morris
Facilities ⊗ �🅙 ▆ ♀ 🄰 📠 ⚌ **Location** 1m E Aberlady
on A198

⸱⸱⸱⸱⸱⸱⸱⸱⸱⸱⸱⸱⸱⸱⸱⸱⸱⸱⸱⸱⸱⸱⸱⸱⸱⸱⸱⸱

Hotel ★★★ 🄰🄰 Greywalls Hotel, Muirfield, GULLANE
☏ 01620 842144 17 en suite 5 annexe en suite

DUNBAR   Map 12 NT67

Dunbar East Links EH42 1LL
☏ 01368 862317 📠 01368 865202
e-mail: secretary@dunbargolfclub.sol.co.uk
**Another of Scotland's old links. It is said that it was
some Dunbar members who first took the game of golf
to the north of England. A natural links course on a
narrow strip of land, following the contours of the sea
shore. There is a wall bordering one side and the shore
on the other side making this quite a challenging course
for all levels of player. The wind, if blowing from the
sea, is a problem.**
*18 holes, 6406yds, Par 71, SSS 71, Course record 64.
Club membership 1000.*
Visitors not Thu, between 12.30-2 weekdays, 12-2
weekends or before 9.30am any day. **Societies** phone in
advance. **Green Fees** £43 per round/£58 per day
(weekend £53/£75). **Cards** 🎴 💳 💳 💳 📧 💳 💳
Prof Jacky Montgomery **Course Designer** Tom Morris
Facilities ⊗ �🅙 🄻 ▆ ♀ 🄰 📠 🚩 ⚌ **Location** 0.5m E off
A1087

Winterfield North Rd EH42 1AU
☏ 01368 863562 📠 01368 863562
e-mail: kevinphillips@tiscali.co.uk
Seaside course with superb views.
*18 holes, 5155yds, Par 65, SSS 64, Course record 61.
Club membership 350.*
Visitors contact in advance. Weekends from 10am-noon &
2pm-4pm **Societies** arrange in advance through
professional, phone or e-mail **Green Fees** not confirmed.
Prof Kevin Phillips **Facilities** ⊗ �🅙 🄻 ▆ ♀ 🄰 📠 🚩 ⚲
⚓ ⚌ **Location** W side of town off A1087

> If the name of the club appears in *italics*, details
> have not been confirmed for this
> edition of the guide.

Continued

GIFFORD
Map 12 NT56

Gifford Edinburgh Rd EH41 4JE
☎ 01620 810267
e-mail: thesecretary@giffordgolfclub.fsnet.co.uk
Parkland course, with easy walking.
9 holes, 6057yds, Par 71, SSS 69.
Club membership 600.
Visitors not 1st Sun of month Apr-Oct. Phone Starter on
01620 810 591 to book tee times. **Societies** phone in
advance. 01620 810 591 **Green Fees** £18 per 18 holes; £12
per 9 holes (£20/£14 weekends). **Facilities** 🅱 💺 ♀ 🛆 ♂
Location 1m SW off B6355

GULLANE See page 335

GULLANE
Map 12 NT48

Gullane West Links Rd EH31 2BB
☎ 01620 842255 📠 01620 842327
e-mail: bookings@gullanegolfclub.com
**Gullane is a delightful village and one of Scotland's
great golf centres. Gullane Golf Club was formed in
1882. There are three Gullane courses of which
numbers 1 and 2 are of championship standard. It
differs most Scottish courses in as much as it is of
the upland links type and really quite hilly. The first tee
is literally in the village. The views from the top of the
course are magnificent and stretch far and wide in
every direction - in fact, it is said that 14 counties can
be seen from the highest spot.**
*Course No 1: 18 holes, 6466yds, Par 71, SSS 72,
Course record 65.*
*Course No 2: 18 holes, 6244yds, Par 71, SSS 71,
Course record 64.*
Course No 3: 18 holes, 5252yds, Par 68, SSS 66.
Club membership 1200.
Visitors advance booking recommended. **Societies**
advance booking advised. **Green Fees** terms on
application. **Cards** 🌐 💳 📇 💳 💷 **Prof** Alasdair Good
Course Designer Various **Facilities** ⊗ 🅼 🅱 💺 ♀ 🛆 🖃
🏌 🎯 🏌 ♂ 🍴 **Location** W end of village on A198
·······································
Hotel ★★★ 🏨 Greywalls Hotel, Muirfield, GULLANE
☎ 01620 842144 17 en suite 5 annexe en suite

HADDINGTON
Map 12 NT57

Haddington Amisfield Park EH41 4PT
☎ 01620 822727 & 823627 📠 01620 826580
e-mail: info@haddingtongolf.co.uk
**Slightly undulating parkland course, within the
grounds of a former country estate running alongside
the River Tyne.**

Continued

18 holes, 6335yds, Par 71, SSS 70, Course record 64.
Club membership 850.
Visitors not 7am-10am & noon-2pm at weekends. Must
contact in advance. **Societies** Mon-Fri, must contact in
advance; deposits required. May play weekdays anytime &
weekends 10-12 & 2-4 **Green Fees** £30 per day, £20 per
round (£40/£30 weekends). **Prof** John Sandilands
Facilities ⊗ 🅼 🅱 💺 ♀ 🛆 🖃 🏌 🎯 ♂ **Leisure** driving
net, practice bunker. **Conf** fac available Corporate
Hospitality Days available **Location** E side of town
centre
·······································
Hotel ★★★ 🏨 Greywalls Hotel, Muirfield, GULLANE
☎ 01620 842144 17 en suite 5 annexe en suite

LONGNIDDRY
Map 12 NT47

Longniddry Links Rd EH32 0NL
☎ 01875 852141 📠 01875 853371
e-mail: secretary@longniddrygolfclub.co.uk
**Undulating seaside links and partial parkland course
with no par 5s. One of the numerous courses which
stretch east from Edinburgh to Dunbar. The inward
half is more open than the wooded outward half, but
can be difficult in prevailing west wind.**
18 holes, 6260yds, Par 68, SSS 70, Course record 63.
Club membership 1140.
Visitors not competition days; deposit required if booking
more than seven days in advance. **Societies** Mon-Thu,
apply in writing, handicap certificate required. **Green Fee**
£55 per day, £37.50 per round (weekends £48 per round).
Cards 🌐 💳 💷 **Prof** John Gray **Course Designer**
HS Colt **Facilities** ⊗ 🅼 🅱 💺 ♀ 🛆 🖃 🏌 🎯 🏌 ♂
Conf Corporate Hospitality Days available
Location N side of village off A198
·······································
Hotel ★★★ 🏨 Greywalls Hotel, Muirfield, GULLANE
☎ 01620 842144 17 en suite 5 annexe en suite

MUSSELBURGH
Map 11 NT37

Musselburgh Monktonhall EH21 6SA
☎ 0131 665 2005 📠 0131 665 4435
e-mail: secretary@themusselburghgolfclub.com
**Testing parkland course with natural hazards includin
trees and a burn; easy walking.**
18 holes, 6725yds, Par 71, SSS 73, Course record 65.
Club membership 1000.
Visitors contact in advance. **Societies** contact in advance.
Green Fees £35 per day; £25 per round (£40/£30
weekends). **Cards** 🌐 💳 💷 **Prof** Fraser Mann **Course
Designer** James Braid **Facilities** ⊗ 🅼 🅱 💺 ♀ 🛆 🖃 🏌
🏌 ♂ **Conf** Corporate Hospitality Days available
Location 1m S on B6415
·······································
Hotel ⓤ Premier Travel Inn Edinburgh (Inveresk),
Carberry Rd, Inveresk, Musselburgh, EDINBURGH
☎ 08701 977092 40 en suite

Musselburgh Links, The Old Golf Course
10 Balcarres Rd EH21 7SD
☎ 0131 665 5438 (starter) 665 6981 (clubhouse)
📠 0131 665 5438
e-mail: info@musselburgholdlinks.co.uk
**A delightful nine-hole links course weaving in and out
of the famous Musselburgh Race Course. This course i
steeped in the history and tradition of golf. Mary Quee
of Scots reputedly played golf at the old course in 1567
but documentary evidence dates back to 1672. The**

Continu

East Lothian

(Honourable Company of Edinburgh Golfers) Muirfield

Gullane

Map 12 NT48

The course at Muirfield was designed by Old Tom Morris in 1891 and is generally considered to be one of the top ten courses in the world. The club itself has an excellent pedigree: it was founded in 1744, making it just 10 years older than the Royal and Ancient but not as old as Royal Blackheath. Muirfield has staged some outstanding Open championships. Perhaps one of the most memorable was in 1972 when Lee Trevino, the defending champion, seemed to be losing his grip until a spectacular shot brought him back to beat Tony Jacklin, who subsequently never won another Open.

Muirfield EH31 2EG
☎ 01620 842123 Fax 01620 842977
e-mail: hceg@muirfield.org.uk

18 holes, 6601yds, Par 70, SSS 73, Course record 63. Club membership 700.
Visitors Tu, Thu only; must contact in advance; handicap certificate (men 18, women 24). **Societies** Tue, Thu; handicap limits (men 18, women 20); members of recognised golf course; groups up to 12 accepted. **Green Fees** £150 per 36 holes, £120 per 18 holes. **Cards** ═ ▬ **Course Designer** Harry Colt
Facilities ⊗ ♨ ♀ ♣ ♒ ⛳
Location NE of village

....

Hotels

★ ★ ★ Greywalls Hotel, Muirfield, GULLANE

☎ 01620 842144 17 en suite 5 annexe en suite

★ ★ ★ 72% The Open Arms Hotel, DIRLETON

☎ 01620 850241 Fax 01620 850570 10 en suite

★ ★ ★ 64% The Marine, Cromwell Rd, NORTH BERWICK

☎ 0870 400 8129 Fax 01620 894480 83 en suite

★ ★ 68% Nether Abbey Hotel, 20 Dirleton Av, NORTH BERWICK

☎ 01620 892802 Fax 01620 895298 13 en suite

1st hole is a par 3 and the next three holes play eastward from the grandstand at the racecourse. The course turns north-west towards the sea then west for the last four holes. Designed by nature and defined over the centuries by generations of golfers, the course boasts many natural features and hazards.
9 holes, 2874yds, Par 34, SSS 34, Course record 29.
Club membership 300.
Visitors book in advance. **Societies** contact in advance in writing or by phone. **Green Fees** £9 per 9 holes, £18 per 18 holes (£9.50/£19 weekends). **Cards** 🏧 💳 📶 ⏿ **Facilities** ⓑ ⌂ 🕈 ⚐ **Conf** fac available
Location 1m E of town off A1

....

Hotel ⏿ Premier Travel Inn Edinburgh (Inveresk), Carberry Rd, Inveresk, Musselburgh, EDINBURGH ☎ 08701 977092 40 en suite

NORTH BERWICK　　　　　　　Map 12 NT58

Glen East Links, Tantallon Ter EH39 4LE
☎ 01620 892726 📄 01620 895447
e-mail: secretary@glengolfclub.co.uk
An interesting course with a good variety of holes including the famous 13th, par 3 Sea Hole. The views of the town, the Firth of Forth and the Bass Rock are breathtaking.

18 holes, 6243yds, Par 70, SSS 70, Course record 67.
Club membership 650.
Visitors booking advisable. **Societies** advance booking recommended. **Green Fees** £42 per day, £32 per round (weekends £54/£44). **Cards** 🏧 💳 📶 ⏿ **Course Designer** Ben Sayers, James Braid **Facilities** ⊗ ⋔ ⓑ ⚑ ⓠ ⌂ 🏠 🕈 ⚐ **Conf** Corporate Hospitality Days available **Location** A1 onto A198 to North Berwick. Right at seabird centre & follow sea-wall road

....

Hotel ★★ 68% Nether Abbey Hotel, 20 Dirleton Av, NORTH BERWICK ☎ 01620 892802 13 en suite

North Berwick Beach Rd EH39 4BB
☎ 01620 892135 📄 01620 893274
e-mail: secretary@northberwickgolfclub.com
Another of East Lothian's famous courses, the links at North Berwick is still popular. A classic championship links, it has many hazards including the beach, streams, bunkers, light rough and low walls. The great hole on the course is the 15th, the famous Redan'.
West Links: 18 holes, 6420yds, Par 71, SSS 72,
Course record 63.
Club membership 730.
Visitors contact in advance 01620 892135 (beyond seven days) or 01620 892666 (within seven days). **Societies**

Continued

contact in advance. **Green Fees** £80 per day; £55 per round (£75 weekends). **Cards** 🏧 💳 📶 ⏿ **Prof** D Huish **Facilities** ⊗ ⋔ ⓑ ⚑ ⓠ ⌂ 🏠 🕈 ⚐ **Location** W side of town on A198

....

Hotel ★★★ 64% The Marine, Cromwell Rd, NORTH BERWICK ☎ 0870 400 8129 83 en suite

Whitekirk Whitekirk EH39 5PR
☎ 01620 870300 📄 01620 870330
e-mail: countryclub@whitekirk.com
Scenic coastal course with lush green fairways, gorse covered rocky banks and stunning views. Natural water hazards and strong sea breezes make this well-designed course a good test of golf.
18 holes, 6526yds, Par 72, SSS 72, Course record 64.
Club membership 400.
Visitors no restrictions. **Societies** apply in writing or phone. **Green Fees** £25 per round/£35 per day (weekend £35/£50). **Cards** 🏧 💳 📶 ⏿ **Prof** Paul Wardell **Course Designer** Cameron Sinclair **Facilities** ⊗ ⋔ ⓑ ⚑ ⓠ ⌂ 🏠 🕈 🎯 ⚐ ⓣ **Conf** fac available **Location** 3m off A1 Edinburgh-Berwick-upon-Tweed, A198 North Berwick

....

Hotel ★★ 68% Nether Abbey Hotel, 20 Dirleton Av, NORTH BERWICK ☎ 01620 892802 13 en suite

PRESTONPANS　　　　　　　Map 11 NT37

Royal Musselburgh Prestongrange House EH32 9RP
☎ 01875 810276 📄 01875 810276
e-mail: royalmusselburgh@btinternet.com
Tree-lined parkland course overlooking Firth of Forth. Well maintained and providing an excellent challenge. The final third of the course can make or break a score. The tough four hole stretches from the long par 4 13th including The Gully, a par 3 14th where to be short is to court disaster, followed by the par 4 15th huddled tight beside trees to the left. A precision drive is required to find the rollercoaster fairway and from there a long iron or fairway wood is played over an uphill approach to a tilting green.
18 holes, 6237yds, Par 70, SSS 70, Course record 64.
Club membership 1000.
Visitors contact professional in advance, restricted Fri pm & weekends. **Societies** should contact in advance through Management secretary **Green Fees** £38 per day; £28 per round (£35 per round weekends). **Prof** John Henderson **Course Designer** James Braid **Facilities** ⊗ ⋔ ⓑ ⚑ ⓠ ⌂ 🏠 🕈 🎯 🛒 ⚐ ⓣ **Conf** fac available Corporate Hospitality Days available **Location** W of town centre on B1361 to North Berwick

....

Hotel ⏿ Premier Travel Inn Edinburgh (Inveresk), Carberry Rd, Inveresk, Musselburgh, EDINBURGH ☎ 08701 977092 40 en suite

EAST RENFREWSHIRE

BARRHEAD　　　　　　　Map 11 NS45

Fereneze Fereneze Av G78 1HJ
☎ 0141 880 7058 📄 0141 881 7149
e-mail: ferenezegc@lineone.net
Hilly moorland course, with a good view at the end of a hard climb to the 3rd, then levels out.

Continued

18 holes, 5962yds, Par 71, SSS 69, Course record 66.
Club membership 750.
Visitors contact in advance; not weekends. Societies apply in writing. Green Fees not confirmed. Prof Haldane Lee Facilities ⊗ ⫚ ⮂ ⣿ ♟ 🏌 📠 ♘ Location NW side of town off B774

Hotel ★★ 76% Uplawmoor Hotel, Neilston Rd, UPLAWMOOR ☎ 01505 850565 14 en suite

CLARKSTON   Map 11 NS55

Cathcart Castle Mearns Rd G76 7YL
☎ 0141 638 9449 📠 0141 638 1201
18 holes, 5832yds, Par 68, SSS 68.
Location 0.75m SW off A726
Phone for further details

Hotel ⏟ Premier Travel Inn Glasgow East Kilbride West, Eaglesham Rd, EAST KILBRIDE ☎ 0870 9906542 40 en suite

EAGLESHAM   Map 11 NS55

Bonnyton Kirktonmoor Rd G76 0QA
☎ 01355 302781 📠 01355 303151
Dramatic moorland course offering spectacular views of beautiful countryside as far as snow-capped Ben Lomond. Tree-lined fairways, plateau greens, natural burns and well-situated bunkers and a unique variety of holes offer golfers both challenge and reward.
18 holes, 6255yds, Par 72, SSS 71.
Club membership 960.
Visitors Mon & Thu, must contact in advance. Societies phone in advance. Green Fees £40 per round. Prof Kendal McWade Facilities ⊗ ⫚ ⮂ ⣿ ♟ 🏌 📠 ♘ Location 0.25m SW off B764

NEWTON MEARNS   Map 11 NS55

East Renfrewshire Pilmuir G77 6RT
☎ 01355 500256 📠 01355 500323
e-mail: secretary@eastrengolfclub.co.uk
Undulating moorland with loch; prevailing south-west wind. Extensive views of Glasgow and the southern Highlands.
18 holes, 6097yds, Par 70, SSS 70, Course record 63.
Club membership 900.
Visitors contact professional in advance Societies contact secretary in advance. Green Fees £40 per round/£50 per day weekends £50/£60). Cards ▦ ▩ ⚏ Prof Stewart Russell Course Designer James Braid Facilities ⊗ ⫚ ⮂ ⣿ ♟ 🏌 ♘ Location 3m SW of Newton Mearns on A77

Hotel ★★ 76% Uplawmoor Hotel, Neilston Rd, UPLAWMOOR ☎ 01505 850565 14 en suite

Eastwood Muirshield, Loganswell G77 6RX
☎ 01355 500280 📠 01355 500333
e-mail: secretary@eastwoodgolfclub.demon.co.uk
An undulating moorland course situated in a scenic setting. Originally built in 1937, the course was redesigned in 2003. The greens are now of modern design, built to USGA specification.
18 holes, 6071yds, Par 70, SSS 70.
Club membership 900.
Visitors contact in advance. Societies contact in advance. Green Fees £40 per day; £30 per round. Cards ▩ ⚏ Prof Iain J Darroch Course Designer Graeme J Webster, Theodore Moone Facilities ⊗ ⫚ ⮂ ⣿ ♟ 🏌 📠 ♘ Location 2.5m S of Newton Mearns, on A77

Continued

Hotel ★★ 76% Uplawmoor Hotel, Neilston Rd, UPLAWMOOR ☎ 01505 850565 14 en suite

UPLAWMOOR   Map 10 NS45

Caldwell G78 4AU
☎ 01505 850366 (secretary) & 850616 (pro)
📠 01505 850604
e-mail: caldwellgolfclub@aol.com
Parkland course.
18 holes, 6294yds, Par 71, SSS 70, Course record 62.
Club membership 600.
Visitors must be with member at weekends & bank holidays. Must contact professional in advance. Societies writing to Secretary. Green Fees £25 per round/£35 per day. Prof Stephen Forbes Course Designer W Fernie Facilities ⊗ ⫚ ⮂ ⣿ ♟ 🏌 📠 ♘ Location 5m SW of Barrhead on A736 Irvine road

Hotel ★★ 76% Uplawmoor Hotel, Neilston Rd, UPLAWMOOR ☎ 01505 850565 14 en suite

FALKIRK

FALKIRK   Map 11 NS88

Falkirk Carmuirs, 136 Stirling Rd, Camelon FK2 7YP
☎ 01324 611061 (club) 📠 01324 639573 (sec)
e-mail: carmuirs.fgc@virgin.net
Parkland course with trees, gorse and streams.
18 holes, 6230yds, Par 71, SSS 70, Course record 65.
Club membership 800.
Visitors phone starter 01324 612219, visiting parties not Sat. Societies phone 01324 612219 in advance. Green Fees £30 per day; £20 per round (£40/£30 Sun). Cards ▦ ▩ ▩ ⚏ Prof Stewart Craig Course Designer James Braid Facilities ⊗ ⫚ ⮂ ⣿ ♟ 🏌 📠 ♘ Conf Corporate Hospitality Days available Location 1.5m W on A9

Hotel ★★★★ 69% The Inchyra, Grange Rd, POLMONT ☎ 01324 711911 109 en suite

LARBERT   Map 11 NS88

Falkirk Tryst 86 Burnhead Rd FK5 4BD
☎ 01324 562054 📠 01324 562054
18 holes, 6053yds, Par 70, SSS 69, Course record 62.
Location On A88 between A9 & A905
Phone for further details

Hotel ★★★★ 69% The Inchyra, Grange Rd, POLMONT ☎ 01324 711911 109 en suite

Glenbervie Stirling Rd FK5 4SJ
☎ 01324 562605 📠 01324 551054
e-mail: secretary@glenberviegolfclub.com
Parkland course with good views of the Ochil Hills.
18 holes, 6438yds, Par 71, SSS 71, Course record 64.
Club membership 600.
Visitors Mon-Fri before 4pm, Societies Tue & Thu only. Apply in writing. Green Fees £40 per day, £30 per round. Cards ▦ ▩ ⚏ Prof David Ross Course Designer James Braid Facilities ⊗ ⫚ ⮂ ⣿ ♟ 🏌 📠 ♘ Conf fac available Corporate Hospitality Days available Location 2m NW on A9

Hotel ★★★★ 69% The Inchyra, Grange Rd, POLMONT ☎ 01324 711911 109 en suite

POLMONT
Map 11 NS97

Grangemouth Polmont Hill FK2 0YE
☎ 01324 503840 📠 01324 503841
Windy parkland course. Testing holes: 3rd, 4th (par 4s); 5th (par 5); 7th (par 3) 216yds over reservoir (elevated green); 8th, 9th, 18th (par 4s).
18 holes, 6314yds, Par 71, SSS 71, Course record 65. Club membership 800.
Visitors contact 24 hours in advance.Must have own golf shoes & clubs, Sat after 4pm. **Societies** contact in writing. **Green Fees** not confirmed. **Prof** Greg McFarlane **Facilities** ⊗ ℍ ఓ ☕ ♀ ♨ 🍴 ♂ **Location** M9 junct 4, 0.5m N

Hotel ★★★★ 69% The Inchyra, Grange Rd, POLMONT
☎ 01324 711911 109 en suite

Polmont Manuelrigg, Maddiston FK2 0LS
☎ 01324 711277 📠 01324 712504
Parkland course, hilly with few bunkers. Views of the River Forth and Ochil Hills.
9 holes, 3073yds, Par 72, SSS 69, Course record 66. Club membership 300.
Visitors no visitors on Sat from Apr-Sep, Mon-Fri. **Societies** apply in writing to club secretary. **Green Fees** terms on applications. **Facilities** ⊗ ℍ ఓ ☕ ♀ ♨
Conf fac available **Location** A805 from Falkirk, 1st right after fire brigade headquarters

Hotel ★★★★ 69% The Inchyra, Grange Rd, POLMONT
☎ 01324 711911 109 en suite

FIFE

ABERDOUR
Map 11 NT18

Aberdour Seaside Place KY3 0TX
☎ 01383 860080 📠 01383 860050
e-mail: aberdourgc@aol.com
Parkland course overlooking the Firth of Forth.

18 holes, 5460yds, Par 67, SSS 66, Course record 59. Club membership 800.
Visitors contact in advance; not Sat. **Societies** phone or write to manager in advance **Green Fees** £30 per day; £22 per round (£35 per day/round Sun). **Cards** 🖃 🖃 🖃 🖃 **Prof** David Gemmell **Facilities** ⊗ ℍ ఓ ☕ ♀ ♨ 🍴 ♂ ♂ **Location** S side of village

Prices may change during the currency of the Guide, please check when booking.

ANSTRUTHER
Map 12 NO50

Anstruther Marsfield, Shore Rd KY10 3DZ
☎ 01333 310956 📠 01333 312283
A tricky links course with some outstanding views of the river Forth. The nine holes consist of four par 4s and five par 3s. The 5th hole is rated one of the hardest par 3s anywhere, measuring 235yds from the white tees.
9 holes, 2266yds, Par 62, SSS 63, Course record 60. Club membership 550.
Visitors advised to phone in advance. **Societies** apply in writing for weekend bookings. **Green Fees** £16 per 18 holes; £10 per 9 holes (£18/£12 weekends). **Course Designer** Tom Morris **Facilities** ⊗ ℍ ఓ ☕ ♀ ♨ ♂
Location Turn right at Craw's Hotel, SW off A917

Hotel ★★ 66% Balcomie Links Hotel, Balcomie Rd, CRAIL ☎ 01333 450237 15 rms (13 en suite)

BURNTISLAND
Map 11 NT28

Burntisland Golf House Club Dodhead, Kirkcaldy Rd KY3 9LQ
☎ 01592 874093 (manager) 📠 01592 873247
e-mail: wktbghc@aol.com
A lush, testing course offering magnificent views over the Forth estuary.

18 holes, 5965yds, Par 70, SSS 70, Course record 62. Club membership 800.
Visitors weekend play may be restricted. Book by telephoning professional or manager. **Societies** apply in writing to manager. **Green Fees** not confirmed. **Cards** 🖃 🖃 🖃 🖃 **Prof** Paul Wytrazek **Course Designer** Willie Park Jnr **Facilities** ⊗ ℍ ఓ ☕ ♀ ♨ 🍴 ♂ ♂ ♂
Conf fac available Corporate Hospitality Days available **Location** 1m E on B923

Hotel ★★ 68% Inchview Hotel, 65-69 Kinghorn Rd, BURNTISLAND ☎ 01592 872239 12 en suite 4 annexe en suite

COLINSBURGH
Map 12 NO40

Charleton Charleton KY9 1HG
☎ 01333 340249 📠 01333 340583
e-mail: bonde@charleton.co.uk
Parkland course with wonderful views over the Firth of Forth.
18 holes, 6216yds, Par 72, SSS 70.
Visitors preferable to contact in advance **Societies** phone or e-mail in advance. **Green Fees** not confirmed. **Cards** 🖃 🖃 🖃 🖃 **Prof** George Finlayson **Course Designer** J Salvesen **Facilities** ⊗ ఓ ☕ ♀ ♨ ♂ ♂
Location Off B942, NW of Colinsburgh

Continued

....
Hotel 🏨 The Inn at Lathones, Largoward, ST
ANDREWS ☎ 01334 840494 13 annexe en suite

Cowdenbeath Seco Place KY4 8PD
☎ 01383 511918
Dora Course: 18 holes, 6201yds, Par 70, SSS 70,
Course record 68.
Location off A92 into Cowdenbeath, 2nd right & course
signed
Phone for further details

Crail Golfing Society Balcomie Clubhouse,
Fifeness KY10 3XN
☎ 01333 450686 & 450960 📄 01333 450416
e-mail: crailgs@hotmail.com
Perched on the edge of the North Sea, the Crail Golfing
Society's courses at Balcomie are picturesque and
sporting. Crail Golfing Society began its life in 1786 and
the course is highly thought of by students of the game
both for its testing holes and the standard of its greens.
Craighead Links has panoramic seascape and
country views. With wide sweeping fairways and
USGA specification greens it is a testing but fair
challenge.
Balcomie Links: 18 holes, 5922yds, Par 69, SSS 70,
Course record 62.
Craighead Links: 18 holes, 6700yds, Par 72, SSS 74,
Course record 69.
Club membership 1735.
Visitors contact in advance, restricted 10am-noon &
2-4.30pm. **Societies** contact in advance, as much notice as
possible for weekend play. **Green Fees** per day
Balcomie/Balcomie £65, Craighead/Balcomie £55; per
round £40 (weekends £78/£68/£50). **Cards** 💳 🖦 💳 💳
💳 🗎 **Prof** Graeme Lennie **Course Designer** Tom Morris
Facilities ⊗ ⅷ 🍸 💺 ♀ 🛆 🖻 ⸕ 🏌 🛒 ♂ ¶
Location 2m NE off A917

....
Hotel ★★ 66% Balcomie Links Hotel, Balcomie Rd,
CRAIL ☎ 01333 450237 15 rms (13 en suite)

....
Additional **Guesthouse** ♦♦♦♦The Spindrift, Pittenweem
Rd, ANSTRUTHER ☎ 01333 310573
📄 01333 310573 8 rms (7 en suite)

Cupar Hilltarvit KY15 5JT
☎ 01334 653549 📄 01334 653549
e-mail: cupargc@fsmail.net
Hilly parkland course with fine views over north-east
Fife. 5th/14th hole is most difficult - uphill and into the
prevailing wind. Said to be the oldest nine-hole club in
the UK.
9 holes, 5153yds, Par 68, SSS 66, Course record 61.
Club membership 400.
Visitors not Sat. **Societies** contact in advance. **Green Fees**
£15 per day. **Course Designer** Allan Robertson **Facilities**
⊗ ⅷ 💺 💺 ♀ 🛆 ⸕ ♂ **Conf** Corporate Hospitality Days
available **Location** 0.75m S off A92

Elmwood Stratheden KY15 5RS
☎ 01334 658780 📄 01334 658781
e-mail: clubhouse@elmwood.co.uk
A new parkland course set in a rural location, offering
fine views of the Lomond Hills to the west and the
Taruit Hills to the east.
18 holes, 5653yds, Par 70, SSS 68.
Club membership 750.
Visitors anytime, bookings available up to 1 week in
advance. **Societies** various packages available. Contact
Golf Administrator in advance. **Green Fees** £19 per round
(£23 weekends & bank holidays). **Cards** 💳 🖾 **Prof**
Graeme McDowall **Facilities** ⊗ ⅷ 💺 ♀ 💺 ♀ 🛆 🖻 ⸕ ♦
🛒 ♂ **Conf** fac available Corporate Hospitality Days
available M90 junct 8, A91 to St Andrews, 0.5m
before Cupar. At Wisemans Dairy right, right at next junct,
course 400yds on left

Canmore Venturefair Av KY12 0PE
☎ 01383 724969 📄 01383 731649
e-mail: canmoregolfclub@aol.com
Parkland course with excellent turf, moderate in
length but a good test of accuracy demanding a good
short game. Ideal for 36 hole play, and suitable for all
ages.
18 holes, 5376yds, Par 67, SSS 66, Course record 61.
Club membership 710.
Visitors Sat not usually available. Limited Sun. Must
contact Professional in advance. **Societies** apply in writing
to secretary. **Green Fees** £25 per day; £19 per round (£25
weekends). **Prof** Gavin Cook **Course Designer** Ben Sayers
& others **Facilities** ⊗ ⅷ 💺 💺 ♀ 🛆 🖻 ⸕ 🛒 ♂
Location 1m N on A823

....
Hotel ★★★ 75% Keavil House Hotel, Crossford,
DUNFERMLINE ☎ 01383 736258 47 en suite

Dunfermline Pitfirrane, Crossford KY12 8QW
☎ 01383 723534 & 729061 📄 01383 723547
e-mail: secretary@dunfermlinegolfclub.com
Gently undulating parkland course with interesting
contours. Five par 5s, five par 3s. No water hazards.
Centre of the course is a disused walled garden, which
is a haven for wildlife.
18 holes, 6121yds, Par 72, SSS 70, Course record 65.
Club membership 720.
Visitors not Sat. Contact to check times. **Societies** contact
in advance. **Green Fees** £38 per day; £27 per round (Sun
£35). **Prof** Chris Nugent **Course Designer** JR Stutt
Facilities ⊗ ⅷ 💺 💺 ♀ 🛆 🖻 ⸕ 🛒 ♂
Location 2m W of Dunfermline on A994

....
Hotel ★★★ 75% Keavil House Hotel, Crossford,
DUNFERMLINE ☎ 01383 736258 47 en suite

Pitreavie Queensferry Rd KY11 8PR
☎ 01383 722591 📄 01383 722591
Picturesque woodland course with panoramic view of
the Forth valley. Testing golf.
18 holes, 6086yds, Par 70, SSS 69, Course record 64.
Club membership 700.
Visitors welcome except for competition days. **Societies**
write or phone in advance. **Green Fees** £30.50 per day;
£20.50 per round (£38.50/£24.50 weekends). **Prof** Paul
Brookes **Course Designer** Dr A MacKenzie **Facilities** ⊗ ⅷ
💺 💺 ♀ 🛆 🖻 ⸕ ♂ **Conf** Corporate Hospitality Days
available **Location** SE side of town on A823

Continued

Hotel ★★★ 65% King Malcolm, Queensferry Rd, DUNFERMLINE ☎ 01383 722611 48 en suite

ELIE   Map 12 NO40

Golf House Club KY9 1AS
☎ 01333 330301 📠 01333 330895
e-mail: sandy@golfhouseclub.freeserve.co.uk
One of Scotland's most delightful holiday courses with panoramic views over the Firth of Forth. Some of the holes out towards the rocky coastline are splendid. This is the course which has produced many good professionals, including James Braid.
18 holes, 6273yds, Par 70, SSS 70, Course record 62.
Club membership 600.
Visitors advisable to contact in advance, limited availability Sat May-Sep & no visitors Sun May-Sep, ballot in operation for tee times during July & August. **Societies** contact in advance. **Green Fees** not confirmed. **Cards** 🔲 🔲 💷 💳 **Prof** Robin Wilson **Course Designer** James Braid **Facilities** ⊗ ⏽ 🏌 💂 ♀ ⛳ 🏠 ✆ 🏐 ⚑ **Leisure** hard tennis courts. **Location** W side of village off A917

Hotel 🏨 The Inn at Lathones, Largoward, ST ANDREWS ☎ 01334 840494 13 annexe en suite

FALKLAND   Map 11 NO20

Falkland The Myre KY15 7AA
☎ 01337 857404
A flat, well-kept course with excellent greens and views of East Lomond Hill and Falkland Palace.
9 holes, 4988yds, Par 67, SSS 65, Course record 62.
Visitors parties by arrangement; check availability weekends. **Societies** contact in advance. **Green Fees** not confirmed. **Facilities** ⊗ by arrangement 🏌 💂 ♀ ⛳ **Location** N side of town on A912

GLENROTHES   Map 11 NO20

Glenrothes Golf Course Rd KY6 2LA
☎ 01592 754561
18 holes, 6444yds, Par 71, SSS 71, Course record 67.
Course Designer JR Stutt **Location** W side of town off B921
Phone for further details

Hotel ★★★★ 🏨 Balbirnie House, Balbirnie Park, MARKINCH ☎ 01592 610066 30 en suite

KINCARDINE   Map 11 NS98

Tulliallan Alloa Rd FK10 4BB
☎ 01259 730798 📠 01259 733950
e-mail: enquires@tulliallangc.f9.co.uk
Pleasant parkland course with scenic views of the Ochil Hills and the River Forth. A burn meanders throughout the course, which combined with maturing trees make this a challenging test of golf. There are a number of slopes which are easily negotiable.
18 holes, 5965yds, Par 69, SSS 69, Course record 63.
Club membership 700.
Visitors restricted at weekends, must contact professional shop. **Societies** contact in advance. **Green Fees** £35 per day, £20 per round (£42/£35 weekends). **Cards** 🔲 🔲 🔳 💷 **Prof** Steven Kelly **Facilities** ⊗ ⏽ 🏌 💂 ♀ ⛳ 🏠 ✆ 🏐 **Conf** fac available Corporate Hospitality Days available **Location** 1m NW on A977

Continued

Hotel ⇧ Premier Travel Inn Falkirk North, Bowtrees Farm, KINCARDINE BRIDGE ☎ 08701 977099 40 en suite

KINGHORN   Map 11 NT28

Kinghorn Macduff Cres KY3 9RE
☎ 01592 890345 & 890978
Municipal course, 300ft above sea level with views over the Firth of Forth and the North Sea. Undulating and quite testing.
18 holes, 5269yds, Par 65, SSS 67, Course record 62.
Club membership 190.
Visitors not 7.30am-10.30am & 12pm-3pm Sat. **Societies** contact in writing. **Green Fees** £13 per round/£20 per day (weekend £17/£25). **Course Designer** Tom Morris **Facilities** ⊗ ⏽ 💂 ♀ ⛳ **Location** S side of town on A921

Hotel ★★★ 67% Dean Park Hotel, Chapel Level, KIRKCALDY ☎ 01592 261635 34 en suite 12 annexe en suite

KIRKCALDY   Map 11 NT29

Dunnikier Park Dunnikier Way KY1 3LP
☎ 01592 261599 📠 01592 642541
e-mail: dunnikierparkgolfclub@btconnect.com
Parkland, rolling fairways, not heavily bunkered, views of the Firth of Forth.
18 holes, 6601yds, Par 72, SSS 72, Course record 65.
Club membership 700.
Visitors visitors must contact course starter in person. **Societies** apply in writing. **Green Fees** terms on application. **Prof** Gregor Whyte **Course Designer** R Stutt **Facilities** ⊗ ⏽ 🏌 💂 ♀ ⛳ 🏠 🚿 🏐 **Location** 2m N on B981

Hotel ★★★ 67% Dean Park Hotel, Chapel Level, KIRKCALDY ☎ 01592 261635 34 en suite 12 annexe en suite

Kirkcaldy Balwearie Rd KY2 5LT
☎ 01592 205240 & 203258 (pro shop) 📠 01592 205240
e-mail: enquiries@kirkcaldygolfclub.co.uk
Challenging parkland course in rural setting, with beautiful views. A burn meanders by five holes. The club celebrated its centenary in 2004.
18 holes, 6086yds, Par 71, SSS 69, Course record 65.
Club membership 822.
Visitors limited play Sat. Advised to contact pro-shop 01592 203258. **Societies** apply in writing or phone. **Green Fees** £30 per day, £24 per round (weekends £38/£30). **Cards** 🔲 🔲 💷 **Prof** Anthony Caira **Course Designer** Tom Morris **Facilities** ⊗ ⏽ 🏌 💂 ♀ ⛳ 🏠 ✆ 🏐 🚿 **Conf** fac available Corporate Hospitality Days available **Location** SW side of town off A910

Hotel ★★★ 67% Dean Park Hotel, Chapel Level, KIRKCALDY ☎ 01592 261635 34 en suite 12 annexe en suite

LADYBANK   Map 11 NO30

Ladybank Annsmuir KY15 7RA
☎ 01337 830814 📠 01337 831505
e-mail: info@ladybankgolf.co.uk
Picturesque classic heathland course of championship status set among heather, Scots pines and silver birch and comprising two loops of nine holes. The drive at the dog-leg 3rd and 9th holes requires extreme care as do

Continued

the 15th and 16th on the back nine. The greens are compact and approach shots require precision to find the putting surface.
18 holes, 6601yds, Par 71, SSS 72, Course record 63. Club membership 1000.
Visitors advance booking weekdays, restricted times at weekends. **Societies** please phone or write in advance. **Green Fees** £60 per day; £45 per round (£55 per round weekends). Reduced rates Apr & Oct. **Cards** 🖃 🖃 🖃 🖃 🖃 **Prof** Sandy Smith **Course Designer** Tom Morris **Facilities** ⊗ ⫙ 🖢 ▣ ♀ ⚐ 🏠 ⚑ ↘ 🚣 ♂ ⚓ **Conf** fac available Corporate Hospitality Days available **Location** onto Kirkcaldy road for 0.5m, at A91/A92 junct

....

Hotel ★★★ 61% Fernie Castle, Letham, CUPAR ☎ 01337 810381 20 en suite

LESLIE   Map 11 NO20

Leslie Balsillie Laws KY6 3EZ
☎ 01592 620040
9 holes, 4686yds, Par 63, SSS 64, Course record 63.
Course Designer Tom Morris **Location** N side of town off A911
Phone for further details

....

Hotel ★★ 77% Rescobie House Hotel & Restaurant, 6 Valley Dr, Leslie, GLENROTHES ☎ 01592 749555 10 en suite

LEUCHARS   Map 12 NO42

Drumoig Hotel & Golf Course Drumoig
KY16 0BE
☎ 01382 541800 📠 01382 542211
e-mail: drumoig@sol.co.uk
A developing but challenging young championship course. Set in a parkland environment, the course is links-like in places. Features include Whinstone Quarries and views over to St Andrews and Carnoustie. Water features are demanding, especially on the 9th where the fairway runs between Drumoig's two tiny lochs.
18 holes, 6835yds, Par 72, SSS 73, Course record 67. Club membership 350.
Visitors advisable to phone in advance. **Societies** phone in advance. **Green Fees** winter £18 per day (weekends £23), summer £31 per day (weekends £36). **Cards** 🖃 🖃 🖃 🖂 🖃 🖃 🖃 **Facilities** ⊗ ⫙ 🖢 ▣ ♀ 🏠 ⚑ 🚣 ♂ ⚓ **Leisure** Scottish National Golf Centre in grounds. **Conf** fac available Corporate Hospitality Days available **Location** on A914 between St Andrews & Dundee

....

Hotel ★★★ 🏌 Rufflets Country House & Garden Restaurant, Strathkinness Low Rd, ST ANDREWS ☎ 01334 472594 19 en suite 5 annexe en suite

St Michaels KY16 0DX
☎ 01334 839365 📠 01334 838789
e-mail: honsec@stmichaelsgolf.co.uk
Parkland course with open views over Fife and Tayside. The undulating course weaves its way through tree plantations. The short par 4 17th, parallel to the railway and over a pond to a stepped green, poses an interesting challenge.
18 holes, 5802yds, Par 70, SSS 68, Course record 66. Club membership 650.
Visitors not Sun am. **Societies** apply in writing, limited weekends. Special deals midweek **Green Fees** terms on application. **Cards** 🖃 🖃 🖃 🖃 **Facilities** ⊗ ⫙ by arrangement 🖢 ▣ ♀ 🏠 ♂ **Location** NW side of village on A919

LEVEN   Map 11 NO30

Leven Links The Promenade KY8 4HS
☎ 01333 428859 & 421390 📠 01333 428859
e-mail: secretary@leven-links.com
Leven has the classic ingredients which make up a golf links in Scotland; undulating fairways with hills and hollows, out of bounds and a burn or stream. Turning into the prevailing west wind at the 13th leaves the golfer with a lot of work to do before one of the finest finishing holes in golf. A top class championship links course used for British Open final qualifying stages, it has fine views over Largo Bay.

18 holes, 6436yds, Par 71, SSS 70, Course record 61. Club membership 1000.
Visitors contact in advance. Limited availability Fri pm & Sat, contact for these times no more than five days in advance. **Societies** apply in advance. **Green Fees** £50 per day, £37 per round (weekends £60/£45). **Cards** 🖃 🖃 🖃 🖃 **Course Designer** Tom Morris **Facilities** ⊗ ⫙ 🖢 ▣ ♀ 🏠 ♂

....

Hotel ★★★ 78% Old Manor Hotel, Leven Rd, LUNDIN LINKS ☎ 01333 320368 24 en suite

Scoonie North Links KY8 4SP
☎ 01333 423437(Starter) & 307007 (Club)
e-mail: manager@scooniegc.fsnet.co.uk
18 holes, 5445yds, Par 67, SSS 65, Course record 63.
Phone for further details

....

Hotel ★★★ 78% Old Manor Hotel, Leven Rd, LUNDIN LINKS ☎ 01333 320368 24 en suite

LOCHGELLY   Map 11 NT19

Lochgelly Cartmore Rd KY5 9PB
☎ 01592 780174
Parkland course with easy walking and often windy.
18 holes, 5491yds, Par 68, SSS 67, Course record 62. Club membership 650.
Visitors no restrictions, parties must book in advance by writing. **Societies** apply in writing. **Green Fees** not confirmed. **Prof** Martin Goldie **Course Designer** Ian Marchbanks **Facilities** ⊗ ⫙ 🖢 ▣ ♀ 🏠 ♂ **Location** W side of town off A910

....

Hotel ★★★ 67% Dean Park Hotel, Chapel Level, KIRKCALDY ☎ 01592 261635 34 en suite 12 annexe en suite

Continued

Lochore Meadows Lochore Meadows Country Park, Crosshill, Lochgelly KY5 8BA
☎ 01592 414300 01592 414345
e-mail: info@lochore-meadows.co.uk
Lochside course with a stream running through it and woodland nearby. Country park offers many leisure facilities.
9 holes, 3207yds, Par 72, SSS 71.
Club membership 240.
Visitors no restrictions. **Societies** contact in advance. **Green Fees** £11 per 18 holes (weekends £14). **Facilities** **Leisure** fishing, outdoor education centre, childrens play park. **Conf** fac available **Location** 2m N off B920

Hotel ★★★ 75% Green Hotel, 2 The Muirs, KINROSS ☎ 01577 863467 46 en suite

LUNDIN LINKS Map 12 NO40

Lundin Golf Rd KY8 6BA
☎ 01333 320202 01333 329743
e-mail: secretary@lundingolfclub.co.uk
The Leven Links and the course of the Lundin Club adjoin each other. The course is part seaside and part inland. The holes are excellent but those which can be described as seaside holes have a very different nature from the inland style ones. The par 3 14th looks seawards across the Firth of Forth towards Edinburgh and the old railway line defines out of bounds at several holes. A number of burns snake across the fairways.
18 holes, 6371yds, Par 71, SSS 71, Course record 63.
Club membership 850.
Visitors visitors welcome weekdays 9-3.30 (3pm Fri) & Sat after 2.30pm, limited times on Sun. Book well in advance. **Societies** book well in advance by telephoning Secretary **Green Fees** £50 per day; £42 per round. (£50 per round weekends). **Cards** **Prof** David Webster **Course Designer** James Braid **Facilities** **Location** W side of village off A915

Hotel ★★★ 78% Old Manor Hotel, Leven Rd, LUNDIN LINKS ☎ 01333 320368 24 en suite

Lundin Ladies Woodielea Rd KY8 6AR
☎ 01333 320832
e-mail: secretary@lundinladies.co.uk
Short, lowland course with Bronze Age standing stones on the second fairway and coastal views.
9 holes, 2365yds, Par 68, SSS 67, Course record 64.
Club membership 400.
Visitors contact in advance. Competition days Wed & some weekends. **Societies** phone secretary. **Green Fees** £12.50 per 18 holes, £8 per 9 holes (£15/£10 weekend). **Course Designer** James Braid **Facilities**

Continued

Location W side of village off A915

Hotel ★★★ 78% Old Manor Hotel, Leven Rd, LUNDIN LINKS ☎ 01333 320368 24 en suite

MARKINCH Map 11 NO20

Balbirnie Park Balbirnie Park KY7 6NR
☎ 01592 612095 & 752006 (tee times)
01592 612383/752006
e-mail: craigfdonnelly@aol.com
Set in the magnificent Balbirnie Park, a fine example of the best in traditional parkland design, with natural contours the inspiration behind the layout.
18 holes, 6214yds, Par 71, SSS 70, Course record 62.
Club membership 900.
Visitors contact in advance. Numbers restricted weekends & visitors must play from yellow tees, smart but casual dress code. **Societies** booking forms sent out on request by professional. **Green Fees** £35 per round/£45 per day (weekends £40/£55). **Cards** **Prof** Craig Donnelly **Course Designer** Fraser Middleton **Facilities** **Conf** fac available **Location** 2m E of Glenrothes, off A92

Hotel ★★★★ Balbirnie House, Balbirnie Park, MARKINCH ☎ 01592 610066 30 en suite

ST ANDREWS See page 343

ST ANDREWS Map 12 NO51

British Golf Museum opp Royal & Ancient Golf Club
☎ 01334 460046
The museum, which tells the history of golf, is of interest to golfers and non-golfers alike. Themed galleries and interactive displays explore the history of the major championships and the lives of the famous players, and trace the development of golfing equipment. An audio-visual theatre shows historic golfing moments.
Open Etr-Oct, Mon-Sat 9.30am-5.30pm, Sun 10am-5pm; Nov-Etr, daily 10am-4pm. **Admission** charge, phone for details.

Duke's Course Craigtoun KY16 8NS
☎ 01334 474371 01334 479456
e-mail: reservations@oldcoursehotel.co.uk
Now owned and managed by the Old Course Hotel, with a spectacular setting above St Andrews. Blending the characteristics of a links course with an inland course, Duke's offers rolling fairways, undulating greens and a testing woodland section, and magnificent views over St Andrews Bay towards Carnoustie.

Continued

St Andrews Links Trust

Fife

St Andrews   Map 12 NO51

Golf was first played here around 1400 and the Old Course is acknowledged worldwide as the home of golf. The Old Course has played host to the greatest golfers in the world and many of golf's most dramatic moments. The New Course (6604yds) was opened in 1895, having been laid out by Old Tom Morris. The Jubilee was opened in 1897, and is 6805yds long from the medal tees. A shorter version of the Jubilee Course is also available, known as the Bronze Course, measuring 5674yds. There is no handicap limit for the shorter course and it is best for lower and middle-handicap golfers. The Eden opened in 1914 and is recommended for middle to high handicap golfers. The Strathtyrum has a shorter, less testing layout, best for high handicap golfers. The nine-hole Balgrove Course, upgraded and re-opened in 1993, is best for beginners and children. The facilities and courses here make this the largest golf complex in Europe.

Pilmour House KY16 9SF
☎ 01334 466666 Fax 01334 479555
e-mail: linkstrust@standrews.org.uk

Old Course: 18 holes, 6609yds, Par 72, SSS 72, Course record 62.
New Course: 18 holes, 6604yds, Par 71, SSS 73.
Jubilee Course: 18 holes, 6742yds, Par 72, SSS 73, Course record 63.
Eden Course: 18 holes, 6112yds, Par 70, SSS 70.
Strathtyrum Course: 18 holes, 5094yds, Par 69, SSS 69.
Balgove Course: 9 holes, 1530yds, Par 30, SSS 30.
Visitors Old Course: not Sun; handicap required (men 24, women 36); daily ballot or 2-year booking. Other courses: 1-month advance booking required for New, Jubilee, Eden, Strath; no advance booking Sat. **Societies** book at least 1 month in advance. **Green Fees** £10–£115 depending on course.
Cards 🖃 💳 💳 💳 💳 💳 **Facilities** ⊗ ⫙ ⌼ ☕ ♀ ⌂ ⌁ 🛺 ✎ ℂ **Conf** Corporate Hospitality Days available
Location off A91

···

Hotels

★ ★ ★ ★ ★ The Old Course Hotel, Golf Resort & Spa, ST ANDREWS

☎ 01334 474371 134 en suite

★ ★ ★ St Andrews Golf Hotel, 40 The Scores, ST ANDREWS

☎ 01334 472611 Fax 01334 472188 21 en suite

★ ★ ★ ★ 71% Macdonald Rusacks Hotel, Pilmour Links, ST ANDREWS

☎ 0870 400 8128 Fax 01334 477896 68 en suite

18 holes, 6749yds, Par 72, SSS 73, Course record 67. Club membership 500.
Visitors booking should be in advance to avoid disappointment through the hotel resort reservations team. **Societies** apply in writing or fax in advance. **Green Fees** from £75 per 18 holes. **Cards** **Prof** Ron Walker **Course Designer** Peter Thomson **Facilities** **Leisure** heated indoor swimming pool, sauna, solarium, gymnasium, computer swing analyses. **Conf** fac available Corporate Hospitality Days available **Location** M90 from Edinburgh onto A91 to Cupar then to St Andrews, turn off for Strathkiness

Hotel ★★★★★ The Old Course Hotel, Golf Resort & Spa, ST ANDREWS ☎ 01334 474371 134 en suite

St Andrews Bay Golf Resort & Spa
KY16 8PN
☎ 01334 837000 🖷 01334 471115
e-mail: info@standrewsbay.com
The Torrance course is a traditional Scottish layout, which works its way around the hotel before bursting open to reveal a cross section of the remaining 12 holes, which wind down towards the coastal edge. The Devlin is a stunning clifftop course with unique characteristics and requiring a well-devised strategy of play. One of the longest courses in the UK.

Torrance: 18 holes, 7037yds, Par 72, SSS 74.
Devlin: 18 holes, 7049yds, Par 72, SSS 74.
Visitors book in advance. **Societies** phone or e-mail in advance. **Green Fees** £30-£95. **Cards** **Prof** John Kerr **Course Designer** Sam Torrance, Gene Sarazen **Facilities** **Leisure** heated indoor swimming pool, sauna, solarium, gymnasium. **Conf** fac available Corporate Hospitality Days available

Hotel ★★★★★ 71% St Andrews Bay Golf Resort & Spa, St Andrews ☎ 01334 837000 209 en suite 8 annexe en suite

SALINE — Map 11 NT09

Saline Kinneddar Hill KY12 9LT
☎ 01383 852591 🖷 01383 853517
e-mail: saline-golf-club@supanet.com
Hillside parkland course with excellent turf and panoramic view of the Forth Valley.
9 holes, 5302yds, Par 68, SSS 66, Course record 62. Club membership 330.
Visitors advisable to contact in advance; not Sat, some restrictions Sun. **Societies** contact in advance.
Green Fees £11 per day (£14 weekends).

Continued

Facilities
Location M90 junct 4, 0.5m E at junct B913 & B914

Hotel ★★★ 65% King Malcolm, Queensferry Rd, DUNFERMLINE ☎ 01383 722611 48 en suite

TAYPORT — Map 12 NO42

Scotscraig Golf Rd DD6 9DZ
☎ 01382 552515 🖷 01382 553130
e-mail: scotscraig@scottishgolf.com
Combined with heather and rolling fairways, the course is part heathland, part links, with the greens being renowned for being fast and true.
18 holes, 6550yds, Par 71, SSS 72, Course record 62. Club membership 900.
Visitors restricted at weekends **Societies** advance booking. **Green Fees** £54 per day, £44 per round (weekends £60/£50). **Cards** **Prof** John Kelly **Course Designer** James Braid **Facilities** **Conf** Corporate Hospitality Days available
Location S side of village off B945

Hotel ★★★ 64% Sandford Country House Hotel, Newton Hill, Wormit, DUNDEE ☎ 01382 541802 16 en suite

THORNTON — Map 11 NT29

Thornton Station Rd KY1 4DW
☎ 01592 771111 🖷 01592 774955
e-mail: johntgc@ic24.net
A relatively flat, lightly tree-lined, parkland course bounded on three sides by a river which comes into play at holes 14-16.
18 holes, 6170yds, Par 70, SSS 69, Course record 61. Club membership 700.
Visitors restricted at weekends before 10am & between 12.30-2pm, also Tue 1-1.30 & Thu 9-10. Booking in advance recommended. **Societies** apply in advance. **Green Fees** £30 per day; £20 per round (£40/£30 weekends). **Facilities** **Location** 1m E of town off A92

Hotel ★★★★ Balbirnie House, Balbirnie Park, MARKINCH ☎ 01592 610066 30 en suite

HIGHLAND

ALNESS — Map 14 NH66

Alness Ardross Rd IV17 0QA
☎ 01349 883877
e-mail: info@alness-golfclub.co.uk
A testing, parkland course with beautiful views over the Cromarty Firth and the Black Isle. It is located on the north west edge of the village of Alness and four holes run parallel to the gorge of the River Averon. Golfers of all abilities will find the course interesting and challenging. A particular test of skill is required at the 14th hole where the tee is located far above the green which lies beside the gorge at a distance of 406yds.
18 holes, 4886yds, Par 67, SSS 64, Course record 62. Club membership 350.
Visitors phone in advance for weekend play, parties must phone for booking **Societies** contact in advance.
Green Fees £20 (£25 weekends). **Cards**
Prof Gary Lister **Facilities**
Leisure fishing. **Conf** fac available Corporate Hospitality Days available **Location** 0.5m N off A9

ARISAIG
Map 13 NM68

Traigh Traigh PH39 4NT
☎ 01687 450337 📄 01678 450293
According to at least one newspaper Traigh is 'probably the most beautifully sited nine-hole golf course in the world'. True or not, Traigh lies alongside sandy beaches with views to Skye and the Inner Hebrides. The feature of the course is a line of grassy hills, originally sand dunes, that rise to some 60ft, and provide a challenge to the keenest golfer.
9 holes, 2456yds, Par 68, SSS 65, Course record 67. Club membership 150.
Visitors no restrictions. Societies contact in advance. Green Fees not confirmed. Course Designer John Salvesen 1994 Facilities ⬛ 🏠 🍴 ⚑ Location A830 to Arisaig, signed onto B8008, 2m N of Arisaig

Hotel ★★ 72% Arisaig Hotel, ARISAIG ☎ 01687 450210
13 en suite

BOAT OF GARTEN
Map 14 NH91

Boat of Garten PH24 3BQ
☎ 01479 831282 📄 01479 831523
e-mail: boatgolf@enterprise.net
This heathland course was cut out from a silver birch forest though the fairways are adequately wide. There are natural hazards of broom and heather, good views and walking is easy. A round provides great variety.

18 holes, 5876yds, Par 70, SSS 69, Course record 67. Club membership 650.
Visitors contact in advance. Handicap certificate required. Play restricted to 10am-4pm weekends & 9.20am-7pm weekdays Societies phone or e-mail in advance. Green Fees £40 per day; £30 per round (£45/£35 weekends). Cards 💳 💳 💳 💳 Course Designer James Braid Facilities ⊗ 🏌 ⬛ ⬛ ♀ ⚑ 🏠 🍴 🛒 🚜 ⚑ Leisure hard tennis courts. Conf Corporate Hospitality Days available Location E side of village

Hotel ★★★ 76% Boat Hotel, BOAT OF GARTEN
☎ 01479 831258 28 en suite

BONAR BRIDGE
Map 14 NH69

Bonar Bridge-Ardgay Midgale Rd IV24 3EJ
☎ 01863 766750 (Sec) & 766199 (Clubhouse)
e-mail: bonarardgaygolf@aol.com
Wooded moorland course with picturesque views of hills and loch.
9 holes, 5162yds, Par 68, SSS 65. Club membership 250.
Visitors no restrictions. Societies apply in writing.

Green Fees £15 per day. Course Designer Various
Facilities ⬛ ⬛ 🛒 🍴 ⚑ Location 0.5m E

Guesthouse ♦♦♦ Kyle House, Dornoch Rd, BONAR
BRIDGE ☎ 01863 766360 6 rms (3 en suite)

BRORA
Map 14 NC90

Brora Golf Rd KW9 6QS
☎ 01408 621417 📄 01408 622157
e-mail: secretary@broragolf.co.uk
Typical seaside links with little rough and fine views. Some testing holes including the 17th Tarbatness, so called because of the lighthouse which gives the line; the elevated tee is one of the best driving holes in Scotland.
18 holes, 6110yds, Par 69, SSS 70, Course record 61. Club membership 704.
Visitors advisable to book in advance May-Oct. Societies advisable to book in advance. Green Fees £30 per round/£35 per day (weekend £35/£40). Cards 💳 💳 Course Designer James Braid Facilities ⊗ 🏌 ⬛ ⬛ ♀ 🏠 🍴 🛒 🚜 ⚑ Location E side of village. Follow signs to Beach Car Park

Hotel ★★★ 73% Royal Marine Hotel, Golf Rd, BRORA
☎ 01408 621252 22 en suite

CARRBRIDGE
Map 14 NH92

Carrbridge Inverness Rd PH23 3AU
☎ 01479 841623 & 0844 414 1415
e-mail: enquiries@carrbridgegolf
Challenging part-parkland, part-moorland course with magnificent views of the Cairngorms.
9 holes, 5402yds, Par 71, SSS 68, Course record 63. Club membership 550.
Visitors during May-Sep, course not open most Sun am. Societies small parties welcome, apply in writing. Green Fees £16 per day (£18 weekends). Facilities ⊗ ⬛ 🛒 ⚑ Location N side of village

Hotel ★★★ 69% Dalrachney Lodge Hotel,
CARRBRIDGE ☎ 01479 841252 11 en suite

DORNOCH
Map 14 NH78

Royal Dornoch Golf Rd IV25 3LW
☎ 01862 810219 ext.185 📄 01862 810792
e-mail: bookings@royaldornoch.com
The Championship course was recently rated 9th among Britain's top courses and is a links of rare subtlety. It appears amicable but proves very challenging in play with stiff breezes and tight lies. The 18-hole Struie links course provides, in a gentler style, an enjoyable test of a golfer's accuracy for players of all abilities.
Championship: 18 holes, 6514yds, Par 70, SSS 73. Struie Course: 18 holes, 6276yds, Par 72, SSS 70. Club membership 1700.
Visitors Recommended to contact in advance for Championship course Societies apply in advance. Green Fees Championship; £72 per round (£82 weekends); Struie £47 per day, £26 per round. Cards 💳 💳 💳 💳 Prof A Skinner Course Designer Tom Morris Facilities ⊗ 🏌 ⬛ ⬛ ♀ 🏠 🍴 🚜 ⚑ Leisure hard tennis courts. Conf Corporate Hospitality Days available Location E side of town

Continued

Continued

The Royal Dornoch Golf Club
Golf Road, Dornoch IV25 3LW

Tel Reservations: 01862 810219 ext 185
Fax: 01862 810792
E-mail: bookings@royaldornoch.com
Website: http://www.royaldornoch.com

Royal Dornoch, regularly in the World's top twenty courses, aims to provide traditional "links golf" of the highest quality on both its Championship and Struie Courses. Golfers and their friends will be made welcome to enjoy "Highland Hospitality" in an informal relaxed style in the clubhouse where they may partake of fine Scottish beverages and food.

Royal Dornoch Golf Club

DURNESS   Map 14 NC46

Durness Balnakeil IV27 4PG
☎ 01971 511364 📠 01971 511321
e-mail: lucy@durnessgolfclub.org
A nine-hole course set in tremendous scenery overlooking Balnakeil Bay. Part links and part inland with water hazards. Off alternative tees for second nine holes giving surprising variety. Tremendous last hole played across the sea to the green over 100yds away.
9 holes, 5555yds, Par 70, SSS 67, Course record 69.
Club membership 150.
Visitors restricted 10am-12.30 on Sun during Jun-Sep.
Societies phone in advance 01971 511364 (ex Sun).
Green Fees £15 per day (£10 after 5pm). **Course Designer** F Keith **Facilities** ⊗ 🛒 ⚲ 🏌 ✓ **Leisure** fishing.

Conf Corporate Hospitality Days available
Location 1m W of village overlooking Balnakeil Bay
Guesthouse ♦♦♦♦ Port-Na-Con House, Loch Eriboll, LAIRG ☎ 01971 511367 3 rms (1 en suite)

FORT AUGUSTUS   Map 14 NH30

Fort Augustus Markethill PH32 4DP
☎ 01320 366660 & 366758
e-mail: alex.barnett@freeuk.com
Moorland course, with narrow fairways and good views. Bordered by the tree-lined Caledonian Canal to the north and heather clad hills to the south.
9 holes, 5379yds, Par 67, SSS 67, Course record 67.
Club membership 170.
Visitors not Sat 1.30-4 & occasional Sun. **Societies** phone in advance. **Green Fees** £15 per day; £12 per round.
Course Designer Colt **Facilities** 🛒 ⚲ 🏌 ✓
Location 1m SW on A82

FORTROSE   Map 14 NH75

Fortrose & Rosemarkie Ness Rd East IV10 8SE
☎ 01381 620529 📄 01381 621328
e-mail: secretary@fortrosegolfclub.co.uk
Links set on a peninsula with the sea on three sides. Easy walking, good views. Designed by James Braid. The club was formed in 1888.
18 holes, 5883yds, Par 71, SSS 69, Course record 63.
Club membership 770.
Visitors restricted 8.45-10.15am & 1-2.15, 4.45-6.30pm.
Societies phone in advance. **Green Fees** not confirmed.
Cards 💳 💳 **Course Designer** James Braid
Facilities ⊗ 🛒 ⚲ 🏌 ✓ **Location** N on A9 over Kessock Bridge, signs to Munlochy and Fortrose

Fortrose & Rosemarkie Golf Club

Hotel ★★★★ 71% Inverness Marriott Hotel, Culcabock Rd, INVERNESS ☎ 01463 237166 76 en suite 6 annexe en suite

FORT WILLIAM   Map 14 NN17

Fort William Torlundy PH33 6SN
☎ 01397 704464
Spectacular moorland location looking onto the cliffs of Ben Nevis. Tees and greens are in excellent condition following major drainage improvements to the fairways.
18 holes, 6217yds, Par 72, SSS 71, Course record 67.
Club membership 420.
Visitors no restrictions. **Societies** contact in writing.
Green Fees £22 per round. **Cards** 💳 💳 💳
Course Designer Hamilton Stutt **Facilities** 🛒 ⚲ ⚲
🏌 ✓ **Location** 3m NE on A82

Continued   *Continued*

....
Hotel ★★★ 75% Moorings Hotel, Banavie, FORT
WILLIAM ☎ 01397 772797 28 en suite

GAIRLOCH   Map 14 NG87

Gairloch IV21 2BE
☎ 01445 712407 📠 01445 712865
e-mail: secretary@gairlochgc.freeserve.co.uk
**Fine seaside links course running along Gairloch Sands
with good views over the sea to Skye. In windy
conditions each hole is affected. The par 5 8th is
described by one of Scotland's teaching professionals as
one of the best natural par 5s in the country.**
9 holes, 4514yds, Par 63, SSS 64, Course record 64.
Club membership 275.
Visitors must be competent golfer & member of a
recognised club. **Societies** apply in writing to secretary.
Green Fees terms on application. **Cards** 🔲 **Course
Designer** Capt Burgess **Facilities** ⊗ 🏌 💺 ♀ ⛳ 🏠 🍴 ⚡
Conf Corporate Hospitality Days available
Location 1m S on A832

....
Hotel ★★ 69% Myrtle Bank, Low Rd, GAIRLOCH
☎ 01445 712004 12 en suite

GOLSPIE   Map 14 NH89

Golspie Ferry Rd KW10 6ST
☎ 01408 633266 📠 01408 633393
e-mail: info@golspie-golf-club.co.uk
**Founded in 1889, Golspie's seaside course offers easy
walking and natural hazards including beach heather
and whins. Spectacular scenery.**
18 holes, 5980yds, Par 68, SSS 68, Course record 64.
Club membership 300.
Visitors all week, contact in advance. **Societies** contact in
advance. **Cards** 🔲 🔲 ⚡
Course Designer James Braid **Facilities** ⊗ 🏌 🏌 💺 ♀ ⛳
🏠 🍴 ⚡ **Location** 0.5m S off A9

....
Hotel ★★★ 73% Royal Marine Hotel, Golf Rd, BRORA
☎ 01408 621252 22 en suite

GRANTOWN-ON-SPEY   Map 14 NJ02

Grantown-on-Spey Golf Course Rd PH26 3HY
☎ 01479 872079 📠 01479 873725
e-mail: secretary@grantownonspeygolfclub.co.uk
**Parkland and woodland course. Part easy walking,
remainder hilly. The 7th to 13th holes really sort out
the golfers.**

18 holes, 5710yds, Par 70, SSS 68, Course record 60.
Club membership 800.
Visitors advisable to contact in advance. No visitors before
10am weekends. **Societies** clubhouse open Apr-Oct,

apply in advance to secretary. **Green Fees** terms on
application. **Cards** 🔲 🔲 🔲 🔲 🔲 ⚡ **Course Designer**
A Brown, W Park, J Braid **Facilities** ⊗ 🏌 by arrangement
🏌 💺 ♀ ⛳ 🏠 🍴 🏐 ⚡ **Location** NE side of town
centre

....
Hotel ★★ 79% Culdearn House, Woodlands Ter,
GRANTOWN ON SPEY ☎ 01479 872106
7 en suite

HELMSDALE   Map 14 ND01

Helmsdale Golf Rd KW8 6JA
☎ 01431 821063
**Sheltered, undulating course following the line of the
Helmsdale River.**
9 holes, 1860yds, Par 62, SSS 61.
Club membership 58.
Visitors no restrictions. **Societies** apply in writing or phone
in advance. **Green Fees** not confirmed. **Facilities** 💺
Location NW side of town on A896

....
Hotel ★★★ 73% Royal Marine Hotel, Golf Rd, BRORA
☎ 01408 621252 22 en suite

INVERGORDON   Map 14 NH76

Invergordon King George St IV18 0BD
☎ 01349 852715 📠 01349 852715
e-mail: invergordongolf@tiscali.co.uk
**Fairly easy but windy 18-hole parkland course, with
woodland, wide fairways and good views over
Cromarty Firth. Very good greens and a fair challenge,
especially if the wind is from the west. Four par 3s and
one par 5.**
18 holes, 6030yds, Par 69, SSS 69, Course record 63.
Club membership 240.
Visitors visitors advised to avoid Tue & Thu 4.30-6, Mon
& Wed 5-6 & Sat 8.30-10 & 1-2pm. **Societies** contact in
advance, call 01349 852715. **Green Fees** £25 per day; £20
per round. **Cards** 🔲 🔲 🔲 ⚡ **Course Designer** A Rae
Facilities 💺 💺 ♀ ⛳ 🍴 ⚡ **Location** W side of town
centre on B817

INVERNESS   Map 14 NH64

Inverness Culcabock IV2 3XQ
☎ 01463 239882 📠 01463 240616
e-mail: igc@freeuk.com
**Fairly flat parkland course with a burn running
through and alongside several of the holes, and also
acting as a lateral water hazard and out of bounds at
several. Considered short by modern day standards, it
is an excellent test of golf rewarding straight drives and
accurate iron play to well-manicured greens.**
18 holes, 6256yds, Par 69, SSS 70, Course record 64.
Club membership 1182.
Visitors booking & handicap certificate required. Limited
play Sat. Dress code in lounge/dining room. **Societies**
apply by phone or write in advance. **Green Fees** £42 per
day, £33 per round. **Cards** 🔲 🔲 🔲 🔲 ⚡ **Prof** Alistair
P Thomson **Course Designer** J Fraser, G Smith
Facilities ⊗ 🏌 💺 💺 ♀ ⛳ 🏠 🍴 ⚡ **Location** 1m E of
town centre on Culcabock Rd

....
Hotel ★★★★ 71% Inverness Marriott Hotel, Culcabock
Rd, INVERNESS ☎ 01463 237166 76 en suite 6 annexe
en suite

Continued

Loch Ness
Fairways, Castle Heather IV2 6AA
☎ 01463 713335 🖶 01463 712695
e-mail: info@golflochness.com
Challenging parkland course with superb views of Inverness, the Beauly Firth and the Black Isle. Built on a gentle slope but none of the holes play uphill. The signature hole is the 14th, only 76yds long, but there is nothing between the green and the tee except a deep gully with a burn at the bottom. The 2nd hole is the longest at over 550yds from the medal tees.

18 holes, 6772yds, Par 73, SSS 72, Course record 67. Club membership 500.
Visitors no restrictions Societies phone for details. Green Fees £25 per day (£30 weekends). Cards ⊞ ▤ ▩ 🔟 Prof Martin Piggot Course Designer Caddies Facilities ⊗ 〣 ⅃ ⚑ ⅄ 🛆 🛋 ⚑ 🍴 📍 🚿 📋 Leisure indoor bowls, petanque. Conf fac available Corporate Hospitality Days available Location SW outskirts of Inverness, along bypass

Hotel ★★★ 63% Loch Ness House Hotel, Glenurquhart Rd, INVERNESS ☎ 01463 231248 21 en suite

Torvean
Glenurquhart Rd IV3 8JN
☎ 01463 711434 (Starter) & 225651 (Office)
🖶 01463 711417
e-mail: info@torveangolfclub.com
Municipal parkland course, easy walking, good views. Boasts one of the longest par 5s in the north at 565yds. Three ponds come into play at the 8th, 15th and 17th holes.
18 holes, 5754yds, Par 69, SSS 68, Course record 64. Club membership 950.
Visitors Advance booking advisable especially at weekends. Societies advance bookings through starter. Green Fees £20 per 18 holes (£25 weekends). Cards ⊞ ▤ 🔟 Course Designer Hamilton Facilities ⊗ 〣 ⅃ ⚑ ⅄ 🛆 🛋 ⚑ 📍 Location 1.5m SW on A82

Hotel ★★★ 63% Loch Ness House Hotel, Glenurquhart Rd, INVERNESS ☎ 01463 231248 21 en suite

KINGUSSIE Map 14 NH70

Kingussie
Gynack Rd PH21 1LR
☎ 01540 661600 🖶 01540 662066
e-mail: kinggolf@globalnet.co.uk
Upland course with natural hazards and magnificent views. Stands about 1000ft above sea level at its highest point, and the River Gynack, which runs through the course, comes into play on five holes.
18 holes, 5500yds, Par 67, SSS 68, Course record 61. Club membership 800.
Visitors advisable to book in advance. Societies contact in advance. Green Fees £22 per round, £27 per day

(weekends £24/£30). Course Designer Vardon, Herd Facilities 〣 ⅃ ⚑ ⅄ 🛆 🛋 ⚑ 🚗 🚿 📍 Location 0.25m N off A86

Hotel 🏠 The Cross, Tweed Mill Brae, Ardbroilach Rd, KINGUSSIE ☎ 01540 661166 8 en suite

LOCHCARRON Map 14 NG83

Lochcarron
IV54 8YS
☎ 01520 722206
e-mail: mail@lochcarrongolf.co.uk
Seaside links course with some parkland with an interesting 1st hole. A short course but great accuracy is required.
9 holes, 3575yds, Par 60, SSS 60, Course record 58. Club membership 130.
Visitors Restricted Sat (club competitions) Societies welcome but restricted Sat 2-5pm. Green Fees £12 per day/ £50 per week. Facilities ⊗ 〣 ⅃ 🛆 ⚑ Location by A896, 1m E of Lochcarron

LYBSTER Map 15 ND23

Lybster
Main St KW3 6AE
☎ 01593 721486 & 721316
Picturesque, short heathland course, easy walking.
9 holes, 1896yds, Par 62, SSS 61, Course record 57. Club membership 140.
Visitors no restrictions. Societies contact in advance. Green Fees £10 per day. Facilities 🛆 Location E side of village

Hotel ★★ 70% Mackay's Hotel, Union St, WICK ☎ 01955 602323 27 rms (19 en suite)

MUIR OF ORD Map 14 NH55

Muir of Ord
Great North Rd IV6 7SX
☎ 01463 870825 🖶 01463 871867
e-mail: muirgolf@supanet.com-email
Long-established (1875) heathland course with tight fairways and easy walking. Testing par 3 13th, Castle Hill.
18 holes, 5596yds, Par 68, SSS 68, Course record 61. Club membership 750.
Visitors not during competitions. Booking required for weekends. Societies write to or phone Secretary Green Fees £18 per round/£22 per day (weekends £25/£30). Course Designer James Braid Facilities ⊗ by arrangement 〣 by arrangement 〣 ⅃ 🛆 🛋 ⚑ ⅄ 🚗 📍 Location S side of village on A862

Hotel ★★★ 72% Priory Hotel, The Square, BEAULY ☎ 01463 782309 34 en suite

NAIRN Map 14 NH85

Nairn
Seabank Rd IV12 4HB
☎ 01667 453208 🖶 01667 456328
e-mail: secretary@nairngolfclub.co.uk
18 holes, 6430yds, Par 71, SSS 73, Course record 64.
Newton: 9 holes, 3542yds, Par 58, SSS 57.
Course Designer A Simpson, Old Tom Morris, James Braid Location 16m E of Inverness on A96
Phone for further details

Booking a tee time is always advisable.

Continued

Nairn Dunbar Lochloy Rd IV12 5AE

☎ 01667 452741 📠 01667 456897

e-mail: secretary@nairndunbar.com

Links course with sea views and testing gorse and whin-ined fairways. Testing hole: Long Peter (527yds).

18 holes, 6765yds, Par 72, SSS 74, Course record 64.
Club membership 1200.

Visitors weekends restricted, contact in advance through Secretary's office. Societies contact in advance. Green Fees £55 per day; £40 per round (£65/£48 weekends). Cards 🌐 💳 💳 Prof David Torrance Facilities ⊗ 〗 🏌 🍴 ♨ ⛳ Conf fac available Corporate Hospitality Days available Location E side of town off A96

··

Hotel ★★ 58% Alton Burn Hotel, Alton Burn Rd, NAIRN
☎ 01667 452051 & 453325 📠 01667 456697
23 en suite

NETHY BRIDGE   Map 14 NJ02

Abernethy PH25 3EB

☎ 01479 821305 📠 01479 821305

e-mail: info@abernethygolfclub.com

Traditional Highland course built on moorland surrounded by pine trees and offering a great variety of shot making for the low handicapped or casual visitor. The 2nd hole, although very short is played across bogland and a B road to a two-tiered green. The small and fast greens are the most undulating and tricky in the valley. The Abernethy forest lies on the boundary and from many parts of the course there are splendid views of Strathspey.

9 holes, 2551yds, Par 66, SSS 66.
Club membership 450.

Visitors contact in advance. Societies contact in advance. Green Fees terms on application. Facilities ⊗ 🏌 ♨ ⛳ Location N side of village on B970

··

Hotel ★★★ ⚓ 71% Muckrach Lodge Hotel, Dulnain Bridge, GRANTOWN-ON-SPEY ☎ 01479 851257
8 en suite 4 annexe en suite

NEWTONMORE   Map 14 NN79

Newtonmore Golf Course Rd PH20 1AT

☎ 01540 673878 📠 01540 670147

e-mail: secretary@newtonmoregolf.com

Inland course beside the River Spey. Beautiful views and easy walking. Testing 17th hole (par 3).

18 holes, 6031yds, Par 70, SSS 69, Course record 64.
Club membership 420.

Visitors contact in advance. Societies apply in writing or by phone to secretary. Green Fees not confirmed. Prof Robert Henderson Facilities ⊗ 〗 🏌 ♨ ⛳ Location E side of town off A9

··

Hotel ★★ 71% The Scot House Hotel, Newtonmore Rd, KINGUSSIE ☎ 01540 661351 9 en suite

REAY   Map 14 NC96

Reay KW14 7RE

☎ 01847 811288 📠 01847 894189

e-mail: info@reaygolfclub.co.uk

Picturesque seaside links with natural hazards, following the contours of Sandside Bay. Most northerly 18-hole links on the British mainland. The 581yd par 5 5th hole Sahara requires a solid tee shot and fairway wood to set up an approach to a sheltered green

protected by a burn. The 196yd par 3 7th Pilkington is a beautiful short hole played across Reay burn to a raised green. The two-tiered 18th protected by its greenside bunkers provides a formidable finishing hole. Unique feature in that it opens and closes with a par 3 and the sea is visible from every hole. An excellent natural seaside links.

18 holes, 5831yds, Par 69, SSS 69, Course record 64.
Club membership 275.

Visitors restricted competition days Societies apply to the secretary in advance. Green Fees £20 per day/round.
Course Designer Braid Facilities ⊗ by arrangement 〗 by arrangement 🏌 by arrangement ♨ 🍴 ⛳
Leisure see web site. Conf Corporate Hospitality Days available Location 11m W of Thurso on A836

··

Hotel ★★★ 60% Royal Hotel, Traill St, THURSO
☎ 01847 893191 102 en suite

STRATHPEFFER   Map 14 NH45

Strathpeffer Spa IV14 9AS

☎ 01997 421219 & 421011 📠 01997 421011

e-mail: mail@strathpeffergolf.co.uk

Beautiful, testing upland course in this historic village. Many natural hazards mean only three sand bunkers on the course and the course's claim to fame is the 1st hole which features the longest drop from tee to green in Scotland. Stunning views.

18 holes, 4792yds, Par 65, SSS 64, Course record 60.
Club membership 400.

Visitors advisable to contact in advance. Societies apply in writing. Green Fees £23 per day; £18 per round. Cards 🌐 💳 💳 🅿 Course Designer Willie Park, Tom Morris
Facilities 🏌 ♨ 🍴 ⛳ Location 0.25m N of village off A834, signed

··

Hotel ★★★ 67% Achilty Hotel, CONTIN
☎ 01997 421355 9 en suite 2 annexe en suite

TAIN   Map 14 NH78

Tain Chapel Rd IV19 1JE

☎ 01862 892314 📠 01862 892099

e-mail: info@tain-golfclub.co.uk

Links course with a river affecting three holes; easy walking, fine views.

18 holes, 6404yds, Par 70, SSS 71, Course record 68.
Club membership 600.

Visitors weekends after 11.30am. Societies book in advance. Green Fees £44 per day, £36 per round (£54/£44 weekends). Cards 🌐 💳 💳 🅿 Course Designer Tom Morris Facilities ⊗ 〗 🏌 ♨ 🍴 ⛳ Conf Corporate Hospitality Days available Location E side of town centre off B9174

Continued

THURSO   Map 15 ND16

Thurso Newlands of Geise KW14 7XD
☎ 01847 893807
18 holes, 5853yds, Par 69, SSS 69, Course record 63.
Course Designer WS Stewart **Location** 2m SW of Thurso
on B874
Phone for further details
....

Hotel ★★★ 60% Royal Hotel, Traill St, THURSO
☎ 01847 893191 102 en suite

WICK   Map 15 ND35

Wick Reiss KW1 4RW
☎ 01955 602726
e-mail: wickgolfclub@hotmail.com
**Typical seaside links course, fairly flat, easy walking. Nine
holes straight out and straight back. Normally breezy.**
*18 holes, 6123yds, Par 69, SSS 71, Course record 63.
Club membership 352.*
Visitors no restrictions. **Societies** apply in writing or phone
in advance. **Green Fees** £20 per day. **Course Designer**
James Braid **Facilities** ⓑ ♥ ♀ ♙ ⚐ ♒ ⎛ **Conf** Corporate
Hospitality Days available **Location** 3.5m N off A9
....

Hotel ★★ 70% Mackay's Hotel, Union St, WICK
☎ 01955 602323 27 rms (19 en suite)

INVERCLYDE

GOUROCK   Map 10 NS27

Gourock Cowal View PA19 1HD
☎ 01475 631001 & 636834 (pro) 🖹 01475 638307
e-mail: adt@gourockgolfclub.freeserve.co.uk
18 holes, 6408yds, Par 73, SSS 72, Course record 64.
Course Designer J Braid, H Cotton **Location** SW side of
town off A770
Phone for further details
....

Hotel ⏏ Premier Travel Inn Greenock, 1-3 James Watt
Way, GREENOCK ☎ 08701 977120 40 en suite

GREENOCK   Map 10 NS27

Greenock Forsyth St PA16 8RE
☎ 01475 720793 🖹 01475 791912
18 holes, 5838yds, Par 69, SSS 69.
Course Designer James Braid **Location** SW side of town
off A770
Phone for further details
....

Hotel ⏏ Premier Travel Inn Greenock, 1-3 James Watt
Way, GREENOCK ☎ 08701 977120 40 en suite

Greenock Whinhill Beith Rd PA16 9LN
☎ 01475 724694 evenings & weekends only
18 holes, 5504yds, Par 68, SSS 68, Course record 64.
Location 1.5m SW off B7054
Phone for further details

KILMACOLM   Map 10 NS36

Kilmacolm Porterfield Rd PA13 4PD
☎ 01505 872139 🖹 01505 874007
e-mail: secretary@kilmacolmgolf.com
**Moorland course, easy walking, fine views. Testing 7th,
13th and 14th holes.**

*18 holes, 5961yds, Par 69, SSS 69, Course record 64.
Club membership 850.*
Visitors weekdays; contact in advance. **Societies** apply in
writing. **Green Fees** £30 per round/£40 per day. **Cards** 💳
💳 💳 💳 **Prof** Iain Nicholson **Course Designer** Willie
Campbell **Facilities** ⊗ ⌘ ⓑ ♥ ♀ ♙ ⚐ ♒ ⎛
Location SE side of town off A761
....

Hotel Ⓤ Gleddoch House Hotel, LANGBANK
☎ 01475 540711 39 en suite

PORT GLASGOW   Map 10 NS37

Port Glasgow Devol Rd PA14 5XE
☎ 01475 704181 & 791214 (Sec)
18 holes, 5712yds, Par 68, SSS 68.
Location 1m S
Phone for further details
....

Hotel Ⓤ Gleddoch House Hotel, LANGBANK
☎ 01475 540711 39 en suite

MIDLOTHIAN

BONNYRIGG   Map 11 NT36

Broomieknowe 36 Golf Course Rd EH19 2HZ
☎ 0131 663 9317 🖹 0131 663 2152
e-mail: administrator@broomieknowe.com
**Easy walking mature parkland course laid out by Ben
Sayers and extended by James Braid. Elevated site with
excellent views.**
18 holes, 6150yds, Par 70, SSS 70, Course record 65.
Visitors contact in advance. **Societies** contact for details.
Green Fees terms on application. **Prof** Mark Patchett
Course Designer B Sayers, J Braid **Facilities** ⊗ ⌘ ⓑ ♥
♀ ♙ ⚐ ♒ ⎛ **Conf** Corporate Hospitality Days available
Location 0.5m NE off B704
....

Hotel ★★★ 75% Dalhousie Castle and Aqueous Spa,
Bonnyrigg, EDINBURGH ☎ 01875 820153 27 en suite
6 annexe en suite

DALKEITH   Map 11 NT36

Newbattle Abbey Rd EH22 3AD
☎ 0131 663 2123 & 0131 663 1819 🖹 0131 654 1810
e-mail: mail@newbattlegolfclub.com
**Gently undulating parkland course, dissected by the
South Esk river and surrounded by woods.**
*18 holes, 6025yds, Par 69, SSS 69, Course record 61.
Club membership 700.*
Visitors Mon-Fri before 4pm. **Societies** welcome
weekdays ex public holidays, before 4pm. **Green Fees** £30
per day; £20 per round. **Prof** Scott McDonald **Course
Designer** S Colt **Facilities** ⊗ ⌘ ⓑ ♥ ♀ ♙ ⚐ ♒ ⎛
Conf Corporate Hospitality Days available
Location SW side of town off A68
....

Hotel ★★★ 75% Dalhousie Castle and Aqueous Spa,
Bonnyrigg, EDINBURGH ☎ 01875 820153 27 en suite
6 annexe en suite

GOREBRIDGE   Map 11 NT36

Vogrie Vogrie Estate Country Park EH23 4NU
☎ 01875 821986
9 holes, 2530yds, Par 33.
Location off B6372
Phone for further details

Continued

PENICUIK   Map 11 NT25

Glencorse Milton Bridge EH26 0RD
☎ 01968 677189 & 676481 🖹 01968 674399
Picturesque parkland course with a burn affecting 10 holes. Testing 5th hole (237yds) par 3.

18 holes, 5217yds, Par 64, SSS 66, Course record 60.
Club membership 700.
Visitors contact secretary, unable to play during club competitions **Societies** contact secretary for details.
Green Fees £32 per day, £25 per round. **Prof** Cliffe Jones
Course Designer Willie Park **Facilities** ⊗ Ⅲ 🄱 🖥 ♀ ⚒ 🏌 🛒 ⚘ **Location** 1.5m N of Penicuik on A701

Inn ♦♦♦ Olde Original Rosslyn Inn, 4 Main St, ROSLIN
☎ 0131 440 2384 6 en suite

MORAY

BUCKIE   Map 15 NJ46

Buckpool Barhill Rd, Buckpool AB56 1DU
☎ 01542 832236 🖹 01542 832236
e-mail: golf@buckpoolgolf.com
Links course with superlative view over Moray Firth, easy walking.
18 holes, 6097yds, Par 70, SSS 69, Course record 63.
Club membership 430.
Visitors parties please apply in advance. **Societies** apply in advance. **Green Fees** £23 per day, £18 per round weekends £28/£23). **Course Designer** JH Taylor
Facilities ⊗ Ⅲ 🄱 🖥 ♀ ⚒ ⚘ **Leisure** squash, snooker. **Location** off A98

Hotel ★★★ 67% The Seafield Hotel, Seafield St,
CULLEN ☎ 01542 840791 19 en suite

Strathlene Portessie AB56 2DJ
☎ 01542 831798 🖹 01542 831798
e-mail: strathgolf@ukonline.co.uk
Raised seaside links course with magnificent view. A special feature of the course is approach shots to raised greens (holes 4, 5, 6 and 13).
18 holes, 5980yds, Par 69, SSS 69, Course record 65.
Club membership 370.
Visitors booking essential at weekends. Contact professional at shop or training facility on arrival or in advance by phone. **Societies** phone for Mon-Fri & apply in writing for weekends. **Green Fees** not confirmed. **Prof** Brian Slorach **Course Designer** George Smith **Facilities** ⊗ 🄱 🖥 ♀ ⚒ 🖰 🏌 ⚘ ℓ **Conf** Corporate Hospitality Days available **Location** 2m E of Buckie on A942

Hotel ★★★ 67% The Seafield Hotel, Seafield St,
CULLEN ☎ 01542 840791 19 en suite

CULLEN   Map 15 NJ56

Cullen The Links AB56 4WB
☎ 01542 840685
e-mail: cullengolfclub@btinternet.com
Interesting links on two levels with rocks and ravines offering some challenging holes. Spectacular scenery.
18 holes, 4610yds, Par 63, SSS 62, Course record 58.
Club membership 500.
Visitors no restrictions but during summer club medal matches given preference on Mon/Wed/Sat. Book tee times advisable. **Societies** advance applications advisable. **Green Fees** Mon-Fri: £16 per round. **Cards** 🔲 🔲 🔲 🄱 **Course Designer** Tom Morris, Charlie Neaves **Facilities** ⊗ ⅢΙ 🄱 🖥 ♀ ⚒ 🏌 ⚘ **Conf** Corporate Hospitality Days available **Location** 0.5m W off A98

Hotel ★★★ 67% The Seafield Hotel, Seafield St,
CULLEN ☎ 01542 840791 19 en suite

DUFFTOWN   Map 15 NJ34

Dufftown Tomintoul Rd AB55 4BS
☎ 01340 820325 🖹 01340 820325
e-mail: marion_dufftowngolfclub@yahoo.com
A short and undulating inland course with spectacular views. The tee of the highest hole, the 9th, is over 1200ft above sea level.
18 holes, 5308yds, Par 67, SSS 67, Course record 64.
Club membership 250.
Visitors tee reserved Tue, Wed 4.30-6.30, Sun 7.30-9, 12.30-2; booking recommended. **Societies** apply in writing or by phone **Green Fees** £15 per round, £20 per day.
Course Designer Members **Facilities** ⊗ by arrangement ⅢΙ by arrangement 🄱 by arrangement 🖥 by arrangement ♀ ⚒ 🏌 🛒 ⚘ **Conf** fac available Corporate Hospitality Days available **Location** 0.75m SW off B9009

Hotel ★★★ 78% Craigellachie Hotel, CRAIGELLACHIE
☎ 01340 881204 25 en suite

ELGIN   Map 15 NJ26

Elgin Hardhillock, Birnie Rd, New Elgin IV30 8SX
☎ 01343 542338 🖹 01343 542341
e-mail: secretary@elgingolfclub.com
Possibly the finest inland course in the north of Scotland, with undulating greens and compact holes that demand the highest accuracy. There are 13 par 4s and one par 5 hole on its parkland layout, eight of the par 4s being over 400yds long.
Hardhillock: 18 holes, 6416yds, Par 68, SSS 69,
Course record 63.
Club membership 1000.
Visitors contact in advance; weekend by arrangement only. **Societies** phone secretary for details. **Green Fees** £40 per day, £30 per round. **Cards** 🔲 🔲 🔲 🄱 🔲 🄱 **Prof** Kevin Stables **Course Designer** John Macpherson
Facilities ⊗ ⅢΙ 🄱 🖥 ♀ ⚒ 🖰 🏌 🛒 ⚘ ℓ
Conf fac available **Location** 1m S on A941

Hotel ★★★ 74% Mansion House Hotel, The Haugh,
ELGIN ☎ 01343 548811 23 en suite

Continued

FORRES
Map 14 NJ05

Forres Muiryshade IV36 2RD
☎ 01309 672250 🖺 01309 672250
e-mail: sandy@forresgolf.demon.co.uk
An all-year parkland course laid on light, well-drained soil in wooded countryside. Walking is easy despite some hilly holes. A test for the best golfers.
18 holes, 6240yds, Par 70, SSS 70, Course record 60.
Club membership 1000.
Visitors welcome although club competitions take priority. Weekends may be restricted in summer. **Societies** advised to phone 2-3 weeks in advance. **Green Fees** £26 per round, £34 per day. **Cards** 🖃 🖃 🖾 💷 **Prof** Sandy Aird
Course Designer James Braid, Willie Park **Facilities** ⊗ ⦾ 🏋 🖢 🍴 ♀ ♨ 🏠 ⛳ 🚶 🛒 ⚲ **Conf** Corporate
Hospitality Days available **Location** SE side of town centre off B9010
....
Hotel ★★★ 68% Ramnee Hotel, Victoria Rd, FORRES
☎ 01309 672410 20 en suite

GARMOUTH
Map 15 NJ36

Garmouth & Kingston Spey St IV32 7NJ
☎ 01343 870388 🖺 01343 870388
e-mail: garmouthgolfclub@aol.com
Flat seaside course with several parkland holes and tidal waters. The 8th hole measures only 328yds from the medal tee but the fairway is bounded by a ditch on either side, the left hand one being out of bounds for the entire length of the hole. The par 5 17th Whinny Side has gorse bordering on both sides of the fairway which can be intimidating to any level of golfer.
18 holes, 5545yds, Par 69, SSS 67.
Club membership 500.
Visitors contact in advance. **Societies** advisable to phone in advance. **Green Fees** £25 per day, £20 per round (£25 weekends). **Cards** 🖃 🖃 🖾 💷 **Course Designer** George Smith **Facilities** ⊗ by arrangement ⦾ by arrangement 🏋 🖢 ♀ ♨ 🏠 ⛳ **Conf** Corporate Hospitality Days available **Location** in village on B9015
....
Hotel ★★★ 74% Mansion House Hotel, The Haugh, ELGIN ☎ 01343 548811 23 en suite

HOPEMAN
Map 15 NJ16

Hopeman Clubhouse IV30 5YA
☎ 01343 830578 🖺 01343 830152
e-mail: hopemangc@aol.com
Links-type course with beautiful views over the Moray Firth. The 12th hole, called the Priescach, is a short hole with a drop of 100ft from tee to green. It can require anything from a wedge to a wood depending on the wind.
18 holes, 5624yds, Par 68, SSS 67.
Club membership 700.
Visitors contact in advance, restricted tee times at weekend & 12.45-1.45 weekdays **Societies** contact in advance. **Green Fees** £18 per round (weekend £23). **Cards** 🖃 🖃 🖾 💷 **Facilities** ⊗ ⦾ 🏋 🖢 ♀ ♨ 🏠 ⛳
Location E side of village off B9040
....
Hotel ★★★ 74% Mansion House Hotel, The Haugh, ELGIN ☎ 01343 548811 23 en suite

KEITH
Map 15 NJ45

Keith Fife Park AB55 5DF
☎ 01542 882469 🖺 01542 888176
e-mail: secretary@keithgolfclub.org.uk
18 holes, 5767yds, Par 69, SSS 68, Course record 65.
Course Designer Roy Phimister **Location** NW of town centre, A96 onto B9014 & 1st right
Phone for further details
....
Hotel ★★★ 78% Craigellachie Hotel, CRAIGELLACHIE
☎ 01340 881204 25 en suite

LOSSIEMOUTH
Map 15 NJ27

Moray Stotfield Rd IV31 6QS
☎ 01343 812018 🖺 01343 815102
e-mail: secretary@moraygolf.co.uk
Two fine Scottish Championship links courses, known as Old and New (Moray), and situated on the Moray Firth where the weather is unusually mild.
Old: 18 holes, 6643yds, Par 71, SSS 73, Course record 65.
New: 18 holes, 6004yds, Par 69, SSS 69, Course record 62.
Club membership 1550.
Visitors contact in advance 01343 812018 Secretary. **Societies** Contact in advance. **Green Fees** terms on applications. **Cards** 🖃 🖃 🖾 💷 **Prof** Alistair Thomson **Course Designer** Tom Morris **Facilities** ⊗ ⦾ 🏋 🖢 ♀ ♨ 🏠 ⛳ 🚶 🛒 ⚲ **Conf** Corporate Hospitality Days available **Location** N side of town
....
Hotel ★★★ 74% Mansion House Hotel, The Haugh, ELGIN ☎ 01343 548811 23 en suite

ROTHES
Map 15 NJ24

Rothes Blackhall AB38 7AN
☎ 01340 831443 (evenings) 🖺 01340 831443
e-mail: rothesgolfclub@netscapeonline.co.uk
9 holes, 4972yds, Par 68, SSS 64.
Course Designer John Souter **Location** SW of town centre
Phone for further details
....
Hotel ★★★ 78% Craigellachie Hotel, CRAIGELLACHIE
☎ 01340 881204 25 en suite

SPEY BAY
Map 15 NJ36

Spey Bay IV32 7PJ
☎ 01343 820424 🖺 01343 829282
e-mail: info@speybay.com
Picturesque, undulating links with a long beach on one side. The fairways are lined with swathes of gorse and heather while shingle and beach form a border at some holes. Each hole requires a good deal of thought from the tee and a deft touch around the greens.
18 holes, 6182yds, Par 70, SSS 70, Course record 65.
Club membership 350.
Visitors phone for details (especially for Sun) **Societies** book by phone. **Green Fees** £25 per round (£30 weekends). **Cards** 🖃 🖾 💷 **Course Designer** Ben Sayers **Facilities** ⊗ ⦾ 🏋 🖢 ♀ ♨ 🏠 ⛳ 🚶 🛒 ⚲ 🍸 **Conf** fac available Corporate Hospitality Days available
Location 4.5m N of Fochabers on B9104

NORTH AYRSHIRE

BEITH   Map 10 NS35

Beith Threepwood Rd KA15 2JR
☎ 01505 503166 & 506814 📠 01505 506814
e-mail: bgc-secretary@hotmail.com
Hilly course, with panoramic views over seven
counties.

9 holes, 5616yds, Par 68, SSS 68.
Club membership 620.
Visitors contact for details. Societies apply in writing to
secretary at least 1 month in advance. Green Fees not
confirmed. Course Designer Members Facilities ⊗ ⅢⅢ ᴸ
ᵂ ♀ ᴸ Location 1.5m NE of town off A737 Beith
bypass

Guesthouse ♦♦♦♦ Whin Park, 16 Douglas St, LARGS
☎ 01475 673437 5 en suite

GREAT CUMBRAE ISLAND   Map 10 NS15
(MILLPORT)

Millport Golf Rd KA28 OHB
☎ 01475 530305 (Prof) 📠 01475 530306
e-mail: secretary@millportgolfclub.co.uk
Pleasantly situated on the west side of Cumbrae looking
over Bute to Arran and the Mull of Kintyre. Exposed
conditions can vary according to wind strength and
direction. A typical seaside resort course.
18 holes, 5828yds, Par 68, SSS 69, Course record 64.
Club membership 460.
Visitors advisable to phone & book tee times especially in
summer. Societies phone or write in advance. Green Fees
not confirmed. Cards 💳 💳 🅿 Course Designer James
Braid Facilities ⊗ ⅢⅢ ᴸ ᵂ ♀ ᴸ 🏠 ✓ Location 4m from
ferry slip

Hotel ★★ 69% Willowbank Hotel, 96 Greenock Rd,
LARGS ☎ 01475 672311 & 675435 📠 01475 689027
30 en suite

IRVINE   Map 10 NS34

Glasgow Gailes KA11 5AE
☎ 0141 942 2011 📠 0141 942 0770
e-mail: secretary@glasgow-golf.com
A lovely seaside links. The turf of the fairways and all
the greens is truly glorious and provides tireless play.
Established in 1882, this is a qualifying course for the
Open Championship.
18 holes, 6535yds, Par 71, SSS 72, Course record 63.
Club membership 1200.

Continued

Visitors booking through secretary recommended; not
before 2.30pm Sat-Sun. Societies initial contact by phone.
Green Fees £70 per day, £55 per round (£60 per round
weekends). Cards 💳 💳 💳 🅿 Prof J Steven Course
Designer W Park Jnr Facilities ⊗ ⅢⅢ by arrangement ᴸ
ᵂ ♀ ᴸ 🏠 🍴 ⅋ 🚜 ✓ Conf Corporate Hospitality Days
available Location off A78 at Newhouse junct, S of
Irvine

Hotel ★★★ 69% Montgreenan Mansion House Hotel,
Montgreenan Estate, KILWINNING ☎ 01294 557733
21 en suite

Irvine Bogside KA12 8SN
☎ 01294 275979 📠 01294 278209
e-mail: secretary@theirvinegolfclub.co.uk
Testing links course; only two short holes.
18 holes, 6400yds, Par 71, SSS 73, Course record 65.
Club membership 450.
Societies are welcome weekdays & pm weekends, phone
in advance. Green Fees terms on application. Cards 💳
💳 Prof Jim McKinnon Course Designer James Braid
Facilities ⊗ ⅢⅢ ᴸ ᵂ ♀ ᴸ 🏠 ✓ Location N side of town
off A737

Hotel ★★★ 69% Montgreenan Mansion House Hotel,
Montgreenan Estate, KILWINNING ☎ 01294 557733
21 en suite

Irvine Ravenspark 13 Kidsneuk Ln KA12 8SR
☎ 01294 271293
e-mail: secretary@irgc.co.uk
Parkland course.
18 holes, 6457yds, Par 71, SSS 71, Course record 65.
Club membership 600.
Visitors not Sat before 2pm. Societies not Sat before 3pm,
contact club steward in advance. Green Fees not
confirmed. Prof Peter Bond Facilities ⊗ ⅢⅢ ᴸ ᵂ ♀ ᴸ
🏠 ✓ Location N side of town on A737

Hotel ★★★ 69% Montgreenan Mansion House Hotel,
Montgreenan Estate, KILWINNING ☎ 01294 557733
21 en suite

Western Gailes Gailes by Irvine KA11 5AE
☎ 01294 311649 📠 01294 312312
e-mail: enquiries@westerngailes.com
A magnificent seaside links with glorious turf and
wonderful greens. The view is open across the Firth of
Clyde to the neighbouring islands. It is a well-balanced
course crossed by three burns. There are two par 5s,
the 6th and 14th, and the 11th is a testing 445yd par 4
dog-leg.
18 holes, 6639yds, Par 71, SSS 74, Course record 65.
Visitors welcome Mon, Wed, Fri. Must contact in advance.
Limited number of times on Sun pm must reserve in
advance Societies Mon, Wed, Fri, Sun pm, contact in
advance. Green Fees £95 per 18 holes, £140 per 36 holes
(both including lunch); £100 Sun (no lunch). Cards 💳
💳 💳 🅿 Facilities ⊗ ⅢⅢ by arrangement ᴸ ᵂ ♀ ᴸ 🏠
✓ Conf Corporate Hospitality Days available
Location 2m S off A737

Hotel ★★★ 69% Montgreenan Mansion House Hotel,
Montgreenan Estate, KILWINNING ☎ 01294 557733
21 en suite

KILBIRNIE

Map 10 NS35

Kilbirnie Place Largs Rd KA25 7AT
☎ 01505 684444 & 683398
e-mail: kilbirnie.golfclub@tiscali.co.uk
Easy walking parkland course. The fairways are generally narrow and burns come into play on five holes.
18 holes, 5543yds, Par 69, SSS 67, Course record 65. Club membership 578.
Visitors contact in advance; not Sat or on competition days. **Societies** phone in advance **Green Fees** £25 per round (£35 Sun). **Facilities** ⊗ ℳ ㏒ ♥ ♀ ⚲ **Conf** Corporate Hospitality Days available **Location** 1m W from Kilbirnie Cross on A760

Hotel ★★ 69% Willowbank Hotel, 96 Greenock Rd, LARGS ☎ 01475 672311 & 675435 🖹 01475 689027 30 en suite

LARGS

Map 10 NS25

Largs Irvine Rd KA30 8EU
☎ 01475 673594 🖹 01475 673594
e-mail: secretary@largsgolfclub.co.uk
A parkland, tree-lined course with views to the Clyde coast and the Arran Isles.
18 holes, 6140yds, Par 70, SSS 71, Course record 63. Club membership 850.
Visitors not competition days. Other times by arrangement with secretary. **Societies** apply in writing. **Green Fees** terms on application. **Cards** 🎴 🎴 🗗 **Prof** Kenneth Docherty **Course Designer** H Stutt **Facilities** ⊗ ℳ ㏒ ♥ ♀ ⚲ 🏠 ⚐ ⚸ **Location** 1m S of town centre on A78

Hotel ★★ 69% Willowbank Hotel, 96 Greenock Rd, LARGS ☎ 01475 672311 & 675435 🖹 01475 689027 30 en suite

Routenburn Routenburn Rd KA30 8QA
☎ 01475 673230 & 686475
Heathland course with fine views over the Firth of Clyde.
18 holes, 5675yds, Par 68, SSS 68, Course record 63. Club membership 450.
Visitors no restrictions. Visitors may request a tee off time, contact Professional (01475 687240) **Societies** apply in writing. **Green Fees** terms on application. **Cards** 🎴 **Prof** J Grieg McQueen **Course Designer** J Braid **Facilities** ⊗ ℳ ㏒ ♥ ♀ ⚲ ⚸ **Conf** Corporate Hospitality Days available **Location** 1m N off A78

Hotel ★★ 69% Willowbank Hotel, 96 Greenock Rd, LARGS ☎ 01475 672311 & 675435 🖹 01475 689027 30 en suite

SKELMORLIE

Map 10 NS16

Skelmorlie Beithglass PA17 5ES
☎ 01475 520152 🖹 01475 521902
e-mail: sec@skelmorliegolf.co.uk
Parkland and moorland course with magnificent views over the Firth of Clyde.
18 holes, 5030yds, Par 65, SSS 65, Course record 63. Club membership 450.
Visitors not before 3pm Sat. **Societies** apply by phone. **Green Fees** terms on application. **Course Designer** James Braid **Facilities** ⊗ by arrangement ℳ by arrangement ㏒ by arrangement ♥ ♀ ⚲ ⚸ **Leisure** fishing. **Location** E side of village off A78

Continued

Hotel ★★ 69% Willowbank Hotel, 96 Greenock Rd, LARGS ☎ 01475 672311 & 675435 🖹 01475 689027 30 en suite

STEVENSTON

Map 10 NS24

Ardeer Greenhead KA20 4LB
☎ 01294 464542 & 465316 🖹 01294 465316
e-mail: peewee_watson@lineone.net
Parkland course with natural hazards, including several water features.
18 holes, 6401yds, Par 72, SSS 71, Course record 66. Club membership 650.
Visitors not Sat. Must contact in advance. **Societies** contact in advance. Special rates for parties of 12 or more. **Green Fees** £40 per day; £25 per round (£50/£35 Sun). **Course Designer** Stutt **Facilities** ⊗ ㏒ ♥ ♀ ⚲ 🏠 ⚐ ⚸ **Leisure** snooker. **Conf** fac available Corporate Hospitalit Days available **Location** 0.5m N off A78

Hotel ★★★ 69% Montgreenan Mansion House Hotel, Montgreenan Estate, KILWINNING ☎ 01294 557733 21 en suite

WEST KILBRIDE

Map 10 NS24

West Kilbride 33-35 Fullerton Dr, Seamill KA23 9HT
☎ 01294 823911 🖹 01294 829573
e-mail: golf@westkilbridegolfclub.com
Seaside links course on the Firth of Clyde, with fine views of Isle of Arran from every hole.
18 holes, 5974yds, Par 70, SSS 70, Course record 63. Club membership 840.
Visitors not weekends or bank holidays, must contact in advance. **Societies** Tue & Thu only; must contact in advance. **Green Fees** £33 per round, £43 per day. **Cards** 🎴 **Prof** Graham Ross **Course Designer** James Braid **Facilities** ⊗ ℳ ㏒ ♥ ♀ ⚲ 🏠 ⚐ **Location** W side of town off A78

Hotel ★★ 69% Willowbank Hotel, 96 Greenock Rd, LARGS ☎ 01475 672311 & 675435 🖹 01475 689027 30 en suite

NORTH LANARKSHIRE

AIRDRIE

Map 11 NS76

Airdrie Rochsoles ML6 0PQ
☎ 01236 762195
18 holes, 6004yds, Par 69, SSS 69, Course record 63.
Course Designer J Braid **Location** 1m N on B802
Phone for further details

Hotel ★★★★ 69% The Westerwood Hotel, 1 St Andrews Dr, Westerwood, CUMBERNAULD ☎ 01236 457171 100 en suite

Easter Moffat Mansion House, Station Rd, Plains ML6 8NP
☎ 01236 842878 🖹 01236 842904
e-mail: secretary@emgc.org.uk
A challenging moorland and parkland course which enjoys good views of the Campsie and Ochil hills. Although fairways are generous, accurate placement from the tee is essential on most holes. The signature hole on the course, the 18th is a truly memorable par 3

Continue

ayed from an elevated tee, to a receptive green in
ont of the clubhouse.
*8 holes, 6221yds, Par 72, SSS 70, Course record 66.
lub membership 500.*
isitors not weekends. Societies contact in advance.
reen Fees £30 per day; £20 per round. Prof Graham
ing Facilities ⊗ ⅢⅢ ⅃⅃ 🍺 ♀ ⌂ 🏠 ✐ Location 2m E of
irdrie on A89

·····

otel ★★★★ 69% The Westerwood Hotel,
St Andrews Dr, Westerwood, CUMBERNAULD
☎ 01236 457171 100 en suite

·ELLSHILL   Map 11 NS76

·ellshill Community Rd, Orbiston ML4 2RZ
☎ 01698 745124 ▤ 01698 292576
ree-lined 18 holes situated in the heart of Lanarkshire
ear Strathclyde Park. First opened for play in 1905
ad extended in 1970. The first five holes are extremely
·emanding but are followed by the gentler birdie alley
·here shots can be recovered. The signature hole is the
·7th, a par 3 which involves a tricky tee shot from an
·evated tee to a small well-bunkered green with out of
·ounds on the right.
*8 holes, 6272yds, Par 70, SSS 69.
lub membership 700.*
isitors apply in writing in advance, not competition Sat &
·un. Societies apply in writing in advance. Green Fees not
·onfirmed. Facilities ⊗ ⅢⅢ ⅃⅃ 🍺 ♀ ⌂ Location 1m SE
·f A721

·····

·otel ⌂ Premier Travel Inn Glasgow (Bellshill),
·elziehill Farm, New Edinburgh Rd, BELLSHILL
☎ 08701 977106   40 en suite

·OATBRIDGE   Map 11 NS76

·rumpellier Drumpellier Av ML5 1RX
☎ 01236 424139 ▤ 01236 428723
·mail: administrator@drumpelliergc.freeserve.co.uk
·arkland course, rolling fairways and fast greens.
*·8 holes, 6227yds, Par 71, SSS 70, Course record 62.
lub membership 827.*
·isitors contact in advance; not Sat. Societies apply in
·dvance. Green Fees £40 per day, £30 per round. Cards
▥ 🔲 🔲 🔳 📧 Prof Jaimie Carver Course Designer
·Fernie Facilities ⊗ ⅢⅢ ⅃⅃ 🍺 ♀ ⌂ 🏠 ✐ 🎯 🦌 🚂 ✐
·onf fac available   Corporate Hospitality Days available
·ocation 0.75m W off A89

·····

·otel ★★★ 68% Bothwell Bridge Hotel, 89 Main St,
·OTHWELL ☎ 01698 852246   90 en suite

·UMBERNAULD   Map 11 NS77

·ullatur 1A Glen Douglas Dr G68 0DW
☎ 01236 723230 ▤ 01236 727271
·mail: carol.millar@dullaturgolf.com
*·arrickstone: 18 holes, 6204yds, Par 70, SSS 70, Course
·cord 68.
·ntonine: 18 holes, 5875yds, Par 69, SSS 68.*
·ourse Designer James Braid Location 1.5m N of A80 at
·umbernauld
·none for further details

·····

·otel ★★★★ 69% The Westerwood Hotel,
·St Andrews Dr, Westerwood, CUMBERNAULD
☎ 01236 457171 100 en suite

Palacerigg Palacerigg Country Park G67 3HU
☎ 01236 734969 & 721461 ▤ 01236 721461
e-mail: palacerigg-golfclub@lineone.net
**Well-wooded parkland course set in Palacerigg
Country Park with good views to the Campsie Hills.**
*18 holes, 6444yds, Par 72, SSS 71, Course record 65.
Club membership 300.*
Visitors anytime except club competitions, advance
booking advisable. Societies apply in writing or by e-mail
to the Secretary. Green Fees £8 per round, £12 per day
(weekend £10 per round). Course Designer Henry Cotton
Facilities ⊗ ⅢⅢ ⅃⅃ 🍺 ♀ ⌂ 🏠 ✐ 🦌 Location 2m SE of
Cumbernauld off B8054

·····

Hotel ★★★★ 69% The Westerwood Hotel,
1 St Andrews Dr, Westerwood, CUMBERNAULD
☎ 01236 457171 100 en suite

Westerwood Hotel 1 St Andrews Dr, Westerwood
G68 0EW
☎ 01236 457171 ▤ 01236 738478
e-mail: westerwood@morton-hotels.com
**Undulating parkland and woodland course designed by
Dave Thomas and Seve Ballastoros. Holes meander
through silver birch, firs, heaths and heather, and the
spectacular 15th, The Waterfall, has its green set
against a 40ft rockface. Buggie track.**

*18 holes, 6616yds, Par 72, SSS 72, Course record 65.
Club membership 1200.*
Visitors advised to book 24hrs in advance. Societies all
bookings in advance to 01236 725281. Green Fees Apr-
Oct £27.50 (£30 weekends), Nov-Mar £15. Cards ▥ ▨
▦ 🔳 📧 Prof Alan Tait Course Designer Seve
Ballastoros, Dave Thomas Facilities ⊗ ⅢⅢ ⅃⅃ 🍺 ♀ ⌂ 🏠
🎯 🍴 🦌 🚂 ✐ Leisure hard tennis courts, heated indoor
swimming pool, sauna, gymnasium, Beauty salon. Conf
fac available   Corporate Hospitality Days available
Location next to A80, 14m from Glasgow

·····

Hotel ★★★★ 69% The Westerwood Hotel,
1 St Andrews Dr, Westerwood, CUMBERNAULD
☎ 01236 457171 100 en suite

GARTCOSH   Map 11 NS66

Mount Ellen Johnston Rd G69 8EY
☎ 01236 872277 ▤ 01236 872249
**Downland course with 73 bunkers. Testing 10th
(Bedlay), 156yds, par 3.**
*18 holes, 5525yds, Par 68, SSS 67, Course record 67.
Club membership 500.*
Visitors may play Mon-Fri 9am-4pm. Must contact in
advance. Societies contact in advance. Green Fees terms
on application. Prof Iain Bilsborough Facilities ⅃⅃ 🍺 ♀
⌂ 🏠 🎯 🦌 ✐ Location 0.75m N off A752

Continued

Hotel ★★★★ 73% Millennium Hotel Glasgow, George Square, GLASGOW ☎ 0141 332 6711 117 en suite

KILSYTH   Map 11 NS77

Kilsyth Lennox Tak Ma Doon Rd G65 0RS
☎ 01236 824115 🖹 01236 823089
18 holes, 5912yds, Par 70, SSS 70, Course record 66.
Location N side of town off A803
Phone for further details

Hotel ★★★★ 69% The Westerwood Hotel,
1 St Andrews Dr, Westerwood, CUMBERNAULD
☎ 01236 457171 100 en suite

MOTHERWELL   Map 11 NS75

Colville Park New Jerviston House, Jerviston Estate, Merry St ML1 4UG
☎ 01698 265779 (pro) 🖹 01698 230418
18 holes, 6250yds, Par 71, SSS 70, Course record 63.
Course Designer James Braid **Location** 1.25m NE of Motherwell town centre on A723
Phone for further details

Hotel ★★★ 68% Bothwell Bridge Hotel, 89 Main St, BOTHWELL ☎ 01698 852246 90 en suite

MUIRHEAD   Map 11 NS66

Crow Wood Garnkirk House, Cumbernauld Rd G69 9JF
☎ 0141 779 1943 🖹 0141 779 9148
e-mail: crowwood@golfclub.fsbusiness.co.uk
Parkland course.
18 holes, 6261yds, Par 71, SSS 71, Course record 62.
Club membership 800.
Visitors contact in advance; not weekends, bank holidays or competition days. **Societies** apply in advance in writing. **Green Fees** not confirmed. **Cards** 🔳 🔳 **Prof** Brian Moffat **Course Designer** James Braid **Facilities** ⊗ ∭ ⅃ 🍺 🍴 ⅄ 🍴 🏌 **Leisure** snooker, pool. **Location** off A80 to Stirling, between Stepps & Muirhead

Hotel ★★★ 75% Malmaison, 278 West George St, GLASGOW ☎ 0141 572 1000 72 en suite

SHOTTS   Map 11 NS86

Shotts Blairhead ML7 5BJ
☎ 01501 822658 🖹 01501 822650
Moorland course with fine panoramic views. A good test for all abilities.
18 holes, 6205yds, Par 70, SSS 70, Course record 63.
Club membership 800.
Visitors booking required. **Societies** apply in writing. **Green Fees** not confirmed. **Prof** John Strachan **Course Designer** James Braid **Facilities** ⊗ ∭ ⅃ 🍺 ⅄ 🍴 🏌 **Location** 2m from M8 off Benhar Road

Hotel ★★★ 68% The Hilcroft Hotel, East Main St, WHITBURN ☎ 01501 740818 32 en suite

---

Looking for a new course? Always telephone ahead to confirm visitor arrangements.

WISHAW   Map 11 NS75

Wishaw 55 Cleland Rd ML2 7PH
☎ 01698 372869 (clubhouse) & 357480 (admin)
🖹 01698 356930
e-mail: jwdouglas@btconnect.com
Parkland course with many tree-lined fairways. Bunkers protect 17 of the 18 greens.
18 holes, 5999yds, Par 69, SSS 69, Course record 62.
Club membership 984.
Visitors contact in advance; not Sat. **Societies** apply in writing. **Green Fees** £22 per round, £32 per day (Sun £27/£37). **Prof** Stuart Adair **Course Designer** James Braid **Facilities** ⊗ ∭ ⅃ 🍺 ⅄ 🍴 🏌 **Location** NW side of town off A721

Hotel ★★★ 72% Popinjay Hotel, Lanark Rd, ROSEBANK ☎ 01555 860441 38 en suite

PERTH & KINROSS

ABERFELDY   Map 14 NN84

Aberfeldy Taybridge Rd PH15 2BH
☎ 01887 820535 🖹 01887 820535
e-mail: abergc@tiscali.com.uk
Founded in 1895, this flat, parkland course is situated by the River Tay near the famous Wade Bridge and Black Watch Monument, and enjoys some splendid scenery.
18 holes, 5283yds, Par 68, SSS 66, Course record 67.
Club membership 250.
Visitors are advised to book in advance especially at weekends. **Societies** contact in advance. **Green Fees** terms on application. **Cards** 🔳 🔳 🔳 **Course Designer** Soutars **Facilities** ⊗ ∭ ⅃ 🍺 ⅄ 🍴 🏌 **Location** N side of town centre

Hotel ★★★ 63% Moness House Hotel & Country Club, Crieff Rd, ABERFELDY ☎ 0870 443 1460 12 en suite

ALYTH   Map 15 NO24

Alyth Pitcrocknie PH11 8HF
☎ 01828 632268 🖹 01828 633491
e-mail: enquiries@alythgolfclub.co.uk
Windy, heathland course with easy walking.
18 holes, 6205yds, Par 71, SSS 71, Course record 64.
Club membership 1000.
Visitors advance booking advisable, handicap certificate required & dress etiquette must be observed. **Societies** phone in advance. **Green Fees** terms on application. **Cards** 🔳 🔳 🔳 **Prof** Tom Melville
Course Designer James Braid

Continued

cilities ⊗ ⚏ ⓛ ♨ ♀ ⚴ ⌂ ⋔ ⚑ ⛟ ⚐ ⵏ
nf fac available **Location** 1m E on B954

tel ★★★ 63% Angus Hotel, Wellmeadow,
AIRGOWRIE ☎ 01250 872455 81 en suite

rathmore Golf Centre Leroch PH11 8NZ
01828 633322 🖷 01828 633533
nail: enquiries@strathmoregolf.com
e Rannaleroch Course is set on rolling parkland and
ath with splendid views over Strathmore. The course
aid out in two loops of nine, which both start and
ish at the clubhouse. It is generous off the tee but
ware of the udulating, links-style greens. Among the
allenging holes is the 480yd 5th with a 180yd carry
er water from a high tee position. The nine-hole
itfie Links has been specially designed with
ginners, juniors and older golfers in mind.

nnaleroch Course: 18 holes, 6454yds, Par 72, SSS 72,
urse record 67.
tfie Links: 9 holes, 1719yds, Par 29, SSS 29.
ıb membership 537.
sitors no restrictions, advised to book in advance.
cieties contact in advance. **Green Fees** £26 per round
eekends £32); Leitfie £10 per round (weekend £11).
rds 💳 💳 💳 🄳 **Prof** Andy Lamb **Course Designer**
n Salvesen **Facilities** ⊗ ⚏ ⓛ ♨ ♀ ⚴ ⋔ ⛟ ⚐ ⵏ
nf Corporate Hospitality Days available
cation 2m SE of Alyth off B954

tel ★★★ 63% Angus Hotel, Wellmeadow,
AIRGOWRIE ☎ 01250 872455 81 en suite

JCHTERARDER   See page 359

JCHTERARDER   Map 11 NN91

chterarder Orchil Rd PH3 1LS
01764 662804 (sec) 🖷 01764 664423 (sec)
nail: secretary@auchterardergolf.co.uk
t parkland course, part woodland with pine, larch
d silver birch. It may be short but tricky with
ining dog-legs and guarded greens that require
uracy rather than sheer power. The 14th Punchbowl
e is perhaps the trickiest. A blind tee shot needs to be
accurately over the left edge of the cross bunker to a
g and narrow green - miss and you face a difficult
vnhill chip shot from deep rough.
holes, 5775yds, Par 69, SSS 68, Course record 61.
ıb membership 820.
itors contact professional/secretary in advance.
ieties contact in advance. **Green Fees** £24 per
nd/£35 per day (weekends £29/£45). **Prof** Gavin Baxter
ırse Designer Ben Sayers **Facilities** ⊗ ⚏ ⓛ ♨ ♀ ⚴

🏠 ⋔ ⚐ **Conf** Corporate Hospitality Days available
Location 0.75m SW on A824

Hotel ★★★★★ The Gleneagles Hotel,
AUCHTERARDER ☎ 01764 662231 270 en suite

BLAIR ATHOLL   Map 14 NN86

Blair Atholl Invertilt Rd PH18 5TG
☎ 01796 481407 🖷 01796 481292
**Parkland course; river runs alongside three holes, easy
walking.**
9 holes, 5816yds, Par 70, SSS 68, Course record 65.
Club membership 460.
Visitors apply in advance to avoid competition times.
Societies apply in writing. **Course Designer** Morriss **Facilities** ⊗ ⚏ ⓛ
♨ ♀ ⚴ ⋔ ⚐ **Location** 0.5m S off B8079

Hotel ★★ 74% Atholl Arms Hotel, Old North Rd, BLAIR
ATHOLL ☎ 01796 481205 30 en suite

BLAIRGOWRIE   Map 15 NO14

Blairgowrie Golf Course Rd, Rosemount PH10 6LG
☎ 01250 872622 🖷 01250 875451
e-mail: admin@blairgowrie-golf.co.uk
Two 18-hole heathland courses, also a nine-hole course.

*Rosemount Course: 18 holes, 6590yds, Par 72, SSS 73,
Course record 64.*
*Lansdowne Course: 18 holes, 6802yds, Par 72, SSS 73,
Course record 67.*
Wee Course: 9 holes, 2327yds, Par 32.
Club membership 1550.
Visitors contact in advance & have handicap certificate,
restricted Wed, Fri & weekends. **Societies** contact in
advance. **Green Fees** Rosemount: £65 per round;
Lansdowne: £50 per round. **Cards** 💳 💳 💳 🄳 **Prof**
Charles Dernie **Course Designer** J Braid, P Allis,
D Thomas, Old Tom Morris **Facilities** ⊗ ⚏ ⓛ ♨ ♀ ⚴ 🏠
⋔ ⚑ ⛟ ⚐ **Conf** Corporate Hospitality Days available
Location Off A93 Rosemount

Hotel ★★★ 63% Angus Hotel, Wellmeadow,
BLAIRGOWRIE ☎ 01250 872455 81 en suite

COMRIE   Map 11 NN72

Comrie Laggan Braes PH6 2LR
☎ 01764 670055
e-mail: enquiries@comriegolf.co.uk
Scenic highland course with two tricky par 3 holes.
9 holes, 6040yds, Par 70, SSS 70, Course record 62.
Club membership 350.
Visitors apply in advance (for party bookings);

Continued   Continued

not Mon & Tue after 4.30pm. **Societies** contact in advance.
Green Fees £20 per day, £16 per 18 holes, £10 per 9 holes
(£25/£20 weekends & bank holidays). **Course Designer**
Col Williamson **Facilities** ⊗ ⬛ ⚒ ⚑ ✓
Location E side of village off A85

....

Hotel ★★★ 68% The Four Seasons Hotel, Loch Earn, ST
FILLANS ☎ 01764 685333 12 en suite 6 annexe en suite

CRIEFF   Map 11 NN82

Crieff Ferntower, Perth Rd PH7 3LR
☎ 01764 652909 📄 01764 655096
e-mail: bookings@crieffgolf.co.uk
**Set in dramatic countryside, Crieff Golf Club was
established in 1891. The Ferntower championship
course has magnificent views over the Strathearn
valley and offers all golfers an enjoyable round.
The short nine-hole Dornoch course, which
incorporates some of the James Braid designed holes
from the original 18 holes, provides an interesting
challenge for juniors, beginners and others short of
time.**

*Ferntower Course: 18 holes, 6427yds, Par 71, SSS 72,
Course record 64.*
Dornock Course: 9 holes, 2372yds, Par 32.
Club membership 720.
Visitors contact professional in advance. **Societies** contact
professional in advance. **Green Fees** Ferntower weekday
per round Mar-Apr £23, May & Oct £26, Jun-Sep £28
(weekends £28/£33/£38); Dornock £9 per 9 holes, £14 for
18 holes. **Cards** 💳 💳 💳 **Prof** David Murchie **Course
Designer** James Braid **Facilities** ⊗ 📶 ⬛ ⬛ ⚒ ⚑ ✓
🔧 ✓ ℂ **Conf** Corporate Hospitality Days available
Location 0.5m NE on A85

....

Hotel ★★★ 74% Royal Hotel, Melville Square, COMRIE
☎ 01764 679200 11 en suite

DUNKELD   Map 11 NO04

Dunkeld & Birnam Fungarth PH8 0HU
☎ 01350 727524 📄 01350 728660
e-mail: richbrnc@aol.com
**Interesting and challenging course with spectacular
views of the surrounding countryside. The original
nine-hole heathland course is now augmented by an
additional nine holes of parkland character close to the
Loch of the Lowes.**
18 holes, 5511yds, Par 70, SSS 67, Course record 63.
Club membership 600.
Visitors contact in advance at weekends, public holidays,
or large parties during the week. **Societies** apply in writing
or phone. **Green Fees** not confirmed. **Cards** 💳 💳 💳

💳 ⬛ 📶 🔧 **Course Designer** DA Tod **Facilities** ⊗ 📶 ⬛
⬛ ⚒ ⚑ 🏠 ⚑ ✓ **Conf** Corporate Hospitality Days
available **Location** 1m N of village on A923

....

Hotel ★★★ 🏠 Kinnaird, Kinnaird Estate, DUNKELD
☎ 01796 482440 9 en suite

DUNNING   Map 11 NO0

Dunning Rollo Park PH2 0QX
☎ 01764 684747
**Parkland course with a series of stone built bridges
crossing a burn meandering over a large part of the
course.**
9 holes, 4836yds, Par 66, SSS 63, Course record 62.
Club membership 580.
Visitors Gents competitions Sat, Ladies Day Tue, no
restrictions otherwise. **Societies** contact in advance in
writing. **Green Fees** not confirmed. **Facilities** ⬛ ⚒ ⚑
Location 1.5m off A9, 4m N of Auchterarder on B9146

....

Hotel ★★★ 69% Lovat Hotel, 90 Glasgow Rd, PERTH
☎ 01738 636555 30 en suite

Whitemoss Whitemoss Rd PH2 0QX
☎ 01738 730300 📄 01738 730490
e-mail: info@whitemossgolf.com

18 holes, 5595yds, Par 68, SSS 68, Course record 63.
Course Designer Whitemoss Leisure **Location** off A9 at
Whitemoss Rd junct, 3m N of Gleneagles
Phone for further details

....

Hotel ★★ 76% Cairn Lodge, Orchil Rd,
AUCHTERARDER ☎ 01764 662634 10 en suite

GLENSHEE (SPITTAL OF)   Map 15 NO1

Dalmunzie Dalmunzie Estate PH10 7QG
☎ 01250 885226 📄 01250 885225
e-mail: enquiries@dalmunziecottages.com
**Well-maintained Highland course with difficult
walking. Testing short course with small but good
greens. One of the highest courses in Britain at 1200f**
9 holes, 2099yds, Par 30, SSS 30.
Club membership 91.
Visitors restricted Sun 10.30-11am. **Societies** advance
contact preferred. **Green Fees** £13 per day. **Course
Designer** Alistair Campbell **Facilities** ⊗ 📶 ⬛ ⬛ ⚒ 🏠
🏠 **Leisure** hard tennis courts, fishing. **Conf** fac availab
Corporate Hospitality Days available
Location 2m NW of Spittal of Glenshee

....

Hotel ★★ 74% Dalmunzie House Hotel, SPITTAL OF
GLENSHEE ☎ 01250 885224 19 rms (16 en suite)

Continued

Gleneagles Hotel

Perth & Kinross

Auchterarder

Map 11 NN91

The PGA Centenary Course, designed by Jack Nicklaus and James Braid, and launched in style in May 1993, has an American-Scottish layout with many water hazards, elevated tees and raised contoured greens. It is the selected venue for the Ryder Cup 2014. It has a five-tier tee structure, making it both the longest and shortest playable course at the resort, as well as the most accommodating to all standards of golfer. The King's Course, with its abundance of heather, gorse, raised greens and plateau tees, is set within the valley of Strathearn with the Grampian mountains spectacularly in view to the north. The shorter Queen's Course, with fairways lined with Scots pines and water hazards, is set within a softer landscape and is considered an easier test of golf. You can improve your game at the golf academy at Gleneagles, where the philosophy is that golf should be fun and fun in golf comes from playing better. A complete corporate golf package is available.

Gleneagles Hotel PH3 1NF
☎ 01764 662231 Fax 01764 662134
e-mail: resort.sales@gleneagles.com

King's Course: 18 holes, 6471yds, Par 70, SSS 73, Course record 60.
Queen's Course: 18 holes, 5965yds, Par 68, SSS 70, Course record 62.
PGA Centenary Course: 18 holes, 6551yds, Par 72, SSS 73, Course record 63.
Visitors 8-week advance booking required; advance payment to secure tee times. **Societies** phone, e-mail or fax. **Green Fees** May-Sept £110 before 3pm, £70 after 3pm, £40 after 5pm; reduced rates Oct-Apr. **Cards** ⚏ 💳 💳 💳 💳 💳 **Prof** Russell Smith **Course Designer** James Braid, Jack Nicklaus
Facilities ⊗ ⚎ ⚏ ⚐ ⚑ ⚒ ⚓ ⚔ ⚕ ⚖ ⚗ ⚘ ⚙
Leisure hard and grass tennis courts, outdoor and indoor heated swimming pools, squash, fishing, sauna, solarium, gymnasium, golf academy, horse riding, shooting, falconry, off road driving.
Conf fac available Corporate Hospitality Days available
Location 2m SW of Auchterarder off A823

....

Hotels

★★★★★ The Gleneagles Hotel, AUCHTERARDER

☎ 01764 662231 270 en suite

★★ 76% Cairn Lodge, Orchil Rd, AUCHTERARDER

☎ 01764 662634 Fax 01764 662866 10 en suite

★★★ 74% Huntingtower Hotel, Crieff Rd, PERTH

☎ 01738 583771 Fax 01738 583777 31 en suite
3 annexe en suite

KENMORE   Map 14 NN74

Kenmore PH15 2HN
☎ 01887 830226 📠 01887 829059
e-mail: golf@taymouth.co.uk
Testing course in mildly undulating natural terrain.
Beautiful setting by Loch Tay. The par 5 4th is 560yds
and only one of the par 4s, the 2nd, is under 400yds -
hitting from the tee out of a mound of trees down a
snaking banking fairway which encourages the ball to
stay on the fairway. The slightly elevated green is
surrounded by banks to help hold the ball on the green.
The fairways are generous and the rough short, which
tends to encourage an unhindered round.
9 holes, 6052yds, Par 70, SSS 69, Course record 67.
Club membership 200.
Visitors advance booking advisable. Societies phone in
advance. Green Fees not confirmed. Cards 💳 💳
Course Designer Robin Menzies Facilities ⊗ ⇞ ⅊ ♨ ♨ ⅊
⅊ 🏠 ⛳ ⋈ ⚲ ⚖ ∅ Leisure fishing.
Location on A827, beside Kenmore Bridge
....
Hotel ★★★ 67% Kenmore Hotel, The Square,
KENMORE ☎ 01887 830205 27 en suite 13 annexe
en suite

Taymouth Castle Taymouth Castle Estate PH15 2NT
☎ 01887 830228 📠 01887 830830
e-mail: taymouth@fishingnet.com
18 holes, 6066yds, Par 69, SSS 69, Course record 62.
Course Designer James Braid Location 1m E on A827,
5m W of Aberfeldy
Phone for further details
....
Hotel ★★★ 67% Kenmore Hotel, The Square,
KENMORE ☎ 01887 830205 27 en suite 13 annexe
en suite

KINROSS   Map 11 NO10

Green Hotel 2 The Muirs KY13 8AS
☎ 01577 863407 📠 01577 863180
e-mail: golf@green-hotel.com
Two interesting and picturesque parkland courses, with
easy walking. Many of the fairways are bounded by
trees and plantations. A number of holes, particularly
on the Blue Course, have views over Loch Leven to the
hills beyond. The 4th is a really challenging par 3. Some
holes have burns or ditches to catch the unwary while
those playing the 6th on the Red Course have to
negotiate a difficult pond, and the Blue's 11th fairway
has a pond on the left.

Red Course: 18 holes, 6256yds, Par 73, SSS 71.
Blue Course: 18 holes, 6438yds, Par 71, SSS 72.
Club membership 600.

Visitors advisable to contact in advance Societies contact
in advance. Green Fees £35 per day, £22 per round
(£45/£33 weekends). Cards 💳 💳 💳 🔲 Prof Stuart
Geraghty Course Designer Sir David Montgomery
Facilities ⊗ ⇞ ⅊ ⇞ ⅊ ⅊ 🏠 ⛳ ⋈ ⚲ ∅ Leisure hard
tennis courts, heated indoor swimming pool, squash,
fishing, sauna, four-sheet curling rink. Conf fac available
Corporate Hospitality Days available Location NE side of
town on B996
....
Hotel ★★★ 75% Green Hotel, 2 The Muirs, KINROSS
☎ 01577 863467 46 en suite

MILNATHORT   Map 11 NO1(

Milnathort South St KY13 9XA
☎ 01577 864069
e-mail: milnathortgolf@ukgateway.net
Undulating inland course with lush fairways and
excellent greens for most of the year. Strategically
placed copses require accurate tee shots. Different tee
and greens for some holes will make for more
interesting play.
9 holes, 5969yds, Par 71, SSS 69, Course record 62.
Club membership 575.
Visitors no restrictions. Societies advisable to book in
advance. Green Fees not confirmed. Facilities ⊗ ⇞ by
arrangement ⅊ ⅊ ⅊ ⚖ ∅ Location S side of town on
A922
....
Hotel ★★★ 75% Green Hotel, 2 The Muirs, KINROSS
☎ 01577 863467 46 en suite

Continued

MUTHILL   Map 11 NN81

Muthill Peat Rd PH5 2DA
☎ 01764 681523 📠 01764 681557
-mail: muthillgolfclub@lineone.net
A nine-hole course which, although short, requires
accurate shot making to match the SSS. The three
par 3s are all challenging holes with the 9th, a 205yd
shot to a small well-bunkered green making a fitting
end to nine holes characterised by great views and
springy well-maintained fairways.
9 holes, 4700yds, Par 66, SSS 63, Course record 62.
Club membership 370.
Visitors no restrictions phone in advance. **Societies** book
in advance. **Green Fees** not confirmed. **Course Designer**
in house **Facilities** ⊗ ⚑ 🍺 ⛿ ⚐ ♂ **Location** W side of
village off A822

Hotel ★★ 76% Cairn Lodge, Orchil Rd,
AUCHTERARDER ☎ 01764 662634 10 en suite

PERTH   Map 11 NO12

Craigie Hill Cherrybank PH2 0NE
☎ 01738 622644 (pro) 📠 01738 620829
-mail: golf@craigiehill.com
Slightly hilly, heathland course. Panoramic views of
Perth and the surrounding hills.
18 holes, 5386yds, Par 66, SSS 67, Course record 60.
Club membership 600.
Visitors Restricted access Sat. Phone up to three days in
advance. **Societies** contact in writing. Restricted play on
Sats. **Green Fees** £30 per day; £20 per round (£30/£25
weekends). **Prof** Kris Esson **Course Designer** Fernie,
Anderson **Facilities** ⊗ 🍴 ⚑ 🍺 ⚑ ⛿ 📷 ⚐ ♂
Conf fac available Corporate Hospitality Days available
Location 1m SW of city centre off A952

Hotel ★★★ 67% Queens Hotel, Leonard St, PERTH
☎ 01738 442222 50 en suite

King James VI Moncreiffe Island PH2 8NR
☎ 01738 445132 (secretary) & 632460 (pro)
📠 01738 445132
-mail: info@kjvigc.fsnet.co.uk
Parkland course, situated on island in the River Tay.
Easy walking.
18 holes, 6038yds, Par 70, SSS 69, Course record 62.
Club membership 650.
Visitors visitors restricted on competition days. Must
contact professional in advance for bookings; not Sat morn.
Societies book by phone. **Green Fees** terms on application.
Cards 💳 💷 **Prof** Andrew Crerar **Course Designer** Tom
Morris **Facilities** ⊗ ⚑ 🍺 ⚑ ⛿ 📷 ⚐ 🛒 ♂
Location SE side of city centre

Hotel ★★★ 67% Queens Hotel, Leonard St, PERTH
☎ 01738 442222 50 en suite

Murrayshall Country House Hotel Murrayshall,
Scone PH2 7PH
☎ 01738 552784 & 551171 📠 01738 552595
-mail: info@murrayshall.com
Murrayshall Course: 18 holes, 6441yds, Par 73, SSS 72.
Lyndoch Course: 18 holes, 5800yds, Par 69.
Course Designer Hamilton Stutt **Location** E side of
village off A94
Phone for further details

Murrayshall Country House Hotel & Golf Course
....

Hotel ★★★ 75% Murrayshall Country House Hotel &
Golf Course, New Scone, PERTH ☎ 01738 551171
27 en suite 14 annexe en suite

North Inch North Inch, off Hay St PH1 5PH
☎ 01738 636481
e-mail: es@pkc.gov.uk
An enjoyable short and often testing course
incorporating mature trees, open parkland with fine
views and attractive riverside. This ancient course has
recently been transformed by a new layout. This has
resulted in one or two more challenging holes. Situated
beside the Tay, this course offers both links and
parkland characteristics.
18 holes, 5442yds, Par 68, SSS 66, Course record 62.
Club membership 459.
Visitors advisable to phone in advance. **Societies** apply in
writing. **Green Fees** not confirmed.

Continued

Continued

Course Designer Tom Morris Facilities ⊗ ⅧⅢ ⅃ ⬛ ♀ ⚲
🏴 ⚙ Leisure squash. Location N of City

Hotel ★★★ 67% Queens Hotel, Leonard St, PERTH
🕾 01738 442222 50 en suite

PITLOCHRY   Map 14 NN95

Pitlochry Golf Course Rd PH16 5QY
🕾 01796 472792 📠 01796 473947
e-mail: pro@pitlochrygolf.co.uk
A varied and interesting heathland course with fine
views and posing many problems. Its SSS permits few
errors in its achievement.
18 holes, 5670yds, Par 69, SSS 69, Course record 63.
Club membership 450.
Societies contact in advance. Green Fees £35 per day, £24
per round (£45/£30 weekends). Cards 🌉 🌉 🌉 💷 Prof
Mark Pirie Course Designer Willy Fernie Facilities ⊗ ⅧⅢ
⅃ ⬛ ♀ ⚲ 🏠 🏴 ⚲ Location off A924 onto
Larchwood Rd

Hotel ★★★ 74% Pine Trees Hotel, Strathview Ter,
PITLOCHRY 🕾 01796 472121 20 en suite

ST FILLANS   Map 11 NN62

St Fillans South Loch Earn Rd PH6 2NJ
🕾 01764 685312 📠 01764 685312
9 holes, 6054yds, Par 69, SSS 69, Course record 73.
Course Designer W Auchterlonie Location E side of
village off A85
Phone for further details

Hotel ★★★ 68% The Four Seasons Hotel, Loch Earn, ST
FILLANS 🕾 01764 685333 12 en suite 6 annexe en suite

STRATHTAY   Map 14 NN95

Strathtay Lyon Cottage PH9 0PG
🕾 01887 840211
Very attractive Highland course in a charming location.
Steep in places but with fine views of surrounding hills
and the Tay valley.
9 holes, 4082yds, Par 63, SSS 63, Course record 61.
Club membership 280.
Visitors welcome, no restrictions Societies in writing or
phone Secretary. Green Fees £12 per day (£15 weekends
& bank holidays). Facilities ⬟ Location off A827, E of
village centre

Hotel ★★★ 63% Moness House Hotel & Country Club,
Crieff Rd, ABERFELDY 🕾 0870 443 1460 12 en suite

RENFREWSHIRE

BISHOPTON   Map 10 NS47

Erskine PA7 5PH
🕾 01505 862108 📠 01505 862302
e-mail: secretaryegc@belb.net
Parkland course on the south bank of the River Clyde,
with views of the river and hills beyond.
18 holes, 6287yds, Par 71, SSS 70.
Club membership 800.
Visitors not weekends. Societies apply in writing or phone
in advance Green Fees £31 per round/£42 per day. Prof
Peter Thomson Facilities ⊗ ⅧⅢ ⅃ ⬛ ♀ ⬟ 🏠 🏴 🦮 ⚲
Location 0.75 NE off B815

BRIDGE OF WEIR   Map 10 NS36

Old Course Ranfurly Ranfurly Place PA11 3DE
🕾 01505 613612 📠 01505 613214
e-mail: secretary@oldranfurly.com
A par 70 course that is both fun and challenging to
play. From the higher, moorland part of the course the
River Clyde comes into view and makes a spectacular
backdrop, with Ben Lomond and the Campsie Fells in
the distance.
18 holes, 6061yds, Par 70, SSS 70, Course record 63.
Club membership 819.
Visitors contact in advance; not weekends. Societies
advisable to contact in advance. Green Fees £35 per day,
£25 per round. Cards 🌉 🌉 🌉 💷 Prof S Thompson
Course Designer W Park Facilities ⊗ ⅧⅢ ⅃ ⬛ ♀ ⬟
Conf Corporate Hospitality Days available Location 6m S
of Glasgow Airport

Hotel ★★★ 70% Lynnhurst Hotel, Park Rd,
JOHNSTONE 🕾 01505 324331 & 324600
📠 01505 324219 21 en suite

Ranfurly Castle The Clubhouse, Golf Rd PA11 3HN
🕾 01505 612609 📠 01505 610406
e-mail: secranfur@aol.com
A picturesque, highly challenging 240-acre moorland
course.
18 holes, 6284yds, Par 70, SSS 71, Course record 65.
Club membership 825.
Visitors members on weekends only. Societies weekdays
only, apply in writing or phone in advance. Green Fees
£30 per round; £40 per day. Cards 🌉 🌉 🌉 💷
Prof Tom Eckford Course Designer A Kirkcaldy,
W Auchterlomie Facilities ⊗ ⅧⅢ ⅃ ⬛ ♀ ⬟ 🏠 🏴 🦮 ⚲
Location 5m NW of Johnstone

Hotel ⬧ Premier Travel Inn Glasgow (Paisley),
Phoenix Retail Park, PAISLEY 🕾 08701 977113
40 en suite

JOHNSTONE   Map 10 NS46

Cochrane Castle Scott Av, Craigston PA5 0HF
🕾 01505 320146 📠 01505 325338
Fairly hilly parkland course, wooded with two small
streams running through it.
18 holes, 6194yds, Par 71, SSS 71, Course record 63.
Club membership 721.
Visitors contact professional for booking, may play at
weekends if introduced by a member. Societies apply in
writing. Green Fees £30 per day; £22 per round. Prof Alan
J Logan Course Designer J Hunter Facilities ⊗ ⅧⅢ ⅃ ⬛
♀ ⬟ 🏠 ⚲ Location 1m from town centre, off Beith Rd

Hotel ★★★ 70% Lynnhurst Hotel, Park Rd,
JOHNSTONE 🕾 01505 324331 & 324600
📠 01505 324219 21 en suite

Elderslie 63 Main Rd, Elderslie PA5 9AZ
🕾 01505 323956 📠 01505 340346
e-mail: eldersliegolfclub@btconnect.com
Parkland course, undulating, with good views.
18 holes, 6175yds, Par 70, SSS 70, Course record 61.
Club membership 940.
Visitors not weekends & bank holidays. Must contact club
in advance & preferably have a handicap certificate.
Societies phone in advance. Green Fees £25 per round/£43
per day. Cards 🌉 🌉 🌉 💷 Prof Richard Bowman

Continued

Course Designer J Braid **Facilities** ⊗ ⟨⟨ ℍ ⬛ ♚ ⚐ ⚑ 🏌
Conf fac available **Location** E side of town on A737

Hotel ★★★ 70% Lynnhurst Hotel, Park Rd,
JOHNSTONE ☎ 01505 324331 & 324600
🖹 01505 324219 21 en suite

LANGBANK   Map 10 NS37

Gleddoch Golf and Country Club PA14 6YE
☎ 01475 540304 🖹 01475 540201
e-mail: golf@gleddochhouse.co.uk
18 holes, 6330yds, Par 71, SSS 71, Course record 64.
Course Designer Hamilton Strutt **Location** off B789 onto
Old Greenock Rd
Phone for further details

Hotel 🆄 Gleddoch House Hotel, LANGBANK
☎ 01475 540711 39 en suite

LOCHWINNOCH   Map 10 NS35

Lochwinnoch Burnfoot Rd PA12 4AN
☎ 01505 842153 & 01505 843029 🖹 01505 843668
**Well-maintained parkland course incorporating
natural burns. Throughout the course the majority of
fairways are wide with tricky greens, but always in
good condition. Very scenic with lots of bunkers.**
18 holes, 6243yds, Par 71, SSS 71, Course record 63.
Club membership 650.
Visitors not weekends & bank holidays unless
accompanied by member (check with pro shop). Restricted
during competition days. **Societies** apply in writing to club
administrator. **Green Fees** not confirmed. **Prof** Gerry
Reilly **Facilities** ⊗ ⟨⟨ ℍ ⬛ ♚ ⚐ ⚑ 🏌 🚲 🏌 **Conf** fac
available Corporate Hospitality Days available
Location W side of town off A760

Guesthouse ♦♦♦♦♦ East Lochhead, Largs Rd,
LOCHWINNOCH ☎ 01505 842610 3 en suite

PAISLEY   Map 11 NS46

Barshaw Barshaw Park PA1 3TJ
☎ 0141 889 2908
18 holes, 5703yds, Par 68, SSS 67, Course record 63.
Course Designer JR Stutt **Location** 1m E off A737
Phone for further details

Hotel ★★★ 70% Glynhill Hotel Leisure Club, Paisley Rd,
RENFREW ☎ 0141 886 5555 145 en suite

Paisley Braehead PA2 8TZ
☎ 0141 884 3903 884 2292 🖹 0141 884 3903
e-mail: paisleygc@onetel.com
**Moorland course with good views which suits all
handicaps. The course has been designed in two loops of
nine holes. Holes feature trees and gorse.**
18 holes, 6466yds, Par 71, SSS 72, Course record 64.
Club membership 850.
Visitors not Sat; handicap certificate; contact in advance.
Societies handicaps certificate essential. Groups over 12
must apply in writing, smaller groups may phone in
advance. **Green Fees** £38 per day; £26 per round. **Cards**
⊟ ▦ ▥ 🆂 **Prof** Gordon Stewart **Course Designer**
JR Stutt **Facilities** ⊗ ⟨⟨ ℍ ⬛ ♚ ⚐ ⚑ 🏌 🚲 🏌
Conf fac available **Location** S side of town off B774

Hotel ★★★ 70% Glynhill Hotel Leisure Club, Paisley Rd,
RENFREW ☎ 0141 886 5555 145 en suite

Ralston Strathmore Av, Ralston PA1 3DT
☎ 0141 882 1349 🖹 0141 883 9837
e-mail: joe@rolstongolf.co.uk
Parkland course.
18 holes, 6071yds, Par 71, SSS 69, Course record 62.
Club membership 750.
Visitors Mon-Fri only & must be accompanied by
member, contact in advance. **Societies** written notice
required **Green Fees** £32 per day; £20 per round. **Cards**
⊟ ▦ 🆂 **Prof** Colin Munro **Course Designer** J Braid
Facilities ⊗ ⟨⟨ ℍ ⬛ ♚ ⚐ ⚑ 🏌 **Conf** fac available
Corporate Hospitality Days available **Location** 2m E off
A737

Hotel 🆄 Premier Travel Inn Glasgow (Paisley), Phoenix
Retail Park, PAISLEY ☎ 08701 977113 40 en suite

RENFREW   Map 11 NS46

Renfrew Blythswood Estate, Inchinnan Rd PA4 9EG
☎ 0141 886 6692 🖹 0141 886 1808
e-mail: secretary@renfrew.scottishgolf.com
Tree-lined parkland course.
18 holes, 6818yds, Par 72, SSS 73, Course record 65.
Club membership 800.
Visitors restricted to Mon, Tue & Thu, apply in advance.
Societies apply in writing in advance. **Green Fees** £40 per
day; £30 per round. **Course Designer** Commander Harris
Facilities ⊗ ⟨⟨ ℍ ⬛ ♚ ⚐ ⚑ 🏌
Location 0.75m W off A8

Hotel ★★★ 70% Glynhill Hotel Leisure Club, Paisley Rd,
RENFREW ☎ 0141 886 5555 145 en suite

SCOTTISH BORDERS

COLDSTREAM   Map 12 NT83

Hirsel Kelso Rd TD12 4NJ
☎ 01890 882678 & 882233 🖹 01890 882233
e-mail: bookings@hirselgc.co.uk
**A beautifully situated parkland course set in the Hirsel
Estate, with panoramic views of the Cheviot Hills. Each
hole offers a different challenge especially the 7th, a
170yd par 3 demanding accuracy of flight and length
from the tee to ensure achieving a par.**
18 holes, 6111yds, Par 70, SSS 70, Course record 65.
Club membership 680.
Visitors contact for details, no restrictions. **Societies** write
or phone the secretary in advance. **Green Fees** £28 per day
(£34 weekends). **Cards** ⊟ ▦ ▥ 🆂 **Facilities** ⊗ ⟨⟨ ℍ
⬛ ♚ ⚐ ⚑ 🏌 🏌 🏌 🏌 **Conf** Corporate Hospitality Days
available **Location** At W end of Coldstream on A697

Hotel ★★★ 71% Ednam House Hotel, Bridge St, KELSO
☎ 01573 224168 30 en suite

DUNS   Map 12 NT75

Duns Hardens Rd TD11 3NR
☎ 01361 882194 🖹 01361 883599
e-mail: secretary@dunsgolfclub.com
**Interesting upland course, with natural hazards of
water and hilly slopes. Views south to the Cheviot Hills.
A burn comes into play at seven of the holes.**
18 holes, 6209yds, Par 70, SSS 70, Course record 67.
Club membership 426.
Visitors welcome except competition days & Mon, Tue &
Wed after 4pm. Advisable to contact in advance Apr-Oct.

Continued

Societies write or phone the secretary in advance for booking details. **Green Fees** not confirmed. **Course Designer** AH Scott **Facilities** ⊗ ⏐Ⅲ ⓑ 🎯 🝙 ⚑ 🛒 🛆 🏌️ 🛒 *⌀* **Conf** Corporate Hospitality Days available **Location** 1m W off A6105

....

Hotel ★★★ 70% Marshall Meadows Country House Hotel, BERWICK-UPON-TWEED ☎ 01289 331133 19 en suite

EYEMOUTH   Map 12 NT96

Eyemouth Gunsgreen Hill TD14 5SF
☎ 01890 750551 (clubhouse) & 750004 (pro shop)
e-mail: eyemouth@gxn.co.uk
A superb course set on the coast, containing interesting and challenging holes, in particular the intimidating 6th hole, a formidable par 3 across a vast gully with the waves crashing below and leaving little room for error. The clubhouse overlooks the picturesque fishing village of Eyemouth and provides panoramic views over the course and the North Sea.
18 holes, 6520yds, Par 72, SSS 72, Course record 66.
Club membership 400.
Visitors May play at any time by arrangement. Some competition restrictions on Sat & Sun am. Phone pro shop. **Societies** apply in writing, e-mail or phone. **Green Fees** not confirmed. **Cards** 🟦 🟥 🟧 💳 **Prof** Paul Terras, Tony McLeman **Course Designer** JR Bain **Facilities** ⊗ ⏐Ⅲ by arrangement ⓑ 🎯 🝙 🛆 🝙 🛒 ⚑ *⌀* **Conf** Corporate Hospitality Days available **Location** E side of town, 2m off A1

....

Hotel ★★★ 70% Marshall Meadows Country House Hotel, BERWICK-UPON-TWEED ☎ 01289 331133 19 en suite

GALASHIELS   Map 12 NT43

Galashiels Ladhope Recreation Ground TD1 2NJ
☎ 01896 753724
Hillside course, superb views from the top; 10th hole very steep.
18 holes, 5185yds, Par 67, SSS 66, Course record 61.
Club membership 311.
Visitors contact the secretary in advance especially for weekends. **Societies** arrangements with secretary especially for weekends. **Green Fees** not confirmed. **Course Designer** James Braid **Facilities** ⊗ ⏐Ⅲ ⓑ 🎯 🝙 🛆 *⌀* **Location** N side of town centre off A7

....

Hotel ★★★ 66% Kingsknowes Hotel, Selkirk Rd, GALASHIELS ☎ 01896 758375   12 en suite

Torwoodlee Edinburgh Rd TD1 2NE
☎ 01896 752260 ▤ 01896 752306
e-mail: thesecretary@torwoodleegolfclub.org.uk
A picturesque course flanked by the River Gala and set among a mix of mature woodland and rolling parkland.
18 holes, 6021yds, Par 69, SSS 70, Course record 64.
Club membership 550.
Visitors restricted Thu, Ladies Day & Sat, men's competitions. **Societies** letter to secretary. **Green Fees** £26 per round/£36 per day. **Cards** 🟦 🟥 🟧 💳 **Course Designer** Willie Park **Facilities** ⊗ ⏐Ⅲ ⓑ 🎯 🝙 🛆 🛒 *⌀* **Location** 1.75m NW off A7

....

Hotel ★★★ 66% Kingsknowes Hotel, Selkirk Rd, GALASHIELS ☎ 01896 758375   12 en suite

HAWICK   Map 12 NT51

Hawick Vertish Hill TD9 0NY
☎ 01450 372293
e-mail: thesecretary@hawickgolfclub.fsnet.co.uk
Hill course with good views.
18 holes, 5929yds, Par 68, SSS 69, Course record 63.
Club membership 600.
Visitors contact in advance. 1st tee off time for visitors on Sun 10.30pm. **Societies** write or phone for booking arrangement. **Green Fees** £35 per day; £27 per round. **Facilities** ⊗ ⏐Ⅲ ⓑ 🎯 🝙 🛆 🝙 🛒 🛒 *⌀* **Location** SW side of town

INNERLEITHEN   Map 11 NT33

Innerleithen Leithen Water, Leithen Rd EH44 6NL
☎ 01896 830951
Moorland course, with easy walking. Burns and rivers are natural hazards. Testing 5th hole (100yds) par 3.
9 holes, 6066yds, Par 70, SSS 69, Course record 65.
Club membership 280.
Visitors advisable to check for availability for weekends. **Societies** by booking. **Green Fees** terms on application. **Course Designer** Willie Park **Facilities** ⓑ 🎯 🝙 🛆 **Conf** Corporate Hospitality Days available **Location** 1.5m N on B709

....

Hotel ★★★★ 70% Peebles Hotel Hydro, PEEBLES ☎ 01721 720602 128 en suite

JEDBURGH   Map 12 NT62

Jedburgh Dunion Rd TD8 6TA
☎ 01835 863587
Mature, undulating parkland course with great views. Some unusual square greens.
9 holes, 5760yds, Par 68, SSS 67, Course record 62.
Club membership 410.
Visitors weekend restrictions; weekdays before 6pm. **Societies** contact at least one month in advance by writing or phone. **Green Fees** not confirmed. **Course Designer** William Park **Facilities** ⊗ ⏐Ⅲ ⓑ 🎯 🝙 🛆 🛒 **Conf** Corporate Hospitality Days available **Location** 1m W on B6358

....

Guesthouse ◆◆◆◆ Crailing Old School B&B, CRAILING ☎ 01835 850382 3 rms (1 en suite)

KELSO   Map 12 NT73

Kelso Racecourse Rd TD5 7SL
☎ 01573 223009 ▤ 01573 228490
18 holes, 6046yds, Par 70, SSS 69, Course record 64.
Course Designer James Braid **Location** N side of town centre off B6461
Phone for further details

....

Hotel ★★★ 68% Cross Keys Hotel, 36-37 The Square, KELSO ☎ 01573 223303 27 en suite

Roxburghe Heiton TD5 8JZ
☎ 01573 450333 ▤ 01573 450611
e-mail: golf@roxburghe.net
An exceptional parkland layout designed by Dave Thomas and opened in 1997. Surrounded by natural woodland on the banks of the River Teviot. Owned by the Duke of Roxburghe, this course has numerous bunkers, wide rolling and sloping fairways and

Continued

:ategically placed water features. The signature hole :the 14th.

The Roxburghe Golf Course

holes, 6925yds, Par 72, SSS 74, Course record 66.
ub membership 310.
sitors dress code (smart casual, no jeans, no training oes). Book in advance **Societies** please phone in vance, a number of packages available. **Green Fees** £80 : day, £60 per round. **Cards** of Craig Montgomerie **Course Designer** Dave Thomas **cilities** **isure** tennis courts, fishing, Clay pigeon shooting, conry, archery, mountain bikes. **Conf** fac available rporate Hospitality Days available **cation** 2m W of Kelso on A698

tel ★★★ 76% The Roxburghe Hotel & Golf urse, Heiton, KELSO ☎ 01573 450331 16 en suite nnexe en suite

AUDER Map 12 NT54

auder Galashiels Rd TD2 6RS
01578 722240 01578 722526
nail: laudergc@aol.com
land course and practice area on gently sloping hill th stunning views of the Lauderdale district. The nature holes are The Wood, a dog-leg par 4 played ınd the corner of a wood which is itself out of ınds, and The Quarry, a 150 yard par 3 played over eral old quarry holes into a bowl shaped green.
oles, 6050yds, Par 72, SSS 69, Course record 66.
ub membership 260.
sitors restricted 4.30-6pm Mon, Tue, Wed & am Sun. **cieties** phone in advance. **Green Fees** £12.50 per /round. **Course Designer** Willie Park Jnr **cilities** **Conf** Corporate Hospitality Days ilable **Location** off A68, 0.5m from Lauder

tel ★★ 67% Lauderdale Hotel, 1 Edinburgh Rd, UDER ☎ 01578 722231 10 en suite

ELROSE Map 12 NT53

elrose Dingleton TD6 9HS
01896 822855
dulating tree-lined fairways with spendid views. ıny bunkers.
oles, 5562yds, Par 70, SSS 68, Course record 61.
ıb membership 380.
sitors competitions all Sats & many Suns Apr-Oct, ies priority Tue, junior priority Wed am in holidays. **cieties** apply in writing. **Green Fees** £20 per day/round. **urse Designer** James Braid **Facilities** **cation** S of town centre on B6359

Hotel ★★★ 71% Burt's Hotel, Market Square, MELROSE ☎ 01896 822285 20 en suite

MINTO Map 12 NT52

Minto TD9 8SH
☎ 01450 870220 01450 870126
e-mail: pat@mintogolfclub.freeserve.co.uk
Pleasant, undulating parkland course featuring mature trees and panoramic views of Scottish border country. Short but quite testing.
18 holes, 5542yds, Par 69, SSS 67, Course record 63.
Club membership 600.
Visitors advisable to phone in advance, & essential for weekends. **Societies** contact in advance. **Green Fees** £30 per day, £27 per round (£38/£32 weekends & bank holidays). **Cards** **Course Designer** Thomas Telford **Facilities** **Conf** Corporate Hospitality Days available **Location** 5m NE from Hawick off B6405

NEWCASTLETON Map 12 NY48

Newcastleton Holm Hill TD9 0QD
☎ 01387 375608
Hilly course with scenic views over the Liddesdale valley and Newcastleton.
9 holes, 5491yds, Par 69, SSS 70, Course record 67.
Club membership 100.
Visitors contact the Secretary in advance. **Societies** contact by phone or in writing in advance. **Green Fees** £10 per day/round. **Course Designer** J Shade **Facilities** **Leisure** fishing. **Location** W side of village

Hotel ★★★ 67% Garden House Hotel, Sarkfoot Rd, GRETNA ☎ 01461 337621 38 en suite

PEEBLES Map 11 NT24

Peebles Kirkland St EH45 8EU
☎ 01721 720197 01721 724441
e-mail: secretary@peeblesgolfclub.co.uk
This parkland course is one of the most picturesque courses in Scotland, framed by the rolling border hills and the Tweed valley and set high above the town. The tough opening holes are balanced by a more generous stretch through to the 14th hole.
18 holes, 6160yds, Par 70, SSS 70, Course record 63.
Club membership 750.
Visitors advisable to ring for information on availability, no visitors on Sat. **Societies** apply by phone or in writing in advance. **Green Fees** £35 per round/£50 per day. **Cards** **Prof** Craig Imlah **Course Designer** HS Colt **Facilities** **Location** W side of town centre off A72

Hotel ★★★★ 70% Peebles Hotel Hydro, PEEBLES ☎ 01721 720602 128 en suite

ST BOSWELLS Map 12 NT53

St Boswells Braeheads TD6 0DE
☎ 01835 823527
Attractive parkland course by the banks of the River Tweed; easy walking.
9 holes, 5274yds, Par 68, SSS 66.
Club membership 320.
Visitors contact in advance. **Societies** booking by writing to secretary. **Green Fees** £20 per round, £12 per 9 holes. **Course Designer** W Park **Facilities** by arrangement **Location** 500yds off A68 east end of village

Continued

Hotel ★★★ ▲▲ 74% Dryburgh Abbey Hotel, ST
BOSWELLS ☎ 01835 822261 37 en suite 1 annexe en suite

SELKIRK   Map 12 NT42

Selkirk Selkirk Hill TD7 4NW
☎ 01750 20621
**Pleasant moorland course with gorse and heather, set
around Selkirk Hill. A testing course for all golfers.
Unrivalled views.**
9 holes, 5620yds, Par 68, SSS 68, Course record 61.
Club membership 349.
Visitors contact in advance; not Mon evening,
competition/match days. Societies phone in advance.
Green Fees £20 per 18 holes, 9 holes on request.
Facilities ⊗ by arrangement ▲ by arrangement
▼ by arrangement ♀ ⌂ ♂ Location 1m S on A7

Hotel ★★★ 71% Burt's Hotel, Market Square,
MELROSE ☎ 01896 822285 20 en suite

WEST LINTON   Map 11 NT15

Rutherford Castle Golf Club EH46 7AS
☎ 01968 661 233 ▤ 01968 661 233
e-mail: info@ruth-castlegc.co.uk
**Undulating parkland set beneath the Pentland Hills.
The many challenging holes are a good test for the
better player while offering great enjoyment to the
average player.**
18 holes, 6525yds, Par 72, SSS 71.
Club membership 120.
Visitors phone booking anytime.application form
forwarded on request. Green Fees terms on application.
Course Designer Bryan Moore Facilities ▼ ♀ ♂
Location on A702 towards Carlisle

Hotel ★★★★ 70% Peebles Hotel Hydro, PEEBLES
☎ 01721 720602 128 en suite

West Linton EH46 7HN
☎ 01968 660256 & 660970 ▤ 01968 660970
e-mail: secretarywlgc@btinternet.com
18 holes, 6132yds, Par 69, SSS 70, Course record 63.
Course Designer Millar, Braid, Fraser Location NW side
of village off A702
Phone for further details

Hotel ★★★★ 70% Peebles Hotel Hydro, PEEBLES
☎ 01721 720602 128 en suite

SOUTH AYRSHIRE

AYR   Map 10 NS32

Belleisle Belleisle Park KA7 4DU
☎ 01292 441258 ▤ 01292 442632
*Belleisle Course: 18 holes, 6431yds, Par 71, SSS 72,
Course record 63.*
Seafield Course: 18 holes, 5498yds, Par 68, SSS 67.
Course Designer James Braid Location 2m S of Ayr on
A719
Phone for further details

Hotel ★★★ 71% Savoy Park Hotel, 16 Racecourse Rd,
AYR ☎ 01292 266112 15 en suite

Dalmilling Westwood Av KA8 0QY
☎ 01292 263893 ▤ 01292 610543
**Meadowland course, with easy walking. Tributaries of
the River Ayr add interest to early holes.**
18 holes, 5724yds, Par 69, SSS 68, Course record 61.
Club membership 260.
Visitors contact in advance. Societies contact in advance.
Green Fees not confirmed. Cards ▦ ▦ ▨ ▧ ▨ Prof
Philip Cheyney Facilities ⊗ ⅷ ▲ ▼ ⌂ 🖥 🏌 ♂
Location 1.5m E of town centre off A77

Hotel ★★★★ 72% Fairfield House Hotel, 12 Fairfield R
AYR ☎ 01292 267461 40 en suite 4 annexe en suite

BARASSIE   Map 10 NS3

Kilmarnock (Barassie) 29 Hillhouse Rd
KA10 6SY
☎ 01292 313920 ▤ 01292 318300
e-mail: secretarykbgc@lineone.net
**The club now has a 27-hole layout. Magnificent seaside
links, relatively flat with much heather and small,
undulating greens.**
18 holes, 6817yds, Par 72, SSS 74, Course record 63.
9 hole course: 2888yds, Par 34.
Club membership 600.
Visitors limited availability Wed & weekends & Fri am.
Contact secretary in advance. Societies phone in advance
& confirm in writing. Green Fees £58 for up to 36 holes.
Cards ▦ ▦ ▨ Prof Gregor Howie Course Designer
Theodore Moone Facilities ⊗ ⅷ ▲ ▼ ♀ ⌂ 🖥 🏌 ♂
Location E side of village on B746, 2m N of Troon

Hotel ★★★★ 69% Marine Hotel, Crosbie Rd, TROON
☎ 01292 314444 90 en suite

GIRVAN   Map 10 NX1

Brunston Castle Golf Course Rd, Dailly KA26 9GD
☎ 01465 811471 ▤ 01465 811545
e-mail: golf@brunstoncastle.co.uk
**Sheltered inland parkland course. A championship
design by Donald Steel, the course is bisected by the
River Girvan and shaped to incorporate all the natura
surroundings. Lined with mature trees and
incorporating a number of water features in addition to
the river.**
*Burns: 18 holes, 6662yds, Par 72, SSS 72,
Course record 63.*
Club membership 400.
Visitors reserved for members at weekends 8-10 & 12.30
1.30. Must contact in advance. Societies phone 01465
811471 to book. Green Fees not confirmed. Cards ▦ ▨
▨ Prof Malcolm Harrison Course Designer Donald Stee
Facilities ⊗ ⅷ ▲ ▼ ♀ ⌂ 🖥 🏌 ▶ ♂ ⚑ Conf fac
available Corporate Hospitality Days available
Location 5m E of Girvan

Hotel ★★★ 75% Malin Court, TURNBERRY
☎ 01655 331457 18 en suite

Girvan Golf Course Rd KA26 9HW
☎ 01465 714346 ▤ 01465 714272
18 holes, 5098yds, Par 64, SSS 65, Course record 61.
Course Designer D Kinnell, J Braid Location N side of
town off A77
Phone for further details

Hotel ★★★ 75% Malin Court, TURNBERRY
☎ 01655 331457 18 en suite

MAYBOLE   Map 10 NS20

Maybole Municipal Memorial Park KA19 7DX
☎ 01655 889770
holes, 2635yds, Par 33, SSS 65, Course record 64.
ocation off A77 S of town
hone for further details

....

otel ★★ Ladyburn, MAYBOLE ☎ 01655 740585
en suite

RESTWICK   Map 10 NS32

restwick 2 Links Rd KA9 1QG
☎ 01292 477404 🖨 01292 477255
mail: bookings@prestwickgc.co.uk
**easide links with natural hazards, tight fairways and
fficult fast undulating greens.**
8 holes, 6544yds, Par 71, SSS 73, Course record 67.
lub membership 575.
Visitors restricted Thu & Sun, no play on Sat. Must
ontact in advance & have a handicap certificate. **Societies**
ontact in writing. **Green Fees** £100 per round/£150 per
ay (Sun £125 per round). **Cards** ▦ ▬ ▦ ▧ 🔲 **Prof**
A Fleming **Course Designer** Tom Morris **Facilities** ⊗ ⓛ
🖤 ♀ ♨ 🛒 🍴 ⏚ **Conf** Corporate Hospitality Days
vailable **Location** in town centre off A79

....

otel ★★★ 70% Parkstone Hotel, Esplanade,
RESTWICK ☎ 01292 477286 22 en suite

restwick St Cuthbert East Rd KA9 2SX
☎ 01292 477101 🖨 01292 671730
mail: secretary@stcuthbert.co.uk
**arkland with natural hazards and sometimes windy.
ree-lined fairways and well bunkered.**
8 holes, 6470yds, Par 71, SSS 71, Course record 64.
lub membership 880.
isitors restricted Thu & Sun & bank
olidays. **Societies** Mon-Fri, apply in writing. **Green Fees**
5 per day. **Cards** ▦ ▬ 🔲 **Course Designer** Stutt & Co
acilities ⊗ ⅏ ⓛ 🖤 ♀ ♨ 🍴 **Conf** Corporate Hospitality
ays available **Location** 0.5m E of town centre off A77

....

otel ★★★ 70% Parkstone Hotel, Esplanade,
RESTWICK ☎ 01292 477286 22 en suite

restwick St Nicholas Grangemuir Rd KA9 1SN
☎ 01292 477608 🖨 01292 473900
mail: secretary@prestwickstnicholas.com
holes, 5952yds, Par 69, SSS 69, Course record 63.
ourse Designer Charles Hunter **Location** S side of town
f A79
one for further details

....

otel ★★★ 70% Parkstone Hotel, Esplanade,
RESTWICK ☎ 01292 477286 22 en suite

ROON See page 369

ROON   Map 10 NS33

roon Municipal Harling Dr KA10 6NE
☎ 01292 312464 🖨 01292 312578
ree links courses, two of championship standard.
*chgreen Course: 18 holes, 6820yds, Par 74, SSS 73.
rley Course: 18 holes, 6360yds, Par 71, SSS 63.
llarton Course: 18 holes, 4870yds, Par 66, SSS 64.*
lub membership 3000.

Visitors no restrictions. **Societies** apply in writing. **Green
Fees** not confirmed. **Cards** ▦ ▬ ▦ 🔲 **Prof** Gordon
McKinlay **Facilities** ⊗ ⅏ ⓛ 🖤 ♀ ♨ 🍴 ⏚
Location 100yds from railway station

....

Hotel ★★★★ 69% Marine Hotel, Crosbie Rd, TROON
☎ 01292 314444 90 en suite

TURNBERRY See page 371

SOUTH LANARKSHIRE

BIGGAR   Map 11 NT03

Biggar The Park, Broughton Rd ML12 6AH
☎ 01899 220618 (club) & 220319 (course)
Flat parkland course, easy walking and fine views.
*18 holes, 5600yds, Par 68, SSS 67, Course record 61.
Club membership 240.*
Visitors contact in advance. Smart casual wear required.
Societies book in advance, observe dress code. **Green Fees**
not confirmed. **Course Designer** W Park Jnr **Facilities** ⊗
⅏ ⓛ 🖤 ♀ ♨ 🛒 🍴 **Leisure** hard tennis courts, boating.
Location S side of town

....

Hotel ★★★ ♨♨ 73% Shieldhill Castle, Quothquan,
BIGGAR ☎ 01899 220035 16 en suite

BOTHWELL   Map 11 NS75

Bothwell Castle Blantyre Rd G71 8PJ
☎ 01698 853177 & 852052 🖨 01698 854052
Flattish tree-lined parkland course in residential area.
*18 holes, 6200yds, Par 70, SSS 70, Course record 63.
Club membership 1000.*
Visitors may only play Mon-Fri 9.30-10.30am & 2-3pm.
Advance booking required. **Societies** Tue, apply in writing.
Green Fees £32 per day; £24 per round. **Prof** Alan
McCloskey **Facilities** ⊗ ⅏ ⓛ 🖤 ♀ ♨ 🍴 ⏚ **Conf**
Corporate Hospitality Days available **Location** NW of
village off B7071

....

Hotel ★★★ 68% Bothwell Bridge Hotel, 89 Main St,
BOTHWELL ☎ 01698 852246 90 en suite

BURNSIDE   Map 11 NS65

Blairbeth Fernbrae Av, Fernhill G73 4SF
☎ 0141 634 3355 & 634 3325 🖨 0141 634 3325
e-mail: committee@blairbethgc.fsnet.co.uk
**Parkland course with some small elevated greens and
views over Glasgow and the Clyde valley.**
*18 holes, 5518yds, Par 70, SSS 68, Course record 63.
Club membership 480.*
Visitors contact in advance; not weekends. **Societies** apply
in advance. **Green Fees** £28 per day; £22 per round. **Cards**
▦ ▬ ▦ 🔲 **Facilities** ⊗ ⅏ ⓛ 🖤 ♀ ♨ 🍴
Conf Corporate Hospitality Days available
Location 2m S of Rutherglen off Burnside Rd

Cathkin Braes Cathkin Rd G73 4SE
☎ 0141 634 6605 🖨 0141 630 9186
e-mail: golf@cathkinbraes.freeserve.co.uk
**Moorland course, 600ft above sea level but relatively
flat with a prevailing westerly wind and views over
Glasgow. A small loch hazard at 5th hole. Very strong
finishing holes.**
*18 holes, 6200yds, Par 71, SSS 71, Course record 63.
Club membership 920.*

Continued   *Continued*

Visitors contact in advance; handicap certificate; not weekends. **Societies** apply in writing or phone. **Green Fees** £33 per round/£43 per day (£45 or £58 incl. food). **Prof** Stephen Bree **Course Designer** James Braid **Facilities** ⊗ ⫼ ⮩ ⫿ ♀ ⚲ 🏠 ⛳ ↘ 🛆 ⛳ **Conf** Corporate Hospitality Days available **Location** 1m S on B759

CARLUKE   Map 11 NS85

Carluke Mauldslie Rd, Hallcraig ML8 5HG
☎ 01555 770574 & 771070
e-mail: admin.carlukegolf@supanet.com
18 holes, 5853yds, Par 70, SSS 68, Course record 63.
Location 1m W off A73
Phone for further details

Hotel ★★★ 72% Popinjay Hotel, Lanark Rd, ROSEBANK ☎ 01555 860441 38 en suite

CARNWATH   Map 11 NS94

Carnwath 1 Main St ML11 8JX
☎ 01555 840251 ⬚ 01555 841070
Picturesque parkland course slightly hilly, with small greens calling for accuracy. Panoramic views.
18 holes, 5222yds, Par 66, SSS 66, Course record 63.
Club membership 586.
Visitors restricted after 5pm, no visitors Sat. **Societies** apply in writing or phone. **Green Fees** £30 per day; £18 per round (£36/£24 Sun). **Facilities** ⊗ ⫼ ⮩ ⫿ ♀ 🛆 ⛳
Location W side of village on A70

Hotel ★★★ 66% Cartland Bridge Hotel, Glasgow Rd, LANARK ☎ 01555 664426 20 rms (18 en suite)

EAST KILBRIDE   Map 11 NS65

East Kilbride Chapelside Rd, Nerston G74 4PF
☎ 01355 247728
18 holes, 6419yds, Par 71, SSS 71, Course record 64.
Location 0.5m N off A749
Phone for further details

Torrance House Calderglen Country Park, Strathaven Rd G75 0QZ
☎ 01355 248638 ⬚ 01355 570916
A mature parkland course.
18 holes, 6476yds, Par 72, SSS 69, Course record 71.
Club membership 700.
Visitors welcome, may book up to six days in advance. **Societies** Mon-Fri. Apply in writing to South Lanarkshire Leisure, Hamilton Palace sports grounds, Hamilton **Green Fees** not confirmed. **Course Designer** Hawtree & Son **Facilities** ⊗ ⫼ ⮩ ⫿ ♀ 🛆 🏠 ⛳ ⛳ **Location** 1.5m SE of East Kilbride on A726

HAMILTON   Map 11 NS75

Hamilton Carlisle Rd, Ferniegair ML3 7UE
☎ 01698 282872 ⬚ 01698 204650
e-mail: secretary@hamiltongolfclub.co.uk
Beautiful parkland course.
18 holes, 6498yds, Par 70, SSS 70, Course record 62.
Visitors contact in advance; not weekends. **Societies** phone secretary in advance. **Green Fees** terms on application.
Cards 🏧 💳 💳 💳 💳 **Prof** Derek Wright **Course Designer** James Braid **Facilities** ⊗ ⫼ ⮩ ⫿ ♀ 🛆 🏠 ↘ ⛳
Location 1.5m SE on A72

Hotel ⚘ Premier Travel Inn Glasgow (Hamilton), Hamilton Motorway Service Area, HAMILTON
☎ 08701 977124 36 en suite

Strathclyde Park Mote Hill ML3 6BY
☎ 01698 429350
Municipal wooded parkland course with views of the Strathclyde Park sailing loch. Surrounded by a nature reserve and Hamilton racecourse.
9 holes, 3113yds, Par 36, SSS 70, Course record 68.
Club membership 140.
Visitors phone, same day booking system in operation. May book up to 1 week in advance in summer months. **Societies** contact in advance for booking. **Green Fees** £3.40 per 9 holes. **Prof** William Walker **Facilities** 🛆 🏠 ⛳ (**Location** N side of town off B7071

Hotel ⚘ Premier Travel Inn Glasgow (Hamilton), Hamilton Motorway Service Area, HAMILTON
☎ 08701 977124 36 en suite

LANARK   Map 11 NS84

Lanark The Moor, Whitelees Rd ML11 7RX
☎ 01555 663219 & 661456 ⬚ 01555 663219
e-mail: lanarkgolfclub@supanet.com
Lanark is renowned for its smooth fast greens, natural moorland fairways and beautiful scenery. The course i built on a substrate of glacial sands, providing a uniqu feeling of tackling a links course at 600ft above sea level. The par of 70 can be a real test when the prevailing wind blows.
Old Course: 18 holes, 6306yds, Par 70, SSS 71, Course record 62.
Wee Course: 9 holes, 1489yds, Par 28.
Club membership 880.
Visitors booking advisable, no visitors weekends. **Societies** apply in advance. **Green Fees** £45 per day; £35 per round. Wee Course; £7 per day. **Prof** Alan White **Course Designer** Tom Morris **Facilities** ⊗ ⫼ ⮩ ⫿ ♀ 🛆 🏠 ↘ 🖊 ⛳ **Conf** Corporate Hospitality Days available **Location** E side of town centre off A73

Hotel ★★★ 66% Cartland Bridge Hotel, Glasgow Rd, LANARK ☎ 01555 664426 20 rms (18 en suite)

LARKHALL   Map 11 NS7:

Larkhall Burnhead Rd ML9 3AA
☎ 01698 889597
9 holes, 6234yds, Par 70, SSS 70, Course record 69.
Location E side of town on B7019
Phone for further details

Hotel ★★★ 72% Popinjay Hotel, Lanark Rd, ROSEBANK ☎ 01555 860441 38 en suite

LEADHILLS   Map 11 NS8

Leadhills 51 Main St ML12 6XP
☎ 01659 74456
9 holes, 4354yds, Par 66, SSS 64.
Location E side of village off B797
Phone for further details

Hotel ★★ 67% Blackaddie House Hotel, Blackaddie Rd, SANQUHAR ☎ 01695 50270 9 en suite

Continued

Royal Troon

South Ayrshire

Troon

Map 10 NS33

Troon was founded in 1878 with just five holes on linksland. In its first decade it grew from five holes to six, then 12, and finally 18 holes. It became Royal Troon in 1978 on its 100th anniversary. Royal Troon's reputation is based on its combination of rough and sandy hills, bunkers, and a severity of finish that has diminished the championship hopes of many. The most successful players have relied on an equal blend of finesse and power. The British Open Championship has been played at Troon eight times - in 1923, 1950, 1962, 1973, 1982, 1989, 1997, and lastly in 2004 when it hosted the 133rd tournament. It has the shortest and longest holes of courses hosting the Open. Ten new bunkers and four new tees were added after the 1997 competition. It is recommended that you apply to the course in advance for full visitor information.

Craigend Rd KA10 6EP
☎ 01292 311555 Fax 01292 318204
e-mail: bookings@royaltroon.com

Old Course: 18 holes, 6641yds, Par 71, SSS 73, Course record 64.
Portland: 18 holes, 6289yds, Par 71, SSS 71, Course record 65. Club membership 800.
Visitors Mon, Tue, Thu only May-Oct; must write in advance; letter of introduction from own club & handicap certificate (men under 20, women under 30). Under 16s may play Portland.
Green Fees £200 day package including coffee & lunch. **Cards** ▦ ▧ ▨ ▩ **Prof** RB Anderson **Course Designer** C Hunter, G Strath, W Fernie **Facilities** ⊗ ┗ ♥ ♀ △ 🗎 ⚐ ✓ ⛳
Location S of town on B749. 5m from Prestwick airport

....

Hotels

★★★★ 69% Marine Hotel, Crosbie Rd, TROON
☎ 01292 314444 90 en suite

★★★ Lochgreen House, Monktonhill Rd, Southwood, TROON
☎ 01292 313343 Fax 01292 318661 32 en suite
8 annexe en suite

★★★ 75% Piersland House Hotel, Craigend Rd, TROON
☎ 01292 314747 Fax 01292 315613 15 en suite
15 annexe en suite

LESMAHAGOW
Map 11 NS83

Holland Bush Acretophead ML11 0JS
☎ 01555 893484 & 893646 📠 01555 893984
e-mail: mail@hollandbushgolfclub.co.uk
18 holes, 6246yds, Par 71, SSS 70, Course record 63.
Course Designer J Lawson, K Pate **Location** 3m S of
Lesmahagow on Coalburn Rd
Phone for further details

Hotel ★★★ 74% Strathaven Hotel, Hamilton Rd,
STRATHAVEN ☎ 01357 521778 22 en suite

RIGSIDE
Map 11 NS83

Douglas Water Ayr Rd ML11 9NP
☎ 01555 880361
9 holes, 5890yds, Par 72, SSS 69, Course record 63.
Location on A70
Phone for further details

Hotel ★★★ 66% Cartland Bridge Hotel, Glasgow Rd,
LANARK ☎ 01555 664426 20 rms (18 en suite)

STRATHAVEN
Map 11 NS74

Strathaven Glasgow Rd ML10 6NL
☎ 01357 520421 📠 01357 520539
e-mail: info@strathavengc.com
Gently undulating, tree-lined, championship parkland
course with views over the town and the Avon valley.
18 holes, 6250yds, Par 71, SSS 71, Course record 65.
Club membership 1050.
Visitors not after 4pm weekdays, weekends; must contact
in advance. **Societies** apply in writing to general manager.
Green Fees £37 per day, £27 per round. **Cards** 💳 💳 🈯
Prof Stuart Kerr **Course Designer** Willie Fernie, J Stutt
Facilities ⊗ ℍ 🄑 🖥 🛒 🄐 🏠 🍴 🛒 ♂ **Conf** fac available
Location NE side of town on A726

Hotel ★★★ 74% Strathaven Hotel, Hamilton Rd,
STRATHAVEN ☎ 01357 521778 22 en suite

UDDINGSTON
Map 11 NS66

Calderbraes 57 Roundknowe Rd G71 7TS
☎ 01698 813425
Parkland course with good view of Clyde valley.
Testing 4th hole (par 4), hard uphill.
9 holes, 5046yds, Par 66, SSS 67, Course record 65.
Club membership 230.
Visitors weekdays before 5pm. **Societies** welcome
Green Fees not confirmed. **Facilities** ⊗ ℍ 🄑 🖥 🛒 🄐
Location 1.5m NW off A74

Hotel ★★★ 68% Bothwell Bridge Hotel, 89 Main St,
BOTHWELL ☎ 01698 852246 90 en suite

STIRLING

ABERFOYLE
Map 11 NN50

Aberfoyle Braeval FK8 3UY
☎ 01877 382493
18 holes, 5210yds, Par 66, SSS 66, Course record 64.
Location 1m E on A81
Phone for further details

Hotel ★★★★ 66% Forest Hills Hotel, Kinlochard,
ABERFOYLE ☎ 01877 387277 54 en suite

BANNOCKBURN
Map 11 NS89

Brucefields Family Golfing Centre
Pirnhall Rd FK7 8EH
☎ 01786 818184 📠 01786 817770
e-mail: brucefields@freenetname.co.uk
Gently rolling parkland with fine views. Most holes can
be played without too much difficulty with the
exception of the 2nd which is a long and tricky par 4
and the 6th, a par 3 which requires exact club selection
and a straight shot.
*Main Course: 9 holes, 2513yds, Par 68, SSS 68,
Course record 66.*
Club membership 300.
Visitors no restrictions **Societies** apply in writing.
Green Fees £17 per 18 holes, £10 per 9 holes (£19/£11
weekends). **Cards** 💳 💳 💳 📇 🈯 **Prof** Gregor Monks
Course Designer Souters Sportsturf **Facilities** ⊗ ℍ 🄑 🖥
🄐 🏠 🍴 🛒 ♂ 🍴 **Leisure** golf academy, nine-hole
par 3 course. **Conf** fac available Corporate Hospitality
Days available **Location** M80/M9 junct 9, A91, 1st left
signed

BRIDGE OF ALLAN
Map 11 NS79

Bridge of Allan Sunnylaw FK9 4LY
☎ 01786 832332
Parkland course, very hilly with good views of Stirling
Castle and beyond to the Trossachs. Testing par 3 1st hole
221yds uphill, with a 6ft wall 25yds before green.
9 holes, 4932yds, Par 66, SSS 66, Course record 59.
Club membership 400.
Visitors restricted Mon & Thu evenings, Sat, contact in
advance. **Societies** contact in advance. **Green Fees** not
confirmed. **Course Designer** Tom Morris **Facilities** ⊗ 🄑
🖥 🄐 🏠 ♂ **Location** 0.5m N off A9

Hotel ★★★ 68% Royal Hotel, Henderson St, BRIDGE OF
ALLAN ☎ 01786 832284 32 en suite

CALLANDER
Map 11 NN60

Callander Aveland Rd FK17 8EN
☎ 01877 330090 & 330975 📠 01877 330062
e-mail: callandergc@nextcall.net
Challenging parkland course with tight fairways and a
number of interesting holes. Designed by Tom Morris
Snr and overlooked by the Trossachs.
18 holes, 5151yds, Par 66, SSS 65, Course record 61.
Club membership 600.
Visitors booking 24-48hrs is advised in the playing season
Handicap certificate Wed/Sun. **Societies** write or phone for
booking form. **Green Fees** £20 per round/£28 per day
(weekends £30/£40). **Cards** 💳 💳 📇 🈯 **Prof** Allan
Martin **Course Designer** Morris, Fernie **Facilities** ⊗ ℍ 🄑
🖥 🄐 🏠 🍴 ♂ 🍴 **Conf** Corporate Hospitality Days
available **Location** E side of town off A84

Hotel ★★★ 77% Roman Camp Country House Hotel,
CALLANDER ☎ 01877 330003 14 en suite

DRYMEN
Map 11 NS48

Buchanan Castle G63 0HY
☎ 01360 660307 📠 01360 660993
e-mail: buchanancastle@sol.co.uk
Parkland course, with easy walking and good views. A
quiet and relaxed place to play golf, with views of the
old castle. Owned by the Duke of Montrose.

Continued

South Ayrshire
Westin Turnberry Resort

Turnberry   **Map 10 NS20**

For thousands of players of all nationalities, Turnberry is one of the finest of all golf destinations, where some of the most remarkable moments in Open history have taken place. The legendary Ailsa Course is complemented by the new highly acclaimed Kintyre Course, while the nine-hole Arran Course, created by Donald Steel and Colin Montgomerie, has similar challenges such as undulating greens, tight tee shots, pot bunkers and thick Scottish rough. With the famous hotel on the left and the magnificent Ailsa Craig away to the right, there are few vistas in world golf to match the 1st tee here. To help you prepare for your game the Colin Montgomerie Links Golf Academy, alongside the luxurious and extensive clubhouse, was opened in April 2000; it features 12 driving bays, four short-game bays, two dedicated teaching rooms and a group teaching room.

Westin Turnberry Resort KA26 9LT
☎ 01655 331000 Fax 01655 331069
e-mail: turnberry@westin.com

Ailsa Course: 18 holes, 6440yds, Par 69, SSS 72, Course record 63.
Kintyre Course: 18 holes, 6376yds, Par 71, SSS 72.
Arran Course: 9 holes, 1996, Par 31, SSS 31.
Visitors residents of the hotel have preferential booking.
Societies apply in writing. Green Fees Ailsa £130 per round (£175 weekends); Kintyre £105 per 18 holes. Cards ▦ ▬ ▬ ▦ ▦ ▦ Prof Paul Burley Course Designer Mackenzie Ross, Donald Steel Facilities ⊗ ⊞ ⓛ ☴ ♀ ♨ ☎ ⌇ 🏠 ♿ ♐ ✝ Leisure hard tennis courts, heated indoor swimming pool, fishing, sauna, solarium, gymnasium, Colin Montgomerie Links Golf Academy. Conf Corporate Hospitality Days available
Location 15m SW of Ayr on A77

....

Hotels

★ ★ ★ ★ ★ The Westin Turnberry Resort, TURNBERRY

☎ 01655 331000 132 en suite 89 annexe en suite

★ ★ ★ 75% Malin Court, TURNBERRY

☎ 01655 331457 Fax 01655 331072 18 en suite

★ ★ Ladyburn, MAYBOLE

☎ 01655 740585 Fax 01655 740580 5 en suite

Buchanan Castle Golf Club

18 holes, 6059yds, Par 70, SSS 69.
Club membership 830.
Visitors contact professional in advance 01360 660330.
Societies contact in advance. **Green Fees** £48 per day; £38
per round. **Cards** ▆▆ **Prof** Keith Baxter **Course Designer**
James Braid **Facilities** ⊗ ⅢⅢ ᴸ ᴸ ᛒ ⅋ ᐃ ᐃ ᛏ ᛤ 𝒸
Conf fac available Corporate Hospitality Days available
Location 1m W
....
Hotel ★★★ 68% Winnock Hotel, The Square, DRYMEN
☎ 01360 660245 48 en suite

Strathendrick G83 8EL
☎ 01360 660695
e-mail: melvinquyn@hotmail.com
**Hillside course with breathtaking views of the Campsie
and Luss Hills and Ben Lomond. Mainly natural
hazards with few bunkers. Greens are comparatively
small but in immaculate condition.**
9 holes, 4982yds, Par 66, SSS 64, Course record 60.
Club membership 470.
Visitors not weekends/evenings. **Societies** apply in
advance. **Green Fees** £18 per day; £15 per 18 holes; £10
per 9 holes. **Facilities** ᐃ 𝒸 **Leisure** hard tennis courts,
driving net. **Location** 0.5m S of Drymen via access lane E
of A811
....
Hotel ★★★★★ 72% De Vere Cameron House,
BALLOCH ☎ 01389 755565 96 en suite

DUNBLANE   Map 11 NN70

Dunblane New Golf Club Perth Rd FK15 0LJ
☎ 01786 821521 ▤ 01786 821522
e-mail: secretary@dngc.co.uk
**Well-maintained parkland course, with reasonably
hard walking. Testing par 3 holes.**
18 holes, 5930yds, Par 69, SSS 69.
Club membership 1000.
Visitors may play 9.30am-noon & 2.30-4pm Mon-Fri.
Must contact in advance. **Societies** welcome Mon, Wed-
Fri, contact in advance. **Green Fees** £35 per day; £25 per
round. **Cards** ▆▆ ▆▆ ▆▆ ▆▆ 𝒹 **Prof** Bob Jamieson
Course Designer James Braid **Facilities** ⊗ ⅢⅢ ᴸ ᛒ ⅋ ᐃ
ᐃ ᛏ 𝒸 **Conf** fac available Corporate Hospitality Days
available **Location** E side of town on A9
....
Hotel ★★★ ♨ Cromlix House Hotel, Kinbuck, Nr
DUNBLANE ☎ 01786 822125 14 en suite

KILLIN   Map 11 NN53

Killin FK21 8TX
☎ 01567 820312 ▤ 01567 820312
e-mail: info@killingolfclub.co.uk
Parkland course at West End of Loch Tay with

outstanding views. Challenging 9-hole course with 14
different tees.

Killin Golf Club

9 holes, 2600yds, Par 66, SSS 65, Course record 61.
Club membership 250.
Visitors not competition days, parties must book in
advance. **Societies** Apply in writing or phone in advance.
Green Fees terms on application. **Cards** ▆▆ ▆▆ ▆▆ ▆▆ 𝒹
Course Designer John Duncan, J Braid **Facilities** ⊗ ⅢⅢ ᴸ
ᛒ ⅋ ᐃ ᐃ ᛏ ᛤ 𝒸 **Location** 0.5m N of village centre
on A827
....
Guesthouse ◆◆◆◆ Fairview House, Main St, KILLIN
☎ 01567 820667 6 en suite

STIRLING   Map 11 NS79

Stirling Queens Rd FK8 3AA
☎ 01786 464098 ▤ 01786 460090
e-mail: enquiries@stirlinggolfclub.tv
**Undulating parkland course with magnificent views of
Stirling Castle and the Grampian Mountains. Testing
15th, Cotton's Fancy, 384yds (par 4).**
18 holes, 6438yds, Par 72, SSS 71, Course record 64.
Club membership 1100.
Visitors may reserve tee off times mid-week 9-4.30pm. At
weekends tee off times may be reserved on day of play
subject to availability. **Societies** apply in writing or phone.
Green Fees £45 per day; £30 per round. **Cards** ▆▆ ▆▆ 𝒹
Prof Ian Collins **Course Designer** James Braid, Henry
Cotton **Facilities** ⊗ ⅢⅢ ᴸ ᛒ ⅋ ᐃ ᐃ ᛏ 🦽 𝒸
Conf Corporate Hospitality Days available
Location W side of town on B8051

WEST DUNBARTONSHIRE

BALLOCH   Map 10 NS48

De Vere Cameron House Hotel Loch Lomond
G83 8QZ
☎ 01389 757211
**Only available for residents of the hotel or a party
booked in advance. A challenging nine-hole course with
water hazards.**
Carrich on Loch Lomond: 18 holes, 7200yds, Par 71.
Wee Demon: 9 holes, 3200yds, Par 32.
Club membership 250.
Visitors contact in advance by writing, phone or e-mail.
Societies apply in writing. **Green Fees** Carrich: £95 per
round, Wee Demon: £18 per day. **Cards** ▆▆ ▆▆ ▆▆ ▆▆
▆▆ ▆▆ 𝒹 **Prof** Stewart Smith **Facilities** ⊗ ⅢⅢ ᴸ ᛒ ⅋ ᐃ
ᛏ ⛵ ⁀ 𝒸 **Leisure** hard tennis courts, heated indoor
swimming pool, squash, fishing, sauna, solarium,
gymnasium. **Conf** fac available Corporate Hospitality

Continued
Continued

ays available **Location** M8 (W) junct 30, towards
rskine Bridge, onto A82 for Crainlarich, course 1m past
alloch rdbt

....

lotel ★★★★ 72% De Vere Cameron House,
ALLOCH ☎ 01389 755565 96 en suite

ONHILL   Map 10 NS37

ale of Leven North Field Rd G83 9ET
☎ 01389 752351 ▤ 0870 749 8950
-mail: clubadministrator@valeoflevengolfclub.org.uk
**loorland course, tricky with many natural hazards -
orse, burns, trees. Overlooks Loch Lomond.**
8 holes, 5277yds, Par 67, SSS 67, Course record 63.
lub membership 750.
isitors not Sat. **Societies** apply to the secretary in writing
r phone call. **Green Fees** £30 per day, £20 per round
£37.50/£25 weekends). **Cards** ▤ ▦ ▤ ▣ ▤ ▤ ▣
rof Barry Campbell **Facilities** ⊗ ⫟ ▯ ♥ ♀ ♨ ☎ ♂ ♂
onf fac available Corporate Hospitality Days available
ocation E side of town off A813

....

lotel ★★★★ 72% De Vere Cameron House,
ALLOCH ☎ 01389 755565 96 en suite

LYDEBANK   Map 11 NS56

lydebank & District Glasgow Rd, Hardgate
81 5QY
☎ 01389 383831 & 383833 ▤ 01389 383831
n undulating parkland course established in 1905,
verlooking Clydebank.
8 holes, 5823yds, Par 68, SSS 68, Course record 64.
lub membership 889.
isitors round only, weekdays only & no bank holidays.
lust tee off before 4.30pm. Apply to professional 01389
83835 **Societies** apply in writing. **Green Fees** terms on
pplication. **Prof** Paul Jamieson **Course Designer** in house
acilities ⊗ ⫟ ▯ ♥ ♀ ♨ ☎ ♂
ocation 2m E of Erskine Bridge

....

lotel � Premier Travel Inn Glasgow (Bearsden),
lilngavie Rd, BEARSDEN ☎ 0870 9906532 61 en suite

lydebank Municipal Overtoun Rd, Dalmuir
81 3RE
☎ 0141 952 6372
8 holes, 5349yds, Par 67, SSS 66, Course record 63.
ocation 2m NW of town centre
hone for further details

....

lotel ★★★★ 74% Beardmore Hotel, Beardmore St,
LYDEBANK ☎ 0141 951 6000 168 en suite

UMBARTON   Map 10 NS37

lumbarton Broadmeadow G82 2BQ
☎ 01389 732830 & 765995 ▤ 01389 765995
lat parkland course.
8 holes, 5992yds, Par 71, SSS 69, Course record 64.
lub membership 700.
isitors may play Mon- Fri only. **Societies** apply in
riting to Secretary. **Green Fees** £30 per day. **Facilities** ⊗
l ▯ ♥ ♀ ♨ **Conf** Corporate Hospitality Days available
ocation 0.25m N off A814

....

uesthouse ♦♦♦♦♦ Kirkton House, Darleith Rd,
ARDROSS ☎ 01389 841951 6 en suite

WEST LOTHIAN

BATHGATE   Map 11 NS96

Bathgate Edinburgh Rd EH48 1BA
☎ 01506 630553 & 652232/630505 ▤ 01506 636775
e-mail: bathgate.golfclub@lineone.net
Moorland course. Easy walking. Testing 11th hole, par 3.
18 holes, 6328yds, Par 71, SSS 70, Course record 58.
Club membership 900.
Visitors casual visitors welcome other than on competition
days. Handicap certificate advisable. **Societies** apply in
writing. **Green Fees** £25 per day; £20 per round (£35/£25
weekends). **Prof** Sandy Strachan **Course Designer** W Park
Facilities ⊗ ⫟ ▯ ♥ ♀ ♨ ☎ ♂ ♠ ⤇ ♂ **Conf** Corporate
Hospitality Days available **Location** E side of town off A89

....

Hotel ★★★ 68% The Hilcroft Hotel, East Main St,
WHITBURN ☎ 01501 740818 32 en suite

BROXBURN   Map 11 NT07

Niddry Castle Castle Rd, Winchburgh EH52 6RQ
☎ 01506 891097 ▤ 01506 891097
**An 18-hole parkland course, requiring accurate golf to
score well.**
18 holes, 5965yds, Par 70, SSS 69, Course record 63.
Club membership 600.
Visitors advisable to contact at weekends, restricted during
competition time. **Societies** contact in advance. **Green
Fees** terms on application. **Course Designer** A Scott
Facilities ⊗ ⫟ ▯ ♥ ♀ ♨ **Conf** Corporate Hospitality
Days available **Location** 9m W of Edinburgh on B9080

....

Hotel ★★★★ 68% Houstoun House, UPHALL
☎ 01506 853831 24 en suite 47 annexe en suite

FAULDHOUSE   Map 11 NS96

Greenburn 6 Greenburn Rd EH47 9HJ
☎ 01501 770292 ▤ 01501 772615
e-mail: administrator@greenburngolfclub.freeserve.co.uk
**Exposed rolling course with sparse tree cover. Water
hazards from a pond and a burn.**
18 holes, 6045yds, Par 71, SSS 70, Course record 65.
Club membership 900.
Visitors contact in advance for details. **Societies** by
arrangement. **Green Fees** terms on application. **Prof** Scott
Catlin **Facilities** ⊗ ⫟ ▯ ♥ ♀ ♨ ☎ ♂
Location 3m SW of Whitburn

....

Hotel ★★★ 68% The Hilcroft Hotel, East Main St,
WHITBURN ☎ 01501 740818 32 en suite

LINLITHGOW   Map 11 NS97

Linlithgow Braehead EH49 6QF
☎ 01506 844356 (Pro) ▤ 01506 842764
e-mail: info@linlithgowgolf.co.uk
**A short but testing undulating parkland course with
panoramic views of the Forth valley.**
18 holes, 5800yds, Par 70, SSS 68, Course record 64.
Club membership 450.
Visitors not Weds & Sat. **Societies** contact in writing.
Green Fees £35 per day; £25 per round (£40/£30 Sun).
Prof Steven Rosie **Course Designer** R Simpson of
Carnoustie **Facilities** ⊗ ⫟ ▯ ♥ ♀ ♨ ☎ ♠ ♂
Location 1m S off A706

....

Hotel ★★★★ 69% The Inchyra, Grange Rd, POLMONT
☎ 01324 711911 109 en suite

West Lothian Airngath Hill EH49 7RH
☎ 01506 825060 📄 01506 826462
Hilly parkland course with superb views of River Forth.
18 holes, 6249yds, Par 71, SSS 70.
Club membership 800.
Visitors weekends by arrangement. Advisable to contact in high season. **Societies** apply in writing. **Green Fees** not confirmed. **Cards** 🔲 🔲 🔲 **Prof** Ian Taylor **Course Designer** Fraser Middleton **Facilities** ⊗ 🍴 ♥ 🔄 △ 🏠 🚩 🏌 🔄 **Conf** Corporate Hospitality Days available
Location 1m N off A706

Hotel ★★★★ 69% The Inchyra, Grange Rd, POLMONT
☎ 01324 711911 109 en suite

LIVINGSTON   Map 11 NT06

Deer Park Golf & Country Club Golf Course Rd EH54 8AB
☎ 01506 446699 📄 01506 435608
e-mail: deerpark@muir-group.co.uk
Long testing course, fairly flat, championship standard.
18 holes, 6690yds, Par 72, SSS 72, Course record 65.
Visitors proper golfing attire to be worn, must book in advance, Sun after 10am. **Societies** phone or write **Green Fees** £28 per 18 holes (£38 weekend play). **Cards** 🔲 🔲 🔲 **Prof** Brian Dunbar **Course Designer** Alliss, Thomas **Facilities** ⊗ 🍴 🍴 ♥ 🔄 △ 🏠 🚩 🔄 **Leisure** heated indoor swimming pool, squash, sauna, solarium, gymnasium, snooker table, ten-pin bowling. **Conf** fac available Corporate Hospitality Days available
Location M8 junct 3, to N side of town

Hotel ⏱ Premier Travel Inn Livingston (Nr Edinburgh), Deer Park Av, Knightsridge, LIVINGSTON
☎ 08701 977161 83 en suite

Pumpherston Drumshoreland Rd, Pumpherston EH53 0LH
☎ 01506 433336 & 433337 (pro) 📄 01506 438250
e-mail: sheena.corner@tiscali.co.uk
Undulating, well-bunkered parkland course with very testing 2nd and 15th holes. The course has water features at five holes and has won several environmental awards. Panoramic views of Edinburgh and the Pentland Hills.
18 holes, 6006yds, Par 70, SSS 72.
Club membership 800.
Visitors pay & play anytime, but confirm in advance if possible **Societies** apply in writing to the secretary. **Green Fees** terms on application. **Cards** 🔲 🔲 🔲 **Prof** Richard Fyvie **Course Designer** G Webster **Facilities** ⊗ by arrangement 🍴 ♥ 🔄 △ 🏠 🔄 **Leisure** Pool table.
Location 1m E of Livingston off B8046

Hotel ⏱ Premier Travel Inn Livingston (Nr Edinburgh), Deer Park Av, Knightsridge, LIVINGSTON
☎ 08701 977161 83 en suite

UPHALL   Map 11 NT07

Uphall EH52 6JT
☎ 01506 856404 📄 01506 855358
e-mail: uphallgolfclub@businessunmetered.com
Windy parkland course, easy walking.
18 holes, 5588yds, Par 69, SSS 67, Course record 61.
Club membership 650.
Visitors contact in advance, restricted weekends.

Societies contact in advance. **Green Fees** terms on application. **Prof** Gordon Law **Facilities** ⊗ 🍴 🍴 ♥ 🔄 △ 🏠 🔄 **Location** W side of village on A899

Hotel ★★★★ 68% Houstoun House, UPHALL
☎ 01506 853831 24 en suite 47 annexe en suite

WEST CALDER   Map 11 NT06

Harburn EH55 8RS
☎ 01506 871131 & 871256 📄 01506 870286
e-mail: info@harburngolfclub.co.uk
Parkland course with a good variety of beech, oak and pine trees. The 11th and 12th holes were extended in 2004. Fine views of the Pentlands

18 holes, 6125yds, Par 71, SSS 70, Course record 64.
Club membership 870.
Visitors contact secretary in advance **Societies** contact by phone. **Green Fees** £30 per day, £25 per 18 holes (Fri £35/£30, Sat-Sun £40/£35). **Prof** Stephen Mills **Facilities** ⊗ 🍴 🍴 ♥ 🔄 △ 🏠 🚩 🔄 **Conf** fac available Corporate Hospitality Days available
Location 2m S of West Calder on B7008

Hotel ★★★ 68% The Hilcroft Hotel, East Main St, WHITBURN ☎ 01501 740818 32 en suite

WHITBURN   Map 11 NS96

Polkemmet Country Park EH47 0AD
☎ 01501 743905 📄 01506 846256
e-mail: mail@beecraigs.com
Public parkland course surrounded by mature woodland and rhododendron bushes and bisected by a river. Interesting and demanding last hole.
9 holes, 3222yds, Par 37.
Visitors no restrictions. **Societies** weekdays only, apply in writing. **Green Fees** 9 holes £5.25; 18 holes £9.10 (weekends & bank holidays £6.15/£10.75). **Cards** 🔲 🔲 🔲 🔲 **Facilities** ⊗ 🍴 🍴 ♥ 🔄 🔄 **Leisure** bowling green.
Location 2m W on B7066

Hotel ★★★ 68% The Hilcroft Hotel, East Main St, WHITBURN ☎ 01501 740818 32 en suite

ARRAN, ISLE OF

BLACKWATERFOOT   Map 10 NR92

Shiskine Shore Rd KA27 8HA
☎ 01770 860226 📄 01770 860205
e-mail: info@shiskinegolf.com
Unique 12-hole links course with gorgeous outlook to the Mull of Kintyre. The course is crossed by two burns and includes the longest par 5 on the island at 509yds.

Continued

Continued

here are several blind holes at which various signals
dicate when the green is clear and it is safe to play.
9 holes, 2990yds, Par 42, SSS 42, Course record 38.
Club membership 670.
Visitors contact in advance. Parties require handicap
rtificates. **Societies** contact in writing in advance. Jul &
ug no parties. **Green Fees** £25 per day; £15 per round
30/£19 weekends & bank holidays). **Course Designer**
rnie of Troon **Facilities** ⊗ � by arrangement ⮐ 💺 🏖️
💺 ⛳ **Leisure** hard tennis courts, bowling green,
lf practice nets. **Conf** Corporate Hospitality Days
ailable **Location** W side of village off A841

otel ★★ 🏩 Kilmichael Country House Hotel, Glen
loy, BRODICK ☎ 01770 302219   4 en suite   3 annexe
suite

RODICK   Map 10 NS03

rodick KA27 8DL
☎ 01770 302349 📠 01770 302349
mail: info@brodickgolfclub.org
9 holes, 4747yds, Par 65, SSS 64, Course record 60.
ocation N side of village, 0.5m N of Brodick Ferry
rminal
hone for further details

otel ★★★ 76% Auchrannie Country House Hotel,
RODICK ☎ 01770 302234   28 en suite

AMLASH   Map 10 NS03

amlash KA27 8JU
☎ 01770 600296 📠 01770 600296
mail: lamlashgolfclub@connectfree.co.uk
ndulating heathland course with magnificent views of
e mountains and sea.
9 holes, 4510yds, Par 64, SSS 64, Course record 58.
Club membership 480.
isitors book in advance by letter **Societies** contact in
riting. **Green Fees** terms on application. **Cards** 💳
ourse Designer Auchterlonie **Facilities** ⊗ � ⮐ 💺 💺 🍴 🏖️
💺 🏌️ ⛳ **Location** 0.75m N of Lamlash on A841

OCHRANZA   Map 10 NR95

ochranza KA27 8HL
☎ 01770 830273 📠 01770 830600
mail: office@lochgolf.demon.co.uk
his course is mainly on the level, set amid spectacular
enery where the fairways are grazed by wild red deer,
hile overhead buzzards and golden eagles may be
en. There are water hazards including the river which
lined by mature trees. The final three holes,
cknamed the Bermuda Triangle, provide an
sorbing finish right to the 18th hole - a 530yd dogleg
rough trees and over the river. The large greens, six
ngle and six double, are played off 18 tees.
9 holes, 5504yds, Par 70, SSS 67, Course record 72.
ub membership 40.
isitors no restrictions; course closed Nov to mid-Apr.
ocieties advance booking preferred. **Green Fees** £16 per
8 holes; £10 per 9 holes; £21 per day. **Course Designer**
laid 1991 I Robertson **Facilities** 💺 🏖️ 🍴 🏌️ ⛳
ocation in Lochranza village

otel ★★ 🏩 Kilmichael Country House Hotel, Glen
loy, BRODICK ☎ 01770 302219   4 en suite   3 annexe
suite

MACHRIE   Map 10 NR83

Machrie Bay KA27 8DZ
☎ 01770 840259 📠 01770 840266
e-mail: office@dougarie.com
**Fairly flat seaside course. Designed at the start of the
20th century by William Fernie.**
9 holes, 4400yds, Par 66, SSS 62, Course record 62.
Club membership 315.
Visitors no restrictions. **Societies** write in advance.
Green Fees not confirmed. **Course Designer** W Fernie
Facilities ⊗ 💺 🏖️ 🍴 ⛳ **Leisure** hard tennis courts.
Location 9m W of Brodick via String Rd

Hotel ★★ 🏩 Kilmichael Country House Hotel, Glen
Cloy, BRODICK ☎ 01770 302219   4 en suite   3 annexe
en suite

SANNOX   Map 10 NS04

Corrie KA27 8JD
☎ 01770 810223 & 810606
**A heathland course on the coast with beautiful
mountain scenery. An upward climb to 6th hole then a
descent from the 7th. All these holes are subject to
strong winds in bad weather.**
9 holes, 1948yds, Par 62, SSS 61, Course record 56.
Club membership 300.
Visitors welcome except Sat pm & first Thu pm of month.
Societies maximum size of party 12, apply in advance.
Green Fees not confirmed. **Facilities** ⊗ � 💺 🏖️
Location 6m N of A841

Hotel ★★★ 76% Auchrannie Country House Hotel,
BRODICK ☎ 01770 302234   28 en suite

WHITING BAY   Map 10 NS02

Whiting Bay KA27 8QT
☎ 01770 700487
18 holes, 4405yds, Par 63, SSS 63, Course record 59.
Location NW side of village off A841
Phone for further details

Hotel ★★ 🏩 Kilmichael Country House Hotel, Glen
Cloy, BRODICK ☎ 01770 302219   4 en suite   3 annexe
en suite

BUTE, ISLE OF

KINGARTH   Map 10 NS05

Bute St Ninians, 32 Marine Place, Ardbeg, Rothesay
PA20 0LF
☎ 01700 502158
e-mail: info@butegolfclub.com
**Flat seaside course with good fenced greens and fine
views over the Sound of Bute to Isle of Arran.**
9 holes, 2582yds, Par 68, SSS 64, Course record 61.
Club membership 250.
Visitors restricted Sat until after 11.30am. **Societies** apply
in advance. **Green Fees** £10 per round/day. **Facilities** 🏖️
Location 6m from Rothesay pier on A845

Hotel ★★ 79% The Royal at Tighnabruaich, Shore Rd,
TIGHNABRUAICH ☎ 01700 811239   11 en suite

PORT BANNATYNE   Map 10 NS06

Port Bannatyne Bannatyne Mains Rd PA20 0PH
☎ 01700 505142
e-mail: macleodbute@btopenworld.com
Seaside hill course with panoramic views. Almost unique in having 13 holes, with the first five being played again before a separate 18th. Difficult 4th (par 3).
13 holes, 5085yds, Par 68, SSS 65, Course record 63.
Club membership 150.
Visitors no restrictions. **Societies** phone in advance. **Green Fees** terms on application. **Course Designer** Peter Morrison **Facilities** ⊗ ⓑ ♥ ♀ 👃 **Location** W side of village off A886

Hotel ★★ 79% The Royal at Tighnabruaich, Shore Rd, TIGHNABRUAICH ☎ 01700 811239 11 en suite

ROTHESAY   Map 10 NS06

Rothesay Canada Hill PA20 9HN
☎ 01700 503554 📄 01700 503554
e-mail: thepro@rothesaygolfclub.com
A scenic island course designed by James Braid and Ben Sayers. The course is fairly hilly, with views of the Firth of Clyde, Rothesay Bay or the Kyles of Bute from every hole. Winds make the two par 5 holes extremely challenging.
18 holes, 5419yds, Par 69, SSS 66, Course record 62.
Club membership 400.
Visitors booking essential for weekends, phone professional 01700 503554. **Societies** contact in advance, booking essential at weekends. **Green Fees** not confirmed. **Cards** 🌐 📇 📇 📇 📇 🔜 🏧 **Prof** James M Dougal **Course Designer** James Braid & Ben Sayers **Facilities** ⊗ ♨ ⓑ ♥ ♀ 👃 🏠 🏌 🏹 👃 ✓ **Conf** Corporate Hospitality Days available **Location** 500yds SE from main ferry terminal

Hotel ★★ 79% The Royal at Tighnabruaich, Shore Rd, TIGHNABRUAICH ☎ 01700 811239 11 en suite

COLONSAY, ISLE OF

SCALASAIG   Map 10 NR39

Colonsay Machrins Farm PA61 7YP
☎ 01951 200364 📄 01951 200312
e-mail: golf@machrin.free-online.co.uk
18 holes, 4775yds, Par 72, SSS 72.
Location 2m W on A870
Phone for further details

ISLAY, ISLE OF

PORT ELLEN   Map 10 NR34

Machrie Hotel Machrie PA42 7AN
☎ 01496 302310 📄 01496 302404
e-mail: machrie@machrie.com
Championship links course opened in 1891, where golf's first £100 Open Championship was played in 1901. Fine turf and many blind holes. Par 4.
18 holes, 6226yds, Par 71, SSS 71, Course record 66.
Club membership 340.

Continued

Visitors no restrictions. **Societies** apply in writing or phone. **Green Fees** £57 per day, £42 per round. **Cards** 🌐 📇 📇 🔜 🏧 **Course Designer** W Campbell **Facilitie** ⊗ ♨ ⓑ ♥ ♀ 👃 🏠 🏌 🏹 ✓ 🍴 **Leisure** fishing, snooker, table tennis. **Conf** fac available
Location 4m N off A846

Inn ♦♦♦♦♦ The Harbour Inn and Restaurant, BOWMORE ☎ 01496 810330 7 en suite

LEWIS, ISLE OF

STORNOWAY   Map 13 NB43

Stornoway Lady Lever Park HS2 0XP
☎ 01851 702240
e-mail: admin@stornowaygolfclub.co.uk
A short but tricky undulating parkland course set in the grounds of Lews Castle with fine views over the Minch to the mainland. The terrain is peat based and there has been substantial investment in drainage works.
18 holes, 5252yds, Par 68, SSS 67, Course record 61.
Club membership 500.
Visitors no golf on Sun. **Societies** apply in writing. **Green Fees** £15 per round/£20 per day. **Facilities** ⓑ ♥ ♀ 👃 🏠 🏌 ✓ **Conf** fac available **Location** 0.5m from town centre off A857

MULL, ISLE OF

CRAIGNURE   Map 10 NM73

Craignure Scallastle PA65 6BA
☎ 01680 300402 📄 01680 300402
e-mail: mullair@btinternet.com
9 holes, 5357yds, Par 69, SSS 66, Course record 72.
Location 1.5m N of Craignure A849
Phone for further details

TOBERMORY   Map 13 NM55

Tobermory PA75 6PG
☎ 01688 302338 📄 01688 302140
e-mail: enquiries@tobermorygolfclub.com
A beautifully maintained hilltop course with superb views over the Sound of Mull. Testing 7th hole (par 3). Often described as the best nine-hole course in Scotland.
9 holes, 4890yds, Par 64, SSS 64, Course record 65.
Club membership 150.
Visitors no restrictions except competition days. **Societies** preferable to contact in advance. **Green Fees** £15 per day. **Course Designer** David Adams **Facilities** ⓑ ♥ ♀ 👃 🏌 🏹 ✓ **Location** 0.5m N off A848

Hotel 🏠 Druimard Country House Hotel, DERVAIG ☎ 01688 400345 5 en suite 2 annexe en suite

ORKNEY

IRKWALL   Map 16 HY41

rkney Grainbank KW15 1RB
☎ 01856 872457
mail: les@orkneygolfclub.co.uk
pen parkland course with few hazards and superb
ews over Kirkwall and the islands. Very exposed to
e elements which can make play tough.
holes, 5411yds, Par 70, SSS 67, Course record 63.
ub membership 350.
sitors not competition days. **Societies** write or phone if
ssible. **Green Fees** £20 per day. **Facilities** ⓑ 🍺 ♀ ⚒
⚿ **Location** 0.5m W off A965

ROMNESS   Map 16 HY20

romness Ness KW16 3DW
☎ 01856 850772
mail: sgc@stromnessgc.co.uk
sting parkland and seaside course with easy walking.
agnificent views of Scapa Flow.
holes, 4762yds, Par 65, SSS 64, Course record 61.
ub membership 350.
sitors no restrictions except during major competitions.
cieties no restrictions. **Green Fees** £20 per day.
cilities ⊗ ⓑ 🍺 ♀ ⚒ ✝ ⚿ **Leisure** hard tennis courts,
wling. **Location** S side of town centre off A965

SHETLAND

ERWICK   Map 16 HU44

hetland PO Box 18, Dale ZE2 9SB
☎ 01595 840369 🖹 840369
mail: clubhousemanager@shetlandgolfclub.co.uk
le Course: 18 holes, 5776yds, Par 68, SSS 68,
urse record 67.
urse Designer Fraser Middleton
cation 4m N on A970
one for further details
....
tel ★★★ 68% Lerwick Hotel, 15 South Rd, LERWICK
01595 692166 34 en suite

WHALSAY, ISLAND OF   Map 16 HU56

Whalsay Skaw Taing ZE2 9AA
☎ 01806 566450 566705
18 holes, 6009yds, Par 70, SSS 68, Course record 65.
Location Whalsay Island
Phone for further details

SKYE, ISLE OF

SCONSER   Map 13 NG53

Isle of Skye IV48 8TD
☎ 01478 650414
e-mail: info@isleofskyegolfclub.co.uk
Seaside course with spectacular views; nine holes with
18 tees. Suitable for golfers of all abilities.
18 holes, 4677yds, Par 66, SSS 64, Course record 62.
Club membership 270.
Visitors during competition play. **Societies** apply in
advance. **Green Fees** £18 per round/£22 per day; 9 holes
£12. **Cards** 🟦 🟥 🔳 🟨 **Facilities** ⊗ ⓑ 🍺 ⚒ 🏠 ✝ ⚿
Location on A87 between Broadford & Portree
....
Hotel ★★ 73% Rosedale Hotel, Beaumont Crescent,
PORTREE ☎ 01478 613131 18 en suite

SOUTH UIST

ASKERNISH   Map 13 NF72

Askernish Lochboisdale PA81 5SY
☎ 01878 700298
e-mail: askernish.golf.club@cwcom.net
18 holes, 5042yds, Par 68, SSS 67, Course record 64.
Course Designer Tom Morris **Location** 5m NW of
Lochboisdale off A865
Phone for further details

If the name of the club appears in *italics*, details
have not been confirmed for this
edition of the guide.

Wales

ANGLESEY, ISLE OF

MLWCH   Map 06 SH49

ll Bay LL68 9RY
☎ 01407 830960 📠 01407 832612
✉ail: secretary@bullbaygolf.freeserve.co.uk
ales's northernmost course, Bull Bay is a pleasant
ıstal, heathland course with natural rock, gorse and
ıd hazards. Views from several tees across the Irish
ı to the Isle of Man, and across Anglesey to Snowdonia.
, holes, 6217yds, Par 70, SSS 70, Course record 60.
ıb membership 700.
ısitors advisable to contact in advance. **Societies** advance
•king essential. **Green Fees** £25 per day (£30 weekends
·bank holidays). **Cards** 🎫 🎫 🎫 🎫 🎫 🎫 **Prof** John
·ms **Course Designer** WH Fowler **Facilities** ⊗ ⅷ ⅃ ⚑
△ 🏠 🏌 🥌 🥌 🥌 **Conf** Corporate Hospitality Days
·ilable **Location** 1m W of Amlwch on A5025

·tel ★★ 70% Lastra Farm Hotel, Penrhyd, AMLWCH
·01407 830906 5 en suite 3 annexe en suite

AUMARIS   Map 06 SH67

·ron Hill LL58 8YW
☎ 01248 810231 📠 01248 810231
✉ail: golf@baronhill.co.uk
·dulating course with natural hazards of rock and
·rse. Testing 3rd and 4th holes (par 4s). Hole 5/14
·ıys into the prevailing wind with an elevated tee
·oss two streams. The hole is between two gorse
·vered mounds.
· oles, 5572yds, Par 68, SSS 68, Course record 65.
·ıb membership 400.
·sitors ladies have priority on Tue am & club
·npetitions Sun, seniors Thu only. **Societies** apply in
·ting to secretary. **Green Fees** £15 per day. **Facilities** ⊗
·⚑ ♀ △ 🏌 🥌 **Conf** Corporate Hospitality Days
·ilable **Location** A545 from Menai Bridge to Beaumaris,
·ırse signed on approach to town

·tel ★★ 75% Ye Olde Bulls Head Inn, Castle St,
·AUMARIS ☎ 01248 810329 12 en suite 1 annexe
·suite

·inces Henllys Hall LL58 8HU
☎ 01248 811717 📠 01248 811511
✉ail: henllys@hpbsite.com
·holes, 6062yds.
·urse **Designer** Roger Jones **Location** A545 through
·aumaris, 0.25m Henllys Hall signed on left
·one for further details

·tel ★★ 75% Ye Olde Bulls Head Inn, Castle St,
·AUMARIS ☎ 01248 810329 12 en suite 1 annexe
·suite

·OLYHEAD   Map 06 SH28

·olyhead Lon Garreg Fawr, Trearddur Bay LL65 2YL
·01407 763279 📠 01407 763279
·ail: mqrsec@aol.com
·eeless, undulating seaside course which provides a
·ied and testing game, particularly in a south wind.
· fairways are bordered by gorse, heather and
·ged outcrops of rock. Accuracy from most tees is

---

paramount as there are 43 fairway and greenside
bunkers and lakes. Designed by James Braid.
18 holes, 6058yds, Par 70, SSS 70, Course record 64.
Club membership 1350.
Visitors contact in advance. **Societies** contact in advance.
Green Fees £25 per day (£30 weekends & bank holidays).
Prof Stephen Elliot **Course Designer** James Braid
Facilities ⊗ ⅷ ⅃ ⚑ ♀ △ 🏠 🏌 🚜 🥌 **Location** A55 to
rdbt at Holyhead, left onto B4545 to Trearddur Bay 1m

Hotel ★★★ 73% Trearddur Bay Hotel, TREARDDUR
BAY ☎ 01407 860301 36 en suite

RHOSNEIGR   Map 06 SH37

Anglesey Station Rd LL64 5QX
☎ 01407 811127 & 811202 📠 01407 811127
e-mail: info@theangleseygolfclub.com
An interesting 18-hole links course set among sand
dunes and heather, renowned for its excellent greens
and numerous streams. The whole course boasts an
abundance of wildlife and is an important conservation
area.
18 holes, 6330yds, Par 70, SSS 71, Course record 64.
Club membership 500.
Visitors phone in advance, some times are reserved for
members. Dress restrictions. **Societies** phone & confirm in
writing. **Green Fees** terms on application. **Cards** 🎫 🎫
🎫 🎫 🎫 **Prof** Mr Matthew Parry **Course Designer**
H Hilton **Facilities** ⊗ ⅷ ⅃ ⚑ ♀ △ 🏠 🏌 🚜 🥌
Location NE side of village on A4080

Hotel ★★★ 73% Trearddur Bay Hotel, TREARDDUR
BAY ☎ 01407 860301 36 en suite

BLAENAU GWENT

NANTYGLO   Map 03 SO11

West Monmouthshire Golf Rd, Winchestown
NP23 4QT
☎ 01495 310233 📠 01495 310361
18 holes, 6300yds, Par 71, SSS 69, Course record 65.
Course Designer Ben Sayers **Location** 0.25m W off A467
Phone for further details

Hotel ★★ 72% Llanwenarth Hotel & Riverside
Restaurant, Brecon Rd, ABERGAVENNY
☎ 01873 810550 17 en suite

TREDEGAR   Map 03 SO10

Tredegar and Rhymney Cwmtysswg, Rhymney
NP2 3BQ
☎ 01685 840743 (club) 07944 843400 (sec)
e-mail: golfclub@tredegarandrhymney.fsnet.co.uk
Mountain course with lovely views. The course has now
been developed into an 18-hole course with easy
walking.
18 holes, 6250yds, Par 67, SSS 67, Course record 68.
Club membership 194.
Visitors cannot play Sun before 12. **Societies** contact in
advance. **Green Fees** £10 per day. **Facilities** ⊗ by
arrangement ⅷ by arrangement ⅃ by arrangement ⚑ by
arrangement △ 🥌 🚜 **Conf** Corporate Hospitality Days
available **Location** 1.75m SW on B4256

Hotel Tregenna Hotel, Park Ter, MERTHYR TYDFIL
☎ 01685 723627 382055 📠 01685 721951 21 en suite

BRIDGEND

BRIDGEND
Map 03 SS97

Coed-Y-Mwstwr The Clubhouse, Coychurch
CF35 6AF
☎ 01656 864934 ▤ 01656 864934
e-mail: secretary@coed-y-mwstwr.co.uk
Challenging holes on this course include the par 3 11th (180yds) involving a drive across a lake and the par 4 5th (448yds) which is subject to strong prevailing winds. Previously 12 holes but extended to 18 holes in 2005.
12 holes, 6144yds, Par 70, SSS 70, Course record 71.
Club membership 300.
Visitors must have handicap certificate, advisable to contact in advance. May only play Sat if with member.
Societies by application. **Green Fees** £18 per 18 holes (£20 weekends). **Cards** ▨ ▭ ▬ ▧ **Course Designer** Chapman, Warren **Facilities** ⊗ ⅷ ᴸ ᵂ ♀ ⅃ ☎ **Conf** fac available Corporate Hospitality Days available
Location M4 junct 35, A473 into Coychurch, course 1m N

···

Hotel ★★★★ 72% Coed-Y-Mwstwr Hotel, Coychurch, BRIDGEND ☎ 01656 860621 28 en suite

Southerndown Ewenny CF32 0QP
☎ 01656 880476 ▤ 01656 880317
e-mail: southerndowngolf@btconnect.com
Downland-links championship course with rolling fairways and fast greens. Golfers who successfully negotiate the four par 3s still face a testing finish with three of the last four holes played into the prevailing wind. The par 3 5th is played across a valley and the 18th, with its split-level fairway, is a demanding finishing hole. Superb views.
18 holes, 6449yds, Par 70, SSS 72, Course record 64.
Club membership 710.
Visitors contact in advance & have handicap certificate.
Societies by arrangement with secretary. **Green Fees** £45 (£60 weekends or 36 holes). **Cards** ▨ ▭ ▬ ▧ **Prof** DG McMonagle **Course Designer** W Park, W Fernie & others **Facilities** ⊗ ⅷ ᴸ ᵂ ♀ ⅃ ☎ ♨ ☞ ✓ ℓ
Location 3m SW of Bridgend on B4524

···

Hotel ★★★ 69% Heronston Hotel, Ewenny Rd, BRIDGEND ☎ 01656 668811 69 en suite 6 annexe en suite

MAESTEG
Map 03 SS89

Maesteg Mount Pleasant, Neath Rd CF34 9PR
☎ 01656 734106 ▤ 01656 731822
e-mail: ijm@fsmail.net
Reasonably flat hill-top course with scenic views.
18 holes, 5929yds, Par 70, SSS 69, Course record 69.
Club membership 789.
Visitors must be a member of a recognised golf club & have a handicap certificate. **Societies** apply in writing.
Green Fees terms on application. **Cards** ▨ ▬ ▧ **Course Designer** James Braid **Facilities** ⊗ ⅷ ᴸ ᵂ ♀ ⅃ ℓ **Conf** fac available **Location** 0.5m W off B4282

···

Hotel ★★★ 68% Aberavon Beach Hotel, PORT TALBOT ☎ 01639 884949 52 en suite

PENCOED
Map 03 SS98

St Mary's Hotel Golf & Country Club St Mar
Hill CF35 5EA
☎ 01656 868900 ▤ 01656 863400
A parkland course with many American-style features. The par 3 10th, called Alcatraz, has a well-deserved reputation.
St Mary's Course: 18 holes, 5291yds, Par 69, SSS 66, Course record 65.
Sevenoaks Course: 12 holes, 3125yds, Par 35.
Club membership 830.
Visitors St. Mary's Course: must contact in advance, handicap certificate not required 9-4 Mon-Fri, after 1pm weekends. Sevenoaks: no restrictions **Societies** phone in advance **Green Fees** not confirmed. **Cards** ▨ ▭ ▬ ▧ ▣ **Prof** John Peters **Course Designer** Peter Johnson **Facilities** ⊗ ⅷ ᴸ ᵂ ♀ ⅃ ☎ ♨ ☞ ✓ ℓ
Leisure tennis courts. **Location** 5m from junct 35 of M4

···

Hotel ★★★ 70% St Mary's Hotel & Country Club, St Marys Golf Club, PENCOED ☎ 01656 861100 & 86028 ▤ 01656 863400 24 en suite

PORTHCAWL
Map 03 SS8

Royal Porthcawl Rest Bay CF36 3UW
☎ 01656 782251 ▤ 01656 771687
e-mail: royalporthcawl@aol. com
One of the great links courses, Royal Porthcawl is unique in that the sea is in full view from every single hole. The course enjoys a substantial reputation with heather, broom, gorse and a challenging wind demanding a player's full skill and attention.
18 holes, 6440yds, Par 72, SSS 73.
Club membership 800.
Visitors contact in advance & produce handicap certifica limit men 20, ladies 30. Restricted at weekends & bank holidays. **Societies** apply in writing, phone or e-mail
Green Fees not confirmed. **Cards** ▨ ▭ ▬ ▧ **Prof** Peter Evans **Course Designer** Ramsey Hunter **Facilities** ⊗ ⅷ ᴸ ᵂ ♀ ⅃ ☎ ♨ ☞ ✓ ℓ
Location M4 J37, proceed to Porthcawl & Rest Bay

···

Hotel ★★★ 65% Seabank Hotel, The Promenade, PORTHCAWL ☎ 01656 782261 67 en suite

PYLE
Map 03 SS8

Pyle & Kenfig Waun-Y-Mer CF33 4PU
☎ 01656 783093 ▤ 01656 772822
e-mail: secretary@pandkgolfclub.co.uk
Links and downland course, with dunes. Easy walking
18 holes, 6776yds, Par 71, SSS 73, Course record 61.
Club membership 950.
Visitors by arrangement weekdays & Sun. **Societies** for large numbers apply in writing, small numbers phone booking accepted. **Green Fees** £45 per day (£65 Sun).
Cards ▨ ▭ ▬ ▧ ▣ **Prof** Robert Evans **Course Designer** Colt **Facilities** ⊗ ⅷ ᴸ ᵂ ♀ ⅃ ☎ ✓ ℓ
Location M4 junct 37, S side of Pyle off A4229.

···

Hotel ★★★ 65% Seabank Hotel, The Promenade, PORTHCAWL ☎ 01656 782261 67 en suite

CAERPHILLY

ARGOED
Map 03 ST19

argoed Heolddu CF81 9GF
☎ 01443 836179 📄 01143 830608
**ountain parkland course, a challenging par 70 with
noramic views. Easy walking.**
* *holes, 6049yds, Par 70, SSS 70, Course record 64.*
lub membership 600.
isitors contact in advance, must play with member at
eekends. **Societies** contact in advance. **Green Fees** not
nfirmed. **Cards** ⬛ ⬛ 🔲 📶 **Prof** Craig Easton
acilities ⊗ ⑂ 🏌 🍴 💂 ⚐ 🏠 ⛳ ✓ **Conf** fac available
orporate Hospitality Days available **Location** NW side of
wn

....

tel ★★★ 68% Maes Manor Hotel, BLACKWOOD
☎ 01495 220011 8 en suite 14 annexe en suite

LACKWOOD
Map 03 ST19

lackwood Cwmgelli NP12 1BR
☎ 01495 222121 (office) & 223152 (club)
**eathland course with sand bunkers. Undulating, with
rd walking. Testing 2nd hole par 4. Good views.**
holes, 5332yds, Par 67, Course record 62.
lub membership 310.
isitors contact club or turn up & pay greens staff; not
eekends & bank holidays unless with member; member
recognised golf club. **Societies** by arrangement for
embers of a recognised golf club. **Green Fees** £14 (£18
eekends). **Facilities** ⊗ 🏌 💂 💂 ⚐ **Location** 0.25m N of
ackwood, off A4048

....

tel ★★★ 68% Maes Manor Hotel, BLACKWOOD
01495 220011 8 en suite 14 annexe en suite

AERPHILLY
Map 03 ST18

aerphilly Pencapel, Mountain Rd CF83 1HJ
☎ 029 20883481 & 20863441 📄 029 20863441
* *holes, 5732yds, Par 71, SSS 69.*
cation 0.5m S on A469
none for further details

....

tel ★★★ 71% Manor Parc Country Hotel & Restaurant,
ornhill Rd, Thornhill, CARDIFF ☎ 029 2069 3723
en suite

ountain Lakes & Castell Heights

aengwynlais CF83 1NG
☎ 029 20861128 & 20886666 📄 029 20863243
nail: sales@golfclub.co.uk
e nine-hole Castell Heights course within the
ountain Lakes complex was established in 1982 on a
-acre site. In 1988 a further 18-hole course, Mountain
kes was designed by Bob Sandow to take advantage
160 acres of mountain heathland, combining both
ountain-top golf and parkland. Most holes are tree-
ed and there are 20 lakes as hazards. Host to major
A tournaments.
ountain Lakes Course: 18 holes, 6612yds, Par 74, SSS
Course record 69.
stell Heights Course: 9 holes, 2812yds, Par 35, SSS 32,
urse record 32.
ub membership 500.
cieties written or phone notice in advance. **Cards** ⬛
⬛ 📶 **Prof** Sion Bebb **Course Designer** Bob

Sandow **Facilities** ⊗ ⑂ 🏌 💂 💂 🏠 ⚐ ⛳ ✓
Conf fac available Corporate Hospitality Days available
Location M4 junct 32, near Black Cock Inn, Caerphilly
Mountain

....

Hotel ★★★ 71% Manor Parc Country Hotel & Restaurant,
Thornhill Rd, Thornhill, CARDIFF ☎ 029 2069 3723
21 en suite

MAESYCWMMER
Map 03 ST19

Bryn Meadows Golf & Country Hotel
CF82 7FN
☎ 01495 225590 or 224103 📄 01495 228272
e-mail: information@brynmeadows.co.uk
**A heavily wooded parkland course with panoramic
views of the Brecon Beacons.**
18 holes, 6132yds, Par 72, SSS 69, Course record 68.
Club membership 540.
Visitors not Sun am. Must contact in advance. **Societies**
Mon-Fri **Green Fees** not confirmed. **Cards** ⬛ ⬛ ⬛
📶 **Prof** Bruce Hunter **Course Designer** Mayo, Jeffries
Facilities ⊗ ⑂ 🏌 💂 💂 🏠 ⚐ ⛳ ✓
Leisure heated indoor swimming pool, sauna, solarium,
gymnasium. **Conf** fac available Corporate Hospitality
Days available **Location** on A4048 Blackwood-Ystrad
road

....

Hotel ★★★ 68% Maes Manor Hotel, BLACKWOOD
☎ 01495 220011 8 en suite 14 annexe en suite

NELSON
Map 03 ST19

Whitehall The Pavilion CF46 6ST
☎ 01443 740245
e-mail: mark@wilde6755.freeserve.co.uk
**Hilltop course. Testing 4th hole (225yds) par 3, and 6th
hole (402yds) par 4. Pleasant views.**
9 holes, 5666yds, Par 69, SSS 68, Course record 63.
Club membership 300.
Visitors must be a member of a recognised golf club &
have a handicap certificate. Must contact in advance to
play at weekends. **Societies** contact in writing four weeks
in advance. **Green Fees** £12 per round. **Facilities** 🏌 💂 💂
⚐ **Leisure** snooker. **Conf** fac available Corporate
Hospitality Days available **Location** 1m SW of Nelson off
A4054

....

Hotel ★★★ 70% Llechwen Hall Hotel, Llanfabon,
PONTYPRIDD ☎ 01443 742050 & 743020
📄 01443 742189 12 en suite 8 annexe en suite

OAKDALE
Map 03 ST19

Oakdale Llwynon Ln NP12 0NF
☎ 01495 220044 220440
**A challenging parkland course for players of all
abilities. Well-maintained and matured greens**
9 holes, 1344yds, Par 28, Course record 27.
Visitors no restrictions pay & play. **Societies** phone in
advance **Green Fees** £5.50 per 9 holes. **Course Designer**
Ian Goodenough **Facilities** 🏌 💂 💂 🏠 ⚐ ⛳ ✓
Leisure fishing, Snooker tables. **Location** off B4251 at
Oakdale

....

Hotel ★★★ 68% Maes Manor Hotel, BLACKWOOD
☎ 01495 220011 8 en suite 14 annexe en suite

Booking a tee time is always advisable.

Continued

CARDIFF

CARDIFF   Map 03 ST17

Cardiff Sherborne Av, Cyncoed CF23 6SJ
☎ 029 20753320 📠 029 20680011
e-mail: cardiff.golfclub@virgin.net
Parkland course, where trees form natural hazards. Interesting variety of holes, mostly bunkered. A stream flows through course and comes into play on nine separate holes.
18 holes, 6099yds, Par 70, SSS 70, Course record 66. Club membership 900.
Visitors contact in advance, only with member at weekends. **Societies** Fri, booking essential. **Green Fees** terms on application. **Cards** ⊞ 🔳 📇 💷 **Prof** Terry Hanson **Facilities** ⊗ 🍴 🏌 💷 ♀ ⌕ 🏠 ⌾ **Leisure** snooker. **Conf** fac available Corporate Hospitality Days available **Location** 3m N of city centre

Hotel ✿ Hotel Ibis Cardiff Gate, Malthouse Av, Cardiff Gate Business Park, Pontprennau, CARDIFF
☎ 029 2073 3222   78 en suite

Cottrell Park Cottrell Park, St Nicholas CF5 6JY
☎ 01446 781781 📠 01446 781187
e-mail: admin@golfwithus.com
Two well-designed courses, opened in 1996, set in historic parkland which was landscaped 200 years ago and offers spectacular views, especially from the Button course. An enjoyable yet testing game of golf for players of all abilities.

Mackintosh: 18 holes, 6397yds, Par 72, SSS 70, Course record 66.
Button: 18 holes, 6156yds, Par 71, SSS 68.
Club membership 1470.
Visitors phone booking advisable. **Societies** contact in advance. **Green Fees** £25 per 18 holes Mon-Thu (£35 Fri-Sun). **Cards** ⊞ 🔳 📇 💷 **Prof** Steve Birch **Course Designer** MRM Sandow **Facilities** ⊗ 🍴 🏌 💷 ♀ ⌕ 🏠 ⌾ 🚬 🏌 ⌾ ⌕ **Conf** fac available Corporate Hospitality Days available **Location** 6.5m W of Cardiff off A48, NW of St Nicholas

Hotel ★★★★ 68% Copthorne Hotel Cardiff-Caerdydd, Copthorne Way, Culverhouse Cross, CARDIFF
☎ 029 2059 9100   135 en suite

Llanishen Cwm Lisvane CF4 5UD
☎ 029 20755078 📠 029 20755078
Sloping course overlooking the Bristol Channel.
18 holes, 5338yds, Par 68, SSS 67, Course record 63.
Club membership 900.
Visitors must play with member at weekends & bank

Continued

holidays, not Wed. Must contact in advance. **Societies** contact in advance. **Green Fees** terms on application. **Prof** Adrian Jones **Facilities** ⊗ 🍴 🏌 💷 ♀ ⌕ 🏠 ⌾ **Conf** fac available **Location** 5m N of city off A469

Hotel ★★★ 65% Quality Hotel & Suites Cardiff, Merthyn Rd, Tongwynlais, CARDIFF ☎ 029 2052 9988
95 en suite

Peterstone Peterstone, Wentloog CF3 2TN
☎ 01633 680009 📠 01633 680563
e-mail: peterstone_lakes@yahoo.com
18 holes, 6555yds, Par 72.
Course Designer Bob Sandow **Location** 3m from Castleton off A48
Phone for further details

Hotel ★★★ 72% St Mellons Hotel & Country Club, Castleton, CARDIFF ☎ 01633 680355   21 en suite 20 annexe en suite

Radyr The Clubhouse, Drysgol Rd, Radyr CF15 8BS
☎ 029 20842408 📠 029 20843914
e-mail: manager@radyrgolf.co.uk
Parkland course that celebrated its centenary in 2002. Good views. Venue for many county and national championships.
18 holes, 6078yds, Par 69, SSS 70, Course record 62.
Club membership 935.
Visitors must play with member at weekends, or by arrangement with Club Office. **Societies** contact in advance. **Green Fees** £40 per day. **Cards** ⊞ 🔳 📇 💷 **Prof** Simon Swales **Course Designer** Colt **Facilities** ⊗ 🍴 🏌 💷 ♀ ⌕ 🏠 🏌 🚬 ⌾ ⌕ **Leisure** Table tennis. **Conf** fac available Corporate Hospitality Days available **Location** M4 junct 32, 4.5m NW of city off A4119

Hotel ★★★ 71% Manor Parc Country Hotel & Restauran Thornhill Rd, Thornhill, CARDIFF ☎ 029 2069 3723
21 en suite

St Mellons St Mellons CF3 2XS
☎ 01633 680408 📠 01633 681219
e-mail: stmellons@golf2003.fsnet.co.uk
Opened in 1936, St Mellons is a parkland course on the eastern edge of Cardiff. The course is laid out in the shape of a clover leaf and provides one of the best tests of golf in south Wales. The course comprises three par 5s, five par 3s and 10 par 4s. The par 3s will make or break your card but the two finishing par 4 holes are absolutely superb.
18 holes, 6275yds, Par 70, SSS 70, Course record 63.
Club membership 700.
Visitors contact in advance. With member only at weekends. **Societies** contact in advance. **Green Fees** £28 per round, £40 per day. **Cards** ⊞ 🔳 📇 💷 **Prof** Barry Thomas **Course Designer** Colt & Morrison **Facilities** ⊗ 🍴 🏌 💷 ♀ ⌕ 🏠 🏌 🚬 ⌾ **Conf** Corporate Hospitality Days available **Location** M4 junct 30, 2m E off A48

Hotel ★★★ 72% St Mellons Hotel & Country Club, Castleton, CARDIFF ☎ 01633 680355   21 en suite 20 annexe en suite

Whitchurch Pantmawr Rd, Whitchurch CF14 7TD
☎ 029 20620985 📠 029 20529860
e-mail: secretary@whitchurchcardiffgolfclub.com
Undulating parkland course providing an oasis within
an urban setting and offering panoramic views of the
city. It is an easy walk and always in good condition
with excellent drainage and smooth, quick greens.
18 holes, 6258yds, Par 71, SSS 71, Course record 62.
Club membership 750.
Visitors contact in advance; not Sat. Societies Thu only.
Must contact in advance. Green Fees £40 per day (£45 per
round weekends). Cards ▩ ▦ ▨ ▧ 🅿 Prof Rhys
Davies Course Designer F Johns Facilities ⊗ ⊪ ⊾ 🍺 ♀
⚒ 🏠 ⛳ 𝒸 Conf Corporate Hospitality Days available
Location M4 junct 32, 0.5m S on A470

Hotel ★★★ 71% Manor Parc Country Hotel & Restaurant,
Thornhill Rd, Thornhill, CARDIFF ☎ 029 2069 3723
21 en suite

CREIGIAU   Map 03 ST08

Creigiau Llantwit Rd CF15 9NN
☎ 029 20890263 📠 20890706
e-mail: manager@creigiaugolf.co.uk
Downland course, with small greens and many
interesting water hazards.
18 holes, 6063yds, Par 71, SSS 70.
Club membership 800.
Visitors contact in advance, must be member of a club, not
at weekends or bank holidays Must contact in advance.
Societies Deposit required.Apply by phone or writing.
Green Fees £35 per day. Cards ▩ ▦ ▨ 🅿 ▧ 🅿
Prof Iain Luntz Facilities ⊗ ⊪ ⊾ 🍺 ♀ ⚒ 🏠 ⛳ 𝒸
Location 6m NW of Cardiff on A4119

Hotel 🅄 Miskin Manor Country Hotel, Pendoylan Rd,
MISKIN ☎ 01443 224204 34 en suite 9 annexe en suite

CARMARTHENSHIRE

AMMANFORD   Map 03 SN61

Glynhir Glynhir Rd, Llandybie SA18 2TF
☎ 01269 851365 📠 01269 851365
e-mail: glynhir.golfclub@virgin.net
Parkland course with good views, last holes close to
Upper Loughor River. The 14th is a 394yd dog-leg.
18 holes, 5917yds, Par 69, SSS 70, Course record 66.
Club membership 700.
Visitors no visitors Sun. Contact professional in advance
(01269 851010). Societies Contact in advance. Green Fees
not confirmed. Prof Duncan Prior Course Designer
F Hawtree Facilities ⊗ ⊪ ⊾ 🍺 ♀ ⚒ 🏠 ⛳ 🍴 ⚓ 𝒸
Conf fac available Corporate Hospitality Days available
Location 2m N of Ammanford

Hotel ★★ 69% Mill at Glynhir, Glynhir Rd, Llandybie,
AMMANFORD ☎ 01269 850672 7 en suite 3 annexe
en suite

> If the name of the club appears in *italics*, details
> have not been confirmed for this
> edition of the guide.

BURRY PORT   Map 02 SN40

Ashburnham Cliffe Ter SA16 0HN
☎ 01554 832269 & 833846
18 holes, 6916yds, Par 72, SSS 74, Course record 70.
Course Designer JH Taylor Location W of town centre on
B4311
Phone for further details

Hotel ★★ 70% Ashburnham Hotel, Ashburnham Rd,
Pembrey, LLANELLI ☎ 01554 834343 & 834455
📠 01554 834483 13 en suite

CARMARTHEN   Map 02 SN42

Carmarthen Blaenycoed Rd SA33 6EH
☎ 01267 281588 📠 01267 281588
e-mail: carmarthengolfc@aol.com
Hilltop course with good views.
18 holes, 6245yds, Par 71, SSS 71, Course record 66.
Club membership 600.
Visitors must have a handicap certificate, phone for times
at weekends. Societies apply in writing minimum of ten
days in advance. Green Fees £20 (£25 weekends). Prof
Pat Gillis Course Designer JH Taylor Facilities ⊗ ⊪ ⊾
🍺 ♀ ⚒ 🏠 ⛳ ⚓ 🍴 𝒸 Conf fac available Corporate
Hospitality Days available Location 4m N of town

Hotel ★★ 70% Falcon Hotel, Lammas St,
CARMARTHEN ☎ 01267 234959 & 237152
📠 01267 221277 14 en suite

Derllys Court Llysonnen Rd SA33 5DT
☎ 01267 211575 📠 01267 211575
e-mail: derllys@hotmail.com
This course has recently been extended to an 18-hole
parkland course. The extra nine holes are of a similar
nature to the existing ones although a little longer in
length and include water hazards and sand bunkers.
18 holes, 5915yds, Par 70, SSS 68, Course record 69.
Club membership 30.
Visitors welcome at all times. Societies phone in advance.
Green Fees terms on application. Cards ▩ ▦ ▨ ▧ 🅿
Course Designer Peter Johnson, Stuart Finney
Facilities ⊗ ⊾ 🍺 ♀ ⚒ 🏠 🍴 𝒸 Conf Corporate
Hospitality Days available
Location off A40 between Carmarthen & St Clears

Hotel ★★ 70% Falcon Hotel, Lammas St,
CARMARTHEN ☎ 01267 234959 & 237152
📠 01267 221277 14 en suite

KIDWELLY   Map 02 SN40

Glyn Abbey Trimsaran SA17 4LB
☎ 01554 810278 📠 01554 810889
e-mail: course-enquiries@glynabbey.co.uk
Beautiful parkland course on the slopes of the
Gwendraeth valley, set in 200 acres with mature
wooded backdrops. USGA greens and tees.
18 holes, 6173yds, Par 70, SSS 70, Course record 70.
Club membership 380.
Visitors phone booking advisable. Societies contact in
advance. Green Fees £15 per round (£20 weekends &
holidays). Cards ▩ ▦ ▨ ▧ 🅿 Prof Darren Griffiths
Course Designer Hawtree Facilities ⊗ ⊪ ⊾ 🍺 ♀ ⚒ 🏠
⛳ 🍴 ⚓ 𝒸 ⛾ Leisure solarium, gymnasium.
Conf fac available Corporate Hospitality Days available

Continued

Location E of Kidwelly on B4317 between Trimsaran & Carway

Hotel ★★ 70% Ashburnham Hotel, Ashburnham Rd, Pembrey, LLANELLI ☎ 01554 834343 & 834455 📠 01554 834483 13 en suite

RHOS
Map 02 SN44

Saron Saron, Penwern SA44 5EL
☎ 01559 370705
e-mail: c9mbl@sarongolf.freereserve.co.uk
Set in 50 acres of mature parkland with large trees and magnificent Teifi valley views. Numerous water hazards and bunkers.
9 holes, 2400yds, Par 32, Course record 34.
Visitors may play at all times no arrangements required. **Societies** phone for details. **Green Fees** £11 per 18 holes, £8 per 9 holes. **Course Designer** Adas **Facilities** 🍺 🔧 🎣 ⚡ **Location** off A484 at Saron, between Carmarthen & Newcastle Emlyn

Hotel ★★ 73% The Penbontbren Farm Hotel, Glynarthen, Llandysul, CARDIGAN ☎ 01239 810248 10 annexe en suite

CEREDIGION

ABERYSTWYTH
Map 06 SN58

Aberystwyth Brynymor Rd SY23 2HY
☎ 01970 615104 📠 01970 626622
e-mail: aberystwythgolf@talk21.com
Undulating meadowland course. Testing holes: 16th (The Loop), par 3; 17th, par 4; 18th, par 3. Good views over Cardigan Bay.
18 holes, 5801yds, Par 70, SSS 69.
Club membership 400.
Visitors contact in advance. **Societies** write or phone in advance. **Green Fees** £20 per round £25 per day (£25/£30 weekends & bank holidays). **Prof** Jim McLeod **Course Designer** Harry Vardon **Facilities** 🍺 🍴 🎣 ⚡ 🔧 **Conf** fac available **Location** N side of town

Hotel ★★★ 66% Belle Vue Royal Hotel, Marine Ter, ABERYSTWYTH ☎ 01970 617558 37 rms (34 en suite)

BORTH
Map 06 SN69

Borth & Ynyslas SY24 5JS
☎ 01970 871202 📠 01970 871202
e-mail: secretary@borthgolf.co.uk
Seaside links over 100 years old. Strong winds at times though part of the course is sheltered among dunes. Some narrow fairways and plenty of natural hazards.
18 holes, 6116yds, Par 70, SSS 70, Course record 61.
Club membership 550.
Visitors contact in advance, may play weekends ring to check no competitions in progress. **Societies** phone in advance. **Green Fees** winter £22 per round/summer £33. **Cards** 💳 💳 💳 💳 **Prof** JG Lewis **Course Designer** Harry Colt **Facilities** 🍴 by arrangement 🎣 ⚡ 🔧 🎣 🚗 **Conf** Corporate Hospitality Days available **Location** 0.5m N on B4353

Hotel ★★★ ⚡ Ynyshir Hall, EGLWYSFACH ☎ 01654 781209 7 en suite 2 annexe en suite

CARDIGAN
Map 02 SN14

Cardigan Gwbert-on-Sea SA43 1PR
☎ 01239 621775 & 612035 📠 01239 621775
e-mail: golf@cardigan.fsnet.co.uk
A links course, very dry in winter, with wide fairways, light rough and gorse. Every hole overlooks the sea.
18 holes, 6687yds, Par 72, SSS 73, Course record 68.
Club membership 600.
Visitors not 1-2pm; handicap certificate preferred; contact in advance. **Societies** phone in advance. **Green Fees** £22 per day (£27.50 weekends & bank holidays). **Cards** 💳 💳 💳 💳 **Prof** Colin Parsons **Course Designer** Grant, Hawtree **Facilities** 🍺 🍴 🎣 ⚡ 🎣 🔧 🚗 **Leisure** squash. **Location** 3m N off A487

GWBERT ON SEA
Map 02 SN15

Cliff Hotel SA43 1PP
☎ 01239 613241 📠 01239 615391
e-mail: cliffhotel@btopenworld.com

9 holes, 1545yds, Par 29.
Location 3m NW of Cardigan off B4548
Phone for further details

LLANGYBI
Map 02 SN65

Cilgwyn SA48 8NN
☎ 01570 493286
9 holes, 5309yds, Par 68, SSS 66, Course record 66.
Course Designer Sandor **Location** 5m N of Lampeter on A485
Phone for further details

Hotel ★★★ 74% Falcondale Mansion, LAMPETER ☎ 01570 422910 20 en suite

LLANRHYSTUD
Map 06 SN56

Penrhos Golf & Country Club SY23 5AY
☎ 01974 202999 📠 01974 202100
e-mail: info@penrhosgolf.co.uk
Beautifully scenic course incorporating lakes and spectacular coastal and inland views.
Championship: 18 holes, 6641yds, Par 72, SSS 73, Course record 71.
Academy: 9 holes, 1827yds, Par 31.
Club membership 300.
Visitors must phone, no jeans allowed on main course. **Societies** phone in advance. **Green Fees** Mon-Thu Championship £20, Academy £5, Fri £25/£5 (weekends & bank holidays £30/£5). **Cards** 💳 💳 💳 💳 **Prof** Paul Diamond **Course Designer** Jim Walters **Facilities** 🍺 🍴 ⚡ 🎣 🎣 🔧 🚗 **Leisure** hard tennis courts, heated indoor swimming pool, sauna, solarium,

Continued

ymnasium, bowling green. **Conf fac available** Corporate Hospitality Days available **Location** A487 onto B4337 in Llanrhystud, course 0.25m on left

....

Hotel ★★★ ≜≜ 75% Conrah Hotel, Ffosrhydygaled, Chancery, ABERYSTWYTH ☎ 01970 617941
1 en suite 6 annexe en suite

CONWY

ABERGELE   Map 06 SH97

Abergele Tan-y-Gopa Rd LL22 8DS
☎ 01745 824034 🖹 01745 824772
e-mail: secretary@abergelegolfclub.freeserve.co.uk
A beautiful parkland course with views of the Irish Sea and Gwyrch Castle. There are splendid finishing holes: a testing par 5 16th; a 185yd 17th to an elevated green; and a superb par 5 18th with out of bounds just behind the green.
18 holes, 6520yds, Par 72, SSS 71, Course record 66.
Club membership 1250.
Visitors contact in advance. Limited play weekends.
Societies contact in advance. **Green Fees** not confirmed.
Prof Iain R Runcie **Course Designer** Hawtree
Facilities ⊗ �🍴 ⓑ 🍺 ♀ ⚲ 🏠 🛒 ⚲
Location 0.5m W off A547

....

Hotel ★★★ 67% Kinmel Manor Hotel, St George's Rd, ABERGELE ☎ 01745 832014 51 en suite

BETWS-Y-COED   Map 06 SH75

Betws-y-Coed LL24 0AL
☎ 01690 710556
e-mail: info@golf-betws-y-coed.co.uk
Attractive flat meadowland course set between two rivers in Snowdonia National Park, known as the Jewel of the Nines.
9 holes, 4998yds, Par 64, SSS 64, Course record 63.
Club membership 300.
Visitors advisable to contact in advance. **Societies** phone in advance. **Green Fees** summer £16 per 18 holes (£21 weekends). **Facilities** ⊗ �🍴 ⓑ 🍺 ♀ ⚲ ⚲
Location NE side of village off A5

....

Hotel ★★★ 71% The Royal Oak Hotel, Holyhead Rd, BETWS-Y-COED ☎ 01690 710219 27 en suite

COLWYN BAY   Map 06 SH87

Old Colwyn Woodland Av, Old Colwyn LL29 9NL
☎ 01492 515581
Hilly, meadowland course with sheep and cattle grazing on parts.
9 holes, 5243yds, Par 68, SSS 66, Course record 62.
Club membership 276.
Visitors welcome ex Sat. Contact in advance. **Societies** contact in advance by phone. **Green Fees** £10 per day (£15 weekends & bank holidays). **Course Designer** James Braid
Facilities ⚲ ⓑ ♀ ⚲ **Location** E of town centre on B5383

....

Hotel ★★★ 68% Hopeside Hotel, 63-67 Princes Dr, West End, COLWYN BAY ☎ 01492 533244 16 en suite

> **Looking for a new course? Always telephone ahead to confirm visitor arrangements.**

CONWY   Map 06 SH77

Conwy (Caernarvonshire) Beacons Way, Morfa LL32 8ER
☎ 01492 592423 🖹 01492 593363
e-mail: secretary@conwygolfclub.co.uk
Founded in 1890, Conwy has hosted national and international championships since 1898. Set among sand hills, possessing true links greens and a profusion of gorse on the latter holes, especially the 16th, 17th and 18th. This course provides the visitor with real golfing enjoyment in stunning scenery.
18 holes, 6647yds, Par 72, SSS 72, Course record 64.
Club membership 1050.
Visitors to contact secretary in advance. Limited play weekends. **Societies** contact in advance. **Green Fees** £42 per day; £35 per round (£48/£42 weekends & bank holidays). **Cards** 🖃 💳 💷 **Prof** Peter Lees **Facilities** ⊗ 🍴 ⓑ 🍺 ♀ ⚲ 🏠 🛒 ⚲ **Location** 1m W of town centre on A55

....

Hotel ★★★ 73% The Groes Inn, Tyn-y-Groes, CONWY ☎ 01492 650545 14 en suite

LLANDUDNO   Map 06 SH78

Llandudno (Maesdu) Hospital Rd LL30 1HU
☎ 01492 876450 🖹 01492 876450
e-mail: george@maesdugolfclub.freeserve.co.uk
Part links, part parkland, this championship course starts and finishes on one side of the main road, the remaining holes, more seaside in nature, being played on the other side. The holes are pleasantly undulating and present a pretty picture when the gorse is in bloom. Often windy, this varied and testing course is not for beginners.
18 holes, 6545yds, Par 72, SSS 72, Course record 62.
Club membership 1120.
Visitors book in advance. **Societies** apply in advance to secretary. **Green Fees** £30 per day, £25 per round (£35/£30 weekends). **Cards** 🖃 💳 💷 **Prof** Simon Boulden **Facilities** ⊗ 🍴 ⓑ 🍺 ♀ ⚲ 🏠 🛒 ⚲ **Leisure** snooker. **Location** S town centre on A546

....

Hotel ★★★ 73% Imperial Hotel, The Promenade, LLANDUDNO ☎ 01492 877466 100 en suite

North Wales 72 Bryniau Rd, West Shore LL30 2DZ
☎ 01492 875325 🖹 01492 873355
e-mail: golf@nwgc.freeserve.co.uk
Challenging seaside links with superb views of Anglesey and Snowdonia. It possesses hillocky fairways, awkward stances and the occasional blind shot. Heather and gorse lurk beyond the fairways and several of the greens are defended by deep bunkers. The first outstanding hole is the 5th, a par 5 that dog-legs into the wind along a rollercoasting, bottleneck fairway. Best par 4s include the 8th, played through a narrow valley menaced by a railway line and the beach and the 11th, which runs uphill into the wind and where the beach again threatens. The finest par 3 is the 16th, with a bunker to the left of a partially hidden, bowl-shape green.
18 holes, 6287yds, Par 71, SSS 71, Course record 66.
Club membership 670.

Continued

Visitors contact in advance. Societies contact in advance.
Green Fees £40 per day, £30 per round (£50/£40
weekends & bank holidays). Mon £20 per round/day.
Cards 💳 💳 💳 💳 💳 🅿 Prof Richard Bradbury
Course Designer Tancred Cummins Facilities ⊗ ⫶ ⬛ ▬
♀ ⬠ ⌂ ⚲ ⬥ ⬥ ♦ Leisure snooker.
Location W side of town on A546

Hotel ★★ St Tudno Hotel and Restaurant, The
Promenade, LLANDUDNO ☎ 01492 874411 19 en suite

Rhos-on-Sea Penrhyn Bay LL30 3PU
☎ 01492 548115 (prof) & 549641 (clubhouse)
📠 01492 549100
18 holes, 6064yds, Par 69, SSS 69, Course record 68.
Course Designer JJ Simpson Location 0.5m W of
Llandudno off A55
Phone for further details

Hotel ★★★ 68% Hopeside Hotel, 63-67 Princes Dr, West
End, COLWYN BAY ☎ 01492 533244 16 en suite

LLANFAIRFECHAN
Map 06 SH67

Llanfairfechan Llannerch Rd LL33 0ES
☎ 01248 680144 & 680524
Hillside course with panoramic views of coast.
9 holes, 3119yds, Par 54, SSS 57, Course record 53.
Club membership 159.
Visitors contact in advance for weekends & bank holidays
Societies apply in writing. Green Fees not confirmed.
Facilities ♀ ⬠ Location W side of town on A55

Hotel ★★ 70% Garden Hotel, 1 High St, BANGOR
☎ 01248 362189 11 rms (10 en suite)

PENMAENMAWR
Map 06 SH77

Penmaenmawr Conway Old Rd LL34 6RD
☎ 01492 623330 📠 01492 622105
Hilly course with magnificent views across the bay to
Llandudno and Anglesey. Drystone wall hazards.
9 holes, 5350yds, Par 67, SSS 66, Course record 62.
Club membership 600.
Visitors advisable to contact in advance; not Sat. Societies
contact in advance. Green Fees £15 per day (£20
weekends & bank holidays). Facilities ⊗ ⫶ ⬛ ▬ ♀ ⬠
⚲ ♦ Location 1.5m NE off A55

Hotel ★★★ 71% Castle Hotel Conwy, High St, CONWY
☎ 01492 582800 28 en suite

Booking a tee time is always advisable.

BODELWYDDAN
Map 06 SJ07

Kimnel Park LL18 5SR
☎ 01745 833548 📠 01745 833544
9 holes, 3100, Par 58, SSS 58.
Phone for further details

Hotel ★★★ 72% Oriel House Hotel, Upper Denbigh Rd,
ST ASAPH ☎ 01745 582716 31 en suite

DENBIGH
Map 06 SJ06

Bryn Morfydd Hotel Llanrhaedr LL16 4NP
☎ 01745 589090 📠 01745 589093
e-mail: reception@brynmorfyddhotelgolf.co.uk
In a beautiful setting in the Vale of Clwyd, the original
nine-hole Duchess Course was designed by Peter Alliss
in 1982. In 1992, the 18-hole Dukes Course was
completed: a parkland course designed to encourage
finesse in play.
*Dukes Course: 18 holes, 5650yds, Par 70, SSS 67, Course
record 74.*
Duchess Course: 9 holes, 2098yds, Par 27.
Club membership 200.
Visitors book in advance, good standards of dress apply.
Societies apply in writing. Green Fees not confirmed.
Cards 💳 💳 💳 💳 🅿 Prof Richard Hughes Course
Designer Peter Allis Facilities ⊗ ⫶ ⬛ ▬ ♀ ⬠ ⌂ ⚲ ⇥
⬥ ⚲ ♦ Conf fac available Corporate Hospitality Days
available Location on A525 between Denbigh & Ruthin

Hotel ★★★ 70% Ruthin Castle, RUTHIN
☎ 01824 702664 58 en suite

Denbigh Henllan Rd LL16 5AA
☎ 01745 814159 📠 01745 14888
e-mail: secretary@denbighgolfclub.fsbusiness.co.uk
Parkland course, giving a testing and varied game.
Good views.
18 holes, 5712yds, Par 69, SSS 68, Course record 64.
Club membership 725.
Visitors contact in advance. Societies apply in writing or
phone. Prof Mike Jones Course Designer John Stockton
Facilities ⊗ ⫶ ⬛ ▬ ♀ ⬠ ⌂ ⚲ ♦ Conf Corporate
Hospitality Days available Location 1.5m NW on B5382

Hotel ★★★ 72% Oriel House Hotel, Upper Denbigh Rd,
ST ASAPH ☎ 01745 582716 31 en suite

LLANGOLLEN
Map 07 SJ24

Vale of Llangollen Holyhead Rd LL20 7PR
☎ 01978 860906
Parkland course, set in superb scenery by the River
Dee.
18 holes, 6705yds, Par 72, SSS 73, Course record 66.
Club membership 800.
Visitors contact in advance. Restricted club competition
days. Handicap certificate required. Societies apply in
writing to the secretary. Green Fees £30 per round (£35
weekends). Cards 💳 💳 💳 💳 🅿 Prof David Vaughan
Facilities ⊗ ⫶ ⬛ ▬ ♀ ⬠ ⌂ ⬥ ⚲ ♦
Location 1.5m E on A5

Hotel ★★★ 66% Bryn Howel Hotel & Restaurant,
LLANGOLLEN ☎ 01978 860331 36 en suite

PRESTATYN
Map 06 SJ08

Prestatyn Marine Rd East LL19 7HS
☎ 01745 854320 📠 01745 854320
e-mail: prestatyngcmanager@freenet.co.uk
Set besides rolling sand dunes and only a few hundred
yards from the sea, this course enjoys a temperate
climate and its seaside location ensures that golfers can
play on superb greens all year round. Some holes of
note are the par 5 3rd with out of bounds on the left
dog-leg followed by the Ridge, a par 4 of 468yds
normally played with the prevailing wind. The pretty
9th is surrounded by a moat where birdies and double
bogies are common followed by the challenging par 4
450yd 10th.

18 holes, 6568yds, Par 72, SSS 72, Course record 65.
Club membership 673.
Visitors welcome except Sat & Tue am. Must contact in
advance. **Societies** booking required. **Green Fees** terms on
application. **Cards** 🔲🔲🔲 **Prof** David Ames
Course Designer S Collins **Facilities** ⊗ �🏊 🍴 ♟ Ⓟ ♿ 🏠
♪ ♦ 🧺 ✓ **Leisure** snooker. **Conf** Corporate Hospitality
Days available **Location** 0.5m N off A548
....
Guesthouse ♦♦♦♦ Barratt's at Ty'N Rhyl, Ty'N
Rhyl, 167 Vale Rd, RHYL
☎ 01745 344138 & 0773 095 4994 📠 01745 344138
3 en suite

St Melyd The Paddock, Meliden Rd LL19 8NB
☎ 01745 854405 📠 01745 856908
e-mail: info@stmelydgolf.co.uk
Parkland course with good views of mountains and
Irish Sea. Testing 1st hole (423yds) par 4. 18 tees.
9 holes, 5829yds, Par 68, SSS 68, Course record 65.
Club membership 400.
Visitors advisable to phone in advance. Restrictions Thu &
Sat. **Societies** phone in advance. **Green Fees** £18 per 18
holes, £9 per 9 holes (£22/£11 weekends). **Prof** Andrew
Barnett **Facilities** ⊗ �🏊 🍴 ♟ Ⓟ ♿ 🏠 ✓ **Leisure** snooker.
Conf Corporate Hospitality Days available
Location 0.5m S on A547

RHUDDLAN
Map 06 SJ07

Rhuddlan Meliden Rd LL18 6LB
☎ 01745 590217 (Sec) & 590898(Pro) 📠 01745 590472
e-mail: golf@rhuddlangolfclub.fsnet.co.uk
Attractive, gently undulating parkland course with
good views. Well bunkered with trees and water
hazards. The 476yd 8th and 431yd 11th require both
length and accuracy.
18 holes, 6471yds, Par 71, SSS 71, Course record 66.
Club membership 1060.

Visitors contact in advance. Restrictions Sat pm. Sun with
member only. **Societies** phone to book reservation. **Green
Fees** £26 per day; £20 per round (£30/£25 Fri, £30 per
round Sat). **Cards** 🔲🔲🔲🔲 **Prof** Andrew Carr **Course
Designer** Hawtree & Son **Facilities** ⊗ �🏊 🍴 ♟ Ⓟ ♿ 🏠
♪ ♦ 🧺 ✓ **Conf** Corporate Hospitality Days available
Location E side of town on A547
....
Hotel ★★★ 67% Kinmel Manor Hotel, St George's Rd,
ABERGELE ☎ 01745 832014 51 en suite

RHYL
Map 06 SJ08

Rhyl Coast Rd LL18 3RE
☎ 01745 353171 📠 01745 360007
e-mail: rhylgolfclub@hotmail.com
Flat links course with challenging holes.
9 holes, 6220yds, Par 70, SSS 70, Course record 65.
Club membership 600.
Visitors contact in advance. **Societies** contact in advance
or see website **Green Fees** terms on application. **Cards** 🔲
🔲🔲🔲 **Prof** John Stubbs **Course Designer** James
Braid **Facilities** ⊗ �🏊 🍴 ♟ Ⓟ ♿ 🏠 ♪ ♦ 🧺 ✓
Conf Corporate Hospitality Days available
Location 1m E on A548
....
Guesthouse ♦♦♦♦ Barratt's at Ty'N Rhyl, Ty'N
Rhyl, 167 Vale Rd, RHYL
☎ 01745 344138 & 0773 095 4994 📠 01745 344138
3 en suite

> In the hotel entries, the percentage figure refers to
> the AA's most recent Quality Assessment Score.

Prestatyn Golf Club

Prestatyn Golf course is the most North
Easterly Links in Wales. A challenge for all
standards of golfers giving a memorable
examination of their game. Visitors and
Societies are welcome on Sundays and
Weekdays except Tuesday am.

To reserve your Golf Day:
Tel/Fax: 01745 854320
E-mail: prestatytngcmanager@freenet.co.uk
Visit our website: www.prestatyngc.co.uk

Continued

RUTHIN
Map 06 SJ15

Ruthin-Pwllglas Pwllglas LL15 2PE
☎ 01824 702296
Hilly parkland course with panoramic views. Stiff climb to 3rd and 9th holes. At 600ft above sea level, the 355yd 5th hole is the highest point at Pwliglas. When the seventh is played the second time - as the 16th - the tee is from a spectacular sheer rock face.
18 holes, 5362yds, Par 66, SSS 66.
Club membership 380.
Visitors welcome except for competition days. Societies apply in writing or phone. Green Fees £16 per day (£22 weekends & bank holidays). Prof M Jones Facilities ⊗ ⅲ ⅃ ⅃ ♀ ⚘ Leisure motorised cart available for disabled.
Conf Corporate Hospitality Days available
Location 2.5m S off A494

Hotel ★★★ 70% Ruthin Castle, RUTHIN
☎ 01824 702664 58 en suite

ST ASAPH
Map 06 SJ07

Llannerch Park North Wales Golf Range, Llannerch Park LL17 0BD
☎ 01745 730805
e-mail: steve@parkgolf.co.uk
Mainly flat parkland course with one dog-leg hole. Fine views towards the Clwydian Range.
9 holes, 1587yds, Par 30.
Visitors pay & play. Societies phone in advance.
Green Fees £3.50 per round. Prof Richard Hughes
Course Designer B Williams Facilities ⚑ 🏠 ⅌ ₹ ₹
Location 200yds S off A525

Hotel ★★ 67% Plas Elwy Hotel & Restaurant, The Roe, ST ASAPH ☎ 01745 582263 & 582089 🗎 01745 583864
7 en suite 6 annexe en suite

FLINTSHIRE

BRYNFORD
Map 07 SJ17

Holywell Brynford CH8 8LQ
☎ 01352 713937 & 710040 🗎 01352 713937
e-mail: holywell_golf_club@lineone.net
Links type course on well-drained mountain turf, with bracken and gorse flanking undulating fairways. 720ft above sea level.
18 holes, 6100yds, Par 70, SSS 70, Course record 67.
Club membership 505.
Visitors advisable to book in advance particularly for weekends. Societies by arrangement with the secretary.
Green Fees not confirmed. Prof Matt Parsleyr Facilities ⊗ ⅲ ⅃ ⚑ ♀ ⚘ 🏠 ⚒ ⚍ Location 1.25m SW off B5121

Hotel ★★ 70% Stamford Gate Hotel, Halkyn Rd, HOLYWELL ☎ 01352 712942 12 en suite

FLINT
Map 07 SJ27

Flint Cornist Park CH6 5HJ
☎ 01352 735645
e-mail: paulm@jcarrins.demon.co.uk
Parkland course incorporating woods and streams. Excellent views of Dee estuary and the Welsh hills.
9 holes, 6984yds, Par 70, SSS 69, Course record 65.
Club membership 300.

Visitors contact in advance, not Sun. Societies apply in writing or phone, not weekends. Green Fees not confirmed. Course Designer HG Griffith Facilities ⊗ ⅃ ⚑ ♀ ⚘ Location 1m W of Flint, signs for Cornist Hall & Flint Golf Club

Hotel ★★★ 66% Mountain Park Hotel, Northop Rd, Flint Mountain, FLINT ☎ 01352 736000 & 730972
🗎 01352 736010 21 annexe en suite

HAWARDEN
Map 07 SJ36

Hawarden Groomsdale Ln CH5 3EH
☎ 01244 531447 & 520809 🗎 01244 536901
18 holes, 5842yds, Par 69, SSS 69.
Location W side of town off B5125
Phone for further details

Hotel ★★ 69% The Gateway To Wales Hotel, Welsh Rd, Sealand, Deeside, CHESTER ☎ 01244 830332
39 en suite

MOLD
Map 07 SJ26

Old Padeswood Station Ln, Padeswood CH7 4JL
☎ 01244 547401 & 547701 🗎 01244 545082
Situated in the beautiful Alyn valley, part bounded by the River Alyn, this challenging course suits all categories of golfers. Nine holes are flat and nine are gently undulating. The signature hole is the 18th, a par 3 that needs a carry to the green as a valley waits below.
18 holes, 6685yds, Par 72, SSS 72, Course record 66.
Club membership 600.
Visitors welcome, subject to tee availability. Societies phone in advance. Green Fees £25 per round (£30 weekends & bank holidays). Prof Tony Davies
Course Designer Jeffries Facilities ⊗ ⅲ ⅃ ⚑ ♀ ⚘ 🏠 ₹ ⚒ ⚍ ⚍ Conf fac available Corporate Hospitality Days available Location 3m SE off A5118

Hotel ★★★ 68% Beaufort Park Hotel, Alltami Rd, New Brighton, MOLD ☎ 01352 758646 106 en suite

Padeswood & Buckley The Caia, Station Ln, Padeswood CH7 4JD
☎ 01244 550537 🗎 01244 541600
e-mail: admin@padeswoodgolf.plus.com
Gently undulating parkland course, with natural hazards and good views of the Welsh hills.
18 holes, 6042yds, Par 70, SSS 69.
Club membership 800.
Visitors weekdays only, contact secretary in advance.
Societies apply in writing or phone. Green Fees £25 per round weekdays. Prof David Ashton Course Designer Williams Partnership Facilities ⊗ ⅲ ⅃ ⚑ ♀ ⚘ 🏠 ₹ ⚍ ⚍ ₹ Leisure snooker (full size tables).
Conf Corporate Hospitality Days available
Location 3m SE off A5118

Hotel ★★★ 68% Beaufort Park Hotel, Alltami Rd, New Brighton, MOLD ☎ 01352 758646 106 en suite

> If the name of the club appears in *italics*, details have not been confirmed for this edition of the guide.

Continued

NORTHOP   Map 07 SJ26

Northop Country Park CH7 6WA
☎ 01352 840440 🗎 01352 840445
Designed by former British Ryder Cup captain, John
Jacobs, the parkland course gives the impression of
having been established for many years. No two holes
are the same and design allows all year play.

*18 holes, 6750yds, Par 72, SSS 73, Course record 64.
Club membership 500.*
Visitors contact in advance and have own equipment.
Societies apply in writing or by phone in advance. Green
Fees not confirmed. Cards 🖸 🖸 🖸 🖸 🖸 🖸 Prof
Keil Sweeney Course Designer John Jacobs Facilities ⊗
🖥 🖥 🖥 🖥 🖥 🖥 🖥 🖥 🖥 Leisure hard tennis
courts, sauna, gymnasium. Conf fac available
Location 150yds from Connahs Quay turning on A55
....
Hotel ★★★★ 70% De Vere St David's Park, St Davids
Park, EWLOE ☎ 01244 520800 145 en suite

PANTYMWYN   Map 07 SJ16

Mold Cilcain Rd CH7 5EH
☎ 01352 741513 🗎 01352 741517
e-mail: info@moldgolfclub.co.uk
Meadowland course with some hard walking and
natural hazards. Fine views.
*18 holes, 5512yds, Par 67, SSS 67, Course record 63.
Club membership 700.*
Visitors contact in advance. Restricted play at weekends
Societies provisional booking by phone. Green Fees
winter £15 per day (£25 weekends & bank holidays) £20
per round. summer £20 per day (£30 weekends & bank
holidays) £25 per round. Cards 🖸 🖸 Prof Mark
Jordan Course Designer Hawtree Facilities ⊗ 🖥 🖥 🖥 🖥
🖥 🖥 🖥 🖥 🖥 Conf fac available Location E side of
village
....
Hotel ★★★ 68% Beaufort Park Hotel, Alltami Rd, New
Brighton, MOLD ☎ 01352 758646 106 en suite

GWYNEDD

ABERDYFI   See page 391

ABERSOCH   Map 06 SH32

Abersoch LL53 7EY
☎ 01758 712622(shop) 712636(office) 🗎 01758 712777
e-mail: admin@abersochgolf.co.uk
18 holes, 5819yds, Par 69, SSS 68, Course record 66.
Course Designer Harry Vardon Location S side of village
Phone for further details

Abersoch Golf Club

....
Hotel ★★ 77% Neigwl Hotel, Lon Sarn Bach,
ABERSOCH ☎ 01758 712363 7 en suite 2 annexe
en suite

BALA   Map 06 SH93

Bala Penlan LL23 7YD
☎ 01678 520359 & 521361 🗎 01678 521361
e-mail: balagolfclub@one-tel.com
Upland course with natural hazards. All holes except
first and last affected by wind. First hole is a most
challenging par 3. Irrigated greens and spectacular
views of surrounding countryside.
*10 holes, 4962yds, Par 66, SSS 64, Course record 64.
Club membership 229.*
Visitors book in advance at weekends. Parties of more than
four people contact the secretary in advance. Societies
contact in advance. Green Fees £20 summer £10 winter.
Prof AR Davies Course Designer Syd Collins Facilities
🖥 🖥 🖥 🖥 🖥 Location 0.5m SW off A494
....
Hotel ★★ 65% Plas Coch Hotel, High St, BALA
☎ 01678 520309 10 en suite

BANGOR   Map 06 SH57

St Deiniol Penybryn LL57 1PX
☎ 01248 353098 🗎 01248 370792
e-mail: secretary@stdeiniol.fsbusiness.co.uk
Elevated parkland course with panoramic views of
Snowdonia, the Menai Strait and Anglesey. Designed by
James Braid in 1906 this course is a test test of accuracy
and course management. The 3rd has a narrow driving
area and a shot to an elevated green. The 4th, one of six
par 3s, provides a choice of pitching the green or
utilising the contours, making it one of the most
difficult holes on the course. The 13th, a dog-leg par 4,
is the last hole of the course's own Amen Corner with
its out of bounds to the right and left. Centenary in
2006.

Continued   Continued

18 holes, 5421yds, Par 68, SSS 67, Course record 61.
Club membership 300.
Visitors contact in advance. **Societies** contact in advance.
Green Fees £19 per day (£23 weekends & bank holidays).
Cards ▭ ▭ ▭ ▭ ▢ **Course Designer** James Braid
Facilities ⊗ ⫴ ⊾ ♥ ⏸ ♀ ⌂ ☞ ⬗ ⫽

Hotel ★★ 67% Anglesey Arms, MENAI BRIDGE
☎ 01248 712305   16 en suite

CAERNARFON   Map 06 SH46

Caernarfon Llanfaglan LL54 5RP
☎ 01286 673783 & 678359 (pro) 🖩 01286 672535
e-mail: caerngc@talk21.com
**Parkland course with gentle gradients. Well kept with
small greens and tree-lined fairways.**
18 holes, 5941yds, Par 69, SSS 68, Course record 63.
Club membership 660.
Visitors contact in advance. **Societies** apply in advance, in
writing or by phone. **Green Fees** £28 per day, £24 per
round (£30 per round weekends). **Cards** ▭ ▭ ▭ ▭ ▢
Prof Aled Owen **Facilities** ⊗ ⫴ ⊾ ♥ ⏸ ♀ ⌂ ➘ ⬗ ⫽
Conf Corporate Hospitality Days available
Location 1.75m SW

Hotel ★★★ 71% Celtic Royal Hotel, Bangor St,
CAERNARFON ☎ 01286 674477 110 en suite

CRICCIETH   Map 06 SH43

Criccieth Ednyfed Hill LL52 0PH
☎ 01766 522154
e-mail: aaguide@criccciethgolfclub.co.uk
**Hilly course on high ground, with generous fairways
and natural hazards. The 16th tee has panoramic views
in all directions.**
18 holes, 5787yds, Par 69, SSS 68.
Club membership 200.
Visitors contact in advance. **Societies** phone in
advance. **Green Fees** £20 per day May-Sep (£15 all
other times). **Facilities** ⊗ ⫴ ⊾ ♥ ⏸ ♀ ⌂ ⫽
Location 1m NE

Hotel ★★★ 🏌 77% Bron Eifion Country House Hotel,
CRICCIETH ☎ 01766 522385 19 en suite

DOLGELLAU   Map 06 SH71

Dolgellau Hengwrt Estate, Pencefn Rd LL40 2ES
☎ 01341 422603 🖩 01341 422603
e-mail: dolgellaugolfclub@hengwrt.fsnet.co.uk
**Undulating parkland course set on former hunting
grounds of the last Welsh prince, with ancient oak and
holly trees. Good views of mountains and Mawddach
estuary.**
9 holes, 4671yds, Par 66, SSS 63, Course record 62.
Club membership 150.
Visitors no restrictions **Societies** contact in advance.
Green Fees not confirmed. **Cards** ▭ ▭ ▭ ▭ ▭
▢ **Course Designer** Jack Jones **Facilities** ⊗ ⫴ ⊾ ♥ ⏸ ♀ ⌂
☞ ⟡ ⫽ ⎰ **Leisure** grass tennis courts, fishing,
gymnasium. **Conf** fac available Corporate
Hospitality Days available **Location** 0.5m N, near Town
Bridge

Hotel ★★★ 74% Plas Dolmelynllyn, Ganllwyd,
DOLGELLAU ☎ 01341 440273 10 en suite

FFESTINIOG   Map 06 SH93

Ffestiniog Y Cefn LL41 4LS
☎ 01766 762637
9 holes, 4570yds, Par 68, SSS 66.
Location 1m E on B4391
Phone for further details

Hotel ★★ 🏌 Maes y Neuadd Country House Hotel,
TALSARNAU ☎ 01766 780200 16 en suite

HARLECH   Map 06 SH53

Royal St Davids LL46 2UB
☎ 01766 780361 🖩 01766 781110
e-mail: secretary@royalstdavids.co.uk
**Championship links with easy walking. Natural
hazards demand strength and accuracy. Under the gaze
of Harlech Castle, with a magnificent backdrop of the
Snowdonia mountains.**
18 holes, 6263yds, Par 69, SSS 71.
Club membership 900.
Visitors pre booking essential, must hold current handicap
certificate. **Societies** contact secretary in advance.
Handicap certificates required. **Green Fees** £52 per day,
£42 per round, £25 after 3pm (£62/£52 weekends &
holidays, £30 after 3pm). Reduced winter rates. **Cards** ▭
▭ ▭ ▢ **Prof** John Barnett **Course Designer** Harold
Finch-Hatton **Facilities** ⊗ ⫴ ⊾ ♥ ⏸ ♀ ⌂ ➘ ⬗ ⫽
Conf fac available Corporate Hospitality Days available
Location W side of town on A496

Hotel ★★ 64% Ty Mawr Hotel, LLANBEDR
☎ 01341 241440 10 en suite

MORFA NEFYN   Map 06 SH24

Nefyn & District LL53 6DA
☎ 01758 720966 🖩 01758 720476
e-mail: nefyngolf@tesco.net
**A 27-hole course played as two separate 18s, Nefyn is a
cliff-top links where you never lose sight of the sea. A
well-maintained course which will be a very tough test
for the serious golfer, but still user friendly for the
casual visitor. Every hole has a different challenge and
the old 13th fairway is some 30yds across from sea to
sea. The course has the bonus of a pub on the beach
roughly halfway round for those whose golf may need
some bolstering.**
*Old Course: 18 holes, 6201yds, Par 71, SSS 71,
Course record 67.*
*New Course: 18 holes, 6317yds, Par 71, SSS 71,
Course record 66.*
Club membership 800.
Visitors contact in advance. **Societies** apply by phone.
Green Fees Sun-Fri £39 per day, £31 per round (£48/£37
Sat & bank holidays). **Cards** ▭ ▭ ▭ ▢ ▢ **Prof** John
Froom **Course Designer** James Braid **Facilities** ⊗ ⫴ ⊾
♥ ♀ ⌂ ⌂ ☞ ⟡ ⬗ ⫽ **Conf** fac available
Location 0.75m NW

Hotel ★★★ 🏌 75% Porth Tocyn Hotel, Bwlch Tocyn,
ABERSOCH ☎ 01758 713303 17 en suite

**In the hotel entries, the percentage figure refers to
the AA's most recent Quality Assessment Score.**

Gwynedd

Aberdovey

Aberdyfi

Map 06 SN69

Golf was first played at Aberdovey in 1886, with the club founded six years later. The links has since developed into one of the finest championship courses in Wales. The club has hosted many prestigious events over the years, and is popular with golfing societies and clubs who regularly return here. Golfers can enjoy spectacular views and easy walking alongside the dunes of this characteristic seaside links. Fine holes include the 3rd, the 11th, and a good short hole at the 12th. The late Bernard Darwin, a former president and captain of the club, was a golf correspondent for the Times. Many of his writings feature the course, which he referred to as, 'the course that my soul loves best of all the courses in the world'; Darwin was a major contributor to its success. He would easily recognise the course today. In 1995 the old clubhouse was destroyed by fire, and rebuilt with the help of a National Lottery grant. The fine new clubhouse was opened by HRH the Duke of York in 1998.

Aberdovey LL35 0RT
☎ 01654 767493 Fax 01654 767027

18 holes, 6454yds, Par 71, SSS 72, Course record 66.
Club membership 1000.
Visitors restricted weekends; handicap certificate; must contact in advance. **Societies** arrangement essential. **Green Fees** £50 per day, £35 per round (£55/£42 weekends). **Cards** ▭ ▬ ▨ ▨ **Prof** John Davies **Course Designer** J Braid **Facilities** ⊗ ⟩⊪ ⤷ ▬ ♀ ⚒ ⋒ ⤵ ▱ ∥ **Leisure** snooker.
Conf fac available **Location** 0.5m W on A493

....

Hotels

★★★ 75% Trefeddian Hotel, ABERDYFI

☎ 01654 767213 59 en suite

★★ 74% Penhelig Arms Hotel Restaurant, ABERDYFI

☎ 01654 767215 Fax 01654 767690 10 en suite
5 annexe en suite

★★ 69% Dovey Inn, Seaview Ter, ABERDOVEY

☎ 01654 767332 Fax 01654 767996 8 en suite

PORTHMADOG   Map 06 SH53

Porthmadog Morfa Bychan LL49 9UU
☎ 01766 514124 📠 01766 514124
e-mail: secretary@porthmadog-golf-club.co.uk
**Seaside links, very interesting but with easy walking
and good views.**
18 holes, 6322yds, Par 71, SSS 71.
Club membership 1000.
Visitors contact in advance. Handicap certificate required.
Societies apply by phone initially. **Green Fees** £28 per
round £35 per day (weekends £35/£42). **Cards** 💳 💳 💳
🔲 **Prof** Peter L Bright **Course Designer** James Braid
Facilities ⊗ 🎵 🔓 🍺 ♀ 🏖 🏠 🐾 🛒 ♂ ℓ
Leisure snooker. **Conf** Corporate Hospitality Days
available **Location** 1.5m SW

Hotel ★★★ ♨ 77% Bron Eifion Country House Hotel,
CRICCIETH ☎ 01766 522385 19 en suite

PWLLHELI   Map 06 SH33

Pwllheli Golf Rd LL53 5PS
☎ 01758 701644 📠 01758 701644
e-mail: admin@pwllheligolfclub.co.uk
**Easy walking on flat seaside course with outstanding
views of Snowdon, Cader Idris and Cardigan Bay.**
18 holes, 6091yds, Par 69, SSS 69, Course record 66.
Club membership 880.
Visitors restricted Tue, Thu & weekends. **Societies** phone
in advance. **Green Fees** £30 per day all week. **Cards** 💳
💳 💳 💳 🔲 **Prof** Stuart Pilkington **Course Designer**
Tom Morris **Facilities** ⊗ 🎵 🔓 🍺 ♀ 🏖 🏠 🛒 ℓ
Location 0.5m SW off A497

Hotel ★★★ ♨ 75% Porth Tocyn Hotel, Bwlch Tocyn,
ABERSOCH ☎ 01758 713303 17 en suite

MERTHYR TYDFIL

MERTHYR TYDFIL   Map 03 SO00

Merthyr Tydfil Cilsanws Mountain, Cefn Coed
CF48 2NT
☎ 01685 723308
**Mountain-top course in the Brecon Beacons National
Park with beautiful views of the surrounding area. The
course plays longer than its card length and requires
accuracy off the tee.**
18 holes, 5625yds, Par 69, SSS 68, Course record 65.
Club membership 160.
Visitors not Sun until after 3pm **Societies** by arrangement.
Green Fees £10 per day (£15 weekends & bank holidays).
Course Designer V Price, R Mathias **Facilities** ⊗ by
arrangement 🎵 by arrangement 🔓 by arrangement 🍺 by
arrangement ♀ 🏖 **Location** off A470 at Cefn Coed

Hotel ★★★ 75% Nant Ddu Lodge, Bistro & Spa, Cwm
Taf, Nant Ddu, MERTHYR TYDFIL ☎ 01685 379111
12 en suite 16 annexe en suite

Morlais Castle Pant, Dowlais CF48 2UY
☎ 01685 722822 📠 01685 388700
e-mail: morlaiscastlegolfclub@uk2.net
**Beautiful moorland course with excellent views of the
Brecon Beacons and surrounding countryside. The
interesting layout makes for a testing game.**

18 holes, 6320yds, Par 71, SSS 71, Course record 64.
Club membership 600.
Visitors contact in advance, especially for weekends.
Societies apply in writing. **Green Fees** terms on
application. **Prof** H Jarrett **Course Designer** James Braid
Facilities ⊗ 🎵 🔓 🍺 ♀ 🏖 🏠 🐾 🛒 ℓ **Conf** fac available
Corporate Hospitality Days available **Location** 2.5m N off
A465. Signs for Mountain Railway, course opp railway car
park

Hotel ★★★ 75% Nant Ddu Lodge, Bistro & Spa, Cwm
Taf, Nant Ddu, MERTHYR TYDFIL ☎ 01685 379111
12 en suite 16 annexe en suite

MONMOUTHSHIRE

ABERGAVENNY   Map 03 SO21

Monmouthshire Gypsy Ln, LLanfoist NP7 9HE
☎ 01873 852606 📠 01873 850470
e-mail: secretary@mgcabergavenny.fsnet.co.uk
**This parkland course is very picturesque, with the
beautifully wooded River Usk running alongside. There
are a number of par 3 holes and a testing par 4 at the
15th.**
18 holes, 5806yds, Par 70, SSS 69, Course record 65.
Club membership 700.
Visitors must play with member at weekends. Must
contact in advance & have handicap certificate.
Societies confirm in writing. **Green Fees** terms on
application. **Prof** B Edwards **Course Designer** James
Braid **Facilities** ⊗ 🎵 by arrangement 🔓 🍺 ♀ 🏠 🐾 ℓ
Location 2m S off B4269

Hotel ★★ 72% Llanwenarth Hotel & Riverside
Restaurant, Brecon Rd, ABERGAVENNY
☎ 01873 810550 17 en suite

Wernddu Golf Centre Old Ross Rd NP7 8NG
☎ 01873 856223 📠 01873 852177
e-mail: info@wernddu-golf-club.co.uk
**A parkland course with magnificent views, wind
hazards on several holes in certain conditions and water
hazards on four holes. This gently undulating course
has a long front nine and a shorter back nine, while the
final hole, a par 3, is an outstanding finish.**
18 holes, 5572yds, Par 69, SSS 67, Course record 63.
Club membership 550.
Visitors advisable to book in advance. **Societies** phone in
advance. **Green Fees** £15 per 18 holes. **Cards** 💳 💳 💳
🔲 **Prof** Tina Tetley **Course Designer** G Watkins **Facilities**
⊗ 🔓 🍺 ♀ 🏠 🐾 🛒 ♂ ℓ **Leisure** fishing, 9-hole pitch
& putt course. **Location** 1.5m NE on B4521

Hotel ★★★ 70% Llansantffraed Court Hotel,
Llanvihangel Gobion, ABERGAVENNY
☎ 01873 840678 21 en suite

BETTWS NEWYDD   Map 03 SO30

Alice Springs Kemeys Commander NP15 1JY
☎ 01873 880708 📠 01873 881075
e-mail: alice@springs18.fsnet.co.uk
Monow Course: 18 holes, 5544yds, Par 69, SSS 69.
Usk Course: 18 holes, 5934, Par 70, SSS 70.
Course Designer Keith R Morgan **Location** N of Usk on
B4598
Phone for further details

Continued   *Continue*

Hotel ★★★ 66% Three Salmons Hotel, Porthycarne St,
USK ☎ 01291 672133 10 en suite 14 annexe en suite

CAERWENT   Map 03 ST49

Dewstow NP26 5AH
☎ 01291 430444 🖹 01291 425816
e-mail: info@dewstow.com
**Two picturesque parkland courses with easy walking
and spectacular views over the Severn estuary towards
Bristol. Testing holes include the par 3 7th, Valley
Course, which is approached over water, some 50ft
lower than the tee, and the par 4 15th, Park Course,
which has a 50ft totem pole in the middle of the
fairway, a unique feature. There is also a 26-bay floodlit
driving range.**
*Valley Course: 18 holes, 6110yds, Par 72, SSS 70, Course
record 64.*
*Park Course: 18 holes, 6226yds, Par 69, SSS 69, Course
record 67.*
Club membership 950.
Visitors advisable to contact in advance. Societies apply in
writing or phone for details. Green Fees £11 per 9 holes,
£18 per 18 holes, £28 per day (£13/£21 weekends). Cards
🖃 🖭 🖾 🖭 🔟 Prof Jonathan Skuse Facilities ⊗ 🖺 🖳
🖳 🛇 🖆 ⛳ 🏌 🚜 🛆 ⛳ Conf fac available Corporate
Hospitality Days available Location 0.5m S of Caerwent

Hotel ✿ Travelodge, Magor Service Area, MAGOR
☎ 08700 850 950 43 en suite

CHEPSTOW   See page 395

CHEPSTOW   Map 03 ST59

Shirenewton Shirenewton NP16 6RL
☎ 01291 641642 🖹 01291 641472
9 holes, 6605yds, Par 72, SSS 72.
Location M48 junct 2, off A48 at Crick
Phone for further details

Hotel ★★ 61% Beaufort Hotel, Beaufort Square,
CHEPSTOW ☎ 01291 622497 22 en suite

MONMOUTH   Map 03 SO51

Monmouth Leasebrook Ln NP25 3SN
☎ 01600 712212 (clubhouse) 🖹 01600 772399
e-mail: sec.mongc@barbox.net
**Parkland course in scenic setting. High, undulating
land with beautiful views. The 8th hole, Cresta Run, is
renowned as one of Britain's most extraordinary golf
holes.**

holes, 5698yds, Par 69, SSS 69, Course record 67.
Club membership 500.

Visitors advisable to contact in advance, bank holidays only
with member. Not before 11.30am on Sun. Societies advance
notice required, write or phone secretary. Green Fees £20
(£24 weekends). Cards 🖃 🖭 🖾 🖭 🔟 Prof Mike
Waldron Course Designer George Walden Facilities ⊗ 🎯
🖺 🖳 🛇 🖆 ⛳ 🏌 🚜 🛆 Conf Corporate Hospitality Days
available Location 1.5m NE off A40

Hotel ★★ 65% Riverside Hotel, Cinderhill St,
MONMOUTH ☎ 01600 715577 & 713236
🖹 01600 712668 17 en suite

Rolls of Monmouth The Hendre NP25 5HG
☎ 01600 715353 🖹 01600 713115
e-mail: enquiries@therollsgolfclub.co.uk
**A hilly and challenging parkland course encompassing
several lakes and ponds and surrounded by woodland.
Set within a beautiful private estate complete with listed
mansion and panoramic views towards the Black
Mountains. The short 4th has a lake beyond the green
and both the 17th and 18th holes are magnificent holes
with which to end your round.**
18 holes, 6733yds, Par 72, SSS 73, Course record 69.
Club membership 160.
Visitors phone in advance. Societies contact in advance.
Green Fees £38 per day (weekends £42) (Mon special, £35
for round + lunch). Cards 🖃 🖭 🖾 🖭 🔟 Facilities ⊗
🎯 🖺 🖳 🛇 🖆 ⛳ 🚜 🛆 Location 4m W on B4233

Hotel ★★ 65% Riverside Hotel, Cinderhill St,
MONMOUTH ☎ 01600 715577 & 713236
🖹 01600 712668 17 en suite

RAGLAN   Map 03 SO40

Raglan Parc Parc Lodge, Station Rd NP5 2ER
☎ 01291 690077
18 holes, 6604yds, Par 72, SSS 73, Course record 67.
Location Off junct A449 & A40
Phone for further details

Hotel ★★★ 70% Llansantffraed Court Hotel,
Llanvihangel Gobion, ABERGAVENNY
☎ 01873 840678 21 en suite

NEATH PORT TALBOT

GLYNNEATH   Map 03 SN80

Glynneath Pen-y-graig, Pontneathvaughan SA11 5UH
☎ 01639 720452 & 720872 🖹 01639 720452
**Attractive hillside golf overlooking the Vale of Neath in
the foothills of the Brecon Beacons National Park.
Reasonably level parkland and wooded course.**
18 holes, 6211yds, Par 71, SSS 71.
Club membership 603.
Visitors restricted starting times at weekend. Societies
contact in advance. Green Fees £17 per day (£22
weekends & bank holidays). £10 Mon. Prof Shane
McMenamin Course Designer Cotton, Pennick, Lawrie,
Williams Facilities ⊗ 🎯 🖺 🖳 🛇 🖆 ⛳ 🚜 🛆
Conf fac available Corporate Hospitality Days available
Location 2m NE of Glynneath on B4242

Hotel ★★★ 66% Castle Hotel, The Parade, NEATH
☎ 01639 641119 & 643581 🖹 01639 641624 29 en suite

Continued

MARGAM   Map 03 SS78

Lakeside Water St SA13 2PA
☎ 01639 899959
18 holes, 4550yds, Par 63, SSS 63, Course record 65.
Course Designer Matthew Wootton **Location** M4 junct
38, off 4283
Phone for further details

Hotel ★★★ 68% Aberavon Beach Hotel, PORT TALBOT
☎ 01639 884949 52 en suite

NEATH   Map 03 SS79

Earlswood Jersey Marine SA10 6JP
☎ 01792 321578
**Earlswood is a hillside course offering spectacular
scenic views over Swansea Bay. The terrain is gently
undulating downs with natural hazards and is designed
to appeal to both the new and the experienced golfer.**
18 holes, 5084yds, Par 68, SSS 68.
Visitors no restrictions. **Societies** advisable to contact in
advance. **Green Fees** £9 per round. **Prof** Mike Day
Course Designer Gorvett Estates **Facilities** ⓑ ♥ ⚐ 🏠
⌢ ⚘ **Location** 4m E of Swansea, off A483

Hotel ★★★ 66% Castle Hotel, The Parade, NEATH
☎ 01639 641119 & 643581 📠 01639 641624 29 en suite

Neath Cadoxton SA10 8AH
☎ 01639 643615 (clubhouse) 📠 01639 632759
**Mountain course, with spectacular views. Testing holes:
10th par 4; 12th par 5; 15th par 4.**
18 holes, 6492yds, Par 72, SSS 72, Course record 66.
Club membership 700.
Visitors with member only at weekends & bank holidays.
Societies should either phone or write in advance. **Green
Fees** Apr-Sep £21; Oct-Mar £11. **Prof** James Braid **Course
Designer** James Braid **Facilities** ⓧ ⫙ ⓑ ♥ ♀ ⚐ 🏠 ⌢ ⚘
Leisure snooker. **Location** 2m NE off A4230

Hotel ★★★ 66% Castle Hotel, The Parade, NEATH
☎ 01639 641119 & 643581 📠 01639 641624 29 en suite

Swansea Bay Jersey Marine SA10 6JP
☎ 01792 812198 & 814153
Fairly level seaside links with part dunes.
18 holes, 6605yds, Par 72, SSS 71, Course record 69.
Club membership 500.
Visitors advisable to contact in advance. **Societies** phone
enquiry or letter stating requirements. **Green Fees** £18 per
round (£25 weekends & bank holidays). **Prof** Mike Day
Facilities ⓧ ⫙ ⓑ ♥ ♀ ⚐ 🏠 ⌢ ⚘
Location M4 junct 42, onto A483, 1st right onto B4290
towards Jersey Marine, 1st right to clubhouse

Hotel ★★★ 66% Castle Hotel, The Parade, NEATH
☎ 01639 641119 & 643581 📠 01639 641624 29 en suite

PONTARDAWE   Map 03 SN70

Pontardawe Cefn Llan SA8 4SH
☎ 01792 863118 📠 01792 830041
e-mail: pontardawe@btopenworld.com
**Meadowland course situated on plateau 600ft above sea
level with good views of the Bristol Channel and the
Brecon Beacons.**
18 holes, 6101yds, Par 70, SSS 70, Course record 64.
Club membership 500.
Visitors contact in advance, but not weekends. **Societies**

phone for availability **Green Fees** £20 per day.
Prof Gary Hopkins **Facilities** ⓧ ⫙ ⓑ ♥ ♀ ⚐ 🏠 ⚘
Leisure snooker & pool rooms.
Location M4 junct 45, off A4067 N side of town centre

Hotel ★★★ 66% Castle Hotel, The Parade, NEATH
☎ 01639 641119 & 643581 📠 01639 641624 29 en suite

PORT TALBOT   Map 03 SS78

British Steel Port Talbot Sports & Social Club,
Margam SA13 2NF
☎ 01639 791938
e-mail: tony.edwards@ntlworld.com
9 holes, 4726yds, Par 62, SSS 63, Course record 60.
Location M4 junct 40
Phone for further details

Hotel ★★★ 68% Aberavon Beach Hotel, PORT TALBOT
☎ 01639 884949 52 en suite

NEWPORT

CAERLEON   Map 03 ST39

Caerleon NP6 1AY
☎ 01633 420342 📠 01633 420342
9 holes, 2900yds, Par 34, SSS 34, Course record 29.
Course Designer Steel **Location** M4 junct 24, B4236 to
Caerleon, 1st left after Priory Hotel, follow road to bottom
Phone for further details

Hotel ★★★★★ 71% The Celtic Manor Resort, Coldra
Woods, NEWPORT ☎ 01633 413000 400 en suite

LLANWERN   Map 03 ST38

Llanwern Tennyson Av NP18 2DY
☎ 01633 412029 (sec) & 413233 (pro) 📠 01633 412029
e-mail: royherbert@btopenworld.com
Mature, parkland course set in a rural environment.
18 holes, 6177yds, Par 70, SSS 69, Course record 66.
Club membership 650.
Visitors welcome, but restrictions at weekends. **Societies**
phone & confirm in writing. **Green Fees** £30 per day (£35
weekends). **Prof** Stephen Price **Facilities** ⓧ ⫙ ⓑ ♥ ♀ ⚐
🏠 ⚘ **Conf** Corporate Hospitality Days available
Location 0.5m S off A455

Hotel ★★★★★ 71% The Celtic Manor Resort, Coldra
Woods, NEWPORT ☎ 01633 413000 400 en suite

NEWPORT   See page 397

NEWPORT   Map 03 ST38

Newport Great Oak, Rogerstone NP10 9FX
☎ 01633 892643 📠 01633 896676
e-mail: newportgolfclub.gwent@euphony.net
**An undulating parkland course on an inland plateau
300ft above sea level with fine views over the
surrounding wooded countryside. There are no blind
holes, but plenty of natural hazards and bunkers.**
18 holes, 6460yds, Par 72, SSS 71, Course record 63.
Club membership 800.
Visitors contact in advance, handicap certificate required.
Not on Sat, limited time Sun. **Societies** contact in writing
or phone **Green Fees** not confirmed. **Prof** Paul Mayo
Course Designer W Fernie **Facilities** ⓧ ⫙ ⓑ ♥ ♀ ⚐ 🏠
Continue

Continued

Monmouthshire

Marriott St Pierre

Chepstow | Map 03 ST59

Set in 400 acres of beautiful parkland, Marriott St Pierre offers two 18-hole courses. The Old Course is one of the finest in the country and has played host to many major championships. The par 3 18th is famous for its tee shot over the lake to an elevated green. The Mathern has its own challenges and is highly enjoyable for golfers of all abilities. The hotel has teaching professionals as well as hire of clubs and equipment. A new 13-bay driving range was added in 1998.

Hotel Country Club
St Pierre Park NP16 6YA
☎ **01291 625261 Fax 01291 627977**
e-mail: golf.stpierre@marriotthotels.co.uk

Old Course: 18 holes, 6733yds, Par 71, SSS 72, Course record 64.
Mathern Course: 18 holes, 5732yds, Par 68, SSS 67.
Club membership 800.
Visitors advisable to contact in advance (up to 10 days).
Societies advance reservation only. **Green Fees** terms on application. Cards ⊟ ▆▆ ▆▆ ▆ ▆▆ ▆▆ ▨ **Prof** Craig Dun
Course Designer H Cotton **Facilities** ⊗ ⫙ ▙ ▆ ♀ ♧ ⯑
⯑ ⯑ ⯑ ⯑ ♂ ⺓ **Leisure** hard tennis courts, heated indoor swimming pool, fishing, sauna, solarium, gymnasium, steam room, health & beauty suite, chipping green. **Conf** fac available
Corporate Hospitality Days available **Location** M48 junct 2, A466 towards Chepstow, onto A48 towards Caldicot

....

Hotels

★★★★ 70% Marriott St Pierre Hotel & Country Club, St Pierre Park, CHEPSTOW

☎ 01291 625261 148 en suite

★★★ 66% The Chepstow Hotel, Newport Rd, CHEPSTOW

☎ 01291 626261 Fax 01291 626263 31 en suite

★★ 68% Castle View Hotel, 16 Bridge St, CHEPSTOW

☎ 01291 620349 Fax 01291 627397 9 en suite 4 annexe en suite

★★ 61% Beaufort Hotel, Beaufort Square, CHEPSTOW

☎ 01291 622497 Fax 01291 627389 22 en suite

Location M4 junct 27, 1m NW on B4591

Hotel ★★★★★ 71% The Celtic Manor Resort, Coldra Woods, NEWPORT ☎ 01633 413000 400 en suite

Parc Church Ln, Coedkernew NP10 8TU
☎ 01633 680933 📄 01633 681011
e-mail: enquiries@parcgolf.co.uk
A challenging but enjoyable 18-hole course with water hazards and accompanying wildlife. The 38-bay driving range is floodlit until 10pm.
18 holes, 5619yds, Par 70, SSS 68, Course record 66.
Club membership 400.
Visitors contact in advance 01633 680933. **Societies** phone in advance. **Green Fees** terms on application. **Cards** 💳 💳 💳 💳 **Prof** M Phillips, R Dinsdale, J Wills **Course Designer** B Thomas, TF Hicks **Facilities** ⊗ ⅏ ᴸ 🍷 ♀ ⚘ 🏠 🍴 🎿 🚲 ⚘ ⚐ **Conf** fac available Corporate Hospitality Days available **Location** 3m SW of Newport, off A48

Hotel ★★★ 66% The Kings Hotel, High St, NEWPORT ☎ 01633 842020 61 en suite

Tredegar Park Parc-y-Brain Rd, Rogerstone NP10 9TG
☎ 01633 894433 📄 01633 897152
e-mail: tpgc@btinternet.com
18 holes, 6150yds, Par 72, SSS 72.
Course Designer R Sandow **Location** M4 junct 27, B4591 N, club signed
Phone for further details

Hotel ★★★ 66% The Kings Hotel, High St, NEWPORT ☎ 01633 842020 61 en suite

PEMBROKESHIRE

HAVERFORDWEST   Map 02 SM91

Haverfordwest Arnolds Down SA61 2XQ
☎ 01437 764523 & 768409 📄 01437 764143
e-mail: haverwestgolf@lineone.net
Fairly flat parkland course, a good challenge for golfers of all handicaps. Set in attractive surroundings with fine views over the Preseli Hills.
18 holes, 5966yds, Par 70, SSS 69, Course record 63.
Club membership 770.
Visitors restricted at weekends. **Societies** apply in writing or phone for booking form. **Green Fees** not confirmed.
Cards 💳 💳 💳 💳 💳 **Prof** Alex Pile
Facilities ⊗ ⅏ ᴸ 🍷 ♀ ⚘ 🏠 🍴 🚲 ⚐ **Conf** fac available
Location 1m E on A40

Hotel ★★ 68% Hotel Mariners, Mariners Square, HAVERFORDWEST ☎ 01437 763353 28 en suite

LETTERSTON   Map 02 SM92

Priskilly Forest Castlemorris SA62 5EH
☎ 01348 840276 📄 01348 840276
e-mail: jevans@priskilly-forest.co.uk
Challenging parkland course with panoramic views and a stunning 18th hole. Immaculate greens and fairways surrounded by rhododendrons, established shrubs and trees. Testing lies.
9 holes, 5874yds, Par 70, SSS 68, Course record 73.
Club membership 150.

Visitors advance booking advisable at weekends during summer. **Societies** phone in advance. **Green Fees** £20 per day, £18 per 18 holes, £12 for 9 holes. **Cards** 💳 💳 💳 💳 **Prof** S Parsons **Course Designer** J Walters **Facilities** ⊗ ᴸ 🍷 ♀ ⚘ 🏠 🍴 🏑 🚲 🎿 ⚘ ⚐ **Leisure** fishing. **Conf** fac available Corporate Hospitality Days available **Location** off B4331 between Letterston & Mathry

Hotel ★★ 74% Wolfscastle Country Hotel, WOLF'S CASTLE ☎ 01437 741688 & 741225 📄 01437 741383 20 en suite 4 annexe en suite

MILFORD HAVEN   Map 02 SM90

Milford Haven Woodbine House, Hubberston SA73 3RX
☎ 01646 697762 📄 01646 697870
e-mail: enquiries@mhgc.co.uk
18 holes, 6030yds, Par 71, SSS 70, Course record 64.
Location 1.5m W of Milford Haven
Phone for further details

Hotel ★★★ 67% Cleddau Bridge Hotel, Essex Rd, PEMBROKE DOCK ☎ 01646 685961 24 en suite

NEWPORT (PEMBROKESHIRE)   Map 02 SN03

Newport (Pemb) The Golf Club SA42 0NR
☎ 01239 820244 📄 01239 820085
e-mail: newportgc@lineone.net
9 holes, 5815yds, Par 70, SSS 68, Course record 64.
Course Designer James Baird **Location** 1.25m N
Phone for further details

Hotel ★★ 69% Trewern Arms, NEVERN ☎ 01239 820395 10 en suite

PEMBROKE DOCK   Map 02 SM90

South Pembrokeshire Military Rd SA72 6SE
☎ 01646 621453 & 682442 📄 01646 621453
A hillside course on an elevated site overlooking the Cleddau and Haven waterway.
18 holes, 6100yds, Par 71, SSS 70, Course record 65.
Club membership 350.
Visitors contact in advance, especially during season. **Societies** apply in advance. **Green Fees** not confirmed. **Cards** 💳 **Prof** Mr Jeremy Tilson **Course Designer** Committee **Facilities** ⊗ ⅏ ᴸ 🍷 ♀ ⚘ 🏠 🍴 ⚐ **Location** SW of town centre off B4322

Hotel ★★ 65% Old Kings Arms, Main St, PEMBROKE ☎ 01646 683611 18 en suite

ST DAVID'S   Map 02 SM72

St David's City Whitesands Bay SA62 6HR
☎ 01437 720572 & 721751
9 holes, 6117yds, Par 70, SSS 70, Course record 68.
Location 2m W overlooking Whitesands Bay
Phone for further details

Hotel ★★★ 77% Warpool Court Hotel, ST DAVID'S ☎ 01437 720300 25 en suite

> **Looking for a new course? Always telephone ahead to confirm visitor arrangements.**

Continued

Celtic Manor Resort

Pembrokeshire

Newport   Map 03 ST38

This relatively new resort has quickly become a world-renowned venue for golf, set in 1400 acres of beautiful, unspoiled parkland at the southern gateway to Wales. Boasting three championship courses, Celtic Manor offers a challenge for all levels of play, complemented by a golf school and one of the largest clubhouses in Europe, as well as extensive leisure facilities. The Wentwood Hills (par 72), a favoured course for championships, is home to the Wales Open and is due to host the Ryder Cup in 2010. Roman Road is a par 70 and is ideal for golfers of all levels, with a variety of tees, generous fairways and deep greens. For shorter round golfers, Coldra Woods, at par 59, is a challenging test of iron play.

Coldra Woods NP18 1HQ
☎ 01633 413000 Fax 01633 410269
e-mail: golf@celtic-manor.com

Roman Road: 18 holes, 6462yds, Par 70, SSS 72, Course record 68.
Coldra Woods: 18 holes, 3807yds, Par 59, SSS 61.
Wentwood Hills: 18 holes, 7097yds, Par 72, SSS 75,
Course record 61.
Club membership 580.
Visitors subject to availability; must book & pay in advance; handicap certificate for Roman Road & Wentwood Hills.
Societies phone for details in advance. **Green Fees** Apr-Oct: Wentworth Hills £95, Roman Road £60, Coldra Woods £25.
Cards 🏧 💳 💳 💳 💳 💳 **Prof** Kevin Carpenter
Course Designer Robert Trent Jones
Facilities ⊗ 🏌 🍴 🍷 🏌 🍴 🚗 🐾 🐕 🚣 🚵 🏌 ♀ ⛳
Leisure hard tennis courts, heated indoor swimming pool, fishing, sauna, solarium, gymnasium, health spa, golf academy with 18 hole course. **Conf** fac available Corporate Hospitality Days available **Location** M4 junct 24, A48 towards Newport, 300yds right

....

Hotels

★★★★★ 71% The Celtic Manor Resort, Coldra Woods, NEWPORT

☎ 01633 413000 400 en suite

★★★ 68% Newport Lodge Hotel, Bryn Bevan, Brynglas Rd, NEWPORT

☎ 01633 821818 Fax 01633 856360 27 en suite

★★★ 66% The Kings Hotel, High St, NEWPORT

☎ 01633 842020 Fax 01633 244667 61 en suite

TENBY
Map 02 SN10

Tenby The Burrows SA70 7NP
☎ 01834 844447 842978 📠 01834 844447
e-mail: tenbygolfclub@ukn.co.uk
The oldest club in Wales, this fine seaside links, with sea views and natural hazards, provides good golf all the year round.
18 holes, 6224yds, Par 69, SSS 71, Course record 65.
Club membership 800.
Visitors subject to competition & tee reservation. **Societies** apply in advance. **Green Fees** not confirmed. **Cards** 📧
📧 📧 📧 📄 **Prof** Mark Hawkey **Course Designer** James Braid **Facilities** ⊗ ⑪ ⓛ ☮ ♀ ⚲ 📧 ☏ ♂ **Conf** Corporate Hospitality Days available **Location** near railway station

Hotel ★★★ 75% Atlantic Hotel, The Esplanade, TENBY
☎ 01834 842881 & 844176 📠 01834 842881 ex 256
42 en suite

Trefloyne Trefloyne Park, Penally SA70 7RG
☎ 01834 842165 📠 01834 842165
18 holes, 6635yds, Par 71, SSS 73.
Course Designer FH Gillman **Location** Trefloyne Park, just W of Tenby
Phone for further details

Hotel ★★★ 70% Fourcroft Hotel, North Beach, TENBY
☎ 01834 842886 40 en suite

POWYS

BRECON
Map 03 SO02

Brecon Newton Park LD3 8PA
☎ 01874 622004
Parkland course, with easy walking. Natural hazards include two rivers on its boundary. Good river and mountain scenery.
9 holes, 5476yds, Par 68, SSS 66, Course record 63.
Club membership 360.
Visitors advisable to contact in advance, limited availability at weekends. **Societies** apply in writing. **Green Fees** not confirmed. **Course Designer** James Braid **Facilities** ⊗ ⑪ ⓛ ☮ ♀ ⚲ 📧 ♂ **Location** 0.75m W of town centre on A40

Hotel ★★ 67% The Castle of Brecon Hotel, Castle Square, BRECON ☎ 01874 624611 31 en suite 12 annexe en suite

Cradoc Penoyre Park, Cradoc LD3 9LP
☎ 01874 623658 📠 01874 611711
e-mail: secretary@cradoc.co.uk
Parkland with wooded areas, ponds and spectacular views over the Brecon Beacons. Challenging golf. New course layout in 2005 included two new holes.
18 holes, 6188yds, Par 71, SSS 71, Course record 65.
Club membership 700.
Visitors contact secretary in advance. Restricted Sun. **Societies** apply in writing or phone in advance to secretary. **Green Fees** £26 per day (£32 weekends & bank holidays). **Cards** 📧 📧 📄 **Prof** Richard Davies **Course Designer** CK Cotton **Facilities** ⊗ ⑪ ⓛ ☮ ♀ ⚲ 📧 ☏ ♂ ⚾ ♂ ☏ **Location** 2m N of Brecon off B4520

Cradoc Golf Club

Hotel ★★ 67% The Castle of Brecon Hotel, Castle Square BRECON ☎ 01874 624611 31 en suite 12 annexe en suite

BUILTH WELLS
Map 03 SO05

Builth Wells Golf Links Rd LD2 3NF
☎ 01982 553296 📠 01982 551064
e-mail: info@builthwellsgolf.co.uk
Well-guarded greens and a stream running through the centre of the course add interest to this 18-hole undulating parkland course. The clubhouse is a converted 16th-century Welsh longhouse.
18 holes, 5376yds, Par 66, SSS 67, Course record 62.
Club membership 380.
Visitors handicap certificate preferred. **Societies** by arrangement. **Green Fees** £27 per day; £21 per round (£30/£25 weekends & bank holidays). **Prof** Simon Edwards **Facilities** ⊗ ⑪ ⓛ ☮ ♀ ⚲ 📧 ☏ ♂ ⚾ ♂ **Conf** Corporate Hospitality Days available **Location** N of A483

Hotel ★★★ ♨ 70% Caer Beris Manor Hotel, BUILTH WELLS ☎ 01982 552601 23 en suite

KNIGHTON
Map 07 SO27

Knighton Ffrydd Wood LD7 1DG
☎ 01547 528046 (Sec) & 528646
Upland course with some hard walking. Fine views over the England border.
9 holes, 5362yds, Par 68, SSS 66, Course record 65.
Club membership 150.
Visitors not Sun until after 4.30pm. **Societies** phone in advance on 01547 528046 **Green Fees** £10 per day (£15 weekends & bank holidays). **Course Designer** Harry Vardon **Facilities** ⊗ ⓛ ☮ ♀ ⚲ **Location** 0.5m S off B4355

Hotel ★★ 80% Milebrook House Hotel, Milebrook, KNIGHTON ☎ 01547 528632 10 en suite

LLANDRINDOD WELLS
Map 03 SO06

Llandrindod Wells The Clubhouse LD1 5NY
☎ 01597 823873 (sec) 📠 01597 823873
e-mail: secretary@lwgc.co.uk
An upland links course, designed by Harry Vardon, with easy walking and panoramic views. One of the highest courses in Wales (1100ft above sea level).
18 holes, 5759yds, Par 69, SSS 69, Course record 65.
Club membership 465.
Visitors no restrictions. **Societies** phone in advance. **Green Fees** not confirmed. **Prof** Philip Davies **Course Designer** H Vardon **Facilities** ⊗ ⑪ ⓛ ☮ ♀ ⚲ 📧 ☏ ♂ ⚾ ♂ ☏ **Conf** fac available **Location** 1m SE off A483

Continued   *Continue*

Iotel ★★★ 73% Hotel Metropole, Temple St,
.LANDRINDOD WELLS ☎ 01597 823700 120 en suite

.LANGATTOCK Map 03 SO21

Old Rectory NP8 1PH
☎ 01873 810373 📠 018373 810373
holes, 2200yds, Par 54, SSS 59, Course record 53.
.ocation SW of village
'hone for further details

Iotel ★★★ 72% Gliffaes Country House Hotel,
:RICKHOWELL
☎ 01874 730371 & 0800 146719 (Freephone)
📠 01874 730463 19 en suite 3 annexe en suite

.LANIDLOES Map 06 SN98

St Idloes Penrallt SY18 6LG
☎ 01686 412559
holes, 5540yds, Par 66, SSS 66, Course record 61.
.ocation 1m N off B4569
'hone for further details

;uesthouse ♦♦♦♦ Old Vicarage, LLANGURIG
☎ 01686 440280 4 en suite

ИACHYNLLETH Map 06 SH70

Machynlleth SY20 8UH
☎ 01654 702000 📠 01654 702928
.owland course with mostly natural hazards.
holes, 5726yds, Par 68, SSS 68, Course record 65.
:lub membership 200.
'isitors Thu Ladies Day, Sun am mens competition.
.ocieties phone in advance. **Green Fees** £15 per day.
:ourse Designer James Braid **Facilities** **Location** 0.5m E off A489

Iotel ★★ 70% Wynnstay Hotel, Maengwyn St,
ИACHYNLLETH ☎ 01654 702941 23 en suite

NEWTOWN Map 06 SO19

St Giles Pool Rd SY16 3AJ
☎ 01686 625844 📠 01686 625844
-mail: st.giles.newtown@euphony.net
nland country course with easy walking. Testing 2nd ıole, par 3, and 4th hole, par 4. River Severn skirts four ıoles.
holes, 6012yds, Par 70, SSS 70, Course record 67.
:lub membership 350.
'isitors advisable to contact in advance. **Societies** contact ı advance. **Green Fees** not confirmed. **Prof** DP Owen **'acilities** by arrangement by arrangement by ırrangement by arrangement **Location** 0.5m NE ın A483

Iotel ★★ 70% Wynnstay Hotel, Maengwyn St,
ИACHYNLLETH ☎ 01654 702941 23 en suite

VELSHPOOL Map 07 SJ20

Welshpool Golfa Hill SY21 9AQ
☎ 01938 850249 📠 01938 850249
-mail: welshpool.golfclub@virgin.net
Undulating, hilly, heathland course with bracing air. 'esting holes are 2nd (par 5), 14th (par 3), 17th (par 3) nd a memorable 18th.
8 holes, 5716yds, Par 71, SSS 68, Course record 68.
:lub membership 400.

Visitors book in advance, restricted some weekends. **Societies** book in advance. **Green Fees** £15.50 per day (£25.50 weekends) (£15.50 winter weekends & bank holidays). **Prof** Bob Barlow **Course Designer** James Braid **Facilities** **Conf** Corporate Hospitality Days available **Location** 3m W off A458

Hotel ★★★ 68% Royal Oak Hotel, The Cross, WELSHPOOL ☎ 01938 552217 25 en suite

RHONDDA CYNON TAFF

ABERDARE Map 03 SO00

Aberdare Abernant CF44 0RY
☎ 01685 872797 📠 01685 872797
Mountain course with parkland features overlooking the Brecon Beacons. Tree-lined with many mature oaks.
18 holes, 5875yds, Par 69, SSS 69, Course record 64.
Club membership 550.
Visitors must have handicap certificate; weekends by arrangment with professional. **Societies** apply in writing in advance to the secretary. **Green Fees** £17 (weekends & bank holidays £21). **Prof** A Palmer **Facilities** **Leisure** 3 practice nets. **Conf** fac available Corporate Hospitality Days available **Location** 1m NE of town centre. Past hospital, 400yds on right

Hotel Tregenna Hotel, Park Ter, MERTHYR TYDFIL
☎ 01685 723627 382055 📠 01685 721951 21 en suite

MOUNTAIN ASH Map 03 ST09

Mountain Ash Cefnpennar CF45 4DT
☎ 01443 479459 📠 01443 479628
e-mail: geoff@magc.fsnet.co.uk
Mountain moorland course with panoramic views of the Brecon Beacons. Not long but testing and demands accuracy from the opening hole, a 390yd par 4 that rises up halfway down its length with woodland on the left and out of bounds on the right. The 10th hole is the highest point, hitting from an elevated platform with woodland on the left below. The 18th is a dramatic finale in the form of a 510yd, par 5, with a carry over gorse, a ditch crossing the fairway and bunkers and sand traps protecting the green.
18 holes, 5553yds, Par 69, SSS 67, Course record 60.
Club membership 560.
Visitors contact in advance for details. **Societies** contact in writing. **Green Fees** £20 (£30 weekend). **Cards** **Prof** Darren Clark **Facilities** **Conf** fac available **Location** 1m NW off A4059

Hotel Tregenna Hotel, Park Ter, MERTHYR TYDFIL
☎ 01685 723627 382055 📠 01685 721951 21 en suite

PENRHYS Map 03 ST09

Rhondda Golf Club House CF43 3PW
☎ 01443 441384 📠 01443 441384
e-mail: rhondda@btinternet.com
18 holes, 6205yds, Par 70, SSS 71, Course record 67.
Location 0.5m W off B4512
Phone for further details

Hotel ★★★ 67% Heritage Park Hotel, Coed Cae Rd, Trehafod, PONTYPRIDD ☎ 01443 687057 44 en suite

Continued

PONTYPRIDD   Map 03 ST08

Pontypridd Ty Gwyn Rd CF37 4DJ
☎ 01443 409904 📄 01443 491622
**Well-wooded mountain course with springy turf. Good
views of the Rhondda Valley and coast.**
18 holes, 5721yds, Par 69, SSS 68, Course record 65.
Club membership 850.
Visitors contact in advance. Must play with member on
weekends & bank holidays. Must have a handicap
certificate. Societies weekdays only. Must contact in
advance. Green Fees £20 per 18 holes. Prof Wade Walters
Facilities ⊗ ⅢⅢ ⅃ △ 🏠 🏐 ⚒ ⚐ Location E of town
centre off A470

Hotel ★★★ 67% Heritage Park Hotel, Coed Cae Rd,
Trehafod, PONTYPRIDD ☎ 01443 687057 44 en suite

TALBOT GREEN   Map 03 ST08

Llantrisant & Pontyclun off Talbot Rd CF72 8AL
☎ 01443 228169 📄 01443 224601
e-mail: lpgc@barbox.net
A scenic, undulating parkland course.
18 holes, 5328yds, Par 68, SSS 66.
Club membership 600.
Visitors must have handicap certificate, must contact in
advance, not at weekends Societies phone in advance
Green Fees not confirmed. Cards 🖾 Prof Steve Hurley
& Matt Vanstone Facilities ⊗ ⅢⅢ ⅃ 🖺 ⛳ ⚘ △ 🏠 ⚐ ⚒
Conf Corporate Hospitality Days available
Location off A4119 Ely Valley Rd to Talbot Green, right
at minirdbt, club 50yds on left

Hotel 🅄 Miskin Manor Country Hotel, Pendoylan Rd,
MISKIN ☎ 01443 224204 34 en suite 9 annexe en suite

SWANSEA

CLYDACH   Map 03 SN60

Inco SA6 5QR
☎ 01792 842929
**Flat meadowland course bordered by meandering
River Tawe and the Swansea valley.**
18 holes, 6064yds, Par 70, SSS 69.
Club membership 450.
Visitors no restrictions. Societies contact in advance.
Green Fees £18 per round (£23 weekend). Facilities ⊗ ⅢⅢ
⅃ ⛳ ⚘ △ Leisure outdoor bowling green.
Conf Corporate Hospitality Days available
Location M4 junct 25, 1.5m NE on A4067

Hotel ⇧ Premier Travel Inn Swansea North, Upper
Fforest Way, Morriston, SWANSEA ☎ 08701 977246
40 en suite

PONTLLIW   Map 02 SS69

Allt-y-Graban Allt-y-Grabam Rd SA4 1DT
☎ 01792 885757
A challenging parkland course with fine panoramic
views, opened in 1993. It is a nine-hole course but with
plans for 12 holes. There are six par 4 holes and three
par 3 holes. The 6th is a challenging hole with a blind
tee shot into the valley and a dog-leg to the left onto an
elevated green.

9 holes, 2210yds, Par 66, SSS 66, Course record 63.
Club membership 158.
Visitors no restrictions. Societies phone in advance. Green
Fees not confirmed. Course Designer FG Thomas
Facilities ⅃ ⛳ ⚘ △ ⚒ ⚐ Location M4 junct 47, A48
towards Pontardulais, left after Glamorgan Arms

Hotel ⇧ Travelodge, Penllergaer, SWANSEA
☎ 08700 850 950 50 en suite

SOUTHGATE   Map 02 SS58

Pennard 2 Southgate Rd SA3 2BT
☎ 01792 233131 & 233451 📄 01792 234797
e-mail: sec@pennardgolfclub.comre
**Undulating, cliff-top seaside links with good coastal
views. At first sight it can be intimidating with steep
hills that make club selection important - there are a
few blind shots to contend with. The difficulties are not
insurmountable unless the wind begins to blow in calm
weather. Greens are slick and firm all year.**
18 holes, 6265yds, Par 71, SSS 72, Course record 69.
Club membership 1020.
Visitors advisable to contact the office in advance; not Tue
Ladies Day. Societies by arrangement, phone or e-mail in
advance. Green Fees £40 per 18 holes (£50 weekends &
bank holidays). Cards 🖾 🖾 🖾 🖾 🖻 Prof MV Bennett
Course Designer James Braid Facilities ⊗ ⅢⅢ ⅃ ⛳ ⚘ △
🏠 ⚒ ⚐ Conf fac available Location 8m SW of Swansea
off A4118

Hotel ★★ ♨ Fairyhill, REYNOLDSTON
☎ 01792 390139 8 en suite

SWANSEA   Map 03 SS69

Clyne 120 Owls Lodge Ln, The Mayals, Blackpyl
SA3 5DP
☎ 01792 401989 📄 01792 401078
e-mail: clynegolfclub@supanet.com
**Challenging moorland course with excellent greens and
scenic views of Swansea Bay and the Gower. Many
natural hazards with a large number of bunkers and
gorse and bracken in profusion,**
18 holes, 6334yds, Par 70, SSS 72, Course record 64.
Club membership 900.
Visitors must be member of a club with handicap
certificate. Groups over eight advised to book in advance.
Societies contact in advance. Green Fees £26 per round
(£32 weekends). Prof Jonathan Clewett Course Designer
HS Colt & Harries Facilities ⊗ ⅢⅢ ⅃ ⛳ ⚘ △ 🏠 ⚒ ⚐ ⚘ ⚐
Leisure chipping green, driving nets, indoor practice net.
Location 3.5m SW on B4436

Hotel ★★★ 65% St Anne's Hotel, Western Ln,
MUMBLES ☎ 01792 369147 33 en suite

Langland Bay Langland Bay SA3 4QR
☎ 01792 361721 📄 01792 361082
e-mail: info@langlandbaygolfclub.com
**Parkland course overlooking the Gower coast. The par
4 6th is an uphill dog-leg open to the wind, and the par
3 16th (151yds) is aptly named Death or Glory.**
18 holes, 5857yds, Par 70, SSS 63.
Club membership 850.
Visitors no restrictions. Tue Ladies Day. Societies not
weekends, phone in advance. Green Fees £30. Prof Mark
Evans Course Designer Henry Cotton Facilities ⊗ ⅢⅢ ⅃
⛳ ⚘ △ 🏠 ⚒ ⚐ Location 6m SW off B4593

Continued   *Continue*

Langland Bay Golf Club

Hotel ★★★ 65% St Anne's Hotel, Western Ln,
MUMBLES ☎ 01792 369147 33 en suite

Morriston 160 Clasemont Rd SA6 6AJ
☎ 01792 796528 📠 01792 796528
e-mail: morristongolf@btconnect.com
**Pleasant parkland course with a very difficult par 3
15th hole, one of the most challenging short holes in
Wales. The 17th is aptly nicknamed Temple of Doom.**
*18 holes, 5891yds, Par 68, SSS 68, Course record 61.
Club membership 700.*
Visitors not Sat; must contact in advance. Societies apply
in writing. **Green Fees** not confirmed. **Prof** M Govier
Facilities ⊗ ⅏ ㄴ ♥ ♀ ♤ 📷 ♂ **Conf** fac available
Corporate Hospitality Days available
Location M4 junct 46, 1m E on A48

Hotel ⇧ Premier Travel Inn Swansea North, Upper
Fforest Way, Morriston, SWANSEA ☎ 08701 977246
40 en suite

THREE CROSSES
Map 02 SS59

Gower Cefn Goleu SA4 3HS
☎ 01792 872480 (Off) 📠 01792 872480
e-mail: info@gowergolf.co.uk
**Set in attractive rolling countryside, this Donald Steel
designed course provides good strategic hazards,
including trees, water and bunkers. Outstanding views
and a challenging game of golf.**
*18 holes, 6441yds, Par 71, SSS 72, Course record 67.
Club membership 500.*
Visitors tee booking up to seven days in advance,
reservations recommended, some weekend vacancies, dress
code & course etiquette must be observed. Societies by
arrangement for established golfers. **Green Fees** Mon-Thu
£20 per 18 holes (£27 weekends). **Cards** ▦ ▤ ▦ ▨ 🔯
Prof Alan Williamson **Course Designer** Donald Steel
Facilities ⊗ ⅏ ㄴ ♥ ♀ ♤ 📷 ⚑ ♙ ♨ ♂ ℓ **Conf** fac
available Corporate Hospitality Days available
Location 6m W from Swansea, signed from Three Crosses

Hotel ★★ 72% Beaumont Hotel, 72-73 Walter Rd,
SWANSEA ☎ 01792 643956 16 en suite

> **If the name of the club appears in *italics*, details
> have not been confirmed for this
> edition of the guide.**

UPPER KILLAY
Map 02 SS59

Fairwood Park Fairwood SA2 7JN
☎ 01792 297849 📠 01792 297849
e-mail: info@fairwoodpark.com
**Parkland championship course on the beautiful Gower
peninsula.**
*18 holes, 6650yds, Par 73, SSS 73, Course record 68.
Club membership 600.*
Visitors welcome except when championship or club
matches are being held. Must contact in advance & provide
handicap certificate. Societies contact in advance. **Green
Fees** terms on application. **Cards** ▬ **Prof** Gary Hughes
Course Designer Hawtree **Facilities** ⊗ ⅏ ㄴ ♥ ♀ ♤ 📷
⚑ ♨ ♂ **Conf** Corporate Hospitality Days available
Location 1.5m S off A4118

TORFAEN

CWMBRAN
Map 03 ST29

Green Meadow Golf & Country Club
Treherbert Rd, Croesyceiliog NP44 2BZ
☎ 01633 869321 & 862626 📠 01633 868430
e-mail: info@greenmeadowgolf.com
**Undulating parkland course with panoramic views.
Tree-lined fairways, water hazards and pot bunkers.
The greens are excellent and are playable all year
round.**
*18 holes, 6029yds, Par 70, SSS 70, Course record 64.
Club membership 400.*
Visitors by arrangement advised especially at weekends,
tel 01633 862626. Correct standard of dress compulsory.
Societies phone for brochure, Golf Shop 01633 862626.
Green Fees £18 per round Tue-Fri (£15 Mon, £22
weekends). **Cards** ▦ ▬ 🔯 **Prof** Dave Woodman **Course
Designer** Peter Richardson **Facilities** ⊗ ⅏ ㄴ ♥ ♀ ♤ 📷
♙ ♨ ℓ ℓ **Leisure** hard tennis courts, sauna, gymnasium.
Conf fac available Corporate Hospitality Days available
Location NE of town off A4042

Hotel ★★★★ 66% Parkway Hotel, Cwmbran Dr,
CWMBRAN ☎ 01633 871199 70 en suite

Pontnewydd Maesgwyn Farm, Upper Cwmbran
NP44 1AB
☎ 01633 482170 📠 01633 838598
e-mail: ct.phillips@virgin.net
**Mountainside course with hard walking. Good views
across the Severn estuary.**
*18 holes, 5278yds, Par 68, SSS 67, Course record 61.
Club membership 502.*
Visitors must be accompanied by a member weekends &
bank holidays. **Green Fees** not confirmed. **Facilities** ⊗ ⅏
ㄴ ♥ ♀ ♤ **Location** N of town centre

Hotel ★★★★ 66% Parkway Hotel, Cwmbran Dr,
CWMBRAN ☎ 01633 871199 70 en suite

PONTYPOOL
Map 03 SO20

Pontypool Lasgarn Ln, Trevethin NP4 8TR
☎ 01495 763655 📠 01495 755564
e-mail: pontypoolgolf@btconnect.com
**Undulating mountain course with magnificent views of
the Bristol Channel.**
*18 holes, 5963yds, Par 69, SSS 69, Course record 64.
Club membership 638.*

Continued

Visitors must have a handicap certificate, restricted availability at weekends, advisable to call in advance. Societies apply in writing or by phone, deposit payable. Green Fees terms on application. Prof James Howard Facilities ⊗ ⅢⅠ ⅃ 昼 ⅀ ♨ ⊡ ⅋ 두 ⅋ Leisure indoor teaching academy with video analysis. Conf Corporate Hospitality Days available Location 1.5m N off A4043

Hotel ★★ 69% Mill at Glynhir, Glynhir Rd, Llandybie, AMMANFORD ☎ 01269 850672 7 en suite 3 annexe en suite

Woodlake Park Golf & Country Club

Glascoed NP4 0TE
☎ 01291 673933 ▤ 01291 673811
e-mail: golf@woodlake.co.uk
Undulating parkland course with magnificent views over Llandegfedd Reservoir. Superb greens constructed to USGA specification. Holes 4, 7 and 16 are par 3s, which are particularly challenging. Holes 6 and 17 are long par 4s, which can be wind affected.
18 holes, 6278yds, Par 71, SSS 72, Course record 67.
Club membership 500.
Visitors book in advance. Societies phone or write for society package. Green Fees £22.50 per 18 holes (£30 weekends & bank holidays). Cards ▤ ▤ Prof Leon Lancey Facilities ⊗ ⅢⅠ ⅃ 昼 ⅀ ♨ ⊡ 두 ♥ ⅋ ⅋ Leisure fishing. Conf fac available Corporate Hospitality Days available Location overlooking Llandegfedd Reservoir

Hotel ★★ 69% Mill at Glynhir, Glynhir Rd, Llandybie, AMMANFORD ☎ 01269 850672 7 en suite 3 annexe en suite

VALE OF GLAMORGAN

BARRY
Map 03 ST16

Brynhill Port Rd CF62 8PN
☎ 01446 720277 ▤ 01446 740422
e-mail: postbox@brynhillgolfclub.co.uk
Meadowland course with some hard walking. Prevailing west wind.
18 holes, 6516yds, Par 72, SSS 71.
Club membership 750.
Visitors not Sun; contact in advance. Societies phone secretary for details. Green Fees £25 per round. Prof Duncan Prior Facilities ⊗ ⅢⅠ ⅃ 昼 ⅀ ♨ ⊡ 두 ⅋ ⅋ Location 1.25m N on B4050

Hotel ★★★ 69% Mount Sorrel Hotel, Porthkerry Rd, BARRY ☎ 01446 740069 42 en suite

RAF St Athan Clive Rd, St Athan CF62 4JD
☎ 01446 797186 & 751043 ▤ 01446 751862
A parkland course with strong winds blowing straight from the sea. Further interest is added by this being a very tight course with lots of trees. Beware of low flying RAF jets.
9 holes, 6480yds, Par 72, SSS 72.
Club membership 450.
Visitors contact in advance, Sun am club competitions only. Societies apply in advance. Green Fees not confirmed. Course Designer the members Facilities ⊗ ⅃ 昼 ⅀ ♨ ⊡ Location between Barry & Llantwit Major

Hotel ★★★ 🏌 74% Egerton Grey Country House Hotel, Porthkerry, BARRY ☎ 01446 711666 10 en suite

St Andrews Major Argae Ln, Coldbrook Rd East, Cadoxton CF63 1BL
☎ 01446 722227 ▤ 01446 748953
e-mail: standrewsmajor@hotmail.co.uk
A scenic 18-hole parkland course, suitable for all standards of golfer. The greens are designed to US specifications. The course provides excellent challenges to all levels of golfers without being physically exerting.
18 holes, 5300yds, Par 69.
Club membership 400.
Visitors advisable to contact in advance. Societies phone in advance. Min 12 people, deposit payable. Green Fees £16 per round (weekends £18). Cards ▤ ▤ ▤ ▤ ▤ Prof Iestyn Taylor Course Designer Richard Hurd Facilities ⊗ ⅃ 昼 ⅀ ♨ 두 ♥ ⊡ ⅋ ⅋
Conf fac available Corporate Hospitality Days available Location 1.5m NE of Barry off A4231

Hotel ★★★ 🏌 74% Egerton Grey Country House Hotel, Porthkerry, BARRY ☎ 01446 711666 10 en suite

DINAS POWYS
Map 03 ST17

Dinas Powis High Walls Av CF64 4AJ
☎ 029 2051 2727 ▤ 029 2051 2727
18 holes, 5486yds, Par 67, SSS 67, Course record 60.
Location NW side of village
Phone for further details

Hotel ★★★ 69% Mount Sorrel Hotel, Porthkerry Rd, BARRY ☎ 01446 740069 42 en suite

PENARTH
Map 03 ST17

Glamorganshire Lavernock Rd CF64 5UP
☎ 029 20701185 ▤ 029 20701185
e-mail: glamgolf@btconnect.com
Parkland course overlooking the Bristol Channel.
18 holes, 6184yds, Par 70, SSS 70, Course record 64.
Club membership 1000.
Visitors contact professional in advance. Societies contact in advance. Green Fees not confirmed. Cards ▤ ▤ ▤ ▤ Prof Andrew Kerr-Smith Course Designer James Braid Facilities ⊗ ⅢⅠ ⅃ 昼 ⅀ ♨ ⊡ 두 ♥ ⅋ ⅋ Location S of town centre on B4267

Hotel ★★★ 69% Mount Sorrel Hotel, Porthkerry Rd, BARRY ☎ 01446 740069 42 en suite

WENVOE
Map 03 ST17

Wenvoe Castle CF5 6BE
☎ 029 20594371
18 holes, 6422yds, Par 72, SSS 71, Course record 64.
Location 1m S off A4050
Phone for further details

Hotel ★★★ 🏌 74% Egerton Grey Country House Hotel, Porthkerry, BARRY ☎ 01446 711666 10 en suite

HENSOL
Map 03 ST07

Vale Hotel Golf & Spa Resort Hensol Park
CF72 8JY
☎ 01443 665899 ▤ 01443 222220
e-mail: golf@vale-hotel.com
Two championship courses set in 200 acres of glorious countryside, with views over Hensol Lake and castle. The Wales National greens are constructed to USGA standard will prove a stern test for even the very best

Continue

yers. **The aptly named Lake course has water**
ning into play on 12 holes. The signature hole, the
h, has an island green reached via a stone bridge.
e club is also home to the Welsh PGA.
les National: 18 holes, 7413yds, Par 73.
ke: 18 holes, 6426yds, Par 72, SSS 71.
nsol: 9 holes, 3115yds, Par 72, SSS 71.
ub membership 1100.
itors must have a handicap certificate. May only play
h member at weekends on Lake course. **Societies** apply
vriting. **Green Fees** not confirmed. **Cards** 🔲 🔲 🔲
🔲 🔲 🔲 **Prof** D Llewellyn, P Johnson, C Coombs
urse Designer Peter Johnson **Facilities** ⊗ ⫪ ⅃ 🍷 ♀
🍴 ⅂ 🐟 🚵 ♂ ⅃ **Leisure** hard tennis courts, heated
oor swimming pool, squash, fishing, sauna, solarium,
nnasium, many facilities in process of being built. **Conf**
available Corporate Hospitality Days available
cation M4 junct 34, 1m SW

....

tel ★★★★ 73% Vale Hotel Golf & Spa Resort, Hensol
k, HENSOL ☎ 01443 667800 29 en suite 114 annexe
suite

WREXHAM

HIRK   Map 07 SJ23

irk Golf Club LL14 5AD
01691 774407 📠 01691 773878
ail: chirkjackbarker@btinternet.com
erlooked by the National Trust's Chirk Castle, a
mpionship-standard 18-hole course with a 664yd
5 at the 9th - one of the longest in Europe. Also a
e-hole course, driving range and golf academy.
holes, 7045yds, Par 72, SSS 73, Course record 69.
ub membership 300.
itors advisable to contact in advance. **Societies** phone
dvance **Green Fees** not confirmed. **Cards** 🔲 🔲 🔲
🔲 **Prof** Rhodri Lloyd Jones **Facilities** ⊗ ⫪ ⅃ 🍷 ♀ ⅃
🐟 🚵 ♂ ⅃ **Leisure** 9-hole par 3 course. **Conf** fac
ilable **Location** 1m NW of Chirk, near Chirk Castle

....

tel ★★★ 66% Moreton Park Lodge, Moreton Park,
drid, CHIRK ☎ 01691 776666 46 en suite

TON   Map 07 SJ34

assey LL13 0SP
01978 780020 📠 01978 781397
turesque nine-hole course in undulating parkland.
oles, 4962yds, Par 66, SSS 64, Course record 62.
ub membership 222.
itors contact in advance to book starting time **Societies**
ne then confirm in writing. **Green Fees** £16 per 18 holes;

Continued

£9.50 per 9 holes (£17.50/£11 weekends & bank holidays).
Cards 🔲 🔲 🔲 🔲 🔲 **Prof** Simon Ward **Course Designer**
Welsh Golf Union **Facilities** ⅃ 🍷 ♀ ⩓ 🍴 ♂ 🚵 ♂
Location 4m S of Wrexham off B5426, signed

....

Hotel ★★★ 68% Cross Lanes Hotel & Restaurant, Cross
Lanes, Bangor Rd, Marchwiel, WREXHAM
☎ 01978 780555 16 en suite

RUABON   Map 07 SJ34

Penycae Ruabon Rd, Penycae LL14 1TP
☎ 01978 810108
9 holes, 2140yds, Par 64, SSS 62, Course record 62.
Course Designer John Day **Location** 1m W off A5
Phone for further details

....

Hotel ★★★ 66% Moreton Park Lodge, Moreton Park,
Gledrid, CHIRK ☎ 01691 776666 46 en suite

WREXHAM   Map 07 SJ35

Clays Bryn Estyn Rd, Llan-y-Pwll LL13 9UB
☎ 01978 661406 📠 01978 661406
e-mail: claysgolf@claysgolf.co.uk
**Gently undulating parkland course in a rural setting
with views of the Welsh mountains. Noted for difficult
par 3s.**
18 holes, 6010yds, Par 69, SSS 69, Course record 62.
Club membership 420.
Visitors book in advance. **Societies** by arrangement in
writing. **Green Fees** £19 per 18 holes (£25 weekends).
Cards 🔲 🔲 🔲 🔲 🔲 🔲 **Prof** David Larvin **Course
Designer** RD Jones **Facilities** ⊗ ⫪ ⅃ 🍷 ♀ ⩓ 🍴 ♂
🚵 ♂ ⅃ **Conf** Corporate Hospitality Days available
Location off A534

....

Hotel ★★★ 68% Llwyn Onn Hall Hotel, Cefn Rd,
WREXHAM ☎ 01978 261225 13 en suite

Wrexham Holt Rd LL13 9SB
☎ 01978 364268 📠 01978 364268
e-mail: info@wrexhamgolfclub.co.uk
**Inland, sandy course with easy walking. Testing dog-leg
7th hole (par 4), and short 14th hole (par 3) with full
carry to green.**
18 holes, 6233yds, Par 70, SSS 70, Course record 64.
Club membership 600.
Visitors not competition days, & are advised to contact in
advance. A handicap certificate is required. **Societies**
welcome Mon & Wed-Fri. Apply in writing **Green Fees**
terms on application. **Prof** Paul Williams **Course Designer**
James Braid **Facilities** ⊗ ⫪ ⅃ 🍷 ♀ ⩓ 🍴 🚵 ♂
Location 2m NE on A534

....

Hotel ★★★ 68% Llwyn Onn Hall Hotel, Cefn Rd,
WREXHAM ☎ 01978 261225 13 en suite

Ireland

NORTHERN IRELAND

CO ANTRIM

NTRIM　　　　　　　　　　　　　　Map 01 D5

Massereene 51 Lough Rd BT41 4DQ
☎ 028 94428096 📠 028 94487661
mail: info@massereene.com
The first nine holes are parkland, while the second,
djacent to the shore of Lough Neagh, have more of a
nks character with sandy ground.
* holes, 6602yds, Par 72, SSS 72, Course record 63.
Club membership 969.
sitors contact in advance. Societies book in advance.
Green Fees £12.50 per 9 holes (£15 weekends); £22 per 18
holes(£28 weekends). Cards 💳💳💳💳 Prof Jim
Smyth Course Designer F Hawtree, H Swan Facilities ⊗
♿ 💷 ♀ ⚲ 🍴 🏌 Conf fac available Corporate
Hospitality Days available Location 1m SW of town

Hotel ★★★★ 59% Galgorm Manor, BALLYMENA
☎ 028 2588 1001 24 en suite

BALLYCASTLE　　　　　　　　　　Map 01 D6

Ballycastle Cushendall Rd BT54 6QP
☎ 028 2076 2536 📠 028 2076 9909
mail: info@ballycastlegolfclub.com
n unusual mixture of terrain beside the sea, lying at
e foot of one of the nine glens of Antrim, with
magnificent views from all parts. The first five holes are
arkland with natural hazards; the middle holes are
nks type and the rest on adjacent upland. Accurate
on play is essential for good scoring while the
ndulating greens will test putting skills.
holes, 5927 metres, Par 71, SSS 70, Course record 64.
Club membership 852.
sitors are welcome during the week. Societies apply in
riting or phone in advance Green Fees £20 per round
£30 weekends & bank holidays). Cards 💳💳💳
of Ian McLaughlin Facilities ⊗ 🍴 ♿ 💷 ♀ ⚲ 🏌
onf fac available Corporate Hospitality Days available
ocation between Portrush & Cushendall (A2)

Hotel ★★★ 70% Bayview Hotel, 2 Bayhead Rd,
PORTBALLINTRAE ☎ 028 2073 4100 25 en suite

BALLYCLARE　　　　　　　　　　Map 01 D5

Ballyclare 23 Springdale Rd BT39 9JW
☎ 028 9332 2696 📠 028 9332 2696
mail: ballyclaregolfclub@supanet
arkland course with lots of trees and shrubs and water
zards provided by the river, streams and lakes. The
ng 3rd hole is played from an elevated tee across a
ke to a curving fairway lined with mature trees,
holes, 5745 metres, Par 71, SSS 71, Course record 66.
ub membership 580.
sitors contact in advance. Societies contact in advance.
reen Fees terms on application. Cards 💳💳💳
of Alan Johnston Course Designer T McCauley
cilities ⊗ 🍴 ♿ 💷 ♀ ⚲ 🏌
nf Corporate Hospitality Days available
cation 1.5m N of Ballyclare

Hotel ★★★★ 59% Galgorm Manor, BALLYMENA
☎ 028 2588 1001 24 en suite

Greenacres 153 Ballyrobert Rd BT39 9RT
☎ 028 9335 4111 📠 028 9335 4166
18 holes, 5819yds, Par 71, SSS 69.
Location 12m from Belfast city centre
Phone for further details

BALLYGALLY　　　　　　　　　　Map 01 D5

Cairndhu 192 Coast Rd BT40 2QG
☎ 028 2858 3324 📠 028 2858 3324
e-mail: cairndhugc@utvinternet.com
Built on a hilly headland, this course is both testing and
scenic, with wonderful coastal views. The par 3 second
hole can require anything from a 9 to a 3 iron
depending on the wind, while the 3rd has a carry of 165
metres over a headland to the fairway. The 10th, 11th
and 12th holes constitute Cairndhu's Amen Corner',
feared and respected by any standard of golfer.
18 holes, 5611 metres, Par 70, SSS 69, Course record 64.
Club membership 905.
Visitors not Sat. Societies apply in writing. Green Fees
not confirmed. Cards 💳💳💳 Prof Robert Walker
Course Designer Mr Morrison Facilities ⊗ 🍴 ♿ 💷 ♀ ⚲
🏠 🏌 ⚲ 🍴 Conf fac available
Location 4m N of Larne on coast road

Guesthouse ♦♦♦♦ Manor Guest House, 23 Older Fleet Rd,
Harbour Highway, LARNE ☎ 028 2827 3305 8 en suite

BALLYMENA　　　　　　　　　　Map 01 D5

Ballymena 128 Raceview Rd BT42 4HY
☎ 028 2586 1487 📠 028 2586 1487
18 holes, 5299 metres, Par 68, SSS 67, Course record 62.
Location 2m E on A42
Phone for further details

Hotel ★★★★ 59% Galgorm Manor, BALLYMENA
☎ 028 2588 1001 24 en suite

Galgorm Castle Golf & Country Club
Galgorm Rd BT42 1HL
☎ 028 2564 6161 📠 028 2565 1151
e-mail: golf@galgormcastle.co.uk
An 18-hole USGA championship course set in 220 acres
of mature parkland in the grounds of one of Ireland's
historic castles. The course is bordered by two rivers
which come into play and includes five lakes. A course
of outstanding beauty offering a challenge to both the
novice and low handicapped golfer.
18 holes, 6736yds, Par 72, SSS 72, Course record 67.
Club membership 450.
Visitors ring to book times. Societies phone in advance to
book tee time. Green Fees £26 (weekends £32). Cards 💳
💳💳 Prof Phil Collins Course Designer Simon
Gidman Facilities ⊗ 🍴 ♿ 💷 ♀ ⚲ 🏠 🏌 ⚲ 🍴
Leisure fishing, PGA-staffed academy.
Conf fac available Corporate Hospitality Days available
Location 1m S of Ballymena on A42

Hotel ★★★★ 59% Galgorm Manor, BALLYMENA
☎ 028 2588 1001 24 en suite

BALLYMONEY　　　　　　　　　　Map 01 D6

Gracehill 141 Ballinlea Rd, Stranocum BT53 8PX
☎ 028 2075 1209 📠 028 2075 1074
e-mail: info@gracehillgolfclub.co.uk
Challenging parkland course with some holes played
over water and many mature trees coming into play.

Continued

18 holes, 6553yds, Par 72, SSS 73, Course record 69.
Club membership 400.
Visitors advisable to contact in advance, especially for weekend play. **Societies** phone in advance for availability & confirm in writing. **Green Fees** £20 per round (£25 weekends). **Cards** ⊞ ▨ 🔀 🗵 **Course Designer** Frank Ainsworth **Facilities** ⊗ ⅢⅡ ㎏ ⚑ ♀ ⚓ ⚘ ⚔ **Conf** fac available Corporate Hospitality Days available
Location M2 N from Belfast, onto A26 N to Ballymoney, signs for Coleraine. At Ballymoney bypass onto B147/A2 to Sranocum/Ballintoy

CARRICKFERGUS
Map 01 D5

Carrickfergus 25 North Rd BT38 8LP
☎ 028 9336 3713 ▤ 028 9336 3023
e-mail: carrickfergusgc@talk21.com
Parkland course, fairly level but nevertheless demanding, with a notorious water hazard at the 1st. Well-maintained, with an interesting in-course riverway and fine views across Belfast Lough.
18 holes, 5768yds, Par 68, SSS 68.
Club membership 850.
Visitors restrictions at weekends. **Societies** contact in advance. **Green Fees** terms on application. **Cards** ⊞ ▨ 🔀 🗵 **Prof** Gary Mercer **Facilities** ⊗ Ⅲ ㎏ ⚑ ♀ ⚒ ♙ ⚘ **Conf** fac available Corporate Hospitality Days available
Location 9m NE of Belfast on A2

Hotel ★★ 67% Dobbins Inn Hotel, 6-8 High St, CARRICKFERGUS ☎ 028 9335 1905 15 en suite

Greenisland 156 Upper Rd, Greenisland BT38 8RW
☎ 028 9086 2236
A parkland course nestling at the foot of Knockagh Hill with scenic views over Belfast Lough.
9 holes, 6045yds, Par 71, SSS 69.
Club membership 660.
Visitors contact club in advance. Play restricted Sat & Thu. **Societies** by arrangement. **Green Fees** £12 (£18 weekends). **Facilities** ⊗ Ⅲ ㎏ ⚑ ♀ ⚒
Location N of Belfast, close to Carrickfergus

Hotel ★★ 67% Dobbins Inn Hotel, 6-8 High St, CARRICKFERGUS ☎ 028 9335 1905 15 en suite

CUSHENDALL
Map 01 D6

Cushendall 21 Shore Rd BT44 0NG
☎ 028 2177 1318
e-mail: cushendallgolfclub@hotmail.com
Scenic course with spectacular views over the Sea of Moyle and Red Bay to the Mull of Kintyre. The River Dall winds through the course, coming into play in seven of the nine holes. This demands a premium on accuracy rather than length. The signature hole is the par 3 2nd, requiring a tee shot across the river to a plateau green with a steep slope in front and out of bounds behind.
9 holes, 4386 metres, Par 66, SSS 63, Course record 62.
Club membership 834.
Visitors Ladies day Thu, time sheet at weekends. **Societies** contact in writing. **Green Fees** £13 per day (£18 weekends & bank holidays). **Course Designer** D Delargy **Facilities** ㎏ ⚑ ♀ ⚒ **Location** in Cushendall beside beach on Antrim coast road

Guesthouse ♦♦♦♦ The Villa Farm House, 185 Torr Rd, CUSHENDUN ☎ 028 2176 1252 3 en suite

LARNE
Map 01 D5

Larne 54 Ferris Bay Rd, Islandmagee BT40 3RT
☎ 028 9338 2228 ▤ 028 9338 2088
e-mail: info@larnegolfclub.co.uk
An exposed part links, part heathland course offering a good test, particularly on the last three holes along the sea shore.
9 holes, 6686yds, Par 70, SSS 70, Course record 64.
Club membership 430.
Visitors not Sat, advisable to avoid Fri. **Societies** apply in writing or phone in advance. **Green Fees** not confirmed.
Course Designer GL Bailie **Facilities** ⊗ Ⅲ ㎏ ⚑ ♀ ⚒
Location 6m N of Whitehead on Browns Bay road

Guesthouse ♦♦♦♦ Drumkeerin, 201A Torr Rd, CUSHENDUN ☎ 028 2176 1554 3 en suite

LISBURN
Map 01 D5

Aberdelghy Bell's Ln, Lambeg BT27 4QH
☎ 028 9266 2738 ▤ 028 9260 3432
e-mail: info@mmsportsgolf.com
This parkland course has no bunkers. The hardest hole on the course is the 340-metre 3rd, a dog-leg through trees to a green guarded by water. The par 3 12th high on the hill and the 14th hole over the dam provide a challenge. The par 4 15th hole is a long dog-leg.
18 holes, 4139 metres, Par 66, SSS 62, Course record 64.
Club membership 200.
Visitors restricted Sat 7.15am-1pm. Ring in advance for Sun. **Societies** phone in advance. **Green Fees** not confirmed. **Cards** ⊞ ▨ 🔀 🗵 **Prof** Ian Murdoch **Course Designer** Alec Blair **Facilities** ⚑ ♀ ⚒ 🏠 ⚘ ⚔
Location 1.5m N of Lisburn off A1

Hotel ★★★ 71% Malone Lodge Hotel, 60 Eglantine Av, BELFAST ☎ 028 9038 8000 51 en suite

Lisburn 68 Eglantine Rd BT27 5RQ
☎ 028 9267 7216 ▤ 028 9260 3608
e-mail: lisburngolfclub@aol.com
Meadowland course, fairly level, with plenty of trees and shrubs. Challenging last three holes, the par 3 finishing hole is a spectacular downhill hole and reaching par is a bonus.
18 holes, 6647yds, Par 72, SSS 72, Course record 67.
Club membership 1200.
Visitors must play with member on Sun. Must tee off before 3pm weekdays unless with a member. **Societies** apply in writing. **Green Fees** not confirmed. **Prof** Stephen Hamill **Course Designer** Hawtree **Facilities** ⊗ Ⅲ ㎏ ⚑ ♀ ⚒ 🏠 ⚘ ♙ 🚜 ⚔ **Conf** Corporate Hospitality Days available **Location** 2m from town on A1

Hotel ★★★ 71% Malone Lodge Hotel, 60 Eglantine Av, BELFAST ☎ 028 9038 8000 51 en suite

MAZE
Map 01 D5

Down Royal Park Dunygarton Rd BT27 5RT
☎ 028 9262 1339 ▤ 028 9262 1339
The nine-hole Valley course and the 18-hole Down Royal Park are easy walking, undulating heathland courses. Down Royal's 2nd hole is 628yds and thought to be among the best par 5 holes in Ireland.
18 holes, 6824yds, Par 72, SSS 72, Course record 69.
Valley Course: 9 holes, 2019, Par 33.

Continue

isitors no restrictions, except dress code. **Societies**
servations in advance. **Green Fees** not confirmed. **Cards**
⌐ 💳 📖 💷 💳 **Prof** P Ball **Facilities** ⊗ by arrangement ⅷ
💻 ♀ ⚒ 🏠 ⚐ 🏴 ❦ 🚲 ♂ ❴ **Location** inside Down
oyal Race Course

....

otel ★★★ 71% Malone Lodge Hotel, 60 Eglantine Av,
ELFAST ☎ 028 9038 8000 51 en suite

EWTOWNABBEY Map 01 D5

allyearl Golf Leisure Centre 585 Doagh Rd,
ossley BT36 5RZ
☎ 028 9084 8287 📠 028 9084 4896
holes, 2520yds, Par 27.
ourse Designer V Lathery
hone for further details

allusk Antrim Rd BT36
☎ 028 90843799
holes, 4444yds, Par 62, SSS 62, Course record 62.
ourse Designer David Fitzgerald
hone for further details

ORTBALLINTRAE Map 01 C6

ushfoot 50 Bushfoot Rd, Portballintrae BT57 8RR
☎ 028 2073 1317 📠 028 2073 1852
mail: bushfootgolfclub@btconnect.com
seaside links course with superb views in an area of
utstanding beauty. A challenging par 3 7th is ringed
y bunkers with out of bounds beyond, while the 3rd
as a blind approach. Also a putting green and pitch
nd putt course.
holes, 6075yds, Par 70, SSS 68, Course record 68.
lub membership 850.
isitors contact in advance. Societies contact in advance.
reen Fees terms on application. Facilities ⊗ ⅷ ⚒ 💻 ♀
⚒ ⚐ ♂ Location off Ballaghmore road

....

otel ★★★ 70% Bayview Hotel, 2 Bayhead Rd,
ORTBALLINTRAE ☎ 028 2073 4100 25 en suite

ORTRUSH See page 409

HITEHEAD Map 01 D5

entra Municipal Slaughterford Rd BT38 9TG
☎ 028 9337 8996
mature course designed with the experienced golfer
nd novice in mind with wide fairways and some
articularly long holes.
holes, 2885 metres, Par 37, SSS 35.
isitors no restrictions. Societies contact in advance.
reen Fees not confirmed. Facilities 💻 ⚒ 🏠 ⚐ ♂ ❴
eisure restaurant on site. Location 6m from
arrickfergus

....

otel ★★ 67% Dobbins Inn Hotel, 6-8 High St,
ARRICKFERGUS ☎ 028 9335 1905 15 en suite

hitehead McCrae's Brae BT38 9NZ
☎ 028 9337 0820 & 9337 0822 📠 028 9337 0825
mail: robin@whiteheadgc.fsnet.co.uk
holes, 6050yds, Par 69, SSS 69, Course record 67.
ourse Designer AB Armstrong Location 1m from town
hone for further details

....

otel ★★ 67% Dobbins Inn Hotel, 6-8 High St,
ARRICKFERGUS ☎ 028 9335 1905 15 en suite

CO ARMAGH

ARMAGH Map 01 C5

County Armagh The Demesne, Newry Rd BT60 1EN
☎ 028 3752 5861 & 3752 8768 📠 028 3752 5861
e-mail: june@golfarmagh.co.uk
18 holes, 6212yds, Par 70, SSS 69, Course record 63.
Phone for further details

....

Hotel ⚐ The Cohannon Inn & Autolodge, 212
Ballynakilly Rd, DUNGANNON ☎ 028 8772 4488
42 en suite

CULLYHANNA Map 01 C5

Ashfield 44 Cregganduff Rd BT35 0JJ
☎ 028 3086 8611
**Parkland course with lakes. The course has seen
continuous improvement over the years with thousands
of trees planted from a wide variety of species.**
18 holes, 5840yds, Par 69.
Visitors contact in advance. **Societies** phone in advance
(028 3086 8180) **Green Fees** not confirmed.
Prof Paddy Gribben **Course Designer** Frank Ainsworth
Facilities ⊗ ⅷ ⚒ 💻 ♀ 🏠 ♂ 🚲 ♂ ❴

....

Hotel ★★ 65% Enniskeen House Hotel, 98 Bryansford
Rd, NEWCASTLE ☎ 028 4372 2392 12 en suite

LURGAN Map 01 D5

Craigavon Golf & Ski Centre Turmoyra Ln,
Silverwood BT66 6NG
☎ 028 3832 6606 📠 028 3834 7272
e-mail: geoffcoupland@craigavon.gov.uk
18 holes, 6496yds, Par 72, SSS 72.
Location 2m N at Silverwood off M1
Phone for further details

Lurgan The Demesne BT67 9BN
☎ 028 3832 2087 📠 028 3831 6166
e-mail: lurgangolfclub@ukinternet.com
**Testing parkland course bordering Lurgan Park Lake
with a need for accurate shots. Drains well in wet
weather and suits a long straight hitter.**
18 holes, 6257yds, Par 70, SSS 70, Course record 66.
Club membership 903.
Visitors not Sat, contact in advance. **Societies** contact in
advance, not Sat. **Green Fees** not confirmed. **Prof** Des
Paul **Course Designer** A Pennink **Facilities** ⊗ ⅷ ⚒ 💻 ♀
🏠 🏴 ♂ **Conf** fac available Corporate Hospitality Days
available **Location** 0.5m from town centre near Lurgan
Park

PORTADOWN Map 01 D5

Portadown 192 Gilford Rd BT63 5LF
☎ 028 3835 5356 📠 028 3839 1394
e-mail: portadowngc@btconnect.com
**Well-wooded parkland course on the banks of the River
Bann, which features among the water hazards.**
18 holes, 6130yds, Par 70, SSS 69, Course record 65.
Club membership 885.
Visitors not Tue & Sat. **Societies** apply in writing or phone
Green Fees £16 (£20 weekends & bank holidays). **Prof**
Paul Stevenson **Facilities** ⊗ ⅷ ⚒ 💻 ♀ 🏠 🏴 ♂ ♂
Leisure squash. **Conf** fac available Corporate Hospitality
Days available **Location** SE via A59

Continued

Hotel The Cohannon Inn & Autolodge, 212 Ballynakilly Rd, DUNGANNON ☎ 028 8772 4488 42 en suite

TANDRAGEE Map 01 D5

Tandragee Markethill Rd BT62 2ER
☎ 028 3884 1272 028 3884 0664
e-mail: office@tandragee.co.uk
18 holes, 5747 metres, Par 71, SSS 70, Course record 65.
Course Designer John Stone **Location** on B3 from Tandragee towards Markethill
Phone for further details

CO BELFAST

BELFAST Map 01 D5

See also **The Royal Belfast**, Holywood, Co Down.

Balmoral 518 Lisburn Rd BT9 6GX
☎ 028 9038 1514 028 9066 6759
e-mail: enquiries@balmoralgolf.com
Parkland course, situated in the suburbs of south Belfast, offering an enjoyable challenge for golfers of all levels.
18 holes, 6276yds, Par 69, SSS 70, Course record 64.
Club membership 912.
Visitors not Sat or Sun before 2.30pm. **Societies** Mon & Thu. Must contact in advance. **Green Fees** not confirmed. **Prof** Geoff Bleakley **Facilities** **Leisure** snooker. **Conf** fac available Corporate Hospitality Days available **Location** 2m S next to Kings Hall

Hotel ★★★ 71% Malone Lodge Hotel, 60 Eglantine Av, BELFAST ☎ 028 9038 8000 51 en suite

Cliftonville 44 Westland Rd BT14 6NH
☎ 028 9074 4158 & 9022 8585
9 holes, 6242yds, Par 70, SSS 70, Course record 65.
Location between Cavehill Rd & Cliftonville Circus
Phone for further details

Hotel ★★★ 66% Jurys Belfast Inn, Fisherwick Place, Great Victoria St, BELFAST
☎ 028 9053 3500 190 en suite

Dunmurry 91 Dunmurry Ln, Dunmurry BT17 9JS
☎ 028 9061 0834 028 9060 2540
e-mail: dunmurrygc@hotmail.com
Maturing very nicely, this tricky parkland course has several memorable holes which call for skilful shots.
18 holes, 6096yds, Par 70, SSS 69, Course record 65.
Club membership 900.
Visitors phone in advance; not Sat. **Societies** contact in writing. **Green Fees** not confirmed. **Prof** John Dolan **Facilities** **Conf** Corporate Hospitality Days available

Hotel ★★★ 71% Malone Lodge Hotel, 60 Eglantine Av, BELFAST ☎ 028 9038 8000 51 en suite

Fortwilliam Downview Av BT15 4EZ
☎ 028 9037 0770 (office) & 9077 0980 (pro)
028 9078 1891
e-mail: fortwilliamgc@utvinternet.com
18 holes, 5993yds, Par 70, SSS 68, Course record 65.
Location off Antrim road
Phone for further details

Hotel ★★★ 66% Jurys Belfast Inn, Fisherwick Place, Great Victoria St, BELFAST
☎ 028 9053 3500 190 en suite

Malone 240 Upper Malone Rd, Dunmurry BT17 9LB
☎ 028 9061 2758 (Office) & 9061 4917 (pro)
028 9043 1394
e-mail: manager@malonegolfclub.co.uk
Two parkland courses, extremely attractive with a larg lake, mature trees and flowering shrubs and bordered by the River Lagan. Very well maintained and offering a challenging round.

Main Course: 18 holes, 6706yds, Par 71, SSS 72.
Edenderry: 9 holes, 6320yds, Par 72, SSS 70.
Club membership 1450.
Visitors advisable to contact pro shop in advance. Main Course: not Sat before 3pm, Sun am, Wed pm, Tue & Fri noon-2pm **Societies** apply in writing or fax to club manager. Large group normally Mon & Thu only.
Green Fees Main Course: £55 per day (£60 weekends); Edenderry: £20 per day (£25 weekends). **Cards** **Prof** Michael McGee **Course Designer** CK Cotton
Facilities
Leisure fishing, Outdoor bowling green.
Conf Corporate Hospitality Days available
Location 4.5m S opposite Lady Dixon Park

Hotel ★★★ 71% Malone Lodge Hotel, 60 Eglantine Av, BELFAST ☎ 028 9038 8000 51 en suite

Mount Ober Golf & Country Club 24 Ballymaconaghy Rd BT8 6SB
☎ 028 9040 1811 & 9079 5666 028 9070 5862
Inland parkland course which is a great test of golf for all handicaps.
18 holes, 5281yds, Par 67, SSS 66, Course record 67.
Club membership 400.
Visitors contact in advance at weekends & bank holidays, may play Sat after 3.30pm & Sun after 10.30am. **Societies** book by phone or fax. **Green Fees** £16 per 18 holes (Sun £18). **Cards** **Prof** Wesley Ramsay **Facilities** **Leisure** American billiards & snooker. **Conf** fac available Corporate Hospitality Days available **Location** off Saintfield Rd

Ormeau 50 Park Rd BT7 2FX
☎ 028 90640700 028 90646250
e-mail: ormeau.golfclub@virgin.net
9 holes, 2688yds, Par 68, SSS 66.
Location S of city centre between Ravenhill & Ormeau roads
Phone for further details

Continued

Championship Course

Co Antrim

Royal Portrush

Portrush

Map 01 C6

This course, designed by Harry S Colt, is considered to be among the best six in the UK. Founded in 1888, it was the venue of the first professional golf event in Ireland, held in 1895, when Sandy Herd beat Harry Vardon in the final. Royal Portrush is spectacular and breathtaking, one of the tightest driving courses known to golfers. On a clear day there's a fine view of Islay and the Paps of Jura from the 3rd tee, and the Giant's Causeway from the 5th. While the greens have to be 'read' from the start, there are fairways up and down valleys, and holes called Calamity Corner and Purgatory (for good reason). The 2nd hole, Giant's Grave, is 509yds, but the 17th is even longer.

Dunluce Rd BT56 8JQ
☎ 028 70822311 Fax 028 70823139
e-mail: rpgc@dnet.co.uk

Dunluce: 18 holes, 6641yds, Par 72, SSS 73.
Valley: 18 holes, 6054yds, Par 70, SSS 72.
Visitors Dunluce restricted am Mon & Sat, pm Wed & Fri; must contact in advance; letter of introduction from own club; handicap certificate. **Societies** apply in writing. **Green Fees** Dunluce £95 per round (£110 weekends); Valley £32.50 per round (£37.50 weekends). **Cards** **Prof** Gary McNeill **Course Designer** H Colt **Facilities** **Location** 0.8km from Portrush on Bushmills road

Hotel

★★★ 70% Bayview Hotel, 2 Bayhead Rd, PORTBALLINTRAE
☎ 028 2073 4100 25 en suite

Shandon Park 73 Shandon Park BT5 6NY
☎ 028 9040 1856
18 holes, 6261yds, Par 70, SSS 70.
Location off Knock road
Phone for further details

DUNDONALD   Map 01 D5

Knock Summerfield BT16 2QX
☎ 028 9048 3251 📠 028 9048 7277
18 holes, 6435yds, Par 70, SSS 71, Course record 66.
Course Designer Colt, Allison & McKenzie
Location 5m E of Belfast
Phone for further details
....
Hotel ★★★ 78% The Old Inn, 15 Main St,
CRAWFORDSBURN ☎ 028 9185 3255 31 en suite
1 annexe en suite

NEWTOWNBREDA   Map 01 D5

The Belvoir Park 73 Church Rd BT8 7AN
☎ 028 9049 1693 📠 028 9064 6113
18 holes, 6516yds, Par 71, SSS 71, Course record 65.
Course Designer H Holt **Location** 2m from city centre off
Saintfield-Newcastle road
Phone for further details
....
Hotel ★★★ 77% Clandeboye Lodge Hotel, 10 Estate Rd,
Clandeboye, BANGOR ☎ 028 9185 2500 43 en suite

CO DOWN

ARDGLASS   Map 01 D5

Ardglass Castle Place BT30 7TP
☎ 028 4484 1219 📠 028 4484 1841
e-mail: info@ardglassgolfclub.com
A scenic clifftop seaside course with championship
standard greens. The first five holes, with the Irish Sea
and cliffs tight to the left, should be treated with respect
as anything resembling a hook will meet with disaster.
The 2nd hole is a daunting par 3. The tee shot must
carry a cliff and canyon - meanwhile the superb views
of the Mountains of Mourne should not be missed.
18 holes, 5498 metres, Par 70, SSS 69, Course record 65.
Club membership 900.
Visitors contact in advance. **Societies** contact in advance,
welcome weekdays & restricted times Sun. **Green Fees**
£32 per round (£45 weekdays). **Cards** 📇 💳 💳 📠
📠 🔲 **Prof** Philip Farrell **Course Designer** David Jones
Facilities ⊗ ℳ ℔ ▆ ♀ ⚑ 🏠 ✲ 🏌 ⚐ **Conf** fac available
Location 7m from Downpatrick on B1
....
Hotel ★★ 65% Enniskeen House Hotel, 98 Bryansford
Rd, NEWCASTLE ☎ 028 4372 2392 12 en suite

ARDMILLAN   Map 01 D5

Mahee Island 14 Mahee Island, Comber BT23 6EP
☎ 028 9754 1234
e-mail: mahee_gents@hotmail.com
An undulating parkland course, almost surrounded by
water, with magnificent views of Strangford Lough and
its islands, with Scrabo Tower in the background. The
greens are small and tricky to play.
9 holes, 5822yds, Par 71, SSS 70, Course record 66.
Club membership 600.

Visitors not Sat before 5pm. **Societies** contact in advance.
Green Fees £12 (weekends & bank holidays £17). **Course**
Designer Mr Robinson **Facilities** ⊗ by arrangement ℳ by
arrangement ℔ by arrangement ▆ by arrangement ▵ 🏠
🏌 ⚐ **Location** off Comber-Killyleagh road 0.5m from
Comber
....
Hotel ★★★ 77% Clandeboye Lodge Hotel, 10 Estate Rd,
Clandeboye, BANGOR ☎ 028 9185 2500 43 en suite

BALLYNAHINCH   Map 01 D5

Spa 20 Grove Rd BT24 8PN
☎ 028 9756 2365 📠 028 9756 4158
e-mail: spagolfclub@btconnect.com
Parkland course with tree-lined fairways and scenic
views of the Mourne Mountains. A long and demanding
course and feature holes include the par 3 2nd and
405yd par 4 11th.

18 holes, 6003yds, Par 72, SSS 72, Course record 66.
Club membership 871.
Visitors contact in advance. No play on Sat. **Societies**
contact in advance. **Green Fees** £18 per round (£23 Sun &
bank holidays). **Cards** 📇 💳 🔲 **Course Designer**
F Ainsworth **Facilities** ⊗ ℳ ℔ ▆ ♀ ▵ 🏠 ✲ 🏌 ⚐
Leisure gymnasium, outdoor bowls. **Conf** fac available
Corporate Hospitality Days available **Location** 1m S
....
Hotel ★★ 65% Enniskeen House Hotel, 98 Bryansford
Rd, NEWCASTLE ☎ 028 4372 2392 12 en suite

BANBRIDGE   Map 01 D5

Banbridge 116 Huntly Rd BT32 3UR
☎ 028 4066 2211 📠 028 4066 9400
e-mail: info@banbridge-golf.freeserve.co.uk
18 holes, 5003 metres, Par 69, SSS 67, Course record 61.
Course Designer F Ainsworth **Location** 0.5m along
Huntly Rd
Phone for further details

BANGOR   Map 01 D5

Bangor Broadway BT20 4RH
☎ 028 9127 0922 📠 028 9145 3394
e-mail: admin@bangorgolfclubni.co.uk
Undulating parkland course in the town. It is well
maintained and pleasant and offers a challenging
round, particularly at the 5th. Scenic views to Scotland
on a clear day.
18 holes, 6410yds, Par 71, SSS 71, Course record 62.
Club membership 1147.
Visitors not Sat & weekdays 1-2 pm. **Societies** contact in
advance, with confirmation by letter. **Green Fees** terms on
application. **Prof** Michael Bannon **Course Designer** James

Continued   *Continue*

Braid **Facilities** ⊗ Ⅲ ⅃ ⅃ ♀ ⅃ 🖳 ⛳ 🚃 ⟋ **Conf**
Corporate Hospitality Days available **Location** 1m from
own centre, 300yds off Donaghadee Rd

Hotel ★★★ 66% Royal Hotel, Seafront, BANGOR
☎ 028 9127 1866 50 en suite

Blackwood Golf Centre 150 Crawfordsburn Rd,
Clandeboye BT19 1GB
☎ 028 9185 2706 📄 028 9185 3785
The golf centre is a pay and play development with a
computerised booking system for the 18-hole
championship-standard Hamilton Course. The course is
built on mature woodland with man-made lakes that
come into play on five holes. The Temple course is an
18-hole par 3 course with holes ranging from the 75yd
1st to the 185yd 10th, which has a lake on the right of
the green. Banked by gorse with streams crossing
throughout, this par 3 course is no pushover.
*Hamilton Course: 18 holes, 6392yds, Par 71, SSS 70,
Course record 62.*
Temple Course: 18 holes, 2492yds, Par 54.
Visitors pay as you play, computerised booking system for
the Hamilton Course, bookable seven days in advance.
Societies phone in advance. **Green Fees** terms on
application. **Cards** 🖮 🖳 🖳 📄 🖳 **Prof** Debbie Hanna
Course Designer Simon Gidman **Facilities** ⊗ ⅃ ♀ ⅃ ⅃
⛳ ⟋ ⟋ **Location** 2m from Bangor off A2 to Belfast

Hotel ★★★ 77% Clandeboye Lodge Hotel, 10 Estate Rd,
Clandeboye, BANGOR ☎ 028 9185 2500 43 en suite

Carnalea Station Rd BT19 1EZ
☎ 028 9127 0368 📄 028 9127 3989
A scenic course on the shores of Belfast Lough.
18 holes, 5647yds, Par 69, SSS 67, Course record 63.
Club membership 1354.
Visitors restricted Sat. **Societies** contact in advance. **Green
Fees** £16.50 (£21 Sun). **Prof** Tom Loughran **Facilities** ⊗
Ⅲ ⅃ ⅃ 🖳 ⛳ ⟋ **Location** 2m W next to railway
station

Hotel ★★★ 78% The Old Inn, 15 Main St,
CRAWFORDSBURN ☎ 028 9185 3255 31 en suite
1 annexe en suite

Clandeboye Tower Rd, Conlig, Newtownards
BT23 3PN
☎ 028 9127 1767 📄 028 9147 3711
e-mail: cgc-ni@btconnect.com
Parkland and heathland courses. The Dufferin is the
championship course and offers a tough challenge
demanding extreme accuracy, with gorse, bracken and
strategically placed trees that flank every hole. Errors
will be punished. The Ava compliments the Dufferin
perfectly. Accuracy is the key on this course with small
targets and demanding tee shots. Outstanding
panoramic views.
Dufferin Course: 18 holes, 6559yds, Par 71, SSS 71.
Ava Course: 18 holes, 5755yds, Par 70, SSS 68.
Club membership 1450.
Visitors contact in advance, weekends after 2.30pm.
Societies Mon-Wed & Fri. Must contact in advance. **Green
Fees** Dufferin £27.50 (£33 weekends); Ava £22 (£27.50
weekends). **Cards** 🖮 🖳 **Prof** Peter Gregory **Course
Designer** Von Limburger, Allis, Thomas **Facilities** ⊗ Ⅲ
⅃ ⅃ ♀ ⅃ 🖳 ⛳ 🚃 ⟋ **Leisure** snooker, table tennis,

indoor bowls. **Conf** fac available Corporate Hospitality
Days available **Location** 2m S on A1 between Bangor &
Newtownards

Hotel ★★★ 66% Royal Hotel, Seafront, BANGOR
☎ 028 9127 1866 50 en suite

Helen's Bay Golf Rd, Helen's Bay BT19 1TL
☎ 028 9185 2815 & 9185 2601 📄 028 9185 2815
e-mail: mail@helensbaygc.com
9 holes, 5161 metres, Par 68, SSS 67, Course record 67.
Location A2 from Belfast
Phone for further details

Hotel ★★★ 78% The Old Inn, 15 Main St,
CRAWFORDSBURN ☎ 028 9185 3255 31 en suite
1 annexe en suite

Rockmount 28 Drumalig Rd, Carryduff BT8 8EQ
☎ 028 9081 2279 📄 020 9081 5851
e-mail: rockmountgc@btconnect.com
A demanding 18-hole course set in open parkland with
mature trees, several streams, and a tricky lake at the
11th hole. Panoramic views.
18 holes, 6373yds, Par 71, SSS 71, Course record 68.
Club membership 750.
Visitors welcome except for Sat or Wed am. **Societies**
welcome except for Wed & Sat, book by phone. **Green
Fees** not confirmed. **Cards** 🖮 🖳 🖳 📄 **Course Designer**
Robert Patterson **Facilities** ⊗ Ⅲ ⅃ ⅃ ♀ ⅃ 🖳 🖳 🚃 ⟋
Conf Corporate Hospitality Days available
Location 10m S of Belfast

Kirkistown Castle 142 Main Rd, Cloughey
BT22 1JA
☎ 028 4277 1233 📄 028 4277 1699
e-mail: kirkistown@supanet.com
A seaside part-links designed by James Braid, popular
with visiting golfers because of its quiet location. The
course is exceptionally dry and remains open when
others in the area have to close. The short but
treacherous par 4 15th hole was known as Braid's
Hole. The 2nd and 10th holes are long par 4s with
elevated greens, which are a feature of the course. The
10th is particularly distinctive with a long drive and a
slight dog-leg to a raised green with a gorse covered
motte waiting for the wayward approach shot. It has
the reputation of being one of the hardest par 4s in
Ireland.
18 holes, 6167yds, Par 69, SSS 70, Course record 65.
Club membership 1012.
Visitors contact in advance, restricted weekends. **Societies**
contact in writing or by phone. **Green Fees** £25 per day
(£30 weekends). **Prof** Richard Whitford **Course Designer**
James Braid **Facilities** ⊗ Ⅲ ⅃ ⅃ ♀ ⅃ 🖳 ⛳ ⟋ **Leisure**
snooker room. **Conf** Corporate Hospitality Days available
Location 16m from Newtownards on A2

Hotel ★★★ 78% The Old Inn, 15 Main St,
CRAWFORDSBURN ☎ 028 9185 3255 31 en suite
1 annexe en suite

Booking a tee time is always advisable.

Continued

DONAGHADEE
Map 01 D5

Donaghadee Warren Rd BT21 0PQ
☎ 028 9188 3624 📄 028 9188 8891
e-mail: deegolf@freenet.co.uk
Undulating seaside course, part links, part parkland, requiring a certain amount of concentration. Splendid views.
18 holes, 5616 metres, Par 71, SSS 69, Course record 64. Club membership 1200.
Visitors contact in advance. **Societies** write or phone in advance. **Green Fees** not confirmed. **Prof** Gordon Drew **Facilities** ⊗ ⅋ ⅃ ⅃ ♂ ⅃ ⅃ ♂ **Conf**
Corporate Hospitality Days available
Location 5m S of Bangor on Coast Rd

Hotel ★★★ 78% The Old Inn, 15 Main St,
CRAWFORDSBURN ☎ 028 9185 3255 31 en suite
1 annexe en suite

DOWNPATRICK
Map 01 D5

Bright Castle 14 Coniamstown Rd, Bright BT30 8LU
☎ 028 4484 1319
18 holes, 7300yds, Par 74, SSS 74, Course record 69.
Course Designer Mr Ennis Snr **Location** 5m S
Phone for further details

Hotel ★★ 65% Enniskeen House Hotel, 98 Bryansford
Rd, NEWCASTLE ☎ 028 4372 2392 12 en suite

Downpatrick 43 Saul Rd BT30 6PA
☎ 028 4461 5947 📄 028 4461 7502
e-mail: info@downpatrickgolfclub.org.com
18 holes, 6100yds, Par 70, SSS 69, Course record 66.
Course Designer Hawtree & Son **Location** 1.5m from town centre
Phone for further details

Hotel ★★ 65% Enniskeen House Hotel, 98 Bryansford
Rd, NEWCASTLE ☎ 028 4372 2392 12 en suite

HOLYWOOD
Map 01 D5

Holywood Nuns Walk, Demesne Rd BT18 9LE
☎ 028 9042 3135 📄 028 9042 5040
e-mail: mail@holywoodgolfclub.co.uk
18 holes, 5480 metres, Par 69, SSS 68, Course record 64.
Location just outside Belfast, off Bangor dual carriageway, behind Holywood
Phone for further details

Hotel ★★★ 78% The Old Inn, 15 Main St,
CRAWFORDSBURN ☎ 028 9185 3255 31 en suite
1 annexe en suite

The Royal Belfast Station Rd, Craigavad BT18 0BP
☎ 028 9042 8165 📄 028 9042 1404
e-mail: royalbelfastgc@btclick.com
On the shores of Belfast Lough, this attractive course consists of wooded parkland on undulating terrain which provides a pleasant, challenging game.
18 holes, 6185yds, Par 70, SSS 69.
Club membership 1200.
Visitors not Wed or Sat before 4.30pm; must be accompanied by a member or present a letter of introduction from their own golf club. Must contact in advance. **Societies** contact in writing or by phone. **Green Fees** £45 (£55 weekends & bank holidays). **Cards** 🔲 🔲
Continued

🔲 🔲 **Prof** Chris Spence **Course Designer** HC Colt **Facilities** ⊗ ⅋ ⅃ ⅃ ♂ ⅃ ⅃ ♂ **Leisure** hard tennis courts, squash. **Conf** Corporate Hospitality Days available **Location** 2m E on A2

Hotel ★★★ 78% The Old Inn, 15 Main St,
CRAWFORDSBURN ☎ 028 9185 3255 31 en suite
1 annexe en suite

KILKEEL
Map 01 D5

Kilkeel Mourne Park BT34 4LB
☎ 028 4176 5095 📄 028 4176 5579
e-mail: kilkeelgolfclub@tinyonline.co.uk
Picturesquely situated at the foot of the Mourne Mountains. Eleven holes have tree-lined fairways with the remainder in open parkland. The 13th hole is testing and a well-positioned tee shot is essential.
18 holes, 6579yds, Par 72, SSS 72, Course record 67. Club membership 750.
Visitors contact in advance, especially for weekend play. **Societies** contact in advance. **Green Fees** terms on application. **Cards** 🔲 🔲 🔲 **Course Designer** Babington, Hackett **Facilities** ⊗ ⅋ ⅃ ⅃ ♂ ⅃ ♂ **Conf** fac available Corporate Hospitality Days available **Location** 3m from Kilkeel on Newry road

Hotel ★★ 65% Enniskeen House Hotel, 98 Bryansford
Rd, NEWCASTLE ☎ 028 4372 2392 12 en suite

KILLYLEAGH
Map 01 D5

Ringdufferin Golf Course 31 Ringdufferin Rd,
Toye BT30 9PH
☎ 028 4482 8812 📄 028 4482 8812
18 holes, 4652 metres, Par 68, SSS 66.
Course Designer Frank Ainsworth **Location** 2m N of Killyleagh
Phone for further details

Hotel ★★★ 69% Portaferry Hotel, 10 The Strand,
PORTAFERRY ☎ 028 4272 8231 14 en suite

MAGHERALIN
Map 01 D5

Edenmore Edenmore House, 70 Drumnabreeze Rd
BT67 0RH
☎ 028 9261 1310 📄 028 9261 3310
e-mail: edenmoregc@aol.com
Edenmore Golf Course: 18 holes, 6244yds, Par 71, SSS 70, Course record 70.
Course Designer F Ainsworth **Location** M1 Moira exit, through Moira towards Lurgan. Turn off in Magheralin & club signed
Phone for further details

Hotel ★★★ 78% The Old Inn, 15 Main St,
CRAWFORDSBURN ☎ 028 9185 3255 31 en suite
1 annexe en suite

NEWCASTLE
See page 413

NEWRY
Map 01 D5

Newry 11 Forkhill Rd BT35 8LZ
☎ 028 3026 3871 📄 028 3026 3871
18 holes, 3000 metres, Par 53, SSS 52, Course record 51.
Course Designer Michael Heaney **Location** 1m from Newry off Dublin road
Phone for further details

Continued

Royal County Down

Co Down

Newcastle   Map 01 D5

The Championship Course is consistently rated among the world's top ten courses. Laid out beneath the imperious Mourne Mountains, the course has a magnificent setting as it stretches out along the shores of Dundrum Bay. As well as being one of the most-beautiful courses, it is also one of the most challenging, with great swathes of heather and gorse lining fairways that tumble beneath vast sand hills, and wild tussock-faced bunkers defending small, subtly contoured greens. The Annesley Links offers a less formidable yet extremely characterful game, played against the same incomparable backdrop. Recently substantially revised under the direction of Donald Steel, the course begins quite benignly before charging headlong into the dunes. Several charming and one or two teasing holes have been carved out amid the gorse, heather and bracken.

36 Golf Links Rd BT33 0AN
☎ 028 43723314 Fax 028 43726281
e-mail: golf@royalcountydown.org

Championship Course: 18 holes, 7065yds, Par 71, SSS 74, Course record 66.
Annesley: 18 holes, 4681yds, Par 66, SSS 63.
Club membership 450.
Visitors not Wed, Sat on Championship Course; not Sat on Annesley; advisable to contact in advance. **Societies** phone for availability & confirm in writing. **Green Fees** Championship Course £115 weekdays, £100 pm (£130 Sun). **Cards** 💳 💳 💳 💳 💳 💳 **Prof** Kevan Whitson **Course Designer** Tom Morris **Facilities** ⊗ 🍴 🍺 🍷 🎱 🏌 🎯 ⌀
Location N of town centre off A2

....

Hotel

★ ★ 65% Enniskeen House Hotel, 98 Bryansford Rd, NEWCASTLE

☎ 028 4372 2392 12 en suite

Hotel ★★ 65% Enniskeen House Hotel, 98 Bryansford Rd, NEWCASTLE ☎ 028 4372 2392 12 en suite

NEWTOWNARDS   Map 01 D5

Scrabo 233 Scrabo Rd BT23 4SL
☎ 028 9181 2355 ▤ 028 9182 2919
e-mail: admin.scrabogc@btconnect.com
Hilly and picturesque, this heathland course stands on a 150-metre hill with rocky outcrops. Accuracy is important. Fine views.
18 holes, 5722 metres, Par 71, SSS 71, Course record 65. Club membership 1002.
Visitors not Sat; contact in advance. Societies contact in advance. Green Fees £19 (£24 Sun). Prof Paul McCrystal Facilities ⊗ ⏍ ⓑ ♟ ⚲ ⚐ ⬠ ⬥ Location outskirts of Newtownards on Ards peninsula, signs for Scrabo Country Park

Hotel ★★★ 77% Clandeboye Lodge Hotel, 10 Estate Rd, Clandeboye, BANGOR ☎ 028 9185 2500 43 en suite

WARRENPOINT   Map 01 D5

Warrenpoint Lower Dromore Rd BT34 3LN
☎ 028 4175 3695 ▤ 028 4175 2918
e-mail: office@warrenpointgolf.com
Parkland course with marvellous views and a need for accurate shots.
18 holes, 6108yds, Par 71, SSS 70, Course record 61. Club membership 1460.
Visitors contact in advance. Societies contact in advance. Green Fees £22 per 18 holes (£30 weekends & bank holidays). Prof Nigel Shaw Course Designer Tom Craddock, Pat Ruddy Facilities ⊗ ⏍ ⓑ ♟ ⚲ ⚐ ⬠ ⬥ Conf fac available Corporate Hospitality Days available Location 1m W

Hotel ★★ 65% Enniskeen House Hotel, 98 Bryansford Rd, NEWCASTLE ☎ 028 4372 2392 12 en suite

CO FERMANAGH

ENNISKILLEN   Map 01 C5

Ashwoods Golf Centre Sligo Rd BT74 7JY
☎ 028 6632 5321 & 6632 2908 ▤ 028 6632 9411
14 holes, 1930yds, Par 42.
Course Designer P Loughran Location 1.5m W of Enniskillen on Sligo road
Phone for further details

Hotel ★★★★ 72% Killyhevlin Hotel, ENNISKILLEN ☎ 028 6632 3481 43 en suite

Castle Hume Castle Hume, Belleek Rd BT93 7ED
☎ 028 6632 7077 ▤ 028 6632 7076
e-mail: info@castlehumegolf.com
Castle Hume is a particularly scenic and challenging course. Set in undulating parkland with large rolling greens, rivers, lakes and water hazards all in play on a championship standard course.
18 holes, 5770 metres, Par 72, SSS 70, Course record 69. Club membership 350.
Visitors may play any time subject to advance arrangement. Societies phone in advance. Green Fees not confirmed. Cards ⚌ ▰ ⬡ Prof Shaun Donnelly Course Designer B Browne Facilities ⊗ ⏍ ⓑ ♟ ⚲ ⚐ ⬠ ⬥ ⬢

🏊 ⬥ ⟨ Leisure fishing. Conf fac available Corporate Hospitality Days available Location 4m from Enniskillen on A46 Belleek-Donegal road

Hotel ★★★★ 72% Killyhevlin Hotel, ENNISKILLEN ☎ 028 6632 3481 43 en suite

Enniskillen Castlecoole BT74 6HZ
☎ 028 6632 5250 ▤ 028 6632 5250
e-mail: enquiries@enniskillengolfclub.com
18 holes, 6230yds, Par 71, SSS 69, Course record 67.
Location 1m E
Phone for further details

Hotel ★★★★ 72% Killyhevlin Hotel, ENNISKILLEN ☎ 028 6632 3481 43 en suite

CO LONDONDERRY

AGHADOWEY   Map 01 C6

Brown Trout Golf & Country Inn
209 Agivey Rd BT51 4AD
☎ 028 7086 8209 ▤ 028 7086 8878
e-mail: bill@browntroutinn.com
A challenging course with two par 5s. During the course of the nine holes, players have to negotiate water seven times and all the fairways are lined with densely packed fir trees.
9 holes, 5510yds, Par 70, SSS 68, Course record 64. Club membership 100.
Visitors no restrictions. Societies contact by phone, restricted tee-off times Sun. Green Fees not confirmed. Cards ⚌ ▰ ⬛ ⬡ ▰ ⬡ Prof Ken Revie Course Designer Bill O'Hara Snr Facilities ⊗ ⏍ ⓑ ♟ ⚲ ⚐ ⬠ ⬢ ⬥ Leisure fishing, gymnasium. Location junct of A54 & B66, 7m S of Coleraine

Hotel ★★ 70% Brown Trout Golf & Country Inn, 209 Agivey Rd, AGHADOWEY ☎ 028 7086 8209 15 en suite

CASTLEDAWSON   Map 01 C5

Moyola Park 15 Curran Rd BT45 8DG
☎ 028 7946 8468 & 7946 8830 (prof) ▤ 028 7946 8626
e-mail: moyolapark@btconnect.com
Parkland championship course with some difficult shots, calling for length and accuracy. The Moyola River provides a water hazard at the 8th. Newly designed par 3 17th demands good shot placement to a green on an island in the Moyola river, when players' capabilities will be tested by the undulating green.
18 holes, 6519yds, Par 71, SSS 71, Course record 67. Club membership 1000.
Visitors contact professional in advance, dress code applies, Ladies Day Wed, Sat & Sun after 1.30pm, book in advance to avoid disappointment. Societies contact in advance, preferably in writing Green Fees Mon-Thu £20 per round; Fri £25; Sat-Sun £30. Cards ⚌ ▰ ⬡ Prof Bob Cockcroft Course Designer Don Patterson Facilities ⊗ ⏍ ⓑ ♟ ⚲ ⚐ ⬠ ⬢ ⬥ Conf fac available Corporate Hospitality Days available Location club signed

Hotel ★★★★ 59% Galgorm Manor, BALLYMENA ☎ 028 2588 1001 24 en suite

CASTLEROCK

Map 01 C6

Castlerock 65 Circular Rd BT51 4TJ
☎ 028 7084 8314 🖶 028 7084 9440
e-mail: info@castlerockgc.co.uk
A most exhilarating course with three superb par 4s,
four testing short holes and five par 5s. After an uphill
start, the hazards are many, including the river and a
railway, and both judgement and accuracy are called
for. The signature hole is the 4th, Leg of Mutton. A
challenge in calm weather, any trouble from the
elements will test your golf to the limits.
*Mussenden Course: 18 holes, 6499yds, Par 73, SSS 71,
Course record 64.*
*Bann Course: 9 holes, 2938yds, Par 34, SSS 33, Course
record 60.*
Club membership 1250.
Visitors contact in advance, limited number of places at
weekends. Must be members of a recognised club. **Societies**
contact in advance. **Green Fees** £50 per day (£70 per round
weekends & bank holidays). **Cards** 🔲 🔲 💷 **Prof** Ian
Blair **Course Designer** Ben Sayers **Facilities** ⊗ ⅷ ⅂ 💷 ♀
♨ 🏠 🏌 ⚑ **Location** 6m from Coleraine on A2
....
Guesthouse ◆◆◆◆◆ Greenhill House, 24 Greenhill Rd,
Aghadowey, COLERAINE ☎ 028 7086 8241 6 en suite

KILREA

Map 01 C5

Kilrea 47a Lisnagrot Rd BT51 5TB
☎ 028 2954 0044
Inland course, winner of an environmental award.
Course development completed spring 2005 made the
par for the course 70.
9 holes, 5578yds, Par 68, SSS 68, Course record 66.
Club membership 300.
Visitors restricted Tue pm, Wed pm during summer & Sat
all year. **Societies** phone in advance, avoid Sun. **Green
Fees** not confirmed. **Facilities** ⊗ ⅷ ⅂ 💷 ♀ △
....
Hotel ★★ 70% Brown Trout Golf & Country Inn, 209
Agivey Rd, AGHADOWEY ☎ 028 7086 8209 15 en suite

LIMAVADY

Map 01 C6

Benone 53 Benone Ave BT49 0LQ
☎ 028 77750555 🖶 028 77750919

Benone Golf Course: 9 holes, 1334 metres, Par 27.
Club membership 100.
Visitors no restrictions. **Societies** contact in advance
during Jul & Aug **Green Fees** not confirmed. **Facilities** △
♨ ⚑ **Leisure** hard tennis courts, heated outdoor swimming
pool. **Location** between Coleraine & Limavady on A2

Benone
Tourist Complex

Benone Golf Course, beside golden Benone Beach,
overlooks the spectacular scenery of the Causeway
Coast at the foot of majestic Binevenagh mountain.
Enjoy picturesque views and stimulating sea air as
you tackle the 9 hole par 3 course, indulge in
on-site facilities, including splash pools, bowling
green and tennis courts, and explore the beautiful
coastline, immersed in history and romantic
legends.

For further information and booking, contact:

The Warden, Benone Tourist Complex,
53 Benone Avenue, Limavady BT49 0LQ
Tel. 028 7775 0555   Fax. 028 7775 0919

***

Radisson Roe Park Hotel & Golf Resort Roe
Park BT49 9LB
☎ 028 7772 2222 🖶 028 7772 2313
e-mail: sales@radissonroepark.com
18 holes, 6318yds, Par 70, SSS 70.
Course Designer Frank Ainsworth **Location** just outside
Limavady on A2 Ballykelly-Londonderry road
Phone for further details
....
Hotel ★★★★ 70% Radisson SAS Roe Park Resort,
LIMAVADY ☎ 028 7772 2222 118 en suite

LONDONDERRY

Map 01 C5

City of Derry 49 Victoria Rd BT47 2PU
☎ 028 7134 6369 🖶 028 7131 0008
e-mail: cityofderry@aol.com
**Two parkland courses on undulating parkland with
good views and lots of trees. The nine-hole course will
particularly suit novices.**
*Prehen Course: 18 holes, 6406yds, Par 71, SSS 71,
Course record 68.*
Dunhugh Course: 9 holes, 2354yds, Par 66, SSS 66.
Club membership 700.
Visitors book for Prehen Course weekends & before
4.30pm weekdays. **Societies** contact in advance. **Green
Fees** not confirmed. **Cards** 🔲 **Prof** Michael Doherty
Facilities ⊗ ⅷ ⅂ 💷 ♀ △ 🏠 🏌 ⚑ **Conf** fac available
Location 2m S
....
Hotel ★★★ 73% Beech Hill Country House
Hotel, 32 Ardmore Rd, LONDONDERRY
☎ 028 7134 9279 17 en suite 10 annexe en suite

Foyle International Golf Centre 12 Alder Rd

BT48 8DB
☎ 028 7135 2222 📠 028 7135 3967
e-mail: mail@foylegolf.club24.co.uk
Foyle International boasts a championship course, a nine-hole par 3 course and a driving range. It is a fine test of golf with water coming into play on the 3rd, 10th and 11th holes. The 6th green overlooks the Amelia Earhart centre.
Earhart: 18 holes, 6678yds, Par 72, SSS 71, Course record 70.
Club membership 320.
Visitors welcome any time, no restrictions. **Societies** booking up to 12 months in advance with deposit. **Green Fees** £14 (£17 weekends). **Cards** 〰️ ▓ ▤ ▨ ⑨ **Prof** Kieran McLaughlin **Course Designer** Frank Ainsworth **Facilities** ⊗ 🍴 🏐 ⬛ ♀ ⛳ 🏠 ⚲ ✓ (**Leisure** 9-hole par 3 course. **Conf** fac available Corporate Hospitality Days available **Location** 1.5m from Foyle Bridge towards Moville

....

Hotel ★★★ 65% White Horse Hotel, 68 Clooney Rd, Campsie, LONDONDERRY ☎ 028 7186 0606 57 en suite

PORTSTEWART Map 01 C6

Portstewart 117 Strand Rd BT55 7PG
☎ 028 7083 2015 & 7083 3839 📠 028 7083 4097
e-mail: bill@portstewartgc.co.uk
Strand Course: 18 holes, 6784yds, Par 72, SSS 72, Course record 67.
Old Course: 18 holes, 4733yds, Par 64, SSS 62.
Riverside: 9 holes, 2622yds, Par 32.
Course Designer Des Giffin
Phone for further details

....

Guesthouse ♦♦♦♦ Harbour Heights, 17 Kerr St, PORTRUSH ☎ 028 7082 2765 10 rms (9 en suite)

CO TYRONE

COOKSTOWN Map 01 C5

Killymoon 200 Killymoon Rd BT80 8TW
☎ 028 8676 3762 & 8676 2254 📠 028 8676 3762
e-mail: killymoongolf@btconnect.com
Parkland course on elevated, well-drained land. The signature hole is the aptly named 6th hole - the Giant's Grave. Accuracy is paramount here and a daunting tee shot into a narrow-necked fairway will challenge even the most seasoned golfer. The enclosing influence of the trees continues the whole way to the green.
18 holes, 6202yds, Par 70, SSS 69, Course record 64.
Club membership 950.
Visitors booking essential through pro shop on 016487 63460. Must contact in advance, have a golf handicap & play after 3.30pm Sat. **Societies** contact in advance. **Green Fees** Mon (except bank holidays) £15 per 18 holes; Tue-Fri £21; Sat-Sun £26. **Prof** Gary Chambers **Course Designer** John Nash **Facilities** ⊗ 🍴 🏐 ⬛ ♀ 🏠 ⚲ ✓ **Leisure** snooker & pool. **Conf** Corporate Hospitality Days available

....

Guesthouse ♦♦♦♦ Grange Lodge, 7 Grange Rd, DUNGANNON ☎ 028 8778 4212 5 en suite

DUNGANNON Map 01 C5

Dungannon 34 Springfield Ln BT70 1QX
☎ 028 8772 2098 📠 028 8772 7338
e-mail: info@dungannongolfclub.com
18 holes, 6046yds, Par 72, SSS 69, Course record 62.
Course Designer Sam Bacon **Location** 0.5m outside town on Donaghmore road
Phone for further details

....

Hotel ⌂ The Cohannon Inn & Autolodge, 212 Ballynakilly Rd, DUNGANNON ☎ 028 8772 4488 42 en suite

FINTONA Map 01 C5

Fintona Ecclesville Demesne, 1 Kiln St BT78 2BJ
☎ 028 8284 1480 & 8284 0777 (office) 📠 028 8284 1480
Attractive nine-hole parkland course with a notable water hazard - a trout stream that meanders through the course causing many problems for badly executed shots.
9 holes, 5765 metres, Par 72, SSS 70.
Club membership 400.
Visitors advised to contact in advance at weekends. **Societies** apply in writing well in advance, weekends not advisable as competitions played. **Green Fees** £10 (£15 weekends). **Prof** Paul Leonard **Facilities** ⊗ by arrangement 🍴 by arrangement 🏐 by arrangement ⬛ ♀ 🏠 **Location** 8m S of Omagh

....

Hotel ★★ 63% Mahons Hotel, Mill St, IRVINESTOWN ☎ 028 6862 1656 24 en suite

NEWTOWNSTEWART Map 01 C5

Newtownstewart 38 Golf Course Rd BT78 4HU
☎ 028 8166 1466 📠 028 8166 2506
e-mail: newtown.stewart@lineone.net
18 holes, 5468 metres, Par 70, SSS 69, Course record 65.
Course Designer Frank Pennick **Location** 2m SW on B84
Phone for further details

OMAGH Map 01 C5

Omagh 83a Dublin Rd BT78 1HQ
☎ 028 8224 3160 📠 028 8224 3160
18 holes, 5683 metres, Par 71, SSS 70.
Course Designer Dun Patterson **Location** S outskirts of town
Phone for further details

STRABANE Map 01 C5

Strabane Ballycolman Rd BT82 9HY
☎ 028 7138 2271 & 7138 2007 📠 028 7188 6514
e-mail: strabanegc@btconnect.com
Testing parkland course with the River Mourne running alongside and creating a water hazard.
18 holes, 5537 metres, Par 69, SSS 69, Course record 62.
Club membership 650.
Visitors by arrangement; not Tue & Sat. **Societies** phone in advance. **Green Fees** terms on application. **Cards** 〰️ ▤ **Course Designer** Eddie Hackett, P Jones **Facilities** ⊗ 🍴 🏐 ⬛ ♀ 🏠 ⚲ ✓ **Conf** fac available **Location** 1m from Strabane on Dublin road

REPUBLIC OF IRELAND

CO CARLOW

BORRIS   Map 01 C3

Borris Deerpark
☎ 059 9773310 ▤ 059 9773750
e-mail: borrisgolfclub@eircom.net
Testing parkland course with tree-lined fairways situated within the McMorrough Kavanagh Estate at the foot of Mount Leinster. Modern sand based greens.
9 holes, 5680 metres, Par 70, SSS 69, Course record 66.
Club membership 718.
Visitors advisable to contact in advance, weekends with member only. **Societies** applications in writing.
Green Fees €25 per 18 holes (€16 with member).
Facilities ⊗ ⅊ ℔ ■ ♀ ⚲ 🏠 ♂

Hotel ★★★★ ♨ Mount Juliet Conrad Hotel,
THOMASTOWN ☎ 056 777 3000 32 en suite 27 annexe en suite

CARLOW   Map 01 C3

Carlow Deerpark
☎ 059 9131695 ▤ 059 9140065
e-mail: carlowgolfclub@eircom.net
Created in 1922 to a design by Cecil Barcroft, this testing and enjoyable course is set in a wild deer park, with beautiful dry terrain and a varied character. With sandy subsoil, the course is playable all year round. There are water hazards at the 2nd, 10th and 11th and only two par 5s, both offering genuine birdie opportunities.
18 holes, 5974 metres, Par 70, SSS 71, Course record 65.
Club membership 1200.
Visitors are welcome, although play is limited on Tue & difficult on Sat & Sun. Must contact in advance. **Societies** book in advance. **Green Fees** not confirmed. **Cards** 🖃
🖃 **Prof** Andrew Gilbert **Course Designer** Cecil Barcroft
Facilities ⊗ ⅊ ℔ ■ ♀ ⚲ 🏠 ♂ **Location** 3km N of Carlow on N9

Hotel ★★★ Seven Oaks Hotel, Athy Rd, CARLOW
☎ 059 913 1308 59 en suite

TULLOW   Map 01 C3

Mount Wolseley Hotel, Golf & Country Club
☎ 059 9151674 ▤ 059 9152123
e-mail: bmurray@mountwolseley.ie
A magnificent setting, a few hundred yards from the banks of the River Slaney with its mature trees and lakes set against the backdrop of the East Carlow and Wicklow mountains. With wide landing areas the only concession for demanding approach shots to almost every green. There is water in play on 11 holes, with the 14th an all-water carry off the tee of 207yds. The 18th is a fine finishing hole - a fairway lined with mature oak trees, then a second shot uphill across a water hazard to green.
18 holes, 6786yds, Par 72, SSS 70, Course record 68.
Club membership 350.
Visitors contact in advance. **Societies** contact in advance.
Green Fees €50 (weekends €70). **Cards** 🖃 🖃 🖃 🖃

Continued

🖃 🖃 🔊 **Course Designer** Christy O'Connor **Facilities**
⊗ ⅊ ℔ ■ ♀ ⚲ 🏠 ♂ **Leisure** hard tennis courts, heated indoor swimming pool, sauna, solarium, gymnasium, treatment rooms. **Conf** fac available Corporate Hospitality Days available **Location** 1.6km from centre of Tullow

Hotel ★★★ Seven Oaks Hotel, Athy Rd, CARLOW
☎ 059 913 1308 59 en suite

CO CAVAN

BALLYCONNELL   Map 01 C4

Slieve Russell Hotel Golf & Country Club
☎ 049 9525090 ▤ 049 9526640
e-mail: slieve-russell@quinn-hotels.com
An 18-hole course opened in 1992 and rapidly establishing itself as one of the finest parkland courses in the country. The complex incorporates a nine-hole par 3 course and driving range. On the main course, the 2nd plays across water while the 16th has water surrounding the green. The course finishes with a 519yd, par 5 18th.
18 holes, 6614yds, Par 72, SSS 72, Course record 65.
Club membership 400.
Visitors book in advance for Sat. Phone in advance.
Societies write or phone in advance **Green Fees** €65 (€80 Sat) (special rates in winter). **Cards** 🖃 🖃 🖃 🖃 🖃
Prof Liam McCool **Course Designer** Paddy Merrigan
Facilities ⊗ ⅊ ℔ ■ ♀ ⚲ 🏠 ♂ 🏌 **Leisure** hard tennis courts, heated indoor swimming pool, sauna, solarium, gymnasium, New spa for 2005. **Conf** fac available Corporate Hospitality Days available **Location** 2.5km E of Ballyconnell

Hotel ★★★★ 70% Slieve Russell Hotel Golf and Country Club, BALLYCONNELL ☎ 049 9526444 157 en suite

BELTURBET   Map 01 C4

Belturbet Erne Hill
☎ 049 9522287 & 049 9524044
Beautifully maintained parkland course with elevated greens on most holes. The 7th hole is a stern test for any golfer.
9 holes, 5480yds, Par 68, SSS 65, Course record 64.
Club membership 200.
Visitors welcome **Societies** contact secretary in advance.
Green Fees €20 per day including weekends. **Course Designer** Eddie Hackett **Facilities** ℔ ■ ♀ ⚲ 🏠 ♂
Location off N3, 0.8km N of town

Hotel ★★★★ 70% Slieve Russell Hotel Golf and Country Club, BALLYCONNELL ☎ 049 9526444 157 en suite

BLACKLION   Map 01 C5

Blacklion Toam
☎ 072 53024 & 53418 ▤ 072 53418
9 holes, 5614 metres, Par 72, SSS 69.
Course Designer Eddie Hackett
Phone for further details

Hotel ★★★ 71% Sligo Park Hotel, Pearse Rd, SLIGO
☎ 071 916 0291 138 en suite

CAVAN   Map 01 C4

County Cavan Drumelis
☎ 049 4331541 & 049 4371313 ▤ 049 31541
e-mail: info@cavangolf.ie
18 holes, 5634 metres, Par 70, SSS 69, Course record 64.
Course Designer Eddie Hackett **Location** on Killeshandra
road out of Cavan
Phone for further details
....

Hotel ★★★ 67% Kilmore Hotel, Dublin Rd, CAVAN
☎ 049 4332288   39 en suite

VIRGINIA   Map 01 C4

Virginia
☎ 049 47235 & 48066
9 holes, 4139 metres, Par 64, SSS 62, Course record 57.
Location By Lough Ramor
Phone for further details
....

Hotel ★★ 67% The Park Hotel, Virginia Park, VIRGINIA
☎ 049 8546100   26 en suite

CO CLARE

BODYKE   Map 01 B3

East Clare ☎ 061 921322 ▤ 061 921717
e-mail: eastclaregolfclub@eircon.net
An 18-hole championship course designed by Arthur
Spring beside Lough Derg, with natural trees and water
on well-drained land. Set on 150 acres of rolling quiet
countryside with superb views of East Clare.
18 holes, 5922yds, Par 71, SSS 71.
Club membership 813.
Visitors no restrictions unless there is a club competition
or a society playing. **Societies** apply in writing, deposit
required. **Green Fees** €30 (€35 weekends & bank
holidays). **Cards** ▤ ▨ ▨ ▨ **Course Designer** Dr
Arthur Spring **Facilities** ⊗ �ℿ ▙ ♥ ♀ ⚐ ⛿ ⛳ ✈ ⚒ ✐
....

Hotel ★★★ 67% Temple Gate Hotel, The Square, ENNIS
☎ 065 682 3300   70 en suite

ENNIS   Map 01 B3

Ennis Drumbiggle
☎ 065 6824074 & 6865415 ▤ 065 6841848
e-mail: egc@eircom.net
On rolling hills, this immaculately manicured course
presents an excellent challenge to both casual visitors
and aspiring scratch golfers, with tree-lined fairways
and well-protected greens.
18 holes, 5612 metres, Par 70, SSS 69, Course record 65.
Club membership 1000.
Visitors advisable to contact in advance, course available
Mon-Sat at most times. **Societies** apply in writing or phone
Green Fees €30 (weekends & bank holidays €35). **Cards**
▤ ▨ ▨ ▨ **Facilities** ⊗ ⅏ ▙ ♥ ♀ ⚐ ⛿ ✈ ⚒ ✐
Conf Corporate Hospitality Days available
Location signed near town
....

Hotel ★★★ 67% Temple Gate Hotel, The Square, ENNIS
☎ 065 682 3300   70 en suite

> **Booking a tee time is always advisable.**

Woodstock Golf and Country Club
Shanaway Rd
☎ 065 6829463 & 6842406 ▤ 065 6820304
e-mail: woodstock.ennis@eircon.net
This parkland course stands on 63 hectares of land and
includes four holes where water is a major hazard. The
course is playable all year and the sand-based greens
offer a consistent surface for putting.
18 holes, 5864 metres, Par 71, SSS 71.
Club membership 350.
Visitors booking advisable at weekends. **Societies**
advisable to phone in advance. **Green Fees** not confirmed.
Cards ▤ ▨ **Course Designer** Arthur Spring **Facilities**
⊗ ⅏ ▙ ♥ ♀ ⚐ ⛿ ⛳ ✈ ⚒ ✐ **Leisure** heated indoor
swimming pool, sauna, gymnasium. **Location** off N85
....

Hotel ★★★ 67% Temple Gate Hotel, The Square, ENNIS
☎ 065 682 3300   70 en suite

KILKEE   Map 01 B3

Kilkee East End
☎ 065 9056048 & 9056977 ▤ 065 9656977
e-mail: kilkeegolfclub@eircom.net
Well-established course on the cliffs of Kilkee Bay.
Mature championship course with a great variety of
challenges - seaside holes, clifftop holes and holes that
feature well-positioned water hazards. The spectacular
3rd hole hugs the cliff top. The ever present Atlantic
breeze provides golfers with a real test.
18 holes, 6075yds, Par 70, SSS 69, Course record 68.
Club membership 710.
Visitors advance booking advisable. **Societies** apply by
writing, phone, fax or e-mail **Green Fees** Sept-June €25
(weekends €30); July-Aug €30/€35. **Cards** ▤ ▨ ▨
▨ **Course Designer** Eddie Hackett **Facilities** ⊗ ⅏ ▙ ♥
♀ ⚐ ⛿ ✈ ⚒ ✐ **Leisure** squash, sauna. **Location** on
Cilff-Edge, East End, Kilkee
....

Hotel ★★ 64% Halpin's Townhouse Hotel, Erin St,
KILKEE ☎ 065 9056032   12 en suite

KILRUSH   Map 01 B3

Kilrush Parknamoney
☎ 065 9051138 ▤ 065 9052633
e-mail: info@kilrushgolfclub.com
18 holes, 5986yds, Par 70, SSS 70, Course record 68.
Course Designer Arthur Spring
Location 0.8km from Kilrush on Ennis road
Phone for further details
....

Hotel ★★ 64% Halpin's Townhouse Hotel, Erin St,
KILKEE ☎ 065 9056032   12 en suite

LAHINCH   Map 01 B3

Lahinch
☎ 065 7081592 ▤ 065 81592
e-mail: info@lahinchgolf.com
Old Course: 18 holes, 6696yds, Par 72, SSS 73.
Castle Course: 18 holes, 5594yds, Par 70, SSS 70.
Course Designer A MacKenzie
Location 3km W of Ennisstymon on N67
Phone for further details
....

Hotel ⌂ Kincora Country House & Gallery Restaurant,
LISDOONVARNA ☎ 065 7074300   14 en suite

MILLTOWN MALBAY   Map 01 B3

Spanish Point
☎ 065 7084198 🖷 065 7084263
-mail: dkfitzgerald@tinet.ie
A nine-hole links course with three elevated greens and
our elevated tees. Overlooking Spanish Point beach.
mprovements to the course are planned, the existing
ourse to be redesigned and lengthened.
 holes, 4600 metres, Par 64, SSS 63, Course record 59.
Club membership 600.
Visitors contact in advance. Not before 1pm Sun. Societies
pply in writing to the secretary. Green Fees not
onfirmed. Cards 🖂 ▦ 🖃 Facilities 🅱 ♥ ♀ ⚐ ❧ ♂
Location 3km SW of Miltown Malbay on N67

....

Hotel ★★ 64% Halpin's Townhouse Hotel, Erin St,
KILKEE ☎ 065 9056032 12 en suite

NEWMARKET-ON-FERGUS   Map 01 B3

Dromoland Castle Golf & Country Club
☎ 061 368444 & 368144 🖷 061 363355/368498
-mail: golf@dromoland.ie
Set in 200 acres of parkland, the course is enhanced by
numerous trees and a lake. Three holes are played
around the lake which is in front of the castle.

8 holes, 6850yds, Par 72, SSS 72, Course record 65.
Club membership 500.
Visitors contact in advance. Societies contact in writing.
Green Fees €110 per day per round. Cards 🖂 ▦ 🖃
📱 Prof David Foley Course Designer Ron Kirby & JB
Carr Facilities ⊗ 沙 🅱 ♥ ♀ ⚐ 🏠 ❧ ♂ ➤ 🚗 ♂
Leisure hard tennis courts, heated indoor swimming pool,
fishing, sauna, solarium, gymnasium. Conf fac available
Corporate Hospitality Days available
Location 3km N on Limerick-Galway road

....

Hotel ★★★★★ Dromoland Castle Hotel,
NEWMARKET-ON-FERGUS ☎ 061 368144
00 en suite

SHANNON AIRPORT   Map 01 B3

Shannon
☎ 061 471849 🖷 061 471507
-mail: shannongolfclub@eircom.net
8 holes, 6874yds, Par 72, SSS 74, Course record 65.
Course Designer John Harris Location 3km from
Shannon Airport
Phone for further details

....

Hotel ★★★ 69% Fitzpatrick Bunratty Hotel, BUNRATTY
☎ 061 361177 115 en suite 4 annexe en suite

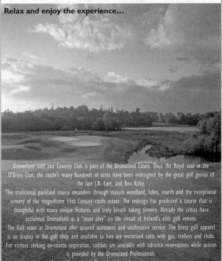

Dromoland Golf and Country Club

Tel: +353 61 368444   Fax: +353 61 368498
Email: golf@dromoland.ie   Web: www.dromoland.ie

Relax and enjoy the experience...

Dromoland Golf and Country Club is part of the Dromoland Estate. Once the Royal seat of the
O'Brien Clan, the castle's many hundreds of acres have been redesigned by the great golf genius of
the late J.B. Carr, and Ron Kirby.
The traditional parkland course meanders through mature woodland, lakes, marsh and the exceptional
scenery of the magnificent 15th Century castle estate. The redesign has produced a course that is
thoughtful with many unique features and truly breath taking scenery. Already the critics have
acclaimed Dromoland as a "must play" on the circuit of Ireland's elite golf venues.
The Golf team at Dromoland offer assured assistance and unobtrusive service. The finest golf apparel
is on display in the golf shop and available to hire are motorised carts with gps, trolleys and clubs.
For visitors seeking on-course inspiration, caddies are available with advance reservations while tuition
is provided by the Dromoland Professionals.
As a golfing retreat, Dromoland is a destination to savour.

CO CORK

BANDON   Map 01 B2

Bandon Castlebernard
☎ 023 41111 🖷 023 44690
e-mail: bandongolfclub@eircom.net
Lovely parkland course in pleasant rural surroundings.
Hazards of water, sand and trees. The course has
recently been extended around the picturesque ruin of
Castle Barnard.
18 holes, 6402yds, Par 71, SSS 71.
Club membership 900.
Visitors not during club competitions; must contact in
advance; no green fees Sun. Societies apply in writing or
phone well in advance. Green Fees €35 (€40 Sat). Cards
🖃 Prof Paddy O'Boyle Facilities ⊗ 沙 🅱 ♥ ♀ ⚐ 🏠 ❧
➤ 🚗 ♂ Leisure hard tennis courts, caddies available.
Location 2.5km W

....

Hotel ★★★ 63% Innishannon House Hotel,
INNISHANNON ☎ 021 4775121 12 en suite

BANTRY   Map 01 B2

Bantry Bay Donemark
☎ 027 50579 🖷 027 53790
e-mail: info@bantrygolf.com
Designed by Christy O'Connor Jnr and extended in
1997 to 18 holes, this challenging and rewarding course
is idyllically set at the head of Bantry Bay. Testing holes
include the par 5 of 487 metres and the little par 3 of
127 metres where accuracy is all-important.
18 holes, 6117 metres, Par 71, SSS 72, Course record 71.

Continued

Club membership 600.
Visitors advance booking recommended. At weekends &
bank holidays visitors between 11.30-1.30pm & 3-4.30pm.
Societies apply in advance by writing or phone **Green
Fees** €40 per 18 holes (€45 weekends), reductions in
winter. **Cards** ▦ ▦ **Course Designer** Christy O'Connor
Jnr, Eddie Hackett **Facilities** ⊗ ∭ ⮂ ♥ ♀ ♨ ♻ ♉
♣ ♦ **Conf** fac available Corporate Hospitality Days
available **Location** 3km N of Bantry town on N71
Glengarrif road

Hotel ★★★ 64% Westlodge Hotel, BANTRY
☎ 027 50360 90 en suite

BLACKROCK Map 01 B2

Mahon Clover Hill
☎ 021 4294280
18 holes, 4862metres, Par 70, SSS 67, Course record 64.
Course Designer Eddie Hackett
Phone for further details

Hotel ★★★★ 72% Rochestown Park Hotel, Rochestown
Rd, Douglas, CORK ☎ 021 4890800 160 en suite

BLARNEY Map 01 B2

Muskerry Carrigrohane
☎ 021 4385297 📠 021 4516860
e-mail: muskgc@eircom.net
**An adventurous game is guaranteed at this course, with
its wooded hillsides and the meandering Shournagh
River coming into play at a number of holes. The 15th
is a notable hole - not long, but very deep - and after
that all you need to do to get back to the clubhouse is
stay out of the water.**
18 holes, 5520 metres, Par 71, SSS 70.
Club membership 851.
Visitors not pm Wed, am Thu; some limited play
weekends after 3.30pm & members hour 12.30-1.30pm
daily; must contact in advance. **Societies** phone in advance
& then confirm in writing. **Green Fees** €35 per
round(€40 weekends). **Cards** ▦ ▦ ▦ **Prof** WM
Lehane **Course Designer** Dr A MacKenzie **Facilities** ⊗ ∭
⮂ ♥ ♀ ♨ ♻ ♉ ♦ **Location** 4km W of Blarney

Hotel ★★★★ Hayfield Manor, Perrott Av, College Rd,
CORK ☎ 021 4845900 88 en suite

CARRIGALINE Map 01 B2

Fernhill Hotel & Golf Club
☎ 021 4372226 📠 021 4371011
e-mail: fernhill@iol.ie
18 holes, 5000 metres, Par 69, SSS 68.
Course Designer ML Bowes **Location** 3km from
Ringaskiddy
Phone for further details

Hotel ★★★★ 72% Rochestown Park Hotel, Rochestown
Rd, Douglas, CORK ☎ 021 4890800 160 en suite

CASTLETOWNBERE Map 01 A2

Berehaven Millcove
☎ 027 70700 📠 027 71957
**Scenic seaside links founded in 1902. Moderately
difficult with four holes over water. Testing nine-hole
course with different tee positions for the back nine.
Water is a dominant feature and comes into play at
every hole.**

Continued

9 holes, 2624 metres, Par 68, SSS 67, Course record 63.
Club membership 150.
Visitors please check for major events. **Societies** phone or
write in advance. **Green Fees** not confirmed. **Cards** ▦
▦ **Course Designer** Royal Navy **Facilities** ⊗ ∭ ⮂ ♥ ♀
♨ ♻ ♉ **Leisure** hard tennis courts, sauna. **Conf** fac
available Corporate Hospitality Days available
Location 3km from Castletownbere on Glen Garriff Rd

Hotel ★★★ ♨ Sea View House Hotel, BALLYLICKEY
☎ 027 50073 & 50462 📠 027 51555 25 en suite

CHARLEVILLE Map 01 B2

Charleville
☎ 063 81257 & 81515 📠 063 81274
e-mail: charlevillegolf@eircom.net

*West Course: 18 holes, 6212yds, Par 71, SSS 69, Course
record 65.*
East Course: 9 holes, 6702yds, Par 72, SSS 72.
Course Designer Eddie Connaughton
Location 3km W of town centre
Phone for further details

Hotel ★★★ ♨ Longueville House Hotel, MALLOW
☎ 022 47156 & 47306 📠 022 47459 20 en suite

CLONAKILTY Map 01 B2

Dunmore Dunmore, Muckross
☎ 023 33352
9 holes, 4464yds, Par 64, SSS 61, Course record 57.
Course Designer E Hackett **Location** 5.5km S of
Clonakilty
Phone for further details

Hotel ★★★★ 75% Inchydoney Island Lodge & Spa,
CLONAKILTY ☎ 023 33143 67 en suite

CORK Map 01 B2

Cork Little Island
☎ 021 4353451 📠 021 4353410
e-mail: corkgolfclub@eircom.net
**This championship-standard course is kept in superb
condition and is playable all year round. Memorable
and distinctive features include holes at the water's
edge and in a disused quarry. The 4th hole is
considered to be among the most attractive and testing
holes in Irish golf.**
18 holes, 5910 metres, Par 72, SSS 72, Course record 67.
Club membership 750.
Visitors not 12.30-2pm or on Thu (Ladies Day), & only
after 2pm Sat & Sun. **Societies** contact in advance. **Green
Fees** €80 (€90 weekends & bank holidays).

Continued

ards 🖾 ▦ ▦ 🖳 Prof Peter Hickey Course Designer
MacKenzie Facilities ⊗ ⅷ ⅃ 🖳 ♀ ⚐ 🖘 ⚐ ⚑ ⚐ ʃ
onf Corporate Hospitality Days available Location 8km
of Cork on N25

....

otel ★★★ 70% WatersEdge Hotel, Yacht Club Quay,
OBH ☎ 021 4815566 19 en suite

ota Island Carrigtwohill
☎ 021 4883700 ▤ 021 4883713
mail: reservations@fotaisland.ie
et in the heart of a 780-acre island in Cork Harbour.
he course is routed among mature woodlands with
ccasional views of the harbour. The traditional design
atures pot bunkers and undulating putting surfaces.
ota hosted the Murphys Irish Open in 2001 and 2002.
8 holes, 6500yds, Par 71, SSS 71, Course record 63.
lub membership 400.
isitors advisable to contact in advance. Metal spikes &
ue jeans not permitted. Societies contact in advance.
reen Fees €62-€98. Cards 🖾 ▦ ▦ Prof Kevin
orris Course Designer Jeff Howes Facilities ⊗ ⅷ ⅃ 🖳
⚐ 🖻 🖘 ⚑ ⚐ ʃ Conf fac available Corporate
ospitality Days available Location off N25 E of Cork
ty. Exit for Cobh, course 500 metres on right

....

otel ★★★ 71% Midleton Park Hotel & Spa,
IDLETON ☎ 021 4631767 40 en suite

he Ted McCarthy Municipal Golf Course
lackrock
☎ 021 294280
8 holes, 4862 metres, Par 70, SSS 66, Course record 63.
ourse Designer E Hackett Location 3km from city centre
hone for further details

....

otel ★★★★ 69% Silver Springs Moran Hotel, Tivoli,
ORK ☎ 021 4507533 109 en suite

ONERAILE   Map 01 B2

oneraile
☎ 022 24137 & 24379
holes, 5528yds, Par 68, SSS 67, Course record 61.
ocation off T11
hone for further details

....

otel ★★★ 65% Springfort Hall Country House Hotel,
IALLOW ☎ 022 21278 49 en suite

OUGLAS   Map 01 B2

ouglas
☎ 021 4895297 ▤ 021 4895297
mail: admin@douglasgolfclub.ie
ell-maintained, very flat parkland course which has
een recently redesigned with panoramic views from
e clubhouse.
8 holes, 5607 metres, Par 72, SSS 69.
lub membership 900.
isitors Contact in advance; not Sat or Sun am or Tue
adies Day). Reserved for members 12.30-2 pm. Societies
ntact in writing, by end of Jan. Green Fees not
onfirmed. Cards 🖾 ▦ Prof Gary Nicholson Course
esigner Peter McEvoy Facilities ⊗ ⅷ ⅃ 🖳 ♀ ⚐ 🖻 🖘
ʃ Location 6km E of Cork city

....

otel ★★★★ 72% Rochestown Park Hotel, Rochestown
d, Douglas, CORK ☎ 021 4890800 160 en suite

FERMOY   Map 01 B2

Fermoy Corrin Cross
☎ 025 32694 (office) & 31472 (shop) ▤ 025 33072
e-mail: fermoygolfclub@eircom.net
**A mature 18-hole heathland course facing the slopes of
Corrin Hill and set in a profusion of natural heather
and gorse and bisected by a road. The course
commands panoramic views over the plains of East
Cork.**
18 holes, 5596 metres, Par 70, SSS 69.
Club membership 820.
Visitors contact in advance, must phone in advance for
weekends bookings Societies advisable to write or phone
in advance. Green Fees €20 (€30 weekends & bank
holidays). Cards 🖾 ▦ Prof Brian Moriarty Course
Designer John Harris Facilities ⊗ ⅷ ⅃ 🖳 ♀ ⚐ 🖻 🖘
⚑ ⚐ Location off N8 S of town, signed

....

Hotel ★★★ ♨♨ Longueville House Hotel, MALLOW
☎ 022 47156 & 47306 ▤ 022 47459 20 en suite

GLENGARRIFF   Map 01 B2

Glengarriff
☎ 027 63150 ▤ 027 63575
9 holes, 2042 metres, Par 66, SSS 62.
Location on N71
Phone for further details

....

Hotel ★★★ 64% Westlodge Hotel, BANTRY
☎ 027 50360 90 en suite

KANTURK   Map 01 B2

Kanturk Fairyhill
☎ 029 50534 ▤ 029 20951
18 holes, 5721 metres, Par 71, SSS 69, Course record 68.
Course Designer Richard Barry **Location** 1m from
Kanturk on Fairyhill road
Phone for further details

....

Guesthouse ◆◆◆◆◆ Assolas Country House,
KANTURK ☎ 029 50015 6 en suite 3 annexe en suite

KINSALE   Map 01 B2

Kinsale Farrangalway
☎ 021 4774722 ▤ 021 4773114
e-mail: office@kinsalegolf.com
**Set in farmland and surrounded by peaceful rolling
countryside, a stiff yet fair challenge to be enjoyed by
all standards of golfers.**
*Farrangalway: 18 holes, 6609yds, Par 71, SSS 71, Course
record 70.*
Ringenane: 9 holes, 5332yds, Par 70, SSS 68.
Club membership 800.
Visitors welcome but may not be able to play at weekends.
Contact in advance. Societies by reservation Green Fees
terms on application. Cards ▦ ▦ Prof Ger Broderick
Course Designer Jack Kenneally Facilities ⊗ ⅷ ⅃ 🖳 ♀
⚐ 🖻 🖘 ⚑ ⚐ Location on Cork-Kinsale road

....

Hotel ★★★ 69% Trident Hotel, Worlds End, KINSALE
☎ 021 4772301 58 en suite

Old Head
☎ 021 4778444 📄 021 4778022
e-mail: info@oldheadgolf.ie

Old Head course is spectacularly situated on a promontory jutting out into the Atlantic. As well as bringing the sea and cliffs into play, you have to contend with strong prevailing winds - a fine test for serious golfers.

18 holes, 6451yds, Par 72, SSS 73.
Club membership 350.
Visitors tee time must be booked in advance. **Societies** pre booking necessary, rates for groups over 24. **Green Fees** 18 holes €250; 36 holes €420. **Cards** 🔷 💳 💳 💳 **Prof** Danny Brassil **Course Designer** R Kirby, J Carr, P Merrigan, E Hackett **Facilities** ⊗ ⌘ ⓛ 🍽 ♀ ♨ 🏠 ⚐ 🏌 ⛳ **Conf** Corporate Hospitality Days available **Location** from Cork R600 to Kinsale, course signed

Hotel ★★★ 73% Actons Hotel, Pier Rd, KINSALE
☎ 021 4772135 76 en suite

LITTLE ISLAND   Map 01 B2

Harbour Point Clash Rd
☎ 021 4353094 📄 021 4354408
e-mail: hpoint@iol.ie

A championship-standard course in rolling countryside on the banks of the River Lee at Cork's scenic harbour. A distinctive and testing course for every standard of golfer, providing for a full range of shots in its design. The large undulating greens and difficult par 3s are a feature of this course.
18 holes, 5883 metres, Par 72, SSS 71, Course record 71.
Visitors contact in advance. **Societies** phone for bookings. **Green Fees** not confirmed. **Cards** 🔷 💳 **Prof** Morgan O'Donovan **Course Designer** Patrick Merrigan **Facilities** ⊗ ⌘ ⓛ 🍽 ♀ ♨ 🏠 ⚐ 🏌 ⛳ 🏌 **Conf** fac available **Location** 8km E of Cork on Rosslare road & exit at Little Island

Hotel ★★★★ 69% Silver Springs Moran Hotel, Tivoli, CORK ☎ 021 4507533 109 en suite

MACROOM   Map 01 B2

Macroom Lackaduve
☎ 026 41072 & 42615 📄 026 41391
e-mail: mcroomgc@iol.ie

A particularly scenic parkland course located on undulating ground along the banks of the River Sullane. Bunkers and mature trees make a variable and testing course and the 12th has a 73-metre carry over the river to the green.

Macroom Golf Clu

18 holes, 5574 metres, Par 72, SSS 70, Course record 67
Club membership 725.
Visitors booking essential for at all times **Societies** Phone in advance. **Green Fees** €35 per day (Mon-Thu early bird until 10.30 €20) (€40 weekends & bank holidays). **Card** 🔷 💳 **Course Designer** Jack Kenneally, Eddie Hackett **Facilities** ⊗ ⌘ ⓛ 🍽 ♀ ♨ 🏠 ⚐ ⛳ **Location** through castle entrance in town square

Hotel ★★★ 70% Castle Hotel, Main St, MACROOM
☎ 026 41074 60 en suite

MALLOW   Map 01 B2

Mallow Ballyellis
☎ 022 21145 📄 022 42501
e-mail: golfmall@gofree.indigo.ie

Mallow Golf Club was first established in the late 19th century. A well-wooded parkland course overlooking the Blackwater Valley, Mallow is straightforward, but no less of a challenge for it. The front nine is by far the longer, but the back nine is demanding in its call for accuracy and the par 3 18th provides a tough finish.

18 holes, 5769 metres, Par 72, SSS 71, Course record 67
Club membership 1250.
Visitors contact in advance. **Societies** apply in advance. **Green Fees** €35 per round (€40 weekends & public holidays). **Cards** 🔷 💳 **Prof** Sean Conway **Course Designer** D W Wishart **Facilities** ⊗ ⌘ ⓛ 🍽 ♀ ♨ 🏠 ⚐ 🏌 ⛳ **Leisure** hard tennis courts, squash. **Location** 1.6km E of Mallow town

Hotel ★★★ 🏌 Longueville House Hotel, MALLOW
☎ 022 47156 & 47306 📄 022 47459 20 en suite

MIDLETON Map 01 C2

East Cork Gortacrue
☎ 021 4631687 & 4631273 🖹 021 4613695
e-mail: eastcorkgolfclub@eircom.net
A well-wooded course calling for accuracy of shots.
18 holes, 5634yds, Par 69, SSS 66, Course record 64.
Club membership 820.
Visitors not Sun am. **Societies** phone. **Green Fees** €25
(weekend €30). **Cards** ▦ 💳 **Prof** Don MacFarlane
Course Designer E Hackett **Facilities** ⊗ ⅷ ▐ ⬛ ♀ ♨ 🏠
🏌 �ℓ ℓ **Location** on A626, 3km N of Midleton on Fermoy
Rd

Hotel ★★★ 71% Midleton Park Hotel & Spa,
MIDLETON ☎ 021 4631767 40 en suite

Water Rock Water Rock
☎ 021 4613499
e-mail: waterrock@eircom.net
**A pay and play parkland course on the banks of the
Owencurra river, employing international standards
and construction including mildly contoured sand
based greens. The course comprises five par 3s and
three par 5s in two loops. The signature hole is known
as Swan Lake, the 240 yard 12th par 3, plays over
water to a contoured green.**
18 holes, 6223yds, Par 70.
Visitors advance booking advisable. **Societies** welcome all
year, may book by phone. **Green Fees** €25 (€30
weekends & bank holidays). **Course Designer** Patrick
Merrilas **Facilities** ⊗ ⅷ ▐ ⬛ ♀ ♨ 🏠 🏌 ⛳ ℓ
Location next to N25 on outskirts of Midleton

Hotel ★★★ 71% Midleton Park Hotel & Spa,
MIDLETON ☎ 021 4631767 40 en suite

MITCHELSTOWN Map 01 B2

Mitchelstown Limerick Rd
☎ 025 24072 & 087 2650110
e-mail: info@mitchelstown-golf.com
**Attractive, gently undulating parkland course set in the
Golden Vale, noted for the quality of the greens, the
magnificent views of the Galtee Mountains and its
friendly atmosphere. Strategically placed sand bunkers
will need accurate play. The course offers woodland
and water in a undulating parkland setting.**
18 holes, 5493 metres, Par 71, SSS 70.
Club membership 600.
Visitors advisable to check in advance (information line
025 24231) **Societies** apply in writing or phone. **Green
Fees** €25 per round (weekends €30). **Course Designer**
David Jones **Facilities** ⊗ ⅷ ▐ ⬛ ♀ ♨ ⛳ ℓ
Location 1km from Mitchelstown on Limerick Rd

Hotel ★★★ 🏌 Longueville House Hotel, MALLOW
☎ 022 47156 & 47306 🖹 022 47459 20 en suite

MONKSTOWN Map 01 B2

Monkstown Parkgariffe, Monkstown
☎ 021 4841376 🖹 021 4841722
e-mail: office@monkstowngolfclub.com
**Undulating parkland course with five tough finishing
holes.**
18 holes, 5441 metres, Par 70, SSS 68, Course record 66.
Club membership 960.

Continued

Visitors contact in advance. Not Tue or before 2pm
weekends. **Societies** apply in writing or phone. Large
groups (24+) should book before Xmas. **Green Fees** €40
per day (weekend €47). **Cards** ▦ 💳 **Prof** Batt Murphy
Course Designer Peter O'Hare & Tom Carey **Facilities** ⊗
ⅷ ▐ ⬛ ♀ ♨ 🏠 🏌 🔊 ℓ ℓ **Conf** Corporate Hospitality
Days available **Location** 0.8km SE of Monkstown

Hotel 🅤 Carrigaline Court Hotel, CARRIGALINE
☎ 021 4852100 91 en suite

OVENS Map 01 B2

Lee Valley Golf & Country Club Clashanure
☎ 021 7331721 🖹 021 7331695
e-mail: leevalleygolfclub@eircom.net
18 holes, 6434yds, Par 72, SSS 70, Course record 62.
Course Designer Christy O'Connor **Location** 13km from
Cork on N22 Cork-Killarney road
Phone for further details

Hotel ★★★ 70% Castle Hotel, Main St, MACROOM
☎ 026 41074 60 en suite

SKIBBEREEN Map 01 B2

Skibbereen & West Carbery Licknavar
☎ 028 21227 🖹 028 22994
e-mail: bookings@skibbgolf.com
18 holes, 6004yds, Par 71, SSS 69, Course record 66.
Course Designer Jack Kenneally **Location** 1.6km W on
Baltimore road
Phone for further details

Hotel ★★★ 67% Baltimore Harbour Hotel Leisure Cntr,
BALTIMORE ☎ 028 20361 64 en suite

YOUGHAL Map 01 C2

Youghal Knockaverry
☎ 024 92787 & 92861 🖹 024 92641
e-mail: youghalgolfclub@eircom.ie
**For many years the host of various Golfing Union
championships, Youghal offers a good test of golf and is
well maintained for year-round play. The Parkland
course has recently been extended with the addition of
two new holes. There are panoramic views of Youghal
Bay and the Blackwater estuary.**
18 holes, 6175 metres, Par 72, SSS 72, Course record 71.
Club membership 994.
Visitors Should contact in advance for weekends & ladies
day (Wed) **Societies** apply in writing a few months in
advance. **Green Fees** €30 per round (€40 weekends).
Cards ▦ 💳 **Prof** Liam Burns **Course Designer** Cd
Harris **Facilities** ⊗ ⅷ ▐ ⬛ ♀ ♨ 🏠 🏌 ⛳ ℓ
Location on N25 from Rosslare, between Waterford &
Cork

Hotel 🏨 Ahernes, 163 North Main St, YOUGAL
☎ 024 92424 13 en suite

CO DONEGAL

BALLYBOFEY Map 01 C5

Ballybofey & Stranorlar Stranorlar
☎ 074 9131093 🖹 074 9130158
A most scenic course incorporating pleasant valleys

Continued

backed by mountains with three of its holes bordered by a lake. There are three par 3s on the first nine and two on the second. The most difficult hole is the long uphill par 4 16th. The only par 5 is the 7th.

18 holes, 5366 metres, Par 68, SSS 68, Course record 64. Club membership 648.

Visitors may play on weekdays. Advisable to book in advance Societies contact golf shop Green Fees €25 (€30 weekends). Cards ▭ Course Designer PC Carr Facilities ⊗ ⅧⓁ ☕♀⚐✿☞ ✓ Conf fac available Corporate Hospitality Days available Location 0.4km from Stranorlar

Hotel ★★★ 70% Kee's Hotel, Stranorlar, BALLYBOFEY ☎ 074 913 1018 53 en suite

BALLYLIFFIN

Ballyliffin Clonmany
☎ 074 9376119 ▤ 074 9376672
e-mail: info@ballyliffingolfclub.com
Old Links: 18 holes, 6604yds, Par 71, SSS 72, Course record 65.
Glashedy Links: 18 holes, 7135yds, Par 72, SSS 74, Course record 68.
Course Designer Tom Craddock, Pat Ruddy Location from Foyle Bridge to Muff & Quigley's Point. Left to Carndonagh, 8km to club
Phone for further details

Guesthouse ♦♦♦♦ Mount Royd Country Home, CARRIGANS ☎ 074 914 0163 4 en suite

BUNCRANA

Buncrana Municipal Railway Rd, Ballymacarry
☎ 074 9362279 & 074 9320749
e-mail: buncranagc@eircom.net
A nine-hole course with a very challenging par 3 3rd with all carry out of bounds on either side. Situated beside the shores of Lough Swilly.
9 holes, 2125yds, Par 62, SSS 60, Course record 59. Club membership 200.
Visitors during open competitions only visitors with club handicaps.Phone in advance to make arrangements for weekends. Societies write in advance or phone. Green Fees €13 per round (€8 ladies). Facilities ⓁⓌ☕♀ Conf fac available

Guesthouse ♦♦♦♦ Mount Royd Country Home, CARRIGANS ☎ 074 914 0163 4 en suite

North West Lisfannon, Fahan, buncrana
☎ 074 9361715 ▤ 074 9363284
e-mail: nwgc@tinet.ie
A traditional links course on gently rolling sandy terrain with some long par 4s. Good judgement is required on the approaches and the course offers a satisfying test coupled with undemanding walking.
18 holes, 5968yds, Par 70, SSS 70, Course record 64. Club membership 580.
Visitors contact in advance for weekends. Wed - Ladies Day Societies phone in advance. Green Fees €25 (€30 weekends). Prof Seamus McBriarty Course Designer Thompson Davy Facilities ⊗ ⅧⓁⓌ☕♀⚐✿ ✓ Location 1.6km S of Buncanna

Guesthouse ♦♦♦♦ Mount Royd Country Home, CARRIGANS ☎ 074 914 0163 4 en suite

BUNDORAN

Bundoran
☎ 071 9841302 ▤ 071 9842014
e-mail: bundorangolfclub@eircom.net
This popular course, acknowledged as one of the best in the country, runs along the high cliffs above Bundoran beach and has a difficult par of 70. Designed by Harry Vardon, it offers a challenging game of golf in beautiful surroundings and has been the venue for a number of Irish golf championships.
18 holes, 5688 metres, Par 70, SSS 70, Course record 67. Club membership 770.
Visitors contact in advance for booking. Societies contact in advance. Green Fees not confirmed. Prof David T Robinson Course Designer Harry Vardon Facilities Ⓛ Ⓦ ♀☕✿☞ ✓ Location off Main St on Sligo-Derry road

Hotel ★★★ 79% Sand House Hotel, ROSSNOWLAGH ☎ 071 985 1777 55 en suite

CRUIT ISLAND

Cruit Island Kincasslagh
☎ 074 9543296 ▤ 074 9548028
A links course on a small island. It is perched along the cliffs overlooking the Atlantic. The course is short but always challenging as the wind blows most of the time. It is crowned by a magnificent 6th hole which is played across a cove to an island green. With the prevailing wind in your face and the Atlantic waves crashing in front, it is not for the fainthearted.
9 holes, 4833 metres, Par 68, SSS 66, Course record 62. Club membership 350.
Visitors restricted Sun & Thu am for Club competitions. Societies apply in writing to secretary. Green Fees not confirmed. Cards ▭ ▭ Course Designer Michael Doherty Facilities Ⓛ Ⓦ♀☕ ✓ Conf Corporate Hospitality Days available Location 8km N of Dungloe

Hotel ★★★ 67% Arnold's Hotel, DUNFANAGHY ☎ 074 913 6208 30 en suite

DUNFANAGHY

Dunfanaghy Kill
☎ 074 9136335 ▤ 074 9136684
e-mail: dunfanaghygolf@eircom.net
Overlooking Sheephaven Bay, the course has a flat central area with three difficult streams to negotiate. At the Port-na-Blagh end there are five marvellous holes, including one across the beach, while at the Horn Head end, the last five holes are a test for any golfer.
18 holes, 5247 metres, Par 68, SSS 66, Course record 63. Club membership 335.
Visitors book in advance, time sheet in operation all year. Societies phone in advance. Green Fees terms on application. Cards ▭ ▭ ▭ Course Designer Harry Vardon Facilities ⓁⓌ♀☕✿☞❀ ✓ Conf fac available Location on N56

Hotel ★★★ 67% Arnold's Hotel, DUNFANAGHY ☎ 074 913 6208 30 en suite

> In the hotel entries, the percentage figure refers to the AA's most recent Quality Assessment Score.

GREENCASTLE · Map 01 C6

Greencastle Geencastle
☎ 074 9381013 📠 074 9381015
mail: info@greencastlegolfclub.net
**links course along the shores of Lough
yle, surrounded by rocky headlands and sandy
aches.**
*holes, 5118 metres, Par 69, SSS 67, Course record 65.
ub membership 750.*
sitors no restrictions. **Societies** phone in advance; not
n. **Green Fees** not confirmed. **Course Designer**
Hackett **Facilities** ⊗ 🍸 ♨ 💪 ♀ 🏌

tel ★★★ 70% Da Vincis Hotel Complex, 15 Culmore
, LONDONDERRY ☎ 028 7127 9111 67 en suite

WEEDORE · Map 01 B6

weedore Derrybeg
075 31140
holes, 6201yds, Par 71, SSS 69.
one for further details

AGHEY · Map 01 B5

onegal Murvagh
☎ 074 9734054 📠 074 9734377
mail: info@donegalgolfclub.ie
**is massive links course was opened in 1973 and
ovides a world-class facility in peaceful surroundings.
is a very long course with some memorable holes,
cluding five par 5s, calling for some big hitting.**
*holes, 6243 metres, Par 73, SSS 73, Course record 69.
ub membership 750.*
sitors restricted Mon, weekends; contact in advance.
cieties contact in advance. **Green Fees** €50 Mon-Thu;
5 Fri-Sun. **Cards** 🔲🔲 **Prof** Leslie Robinson **Course
signer** Eddie Hackett **Facilities** ⊗ 🍸 💪 ♨ ♀ 🏌
. 🏌 **Conf** Corporate Hospitality Days available
cation 9.5km S of Donegal on Ballyshannon road

tel ★★★ 79% Sand House Hotel, ROSSNOWLAGH
071 985 1777 55 en suite

ETTERKENNY · Map 01 C5

etterkenny Barnhill
074 9121150 📠 074 9121175
**e fairways are wide and generous, but the rough,
en you find it, is short, tough and mean. The flat and
tiring terrain on the shores of Lough Swilly provides
od holiday golf. Many interesting holes include the
imidating 1st with its high tee through trees, and the
cky dog-leg of the 2nd hole. The last seven holes are
undulating ground; steep climb from 11th green to
th tee.**
*holes, 6239yds, Par 70, SSS 71, Course record 65.
ub membership 700.*
sitors preferred Mon-Fri, except Wed evenings after
m. Advisable to contact in advance for weekends & bank
lidays. **Societies** apply by writing or phone. **Green Fees**
t confirmed. **Course Designer** Eddie Hacket
cilities ⊗ 🍸 💪 ♨ ♀ 🏌 **Conf** fac available
cation 3km from town on Rathmelton road

tel ★★★ 70% Kee's Hotel, Stranorlar, BALLYBOFEY
074 913 1018 53 en suite

MOVILLE · Map 01 C6

Redcastle Redcastle
☎ 074 9382073 📠 074 9382214
e-mail: redcastle.hotel@oceanfree.net
**A testing course enjoying a picturesque setting on the
shores of Loch Foyle. The two challenging par 3 holes
should be approached with the necessary respect.**
*9 holes, 3076yds, Par 36.
Club membership 200.*
Visitors welcome except club times, advisable to phone.
Societies enquiries welcome by phone or in writing. **Green
Fees** not confirmed. **Cards** 🔲🔲🔲 **Facilities** ⊗ 🍸
💪 ♀ ♨ 🏌 🏊 🏌 **Leisure** hard tennis courts, heated
indoor swimming pool, fishing, sauna, gymnasium. **Conf**
fac available **Location** on Londonderry-Moville road

NARIN · Map 01 B5

Narin & Portnoo
☎ 074 9545107 📠 074 9545994
e-mail: narinportnoo@eircom.net
**Seaside links with every hole presenting its own special
feature, the signature hole being the chasm-crossing
8th. One of the few natural links layouts remaining,
with undulating fairways and greens. Fine views of
Gweebarra Bay are visible from the course with an
adjacent award winning beach. The links will test a
player's iron play, with raised greens a common
feature.**
*18 holes, 5322 metres, Par 69, SSS 68, Course record 63.
Club membership 150.*
Visitors contact in advance for weekend tee times (e-mails
welcome). **Societies** phone or e-mail in advance. **Green
Fees** €30 per day (€35 weekends & bank holidays).
Cards 🔲🔲🔲🔲🔲 **Course Designer** Leo
Wallace, Hugh McNeill **Facilities** 💪 ♨ ♀ 🏊 🍸 🏌
Leisure blue flag standard beach 200 metres away.
Location 9.5km from Ardara

PORTSALON · Map 01 C6

Portsalon
☎ 074 9159459 📠 074 9159919
e-mail: portsalongolfclub@eircom.net
**Another course blessed by nature. The golden beaches
of Ballymastocker Bay lie at one end, while the beauty
of Lough Swilly and the Inishowen Peninsula beyond is
a distracting but pleasant feature to the west. Situated
on the Fanad Peninsula, this lovely links course
provides untiring holiday golf at its best.**
*18 holes, 6185 metres, Par 72, SSS 72, Course record 71.
Club membership 500.*
Visitors phone in advance. **Societies** phone in advance.
Green Fees €35 (€40 weekends & bank holidays). **Cards**
🔲🔲🔲 **Course Designer** Pat Ruddy **Facilities** ⊗ by
arrangement 🍸 by arrangement 💪 by arrangement ♨ by
arrangement ♀ 🏊 🏌 **Conf** Corporate Hospitality Days
available **Location** 32km N of Letterkenny

RATHMULLAN · Map 01 C6

Otway Saltpans
☎ 074 58319
e-mail: otway_golf_club@iolfree.ie
**One of the oldest courses in Ireland, created in 1861
by British military personnel as a recreational
facility.**

Continued

9 holes, 4234yds, Par 64, SSS 60, Course record 60.
Club membership 112.
Visitors welcome. **Societies** contact for details. **Green Fees** €15 per day (€20 weekends). **Facilities** ♀ ⅄ **Conf** Corporate Hospitality Days available **Location** W shore of Loch Swilly

Guesthouse ♦♦♦ Ballyraine Guest House, Ramelton Rd, LETTERKENNY ☎ 074 912 4460 & 912 0851 ▤ 074 912 0851 8 en suite

ROSAPENNA   Map 01 C6

Rosapenna Downings
☎ 074 9155301 ▤ 074 9155128
e-mail: rosapenna@tinet.ie
Dramatic links course offering a challenging round. Originally designed by Tom Morris and later modified by James Braid and Harry Vardon, it includes features such as bunkers in mid-fairway. The best part of the links runs in the low valley along the ocean.
Old Tom Morris: 18 holes, 6271yds, Par 70, SSS 71.
Sandy Hills Links: 18 holes, 6356yds, Par 71.
Club membership 400.
Visitors no restrictions. **Societies** contact in advance.
Green Fees Old Tom Morris: €45 per round (€50 weekend & bank holiday); Sandy Hills Links €60 per round. **Cards** ⊞ ▦ ▨ ▣ **Prof** Brian Patterson **Course Designer** Old Tom Morris **Facilities** ⊗ ⅏ ⅃ ♨ ♀ ⅄ 🏠 ⑂ ⛳ ⛴ ⚓ ⚘ ⎓ ⎔ **Leisure** hard tennis courts, heated indoor swimming pool. **Conf** fac available **Location** 40km N of Letterkenny

Hotel ★★★ 67% Arnold's Hotel, DUNFANAGHY ☎ 074 913 6208 30 en suite

CO DUBLIN

BALBRIGGAN   Map 01 D4

Balbriggan Blackhall
☎ 01 8412229 ▤ 01 8413927
e-mail: balbriggangolfclub@eircom.net
A parkland course with great variations and good views of the Mourne and Cooley mountains.
18 holes, 5922 metres, Par 71, SSS 71.
Club membership 650.
Visitors contact in advance. With member only at weekends. Tue Ladies Day. **Societies** apply in writing.
Green Fees terms on application. **Prof** Nigel Howley **Course Designer** Paramoir **Facilities** ⊗ ⅏ ⅃ ♨ ♀ ⅄ ⚓ ⎓ **Location** 1km S off Balbriggan on N1

Hotel ★★★ 67% Boyne Valley Hotel & Country Club, Stameen, Dublin Rd, DROGHEDA ☎ 041 9837737 73 en suite

BALLYBOUGHAL   Map 01 D4

Hollywood Lakes
☎ 01 8433406 ▤ 01 8433002
e-mail: hollywoodlakesgc@eircom.net
A parkland course opened in 1992 with large USGA-type, sand-based greens and tees. There are water features on seven holes. The front nine requires accuracy while the second nine includes a 581-metre par 5.

Hollywood Lakes Golf Club

18 holes, 6246 metres, Par 72, SSS 72, Course record 67.
Club membership 780.
Visitors welcome Mon-Fri but may only play weekends from 2pm. **Societies** phone then write in advance. **Green Fees** €35 per round (€45 weekends). **Cards** ⊞ ▨ **Prof** Sid Baldwin **Course Designer** Mel Flanagan **Facilities** ⊗ ⅏ ⅃ ♨ ♀ ⅄ 🏠 ⑂ ⛳ ⚓ ⎓ **Location** 5km off Dublin Belfast road

Hotel ★★★ 71% Marine Hotel, Sutton Cross, DUBLIN 1 ☎ 01 8390000 48 en suite

BRITTAS   Map 01 D4

Slade Valley Lynch Park
☎ 01 4582183 & 4582739 ▤ 01 4582784
18 holes, 5388 metres, Par 69, SSS 68, Course record 65.
Course Designer W Sullivan & DO Brien
Location 14.5km SW of Dublin on N81
Phone for further details

Hotel ★★★ 66% Downshire House Hotel, BLESSINGTON ☎ 045 865199 14 en suite 11 annexe en suite

CASTLEKNOCK   Map 01 D4

Elm Green
☎ 01 8200797 ▤ 01 8226662
e-mail: elmgreen@golfdublin.com
18 holes, 5796yds, Par 71, SSS 66, Course record 65.
Course Designer Eddie Hackett **Location** off Navan Rd
Phone for further details

Hotel ★★★ 70% Finnstown Country House Hotel, Newcastle Rd, Lucan, DUBLIN ☎ 01 6010700 25 en suite 28 annexe en suite

Luttrellstown Castle Dublin15
☎ 01 8089988 ▤ 01 8089989
e-mail: golf@luttrellstown.ie
18 holes, 6032 metres, Par 72, SSS 73, Course record 66.
Course Designer N Bielenberg **Location** Porterstown Rd
Phone for further details

Hotel ★★★ 70% Finnstown Country House Hotel, Newcastle Rd, Lucan, DUBLIN ☎ 01 6010700 25 en suite 28 annexe en suite

> **Looking for a new course? Always telephone ahead to confirm visitor arrangements.**

:LOGHRAN
Map 01 D4

orrest Little
☎ 01 8401183 & 8401763 🖷 01 8401000
e-mail: office@forrestlittle.com
**well-manicured and mature parkland with water on
ur holes to test any golfer.**
*8 holes, 5902 metres, Par 71, SSS 72, Course record 68.
lub membership 1000.*
isitors preferred am weekdays. **Societies** welcome Mon/
hu/Fri. Apply in advance by writing or phone. **Green
ees** €50 per 18 holes. **Cards** 💳 **Prof** Tony Judd **Course
esigner** Mr Hawtree snr **Facilities** ⊗ �𝄞 🛏 💷 ♀ 🛆 🏠
⌇ 🏌 **Conf** Corporate Hospitality Days available **Location**
5km N of Dublin on N1, next to Dublin Airport

otel ★★★ 71% Marine Hotel, Sutton Cross, DUBLIN 13
☎ 01 8390000 48 en suite

:ONABATE
Map 01 D4

alcarrick Corballis
☎ 01 8436957 🖷 01 8436228
e-mail: balcarr@iol.ie
**plendid 18-hole semi-links course with many
allenging holes, located close to the sea. A strong
revailing wind often plays a big part on every hole and
any of the par 3s are fronted by water.**
*8 holes, 6273 metres, Par 73, SSS 71.
lub membership 750.*
isitors contact in advance. **Societies** phone in advance.
reen Fees terms on application. **Cards** 💳 **Prof**
ephen Rayfus **Course Designer** Barry Langan **Facilities**
⊗ �𝄞 🛏 💷 ♀ 🛆 🏠

otel ★★★ 67% Deer Park Hotel & Golf Courses,
OWTH ☎ 01 8322624 80 en suite

onabate Balcarrick
☎ 01 8436346 🖷 01 8434488
e-mail: info@donabategolfclub.com
**ater comes into play on eight holes. All greens
ow USGA standard. Sand based course playable all
ear.**
*7 holes, 6068 metres, Par 72, SSS 73, Course record 66.
lub membership 1200.*
isitors phone in advance, restricted Tue/Wed &
eekends. **Societies** phone in advance **Green Fees** not
onfirmed. **Cards** 💳 **Prof** Hugh Jackson
ourse Designer Pat Suttle **Facilities** ⊗ ⟨⟩ 🛏 💷 ♀ 🛆 🏠
🔗 🏌 **Conf** Corporate Hospitality Days available
ocation off R132 1.5km N of Swords & signed

otel ★★★ 67% Deer Park Hotel & Golf Courses,
OWTH ☎ 01 8322624 80 en suite

sland Corballis
☎ 01 8436205 🖷 01 8436860
e-mail: info@theislandgolfclub.com
**n old links course surrounded by the Irish Sea,
onabate beach and the Broadmeadow estuary,
estling between the highest sand dunes of any links
urse in Ireland. The rugged beauty cannot fail to
apress. An Irish qualifying course for the Open
hampionship from 2005.**
*9 holes, 6206 metres, Par 71, SSS 63.
lub membership 1020.*

Continued

The Island Golf Club

Visitors contact in advance. **Societies** Contact club office
Green Fees €110 per 18 holes. **Cards** 💳 📇 🪪 🏧
Prof Kevin Kelliher **Course Designer** Martin Hawtree
Facilities ⊗ ⟨⟩ 🛏 💷 ♀ 🛆 🏠 🏌 ⚐ 🔗 🏌 **Conf** fac
available Corporate Hospitality Days available
Location on N1 Dublin-Belfast road, pass airport, turn for
Donabate/Portrane, signed

Hotel ★★★ 67% Deer Park Hotel & Golf Courses,
HOWTH ☎ 01 8322624 80 en suite

Turvey Golf Hotel Turvey Av
☎ 01 8435169 🖷 01 8435179
e-mail: turveygc@eircom.net
**A mature parkland course with oak trees over 220
years old. A test of golf for all levels of golfer.**
*18 holes, 6068 metres, Par 71, SSS 72.
Club membership 500.*
Visitors contact in advance by phone, writing or e-mail.
No visitors before 1pm weekends. **Societies** apply by
phone, writing or e-mail. May only play after 1pm
weekends. **Green Fees** €30 per 18 holes, €15 per 9
holes (€35/€20 weekends). **Cards** 💳 🏧 **Course
Designer** P McGurk **Facilities** ⊗ ⟨⟩ 🛏 💷 ♀ 🛆 🏘 🏌
🔗 🏌 **Conf** fac available Corporate Hospitality Days
available **Location** M1, 1st junct N after Dublin airport,
1m Turvey signed on right

Hotel ★★★ 67% Deer Park Hotel & Golf Courses,
HOWTH ☎ 01 8322624 80 en suite

DUBLIN
Map 01 D4

Carrickmines Carrickmines
☎ 01 2955972
Meadowland and partly hilly gorseland course.
*9 holes, 6063yds, Par 71, SSS 69.
Club membership 600.*
Visitors not Wed, Sat or bank holidays. **Societies** contact
for details. **Green Fees** terms on application.
Facilities 🛏 💷 ♀ 🛆 🏌 **Location** 11km S of Dublin

Hotel ★★★ 68% The Gresham Royal Marine Hotel,
Marine Rd, DUN LAOGHAIRE
☎ 01 2801911 103 en suite

Castle Woodside Dr, Rathfarnham
☎ 01 4904207 🖷 01 4920264
e-mail: office@castlegc.ie
**A tight, tree-lined parkland course which is very highly
regarded by all who play there.**
*18 holes, 5732 metres, Par 70, SSS 70, Course record 63.
Club membership 1350.*

Continued

Visitors not weekends & bank holidays. **Societies** phone or write in advance. **Green Fees** €60 per 18 holes. **Cards** ⊟ ⊞ **Prof** David Kinsella **Course Designer** Barcroft-Pickman & Hood **Facilities** ⊗ ⅢⅡ ᴸᴵ 🍴 ♀ ⌂ 🏠 ♂ **Location** off Dodder Park Rd

Hotel ★★★★ 72% Jurys Hotel and Towers, Pembroke Rd, Ballsbridge, DUBLIN 4 ☎ 01 660 5000 303 en suite

Clontarf Donnycarney House, Malahide Rd
☎ 01 8331892 & 8331520 ▤ 01 8331933
e-mail: info.cgc@indigo.ie

18 holes, 5317 metres, Par 69, SSS 68, Course record 64.
Course Designer Harry Colt **Location** 4km N via Fairview
Phone for further details

Hotel ★★★ 63% McEniff Skylon Hotel, Drumcondra Rd, DUBLIN 9 ☎ 01 8379121 88 en suite

Corrstown Corrstown, Kilsallaghan
☎ 01 8640533 & 8640534 ▤ 01 8640537
e-mail: info@corrstown.com
The 18-hole course has a small river meandering through, coming into play at several holes culminating in a challenging island green finish. Orchard course has mature trees and rolling pastureland offering golfers a relaxing enjoyable game.
River Course: 18 holes, 6077 metres, Par 72, SSS 71, Course record 69.
Orchard Course: 9 holes, 2792 metres, Par 35, SSS 69.
Club membership 1050.
Visitors advisable to contact in advance. May play weekends after 3pm on River Course. Visitors welcome anytime on Orchard Course. **Societies** phone or write in advance. **Green Fees** £50 per 18 holes (£60 weekends). Orchard course £25 (£30 weekends). **Cards** ⊟ ⊞ ⊞ **Prof** Pat Gittens **Course Designer** Eddie Connaughton **Facilities** ⊗ ⅢⅡ ᴸᴵ 🍴 ♀ ⌂ 🏠 ⚲ 🚜 ♂ **Location** W of Dublin Airport via St Margarets

Hotel ★★★ 63% McEniff Skylon Hotel, Drumcondra Rd, DUBLIN 9 ☎ 01 8379121 88 en suite

Deer Park Hotel & Golf Course Howth D13
☎ 01 8322624 ▤ 01 8392405
e-mail: sales@deerpark.iol.ie
Claiming to be Ireland's largest golf-hotel complex, Deer Park offers a challenge to all levels of golfer. Spectacular scenery within the parkland setting surrounding Howth Castle.
St Fintans: 9 holes, 3373yds, Par 37.
Deer Park: 18 holes, 6830yds, Par 72.
Grace O'Malley: 9 holes, 3130yds, Par 35.
Short Course: 12 holes, 1810yds, Par 36.

Deer Park Hotel & Golf Course

Club membership 350.
Visitors no restrictions. There may be delays especially Sun am. **Societies** contact by phone. **Green Fees** 18 holes€25; 9 holes €17. **Cards** ⊟ ⊞ ⊞ ▣ **Course Designer** Fred Hawtree **Facilities** ⊗ ⅢⅡ ᴸᴵ 🍴 ♀ ⌂ ⚐ 🏠 ♂ **Leisure** hard tennis courts, heated indoor swimming pool, sauna. **Conf** fac available Corporate Hospitality Days available **Location** 14.4km from Dublin, follow coast road, 0.8km before Howth Harbour

Hotel ★★★ 67% Deer Park Hotel & Golf Courses, HOWTH ☎ 01 8322624 80 en suite

Edmondstown Edmondstown Rd, Edmondstown
☎ 01 4931082 & 4932461 ▤ 01 4933152
e-mail: info@edmondstowngolfclub.ie
A popular and testing parkland course situated at the foot of the Dublin Mountains in the suburbs of the city. Recently completely renovated and redesigned. All greens are now sand based to the highest standard. An attractive stream flows in front of the 4th and 6th greens calling for an accurate approach shot. The par 3 17th will test the best golfers and the 5th and 12th require thoughtful club selection to the green.

18 holes, 6111 metres, Par 71, SSS 73, Course record 66.
Club membership 750.
Visitors contact in advance as there are daily times reserved for members. Limited times after 3.30pm weekends. **Societies** contact Angela Sterling (marketing manager) in advance. **Green Fees** €55 per round (€65 weekends). **Cards** ⊟ ⊞ ⊞ ▣ **Prof** Gareth McShea **Course Designer** McEvoy, Cooke **Facilities** ⊗ ⅢⅡ ᴸᴵ 🍴 ♀ ⌂ 🏠 ⚐ ⚲ 🚜 ♂ **Conf** fac available Corporate Hospitality Days available **Location** M50 junct 12

Hotel ★★★ 67% Jurys Montrose Hotel, Stillorgan Rd, DUBLIN ☎ 01 2693311 178 en suite

Continued

lm Park Golf & Sports Club Nutley House,
utley Ln, Donnybrook
☎ 01 2693438 🗎 01 2694505
mail: office@elmparkgolfclub.ie
teresting parkland course requiring a degree of
curacy, particularly as half of the holes involve
ossing the stream.
8 holes, 5380 metres, Par 69, SSS 69, Course record 64.
lub membership 1900.
isitors contact in advance. **Societies** apply in advance.
reen Fees terms on application. **Cards** 🖩 🖩 🖩 🖳
rof Seamus Green **Course Designer** Paytrick Merrigan
acilities ⊗ 🎵 🖳 🛒 ♀ 🛆 🏠 🍴 🏌 🏇 ♂ ⚑ **Leisure** hard &
ass tennis courts. **Location** 5km from city centre

tel ★★★★ 72% Jurys Hotel and Towers, Pembroke
d, Ballsbridge, DUBLIN 4 ☎ 01 660 5000 303 en suite

range Rathfarnham
☎ 01 4932889
8 holes, 5517 metres, Par 68, SSS 69.
ocation 9.5km from city centre
hone for further details

tel ★★★ 67% Jurys Montrose Hotel, Stillorgan Rd,
UBLIN ☎ 01 2693311 178 en suite

ollystown Hollystown
☎ 01 8207444 🗎 01 8207447
mail: info@hollystown.com
et in the Dublin countryside, this mature parkland
urse incorporates the natural features of trees, lakes
d streams. Three loops of nine holes provide three
stinctly different 18-hole combinations, each offering
unique challenge to all golfing standards.
ed/Yellow: 18 holes, 5829yds, Par 70, SSS 69.
ellow/Blue: 18 holes, 6216yds, Par 71, SSS 69.
ue/Red: 18 holes, 6201yds, Par 71, SSS 69.
lub membership 690.
isitors no restrictions **Societies** contact in advance.
reen Fees €26 (€36 weekends & bank holidays). **Cards**
🖩 🖩 **Prof** Joe Murray **Course Designer** Eddie Hackett
acilities ⊗ 🖳 🛒 ♀ 🛆 🍴 🏇 ♂ ⚑ **Conf** fac available
orporate Hospitality Days available **Location** 13km off
8 Dublin-Cavan road at Mulhuddart

tel ⏚ Travelodge Dublin (Navan Road), Auburn Av
oundabout, Navan Rd, ☎ 08700 850 950 100 en suite

owth St Fintan's, Carrickbrack Rd, Sutton
☎ 01 8323055 🗎 01 8321793
mail: secretary@howthgolfclub.ie
hilly heathland course with scenic views of Dublin
ay. It presents a good challenge to the novice or expert
olfer.
8 holes, 5618 metres, Par 72, SSS 69.
lub membership 1200.
isitors contact in advance; not Wed & weekends.
cieties contact in advance. **Green Fees** not confirmed.
ards 🖩 🖩 🖩 🖳 **Prof** John McGuirk **Course**
esigner James Braid **Facilities** ⊗ by arrangement 🎵 by
rrangement 🖳 🛒 ♀ 🛆 🏠 🏇 ♂ ⚑ **Conf** fac available
orporate Hospitality Days available **Location** 14.4km NE
city, 3km from Sutton Cross on Sutton side of Hill of
owth

tel ★★★ 71% Marine Hotel, Sutton Cross, DUBLIN 13
01 8390000 48 en suite

Milltown Lower Churchtown Rd, Dublin 14
☎ 01 4976090 🗎 01 4976008
e-mail: info@milltowngolfclub.ie
Level parkland course on the outskirts of the city.
18 holes, 5638 metres, Par 71, SSS 69, Course record 64.
Club membership 1400.
Visitors contact in advance; not weekends. **Societies** apply
in writing. **Green Fees** €80 per 18 holes. **Cards** 🖩 🖩
Prof John Harnett **Course Designer** Freddie Davis
Facilities ⊗ 🎵 🖳 🖳 ♀ 🛆 🏠 🍴 ♂

Hotel ★★★★ 72% Jurys Hotel and Towers, Pembroke
Rd, Ballsbridge, DUBLIN 4 ☎ 01 660 5000
303 en suite

Newlands Clondalkin
☎ 01 4593157 & 4593498 🗎 01 4593498
18 holes, 5714 metres, Par 71, SSS 70.
Course Designer James Braid
Phone for further details

Hotel ★★★ 70% Lynch Green Isle Hotel, Naas Rd,
DUBLIN 22 ☎ 01 4593406 90 en suite

Rathfarnham Newtown
☎ 01 4931201 & 4931561 🗎 01 4931561
e-mail: rgc@oceanfree.net
Parkland course designed by John Jacobs in 1962.
14 holes, 5815 metres, Par 71, SSS 70, Course record 69.
Club membership 685.
Visitors contact in advance, by arrangement only.
Societies restricted to Mon, Thu & Fri. **Green Fees** €40
per 18 holes. **Prof** Brian O'Hara **Course Designer** John
Jacobs **Facilities** 🖳 🖳 ♀ 🛆 🏠 ♂ ⚑
Location M50 Firhouse/Knocklyon exit

Hotel ★★★★ 72% Jurys Hotel and Towers, Pembroke
Rd, Ballsbridge, DUBLIN 4 ☎ 01 660 5000 303 en suite

Royal Dublin North Bull Island Reserve, Dollymount
☎ 01 8336346 🗎 01 8336504
e-mail: jlambe@theroyaldublingolfclub.com
**A popular course with visitors, for its design subtleties,
the condition of the links and the friendly atmosphere.
Founded in 1885, the club moved to its present site in
1889 and received its Royal designation in 1891. A
notable former club professional was Christy
O'Connor, who was appointed in 1959 and immediately
made his name. Along with its many notable holes,
Royal Dublin has a fine and testing finish. The 18th is a
sharp dog-leg par 4, with out of bounds along the right-
hand side. The decision to try the long carry over the
'garden' is one many visitors have regretted.**
18 holes, 6002 metres, Par 72, SSS 71, Course record 63.
Club membership 1250.
Visitors contact in advance; handicap certificate; not Wed,
Sat until 4pm, restricted Sun. **Societies** book one year in
advance. **Green Fees** €125 all week. **Cards** 🖩 🖩 🖩
Prof Leonard Owens **Course Designer** HS Colt **Facilities**
⊗ 🎵 🖳 🖳 ♀ 🛆 🏠 🍴 🏇 ♂ ⚑ **Conf** fac available
Corporate Hospitality Days available **Location** 5.5km NE
of city centre

Hotel ★★★ 67% Longfield's Hotel, Fitzwilliam St Lower,
DUBLIN 2 ☎ 01 6761367 26 en suite

St Margaret's Golf & Country Club St
Margaret's
☎ 01 8640400 📠 01 8640289
e-mail: sales@stmargaretsgolf.com
18 holes, 6917yds, Par 73, SSS 73, Course record 69.
Course Designer Craddock, Ruddy **Location** from airport
rdbt exit for Belfast, 500 metres 1st exit from rdbt to St
Margarets just passed Coachman's Innbo
Phone for further details

Hotel ★★★ 71% Marine Hotel, Sutton Cross, DUBLIN 13
☎ 01 8390000 48 en suite

Stackstown Kellystown Rd, Rathfarnham
☎ 01 4942338 & 4941993 📠 01 4933934
e-mail: stackstowngc@eircom.net
**Pleasant course in the foothills of the Dublin mountains,
affording breathtaking views of Dublin city and bay.
Mature woodland borders every hole and premium is
placed on accuracy off the tee. In 1999 the course was
remodelled and the mountain streams which run
through the course were harnessed to bring them into
play and provide attractive on-course water features.**
*18 holes, 6152yds, Par 72, SSS 72, Course record 68.
Club membership 1092.*
Visitors preferred Mon, Thu-Fri & Sun pm. **Societies**
phone in advance and confirm in writing. **Green Fees** €35
(€45 Sun). **Prof** Michael Kavanagh **Course Designer**
Shaftrey **Facilities** ⊗ ⟫Ⅲ ⅃ ♭ 🛒 ♀ ♨ 👜 ⏲ ⌇ 🏌 🔶 ⌀
Conf fac available Corporate Hospitality Days available
Location M50 junct 13, signs for Rathfarnham. 3rd lights
left for Leopardstown & Ticknock. Next lights follow road
under M50, club 300 metres

Hotel ★★★ 67% Jurys Montrose Hotel, Stillorgan Rd,
DUBLIN ☎ 01 2693311 178 en suite

DUN LAOGHAIRE   Map 01 D4

Dun Laoghaire Eglinton Park, Tivoli Rd
☎ 01 2803916 📠 01 2804868
e-mail: dlgc@iol.ie
**This is a well-wooded parkland course, not long, but
requiring accurate club selection and placing of shots.
The course was designed by Harry Colt in 1918.**

*18 holes, 5313 metres, Par 69, SSS 68, Course record 63.
Club membership 1118.*
Visitors restricted Thu, Sat & Sun. Phone pro 2801694 in
advance **Societies** apply in writing. **Green Fees** not
confirmed. **Cards** 🟰 💳 **Prof** Vincent Carey **Course
Designer** Harry Colt **Facilities** ⊗ ⟫Ⅲ ⅃ ♭ 🛒 ♀ ♨ 👜 ⏲ ⌀
Conf fac available **Location** 1.2km from town centre &
ferry port

Continued

Hotel ★★★ 68% The Gresham Royal Marine Hotel,
Marine Rd, DUN LAOGHAIRE
☎ 01 2801911 103 en suite

KILLINEY   Map 01 D4

Killiney Ballinclea Rd
☎ 01 2852823 📠 01 2852861
e-mail: killineygolfclub@eircom.net
**The course is on the side of Killiney Hill with
picturesque views of south Dublin and the Wicklow
Mountains.**
*9 holes, 5655 metres, Par 70, SSS 70.
Club membership 450.*
Visitors not Tue, Thu, Sat, Sun am. **Societies** Apply in
writing. **Green Fees** €50. **Cards** 🟰 💳 **Prof** P O'Boyle
Facilities ♭ 🛒 ♀ ♨ 👜 ⏲ 🏌 🔶 ⌀ **Conf** fac available

Hotel ★★★★ 69% Fitzpatrick Castle Hotel, KILLINEY
☎ 01 2305400 113 en suite

LUCAN   Map 01 D4

Hermitage Ballydowd
☎ 01 6265049 📠 01 6238881
e-mail: hermitagegolf@eircom.net
**Part level, part undulating course bordered by the
River Liffey and offering some surprises.**
*18 holes, 6034 metres, Par 71, SSS 71.
Club membership 1100.*
Visitors contact in advance. **Societies** phone well in
advance. **Green Fees** €80 per 18 holes. **Cards** 💳 **Prof**
Simon Byrne **Course Designer** J McKenna **Facilities** ⊗
⟫Ⅲ ♭ 🛒 ♀ ♨ 👜 ⏲ 🔶 ⌀ **Location** on N4

Hotel ★★★ 70% Finnstown Country House Hotel,
Newcastle Rd, Lucan, DUBLIN ☎ 01 6010700
25 en suite 28 annexe en suite

Lucan Celbridge Rd
☎ 01 6282106 📠 01 6282929
e-mail: luncangolf@eircom.net
**Founded in 1897 as a nine-hole course and extended to
18 holes in 1988, Lucan involves playing over a lane
which bisects the 1st and 7th holes. The front nine is
undulating while the back nine is flatter and features
water hazards and a 538-metre par 5 18th hole.**
*18 holes, 5958 metres, Par 71, SSS 71, Course record 67
Club membership 780.*
Visitors may play Mon, Tue & Fri. **Societies** apply in
writing. **Green Fees** €45. **Course Designer** Eddie Hacke
Facilities ⊗ ⟫Ⅲ ♭ 🛒 ♀ ♨ 🏌 👜 ⌀ **Location** N4 W to
Celbridge at rear of Spa Hotel

Hotel ★★★ 64% Lucan Spa Hotel, LUCAN
☎ 01 6280494 71 rms (61 en suite)

MALAHIDE   Map 01 D4

Malahide Beechwood, The Grange
☎ 01 8461611 📠 01 8461270
e-mail: malgc@clubi.ie
Main Course: 18 holes, 6066 metres, Par 71.
Course Designer E Hackett **Location** 1.6km from coast
road at Portmarnock
Phone for further details

Hotel ★★★★ Portmarnock Hotel & Golf Links, Strand
Rd, PORTMARNOCK ☎ 01 8460611 99 en suite

Continue

Malahide Golf Club

PORTMARNOCK   See page 433

PORTMARNOCK   Map 01 D4

Portmarnock Hotel & Golf Links Strand Rd
☎ 01 8460611 📠 01 8462442
e-mail: sales@portmarnock.com
This links course makes full use of the dunes and
natural terrain to provide an authentic links layout.
The elevated tees and greens, blind approaches and
doglegs - not to mention sea breezes, will keep the golfer
thinking through every round. Gently undulating
fairways leading to large fast greens must be negotiated
through 98 strategically placed bunkers, while hillocks,
wild grasses and gorse await wayward shots.
18 holes, 5992 metres, Par 71, SSS 72, Course record 67.
Visitors welcome anytime except 25 Dec, subject to
availability. Societies apply in advance by phone or in
writing to check availability. **Green Fees** €125 per round.
Course Designer Bernhard Langer **Facilities** ⊗ ⅷ 🍴 ⬛️
🍸 🏠 🛈 🏌 🏑 ♿ 🏌 **Leisure** sauna, gymnasium.
Conf fac available Corporate Hospitality Days available

Hotel ★★★★ Portmarnock Hotel & Golf Links, Strand
Rd, PORTMARNOCK ☎ 01 8460611 99 en suite

RATHCOOLE   Map 01 D4

Beech Park Johnstown
☎ 01 4580522 📠 01 4588365
e-mail: info@beechpark.ie
Relatively flat parkland with heavily wooded fairways.
Famous for its Amen Corner (holes 10 to 13).
*Beech Park: 18 holes, 5753 metres, Par 72, SSS 70,
Course record 67.*
Club membership 1038.
Visitors not weekends, phone in advance. **Societies** apply
in writing. **Green Fees** not confirmed. **Cards** 🔲 🔲 🔲
Course Designer Eddie Hackett **Facilities** ⊗ ⅷ 🍴 ⬛️ ♿
🏌 ♿ **Conf** Corporate Hospitality Days available

Hotel ★★★ 70% Finnstown Country House Hotel,
Newcastle Rd, Lucan, DUBLIN ☎ 01 6010700
45 en suite 28 annexe en suite

RUSH   Map 01 D4

Rush
☎ 01 8438177 (Office) 8437548 (Clubhouse)
📠 01 8438177
e-mail: info@rushgolfclub.com
Seaside borders three fairways on this links course.
There are 28 bunkers and undulating fairways to add

to the challenge of the variable and strong winds that
blow at all times and change with the tides. There are
no easy holes.
9 holes, 5598 metres, Par 70, SSS 69.
Club membership 500.
Visitors restricted Wed, Thu, weekends & bank holidays.
Societies phone or apply in writing. **Green Fees** €32 per
round. **Facilities** ⊗ ⅷ 🍴 ⬛️ ♿ 🏌 **Location** M1 N, exit
for Rush

Hotel 🏠 Redbank House & Restaurant, 5-7 Church St,
SKERRIES ☎ 01 8491005 8490439 📠 01 8491598
7 en suite 5 annexe en suite

SAGGART   Map 01 D4

City West Hotel & Golf Resort
☎ 01 4010500 & 4010878 (shop) 📠 01 4588565
e-mail: info@citywest-hotel.iol.ie
Course west of Dublin comprising 142 acres at the
foothills of the Dublin mountains and built on fine
parkland. Well wooded and enjoys natural drainage.
*Championship: 18 holes, 6314yds, Par 70, SSS 70,
Course record 65.*
Executive: 18 holes, 5154yds, Par 65, SSS 69.
Visitors time sheet in operation, phone in advance.
Societies apply in writing or phone in advance. **Green
Fees** not confirmed. **Cards** 🔲 🔲 🔲 🔳 **Course
Designer** Christy O'Connor Jnr **Facilities** ⊗ ⅷ 🍴 ⬛️ ♿
🏠 🏠 🍴 🏌 🏑 **Leisure** heated indoor swimming pool,
fishing, sauna, solarium, gymnasium. **Conf** fac available
Corporate Hospitality Days available **Location** Naas road,
N7 S

Hotel ★★★ 65% Bewley's Hotel Newlands Cross,
Newlands Cross, Naas Rd, DUBLIN 22
☎ 01 4640140 258 en suite

SKERRIES   Map 01 D4

Skerries Hacketstown
☎ 01 8491567 📠 01 8491591
e-mail: skerriesgolfclub@eircom.net
Tree-lined parkland course on gently rolling
countryside, with sea views from some holes. The 1st
and 18th are particularly challenging.
18 holes, 6081 metres, Par 73, SSS 72, Course record 67.
Club membership 800.
Visitors contact in advance; not weekends. **Societies**
contact well in advance in writing. **Green Fees** €50 per
round. **Cards** 🔲 🔲 **Prof** Jimmy Kinsella
Facilities ⊗ ⅷ 🍴 ⬛️ ♿ 🏠 🏌 ♿
Location E of Dublin-Belfast road

Hotel ★★★ 67% Boyne Valley Hotel & Country Club,
Stameen, Dublin Rd, DROGHEDA ☎ 041 9837737
73 en suite

SWORDS   Map 01 D4

Swords Open Golf Course Balheary Av, Swords
☎ 01 8409819 & 8901030 📠 01 8409819
e-mail: info@swordsopengolfcourse.com
Parkland course situated in countryside, beside the River
Broadmeadow 16km from Dublin.
18 holes, 5612 metres, Par 70, SSS 70, Course record 73.
Club membership 475.
Visitors timesheet bookings available all year, phone to
book, may play at any time **Societies** phone well in
advance. **Green Fees** €18 per 18 holes (€25 weekends).

Continued   Continued

Course Designer T Halpin **Facilities** ⛳ 🍽 🏕 ⛳ 🏌

Swords Open Golf Course

Hotel ★★★ 63% McEniff Skylon Hotel, Drumcondra Rd, DUBLIN 9 ☎ 01 8379121 88 en suite

TALLAGHT   Map 01 D4

Dublin City Ballinascorney
☎ 01 4516430 📠 01 4598445
e-mail: info@dublincitygolf.com
Set in the valley of Glenasmole, this very scenic course offers a variety of terrain, where every hole is different, many would be considered feature holes.
18 holes, 5535yds, Par 69, SSS 67, Course record 63. Club membership 350.
Visitors please contact in advance, welcome weekdays & weekends at any time. **Societies** contact for details. **Green Fees** not confirmed. **Cards** 💳 💳 **Course Designer** Eddie Hackett **Facilities** ⛳ 🍽 🏌 🏕 🏌 🐾 🛺 ⛳ **Conf** fac available **Location** 13km SW of Dublin, M50 junct 11 (Firhouse), on R114

Hotel ★★★ 70% Lynch Green Isle Hotel, Naas Rd, DUBLIN 22 ☎ 01 4593406 90 en suite

CO GALWAY

BALLINASLOE   Map 01 B4

Ballinasloe Rosglos
☎ 090 9642126 📠 090 9642538
e-mail: ballinasloegolfclub@eircom.net
Well-maintained parkland course, extended from a par 68 to a par 72. With a number of feature holes and two water hazards.
18 holes, 5865 metres, Par 72, SSS 70, Course record 69. Club membership 884.
Visitors preferably Mon-Sat, contact in advance. **Societies** contact in advance. **Green Fees** not confirmed. **Cards** 💳 💳 **Prof** n **Course Designer** E Hackett, E Connaughton **Facilities** ⊗ by arrangement 🍽 by arrangement ⛳ by arrangement 🍽 by arrangement 🏌 🏕 🏌 ⛳ 🏌 **Conf** Corporate Hospitality Days available
Location 3km from Ballinasloe, on Portumna road

BALLYCONNEELY   Map 01 A4

Connemara
☎ 095 23502 & 23602 📠 095 23662
e-mail: links@iol.ie
This championship links course is situated by the Atlantic Ocean in a most spectacular setting, with the

Continued

Twelve Bens Mountains in the background. Established in 1973, it is a tough challenge, due in no small part to its exposed location, with the back nine the equal of any in the world. The last six holes are exceptionally long and offer a great challenge to golfers of all abilities. When the wind blows, club selection is crucial. Notable holes are the 13th (200yd par 3), the long par 5 14th, the 15th with a green nestling in the hills, the 16th guarded by water and the 17th and 18th, both par 5s over 500yds long.

Championship: 18 holes, 6666yds, Par 72, SSS 73, Course record 64.
New: 9 holes, 3012yds, Par 35.
Club membership 970.
Visitors advisable to book in advance. Sun am members only **Societies** phone or e-mail in advance. **Green Fees** not confirmed. **Cards** 💳 💳 **Prof** Hugh O'Neill **Course Designer** Eddie Hackett **Facilities** ⊗ 🍽 ⛳ 🍽 🏌 🏕 ⛳ 🏌 🐾 🛺 ⛳ 🍴 **Conf** Corporate Hospitality Days available
Location 14.5km SW of Clifden

Hotel ★★★★ 69% Abbeyglen Castle Hotel, Sky Rd, CLIFDEN ☎ 095 21201 44 en suite

BEARNA   Map 01 B3

Bearna Golf and Country Club Corboley
☎ 091 592677 📠 091 592674
e-mail: info@bearnagolfclub.com
Set amid the beautiful landscape of the west of Ireland and enjoying commanding views of Galway Bay, the course covers more than 100 hectares of countryside. This has resulted in generously proportioned fairways, many elevated tees and some splendid carries. Water comes into play at thirteen holes and the final four holes provide a memorable finish.
18 holes, 5746 metres, Par 72, SSS 72, Course record 68. Club membership 600.
Visitors phone in advance. Can play at any time **Societies** contact in advance. **Green Fees** €35 Mon-Thu (€40 Fri, €50 Sat-Sun & bank holidays). **Cards** 💳 💳 💳 **Prof** Declan Cunningham **Course Designer** Robert J Brown **Facilities** ⊗ 🍽 ⛳ 🍽 🏌 🏕 🏠 🏌 🐾 🛺 ⛳ **Conf** fac available **Location** 8km W of Galway on Spiddal Rd

Hotel ★★★★ 70% Galway Bay Hotel Conference Leisure Centre, The Promenade, Salthill, GALWAY ☎ 091 520520 153 en suite

Championship Course

Portmarnock

Co Dublin

Portmarnock Map 01 D4

U niversally acknowledged as one of the truly great links courses, Portmarnock has hosted many great events from the British Amateur Championships of 1949 and the Canada Cup in 1960, to 12 stagings of the revised Irish Open. Founded in 1894, the serpentine championship course offers a classic challenge: surrounded by water on three sides, no two successive holes play in the same direction. Unlike many courses that play nine out and nine home, Portmarnock demands a continual awareness of wind direction. Extraordinary holes include the 14th, which Henry Cotton regarded as the best hole in golf; the 15th, which Arnold Palmer regards as the best par 3 in the world; and the 5th, regarded as the best on the course by the late Harry Bradshaw. Bradshaw was for 40 years Portmarnock's golf professional and runner-up to AD Locke in the 1949 British Open, playing his ball from an empty bottle of stout.

☎ 01 8462968 Fax 01 8462601
e-mail: emer@portmarnockgolfclub.ie

Old Course: 18 holes, 7182yds, Par 72, SSS 73.
New Course: 9 holes, 3370yds, Par 37.
Club membership 1100.
Visitors not Wed; restricted Sat, Sun, public holidays; contact in advance & confirm in writing; handicap certificate.
Societies must contact in advance in writing. **Green Fees** £165 (£190 weekends & public holidays). **Cards**
Prof Joey Purcell **Course Designer** W Pickeman
Facilities ⊗ ╳ by prior arrangement 🏌 🍽 ♀ 🏌 🏠 ⛳ 🏌
🛺 ⛳ **Location** 13km NE of Dublin. 8km E of Dublin Airport

....

Hotel

★ ★ ★ ★ Portmarnock Hotel & Golf Links, Strand Rd,
PORTMARNOCK

☎ 01 8460611 99 en suite

GALWAY — Map 01 B4

Galway Blackrock, Salthill
☎ 091 522033 📠 091 529783
e-mail: galwaygolf@eircom.net
Designed by Dr A McKenzie, this course is inland by nature, although some of the fairways run close to the ocean. The terrain is of gently sloping hillocks with plenty of trees and furze bushes to catch out the unwary. Although not a long course, it continues to delight the visiting golfer.
18 holes, 6376yds, Par 70, SSS 71, Course record 67.
Club membership 1050.
Visitors preferred on weekdays, except Tue. Societies apply in writing. Green Fees not confirmed. Cards ▦ ▦
Prof Don Wallace Course Designer Dr A MacKenzie
Facilities ⊗ ⅷ ⅬⅬ 🍺 ♀ △ 🏠 🛠 🐟 ⊘ Conf Corporate Hospitality Days available Location 3km W in Salthill

Hotel ★★★ 60% Lochlurgain Hotel, 22 Monksfield, Upper Salthill, GALWAY ☎ 091 529595 13 en suite

Glenlo Abbey Bushypark
☎ 091 526666 📠 091 527800
e-mail: glenlo@iol.ie
9 holes, 6009 metres, Par 71, SSS 71.
Course Designer Jeff Howes Location on N59 Galway-Clifden road 4km from Galway
Phone for further details

Hotel ★★★★ ♨ 77% Glenlo Abbey Hotel, Bushypark, GALWAY ☎ 091 526666 46 en suite

GORT — Map 01 B3

Gort Castlequarter
☎ 091 632244 📠 091 632387
e-mail: info@gortgolf.com
Set in 65 hectares of picturesque parkland. The 515-metre 9th and the 472-metre 17th are played into a prevailing wind and the par 4 dog-leg 7th will test the best.
18 holes, 5705 metres, Par 71, SSS 69.
Club membership 1060.
Visitors advisable to contact in advance. Sun am reserved for members. Societies apply in writing, phone, fax or e-mail. Green Fees €25 per day (€30 weekends). Cards ▦ ▦ ▦ Course Designer Christy O'Connor Jnr
Facilities ⊗ by arrangement ⅷ by arrangement ⅬⅬ ♀ △ 🏠 🛠 🐟 ⊘

LOUGHREA — Map 01 B3

Loughrea Bullaun Rd, Graigue
☎ 091 841049 📠 091 847472
18 holes, 5261 metres, Par 69, SSS 67, Course record 68.
Course Designer Eddie Hackett
Phone for further details

Hotel ★★★ 68% Meadow Court Hotel, LOIGHREA ☎ 091 841051 21 rms

MOUNTBELLEW — Map 01 B4

Mountbellew Ballinasloe
☎ 0905 79259 📠 0905 79274
9 holes, 5143 metres, Par 69, SSS 66, Course record 63.
Location off N63 midway between Roscommon & Galway
Phone for further details

ORANMORE — Map 01 B3

Athenry Palmerstown
☎ 091 794466 📠 091 794971
e-mail: athenrygc@eircom.net
A mixture of parkland and heathland built on a limestone base against the backdrop of a large pine forest. The par 3 holes are notable with a feature hole at the 12th - from an elevated tee played between beech and pine trees.
18 holes, 5687 metres, Par 70, SSS 70, Course record 67.
Club membership 1000.
Visitors advisable to phone in advance; not Sun or Sat am. Societies apply in writing, phone or e-mail. Green Fees not confirmed. Cards ▦ ▦ ▦ Prof Raymond Ryan Course Designer Eddie Hackett Facilities ⊗ ⅷ ⅬⅬ ♀ △ 🏠 🛠 🐟 ⊘ Ⓒ Conf Corporate Hospitality Days available Location on R348 to Athenry, 10km E of Galway

Galway Bay Golf & Country Club Renville
☎ 091 790503 📠 091 792510
e-mail: gbaygolf@iol.ie
18 holes, 6533 metres, Par 72, SSS 73, Course record 68.
Course Designer Christy O'Connor Jnr
Location N18 S towards Limerick, right for Oranmore at rdbt, through village, signed
Phone for further details

OUGHTERARD — Map 01 B4

Oughterard
☎ 091 552131 📠 091 552377
e-mail: golfough@iol.ie
18 holes, 6660yds, Par 70, SSS 69, Course record 67.
Course Designer P Merrigan Location 1.5km from Oughterard on N59 from Galway
Phone for further details

Hotel ★★★ ♨ 77% Lough Inagh Lodge Hotel, Inagh Valley, RECESS ☎ 095 34706 & 34694 📠 095 34708 12 en suite

PORTUMNA — Map 01 B3

Portumna
☎ 090 9741059 📠 090 9741798
e-mail: portumnagc@eircom.net
Parkland course with mature trees.
18 holes, 6225 metres, Par 72, SSS 72.
Club membership 900.
Visitors restricted Sat, no green fees Sun. Societies contact in writing. Green Fees not confirmed. Cards ▦ ▦
Prof Richard Clarke Course Designer E Connaughton
Facilities ⊗ ⅷ ⅬⅬ ♀ △ 🏠 🛠 🐟 ⊘
Location 4km from town on Woodford-Ennis road

Hotel ★★★ 63% County Arms Hotel, BIRR ☎ 0509 20791 24 en suite

RENVYLE — Map 01 A4

Renvyle House Hotel
☎ 095 43511 📠 095 43515
e-mail: renvyle@iol.ie
Pebble Beach: 9 holes, 3500yds, Par 36,
Course record 34.
Location from N59 W, right into Recess, left at Kylemore, right at Letterfrack, continue 5m
Phone for further details

Continued

otel ★★★ 70% Renvyle House Hotel, RENVYLE
☎ 095 43511 68 en suite

UAM   Map 01 B4

'uam Barnacurragh
☎ 093 28993 🖹 093 26003
8 holes, 5513 metres, Par 72, SSS 69.
ourse Designer Eddie Hackett **Location** 0.8km from
wn on Athenry road
hone for further details

CO KERRY

ALLYBUNION See page 437

ALLYFERRITER   Map 01 A2

ingle Links
☎ 066 9156255 🖹 066 9156409
-mail: dinglegc@iol.ie
his most westerly course in Europe has a
agnificent scenic location. It is a traditional links
urse with beautiful turf, many bunkers, a stream that
mes into play on 14 holes and, usually, a prevailing
ind.
8 holes, 6700yds, Par 72, SSS 71, Course record 72.
'lub membership 432.
isitors phone in advance. **Societies** contact in advance.
reen Fees Nov-Feb €40 per 18 holes (weekends €40);
ar, Apr, Oct €50 (€60); May-Sep €65 (€75). **Cards**
🟦 ▓▓ ▭ **Course Designer** Hackett, O'Connor Jnr
acilities ⊗ ⊪ ⅃ 🍺 ♀ ⚘ 🏠 ⛳ ♂ **Leisure** buggies for
re May-Oct. **Location** 2.5m from Ballyferriter

uesthouse ♦♦♦♦♦ Gormans Clifftop House &
estaurant, Glaise Bheag, Ballydavid, DINGLE
☎ 066 9155162 9 en suite

ASTLEGREGORY   Map 01 A2

astlegregory Stradbally
☎ 066 7139444 🖹 066 7139958
mail: castlegregorygolf@oceanfree.net
links course sandwiched between the sea and a
eshwater lake and mountains on two sides. The 3rd
ole is visually superb with a 334-metre drive into the
ind.
holes, 2569 metres, Par 68, SSS 68, Course record 67.
'lub membership 378.
isitors advisable to contact in advance. Restrictions at
eekends. **Societies** apply in advance. **Green Fees** €28
er 18 holes, €18 per 9 holes. **Course Designer** Dr Arthur
pring **Facilities** 🍺 ♀ ⚘ ⛳ ♂ **Leisure** fishing.
ocation on Tralee-Castlegregory-Conor pass road, 1km
om Stradbally

lotel ★★★ 67% Abbey Gate Hotel, Maine St, TRALEE
☎ 066 7129888 100 en suite

LENBEIGH   Map 01 A2

ooks
☎ 066 9768205 🖹 066 9768476
mail: office@dooks.com
ong-established course on the shore between the
erry mountains and Dingle Bay. Sand dunes are a

Continued

feature (the name Dooks is a derivation of the Gaelic
word for sand bank) and the course offers a fine
challenge in a superb Ring of Kerry location. Recently
redesigned by Martin Hantree.
18 holes, 6271yds, Par 72, SSS 70.
Club membership 900.
Visitors contact in advance. Members time reserved.
Societies contact in advance. **Green Fees** €58 per 18
holes. **Cards** 🟦 ▓▓ ▭ **Course Designer** Martin Hantree
Facilities ⊗ ⊪ 🍺 ♀ ⚘ 🏠 ⛳ ♂ **Conf** Corporate
Hospitality Days available **Location** on N70 between
Killorglin & Glenbeigh

Hotel ★★★ 70% Gleneagle Hotel, KILLARNEY
☎ 064 36000 250 en suite

KENMARE   Map 01 B2

Ring of Kerry Golf & Country Club
Templenoe
☎ 064 42000 🖹 064 42533
e-mail: reservations@ringofkerrygolf.com
A world class golf facility with spectacular views across
Kenmare Bay. Opened in 1998, the club has gone from
strength to strength and is fast becoming a must-play
course for golfers visiting the area. Every hole is
memorable.

18 holes, 6330yds, Par 72, SSS 73, Course record 68.
Club membership 250.
Visitors advisable to book for weekends. **Societies** book
beforehand by phone, in writing or by e-mail. **Green Fees**
18 holes €80; 36 holes €120 any day. **Cards** 🟦 ▓▓ ▭
Prof Adrian Whitehead **Course Designer** Eddie Hackett
Facilities ⊗ ⊪ 🍺 ♀ ⚘ 🏠 ⛳ 🛒 ♂ ⛳
Conf fac available Corporate Hospitality Days available
Location 6.5km W of Kenmare

Hotel ★★★★ ♨ Sheen Falls Lodge, KENMARE
☎ 064 41600 66 en suite

KILLARNEY   Map 01 B2

Beaufort Churchtown, Beaufort
☎ 064 44440 🖹 064 44752
e-mail: beaufortgc@eircom.net
A championship standard par 71 parkland course
designed by Dr Arthur Spring. This course is in the
centre of south-west Ireland's golfing mecca. Ruins of a
medieval castle dominate the back nine and the whole
course is overlooked by the MacGillycuddy Reeks. The
par 3 8th and par 4 11th are two of the most memorable
holes.
18 holes, 6600yds, Par 71, SSS 72, Course record 68.
Club membership 350.

Continued

Beaufort Golf Course

Visitors booking advisable for weekends. **Societies** advance booking essential. **Green Fees** €50 (€60 weekends). **Cards** 🔲 🔲 🔲 🔲 🔲 **Course Designer** Arthur Spring **Facilities** ⊗ ℳ ⅃ ⬛ ♀ △ ⬒ ⛳ ⚒ ♂ **Conf** Corporate Hospitality Days available **Location** 11km W of Killarney, off N72 W
....
Hotel ★★★ 69% Castlerosse Hotel, KILLARNEY ☎ 064 31144 121 en suite

Castlerosse Hotel ☎ 064 31144 🗎 064 31031
e-mail: golf@crhk.ie
Set in mature parkland, the course commands fine views and has fully irrigated USGA standard greens plus a practice green.
9 holes, 3020yds, Par 36.
Club membership 96.
Visitors contact for availability. **Societies** apply in writing **Green Fees** €28 for 18 holes, €17 for 9 holes. **Cards** 🔲 🔲 🔲 🔲 **Course Designer** H Wallace **Facilities** ℳ ⅃ ⬛ ♀ △ ⛳ ⬒ ♂ ⚒ ♂ **Leisure** hard tennis courts, heated indoor swimming pool, sauna, gymnasium.
....
Hotel ★★★ 69% Castlerosse Hotel, KILLARNEY ☎ 064 31144 121 en suite

Killarney Golf & Fishing Club Mahony's Point
☎ 064 31034 🗎 064 33065
e-mail: reservations@killarney-golf.com
The three courses are parkland with tree-lined fairways; many bunkers and small lakes provide no mean challenge. Mahoney's Point Course has a particularly testing par 5, 4, 3 finish and the courses call for great skill from the tee. Killarney has been the venue for many important events and is a favourite of many famous golfers.
Mahony's Point: 18 holes, 5826 metres, Par 72, SSS 72, Course record 64.
Killeen: 18 holes, 6001 metres, Par 72, SSS 72, Course record 68.
Lackabane: 18 holes, 6011 metres, Par 72, SSS 72.
Club membership 1600.
Visitors advisable to contact in advance. Neat casual dress required in the clubhouse & on the course. **Societies** phone in advance or apply in writing. **Green Fees** per 18 holes: Mahony's Point €80, Killeen €85, Lackabane €60.
Cards 🔲 🔲 🔲 🔲 **Prof** Tony Coveney **Course Designer** H Longhurst, Sir Guy Campbell **Facilities** ⊗ ℳ ⅃ ⬛ ♀ △ ⬒ ⛳ ♂ ⚒ ♂ ⅃ **Leisure** sauna, gymnasium. **Conf** Corporate Hospitality Days available **Location** on N72, Ring of Kerry road
....
Hotel ★★★★ Aghadoe Heights Hotel, KILLARNEY ☎ 064 31766 75 en suite

Killorglin Stealroe
☎ 066 9761979 🗎 066 9761437
e-mail: kilgolf@iol.ie
A parkland course designed by Eddie Hackett as a challenging but fair test of golf, surrounded by magnificent views.
18 holes, 6497yds, Par 72, SSS 71, Course record 68.
Club membership 510.
Visitors pre booking of tee time advisable. Deposit required for groups. **Societies** book by phone, confirm in writing. **Green Fees** €30 (weekends & bank holidays €35). **Cards** 🔲 🔲 🔲 🔲 **Prof** Hugh Duggan **Course Designer** Eddie Hackett **Facilities** ⊗ ℳ ⅃ ⬛ ♀ △ ⬒ ⛳ ♂ ⚒ ♂ **Leisure** fishing. **Location** 3km from Killorglin, on N70 to Tralee
....
Guesthouse ◆◆◆◆ The Grove Lodge, Killarney Rd, KILLORGLIN ☎ 066 9761157 10 en suite

Parknasilla
☎ 064 45122 🗎 064 45323
9 holes, 5400 metres, Par 70, SSS 69.
Course Designer Arthur Spring **Location** 3km E of Sneer on Ring of Kerry road
Phone for further details
....
Hotel ★★★★ 75% Great Southern Hotel, PARKNASILLA ☎ 064 45122 24 en suite 59 annexe en suite

Tralee West Barrow
☎ 066 7136379 🗎 066 7136008
e-mail: info@traleegolfclub.com
The first Arnold Palmer designed course in Europe, this magnificent 18-hole links is set in spectacular scenery on the Barrow peninsula, surrounded on three sides by the sea. Perhaps the most memorable hole is the par four 17th which plays from a high tee, across a deep gorge to a green perched high against a backdrop of mountains. The back nine is very difficult and challenging. Not suitable for beginners.
18 holes, 5970 metres, Par 71, SSS 71, Course record 66.
Club membership 1306.
Visitors not after 4.20pm weekdays, only 7.30-10.30am Wed, 11am-1.30pm Sat, 11.30-1pm bank holidays, not Sun; handicap certificate; contact in advance. **Societies** weekdays only; must contact in writing. **Green Fees** €160 per round. **Cards** 🔲 🔲 🔲 **Prof** David Power **Course Designer** Arnold Palmer **Facilities** ⊗ ℳ ⅃ ⬛ ♀ △ ⬒ ⛳ ♂ **Location** 13km NW of Tralee off Spa-Fenit road
....
Hotel ★★★ 69% Meadowlands Hotel, Oakpark, TRALEE ☎ 066 7180444 58 en suite

Waterville House & Golf Links
☎ 066 9474102 🗎 066 9474482
e-mail: wvgolf@iol.ie
On the western tip of the Ring of Kerry, this course is highly regarded by many top golfers. The feature holes are the par 5 11th, which runs along a rugged valley

Continue

Ballybunion

Co Kerry

Ballybunion

Map 01 A3

Having excellent links, Ballybunion is recognised for its fine development of the natural terrain. Mr Murphy built the Old Course in 1906. With large sand dunes and an Atlantic backdrop, Ballybunion offers the golfer an exciting round of golf in a scenic location. But be warned, the Old course is difficult to play in the wind. President Clinton played Ballybunion on his historic visit to Ireland in 1998. Although overshadowed by the Old Course, the Cashen Course designed by Robert Trent Jones is also world class, characterised by narrow fairways, small greens and large dunes.

Sandhill Rd
☎ 068 27146 Fax 068 27387
e-mail: bbgolfgc@ioe.ie

Old Course: 18 holes, 6603yds, Par 71, SSS 72, Course record 67.
Cashen: 18 holes, Par 72, SSS 71, Course record 69.
Club membership 1500.
Visitors not weekends; contact in advance. **Societies** apply in advance. **Green Fees** Old Course £135 per round; Cashen Course £95 per round; both courses £180. **Cards** ⚌ 💳 ⚌
Prof Brian O'Callaghan **Course Designer** Simpson
Facilities ⊗ ♨ ┗ ♥ ♀ ♨ 🏠 ⚐ ⚑ ∫ **Leisure** sauna.
Location 2km S

....

Guesthouses

♦♦♦♦♦ Cashen Course House, Golf Links Rd, BALLYBUNION
☎ 068 27351 9 en suite

♦♦♦♦ The Tides Guest House, BALLYBUNION
☎ 068 27980 Fax 068 27923 5 en suite

Hotels

★★★ 68% The White Sands Hotel, BALLYHEIGUE
☎ 066 7133102 Fax 066 7133357 81 en suite

★★★★ 70% Ballygarry House Hotel, Killarney Rd, TRALEE
☎ 066 7123322 Fax 7127630 46 en suite

★★★ 67% Abbey Gate Hotel, Maine St, TRALEE
☎ 066 7129888 Fax 066 7129821 100 en suite

between towering dunes, and the par 3 17th, which features an exceptionally elevated tee. Needless to say, the surroundings are beautiful.
18 holes, 6640yds, Par 72, SSS 72, Course record 65.
Visitors preferable to contact in advance. **Societies** contact secretary or manager in advance. **Green Fees** not confirmed. **Cards** ▩ ▩ ▩ ▨ **Prof** Liam Higgins **Course Designer** Eddie Hackett, Tom Fazio **Facilities** ⊗ ⋔ ⓑ ⓡ ♀ ⓓ ⓐ ⓣ ⓜ ⬟ ♣ ♂ ♪ **Leisure** heated outdoor swimming pool, fishing, sauna. **Location** on Ring of Kerry road (N70) 0.5km from Waterville

Hotel ★★★ 66% Derrynane Hotel, CAHERDANIEL
☎ 066 9475136 73 en suite

CO KILDARE

ATHY
Map 01 C3

Athy Geraldine
☎ 059 8631729 ▤ 059 8634710
e-mail: info@athygolfclub.com
The course was upgraded in 2003 to include new tees, new bunkers, a new par 5 with a lake feature and trees have been planted to create a more exacting course. The last five holes are now more demanding and the 16th and 17th are considered to be among the most difficult consecutive par 4s found anywhere. The 18th is a testing finishing hole with bunkers off the tee and also for the next two shots.
18 holes, 6475yds, Par 72, SSS 71.
Club membership 800.
Visitors advisable to call in advance, no green fees on Sun. **Societies** apply in writing or e-mail to the Hon Secretary **Green Fees** €25 per 18 holes (€35 Sat & bank holidays). **Cards** ▩ ▩ **Course Designer** Jeff Howes **Facilities** ⊗ ⋔ by arrangement ⓑ ♀ ♀ ⓐ ♣ ♂ ♪ **Conf** fac available Corporate Hospitality Days available **Location** 1.5km N of Athy on Kildare road

Guesthouse ◆◆◆◆◆ Coursetown Country House, Stradbally Rd, ATHY ☎ 059 8631101 5 en suite

CARBURY
Map 01 C4

Highfield Highfield House
☎ 046 9731021 ▤ 046 9731021
e-mail: highfieldgolf@eircom.ie
A relatively flat parkland course but with interesting undulations, enhanced by the fast flowing stream which runs through many holes. The 4th dog-legs over the lake, the 7th is a great par 5 with a challenging green, the 10th par 3 is over rushes onto a plateau green (out of bounds on left). The 1st tee is situated on top of the new cedar log clubhouse, which provides a spectacular starting point.
18 holes, 6007yds, Par 70, SSS 69.
Club membership 500.
Visitors welcome, must contact in advance for weekend play. **Societies** phone or apply in writing. **Green Fees** Mon-Fri €20-£30 per day (€30-€40 weekends). **Cards** ▩ ▩ **Prof** Barry Hamill **Course Designer** Alan Duggan **Facilities** ⊗ ⋔ ⓑ ♀ ♀ ⓐ ⓐ ♂ ♪ **Conf** fac available Corporate Hospitality Days available **Location** take M4 from Dublin, 14.5km S of Enfield

Hotel ★★★★ 72% Keadeen Hotel, NEWBRIDGE
☎ 045 431666 75 en suite

CASTLEDERMOT
Map 01 C3

Kilkea Castle ☎ 0503 45555 ▤ 0503 45505
e-mail: kilkeagolfclub@eircom.net
18 holes, 6200 metres, Par 71, SSS 71.
Phone for further details

Hotel ★★★ Seven Oaks Hotel, Athy Rd, CARLOW
☎ 059 913 1308 59 en suite

DONADEA
Map 01 C4

Knockanally Golf & Country Club
☎ 045 869322 ▤ 045 869322
e-mail: golf@knockanally.com
18 holes, 6485yds, Par 72, SSS 72, Course record 66.
Course Designer Noel Lyons **Location** 5km off Dublin-Galway road between Kilcock & Enfield
Phone for further details

Hotel ★★★ 64% Lucan Spa Hotel, LUCAN
☎ 01 6280494 71 rms (61 en suite)

KILDARE
Map 01 C3

Cill Dara Cill Dara, Little Curragh
☎ 045 521295 & 521433
e-mail: cilldaragolfclub@ireland.com
9 holes, 5852 metres, Par 71, SSS 70, Course record 64.
Location 1.6km E of Kildare
Phone for further details

Hotel ★★★★ 72% Keadeen Hotel, NEWBRIDGE
☎ 045 431666 75 en suite

The Curragh Curragh
☎ 045 441238 & 441714 ▤ 045 441714
A particularly challenging course, well wooded and with lovely scenery all around.
18 holes, 6035 metres, Par 72, SSS 71, Course record 63.
Club membership 1040.
Visitors contact in advance, preferred on Mon, Wed, Thu & Fri. **Societies** apply in writing. **Green Fees** not confirmed. **Prof** Gerry Burke **Facilities** ⊗ ⋔ ⓑ ♀ ♀ ⓐ ⓐ ♣ ♪ **Location** off N7 between Newbridge & Kildare

Hotel ★★★★ 72% Keadeen Hotel, NEWBRIDGE
☎ 045 431666 75 en suite

KILL
Map 01 D4

Killeen
☎ 045 866003 ▤ 045 875881
e-mail: admin@killeengc.ie
18 holes, 5561 metres, Par 71, SSS 71, Course record 70.
Course Designer Pat Ruddy, M Kelly **Location** signed off N7 at Kill
Phone for further details

Hotel ★★★ 77% Barberstown Castle, STRAFFAN
☎ 01 6288157 58 en suite

MAYNOOTH
Map 01 D4

Carton House
☎ 01 5052000 ▤ 01 6286555
e-mail: reservations@carton.ie
The O'Meara is a parkland course surrounded by the

Continued

Continued

ancient specimen trees of this fine estate. Feature holes include the 14th, 15th and 16th - a pair of par 5 wrapped around a par 5 crossing the loops of the river Rye. The Montgomerie plays like a links course with bunker hazards and a prevailing wind. The fairways run firm and fast and the bunker complexes demand strategic and shot making excellence and the ground game is always in play.

O'Meara: 18 holes, 6608yds, Par 72, SSS 72.
Montgomerie: 18 holes, 6821yds, Par 72, SSS 73, Course record 68.

Visitors contact reservations by phone or e-mail. **Societies** phone Group Sales Co-ordinator 01 5052000 **Green Fees** Apr: €85 per round, May-Oct: €115 per round (€95/€135 Fri-Sun). **Cards** 🖃 💳 💳 **Prof** Francis Howley **Course Designer** O'Meara, Lobb & Montgomerie, Edy **Facilities** ⊗ ⅋ 🗽 💄 💷 🍴 🕰 🏌 🏌 🚵 ∅ ⌀ **Leisure** fishing. **Conf** Corporate Hospitality Days available **Location** from Dublin N4 W & exit for Leixlip West. Signs for Carton House

Hotel ★★★ 75% Moyglare Manor, Moyglare, MAYNOOTH ☎ 01 6286351 17 en suite

NAAS   Map 01 D4

Craddockstown Blessington Rd
☎ 045 897610 🖷 045 896968
e-mail: gaynolan@craddockstown.com
A parkland course with easy walking. A major redevelopment was completed in 2004 with new tee boxes, two new greens, many water features, fairway improvements and the redevelopment of all greenside bunkers.
18 holes, 5726 metres, Par 71, SSS 69, Course record 66.
Club membership 800.
Visitors should ring in advance to verify tee times available, limited at weekends. **Societies** apply in writing. **Green Fees** 18 holes €35 Mon-Thu, €40 Fri, €45 weekends. **Cards** 🖃 💳 **Course Designer** A Spring **Facilities** ⊗ ⅋ 🗽 💄 💷 🍴 🏌 🚵 ∅ **Conf** fac available Corporate Hospitality Days available **Location** off N7/N97 towards Naas, left onto Blessington Rd

Hotel ★★★ 59% Ambassador Hotel, KILL
☎ 045 877064 36 en suite

Naas Kerdiffstown
☎ 045 897509 & 874644 🖷 045 896109
e-mail: naasgolfclubisdn@eircom.net
Recent completed renovations have made this course a truly unique challenge. The par 3 17th hole is now one of the most challenging tee shots where a round of golf can be won or lost.
18 holes, 5663 metres, Par 71, SSS 69, Course record 65.
Club membership 1200.
Visitors not Sun, Tue or Thu. **Societies** contact in advance by phone. **Green Fees** €35 per round (€42 weekends & bank holiday). **Cards** 🖃 💳 **Course Designer** E Hackett, A Spring, J Howes **Facilities** ⊗ ⅋ 🗽 💄 💷 🏌 ∅ **Location** 1.5km from town on N7 Sallins-Johnstown road

Hotel ★★★ 66% Downshire House Hotel, BLESSINGTON ☎ 045 865199 14 en suite 11 annexe en suite

STRAFFAN   See page 441

STRAFFAN   Map 01 D4

Castlewarden
☎ 01 4589254 & 4589838 🖷 01 4588972
e-mail: info@castlewardengolfclub.com
18 holes, 6496yds, Par 72, SSS 70.
Course Designer Tommy Halpin **Location** between Naas & Rathcoole
Phone for further details

Hotel ★★★ 59% Ambassador Hotel, KILL
☎ 045 877064 36 en suite

CO KILKENNY

CALLAN   Map 01 C3

Callan Geraldine
☎ 056 25136 & 25949 🖷 056 55155
e-mail: info@callangolfclub.com
18 holes, 6422yds, Par 72, SSS 70, Course record 66.
Course Designer B Moore, J Power **Location** 1.5km from Callan on Knocktopher road
Phone for further details

Hotel ★★★ 75% Newpark Hotel, KILKENNY
☎ 056 776 0500 111 en suite

KILKENNY   Map 01 C3

Kilkenny Glendine
☎ 056 7765400 🖷 056 7723593
e-mail: enquiries@kilkennygolfclub.com
One of Ireland's most pleasant inland courses, noted for its tricky finishing holes and its par threes. Features of the course are its long 11th and 13th holes and the challenge increases year by year as thousands of trees planted over the last 30 years or so are maturing. As host of the Kilkenny Scratch Cup annually, the course is permanently maintained in championship condition.
18 holes, 5925 metres, Par 71, SSS 70, Course record 68.
Club membership 1368.
Visitors contact in advance. **Societies** contact in advance. **Green Fees** not confirmed. **Cards** 🖃 💳 **Prof** Jimmy Bolger **Facilities** ⊗ ⅋ 🗽 💄 💷 🍴 🏌 🕰 🚵 ∅ ⌀ **Location** 1.5km from centre on Castlecomer road

Hotel ★★★ 65% Langtons Hotel, 69 John St, KILKENNY ☎ 056 776 5133 14 en suite 16 annexe en suite

THOMASTOWN   See page 443

CO LAOIS

ABBEYLEIX   Map 01 C3

Abbeyleix Rathmoyle
☎ 0502 31450 🖷 0502 30108
e-mail: info@abbeyleixgolfclub.ie
A pleasant, parkland 18-hole course. Undulating with water features at five holes.
18 holes, 5557 metres, Par 72, SSS 70.
Club membership 470.

Continued

Visitors welcome weekdays. **Societies** apply in writing.
Green Fees €20 per round(€30 weekends). **Course
Designer** Mel Flanagan **Facilities** ⊗ 🏠 💺 ♀ ♨ ♂
Location 0.6km outside town on Ballyroaw road

Hotel ★★★ 75% Newpark Hotel, KILKENNY
☎ 056 776 0500 111 en suite

MOUNTRATH   Map 01 C3

Mountrath Knockanina
☎ 0502 32558 & 32643 (office) 📠 0502 32643
e-mail: info@mountrathgolfclub.ie
**A picturesque course at the foot of the Slieve Bloom
Mountains in central Ireland. The 18-hole course has
fine fairways and well-bunkered greens, the River Nore
flows through the course.**
18 holes, 5732 metres, Par 71, SSS 70, Course record 68.
Club membership 600.
Visitors check for availability at weekends, other days no
problem but safer to check. **Societies** contact in advance.
Green Fees 18 holes €20 (weekends €30); (Dec-Feb
€15). **Facilities** ⊗ by arrangement 🏠 💺 ♀ ♨ ♂
Location 2.5km from town on Dublin-Limerick road

Hotel ★★★★ 72% Keadeen Hotel, NEWBRIDGE
☎ 045 431666 75 en suite

PORTARLINGTON   Map 01 C3

Portarlington Garryhinch
☎ 0502 23115 📠 0502 23044
e-mail: portalingtongc@eircom.net
18 holes, 5723 metres, Par 71, SSS 70, Course record 66.
Course Designer Eddie Hackett **Location** 6.5km from
town on Mountmellick road
Phone for further details

Hotel ★★★★ 72% Keadeen Hotel, NEWBRIDGE
☎ 045 431666 75 en suite

PORTLAOISE   Map 01 C3

The Heath
☎ 0502 46533 & 46045 (office) 📠 0502 46866
e-mail: info@theheathgc.ie
**Course noted for its rough heather and gorze furze and
scenic views of the rolling hills of Co Laois. Remarkably
dry conditions all year round.**
18 holes, 5857 metres, Par 71, SSS 70, Course record 67.
Club membership 950.
Visitors contact in advance, preferred on weekdays.
Societies apply in writing to the Administrator **Green Fees**
not confirmed. **Cards** 📖 💳 💳 💳 **Prof** Mark O'Boyle
Facilities ⊗ ⨝ 🏠 💺 ♀ ♨ 🏠 ♨ ♂ ♟
Location 6.5km N on N7

Hotel ★★★★ 72% Keadeen Hotel, NEWBRIDGE
☎ 045 431666 75 en suite

RATHDOWNEY   Map 01 C3

Rathdowney
☎ 0505 46170 📠 0505 46065
e-mail: rathdowneygolf@eircom.net
**An 18-hole parkland course, with undulating terrain.
The 17th hole is a tricky par 3, 12th and 15th are
particularly tough par 4s and the 6th is a challenging
par 5 (503 metres) into the prevailing wind. A good test
for golfers of all abilities.**

Continued

18 holes, 5894 metres, Par 71, SSS 70, Course record 67.
Club membership 500.
Visitors. Ladies have priority on Wed, Sat & Sun am are
reserved for member & societies. **Societies** apply in writing
& pay deposit to confirm booking. **Green Fees** €20 (€25
weekends). **Course Designer Facilities** ⊗
by arrangement 🏠 💺 ♀ ♨ 🏠 ♂ **Conf** Corporate
Hospitality Days available **Location** 0.8km SE. Follow
Johnstown signs from town square

Hotel ★★★ 75% Newpark Hotel, KILKENNY
☎ 056 776 0500 111 en suite

CO LEITRIM

BALLINAMORE   Map 01 C4

Ballinamore
☎ 071 9644346
**A very dry and very testing nine-hole parkland course
along the Ballinamore-Ballyconnell Canal. Not busy on
weekdays which makes it ideal for high handicap
golfers, while at the same time it tests the ability of even
a scratch golfer.**
9 holes, 5680yds, Par 70, SSS 68, Course record 66.
Club membership 300.
Visitors competition day Sun. Visitors welcome to play in
open competitions. **Societies** contact in writing or phone
secretary. **Green Fees** not confirmed. **Course Designer**
A Spring **Facilities** 💺 ♀ ♨ **Leisure** fishing.
Location 3km from Ballinamore, along Shannon-Erne
canal

Hotel ★★★★ 70% Slieve Russell Hotel Golf and Country
Club, BALLYCONNELL ☎ 049 9526444 157 en suite

CARRICK-ON-SHANNON   Map 01 C4

Carrick-on-Shannon Woodbrook
☎ 071 9667015 📠 071 9667015
e-mail: ckgc@eircom.net
9 holes, 5545 metres, Par 70, SSS 68.
Course Designer Eddie Hackett **Location** 6.5km W by N4
Phone for further details

Hotel ★★★★ 70% Slieve Russell Hotel Golf and Country
Club, BALLYCONNELL ☎ 049 9526444 157 en suite

CO LIMERICK

ADARE   Map 01 B3

Adare Manor
☎ 061 396204 📠 061 396800
e-mail: info@adaremanorgolfclub.com
**An 18-hole parkland course, par 69, in an unusual
setting. The course surrounds the ruins of a 13th-
century castle and a 15th-century abbey.**
18 holes, 5800yds, Par 69, SSS 69, Course record 63.
Club membership 750.
Visitors welcome weekdays, weekends only by
arrangement & subject to availability. Advisable to contact
in advance. **Societies** apply in writing or e-mail **Green
Fees** not confirmed. **Cards** 📖 💳 **Course Designer** Ben
Sayers, Eddie Hackett **Facilities** ⊗ ⨝ 🏠 💺 ♀ ♨ 🏠 ♂ ♂
Location 16km from Limerick on Killarney road

Hotel ★★★★ 70% Dunraven Arms Hotel, ADARE
☎ 061 396633 75 en suite

Championship Course

Co Kildare

The K Club

Straffan

Map 01 D4

The K Club is the venue for the Ryder Cup in 2006, the first time that Ireland has hosted the event. The course reflects the personality of its architect, Arnold Palmer, covering 220 acres of Kildare woodland, with 14 man-made lakes and the River Liffey providing the water hazards. From the instant you arrive at the 1st tee, you are enveloped by a unique atmosphere: the courses are both cavalier and charismatic. The Palmer Course is one of Europe's most spectacular courses, charming, enticing, and invariably bringing out the very best in your game. The best way to describe the Smurfit Course is that of an inland links, but its attributes do not stop there. The course has many dramatic landscapes with dunes moulding throughout, while some 14 acres of water have been worked in to the design, especially through the final holes 13-18; a watery grave awaits many on the home stretch. The course is entirely different from the Palmer Course located just across the River Liffey.

☎ 01 6017300 Fax 01 6017399
e-mail: golf@kclub.ie

Palmer Course: 18 holes, 6526 metres, Par 74, SSS 72, Course record 65.
Smurfit Course: 18 holes, 6636 metres, Par 72, SSS 72.
Club membership 540.
Visitors restricted at members' times; contact in advance to book tee times. **Societies** phone & write in advance. **Green Fees** terms on application. **Cards** ▦ ▬ ▭ ▣ **Prof** John McHenry, Peter O'Hagan **Course Designer** Arnold Palmer **Facilities** ⊗ ⅏ ⤫ ♥ ♀ ⚘ 🏠 🍴 🛒 🍽 🚲 ⚙ ⚑
Leisure heated indoor swimming pool, fishing, sauna, solarium, gymnasium. **Conf** fac available Corporate Hospitality Days available **Location** M4 junct 3, R406 to Straffan, entrance to hotel on right in village

Hotel

★ ★ ★ ★ ★ The K Club, STRAFFAN

☎ 01 6017200 69 en suite 10 annexe en suite

LIMERICK
Map 01 B3

Castletroy Castletroy
☎ 061 335753 & 335261 🖹 061 335373
e-mail: cgc@iol.ie
Parkland course with out of bounds on the left of the first two holes. The long par five 10th features a narrow entrance to a green guarded by a stream. The par three 13th has a panoramic view of the course and surrounding countryside from the tee and the 18th is a daunting finish, with the drive played towards a valley and the ground rising towards the green which is protected on both sides by bunkers.
18 holes, 5854 metres, Par 71, SSS 70, Course record 65. Club membership 1062.
Visitors contact in advance; handicap certificate; not Sun or 1-2.30pm weekdays. **Societies** apply in writing. **Green Fees** €40 per 18 holes (€50 Fri-Sun & bank holidays).
Cards 🔲 🔲 🔲 **Course Designer** Eddie Connaughton
Facilities ⊗ ⠀⠀⠀⠀⠀⠀⠀⠀⠀⠀⠀
Conf Corporate Hospitality Days available
Location 5km from city on Dublin road

Hotel ★★★★ 70% Castletroy Park Hotel, Dublin Rd, LIMERICK ☎ 061 335566 107 en suite

Limerick Ballyclough
☎ 061 415146 🖹 061 319219
e-mail: pat.murray@limerickgc.com
Tree-lined parkland course. The club is the only Irish winner of the European Cup Winners Team Championship.
18 holes, 5938 metres, Par 72, SSS 71, Course record 63. Club membership 1300.
Visitors not after 5pm on Tue & weekends. **Societies** contact in writing. **Green Fees** €50 Mon-Thu (€60 Fri-Sun & bank holidays). **Cards** 🔲 🔲 🔲 **Prof** Lee Harrington **Course Designer** A MacKenzie **Facilities** ⊗ ⠀⠀⠀⠀⠀⠀⠀⠀⠀⠀ **Conf** Corporate Hospitality Days available **Location** 5km S on Fedamore Rd

Hotel ★★★ 73% Limerick Strand, Ennis Rd, LIMERICK ☎ 061 327777 95 en suite

Limerick County Golf & Country Club
Ballyneety
☎ 061 351881 🖹 061 351384
e-mail: lcgolf@ioi.ie
Limerick County was designed by Des Smyth and presents beautifully because of the strategic location of the main features. It stretches over undulating terrain with one elevated section providing views of the surrounding countryside. It features over 70 bunkers with six lakes and several unique design features.
18 holes, 6712yds, Par 72, SSS 74, Course record 70. Club membership 800.
Visitors booking essential. **Societies** book by phone or in writing. **Green Fees** €30 per round (€50 weekends).
Cards 🔲 🔲 🔲 📇 **Prof** Donal McSweeney **Course Designer** Des Smyth **Facilities** ⊗ ⠀⠀⠀⠀⠀⠀⠀⠀⠀⠀⠀ **Conf** fac available Corporate Hospitality Days available **Location** 8km SE of Limerick on R512

Hotel ★★★ 65% Hotel Greenhills, Caherdavin, LIMERICK ☎ 061 453033 18 rms (13 en suite)

NEWCASTLE WEST
Map 01 B3

Killeline Cork Rd
☎ 069 61600 🖹 069 77428
e-mail: killeline@eircom.net
18 holes, 6671yds, Par 72, SSS 68.
Location 0.4km off Limerick-Killarney route
Phone for further details

Hotel ★★★★ 70% Dunraven Arms Hotel, ADARE ☎ 061 396633 75 en suite

Newcastle West Ardagh
☎ 069 76500 🖹 069 76511
e-mail: ncwgolf@eircom.net
Course set in 150 acres of unspoiled countryside, built to the highest standards on sandy free draining soil. A practice ground and driving range are included. Hazards on the course include lakes, bunkers, streams and trees. A signature hole is the par 3 6th playing 185yds over a lake.

18 holes, 6141yds, Par 71, SSS 72, Course record 67. Club membership 1019.
Visitors advisable to contact in advance, but available most days. **Societies** contact in advance. **Green Fees** not confirmed. **Cards** 🔲 🔲 **Prof** Tom Murphy **Course Designer** Dr Arthur Spring **Facilities** ⊗ ⠀⠀⠀⠀⠀⠀⠀⠀⠀⠀⠀ **Conf** fac available Corporate Hospitality Days available **Location** 2m off N21 between Limerick & Killarney

Hotel ★★★★ 70% Dunraven Arms Hotel, ADARE ☎ 061 396633 75 en suite

CO LONGFORD

LONGFORD
Map 01 C4

County Longford Glack, Dublin Rd
☎ 043 46310 🖹 043 47082
e-mail: colonggolf@eircom.net
A lovely 18-hole parkland course with lots of trees.
18 holes, 6300 metres, Par 72, SSS 69, Course record 69. Club membership 819.
Visitors very welcome, but advisable to phone in advance for Tue, Thu & Sun play. **Societies** by arrangement. **Green Fees** not confirmed. **Course Designer** Irish Golf Design
Facilities ⊗ ⠀⠀⠀⠀⠀⠀⠀⠀⠀⠀⠀
Location E of town

Hotel ★★★ 70% Abbey Hotel, Galway Rd, ROSCOMMON ☎ 090 662 6240 50 en suite

Mount Juliet

Co Kilkenny

Thomastown   Map 01 C3

Venue for the American Express Championship in 2002 and 2004, Mount Juliet's superb 18-hole course was designed by Jack Nicklaus. It has also hosted many prestigious events including the Irish Open on three occasions. The course has a cleverly concealed drainage and irrigation system, perfect even when inclement weather would otherwise halt play. It takes advantage of the estate's mature landscape to provide a world-class 72-par challenge for professionals and high-handicap golfers alike. A unique three-hole golfing academy has been added to allow novice and experienced players ample opportunity to improve their game, while a new 18-hole putting course provides an extra dimension of golfing pleasure and is the venue for the National Putting Championship.

Hotel & Golf Club
☎ 056 7773064 Fax 056 7773078
e-mail: golfinfo@mountjuliet.ie

18 holes, 6926yds, Par 72, SSS 73, Course record 62. Club membership 500.
Visitors must contact in advance. **Societies** book in advance by phone or writing. **Green Fees** £140 (£155 weekends). **Cards** ▭ ▬ ▬ 🔒 **Prof** Sean Cotter **Course Designer** Jack Nicklaus **Facilities** ⊗ ⅏ ⬥ 🏌 ♀ ♨ 🏠 🍴 🛏 🐎 🚵 ⚲ ⛳ **Leisure** hard tennis courts, heated indoor swimming pool, fishing, sauna, solarium, gymnasium, archery, clay shooting, equestrian. **Conf** fac available Corporate Hospitality Days available **Location** 4km S of Thomastown off N9

....

Hotels

★ ★ ★ ★ Mount Juliet Conrad Hotel, THOMASTOWN

☎ 056 777 3000 32 en suite 27 annexe en suite

★ ★ ★ ★ 71% Kilkenny River Court Hotel, The Bridge, John St, KILKENNY

☎ 056 772 3388 Fax 056 772 3389 90 en suite

★ ★ ★ 75% Newpark Hotel, KILKENNY

☎ 056 776 0500 Fax 056 776 0555 111 en suite

★ ★ ★ 65% Langtons Hotel, 69 John St, KILKENNY

☎ 056 776 5133 Fax 056 776 3693 14 en suite 16 annexe en suite

CO LOUTH

ARDEE   Map 01 D4

Ardee Townparks
☎ 041 6853227 📠 041 6856137
e-mail: ardeegolfclub@eircom.net
Pleasant parkland course with mature trees and a stream. The 13th hole is a par 3 over water and is the main feature of the course.
18 holes, 6464yds, Par 71, SSS 72, Course record 64. Club membership 680.
Visitors contact pro 041 6853227. **Societies** apply by writing, e-mail or phone to Secretary/Manager **Green Fees** not confirmed. **Cards** 🔲 🔲 **Prof** Scott Kirkpatrick **Course Designer** Eddie Hackett & Declan Branigan **Facilities** ⊗ 🖢 ⚑ 🖵 🎿 🏠 🖢 🛒 🛺 🎿 ⛷ **Conf** Corporate Hospitality Days available **Location** N33 to Ardee, 400 metres from Fair Green

Hotel ★★★ 73% Ballymascanlon House Hotel, DUNDALK ☎ 042 9358200 90 en suite

BALTRAY   Map 01 D4

County Louth
☎ 041 9881530 📠 041 9881531
e-mail: reservations@countylouthgolfclub.com
Generally held to have the best greens in Ireland, this links course was designed by Tom Simpson to have well-guarded and attractive greens without being overly dependant on bunkers. It provides a good test for the modern champion, notably as the annual venue for the East of Ireland Amateur Open.
18 holes, 6673yds, Par 72, SSS 72, Course record 64. Club membership 1342.
Visitors contact in advance. **Societies** by arrangement. **Green Fees** €110 per round (€130 weekends). **Cards** 🔲 🔲 🔲 **Prof** Paddy McGuirk **Course Designer** Tom Simpson **Facilities** ⊗ 🖢 🖢 🖵 🎿 🏠 🛒 🛺 🎿 ⛷ **Leisure** hard tennis courts. **Location** 8km NE of Drogheda

DUNDALK   Map 01 D4

Ballymascanlon House Hotel
☎ 042 9358200 📠 042 9371598
e-mail: info@ballymascanlon.com
A testing 18-hole parkland course with numerous water hazards and two difficult holes through woodland, this very scenic course is set at the edge of the Cooley Mountains.

18 holes, 5548yds, Par 68, SSS 66.
Visitors phone in advance to check availability. **Societies** booking by phone or letter. **Green Fees** terms on

Continued

application. **Cards** 🔲 🔲 🔲 📠 🔲 **Course Designer** Craddock, Ruddy **Facilities** ⊗ 🖢 🖢 🖢 🖵 🎿 🏠 🛒 🛺 🎿 ⛷ **Leisure** hard tennis courts, heated indoor swimming pool, sauna, gymnasium. **Conf** fac available Corporate Hospitality Days available **Location** 5km N of Dundalk on Carlingford road

Hotel ★★★ 73% Ballymascanlon House Hotel, DUNDALK ☎ 042 9358200 90 en suite

Dundalk Blackrock
☎ 042 9321731 📠 9322022
e-mail: manager@dundalkgolfclub.ie
A championship course with fine views of mountain and sea.
18 holes, 6028 metres, Par 72, SSS 71. Club membership 1500.
Visitors contact in advance; not Tue, Sun. **Societies** apply in writing in advance. **Green Fees** €55 per day. **Cards** 🔲 🔲 **Prof** Leslie Walker **Facilities** ⊗ 🖢 🖢 🖵 🎿 🏠 🛺 🎿 ⛷ **Leisure** sauna. **Conf** Corporate Hospitality Days available **Location** 4km S on coast road from Dundalk

Hotel ★★★ 73% Ballymascanlon House Hotel, DUNDALK ☎ 042 9358200 90 en suite

Killin Park Killin Park
☎ 042 9339303 📠 042 9331412
Opened in 1991 and designed by Eddie Hackett, this undulating 18-hole parkland course has mature woodland and river features. It provides challenging golf and breathtaking scenery. Bordered on the north side by Killin Wood and on the south by the Castletown River.
18 holes, 5293yds, Par 69, SSS 65, Course record 65. Club membership 300.
Visitors no restrictions. **Societies** apply by phone or in writing in advance. **Green Fees** not confirmed. **Course Designer** Eddie Hackett **Facilities** ⊗ 🖢 by arrangement 🖢 🖢 🖵 🎿 🏠 🛒 🛺 🎿 ⛷ **Location** onto Castle Blaney road from Dundalk, right at Fagans Lounge to river bridge, course on left

Hotel ★★★ 73% Ballymascanlon House Hotel, DUNDALK ☎ 042 9358200 90 en suite

GREENORE   Map 01 D4

Greenore
☎ 042 9373212 & 9373678 📠 042 9383898
e-mail: greenoregolfclub@eircom.net
Situated amidst beautiful scenery on the shores of Carlingford Lough, with views of the Mourne Mountains. The pine trees here are an unusual feature on a part-links course. There are quite a number of water facilities, tight fairways and very good greens.
18 holes, 6647yds, Par 71, SSS 73, Course record 69. Club membership 1035.
Visitors contact in advance at weekends. **Societies** contact in advance especially for weekend play. **Green Fees** not confirmed. **Cards** 🔲 🔲 🔲 **Prof** Robert Giles **Course Designer** Eddie Hackett **Facilities** ⊗ 🖢 🖢 🖢 🖵 🎿 🏠 🛺 🎿 ⛷ **Leisure** Golf lessons available on request but must be pre booked. **Conf** Corporate Hospitality Days available **Location** M1 exit Dundalk, 16km on E coast road to Earlingford/Greenmore

Hotel ★★★ 73% Ballymascanlon House Hotel, DUNDALK ☎ 042 9358200 90 en suite

TERMONFECKIN   Map 01 D4

Seapoint
☎ 041 9822333 🖷 041 9822331
e-mail: golflinks@seepoint.ie
**A premier championship links course of 6470 metres
with a particularly interesting 17th hole.**
18 holes, 6470 metres, Par 72, SSS 74.
Club membership 580.
Visitors phone in advance for restrictions. **Societies** phone
in advance. **Green Fees** €50 (€60 weekends). Half price
for 9 holes. **Cards** 🔲 🔲 🔲 **Prof** David Carroll **Course
Designer** Des Smyth **Facilities** ⊗ ⊁ 🖳 ⏆ ♀ 🛆 🖻 ⸀ ⸜
🚜 ⸌ ⸀ **Location** 6.5km NE of Drogheda

Hotel ★★★ 67% Boyne Valley Hotel & Country Club,
Stameen, Dublin Rd, DROGHEDA ☎ 041 9837737
73 en suite

CO MAYO

BALLINA   Map 01 B4

Ballina Mossgrove, Shanaghy
☎ 096 21050 🖷 096 21718
e-mail: ballinagc@eircom.net
Undulating but mostly flat inland course.
18 holes, 6103yds, Par 71, SSS 69, Course record 69.
Club membership 520.
Visitors not Sun before 11.30am. **Societies** apply in
writing or phone in advance. **Green Fees** terms on
application. **Cards** 🔲 🔲 🔲 **Course Designer**
E Hackett **Facilities** 🖳 ⏆ ♀ 🛆 ⸀ 🚜 ⸌
Location 1.5km outside town on Bonnocolon Rd

BALLINROBE   Map 01 B4

Ballinrobe Cloonacastle
☎ 094 9541118 🖷 094 9541889
e-mail: bgcgolf@iol.ie
**A championship parkland 18-hole course, set in the
mature woodlands of a historic estate at Cloonacastle.
The layout of the course incorporates seven man-made
lakes with the River Robe flowing at the back of the 3rd
and 5th greens. Ballinrobe is full of character, typified
by the 19th-century residence now used as the
clubhouse.**
18 holes, 6043 metres, Par 73, SSS 72, Course record 67.
Club membership 650.
Visitors welcome daily, phone to reserve tee time.
Societies phone or write to Secretary in advance. **Green
Fees** not confirmed. **Cards** 🔲 🔲 **Prof** Courtney Cougar
Course Designer Eddie Hackett **Facilities** ⊗ ⊁ 🖳 ⏆ ♀
🛆 🖻 ⸀ 🚜 ⸌ ⸀ **Conf** Corporate Hospitality Days
available **Location** N84 onto R331 to Claremorris

BALLYHAUNIS   Map 01 B4

Ballyhaunis Coolnaha
☎ 0907 30014 🖷 094 81829
e-mail: tmack@tinet.ie
9 holes, 5413 metres, Par 70, SSS 68, Course record 68.
Location 5km N on N83
Phone for further details

> **Prices may change during the currency of the
> Guide, please check when booking.**

BELMULLET   Map 01 A5

Carne Carne
☎ 097 82292 🖷 097 81477
e-mail: carngolf@iol.ie
**A wild tumultuous roller-coaster landscape, which has
been shaped into an inspirational links course by Eddie
Hackett.**

18 holes, 6119 metres, Par 72, SSS 72, Course record 66.
Club membership 460.
Visitors welcome, booking essential to guarantee tee-time.
Societies booking advisable. **Green Fees** €55 per day
(weekends & bank holidays €55 per round). **Cards** 🔲
🔲 🔳 **Course Designer** Eddie Hackett **Facilities** ⊗ ⊁ 🖳
⏆ ♀ 🛆 🖻 ⸀ 🚜 ⸌ **Location** 3km from Belmullet

CASTLEBAR   Map 01 B4

Castlebar Hawthorn Av, Rocklands
☎ 094 21649 🖷 094 26088
e-mail: info@castlebargolfclub.ie
**Course opened September 2000. Fast greens with severe
borrows. Accuracy is essential from the tee on most
holes. Long difficult course from blue (championship)
tees.**
18 holes, 5698 metres, Par 71, SSS 70.
Club membership 650.
Visitors must contact in advance for weekend play. No
vistors on Sun. **Societies** contact in advance. **Green Fees**
€25 per day (€32 Fri, Sat & Sun). **Cards** 🔲 🔲 **Course
Designer** Peter McEvoy **Facilities** ⊗ 🖳 ⏆ ♀ 🛆 ⸀ 🚜 ⸌
Location 1.6km from town on Belcarra road

Hotel ★★ 64% Welcome Inn Hotel, CASTLEBAR
☎ 094 902 2288 & 902 2054 🖷 094 902 1766 40 en suite

CLAREMORRIS   Map 01 B4

Claremorris Castlemacgarrett
☎ 094 93 71527 🖷 094 93 72919
e-mail: info@claremorrisgolfclub.com
**A 18-hole parkland course designed by Tom Craddock,
designer of Druids Glen. It consists of many eye-
catching water features, bunkers, trees and wooded
backgrounds. The feature hole is the short par 4 14th
with its island green.**
18 holes, 6600 metres, Par 73, SSS 70, Course record 68.
Club membership 600.
Visitors contact club for availability. **Societies** contact 094
9371527 for details. **Green Fees** Oct-Mar €26/€32 per
round; Apr-Sep €32/€40. **Cards** 🔲 🔲 **Course
Designer** Tom Craddock **Facilities** ⊗ by arrangement ⊁
by arrangement 🖳 ⏆ ♀ 🛆 ⸀ 🚜 ⸌ **Location** 1.5m S of
town on N17

Continued

Hotel ★★★ 63% Belmont Hotel, KNOCK
☎ 094 938 8122 63 en suite

KEEL Map 01 A4

Achill Achill Island, Westport
☎ 098 43456
e-mail: achillgolfclub@eircom.net
Seaside links in a scenic location by the Atlantic Ocean.
9 holes, 2723 metres, Par 70, SSS 66, Course record 69.
Club membership 240.
Visitors welcome but cannot play on some Sun. **Societies** write or phone in advance. **Green Fees** terms on application. **Course Designer** Paddy Skirrit
Facilities **Location** 15km from Keel

Hotel ★★★ 76% Hotel Westport Conference Leisure Centre, Newport Rd, WESTPORT
☎ 098 25122 129 en suite

SWINFORD Map 01 B4

Swinford Brabazon Park
☎ 094 92 51378 📠 094 92 51378
e-mail: regantommy@eircom.net
A pleasant parkland course with good views of the beautiful surrounding countryside. Tough par 3s.
9 holes, 5542 metres, Par 70, SSS 68.
Club membership 300.
Visitors contact for Sun play during peak season. **Societies** apply in writing or phone in advance. **Green Fees** €15 per day. **Facilities** **Location** on old Kiltimagh road, 8 km from town

Hotel ★★ 64% Welcome Inn Hotel, CASTLEBAR
☎ 094 902 2288 & 902 2054 📠 094 902 1766 40 en suite

WESTPORT Map 01 B4

Westport Carrowholly
☎ 098 28262 & 27070 📠 098 27217
e-mail: wpgolf@eircom.net
This is a beautiful course with wonderful views of Clew Bay, with its 365 islands, and the holy mountain called Croagh Patrick, famous for the annual pilgrimage to its summit. Golfers indulge in a different kind of penance on this challenging course with many memorable holes. Perhaps the most exciting is the par five 15th, 580yds long and featuring a long carry from the tee over an inlet of Clew Bay.
18 holes, 6667yds, Par 73, SSS 71, Course record 65.
Club membership 600.
Visitors contact in advance. **Societies** apply in writing or phone or e-mail well in advance. **Green Fees** €38/€45 per round (weekends €42/€55). **Cards**
Prof Alex Mealia **Course Designer** Fred Hawtree
Facilities
Conf Corporate Hospitality Days available
Location 4 km from town on Newport road

Hotel ★★★ 76% Hotel Westport Conference Leisure Centre, Newport Rd, WESTPORT
☎ 098 25122 129 en suite

Where to stay, where to eat?
Visit www.theAA.com

CO MEATH

BETTYSTOWN Map 01 D4

Laytown & Bettystown
☎ 041 9827170 📠 041 28506
e-mail: bettystowngolfclub@utvinternet.com
A very competitive and trying links course.
18 holes, 5652 metres, Par 71, SSS 70, Course record 65.
Club membership 950.
Visitors not 1-2pm; advisable to contact in advance. **Societies** contact in writing. **Green Fees** not confirmed. **Cards** **Prof** Robert J Browne **Facilities** **Leisure** hard tennis courts.
Location off N1(M1) at signs for Julianstown/Laytown/Bettystown

Hotel ★★★ 64% Ardboyne Hotel, Dublin Rd, NAVAN
☎ 046 902 3119 29 en suite

DUNSHAUGHLIN Map 01 D4

Black Bush Thomastown
☎ 01 8250021 📠 01 8250400
e-mail: golf@blackbush.iol.ie

Black Bush: 18 holes, 6930yds, Par 73, SSS 72.
Agore: 18 holes, 6598yds, Par 71, SSS 69.
Thomastown: 18 holes, 6433yds, Par 70, SSS 68.
Course Designer Bobby Browne **Location** 2.5km from village on Dunshaughlin-Ratoath road
Phone for further details

Hotel ★★★ 70% Finnstown Country House Hotel, Newcastle Rd, Lucan, DUBLIN ☎ 01 6010700
25 en suite 28 annexe en suite

KELLS Map 01 C4

Headfort
☎ 046 9240146 📠 046 9249282
e-mail: hgcadmin@eircom.net
The Old Course is a delightful parkland course which is regarded as one of the best of its kind in Ireland. There are ample opportunities for birdies, but even if these are not achieved, provides for a most pleasant game. The New Course is a challenging course with water featuring on 13 of its 18 holes. Not a course for the faint hearted, this is a course for the thinking golfer.
Old Course: 18 holes, 5973 metres, Par 72, SSS 71.
New Course: 18 holes, 6164, Par 72, SSS 74.
Club membership 1608.
Visitors contact in advance, timesheets in operation

Continued

Societies apply in writing. **Green Fees** Old Course: €45 per round (€50 Fri-Sun). New Course; €60 per round €65 Fri-Sun). **Cards** 〰️ 📇 💳 **Prof** Brendan McGovern **Course Designer** Christy O'Connor jnr **Facilities** ⊗ 〽️ 🏌️ 🍴 ♀ ⛳ 🏠 ⛳ 🛒 🏌️ ♂ **Location** 0.8km E of Kells on N3

Hotel ★★★ 64% Ardboyne Hotel, Dublin Rd, NAVAN ☎ 046 902 3119   29 en suite

KILCOCK   Map 01 C4

Kilcock Gallow
☎ 01 6287592 📠 01 6287283
e-mail: kilcockgolfclub@eircom.net
A parkland course with generous fairways, manicured greens and light rough only.
*18 holes, 5775 metres, Par 72, SSS 70, Course record 69.
Club membership 700.*
Visitors contact in advance for weekends, no problem weekdays. **Societies** phone for dates available. **Green Fees** not confirmed. **Cards** 💳 **Course Designer** Eddie Hackett **Facilities** ⊗ 〽️ 🏌️ 🍴 ♀ ⛳ 🛒 ♂ **Location** 3km from end of M4

Hotel ★★★ 64% Lucan Spa Hotel, LUCAN ☎ 01 6280494   71 rms (61 en suite)

NAVAN   Map 01 C4

Royal Tara Bellinter
☎ 046 25508 & 25244 📠 046 25508
e-mail: info@royaltaragolfclub.com
*18 holes, 5757 metres, Par 71, SSS 70.
Bellinter Nine: 9 holes, 3184yds, Par 35, SSS 35.*
Course Designer Des Smyth **Location** 9.5km from town on N3
Phone for further details

Hotel ★★★ 64% Ardboyne Hotel, Dublin Rd, NAVAN ☎ 046 902 3119   29 en suite

TRIM   Map 01 C4

County Meath Newtownmoynagh
☎ 046 31463 📠 046 37554
18 holes, 6720 metres, Par 73, SSS 72, Course record 68.
Course Designer Eddie Hackett, Tom Craddock
Location 5km outside Trim on Trim-Longwood road
Phone for further details

Hotel ★★★ 64% Ardboyne Hotel, Dublin Rd, NAVAN ☎ 046 902 3119   29 en suite

CO MONAGHAN

CARRICKMACROSS   Map 01 C4

Mannan Castle Donaghmoyne
☎ 042 9663308 📠 042 9663308
e-mail: mannancastlegc@eircom.net
Parkland and picturesque, the course features the par 3 and to an island green. The short par 4 12th through the woods and the 14th to 18th, all crossing water at least once. A test of golf for both amateur and professional.
*18 holes, 6500yds, Par 70, SSS 69.
Club membership 700.*

Visitors may play anytime except competition times Sat, Sun & Wed. **Societies** apply in writing to the secretary. **Green Fees** €25 (€35 weekends). **Course Designer** F Ainsworth **Facilities** ⊗ 〽️ 🏌️ ♀ ⛳ 🍴 🏌️ ♂ **Location** 6.5km N

Hotel ★★★ 73% Ballymascanlon House Hotel, DUNDALK ☎ 042 9358200   90 en suite

Nuremore
☎ 042 9671368 📠 042 9661853
e-mail: nuremore@eircom.net
Picturesque parkland course of championship length incorporating the drumlins and lakes that are a natural feature of the Monaghan countryside. Precision is required on the 10th to drive over a large lake and between a narrow avenue of trees. Signature hole 18th.

*18 holes, 6400yds, Par 71, SSS 69, Course record 64.
Club membership 250.*
Visitors welcome all times but must contact Maurice Cassidy in advance. **Societies** contact in advance. **Green Fees** not confirmed. **Cards** 〰️ 📇 💳 📱 **Prof** Maurice Cassidy **Course Designer** Eddie Hackett **Facilities** ⊗ 〽️ 🏌️ ♀ ⛳ 🍴 🏌️ 🐟 🛒 ♂ **Leisure** hard tennis courts, heated indoor swimming pool, squash, fishing, sauna, gymnasium. **Conf** fac available   Corporate Hospitality Days available **Location** 1.5km S of Carrickmacross on N2

Hotel ★★★★ 75% Nuremore Hotel, CARRICKMACROSS ☎ 042 9661438   72 en suite

CASTLEBLAYNEY   Map 01 C4

Castleblayney Onomy
☎ 042 9740451 📠 042 9740451
e-mail: rayker@eircom.com
9 holes, 5378yds, Par 68, SSS 66, Course record 65.
Course Designer Bobby Browne **Location** on Hope Castle Estate in Castleblayney
Phone for further details

Hotel ★★★ 73% Ballymascanlon House Hotel, DUNDALK ☎ 042 9358200   90 en suite

CLONES   Map 01 C5

Clones Hilton Park
☎ 047 56017 & 56913 📠 047 56913
e-mail: clonesgolfclub@eircom.net
Parkland course set in drumlin country and renowned for the quality of the greens and the wildlife. Due to limestone belt, the course is very dry and playable all year round.
*18 holes, 5549 metres, Par 69, SSS 69, Course record 62.
Club membership 450.*

Continued   *Continued*

Visitors contact in advance. Timesheets in operation at weekends. **Societies** phone in advance. **Green Fees** €25 per round. **Cards** ▆▆ ▆▆ **Course Designer** Dr Arthur Spring **Facilities** ⊗ ℳ ㏒ ▆ ♀ ⚒ ♦ ♣ ⚔ **Conf** Corporate Hospitality Days available **Location** 5km from Clones on Scotshouse road

Hotel ★★★★ 61% Hillgrove Hotel, Old Armagh Rd, MONAGHAN ☎ 047 81288 44 en suite

MONAGHAN   Map 01 C5

Rossmore Rossmore Park, Cootehill Rd
☎ 047 81316
An undulating 18-hole parkland course amid beautiful countryside.
18 holes, 5590 metres, Par 70, SSS 69, Course record 68.
Club membership 600.
Visitors contact in advance. **Societies** apply in writing or phone in advance **Green Fees** terms on application. **Cards** ▆▆ ▆▆ **Course Designer** Des Smyth **Facilities** ㏒ ▆ ♀ ㏒ ⚔ ♣ **Leisure** snooker. **Location** 3km S

Hotel ★★★★ 61% Hillgrove Hotel, Old Armagh Rd, MONAGHAN ☎ 047 81288 44 en suite

CO OFFALY

BIRR   Map 01 C3

Birr The Glenns
☎ 0509 20082 📠 0509 22155
e-mail: birrgolfclub@eircom.net
The course has been laid out over undulating parkland utilising the natural contours of the land, which were created during the ice age. The sandy subsoil means that the course is playable all year round.
18 holes, 5700 metres, Par 70, SSS 70, Course record 62.
Club membership 800.
Visitors contact in advance. **Societies** advance contact to secretary. **Green Fees** €25. **Course Designer** Eddie Connaughton **Facilities** ⊗ ℳ ㏒ ▆ ♀ ㏒ ⚔ ♣ ⚔ **Location** 3km W of Birr to Banagher

Hotel ★★★ 63% County Arms Hotel, BIRR
☎ 0509 20791 24 en suite

DAINGEAN   Map 01 C4

Castle Barna
☎ 0506 53384 📠 0506 53077
e-mail: info@castlebarna.ie
Parkland course on the bank of the Grand Canal. Many mature trees, natural streams and the naturally undulating landscape provide a great challenge for golfers of all abilities.
18 holes, 5798 metres, Par 72, SSS 69, Course record 66.
Club membership 600.
Visitors not Sun am. **Societies** phone to check availability. **Green Fees** €20 per round (€29 weekends & bank holidays). **Cards** ▆▆ ▆▆ **Course Designer** Alan Duggan, Kieran Monahan **Facilities** ⊗ by arrangement ℳ by arrangement ㏒ ▆ ♀ ㏒ ⚔ ♣ ♦ ⚔ **Conf** Corporate Hospitality Days available **Location** 11km off N6 at Tyrellspass

EDENDERRY   Map 01 C4

Edenderry
☎ 046 9731072 📠 046 9733911
e-mail: enquiries@edenderrygolfclub.com
18 holes, 6029 metres, Par 72, SSS 72, Course record 66.
Course Designer Havers, Hackett **Location** 1.2km outside Edenderry off Dublin route
Phone for further details

Hotel 🏠 Crookedwood House, Crookedwood, MULLINGAR ☎ 044 72165 8 en suite

TULLAMORE   Map 01 C4

Tullamore Brookfield
☎ 0506 21439 📠 0506 41806
e-mail: tullamoregolfclub@eircom.net
Course set in mature parkland of oak, beech and chestnut. The original design was by James Braid and this has been radically altered to meet the highest standards of the modern game, with new sand-based undulating greens, lakes, bunkering, mounding and more trees.
18 holes, 6196yds, Par 70, SSS 71, Course record 68.
Club membership 1000.
Visitors contact in advance, restricted on Tue & at weekends. **Societies** contact in advance. **Green Fees** Mon-Fri €37 per 18 holes (€48 Sat). **Cards** ▆▆ ▆▆ **Prof** Donagh McArdle **Course Designer** James Braid, Paddy Merrigam **Facilities** ⊗ ℳ ㏒ ▆ ♀ ㏒ ⚔ ♣ ♦ ⚔ **Location** 4km SW on Kinnitty road

Hotel ★★★ 70% Hodson Bay Hotel, Hodson Bay, ATHLONE ☎ 090 6442000 133 en suite

CO ROSCOMMON

ATHLONE   Map 01 C4

Athlone Hodson Bay
☎ 0902 92073 📠 0902 94080
18 holes, 5854 metres, Par 71, SSS 71, Course record 66.
Course Designer J McAllister **Location** 6.5km from town beside Lough Ree
Phone for further details

Hotel ★★★ 70% Hodson Bay Hotel, Hodson Bay, ATHLONE ☎ 090 6442000 133 en suite

Booking a tee time is always advisable.

BALLAGHADERREEN

Map 01 B4

Ballaghaderreen
☎ 094 9860295
Mature nine-hole course with an abundance of trees. Accuracy off the tee is vital for a good score. Small protected greens require a good short-iron plan. The par 3, 5th hole at 178yds has ruined many a good score.
9 holes, 5727yds, Par 70, SSS 67, Course record 68.
Club membership 250.
Visitors no restrictions. Societies apply in writing or phone during office hours. Green Fees €15 per day. Course Designer Paddy Skerritt Facilities ⓑ ☕ ♀ ⚒ ∅
Location 3km S of town

BOYLE

Map 01 B4

Boyle Roscommon Rd
☎ 071 9662594
Situated on a low hill and surrounded by beautiful scenery, this is an undemanding course where, due to the generous fairways and semi-rough, the leisure golfer is likely to finish the round with the same golf ball.
9 holes, 5324 metres, Par 67, SSS 66, Course record 65.
Club membership 621.
Visitors no restrictions. Societies contact in writing. Green Fees not confirmed. Course Designer E Hackett Facilities ⊗ by arrangement ∭ by arrangement ⓑ ☕ ♀ ⚒ ⛳ Location 3km from Boyle on Roscommon road

CASTLEREA

Map 01 B4

Castlerea Clonalis
☎ 094 9620068
The clubhouse is virtually at the centre of Castlerea course with seven tees visible. A pleasant parkland course incorporating part of the River Francis very near the centre of town.
9 holes, 4974 metres, Par 68, SSS 66, Course record 62.
Club membership 837.
Visitors welcome, but Sun by arrangement only. Societies contact for details. Green Fees €15 per day. Facilities ⓑ ☕ ♀ ⚒ ∅ Location on Dublin-Castlebar road

Hotel ★★★ 70% Abbey Hotel, Galway Rd, ROSCOMMON ☎ 090 662 6240 50 en suite

ROSCOMMON

Map 01 B4

Roscommon Mote Park
☎ 090 6626382 ▤ 090 6626043
e-mail: rosegolfclub@eircom.net
Located on the rolling pastures of the Mote Park estate. Numerous water hazards, notably on the tricky 13th, multi-tiered greens and an excellent irrigation to give an all-weather surface.
18 holes, 6290 metres, Par 72, SSS 70.
Club membership 700.
Visitors contact in advance, especially Sun. Societies apply in writing or phone. Green Fees €30 (€35 weekends). Course Designer E Connaughton Facilities ⊗ ∭ ⓑ ☕ ♀ ⚒ ⛳ ∅ Location 08km S of Roscommon

Hotel ★★★ 70% Abbey Hotel, Galway Rd, ROSCOMMON ☎ 090 662 6240 50 en suite

STROKESTOWN

Map 01 C4

Strokestown Bumlin
☎ 078 33528
Picturesque nine-hole course set in parkland with fine views.
9 holes, 2615 metres, Par 68.
Club membership 250.
Visitors may play any times except during competitions. Societies apply in writing or phone at least two weeks in advance. Green Fees not confirmed. Course Designer Mel Flanagan Facilities ⚒ Location 2.5m from Strokestown

Hotel ★★★ 70% Abbey Hotel, Galway Rd, ROSCOMMON ☎ 090 662 6240 50 en suite

CO SLIGO

BALLYMOTE

Map 01 B4

Ballymote Ballinascarrow
☎ 071 9183089 ▤ 071 9189210
e-mail: jocon@iol.ie
Although Ballymote was founded in 1940, the course dates from 1993 and has matured well into a parkland with ample fairways and large greens. The feature par 4 7th hole has the green surrounded by water and Ballinascarrow Lake in the background. A challenging course set in breathtaking scenery.
9 holes, 5302 metres, Par 70, SSS 68.
Club membership 250.
Visitors no restrictions Societies phone in advance. Green Fees not confirmed. Course Designer Eddie Hacket, Mel Flanagan Facilities ☕ ⚒ ⛳ ∅ Leisure fishing. Location 1.5km N

Hotel ★★★ 71% Sligo Park Hotel, Pearse Rd, SLIGO ☎ 071 916 0291 138 en suite

ENNISCRONE

Map 01 B5

Enniscrone
☎ 096 36297 ▤ 096 36657
e-mail: enniscronegolf@eircom.net
27 holes, 6698yds, Par 73, SSS 72, Course record 70.
Course Designer E Hackett, Donald Steel
Location 0.8km S on Ballina road
Phone for further details

SLIGO

Map 01 B5

County Sligo Rosses Point
☎ 071 9177134 or 9177186 ▤ 071 9177460
e-mail: cosligo@iol.ie
Now considered to be one of the top links courses in Ireland, County Sligo is host to a number of competitions, including the West of Ireland championships and internationals. Set in an elevated position on cliffs above three large beaches, the prevailing winds provide an additional challenge. Tom Watson described it as 'a magnificent links, particularly the stretch of holes from the 14th to the 17th'.
18 holes, 6043 metres, Par 71, SSS 72, Course record 67.
Bomore: 9 holes, 2785 metres, Par 35, SSS 69.
Club membership 1175.

Continued

Visitors contact in advance, available most days except Captains or Presidents days.Deposit required to secure. **Societies** contact in writing & pay a deposit. **Green Fees** Championship Course:€65 per 18 holes Mon-Thu (€80 Fri-Sun & bank holidays). **Cards** 🖷 📰 🔜
Prof Jim Robinson **Course Designer** Harry Colt
Facilities ⊗ ⅲ 🖢 🖳 ♀ ♨ 🖻 ⅞ ❦ 🏂 ⸗
Conf fac available Corporate Hospitality Days available **Location** off N15 to Donegal

Strandhill Strandhill
☎ 071 91 68188 📄 071 91 68811
e-mail: strandhillgc.eircom.net
This scenic course is situated between Knocknarea Mountain and the Atlantic, offering golf in its most natural form amid the sand dunes of the West of Ireland. The 1st, 16th and 18th are par 4 holes over 364 metres; the 2nd and 17th are testing par 3s which vary according to the prevailing wind; the par 4 13th is a testing dogleg right. This is a course where accuracy will be rewarded.
18 holes, 5516 metres, Par 69, SSS 68.
Club membership 450.
Visitors contact in advance. **Societies** apply in advance. **Green Fees** not confirmed. **Cards** 🖷 📰 **Facilities** ⊗ ⅲ 🖢 🖳 ♀ ♨ 🖻 ⅞ 🏂 ⸗ **Location** 8km from town

Hotel ★★★ 71% Sligo Park Hotel, Pearse Rd, SLIGO
☎ 071 916 0291 138 en suite

TOBERCURRY   Map 01 B4

Tobercurry
☎ 071 85849
e-mail: contacttubbercurry@eircom.net
A nine-hole parkland course designed by Edward Hackett. The 8th hole, a par 3, is regarded as being one of the most testing in the west of Ireland. An exceptionally dry course, playable all year round.
9 holes, 5490 metres, Par 70, SSS 69, Course record 65.
Club membership 300.
Visitors Advisable to contact in advance of wishing to play at weekends **Societies** phone in advance **Green Fees** not confirmed. **Course Designer** Eddie Hackett **Facilities** ⊗ ⅲ 🖢 🖳 ♀ ♨ ⸗ **Conf** Corporate Hospitality Days available **Location** 0.4km from Tobercurry

CO TIPPERARY

CAHIR   Map 01 C3

Cahir Park Kilcommon
☎ 052 41474 📄 052 42717
e-mail: management@cahirparkgolfclub.com
Parkland course dissected by the River Suir which adds a challenge to the par 4 8th and par 3 16th. Water in play on seven holes.
18 holes, 6350yds, Par 71, SSS 71, Course record 66.
Club membership 750.
Visitors may play any time except during competitions. **Societies** by arrangement, apply in writing. **Green Fees** €25 (€30 weekends). **Course Designer** Eddie Hackett **Facilities** 🖢 🖳 ♀ ♨ 🖻 🏂 ⸗ ⏾ **Location** 1.6km from Cahir on Clogheen road

CARRICK-ON-SUIR   Map 01 C2

Carrick-on-Suir Garvonne
☎ 051 640047 📄 051 640558
e-mail: cosgc@eircom.net
18 holes, 6061 metres, Par 72, SSS 71, Course record 69.
Course Designer Eddie Hackett **Location** 3km SW
Phone for further details

Hotel ★★★ 74% Hotel Minella, CLONMEL
☎ 052 22388 70 en suite

CLONMEL   Map 01 C2

Clonmel Lyreanearla, Mountain Rd
☎ 052 24050 & 21138 📄 052 83349
e-mail: cgc@indigo.ie
Set in the scenic, wooded slopes of the Comeragh Mountains, this is a testing course with lots of open space and plenty of interesting features. It provides an enjoyable round in exceptionally tranquil surroundings.
18 holes, 6347yds, Par 72, SSS 71.
Club membership 950.
Visitors contact in advance. **Societies** apply in advance by writing or phone. **Green Fees** not confirmed. **Cards** 📰
Prof Robert Hayes **Course Designer** Eddie Hackett
Facilities ⊗ ⅲ by arrangement 🖢 🖳 ♀ ♨ 🖻 ⅞ 🏂 ⸗
Location 5km from Clonmel off N24

Hotel ★★★ 74% Hotel Minella, CLONMEL
☎ 052 22388 70 en suite

MONARD   Map 01 B3

Ballykisteen Ballykisteen, Limerick Junction
☎ 062 33333 📄 062 52457
18 holes, 6765yds, Par 72, SSS 72.
Course Designer Des Smith **Location** on N24 3km from Tipperary towards Limerick
Phone for further details

Guesthouse ◆◆◆ Ach-na-Sheen Guesthouse, Clonmel Rd, TIPPERARY ☎ 062 51298 8 en suite

NENAGH   Map 01 B3

Nenagh Beechwood
☎ 067 31476 📄 067 34808
e-mail: nenaghgolfclub@eircom.net
The sand-based greens guarded by intimidating bunkers are a challenge for even the most fastidious putters. Excellent drainage and firm surfaces allow play all year round.
18 holes, 6009 metres, Par 72, SSS 72, Course record 71.
Club membership 1100.
Visitors Mon-Fri only, must contact in advance. **Societies** apply in writing. **Green Fees** €30 per 18 holes. **Cards** 📰
Prof Robert Kelly **Course Designer** Patrick Merrigan
Facilities ⊗ ⅲ 🖢 🖳 ♀ ♨ 🖻 ⅞ ❦ 🏂 ⸗
Location 5km from town on old Birr road

Guesthouse ◆◆◆ Ashley Park House, NENAGH
☎ 067 38223 & 06738013 📄 067 38013 5 en suite

ROSCREA   Map 01 C3

Roscrea Golf Club Derryvale
☎ 0505 21130 🖹 0505 23410
Course situated on the eastern side of Roscrea in the shadows of the Slieve Bloom mountains. A special feature of the course is the variety of the par 3 holes, most noteworthy of which is the 165-metre 4th, which is played almost entirely over a lake. It is widely recognised that the finishing six holes will prove a worthy challenge to even the best players. The most famous hole on the course in the 7th. referred to locally as the Burma Road, a par 5 of over 457 metres with the fairway lined with trees and out of bounds on the left side.
18 holes, 5809 metres, Par 71, SSS 70, Course record 66. Club membership 600.
Visitors phone in advance, on Sun by arrangement. Societies apply in writing to Hon Secretary. Green Fees €20 (€25 weekends). Cards 🖳 📖 Course Designer A Spring Facilities ⊗ ⅏ ⅃ ♥ ♀ ♨ ♣ ♿ Conf Corporate Hospitality Days available Location N7, Dublin side of Roscrea

Hotel ★★★ 63% County Arms Hotel, BIRR
☎ 0509 20791 24 en suite

TEMPLEMORE   Map 01 C3

Templemore Manna South
☎ 0504 31400 & 32923 🖹 0504 35450
Parkland course with many mature and some newly planted trees which offers a pleasant test to visitors without being too difficult. The course is undergoing changes with three new holes being brought into play, although it will remain a nine-hole course.
9 holes, 5443 metres, Par 70, SSS 69, Course record 68. Club membership 330.
Visitors not during events. Societies contact in advance. Green Fees €15 per day(€20 weekends). Cards 🖳 Facilities ⊗ ⅏ ⅃ ♥ ♀ ♿ Leisure hard tennis courts. Location 0.8km S of town by N62

Hotel ★★★ 63% County Arms Hotel, BIRR
☎ 0509 20791 24 en suite

THURLES   Map 01 C3

Thurles Turtulla
☎ 0504 21983 & 24599 🖹 0504 24647
18 holes, 5904 metres, Par 72, SSS 71, Course record 67.
Course Designer J McMlister Location 1.5km from town on N62 Cork road
Phone for further details

Guesthouse ♦♦♦ Ach-na-Sheen Guesthouse, Clonmel Rd, TIPPERARY ☎ 062 51298 8 en suite

TIPPERARY   Map 01 C3

County Tipperary Golf & Country Club
Dundrum House Hotel, Dundrum
☎ 062 71717 🖹 062 71718
e-mail: dundrumh@id.ie
18 holes, 7050yds, Par 72, SSS 72, Course record 70.
Course Designer Philip Walton Location 11km W of Cashel off N8
Phone for further details

Guesthouse ♦♦♦ Ach-na-Sheen Guesthouse, Clonmel Rd, TIPPERARY ☎ 062 51298 8 en suite

Tipperary Rathanny
☎ 062 51119 🖹 062 51119
e-mail: tipperarygolfclub@eircom.net
18 holes, 5761 metres, Par 71, SSS 71, Course record 66.
Location 1.6km S
Phone for further details

Guesthouse ♦♦♦ Ach-na-Sheen Guesthouse, Clonmel Rd, TIPPERARY ☎ 062 51298 8 en suite

CO WATERFORD

DUNGARVAN   Map 01 C2

Dungarvan Knocknagranagh
☎ 058 41605 & 43310 🖹 058 44113
e-mail: dungarvangc@eircom.net
A championship-standard course beside Dungarvan Bay, with seven lakes and hazards placed to challenge all levels of golfer. The greens are considered to be among the best in Ireland.
18 holes, 6560yds, Par 72, SSS 71, Course record 66. Club membership 900.
Visitors welcome weekdays, booking advisable weekends. Societies phone then write to confirm booking. Green Fees not confirmed. Cards 🖳 📖 Prof David Hayes Course Designer Moss Fives Facilities ⊗ ⅏ ⅃ ♥ ♀ ♨ ⌂ ⅂ ♣ ♣ ♿ Leisure snooker. Location off N25 between Waterford & Youghal

Hotel ★★★ 61% Lawlors Hotel, DUNGARVAN
☎ 058 41122 & 41056 🖹 058 41000 89 en suite

Gold Coast Golf Leisure Ballinacourty
☎ 058 44055 🖹 058 44055
e-mail: info@goldcoastgolfclub.com
A parkland course bordered by the Atlantic Ocean with unrivalled views of Dungarvan Bay. The mature tree-lined fairways of the old course are tastefully integrated with the long and challenging newer holes to create a superb course.
18 holes, 6171 metres, Par 72, SSS 72, Course record 70. Club membership 600.
Visitors book in advance, times available throughout the week. Societies apply by phone in advance. Green Fees €35 per 18 holes (€45 weekends). Cards 🖳 📖 📖 ▦ Course Designer Maurice Fives Facilities ⊗ ⅏ ⅃ ♥ ♀ ♨ ⌂ ⅂ ⚐ ♣ ♣ ♿ ⚲ Leisure hard tennis courts, heated indoor swimming pool, sauna, gymnasium. Conf fac available Location off N25 3km N of Dungarvan

Hotel ★★★ 61% Lawlors Hotel, DUNGARVAN
☎ 058 41122 & 41056 🖹 058 41000 89 en suite

West Waterford
☎ 058 43216 & 41475 🖹 058 44343
e-mail: info@westwaterfordgolf.com
Designed by Eddie Hackett, the course is on 150 acres of rolling parkland by the Brickey River with a backdrop of the Comeragh Mountains, Knockmealdowns and Drum Hills. The first nine holes are laid out on a large plateau featuring a stream which comes into play at the 3rd and 4th holes. The river at the southern boundary affects several later holes.
18 holes, 6712yds, Par 72, SSS 72, Course record 70. Club membership 400.
Visitors pre book for tee times. Societies phone or write in advance. Green Fees €30 per 18 holes (€40 weekends &

Continued

bank holidays). **Cards** ⊞ 📧 **Course Designer** Eddie Hackett **Facilities** ⊗ ⫿ 🍴 🍺 💺 ♀ 👤 🏠 🚩 🐕 🚜 𝄞 **Leisure** hard tennis courts. **Location** 5km W of Dungarvan off N25

....

Hotel ★★★ 61% Lawlors Hotel, DUNGARVAN
☎ 058 41122 & 41056 📄 058 41000 89 en suite

DUNMORE EAST   Map 01 C2

Dunmore East
☎ 051 383151 📄 051 383151
e-mail: dunmoregolf@eircom.net
Overlooking the village, bay and the Hook peninsula, this course promises challenging golf for the high or low handicap golfer.
18 holes, 5400 metres, Par 72, SSS 69, Course record 65. Club membership 500.
Visitors welcome, no restrictions. **Societies** phone in advance. **Green Fees** not confirmed. **Cards** ⊞ 📧
Prof James Kane-Nash **Course Designer** WH Jones
Facilities ⊗ ⫿ 🍺 💺 ♀ 👤 🏠 🚩 🐕 𝄞 **Location** into Dunmore East, left after fuel station, left at Strand Inn & 1st right

....

Hotel ★★★ 65% Majestic Hotel, TRAMORE
☎ 051 381761 60 en suite

LISMORE   Map 01 C2

Lismore Ballyin
☎ 058 54026 📄 058 53338
e-mail: moynihan@eircom.net
Picturesque, tree-dotted, sloping, nine-hole parkland course on the banks of the Blackwater River.
9 holes, 2748 metres, Par 69, SSS 68.
Club membership 350.
Visitors phone in advance, especially weekends. **Societies** apply in writing or phone. **Green Fees** not confirmed.
Course Designer Eddie Hackett **Facilities** 🍺 💺 ♀ 👤 𝄞 ⚑ **Location** 1.5km from Lismore on Ballyduff road

....

Hotel ★★★ 61% Lawlors Hotel, DUNGARVAN
☎ 058 41122 & 41056 📄 058 41000 89 en suite

TRAMORE   Map 01 C2

Tramore Newtown Hill
☎ 051 386170 📄 051 390961
e-mail: tragolf@iol.ie
18 holes, 5918 metres, Par 72, SSS 72, Course record 65.
Course Designer Capt HC Tippet **Location** 0.8km from Tramore on Dungaruan coast road
Phone for further details

....

Hotel ★★★ 65% Majestic Hotel, TRAMORE
☎ 051 381761 60 en suite

WATERFORD   Map 01 C2

Faithlegg Faithlegg
☎ 051 382241 & 086 3840215 📄 051 382664
e-mail: golf@faithlegg.com
Some wicked slopes and borrows on the immaculate greens, a huge 432yd 17th that has a host of problems, and a dog-leg approach to the two-tier 18th green are just some of the novel features on this course. Set on the banks of the River Suir, the course has been integrated into a landscape textured with mature trees, flowing parkland and five lakes.
18 holes, 6629yds, Par 72, SSS 72, Course record 69. Club membership 440.
Visitors subject to availability, booking advised **Societies** apply in writing or phone at least a month in advance.
Green Fees not confirmed. **Cards** ⊞ 📧 📧 💳 **Prof** Darragh Tighe **Course Designer** Patrick Merrigan
Facilities ⊗ ⫿ by arrangement 🍺 💺 ♀ 👤 🏠 🚩 🐕
🚜 𝄞 **Leisure** hard tennis courts, heated indoor swimming pool, sauna, solarium, gymnasium, full PGA club repair & custom fitting service available. **Conf** fac available **Location** onto Dunmore East road from Waterford, pass hospital, left for Cheekpoint, 300 metres turn right under bridge, club 3km

....

Hotel ★★★ 64% McEniff Ard Ri Hotel, Ferrybank,
WATERFORD ☎ 051 832111 98 en suite

Waterford Newrath
☎ 051 876748 📄 051 853405
e-mail: info@waterfordgolfclub.com
One of the finest inland courses in Ireland. This is exemplified by the spectacular closing stretch, in particular the downhill 18th with its elevated tee, a wonderful viewpoint and a narrow gorse lined fairway demanding a very accurate tee shot.
18 holes, 5722 metres, Par 71, SSS 70, Course record 64. Club membership 1102.
Visitors contact in advance. **Societies** apply in writing.
Green Fees terms on application. **Course Designer** W Park, J Braid **Facilities** ⊗ ⫿ 🍺 💺 ♀ 👤 🏠 🚩 🚜 𝄞 **Location** 1.5km N

....

Hotel ★★★ 64% McEniff Ard Ri Hotel, Ferrybank,
WATERFORD ☎ 051 832111 98 en suite

Waterford Castle The Island, Ballinakill
☎ 051 871633 📄 051 871634
e-mail: golf@waterfordcastle.com
A unique 130-hectare island course in the River Suir and accessed by private ferry. The course has four water features on the 2nd, 3rd, 4th and 16th holes with a Swilken Bridge on the 3rd hole. Two of the more challenging holes are the par 4s at the 9th and 12th, the 9th being a 379-metre uphill, dog-leg right. The 417-metre 12th is a fine test of accuracy and distance. The views from the course are superb.
18 holes, 5827 metres, Par 72, SSS 71, Course record 70. Club membership 770.
Visitors contact in advance, pre booking required.
Societies apply in advance. **Green Fees** winter €45-€50; summer €50-€60. **Cards** ⊞ 📧 📧 **Course Designer** Des Smyth **Facilities** ⊗ ⫿ 🍺 💺 ♀ 👤 🚩 🏠 🐕 🚜 𝄞 ⚑ **Leisure** hard tennis courts. **Conf** fac available Corporate Hospitality Days available **Location** 3km E of Waterford via private ferry

....

Hotel ★★★★ Waterford Castle Hotel, The Island,
WATERFORD ☎ 051 878203 19 en suite

> **If the name of the club appears in *italics*, details have not been confirmed for this edition of the guide.**

Continued

CO WESTMEATH

ATHLONE   Map 01 C4

Glasson Golf & Country Club Glasson
☎ 090 6485120 📠 090 6485444
e-mail: info@glassongolf.ie
Opened in 1993 the course has earned a reputation for
being one of the most challenging and scenic courses in
Ireland. Designed by Christy O'Connor Jnr it is
reputedly his best yet. Surrounded on three sides by
Lough Ree the views from everywhere on the course
are breathtaking.
18 holes, 6671yds, Par 72, SSS 72, Course record 65.
Club membership 220.
Visitors book in advance. Societies book in advance.
Green Fees not confirmed. Cards 🔲 🔳 🔳 🔳 🔳
Course Designer Christy O'Connor Jnr Facilities ⊗ ⍾ ⅃
♥♀⅄⌂♟🏴 ➘⚒ ✐ Leisure chipping green.
Conf fac available Corporate Hospitality Days available
Location 9.5km N of Athlone on N55
....
Hotel ★★★ 70% Hodson Bay Hotel, Hodson Bay,
ATHLONE ☎ 090 6442000 133 en suite

DELVIN   Map 01 C4

Delvin Castle Clonyn
☎ 044 64315 & 64671 📠 044 64315
18 holes, 5800 metres, Par 70, SSS 68.
Course Designer John Day Location on N52 Dundalk-
Mullingar road
Phone for further details
....
Hotel ★★★ 64% Ardboyne Hotel, Dublin Rd, NAVAN
☎ 046 902 3119 29 en suite

MOATE   Map 01 C4

Moate
☎ 090 6481271 📠 090 6482645
A parkland course with trees, lakes and many bunkers.
18 holes, 5742 metres, Par 72, SSS 70, Course record 67.
Club membership 650.
Visitors welcome, advisable to phone in advance.
Societies contact in advance. Green Fees €25 (€30
weekends & bank holidays). Prof Paul Power Course
Designer B Browne Facilities ⊗ ⍾ ⅃ ♥♀⅄⌂ ✐
Location 1.5km N
....
Hotel ★★★ 70% Hodson Bay Hotel, Hodson Bay,
ATHLONE ☎ 090 6442000 133 en suite

Mount Temple Mount Temple
☎ 0902 81841 & 81545 📠 0902 81957
e-mail: mttemple@iol.ie
18 holes, 6020 metres, Par 72, SSS 72, Course record 71.
Course Designer Michael Dolan Location 5km off N6 to
Mount Temple
Phone for further details
....
Hotel ★★★ 70% Hodson Bay Hotel, Hodson Bay,
ATHLONE ☎ 090 6442000 133 en suite

> Prices may change during the currency of the
> Guide, please check when booking.

MULLINGAR   Map 01 C4

Mullingar
☎ 044 48366 📠 044 41499
18 holes, 6406yds, Par 72, SSS 71, Course record 63.
Course Designer James Braid Location 5km S
Phone for further details
....
Hotel 🏠 Crookedwood House, Crookedwood,
MULLINGAR ☎ 044 72165 8 en suite

CO WEXFORD

ENNISCORTHY   Map 01 D3

Enniscorthy Knockmarshall
☎ 054 33191 📠 054 37367
18 holes, 6115 metres, Par 72, SSS 72.
Course Designer Eddie Hackett Location 1.5km from
town on New Ross road
Phone for further details
....
Hotel ★★★ 70% Riverside Park Hotel, The Promenade,
ENNISCORTHY ☎ 054 37800 60 en suite

GOREY   Map 01 D3

Courtown Kiltennel
☎ 055 25166 📠 055 25553
e-mail: courtown@iol.ie
18 holes, 5898 metres, Par 71, SSS 71, Course record 65.
Course Designer Harris & Associates Location 5km from
town off Courtown road
Phone for further details
....
Hotel ★★★ ⚑ Marlfield House Hotel, GOREY
☎ 055 21124 20 en suite

NEW ROSS   Map 01 C3

New Ross Tinneranny
☎ 051 421433 📠 051 420098
This well-kept parkland course has an attractive
backdrop of hills and mountains. Straight hitting and
careful placing of shots is very important, especially on
the 2nd, 6th, 10th and 15th, all of which are challenging
holes.
18 holes, 5751yds, Par 70, SSS 70.
Club membership 700.
Visitors welcome, booking required for weekend play.
Societies apply to secretary/manager. Green Fees €30 per
round(€40 weekends & bank holidays). Cards 🔲 🔳
Course Designer Des Smith Facilities ⊗ ⅃ ♥♀⅄⌂
➘⚒ ✐ Location 5km from town centre
....
Guesthouse ♦♦♦♦ Oakwood House, Ring Rd,
Mountgarrett, NEW ROSS ☎ 051 425494 4 en suite

ROSSLARE   Map 01 D2

Rosslare Rosslare Strand
☎ 053 32203 📠 053 32263
e-mail: office@rosslare.com
This traditional links course is within minutes of the
ferry terminal at Rosslare. Many of the greens are
sunken and are always in beautiful condition, but the

Continued

semi-blind approaches are among features of this course which provide a healthy challenge. Celebrating 100 years of golf in 2005.
Old Course: 18 holes, 6608yds, Par 72, SSS 72, Course record 66.
Burrow: 12 holes, 3956yds, Par 46.
Club membership 1000.
Visitors phone 053 32203 ext3 in advance. **Societies** apply in writing or phone. **Green Fees** terms on application.
Cards ⊞ ▩ **Prof** Johnny Young **Course Designer** Hawtree, Taylor **Facilities** ⊗ ⅷ ⅊ ☕ ⅊ ⅄ ⚑ ⛳ 🏌 ⚒ 𝒻 **Leisure** sauna. **Conf** Corporate Hospitality Days available **Location** 9.6km N of Rosslare ferry terminal

Hotel ★★★★ Kelly's Resort Hotel, ROSSLARE ☎ 053 32114 118 annexe en suite

St Helen's Bay Golf & Country Club St

Helens, Kilrane
☎ 053 33234 🖹 053 33803
e-mail: sthelens@iol.ie
27 holes, 5813 metres, Par 72, SSS 72, Course record 69.
Course Designer Philip Walton **Location** 5 mins from Rosslare ferry terminal
Phone for further details

Hotel ★★★★ 70% Ferrycarrig Hotel, Ferrycarrig Bridge, WEXFORD ☎ 053 20999 102 en suite

WEXFORD   Map 01 D3

Wexford Mulgannon
☎ 053 42238 🖹 053 42243
e-mail: info@wexfordgolfclub.ie
Parkland course with panoramic view of the Wexford coastline and mountains.
18 holes, 6100yds, Par 72, SSS 70.
Club membership 800.
Visitors contact in advance; not Thu & Sun. **Societies** contact in writing. **Green Fees** €32 per 18 holes, summer, €27 winter (€38 weekends & bank holidays).
Cards ⊞ ▩ **Prof** LIam Bowler **Facilities** ⊗ ⅷ ⅊ ☕ ⅊ ⅄ ⚑ 🏌 ⚒ 𝒻

Hotel ★★★ 74% Talbot Hotel Conference Leisure Centre, The Quay, WEXFORD ☎ 053 22566 98 en suite

CO WICKLOW

ARKLOW   Map 01 D3

Arklow Abbeylands
☎ 0402 32492 🖹 0402 91604
e-mail: arklowgolflinks@eircom.net
18 holes, 5802 metres, Par 69, SSS 68, Course record 64.
Course Designer Hawtree & Taylor **Location** 0.8km from town centre
Phone for further details

Hotel ★★★ ♨ Marlfield House Hotel, GOREY ☎ 055 21124 20 en suite

BALTINGLASS   Map 01 D3

Baltinglass Dublin Rd
☎ 059 6481350 🖹 059 6481842
e-mail: baltinglassgc@eircom.net
An 18-hole course overlooking Baltinglass town with breathtaking views of the Wicklow Mountains.

Continued

Abundant mature trees make this course a good test of golf for all levels of handicap.
18 holes, 5912 metres, Par 71, SSS 71, Course record 68.
Club membership 600.
Visitors advisable to check availability for weekends. **Societies** apply in writing or by phone. **Green Fees** not confirmed. **Course Designer** Lionel Hewston **Facilities** ⊗ ⅊ ☕ ⅊ ⅄ ⚑ ⚒ 𝒻 **Location** 500 metres N of Baltinglass

Hotel ★★★ Seven Oaks Hotel, Athy Rd, CARLOW ☎ 059 913 1308 59 en suite

BLAINROE   Map 01 D3

Blainroe
☎ 0404 68168 🖹 0404 69369
e-mail: blainroegolfclub@eircom.net
Parkland course overlooking the sea on the east coast, offering a challenging round to golfers of all abilities. Some holes are situated right on the coast and two holes worth noting are the 14th, played over the sea from a cliff promontory and the par 3 15th over the lake.
18 holes, 6175 metres, Par 72, SSS 72, Course record 71.
Club membership 1140.
Visitors contact in advance. **Societies** phone in advance. **Green Fees** €50 (€65 weekends). **Cards** ⊞ ▩ **Prof** John McDonald **Course Designer** Fred Hawtree **Facilities** ⊗ ⅷ ⅊ ☕ ⅊ ⅄ ⚑ 🏌 ⚒ ⚑ 𝒻 **Conf** Corporate Hospitality Days available **Location** 5km S of Wicklow on coast road

Farmhouse ♦♦♦♦ Kilpatrick House, Redcross, WICKLOW ☎ 0404 47137 4 rms (3 en suite)

BLESSINGTON   Map 01 D3

Clarian Tulfarris House Hotel & Country Club
☎ 045 867644 & 867600 🖹 045 867000
e-mail: info@tulfarris.com
18 holes, 7116yds, Par 72, SSS 74, Course record 68.
Course Designer Patrick Merrigan **Location** via N81 3km from Blessington
Phone for further details

Hotel ★★★ 66% Downshire House Hotel, BLESSINGTON ☎ 045 865199 14 en suite 11 annexe en suite

BRAY   Map 01 D4

Bray Greystones Rd
☎ 01 2763200 🖹 01 2763262
e-mail: braygolfclub@eircom.net
A USGA standard parkland course of nearly 81 hectares, combines stunning scenery with a classic layout. The 11th par 4 signature hole provides a fine view of the coastline.
18 holes, 5991 metres, Par 71, SSS 72.
Club membership 812.
Visitors welcome Mon, Thu & Fri. Restricted play weekends **Societies** contact in advance. **Green Fees** €50 per 18 holes (€70 weekends). **Cards** ⊞ ▩ ▩ ▩ 🔂 **Prof** Ciaran Carroll **Course Designer** Smyth, Brannigan **Facilities** ⊗ ⅷ ⅊ ☕ ⅊ ⅄ ⚑ 🏌 ⚒ 𝒻 ☏ **Conf** fac available Corporate Hospitality Days available **Location** N11 from Dublin, exit Bray/Greystones

Hotel ★★★ 65% Royal Hotel Leisure Centre, Main St, BRAY ☎ 01 2862935 91 en suite

ld Conna Ferndale Rd
☎ 01 2826055 & 2826766 🖹 01 2825611
✉mail: info@oldconna.com
arkland course set in wooded terrain with panoramic
ews of the Irish Sea and the Wicklow mountains.
holes, 6550yds, Par 72, SSS 72, Course record 68.
lub membership 1000.
isitors advisable to contact in advance; not weekends;
ess code. **Societies** phone well in advance. **Green Fees**
ot confirmed. **Cards** 🖃 🖃 **Prof** Michael Langford
ourse Designer Eddie Hackett **Facilities** ⊗ ⋔ ⮾ ♨ ♥ ♀
s ☎ ⋔ ♥ ⤫ ♂ **Conf** fac available Corporate
ospitality Days available **Location** 2m from Bray

otel ★★★ 65% Royal Hotel Leisure Centre, Main St,
RAY ☎ 01 2862935 91 en suite

Woodbrook Dublin Rd
☎ 01 2824799 🖹 01 2821950
✉mail: golf@woodbrook.ie
erched on top of 30-metre seacliffs, the course has
cently been redesigned with 18 new sand-based, bent-
rass greens of varying sculpture and built to USGA
pecification. Cunning placement of fairway and
reenside bunkers call for shot making virtuosity of the
ghest calibre.
holes, 6017 metres, Par 72, SSS 71, Course record 65.
lub membership 1200.
isitors contact in advance & have a handicap certificate.
ocieties contact in advance. **Green Fees** €90 per 18 holes
€95 weekends & bank holidays). **Cards** 🖃 🖃
rof Billy Kinsella **Course Designer** Peter McEvoy
acilities ⊗ ⋔ ⮾ ♨ ♀ ♏ ☎ ⋔ ♥ ⤫ ♂
ocation 17.5km S of Dublin on N11

otel ★★★ 65% Royal Hotel Leisure Centre, Main St,
RAY ☎ 01 2862935 91 en suite

RITTAS BAY Map 01 D3

he European Club
☎ 0404 47415 🖹 0404 47449
✉mail: info@europeanclub.com
links course that runs through a large dunes system.
nce it was opened in 1992 it is rapidly gaining
cognition as one of Irelands best courses. Notable
oles include the 7th, 13th and 14th.
) holes, 7210yds, Par 71, SSS 73, Course record 67.
lub membership 100.
isitors booking advised for weekends; dress code.
ocieties book in advance. **Green Fees** not confirmed.
ards 🖃 🖃 **Course Designer** Pat Ruddy **Facilities** ⊗
♨ ⮾ ♨ ☎ ⋔ ♥ ⤫ ♂ **Conf** Corporate Hospitality
ays available **Location** 1.5km from Brittas Bay Beach

armhouse ♦♦♦♦ Kilpatrick House, Redcross,
ICKLOW ☎ 0404 47137 4 rms (3 en suite)

ELGANY Map 01 D3

elgany
☎ 01 2874536 🖹 01 2873977
✉mail: delganygolf@eircom.net
n undulating parkland course amidst beautiful
enery. Remodelled in 2002 with sand-based greens
d tees to USGA specifications.
holes, 5473 metres, Par 69, SSS 68.
lub membership 1070.

Visitors may play Mon, Thu & Fri. Contact in advance.
Societies contact in advance. **Green Fees** €45 per 18 holes
(€55 weekends). **Cards** 🖃 🖃 **Prof** Gavin Kavanagh
Course Designer H Vardon **Facilities** ⊗ ⋔ ⮾ ♨ ♥ ♀ ♨ ♏
♥ ⤫ ♂ **Location** 1.2km from village

Hotel ★★★★ 64% Glenview Hotel, Glen O' the Downs,
DELGANY ☎ 01 2873399 70 en suite

Glen of the Downs Coolnaskeagh
☎ 01 2876240 🖹 01 2870063
e-mail: info@glenofthedowns.com
A parkland course that plays much like a links course
with sand-based greens and tees. Among its features is a
five-tier double green, which is shared by the 8th and
10th holes. Sandwiched in between is a fine par 5, the
9th, which measures 500yds off the back.
18 holes, 5980yds, Par 71, SSS 70.
Club membership 650.
Visitors booking necessary. **Societies** booking in advance
essential. **Green Fees** from €35-€85. **Cards** 🖃 🖃
Course Designer Peter McEvoy **Facilities** ⊗ ⋔ ⮾ ♨ ♥ ♀
♨ ☎ ⋔ ♥ ⤫ ♂ **Conf** fac available Corporate
Hospitality Days available **Location** off N11 S, 4m from
Bray

Hotel ★★★★ 64% Glenview Hotel, Glen O' the Downs,
DELGANY ☎ 01 2873399 70 en suite

DUNLAVIN Map 01 D3

Rathsallagh
☎ 045 403316 🖹 045 403295
e-mail: info@rathsallagh.com
Designed by Peter McEvoy and Christy O'Connor Jnr,
this is a spectacular course which will test the pro's
without intimidating the club golfer. Set in 252 acres of
lush parkland with thousands of mature trees, natural
water hazards and gently rolling landscape. The greens
are of high quality, in design, construction and
condition.
18 holes, 6916yds, Par 72, SSS 74, Course record 68.
Club membership 410.
Visitors booking & neat dress is essential. Metal spikes are
prohibited. **Societies** apply in writing or by phone or e-
mail. **Green Fees** €60 per round (€75 Fri-Sat & bank
holidays). Reduced rates for hotel residents;. **Cards** 🖃
🖃 🖃 **Prof** Brendan McDaid **Course Designer** McEvoy,
O'Connor **Facilities** ⊗ ⋔ ⮾ ♨ ♥ ♀ ♨ ☎ ⋔ ♥ ♂ ♥ ⤫
♂ ⓘ **Leisure** hard tennis courts, sauna, private Jacuzzi
steam room, croquet lawn, walled garden. **Conf** fac
available Corporate Hospitality Days available **Location**
24km SE of Naas off Dublin-Carlow road

Guesthouse ♦♦♦♦ Rathsallagh House, DUNLAVIN
☎ 045 403112 29 en suite

ENNISKERRY Map 01 D4

Powerscourt Powerscourt Estate
☎ 01 2046033 🖹 01 2761303
e-mail: golfclub@powerscourt.ie
A free-draining course with links characteristics. This
championship course with top quality tees and
exceptional tiered greens, is set in some of Ireland's
most beautiful parkland. The course has an abundance
of mature trees and natural features, with stunning
views of the sea and the Sugarloaf mountain.

Continued

Continued

Powerscourt Golf Club

East Course: 18 holes, 5930 metres, Par 72, SSS 72.
West Course: 18 holes, 5906 metres, Par 72, SSS 72.
Club membership 920.
Visitors necessary to book in advance. **Societies** necessary
to book in advance. **Green Fees** terms on application.
Cards 🌐 💳 💳 💳 💳 💳 💳 **Prof** Paul Thompson
Course Designer Peter McEvoy **Facilities** ⊗ ⅷ ⅆ ⚑ ♀
⚐ ⌂ ⅋ ⌷ ⚒ ♨ ⚷ ⌇ **Conf** fac available Corporate
Hospitality Days available **Location** 19km S of Dublin off
N11 to Enniskerry, signs for Powerscourt Estate
....
Hotel ★★★ 65% Royal Hotel Leisure Centre, Main St,
BRAY ☎ 01 2862935 91 en suite

GREYSTONES   Map 01 D3

Charlesland Golf & Country Club Hotel
☎ 01 2874350 & 2878200 📠 01 2874360
e-mail: teetimes@charlesland.com
18 holes, 5963 metres, Par 72, SSS 72.
Course Designer Eddie Hackett **Location** 1.5km S of
Greystones on Delgany road
Phone for further details
....
Hotel ★★★★ 64% Glenview Hotel, Glen O' the Downs,
DELGANY ☎ 01 2873399 70 en suite

Greystones ☎ 01 2874136 📠 01 2873749
e-mail: secretary@greystonesgc.com
18 holes, 5322 metres, Par 69, SSS 68.
Course Designer P Merrigan
Phone for further details
....
Hotel ★★★★ 64% Glenview Hotel, Glen O' the Downs,
DELGANY ☎ 01 2873399 70 en suite

KILCOOLE   See page 457

KILCOOLE   Map 01 D3

Kilcoole
☎ 01 2872066 2872070 📠 01 2010497
e-mail: admin.kg@eircom.net
9 holes, 5506 metres, Par 70, SSS 69, Course record 70.
Location N11 Kilcoole-Newcastle, opp Druids Glen golf
club
Phone for further details
....
Hotel ★★★★ 64% Glenview Hotel, Glen O' the Downs,
DELGANY ☎ 01 2873399 70 en suite

RATHDRUM   Map 01 D3

Glenmalure Greenane
☎ 0404 46679 📠 0404 46783
e-mail: golf@glenmalure-golf.ie
18 holes, 5300yds, Par 71, SSS 67, Course record 71.
Course Designer P Suttle **Location** 3km W
Phone for further details
....
Hotel ★★★ 67% Woodenbridge Hotel, WOODEN
BRIDGE ☎ 0402 35146 23 en suite

ROUNDWOOD   Map 01 D3

Roundwood Newtown, Mountkennedy
☎ 01 2818488 & 2802555 📠 01 2843642
e-mail: rwood@indigo.ie
18 holes, 6685yds, Par 72, SSS 72.
Location 4km off N11 at Newtown Mount Kennedy on
N765
Phone for further details
....
Hotel ★★★ 65% The Glendalough Hotel,
GLENDALOUGH ☎ 0404 45135 44 en suite

SHILLELAGH   Map 01 D3

Coollattin Coollattin
☎ 055 29125 📠 055 29125
18 holes, 6148yds, Par 70, SSS 68, Course record 70.
Course Designer Peter McEvoy
Phone for further details
....
Hotel ★★★ ♨ Marlfield House Hotel, GOREY
☎ 055 21124 20 en suite

WICKLOW   Map 01 D3

Wicklow Dunbur Rd
☎ 0404 67379 📠 64756
e-mail: info@wicklowgolfclub.ie
**Situated on the cliffs overlooking Wicklow Bay, this
parkland course does not have many trees. It provides
challenging test of golf with each hole having its own
individual features.**
18 holes, 5946yds, Par 71, SSS 70.
Club membership 700.
Visitors restrictions Wed/Thu evening & Sun.
Recommended to call in advance for times **Societies**
contact for details or availability **Green Fees** €40 per
round. **Cards** 🌐 💳 **Prof** Darren McLoughlin **Course
Designer** Craddock & Ruddy **Facilities** ⊗ ⅷ ⅆ ⚑ ♀ ⚐
⌂ ♨ ⅋ **Location** off N11 48km S of Dublin
....
Farmhouse ♦♦♦♦ Kilpatrick House, Redcross,
WICKLOW ☎ 0404 47137 4 rms (3 en suite)

WOODENBRIDGE   Map 01 D3

Woodenbridge Woodenbridge, Arklow
☎ 0402 35202 📠 0402 35754
e-mail: wgc@eircom.net
18 holes, 6400yds, Par 71, SSS 70, Course record 71.
Course Designer Patrick Merrigan **Location** 6.5km NW
of Arklow
Phone for further details
....
Hotel ★★★ 67% Woodenbridge Hotel, WOODEN
BRIDGE ☎ 0402 35146 23 en suite

Co Wicklow

Druid's Glen

Kilcoole

Map 01 D3

Druid's Glen from the 1st tee to the 18th green creates an exceptional golfing experience, with its distinguished surroundings and spectacular views. This masterpiece of inspired planning and golfing architecture was designed by Tom Craddock and Pat Ruddy. It is the culmination of years of preparation, creating a unique inland course that challenges and satisfies in equal parts. Special features include an island green on the 17th hole and a Celtic Cross on the 12th. Druid's Glen hosted the Murphy's Irish Open in 1996, 1997, 1998 and for an unprecedented fourth time in 1999. In 2000 Druid's Glen won the title of European Golf Course of the Year and in 2002 it hosted the Seve Trophy. The world's top professionals and club golfers alike continue to enjoy the challenge here. A variety of teeing positions are available and there is a practice area, including three full-length academy holes. Individual and corporate members enjoy generous reserved tee times; visitors are very welcome but it is recommended that you book well in advance.

Druid's Glen Golf Club
Newtown Mount Kennedy
☎ 01 2873600 Fax 01 2873699
e-mail: info@druidsglen.ie

18 holes, 6547yds, Par 71, SSS 73, Course record 62.
Club membership 219.
Visitors advance booking essential. Societies advance booking essential. Green Fees terms on application. Cards ▧ ▦ ▤ ▨ ▩ ▨ Prof George Henry Course Designer Tom Craddock, Pat Ruddy Facilities ⊗ ⏐ ⛶ ⚑ ⛳ ⛴ ⛱ ⛲ ⛳ ⛴ ⛷ ⛸ ⚒ ⛏
Leisure heated indoor swimming pool, sauna, gymnasium.
Location 5km off N11, S of Glen of the Downs

....

Hotels

Marriott Druids Glen Hotel & Country Club,
NEWTOWN MOUNT KENNEDY
☎ 01 2870800 148 en suite

★★★ 67% Hunter's Hotel, RATHNEW
☎ 0404 40106 Fax 0404 40338 16 en suite

★★★★ 64% Glenview Hotel, Glen O' the Downs, DELGANY
☎ 01 2873399 Fax 01 2877511 70 en suite

Business and Pleasure

(At Powerscourt you don't have to separate them)

With so much time given over to work it's important to keep your eye on the ball when it comes to the social side of business. So whether entertaining staff, colleagues or clients, hit the right note and bring them to Powerscourt Golf Club. Located just half an hour from Dublin, not only can we boast 2 of the finest courses in the country but we're also open to visitors every day of the week. Come to Powerscourt and see how we've got corporate hospitality down to a tee.

POWERSCOURT
GOLF CLUB

Powerscourt Estate, Enniskerry, Co. Wicklow Tel: +353 1 204 6033   Fax: +353 1 276 1303

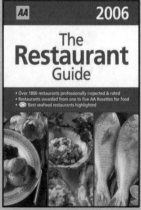

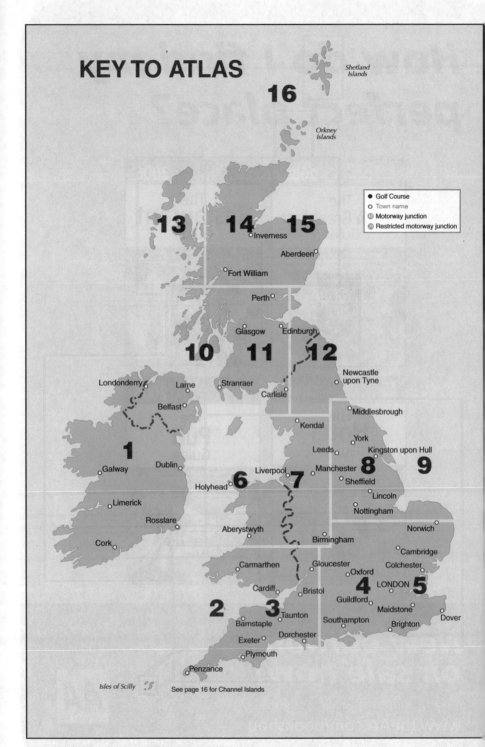

KEY TO ATLAS

Shetland Islands

Orkney Islands

- ● Golf Course
- ○ Town name
- Ⓜ Motorway junction
- Ⓡ Restricted motorway junction

Isles of Scilly   See page 16 for Channel Islands

© Automobile Association Developments Limited 2005

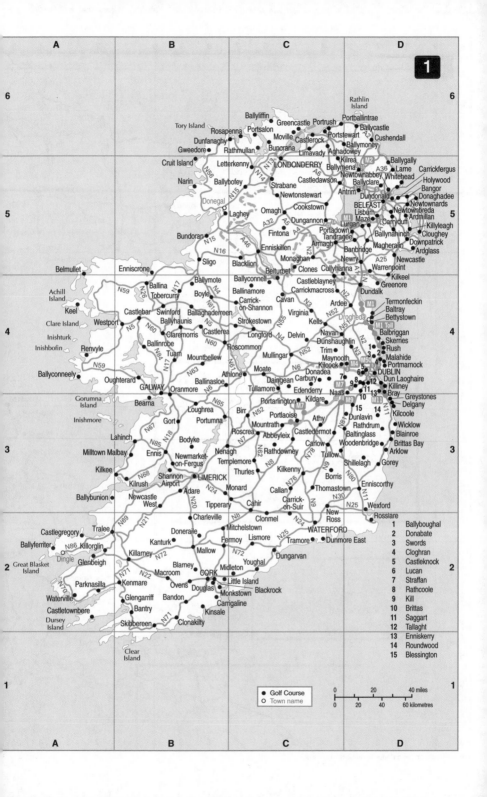

1

Grid reference letters
A   B   C   D

Grid reference numbers
6   5   4   3   2   1

Rathlin Island
Ballyliffin
Tory Island
Rosapenna   Portsalon   Greencastle   Portrush   Portballintrae
Dunfanaghy   Moville   Castlerock   Portstewart   Ballycastle
Gweedore   Rathmullan   Buncrana   Limavady   Ballymoney   Cushendall
Cruit Island   Letterkenny   LONDONDERRY   Kilrea   Aghadowey   Ballygally
Narin   Ballybofey   Strabane   Ballymena   Newtownabbey   Lame   Carrickfergus
Castledawson   Antrim   Ballyclare   Whitehead   Holywood
Newtonstewart   Dundonald   Bangor   Donaghadee
Laghey   Omagh   Cookstown   BELFAST   Newtownards
Bundoran   Dungannon   Lisburn   Maze   Carryduff   Newtownbreda   Ardmillan
Portadown   Lurgan   Killyleagh
Fintona   Tandragee   Ballynahinch   Cloughey
Enniskillen   Monaghan   Armagh   Magheralin   Downpatrick
Sligo   Blacklion   Banbridge   Ardglass
Belturbet   Clones   Cullyhanna   Newry   Newcastle
Warrenpoint   Kilkeel
Ballyconnell   Castleblayney   Greenore
Ballymote   Ballinamore   Carrickmacross   Dundalk
Tobercurry   Boyle   Carrick-on-Shannon   Cavan   Ardee   Termonfeckin
Ballina   Virginia   Baltray
Castlebar   Swinford   Ballaghaderreen   Strokestown   Kells   Bettystown
Westport   Ballyhaunis   Castlerea   Longford   Delvin   Navan   Balbriggan
Claremorris   Roscommon   Mullingar   Dunshaughlin   Skerries
Ballinrobe   Tuam   Mountbellew   Moate   Trim   Rush
Renvyle   Roscommon   Athlone   Daingean   Maynooth   Malahide
Oughterard   Ballinasloe   Tullamore   Carbury   Kilcock   Portmarnock
GALWAY   Oranmore   Edenderry   Donadea   DUBLIN
Bearna   Loughrea   Portarlington   Kildare   Naas   Dun Laoghaire
Gort   Portumna   Portlaoise   Athy   Killiney
Inishmore   Lahinch   Bodyke   Birr   Mountrath   Castledermot   Bray
Milltown Malbay   Newmarket-on-Fergus   Roscrea   Abbeyleix   Carlow   Dunlavin   Greystones
Ennis   Nenagh   Templemore   Rathdowney   Tullow   Rathdrum   Delgany
Kilkee   Thurles   Kilkenny   Baltinglass   Kilcoole
Shannon Airport   Monard   Callan   Borris   Woodenbridge   Wicklow
Ballybunion   LIMERICK   Adare   Carrick-on-Suir   Shillelagh   Blainroe
Newcastle West   Tipperary   Thomastown   Enniscorthy   Brittas Bay
Charleville   Cahir   New Ross   Gorey   Arklow
Castlegregory   Tralee   Doneraile   Clonmel   WATERFORD   Wexford
Ballyferriter   Killorglin   Mitchelstown   Lismore   Tramore   Rosslare
Glenbeigh   Kanturk   Fermoy   Dunmore East
Parknasilla   Mallow   Youghal   Dungarvan
Killarney   Blarney   Midleton
Waterville   Macroom   CORK   Little Island   Blackrock
Kenmare   Ovens   Douglas   Monkstown
Castletownbere   Glengarriff   Bandon   Carrigaline
Dursey Island   Bantry   Kinsale
Skibbereen   Clonakilty
Clear Island

Belmullet   Enniscrone
Achill Island
Keel
Clare Island
Inishturk
Inishbofin
Ballyconneely
Gorumna Island
Great Blasket Island
Dingle

1	Ballyboughal
2	Donabate
3	Swords
4	Cloghran
5	Castleknock
6	Lucan
7	Straffan
8	Rathcoole
9	Kill
10	Brittas
11	Saggart
12	Tallaght
13	Enniskerry
14	Roundwood
15	Blessington

● Golf Course
○ Town name

0   20   40 miles
0   20   40   60 kilometres

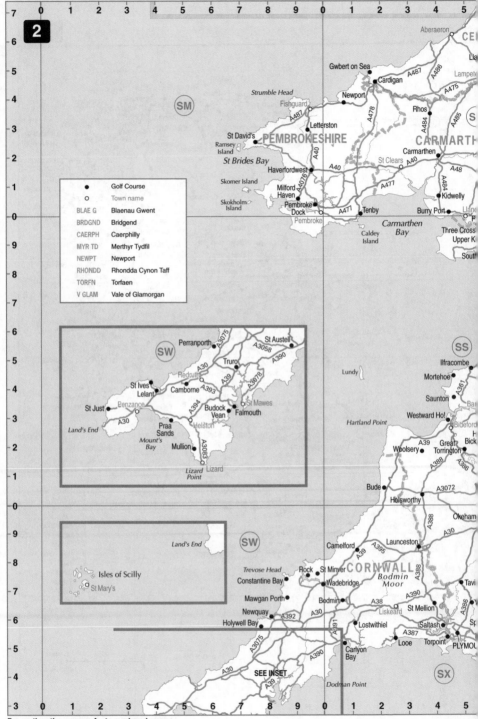

2

●		Golf Course
○		Town name
BLAE G		Blaenau Gwent
BRDGND		Bridgend
CAERPH		Caerphilly
MYR TD		Merthyr Tydfil
NEWPT		Newport
RHONDD		Rhondda Cynon Taff
TORFN		Torfaen
V GLAM		Vale of Glamorgan

SM

SW

SW

SS

SX

Aberaeron
CEI
Llan
Gwbert on Sea
Cardigan
A487
A486
Lampete
A475
Newport
A478
Rhos
A484
A485
S
Strumble Head
Fishguard
A487
Letterston
PEMBROKESHIRE
CARMARTH
St David's
Ramsey
Island
St Clears
A40
Carmarthen
St Brides Bay
Haverfordwest
A48
A484
Skomer Island
A4076
A40
Kidwelly
Milford
Haven
A477
Skokholm
Island
Pembroke
Dock
A471
Tenby
Burry Port
Llane
P
Pembroke
Carmarthen
Bay
Three Cross
Upper K
Caldey
Island
South

Perranporth
A3075
St Austell
A3058
A390
Truro
Redruth
A30
A39
A3078
St Ives
Lelant
Camborne
A393
St Austell
Ilfracombe
Mortehoe
St Just
Penzance
A394
Budock
Vean
St Mawes
Falmouth
Saunton
Bar
Land's End
A30
Praa
Sands
Helston
Hartland Point
Westward Ho!
Bideford
H
Mount's
Bay
Mullion
A3083
Lundy
Great
Torrington
Bick
Woolsery
A388
A386
Lizard
Point
Lizard

Land's End
Isles of Scilly
St Mary's
Bude
A3072
Holsworthy
A388
Okeham
A30
Camelford
A395
Launceston
A388
A30
Trevose Head
Rock
St Minver
CORNWALL
Bodmin
Moor
A388
Tavi
Constantine Bay
Wadebridge
A39
A390
A386
Mawgan Porth
Bodmin
A38
St Mellion
Sp
Newquay
A392
A30
Liskeard
St Mellion
Saltash
Holywell Bay
A391
Lostwithiel
Looe
Torpoint
PLYMOU
A3075
A390
Carlyon
Bay
SEE INSET
A39
Dodman Point
SX

For continuation pages refer to numbered arrows

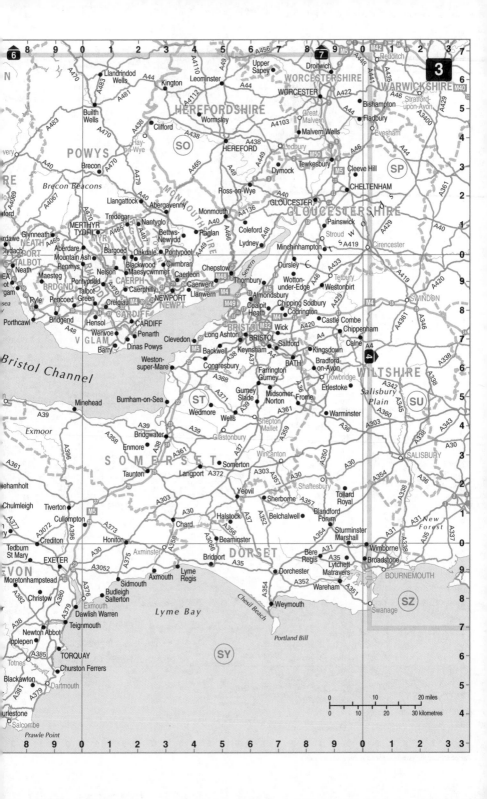

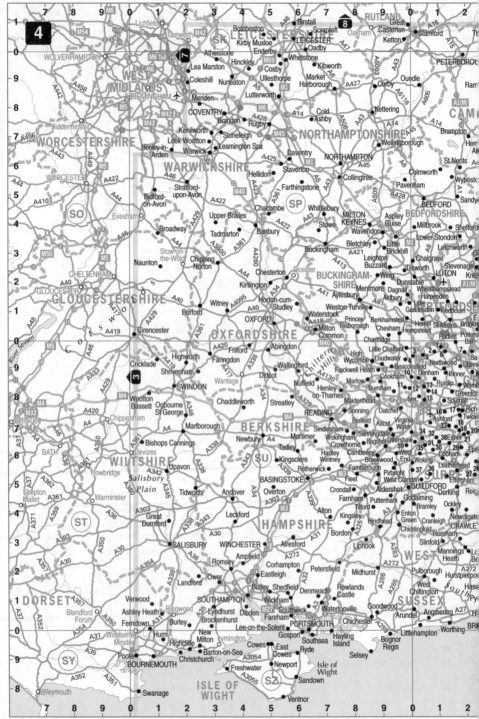

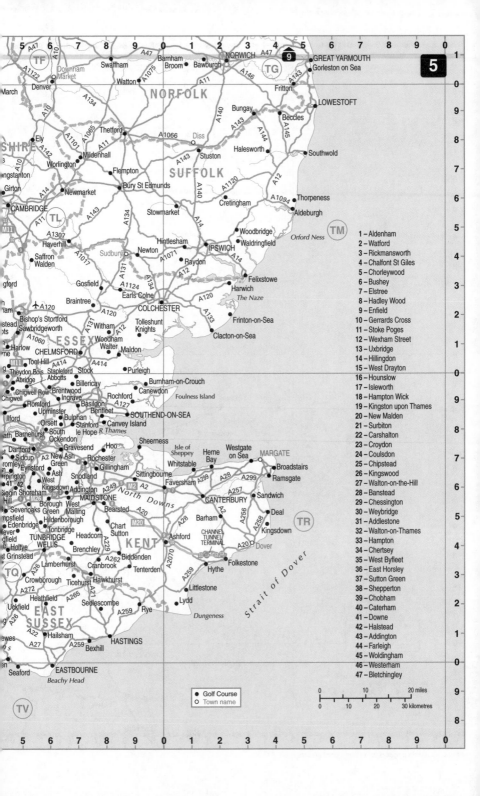

5

Map Labels and Place Names

Numbered locations (golf courses):

1 – Aldenham
2 – Watford
3 – Rickmansworth
4 – Chalfont St Giles
5 – Chorleywood
6 – Bushey
7 – Elstree
8 – Hadley Wood
9 – Enfield
10 – Gerrards Cross
11 – Stoke Poges
12 – Wexham Street
13 – Uxbridge
14 – Hillingdon
15 – West Drayton
16 – Hounslow
17 – Isleworth
18 – Hampton Wick
19 – Kingston upon Thames
20 – New Malden
21 – Surbiton
22 – Carshalton
23 – Croydon
24 – Coulsdon
25 – Chipstead
26 – Kingswood
27 – Walton-on-the-Hill
28 – Banstead
29 – Chessington
30 – Weybridge
31 – Addlestone
32 – Walton-on-Thames
33 – Hampton
34 – Chertsey
35 – West Byfleet
36 – East Horsley
37 – Sutton Green
38 – Shepperton
39 – Chobham
40 – Caterham
41 – Downe
42 – Halstead
43 – Addington
44 – Farleigh
45 – Woldingham
46 – Westerham
47 – Bletchingley

Legend:
- ● Golf Course
- ○ Town name

0   10   20 miles
0   10   20   30 kilometres

Map place names:

NORWICH, GREAT YARMOUTH, Gorleston on Sea, Swaffham, Barnham Broom, Bawburgh, TF, TG, Downham Market, Denver, A1122, A47, A1075, Watton, A11, A146, Fritton, A143, LOWESTOFT, March, NORFOLK, A134, A140, Bungay, Beccles, A143, A145, Thetford, A1066, Diss, Halesworth, Southwold, Ely, A1101, A1065, A11, Mildenhall, Stuston, A1120, A12, SHIRE, Worlington, A142, A143, SUFFOLK, Flempton, Kingstanton, Girton, A14, Newmarket, Bury St Edmunds, A140, Cretingham, A1094, Thorpeness, CAMBRIDGE, TL, Stowmarket, A14, Aldeburgh, Orford Ness, TM, A11, A1307, A143, A134, Woodbridge, Haverhill, Hintlesham, Newton, Waldringfield, IPSWICH, Saffron Walden, A1017, Sudbury, A131, Raydon, A14, Felixstowe, Gosfield, A1124, A134, Harwich, The Naze, gford, Earls Colne, A12, Braintree, A120, COLCHESTER, A120, ham, Bishop's Stortford, A120, Tolleshunt Knights, Frinton-on-Sea, stead, Sawbridgeworth, Witham, Woodham Walter, Clacton-on-Sea, ts, A1060, Harlow, CHELMSFORD, Maldon, A12, ESSEX, rne, M11, Toot Hill, A414, A414, g, Theydon Bois, Stapleford, Stock, Purleigh, Abridge, Abbotts, Billericay, Burnham-on-Crouch, Chigwell Row, Brentwood, Rochford, Canewdon, Chigwell, Romford, Ingrave, Basildon, A127, Foulness Island, Upminster, Bulphan, Benfleet, llford, Orsett, Stanford, Canvey Island, SOUTHEND-ON-SEA, ath, Barnehurst, South Ockendon, le Hope, R Thames, Dartford, Hoo, Sheerness, Sidcup, A2, New Ash Green, Rochester, Isle of Sheppey, Westgate on Sea, MARGATE, romley, Eynsford, Ash, Snodland, Gillingham, Whitstable, Herne Bay, Broadstairs, rpington, West Kingsdown, Addington, A249, Sittingbourne, A28, A299, Ramsgate, Biggin Shoreham, M26, Borough Green, A2, Faversham, A299, Sandwich, Hill, Sevenoaks, West Malling, MAIDSTONE, Bearsted, A20, CANTERBURY, A257, Deal, mpsfield, Edenbridge, Hildenborough, Chart Sutton, M20, Barham, A256, A258, Kingsdown, lever, gfield, TUNBRIDGE WELLS, Tonbridge, Headcorn, A229, Ashford, CHANNEL TUNNEL TERMINAL, Dover, Holtye, Brenchley, KENT, A28, A20, t Grinstead, A26, Lamberhurst, Biddenden, A2070, Hythe, Folkestone, TQ, Crowborough, Ticehurst, Cranbrook, Tenterden, A259, Littlestone, A272, Hawkhurst, Heathfield, A265, Sedlescombe, Lydd, Dungeness, Uckfield, A259, Rye, A26, EAST SUSSEX, A22, Hailsham, Strait of Dover, ewes, A259, HASTINGS, s, A27, Bexhill, Seaford, EASTBOURNE, Beachy Head, TV

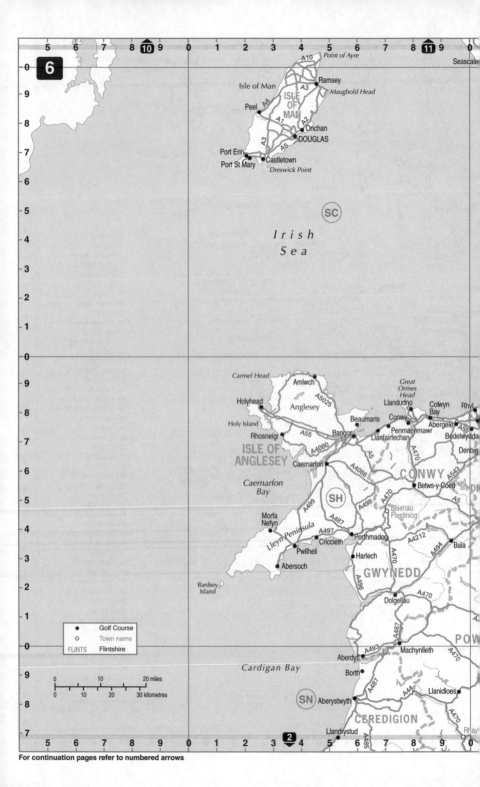

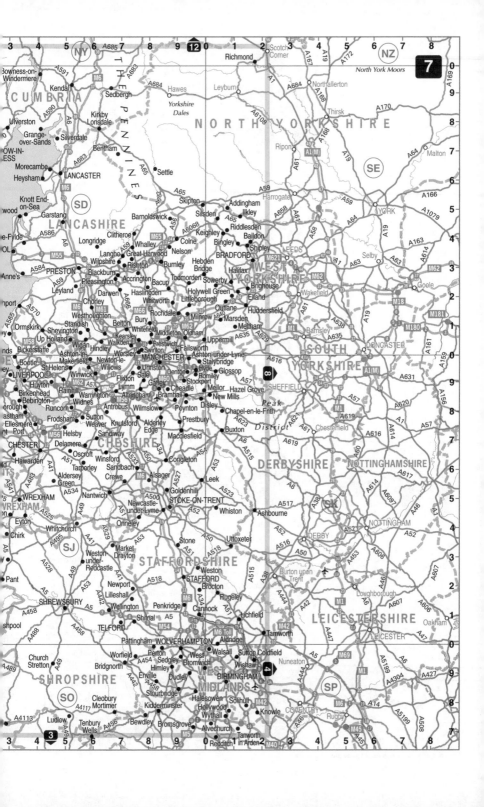

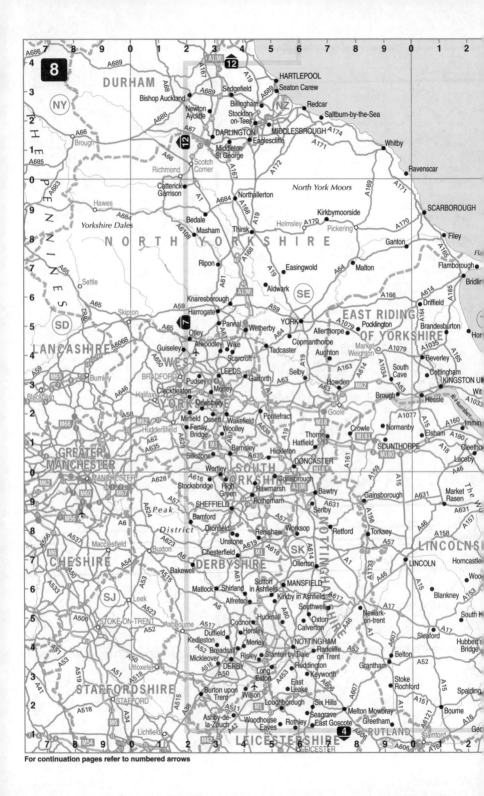

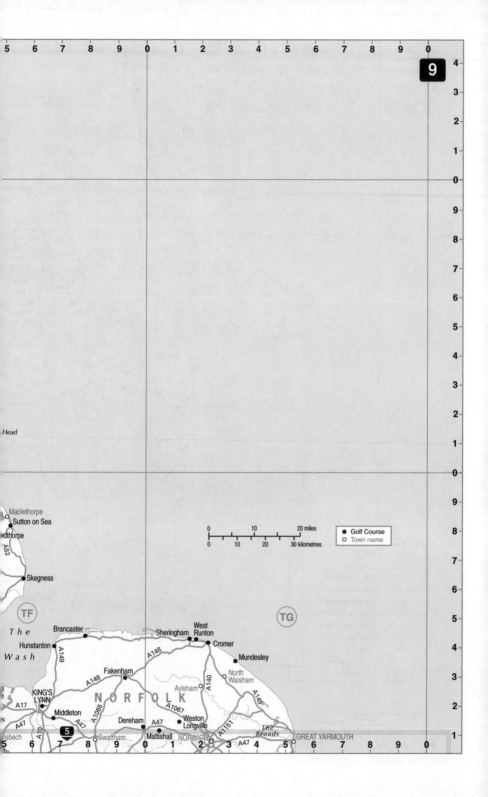

9

5 6 7 8 9 0 1 2 3 4 5 6 7 8 9 0

4
3
2
1
0
9
8
7
6
5
4
3
2
1
0
9
8
7
6
5
4
3
2
1
0
9
8
7
6
5
4
3
2
1

Head

Mablethorpe
Sutton on Sea
dthorpe
A52
Skegness

TF
The
Brancaster
Sheringham
West Runton
Cromer
Wash
Hunstanton
A149
A148
Mundesley
Fakenham
A148
North Walsham
A1067
Aylsham
A140
NORFOLK
A149
A1065
KING'S LYNN
A17
Middleton
Dereham
A47
Weston Longville
A1151
The Broads
A10
A47
5
A47
Swaffham
Mattishall
NORWICH
A47
GREAT YARMOUTH
isbech

0   10   20 miles
0   10   20   30 kilometres

● Golf Course
○ Town name

5 6 7 8 9 0 1 2 3 4 5 6 7 8 9 0

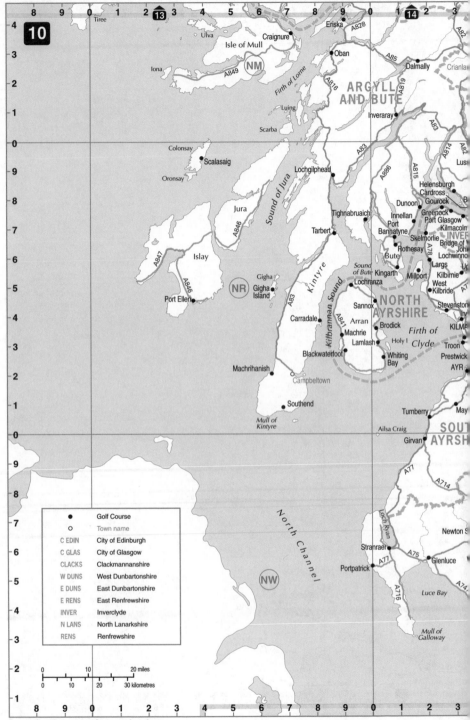

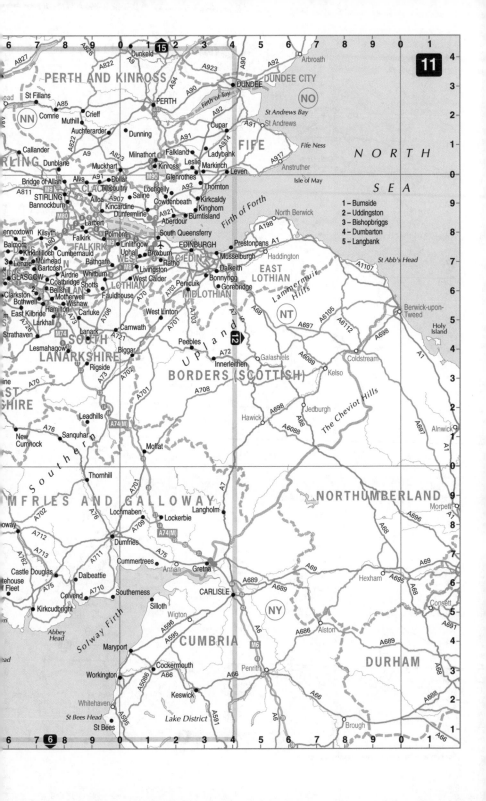

For continuation pages refer to numbered arrows

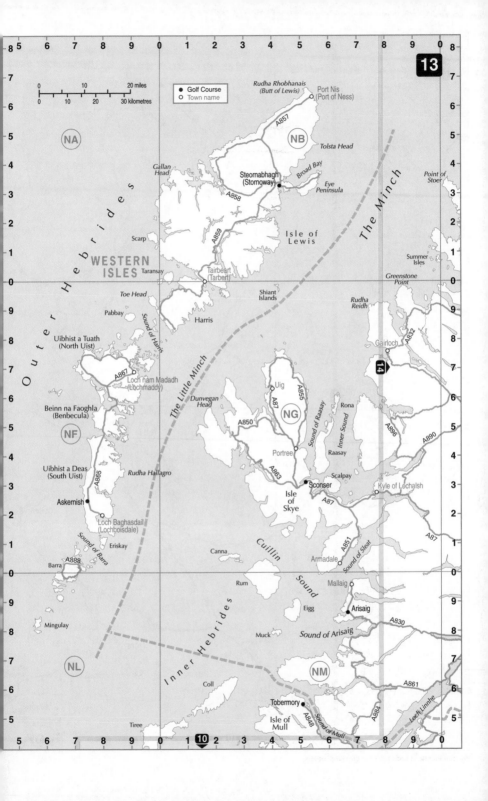

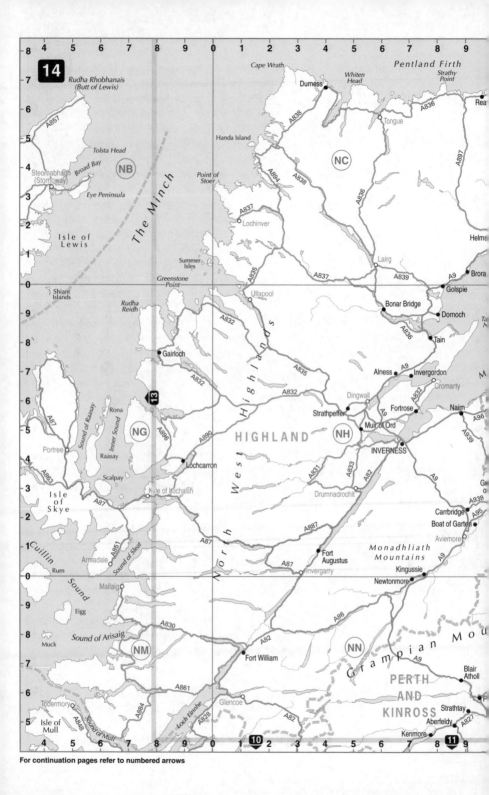

Island of Stroma
Duncansby Head
John o'Groats
A836

Noss Head
A882
Wick

ND

A9
A99

Lybster

ossiemouth
Spey Bay   Cullen
an   Garmouth   Buckie   Banff Macduff   Fraserburgh
lgin   Inverallochy
A96   A98
A941   A95   A98
RAY   Keith   Turriff   A950
Rothes   A97   A952   Peterhead
NJ   NK
A95   Dufftown   Huntly   A947   A948
A920   A96   A975   Cruden Bay
A941   A920   Ellon
omintoul   Insch   Oldmeldrum   Newburgh
939   Inverurie   A90
ABERDEENSHIRE   Newmachar
Kennay   Kintore   Balmedie
Alford   A944   ABERDEEN CITY
A944   ABERDEEN
A938   A97   A980
A97   Tarland   Torphins   A93
A93   Aboyne   Peterculter
Ballater   Banchory   Portlethen
S   A957   A90
                              Stonehaven

al of
shee   Auchenblae   A92

NO   ● Golf Course
                                            ○ Town name
al of
shee   Edzell A90
ANGUS
Kirriemuir   Brechin A935
A926   A932   Montrose
Alyth   A934
rie   Forfar   A933   Lunan Bay
                                  0   10   20 miles
                                  0   10   20   30 kilometres

12

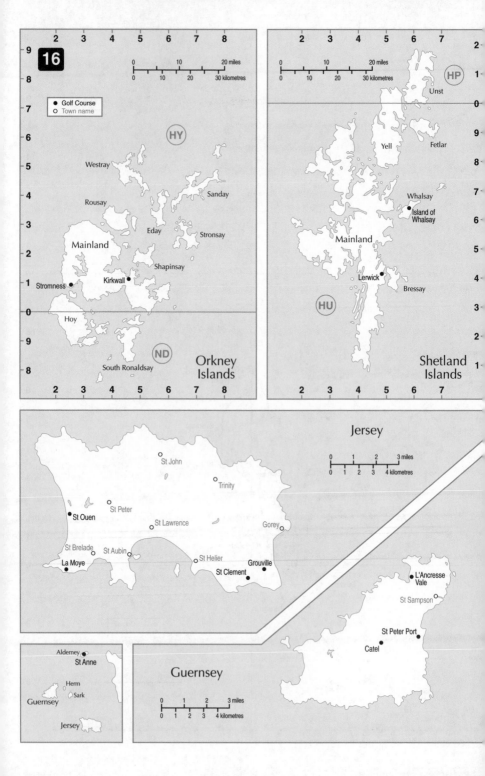

Index

Index

Notes

 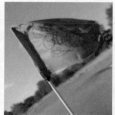  

WIN A GOLF BREAK FOR TWO

with AA Lifestyle Guides
in association with

DE VERE 🦁 HOTELS

Hotels of character, run with pride

**AA Lifestyle Guides has five golf breaks to give away.
We invite you to enter one of five free prize draws*.
The winner of each prize draw will enjoy a complimentary
golf break consisting of a two night stay including
breakfast and dinner at a De Vere Golf Hotel of your
choice PLUS a free round of golf on a specified course.**

For more information on golf breaks at De Vere Hotels visit: www.DeVereGolf.co.uk
or call 01928 714 068 for a copy of our Golf Leisure Breaks Brochure.

Please complete (in capitals please) and return this page to:

AA Golf Guide Prize Draw
AA Publishing
Fanum House (14)
Basing View
Basingstoke RG21 4EA

Title Mr/Mrs/Miss/Ms/other, please state

Initial _____ Surname _____

House Name or Number _____

Street _____

Town _____

County _____

Postcode _____

Telephone Number _____

Email _____

1. Gender male ☐   female ☐

2. Age   18-24 ☐ 25-44 ☐ 45-65☐ 65+ ☐

3. Age of children in the household

           under 10 yrs ___ 10-17 yrs ___

4. Do you have any pets in your household?   yes ☐   no ☐

5. AA Membership no. (if applicable) _____

6. Have you bought any other travel guides in the last 12 months?   yes ☐   no ☐

7. Please select any of the following leisure activities that are of interest to you:

Eating out   ☐

Walking   ☐

Short breaks in the UK   ☐

Short breaks overseas   ☐

Longer breaks in the UK   ☐

Longer breaks overseas   ☐

The information we hold about you will be used to provide the product(s) and service(s) requested and for identification, account administration, analysis, and fraud/loss prevention purposes. More details about how the information is used is in our privacy statement, which you'll find under the heading "Personal Information" in our terms and conditions and on our website. Copies are also available from us by post, by contacting our Data Protection Compliance Officer, The AA, Fanum House, Basingstoke, Hampshire, RG21 4EA

In addition, we may want to contact you about the other products and services from us or our partners. Please tick here if you do NOT want to hear about such products. (   )

Finally, we may want to contact you about other products and services from us or our partners by email, text or multi-media message.

Please tick here if you want to hear about such products. (   )

*Terms and conditions

1. A winner will be drawn from each of the five draws to take place on the first Monday in each of the following months, January, March, May, July and September 2006. 2. Closing date for receipt is midday on the relevant draw date. Final closing date for receipt of entries for the final draw is 1st September 2006. 3. Entries recieved after any draw date, other than the final one, will go forward into the next available draw. Each entry will only be entered in one draw. Only one entry per household (per draw) will be accepted (in relation to all the draws).4. Winner will be notified by post with 14 days of the relevant date. 5. Prizes must be booked within date specified on the letter detailing how to redeem the prize. Prizes are non transferable and no cash alternative is available.6. This prize cannot be used in conjunction with any other discount, promotions or special offers. 7. Each prize consists of 2 nights accommodation for two people in standard twin/double room, including breakfast and dinner from the table d'hote menu or equivalent, plus one round of golf on a specified course. 8. De Vere Hotels provide all hotel accommodation, services and facilities and AA Publishing is not party to your agreement with De Vere Hotels in this regard. 9. No purchase of any AA products is necessary to enter the draws. 10. The prize draw is open to UK residents over the age of 18, other than employees and agents of the Automobile Association or De Vere Hotels, members of their households or anyone else connected with the promotion. 11. Golf Breaks must be pre-booked via the number detailed on the competition letter. All breaks are subject to promotional availability and tee times at the club.12. For a list of winners, please send a stamped, self addressed envelope to AA Lifestyle Guide Winners 2006, AA Publishing, Fanum House 14, Basing View, Basingstoke, Hampshire, RG21 4EA. 13. Winners may be asked to participate in draw-related publicity. 14. AA Publishing does not accept any liability for other parties failure to provide any of the prizes which are the subject of this prize draw.